Accounting

A Management Approach

The Robert N. Anthony / Willard J. Graham Series in Accounting

Accounting

A Management Approach

Gordon Shillinglaw
Professor of Accounting
Graduate School of Business
Columbia University

Philip E. Meyer
Professor of Accounting
School of Management
Boston University

Eighth Edition   1986

IRWIN
Homewood, Illinois   60430

Preface

Our title, *Accounting: A Management Approach,* expresses both the objective and the message of this book—to describe the nature, techniques, and uses of accounting from the perspective of people who manage businesses and investments in businesses.

Although our subject, *accounting,* has undergone an unending series of modifications and refinements over time, its essential character has remained intact. We think that *Accounting: A Management Approach* has had a parallel experience during its 35-year publishing history. While the book's tradition has been our guiding force, we've recognized the need for this eighth edition to update, refine, and improve upon the earlier editions.

Emphasis and Approach

This text emphasizes conceptual understanding, but it is by no means all theory and no practice. We never lose sight of the fact that accounting exists because people need to use it. As a result, we concentrate on the significance, meaning, and implications of accounting concepts and practices—rather than on techniques and procedural rules. Although we examine the accounting model as it now exists, we don't hesitate to identify shortcomings and alternative approaches.

Despite the many significant changes in both structure and content in this edition, its objective is essentially the same as that of the previous seven editions—to enable the reader to understand the concepts on which accounting information is based and the meaning of the amounts presented in both financial statements prepared for outside parties and accounting reports prepared for management's use. This approach enables us to describe the choices accountants and managers must make, *and* to examine the reasons for choosing one measurement or presentation basis instead of others. While we do cover recordkeeping procedures and authoritative pronouncements, they are not emphasized.

Adaptability

One of this book's distinctive features is the *adaptability* of its 24 chapters to either one- *or* two-term courses which cover both financial and managerial accounting or financial accounting alone:

The comprehensive two-semester/two-quarter course can cover 10 to 13 chapters each term.

The comprehensive one-semester course can cover as few as 14 or as many as 19 chapters.

The one-term financial accounting course can cover as few as 12 of the 15 accounting-basics and financial-accounting chapters or as many as all of them.

The Eighth Edition

Although this edition incorporates the strengths of previous editions, we've strived to introduce a fresh perspective. We've been mindful of the changes that have occurred in the business environment and of the accounting profession's responses. We've also recognized the need to relate accounting to the economic conditions of the 1980s. We use the corporate form of enterprise as our focal point from the very outset, and we give considerable attention to the importance of the aftertax perspective, the increasing emphasis on cash flow, and the problems created by changing prices.

The Financial Coverage

In Part 1, **Accounting Basics** (six chapters), the opening chapter now provides both an overview of accounting *and* the first exposure to financial statements and their components. The coverage of end-of-period adjustments is now the entire focus of Chapter 4; the material on nonordinary components of income has been shifted to the financial-statement analysis chapter. Significant changes have been introduced in our treatment of the time-value-of-money concept (Chapter 6): future values have been deleted, and the discussion of financial statements based on present values is no longer included in this early chapter.

Financial Accounting is covered in Part 2 (nine chapters). While the inventory discussion revolves around historical-costing methods and their managerial implications, Chapter 8 also compares and contrasts historical-costing and current-costing. The plant asset coverage includes the current-costing dimension as well (Chapter 9), and pension accounting is now afforded substantive—but not overwhelming—treatment as part of the discussion of liabilities (Chapter 10). Perhaps the most significant change in Part 2 is in the handling of funds flow analysis. Chapter 13 covers only the *cash flow* definition of funds, reflecting the trend that has developed in the corporate community during the 1980s. The notion of working capital is limited to discussion in the context of financial-statement analysis.

The discussion of changing prices and financial reporting (Chapter 14) now covers financial statements prepared on a present-value basis, constant-dollar measurements, and a new section on foreign-currency accounting. Our coverage of financial statement analysis now includes live business- and geographic-segment illustrations as well as the components-of-income material; the discussion of pretax and aftertax leverage calculations now appears as an appendix to the chapter.

The Managerial Coverage

The sequence of the nine chapters in Part 3, **Managerial Accounting,** has been changed in response to helpful suggestions from several adopters of the seventh edition. Part 3 begins with two chapters on the fundamentals of decision analysis, with cost-volume-profit analysis now integrated into the incremental analysis discussion. This initial exposure to cost concepts is followed by coverage of product costing. The two product-costing chapters cover both process costing and job order costing—both full-costing and variable-costing. The focus is on the structure and meaning of product cost measurement, not on debits and credits or on the flow of costs through a set of factory accounts.

Attention then shifts to specific planning and control topics—beginning with short-term budgetary planning (Chapter 20) and capital-expenditure analysis (Chapter 21). Part 3 then turns to control reporting to management, and here too we've adopted a novel approach. We first discuss profit reporting in a profit-center environment—and include basic coverage of transfer pricing. We have two reasons for beginning with internal profit reporting: (1) it is more comprehensive than departmental cost reporting (which is the conventional point of entry into control accounting), and (2) it provides a substantive link between product costing/budgetary planning and the remaining chapters on control reporting.

We discuss cost-control reporting primarily at the departmental and project levels, beginning with basic concepts and reporting objectives, implemented by standard costing and flexible budgeting. An important innovation is the expansion of the concept of flexible budgeting to resolve the long-standing question of how to integrate direct labor and direct materials usage and price variances into the analysis of overhead spending variances. Detailed journal entries and the use of accounts to derive cost variances have been omitted to make way for this integrative approach; since such material is essentially procedural, it can best be covered in second-level courses.

The text concludes with an examination of cost-control reporting in service industries and with a review of the behavioral issues arising in the design and implementation of control systems generally.

Overall Teachability

Understandability of the text has been enhanced by the extensive use of numerical examples throughout the narrative, and numerous exhibits, tables, and diagrams. We continue to use a conversational writing style, highlight key technical terms, and provide study-reminders at appropriate points.

Given the vital importance of having end-of-chapter material reinforce understanding, address nuances and subtleties, and arouse interest in the subject, we offer a set of rich and varied exercises and problems which both challenge the student and provide the basis for wholesome classroom discussion. Each chapter's problems implement and complement its text, and each chapter has a series of independent study problems for which solutions are provided in Appendix B.

A Word to Students

Although we've made every effort to make this book clear and readable, it's still no novel. In our own teaching, we encourage our students to study the illustrations carefully, verify each amount, and even replicate the calculations. The next step is to solve the independent study problems which are found at the end of each chapter. Once this has been done, the student should be in an excellent position to prepare solutions for the problems assigned by the instructor.

To help the student master the material, a study guide is available for use with this book. The guide provides a detailed study outline for each chapter, a concise definition for each of the book's 350+ key terms, and a variety of self-study exercises with solutions (of course). While the study guide is not a substitute for a diligent review of the text and the end-of-chapter exercises and problems, it does provide an additional medium through which basic understanding can be enhanced and solidified.

Acknowledgments

We are grateful to our constituency for the success of the previous editions and for the many helpful suggestions that have been offered over the years. These contributors are too numerous to list in detail, but we are particularly grateful for the help and encouragement we have received from our former co-author, Myron J. Gordon, and the suggestions and comments provided by William Baber, Da-hsien Bao, Larry Grasso, Philip

T. Meyers, Carl L. Nelson, Hugo Nurnberg, Joel Siegel, and Abraham Simon.

A special vote of thanks goes to Robert M. Bowen, John M. Lacey, Glenn M. Pfeiffer, William Rotch, and Arnold Wright, who prepared particularly insightful and thoughtful reviews of the seventh edition. Their comments led to major changes in content and presentation in this edition. We are grateful to them for giving so generously of their time and wisdom. Obviously, any defects and shortcomings that remain are our own.

Material from the Uniform CPA Examinations (American Institute of Certified Public Accountants) and Certificate in Management Accounting Examinations (Institute of Management Accounting) has been adapted or reproduced with permission, for which we are most grateful. We express our appreciation to Charles W. Bastable, John C. Burton, Eric G. Flamholtz, Michael J. Ginzberg, and Carl L. Nelson for permission to use or adapt a number of their problems, and to the IMEDE management development institute in Lausanne, Switzerland, for permission to reproduce a number of cases from its collection.

Gordon Shillinglaw
Philip E. Meyer

Contents

Part 1

Accounting Basics

Chapter 1

The Accounting Framework

Accountability has been a fact of life since civilization began. Accountability for participation in economic events is effected through the practice of accounting, the process of identifying, measuring, and communicating economic information to permit informed judgments and decisions by users of the information.[1]

As this definition implies, the importance of accounting for business organizations lies in its usefulness to decision makers: to investors seeking opportunities to earn returns on their investments; to suppliers seeking assurance that they will be paid for their goods or services; to company managers whose job is to generate income for the enterprise that employs them; and to employees and other interested groups.

In this chapter we'll describe, in an introductory way, what accounting tries to do, why it does it, and who decides how it is to be done. Although the same information may be useful both to external investors and to internal managers, in many instances different types of users need different kinds of information. In most of this chapter, we'll take a preliminary look at accounting measurements intended primarily for investors and other outsiders—**financial accounting.**

This done, we'll identify some of the distinctive features of that portion of accounting which is directed to a company's managers—that is, **managerial accounting.** Finally, we'll wrap up the chapter with some discussion of who the accountants are and who decides how they will do their work. Before we can do any of those things, however, we need to identify the economic phenomena accounting attempts to measure.

---

[1] American Accounting Association, *A Statement of Basic Accounting Theory* (Sarasota, Fla., 1966, p. 1).

The Underlying Economic Phenomena

Accounting measurements deal with real economic quantities—assets, liabilities, and the equity of the owners of a specific business. We'll start by looking at each of these underlying realities.

Business Assets

A business enterprise gets its first resources when the owners invest cash or other property in the business. They then appoint managers. In some cases, the owners may be their own managers, but this is rare in large businesses. The managers then obtain the use of physical property, such as buildings and machinery, and hire any other people they need to get the business going.

Both the initial investment by the owners and subsequent actions taken by the managers provide the business with **assets,** which are objects, claims, and other rights owned by and having value to the organization. They have value either because they can be exchanged for cash or other goods or services in the future or because the company can use them to increase the amount of cash or other assets at its disposal in the future.

Some assets are **monetary assets,** representing enforceable claims on others for specified amounts of money. The first of these is cash, the money the company has in its cash registers ("cash on hand") and in its bank accounts ("cash in bank"). Another monetary asset, accounts receivable, consists of the claims the company has against its customers for goods or services provided to them.

Almost every business has at least some **nonmonetary assets** as well. Some of these are tangible physical assets. Inventories, for example, are physical items the company intends to sell to its customers (merchandise) or consume in operating the business (office supplies, raw materials, and so forth). Plant assets (known also by such names as fixed assets, long-lived assets, or property, plant, and equipment) consist of any land, buildings, and machinery the company owns and intends to use rather than sell.

Finally, many businesses have **intangible assets** that enable them to compete in the marketplace on favorable terms. The exclusive right to use a well-known trademark is an example of an intangible asset.

Sources of Business Assets

A business's assets are provided by its owners and by its creditors, who thereby become equityholders in the business. A creditor is someone (an individual, a group of individuals, or another company) from whom the company has acquired assets or services in exchange for the company's obligation to make payment or provide services in the future. A creditor who has provided cash to the enterprise is known as a lender. An owner, in contrast, is someone who has invested resources in the company—usually cash—in exchange for the rights and risks of ownership.

The main differences in the contractual relationships of creditors and owners are summarized in Exhibit 1–1. The general idea is that creditors

EXHIBIT 1–1
Simplified Comparison of Owners and Creditors

Creditors	Owners
1. Make no decisions on how the company's resources are used.	1. Decide, either directly or through representatives they elect or appoint, how the company's resources are used.
2. Have a right to specified payments on specified dates and can bring legal action if a payment is not made when it is due.	2. Are entitled to receive payments only after the company has provided adequately for the amounts due its creditors.
3. Will receive no more than the specified amounts, no matter how prosperous the company becomes.	3. Can receive very large amounts if the company prospers.
4. Have the right to receive specified amounts, and no more, if the company is dissolved.	4. Have the right to receive whatever is left over after all creditors' claims have been met; will receive nothing if the creditors' claims are not met in full.

accept limits on the rewards they will receive and, in return, assume relatively smaller risks than owners. In practice, both the legal and risk/reward relationships are less clear-cut than this discussion suggests, but these variations are insignificant for our purposes.

A company's obligations to its creditors are its **liabilities.** Four important kinds of liabilities are:

1. *Accounts payable,* measuring the amounts due to people or organizations for goods or services they have supplied to the company.
2. *Notes payable,* measuring the amounts lent to the company by banks and others, usually for short periods of time.
3. *Wages and salaries payable,* measuring the amounts due to employees for services rendered to the company.

4. *Bonds payable,* a form of long-term debt, arising from the amounts lent to the company by outsiders for relatively long periods of time in exchange for the company's agreement to pay specified amounts at specified future dates.

The amounts the owners provide to the business in exchange for their ownership rights constitute the **owners' equity.** In some cases, the original owners may transfer all or part of their ownership rights to others, who thereby become owners of the business. These transfers of ownership don't change the assets, liabilities, or owners' equity of the business, however. Not until the new owners either invest new resources in the business (as opposed to buying ownership rights from other owners) or withdraw resources already there, will the change of ownership have a direct effect on the company.

Business Income

Owners invest in a business because they want the investment to increase their wealth. If the business does this, we say it has generated a *profit, income,* or *earnings* (the terms are used interchangeably). If the activities of the business reduce the owners' wealth, we say it has operated at a *loss.*

One of the accountant's most important tasks is to measure the amount of profit or loss the business generates each year or in any other relevant time period. The accounting measure of a company's profit during a particular time period is known as **net income** or **net loss.** This amount reflects the effects of *changes during a period of time.* A list of assets, liabilities, and owners' equity, in contrast, always refers to their *status on a particular date.*

Accountants measure the net income of a specified time period by subtracting the expenses of the period from the revenues of that period. These terms can be defined as follows:

1. The **revenues** of a period are the resources received by the business as a result of providing products or services to outsiders during that period.
2. The **expenses** of a period are the resources consumed by the company to generate the revenues of that period.

Revenues measure accomplishment, while expenses measure efforts. Revenues come from sales of merchandise to customers and from fees earned from services performed for clients or others. Expenses are the costs incurred by the business to enable it to generate the period's revenues. Some common expenses are the cost of the merchandise sold, the cost of employees' salaries, the cost of renting a building, and the cost of insurance coverage.

Proprietorships, Partnerships, and Corporations

In setting up a business, the owners have to choose the legal form the business will take. Many small businesses and many professional firms, both large and small, are formed as *individual proprietorships* or as *partnerships* of two or more people. Businesses can be set up in either form very simply, with few formalities and little red tape. No permission needs to be obtained; from a legal point of view, the activities of the business are regarded as simply one portion of the activities of the individual owner or owners.

The other major form of business organization is the **corporation.** A corporation is established by the issuance of a corporate charter by a government body; in the United States, corporate charters are usually issued by state governments.

The property of the corporation is legally separate from that of its owner(s). If an owner dies, the corporation lives on because the ownership interest is simply transferred to a new owner or owners. Furthermore, the corporation, not its owner(s), is legally liable for the corporation's debts. This *limited liability* feature means that once the owners of the corporation have invested their funds in the corporation, they as individuals have no further obligation to the corporation's creditors. If the corporation fails to pay its bills, the creditors can't demand that the owners pay these bills with their personal assets.

Limited liability makes investment in a business feasible for many people who have confidence in its future but don't wish to be active in its management *and* do want to limit their risks. In fact, the development of large-scale industry in the Western world was made possible largely because of the corporate form of organization.

In exchange for their investment, the owners of a corporation receive shares of capital stock and are called stockholders, shareholders, or shareowners. The shareholders elect a group of people to serve as the company's *board of directors*. This board represents the shareholders between shareholder meetings, in whatever ways the shareholders agree to. Among other things, it appoints the company's top managers, establishes the basic policies that management is expected to observe in operating the business, and reviews management's performance on the stockholders' behalf.

Financial Accounting	The assets, liabilities, owners' equity, and net income of a business are listed periodically in a set of reports known as **financial statements.** These statements, the focus of financial accounting, are prepared mainly to help investors evaluate the performance of the company's managers and decide whether to let the company use their goods or money, and on what terms.

A full set of financial statements is usually issued once a year, with summary statements every quarter. Most publicly owned companies prepare three major financial statements:

1. An **income statement** (also known as a profit and loss statement)—listing the company's revenues, expenses, and net income for a period of time.
2. A **balance sheet** (statement of financial position)—listing the company's assets, liabilities, and owners' equity at the end of the period.
3. A **statement of changes in financial position**—showing all the inflows and outflows of cash or working capital during the period.

The Income Statement

A company's income statement lists its revenues and expenses during the period; the difference between the total of the revenues and the total of the expenses is the company's net income of that period.

Exhibit 1–2 shows the income statement of Clark Hardware Company for the year 19x5. The first line shows the company's revenues from the

EXHIBIT 1–2

CLARK HARDWARE COMPANY
Income Statement
For the Year Ended December 31, 19x5

Sales revenues		$846,000
Cost of goods sold.		502,000
Gross margin		344,000
Operating expenses:		
Salaries and wages.	$143,000	
Other operating expenses	96,000	
Total operating expenses.		239,000
Income before income taxes.		105,000
Income tax expense		42,000
Net income		$ 63,000

sale of merchandise during the year, while the second line shows the cost of this merchandise. The difference between these two amounts is the *gross margin,* shown on the third line.

The next two lines show the cost of employees' services to the company during the year and the cost to the company of owning or renting its store, advertising its wares, using telephone and electric utilities, and so forth. The total of these expenses was $239,000 in 19x5, $105,000 less than the gross margin. Income taxes took $42,000 of that, leaving net income of $63,000 for the owners. This $63,000 increase in the owners' equity represented funds that either could be reinvested in the business or could be withdrawn from the company by the shareholders, usually in the form of cash. For a U.S. corporation, the decision to reinvest or withdraw is made by the board of directors.

Income and the Income Tax

Income statements prepared as part of financial accounting are *not* income tax returns. The purpose of an income tax return is to enable the government to determine the amount of income tax the company must pay; the final income number on an income tax return is **taxable income,** the amount subject to income tax. In contrast, the final number on an income statement is **net income,** the amount left after all losses and expenses, including income tax expense, have been deducted from the revenues and gains of the period.

Taxable income in the United States and many other countries often differs substantially even from pretax accounting income. The reason is that some of the rules used in calculating taxable income aren't the same as those used in financial accounting. Legislatures often use income taxation as a way of influencing the actions of managers and investors. For example, if the government wishes to encourage investments in oil exploration, it can rule that part of the spread between the revenues and expenses of this kind of activity *isn't* "income" for tax purposes. Or, if the legislature wants to discourage political lobbying by businesses, it can rule that the costs of lobbying activities aren't deductible from revenues for tax purposes.

In both of these situations, adoption of tax definitions of revenues and expenses for financial reporting might mislead investors. As a result, in measuring financial performance for reporting to investors, accountants include the amounts of all resources earned during the period and the amounts of all resources sacrificed to obtain them, even if these amounts differ from those shown on the income tax return. Differences between a properly prepared income statement and a properly prepared tax return therefore aren't fraudulent, either in intent or in result.

What this means is that *income tax questions aren't what we'll be studying in this book.* Our concern will be to try to identify what "good accounting" means, not what will minimize income taxes. At appropriate places in the text, however, we'll allude to pertinent tax considerations insofar as they might affect managers' decisions or the accounting treatment of some transactions.

The Balance Sheet

A balance sheet is a list of a company's assets, liabilities, and owners' equities on a specific date. Exhibit 1–3 shows two balance sheets for

EXHIBIT 1–3

CLARK HARDWARE COMPANY
Comparative Balance Sheets
As of December 31, 19x4 and 19x5

	19x4	19x5
Assets		
Current assets:		
Cash	$ 15,000	$ 33,000
Accounts receivable	62,000	85,000
Inventories	126,000	121,000
Total current assets	203,000	239,000
Land, buildings, and equipment	295,000	275,000
Total assets	$498,000	$514,000
Liabilities and Owners' Equity		
Current liabilities		
Accounts payable	$ 75,000	$ 56,000
Notes payable to banks	—	10,000
Total current liabilities	75,000	66,000
Mortgage loan payable	100,000	100,000
Total liabilities	175,000	166,000
Owners' equity:		
Capital stock	261,000	261,000
Retained earnings	62,000	87,000
Total owners' equity	323,000	348,000
Total liabilities and owners' equity	$498,000	$514,000

Clark Hardware Company, one for the beginning of the year and the other for the year-end.

The Accounting Equation.   Perhaps the most obvious feature of these balance sheets is that the total of the assets is equal to the total of the liabilities and the owners' equity. This equality is no coincidence. In the accounting systems used today, *the asset total must be identical to the total of the equities,* with **equities** being the sum of total liabilities and owners' equity. This identity is referred to as the **accounting equation:**

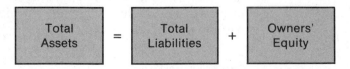

The accounting equation holds true for all organizations at all times. It holds true because the list of assets and the list of liabilities and owners'

equity are merely two ways of looking at the same set of resources. The list of equities classifies the resources according to their source—that is, it answers the question: where did the resources come from? The list of assets, on the other hand, classifies the same set of resources according to their nature—that is, it answers the question: what form did the resources take?

Order of Presentation. The assets in the balance sheets in Exhibit 1–3 are listed in order of their closeness to cash. The first asset to be listed after cash is accounts receivable, on the grounds that this amount will be converted into cash sooner than the inventories and plant assets (land, buildings, and equipment) that are listed below it.

The liabilities are also listed roughly in the order in which they will have to be paid. Accounts payable and notes payable are listed before the mortgage loan because they will be paid before the mortgage loan becomes due.

Since Clark Hardware Company is a corporation, its balance sheet lists two items under owners' equity. The amount shown opposite **capital stock** is the amount the owners have paid the company for their shares of the company. **Retained earnings** is the cumulative excess of the company's net income in all the years since it was formed over the total amount of resources the company has distributed to its owners (dividends) in that same interval. In this case, the amount of retained earnings increased by $25,000 in 19x5, indicating that the company paid the owners $25,000 less than the net income earned during the year.

Current Assets and Current Liabilities. Both the assets and the liabilities are divided in Exhibit 1–3 into two groups, current and noncurrent. This distinction is based on the relationship of the assets and liabilities to the **operating cycle.** The operating cycle of a retail store begins when the managers buy merchandise that they plan to offer for sale to potential customers. This has two consequences: (1) the store has something to offer its customers, and (2) the company has an obligation to pay its suppliers at an appropriate time. These two effects are shown in the two rectangular blocks at the left of center in Exhibit 1–4.

The operating cycle continues as the store sells merchandise to a customer. This reduces the amount of merchandise available for sale to other customers, but it does give the company the right to receive money from the customer who bought the merchandise. This change is indicated by the arrow at the top of the diagram. In the next stage the customer pays and the company receives cash. This cash can then be used to pay suppliers, and the operating cycle is complete. If the company is successful, the operating cycle will also generate enough cash to pay the owners for the use of their money and allow the operating cycle to begin again.

The assets classified as **current assets** are cash and all other assets

EXHIBIT 1–4
Operating Cycle of a Retail Store

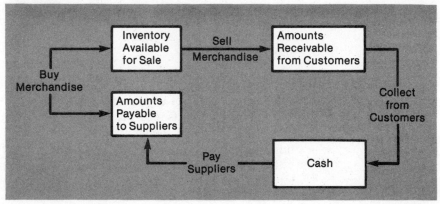

management reasonably expects to convert into cash within one operating cycle. In most cases, this is a year or less. **Current liabilities** are those obligations that are expected to be eliminated by the use of assets that are classified as current in the same balance sheet. Current liabilities include all liabilities that will become payable during the next 12 months, no matter how short the operating cycle may be. For example, if a company has a liability that will be paid off in installments spread over several years, the portion that will have to be paid during the next 12 months will be classified as a current liability.

Working Capital.   The difference between the total amount of current assets and the total of the current liabilities is known as the **working capital.** Clark Hardware Company's working capital increased substantially between the beginning of 19x5 and the end of the year:

	19x4	19x5
Current assets	$203,000	$239,000
Current liabilities	75,000	66,000
Working capital	$128,000	$173,000

Working capital measures the amounts of the current assets that must be financed from long-term sources. It reflects the idea that increases in the company's needs for current assets are likely to be met largely by increases in its current liabilities; only the gap between the two totals has to be financed from long-term sources.

Working capital is also a commonly used measure of the company's *liquidity,* that is, the ability to meet cash obligations when they come due. Most of us think of liquidity in terms of *cash*—in the pocket, in a checking account, in a cookie jar, and so forth. Businesses tend to take a longer view, in deference to seasonal patterns and the length of their operating cycles. This means that their notion of liquidity can include accounts receivable and other assets that will bring in cash in the near future.

Clark Hardware had a strong working capital position at the end of 19x5, much stronger than at the beginning of the year. Why this happened is a question we can only answer after further analysis of the company's situation and its actions during the year. We will discuss this kind of analysis in Chapter 13.

Bases of Asset Measurement. The balance sheets in Exhibit 1–3 list the company's two monetary assets (cash and accounts receivable) at their *value* to the company, that is, the amount of cash the company has on hand or expects to collect from its customers for goods or services it has provided them. The nonmonetary assets (inventories and land, buildings, and equipment) are measured on the basis of their *historical cost,* that is, the amounts the company has expended to acquire them.

What we see, then, is a mixed bag: some of the assets are measured by what they are worth to the company on the balance sheet date; others are listed at their cost. When the items in these two groups are added together, as they are on every balance sheet, the total represents neither the cost nor the value of the company's assets, but a mixture of the two. Given this, it should be no surprise that the reported owners' equity doesn't measure the value of the owners' interest in the business. *The amount shown as the owners' equity in the usual balance sheet won't equal the value of the owners' equity except by coincidence.*

The accountant usually uses the term *basis of valuation* to refer to the quantity an asset dollar amount represents; we prefer the term **basis of measurement** because many items are not measured at their values. We'll provide a more complete discussion of the concept of value in Chapter 6.

The Statement of Changes in Financial Position

The third major financial statement is the *statement of changes in financial position,* or **funds statement.** This shows where the company has obtained financial resources during the period and what it has done with them.

A simple funds statement for Clark Hardware Company for 19x5 is shown in Exhibit 1–5. Since Clark measures changes in its financial resources in terms of their effects on cash—as opposed to their effects on working capital, for instance—the statement identifies the transactions that were the company's sources and uses of cash. In this case, most of the new cash came from the operation of the company's store. This amount was more than enough to cover the dividend payments to the

EXHIBIT 1–5

CLARK HARDWARE COMPANY
Statement of Changes in Financial Position
For the Year Ended December 31, 19x5

Sources of cash:		
By operating the business.........		$54,000
From bank borrowing		10,000
From sale of equipment...........		5,000
Total sources of cash...........		$69,000
Uses of cash:		
To buy equipment................	$13,000	
To pay dividends to owners	38,000	
Total uses of cash.............		51,000
Increase in cash balance...........		$18,000

owners and buy some new equipment. As a result, the company was able to increase its cash balance substantially. Investors had to decide for themselves whether this was an appropriate set of actions, given the conditions in 19x5.

The statement of changes in financial position ties into the balance sheet and the income statement. It shows, for example, what the company has done to get from its $15,000 cash balance at the beginning of the year to its $33,000 cash position at the end of the year. Like the income statement, therefore, it links two balance sheets together. We're not quite ready to deal with these interrelationships yet, but we'll place a good deal of stress on them in later chapters.

The Economic Role of Financial Accounting

Business financial statements have impacts far beyond their effects on the decisions of individual investors and financial institutions such as banks. In fact, it can be maintained that the widespread availability of reliable financial statements is essential to the efficient allocation of resources in a market-based economic system. To demonstrate this, let's look briefly at some of the determinants of capital flow in a free economy, beginning with the relationships between a company's owners and its managers.

Agents and Principals

As we pointed out earlier, most investors who wish to own shares of business corporations don't wish to help manage these companies. Instead, they elect representatives who hire managers to run the companies for them. These managers act as **agents** for the owners, who may also be thought of as the **principals** for whom the agents act.

Principals hire agents with the understanding, contractual or otherwise, that the agents will take actions that will benefit the principals. Agents also have their own objectives, however, and these may conflict with those of their principals. Managers, for example, may negotiate large salaries for themselves, thereby reducing the profits available to the owners. Alternatively, managers may pocket their salaries without exerting the efforts the owners expect of them.

These inherent conflicts in the interests of owners and managers are resolved in various ways. One way is for the owners to *observe* the managers' actions, either continuously or in a random pattern. Most owners have neither the time to do this nor the ability to evaluate what they would see, so this approach is seldom feasible. Another way is to draw up contracts between owners and managers that will provide *incentives* for the managers to take actions that will benefit the owners. Accounting data usually enter into these contracts, as we'll see in a moment. Still another way is to require the managers to *report* periodically, revealing the results they have achieved.

This is where financial accounting comes in. Owners entrust their resources to the managers, who therefore become *stewards* of those resources, responsible for using them prudently and effectively. Owners pay for accounting reports so that they can evaluate the managers' performance as stewards of the owners' resources. This is known as the **stewardship function** of accounting. Conversely, only by promising to issue periodic accounting reports can the managers get others to make ownership investments in the business.

This is the crucial point. Without those investments, each company's size would be limited to the amount the managers could finance from their own resources. Given the huge amounts of capital required by modern technology, the industrial economies of today simply could not exist if all companies had to get all of their ownership capital from their managers.

Impact on Investor Decisions

Business financial statements also serve a second purpose, to help investors direct the flow of capital to enterprises which can use it most efficiently. The prudent investor uses financial data to identify companies and industries in which future economic performance is likely to be strong. In general, companies with strong financial statements are usually far more successful in raising funds than companies with poor recent financial performance. In other words, financial statements have an effect on the allocation of available investment capital.

This claim may appear to be exaggerated. By the time companies publish the formal statements that summarize the financial effects of their operations and the other events of a period, the best-informed investors ordinarily have obtained most of the information the statements contain, at least in qualitative form. Only in unusual situations do the statements contain major surprises.

Even so, the published statements are both necessary and important. The first—and perhaps the most obvious—reason is that they provide quantitative confirmation of the judgments and estimates outside investors and analysts have made on the basis of previously available information. The variables investors try to forecast are either directly reported in financial statements (e.g., sales volume) or closely related to them (e.g., share of the market).

Second, the financial statements provide a great deal of detail, particularly in the accompanying technical narrative (called *notes*), which investors can use in analyzing the company and preparing estimates of its future progress. Investors' estimates of key financial quantities are likely to be considerably less accurate in the absence of credible financial statements.

Effect on Liquidity

We don't claim, of course, that a company's promise to issue financial statements will automatically ensure that it receives the funds it needs. Our point is that the issuance of financial statements based on a set of mutually understood measurement principles is a *prerequisite* to access to capital markets. In fact, we'd maintain that these statements are a prerequisite to the existence of efficient capital markets themselves.

Capital markets consist largely of financial intermediaries that stand ready to bring those who have capital together with those who need it. They thus serve a matchmaking purpose—that is, both suppliers and demanders of capital know where to go to meet their needs.

Capital markets also serve another purpose in that they provide investors with *liquidity*. The fact that investors need help in deciding where to place the funds at their disposal implies that they are willing to take those funds from one company and give them to another, under certain circumstances. Before committing themselves to any one company, therefore, they need to have some assurance that if they aren't satisfied with management's performance or the company's future prospects, or if they want to spend some of their funds on current consumption, they will be able to find others who will be willing to buy their interests in that company. This requires organized markets.

The financial intermediaries that constitute the financial marketplace must have information about the companies whose investment shares are to be traded. To a large extent, their needs for information arise from the same sources as the needs of owners and lenders, primarily the need for data on which to base decisions. They also can be said to have *fiduciary* or *trust* responsibilities toward those whose funds they are placing. Corporate financial statements provide them with a good part of the information on which to prepare their fiduciary evaluations.

Contractual Arrangements

We have already referred to the fact that some contracts between managers and their companies incorporate accounting numbers. Bonuses, for example, may be pegged to the amount of accounting net income.

Other kinds of contracts also use accounting numbers to establish important contractual requirements. An agreement between a lender and the company, for example, may require the company to maintain a specified amount of working capital, or it may prohibit withdrawals by the owners unless accounting income reaches a specified level.

These covenants play the same kind of role in enabling the corporation to borrow large sums as the reporting requirement plays in enabling it to attract owner investments. Without the restrictive covenants, lenders' risks would seem greater, and this would induce potential lenders to demand higher rewards or to withhold their funds entirely.

Managerial Accounting

The second major branch of accounting is **managerial accounting.** Managerial accounting consists of the means by which an organization's accounting staff helps management plan and control the organization's activities. Our introductory description of managerial accounting will be brief because we won't take up the main threads of the discussion again until Part III. Some explanation is necessary here, however, not only to put financial accounting in perspective but also because many aspects of financial accounting have managerial implications.

Planning and Control Processes

Planning can be defined as the process of deciding how to use available resources. The key word in this definition is "deciding," because planning is essentially a matter of choosing the set of alternatives which seem most likely to enable the organization to meet its objectives. Several different kinds of planning processes can be identified, but the most important for our purposes is comprehensive, periodic planning for the activities of the organization as a whole.

Control is the complement of planning. It consists of management's efforts to prevent undesirable departures from planned results, to keep track of what is happening, to interpret this information, and to take action in response to it.

The main relationship between planning and control is diagrammed in

EXHIBIT 1–6
Planning and Control Loops

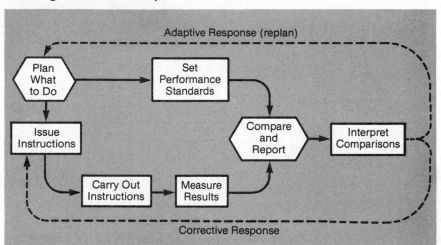

Exhibit 1–6. Planning produces a plan. This becomes a set of instructions to be executed. The results of the actions taken on the basis of the plan are then compared with the planned results. The differences from the plan are interpreted to determine what kind of response is appropriate. A corrective response requires a change in the way the plan is carried out, while an adaptive response requires replanning. Each of these leads back to an earlier phase of the process, and the loop is completed.

Accounting's Role

Accounting's most visible contribution to planning and control processes is in the accumulation of data and preparation of reports on the results of operations. For example, many companies have their accountants prepare income statements for individual groups of products or market segments.

Exhibit 1–7 summarizes one month's revenues and expenses in Clark Hardware Company's equipment rental department, which the company set up in 19x6. This statement is generally similar in structure to the income statement for the company as a whole; the main difference is that it stresses differences from planned results rather than the absolute amounts. Management's job is to determine the causes of the variations from plan and to decide what action, if any, to take.

In larger companies, control reporting of this sort seldom stops with the departmental income statement. Other, more detailed, statements are prepared for managers bearing responsibilities at each organizational

EXHIBIT 1–7

CLARK HARDWARE COMPANY
Equipment Rental Department
Income Statement
For the Month Ended March 31, 19x7

	Actual	Plan	Difference
Revenues	$7,000	$8,000	−$1,000
Expenses:			
Salaries	3,000	4,500	− 1,500
Supplies	1,000	800	+ 200
Other expenses	2,000	2,300	− 300
Total expense	6,000	7,600	− 1,600
Departmental income	$1,000	$ 400	+$ 600

level. Some of these managers may have responsibility for revenues as well as for costs; others have cost responsibility only. In each case, the content of the report should correspond to the scope of the manager's responsibility.

Managerial accounting also has an important role to play in the *planning* process. For one thing, accounting data on the results of activities carried out in the past often prove very helpful to anyone trying to estimate the future effects of management's present decisions. Exhibit 1–8, for example, lists the costs incurred by Clark Hardware Company's service department in installing lighting fixtures for one of its customers. A file of records of this sort, properly analyzed and interpreted, can help management estimate costs of future jobs with characteristics similar to those of jobs performed in the past.

Managerial accounting makes another major contribution to the plan-

EXHIBIT 1–8

CLARK HARDWARE COMPANY
Equipment Service Department
Cost Summary, Customer Job No. 1776

	Hours	Cost
Labor:		
Jones	4	$ 40
Smith	18	216
Brown	6	48
Total labor	28	304
Materials		178
Total cost		$482

ning process. The accounting staff is ordinarily responsible for assembling, consolidating, and testing the tentative plans drawn up at the beginning of each period by the managers of the various segments of the organization. Inconsistencies must be identified and corrected, and the consolidated plan must be tested for feasibility and consistency with top management's objectives.

Accountants and Accounting Standards

Both a company's employees and outsiders play roles in the accounting process. In this section, we'll examine the roles played by company employees and by two kinds of outsiders: (1) financial accounting standard-setting bodies and (2) independent accountants known as *auditors*. We'll also explain why outside standard-setting bodies have little to say about how company accountants fulfill their *managerial accounting* responsibilities.

The Company's Accounting Staff

Most people who work in accounting are employed directly by the businesses and other organizations to which the accounting data apply. They prepare payrolls, record purchases and sales, and keep track of their employer's property. They prepare financial statements and help management plan for the future. They participate in the design of systems to do all this and help managers interpret the information that emerges from these systems.

Most activities of the accounting staff are routine clerical functions. Accounting is far more than this, however. It consists primarily of highly varied analytical tasks requiring a good deal of technical training and understanding of business operations. Most of the people who perform these tasks have college or graduate degrees.

Overseeing and coordinating all these people is the chief accounting officer or **controller,** usually a person with many years of experience in subordinate positions. In a large company, the controller will have a number of immediate subordinates or lower-level counterparts with titles such as assistant controller, plant controller, or divisional controller.

Many of the people now moving toward higher positions of this sort in the United States have **certificates in management accounting** (CMA). The CMA designation is granted to those who meet the experience, educational, and examination requirements of the Institute of Management Accounting, an offshoot of a professional society of managerial accountants, the National Association of Accountants. Comparable certification arrangements exist in other countries. In Canada, for example, the Society of Management Accountants of Canada awards the Registered Industrial Accountant (RIA) certificate.

Possession of one of these certificates isn't an official requirement for advancement in controllership unless the company itself makes such a requirement, but it does provide evidence of knowledge and skills that management may find useful in its employment and promotion decisions.

Financial Accounting Policies and Standards

As we'll see in Part II, accounting measurements aren't always as precise as they're often imagined to be. Surprising though it may seem at this stage, some financial quantities can be measured in two or more different ways. Management, with the help of the company's accountants, decides which measurement alternatives are to be used. These choices, known as **accounting policies,** therefore may differ from company to company. To reduce the danger that a particular company's statements will be misinterpreted, each U.S. corporation must disclose its accounting policies in the notes to its financial statements, and can change these policies only infrequently and by justifying the reasons for any such change.

Management doesn't have a completely free hand in choosing accounting policies. The chosen policies must fit within the limits set by the measurement guidelines known collectively as **generally accepted accounting principles.** Generally accepted accounting principles evolved gradually and informally during several centuries, but further development is now entrusted in most countries to formal rule-making bodies. In the United States, for example, responsibility for specifying how accounting measurements are to be made is vested in the Financial Accounting Standards Board (FASB), created in 1973 with the support of the major professional associations of accountants and financial executives. The FASB's major pronouncements are called **statements of financial accounting standards.**

The FASB is a creature of the private sector, sponsored and financed primarily by corporations, accounting firms, and other nongovernment organizations. Governments also have an interest in private-sector accounting; the major federal government body with the power to influence financial accounting standards in the United States is the Securities and Exchange Commission (SEC). The SEC has generally interpreted its role as deciding what must be disclosed and reported, usually allowing the FASB and its predecessors to determine how accounting variables are to be measured.

Financial accounting and reporting by nonbusiness organizations in the United States attracted little public interest until relatively recently. Responsibility for measurement and reporting standards for private-sector, not-for-profit organizations has been assumed by the FASB, and a new Government Accounting Standards Board was organized in 1984 to play a comparable role for public-sector organizations.

Auditing

Investors accept financial statements because they know they are based on generally accepted accounting principles. They know this because the statements have been reviewed by independent accountants known as *auditors*—trained professionals who are *not* employees of the company being audited. **Auditing** for this purpose can be defined as a systematic process of obtaining, evaluating, and reporting evidence on how well procedures or tested information satisfy previously established criteria (such as generally accepted accounting principles), or how valid a set of tested assertions appears to be.

To make the comparisons required by an audit, auditors must examine not only the statements themselves but also the records on which they have been based and the company's system of **internal controls,** including **internal audits.** Internal controls are procedures and rules the business managers establish to assure that the assets are protected from loss as a result of carelessness, dishonesty, or poor judgment, and that data are recorded accurately and in a timely fashion. Internal audits, which are performed by company employees, test whether established procedures are being followed and controls are operating properly. The better the control system and the more thorough the internal audits, the less work the independent auditors have to do to assure themselves that the financial statements are fairly presented.

Internal control systems in the United States are shaped to some extent by the requirements of the Foreign Corrupt Practices Act of 1977.[2] Beyond that, internal controls are established because management is convinced they will produce benefits that exceed their costs. Furthermore, exercising internal control is clearly a responsibility of management at all levels. Although the company's accountants and financial managers design and administer the system, effective internal control requires continual managerial participation throughout the company.

We should emphasize that management, not the auditors, prepares a company's financial statements. The auditors *examine* the underlying accounting assumptions, principles, and procedures management has adopted, but the statements themselves are management's responsibility. This is made clear in the declaration in the upper part of Exhibit 1–9. This declaration was published by the management of Uniroyal, Inc., as part of its financial statements for 1984. The declaration in the lower part is the report (known as the *audit opinion*) the company's auditors pre-

---

[2] This act prohibited companies or their employees from engaging in transactions with companies and persons located in foreign countries, which transactions would be illegal in the United States. To deal with the issue of how to monitor its employees' activities, the act prescribed that each company maintain a system of internal controls. Although auditors had always looked favorably on the existence of these controls, the 1977 legislation was the first time a universal requirement was established.

EXHIBIT 1–9
Illustrative Management Declaration and Auditors' Opinion

**Responsibility for
Financial Reporting**

The accompanying financial statements have been prepared by management in conformity with generally accepted accounting principles and include certain estimates based on management judgments. Financial information included throughout this Annual Report is consistent with the financial statements.

Management maintains a system of internal accounting controls which is designed to provide reasonable assurance that assets are safeguarded and that transactions are executed in accordance with management's authorization and are recorded in reasonable detail and completeness to permit preparation of financial statements. The system is continually monitored for its adequacy and effectiveness.

The Audit/Pension Committee, composed of outside directors, meets with management, the internal auditors and with Deloitte Haskins & Sells, the company's external auditors, a minimum of three times each year to review pertinent auditing and financial reporting matters, and to satisfy itself that all are properly discharging their responsibilities. The internal and external auditors have free access to this Committee to discuss, without management present, the results of their audits and their opinions on the adequacy of internal accounting controls and the quality of the company's financial reporting.

John R. Graham
Vice President, Finance and
Chief Financial Officer

Auditors' Opinion

**Deloitte
Haskins+Sells**

To The Board of Directors and Stockholders of Uniroyal, Inc.:

We have examined the consolidated balance sheets of Uniroyal, Inc. and its subsidiaries as of December 30, 1984 and January 1, 1984 and the related consolidated statements of income, changes in stockholders' equity and changes in financial position for each of the three fiscal years in the period ended December 30, 1984. Our examinations were made in accordance with generally accepted auditing standards and, accordingly, included such tests of the accounting records and such other auditing procedures as we considered necessary in the circumstances.

In our opinion, such consolidated financial statements present fairly the financial position of the companies at December 30, 1984 and January 1, 1984 and the results of their operations and the changes in their financial position for each of the three fiscal years in the period ended December 30, 1984, in conformity with generally accepted accounting principles consistently applied during the period except for the change, with which we concur, in 1984 in the method of accounting for pension costs related to plant closings.

Deloitte Haskins & Sells
195 Church Street
New Haven, Connecticut 06510

February 20, 1985

pared upon completion of their audit examination. It shows that they were satisfied that the statements conformed to generally accepted accounting principles.

The audit opinion in Exhibit 1–9 is known as a *qualified opinion,* and the nature of the qualification is stated in the opinion's last sentence. Although the financial statements are fairly presented, the auditors point out that interperiod comparability has been affected by a change in an accounting method. A qualification of a more serious nature would have occurred if the auditors had been dissatisfied with some major aspect of the financial statements or the system used to generate the underlying data. Auditors issue *unqualified* (or "clean") *opinions* when there are no qualifications at all. Qualified opinions expressing major reservations as to the financial statements of large business enterprises in the United States are extremely rare: management will either make the changes the auditors call for or provide enough evidence to convince the auditors to withdraw their objections.

The audits of most published financial statements are performed by organizations known as public accounting firms. The firms with headquarters in the United States are organized as partnerships; each of the largest among them has more than 1,000 partners and operates in offices throughout the United States and in many other countries. As Exhibit 1–10 shows, each firm has three major divisions—audit, tax, and management consulting—but the audit division is the largest by far.

EXHIBIT 1–10
Divisions of Major Public Accounting Firms

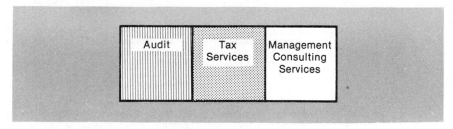

All the partners in the audit divisions of these large firms and most of the professional staff are professionally certified. Those with certificates issued in the United States are known as **certified public accountants** (CPAs); in Canada and the United Kingdom they are called **chartered accountants** (CAs). These people have satisfied the educational, experience, and examination requirements established by the states, provinces, or other jurisdictions in which they practice.

In performing an independent audit, the auditor of a U.S. business is guided by auditing standards and procedures based in part on long-standing practices and in part on pronouncements of the American Institute of Certified Public Accountants (AICPA), the professional organization of licensed CPAs in the United States.

Influences on Managerial Accounting

Management generally gets much more information from the company's accounting system than is prepared for external financial reporting. In general, outsiders have no authority to limit management's freedom to design the portion of its accounting system that provides this additional information. There is no Managerial Accounting Standards Board. The Management Accounting Practices Committee of the National Association of Accountants does issue guidelines on these matters from time to time, but it has no enforcement power. The Society of Management Accountants of Canada publishes monographs on managerial accounting topics periodically, but again its recommendations aren't binding.

Government has had a relatively minor influence on accounting for internal use. Statistical reporting requirements on such matters as employees' wages have undoubtedly affected the information base that is available to management, and income taxation also has affected the measurements of some variables, but the government's influence in a broad sense has been limited mainly to companies in regulated industries such as transportation and electric utility companies, and to companies with substantial government contracts.

The main constraint on management's freedom in system design is **cost.** To avoid the costs of measuring an item such as the company's inventories in more than one way, management may be tempted to use financial accounting numbers for all purposes, even if they are poorly suited to some managerial needs. Cost certainly can't be ignored, of course, but management should approach this issue with an open mind, deciding in each case whether the benefits of separate measurements for managerial uses exceed the costs of making them.

Accounting: A Management Approach

The title of this book is *Accounting: A Management Approach.* How do we reconcile this with the fact that we'll spend about two thirds of our time on financial accounting and only one third on managerial accounting? The answer is that both financial accounting and managerial accounting can be approached from either of two directions. The one we have chosen, a *management* approach, looks at accounting from the manager's viewpoint—what accounting data mean and how managers can use them. The alternative, which might be called a *technical* approach, would emphasize the techniques available to the accountant for accumulating accounting data, processing these data, and communicating information drawn from them. A management approach is more useful than a technical approach for the managers and future managers to whom this book is addressed.

Second, managers need to understand financial accounting because they often have to negotiate with bankers, lawyers, and others in connection with obtaining capital funds from investors or with restructuring the company's financial relationships with its owners and creditors. They need to be able to discuss accounting issues with the company's accountants, because some of the actions management takes may depend on how they will be accounted for. In addition, accountants' measurements often call for the use of professional judgment, and input from managers may be important—hence the managers' need to understand the issues.

Underlying both of these reasons is one that may be even more basic. A company's financial accounting system can be regarded as a model of the business as a whole. A manager who understands how these events affect this model is likely to understand how these events affect the business itself.

Finally, many concepts in financial accounting apply to managerial accounting as well. Seeing their origins in financial accounting therefore is a useful way to understand their use in managerial accounting.

Summary

Accounting is the primary means of organizing and reporting information, mostly in financial terms, for the use of an organization's management and outsiders. Accounting designed for outsiders is known as *financial accounting;* measurement and reporting for internal consumption are the domain of *managerial accounting.*

From a financial accounting standpoint, a business enterprise can be viewed as a set of resources assembled under a common control for the purpose of generating income for the owners. Financial accounting produces financial statements—primarily balance sheets, income statements, and statements of changes in financial position. Balance sheets measure and report the company's assets, liabilities, and owners' equity on a particular date. Income statements measure the economic productivity of the company's resources. The statement of changes in financial position reveals where the company has obtained resources during the period and what it has done with them.

Company financial statements serve private purposes in that they give investors information for use in evaluating the performance of company managers and in estimating the company's future prospects. They also serve broader social purposes, by providing a basis on which investors other than company managers will be willing to invest their funds. Without that willingness, the aggregations of capital required by modern technology could never be assembled.

Financial accounting measurements must follow financial accounting standards. In the United States, these are issued by the Financial Accounting Standards Board. These standards are intended to apply to all companies in like situations, and the certified public accountants who audit financial statements attest to whether they have been followed.

A company's in-house accountants aren't subject to external constraints for internal managerial accounting. Managerial accounting is designed to provide management at all levels with information useful in planning and controlling the company's operations. Accounting measurements for these purposes can take any form as long as they give management the information it wants at a price it is willing to pay.

Accounting also has other branches, the most important of which is tax accounting. Tax accounting consists both of tax planning, designed to anticipate the effects of taxation on the company's future, and tax compliance, the calculation of the amount of past income subject to tax. Contrary to popular belief, financial accounting is not tax accounting, although there are many common elements. In the chapters that follow, we'll point out some of the differences between financial accounting and tax accounting, and attempt to establish their significance to investors and to management.

Key Terms

Accounting policies
Asset
Auditing
Balance sheet
Capital stock
Certificate in management
  accounting
Certified public accountant
Controller
Corporation
Cost
Current assets
Current liabilities
Equities
Expense
Financial accounting
Financial statements
Generally accepted accounting
  principles
Income statement

Intangible asset
Internal audit
Internal controls
Liability
Managerial accounting
Monetary assets
Net income
Nonmonetary assets
Operating cycle
Owners' equity
Retained earnings
Revenue
Statement of changes in financial
  position
Statements of financial accounting
  standards
Stewardship function
Taxable income
Working capital

Independent Study Problems (Solutions in Appendix B)

1. Organizing a Balance Sheet. The following are all the assets, liabilities, and owners' equities of Bolter Company on December 31, 19x1:

Accounts payable...............	$13,300
Accounts receivable.............	8,120
Bonds payable	40,200
Buildings......................	65,760
Capital stock..................	35,000
Cash on hand and in bank	6,600
Equipment.....................	4,450
Inventory of merchandise	11,200
Land..........................	18,000
Notes payable (due in 19x2)	9,000
Retained earnings...............	To be derived
Wages payable	1,770

a. Calculate the amount of Bolter Company's retained earnings on December 31, 19x1.
b. Prepare a correctly structured balance sheet for Bolter Company as of December 31, 19x1.

2. Calculating Income from Balance Sheet Changes. Art Company had total assets of $846,000, total liabilities of $237,000, and capital stock of $400,000 on December 31, 19x1. The company paid dividends of $45,000 to its shareowners in 19x2, and had total assets of $798,000 and total liabilities of $169,000 on December 31, 19x2. No additional capital stock was issued during 19x2.

a. Calculate the company's retained earnings on December 31, 19x1 and on December 31, 19x2.
b. Calculate the company's net income for 19x2.

3. Organizing an Income Statement. Morgan Corporation sells personal computers and computer software in a retail store. Each amount in the following table belongs either in the income statement for the year that ended on December 31, 19x4 or in the balance sheet as of December 31, 19x4:

Cost of advertising during 19x4.................	$ 14,500
Capital stock at December 31, 19x4..............	50,000
Cost of goods sold in 19x4.....................	326,700
Income taxes on 19x4 income	37,500
Cost of real estate owned by the company.........	15,500
Cost of renting the company's store in 19x4	12,600
Employees' salaries and wages	82,400
Sales of computers and software................	521,600
Supplies and repair parts used..................	4,100
Cash in bank, December 31, 19x4	18,600

Select those items that are determinants of income and prepare an income statement for the year ended December 31, 19x4.

Exercises and Problems

4. Financial versus Managerial Accounting. Distinguish between financial accounting and managerial accounting. How does managerial accounting differ from a "management approach" to accounting?

5. Setting Accounting Standards. What are the reasons for the practice in the United States of having a private-sector body (the Financial Accounting Standards Board) rather than a government body codify accounting rules? What arguments can you advance against this practice?

6. Economic Role of Financial Statements. What is the economic role of reports that attempt to tell investors what resources companies have and how effectively they have used these resources? What economic effects would you expect to result from a government ban on the publication of these reports?

7. Role of Independent Auditors. What is the role of the external (independent) auditors who attest to the financial reports issued by investor-owned business corporations? Could these reports play the economic role you assigned to them in answer to question 6 if the external auditors' functions were abolished?

8. Flexibility in Managerial Accounting. Why do companies have more flexibility in managerial accounting than in financial accounting? Is this flexibility desirable?

9. Incentives for Corporate Reporting. Discuss the proposition that the reason corporate stockholders bear the cost of preparing and issuing periodic, audited financial statements is that they can't observe the work of the managers they hire.

10. Incentives for Corporate Reporting. Corporations in the imaginary republic of Euphoria are not required by law to issue periodic, audited financial reports. Explain why you either do or do not believe corporations in Euphoria would still issue such reports.

11. Flexibility in Financial Accounting. Generally accepted accounting principles vary from country to country. In some countries, these principles are flexible enough to allow management to calculate net income at almost any level it chooses, at least for a year or so. What effects, if any, is this flexibility likely to have?

12. Tax Accounting versus Financial Accounting. Government bodies that levy taxes on businesses generally provide their own definitions of how pretax performance is to be measured. Some countries require companies to use these same definitions when they prepare their reports to investors; in other countries, including the United States, accountants insist on maintaining significant differences between tax reporting and investor reporting. What arguments can you think of to support each of these positions?

13. Flexibility in Financial Accounting.   It has sometimes been argued that each business should be free to make accounting measurements in any way it chooses as long as it makes full accounting disclosure. Others have argued that all enterprises should make their accounting measurements in identical ways. What are the differences between accounting measurement and accounting disclosure? What are the relative advantages of the two positions?

14. Accountants' Responsibilities.   Prepare a brief list of the rights and responsibilities to the public you believe lawyers and physicians have. Should independent public accountants or managerial accountants have rights and public responsibilities similar to those you have listed? Why should they be alike or different?

15. Certification of Accountants.   Why is certification as a certified public accountant or chartered accountant required of those who issue opinions on the financial statements of investor-owned companies, while possession of the certificate in management accounting or certification as a registered industrial accountant isn't always required of those who prepare financial statements for use by management?

16. Use of Accounting Information.   Think of an organization you have been closely associated with, such as a business, club, or religious group. Who used information on that organization's resources and economic performance? What information was provided? Why was this information considered necessary?

17. True or False.   State whether each of the following is true, false, or doubtful. Give reasons.

a. The total assets of a business are increased by the purchase of goods on credit.
b. Cash and owners' equity are the same.
c. The total of a company's assets occasionally may exceed the total of its liabilities and owners' equity.
d. Since long-term debt and owners' investments are both sources of assets, they may be considered as essentially identical.
e. Income is a source of assets.

f. When a company owes taxes to a government body, that government body is, in effect, providing some of the resources used by the company.

18. The Nature of Assets.   Identify corporate assets that aren't included in end-of-year balance sheets. Why are such assets excluded, and how does their omission affect corporate financial statements?

19. Notes to Financial Statements.   In addition to a company's balance sheet, income statement, and statement of changes in financial position, what additional financial information would a commercial loan officer or securities analyst want to see included in the notes to a set of financial statements?

20. Net Assets and Owners' Equity.   "Although the accountant chooses to derive the net income amount by measuring changes in the owners' equity, net income in reality consists of an increase in the company's net assets (total assets minus total liabilities)."

Is this statement true? Describe a transaction that increases net assets without producing income. Does this disprove the statement?

21. Net Income and Cash on Hand.   "I don't get it! My company had record earnings this year, retained earnings grew, and total assets are at an all-time high. How is it possible that there's less cash on hand now than there was at the end of last year?"

Is this a plausible scenario? Does it reflect a flaw in accounting techniques or a failure to understand accounting data? Reconcile the apparent anomaly for the perplexed entrepreneur.

22. Earnings Forecasts.   Arch Lancester, chairman of the board of High Tech, Inc., seeks your opinion on how to respond to the following excerpt from a disgruntled stockholder's recent letter. "Reading High Tech's financial statements is like driving a sports car using only the rearview mirror. To beat the market, I need to know what will happen in the future—not a history of bygones. Publish the company's projected financial statements for those of us interested in the future, and give the historians photocopies of past tax returns."

23. Calculating Net Income from Balance Sheet Changes.   The XYZ Company balance sheet on January 1, 19x1, listed assets of $1.1 million, liabilities of $100,000, and capital stock for which the company had received $300,000.

During the year, $140,000 was received from the sale of additional capital stock, and dividends of $40,000 were declared and paid. The balance sheet on December 31, 19x1, showed assets of $1.5 million and liabilities of $350,000.

a. Calculate retained earnings, January 1, 19x1.
b. Calculate retained earnings, December 31, 19x1.
c. Calculate net income for the year ended December 31, 19x1.

24. Preparing a Balance Sheet. Although Robinson, Inc.'s $42,000 cash on hand as of December 31, 19x1, was far greater than the wages payable of $11,000, there was concern about the $56,000 accounts payable being twice the size of accounts receivable. Total liabilities were 80 percent of total assets, and retained earnings were three times as large as capital stock. Inventory on hand had cost $70,000, liabilities including a bank note due in July 19x3 totaled $192,000, and Robinson's assets also included machinery.

Prepare Robinson, Inc.'s December 31, 19x1, balance sheet.

25. Preparing a Balance Sheet. Sorkin Company had the following assets, liabilities, and owners' equity on December 31, 19x1:

Accounts payable......................	$ 40,000
Accounts receivable....................	60,000
Capital stock..........................	300,000
Cash.................................	To be derived
Inventories...........................	90,000
Mortgage loan payable (long-term)	100,000
Plant assets...........................	375,000
Retained earnings	125,000
Salaries payable	10,000

Prepare a balance sheet for Sorkin Company as of December 31, 19x1.

26. Organizing an Income Statement. Daley Company operates an automobile repair business. The boss has handed you a smudgy piece of paper containing the following data:

Cost of repair parts used	$ 33,900
Accounts receivable from customers	5,700
Wages earned by employees	41,300
Charges to customers for repair work	151,500
Cost of repair parts inventory	42,600
Rental cost of garage	15,600
Cost of telephone and electric service used	1,400
Accounts payable to parts suppliers.............	8,100

This list contains all the data needed to prepare an income statement for the year that ended on December 31, 19x1, together with some data that are irrelevant to that purpose. Prepare an income statement for the year, including a heading, modeled on the one in Exhibit 1–2.

27. Balance Sheet Exercises. In each of the following independent cases, calculate the December 31, 19x2, assets, liabilities, and owners' equity, and prepare a table showing the amount of retained earnings on January 1, 19x2, the amount at the end of 19x2, and additions to and subtractions from retained earnings during the year. In each case, capital stock amounted to $5,000, both on January 1, 19x2 and at year-end.

a. On December 31, 19x2, Gray Company had owners' equity of $27,600, compared with $25,400 on January 1. Total assets at year-end were $51,900, and 19x2 dividends were $8,500.

b. Blue, Ltd., began the year 19x2 with owners' equity of $51,300. During 19x2, net income was $6,600. At year-end, assets were $63,300 and liabilities were $14,800.

c. Black, Inc., had liabilities of $69,400 and owners' equity of $48,800 on December 31, 19x2. During 19x2, it had a net loss of $18,400 and distributed dividends of $14,700.

d. The owners' equity of Green Corporation increased by $15,800 during 19x2. At year-end, liabilities were $22,400 and assets were $51,300. Dividends during 19x2 were $13,900.

28. Measuring and Interpreting Financial Results. Stanley Throckmorton, who sells popcorn at public events, has no capital invested in his business other than the cash he keeps in his "business" wallet and a pushcart he bought five years ago for $200. This pushcart contains a corn-popping machine, a fuel tank, storage space for materials (unpopped corn, butter, and salt), and a compartment in which the popped corn can be kept warm until a customer buys it.

One morning, Throckmorton left home with $100 in cash in his business wallet. Contemplating an unusually busy day, he bought materials (corn, butter, and salt) costing $120. Although he usually paid cash for his purchases, this was an exceptionally large one for him. Being a regular customer of his supplier, he was permitted to charge $50 of the total amount and pay cash for the rest.

He then attended a baseball game where he sold three quarters of his purchases for $135, all in cash. At the end of the day, he returned home with his unsold stock, planning to replenish his inventory, pay his bill, and obtain fuel for his corn popper on the following morning. (He normally bought fuel on alternate business days at a cost of about $4. A purchase of this size was enough for two days' operation of the corn popper.)

a. How would you measure the results of Throckmorton's operations for this day? Quantify your answer as much as possible and list the items, if any, that you found difficult to quantify.

b. Why should Throckmorton be interested in a measure of his operating results, defined as in *a*? How might knowledge of operating results affect his business actions?

c. What other information might Throckmorton want to be able to get from his accounting records?

29. Data for Owners' Decision. Angus MacTavish scratched his head in bewilderment. "I can't figure it out," he said. "I've been running this business for almost a year, and I have more customers by far than I had expected when I started. I have had to hire a new bookkeeper just to get out the bills to my customers and to record their payments when they come in. Yet here I am, just before Christmas, and I don't have enough cash in the bank to pay for that new coat I promised to buy my wife if the business did well. I wonder what has gone wrong."

MacTavish went into business for himself on January 1, 19x1. He took $30,000 from his savings, rented a store, bought a stock of merchandise from a wholesaler, hired a shop assistant, and opened his doors for business. The store proved to be in an excellent location, and MacTavish quickly earned a reputation of being an honest merchant with good-quality merchandise and favorable prices. As the year wore on, his store became more and more crowded with customers, and he had to add an extra clerk to handle the business.

During the year, he bought one additional display cabinet to display his stock of a new line of products that a manufacturer's representative offered to him. Other than this, he didn't recall any major purchases of furniture or equipment. It seemed to him, however, that the better his business became, the less cash he had in the bank.

MacTavish was confident that his December business would bring in enough cash so that he needn't worry about not being able to meet the payroll at the end of December, but, even so, he would have a good deal less cash in the bank at the end of the year than he had when he started in business. This disturbed him because, as he put it, "I have sunk everything I have into this business, given up a good steady job with a strong company, and have worked day and night to make a go of it. If it's not going to pay off, I'd like to know it soon so that I can sell out and go back to work with someone else. I've made a lot of sacrifices this past year to go into business for myself, and I'd like to know whether it was all worthwhile."

This statement was made by MacTavish to Nancy Carr, a local public accountant to whom he had turned for advice. Carr replied that the first thing she would have to do would be to try to draw up a set of financial statements for the MacTavish store that would summarize the results of the first year's operations to date.

a. To what extent does the decline in MacTavish's cash balance indicate the success or failure of his business operations during this period?

What other explanations can you offer for this change? How would you measure the degree of success achieved by the store during its first year?

b. If you were MacTavish, what kinds of information would you need before you could decide whether to stay in business or to sell out? How much of this information would you expect Carr to be able to supply?

c. Assuming that MacTavish decides to stay in business and decides that he needs a bank loan to provide him with additional cash, what kinds of information do you think the banker would have to have before approving the loan? Would this necessarily be the same as the information needed by Carr?

30. Data for Owners' Decisions. "We can't do business if you don't give me any more to go on than that," said Claude Montrone. After 15 years on the marketing staff of a large manufacturer of office supplies and equipment, Montrone was thinking of going into business for himself. A small inheritance, added to the accumulated savings of the past 15 years, gave him approximately $70,000 to invest. His older sister had indicated that she would be willing to invest up to $15,000 if she felt that the business venture was sound. Montrone also hoped to borrow from his bank additional amounts as needed. These amounts would be repaid during the first five years of the new venture. The manager of his bank had said that the bank would be happy to consider a loan application, but of course the actual granting of the loan would depend on the bank's appraisal of the ability of the business to generate enough funds to pay back the loan plus interest.

The statement quoted at the beginning of this case was directed to Paul Alain, owner of a store in Nutley, New Jersey. Alain owned several enterprises, and as he approached retirement age, he found it increasingly difficult to do an adequate management job in each one. Therefore, he had decided to sell his most important business, the Alain Stationery Store, and he was offering to sell the store's assets for $150,000. The buyer would also have to accept the obligation to pay the amounts owed to the store's suppliers (accounts payable), amounting to about $20,000.

Montrone thought he might be able to persuade Alain to spread some of the purchase price over a five-year period, but he doubted Alain would come down in his price as a result of bargaining. The purchaser would receive a five-year renewable lease on the store itself, the goods in inventory, and the amount owed to the store by some of its customers. If he bought the store, Montrone would have Alain's list of customers, and he saw no reason why he would not be able to keep the two store clerks who had been working in the store for more than five years.

Montrone had inspected the store and toured the area in and around Nutley to get some idea of the location of his customers and potential customers and the quality of the competition. He was generally familiar with the competitive situation in the area and felt that he could develop considerable business with small and medium-sized commercial and industrial companies in the area. Alain gave him the names of several of his larger customers but was unwilling to show Montrone any details on his business with these customers.

The only data Montrone had were the following, all supplied to him by Alain:

Year	Sales to Customers	Salary and Dividends Paid to Alain
1973	$155,000	$17,000
1974	150,000	17,000
1975	165,000	17,000
1976	195,000	20,000
1977	190,000	20,000
1978	180,000	19,000
1979	195,000	22,000
1980	210,000	25,000
1981	220,000	27,000
1982	205,000	26,000

a. What additional information would Montrone want to have before deciding whether to buy this business? How much of his information would you expect to find in the accounting records of Alain Stationers, Inc.?

b. If you were Montrone's banker, what information would you want to have to assist you in evaluating a loan request from Montrone? Would this information be any different from the information Montrone would want for deciding whether to buy the business?

c. To what extent would you expect accounting data to have entered into Alain's decision to sell the store and to set the price at $150,000? What kind of data should be looked for in making these decisions?

d. If you were Montrone, what services would you expect an independent accountant—that is, an accountant not in Alain's employ—to render in connection with this acquisition?

Chapter 2

Transactions Analysis

An accounting system is a model of the real resources and actual events in the life of a business enterprise. Once the model has been set up, each action the company takes is mirrored in the model as the system reflects the effects of this action on the company's resources.

The accountant's raw materials, in other words, are the company's **transactions,** the actions and events in which the business had a direct part. Accounting measurements of assets, liabilities, owners' equity, and net income or loss are derived indirectly, the net results of the company's accountants' analyses of the economic effects of hundreds, thousands, or millions of individual transactions. Our task in this chapter is to illustrate this process by examining how accountants might analyze the transactions arising in the formation and operation of a small retail store.

Transactions Analysis: An Illustration

In June 19x1, the sales manager of Ajax Manufacturing Company offered Charles Erskine the exclusive dealership rights in his community for the Ajax line of refrigerators and other electrical appliances. Erskine, then a salesman for a wholesale distributorship of a competing line of appliances, decided that he had a good chance of succeeding. He obtained a corporate charter in the name of Erskine Appliances, Inc., gave up his old job, and began to devote himself full-time to the new business.

Let's see how the accountant for this new business might have analyzed its first sets of transactions.

```
┌─────────────────────────────────────────────────────────────────┐
│                    TERMINOLOGY REMINDER                           │
│  Equities is the sum of liabilities and owners' equity—by         │
│  definition, the total of the equities is equal to total assets.  │
└─────────────────────────────────────────────────────────────────┘
```

Investment Transactions

On June 30, 19x1, Erskine and two of his friends purchased all the shares (certificates of ownership) of the new corporation, paying a total of $30,000 in cash ($20,000 from Erskine and $5,000 from each of the others). Their purchase of these shares made the three friends shareowners or *stockholders* in the corporation. They had a stockholders' meeting and elected themselves members of the *board of directors*. The first acts of the Erskine Appliances board were to appoint Erskine president of the company and to authorize him to open a bank account in the company's name. Erskine then deposited the $30,000 in this account.

The exchange of shares of the company's stock for $30,000 provided the company with its first asset, $30,000 in cash. In return, Erskine and his two friends obtained equity in the new company. Accounting systems measure owners' equity by the amount the owners invest in the business. The full analysis of this first transaction therefore can be written as follows:

Asset Increase	(1)	Owners' Equity Increase
Cash $30,000		Capital stock $30,000

This analysis shows what happened to the assets and the equities of the *business,* as something separate and distinct from the owners' other interests and activities. For example, suppose Erskine bought his shares of stock in the new corporation by taking $20,000 from his personal bank account. From his point of view, he simply decreased one asset (cash in his personal bank account) and established another (investment in Erskine Appliances, Inc.). His total wealth didn't change.

This illustrates an important point. Financial statements always relate to a specific set of resources. The set of resources being reported on constitutes the *accounting entity.* To avoid confusion, therefore, accountants have to begin with a clear definition of the accounting entity with which they are working. They can then exclude any transactions that don't affect this entity. For example, if Erskine were to take another $5,000 from his personal savings account to buy a new automobile for family use, that transaction wouldn't be reflected in the financial statements of Erskine Appliances, Inc.

The result of this investment transaction illustrates another point: *Every equity in one accounting entity is an asset in some other accounting*

EXHIBIT 2–1
Relationship between Accounting Entities

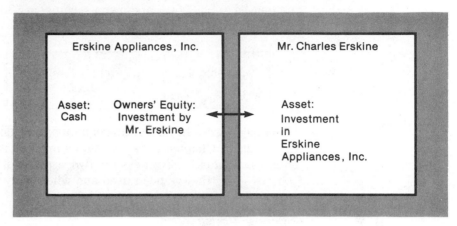

entity. This shows up clearly in Exhibit 2–1. An investor looking at Erskine as an accounting entity would regard his or her investment in the store as an asset. The same investor looking at the store as an accounting entity would see this same investment as a component of the owners' equity.

A Payment Transaction

Immediately after opening the company's checking account, Erskine signed the Ajax franchise agreement and entered into a two-year lease (starting July 1) on a store containing ample office, storage, and display space. The rent on the store was $1,200 a month, and he paid the rent for three months in advance by writing a check for $3,600 against the company's balance in its checking account. A payment of cash is known as a **disbursement.**

How did the payment to the landlord affect the company's assets, liabilities, and owners' equity? First, we know that the amount in the checking account was $3,600 less than it had been. This means that the transaction reduced the size of the asset, cash, by $3,600. Second, by paying the landlord $3,600, the company acquired the exclusive right to use the store for three months. This right, which accountants called **prepaid rent,** was an asset—the company owned it and clearly expected to use it to carry out operations that would benefit the business (otherwise, the company wouldn't have paid $3,600 for it). In other words, the transaction was analyzed as follows:

Asset Increase	(2)	Asset Decrease
Prepaid rent $3,600		Cash $3,600

In this transaction, one asset was exchanged for another with no change in the owners' equity. The transaction therefore left total assets unchanged at $30,000—and owners' equity at $30,000 as well—producing the following equation:

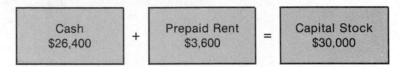

In other words, the accounting equation remained balanced, as it must. As we said in Chapter 1, the asset total must be equal to the total of the equities, because they measure two aspects of the same set of resources—how they've been used and where they've come from.

Purchase Transactions

Immediately after the lease was signed, Ajax Manufacturing Company delivered merchandise to Erskine Appliances, for which Erskine agreed to pay $13,000 within the next 30 days. By this transaction, the store acquired an asset, merchandise inventory, at a cost of $13,000. No asset was given up immediately, however, because Ajax agreed to wait 30 days for its money. In other words, Ajax in effect made a short-term investment in Erskine Appliances, and the company had its first creditor.

As a result of this transaction, Ajax had a claim against Erskine Appliances, and it regarded this claim as an asset. To Erskine Appliances, however, this same claim appeared as a liability because it would have to be settled by the payment of cash within 30 days. The store accepted this liability in exchange for the assets received from Ajax, and the transaction was viewed as follows:

Asset Increase	**(3)**	**Liability Increase**
Inventory. $13,000		Accounts payable $13,000

The accounting equation now has *two* equities. The $30,000 capital stock represents the *owners' equity* and the $13,000 accounts payable signifies the existence of liabilities or *creditor's equity*. Charles Erskine and the other stockholders are *owner* equityholders while Ajax Manufacturing is a *creditor* equityholder. Each of these parties is an equityholder because each represents a source of Erskine Appliances, Inc.'s assets. In the accounting equation, total assets equals total equities.

Next, Erskine bought secondhand equipment for the store, paying $9,000 in cash from the store's bank account. This transaction was just like the prepayment of rent: one asset, cash, was exchanged for another asset, equipment. The equipment was measured for accounting purposes just as the prepaid rent had been, at its cost—that is, by the amount of cash given up to acquire it. The transaction therefore was interpreted in the following way:

Asset Increase	(4)	Asset Decrease
Equipment $9,000		Cash $9,000

This left the total asset amount at $43,000, and the accounting equation remained in balance.

Erskine's final act on June 30 was to hire Karen Watson to work with him in the store at a salary of $1,400 a month. She was to start work the next morning. This had no effect on the June 30 assets and equities, however. Because Watson would be paid only if she actually showed up for work, the business owed her nothing on June 30. No asset was created because the company had no ownership right to Watson's future services.

Maintaining the Accounting Equation

Transactions analysis is governed by one basic rule—the accounting equation must always remain balanced. This means the accounting analysis of *each* transaction must also be balanced—that is, a change in one item must be accompanied by a change in one or more other items so that the total of the assets remains equal to the total of the liabilities and owners' equity.

These specifications are met by the table in Exhibit 2–2, which shows the effects of Erskine Appliances' first four transactions. Notice particularly that the accounting equation remained balanced after each transaction. The total of the amounts shown for the store's four assets at the end of June was $43,000, and the amounts shown for the liabilities and owners' equity added up to the same total. Of this, $30,000 had been supplied by the owners and $13,000 by a creditor, the supplier of merchandise.

EXHIBIT 2–2

ERSKINE APPLIANCES, INC.
Assets, Liabilities, and Owners' Equity
June 30, 19x1

	Cash	+	Inventory	+	Prepaid Rent	+	Equipment	=	Accounts Payable	+	Capital Stock
(1)	+$30,000										+$30,000
(2)	− 3,600			+	$3,600						
Bal.	26,400			+	3,600			=			30,000
(3)		+	$13,000						+$13,000		
Bal.	26,400	+	13,000	+	3,600			=	13,000	+	30,000
(4)	− 9,000					+	$9,000				
Bal.	$17,400	+	$13,000	+	$3,600	+	$9,000	=	$13,000	+	$30,000

Sale Transactions: Revenues and Expenses

Nothing the business did during June produced measurable income. When the store opened for business in July, however, Erskine hoped the events of that month would produce net income.

TERMINOLOGY REMINDER

1. The *revenues* of a period are the resources received by the business as a result of providing products or services to outsiders during that period.
2. The *expenses* of a period are the resources consumed by the company to generate the revenues of that period.

Erskine Appliances sold merchandise to its customers in July for $16,200. Of this, $2,800 was for cash, and the remaining $13,400 was sold on credit.[1] The merchandise covered by these sales had been part of the first shipment received from Ajax Manufacturing Company on June 30. The items sold had cost $10,600.

Notice what happened: The company exchanged one group of assets (merchandise) for another (cash and accounts receivable). As a result of these exchanges, total assets increased by $5,600, as follows:

Cash received	+$ 2,800
Receivables increased	+ 13,400
Inventory decreased	− 10,600
Assets increased	+$ 5,600

Since the liabilities went neither up nor down, the owners' equity increased by $5,600 as well.

We can see this more clearly if we restate the accounting equation in the following form:

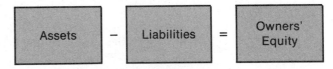

The quantity on the left side of this revised equation (assets minus liabilities) is sometimes called **net assets.** Obviously, anything that increases net assets also increases owners' equity, or vice versa. This is

---

[1] The terms **on credit** and **on account** are used interchangeably to mean that payment for goods or services purchased or sold is to be made at some date later than the date of the delivery of the goods or the performance of the service.

crucial. A business has net income only to the extent that it uses its resources to increase its net assets. If there is no increase in net assets, there is no income. And if the net assets increase, then the owners' equity also increases.

We are now able to summarize Erskine Appliances' July sale transactions in terms of the accounting equation:

Asset Increases		**(5)**	**Asset Decrease**	
Cash	$ 2,800		Inventory	$10,600
Accounts receivable ...	13,400		**Owners' Equity Increase**	
			Income	5,600
	$16,200			$16,200

This analysis measures the margin between sales revenue and the cost of the merchandise that was sold, usually referred to as the *gross margin.* It doesn't tell us, however, whether this was a large or a small percentage of revenue. To provide a basis for percentage calculations of this kind, accountants always divide the analysis of sale transactions into two parts, one dealing with the revenue and the other dealing with the expense (*cost of goods sold*). The analysis of Erskine Appliances' first set of sale transactions therefore showed the following:

Asset Increases		**(5a)**	**Owners' Equity Increase**	
Cash	$ 2,800		Revenues	$16,200
Accounts receivable ...	13,400			
	$16,200			

The items on the left are the assets the store received from its customers during the month; the item on the right shows that assets worth $16,200 were provided for the owners' benefit. Taken by themselves, in other words, these sale transactions increased the owners' equity by $16,200.

We know, of course, that owners' equity didn't increase by the full $16,200. To earn this revenue, Erskine had to deliver merchandise which had cost the store $10,600—this is the *second* aspect of Erskine's first sale transactions. Since this removed merchandise from the company's inventory, that asset decreased in size and so did the owners' equity. This analysis can be summarized as follows:

		(5b)	**Asset Decrease**	
Expenses	$10,600		Inventory	$10,600

Taken together, these two analyses show the same changes in assets and owners' equity as analysis (5); the only difference is that two amounts, +$16,200 and −$10,600, have been substituted for the +$5,600 in analysis (5).

Terminology: Cost and Expense

Two terms used in this illustration are often misused in practice, even by experienced analysts of financial statements. The terms are *cost* and *expense*. Cost is the broader term, and Exhibit 2–3 shows how costs flow

EXHIBIT 2–3
Distinction between Cost and Expense

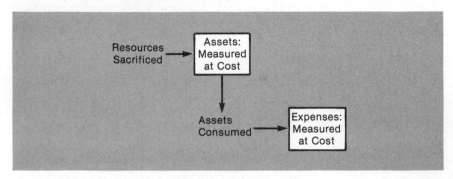

through the company. First, resources are used to acquire assets (for example, inventories). These assets are measured by the amount of resources sacrificed to obtain them (their cost). When the assets are used to produce revenue, their costs measure the company's expenses.

> **TERMINOLOGY**
>
> *Cost* is the amount of resources sacrificed to obtain something or achieve some objective.
> *Expense* is the cost of resources given up to obtain revenues of the current period; a cost subtracted from revenues on the income statement.

In other words, cost is the basis of measurement, and asset and expense are two stages in the life cycle of a cost. Nonmonetary assets such as inventory are resources the company still has, measured at their cost. Expenses such as the cost of goods sold are resources the company has used up in producing the revenues of a particular time period, measured at their cost. (In contrast, *monetary assets,* which enable the company to buy assets and pay debts, are ordinarily measured at their value to the company.)

The term *expense* should also be distinguished from the terms *expenditure, disbursement,* and *loss:*

1. An **expenditure** is any use of resources. Companies make expenditures when they acquire inventories, when they sell inventories, or when they use their employees' services. Some expenditures lead to expenses of the current period; others do not.
2. A **disbursement** is an immediate outlay of cash.
3. A **loss** is a reduction in an asset that does not have a related revenue benefit. Whereas use of office supplies is an expense, uninsured destruction of office supplies by fire would be classified as a loss on the income statement.

When a cost is incurred (that is, when resources are used for a purpose), the key question is: when is the company likely to reap the benefits resulting from the cost? If the benefits all materialize in the period in which the cost is incurred, the cost should be recognized as an expense immediately. If the benefits are expected to occur in the future, then the cost should be identified as an asset. The cost of merchandise purchased, for example, is treated as the cost of an asset until it generates revenue. At that time it becomes an expense, because it will then have produced all the benefit management can reasonably expect from it.

Other Operating Transactions

Subtracting the cost of goods sold from sales revenues *doesn't* yield the company's net income. Many other goods and services are consumed each period to create the period's revenues. Their costs also are expenses of the period.

For example, Erskine Appliances used Watson's services during the month of July at a cost of $1,400. One clear effect of this transaction was to create a liability—by using Watson's services, the store acquired a legal obligation to pay her for those services.

What else did this transaction (use of Watson's services) do? Its purpose was to help the company sell merchandise, create net income, and thereby increase owners' equity. Erskine saw no reason why Watson's work this month would benefit any period in the future. This means that the entire cost was a cost of generating revenues in July. Since revenues are increases in owners' equity, the costs incurred to produce them are reductions in owners' equity. In sum, using Watson's services had the following effects:

Owners' Equity Decrease	(6)	Liability Increase
Expenses $1,400		Salaries payable. $1,400

Another group of items had similar effects. Electricity, telephone, and other costs of operating the store and office during the month amounted to $700. Since these costs related to current operations, they were regarded as having been consumed in the creation of current revenues—in other words, treated as expense:

Owners' Equity Decrease	(7)	Liability Increase
Expenses.............. $700		Accounts payable....... $700

Once again, the use of these services reduced the owners' equity while increasing the company's liabilities.

CARDINAL RULES OF TRANSACTIONS ANALYSIS

1. The accounting equation must remain balanced at all times; the changes resulting from each transaction must also balance each other.
2. Expenses are recognized when resources are used up to create current revenues; *whether cash is paid for these resources at the time they are used, or earlier, or later has no bearing on the question of when the costs of the resources become expenses.*

Other Transactions

A number of other transactions took place during July. First, additional merchandise was purchased on credit at a cost of $6,400:

Asset Increase	(8)	Liability Increase
Inventory.............. $6,400		Accounts payable $6,400

The owners' equity was not affected by this transaction. Acquisition of the assets was financed temporarily by an increase in a liability.

Second, collections from customers on credit sales [see transaction (5a)] totaled $2,500. These were pure exchange-of-asset transactions and had no effect on the owners' equity. The analysis was:

Asset Increase	(9)	Asset Decrease
Cash $2,500		Accounts receivable $2,500

Third, the company paid Ajax Manufacturing Company, the electric company, the telephone company, and other suppliers $12,500, part of the money owed to them as a result of transactions (3) and (7). This is known as paying money "on account." In other words, an asset (cash) was surrendered to reduce some of the company's liabilities (accounts payable). These transactions were analyzed in the following terms:

Liability Decrease	(10)	Asset Decrease
Accounts payable..... $12,500		Cash............... $12,500

Fourth, the store paid Watson her salary. This had exactly the same effect as the payment to suppliers—an asset was used to reduce a liability:

Liability Decrease	**(11)**	**Asset Decrease**
Salaries payable $1,400		Cash $1,400

Payment of Watson's salary canceled the liability we identified in our analysis of transaction (6).

Finally, the company paid Charles Erskine an $1,800 salary for July. This was the amount he would have earned if he had continued working for his former employer. Payment of the salary reduced both the company's assets and its owners' equity by $1,800:

Owners' Equity Decrease	**(12)**	**Asset Decrease**
Expenses $1,800		Cash $1,800

Rent Expense

The data for each of the transaction analyses described above were found in documents that were prepared or received by Erskine Appliances as a matter of routine. Data for the analysis of merchandise purchases, for example, came from the bills or *invoices* received from the store's suppliers.

Not all the facts relevant to the preparation of periodic financial statements were in documents of this sort, however. For example, a portion of the asset *prepaid rent* was consumed during the month, but the landlord had no reason to send the company a document conveying that information. Erskine's accountant therefore had to be alert to make sure that the cost of the store rental for July wasn't overlooked.

Going back to the documents underlying transaction (2), the accountant found that the rental payment of $3,600 had covered a period of three months beginning July 1 at a cost of $1,200 a month. Since one month had gone by, one third of the total prepayment, or $1,200, had been consumed during July:

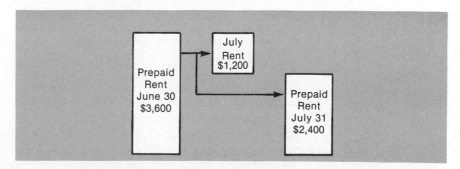

Whatever benefits were to be obtained from use of the store in July *were* obtained in July. Management couldn't reasonably expect to gain any substantial benefit in future periods as a result of the July rental cost. The $1,200 therefore was an operating expense of the month; both the assets and the owners' equity had been reduced by $1,200. This analysis can be summarized as follows:

Owners' Equity Decrease	(13)	Asset Decrease
Expenses $1,200		Prepaid rent $1,200

Depreciation Expense

One other resource was used in the business during July: the equipment the company had bought on June 30. The question was whether any of the $9,000 cost of this equipment had become an expense during the month.

This is a more complicated question than the one we answered in connection with the prepaid rent. As far as Erskine and Watson could see, the equipment was in just as good condition at the end of July as at the beginning. They knew it wouldn't last forever, however. It would have to be replaced sometime. Its benefits would be limited to the period between the date of purchase and the date of replacement. The costs, therefore, would be an expense of this long period. The problem was how much of this expense applied to the month of July and how much would apply to the other months that would benefit from the use of the equipment.

To resolve this issue, Erskine asked an equipment dealer how long he could expect to use the equipment in the store. They finally decided that five years (60 months) was a reasonable estimate and that 1/60 of the $9,000 cost ($150) should be considered a cost of producing revenue each month for 60 months.

This cost is called **depreciation.** The accountant defines depreciation as the portion of the cost of a plant asset, useful for two or more periods, that is attributable to the operations of each of those periods. Depreciation of the equipment in July had the following effects on the company's assets and equities:

Owners' Equity Decrease	(14)	Asset Decrease
Expenses $150		Equipment $150

The item on the right says that part of the asset (equipment) was used up during the month; the item on the left says this happened because the equipment was used to help produce revenues for the store during July—that is, the owners' equity was $150 less than if no equipment depreciation had taken place.

The process of transferring costs from asset to expense in this way is known as cost **amortization.** Amortization is necessary whenever an asset is expected to produce benefits in two or more periods and will be wholly or partially consumed as it does this. Under most circumstances, land doesn't depreciate because it makes its contribution without losing any of its power to contribute in the future. Equipment depreciates because it loses its usefulness sooner or later—usually due to physical deterioration and technological obsolescence. The cost of anything that depreciates must be amortized—that is, assigned in some systematic way to the operations of the period between the date the asset is acquired and the date it is disposed of.

Cash Dividends

When the owner of an individual proprietorship withdraws cash from the business for his or her own use, this action reduces both the company's assets and the owner's equity in the company. When the owners of a corporation withdraw cash for their own use, this withdrawal, called a **cash dividend,** reduces both the business's assets and the owners' equity.

Although all the data on the store's operations in July weren't yet available on the final day of the month, Erskine knew that sales volume in the first month had been far greater than he had expected. He was confident that the store had earned net income and therefore had operated profitably at this volume. Furthermore, the company had more than enough cash in the bank to meet the needs of the operating cycle in the next few months. To celebrate, the members of the board of directors declared a $300 cash dividend on July 31, payable on August 10, 19x1.[2] This transaction had the following effects:

Owners' Equity Decrease	(15)	Liability Increase	
Retained earnings	$300	Dividends payable	$300

This analysis reveals a peculiarity of the corporate form of organization. The act of declaring a cash dividend makes it a legal obligation of the corporation. The stockholders of Erskine Appliances, Inc., therefore became creditors of the corporation to the tune of $300. At the same time, their owners' equity in the corporation was reduced by $300.

The Financial Statements	After these transactions were analyzed, the assets, liabilities, and owners' equity of Erskine Appliances appeared as in Exhibit 2–4. The numbers in parentheses refer to the transaction numbers in the preceding

---

[2] In the United States, the power to declare dividends is vested in the board of directors. The directors of companies in which shares are owned by the general public ordinarily meet to declare dividends four times a year. In Europe and much of the rest of the world, dividends are declared once each year by a formal vote of the shareholders at the annual shareholders' meeting.

EXHIBIT 2–4

ERSKINE APPLIANCES, INC.
Assets, Liabilities, and Owners' Equity
For the Month Ended July 31, 19x1

Assets:

Cash

Bal. 7/1	17,400
(5a)	+ 2,800
(9)	+ 2,500
(10)	−12,500
(11)	− 1,400
(12)	− 1,800
Bal 7/31	7,000

Accounts Receivable

Bal. 7/1	—
(5a)	13,400
(9)	− 2,500
Bal. 7/31	10,900

Inventory

Bal. 7/1	13,000
(5b)	−10,600
(8)	+ 6,400
Bal. 7/31	8,800

Prepaid Rent

Bal. 7/1	3,600
(13)	−1,200
Bal. 7/31	2,400

Equipment

Bal. 7/1	9,000
(14)	− 150
Bal. 7/31	8,850

Liabilities:

Accounts Payable

Bal. 7/1	13,000
(7)	+ 700
(8)	+ 6,400
(10)	−12,500
Bal. 7/31	7,600

Salaries Payable

(6)	+1,400
(11)	−1,400
Bal. 7/31	—

Dividends Payable

Bal. 7/1	—
(15)	+300

Owners' Equity:

Capital Stock

Bal. 7/1	30,000

Income

Bal. 7/1		—
(5a)	Sales revenue	+16,200
(5b)	Cost of goods sold	−10,600
(6)	Salary expense	− 1,400
(7)	Miscellaneous expense	− 700
(12)	Salary expense	− 1,800
(13)	Rent expense	− 1,200
(14)	Depreciation expense	− 150
Bal. 7/31		350

Retained Earnings

Bal. 7/1	—
(15)	−300

discussion. The plus and minus signs beside the various owners' equity elements identify them as positive or negative components of the total owners' equity.

Erskine's accountant prepared two financial statements from the information in Exhibit 2–4: (1) an income statement for the month and (2) a balance sheet as of July 31, 19x1.

The Income Statement *for a period of time*

The company's accountant arranged the month's revenues and expenses in the income statement shown in Exhibit 2–5. Since the reve-

EXHIBIT 2–5

ERSKINE APPLIANCES, INC.
Income Statement
For the Month Ended July 31, 19x1

Sales revenues.		$16,200
Cost of goods sold		10,600
Gross margin		5,600
Operating expenses:		
Salaries	$3,200	
Rent.	1,200	
Depreciation	150	
Other	700	
Total operating expenses		5,250
Net income.		$ 350

nues exceeded the expenses by $350, this was the company's net income for the month. Net income is the accountant's measure of the increase in the owners' equity as a result of their ownership of Erskine Appliances during July 19x1. Owners expect that increases in their equity in a business will result in increases in their wealth—through the receipt of cash dividends or increases in the market value of their shares, or both.

Notice that the $300 dividend *isn't* shown as an expense. Net income measures the increase in the owners' equity resulting from revenue-producing activities. Dividends aren't contractual payments for revenue-producing services used. The declaration and distribution of a dividend merely reduces one of the owners' assets—their investment in the company—and increases another—first the amount receivable by the owners from the company and then cash in their possession when the dividend is actually paid.

The Balance Sheet *@ a point in time*

Exhibit 2–6 shows the balance sheet of Erskine Appliances, Inc., as of July 31, 19x1. Except for the $50 retained earnings, the numbers in this balance sheet come directly from Exhibit 2–4, which summarized the assets, liabilities, and owners' equity the company had at the beginning of the month and the effects of the month's transactions on these quantities.

EXHIBIT 2–6

ERSKINE APPLIANCES, INC.
Balance Sheet
As of July 31, 19x1

Assets

Current assets:

Cash	$ 7,000
Accounts receivable	10,900
Inventory	8,800
Prepaid rent	2,400
Total current assets	29,100
Equipment	8,850
Total assets	$37,950

Liabilities and Owners' Equity

Current liabilities

Accounts payable	$ 7,600
Dividends payable	300
Total current liabilities	7,900

Owners' equity:

Capital stock	30,000
Retained earnings	50
Total owners' equity	30,050
Total liabilities and owners' equity	$37,950

Actually, the $50 retained earnings amount also comes from Exhibit 2–4. It has to, because that exhibit shows *all* the company's recognized assets, liabilities, and owners' equity amounts as well as *all* the effects of the July transactions. Retained earnings at the end of the month therefore has to be there somewhere.

Remember from Chapter 1 that retained earnings is the accountants' name for the *cumulative* difference between net income and the amount of dividends declared since the company was formed. Since July was Erskine's first month of operations, it began the month with no net income and no dividend history—that is, the cumulative amount of retained earnings was zero at the beginning of July. This means that the retained earnings at the end of July had to be the difference between net income and dividends declared in July only. The $300 dividend was shown as a negative amount in the Retained Earnings category in Exhibit 2–4; by combining this with the $350 from the Income category just above it in the exhibit, Erskine's accountant was able to determine that retained earnings amounted to $50 at the end of the month.

These relationships are summarized in the following table:

Retained earnings, July 1, 19x1.	$ 0
Add: Net income for the month.	350
Less: Dividends declared during the month	(300)
Retained earnings, July 31, 19x1.	$ 50

If income and dividends for the period are shown as separate items in a listing such as the one in Exhibit 2–4, the amount shown for retained earnings in that list will represent the retained earnings at the *beginning* of the period.

Omissions from Financial Statements

As we have already said, a company's balance sheet doesn't pretend to show how much the company is worth, nor does the income statement profess to tell how much the value of the owners' equity has increased during the period. What we haven't yet mentioned is that the financial statements may not even identify some aspects of wealth or economic performance which in some cases may be even more important than the items that are reported. In a high-technology company, for example, the most important asset may be the talent and loyalty of the professional staff, but this asset never appears on a conventional balance sheet.

Charles Erskine became especially aware of some of these omissions when he planned to approach a local bank for a loan, because he was anxious that the balance sheet present every justifiable evidence of financial strength. He was concerned, for example, because the balance sheet failed to list the three resources he considered to be the company's most valuable assets: the dealership franchise, his customer following in the trade, and the lease on the store which he had obtained on very favorable terms.

The franchise and customer loyalty are our first examples of intangible assets, which enable a business to earn higher income than its investment in tangible assets would normally produce. There is no question that items such as these are important. Erskine certainly should have emphasized them in his discussions with the bank's lending officers. Accountants exclude them from the balance sheet, however, because they can't verify the evidence on which measurements of these quantities as assets would have to be based. This kind of asset appears on the balance sheet only if the company *buys* a franchise or *buys* access to a group of customers. In such cases, the asset is measured at its cost because the purchase price can be verified fairly easily.

The financial statements also ignored the two-year lease on the store. This lease gave Erskine Appliances the right to use the store building for two years at a fixed rental; it also committed the company to a series of fixed payments to the landlord. This agreement was an important factor: favorable if property values went up and unfavorable if they went down. Even so, the accounting profession doesn't regard the signing of this sort of lease as an exchange of resources that should be recognized in a balance sheet. The leased property enters the accounting system only as the property is used or as payments are made.

Summary

Accounting measures of income and financial position are based on summaries of the accountant's analyses of individual transactions. The analysis of a transaction consists of identifying its effects on the company's assets, liabilities, and owners' equity. Each transaction affects at least two kinds of assets, liabilities, or owners' equity. For each transaction, the sum of the asset changes must equal the sum of the changes in liabilities and owners' equity, as in the list in Exhibit 2–7. As a result, the accounting equation always remains balanced.

EXHIBIT 2–7
Balanced Transactions Analyses

An asset increases, another asset decreases.
An asset increases, a liability increases.
An asset increases, owners' equity increases.
An asset decreases, a liability decreases.
An asset decreases, owners' equity decreases.
A liability increases, another liability decreases.
A liability increases, owners' equity decreases.
A liability decreases, owners' equity increases.
One part of owners' equity increases, another part decreases.

The income statement and balance sheet don't necessarily reflect all the available information about the financial status and performance of the business enterprise because accountants are generally unwilling to use estimates that can't be verified readily. This means that both management and outsiders must be alert, ready to recognize situations in which information on unmeasured quantities is vital to an understanding of the company and its operations.

Key Terms

Amortization
Cost of goods sold
Depreciation
Disbursement
Expenditure
Gross margin

Loss
Net assets
On account
Prepaid rent
Transaction

STUDY AID: THE TRANSACTIONS EQUATION

Solutions to many problems in transactions analysis require a thorough understanding of the relationship we refer to as the transactions equation:

| Ending Balance | = | Beginning Balance | + | Additions during the Period | − | Subtractions during the Period |

This equation applies to any statement component. Any of the four elements in this equation can be calculated if the other three are known.

Independent Study Problems (Solutions in Appendix B)

1. Income, Dividends, and Balance Sheet Changes. Two sisters formed a corporation on January 1, 19x1, each of them investing $10,000 and receiving 1,000 shares of the corporation's capital stock in exchange. The corporation issued no more shares of capital stock during the next three years, and on January 1, 19x4, the company had total assets of $120,000 and total liabilities of $64,000.

During 19x4, the corporation issued 100 additional shares of its capital stock to a friend of the two sisters, receiving in exchange $6,000 in cash. Cash dividends amounting to $24,000 were declared and paid during the year. On December 31, 19x4, the company had assets amounting to $140,000 and liabilities of $68,000.

a. Calculate net income for 19x4.
b. Present the owners' equity section of the company's balance sheet on December 31, 19x4.

2. Transactions Equation. Each of the following describes an asset or liability of Egbert Company, including certain transactions during a recent year:

1. Accounts receivable: beginning balance, $100; sales on account, $500; ending balance, $80.

2. Accounts payable: beginning balance, $50; payments to suppliers, $250; ending balance, $40.
3. Wages payable: beginning balance, $20; wages earned by employees, $300; wages paid to employees, $295.
4. Merchandise inventory: ending balance, $90; cost of goods purchased, $240; cost of goods sold, $265.
5. Prepaid rent: beginning balance, $45; ending balance, $60; rent paid, $130.

For each of these, use the transactions equation to calculate the missing amount. Explain in a word or brief phrase what each of these missing amounts represents.

3. Transactions Analysis; Income Statement. A store had the following transactions in 19x1:

1. It bought merchandise on account for $1 million.
2. It sold merchandise on account for $1.5 million.
3. It used the services of its employees; these employees earned salaries totaling $300,000 by providing these services.
4. It received invoices totaling $100,000 from the electric company, the telephone company, and other outside companies for services used during 19x1.
5. It paid $1,050,000 to merchandise suppliers, utility companies, and other outside service companies.
6. It paid its employees $280,000.
7. It collected $1.6 million in cash from its customers.
8. It bought display cabinets and other store equipment for $40,000, paying $25,000 in cash and promising to pay the balance early in 19x2.
9. It determined that the cost of the merchandise sold (item 2) was $940,000.
10. It estimated that depreciation of store fixtures and equipment during the year amounted to $18,000.
11. It declared cash dividends to its stockholders amounting to $10,000.
12. It paid previously declared cash dividends of $7,500 to its stockholders.

a. Identify the effects of each of these transactions and other events on the company's assets, liabilities, and owners' equity. For each change, state both the amount in dollars and the direction of the change (+ or −).
b. Prepare an income statement for the year.

4. Analyzing Transactions. A furniture store opened for business on January 1, 19x1. The store's transactions in 19x3, its third year of operations, included the following, among others:

1. The company purchased office furniture on July 1, 19x3, $4,200. The supplier was paid on October 1, 19x3. Office furniture in this company has a 12-year life.
2. Management hired a sales representative on October 1 at a salary of $1,500 a month. The representative started work immediately and remained in the company's employ until January 31, 19x4. Each sales representative's salary is paid on the 15th of each month, covering work done in the preceding month. All salary payments due in 19x3 were made on the specified dates.
3. The company sold merchandise on account for $300,000. This merchandise had been purchased and placed in inventory in 19x2. It had cost $220,000 at that time.
4. The company paid a supplier $24,000 for merchandise received in 19x2.
5. The company paid $22,500 on November 1, 19x3, for store rental covering the period from October 1, 19x3, through March 31, 19x4.

a. How much expense should have been recognized in the store's 19x3 income statements as a result of each of these transactions in 19x3?
b. Identify the effects of each of these transactions on the store's assets, liabilities, and owners' equity in 19x3.

5. Transactions Analysis; Financial Statements. Handyman Tool Shop, Inc. is an incorporated retailer of hardware supplies. Its balance sheet on December 31, 19x1, showed the following:

HANDYMAN TOOL SHOP, INC.
Balance Sheet
December 31, 19x1

Assets		Liabilities and Owners' Equity		
Current assets:		Current liabilities:		
Cash	$ 12,510	Accounts payable		$ 35,180
Accounts receivable	23,060	Salaries payable		1,400
Merchandise inventory	67,200	Total current		
Total current assets	102,770	liabilities		36,580
Equipment	19,020	Owners' equity:		
		Capital stock	$50,000	
		Retained earnings	35,210	
		Total owners' equity		85,210
		Total liabilities and		
Total assets	$121,790	owners' equity		$121,790

The store's transactions for the year 19x2 are summarized in the following items:

1. Sold merchandise on account at a total price of $301,000. The cost of the merchandise was $181,000.

2. Collected $296,000 in cash from customers.
3. Purchased merchandise from suppliers on account at a cost of $246,300.
4. Bought a secondhand delivery truck on account, $3,800.
5. Occupied the store for the entire year at a monthly rental of $1,250.
6. Used telephone, electricity, and other miscellaneous services costing $21,000.
7. Made cash salary payments to employees, $44,400. The company owed nothing to its employees at the end of 19x2.
8. Made other cash payments totaling $248,850, as follows:
   To suppliers of merchandise, $209,000.
   To seller of secondhand delivery truck, $3,800.
   To landlord for use of the store, $13,750.
   To suppliers of electricity and other miscellaneous services, $22,300.
9. Calculated the year's depreciation on the equipment, $4,800.
10. Issued 1,000 additional shares of capital stock to local investors in exchange for $60,000 in cash.
11. Declared a cash dividend of $25,000, to be paid to shareowners on January 20, 19x3.

a. Set up a table of the company's assets, liabilities, and owners' equity on January 1, 19x2, using the format of Exhibit 2–4.
b. Identify the effects of each of the year's transactions on the company's assets, liabilities, and owners' equity, and insert these in the table you set up in part a. Be sure to identify the direction of each change (+ or −).
c. Prepare an income statement for the year and a balance sheet as of December 31, 19x2.

Exercises and Problems

6. Measuring Expense.   Andrew Jenkins worked 100 hours in the Acme Hardware Store during June. He was paid $450 during July for these services. How much of this amount was an expense of the store in June? How much was an expense in July? How much was income to Jenkins in June, and how much in July? Explain.

7. Concepts of Wealth and Income.   Eugene and Janet Bronson own and operate a farm. Their title to the land includes the rights to any mineral wealth it contains. They have just discovered that a rich oil field recently found nearby extends far into their property. Drilling wells and selling the oil from these wells will be very worthwhile.

a. Did the discovery lead to an immediate increase in the known assets of this farm? Is it likely that the farm's market value increased as a result of the discovery? Did the discovery add to the Bronsons' income of the period in which the discovery was made?

b. Would the accountant report an immediate increase in assets on the farm's balance sheet or on the income statement for the period in which the discovery was made?

8. Analyzing a Sales Transaction. Merchandise costing $4,000 is sold from inventory, on account, for $5,200.

a. Analyze the effects of this transaction on the assets, liabilities, and owners' equity.

b. What expenses connected with this transaction are known at the time the sale takes place? What expenses are not known?

c. How and when will the profit or loss resulting from this transaction be determined?

9. Accounting Equation. Analyze each of the following December, 19x4, events to determine its effect on the accounting equation.

a. Bought inventory on account for $4,000.
b. Paid rent in advance, $1,800.
c. Salaries earned and paid, $975.
d. Issued new capital stock for $10,000 cash.
e. Sold $600 inventory for $900 cash.
f. One third of the prepaid rent expired.
g. Agreed to commit $1,500 to an advertising campaign next month.
h. Paid an outstanding bank loan, $500.
i. Declared and paid a cash dividend, $400.
j. Depreciation on machinery during December, $375.

Use a matrix consisting of 10 rows (*a* through *j*) and the following four columns: *Assets, Liabilities, Capital Stock,* and *Retained Earnings.* In each of the 40 cells, place the appropriate letter as follows: I = increase, D = decrease, N = no effect.

10. Identifying Income Statement Elements; Balance Sheets. The following list includes all the items that should appear on the income statement for Omega Stores for the year 19x1, together with all the necessary information to prepare balance sheets as of the beginning and the end of the year:

Accounts payable, beginning of year.	70
Accounts payable, end of year	90
Accounts receivable, beginning of year.	200
Accounts receivable, end of year	210
Cash on hand, beginning of year.	70
Cash on hand, end of year	80

Cost of merchandise purchased during 19x1........	630
Cost of merchandise sold during 19x1............	600
Dividends declared and paid to owners in 19x1.....	20
Merchandise inventory, beginning of year.........	120
Merchandise inventory, end of year..............	?
Miscellaneous expenses during 19x1.............	60
Owners' equity, beginning of year..............	320
Owners' equity, end of year...................	?
Rent expense for 19x1.........................	40
Salaries and wages expense for 19x1.............	110
Sales revenues for 19x1........................	1,000
Tax expense for 19x1..........................	140

a. Using the relevant data from this list, prepare an income statement for the year 19x1.

b. Prepare balance sheets as of January 1 and December 31, 19x1.

11. Supplying Missing Information. From the following financial data for four businesses (I, II, III, and IV), determine the amount of each item missing:

	I	II	III	IV
Assets, 1/1/x1	$ 60,000	$100,000	$ 80,000	$　J
Liabilities, 1/1/x1..........	25,000	D	20,000	100,000
Assets, 12/31/x1	70,000	E	G	600,000
Liabilities, 12/31/x1........	26,000	29,000	16,000	K
Owners' equity, 1/1/x1.....	A	70,000	H	400,000
Owners' equity, 12/31/x1 ...	B	74,000	I	420,000
Revenues, 19x1...........	350,000	500,000	400,000	L
Expenses, 19x1	337,000	F	380,000	1,500,000
Dividends declared, 19x1...	C	5,000	8,000	15,000

12. Preparing Financial Statements from Account Balances. The financial records of Fox Automobile Repair Shop, Inc., showed the following amounts on December 31, 19x6:

Accounts payable.................	$ 22,100
Accounts receivable..............	41,000
Buildings.......................	120,000
Capital stock....................	50,000
Cash...........................	6,400
Dividends declared during 19x6.....	30,000
Equipment......................	121,300
General expenses.................	31,400
Inventory of repair parts	42,500
Repair parts used during 19x6......	35,600
Retained earnings	?
Revenues.......................	289,400
Wages expense	150,900
Wages payable..................	3,800

a. Prepare an income statement for 19x6 and a balance sheet as of December 31, 19x6.

    b. Explain why the amounts shown for wages expense and wages payable aren't identical.

    c. The stockholders invested no money in the business during 19x6. Calculate their equity in the business on January 1, 19x6 (the beginning of the year).

13. Transactions Analysis. Listed here are Oliver Company's balance sheet amounts at seven successive times. Identify the reason for the change from each amount to its successor.

	A	B	C	D	E	F	G
Assets:							
Cash	$ 10	$ 10	$ 25	$ 25	$ 37	$ 37	$ 15
Receivables.	20	20	43	43	31	31	31
Inventory	30	44	23	23	23	23	23
Machinery	40	40	40	45	45	42	42
Total	$100	$114	$131	$136	$136	$133	$111
Equities:							
Payables	$ 50	$ 64	$ 64	$ 64	$ 64	$ 75	$ 53
Capital stock.	20	20	20	25	25	25	25
Retained earnings . . .	30	30	47	47	47	33	33
Total	$100	$114	$131	$136	$136	$133	$111

14. Correcting Errors in Financial Statements. Cronin Corporation was founded at the end of 19x3 by a group of investors who invested a total of $100,000 in the business. During 19x4, the company engaged in its first revenue-producing activities. At the end of the year, the company's payroll clerk prepared the following financial statements:

CRONIN CORPORATION
Income Statement
For the Year Ended December 31, 19x4

Collections from customers	$229,500	
Refund from income tax bureau	17,800	
Proceeds from six-month bank loan	20,000	
Total revenues		$267,300
Salary payments	49,700	
Utility payments	8,500	
Cash paid for merchandise	89,800	
Legal fees paid	2,800	
Rent, insurance, and advertising payments	22,400	
Cash dividends	55,000	
Income taxes paid	28,500	
Total expenses		256,700
Net income		$ 10,600

CRONIN CORPORATION
Balance Sheet
As of December 31, 19x4

Cash	$110,600	Capital stock............	$100,000
		Retained earnings	10,600
Total assets	$110,600	Total equities..........	$110,600

Upon inquiry from a bank loan officer, the company's president acknowledged that some information may have been overlooked, as follows:

1. Although the company owed its suppliers $15,600 on December 31, 19x4, it was owed $43,700 by its customers on that date.
2. The payroll clerk had failed to record the purchase of land for $40,500 cash.
3. At year-end, the cost of the merchandise on hand was $20,700, and the appraised value of the land was $49,500.
4. At the close of the year, a $700 electric company bill hadn't been paid, and Cronin's employees were owed $3,100 for work they had performed in 19x4.
5. No income taxes remained unpaid at the end of 19x4.

In the light of this additional information, prepare Cronin Corporation's 19x4 income statement and its end-of-year balance sheet.

15. Identifying Transactions. McIntyre Company is engaged in wholesaling. The following are just a few of the many events that took place in 19x1:

1. A forklift truck was bought from Warehouse Machinery Company; payment was deferred until 19x2, but the truck was delivered and placed in service in one of McIntyre's warehouses in December 19x1.
2. A bookkeeper was hired, employment to begin on January 2, 19x2. One month's salary was paid in December 19x1 to help the bookkeeper pay off some outstanding personal debts before starting on the new job; this advance was to be deducted in installments from the bookkeeper's salary in 19x2.
3. The market value of the owners' equity in this company increased by 20 percent in 19x1.
4. Completion of a highway interchange in 19x1 doubled the market value of a parcel of land owned by the company.
5. A routine audit revealed that the company's cash balance at the end of 19x1 was $250,000 less than the amount shown in the company's records and that no insurance was carried against cash shortages of this kind.

6. An office machine was leased from Rothwell Service Company in December 19x1; payments were to be made annually for five years, and the first payment was made in January 19x2. At the end of the five-year lease period, the machine was to be returned to Rothwell.
7. One of McIntyre's research engineers was finally able to solve a difficult repackaging problem after several weeks of work in 19x1, paid for by McIntyre. McIntyre patented the solution in 19x1 and prepared to offer it commercially in exchange for annual royalty payments. A substantial number of royalty agreements were anticipated, but none was signed in 19x1.

Using what you have already learned about accounting, together with a dash of logic and a sprinkle of imagination, identify the immediate effect, if any, of each of these events on the accountant's measurements of the company's assets, liabilities, and owners' equity in 19x1. If the event had no effect, explain why.

16. Transactions Analysis. The following events took place in Appliance Repair Corporation in August 19x1:

1. Performed services and billed the customer for $700.
2. Ordered an electric typewriter for the office, to be delivered in October 19x1, price $920 to be paid at delivery.
3. Purchased and paid for a two-year supply of office stationery, price $380.
4. Hired a new secretary on August 31 at a salary of $1,500 a month. The secretary started work on September 1, 19x1.
5. Paid a clerk a $1,000 salary for work performed in the company's office in July 19x1.
6. Paid the owner's salary for the month of August 19x1, $2,500. (The business operated as a corporation, and the owner worked full-time as its president.)
7. Collected cash from a customer, $1,800, for services rendered in June 19x1.
8. Calculated the depreciation of store equipment in August 19x1, $360.

All transactions of previous months were analyzed correctly and recorded properly; no analyses of August 19x1 transactions have been made.

Indicate the effects, if any, of each of the foregoing events on the assets, liabilities, and owners' equity of this business. (Be sure to state whether the effect in each case was an increase or a decrease.)

17. Supplying Missing Data. You have the following balance sheets for last year for a small retail store:

	January 1	December 31
Cash	$ 10	$ 14
Accounts receivable from customers	20	25
Merchandise inventory	30	32
Current assets...........................	60	71
Plant and equipment......................	50	52
Total assets	$110	$123
Accounts payable to suppliers of merchandise...	$ 15	$ 22
Dividends payable	—	2
Current liabilities	15	24
Owners' equity:		
Capital stock..............................	60	60
Retained earnings	35	39
Total liabilities and owners' equity	$110	$123

You are given the following additional data on the year's transactions:

1. Collections from customers, $145.
2. Payments to suppliers of merchandise, $95.
3. Purchases of equipment (all paid in cash), $6.
4. Dividends declared, $5.
5. Selling and administrative expenses, $37.
6. Plant and equipment retired or sold, none.
7. The only expenses last year were the cost of merchandise sold, depreciation, and selling and administrative expenses.

a. Calculate sales revenues for the year.
b. Calculate the cost of merchandise sold during the year.
c. Calculate depreciation for the year.
d. Calculate net income for the year.

18. Supplying Missing Information. The owners of M Wholesale Company prepared the following table of their company's assets and liabilities:

	December 31	
	19x8	19x9
Cash..................................	$ 2,000	$ 4,200
Merchandise inventory...................	12,300	15,000
Accounts receivable....................	7,000	5,000
Accounts payable for merchandise	8,000	10,100
Furniture and fixtures (net after deduction of accumulated depreciation)	3,000	2,600

Expenses for 19x9 consisted of the cost of goods sold, depreciation, and miscellaneous selling and administrative expenses. The goods and services classified as miscellaneous selling and administrative expenses were all bought and paid for in cash during 19x9.

A further analysis of the company's checkbook for 19x9 shows two more groups of transactions: (1) deposits of all amounts received from customers during the year, $50,000, and (2) payments to suppliers for merchandise amounting to $33,000. No other receipts or payments occurred during 19x9.

For 19x9, what were the:

a. Sales revenues?

b. Purchases of merchandise?

c. Cost of merchandise sold?

d. Other expenses?

e. Net income?

f. Owners' equity, 12/31/x8?

g. Owners' equity, 12/31/x9?

19. Transactions Analysis. Grafton Company is organized as a corporation. The following transactions took place during 19x2. These transactions are completely independent and do not represent all the year's transactions of this company.

1. Purchase of merchandise on account, placed in inventory, $450.
2. Payment to supplier for merchandise received and placed in inventory in 19x1, $884. The purchase was recorded correctly in 19x1.
3. Issue of additional shares of capital stock to T. O. Pitt, principal stockholder, in exchange for $8,500 cash.
4. One month's salary earned by T. O. Pitt for his services as company president during December 19x2, $2,000, paid in cash on December 31.
5. Sale of merchandise from inventory on credit: sale price $1,200, cost $920.
6. Store clerks' wages earned during December 19x2, but not paid before the end of the month, $2,800.
7. Receipt of bill for electricity used in store and office during 19x2, $87.
8. Collection of $1,106 on accounts receivable.
9. Portion of store rent prepaid in 19x1 which applied to Grafton's use of the store in 19x2, $3,000.

Identify the effects of each of these transactions on the company's assets, liabilities, and owners' equity in 19x2. Be sure to indicate whether each effect is an increase or a decrease.

20. Transactions Analysis. Gee Corporation operates a retail business. The company engaged in the following transactions, among others, in 19x2. Each transaction was completely independent of the others in this list.

1. Purchase of merchandise on an extended-payment contract, $2,100. The merchandise was placed in inventory, one third of the price was paid at the time of purchase, and the note for the remainder was to be paid in installments beginning in 19x3.
2. Payment of $15,000 to suppliers of merchandise on account.
3. Payment of $600 for insurance coverage for the year 19x2.
4. Sale of merchandise from inventory, $8,300 for cash and $13,700 on account; cost of merchandise sold, $16,400.
5. Purchase of land and building on December 31, 19x2, $22,000 for the land and $140,000 for the building; $80,000 was paid in cash and the remainder was financed by borrowing from a bank, giving in exchange a six–year note payable.
6. Collection of $18,300 on customers' accounts.
7. Use of office supplies costing $800 from the office supplies inventory.
8. Depreciation of delivery equipment, $1,550.
9. Accountant's fee for services rendered in 19x2, $700, to be paid in 19x3.
10. Declaration and payment in cash of cash dividends to owners of the company's capital stock, $5,600.

Identify the effects of each of these transactions on the company's assets, liabilities, and owners' equity in 19x2. Be sure to indicate whether each effect was an increase or a decrease.

21. Transactions Analysis; Financial Statements. S&R Auto Parts Company operates an automobile supplies store. It had the following assets, liabilities, and owners' equity on January 1, 19x1:

Cash	$ 3,200	Accounts payable	$ 3,700
Accounts receivable	1,400	Bank loan payable	10,000
Inventory	22,000	Capital stock	11,000
Prepaid rent	800	Retained earnings	4,700
Equipment	2,000		
Total	$29,400	Total	$29,400

The company had the following transactions in January 19x1:

1. Bought merchandise on account, $3,300, and placed it in inventory.
2. Sold merchandise from inventory: price to customers, $8,100 cash and $2,300 on account.
3. Collected $850 cash from customers, on account.
4. Used store clerks' services costing $1,840.
5. Made payments, as follows:
    To store clerks, $1,840.
    To merchandise suppliers, on account, $3,500.
    To landlord, for rent for February, March, and April 19x1, $2,400.

> To owner of a majority of the capital shares as a salary for services as
> president of the corporation, $1,500.
> To electric and telephone companies for services in January, $200.
> To local newspaper for advertising space used in January, $150.

6. Calculated the cost of the merchandise sold from inventory in January, $4,200.
7. Calculated the month's depreciation on the equipment, $50.
8. Paid the bank $100 for interest on the bank loan payable, covering the period from January 1 to January 31, 19x1.
9. Declared dividends of $1,000 to be paid in cash to stockholders on February 10, 19x1.

a. For each transaction or other event, identify the effects on the company's assets, liabilities, and owners' equity in January 19x1, using the format illustrated in Exhibit 2–2. (Add a column headed "Retained Earnings" to receive elements of net income and dividends.)
b. Prepare an income statement for the month of January 19x1 and a balance sheet as of January 31, 19x1, distinguishing between current and noncurrent items in the balance sheet. (The bank loan and prepayment should be classified as current items.)
c. C. Rowe, the company's president and majority stockholder, claims that the change in the cash balance each month is a better measure of the company's income or loss than the net income or loss you calculated as part of your answer to part b. Using numbers from this problem, prepare an analysis of this argument.

22. Transactions Analysis; Financial Statements.   On January 1, 19x1, Jane Doe formed Doe Stores, Inc., a merchandising company. This company had the following transactions during its first month:

1. Ms. Doe and a group of her friends made a cash investment of $90,000 in the business, receiving 10,000 shares of capital stock in exchange.
2. Land, $30,000, a building, $60,000, and equipment, $24,000, were purchased on January 1. Cash in the amount of $89,000 was paid for these items. The balance was owed on a five-year note payable.
3. Merchandise costing $40,000 was purchased on credit and placed in inventory.
4. Merchandise costing $30,000 was sold from inventory for $50,000. Of this latter amount, $21,000 was for cash and the balance was sold on credit.
5. Salaries and wages totaled $13,500 for the month. This entire amount was paid in cash.
6. Miscellaneous expenses amounted to $4,200. Of this amount, $3,300 was paid in cash; the rest was paid in February.
7. The depreciation for the month was $150 on the building and $200 on the equipment.

8. The company paid $200, covering interest charges on the note payable for the month of January.

a. Analyze each of Doe Stores' transactions in January, identifying their effects on the following assets, liabilities, and owners' equity of the company, using the format illustrated in Exhibit 2–2.

Cash	Equipment
Accounts receivable	Accounts payable
Inventory	Notes and interest payable
Land	Capital stock
Buildings	Retained earnings

Label each of these to identify it as an asset (*A*), a liability (*L*), or an owners' equity (*OE*).

b. Prepare an income statement for the month.
c. Prepare a balance sheet as of January 31.

23. Transactions Analysis; Financial Statements. Westbridge, Inc., buys and sells iron pipe. On January 1, the business had the following assets, liabilities, and owners' equity:

Cash, $3,000; receivables, $50,000; inventories, $136,000; store equipment, $74,800; accounts payable, $33,800; wages payable, $0; taxes payable, $9,300; note payable, $0; capital stock, $150,000; retained earnings, $70,700.

The following transactions took place in January:

1. Merchandise costing $78,800 was purchased on account and placed in inventory.
2. Merchandise with a cost of $82,100 was taken from inventory and sold on account for $106,300.
3. The company's employees earned salaries totaling $5,000 by working for the company in January.
4. The costs of telephone service, electricity, and other supporting services provided by outside suppliers and bought on account amounted to $11,200.
5. Tax expense applicable to the month of January was estimated to be $2,000, but no taxes were paid during the month.
6. Customers paid bills amounting to $125,100.
7. Westbridge paid $5,000 to its employees, $109,700 to its suppliers of merchandise, and $9,700 to suppliers of supporting services.
8. Depreciation of store equipment amounted to $300.
9. Westbridge purchased and received new store equipment costing $20,000; payment for this equipment was to be made in March.
10. On January 31, Westbridge borrowed $6,500 from a bank and deposited this amount in the company's bank account. The company's president signed a note promising to repay this amount to the bank at the end of April.

a. List the January 1 assets, liabilities, and owners' equity, using the format illustrated in Exhibit 2–2. Then show the financial effects of the month's transactions, using only the 10 categories listed at the beginning of this problem.

b. Prepare an income statement for the month of January and a balance sheet as of January 31.

24. Transactions and Financial Statements. On December 31, Grace Harvey completed her first year as owner-manager of Harvey's Sportswear, Inc. The following data summarize the first year's transactions:

1. Harvey invested $70,000 cash in the business, receiving 10,000 shares of the company's capital stock in exchange.
2. In January, the company borrowed $30,000 cash from a bank. The loan was to be repaid within 18 months.
3. In January, the company secured a five-year lease on shop space, with rental charges to be based on sales volume in the store. Rent for the 12 months that ended on December 31 amounted to $11,460, paid entirely in cash.
4. The company bought furniture and store equipment for $37,500 cash.
5. The company bought merchandise on credit for $142,925.
6. During the year, the company sold some of the merchandise described in item 5. The cost of the merchandise sold was $108,450 and its selling price totaled $161,000, of which $85,500 was cash and $75,500 was on credit.
7. Grace Harvey received a salary of $30,000 cash from the company. The company also paid $3,210 as wages to part-time employees, and paid $10,110 cash for other goods and services used in running the business during the year.
8. The company returned defective merchandise to a supplier for full credit, $4,405.
9. Harvey's Sportswear, Inc., collected $22,130 of the amounts owed it by customers who had bought merchandise on credit.
10. The company made payments to suppliers on account, $107,600.
11. A shoplifter stole merchandise that had cost $410.
12. On December 31, the company repaid $1,500 of the amount it had borrowed from the bank (item 2), plus an additional $3,600 representing one year's interest on the amount borrowed.
13. Harvey decided to depreciate the cost of the furniture and equipment evenly over a five-year period. She didn't believe that any salvage value would be left at the end of that time.

a. Analyze the effects of the above transactions on the assets, liabilities, and owners' equity of Harvey's Sportswear, Inc., using the format illustrated in Exhibit 2–2, including a "Retained Earnings" column for net income and dividend items.

b. Prepare an income statement for the year and a year-end balance sheet.

c. What further information would you want to have before you could tell Harvey whether her business venture was a success from a financial viewpoint?

25. Transactions and Financial Statements.   In January, Alan Bucknell formed Bucknell Corporation to own and operate a new retail grocery store. The following list summarizes the transactions of the new corporation's first year of business:

1. Bucknell invested $180,000 cash in the business, receiving shares of stock in the new corporation in exchange.

2. The company bought land and a store building for $80,000 and equipment for $10,000, paying $50,000 cash and borrowing the remaining $40,000 from a bank. Land accounted for $15,000 of the cost of land and building.

3. The company bought on account merchandise costing $110,625 and placed it in inventory.

4. The company sold merchandise from inventory. This merchandise had cost the company $94,550 and was sold for $118,625, of which $62,750 was for cash and the balance was on credit.

5. The company paid employees' wages in cash, $21,225.

6. Bucknell Corporation paid $7,875 cash for other operating expenses.

7. The company received $750 cash for rent of storage space in its store loft during the year.

8. The company suffered an uninsured loss by fire of merchandise inventory that had cost $5,000 and equipment that had cost $2,600.

9. The company paid $98,750 of its accounts payable, $86,250 with cash and $12,500 with short-term notes payable.

10. Customers paid the company $53,750 of the amounts they owed it.

11. During the year, Bucknell had the company pay him a salary of $14,625, $12,000 in cash and merchandise that had cost $2,625. He calculated that if he hadn't gone into business for himself, he would have received a salary of $28,000 from his former employer.

12. Bills for expenses incurred in December but still unpaid on December 31 amounted to $550.

13. Depreciation during the year was estimated to be $2,000 for the building and $1,000 for the equipment.

14. On December 31, the company paid the bank $4,800 interest on the bank loan, covering the period from the time of the loan to the end of the year.

a. Analyze the effects of the above transactions on the assets, liabilities, and owners' equity of Bucknell Corporation, using the format illustrated in Exhibit 2–2, including a "Retained Earnings" column for net income and dividend items.

b. Prepare an income statement for the year and a balance sheet as of December 31.

Chapter 3

Accounting Recordkeeping

The transactions analyses we described in Chapter 2 are the first stage in what is known as the **accounting cycle**—the operations accountants perform to provide a cumulative record of their analyses of individual transactions and to prepare financial statements. We'll begin this chapter by presenting an overview of the procedures accountants use to take their transactions analyses into the next stages of the accounting cycle, continue by examining some special procedures used to record depreciation, and conclude by applying these procedures to a simple set of transactions.

The Bookkeeping Process

The means by which the accounting analyses of transactions are recorded in a formal way are known as **bookkeeping** systems. We'll discuss the following five components of bookkeeping systems:

1. Accounts.
2. Documents, journals, and ledgers.
3. Double-entry bookkeeping.
4. Debit/credit notation.
5. Closing entries.

Accounts

An **account** is simply a record in which to enter the effects of a company's transactions on one of its assets, liabilities, or components of owners' equity. Each account shows three kinds of facts: *increases* in the quantity represented by the account, *decreases* in the quantity represented by the account, and the *balance* in the account after all transactions have been recorded. The balance in an account on any date is the *cumulative* difference between the increases and the decreases that have been recorded in the account since it was created.

For example, suppose a new company has two transactions affecting cash on June 6, 19x1, its first day in business:

1. Issuance of capital stock for $100,000 cash.
2. Payment of $25,000 for equipment.

The Cash account will show the following:

Cash

Date	Description	Amount
6/6	Issuance of capital stock.........	+$100,000
6/6	Payment for equipment........	− 25,000
6/6	Balance.....................	+$ 75,000

The Chart of Accounts

A list of titles of a company's accounts is known as its **chart of accounts.** Exhibit 3–1 shows the chart of accounts Charles Erskine set up to record the transactions we analyzed in Chapter 2.

EXHIBIT 3–1
Erskine Appliances, Inc.: Initial Chart of Accounts

Assets	Cash Accounts receivable Inventory Prepaid rent Equipment
Liabilities	Accounts payable Salary payable Dividend payable
Owners' Equity	Capital stock Retained earnings Sales revenue Cost of goods sold Salary expense Rent expense Depreciation expense Miscellaneous expense Dividends declared

Each company decides which accounts it wants to use. These decisions depend on the information management wants to or must obtain from the accounting records for various purposes. For this reason, even different companies in the same business are likely to have very different sets of accounts.

For example, suppose management wants to know the cost of telephone service each month. If telephone costs are included with the costs of water and electric power in an account titled "Utilities Expense," the accountant would have to review all the transactions affecting that account to isolate the telephone service component. To avoid that chore, the accountant will probably set up three separate accounts, one for each kind of utility service. The balances in these accounts can then be used to give management the information it wants. In another company, however, management may not need separate information on telephone costs and a single utilities expense account will be used.

The chart of accounts in Exhibit 3–1 is much shorter than even the smallest businesses are likely to use. We'll add account titles in this chapter as we need them, but even our finished list will be far from complete. The important point is to use titles that describe the assets, liabilities, and owners' equity items clearly, and then use these account titles consistently.

Documents, Journals, and Ledgers

Data usually enter the accounting system on documents that are prepared or received at the time the transactions take place. Most of these documents are prepared initially for some other purpose: The main purpose of a sales slip or invoice, for example, is to tell the customer how much to pay; similarly, the main purpose of a bill or invoice received from a supplier is to tell the company how much the supplier expects the company to pay, and for what. A company's accountants read these documents with something else in mind—namely, to decide which assets and equities have been affected and which accounts should be used to record these effects.

These analyses are typically assembled ("entered") first in a **journal,** a chronological record of the transactions represented by the documents. A journal is a book, file of papers, reel of magnetic tape, or other medium in which the accounting analysis of each transaction is recorded *in its entirety.* In some cases, a file of the documents themselves may serve as a journal. The record of an individual transaction in a journal is known as a **journal entry.**

A journal entry identifies the document from which the entry is prepared, lists the accounts affected and by what amounts, and explains the nature of the transaction. For example, the journal entry to record the analysis of the issuance of stock for $100,000 cash shows the following:

1. Cash account increased by $100,000.
2. Capital Stock account increased by $100,000.
3. Explanation: to record the issuance of capital stock for cash (reference: stock purchase ticket number 1).

A company is likely to use several journals. A *payroll journal*, for example, is used to record all the details of the amounts earned by each employee, together with the deductions from these amounts for withheld taxes and other items. A separate line is provided for each employee each pay period. Similarly, a *sales journal* is used exclusively to record sales of merchandise. Some reasons for this specialization will become apparent in a moment, but for now we'll ignore these special journals and assume that all transactions are recorded in a single journal, known as the **general journal.** In practice, this journal is used to record every transaction for which no special journal has been established. If a company has only one journal, it will be a general journal.

Documents and journal entries are the first two stages in the diagram in Exhibit 3–2. To complete the recording process, the amounts entered

EXHIBIT 3–2
The Flow of Transactions Data

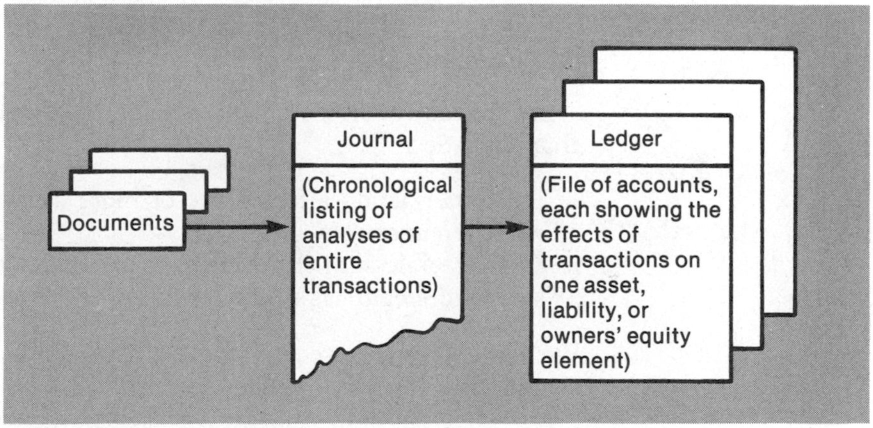

in the journals are transferred or *posted* to the individual accounts. The file of accounts is called the **ledger,** with each account appearing on a separate page or computer storage section. Since every transaction affects at least two categories of assets, liabilities, or owners' equity, each journal entry of necessity leads to two or more amounts posted to the ledger. In the ledger, the individual transaction no longer appears as a complete unit; instead, its component parts are scattered in two or more accounts. For example, the issuance of stock for cash appears in two accounts:

Cash		Capital Stock	
6/6	+$100,000	6/6	+$100,000

Looking at only one ledger account will reveal only one aspect of this transaction, whereas in the general journal both aspects are visible together.

The main file of accounts is known as the *general ledger.* Many accounts in the general ledger are likely to be *control accounts,* which represent a whole class of assets, liabilities, or owners' equity; the detailed listing is in a separate file, known as a *subsidiary ledger.*

For example, if the general ledger has a single Accounts Receivable account, it will undoubtedly be supported by a subsidiary ledger showing the amounts owed by individual customers. A subsidiary ledger may take the form of a file of cards (one for each customer), a file of unpaid invoices (one for each purchase from a supplier), or a section of computer memory.

In summary, a transaction evidenced by a document is recorded in a journal by a journal entry. Every journal entry contains at least two amounts, and the amounts entered in a journal are subsequently posted to the designated accounts in the ledger.

Double-Entry Bookkeeping

Each of our analyses of transactions in Chapter 2 had two essential characteristics:

1. Each transaction affected two or more assets, liabilities, or owners' equity components; and
2. The algebraic sum of the changes in the assets equaled the algebraic sum of the changes in the liabilities and owners' equity.

We can express the second of these features mathematically, using the symbol Δ to denote a change:

$$\Delta \text{ Total assets} = \Delta \text{ Total liabilities} + \Delta \text{ Owners' equity}$$

This second feature is essential for the accounting equation to stay balanced at all times. If every change is balanced in this way, then the accounting equation itself can never get out of balance.

These two features in the journal-entry process give us the system known as **double-entry bookkeeping.** Every journal entry in double-entry bookkeeping contains a symmetrical set of changes that affect the balances of at least two accounts. For example, the two cash transactions we described earlier affect three accounts: Cash, Capital Stock, and

Equipment. Expressed in plus-and-minus notation, these transactions have the following effects on the accounts:

Cash   + Equipment = Capital Stock

Entry no.:			
(1)	+$100,000		+$100,000
(2)	− 25,000	+$25,000	
Balances	$ 75,000 +	$25,000 =	$100,000

In each of these two entries, the net change in the accounts on the left of the equal sign is the same as the net change in the account on the right.

T-accounts

Each of the accounts we've been using has had a single column of amounts, each accompanied by a plus or a minus sign. Although the form of the accounts may vary from company to company, each account can be visualized as the letter **T**. This schematic representation is known as a **T-account.** Additions and the account balance appear on one side of the T; subtractions appear on the other side. A T-account representing our Cash account and including the effects of the first two cash transactions looks like this:

Cash

(+)		(−)	
Beginning balance	0	Payment	25,000
Receipt	100,000		
Ending bal. 75,000			

The balance in this account can be obtained at any time by subtracting the sum of the amounts on the right from the sum of the amounts on the left.

Putting the positive amount on the left side and the negative quantity on the right side of the Cash T-account follows a centuries-old tradition: Positive balances in asset accounts and amounts signifying increases in assets appear on the left in asset accounts, while amounts representing decreases in assets appear on the right side. In contrast, positive balances and increases in liability and owners' equity accounts appear on the right side; decreases appear on the left. The Capital Stock account therefore shows the following:

Capital Stock

(−)		(+)	
		Beginning balance	0
		Issue of stock	100,000
		Ending bal. 100,000	

The main benefit of this left/right arrangement is that the nature of account balances and the effects of transactions are indicated clearly by the *positions* of the amounts, with no need for further verbal description. Furthermore, when we list all of the accounts' balances, we find that the total of the left-side balances equals the total of the right-side balances. In our example so far, we have:

	Left	**Right**
Cash..................	$ 75,000	
Equipment.............	25,000	
Capital Stock..........		$100,000
Total	$100,000	$100,000

This equality is simply another result of the accounting equation. Positive balances in liability and owners' equity accounts are on the right side; positive balances in asset accounts are on the left. Since total assets must equal the total of the liabilities and the owners' equity, the left-side total must equal the right-side total.

RULES GOVERNING THE USE OF T-ACCOUNTS

1. An *increase* in an *asset* is entered on the *left* side of the T, as is the balance in the asset account.
2. A *decrease* in an *asset* is entered on the *right* side of the T.
3. An *increase* in a liability or owners' *equity* is entered on the *right* side of the T, as is the balance in the liability or owners' equity account.
4. A *decrease* in a liability or owners' *equity* is entered on the *left* side of the T.

Debit and Credit Notation

Just as it is not precise to use the terms *plus* and *minus* without also specifying the kind of account, so is it also a bit cumbersome to use the terms *left side* and *right side* repeatedly. Accountants therefore have adopted a more concise notation:

1. **Debit** (abbreviated as *Dr.*) is an amount on the *left* side, indicating a positive balance in an asset account, an increase in an asset, or a decrease in a liability or owners' equity.
2. **Credit** (abbreviated as *Cr.*) is an amount on the *right* side, indicating either a positive balance or an increase in a liability or owners' equity, or a decrease in an asset.

In a transaction that brings cash into the company, the increase in cash is recorded by a debit to the Cash account; the payment of cash requires a credit to Cash.

All this is summarized in schematic terms as follows:

Asset		Liability		Owners' Equity	
(+)	(−)	(−)	(+)	(−)	(+)
Dr.	Cr.	Dr.	Cr.	Dr.	Cr.

This terminology is likely to be confusing at first. For one thing, the terms *debit* and *credit* are both *nouns* and *verbs*. Accountants enter debits and credits (nouns) in journals and ledger accounts. They also debit and credit (verbs) specific accounts. The terms are even more confusing when one party to a transaction describes it to another. For example, your bank *credits* your deposit to your account because the balance in your account at the bank is one of the bank's liabilities and your deposit has increased that amount. If you keep your own double-entry books, however, you will record the deposit as a *debit* to an asset account such as Cash in Bank.

The debit/credit notation gives accountants a more compact way to present the analyses of transactions than the increase/decrease notation we used in Chapter 2. For example, the analysis of a $10,000 purchase of merchandise on credit can be presented in the following way:

Accounts	Debit	Credit
Inventory	10,000	
Accounts Payable		10,000
To record the purchase of merchandise on credit.		

In this form, debits are written first; credits are written underneath, with both the account titles and amounts *indented to the right*. This is a journal entry, written in what is called a *general journal form*.

The entry above is known as a *simple entry* because it contains only one debit and one credit. A *compound entry*, in contrast, contains more than two amounts. To keep the accounting equation in balance, the sum of the debit amounts must equal the sum of the credits. For example, if cash had been paid immediately for 30 percent of the $10,000 purchase of merchandise, the following compound entry would have been prepared:

Inventory	10,000	
Cash		3,000
Accounts Payable		7,000

The sum of the two credits is $10,000, just equal to the amount of the debit to Inventory.

Revenue and Expense Accounts

To prepare an income statement, the accountant has to separate the revenue amounts and expense amounts from other amounts that also affect the owners' equity. A separate account is therefore set up for each type of revenue and each kind of expense management wishes to identify.

To illustrate the use of revenue and expense accounts, let's assume a company sells merchandise from its inventory. The selling price is $6,000, the sale is for cash, and the merchandise was purchased earlier at a cost of $4,000. The company has one revenue account, Revenue from Sales. The journal entry recording the sale must reflect two basic facts: (1) The asset (cash) is increased by $6,000; and (2) the owners' equity (revenue) is increased by the same amount. The entry in general journal form is as follows:

```
Cash................................................. 6,000
    Revenue from Sales ................................        6,000
```

The first amount is a debit, denoting the increase in cash; the second amount, indented to the right, is a credit, identifying an increase in the owners' equity. Since revenues are increases in owners' equity and increases in owners' equity appear on the right side of owners' equity accounts, it follows that increases in revenues should appear on the right side of revenue accounts.

A second journal entry is necessary to record the company's $4,000 cost of the merchandise. This entry must show (1) a $4,000 reduction in the company's inventory asset *and* (2) a $4,000 reduction in the owners' equity. Since revenues increase owners' equity and one of the costs incurred to generate these revenues is the cost of the merchandise delivered to the customer, it follows that the cost of the merchandise sold is a reduction in the owners' equity.

The company in this illustration uses the expense account, Cost of Goods Sold, to record the costs of merchandise sold during a period. Because this is an owners' equity account and because reductions in owners' equity are shown on the left side of owners' equity accounts, the Cost of Goods Sold account has a left-side (debit) balance. The entry in general journal form is:

```
Cost of Goods Sold ................................... 4,000
    Inventory........................................        4,000
```

The debit shows the expense (reduction in owners' equity); the credit shows the reduction in the asset.

We have now illustrated three owners' equity accounts; they can be grouped as follows:

Owners' Equity

(−) Cost of Goods Sold		(+) Capital Stock	
Dr.	Cr.	Dr.	Cr.
4,000			100,000

		Revenue from Sales	
		Dr.	Cr.
			6,000

These three accounts are shown as components of a giant T-account. Accounts that have positive balances (*Capital Stock* and *Revenue from Sales*) are shown on the positive (right-hand) side of the large T. The account that has a negative owners' equity balance (*Cost of Goods Sold*) appears on the negative (left-hand) side.

Other Owners' Equity Accounts

Some owners' equity accounts accumulate the amounts contributed to the corporation by investors who have purchased shares of stock from the corporation. These amounts are referred to as the corporation's **paid-in capital,** contributed capital, or invested capital. In Chapter 11 we'll explain how paid-in capital can be recorded in more than one account, but in this chapter we're using only one, the Capital Stock account.

A second type of owners' equity account measures the company's *earned* capital. Earned capital goes under the name of **retained earnings.** As we pointed out in Chapter 2, it measures the amount by which the company's net income has exceeded the dividends distributed to the stockholders since the company was formed. Net income increases the owners' equity; it therefore appears on the credit side of the Retained Earnings account. Dividends, on the other hand, decrease owners' equity. When a dividend is declared, Retained Earnings must be debited.

For example, suppose the company had a net income of $10,000 in its first year and $30,000 in its second year. It paid no dividends to its shareholders the first year but declared dividends of $5,000 at the end of the second year. Before the second-year dividends were debited to it, the Retained Earnings account had a credit balance of $40,000:

Retained Earnings

Net income, year 1	10,000
Net income, year 2	30,000
	40,000

The declaration of the $5,000 dividend could be recorded by the following journal entry:

```
Retained Earnings ....................................  5,000
        Dividends Payable...................................        5,000
```

The debit to Retained Earnings records the reduction in owners' equity that takes place when the dividend is declared; the credit to Dividends Payable records the increase in the company's liabilities, in this case its liabilities to its owners for the amount of the dividend. Now the Retained Earnings account shows a $35,000 balance:

Retained Earnings

Dividend, year 2	5,000	Net income, year 1	10,000
		Net income, year 2	30,000
			40,000
		Bal. 35,000	

REMINDER

The declaration of a dividend is the act that reduces owners' equity. Later payment of that dividend has no further effect on owners' equity. It simply reduces both an asset (cash) and a liability (dividends payable).

Continuing Accounts and Transitory Accounts

Revenue and expense accounts are *transitory* accounts—that is, they accumulate the effects of transactions for one period only. Having these accounts makes it easier for accountants to prepare income statements—the income statement is simply a summary of the balances in the revenue and expense accounts at the end of the period.

Accountants may also choose to set up another transitory account, Dividends Declared, to record the effect on owners' equity of declarations of dividends during the year. If this account is used, the entry to record the declaration of a $5,000 dividend is:

```
Dividends Declared ....................................  5,000
        Dividends Payable...................................        5,000
```

Exhibit 3–3 illustrates the relationship between these transitory accounts and the *continuing* owners' equity accounts (those that carry their balances forward from period to period), in this case, Capital Stock and Retained Earnings. Notice how the revenue and expense accounts are

EXHIBIT 3–3
Relationship of Transitory Owners' Equity Accounts to the Continuing Accounts

Capital Stock		Retained Earnings			
(−) Dr.	(+) Cr.	(−) **Dividends Declared**		(+) **Net Income**	
		Dr.		(−) **Dr. Expenses**	(+) **Cr. Revenues**
				Dr.	Cr.

brought together schematically as net income, represented by a larger T-account on the right side of the even larger T-account labeled Retained Earnings. In other words, all of the transitory accounts we have introduced so far are really subdivisions of the continuing account entitled Retained Earnings.

These relationships take some getting used to. The following list may be a useful means of understanding them:

1. Capital Stock and Retained Earnings are the two primary continuing components of owners' equity and therefore are increased with credits and decreased with debits.
2. Retained Earnings *increases* as a result of profitable operations, as measured by net income. Retained Earnings *decreases* when dividends are declared.
3. Net Income is the positive component of Retained Earnings and therefore appears on the right side of the Retained Earnings T-account in Exhibit 3–3. Increases in net income are shown as credits; decreases are shown as debits.
4. Dividends Declared is the negative component of Retained Earnings and therefore appears on the debit ("negative") side of the larger Retained Earnings T-account in Exhibit 3–3. Dividends Declared has either a debit balance or a zero balance.
5. Revenues, the positive component of net income, are represented by credits. Expenses, the negative components of net income, are represented by debits.
6. The net effect on owners' equity of the revenues, expenses, and dividends declared in the current period is merged with the effects of similar transactions in previous periods to constitute the end-of-period Retained Earnings balance.

Closing Entries

All accounts whose balances appear in end-of-period balance sheets are continuing accounts. By contrast, the revenue, expense, and dividend accounts are transitory accounts. At the end of each period, all transitory accounts' balances are transferred to Retained Earnings, so that the balance in that account measures the amount of retained earnings at year-end.

These transfers are accomplished by **closing entries.** A closing entry is made to transfer the balance in one account to another account, according to the following rules:

1. If the account from which the transfer is made has a *credit* balance, that account is *debited* with an amount equal to the account balance; an identical amount is credited to the account to which the transfer is made.
2. If the account from which the transfer is made has a *debit* balance, that account is *credited* with an amount equal to the account balance; an identical amount is debited to the account to which the transfer is made.

For example, suppose our company has the following balances in its transitory accounts at the end of the year:

	Debit	Credit
Revenue from sales		$300,000
Cost of goods sold	$180,000	
Selling expenses	50,000	
Administrative expenses	40,000	
Dividends declared	5,000	

(In practice, and in the problems in this book, many more transitory accounts will be used; we've kept the number to five to avoid unnecessary complexity in this first illustration.)

The first closing entry removes the credit balance in the Revenue from Sales account by debiting that account by an amount equal to the account balance. The entry is:

Revenue from Sales	300,000	
Income Summary		300,000

The debit to Revenue from Sales reduces the balance in that account to zero; it is ready to receive the next year's postings:

Revenue from Sales			
Closing entry	300,000	Revenue transactions	300,000

Our newly created **Income Summary account** is also a transitory account, used solely to assemble the revenues and expenses in one place at the end of the period. The $300,000 credit to this account indicates that sales revenues have increased the owners' equity.

Next, the debit balances in the three expense accounts are eliminated by crediting them with amounts equal to the account balances:

Income Summary...	270,000	
Cost of Goods Sold..............................		180,000
Selling Expenses................................		50,000
Administrative Expenses		40,000

This entry transfers the debit balances from three owners' equity accounts (Cost of Goods Sold, Selling Expenses, and Administrative Expenses) to the Income Summary. The credits to the expense accounts reduce the balances in those accounts to zero, so they are ready to receive the next year's postings. The debit to Income Summary reduces the credit balance in that account to $30,000, the net income for the year.

The third closing entry transfers the net income to Retained Earnings:

Income Summary...................................	30,000	
Retained Earnings.............................		30,000

The debit to Income Summary reduces the balance in that account to zero:

Income Summary

Expenses	270,000	Revenues	300,000
Closing entry	30,000		

The credit to Retained Earnings shows that the company's operations this year have been profitable, increasing the owners' equity by $30,000.

The fourth and final closing entry removes the balance in the Dividends Declared account:

Retained Earnings	5,000	
Dividends Declared............................		5,000

The credit to Dividends Declared reduces the balance in that account to zero. The debit to Retained Earnings shows that the dividends reduced the owners' equity by $5,000. With income of $30,000 and dividends of $5,000, the company has increased its owners' equity this year, by retaining $25,000 of its net income in the business:

Retained Earnings

Dividends declared	5,000	Beginning balance	10,000
		Net income	30,000
		Ending bal. 35,000	

As long as the company's total net income to date exceeds the company's total dividends to date, the Retained Earnings account will have a credit balance, because credits represent increases (income) and debits represent decreases (dividends and losses). Our $35,000 credit balance shows that this company's activities since its inception have had a positive effect on the owners' equity.

There is nothing sacred about the closing entries we've used in this illustration. For example, we could have omitted the Income Summary account, or we could have had a separate closing entry for each expense account instead of putting them together in a single compound entry. We could even have used one compound closing entry to close all the transitory accounts at once:

Revenue from Sales...............................	300,000	
Cost of Goods Sold.............................		180,000
Selling Expenses................................		50,000
Administrative Expenses		40,000
Dividends Declared.............................		5,000
Retained Earnings..............................		25,000
To close all transitory accounts and bring Retained Earnings to its correct balance.		

Any combination of entries that reduces the transitory accounts to zero balances and adds $25,000 to Retained Earnings is acceptable.

Bookkeeping Summary

Bookkeeping consists of a series of steps through which the effects of transactions are recorded in a company's accounting system. Although various types of mechanical and electronic devices may be used, bookkeeping's basic elements encompass these salient features:

1. *Accounts* are used to group the effects of transactions on individual assets, liabilities, and owners' equity components.
2. *Documents* provide the data that are analyzed and then entered in *journals* and subsequently posted to *ledger* accounts.
3. *Double-entry bookkeeping* entails recognizing that every transaction affects at least two components of the *accounting equation* and that there must always be equality between assets and the sum of liabilities and owners' equity.
4. *Debit/credit notation* prescribes the manner in which increases, decreases and balances are positioned in asset, liability, and owners' equity ledger accounts.
5. *Closing entries* enable the end-of-period Retained Earnings account balance to include the effects of the period's revenues, expenses, and dividends.

**Accounts for
Depreciable Assets**

Land, buildings, equipment, and other tangible assets provide operating capacity for several accounting periods into the future. Those that lose their usefulness due to physical deterioration or technological obsolescence are known as **depreciable assets**. We'll now see which accounts are used to record (1) property acquisitions and depreciation and (2) sales of depreciable assets.

Property Acquisition and Depreciation

When a business buys equipment, it acquires an asset. Suppose, for example, a company paid $8,000 in cash for office equipment it expected to use for eight years. This transaction increased one asset (equipment) and decreased another (cash). The entry to record the purchase was:

Equipment.. 8,000
    Cash 8,000

The debit to the Equipment account recorded the increase in the asset; the credit to Cash recorded the decrease in that asset.

At the time of the purchase, the company estimated that depreciation on this equipment would amount to $1,000 a year. At the end of the first year, therefore, the company's accountants made the following analysis:

Decrease in owners'   Decrease in asset
  equity (Expense) ..... $1,000   (Equipment) $1,000

This could be translated into an entry of the following form:

Depreciation Expense 1,000
    Equipment 1,000
  To record one year's depreciation on equipment.

If the entries recording depreciation were actually made this way, the accounts would show the following preclosing balances at the end of the third year:

Equipment

Original cost of		Depreciation, year 1	1,000
equipment purchased	8,000	Depreciation, year 2	1,000
		Depreciation, year 3	1,000
			3,000

Bal. 5,000

Depreciation Expense

Depreciation, year 3	1,000	

The $5,000 balance in the Equipment account shows the portion of the original cost that had not yet been charged to expense. The balance in the Depreciation Expense account relates only to the third year, however. It represents the cost of only that portion of the asset's life that was consumed *during that year,* because expense accounts accumulate costs for one accounting period only and are closed out at the end of each period.

Since under this approach the Equipment account balance would disclose only the equipment's yet-to-be-depreciated cost, no one who was unwilling or unable to make a detailed search through the company's records could identify the equipment's original cost. Because information on the original cost of equipment and other plant assets is generally thought to be useful (and is often required by law), the more common treatment is to use a separate account to accumulate the amounts reflecting the consumed portion of the original cost. This account is called **Accumulated Depreciation;** the amounts that accumulate on the right side of this account are those we posted to the right side of the Equipment account we used earlier in this illustration. The two accounts now show the following:

Equipment	Accumulated Depreciation
Original cost of equipment purchased 8,000	Depreciation, year 1 1,000 Depreciation, year 2 1,000 Depreciation, year 3 1,000 Bal. 3,000

The entry to record depreciation for the third year therefore is:

Depreciation Expense	1,000	
Accumulated Depreciation.		1,000

As before, the debit records the reduction in the owners' equity, while the credit to Accumulated Depreciation records the consumption of the asset.

The Accumulated Depreciation account is our first example of a **contra account.** A contra account is always paired with some other account and serves to accumulate some or all of the effects of transactions on the asset, liability, or owners' equity component to which it is coupled. Thus, the Accumulated Depreciation account is a deduction-from-asset contra account, or contra-asset account. Since the related asset account has a debit balance, the contra account has a credit balance. In financial statements, the balance in the contra account should always be deducted from the balance in its parent account, as follows:

Equipment, at original cost (parent account)	$8,000
Less: Accumulated depreciation (contra account)	3,000
Equipment, net	$5,000

The *net* amount is the asset's unamortized cost, that is, the amount that hasn't yet been amortized (i.e., depreciated). It is usually referred to as the asset's **book value.**

We should emphasize that although the Accumulated Depreciation account has a credit balance, it is neither a liability nor an owners' equity account. When the balance in this account is subtracted from the balance in the related plant asset account, it shows that some of the original cost of the plant asset has been consumed. The portion of the cost that is expected to be consumed in future periods is the difference between the balances in these two accounts.

A credit to the Accumulated Depreciation account therefore records a *decrease* in the plant asset. It doesn't record an increase in a contra asset because there is no such thing as a contra-asset. *Contra-asset* is a term used to describe a certain kind of *account*. The balance in that account must be regarded as part of the description of the asset the contra account is attached to. It has no separate existence apart from the asset itself.

The balance in the Accumulated Depreciation account can be used as a rough index of the age of the company's equipment—the older the equipment, the higher the ratio of accumulated depreciation to original cost. An increase in this ratio usually means that the company is riding on its past investments in facilities; a reduction in the ratio is likely to reflect a modernization or expansion program.

Disposition of Depreciable Assets

From time to time companies dispose of depreciable assets by selling them, trading them for newer models, or losing them through involuntary destruction. The first step in recording a disposition is to recognize the depreciation between the beginning of the year in which the disposition was made and the disposition date. For example, suppose a machine costing $8,000 had accumulated depreciation of $3,000 in its first three years at the rate of $1,000 a year. The machine was sold for $2,300 in cash at the end of the first three months of year 4. This means that depreciation expense of $250 (3/12 of the annual amount) should be recorded in year 4. The entry is:

```
Depreciation Expense .....................................  250
    Accumulated Depreciation..............................       250
```

(To reduce recordkeeping, some companies might adopt a reasonable assumption about the length of the interval—such as that all retirements take place at midyear.)

The second step in recording a disposition is to remove both the asset's original cost and its accumulated depreciation from the accounts. In our example, the original cost was $8,000 and the accumulated depreciation was $3,250. Before we can prepare the entry to remove these amounts from the accounts, however, we must find out whether the assets received from the sale of the machine were equal to, greater than, or less than the machine's undepreciated cost (book value). In this case, the amount received was $2,300 and the book value was $4,750 ($8,000 − $3,250). The difference between these two amounts is the *loss* on the sale, calculated as follows:

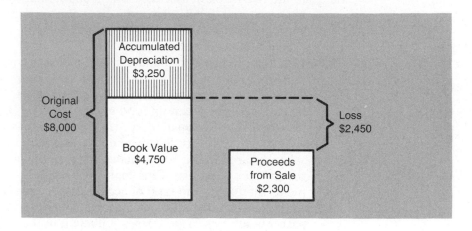

The entry to record the sale is:

```
Cash.................................................  2,300
Accumulated Depreciation .............................  3,250
Loss on Sale of Equipment.............................  2,450
    Equipment ........................................        8,000
```

In this entry, the credit of $8,000 removed the original cost of the machine from the asset account, while the debit of $3,250 did the same for the accumulated depreciation applicable to it. The debit to cash recorded the inflow of this asset, and the debit to the loss account recorded the decrease in the owners' equity that was recognized at the time of the sale.

If the machine had been sold for $6,300—instead of $2,300—the company would have recorded a $1,550 *gain*. Receiving cash of $6,300 in exchange for an asset with a book value of $4,750 means that *total* assets increased by $1,550, and that owners' equity increased by $1,550 as well.[1]

---

[1] An entry in general journal form would be:

```
Cash.................................................  6,300
Accumulated Depreciation .............................  3,250
    Equipment ........................................        8,000
    Gain on Sale of Equipment ........................        1,550
```

The gain or loss on a disposition is recognized in the year the asset is disposed of, but it actually results from an incorrect estimate of either the asset's lifetime or its ultimate resale value. For our machine on which we recognized a $2,450 loss, if the lifetime and resale value had been fore-casted correctly when the machine was acquired, a total of $5,700 would have been charged as depreciation during the first 3¼ years. As Exhibit 3–4 shows, this would have been just enough to bring the book value down to the ultimate $2,300 sale price in year 4.

EXHIBIT 3–4
Lifetime Depreciation

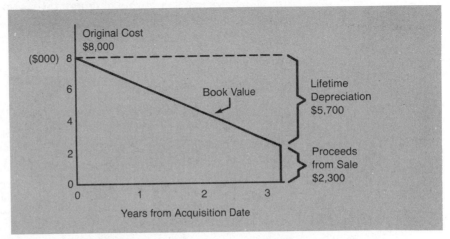

It can be argued that the proper treatment of the loss would be to go back and restate the company's earnings for the first three years. Unfor-tunately, the income statements of prior years are past history, and re-peated correction of prior years' earnings can be very confusing. The company therefore reported the entire loss in the income statement for year 4, with no attempt to prorate any portion of it to earlier years.

An Integrative Illustration

The portion of the accounting cycle we've seen so far appears in Ex-hibit 3–5. We'll complete this diagram in Chapter 4 by inserting several additional operations we haven't described yet. To reinforce our under-standing of the parts of the cycle we've explained so far, however, we'll apply these procedures to a set of transactions for Saturn Stores, Inc., for the year 19x1.

Saturn Stores, Inc., began the year 19x1 with the following account balances:

	Debit	Credit
Cash	$ 100,000	
Accounts receivable	300,000	
Inventory.....................	400,000	
Prepaid rent	50,000	
Equipment	800,000	
Accumulated depreciation		$ 350,000
Accounts payable..............		200,000
Capital stock..................		850,000
Retained earnings		250,000
Total......................	$1,650,000	$1,650,000

For simplicity, we'll continue to ignore taxes. Notice that the sum of the debit balances at the beginning of the year equals the sum of the credit balances; this is necessary if the accounting equation is to balance.

EXHIBIT 3–5
Partial Diagram of Accounting Cycle

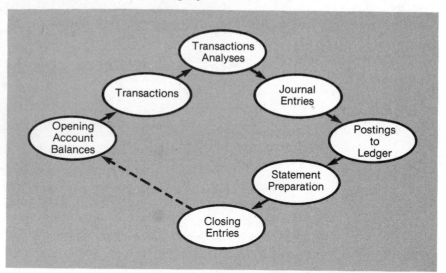

The Transactions

The company's transactions during the year can be summarized as follows:

1. Sales on account, $2,200,000.
2. Collections from customers, on account, $2,150,000.
3. Purchases of merchandise, on account, $1,300,000.
4. Payments to suppliers of merchandise, on account, $1,375,000.
5. Cost of merchandise sold, $1,400,000.

6. Salaries earned by employees, $320,000.
7. Salaries paid to employees, $310,000.
8. Cost of other services purchased on account and used, $90,000.
9. Payments to suppliers of other services purchased on account, $85,000.
10. Rental payments for right to use store premises during the period from July 1, 19x1, to June 30, 19x2, $120,000.
11. Rental costs applicable to 19x1, $110,000 ($50,000 for the period from January 1 to June 30, 19x1, and $60,000 for the period from July 1 to December 31, 19x1).
12. Equipment purchased (paid for in cash), $100,000.
13. Depreciation on equipment, $82,000.
14. Proceeds from sale of equipment, $15,000 (original cost of equipment sold, $40,000; accumulated depreciation on equipment sold, $22,000).
15. Dividends declared, $60,000.
16. Dividends paid, $45,000.

REMINDER: CUSTOMARY ACCOUNT BALANCES

Accounts Usually Having Debit Balances	**Accounts Usually Having Credit Balances**
Asset	Contra-asset
Expense	Revenue
Loss	Gain
Dividends declared	Liability
	Contributed capital
	Retained earnings

Journal Entries

The following journal entries identify and record the effects of these transactions on the company's assets, liabilities, and owners' equity. Each entry has an identifying number keyed to the list of transactions above and an explanation of the entry. In practice, each entry would also identify the document on which it is based, but we've omitted this because it would add nothing to our discussion.

1.	Accounts Receivable	2,200,000	
	Revenue from Sales.		2,200,000

To record increases in accounts receivable (asset) and in revenue (increase in owners' equity) resulting from sales.

2. Cash....................................... 2,150,000
        Accounts Receivable....................   2,150,000
        To record increases in cash (asset) and de-
        crease in accounts receivable (asset) resulting
        from collections from customers.

3. Inventory................................. 1,300,000
        Accounts Payable   1,300,000
        To record increases in inventory (asset) and in
        accounts payable (liability) resulting from pur-
        chases of merchandise.

4. Accounts Payable......................... 1,375,000
        Cash   1,375,000
        To record decreases in accounts payable (liabil-
        ity) and in cash (asset) resulting from payments
        to suppliers of merchandise.

5. Cost of Goods Sold 1,400,000
        Inventory.............................   1,400,000
        To record expense (decrease in owners' equity)
        and decrease in inventory (asset) resulting from
        sales of merchandise to customers.

6. Salaries Expense.......................... 320,000
        Salaries Payable......................   320,000
        To record expense (decrease in owners' equity)
        and increase in salaries payable (liability) result-
        ing from use of employees' services.

7. Salaries Payable 310,000
        Cash   310,000
        To record decreases in salaries payable (liabil-
        ity) and in cash (asset) resulting from salary pay-
        ments to employees.

8. Miscellaneous Expenses   90,000
        Accounts Payable   90,000
        To record expense (decrease in owners' equity)
        and increase in accounts payable (liability) re-
        sulting from purchase and use of miscellaneous
        services.

9. Accounts Payable..........................   85,000
        Cash   85,000
        To record decreases in accounts payable (liabil-
        ity) and in cash (asset) resulting from payments
        to suppliers of miscellaneous services.

10. Prepaid Rent.............................. 120,000
        Cash   120,000
        To record increase in prepaid rent (asset) and
        decrease in cash (asset) resulting from rental
        payments covering the period from July 1, 19x1,
        to June 30, 19x2.

11.	Rent Expense	110,000	
	Prepaid Rent.........................		110,000

To record expense (decrease in owners' equity) and decrease in prepaid rent (asset) resulting from use of store premises.

12.	Equipment................................	100,000	
	Cash		100,000

To record increase in equipment (asset) and decrease in cash (asset) resulting from purchase of store equipment and payment of cash.

13.	Depreciation Expense.......................	82,000	
	Accumulated Depreciation		82,000

To record expense (decrease in owners' equity) and decrease in equipment (asset) resulting from depreciation of store equipment.

14.	Cash	15,000	
	Accumulated Depreciation...................	22,000	
	Loss on Sale of Equipment	3,000	
	Equipment		40,000

To record increase in cash (asset), decrease in equipment (asset), and loss (decrease in owners' equity) resulting from sale of store equipment for $3,000 less than its book value.

15.	Dividends Declared.........................	60,000	
	Dividends Payable		60,000

To record increase in dividends declared (decrease in owners' equity) and increase in dividends payable (liability) resulting from declaration of dividends to stockholders.

16.	Dividends Payable.........................	45,000	
	Cash		45,000

To record decreases in dividends payable (liability) and in cash (asset) resulting from payment of cash dividends to stockholders.

Ledger Posting

Each number in the journal entries must be posted to the appropriate ledger account. The accounts showing these postings, together with their opening balances, are presented in Exhibit 3–6. Notice that each debit and each credit is accompanied by a number identifying the transaction from which it arose. This is essential because the accountant must leave a *trail* in case someone wants to verify an entry or trace an error to its source.

Closing Entries

The transitory accounts can be returned to zero balances by a series of closing entries like those illustrated earlier in this chapter:

EXHIBIT 3–6
Saturn Stores, Inc.: Ledger Accounts

Cash			
Bal. 1/1	100,000	(4)	1,375,000
(2)	2,150,000	(7)	310,000
(14)	15,000	(9)	85,000
		(10)	120,000
		(12)	100,000
		(16)	45,000
Bal. 230,000			

Prepaid Rent			
Bal. 1/1	50,000	(11)	110,000
(10)	120,000		
Bal. 60,000			

Accounts Receivable			
Bal. 1/1	300,000	(2)	2,150,000
(1)	2,200,000		
Bal. 350,000			

Equipment			
Bal. 1/1	800,000	(14)	40,000
(12)	100,000		
Bal. 860,000			

Accumulated Depreciation			
(14)	22,000	Bal. 1/1	350,000
		(13)	82,000
		Bal. 410,000	

Inventory			
Bal. 1/1	400,000	(5)	1,400,000
(3)	1,300,000		
Bal. 300,000			

Salaries Payable			
(7)	310,000	(6)	320,000
		Bal. 10,000	

Accounts Payable			
(4)	1,375,000	Bal. 1/1	200,000
(9)	85,000	(3)	1,300,000
		(8)	90,000
		Bal. 130,000	

Dividends Payable			
(16)	45,000	(15)	60,000
		Bal. 15,000	

Capital Stock			
		Bal. 1/1	850,000

Depreciation Expense			
(13)	82,000		

Retained Earnings			
		Bal. 1/1	250,000

Rent Expense			
(11)	110,000		

Revenue from Sales			
		(1)	2,200,000

Miscellaneous Expenses			
(8)	90,000		

Cost of Goods Sold			
(5)	1,400,000		

Loss on Sale of Equipment			
(14)	3,000		

Salaries Expense			
(6)	320,000		

Dividends Declared			
(15)	60,000		

17. Revenue from Sales 2,200,000
        Income Summary........................   2,200,000
    To close the revenue account and transfer the
    balance to the Income Summary account.

18. Income Summary 2,005,000
        Cost of Goods Sold.....................   1,400,000
        Salaries Expense   320,000
        Depreciation Expense...................   82,000
        Rent Expense...........................   110,000
        Miscellaneous Expenses.................   90,000
        Loss on Sale of Equipment   3,000
    To close expense and loss accounts and trans-
    fer balances to the Income Summary account.

19. Income Summary   195,000
        Retained Earnings......................   195,000
    To close the Income Summary account and
    transfer the net income to Retained Earnings.

20. Retained Earnings.........................   60,000
        Dividends Declared   60,000
    To close the Dividends Declared account and
    transfer its balance to Retained Earnings.

After these closing entries have been posted, the following balances remain in the ledger accounts:

	Debit	Credit
Cash	$ 230,000	
Accounts receivable	350,000	
Inventory.....................	300,000	
Prepaid rent	60,000	
Equipment	860,000	
Accumulated depreciation		$ 410,000
Accounts payable..............		130,000
Salaries payable...............		10,000
Dividends payable		15,000
Capital stock..................		850,000
Retained earnings		385,000
Total.....................	$1,800,000	$1,800,000

Once again the total debit balance equals the total credit balance. This doesn't necessarily mean we've made no errors in analyzing the effects of transactions, but at least we haven't violated the accounting equation.

Financial Statements

Financial statements can be prepared directly from the accounts. Income statements include not only revenues and their related expenses but also any gains or losses that have occurred during the period. A gain or loss measures the effect on owners' equity of an event that isn't directly related to the company's revenue-generating activities, such as an uninsured fire loss or a gain from the sale of a depreciable asset. Gains and

losses can be listed in the income statement with the ordinary revenues
and expenses. Alternatively, the company may disclose the gains and
losses as separate determinants of net income.

Saturn Stores' income statement for 19x1 is shown in Exhibit 3–7. The
numbers in this financial statement have been taken from the Income
Summary account, which was set up expressly for this purpose. In this
statement, operating income measures the effect of the company's operations before considering gains and losses.

EXHIBIT 3–7

SATURN STORES, INC.
Income Statement
For the Year Ended December 31, 19x1
(in thousands of dollars)

Revenues from sales.............		$2,200
Cost of goods sold		1,400
Gross margin		800
Operating expenses:		
Salaries	$320	
Rent........................	110	
Depreciation.................	82	
Miscellaneous................	90	
Total operating expenses		602
Operating income		198
Loss on sale of equipment........		3
Net income.....................		$ 195

EXHIBIT 3–8

SATURN STORES, INC.
Balance Sheet
As of December 31, 19x1
(in thousands of dollars)

Assets			**Liabilities and Owners' Equity**		
Current assets:			Current liabilities:		
Cash		$ 230	Accounts payable		$ 130
Accounts receivable		350	Salaries payable............		10
Inventory.................		300	Dividends payable		15
Prepaid rent		60	Total current		
Total current assets		940	liabilities.............		155
			Capital stock	$850	
Equipment	$860		Retained earnings............	385	
Less: Accumulated			Total owners' equity.....		1,235
depreciation	410	450	Total liabilities and		
Total assets		$1,390	owners' equity......		$1,390

The company's balance sheet as of the end of 19x1 is shown in Exhibit 3–8. The amounts in this financial statement have been drawn from the final account balances at the end of the year, after all closing entries were posted. We'll take a closer look at statement preparation in Chapter 4.

Summary

Accountants have developed a concise form of notation to identify the results of transactions analyses. The term *debit* is used to describe an increase in an asset or a decrease in a liability or in a component of owners' equity. The term *credit* describes a decrease in an asset or an increase in a liability or owners' equity. To summarize a transaction analysis in written form, the accountant merely has to write the names and amounts of the affected items in a journal, with the debits first and credits below and indented to the right.

Consistent with this notation, *accounts* are generally represented schematically by diagrams in the shape of the letter T. Debits are on the left side of the T, credits on the right. When the amounts credited to an account exceed the amounts debited to it, the account is said to have a credit balance; an excess of debits over credits produces a debit balance.

The debit/credit scheme affects all accounts. As a result, accountants strive to have all accounts *in balance* at all times. By seeing that the total of the debit balances equals the total of the credit balances, accountants know that the accounting equation—*assets equal equities*—is in balance.

This system provides a basis for subdividing some accounts into positive and negative components. If the account normally has a debit balance, then its companion, known as a *contra account,* will have a credit balance. The Accumulated Depreciation account, for example, is a contra-asset account with a credit balance, representing the portion of the cost of depreciable assets that has been charged to operations since the asset was originally acquired.

Key Terms

Account	Double-entry bookkeeping
Accounting cycle	General journal entry
Accumulated depreciation	Income Summary account
Book value	Journal
Chart of accounts	Ledger
Closing entry	Paid-in capital
Contra account	T-account
Debit and credit	

Independent Study Problems (Solutions in Appendix B)

1. Continuation of Integrative Illustration. Saturn Stores, Inc., the company for which we constructed the integrative illustration in this chapter, had the following transactions in 19x2:

1. Sales on account, $2,500,000.
2. Collections from customers, on account, $2,400,000.
3. Purchases of merchandise, on account, $1,600,000.
4. Payments to suppliers of merchandise, on account, $1,525,000.
5. Cost of merchandise sold, $1,550,000.
6. Salaries earned by employees, $380,000.
7. Sales paid to employees, $385,000.
8. Cost of other services purchased on account and used, $130,000.
9. Payments to suppliers of other services purchased on account, $125,000.
10. Rental payments for the right to use store premises during the period from July 1, 19x2 to June 30, 19x3, $132,000.
11. Rental costs applicable to 19x2, ???.
12. Equipment purchased for cash, $80,000.
13. Depreciation on equipment, $88,000.
14. Proceeds from sale of equipment, $32,000; original cost of this equipment was $100,000, and its accumulated depreciation was $82,000.
15. Dividends declared, $80,000.
16. Dividends paid, $75,000.

a. Set up T-accounts and enter the opening balances from the information provided in the integrative illustration in this chapter.
b. Prepare journal entries in general journal form for Saturn Stores' transactions in 19x2, using the account titles provided in the illustration and any new accounts you find necessary.
c. Post these entries to the appropriate T-accounts.
d. Prepare appropriate closing entries as of December 31, 19x2.
e. Prepare an income statement for the year 19x2 and a balance sheet as of December 31, 19x2.

2. Interpreting Changes in Account Balances. Yolande Company's ledger included the following correct preclosing account balances, among others, at the close of business:

	On December 31, 19x1		On December 31, 19x2	
	Debit	**Credit**	**Debit**	**Credit**
Cash...................	$ 50		$ 75	
Merchandise inventory....	150		115	
Cost of goods sold.......	640		700	
Accounts payable to merchandise suppliers..		$80		$90

a. Calculate the cost of merchandise purchased in 19x2.
b. Calculate the amount of cash paid to merchandise suppliers in 19x2.

3. Journal Entries; Ledger Accounts. Kelly Company's ledger includes the following eight accounts, among others:

Account	Balance March 1, 19x1
Cash	$ 13,200
Accounts receivable	72,000
Merchandise inventory	92,000
Salaries and wages payable	450
Accounts payable	65,000
Sales revenues	130,000
Cost of goods sold	79,000
Salaries and wages expense	14,500

Kelly Company had the following transactions, among others, in March 19x1:

1. It bought merchandise costing $46,500 on account and placed this merchandise in inventory.
2. It sold merchandise from inventory for $57,000 on account; the cost of this merchandise was $36,000.
3. It collected $60,000 in cash on account from its customers.
4. It paid its merchandise suppliers $61,300 on account.
5. Its employees earned salaries and wages of $7,200 in March.
6. Store employees were paid $7,500; this included the March 1 liability.

a. Prepare T-accounts representing the eight ledger accounts listed and enter the March 1 balances. Be careful to place these balances on the correct sides of the T-accounts.
b. Prepare entries in general journal form to record your analyses of the six transactions listed.
c. Post these entries to the T-accounts.
d. Calculate the March 31 balance in each of these accounts and state what each balance represents.

4. Depreciable Assets; Journal Entries. Alpha Company bought a truck on January 1, 19x6, for $10,000 in cash. Management decided to recognize depreciation of $2,000 each year for five years. The truck was placed in service immediately and was used until January 1, 19x9, when it was sold for $2,500 cash.

a. Prepare entries in general journal form to record the purchase of the truck and depreciation for 19x6.
b. Set up two T-accounts—*Truck* and *Accumulated Depreciation*—and enter the balances that should have appeared in these accounts on December 31, 19x8, just before the truck was sold.
c. Prepare an entry in general journal form to record the sale of the truck on January 1, 19x9.

5. Transactions Analyses; Journal Entries. Harrell Corporation owns and operates a retail store. The following events took place last month:

1. The company purchased merchandise for $5,000; the supplier accepted, as payment for this purchase, the company's written promise (its *note*) to pay this amount next month.
2. The company received $4,000 from customers to pay for goods purchased by them in transactions recorded during the previous month.
3. The company paid previously recorded accounts payable of $6,000.
4. Store employees earned salaries of $1,000 during the month.
5. Store employees were paid $900 of the amounts they had earned.
6. The company borrowed $50,000 by signing a long-term note.
7. The company sold merchandise on account for $8,000; the cost of this merchandise, purchased in a previous period, was $6,000.
8. The company purchased a parcel of land at a cost of $7,000 cash.
9. The board of directors declared a dividend of $3,000, to be paid in cash to its shareholders next month.
10. Office stationery costing $60 was purchased on credit for current use.
11. Someone stole $100 in cash from the company. The loss is fully covered by insurance, but nothing has yet been received from the insurance company.

Prepare journal entries in conventional debit-and-credit notation, using account titles similar to those used in this chapter, including appropriately titled revenue and expense accounts. For each debit or credit, indicate whether it represented an increase ($+$) or a decrease ($-$) in an asset (A), a liability (L), or the owners' equity (OE). You may assume that all transactions of previous months were recorded correctly.

6. Journal Entries; Closing Entries. The balance sheet of Handyman Tool Shop and its transactions in the year 19x2 are listed in problem 5 at the end of Chapter 2. The company maintains accounts with the titles listed in the December 31, 19x1, balance sheet, plus the following: Dividends Payable, Sales Revenues, Rental Expense, Salaries Expense, Depreciation Expense, Cost of Goods Sold, Miscellaneous Expenses, and Dividends Declared. The original cost of the equipment was $36,140, and the accumulated depreciation was $17,120 as of December 31, 19x1.

a. Establish T-accounts and enter the December 31, 19x1, balances.
b. Prepare entries in general journal form to record the company's transactions in 19x2, using only the accounts specified in this problem.
c. Post the amounts from the journal entries to the T-accounts and calculate the December 31, 19x2, account balances.
d. Prepare closing entries in general journal form.

Exercises and Problems

7. Converting Account Balances to Income Statement. A fire damaged the accounting records of the Andy Hobby Emporium. The bookkeeper was able to assemble some of the ledger sheets, which fortunately included all the accounts relevant to the preparation of an income statement. Based on the following account balances, prepare an income statement for the period covered by these records.

	Debit	Credit
Accounts receivable..........	$14,800	
Accumulated depreciation.....		$ 5,100
Advertising expense..........	3,300	
Cost of goods sold...........	28,700	
Depreciation expense.........	1,700	
Dividends declared...........	2,500	
Gain on sale of machinery.....		700
Merchandise inventory........	9,100	
Retained earnings............		7,000
Salaries expense.............	11,100	
Sales revenue		64,200

8. Interpreting Changes in Account Balances. M. L., Inc., rents a warehouse at a cost of $900 a month for which several months' rent must be paid in advance. M. L. also leases office space from another landlord for $800 a month for which late payments are accepted without a penalty. M. L., Inc.'s balance sheets at December 31, 19x8 and 19x9 contained the following amounts:

	December 31	
	19x8	19x9
Prepaid rent	$2,700	$1,800
Rentals payable	1,600	2,000

a. What was the rent expense in 19x9?
b. How much cash was paid to landlords in 19x9?

9. Equipment Retirement. A company uses an Accumulated Depreciation account. One of its machines was scrapped last month. This machine cost $1,000 initially and had a book value of $200 at the time it was scrapped. The company gave the machine to a scrap dealer, who paid the costs of removing it. Someone has suggested that the following entry be made to record the disposition of the machine:

Loss on Equipment Retirement 200
        Equipment   200

a. Why would this be wrong?
b. What entry would be correct?

10. Equipment Accounts. The opening balance in an Equipment account was $300, with accumulated depreciation totaling $100 shown in a separate account.

Depreciation for the year is $50, equipment purchases during the year amount to $250, and items originally costing $75 are sold for $20, resulting in a retirement loss of $40.

a. What is the correct ending balance in the Accumulated Depreciation account?

b. Prepare journal entries to record the events described. You may assume that all purchases and sales of equipment were cash transactions.

11. Interpreting Year-End Owners' Equity Account Balances.   After all transactions for the year had been recorded, the following balances were found in the owners' equity accounts of a small corporation (the sequence of the accounts in the list is alphabetical and has no other significance):

	Debit	**Credit**
Capital stock..........		$ 20,000
Cost of goods sold.....	$70,000	
Dividends declared.....	6,000	
Other expenses........	21,000	
Retained earnings		1,000
Sales revenue		100,000

a. What does the $6,000 opposite "Dividends declared" mean? Were these dividends paid in cash during the year?

b. What does the $1,000 opposite "Retained earnings" mean?

c. What balance would you show opposite "Retained earnings" on the year-end balance sheet?

12. Equipment Accounts; Journal Entries.   The balance sheet in Johnson Company's annual report for the year ended December 31, 19x1, showed the following amounts for plant and equipment:

	January 1	**December 31**
Plant and equipment..................	$400,000	$440,000
Less: Accumulated depreciation	180,000	190,000
Plant and equipment (net)	$220,000	$250,000

The income statement for the year showed depreciation expense of $30,000 and a gain of $10,000 on the sale of equipment. This equipment had a book value of $40,000, and it was sold for cash.

a. Calculate the cost of plant and equipment purchased during the year.

b. Prepare the appropriate journal entries to record the purchase of plant and equipment, the sale of equipment, and depreciation expense for the year. All plant and equipment purchases were cash transactions.

13. Equipment Accounts. During 19x4, Ken Company bought equipment for cash of $95,000. During the year, Ken sold equipment that it had been using for several years; the cash proceeds of $17,000 resulted in Ken recording a $5,000 loss. Ken Company's balance sheets at December 31, 19x3 and 19x4, contained the following amounts:

	December 31	
	19x3	**19x4**
Equipment	$143,000	$192,000
Less: Accumulated depreciation	99,000	107,000

a. What was the depreciation expense in 19x4?
b. What was the original cost of the sold equipment?

14. Supplying Missing Amounts. Sardis Company's bookkeeper burned the company's journals and spilled acid on the ledger in a moment of pique. Fortunately, the acid destroyed only the amounts missing from the following table:

	Beginning Balance	Transactions		Ending Balance
		Debits	**Credits**	
Accounts receivable	$35,000	$40,000	A	$36,000
Merchandise inventory	48,000	B	$26,000	42,000
Prepaid rent	3,000	1,000	2,000	C
Equipment	D	10,000	6,000	79,000
Accumulated depreciation	25,000	E	7,000	28,000
Wages payable	100	7,700	F	400
Accounts payable	G	19,000	H	25,000

The Accounts Payable account is used only in connection with transactions between Sardis Company and its suppliers of merchandise inventory.

a. Make the necessary calculations to determine the amounts missing from the table.
b. After you have answered part *a*, the table has seven debits and seven credits arising from transactions of the current period. For each debit and each credit, prepare an entry in general journal form that in your judgment was the entry in which the company originally recorded that debit or credit. If the debit or credit is to an account not included in the table, use any suitably descriptive account title.

15. Supplying Missing Amounts. Six accounts from Lea Corporation's ledger are presented in alphabetical order. All sales are on account, and all revenues and expenses are included in the transactions identified below.

	Beginning Balance	Transactions		Ending Balance
		Debits	Credits	
Accounts receivable	$ 17,000	A	$140,000	$ 22,000
Dividends declared		B		
Merchandise inventory	40,000	$93,000	C	45,000
Prepaid rent	1,500	4,100	D	1,200
Retained earnings	114,500	E	F	126,700
Wages payable	1,900	28,100	G	2,200

Make the necessary calculations to determine the amounts missing from the table.

16. Journal Entries; Ledger Accounts. Bellagio Company's ledger included the following eight accounts, among others, with these account balances at the beginning of April 19x1:

Cash	$ 45,600
Accounts receivable	83,500
Merchandise inventory	93,400
Salaries and wages payable........	800
Accounts payable	49,100
Sales revenues..................	213,900
Cost of goods sold	149,200
Salaries and wages expense	19,700

Bellagio Company had the following transactions, among others, in April 19x1:

1. It bought merchandise costing $55,900 on account and placed this merchandise in inventory.
2. It sold merchandise from inventory for $53,400 on account; the cost of this merchandise was $33,300.
3. It collected cash amounting to $81,000 on account from its customers.
4. It paid its merchandise suppliers $46,200 on account.
5. Its employees earned salaries and wages amounting to $6,500 in April.
6. Store employees were paid $6,200; this included the liability as of April 1.

a. Prepare T-accounts representing the eight ledger accounts listed and enter the April 1 balances. Be careful to place the balances on the correct sides of the T-accounts.
b. Prepare entries in general journal form to record your analyses of the six transactions listed.
c. Post these entries to the T-accounts.
d. Calculate the April 30 balance in each account and state what each balance represents.

17. Closing Entries. The accounts of Wolf Repair Service, Inc., had the following balances on December 31, 19x1:

	Debit	**Credit**
Accounts payable		$ 11,050
Accounts receivable	$ 31,000	
Accumulated depreciation		40,000
Capital stock		60,000
Cash	7,050	
Depreciation expense	15,000	
Dividends declared	10,000	
Dividends payable		2,500
Miscellaneous expenses	5,000	
Parts expenses	25,000	
Parts inventory	5,250	
Plant assets	140,000	
Prepaid rent	3,000	
Rent expense	9,000	
Retained earnings		40,050
Salaries and wages expense	96,000	
Salaries and wages payable		2,700
Sales revenues		190,000
Total	$346,300	$346,300

Prepare entries in general journal form to close all transitory accounts in preparation for recording transactions in 19x2.

18. Interpreting Entries in Accounts. Explain the most probable meaning of each number in the following T-accounts (beginning balances, ending balances and other entries have been omitted):

Accounts Receivable				**Merchandise Inventory**		
. . .	. . .	. . .		. . .	. . .	. . .
. . .	. . .	. . .		. . .	. . .	. . .
. . .	. . .	. . .		. . .	. . .	. . .
June 6	712	July 17	1,019	April 28	297	March 15	990

Store Equipment				**Accumulated Depreciation**		
. . .	. . .	. . .		. . .	. . .	. . .
. . .	. . .	. . .		. . .	. . .	. . .
. . .	. . .	. . .		. . .	. . .	. . .
March 12	3,241	Nov. 29	2,062	Nov. 29	1,445	Dec. 31	865

19. Plant Asset Accounts; Journal Entries. On January 2, 19x1, Febrile Company bought an electric typewriter for office use, paying $630 in cash. Management decided to recognize depreciation of $90 each year for six years.

a. What was the correct preclosing balance in the Accumulated Depreciation account as of December 31, 19x3?

   b. What was the correct preclosing balance in the Depreciation Expense account as of December 31, 19x3?

   c. What was the "book value" of the typewriter on December 31, 19x3?

   d. What entry would be required on December 31, 19x7, if the typewriter were sold on that date for $90 cash?

   e. What entry would be required on December 31, 19x4, if the typewriter were sold on that date for $80 cash?

20. Identifying Plant Asset Transactions from Financial Statement Data. Two successive balance sheets showed the following amounts:

	End of 19x1	End of 19x2
Property, plant, and equipment (cost)	$10,000	$11,200
Less: Accumulated depreciation	4,000	4,500
Property, plant, and equipment (net)	$ 6,000	$ 6,700

The income statements for the two years included the following items:

	19x1	19x2
Depreciation	$1,000	$ 900
Gain (loss) on the sale of property, plant, and equipment	100	(200)

The notes to the financial statements reported that the original cost of property, plant, and equipment sold for cash amounted to $800 in 19x1 and $700 in 19x2.

   a. Describe the transactions that led to changes in the *Property, Plant, and Equipment* and *Accumulated Depreciation* accounts *during 19x2.* Quantify the effects of these transactions on the company's accounts. (If you decide to do this by means of journal entries, give a brief verbal explanation of the meaning of each entry line.)

   b. Calculate the amounts in the balance sheet at the beginning of *19x1.* The proceeds from sales of property, plant, and equipment in 19x1 totaled $300. No property, plant, or equipment was bought in 19x1.

21. Transactions Analysis; Journal Entries. A number of transactions of an appliance repair business are described in problem 16 at the end of Chapter 2. Prepare entries in general journal form to record your analyses of these transactions.

22. Transactions Analysis; Journal Entries. A number of Grafton Corporation's transactions in 19x2 are described in problem 19 at the end of Chapter 2. Prepare entries in general journal form to record your analyses of these transactions.

23. Transactions Analysis; Journal Entries. A number of Gee Corporation's transactions in 19x2 are described in problem 20 at the end of Chapter 2. Prepare entries in general journal form to record your analyses of these transactions.

24. Transactions Analysis; Journal Entries. Woods Company is organized as a corporation and is engaged in retail trade. The owners' equity section of the ledger contains one revenue account (Sales Revenue), a number of expense accounts, and two balance sheet accounts (Capital Stock and Retained Earnings).

Woods Company had the following transactions, among others, this month (each transaction was independent of the others in this list):

1. Purchased office equipment on account, $4,700.
2. Received bill from plumbing contractor for repairs performed this month, $225.
3. Sold merchandise from inventory on account, $22,400; cost of merchandise was $16,700.
4. Issued 100 shares of the company's capital stock for $5,000 cash.
5. Hired clerk to start work the first of next month, salary $560 a month.
6. Collected $26,200 from customers on account.
7. Borrowed $1,000 cash from a bank.
8. Ordered a carload of bagged charcoal for sale to customers, $24,000.
9. Recorded $1,400 depreciation and $2,200 expiration of prepaid rent.
10. Recognized $1,500 salary earned this month by Mr. N. A. Woods, president of the company and owner of 75 percent of the corporation's capital stock.
11. Received bills, as follows:
    For new delivery truck, $19,500.
    For a one-year property insurance policy to be effective the first of next month, $1,600.
    For this month's telephone service, $85.
    These bills will be paid next month. The dealer will not deliver the new delivery truck until it has been paid for:

a. Prepare a journal entry or entries for each transaction.
b. For each debit and each credit, indicate (1) whether it represents an increase or a decrease in an asset, a liability, or the owners' equity, and (2) whether the amount would appear in full on the income statement for this month.

25. Erroneous Journal Entries. Auld Sod Company sells seeds, garden tools and supplies, and outdoor furniture to retail customers. Four of the company's transactions during 19x5 were as follows:

1. It agreed to rent a warehouse from Park Enterprises for three years, effective January 1, 19x6. The monthly rental payment was $950, and the first month's and final two months' rent was paid immediately.
2. It bought desk calculators for $990. Payment was made in cash and the calculators were distributed to the company's administrative personnel.
3. It paid cash, $167, for bunting, banners, displays, and refreshments purchased for use in a special sales promotion event taking place that same day.
4. It sold seeds, fertilizer, a garden tractor, and hand tools to Talbot Textile Company on account at a price of $850 for Talbot's use in landscaping its new office building. These products had cost Auld Sod $650.

The company's clerical personnel made one entry to record each of these transactions as it took place, as follows:

(1)	Rent expense	2,850	
	Accounts Payable		2,850
(2)	Office Supplies Expense	990	
	Accounts Payable		990
(3)	Advertising Expense	167	
	Inventories		167
(4)	Accounts Receivable	850	
	Inventories		850

a. Disregarding the entries made by the company's clerical personnel, indicate how each of these four transactions affected the company's assets, liabilities, and owners' equity. You should use the words *increase* and *decrease* rather than *debit* and *credit*.

b. For each transaction, indicate whether the correct entry was made. If not, state why the entry was incorrect and construct the entry the company should have made, using suitable account titles similar to those used in this chapter.

26. T-Accounts, Journal Entries, Statements, Closing Entries. Freemont Hardware Store, Inc., had the March 31, 19x1, balance sheet shown at the top of p. 111. The following items summarize the company's transactions for the month of April:

1. Purchased merchandise on account at a total cost of $67,500 and placed it in inventory.
2. Purchased an electric warehouse truck on account at a cost of $8,000.
3. Sold merchandise on account for $91,000; cost, $57,500.
4. Collected $75,000 on accounts receivable.

FREEMONT HARDWARE STORE, INC.
Balance Sheet
March 31, 19x1

Assets			Liabilities and Owners' Equity		
Current assets:			Current liabilities:		
Cash		$ 55,000	Notes payable		$ 15,000
Accounts receivable		120,500	Accounts payable		79,000
Merchandise inventory		108,500	Total current liabilities		94,000
Total current assets		284,000	Long-term debt		60,000
Plant assets:			Total liabilities		154,000
Land	$ 20,000		Owners' equity:		
Building	130,000		Capital stock	$200,000	
Equipment	54,000		Retained earnings	89,000	
Total	204,000		Total owners' equity		289,000
Accumulated					
depreciation	45,000	159,000	Total liabilities and		
Total assets		$443,000	owners' equity		$443,000

5. Received invoices covering telephone service, electricity, and other services bought and used during April, $5,700 (credit Accounts Payable).
6. Recorded employees' salaries for the month of April, $14,000.
7. Rented a small storeroom in a nearby building for 12 months, beginning April 1, 19x1, at a monthly rental of $550. Paid six months' rent in cash.
8. Paid $91,700 on accounts payable, $14,000 in salaries to employees, and $750 to holders of the company's notes payable and long-term debt, covering interest for the use of their money during April.
9. Calculated depreciation for the month of April: equipment, $800; building, $250.
10. The board of directors declared a dividend in the amount of $2,500 to be paid to shareholders in cash on May 15, 19x1.

a. Set up T-accounts for the items shown on the balance sheet and enter the March 31 balances.

b. Analyze each transaction and prepare journal entries using the account titles you adopted in part *a* plus any others required by your analyses.

c. Set up additional T-accounts, as required, and post your entries from part *b.*

d. Determine the April 30 balance in each account. Using these balances, prepare an income statement for the month of April and a balance sheet as of April 30. (Ignore income taxes.)

e. Prepare an appropriate closing entry or entries as of April 30.

27. Comprehensive Problem. Wentworth Petroleum Company provides fuel oil and oil burner maintenance services to retail customers. Its fiscal year begins on July 1 each year, after the end of the heating season, and ends the following June 30. The company's account balances at the start of business on July 1, 19x1, were as follows:

	Debit	Credit
Cash	$250,000	
Accounts receivable	50,000	
Inventory	200,000	
Prepaid rent	60,000	
Equipment	300,000	
Accumulated depreciation		$125,000
Accounts payable		150,000
Salaries payable		25,000
Dividends payable		10,000
Capital stock		375,000
Retained earnings		175,000

The company maintained no inventories of office supplies or repair parts for maintenance services. Purchases of these items are recorded as expenses.

The following information relates to the 12-month period that began on July 1, 19x1, and ended on June 30, 19x2:

1. Sales of fuel oil on account, $2,500,000.
2. Amount billed to customers for maintenance services provided on account, $250,000.
3. Salaries earned by employees, $500,000.
4. Purchases on account: fuel oil, $2,000,000; repair parts for maintenance service work, $25,000; office supplies and postage, $12,500; maintenance of delivery vehicles, $20,000; gasoline and oil for delivery vehicles, $75,000; new delivery truck, $50,000; telephone, electricity, and other miscellaneous services, $15,000.
5. Dividends declared, $100,000.
6. Cash collections from customers, $2,700,000.
7. Payments on account: to suppliers, $2,075,000; to employees for salaries, $515,000; to landlord for 12 months' rent from January 1 to December 31, 19x2, $135,000; to shareholders for dividends, $110,000.
8. Cash received from sale of old delivery truck, $5,000. This truck had been bought for $20,000 many years earlier and was fully depreciated at the time it was sold.
9. Cash received from the issuance of additional shares of capital stock, $90,000.
10. Depreciation for the year, $60,000.
11. Recorded cost of fuel oil sold. The cost of fuel oil in inventory on June 30, 19x2, was $450,000.

12. Recorded rent expense.

a. Draft a chart of accounts for Wentworth Petroleum Company, Inc., including appropriate revenue and expense accounts.

b. Set up T-accounts and enter the July 1, 19x1, balances.

c. Prepare journal entries to record your analyses of the information provided. For each debit and each credit, indicate whether it represents an increase or a decrease in an asset, liability, or owners' equity.

d. Post your entries to the T-accounts and calculate the June 30, 19x2, balances.

e. Prepare an income statement for the year ended June 30, 19x2, and a balance sheet as of June 30, 19x2.

f. Prepare a closing entry or entries to prepare the accounts to receive entries recording transactions in the 19x2–x3 fiscal year.

28. Comprehensive Problem: Profit-Seeking School. The Greeley School, a private preparatory day school, accepted its first students and held it first classes in September 19x1. The school was founded by Jonathan Greeley, the former senior tutor of a large eastern preparatory school.

Greeley was anxious to try out a new system of instruction and had persuaded a group of wealthy businesspeople to supply most of the capital he needed to finance the new venture. He intended to operate the school for profit, partly to demonstrate that it could be done, and partly because this seemed to him the best basis on which to attract the required capital.

As expected, enrollment was below capacity during the first year, but by May 19x2, applications for September enrollment were so numerous that Greeley believed his classes would be filled during the second year.

His backers were impressed by the file of admission applications and pleased by the competence Greeley seemed to have shown in administering the school, but they were anxious to find out how much money the school had lost during its initial year of operations. As one of the shareholders said, "The enrollment figures are impressive, but so are those at the university, and they have to tap us alumni every year just to meet the payroll. I don't expect we'll show a profit at Greeley this year, but if the loss is much larger than we had expected we ought to think seriously of closing up shop or selling our shares for whatever we can get for them."

The school started its formal existence on July 1, 19x1, with the issuance of a corporate charter. The following transactions took place during its first 12 months:

1. Two hundred shares of capital stock were issued on July 1, 19x1, for $90,000 cash.

2. At the same time, the shareholders deposited an additional $30,000 in the corporation's bank account, receiving, in exchange, notes payable in this amount (payable before December 31, 19x2).

3. A two-year lease was signed, giving the school the right to use a large mansion and its grounds from July 1, 19x1, to June 30, 19x3. The monthly rental was $6,000. An initial cash payment of $18,000 was made on July 1, 19x1 covering the first month's rent and a two-month refundable security deposit, and cash payments of $6,000 each were made on the first of each succeeding month, through June 1, 19x2.

4. Classroom blackboards were purchased on credit for $10,800. Other private schools in the area estimated that, on the average, blackboards could be used for 12 years before replacement was necessary.

5. Classroom furniture costing $27,000 was purchased from the Tower Seating Company, which accepted a down payment of $12,000 in cash and a note payable for the balance (payable before May 1, 19x3). Classroom furniture was expected to have an eight-year life on the average.

6. Equipment of various kinds, with an expected average life of five years, was purchased for $21,000 cash.

7. Students' tuition and other fees amounted to $234,000. Of this amount, $18,000 had not yet been collected by June 30, 19x2, but Greeley was confident that this amount would be received before the new school year began in September.

8. Salaries were paid in cash:
   Teaching staff, $162,000.
   Office staff, $33,000.

9. On June 15, 19x2, two parents paid tuition for the 19x2–x3 school year, amounting to $10,200.

10. Various school supplies were bought on credit for $12,300. Of these, $600 were still in the school's storeroom unused on June 30, 19x2.

11. Utility bills and other miscellaneous operating costs applicable to the year ending June 30, 19x2, were paid in cash, $11,400.

12. Payments amounting to $13,500 were made on account to suppliers of items referred to in 4 and 10 above.

13. The holders of the school's notes were paid interest of $2,700. In addition, the Tower Seating Company was paid $4,500 of the amount borrowed (item 5).

a. Prepare a list of account titles you think would be useful for recording these transactions, including revenue and expense accounts and an accumulated depreciation account. Then analyze the transactions in debit and credit form. For each debit and each credit indicate (1) whether the effect is to increase or to decrease an asset (*A*), liability (*L*), or owners' equity (*OE*), and (2) whether the amount would appear in full on the income statement for the current year. For example:

```
Cash  . . . . . . . . . . . . . . . . . . . . . . . . . . . . . . . . . . . . . . . . . . . . . . . .    XXX
      Capital Stock. . . . . . . . . . . . . . . . . . . . . . . . . . . . . . . . . . . . .           XXX
```
Increase *A*; increase *OE*; no effect on current income.

Don't forget to record depreciation for the year.

b. Post these amounts to T-accounts.

c. Prepare an income statement for the year and a balance sheet as of June 30, 19x2.

d. Upon seeing your figures, Greeley objected to the depreciation charge. "We just can't afford to write off any of those costs this year," he said. "Next year our tuition will be up, and we can start recovering depreciation." Do you agree with Greeley, or do you have a different concept of depreciation? Defend your position.

e. If you were a shareholder, how would you use the financial statements in your evaluation of the financial success or failure of this new enterprise? Assuming your decision to retain your shares or sell them would be based on your forecast of future financial statements, would the financial statements of a period in the past be of any relevance to you?

Chapter 4

Accruals and Deferrals

The accounting cycle begins with the analysis of transactions and ends with closing entries that allow the transitory accounts to receive the record of the next period's transactions. In this chapter, we'll examine several steps in the accounting cycle that we didn't discuss in Chapter 3, especially the construction of **adjusting entries** that must be made at the end of each period before the financial statements can be prepared. We'll begin the chapter, however, with a brief review of the general concept of *accrual accounting,* the measurement system in general use today.

Accrual Accounting   Just as Moliere's bourgeois gentleman was delighted to learn that he had been speaking prose all his life, we are happy to note that while we have been learning the fundamentals of transactions analysis, we have been practicing **accrual accounting.** Accrual accounting is any system in which changes in assets, liabilities, and owners' equity are measured by flows of resources of all kinds rather than by flows of cash alone. The alternative to accrual accounting is *cash-basis accounting.*[1]

We can best illustrate the fundamental differences between accrual accounting and cash-basis accounting by a simple example.

John Appleby operates a small management consulting business under the name of Appleby Associates. On January 25, he purchased and received materials costing $1,000 for use on an assignment. He paid for the

---

[1] The word *accrue* literally means to accumulate or to arise. Accountants use it to signify that an accountable event has occurred, even though there has been no routinely recorded transaction.

116

materials on February 9 and started to work on the assignment on March 5. The project was completed on March 28, and Jones Company was billed for the contract price of $12,000 on that date. Salaries of employees who worked on the assignment during March totaled $4,000, and this amount was paid on March 31.

This series of transactions is summarized in Exhibit 4–1. An expenditure in January was followed by a cash disbursement of $1,000 in February, another disbursement of $4,000 in March, and a cash receipt of $12,000 in April. Cash-basis accounting would indicate that the company lost $1,000 in February and $4,000 in March, and earned $12,000 in April, when cash was finally received from the client.

EXHIBIT 4–1
Appleby Associates: Timing of Events

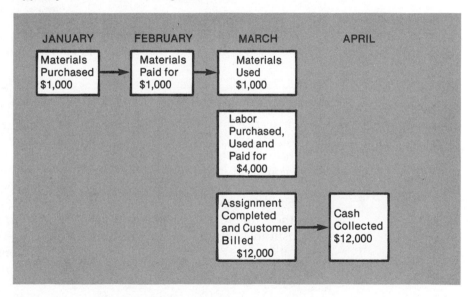

Anyone who has mastered the first three chapters of this book will recognize quickly that income or loss calculated on a cash basis ignores many significant resource flows. For example, accrual accounting for Appleby Associates brings *all* the resource flows together in the income statement for March, when all the work was done—that is, Appleby Associates had to recognize income of $7,000 on this contract in March ($12,000 − $4,000 − $1,000), even though the company had paid out $5,000 in cash by the end of the month with no cash inflows.

While this example illustrates the basic nature of accrual accounting, implementing accrual accounting is more complicated. No method of routine, day-by-day recording of transactions can make a fully adequate identification of income, assets and liabilities. Adjustments must be made at the end of the year, necessitated by circumstances that either arise only at year-end or can be dealt with more efficiently once a year (or once a month or quarter) than on a continuing basis.

In the next nine sections, we'll describe nine adjustments that are frequently made so that the accounts will conform to the precepts of accrual accounting. Three of these adjustments focus on the revenue accounts; the other six are designed to bring expense totals to accrual-basis levels. The nine adjustments are:

Adjustments to Revenues	Adjustments to Expenses
Interest revenue	Interest expense
Revenue deferral	Wage and salary accrual
Uncollectible receivables	Product warranties
	Inventory adjustment
	Depreciation
	Amortization of prepaid costs

These aren't the only adjustments companies make, but they illustrate the general principles that govern all adjustments.

Interest Revenue Accrual

Appropriately enough, the first adjustment we'll discuss is an **accrual.** An accrual is an entry made to recognize a revenue or expense, together with its related effect on an asset or liability, when the accounting period ends before the revenue or expense is recorded as part of the ordinary recordkeeping routine.

The first accrual we'll illustrate is a revenue accrual, the recognition of accrued interest on the loans a company has made to its customers and others. Interest accruals are made not only by banks and other financial institutions, which make loans as their main line of business; commercial businesses also make loans, usually by accepting promissory notes from customers when payment is to be deferred beyond the normal credit period.

TERMINOLOGY

A **promissory note** is a written promise to pay a set amount of money on a specified date known as the *maturity date.* The amount borrowed is termed the *proceeds,* the amount paid for the use of the proceeds is called **interest,** and the amount to be repaid to the lender on the maturity date is the *maturity value* or face value.

For example, in 19x7, Baxter Stores, a large distributor of home appliances and equipment, supplied all the major appliances for a new apartment building. The price agreed upon was $110,000, and the transaction was recorded by the following entry:

Accounts Receivable	110,000	
Sales Revenues		110,000

Baxter's terms of sale required the contractor who was building the apartments to pay the full price on or before November 16, 19x7. When that day arrived, however, the contractor was short of cash and offered to pay $15,000 in cash and give a 180-day promissory note with a maturity value of $100,000, including interest, to cover the $95,000 balance of the invoice price. Baxter's management agreed, and accepted the contractor's note.

Taking a note for a larger maturity value ($100,000) than the amount exchanged for it ($95,000) is known as *discounting* the note. In discounting a note, the lender calculates the amount due at the maturity date (including interest) and then deducts interest on this amount to determine the sum to be made available to the borrower.

In this case, Baxter Stores and the contractor agreed that $5,000 was an appropriate amount of interest on $95,000 for 180 days. This is roughly the same as interest of $10,000 for a full year, or about 10 percent. Baxter therefore was discounting the contractor's note at 10 percent.[2]

Baxter Stores made the following entry to record its receipt of $15,000 cash and acceptance of the note:

Cash	15,000	
Notes Receivable	95,000	
Accounts Receivable		110,000[3]

This entry shows that Baxter simply exchanged one asset (an account receivable) for two others (cash and a note receivable).

Even though the contractor wouldn't *pay* Baxter any interest until the end of the 180-day period, Baxter *earned* interest every day because the contractor had the use of Baxter's money every day. Since the note was dated November 16, 19x7, Baxter earned interest on this note for 45 days

---

[2] The contractor in this case actually paid interest at a rate slightly higher than 10 percent a year. In discounting transactions, the quoted interest rate is applied to the maturity value rather than to the amount actually borrowed. Since the contractor paid $5,000 for the use of $95,000 for approximately six months, the effective rate of interest was approximately $2 \times \$5,000/\$95,000$, or 10.5 percent a year.

[3] An equivalent alternative is to record the note at its face value, with the discount credited to a contra account:

Cash	15,000	
Notes Receivable	100,000	
Discount on Notes Receivable		5,000
Accounts Receivable		110,000

in 19x7 (14 days in November and 31 days in December), as in the following diagram:[4]

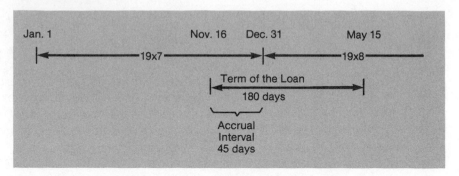

This means that 45/180, or one fourth, of the full loan period fell in 19x7. Interest revenue for 19x7 therefore was one fourth of the interest for 180 days:

$$\text{Interest revenue} = 1/4 \times \$5,000 = \$1,250$$

The adjusting entry to accrue this interest was as follows:[5]

(1)

Notes Receivable	**1,250**	
Interest Revenue		**1,250**

The credit to Interest Revenue, a transitory owners' equity account, shows that this transaction increased Baxter's owners' equity in 19x7. The debit to Notes Receivable shows that the amount owed by the contractor at the end of the year included both the invoice price of the merchandise ($95,000) and interest for the use of Baxter's money for 45 days ($1,250). If Baxter had had an Interest Receivable account in its chart of accounts, the accountant would have debited that instead.

Revenue Deferral   A second kind of end-of-period adjustment to recorded revenues is a **revenue deferral,** designed to remove from current revenues amounts that won't be earned until a future period.

---

[4] In determining the maturity date of the note, the day the loan is made isn't counted. In this case, interest started on November 17, the day after the date on the note. The maturity date was May 15, 19x8 (14 days in November, 31 in December, 31 in January, 28 in February, 31 in March, 30 in April, and 15 in May).

[5] The nine adjusting entries that are discussed in this chapter are numbered so that they can be referred to relatively easily later on. They are displayed in boldface type to distinguish them from other entries that are part of the explanation but aren't adjusting entries.

A revenue deferral is necessary when revenue has been recorded before it is earned. For example, when customers pay in advance for goods or services, no revenue is created. A revenue account may be credited, however, either because the bookkeeping routine requires it or because, in most cases, the revenue will be earned before the financial statements are prepared. When this is done, an adjusting entry may have to be made at the end of the period if the revenue hasn't been earned by that time.

At the beginning of December 19x7, a customer paid Baxter Stores $25,000 for merchandise to be delivered later. A clerk in Baxter's accounting department recorded the transaction as an ordinary sale, as follows:

Cash. 25,000
    Sales Revenues   25,000

Baxter delivered 40 percent of this order on December 29, 19x7, and made no entry at that time. The result was that the year-end balance in Sales Revenues was $15,000 too large (60 percent of $25,000), and Baxter had an unrecorded liability of $15,000—its obligation to deliver the rest of the merchandise later.

To avoid overstating sales revenues and understating liabilities, Baxter made the following adjusting entry at the end of 19x7:

(2)

Sales Revenues. **15,000**
    Advances from Customers **15,000**

The debit to Sales Revenues reduced the balance in that account to the amount earned in 19x7; the credit to Advances from Customers recognized Baxter's liability to deliver merchandise to the customer in 19x8.

A liability for advances from customers is sometimes called *deferred revenue, unearned revenue,* or a *deferred credit.* No matter what it is called, however, it is a liability the company must meet, either by delivering goods as promised or by returning the customer's money.

Uncollectible Receivables

The third major kind of adjustment to recorded revenues is the adjustment to allow for the fact that some outstanding receivables will never be paid. These uncollectible accounts, or **bad debts,** are a fact of life in most businesses. We need to examine carefully why this is so and how the adjustment is usually made.

Measuring Revenues and Receivables from Credit Sales

The amount of revenue arising from a group of ordinary sale transactions is the amount the seller will collect from this group of customers. Furthermore, generally accepted accounting principles require that the company report its receivables at their value to the company—that is, the amount the company will be able to collect in the normal course of business.

In most businesses, the seller knows that *some* customers will never pay the full amounts they agree to pay for the goods or services they buy. This means that the real revenues are the amounts billed all customers in the group, less the amounts the seller won't be able to collect. It also means that the value of the receivables on any date will be their *face value* (the amount the customers owe), *less* the amounts that will eventually prove to be uncollectible.

These relationships are illustrated in Exhibit 4–2. The shaded blocks at the left represent the total amounts billed to customers in the current

EXHIBIT 4–2
Gross versus Net Revenues and Receivables

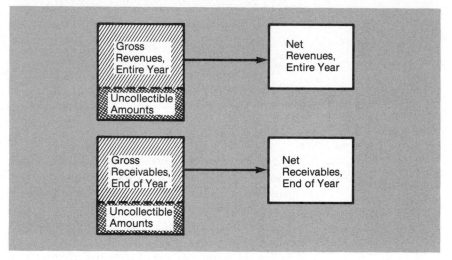

period and the total amounts still listed as due from customers at the end of the year. Subtracting the uncollectible portions of these amounts yields the net revenues and net receivables, represented by the unshaded blocks at the right.

Sales revenues are usually recorded at their face value. After all, management doesn't know which customers will eventually default, so it records all revenues and receivables initially as if it believes no one will default. Baxter Stores' credit sales in 19x7 amounted to $1 million, and its entries to record these sales can be summarized as follows:

```
Accounts Receivable ............................  1,000,000
        Sales Revenues ..............................              1,000,000
```

The debit to Accounts Receivable represents an increase in that asset; the credit to Sales Revenues recorded an increase in owners' equity.

The company also received $850,000 from its credit customers in 19x7 in payment of amounts they owed on account. A summary of the entries the company made to record these receipts is as follows:

```
Cash...............................................  850,000
      Accounts Receivable...........................           850,000
```

After these entries were made, Baxter's Sales Revenues account had a credit balance of $1 million, while its Accounts Receivable account had a debit balance of $150,000 ($1,000,000 − $850,000). (For simplicity, we're assuming for the moment that Baxter had never sold on credit before 19x7, so it started the year with no accounts receivable.)

Both of these numbers are overstated, however. Management knew that some of its 19x7 customers would never pay the amounts they owed. In fact, the company's credit manager estimated that $12,200 of the receivables arising from 19x7 sales would never be paid. In other words, total revenue from 19x7 sales was really only $1,000,000 − $12,200 = $987,800, and the value of the receivables on December 31, 19x7, was only $150,000 − $12,200 = $137,800. An entry of some sort had to be made to reflect that fact.

The Adjusting Entry

The adjustment at the end of 19x7 to correct the overstatements of revenues and receivables could have been made as follows:

```
Sales Revenues....................................  12,200
      Accounts Receivable...........................           12,200
```

This entry would have reduced the owners' equity *and* receivables asset totals to their correct levels.

The entry wasn't made this way, however, for two reasons. One reason is that management doesn't know which customers will default when it makes sales. This means that the accountant can't remove any individual accounts from the accounts receivable file. Crediting the Accounts Receivable account therefore would make the balance in that account unequal to the sum of the balances in the individual accounts receivable. That would be unacceptable, because the balance in the Accounts Receivable ledger account is supposed to be a control total for the individual accounts.

The secondary reason why this entry is often unacceptable is that management may want to calculate certain financial ratios, such as the ratio of the cost of goods sold to sales, as percentages of *gross* revenues, that is, *before* deducting uncollectible amounts. If the balance in the

Sales Revenues account were reduced by the amount of this adjustment, the amount of gross revenues could not be derived from the ledger account balances.

For these reasons, Baxter Stores set up two new accounts—**Bad Debts** and **Allowance for Uncollectibles**—and made the following entry:

(3)

Bad Debts...	12,200	
Allowance for Uncollectibles		12,200

These two accounts were contra accounts—to Sales Revenues and Accounts Receivable, respectively. The debit to Bad Debts corrected the overstatement of revenues in the Sales Revenues account; the credit to Allowance for Uncollectibles brought the accounts receivable asset down to its correct level. Once this adjustment was made, the financial statements disclosed the following amounts:

Income statement:

Gross sales............................	$1,000,000
Less: Bad debts.......................	12,200
Net sales..............................	$ 987,800

Balance sheet:

Accounts receivable, gross	$ 150,000
Less: Allowance for uncollectibles	12,200
Accounts receivable, net	$ 137,800

TERMINOLOGY REMINDER: CONTRA ACCOUNT

A *contra account* is an account established to accumulate a specific class of deductions from the gross amount of some asset, liability, owners' equity, revenue, or expense. For presenting financial statements, the balance in the contra account should always be deducted from the gross amount with which it is paired.

The $12,200 shown in the income statement as estimated bad debts is a *sales deduction,* which must be subtracted from gross sales to reflect the fact that the amount to be collected from customers will be less than the gross sales amount. Sales deductions are like expenses in that both are subtracted from gross revenues in the determination of net income. Expenses, however, are *costs* of resources used to obtained revenues, while sales deductions are *corrections* of the gross revenue amounts. Therefore, although bad debts are often listed among expenses (and are called *bad debt expense* in those cases), they really belong in the revenue section of the income statement, as in the preceding table.

Write-Offs of Specific Uncollectible Accounts

At some point, management will identify specific customers' receivables as being, in fact, uncollectible. Since amounts were put in the Allowance for Uncollectibles account because management knew that this would happen some day, the balance in this account is reduced when it actually does happen—that is, when specific receivables are identified as uncollectible.

> TERMINOLOGY REMINDER
>
> *Write-off* means the reduction in an asset due to a determination that its value is less than its recorded amount. It can also be used as a verb, as in "*writing off* a receivable."

In our example, the entry to record the write-off of a $1,000 account would be as follows:

```
Allowance for Uncollectibles............................  1,000
     Accounts Receivable................................          1,000
```

The credit to Accounts Receivable reduces the balance in this account, and the debit to the allowance reduces its balance by the same amount.

This entry doesn't record a reduction in the asset, because the value of the receivables as a whole has not decreased. *The asset reduction actually took place when the sale took place, and was recorded when the bad debt adjustment was made.* The only change at the time of the write-off is that a *specific* receivable is identified as one of those for which the *general* provision was made in the first place.

These facts are reflected in the following table:

	Before Adjustment	After Adjustment	After Write-Off
Receivables, gross	$150,000	$150,000	$149,000
Less: Allowance	—	12,200	11,200
Receivables, net	$150,000	$137,800	$137,800
Decrease in receivables......	—	$ 12,200	—

The left-hand column shows the initial record of the receivables. The middle column shows what really happened—that is, the receivables were worth $12,200 less than the initial record indicated. Finally, the right-hand column shows why the $1,000 write-off had *no effect on net receivables.*

Aging the Accounts

Management can't defer preparing its financial statements until all receivables arising from the period's sales have either been collected or written off. The year-end adjustment therefore has to reflect an estimate of the amounts customers won't pay in the future.

A common technique for estimating bad debts is known as **aging the accounts.** This is based on the premise that the older the claim, the less likely it is to be collected. The analysis is performed as follows:

1. Customer account balances are classified by age—that is, by the length of time since the invoice date.
2. An estimated bad debts percentage is developed for each age group, partly from historical experience and partly from a qualitative examination of a sample of accounts in the group.
3. These bad debts percentages are multiplied by the amounts receivable in their respective age brackets.
4. The products of these calculations are added, and the total is used to adjust the appropriate account balances.

Remember that Baxter's credit manager estimated that $12,200 of its year-end accounts receivable would never be collected. The credit manager derived this number by aging these receivables and applying bad-debt ratios similar companies were experiencing. This analysis shows the following:

Age (Days)	Amount Receivable	Percent Uncollectible	Amount Uncollectible
1–30	$100,000	0.8	$ 800
31–60	35,000	4.0	1,400
61–120	10,000	55.0	5,500
121 and older	5,000	90.0	4,500
Total	$150,000		$12,200

Receivables from Previous Years

In setting up our illustration, we made one simplifying assumption—that Baxter Stores had made no credit sales before 19x7 and therefore had no uncollectible accounts as of January 1, 19x7. For this reason, Baxter Stores' estimated bad debts for 19x7 and the balance in the Allowance for Uncollectibles account at the end of 19x7 were identical: $12,200.

Let's extend this illustration to the more general case by considering the following information for the next year, 19x8:

Credit sales	$1,200,000
Collections on accounts receivable	1,150,000
Write-offs of specific uncollectible accounts.	10,300
Estimated uncollectible amounts, December 31, 19x8	14,700

Before adjusting entries were made at the end of 19x8, the receivables accounts showed the following:

Accounts Receivable

Bal. 1/1	150,000	Collections	1,150,000
Sales	1,200,000	Write-offs	10,300
Bal. 12/31	189,700		

Allowance for Uncollectibles

Write-offs	10,300	Bal. 1/1	12,200
		Bal. 12/31	1,900

We know from the table preceding the T-accounts, however, that the balance in the Allowance for Uncollectibles account at the end of 19x8 should have been $14,700. The company therefore had to add $12,800 to the $1,900 credit balance in this account to bring it to the correct level. The adjusting entry was:

Bad Debts	12,800	
Allowance for Uncollectibles		12,800

Gross sales revenues were reduced by $12,800; net accounts receivable were reported to be $14,700 less than their gross amount.

This entry implies that $12,800 of the estimated uncollectibles arose from sales in 19x8 and that the other $1,900 arose from sales made in 19x7. In fact, the $12,800 is likely to be the sum of the estimated defaults on current sales *and* the correction of the estimate Baxter's management made at the end of the previous year. Accountants don't usually try to separate these two components; it's usually accurate enough to refer to the combined total as the effect of the current year's sales.

Interest Expense Accrual

The three previous adjustments were designed to bring the balances in revenue accounts to correct accrual-accounting levels. Now we'll turn to six adjustments that are designed to bring the balances in expense accounts to their proper levels.

To begin with, remember that in accrual accounting, the cost of any goods or services consumed is an expense in the period in which the related revenue benefit occurs, no matter when the related disbursement is made—past, present, or future. When routine, day-by-day recording of transactions doesn't measure an expense according to this principle, an end-of-period adjustment has to be made.

One such adjustment is the accrual of interest expense by companies that have borrowed money from banks or other lenders. This accrual is exactly the same as the accrual of interest revenue Baxter accomplished by entry (1). The accrual is necessary because although the borrowing company incurs interest expense every day it uses money, it makes interest *payments* less frequently. When time has elapsed between the most recent payment date and the end of the accounting period, an accrual is necessary to include interest for that interval in the financial statements for the period.

For example, Baxter Stores borrowed $30,000 from a bank on December 1, 19x7, promising to repay this amount, plus interest, 90 days later. Since Baxter paid no interest before the end of the year, its accountants had to accrue interest expense on this loan before they could prepare the financial statements for 19x7.

MORE TERMINOLOGY

The interval between the borrowing and maturity dates is the *life* or *term* of the loan—90 days in this case. The *proceeds* is the amount received from the lender when the loan is made. The *interest rate* is the percentage which, when multiplied by the proceeds, determines the amount of interest the borrower would pay if the loan were for a one-year term. In this case, $30,000 was the proceeds and the interest rate was 12 percent.

In exchange for the loan, Baxter gave the bank a 90-day, 12 percent promissory note. Baxter's bank followed customary banking practice by calculating interest on its short-term loans as if the year were 360 days long. The 90-day note therefore required interest at 90/360, or one fourth, of the annual rate. Baxter Stores, in other words, agreed to pay the bank $30,000 plus interest of $900 (1/4 × 12 percent × $30,000) on March 1, 19x8, exactly 90 days from the date of the loan.

The next transaction to be recorded in Baxter's normal bookkeeping routine was the repayment of the loan plus interest on March 1, 19x8. The company had to issue financial statements as of December 31, 19x7, however. It had used the bank's money for 30 days by that date, and the cost of using it for this period was a cost of doing business in 19x7. Again we can show the accrual interval in a diagram:

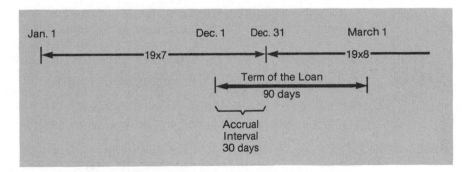

This means that 30/90 of the $900 total interest cost, $300, was a 19x7 expense. The adjusting entry was:

(4)

Interest Expense	**300**	
Notes Payable		**300**

The debit to the expense account recorded a reduction in the owners' equity; the credit to Notes Payable recorded the increase in the amount owed to the bank. (A credit to Interest Payable instead of to Notes Payable would have been appropriate if the chart of accounts had included that account.)

When the note matured on March 1, 19x8, the entry to record the payment of the amount borrowed and 90 days' interest was:

Notes Payable	30,300	
Interest Expense	600	
Cash		30,900

The debit to Notes Payable recorded the repayment of the amount that had been owed at the beginning of the year, including the $300 liability that had been recorded in the December 31, 19x7, adjustment. The $600 interest expense was the cost of using the bank's money during January and February 19x8, and the $30,900 reduction in cash was the sum of the $30,000 original proceeds of the loan and the $900 interest cost for 90 days.

Accruing Wages and Salaries

Some salaries and wages are paid weekly. This means that the accounting period may end on a day other than the last day of a weekly payroll period. When this happens, an accrual must be made so that the cost of all the employees' time used during the accounting period will be reflected in the financial statements for the period.

For example, Baxter Stores' last weekly payroll period of 19x7 ended on Saturday, December 28. Monday and Tuesday, December 30 and 31, were full working days, which means that some wages were earned by employees in 19x7 but were not recorded in the accounts as part of the normal bookkeeping process until the next year. These amounts were paid as part of the first weekly payroll of 19x8, but part of that payroll was really a cost applicable to 19x7.

Employees in the company's stores and offices earned $5,000 and $1,000, respectively, on the two working days between the end of the last weekly payroll period and the end of the year. The entry to accrue these costs was:

(5)

Salaries and Wages Expense	6,000	
Salaries and Wages Payable		6,000

The debit to Salaries and Wages Expense recorded the December 30 and 31 portion of the payroll as a cost of generating revenue benefits in 19x7; the credit to Salaries and Wages Payable recognized the company's liability on December 31, 19x7, to pay its employees in 19x8 for work done in 19x7.

If the first payroll in 19x8 amounted to $16,000, Baxter would record the following entry at that time:

Salaries and Wages Payable	6,000	
Salaries and Wages Expense	10,000	
Cash		16,000

This entry would recognize the payment of both the $6,000 end-of-19x7 liability and the $10,000 expense incurred in 19x8.

Product Warranties

Some costs arising from the sale of merchandise may not be incurred until *after* the merchandise is delivered to customers. A prime example is the cost of doing work under the terms of a product warranty.

Recognizing Warranty Expense

Warranties help the company make sales by reassuring potential customers that the company's products are of high quality and any defects will be corrected. The cost of performing warranty service on goods sold in any period, therefore, is part of the cost of securing the revenues of that period. For this reason, warranty costs should be recognized as expenses in the period in which revenues are recorded, even though the exact amount of these costs won't be known until later.

Exhibit 4–3 shows how the expense to be recognized in the delivery period includes warranty costs, represented by the block at the right, as well as costs incurred both currently and in previous periods.

EXHIBIT 4–3
Classifying Costs as Expenses: Revenues Recognized at Delivery

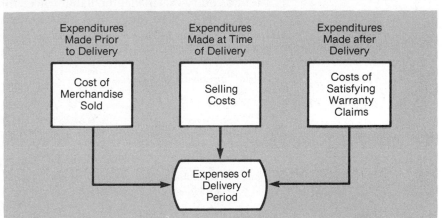

Suppose Baxter Stores decided in March 19x7 that, for all future sales, it would stand ready to repair or replace defective appliances without charge to its customers, even after the manufacturers' warranty periods expired. The costs of providing these services enter the accounting system in two stages:

1. As an end-of-period adjustment, Baxter recognizes the expected future costs of service on these products as a current expense *and* as an end-of-period liability.
2. By providing warranty services to customers in a later period, Baxter reduces its liability to its appliance customers. The company measures the reduction in this liability by the actual cost of providing the warranty service.

Baxter Stores' management estimated that the warranties in force at the end of 19x7 would lead to future expenditures of about $16,500. These were costs of 19x7 revenues, and $16,500 was also the company's estimated liability at the end of 19x7. To enter these amounts in the financial statements for 19x7, the company made the following adjusting entry:

(6)

Warranty Expense.....................................	**16,500**	
Liability for Service Warranty......................		**16,500**

The $16,500 debit recorded the expected future expenditure as a current-period expense; the credit amount established Baxter's end-of-19x7 liability to its customers.

Actual Warranty Expenditures

After this entry was made, the liability account was ready for use in the next year (19x8). Warranty claims in 19x8 were satisfied by payment of $5,000 in cash and the use of merchandise from inventory, at a cost of $10,000. This required the following entry in 19x8:

Liability for Service Warranty	15,000	
Cash		5,000
Inventory		10,000

The liability account then showed the following:

Liability for Service Warranty

Expenditures in 19x8	15,000	Bal. 1/1/x8	16,500
		Bal. 1,500	

At the end of 19x8, Baxter estimated that warranties then in force would lead to future costs of approximately $21,400. This required the following adjusting entry as of December 31, 19x8:

Warranty Expense	19,900	
Liability for Service Warranty		19,900

Since the liability had been reduced in 19x8 to $1,500, the amount needed to reach the desired $21,400 level was $19,900 ($21,400 − $1,500).

Nature of the Warranty Liability

The liability for service warranty is a different kind of liability from any we've seen up to now, for two reasons. First, this liability is often discharged by performing services or replacing parts or merchandise, not by paying cash to a creditor. Advances from customers was the closest to this among the liabilities we studied earlier. Second, the amount of the liability is uncertain. If the actual warranty claims turn out to be different from the estimated amounts, the expense that was recorded will be corrected in a subsequent period—that is, when the claims are ascertained and discharged.

For example, suppose the $21,400 estimated liability at the end of 19x8 included $2,400 in connection with merchandise the company sold in 19x7 and $19,000 in connection with 19x8 sales. This means that the $19,900 recognized as expense in 19x8 included $900 ($19,900 − $19,000) to correct the understatement of expense in 19x7.

TYPES OF EXPENSE ADJUSTMENTS

Our illustration includes six expense adjustments. The three expense adjustments we've discussed so far have been (1) accruing interest, (2) accruing wages and salaries, and (3) providing for product warranties. They all arise from the need to recognize previously unrecorded usage of goods or services. In all three cases, the year-end adjusting entries recognize as expenses never-recorded costs that were incurred to help generate the current period's revenues.

The three remaining expense adjustments differ from the first three because they arise from costs that were recorded previously. These last three adjustments serve to reclassify portions of those costs as determinants of the current period's net income.

Inventory and the Cost of Goods Sold

The sale of merchandise requires removing the cost of the goods sold from the Inventory account. The amount to be removed can be determined by either the *periodic inventory method* or the *perpetual inventory method.*

Periodic Inventory Method

Under the **periodic inventory method,** an account called Purchases is ordinarily used. Although it represents neither an asset nor an expense, Purchases is the debit-balance account in which the company records the cost of merchandise acquired as purchase transactions occur.

In periodic inventory accounting, inventories still on hand are counted and their costs are determined at the end of the year. The cost of the goods sold is then determined by subtracting the cost of the ending inventory from the sum of the cost of the beginning inventory and the cost of goods purchased during the period:

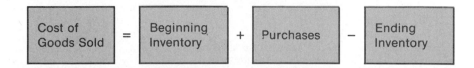

This is shown more clearly in the diagram on the left side of Exhibit 4–4. The height of the large column represents the cost of all the goods available for sale during the period. After the ending inventory has been counted and subtracted from the total, what's left is the cost of goods sold. An adjusting entry brings the Purchases account to a zero balance and the Inventory account to its end-of-year level.

EXHIBIT 4–4
Calculating the Cost of Goods Sold

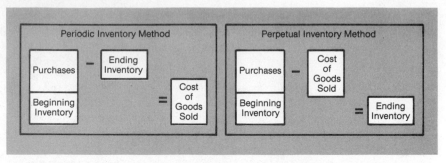

To illustrate, suppose the cost of Baxter's inventory on January 1, 19x7, was $82,000. Since one period's ending inventory is the following period's beginning inventory, this amount was based on the physical count at the end of 19x6. Purchases during 19x7 were $457,000, and the year-end count indicated that goods costing $89,000 were on hand.

The $82,000 beginning balance in Inventory was unaffected by entries made during 19x7. The costs of the goods acquired were entered in the Purchases account by the following entry:

Purchases	457,000	
Accounts Payable		457,000

Baxter made no entry to the inventory and expense accounts when merchandise was sold. Instead, company personnel counted the inventory at the end of the year and determined that goods costing $89,000 were on hand at that time. In other words, inventory increased by $7,000 between the beginning and end of 19x7, meaning that purchases had exceeded the cost of goods sold by that amount. To reflect this information, the accountants made the following adjusting entry:

(7)

Inventory	**7,000**	
Cost of Goods Sold	**450,000**	
Purchases		**457,000**

The $7,000 debit to Inventory increased the year-end asset balance to its correct level ($89,000), and the debit to Cost of Goods Sold established the $450,000 expense that would appear in the income statement. The $457,000 credit to Purchases reduced its balance to zero, thus enabling it to begin receiving new debit amounts to record the following year's acquisitions of merchandise.

Perpetual Inventory Method

The **perpetual inventory method** requires that the cost of purchased goods be added (debited) to the Inventory account at the time they are received. No Purchases account is used. Each time an item is sold, an entry is made to transfer its cost from Inventory to the Cost of Goods Sold account. The right side of Exhibit 4–4 diagrams this sequence.

If Baxter Stores had used the perpetual inventory method, it would have recorded its purchases of merchandise as follows:

Inventory	457,000	
Accounts Payable		457,000

Each time the company sold merchandise, someone would have had to determine the cost of the merchandise sold. Let's suppose the total of these costs came to $449,000 in 19x7. A summary entry to record this amount would have been:

Cost of Goods Sold	449,000	
Inventory.		449,000

As a result of these transactions, the Inventory account had a $90,000 balance as of December 31.

Inventory			
Jan. 1	82,000	Cost of goods sold	449,000
Purchases	457,000		
	539,000		449,000
Bal. 90,000			

Barring error, theft, or decay, the balance in the Inventory account should always equal the cost of the goods on hand. To verify this, however, a physical count is taken periodically. Any difference between the cost of the inventory actually on hand at that time and the amount shown in the Inventory account is the cost of lost, stolen, or spoiled goods or the result of bookkeeping errors.

In our illustration, the tally on December 31 located merchandise with a total cost of only $89,000. The $1,000 difference between this and the $90,000 indicated by the inventory records became the basis for an inventory adjustment. Lacking any way of separating the amounts due to the various causes, Baxter's accountants would have charged off the entire amount with the following entry:

Inventory Shrinkage Expense	1,000	
Inventory.		1,000

The credit to Inventory recognized the reduction in this asset that was revealed by the annual count; the debit to Inventory Shrinkage Expense recorded the accompanying reduction in owners' equity. If the count had exceeded the book value of the merchandise on hand, indicating that errors had been made in recording the cost of goods sold, that account would have been credited.

In a published income statement, the adjustment to the recorded inventory is ordinarily reported as part of the cost of goods sold, leading to the same reported cost of goods sold as in the periodic inventory method.

Depreciation of Plant Assets

A second type of expense-oriented adjustment which measures the consumption of an existing asset is **depreciation.** Recall from Chapter 2 that the objective of depreciation is to allocate the cost of plant assets systematically to the operations of the future periods that benefit from the assets' use. Even though depreciation occurs throughout the year, it is usually recorded at the end of each accounting period as part of the adjustment process.

Baxter Stores had furniture and equipment on hand at the end of 19x7 with a total original cost of $144,000, of which $39,000 had been depreciated in previous years. The company's property records showed the location and annual depreciation rate on each asset. From these records, the accountants found that depreciation amounted to $6,000 in 19x7 on the furniture and equipment in the stores, and $3,000 on office furniture and equipment, a total of $9,000. They made the following adjusting entry:

(8)

Depreciation Expense.....................................	9,000	
Accumulated Depreciation		9,000

The debit recognized the decrease in owners' equity resulting from the effect of the passage of time on the company's furniture and equipment. The credit to Accumulated Depreciation measured an asset reduction, reflecting the decline in the remaining usefulness of this group of assets.[6]

Amortization of Prepaid Costs

Baxter's final adjustment is another instance of recognizing the consumption of an asset that the company had acquired previously. Although we saw a simplified prepaid rent example of this kind in Chapter 2, we'll now consider *prepaid insurance* (sometimes called *unexpired insurance*).

The balance in Baxter Stores' Prepaid Insurance account was $6,000 at the end of 19x7. A review of the insurance file revealed that this amount could be traced to five policies that had been in force for all or part of 19x7. This information is summarized in Exhibit 4–5.

The total at the bottom of column (4) is the balance in the Prepaid

---

[6] In practice, a variety of acceptable methods can be used to estimate depreciation expense. These will be discussed at length in Chapter 9.

EXHIBIT 4–5
Data for Insurance Expense Adjustment

(1) Policy No.	(2) Effective Date	(3) Expiration Date	(4) Un-adjusted Balance	(5) Monthly Premium Cost	(6) Months this Year	(7) Premiums Expired (5) × (6)	(8) Un-expired Premiums (4) − (7)
AB 406–721	1/1/x4	12/31/x7	$ 540	$ 45	12	$ 540	—
CD 492–881	4/1/x6	3/31/x7	60	20	3	60	—
XL 172–008	7/1/x5	12/31/x8	2,400	100	12	1,200	$1,200
CD 712–654	4/1/x7	3/31/x8	300	25	9	225	75
PL 202–903	1/1/x7	12/31/x9	2,700	75	12	900	1,800
Total			$6,000			$2,925	$3,075

Insurance asset account. Column (5) shows the monthly premium for each of these policies, taken from information in the policies themselves. Column (6) shows how many months each policy was in force between January 1 and December 31, 19x7. The cost of insurance coverage for the year [column (7)] was then calculated by multiplying the monthly premium by the number of months. The total of these amounts, $2,925, had to be transferred from the Prepaid Insurance account to an appropriate expense account. The adjusting entry was:

(9)

| Insurance Expense . . . . | 2,925 | |
| Prepaid Insurance . . . . | | 2,925 |

This entry reduced the balance in the Prepaid Insurance account to $3,075, the total at the bottom of column (8). This represented the unexpired premiums on the three policies still in force on January 1, 19x8.

SUMMARY: THE ROLE OF ADJUSTING ENTRIES

Accrual accounting necessitates making revenue and expense adjustments at the end of every accounting period. Under accrual accounting, *income* is the net increase in net assets resulting from operations. Since *net assets* are the excess of assets over liabilities, accountants determine income by measuring the changes in *all* assets and liabilities resulting from operations—not just changes in Cash.

End-of-period adjustments represent the culmination of that process. Despite accountants' adherence to the rules of accrual accounting throughout the year, year-end adjustments are always necessary. They are an integral part of accrual accounting, not a way to compensate for carelessness. If it is determined that substantive accounting errors or arithmetic mistakes have been made during the year, however, correcting entries are made at the same time the recurring adjustments are recorded.

Trial Balances   The adjusting entries we described in the preceding sections follow the journalizing and posting stages in the accounting cycle we described in Chapter 3. Before and after these adjustments are made, the accountants are likely to prepare **trial balances.** In this section, we'll explain what these trial balances are and describe their place in the accounting cycle.

Unadjusted Trial Balance

A trial balance is a list of every account title in the ledger and its balance on a specified date, with all debit balances arranged in one column and all credit balances in another. The first trial balance taken as of a given date is the **unadjusted trial balance,** which shows the account balances after all routine bookkeeping operations have been completed but before any adjusting entries have been entered. Its purpose is to make sure that the accounting equation has remained balanced throughout the journalizing and posting stages of the accounting cycle—that is, that the sum of the balances in all accounts with debit balances is equal to the sum of all the balances in accounts with credit balances.

Exhibit 4–6 presents Baxter Stores' unadjusted trial balance as of December 31, 19x7. Notice that this trial balance lists both balance sheet and income statement accounts. The only aspects of an account that have any relevance at this point are its balance and whether it is a debit or credit balance.

Fortunately, the column totals in Exhibit 4–6 are equal. This doesn't necessarily mean that the accounting is free of errors, however. A balanced trial balance indicates only that the sum of the posted debits equals the sum of the posted credits. It won't disclose that a correct debit in the journal was posted as a debit to the wrong ledger account, or that a balanced journal entry contained incorrect amounts, or that one or more transactions weren't journalized and posted at all. Accountants must remain alert to the possibility of substantive errors of this sort, even if the trial balance is balanced.

Adjusted Trial Balance

A second trial balance is prepared after all adjusting entries have been posted and account balances have been recalculated.[7] Again, the main purpose is to make sure that the equality of debits and credits has been maintained. A second purpose is to bring all account balances together in

---

[7] For convenience, the adjustments may be made outside the ledger, in a columnar worksheet or computer spreadsheet, in which case the adjusted trial balance can be prepared before the entries have been posted to the ledger. The process is essentially the same, however.

a compact list, to make it easier for accountants to prepare the financial statements.

Exhibit 4–7 presents Baxter's **adjusted trial balance,** based on ledger account balances that include the nine year-end adjustments discussed in this chapter. The adjusted trial balance amounts that differ from those in the earlier trial balance appear in boldface.

Baxter's nine adjusting entries are summarized in Exhibit 4–8. Since Baxter Stores used the periodic inventory method, its trial balance contained a Purchases account, and the inventory adjustment was used to determine the cost of goods sold. Readers who take a few minutes to return to the discussion of the adjustments will be able to follow those amounts into the adjusted trial balance.

| Financial Statements | Once the adjusted trial balance has been prepared, the next stage in the accounting cycle is the preparation of financial statements. The account balances in Exhibit 4–7 don't pose any problems we didn't discuss earlier, so we can present Baxter Stores' balance sheet and income statement for 19x7 with relatively few explanatory comments. |

Income Statement

Exhibit 4–9 presents Baxter's income statement for the year. The only new features here are (1) the deduction of the estimate of bad debts from gross revenues, (2) the separation of interest revenue and interest expense from income from commercial operations, and (3) the deduction of income tax expense at the bottom.[8]

Income statements may be further segmented in some circumstances, but we'll defer any discussion of these situations to Chapter 15.

Balance Sheet

Baxter Stores' year-end balance sheet is shown in Exhibit 4–10. The asset and liability balances in this statement were copied from the adjusted trial balance in Exhibit 4–7. They have been arranged in current and noncurrent categories, as in the illustrations in previous chapters. Baxter Stores had noncurrent assets in 19x7, but no noncurrent liabilities.

The retained earnings amount in this balance sheet differs from the balance in the Retained Earnings account in the adjusted trial balance. The latter number, it will be remembered, was the balance in that ac-

---

[8] The accrual of income tax expense is usually entered as a year-end adjusting entry. We omitted that step, however, because discussion of the income tax implications of some of Baxter Stores' transactions would have lengthened the presentation intolerably.

EXHIBIT 4–6

BAXTER STORES, INC.
Unadjusted Trial Balance
As of December 31, 19x7

Account	Debit	Credit
Cash........................	$ 64,000	
Notes receivable...............	95,000	
Accounts receivable............	150,000	
Allowance for uncollectibles.....		$ —
Inventory....................	82,000	
Prepaid insurance	6,000	
Furniture and equipment........	144,000	
Accumulated depreciation		39,000
Notes payable.................		30,000
Accounts payable..............		91,200
Salaries and wages payable		—
Taxes payable.................		19,625
Dividends payable		4,000
Advances from customers.......		—
Liability for service warranty.....		—
Capital stock..................		200,000
Retained earnings		44,150
Sales revenues		1,015,000
Interest revenue		—
Bad debts	—	
Purchases....................	457,000	
Cost of goods sold.............	—	
Salaries and wages expense.....	274,000	
Depreciation expense	—	
Rent expense	80,000	
Utilities expense...............	23,000	
Warranty expense..............	—	
Insurance expense.............	—	
Interest expense...............	1,200	
Income tax expense............	31,600	
Miscellaneous expense	19,175	
Dividends declared.............	16,000	
Totals.....................	$1,442,975	$1,442,975

EXHIBIT 4–7

BAXTER STORES, INC.
Adjusted Trial Balance
As of December 31, 19x7

Account	Debit	Credit
Cash.........................	$ 64,000	
Notes receivable...............	**96,250**	
Accounts receivable............	150,000	
Allowance for uncollectibles.....		$ 12,200
Inventory....................	**89,000**	
Prepaid insurance	**3,075**	
Furniture and equipment........	144,000	
Accumulated depreciation		**48,000**
Notes payable.................		**30,300**
Accounts payable..............		91,200
Salaries and wages payable		**6,000**
Taxes payable.................		19,625
Dividends payable		4,000
Advances from customers.......		**15,000**
Liability for service warranty.....		**16,500**
Capital stock.................		200,000
Retained earnings		44,150
Sales revenues		**1,000,000**
Interest revenue		**1,250**
Bad debts	12,200	
Purchases	—	
Cost of goods sold............	450,000	
Salaries and wages expense.....	280,000	
Depreciation expense	**9,000**	
Rent expense	80,000	
Utilities expense..............	23,000	
Warranty expense.............	**16,500**	
Insurance expense............	**2,925**	
Interest expense..............	**1,500**	
Income tax expense...........	31,600	
Miscellaneous expense	19,175	
Dividends declared............	16,000	
Totals	**$1,488,225**	**$1,488,225**

EXHIBIT 4–8
Baxter Stores, Inc.: Adjusting Entries

(1)	Notes receivable............................	1,250	
	Interest Revenue		1,250
	To record accrued interest revenue.		
(2)	Sales Revenues.............................	15,000	
	Advances from Customers		15,000
	To reclassify funds received in advance.		
(3)	Bad Debts	12,200	
	Allowance for Uncollectibles		12,200
	To record estimated uncollectibles.		
(4)	Interest Expense............................	300	
	Notes Payable		300
	To record accrued interest expense.		
(5)	Salaries and Wages Expense	6,000	
	Salaries and Wages Payable		6,000
	To record accrued payroll expense.		
(6)	Warranty Expense...........................	16,500	
	Liability for Service Warranty..............		16,500
	To record estimated cost of servicing warranty claims.		
(7)	Inventory	7,000	
	Cost of Goods Sold	450,000	
	Purchases...............................		457,000
	To record cost of goods sold and cost of goods on hand.		
(8)	Depreciation Expense	9,000	
	Accumulated Depreciation................		9,000
	To record depreciation of plant assets.		
(9)	Insurance Expense..........................	2,925	
	Prepaid Insurance		2,925
	To record expiration of insurance coverage.		

EXHIBIT 4–9

BAXTER STORES, INC.
Income Statement
For the Year Ended December 31, 19x7

Gross revenue from sales		$1,000,000
Less: Bad debts.		12,200
Net revenue from sales.		987,800
Cost of goods sold		450,000
Gross margin.		537,800
Operating expenses:		
Salaries and wages	$280,000	
Rent.	80,000	
Utilities	23,000	
Depreciation.	9,000	
Warranties	16,500	
Insurance	2,925	
Miscellaneous	19,175	
Total		430,600
Operating income before taxes.		107,200
Other revenue and expense:		
Interest revenue.	1,250	
Interest expense	1,500	
Net other expense		250
Income before income taxes		106,950
Income tax expense		31,600
Net income.		$ 75,350

count at the *beginning* of the year. The year-end balance was obtained by adding the net income for the year and subtracting the dividends, as follows:

Retained earnings, beginning of year	$ 44,150
Add: Net income.	75,350
	119,500
Less: Cash dividends declared.	16,000
Retained earnings, end of year.	$103,500

The balance sheet includes two contra-account balances. As was the case in the income statement, each contra-account balance appears with the gross amount to which it relates. Accounts receivable appears as $150,000 gross and $137,800 net, "net" meaning after deducting the allowance for uncollectibles. Furniture and equipment are disclosed on a dual basis as well—cost is $144,000 and book value is $96,000.

The balance sheet also includes one *combined* item, "other current liabilities." This sum appears as two separate amounts in the adjusted

EXHIBIT 4–10

BAXTER STORES, INC.
Balance Sheet
As of December 31, 19x7

Assets

Current assets:

Cash		$ 64,000
Notes receivable.......................		96,250
Accounts receivable	$150,000	
Less: Allowance for uncollectibles......	12,200	137,800
Inventory.............................		89,000
Prepaid insurance		3,075
Total current assets		390,125

Plant assets:

Furniture and equipment	144,000	
Less: Accumulated depreciation	48,000	96,000
Total assets		$486,125

Liabilities and Owners' Equity

Current liabilities:

Notes payable........................		$ 30,300
Accounts payable.....................		91,200
Taxes payable........................		19,625
Advances from customers		15,000
Liability for service warranty		16,500
Other current liabilities		10,000
Total current liabilities..............		182,625

Owners' equity:

Capital stock..........................	$200,000	
Retained earnings	103,500	
Total owners' equity................		303,500
Total liabilities and owners' equity..		$486,125

trial balance—$6,000 salaries and wages payable and $4,000 dividends payable. These amounts were combined because neither, taken by itself, was big enough to have a material effect on the company's financial position.

Closing Entries

Exhibit 4–11 shows the various stages in the accounting cycle, including both those described in Chapter 3 and those described here. As this indicates, once the financial statements have been prepared, the only remaining stage in the accounting cycle is the preparation of closing entries. Completion of this final stage is represented in Exhibit 4–11 by the dashed line from the "closing entries" oval to the "opening account balances" oval we started with.

EXHIBIT 4–11
The Accounting Cycle

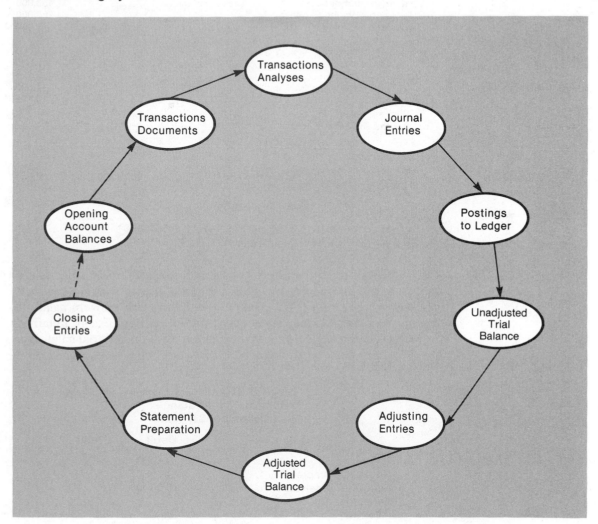

Recall from Chapter 3 that closing entries are made to reduce each of the transitory accounts to a zero balance—that is, each income statement account and the Dividends Declared and Income Summary accounts. Baxter Stores' closing entries for 19x7 were as follows:

(a)

Sales Revenues	1,000,000	
Interest Revenue.	1,250	
Bad Debts		12,200
Income Summary		989,050
To close the revenue-related accounts.		

(b)

Income Summary	913,700	
Cost of Goods Sold		450,000
Salaries and Wages Expense		280,000
Depreciation Expense		9,000
Rent Expense		80,000
Utilities Expense		23,000
Warranty Expense		16,500
Insurance Expense		2,925
Interest Expense		1,500
Miscellaneous Expense		19,175
Income Tax Expense		31,600

To close the expense accounts.

(c)

Income Summary	75,350	
Retained Earnings		75,350

To close the Income Summary account.

(d)

Retained Earnings	16,000	
Dividends Declared		16,000

To close the Dividends Declared account.

Once the closing entries were posted and new account balances were calculated, the accountant was able to prepare the *postclosing trial balance* shown in Exhibit 4–12. The only accounts with nonzero balances are the continuing balance sheet accounts. All of these except Retained Earnings have the same balances they had in the adjusted trial balance of

EXHIBIT 4–12

BAXTER STORES, INC.
Postclosing Trial Balance
As of December 31, 19x7

Account	Debit	Credit
Cash	$ 64,000	
Notes receivable	96,250	
Accounts receivable	150,000	
Allowance for uncollectibles		$ 12,200
Inventory	89,000	
Prepaid insurance	3,075	
Furniture and equipment	144,000	
Accumulated depreciation		48,000
Notes payable		30,300
Accounts payable		91,200
Salaries and wages payable		6,000
Taxes payable		19,625
Dividends payable		4,000
Advances from customers		15,000
Liability for service warranty		16,500
Capital stock		200,000
Retained earnings		103,500
Totals	$546,325	$546,325

Exhibit 4–8. The Retained Earnings account has a balance of $103,500, the amount reported in the December 31 balance sheet. All the transitory accounts have zero balances and the accounting cycle is complete.

Summary

Most bookkeeping is initiated by action documents such as payroll checks and customer invoices. Data for financial reporting are derived as a by-product of these important but routine activities.

Because the initial impetus for bookkeeping arises from needs other than the need to prepare financial statements, it probably isn't surprising that the bookkeeping results fail to consider all of the factors that have a bearing on accrual-basis financial statements. The accounting cycle continues, therefore, with the preparation of end-of-period adjusting entries, initiated by accountants for the sole purpose of deriving financial statements. This chapter has illustrated nine common adjusting entries; in practice, many more might be necessary.

Once adjusting entries have been made, accountants use the adjusted account balances to prepare financial statements. This done, they then close the transitory owners' equity accounts, thus setting the stage for the next accounting cycle.

Key Terms

Accrual	Inventory shrinkage
Adjusting entry	Periodic inventory method
Allowance for uncollectibles	Perpetual inventory method
Bad debts	Promissory note
Interest	Trial balance

TECHNICAL NOTE: MAKING CORRECTING ENTRIES

Before making a correcting entry, (1) determine the entry that should have been made, (2) identify any differences between that entry and the entry that was made, (3) debit any account that was underdebited or overcredited with the amount underdebited or overcredited, and (4) credit any account that was undercredited or overdebited with the amount undercredited or overdebited.

Independent Study Problems (Solutions in Appendix B)

1. Bad Debts. Reilly Company recognizes revenues at the time it delivers products to its customers. You have the following information for the month of June:

1. Opening balances:
Accounts Receivable, $950,000.
Allowance for Uncollectibles, $25,000.

2. Gross sales, $500,000.
3. Collections from customers, $510,000.
4. Write-offs of specific uncollectibles, $8,000.
5. Estimated uncollectible amounts, June 30, $28,200.

a. Analyze the effects of items 2, 3, 4, and 5 on the company's assets, liabilities, and owners' equity. (Use +/− notation.)
b. Prepare journal entries to reflect your analyses in part *a*.
c. What amount should be reported to the shareholders for accounts receivable at the end of June?
d. What amount should be shown for bad debts on the income statement for the month of June?

2. Interest Accrual. On September 15, Calhoun Company borrowed $6,000 from the bank, promising to pay $6,000 plus accrued interest at 14 percent 60 days from the date of the note. On November 14, the company paid the accrued interest and renewed the note for an additional 30 days. At the second maturity, on December 14, Calhoun paid $4,000 in cash and gave a new 30-day, 14 percent note for the remaining amount due. This last note was paid in full when due.

a. Calculate Calhoun's interest expense for the year that ended December 31.
b. Prepare a journal entry to record the December 31 accrual.
c. Assuming that no additional entry was made between the accrual entry and the repayment date in January, prepare a journal entry to record the January payment.

3. Warranty Accrual. For many years, Philox Corporation has given each of its customers a two-year warranty on all purchases of Philox products. Management estimated that it would cost $55,000 to carry out its future obligations under the warranties in force on December 31, 19x1, and this amount was reflected in the company's ledger.

During 19x2, Philox paid $40,000 for warranty claims: three quarters in parts and complete units of merchandise, one quarter in cash. As of the end of 19x2, management estimated its warranty liability to be $83,500.

a. Calculate the amount of warranty expense to be shown on the company's income statement for 19x2.
b. Using whatever accounts are appropriate, prepare journal entries to record the warranty expense and other warranty-related transactions in 19x2.

4. Revenues and Expenses; Missing Amounts. The following table contains amounts relating to Patey Corporation's 19x8 operations. All purchases and sales were on account. No debits or credits other than those indicated were made in the accounts listed in this table.

	Postclosing Trial Balance, December 31, 19x7	Debits	Credits	Adjusted Trial Balance, December 31, 19x8
Accounts receivable.........	$82,400	A	B	$ 96,700
Rent expense		$ 21,600		C
Sales revenue			D	317,300
Cost of goods sold..........		E		206,200
Bad debts		F		G
Allowance for uncollectibles..	3,300	H	$4,500	5,100
Prepaid rent................	I	24,800	J	7,500
Merchandise inventory.......	31,800	194,900	K	L

  a. Determine and label the missing amounts.
  b. Which of the missing amounts probably arose from adjusting entries?

5. Adjusting Entries; Financial Statements. The December 31, 19x3, trial balance of Guyton Company is as follows:

GUYTON COMPANY
Trial Balance
As of December 31, 19x3

Account	Debit	Credit
Cash.....................................	$ 30,900	
Notes receivable...........................	17,700	
Accounts receivable........................	91,600	
Allowance for uncollectibles.................		$ 1,500
Inventory of merchandise, January 1, 19x3.....	89,000	
Prepaid insurance	2,425	
Other prepayments.........................	1,340	
Land.....................................	16,000	
Building and equipment	45,800	
Accumulated depreciation		8,100
Accounts payable...........................		18,800
Mortgage payable..........................		45,000
Capital stock..............................		150,000
Retained earnings		53,720
Sales revenues		400,000
Interest revenue		480
Purchases	344,500	
Advertising expense........................	1,200	
Salaries and wages expense..................	16,400	
Miscellaneous selling expense...............	5,800	
Property tax expense.......................	3,300	
Miscellaneous general expenses	8,435	
Interest expense...........................	3,200	
Totals.................................	$677,600	$677,600

The following information had not been recorded in the accounts when the trial balance was prepared:

1. A customers' account amounting to $165 was 18 months overdue, with little chance it would ever be collected; management decided to write it off.
2. Aging of the accounts receivable remaining on the books after the write-off in item 1 indicated that receivables amounting to $89,315, measured at gross invoice prices, probably were collectible.
3. The cost of the merchandise in the inventory on December 31, 19x3, was $86,440.
4. Merchandise costing $975 was received on December 31, 19x3, but was still in the receiving room and therefore wasn't included in the inventory count (item 3). The invoice covering this shipment wasn't reflected in the trial balance.
5. $1,725 of the insurance premiums paid before December 31, 19x3, were for insurance coverage in 19x4.
6. Depreciation for the year was $1,240.
7. Unrecorded interest accrued on the mortgage payable since the last interest payment amounted to $400.
8. Unrecorded wages earned by employees between the end of the last payroll period of 19x3 and the end of the year amounted to $240.

a. Prepare a journal entry for each year-end adjustment.
b. Prepare an adjusted trial balance.
c. Prepare an income statement for 19x3 and a year-end balance sheet.

Exercises and Problems

6. Interest Expense Accrual. Peterson Company borrowed $20,000 from a bank on January 21, giving in exchange a 90-day, 15 percent note.

a. Prepare an entry to record the borrowing.
b. Prepare whatever entry this transaction would make necessary on January 31 if Peterson Company wished to prepare a set of accrual-basis financial statements as of the close of business on that date.
c. What entry would be necessary on January 31 if Peterson Company prepared financial statements quarterly instead of monthly, the first quarter of the year ending on March 31? What entry would be made on February 28? On March 31?

7. Prepaid Insurance and Insurance Expense. As of January 1, 19x4, Abigail Corporation's Prepaid Insurance account contained a $3,857 balance representing two policies: 3 months of fire and theft insurance and 14 months of motor vehicle insurance. The following insurance-related transactions occurred during 19x4.

Feb. 20: Paid a $3,000 premium for one-year life insurance coverage for key company executives, effective March 1.
Mar. 29: Paid $7,200 for three-year renewal of fire and theft coverage,

effective upon March 31 expiration of the two-year policy that had cost $4,200.

Aug. 24:   Purchased business interruption insurance at a three-year cost of $4,860, effective September 1. Paid $1,620 immediately for the first year's coverage.

Oct. 1:   Paid $2,400 to increase the fire and theft coverage for the duration of the existing policy, effective October 1.

An entry debiting Prepaid Insurance was made for each of these transactions.

a. What was Abigail Corporation's insurance expense in 19x4?

b. What was Abigail Corporation's prepaid insurance as of January 1, 19x5?

c. What adjusting entry did Abigail make as of December 31, 19x4?

8. Interpreting Account Entries; Adjusting Entry.   The following amounts appeared in the Prepaid Rent account of a motion picture theater during 19x1:

Prepaid Rent	
Bal. 1/1	10
Debits	75

Investigation shows that the balance in this account on December 31, 19x1, should have been $25, debit.

a. How much money was paid to the landlord in 19x1?

b. What was the rent expense for 19x1?

c. What adjusting entry had to be made before the books could be closed at the end of 19x1?

9. Warranty Accrual.   Peale Company makes oil burners, which it warrants for parts and labor for 12 months after installation by retail dealers. At the end of 19x1, Peale's management estimated that the company would have to spend $57,000 in the future to fulfill the terms of its warranties on products it had sold to dealers on or before December 31, 19x1.

In 19x2, Peale had sales revenues of $1 million and income of $150,000 before warranty expense and income taxes. The company spent $60,000 in 19x2 to make good on warranties outstanding. At the end of 19x2, Peale's management estimated that the company would have to spend $78,000 in 19x3 and 19x4 to fulfill the terms of its warranties on products it shipped to dealers in 19x1 and 19x2.

a. Calculate warranty expense for 19x2.

b. How important to Peale Company is the requirement that it account for warranty costs on an accrual basis in 19x2?

c. Peale Company is growing from year to year and the income tax-levying authorities allow the deduction of warranty costs only as warranty expenditures are made. How does this rule of taxation affect Peale Company?

10. Interest Revenue, Interest Expense. McKay Company borrowed $40,000 from a bank on June 10, 19x2. The loan matured on February 5, 19x3, at which time McKay paid both the principal and 15 percent interest.

On September 27, 19x3, McKay lent $9,000 to Gardner, Ltd. Gardner paid the $9,000 note on February 24, 19x4, together with interest at an annual rate of 12 percent.

On December 11, 19x3, McKay accepted a customer's 60-day note to satisfy a past-due account. McKay recorded the note at the $62,000 amount of the unpaid balance even though its maturity value was $65,000. The customer paid the full amount on February 9, 19x4.

Prepare McKay Corporation's journal entries relating to these transactions, as well as year-end adjusting entries.

11. Interpreting Accounting Entries; Adjusting Entry. The following amounts appeared in the *Salaries Payable* account of an advertising firm during 19x2:

Salaries Payable			
(2)	1,360	Bal. 1/1	50
		(1)	1,400
		Bal. 12/31	90

The debit and credit shown here represent the many debits and credits that were actually entered in this account during the year.

All these amounts were correct, and no further adjustments were necessary. Payroll taxes were zero, and all salary costs passed through this account.

a. Calculate salary expense for the year.
b. How much of the salaries earned by employees in 19x2 were paid in cash during the year?
c. How much was paid to employees during 19x2 for work done in 19x1?
d. How much will be paid to employees in 19x3 for work done in 19x2?

12. Missing Amounts. Bell Company's ledger included the following four accounts:

	Postclosing Trial Balance, December 31, 19x4	Debits	Credits	Adjusted Trial Balance, December 31, 19x5
Bad debts		A		$ 4,200
Accounts receivable	$75,000	B	$464,000	C
Allowance for uncollectibles . .	3,200	D	E	3,900
Sales revenues			F	450,000

The debits and credits represented in this table are the only entries made in these four accounts. All of the company's sales during the year were on credit.

Determine and label the missing amounts.

13. Revenues and Expenses.   During 19x1, Arkin Company had sales of $450,000, its accounts receivable increased by $22,400, and its allowance for uncollectibles increased by $3,800. Its December 31 adjustments included recording cost of goods sold for $310,000 and its $14,700 estimate of bad debts.

a. How much cash did Arkin Company receive from its customers during 19x1?

During 19x2, Brockton Corporation had sales of $252,000, which represented a 50 percent markup over the goods' cost. Brockton's accounts payable to its merchandise suppliers increased by $18,700, while the cost of the year-end inventory was $16,500 less than it had been 12 months earlier.

b. How much cash did Brockton Corporation pay to its suppliers during 19x2?

During 19x3, Carter, Inc., had a $5,000 increase in capital stock and a $14,700 decrease in total liabilities. Carter's directors declared and paid a $2,500 cash dividend, expenses were $97,300, and assets increased by $43,300.

c. What was the amount of Carter, Inc.'s sales revenue in 19x3?

14. Preparing Financial Statements.   Listed below are account balances relating to Rogers Corporation's 19x3 financial statements.

Machinery	$ 20,000	Depreciation expense	$ 600
Prepaid insurance	400	Accounts payable	12,600
Notes payable (due 19x6)	12,400	Insurance expense	1,400
Bad debts	200	Allowance for uncollectibles . .	300
Land	4,400	Retained earnings,	
Cash	4,600	Jan. 1, 19x3	18,000
Interest expense	1,300	Accumulated depreciation	5,400
Capital stock	1,500	Accounts receivable	14,000
Dividends declared	7,500	Merchandise inventory,	
Revenue from sales	141,500	Dec. 31, 19x3	4,300
Purchases of merchandise . . .	22,900	Interest revenue	900
Wages and salaries expense . .	103,600	Income tax expense	1,800
Merchandise inventory,		Notes receivable (due in 19x4)	5,000
Jan. 1, 19x3	6,100	Wages and salaries payable . .	1,200

a. Prepare the 19x3 income statement.

b. Prepare the December 31, 19x3, balance sheet.

15. Accruals and Adjustments.   During 19x3, Carlton, Ltd., paid cash of $24,000 for insurance, $82,500 for rent, $196,000 for salaries, and $17,100 for warranty claims. Carlton's end-of-year unadjusted trial balance included $58,000 of rent expense and $196,000 of salaries expense.

After all adjusting entries were made, Carlton's balance sheet showed changes from December 31, 19x2, in the following four accounts:

Prepaid rent, increase	$ 3,200
Prepaid insurance, decrease	12,200
Salaries payable, increase	6,300
Liability for warranty claims, decrease	3,300

You discover that when payment was made each month for that month's computer rental, the expense was recorded immediately. Rental payments for office space were made in advance and were recorded as prepaid rent.

a. What was Carlton's insurance expense for 19x3?

b. What was Carlton's rent expense for 19x3?

c. What was Carlton's warranty expense for 19x3?

d. What was Carlton's salaries expense for 19x3?

16. Revenues, Expenses, and Adjustments.   Universal Corporation paid Dillon, Inc., $45,000 cash on August 1, 19x1, for the exclusive right to use Universal's computer from then until February 1, 19x3. Dillon recorded this transaction in a Revenue Received in Advance liability account.

About a year later, on August 4, 19x2, Universal bought merchandise for $13,000 cash, and it used the perpetual method of inventory recordkeeping to record the transaction. On September 14, 19x2, Universal sold the merchandise to Dillon; Dillon issued a 15 percent, 120-day note for the $18,000 invoice price, and it used the periodic method of inventory recordkeeping to record the transaction.

Dillon sold one third of the merchandise on December 10, 19x2, for $11,500 cash, and the remainder on March 2, 19x3, for $24,000 cash. On January 12, 19x3, Dillon paid Universal the full amount owed on the September 19x2 note.

Using parallel columns for Universal and Dillon, prepare the journal entries that each company recorded in 19x1, 19x2, and 19x3.

17. Effects of Recordkeeping Errors.   Craft Company used the periodic method of inventory recordkeeping. An audit early in 19x5 established that the company had made the following eight recordkeeping errors in 19x3 and 19x4:

1. Failed to record accrued salaries in 19x3. These salaries were paid in 19x4.
2. Overstated cost of December 31, 19x3, inventory.
3. Forgot to record depreciation expense in 19x3.
4. Treated December 31, 19x3, prepaid rent as a 19x3 rent expense.
5. Recorded interest earned in 19x3 as revenue in 19x4.
6. Recorded January 19x4 advertising cost as expense when paid for in 19x3.
7. Recorded $9,280 estimated bad debts as $19,280 on December 31, 19x4.
8. In 19x4, bought land, recorded it as a machine, and recognized depreciation expense in 19x4.

Determine the effects of each error on the following financial statement elements:

a. 19x3 income.
b. December 31, 19x3, assets.
c. December 31, 19x3, liabilities.
d. 19x4 income.
e. December 31, 19x4, owners' equity.

To answer this, you should set up a five-column table and use *O* to signify overstatement, *U* for understatement, and *X* for no effect.

18. Revenues and Receivables.   Davis Company started operations early in 19x1. You have the following data for 19x1 and 19x2:

	19x1	19x2
Sales on credit	$320,000	$500,000
Collections from credit customers	260,000	480,000
Write-offs of specific accounts receivable	—	3,900
Amounts of gross receivables at year-end management expects to be uncollectible (after specific write-offs)	5,000	6,000

a. Prepare entries in general journal form to reflect your analysis of this information, including closing entries for each year.
b. Calculate the company's net revenues as they should be shown on each year's income statement.
c. Show how accounts receivable should be reported on the year-end balance sheets for 19x1 and 19x2.

19. Revenues and Receivables: Missing Data. You have the following partial data on two companies' revenues in a recent year and their receivables at the beginning and end of that year. All sales are on account. Supply the amounts missing from this table.

	Company A	Company B
Allowance for uncollectibles:		
January 1	$ 4	$ 10
December 31	5	F
Collections from customers	A	545
Estimated bad debts	B	6
Gross accounts receivable:		
January 1	50	G
December 31	C	90
Gross sales	370	H
Net accounts receivable:		
January 1	D	70
December 31	35	79
Net sales	E	I
Write-offs of specific uncollectibles	6	J

20. Recordkeeping Errors. Crown Company uses the periodic inventory method. The annual inventory count was made at the end of 19x1 and was reflected in the ledger at that time. Subsequently, the following recordkeeping errors were discovered:

1. A purchase of merchandise for $4,200 was incorrectly debited to Furniture and Fixtures.
2. Cash of $1,300 received from a customer on account was incorrectly credited to Sales.
3. A $400 payment to a vendor on account was incorrectly debited to Merchandise Inventories.
4. A sales invoice for $400 was not recorded; payment was not received from the customer before the end of the year, but Crown's management anticipated no difficulty in collecting it early in 19x2.
5. A $100 telephone bill was incorrectly charged to Entertainment Expense instead of to Telephone Expense.

a. For each of these, construct the adjusting entry that would have been made if the error had been discovered *before* the financial statements were prepared and *before* the year-end closing entries were made.

b. How would your answer to part *a* differ if these errors had been discovered *after* the closing entries had been made and *after* the financial statements for the year had been published?

21. Preparing an Income Statement. Mountain Corporation was created in January 19x3. Its unconventional bookkeeping system produced the following data:

	Cash Exchanged	No Cash Exchanged
Rent of store location	$ 9,000	
Cost of merchandise purchased	83,500	$66,200
Salaries and wages	28,900	1,300
Sales of merchandise	98,800	83,100
Store fixtures acquired		14,000
Insurance cost	1,500	

Your investigation of 19x3's transactions reveals that rent was paid covering the period from January 1, 19x3, through March 31, 19x4; the insurance policy covers the 12 months that began February 1, 19x3; the store fixtures are likely to last 10 years; and the year-end inventory had cost $23,200.

Prepare Mountain Corporation's 19x3 income statement. Ignore income taxes.

22. Corrections; Adjusting Entries. The information that follows was collected by the companies' accountants before their companies' financial statements for the year 19x1 were prepared and before the closing entries for the year were made. Each company was engaged in wholesaling, with a fiscal year ending on December 31, 19x1.

For each company, prepare the journal entry necessary to adjust the accounts as of the end of the fiscal year. If no entry is necessary, write "no entry."

a. In Company A, local property taxes covering the period October 1, 19x1, through September 30, 19x2, were expected to amount to $30,000. These would be paid in July 19x2.

b. Company B received invoices on January 10, 19x2, covering telephone and electric service for the month of December 19x1, totaling $1,000.

c. Company C's perpetual inventory records and Inventory account balance indicated that the cost of merchandise on hand on December 31, 19x1, was $50,500. A physical count revealed that the amount actually on hand had cost $48,500.

d. Company D's last weekly payroll period of 19x1 ended on December 26. The next weekly payroll covered the five working days from December 27, 19x1, through January 2, 19x2, holidays being counted as "working days" for this purpose. The total January 2 payroll was

$25,000, of which $5,000 was for office employees and $20,000 was for store employees. The company uses a separate salary expense account for each department. Employer payroll taxes may be ignored.

e. In 19x0, Company E bought merchandise for inventory amounting to $10,000, but at the time of acquisition the purchase was incorrectly debited to Office Supplies Expense. The merchandise itself was placed in the storeroom, however, and was counted properly in the annual physical inventory taken at the end of 19x0. In reviewing certain records now, just after the end of 19x1, the earlier error has been discovered.

f. A machine that had cost Company F $11,000 when new was sold during 19x1 for $5,000. At the time of the sale, its book value was $3,000. To record the sale, an accounting clerk debited Cash and credited Other Income $5,000.

23. Correcting Journal-Entry Errors. Commonmarket Corporation had calculated its 19x2 net income to be $94,800. It used the perpetual method of inventory recordkeeping. Before making year-end closing entries, Commonmarket's accountants determined that the following eight errors had been made during the year:

1. $42,000 cash sales were recorded as sales on account.
2. $11,000 payment for prepaid rent was recorded as the payment of accounts payable.
3. The $7,400 salaries earned by employees in 19x2, but not paid as of the end of 19x2, were recorded as: Dr. Salaries Expense 5,400, Cr. Accounts Payable, 5,400.
4. Collection of $9,600 accounts receivable was recorded: Dr. Sales Revenues 9,600, Cr. Cash 9,600.
5. The issuance of $15,000 of new shares of Commonmarket Corporation's capital stock was recorded as a $15,000 loan from a bank.
6. A delivery truck, with original cost of $20,000 and three fourths depreciated, was sold for $6,500 cash; the bookkeeper incorrectly assumed that the truck's accumulated depreciation was $14,000 at the time of the sale.
7. A $3,400 dividend declared and paid was recorded as: Dr. Dividend Expense 3,400, Cr. Cash 3,400.
8. $17,000 of inventory sold for $21,500 cash was recorded as: Dr. Cash 21,500, Cr. Merchandise Inventory 17,000, Cr. Net Income 4,500.

a. What is the correct amount of Commonmarket's 19x2 net income? Ignore income taxes.
b. Prepare the journal entries needed to correct Commonmarket's ledger accounts.

24. Correcting Journal-Entry Errors.   Acton Company uses the perpetual method of inventory recordkeeping. During the bookkeeper's vacation, the company's payroll clerk prepared and posted journal entries to record the company's transactions. Upon returning to work, the bookkeeper reviewed the entries and identified the following items as candidates for correction:

1. When goods costing $3,200 were bought on account, the entry was: Dr. Cost of Goods Sold $3,200, Cr. Cash $3,200.
2. Upon selling half the above merchandise for $2,500 cash, the entry was: Dr. Income $700, Dr. Cash $2,500, Cr. Sales Revenues $1,600, Cr. Inventory $1,600.
3. The declaration and immediate payment of a $1,000 dividend was recorded as: Dr. Capital Stock $1,000, Cr. Dividends Declared $1,000.
4. When the company paid $1,100 in commissions to its sales personnel, the following entry was made: Dr. Selling Expenses $1,100, Cr. Sales Revenue $1,100.
5. Depreciation was recorded on office furniture: Dr. Depreciation Expense $700, Cr. Office Furniture $700.
6. Acton bought a delivery truck for $14,000. It paid $10,000 immediately and signed a note for the balance, due in six months. The entry was: Dr. Truck $10,000, Dr. Depreciation Expense $4,000, Cr. Cash $6,000, Cr. Accumulated Depreciation $4,000, Cr. Accounts Payable $4,000.
7. Receipt of a $900 bill from the electric company was recorded as follows: Dr. Utilities Expense $900, Cr. Accounts Payable $900.
8. An $1,800 payment to the landlord for next year's rent was recorded as: Dr. Rent Expense $1,800, Cr. Prepaid Rent $1,800.
9. Salaries of $2,100 were paid for five days' work ending on the day the payment was made. No previous entry had been made with respect to these salaries. The entry was: Dr. Cash $2,100, Cr. Salaries Payable $2,100.

a. Analyze each of the nine transactions and prepare the journal entry that should have been made to record it.
b. For each transaction, prepare a journal entry to *correct* the error that was made.

25. Revenues and Expenses: Missing Amounts.   The following table contains amounts relating to Dixon Company's 19x6 operations. Dixon sells tennis equipment on account. It also has just begun operating tennis courts for which it sells a 15-month membership plan: cash fees (rentals) are collected in advance, and members have unlimited access to tennis courts on a reservations basis.

	Postclosing Trial Balance, Dec. 31, 19x5	Debits	Credits	Adjusted Trial Balance, Dec. 31, 19x6
Wages payable	$14,900	$92,700	A	$ 12,600
Inventory	B	78,700	$ 75,200	13,400
Rentals received in advance			14,500	C
Interest revenue			D	36,900
Allowance for uncollectibles	14,200	E	26,600	34,400
Warranty expense		F		6,600
Interest payable	G	21,200	26,100	30,500
Liability for warranty claims	H	4,200	I	19,800
Accumulated depreciation	93,000	52,200	J	103,300
Interest receivable	14,500	K	L	16,100
Accounts receivable	35,400	M	306,500	38,900

a. Determine and label the missing amounts.

b. Using the amounts in the table, prepare Dixon Company's income statement for 19x6. Ignore income taxes.

26. Misstated Income, Accounting Errors. Arlington Company reported net income of $62,000 for 19x2 and $93,000 for 19x3. Based on the information that follows, determine the correct amount of income for each year.

a. The $15,000 wages paid on January 6, 19x3, were recorded as an expense even though 35 percent related to work performed in December 19x2.

b. On November 16, 19x2, Arlington lent $8,400 to a supplier for 60 days at 16 percent. Arlington recorded $224 interest revenue in 19x2.

c. Arlington paid $3,600 during March 19x2 for a life insurance policy that would be effective April 1, 19x2, and run for two years. Prepaid insurance was increased by $3,600 in 19x2 and reduced by $3,600 in 19x4.

d. In December 19x2, Arlington introduced a warranty reimbursement program. Since Arlington would honor claims relating to merchandise sold anytime in 19x2, it recognized $5,200 of warranty expense in 19x2. Warranties were also given on merchandise sold in 19x3. When warranty claims were presented in 19x3, the $4,300 paid in cash was recorded as an expense. At the end of 19x3, Arlington determined that future claims would likely be $5,900, and it therefore recorded additional warranty expense of $1,600 in 19x3 ($5,900 − $4,300).

e. As a friendly gesture to a landlord who was in dire financial straits, in December 19x2 Arlington prepaid rent for the first four months of 19x3 at the rate of $550 a month and recorded the payment as rent expense.

f. On April 1, 19x2, Arlington bought a delivery truck for $15,300, which it expected to use until the end of 19x5. Since all 12 months of 19x2 would not benefit from the truck, the bookkeeper decided to record depreciation so that 19x3, 19x4, and 19x5 would each be charged with one third of the vehicle's cost.

g. In 19x2, Arlington began making credit sales for the first time. The year-end aged accounts receivable indicated that $8,200 would probably never be collected. Since no accounts were written off during that year, the bookkeeper saw no sense in even recording the $8,200 estimate. When $5,600 of accounts were judged to be definitely worthless during 19x3, the following entry was recorded:

Loss	5,600	
Accounts Receivable.		5,600

Although the end-of-19x3 aged receivables indicated that specific accounts totaling $9,700 would likely be written off as uncollectible in 19x4, the bookkeeper believed that consistency dictated that no entry be made to record this estimate.

27. Adjusting Entries.   Melton Corporation had the following preadjustment balances in certain credit-balance accounts as of December 31, 19x3:

Accumulated depreciation	$1,900
Advances from customers	0
Allowance for uncollectibles	500
Interest payable	0
Liability for warranty claims.	1,000
Notes payable	2,000
Wages payable.	0

1. Management determined that the year-end warranty claims liability should be equal to 4 percent of 19x3's $140,000 gross sales revenues plus $800 for prior years' sales.
2. As of year-end, $12,250 of 19x3's $63,500 service revenues represented collections of 19x4 revenues.
3. The note payable was a December 1, 19x3 agreement to pay $2,060 on March 2, 19x4, to settle a $2,000 debt to a supplier.
4. Depreciation expense for 19x3 was $3,500, and a machine—which had cost $2,000 and which was 30 percent depreciated—was sold in 19x3 for $1,750. Neither of these transactions had been recorded.
5. During 19x3, $3,100 of insurance coverage expired; as of year-end, $600 had been prepaid for 19x4 insurance coverage.
6. Melton Corporation paid wages of $11,000 to its employees on January 4, 19x4. Of this amount, 40 percent related to work these employees performed in the company's offices and salesroom in 19x4, and 60 percent was for 19x3 work. The company also paid its employees $82,000 in 19x3 as wages for work they performed in 19x3.

7. Management estimated that 13 percent of the $20,000 year-end receivables would never be collected.

a. For each of the seven indicated ledger accounts, calculate the amount that should appear in the December 31, 19x3 balance sheet.

b. For each of the following nine items, calculate the amount that should appear in the 19x3 income statement:
> Bad debts
> Depreciation expense
> Gain or loss on sale of machine
> Insurance expense
> Interest expense
> Sales revenues, gross
> Service revenues
> Wages expense
> Warranty expense

28. Adjusting Entries and Financial Statements. Broden Company's unadjusted trial balance as of December 31, 19x4, is as follows:

BRODEN COMPANY
Unadjusted Trial Balance
As of December 31, 19x4

Cash........................	$ 46,200	Allowance for uncollectibles..	$ 1,300
Accounts receivable.........	124,600	Accumulated depreciation....	39,900
Notes receivable............	10,000	Accounts payable...........	42,400
Interest receivable	900	Liability for warranty claims ..	1,100
Inventory	31,600	Notes payable	60,000
Prepaid insurance...........	2,000	Capital stock...............	280,000
Land........................	60,000	Retained earnings...........	541,300
Buildings	838,000	Sales......................	724,500
Machinery	86,700		
Cost of goods sold..........	219,800		
Salaries and wages expense..	188,400		
Utilities expense	40,300		
Dividends declared..........	42,000		
Total	$1,690,500	Total	$1,690,500

The following information became known shortly after year-end:

1. The company uses the perpetual method of inventory recordkeeping, and the year-end inventory count indicates that the cost of the goods on hand was $26,900.

2. The $10,000 note receivable is a 12 percent, two-year note which was received from a customer on April 1, 19x3. The customer will pay the amount due Broden Company, including interest for the full two years, when the note matures in 19x5. Interest in each of the two years is based on the $10,000 original amount of the note.

3. Management estimates that 7 percent of year-end accounts receivable will probably never be collected.
4. Salaries and wages of $2,700 were earned in 19x4 for which payment will be made on January 6, 19x5. No entry has been made to record these salaries and wages.
5. Depreciation for the year was calculated to be $31,778.
6. The company owes a bank $60,000. Although this amount is due in February 19x6, each year's interest must be paid within 15 days after the close of the calendar year. The $60,000 was borrowed on October 2, 19x4, and the interest rate is 14 percent.
7. The engineering department estimates that future warranty claims are likely to be $24,000.
8. A review of the insurance file indicates that as of January 1, 19x5, prepaid premiums total $200.

a. Prepare adjusting journal entries and an adjusted trial balance.
b. Prepare Broden Company's 19x4 income statement and its balance sheet as of December 31, 19x4.
c. Prepare the year-end closing entries.

29. Adjusting Entries, Financial Statements. Dover Corporation sells merchandise and publishes an industry newsletter. Its December 31, 19x5, trial balance is as follows:

DOVER CORPORATION
Trial Balance
As of December 31, 19x5

Account	Debit	Credit
Cash........................	$ 24,600	
Accounts receivable............	51,300	
Allowance for uncollectibles.....		$ 1,800
Notes receivable...............	12,000	
Interest receivable	300	
Merchandise inventory	14,600	
Prepaid rent	3,500	
Prepaid insurance	1,700	
Machinery	16,600	
Accumulated depreciation		3,400
Accounts payable..............		7,700
Liability for warranty claims		900
Notes payable.................		5,000
Capital stock.................		4,000
Retained earnings		32,600
Revenue from sales		176,900
Revenue from subscriptions.....		14,300
Purchases	73,400	
Salaries and wages expense.....	44,600	
Dividends declared.............	4,000	
Totals	$246,600	$246,600

The following information had not yet been recorded when the trial balance was prepared:

1. Accrued interest on the notes receivable was $900 at year-end. The interest will be received when the notes mature in 19x6. Accrued interest on the notes payable was $400. Although the notes will mature in 19x7, Dover is required to pay the interest accrued in 19x5 in January 19x6.
2. Management's assessment of sales and year-end receivables determined that future warranty costs will probably amount to $2,500 and that $3,100 of the receivables will likely not be collectible.
3. Dover's rental cost was $250 a month, and its depreciation was $150 a month.
4. Based on newsletters Dover delivered during the year, only $11,900 of the amounts recorded as revenue from subscriptions in 19x5 was earned during 19x5.
5. Salaries and wages earned but unpaid as of December 31 totaled $900.
6. An examination of the insurance file indicates that Dover will begin 19x6 with $300 of prepaid coverage.
7. A physical count of the merchandise at year-end reveals that goods that had cost Dover $15,900 are on hand.

a. Prepare a journal entry for each year-end adjustment.
b. Prepare an adjusted trial balance.
c. Prepare Dover Corporation's 19x5 income statement and the balance sheet as of December 31, 19x5.
d. Prepare the closing entries that assume the adjusting entries had already been posted to Dover's ledger accounts.

30. Adjustments and Closing Entries.   Towle Company's December 31, 19x4, unadjusted trial balance is presented:

TOWLE COMPANY
Unadjusted Trial Balance
As of December 31, 19x4

Account	Debit	Credit
Cash	$ 14,400	
Accounts receivable	81,600	
Allowance for uncollectibles		$ 700
Merchandise inventory, January 1, 19x4	11,200	
Prepaid rent	1,300	
Machinery and equipment	9,500	
Accumulated depreciation		2,200
Accounts payable		41,800
Wages and salaries payable		1,900
Capital stock		5,000
Retained earnings, January 1, 19x4		49,600
Sales		216,600
Purchases	114,200	
Wages and salaries expense	59,900	
Rent expense	15,700	
Dividends declared	10,000	
Totals	$317,800	$317,800

Towle's accountants prepared a number of adjusting entries and posted them to the accounts. Once they had done this, they prepared and recorded the following closing entries as of December 31, 19x4:

Sales	216,600	
Bad Debts		1,700
Income Summary		214,900
Income Summary	195,000	
Cost of Goods Sold		116,300
Wages and Salaries Expense		61,300
Rent Expense		16,500
Depreciation Expense		900
Income Summary	19,900	
Retained Earnings		19,900
Retained Earnings	10,000	
Dividends Declared		10,000

Based on this information, prepare Towle Company's December 31, 19x4, balance sheet.

Chapter 5

Manufacturing Cost Flows

Accrual accounting is appropriate to all kinds of organizations, not just to the merchandising companies that have been our focus so far. Banks, insurance companies, manufacturers, real estate developers, research laboratories—all have industry-specific accounting measurement problems.

Of all of these, manufacturing operations probably best exemplify the differences between accrual accounting and cash-basis accounting. Our purpose in this chapter is to show how the principles of accrual accounting can be applied to the manufacturing operations of an income-seeking business.

The Manufacturing Cycle

Manufacturing is the process by which companies convert one set of goods (materials) into another set of goods (finished products). Manufacturing takes place in physical facilities, which are most commonly known as *factories*.

The sequence of events from the purchase of materials to the completion of finished products is known as the **manufacturing cycle,** illustrated in Exhibit 5–1. As this shows, the cycle begins with the purchase of materials. These are generally placed in storerooms or stockpiles when they are received. The quantities in these locations are known as *materials inventories*. When some of them are needed in production, they are transferred from the storeroom or stockpile to appropriate locations in the factory. When this happens, we say that materials have been *issued*. They then become part of the **work in process.**

Work in process is a form of inventory—an inventory of partly processed products. This inventory doesn't consist of the original **factory**

EXHIBIT 5–1
The Manufacturing Cycle

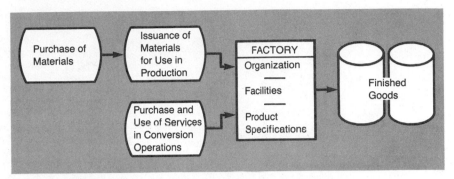

materials alone, however. It also includes the other factory resources that have been used to convert the materials into their partly processed state. The most obvious other factory resource is *labor time*—the amount of time factory employees have spent working on the materials. **Factory labor** time and the other factory resources used in production are just as much a part of the work in process as the materials because they are just as necessary to bring the items in process to their present state.

The manufacturing cycle ends when the last operations have been performed on the product and it is placed in a warehouse or other location, ready for delivery to a customer. This product then becomes part of the **finished goods** inventory. Materials, work in process, and finished goods are all assets. More precisely, they are three different kinds of inventory assets, all of which appear in a company's balance sheet among its current assets. Finished goods remain assets until they are shipped to customers, lost, or disposed of in some way. Materials and work in process are assets that are transformed into other assets as they proceed to the next stage of the manufacturing cycle.

Manufacturing Cost Flows

To apply the accrual concept to manufacturing operations, accountants trace the flow of manufacturing costs through an account structure that parallels the flow of resources through the manufacturing cycle.

Exhibit 5–2 illustrates this flow of costs in a schematic diagram. The left block in this exhibit shows that when materials are purchased, their costs become the costs of the materials inventory. When some of these materials are placed in production, their costs are transferred to the work in process inventory, represented by the block in the middle of the exhibit. The costs of labor time (labor cost) and the costs of other factory resources consumed in manufacturing are included in the costs of the work in process inventory as they are incurred in production. When the

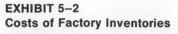

EXHIBIT 5–2
Costs of Factory Inventories

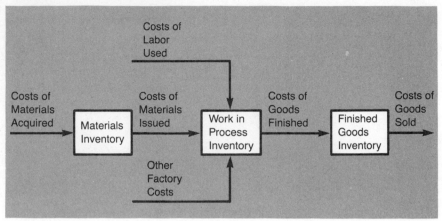

manufacturing cycle ends, the costs of the completed products are transferred from the work in process category to the finished goods category, as shown in the right of Exhibit 5–2.

In this section, we'll use a simple example to show how a manufacturing company might use accounts to accumulate the costs of manufacturing operations and divide them between the costs of goods sold and the costs of the ending inventory for financial accounting purposes.

Preproduction Transactions

Strong Cabinets, Inc., was founded by David Strong on July 1, 19x1, to manufacture bookshelves, cabinets, and other wooden furniture. Some of this furniture was made in standard designs to be sold to retail stores; the rest was of very high quality to fill the orders of specific customers.

Strong Cabinets began operations with $200,000 in cash, provided by Strong in exchange for shares of the company's capital stock. The entry was:

(1)

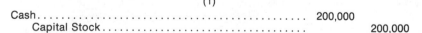

Cash... 200,000
     Capital Stock.................................   200,000

This showed the increase in the company's assets and the creation of owners' equity.

Strong hired skilled cabinetmakers, carpenters, and office workers as the company began operations. The company expended no resources in hiring these resources and acquired no property rights. Nor did the company incur a liability—the liability would be created only as the employees did their work, providing services to the company. As a result, no entry was made in the accounts to record the hiring of these employees.

Three other transactions took place before manufacturing operations began: (1) prepayment of rent, (2) purchase of factory equipment, and (3) purchases of materials. The accounting treatment of these is familiar to us from previous chapters, so we'll describe them very briefly.

The rental on the factory space amounted to $84,000 a year, and Strong Cabinets paid a year's rent in advance on July 1, 19x1. The entry recording this transaction showed the acquisition of one asset in exchange for another:

(2)

Prepaid Rent......................................	84,000	
Cash		84,000

Next, tools and equipment were bought on account for $100,000, and their cost was entered in a new asset account, Factory Equipment. The accompanying liability was also recognized at this time by an entry in the Accounts Payable account. The record of this transaction therefore showed the following changes:

(3)

Factory Equipment.................................	100,000	
Accounts Payable		100,000

Third, the company bought lumber and other materials for use in the factory. These materials were bought on credit at a total cost of $220,000. The entries recording these purchases showed that both assets and liabilities increased:

(4)

Factory Materials Inventory..........................	220,000	
Accounts Payable		220,000

The only difference between these purchases and the inventory purchases we discussed in previous chapters is that these are materials to be used in manufacturing processes, not merchandise ready for resale without further processing.

Recording the Issuance of Materials

When production materials are *issued,* they are merely transferred from one asset category to another. For example, Strong Cabinets issued materials from inventory with a total cost of $140,000 during the last six months of 19x1. In this company's highly simplified accounting system, a single account, Work in Process Inventory, is used to accumulate all the costs assignable to the in-process inventory assets. The entries that recorded the issuance of materials in 19x1, summarized in entry (5), showed increases in the work in process inventory and decreases in the quantity of unissued materials on hand:

(5)

Work in Process Inventory   140,000
    Factory Materials Inventory   140,000

The costs of materials issued are still the costs of inventory assets. Issuance merely changes the physical location of these assets. Issuance creates no revenues, and the costs of materials issued therefore remain in inventory. Entry (5) recognized their change in status by transferring the costs from one inventory account to another.

Recording Factory Labor Costs

Factory labor costs are incurred to produce assets—finished goods inventories—that will produce sales revenues greater than the costs required to produce them. During the second half of 19x1 (the first six months of operations), wages and salaries in Strong Cabinets' factory amounted to $200,000. The entries recording these payrolls can be summarized as follows:

(6)

Work in Process Inventory   200,000
    Wages and Salaries Payable   200,000

The debit to the Work in Process Inventory account recorded an increase in the cost of this inventory asset. Factory labor costs add to the asset because they bring it closer to the form in which it will be useful to customers. Treating factory labor costs as the cost of an asset is called **capitalization of costs.**

Factory labor costs don't become expenses until revenues are earned and appear in an income statement, either later in the same period or in some subsequent period. Factory labor costs therefore differ from the costs of the wages and salaries of office and store employees, which are generally recognized as expenses immediately on the grounds that they are costs of generating the revenues of the current period.

Recognize that we have here a very logical application of accrual accounting. Although the payroll costs are costs of doing business, they become determinants of net income only when the company derives the benefits they help bring about. This identification of costs with benefits is accomplished by *deferring* their expense recognition, effected by initially classifying these costs as the creation of an inventory asset.

Recording Depreciation

A third element of factory cost is depreciation of factory facilities. Depreciation is ordinarily treated as a current expense when it relates to facilities used for administrative or marketing activities. When it relates to manufacturing facilities, however, it is treated as a cost of producing inventory assets—work in process inventory initially and finished goods later on.

This treatment again reflects the idea that the asset has merely been converted from one form to another; the services formerly embodied in a machine are now embodied in the goods produced during the period. Factory depreciation therefore doesn't become an expense until revenues from the sale of the resulting products are recognized in the income statement. Depreciation on Strong Cabinets' factory tools and equipment amounted to $8,000 in the second half of 19x1, and the entry was as follows:

(7)

Work in Process Inventory	8,000	
Accumulated Depreciation.		8,000

The credit to Accumulated Depreciation records the decrease in the company's equipment assets. This is a contra-asset account, as we explained in Chapter 3, and its end-of-period balance appears on the balance sheet as a deduction from the original cost of factory plant assets.

Other Factory Costs

Running a factory calls for the use of many more resources than materials, labor, and equipment. In the second half of 19x1, Strong Cabinets bought various services on account from outside suppliers—electric power and telephone service, for example—for immediate use in the factory's production operations. The total cost of these services was $70,000, and the entries to record these transactions can be summarized as follows:

(8)

Work in Process Inventory	70,000	
Accounts Payable		70,000

The debits to the inventory account showed that these costs were incurred to produce inventory assets: costs of resources such as these are just as much part of the cost of production as materials, labor, and factory depreciation costs.

Strong Cabinets had one other factory cost in the first half of 19x1, the cost of the space the cabinet shop occupied. Rent of $84,000 had been paid on July 1, 19x1 [entry (2)], covering the ensuing 12 months. Six months of this period had elapsed by the end of the year, and six months' rent therefore had to be treated as a cost of factory operations in 19x1. The accountants' analysis showed the following asset changes:

(9)

Work in Process Inventory	42,000	
Prepaid Rent		42,000

This signifies that the prepaid rent asset decreased and that the rent cost became a cost of the work in process inventory asset.

Cost of Goods Finished

Entry (9) completed the recognition of the 19x1 costs of production. The Work in Process Inventory account then contained the following costs:

Work in Process Inventory	
(5) Materials	140,000
(6) Labor	200,000
(7) Depreciation	8,000
(8) Services	70,000
(9) Rent	42,000
	460,000

Some products Strong Cabinets' factory began working on in 19x1 were still unfinished at the end of the year. Work on other products was completed, however, and the finished units were placed in Strong Cabinets' shipping room. In examining the records, the accountants found that of the total cost incurred ($460,000), the portion associated with the finished units amounted to $350,000.[1] The entry to record the completion of these units was:

(10)

Finished Goods Inventory 350,000
     Work in Process Inventory   350,000

Both of these are asset accounts; the entry merely indicated the change in the inventory from an unfinished to a finished form.

The Work in Process Inventory account showed the following after this entry was made:

Work in Process Inventory			
(5)	140,000	(10)	350,000
(6)	200,000		
(7)	8,000		
(8)	70,000		
(9)	42,000		
	460,000		
Bal. 110,000			

In other words, the cost of unfinished furniture still in process on December 31, 19x1, was $110,000.

---

[1] We'll explain in Chapters 18 and 19 how accountants assign factory costs to individual units of product and thereby determine the total cost of all the products finished in a given period.

Cost of Goods Sold

The Finished Goods Inventory account plays the same role in a manufacturing company as the Merchandise Inventory account plays in a retailing or wholesaling company. It identifies the costs of salable products as balance sheet assets until revenues from the sale of the goods are reported in some period's income statement.

Strong Cabinets, Inc., has perpetual inventory records for its inventory of finished products. A separate computer file is set up for each kind of finished product. When units are finished, the costs assigned to them are entered in this file. When goods are sold and shipped to a customer, the costs assigned to the shipped units are subtracted from the balance in the file and identified as the cost of goods sold.

Using this system, Strong Cabinets determined that the sum of the factory costs of the items the company sold in 19x1 was $280,000. The delivery of these items to the company's customers constituted transfers of company-owned resources to these customers. The cost of these resources, the cost of goods sold, is shown in the income statement as an expense, just as the costs of advertising and sales salaries are classified as expenses—that is, all were costs incurred to create the revenues earned and recognized in this period. Strong Cabinets recorded this transfer of costs in 19x1 by the following entry:

(11)

Cost of Goods Sold	280,000	
Finished Goods Inventory		280,000

The debit to the Cost of Goods Sold account recorded a decrease in the company's owners' equity (an offset against the increase in owners' equity contributed by sales revenues). The credit to Finished Goods Inventory recorded the accompanying decrease in that asset.

Recognition of these transactions left a balance of $70,000 in the Finished Goods Inventory account, the cost of the finished furniture still in the storeroom at the end of 19x1:

Finished Goods Inventory

(10)	350,000	(11)	280,000
Bal. 70,000			

Schedule of Manufacturing Costs

The flow of manufacturing costs through the accounts is diagrammed in Exhibit 5–3. Notice that inventories are found in three stages—$80,000 unprocessed, $110,000 partly processed, and $70,000 finished. Each dollar amount identified with a cost flow in this diagram came from one of the entries in the illustration.

EXHIBIT 5–3
Manufacturing Cost Flows for Income Reporting

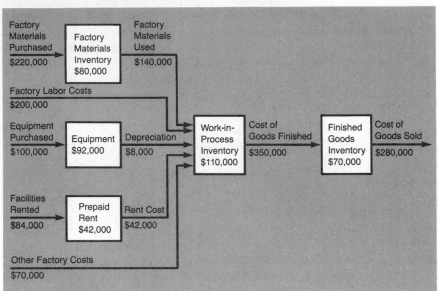

These cost flows are summarized in tabular form in Strong Cabinets' Schedule of Manufacturing Costs and Cost of Goods Sold in Exhibit 5–4. This shows that of the $460,000 of total factory cost actually applicable to factory operations during 19x1, only $280,000—the amount on the right-most arrow—was transferred to expense in the income statement for the year. The remaining $180,000 had become the costs of the work in process inventory ($110,000) and the finished goods inventory ($70,000). The schedule also shows that the materials inventory had a year-end balance of $80,000.[2]

We started with zero inventories in this illustration because we wanted to show how manufacturing inventories are created. The manufacturing-cost schedule in Exhibit 5–4 shows how beginning inventories can be inserted. Later in this chapter, we'll illustrate the impact of beginning inventories on the determination of the cost of goods finished and the cost of goods sold.

Notice that nowhere in this illustration have we referred to the payment of cash. The timing of cash payments has no bearing on the apportionment of costs among the various categories of assets and expenses.

_____

[2] The year-end balance sheet also contains other factory-related costs not classified as inventory: (1) rent prepayments of $42,000 (6/12 of $84,000), and (2) factory equipment cost of $92,000 [because only $8,000 (entry 7) of its $100,000 original cost (entry 3) was used in the manufacturing process in 19x1].

EXHIBIT 5–4

STRONG CABINETS, INC.
Schedule of Manufacturing Costs and Cost of Goods Sold
For the Six Months Ended December 31, 19x1

Factory costs:		
Materials costs:		
Materials on hand, July 1, 19x1	$ 0	
Materials purchased	220,000	
Cost of materials available for use.	220,000	
Less: Materials on hand, December 31, 19x1.	80,000	
Cost of materials used.		$140,000
Factory labor cost		200,000
Other factory costs:		
Depreciation.	8,000	
Rent.	42,000	
Miscellaneous.	70,000	120,000
Total factory cost		460,000
Add: Work in process, July 1, 19x1.		0
Total cost in production.		460,000
Less: Work in process, December 31, 19x1.		110,000
Cost of goods finished		350,000
Add: Finished goods inventory, July 1, 19x1.		0
Cost of goods available for sale		350,000
Less: Finished goods inventory, December 31, 19x1		70,000
Cost of goods sold		$280,000

Eliminating cash transactions from the illustration interfered in no way with our ability to trace the manufacturing costs through the accounts.

Nonmanufacturing Costs and the Income Statement

Every manufacturer incurs many costs for activities other than manufacturing. Advertising costs, the president's salary, and expenditures for research and development are only a few examples of costs that are incurred for purposes other than the actual conversion of raw materials into finished products.

All such costs are accounted for just as they would be in a retailing or wholesaling business. Sales office rental costs and advertising costs are recognized as expense when the space and advertising services are provided, whether products have been sold or not. They aren't part of the cost of manufacturing products and therefore they don't enter the factory cost accounts in any way. They go directly to expense without passing through the Work in Process Inventory and the Finished Goods Inventory accounts along the way.

Strong's salary and the salaries of the rest of the selling and administrative work force in 19x1 amounted to $170,000. The entries to accrue these payrolls can be summarized as follows:

(12)

Selling and Administrative Salaries Expense	170,000	
Wages and Salaries Payable		170,000

The effect of these transactions, in other words, was to decrease the owners' equity and increase the company's liabilities.

Transactions giving rise to other selling and administrative costs had similar effects. They amounted to $31,000 and can be summarized as follows:

(13)

Other Selling and Administrative Expenses	31,000	
Accounts Payable		31,000

To complete the illustration of the operating cycle, we need to identify the revenues of the period and show what accounts they affected. Finished furniture was sold on account in 19x1 for a total of $500,000, thereby increasing the company's assets and its owners' equity:

(14)

Accounts Receivable	500,000	
Sales Revenue		500,000

Finally, the company made provision for income taxes attributable to the operation of the business in 19x1. The effective tax rate that year was 40 percent, and the income tax accrued at that rate was $7,600. The entry was:

(15)

Income Tax Expense	7,600	
Income Tax Payable		7,600

After all these entries were made, the company's accountants prepared the income statement shown in Exhibit 5–5.

EXHIBIT 5–5

STRONG CABINETS, INC.
Income Statement
For the Six Months Ended December 31, 19x1

Sales		$500,000
Operating expenses:		
Cost of goods sold (from Exhibit 5–4).	$280,000	
Selling and administrative salaries.	170,000	
Other selling and administrative expenses	31,000	481,000
Income before income taxes.		19,000
Income tax expense.		7,600
Net income		$ 11,400

Illustration Including Beginning Inventories

Strong Cabinets began the year 19x2 with the following balances in its manufacturing cost accounts (from Exhibit 5–4):

Factory materials inventory	$ 80,000
Work in process inventory	110,000
Finished goods inventory	70,000

During the year 19x2, the factory had the transactions recorded in the following entries:

a.	Factory Materials Inventory	400,000	
	Accounts Payable		400,000
	To record the purchase of factory materials on credit.		
b.	Work in Process Inventory	390,000	
	Factory Materials Inventory		390,000
	To record issuance of factory materials for use in production.		
c.	Work in Process Inventory	450,000	
	Wages and Salaries Payable		450,000
	To record the use of factory labor.		
d.	Work in Process Inventory	16,000	
	Accumulated Depreciation		16,000
	To record depreciation on factory equipment.		
e.	Prepaid Rent	63,000	
	Cash		63,000
	To record the payment of nine months' rent on the factory building.		
f.	Work in Process Inventory	84,000	
	Prepaid Rent		84,000
	To record use of the factory building.		
g.	Work in Process Inventory	130,000	
	Accounts Payable		130,000
	To record other factory costs in 19x2.		
h.	Finished Goods Inventory	1,100,000	
	Work in Process Inventory		1,100,000
	To record the completion of product units in 19x2.		
i.	Cost of Goods Sold	1,050,000	
	Finished Goods Inventory		1,050,000
	To record the cost of the goods sold in 19x2.		

The flow of costs through the manufacturing cost accounts in 19x2 is shown in T-account form in Exhibit 5–6. Cash, Accounts Payable, and other accounts whose balances don't enter into the schedule of manufacturing costs are omitted from this exhibit. Notice that the balance in

EXHIBIT 5–6
Strong Cabinets, Inc.: Factory Cost Accounts in 19x2

Factory Materials Inventory			Work in Process Inventory		
Bal.	80,000	(b) 390,000	Bal.	110,000	(h) 1,100,000
(a)	400,000		(b)	390,000	
Bal. 90,000			(c)	450,000	
			(d)	16,000	
			(f)	84,000	
			(g)	130,000	
			Bal. 80,000		

Finished Goods Inventory			Cost of Goods Sold		
Bal.	70,000	(i) 1,050,000	(i)	1,050,000	
(h)	1,100,000				
Bal. 120,000					

Factory Materials Inventory increased by $10,000 during the year, as the amount of materials issued was less than the amount purchased. The Work in Process balance decreased by $30,000, as the cost of the units completed exceeded the cost of the work done. The balance in the Finished Goods Inventory account increased, however, as the sales volume fell slightly short of the volume of goods finished during the year.

Other Applications of Accrual Accounting

Manufacturing activities aren't the only ones to require placing some operating costs on the end-of-period balance sheet. In principle, the costs of any activity designed to create or help a company generate the revenues of future periods should be *capitalized* (placed on the balance sheet as the costs of assets) until the period in which revenues are recognized.

A good example of this kind of activity is real estate development. A real estate developer usually makes substantial expenditures—for such services as surveys, legal advice, architects' designs, and site preparation—before any revenues are recognized. All those costs should be capitalized when they are incurred because they apply to future revenues rather than to the revenues of the current period.[3]

Oil and gas exploration companies also must capitalize the costs of their successful exploration activities. These activities are designed to

---

[3] The factors affecting accountants' decisions whether to capitalize such costs are discussed in detail in Chapter 9.

discover oil and gas reserves large enough to justify oil and gas production in future periods. Their costs therefore aren't recognized as expenses until the future periods in which the revenues are recognized (or in which it becomes clear that revenues will not ensue).

Oil and gas accounting has been the subject of extensive study and discussion in connection with the costs of *unsuccessful* wells: should the costs of unsuccessful drilling be expensed immediately, or should they be capitalized (i.e., be treated as the cost of an asset)? Proponents of capitalization emphasize that oil and gas companies consciously accept the risk of "dry holes" because the costs of dry holes are part of the cost of discovering successful wells. This point of view reflects the same reasoning as the premise underlying the (noncontroversial) capitalization of successful wells' exploration costs—namely, that accountants capitalize costs that are expected to contribute to future revenues. The wells being explored therefore are treated in very much the same manner as work in process inventories in manufacturing.

Readers of financial statements need to be aware of the importance of capitalized operating costs in each company in which they are interested. Companies that capitalize substantial portions of their operating costs in any period will report more net income than they would have reported if they had recognized these costs as current expenses. Net income for these companies also is very likely to be substantially larger than the amount of cash the company is generating for dividends and other purposes. We'll be discussing these two aspects of accrual accounting in Chapters 9 and 13.

Summary

Accounting treatment of manufacturing costs is an excellent illustration of the application of the accrual concept. Accounting views manufacturing as a process of adding the costs of manufacturing labor and other manufacturing services to the cost of purchased materials. The costs of manufacturing follow the flow of the goods themselves, from raw materials inventory to work in process to finished goods and finally to goods sold.

The costs of the goods at all these stages except the last are regarded as costs of assets and therefore are included in the inventory section of the balance sheet. Only when the goods are sold do these costs become expenses, identified in the income statement as the cost of goods sold. Costs of administering the company and of selling and distributing its products are recognized immediately as expenses, just as in a wholesaling or retailing business.

Accrual accounting also requires companies to capitalize the costs of activities other than manufacturing. Real estate development and oil and gas exploration are two kinds of activities which require capitalization of substantial amounts of a company's operating costs.

Key Terms	Capitalization of costs	Finished goods
	Factory labor	Manufacturing cycle
	Factory materials	Work in process

Independent Study Problems (Solutions in Appendix B)

1. Manufacturing Cost Schedule. Using the data in Exhibit 5–6, prepare a schedule of Strong Cabinets' manufacturing costs and the cost of goods sold for the year 19x2.

2. Cost Flow Diagram. Buildmore Manufacturing Company had the following inventories on September 1 and September 30, 19x1:

	September 1	September 30
Raw materials	$20,000	$25,000
Work in process	30,000	20,000
Finished goods	12,000	20,000

During the month of September, the cost of raw materials purchased was $60,000, factory labor costs totaled $80,000, and other costs applicable to production amounted to $30,000.

Prepare a diagram showing the flow of costs through the inventories to the cost of goods sold.

3. T-accounts; Journal Entries. All Buildmore Manufacturing Company's purchases of factory materials in the month of September 19x1 (see problem 2) were purchased on account. Factory labor costs for the month were accrued, with payments to be made in October. All resources used in production in September, other than materials and labor, were purchased on credit during the month.

a. Set up inventory T-accounts similar to those used in this chapter and enter the opening balances.
b. Prepare a set of journal entries to record the factory's transactions in September, using account titles similar to those used in this chapter.
c. Post the amounts shown in the journal entries to T-accounts.

4. Manufacturing Cost Flows; Income Statement. King Manufacturing Company had the following inventories on October 1:

Materials	$11,650
Work in process	8,320
Finished goods	11,100

The following transactions took place in October:

1. Purchases of factory materials on account at a cost of $4,500.
2. Issues of factory materials to production departments, $7,250.

3. Use of factory labor, $5,100; selling and administrative salaries, $2,600.
4. Depreciation: on manufacturing facilities, $400; on administrative office equipment, $100.
5. Purchases of miscellaneous goods and services on account for immediate use: in the factory, $1,820; by sales and administrative personnel, $1,735.
6. Completion of all manufacturing operations on products costing $12,650 and the transfer of these products to the finished goods storeroom.
7. Sales revenues from manufactured goods sold on credit, $19,350.

   The company determined that the cost of the finished goods inventory on hand on October 31, 19x1, was $9,250.

a. Calculate (1) the total factory cost, (2) the cost of goods finished, and (3) the cost of goods sold in October.
b. Account for these transactions using T-accounts, and establish the closing balances in the inventory accounts. Use a single account for selling and administrative expenses.
c. Prepare an income statement for the month. Ignore income taxes.

5. Supplying Missing Information.   The following data were taken from the ledger accounts of Abcess Manufacturing Company for the most recent month:

Factory materials inventory, beginning of month . .	$ 0
Work in process inventory, beginning of month. . .	0
Finished goods inventory, beginning of month . . .	5,000
Purchases of factory materials	360,000
Depreciation on factory and factory equipment . . .	15,000
Factory materials placed in production	290,000
Depreciation on office equipment	2,000
Sales and administrative salaries	59,000
Factory labor	140,000
Other selling and administrative expense	29,000
Other production costs for the month	135,000
Revenue from sales	525,000
Income taxes on taxable income for the month . . .	24,000
Dividends declared during the month	35,000
Work in process inventory, end of month	115,000
Finished goods inventory, end of month	85,000
Retained earnings, beginning of month.	40,000

Compute the following amounts:

a. Total production costs for the month.
b. Total cost of goods finished during the month.
c. Cost of goods sold during the month.
d. Net income for the month.

e. Retained earnings, end of month.

f. Raw materials inventory, end of month.

6. Discussion. A computer software development company spent $380,000 in 19x1 to develop a new software package. At the end of 19x1, management estimated that an additional $200,000 would have to be spent in 19x2 to develop the instruction manual and introduce the package to potential customers.

This company had income of $1 million from other sources in 19x1. The new package seemed likely to have a good deal of market appeal because it combined word processing and spreadsheet calculations in a much faster, more versatile format than any software package then on the market.

Discuss the arguments for and against capitalizing the $380,000 development cost in 19x1. The decision will not affect the company's income taxes.

7. Analogy to Manufacturing: Discussion. The Belmont Bruisers, one of the original teams in the Continental Rugby League, pays bonuses to induce young players to sign multiyear contracts with the team. Most of these players spend a few years playing for the Bruisers' minor-league teams, where their salaries are higher than their skills warrant. Each farm team has a special talent-development instructor to coach the bonus players on the roster.

a. Describe how these costs could be accounted for in the same manner as manufacturing costs, with three asset stages preceding the classification of costs as expenses.

b. Discuss the difficulties of applying this method of accounting in this kind of operation.

8. Classifying Costs as Current Expenses. A manufacturing company incurs the following costs in the current month:

a. Depreciation on office equipment.

b. Production superintendent's salary.

c. Raw materials purchased for the factory.

d. Factory labor on work shipped to customers this month.

e. Depreciation on factory machinery.

f. Materials used this month to package finished products.

g. Cartons used this month to ship products to customers.

h. Sales brochures purchased for use during the next six months.

i. Wages of raw materials stockroom clerk.

j. Wages of shipping department manager.

k. Freight charge on materials received.

l. Freight charge on products shipped.

m. Factory labor used to build new long-lived storage cabinets in sales showroom.

n. Factory labor used to repair water cooler in sales showroom.

o. Factory labor used to repair factory water cooler.

p. Outside contractor's fee for repairing factory machine.

Which of these costs are expenses of the current month, in their entirety?

9. Calculating the Cost of Goods Finished. Manufacturing costs for a period totaled $300,000, the work in process inventory increased from $250,000 at the beginning of the period to $280,000 at the end, and the cost of goods sold during the period amounted to $310,000.

a. Calculate the cost of goods finished during the period.

b. By how much did the cost of finished goods on hand increase or decrease during the period?

10. Supplying Missing Information. The following data are available for a manufacturing operation:

Balance sheet data:

	December 31, 19x1	December 31, 19x2
Raw materials inventory.......	$240	$285
Work in process inventory.....	128	271
Finished goods inventory	87	172
Factory plant and equipment (net)............	492	476

Totals for the year 19x2:

1. Purchases of raw materials, $1,250.
2. Purchases of factory plant and equipment, $23.
3. Wages earned by factory employees, $566.
4. Production costs other than raw materials, labor, and depreciation, $2,418.
5. Factory plant and equipment sold, none.

a. Calculate the cost of raw materials used during the year.

b. Calculate factory depreciation for the year.

c. Calculate the cost of goods finished during the year.

d. Calculate the cost of goods sold during the year.

(Prepared by Charles Boynton)

11. Statement of Manufacturing Costs. Albatross Corporation is engaged in the manufacture and sale of plastic water toys. Its inventories were as follows:

	January 1	June 30
Raw materials	$10,000	$16,000
Work in process	40,000	50,000
Finished goods	20,000	10,000

The following costs were incurred between these two dates:

Factory raw materials purchased	$90,000
Factory labor	40,000
Factory depreciation	7,000
Factory utilities and other costs	13,000
Sales salaries	5,000
Office salaries	8,000
Other selling and office costs	4,000

Prepare a schedule of manufacturing costs and cost of goods sold for the six months ended June 30.

12. Elements of Cost of Goods Manufactured and Sold. Scotch Company's inventories experienced the following changes during 19x3:

Materials	$14,300 increase
Work in process	2,900 decrease
Finished goods	11,800 increase

Factory costs other than materials and labor were $215,600, which was 140 percent of the labor cost. The cost of materials used was 20 percent of the total factory cost.

a. What was the total factory cost?
b. What was the cost of materials purchased?
c. What was the cost of goods finished?
d. What was the cost of goods sold?

13. Supplying Missing Information. Sandra Manufacturing Company reported the following data in three recent but nonconsecutive periods:

	Period 1	Period 2	Period 3
Cost of goods sold	A	$850	$1,050
Selling and administrative expense	$ 230	220	225
Cost of goods finished	B	880	1,000
Total factory cost	1,030	905	I
Net income	C	E	195
Sales revenue	1,500	F	1,600
Income before taxes	D	130	J
Income tax expense	100	50	K

Work in process inventory, beginning of period	100	60	90
Work in process inventory, end of period	120	G	65
Finished goods inventory, beginning of period	200	H	210
Finished goods inventory, end of period	210	270	L

All of the company's revenues and expenses are included in these tables.

Make the calculations necessary to complete each of these tables.

14. Forecasting the Cost of Goods Sold. Velting Corporation manufactures and sells only one product. Management estimates that the company will sell 200,000 units of this product next year. You have been asked to estimate the cost of goods sold at this volume, based on the following information:

1. Each unit of the product requires approximately 4 pounds of material A and 0.1 pound of material B.
2. The company has no inventory of material A, which is highly perishable and is delivered to the factory daily in quantities sufficient for the day's production. Purchase prices during the coming year are expected to average 60 cents a pound.
3. The company will have 25,000 pounds of material B on hand at the beginning of the year and will buy no more until this stock has been exhausted. The material now in stock was purchased at a cost of $4 a pound. The purchase price of material B is now $4.50 a pound and is expected to hold constant at that level throughout the coming year.
4. It is estimated that two hours of labor at $8 an hour will be required to produce each finished unit.
5. Annual depreciation on factory buildings and equipment will be $136,000.
6. Other factory costs are expected to total $40,000 plus an additional $2,000 for every 10,000 units finished.
7. Production is of such a nature that there will be no beginning or ending inventories of work in process.
8. The company will have 20,000 units of finished products in inventory at the beginning of the year, at a cost of $19 each.
9. A partially completed study by a research team leads you to feel that the final inventory at the close of the year should be 40,000 finished units.
10. Due to a design change, the units produced during the year will be slightly different from those in stock at the beginning of the year. For

this reason, the units in the beginning inventory will be sold before any units produced during the coming year are placed on sale.

You have decided to perform the calculations in the sequence listed below. To help management understand these calculations, identify the steps you take and label each amount clearly.

a. Calculate the number of finished units to be produced next year.
b. Calculate the estimated cost of the raw materials to be used for the desired production.
c. Calculate the estimated cost of goods to be manufactured next year.
d. Calculate the estimated cost of goods to be sold next year.
e. Calculate the estimated cost of all materials and finished goods that will remain in inventory at the end of the coming year.

15. Journal Entries; Net Income.   Poirot Manufacturing Company has a very simple accounting system. It uses only 18 accounts, which had the following balances at the start of business on September 1, 19x1, the start of the company's fiscal year:

Cash	$ 20,000	
Accounts receivable	95,000	
Materials inventory	62,000	
Work in process	28,000	
Finished goods inventory	122,000	
Machinery and equipment	100,000	
Accumulated depreciation		$ 32,000
Accounts payable		38,000
Wages and salaries payable		—
Dividends payable		—
Notes payable		—
Capital stock		200,000
Retained earnings		157,000
Sales revenues		—
Cost of goods sold	—	
Selling and administrative expenses	—	
Nonoperating gains and losses	—	
Dividends declared	—	

The company completed the following transactions during the month of September:

1. Factory materials purchased on account and placed in the materials storeroom, $34,000.
2. Materials issued from materials storeroom to factory production departments, $35,000.
3. Wages and salaries accrued: factory labor, $20,000; selling and administrative salaries, $4,000.
4. Depreciation: factory machinery, $500; administrative office equipment, $300.

5. Costs of other goods and services acquired on account and used immediately: manufacturing, $8,000; selling and administrative, $3,800.
6. Products completed and transferred to finished goods inventories, $62,000.
7. Sales on account, $78,000.
8. The balance in the Finished Goods Inventory account was $1,000 more on September 30 than on September 1, after all appropriate entries for September were recorded.
9. Cash dividends declared, $20,000.
10. Collections from customers on account, $65,000.
11. Cash payments: to employees, $23,700; to suppliers on account, $69,600; to shareowners (dividends), $20,000.
12. Cash borrowed from the bank on September 30, $5,000.
13. Cost of factory equipment purchased on account and installed on September 30, $30,000.
14. Equipment sold for cash, $500. This equipment had an original cost of $9,000 and accumulated depreciation of $7,000.
15. Additional shares of capital stock issued in exchange for $50,000 cash.

a. Establish T-accounts to present the 18 accounts identified at the beginning of this problem, and enter the September 1 balances.
b. Prepare journal entries to record these transactions, using only the 18 account titles listed.
c. Post the amounts in your journal entries to the T-accounts.
d. Prepare a schedule of manufacturing costs and an income statement for September.

16. Supplying Missing Information; Unit Cost.   Peerless Cloak Company manufactures silk-lined evening cloaks. The company filed a claim with its insurance company under its burglary insurance policy, stating that on the night of September 10, its workroom was burglarized. Compensation was claimed for the loss of 400 cloaks ($12,000) and 1,000 yards of silk ($3,500). An insurance claims adjuster analyzed the company's records and assembled the following information for the period from January 1 to September 10:

1. Inventories of cloaks, cloth, and silk had a cost of $211,200 on January 1.
2. Purchases were: cloth, 38,000 yards at $2 a yard; silk, 11,000 yards at $3.50 a yard.
3. 6,000 cloaks were manufactured, consuming 39,500 yards of cloth and 10,000 yards of silk.
4. 9,000 cloaks were sold.
5. Manufacturing costs for all elements other than materials totaled $42,000.

6. Materials and manufacturing costs per unit were approximately the same as during the preceding year.
7. A physical count of the inventories on September 11 yielded the following cost totals, approved by the adjuster: 13,000 yards of cloth, $26,000; and 6,000 yards of silk, $21,000. The inventory also contained 3,000 finished cloaks.
8. The insurance policy provided for compensation equal to the cost of any items stolen.

If you were the claims adjuster, how much of the company's claim would you approve for payment? (Suggestion: As one step in your analysis, you need to calculate the average unit cost of the cloaks manufactured.)

17. Transactions Analysis; Financial Statements. On February 1, 19x1, Paltry Corporation's accounts showed the following balances (all accounts not shown had zero balances):

Cash	$ 9,200	
Accounts receivable	13,000	
Raw materials	3,500	
Work in process	5,000	
Finished goods	6,200	
Prepaid insurance	1,000	
Plant and equipment	62,000	
Accumulated depreciation		$22,000
Accounts payable		13,900
Capital stock		34,000
Retained earnings		30,000

Paltry Corporation completed the following transactions during February:

1. Purchased materials on account, $42,000.
2. Issued materials to factory for use on month's production, $38,500.
3. Sold merchandise: for cash, $10,000; on credit, $90,000.
4. Collected $93,000 on accounts receivable.
5. Paid rent on office equipment for February, March, and April, $900.
6. Purchased factory equipment on account, $9,000.
7. Purchased office furniture on account, $1,000.
8. Accrued employees' wages and salaries for the month: factory labor, $20,000; office and sales force, $8,000.
9. Received invoices for various goods and services bought on account and used during the month: factory, $25,200; office and sales departments, $15,000.
10. Recognized depreciation for February: factory, $300; office, $100.
11. Paid sales representatives and executives: for travel and entertainment expenses during month, $2,000; as advances against March expenses, $1,050.
12. Paid employees (for wages and salaries), $27,300.

13. Paid suppliers on account, $75,200.
14. Sold a piece of factory equipment for $500 cash; its original cost was $3,000, and it had accumulated depreciation of $2,100 at the date of sale.
15. Noted expiration of insurance premiums: on office, $50; on factory, $250.
16. Finished and transferred to warehouse goods costing $68,000.
17. Declared cash dividend to shareholders, $2,000, payable on March 15.
18. Counted inventories on February 28; cost of finished goods on hand was $5,800.

a. Prepare journal entries to record all this information. To accomplish this, you will need to use accounts other than those listed at the beginning of this problem.
b. Set up T-accounts, enter the February 1 balances, and post the journal entries to these T-accounts.
c. Using the balances in the T-accounts, prepare an income statement for the month of February and a balance sheet as of February 28.

18. Transactions Analysis; Financial Statements. On May 1, 19x1, Deppe Company's accounts had the following balances (all accounts not listed had zero balances):

Cash	$ 25,600	
Accounts receivable	11,800	
Materials and supplies	7,200	
Work in process................	6,500	
Finished goods	12,900	
Prepaid insurance	1,200	
Plant and equipment............	156,000	
Accumulated depreciation		$76,000
Accounts payable...............		15,400
Capital stock..................		80,000
Retained earnings		49,800

The following transactions took place during May:

1. Materials and supplies purchased on account, $30,300.
2. Wages and salaries earned by employees during month: factory labor, $34,600; sales and office salaries, $23,400. (Note: Cash payments occasioned by employee payrolls are described in item 13 below.)
3. Materials issued for use in production, $18,800.
4. Equipment purchased in exchange for Deppe's promissory note, calling for one payment of $2,500 before May 31 and quarterly payments thereafter of $2,500 each, plus interest on the $7,500 outstanding on May 31. (See item 13 below for payment information.)
5. Goods sold on account for $110,000.

6. Supplies issued from storeroom and used: factory, $3,200; office, $2,700.
7. Costs of miscellaneous goods and services bought on account and used during May:
    Office rental, $2,300.
    Repairs of factory equipment, $600.
    Electricity and other utilities: factory, $3,600; office, $500.
    Newspaper advertising, $300.
    Other: factory, $11,860; office, $13,740.
8. Paid property taxes on factory, May 1 through October 31, 19x1, $1,200.
9. Insurance premiums expired: factory, $200; office, $100.
10. Depreciation: factory, $800; office, $160.
11. Collections from customers, $106,000.
12. Sale of capital stock for cash, $10,000.
13. Payments made:
    To suppliers of materials and other goods and services, on account, $61,260.
    To equipment manufacturer, on promissory note (see 4 above), $2,500.
    To employees, $57,740.
14. Equipment sold, $300 cash (original cost, $5,000; book value $800).
15. Dividends declared, $3,000, to be paid on June 15.
16. Cost of goods finished, $64,200.
17. Finished goods on hand, May 31, $11,800.

a. Prepare journal entries to record all this information in accrual-basis accounts. You will need to open accounts in addition to those listed at the beginning of this problem. (For simplicity, you may wish to set up a single expense account for all selling and administrative expenses.)
b. Set up T-accounts, enter the May 1 account balances, and post your journal entries to these accounts.
c. Prepare an income statement for May and a balance sheet as of May 31. Ignore any income taxes that might be levied on Deppe Company's income for the month.

Chapter 6

The Present-Value Concept

Before we go further in our study of accounting, we need to study the concept of *value* in some depth. The first reason is that assets have no place on the balance sheet if they have no value, nor should a company report net income if no value change has taken place. Second, value is much more relevant to the decisions management and investors must make than are the historical costs of the company's assets or the historical amounts creditors and owners have invested in them. Third, value-based measurements do enter into some conventional accounting calculations, and we can't understand these calculations unless we know what value is all about.

In this chapter, we'll explain what value means, how it can be calculated, and why it isn't the primary basis for conventional financial statements.

Sources of Economic Value

The economic value of any asset stems from its ability to provide the company with *cash*. Cash is the only universally useful asset, the only asset that can always be used to buy other assets or to pay creditors or owners. An oil well, for example, is a resource that could be measured in many ways—by the amount of oil it is capable of tapping, for example—but it only has value if it can generate cash. The well has no value at all if the company would have to pay more to extract the oil than customers would pay for it.

One measure of an asset's value is the amount of cash the asset could bring in immediately, or nearly so, from an orderly sale to an independent outside buyer. This is the asset's **market value.** Market value is seldom the appropriate measure of an asset's value for an ongoing business because most of the assets of an ongoing business *aren't* intended for immediate sale. Instead, they are held because the company intends to sell them or use them to generate cash receipts in some future period or periods—referred to as *positive cash flows,* or just **cash flows**. Presumably, the perceived value of the cash flows to be generated in one of these ways is greater than the asset's current market value—otherwise, the company would sell the asset immediately.

The value of assets which are held for future use or sale stems from any of four sources:

1. The asset may give the business an immediate ability to pay for goods and services (cash).
2. The asset may be exchangeable for cash in the very near future (accounts receivable).
3. The business may be able to sell the asset and receive cash in the very near future (merchandise inventory).
4. The business may be able to use the asset to produce goods or services for which outsiders will pay more cash in one or more future periods than the business will have to pay to produce them (factory equipment, prepaid rent, etc.).

Our task in the next section will be to see how estimates of the cash flows from these sources can be translated into a measure of value.

The Time Value of Money

The economic value of an asset depends not only on the amount of cash the asset will generate, but also on *when* the cash will be generated. Other things being equal, a dollar now is always worth more than a dollar sometime in the future. This phenomenon is known as the *time value of money*. The reason is that cash available on one date can be invested to yield a greater amount at a future date. This fact is reflected in the concepts of **future value** and **present value.**

We'll introduce five mathematical formulas as part of the explanation in this section. We're presenting them because they will help many readers understand the time value of money more easily. Anyone who finds the formulas to be more of an obstacle than an aid needn't worry, however. The narrative alone, without the formulas, provides everything most people will need to understand the subject and to solve the problems at the end of this chapter.

Future Value

The future value of a sum of cash is the amount to which that sum will grow if it is invested at a specified interest rate for a specified period of time. This relationship can be expressed mathematically as follows:

$$F_1 = P(1 + r) \tag{1}$$

in which P = the present sum of money, r = the rate of interest, and F_1 = the future value one year from now.

Suppose, for example, that a bank will pay $1,150 one year from now in return for a $1,000 deposit today. We say that this bank is paying interest at the rate of 15 percent a year. Using equation (1), with P = $1,000 and r = 0.15:

$$F_1 = \$1,000 \times (1 + 0.15) = \$1,000 + \$150 = \$1,150$$

Continuing the example, if the $1,150 is left in the bank for a second year, it will build up by the end of the two years to a balance of $1,150 + ($1,150 × 0.15) = $1,322.50. Interest in the second year amounts to $172.50 and is greater than the first year's interest because the bank is now paying interest not only on the original investment but also on the interest earned during the first year. The mathematical formula for computing the future value of a present sum two years later is:

$$F_2 = F_1(1 + r) = P(1 + r)(1 + r) = P(1 + r)^2 \qquad (2)$$

If r = 0.15, $(1 + r)^2$ will be 1.3225 and the future value of $1,000 now will be $1,322.50. The 1.3225 amount is called the *multiplier*; it is the amount that links the beginning and the end of the interest-earning interval.

Equation (2) can be extended to a more general formula. If an amount P is invested at interest of r percent a year, with interest added once a year at the end of the year, the amount will have grown at the end of n years to a future value (F_n) of the following amount:

$$F_n = P(1 + r)^n \qquad (3)$$

Using this equation to extend our illustration beyond two years gives us the future amounts represented by the heights of the vertical bars in Exhibit 6–1. Starting with $1,000, the depositor's account will build at 15 percent each year—to $1,150 in one year, $1,322.50 in two years, and so on, up to $16,366.54 at the end of 20 years.

This form of interest calculation, in which interest is earned on previously earned interest, is known as **compounding.** In this case, interest has been compounded annually, meaning that interest is added to the bank balance only once a year. In practice, interest can be compounded quarterly, daily, or even continuously. We'll study the effects of varying the compounding interval shortly.

Present Value

The time value of money can also be viewed from another perspective—to focus attention on the present value of a future amount. *The*

EXHIBIT 6–1
Future Values Equivalent to a Present Value of $1,000 (Annual Compounding at 15 Percent a Year)

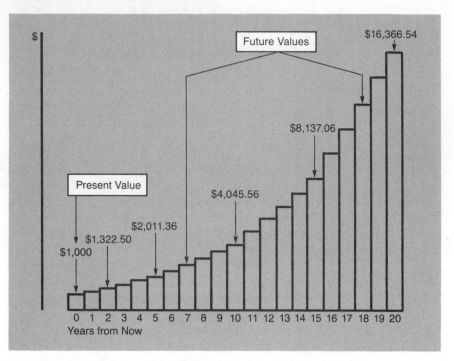

present value of a future sum of cash is the amount that must be invested now at the specified rate of compound interest to grow to an amount equal to the future sum at the specified future date.

Present value and future value, in other words, are just two ends of the same relationship. An investor who considers 15 percent annual compound interest a satisfactory reward will regard $1,322.50 two years from now as exactly equivalent to $1,000 now.

The formula to compute present value from known or estimated future values can be found by turning equation (3) around. Since $F_n = P(1 + r)^n$, then

$$P = \frac{F_n}{(1 + r)^n} = F_n(1 + r)^{-n} \qquad (4)$$

This shows that the present value of any future sum can be determined by multiplying the latter by $(1 + r)^{-n}$ or by dividing it by $(1 + r)^n$.

For example, if r is 15 percent a year, and an asset is expected to yield a cash inflow of $1,000 one year from now, the present value of this cash inflow is:

$$P = \frac{\$1,000}{(1.15)^1} = \$869.57$$

This calculation shows us that $869.57 is the amount that will grow to $1,000 in one year if it is invested now at 15 percent interest compounded annually ($869.57 + 0.15 × $869.57 = $1,000). $869.57 therefore is the present value of $1,000 a year from now.

Similarly, if the cash flow is $1,000, *n* is two years, and *r* is 15 percent, equation (4) reveals that the present value of the cash inflow is:

$$P = \frac{\$1,000}{(1.15)^2} = \frac{\$1,000}{1.3225} = \$756.14$$

In other words, we'll have to invest only $756.14 instead of $869.57 if we're willing to wait two years instead of one for the promised $1,000 cash flow.

If we repeat our present value calculations for amounts to be received 5, 10, 15, and 20 years from now, we get the values shown in Exhibit 6–2, rounded to the nearest cent. The basic conclusion from this illustra-

EXHIBIT 6–2
Present Values of Future Cash Flows of $1,000 (Annual Compounding at 15 Percent a Year)

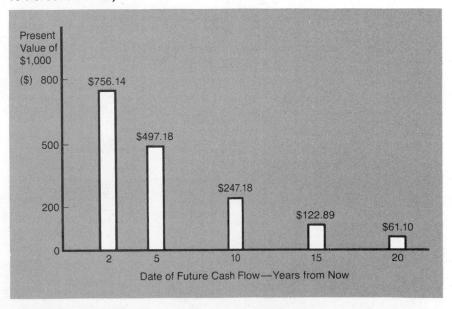

tion is that cash available in the near future is worth more than the same amount of cash at a more distant date. The sooner the cash is available, the sooner it can be invested to earn more cash—this makes it more valuable.

In our illustration, the $1,000 to be received two years from now was divided by the 1.3225 multiplier we derived from equation (2). The more common technique is to determine the **present-value multiplier**—the reciprocal of the future-value multiplier—and multiply this by the amount of the future cash flow. To calculate the present value of a cash flow two years from now at a 15 percent annual rate of interest, the present-value multiplier is 1/1.3225 = 0.75614. Using this multiplier to determine present value is equivalent to dividing the future cash flow by the future-value multiplier.

The Present Value of a Series of Cash Flows

While some assets derive all their value from the expectation of a single cash receipt at some point in the future, the value of other assets stems from a *series* of future cash receipts. The present value of an asset of this kind is the sum of the present values of the various cash flows.

This idea is illustrated in Exhibit 6–3. The two blocks at the right represent two cash sums a franchising company (the franchisor) expects to receive from one of its franchise operators (the franchisee). The first of these sums, $5,000, will be received one year from now; the other, $10,000, will be received two years from now. The two blocks joined on the left side of the diagram are the present values of these two cash flows,

EXHIBIT 6–3
Present Value of a Series of Cash Flows (Annual Compounding at 15 Percent a Year)

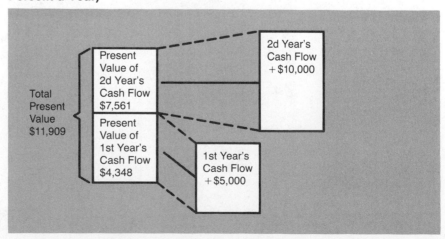

calculated on the basis of a 15 percent interest rate. Since the franchisor's ownership of this franchise contract gives it the right to receive both these future amounts, the present value of the asset must be the *sum* of the present values of the two amounts.

The calculations behind this exhibit are summarized in the following **cash-flow timetable**, using the present-value multipliers we derived in the preceding section:

(1) Years from Now	(2) Cash Receipt	(3) Multiplier	(4) Present Value at 15% (2) × (3)
1	$ 5,000	0.8696	$ 4,348
2	10,000	0.7561	7,561
Total			$11,909

The present-value multipliers are rounded off to four digits; further precision is seldom warranted.

Present Value of an Annuity

A series of *equal* periodic cash flows is known as an **annuity.** The present value of a five-year annuity of $1,000 a year can be calculated by multiplying each of the five cash flows by the appropriate present-value multiplier:

(1) Years from Now	(2) Cash Receipt	(3) Multiplier	(4) Present Value at 15% (2) × (3)
1	$1,000	$1/1.15 = 0.8696$	$ 869.60
2	1,000	$1/(1.15)^2 = 0.7561$	756.10
3	1,000	$1/(1.15)^3 = 0.6575$	657.50
4	1,000	$1/(1.15)^4 = 0.5718$	571.80
5	1,000	$1/(1.15)^5 = 0.4972$	497.20
Total		3.3522	$3,352.20

A much simpler method is to add the annual multipliers and multiply this sum by the amount of the annuity. This sum can be expressed mathematically as follows:

$$P = A \times \left[\frac{1 - (1 + r)^{-n}}{r} \right] \tag{5}$$

in which A is the size of the annual cash flow. In our example, the sum of the present-value multipliers is 3.3522; multiplying this sum by the

$1,000 annual cash flow gives us the same total present value, $3,352.20, we got by using the annual present-value multipliers.

Annuity multipliers enter into a variety of calculations. For example, we might want to know how large a five-year annuity $10,000 can buy if interest is compounded annually at 15 percent. In other words, by investing $10,000 today, what constant amount would we receive at the end of each year for the next five years? The relationship is:

$$\text{Present value} = \text{Annual cash flow} \times \text{Present-value multiplier}$$

This is equivalent to:

$$\text{Annual cash flow} = \frac{\text{Present value}}{\text{Present-value multiplier}}$$

Using the present-value multiplier for a five-year annuity at 15 percent, we get:

$$\text{Annual cash flow} = \frac{\$10,000}{3.3522} = \$2,983.12 \text{ a year}$$

CALCULATING PRESENT VALUE

1. Estimate the amount of each future cash flow and the date or period when it will take place.
2. Enter these amounts in a *cash-flow timetable*.
3. Choose an appropriate interest rate.
4. Identify the present-value multiplier at this rate for each amount in the timetable and enter these multipliers in the next column of the timetable.
5. Multiply each cash-flow amount by the appropriate present-value multiplier and enter these amounts in the last column of the timetable.
6. Add the amounts in the last column to obtain the asset's total present value.

Interest Tables

The calculation of present-value multipliers [for example, $1/(1.15)^5 = 0.4972$] is time-consuming. Fortunately, we don't have to make these calculations by hand. We can use an electronic computer, if we have one, or a calculator containing a compound-interest program. If we don't have ready access to either of these, we can consult published **interest tables** which contain the present-value and future-value multipliers for many interest rates (r) and time periods (n).

Although the remainder of this chapter can be read and understood without special aids, few of the problems and exercises at the end of this chapter can be solved efficiently unless a calculator or a set of interest tables is used. To meet the need for computational aids, we have provided an abbreviated set of interest tables in Appendix A at the end of the book, together with instructions for using them.

Determinants of Present Value

The present value of an asset depends on four factors: the amounts of future cash flows, their timing, the applicable interest rate, and the length of the compounding interval. Let's examine each of these, in turn.

Amounts and Timing of Future Cash Flows

The significance of amounts and timing can be summarized in two observations. First, the greater the cash flow in any future period, the greater is its present value at a specified interest rate. Second, the closer a given cash flow is to the present, the greater is its present value at a specified interest rate.

For example, suppose the interest rate is 15 percent and we have four assets, with the following streams of future cash flows:

Years from Now	Asset A	Asset B	Asset C	Asset D
1.........	+$24,000	+$30,000	+$10,000	−$10,000
2........	+ 16,000	+ 20,000	+ 20,000	0
3........	+ 8,000	+ 10,000	+ 30,000	+ 70,000
Total	+$48,000	+$60,000	+$60,000	+$60,000

All but one of the cash flows are cash receipts (*positive* cash flows). Asset D has a cash disbursement in year 1, but a positive *net* cash flow for the three-year period as a whole. Asset B has the same time pattern of cash flows as Asset A, but each cash receipt is 25 percent greater. Assets B, C, and D have identical net lifetime cash-flow totals (+$60,000), but they differ in the timing of the cash flows. Asset D even requires us to pay an additional $10,000 a year from now to obtain even greater cash receipts in the third year.

The present values of these four assets are shown in Exhibit 6–4. The present-value multipliers are multiplied by each asset's future cash flows to derive the present value amounts in the last four columns. The present value of Asset B is exactly 25 percent greater than the present value of Asset A because each of its cash flows in 25 percent greater. Asset B is more valuable than either Asset C or Asset D because its positive cash flows will occur sooner than those of either of the other two.

EXHIBIT 6–4
Present Values of Four Assets

Years from Now	Multiplier at 15% $[1/(1.15)^n]$	Present Value at 15%			
		Asset A	Asset B	Asset C	Asset D
1......	0.8696	+$20,870	+$26,088	+$ 8,696	−$ 8,696
2......	0.7561	+ 12,098	+ 15,122	+ 15,122	0
3......	0.6576	+ 5,260	+ 6,575	+ 19,725	+ 46,025
Net present value		+$38,228	+$47,785	+$43,543	+$37,329

Interest Rate

An important aspect of the time value of money is that the higher the interest rate applied to future cash flows, the smaller is the present value of a given stream of cash flows. For example, in our earlier franchising company illustration (Exhibit 6–3), the franchise agreement was expected to produce one cash receipt of $5,000 one year from now and another of $10,000 one year after that. If the interest rate is 10 percent, the present value of these cash flows is $12,809, the amount shown at the bottom of the 10 percent column in Exhibit 6–5. If the interest rate is 15 percent, the present value is $11,909 (taken from the right-hand column).

EXHIBIT 6–5
Present Values at Two Different Rates

Years from Now	Cash Receipt	10%		15%	
		Multiplier	Present Value	Multiplier	Present Value
1.......	$ 5,000	1/1.10 = 0.9091	$ 4,545	1/1.15 = 0.8696	$ 4,348
2.......	10,000	$1/(1.10)^2$ = 0.8264	8,264	$1/(1.15)^2$ = 0.7561	7,561
Total			$12,809		$11,909

The reason for this relationship is that as the rate of interest increases, more of each cash flow will go to pay interest on the amount invested, leaving less to repay the investment itself. A given cash flow therefore can support a smaller investment if the interest rate is high than if it is low.

For example, at an interest rate of 10 percent, the two cash flows are big enough to support an investment outlay of $12,809. The calculations behind this statement are shown in the first two lines of Exhibit 6–6. If $12,809 is spent to acquire the asset, interest at 10 percent will take

EXHIBIT 6–6
Effect of Interest Rate on Recoverable Amount

Year	(1) Beginning Investment	(2) Interest Rate	(3) Interest (1) × (2)	(4) Cash Receipt	(5) Available for Recovery of Investment (4) − (3)	(6) Ending Investment (1) − (5)
1	$12,809	0.10	$1,281	$ 5,000	$3,719	$ 9,090
2	9,090	0.10	909	10,000	9,091	(1)
1	11,909	0.15	1,786	5,000	3,214	8,695
2	8,695	0.15	1,304	10,000	8,696	(1)
1	11,909	0.10	1,191	5,000	3,809	8,100
2	8,100	0.10	810	10,000	9,190	(1,090)

$12,809 × 0.10 = $1,281 of the first year's cash flow. This amount is shown in the first line of column (3). In column (5), we see that this leaves $3,719 of the $5,000 cash flow to provide a partial repayment of the initial outlay itself. After this repayment, $12,809 − $3,719 = $9,090 of the initial outlay, the amount shown in column (6), has yet to be recovered.

The calculations on the second line of the exhibit show that interest on the $9,090 unrecovered portion of the initial outlay amounts to $909 in the second year. When we subtract this from the $10,000 cash receipt at the end of the second year, we see that $9,091 is left to repay the initial outlay. This differs from the amount unrecovered at the beginning of the year only by a $1 rounding error, the number on the second line in column (6) in Exhibit 6–6. This shows that the cash flows from the franchise contract are just adequate to pay interest at the rate of 10 percent on an initial investment outlay of $12,809.

The situation is different if the interest rate is 15 percent. In this case, the cash flows are only worth $11,909. The calculations to demonstrate this are shown in the third and fourth lines in Exhibit 6–6. Once again, after interest is taken out, just enough of the cash flows is left to pay for a $11,909 asset, with only a $1 rounding error.

What would happen if the company could obtain this asset for $11,909, but only had to pay interest at a rate of 10 percent? As the final two rows in Exhibit 6–6 show, since interest now takes a smaller portion of each cash flow, the cash flows will give the company $1,090 more than it needs to pay interest and recover its initial outlay. The asset is obviously worth more than the $11,909 the company has to pay for it, because it is expected to generate more cash flows than the company will need to compensate its investors at an interest rate of 10 percent. To repeat, the higher the interest rate, the lower the present value of a given set of cash flows.

The Compounding Interval

The fourth factor affecting an asset's present value is the length of the compounding interval. The more frequently interest must be compounded, the less a given stream of future cash flows is worth today.

Suppose we want to know the present value of an asset that is expected to generate a single cash inflow of $10,000 two years from now. If the interest rate is 10 percent a year and interest is compounded once a year, the present value of the asset will be $10,000/(1.10)^2 = $8,264$. The interest earned in the two-year period will be $10,000 - $8,264 = $1,736$.

If the compounding interval is cut in half (to six months), the interest rate per period is also cut in half (to 5 percent each six-month period). The present value of this asset therefore will be $10,000/(1.05)^4 = $8,227$. The interest earned in this case is $10,000 - $8,227 = $1,773$. The present value is $37 less than under annual compounding, because the investors demand that interest be compounded twice a year—therefore, $37 more of the future cash flow must be given to them as interest.

TERMINOLOGY: NOMINAL AND EFFECTIVE INTEREST RATES

A **nominal interest rate** is the stated annual percentage divided by the number of compounding periods occurring each year. For example, if the nominal interest rate is 10 percent a year and interest is compounded every six months, the nominal interest rate for each half-year interval is 5 percent (10 percent divided by 2).

An **effective interest rate** is the ratio of (1) the actual interest earned in a year to (2) the debt's beginning-of-year present value (assuming no cash additions or reductions during the year). When interest is compounded more than once a year, the effective interest rate is slightly higher than the nominal rate. This happens because interest in all compounding periods except the first is earned not only on the beginning-of-year present value, but also on interest accrued in preceding compounding periods during the year. For example, a 10 percent nominal annual rate compounded semiannually results in a 5 percent nominal rate every six months and an effective annual rate of interest of 10.25 percent (5 percent + 5 percent × 1.05).

Most of us are familiar with a calculation that is closely related to the one summarized in the preceding paragraph: the compounding of interest on certain kinds of bank deposits. If one bank compounds interest *daily* at a chosen nominal annual rate (e.g., 10 percent), a given deposit will earn more interest and grow faster than the same deposit in another bank that compounds interest *quarterly* at the same nominal annual rate.

Notice the difference between these two examples. In the first example in which the future value was known ($10,000), the length of the compounding interval affected the *present value* ($8,264 versus $8,227). In the bank example, the present value was known (the initial deposit), and the compounding interval affected the *future value*.

In most money market operations today, daily compounding is commonplace, because money can be invested or borrowed for a period as short as a single day. To avoid unnecessary confusion, however, we'll stick to annual compounding in this chapter.

Applications of the Time-Value-of-Money Concept

The time-value-of-money concept pervades all facets of economic life. We'll return to it many times in future chapters, but for the moment let's look closely at two applications and superficially at a few others.

Evaluating Deferred-Payment Assets

Accountants record all asset expenditures at their cost. When the disbursement of cash is deferred, however, the sum of the future payments does *not* measure accurately the cost of the asset acquired. For example, suppose Bradley Corporation bought a parcel of land on January 1, 19x1, agreeing to pay a total of $26,000: $8,000 down and $9,000 at the end of each of the next two years. We'll assume the applicable interest rate was 14 percent, compounded annually; in practice, if the rate wasn't explicitly cited by the seller, it would be based on the rate the buyer would pay to borrow money.

Generally accepted accounting principles require Bradley to record the cost of the land at the present value of the three payments it is required to remit. Since the amount of the down payment is its present value (because this payment is made immediately), the company must calculate only the present value of the two deferred payments. Since each of those payments is $9,000, we use the present-value multiplier for a two-period annuity—1.6467—from the 14 percent column and 2-period row of Table 2 in Appendix A. The sum of the present values of the three payments, therefore, is:

$$\$8,000 + \$9,000 \times 1.6467 = \$22,820$$

The cost of the land, therefore, is $22,820, and this is the amount at which Bradley records this asset. The $3,180 difference between this cost and the $26,000 cash Bradley will eventually pay is the interest cost

Bradley will incur and recognize as expense during the two-year loan period.

Bradley could use a variety of different account structures to account for the acquisition of this asset, but the following entry reflects the essence of the transaction:

January 1, 19x1

Land...	22,820	
Cash		8,000
Notes Payable		14,820

This entry identifies the increase in the land asset, the decrease in the cash asset, and the increase in Bradley's notes payable liability.

If this account structure is used, the following entries illustrate how Bradley would record the loan payments and each year's interest expense:

December 31, 19x1

Interest Expense (0.14 × $14,820)	2,075	
Notes Payable.......................................	6,925	
Cash		9,000

December 31, 19x2

Interest Expense [0.14 ×($14,820 − $6,925)]	1,105	
Notes Payable.......................................	7,895	
Cash		9,000

Calculation of the 19x1 interest expense is based on the amount of the loan outstanding at the beginning of the year—that is, the present value of the two deferred payments, $14,820 ($9,000 × 1.6467). Interest expense for 19x1, therefore, is $2,075, as shown in the entry. This means that $6,925 of the first $9,000 payment ($9,000 − $2,075) constitutes a partial repayment of the $14,820 loan. The liability that appears in the balance sheet as of the end of 19x1 therefore is $7,895 ($14,820 − $6,925). The proof is that $7,895 is the present value of the $9,000 due one year later ($9,000 × 0.8772, from Table 1, $r = 0.14$, $n = 1$).

Similarly the interest expense in 19x2 is based on the amount of the loan outstanding at the beginning of that year, $7,895. Interest at 14 percent on that amount is $1,105, leaving exactly $7,895 of the final $9,000 payment to repay the last portion of the loan.

Calculating an Unspecified Interest Rate

To record Bradley Corporation's purchase of land, the accountants had to know (1) the amounts and timing of the future payments and (2) the appropriate interest rate to be able to calculate (3) the present value of these future payments at this rate. An important variation of this procedure in practice is to calculate (1) the interest rate implicit in a transaction when (2) an asset's cash price and (3) the amounts and timing of a future series of payments are known.

For example, on January 1, 19x4, Lincoln Company bought land that had a cash price of $50,000. Instead of paying cash, Lincoln agreed to remit $29,197 at the end of each year for two years. In this case, Lincoln didn't have to make any compound-interest calculations to record its acquisition:

January 1, 19x4

Land. 50,000
    Notes Payable   50,000

The amount of the liability was automatically determined by the price of the asset Lincoln received in exchange for its promise to make payments to the seller in the future.

When Lincoln remitted its first payment on December 31, 19x4, it had to recognize the interest expense pertaining to 19x4. Although the interest rate wasn't stated explicitly by the seller, the **implicit rate of interest** can be calculated on the basis of the information already at hand. Lincoln could have acquired the asset either by paying $50,000 immediately or by paying $29,197 a year for two years. The seller apparently regarded those two arrangements as equivalent to each other—in other words, the present value of the two deferred payments must have been $50,000.

We know that the total interest cost over the term of the loan is $8,394 (2 × $29,197 − $50,000), but we don't know how much of that was interest expense in 19x4. In our Bradley Corporation example, we knew the interest rate and therefore could make the interest calculation directly. Now we have to approach the problem from the other side: first, we'll calculate the present-value multiplier, and then we'll use that to determine the interest rate.

For an annuity, the present-value multiplier expresses the relationship between the annuity's present value and the amount of each payment:

$$\$29,197 \times \text{Multiplier} = \$50,000$$

which converts to:

$$\frac{\$50,000}{\$29,197} = \text{Multiplier} = 1.7125$$

In Table 2 of Appendix A, because we assume *annual* compounding, we look in the $n = 2$ row for a 1.7125 multiplier and find it in the $r = 0.11$ column. This tells us that the two future payments of $29,197 each have a total present value of $50,000 only if an 11 percent multiplier is used.

In other words, 11 percent is the rate of interest implicit in Lincoln's arrangement with the seller of the land.

Given this, interest expense for 19x4 is 11% × $50,000 = $5,500, and the amount repaid on the loan is $29,197 − $5,500 = $23,697. The end-of-year entry for 19x4 is as follows:

December 31, 19x4

Interest Expense (0.11 × $50,000)	5,500	
Notes Payable ($29,197 − $5,500)	23,697	
Cash		29,197

Since the loan balance was reduced by $23,697 at the end of 19x4, the amount of the loan on January 1, 19x5 was $50,000 − $23,697 = $26,303. Interest expense for 19x5 was $26,303 × 0.11 = $2,893. This left $26,304 of the second $29,197 payment to repay the remainder of the original loan. The $1 difference between this amount and the January 1, 19x5 liability is a rounding error in our calculations.

Capital Expenditure Decisions

A major use of present-value calculations is in the evaluation of capital expenditure proposals—proposals to build factories, buy equipment, introduce new products, or buy other companies. Here, the cash outflows (disbursements) are concentrated in the near future, with the compensating cash inflows (receipts) further in the future.

The question is whether the present value of the distant cash receipts is at least as great as the present value of the near-term cash outflows. We'll devote an entire chapter, Chapter 21, to a review of this kind of problem.

Leasing, Lending, and Borrowing Decisions

The time-value-of-money concept is always applied in decisions to lend or borrow money or to lease property. Calculations in the financial services industries are likely to be highly precise, with interest rates in many instances carried to two or more decimal places. We'll review some of these applications in Chapter 10.

Valuing a Company

Present-value calculations are often used by investors seeking to appraise companies they are interested in buying. The issue here is often to identify values that conventional balance sheets fail to disclose. Often, this means estimating the value of the company's intangible assets. We'll study this application in the next section, partly because it is important in itself and partly because it identifies the problems we would encounter if we tried to adopt a *value* basis for financial reporting generally.

Economic Income   Although most present-value calculations apply to individual assets, liabilities, or decisions, the concept can also be applied to the measurement of a company's **economic income.** Economic income is the amount an individual or business can afford to spend during a period and be as well off at the end of the period as at the beginning. *How well off the individual or business is* can be measured either by market value or by the present value of future net cash inflows. In this section, we'll explain how these concepts can be used in the measurement of economic income.

Economic Income: Market Value Basis

An individual shareowner is likely to measure economic value by the market value of his or her shares. From this standpoint, the individual's income from the shares is the sum of (1) the dividends received during the period, and (2) the change in the market value of the shares. Both *dividends* and an *increase* in the shares' market value increase the owners' wealth. If income is defined as the increase in the owner's wealth—that is, how well off the owner is—then both the dividends and the increase in market value are income to the owner. Conversely, if the owner receives dividends but the value of the shares falls by an equal amount, the owner's wealth hasn't increased and there is no income.

For example, suppose Lucy Strong owns 100 shares of Star Company's stock. The market price of this stock was $27 on January 1, 19x1 and $30 on December 31, 19x1; dividends of $2 a share were declared and paid in 19x1. Strong's economic income from this asset, therefore, was $2 + ($30 − $27) = $5 a share, or $500 in total. Both the dividend and the increase in market value added to her wealth; therefore, both were components of her *economic income.* This also means that Strong's *economic wealth* consisted of the sum of the cash already received and the market value of the shares owned.

Although the concepts of economic income and economic wealth are employed in investment decision making, neither concept has been adopted either by the accounting profession or in tax law in the United States. In other words, income statements and tax returns include in income only dividends and gains or losses on *sales* of shares, and balance sheets usually measure only the original cost of owned shares.[1]

Economic Income: Present Value Basis

A company's economic income and economic wealth are measured by the present value of the stream of anticipated future net cash inflows

---

[1] Investment companies (i.e., mutual funds) are the major exceptions to this rule. They recalculate the values of their investment portfolios every day.

accruing to the owners. By *net cash inflows,* we're referring to all future cash flows—the difference between cash inflows and cash outflows. This includes both the amounts that will be paid out as dividends and the amounts that will be retained and reinvested in the business. While the market-value approach to economic income is particularly useful to an investor in shares of stock, the present-value basis is more appropriate for measuring the economic income of business enterprises.

When this approach is taken, economic income is the increase in the present value of the anticipated stream of future net cash inflows, plus any amounts distributed to the owners during the period. Presumably, if no cash had been distributed, the end-of-period present value would have been that much greater. The amount distributed therefore is part of the change in value, which is the measure of economic income.

For example, suppose Star Company began the year 19x1 with an expectation of a 20-year annuity of net cash inflows amounting to $1 million a year. The interest rate was 15 percent. During the year, the net cash inflow amounted to $1 million, as anticipated, of which $800,000 was distributed to the owners as cash dividends. The other $200,000 was reinvested by the company in plant assets and working capital to provide for future growth. At the end of the year, the new expectation was that the future net cash inflow would be $1,050,000 a year for 25 years; the interest rate was 14 percent. (A possible explanation is that the company is in the oil-producing business, and operations in 19x1 revealed a richer and longer-lasting underground oil deposit in the company's drilling area; a reduction in the rate of inflation was accompanied by a reduction in the interest rate.)

The income calculated under these circumstances is diagramed in Exhibit 6–7. Block A at the left shows the present value of the 20-year annuity at the beginning of the year: $1,000,000 × 6.2593 = $6,259,300.

EXHIBIT 6–7
Income on a Present-Value Basis

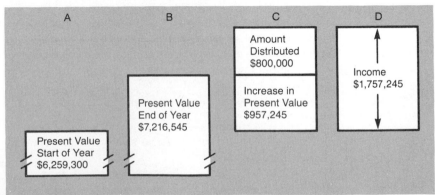

The 6.2593 multiplier comes from the 20-year row of the 15 percent column in Table 2 of Appendix A. Block B shows the present value of the $1,050,000, 25-year annuity at the end of the year: $1,050,000 × 6.8729 = $7,216,545. The 6.8729 present-value multiplier comes from the 25-year row of the 14 percent column in Table 2 of Appendix A.

The difference between these two present values is $957,245 and is shown in the lower portion of block C. Economic income for the period, represented by block D, was the sum of this increase in present value and the dividends of $800,000 that were distributed during the year, a total of $1,757,245.

Economic versus Accounting Income

Since economic income is based on present-value calculations while accounting income is based on the analysis of historical transactions, they are highly unlikely to be identical. First, many of the conventional determinants of accounting net income are measured differently in calculating economic income. For example, in the calculation of economic income, the cost of goods sold is measured at the goods' value on the date of sale rather than at their historical cost. Second, economic income includes recognition of changes in value in assets and liabilities that aren't yet realized in transactions with outsiders, such as changes in the value of inventory on hand.

We'll discuss some of the reasons for these differences in Chapters 8 and 9, as changes in the current replacement costs of inventories and plant assets don't enter the calculation of accounting net income. In Chapter 10, we'll describe changes in the present value of the company's liabilities that aren't reflected in accounting net income. Finally, in Chapter 14, we'll examine these effects in the context of the effects of changes in general price levels.

Inapplicability of Value Basis for Financial Reporting

It is hard to challenge the argument that managers and investors are likely to judge the company's performance by the increase or decreases in its value. In fact, that is precisely how investment companies (i.e., mutual funds) measure their income. Despite its conceptual advantages, however, the *value* basis for calculating income, assets, liabilities and owners' equity is not used in most industries, mainly for two reasons:

1. The cash-flow estimates in most situations can't be verified satisfactorily.
2. The appropriate interest rate isn't known with certainty.

The amount, timing, and duration of the future cash flows of a business are highly uncertain, to say the least. Accountants can verify management's past estimates of future cash flows to some extent, but their ability to verify current estimates is much more limited. Present value-based financial statements therefore would summarize management's estimates, relatively unrestrained by objective tests applied by outsiders. The most accountants could do would be to review the assumptions on which management based its estimates, using available information on economic conditions and the political climate. The credibility of statements prepared on a present-value basis probably would be quite low.

The second obstacle to financial reporting on a present-value basis is that estimates of the appropriate interest rate to apply to the estimated future cash flows are far from precise. Errors in the rate can have significant effects on estimates of present value and on income amounts based on these estimates. For example, we found that the present value of a 20-year, $1 million annuity at 15 percent interest is $6,259,300. If we vary the interest rate just one percentage point, to 14 percent or 16 percent, we change the present value by more than $300,000—to $6,623,100 or $5,928,800 (based on the present-value multipliers in Table 2 of Appendix A). Reducing the interest rate to 10 percent increases the present value to $8,513,600; increasing the rate to 20 percent reduces the present value to $4,870,000.

The choice of the interest rate would also affect the relevance of the statements to individual investors. Some investors may wish to capitalize future cash flows at 15 percent, some may wish to use 12 percent, and others may prefer to adjust for perceived differences in future cash flows by applying different interest rates to different portions of the cash-flow stream. No matter which rate or set of rates is chosen, it won't meet everyone's needs.

As a result of these difficulties, the present-value basis has been ruled out for routine financial reporting. It is a powerful and useful concept, however, and we'll return to it time and again as we expand our understanding of accounting measurements in later chapters.

Summary

The value of a business asset depends on the amount and timing of the net cash inflows it can produce in the future *and* on the rate of interest the owners expect to earn from these future cash flows. Distant cash flows are less valuable than those expected to take place in the near future; these differences in timing require that all cash flows be expressed at their present values at a single point in time. The present value of a cash flow is the amount which, if invested at the specified interest rate for the specified period of time, will grow to equal the cash flow when it occurs. The present-value multipliers in Appendix A make the calculations easier.

A conventional business balance sheet doesn't pretend to measure the value of the business, nor does a conventional income statement measure all the changes in value arising during the period. In this chapter, we've shown how the present-value concept can be used to calculate income in a very different way from the method accountants use. Economic income is the sum of the change in the company's present value from the beginning to the end of the period and the dividends distributed during the period.

Although these calculations are highly useful in various contexts, accountants don't use them in conventional financial reporting because they would require the use of judgment that can't be verified satisfactorily by objective tests.

Accountants do use the present-value concept in a number of ways—calculating the value of a deferred-payment asset, for example, or calculating the interest rate implicit in certain deferred-payment transactions. Accountants, managers, and economists also apply the present-value concept in many other ways, and we'll examine several of these applications in later chapters.

Key Terms

Annuity	Implicit interest
Cash flow	Interest tables
Cash-flow timetable	Market value
Compound interest	Net cash inflow
Deferred-payment asset	Nominal interest rate
Economic income	Present value
Effective interest rate	Present-value multiplier
Future value	

> ### STUDY SUGGESTION
>
> Before attempting the problems and exercises that follow, the reader should study and understand Appendix A, omitting only the section on "Bond Yield Tables."

Independent Study Problems (Solutions in Appendix B)

1. Present-Value Exercises. Calculate the value on January 1, 19x1, of assets that have the following cash flows, with interest at 12 percent compounded annually:

a. Outlay: $35,000 on January 1, 19x1.
   Receipt: $100,000 on January 1, 19x11.
b. Outlays: $80,000 on January 1, 19x1; $20,000 on January 1, 19x6.
   Receipts: $10,000 on each January 1, 19x2 through 19x7; $20,000 on each January 1, 19x8 through 19x17.

c. Outlays: $20,000 on each January 1, 19x1 through 19x11.
Receipt: $250,000 on January 1, 19x13.

2. Equivalent Annuities. Present Company borrowed $1 million today at a nominal annual interest rate of 10 percent. Present Company plans to make a series of five equal annual payments to the lender, the first payment to be made a year from today. Part of each payment will cover interest for the year; the remainder will be used to repay part of the amount borrowed from the lender. The amount of the payment is to be calculated in such a way that Present Company will owe the lender exactly nothing when the final payment in the series has been made.

a. How much will Present Company have to pay the lender at the end of each of the next five years?
b. Prove your answer by preparing a schedule that shows how much of each year's payment is needed to cover the interest and how much is left over to repay the amount borrowed.
c. How much would Present Company have to pay at the end of each period for five years if payments to the lender were made semiannually instead of annually, at a nominal annual interest rate of 10 percent, compounded semiannually?
d. Suppose that Present Company determines it will have no more than $200,000 available at the end of each of the next five years to pay the lender. How much can Present Company borrow now if this series of $200,000 payments will be made to the lender, with interest compounded annually at 10 percent?

3. Deferred-Payment Asset. Menlo Company purchased equipment on July 1, 19x7, for which it agreed to pay $96,000, as follows:

1. $16,000 to be paid immediately.
2. Four $15,000 payments, one every three months beginning October 1, 19x7.
3. Five $4,000 payments, one every three months beginning October 1, 19x8.

Since the seller didn't identify the applicable interest rate, Menlo used the 20 percent nominal annual rate, compounded quarterly, which it would have had to pay for a bank loan reflecting similar loan conditions.

a. At what amount should Menlo have recorded the cost of the equipment?
b. What was Menlo's interest expense for 19x7?

4. Semiannual versus Annual Compounding. The Superhighway Sweepstakes Commission plans to offer a special once-a-year winning jackpot in the amount of $30 million each New Year's Eve. The jackpot will be paid at the rate of $600,000 each June 30 and December 31 for the next 25 years. The Commission will also be required to contribute $5 million to the State Highway Fund on the first July 1 after the drawing.

a. Assuming the Commission can earn interest at a nominal annual rate of 14 percent, compounded *semiannually* (7 percent every six months), what amount of cash receipts must it collect from sweepstakes ticket sales by New Year's Eve to meet its cash payment obligations?

b. Assume that the jackpot is to be paid at the rate of $1.2 million each December 31 for 25 years, the first payment is to be made 12 months after the drawing, and the Highway Fund is to receive its $5 million on December 31 (12 months after the drawing). If the Commission were to earn 14 percent annual interest compounded *annually*, what amount of receipts would be necessary?

c. Suppose the facts were as in *b* except that the first payment to the jackpot winner would be made immediately. What amount of receipts would be necessary?

5. Calculating Income on a Present-Value Basis.   William Appersham operates a ferry service across Deepwater Bay. A bridge is now being built across the bay. When it is completed two years from now, Appersham will close the ferry service and retire to his plantation in the Virgin Islands. He expects the following cash flows from the ferry operation:

Year	Cash Receipts	Cash Disbursements	Net Cash Receipts
1.......	$350,000	$200,000	$150,000
2.......	400,000	220,000	180,000

At the end of each year he will withdraw the year's net cash receipts and invest them in highway bonds where they will earn interest at an annual rate of 12 percent, compounded annually. In addition, at the end of year 2, he will be able to withdraw the $50,000 he must now maintain as a working cash fund to keep his ferry service going.

The sale value of his ferry boats two years from now will be virtually zero.

a. What is the present value of the ferry service to Appersham now?

b. Assuming that all forecasts are correct, what will be the present value of the assets of the ferry service a year from now, before Appersham withdraws the net cash receipts of the first year's operations?

c. Calculate the net income of the ferry service for the first year on a present-value basis, assuming that all forecasts are correct.

d. Calculate the ferry service's income for the second year on a present-value basis, again assuming that all forecasts are correct.

e. Appersham has just discovered that he can invest his available cash at 15 percent, compounded annually, instead of at 12 percent. How would this affect your analysis?

---

6. Valuation Differences. The management of Gupta Corporation has recently been cited by a national society of industrial engineers for its efficiency in organizing and controlling the company's affairs. The aggregate market value of the company's stock, based on the current market price per share, is $10 million; the balance sheet owners' equity is only $4 million.

Management's own forecast of future cash flows, converted to present value at an interest rate that seems appropriate for a company of its size and class, is $9 million. The board of directors of the Marshall Company has just made a cash offer of $12 million for the outstanding stock in the Gupta Corporation.

What might account for the differences among the four measures of the value of Gupta Corporation?

7. Valuing a Lottery Prize. Sander van Euler recently held the winning combination of numbers in a state lottery. The prize consisted of 21 annual payments of $952,000 each, the first payment being made immediately in front of television cameras. The prize was announced to the press as the first $20 million lottery prize ever.

Van Euler had the right to sell his rights to the 21 payments to which this prize entitled him. One opportunity to do this was presented by a group of potential buyers who were willing to pay Van Euler a price that would earn them a return of 12 percent compounded annually.

a. What was the prize worth to the potential buyers?
b. Was the state justified in announcing this as a $20 million prize? Why or why not?
c. Van Euler accepted the buyers' offer because he wanted to use $7 million of the proceeds to buy an annuity that would give him a fixed amount of cash each year for 40 years, the first receipt to come six years after the prize date. What would be the amount of each of these annual receipts if Van Euler's investment in the annuity were to earn 10 percent interest compounded annually?

8. Cost of New Bridge: Discussion Question. A state government recently issued $10 million of bonds, bearing interest of 10 percent a year for 20 years, and used the $10 million to repair a large suspension bridge. A group of legislators had argued against the sale of the bonds, saying that this action would increase the cost of the bridge from $10 million to $30 million. They believed the bridge repair should have been financed from current state tax revenues. By law, the state had to have a balanced operating budget each year.

Do you agree with the legislators? Be prepared to justify your position, giving due consideration to opposing views.

9. Calculating Present Value Without Interest Tables. Without using the interest tables or the present value key on a calculator, calculate the present value at 10 percent of a single sum of $100 to be received six years from now. Then verify your answer by using the appropriate table in Appendix A.

10. Present-Value Exercise. Using Table 2 in Appendix A, determine the present value of a series of payments of $100 a year for each of the next six years. Assume that the first payment is received one year from now and the interest rate is 12 percent, compounded annually.

11. Present-Value Exercise. Check your answer to Problem 10 by using Table 1.

12. Calculating Present Value. You are considering the purchase of six promissory notes. The issuers of these notes will pay you nothing until the notes mature, at which time they will pay the face value of the notes. Three of the notes have face values of $100 and will come due one each at the end of years 3, 4, and 5. The other three have face values of $150 and come due one each at the end of years 6, 7, and 8.

If your interest rate is 15 percent, what will you be willing to pay for the full set of six notes at the beginning of year 1? Table 1 in Appendix A is available for your use in solving this problem; Table 2 is not available.

13. Verifying Present Value Calculation. Use Table 2 to solve Problem 12.

14. Determinants of Present Value. Dolly Company has an asset that is expected to generate future net cash receipts of $100,000 during its lifetime. Calculate the present value of this asset under each of the following assumptions:

a. Receipts of $10,000 a year for 10 years, beginning one year from today; interest rate 10 percent, compounded annually.
b. Receipts of $10,000 a year for 10 years, beginning five years from today; interest rate 10 percent, compounded annually.
c. Receipts of $20,000 a year for five years, beginning today; interest rate 10 percent, compounded annually.
d. Additional outlay of $50,000 one year from today; receipts of $25,000 a year for six years, beginning one year from today; interest rate 10 percent, compounded annually.

e. Receipts of $10,000 a year for 10 years, beginning one year from today; interest rate 20 percent, compounded annually.

f. Receipts of $5,000 every six months for 10 years, beginning six months from today; nominal interest rate 20 percent a year, compounded semiannually.

g. Receipts of $2,500 every three months for 10 years, beginning three months from today; nominal interest rate 20 percent a year, compounded quarterly.

15. Present Value Exercises.   Calculate the present value of each of the following at 10 percent, using the interest tables in Appendix A:

a. $100,000 to be received 10 years from now; interest compounded annually.

b. $10,000 to be received at the end of each of the next 10 years; interest compounded annually.

c. $5,000 to be received at the end of each of the next five years, plus $15,000 to be received at the end of each of the five years after that; interest compounded annually.

d. $15,000 to be received at the end of each of the next five years, plus $5,000 to be received at the end of each of the five years after that; interest compounded annually.

e. $5,000 to be received at the end of each of the next 20 six-month periods; interest compounded semiannually at 5 percent each six-month period.

16. Deferred Salary Payments.   The Roadside Rogues professional basketball club chose the date of Dunk Doolittle's 30th birthday to present him with a deferred-payment contract that earned him the title, "the $10 million man." The agreement called for a $750,000 payment every half year beginning in six months, for the next six years (12 payments in all). Dunk would also receive $500,000 "retirement" payments on his 50th and 65th birthdays.

a. Determine the present value of the payments, assuming a nominal annual interest rate of 12 percent, compounded semiannually.

b. Before signing the agreement, Dunk decided that he'd rather receive semiannual payments every half year, beginning six months from then and continuing until his 55th birthday, with no "retirement" payments then or later. Since he and the Rogues had already agreed on the present-value amount derived in part *a*, what would be the amount of each semiannual payment?

17. Timing of Gift: Donor versus Recipient.   Soon after graduating from college, Audrey Worthington and a group of friends decided to endow a "chair" to honor their favorite accounting professor. Their alma mater's treasurer indicated that for the chair to be established four years from today, funding could be effected three different ways:

1. Pay $2 million two years from today.
2. Remit five $400,000 payments, one every half year, beginning today.
3. Pay $1 million six months from today, and remit five $200,000 payments, one every half year, beginning 18 months from today.

Assuming a 10 percent nominal annual interest rate compounded semiannually, which one of the three payment plans would be the most attractive to the donors, and which would be the most desired by the university?

18. Deferred-Payment Asset. On July 1, 19x1, Eagle Enterprises bought property which had a cash purchase price of $125,000. In lieu of paying cash immediately, Eagle gave the seller a noninterest-bearing note with a face value that reflected 12 percent nominal annual interest compounded semiannually; the one and only payment was due June 30, 19x4.

a. What was the face value of the note?
b. What was the interest expense in 19x1?
c. What was the interest expense in 19x2?

19. Deferred-Payment Asset. On January 2, 19x3, Essex, Ltd., bought a word processor, for which it agreed to remit five $2,956.53 payments, one every six months beginning June 30, 19x3. The cash purchase price of the word processor was $11,500. Essex depreciated the equipment by an equal amount each year for five years and anticipated no salvage value.

What amounts should have appeared in Essex, Ltd.'s December 31, 19x3, balance sheet and in its 19x3 income statement as a result of buying the word processor?

20. Calculating Annuity Equivalent to Present Value. A pension fund not subject to income taxes plans to buy a piece of equipment for $10,000 and lease it to a manufacturer. The equipment has an estimated useful life of 10 years and is to be leased to the manufacturer for that time. It will have no salvage value at the end of its ten-year life. The pension fund's management wishes to charge the manufacturer an annual rental that will enable the fund to recover the purchase price of the equipment during the ten years and earn 8 percent a year on its investment.

a. What is the lowest annual rental the pension fund should accept if the rental is received at the end of each year for ten years?
b. What is the lowest annual rental the pension fund should accept if the rental is received at the beginning of each year for ten years?

(Prepared by Carl L. Nelson)

21. Value of Asset to Buyer and Seller. A boat can be bought for $21,000, payable in cash immediately. Alternatively, the seller will accept a series of cash payments, starting with $10,000 immediately and then $2,000 at the end of each of the next eight years.

a. If buyers can always invest their money at 10 percent compounded annually, which of these alternatives should they prefer?

b. Assuming that sellers can invest their money at 8 percent compounded annually, what is the series of payments worth to them?

22. Comparability of Values at Different Times. You have three assets for which you forecast the following cash flows:

Years from Now	Asset A	Asset B	Asset C
1	+$1,000		
2	+ 1,000		
3	+ 1,000	+$1,700	
4	+ 1,000	+ 1,700	
5	+ 1,000	+ 1,700	+$2,000
6			+ 2,000
7			+ 2,000

Each of these assets is being managed by one of your company's trainees. You have asked them to calculate the values of these assets, assuming that money is worth 10 percent, compounded annually. They have given you the following estimates:

Asset A: present value today, $3,791.

Asset B: present value three years from now, $4,650.

Asset C: future value seven years from now, $6,620.

Which of these assets is the most valuable? Which is the least valuable? Show your calculations.

23. Comparing Two Short-Term Investments. A bank offers a $20 immediate cash bonus to anyone who deposits $1,000 in the bank today and leaves it on deposit for a year. The bank will add interest to this deposit at the end of each three-month period at a nominal annual rate of 11 percent, compounded quarterly.

If you don't accept the bank's offer, you will invest $1,000 in a money market fund which will add interest to your investment monthly, at a nominal annual rate of 12 percent, compounded monthly.

If you accept the bank's offer, you will invest the $20 cash bonus in the money market fund described in the preceding paragraph.

Which of these opportunities should you accept? Quantify the advantage this opportunity has over the other. (Note: you will not be able to use the interest tables in Appendix A to solve this problem. You can solve it either by performing a sequence of operations or by using one or more of the mathematical formulas in this chapter.)

24. Calculating the Value of an Asset. Thomas Peterson is an investor who expects to earn at least 8 percent a year on his investments. He estimates that an investment in a new mine will bring him $10,000 in cash at the end of each of the next 15 years. At the end of that time, the mine will be worthless.

a. How much is the mine worth to Peterson?
b. How much would the mine be worth to Peterson today if it were expected to produce $10,000 a year for 25 years? For 40 years? For 50 years?
c. Prepare a diagram with "values" on the vertical scale and the number of years on the horizontal scale. Enter your answers to parts *a* and *b* on this diagram. From the diagram, try to estimate how much the mine would be worth if it were to be productive at the present rate for 100 years. What other method or methods could you have used to calculate this amount?

25. Discussion Question: Effects of Purchase and Sale on Income. On July 1, 19x1, Ruth Norris bought 500 shares of stock in the Parkway Corporation at a price of $20 a share. She estimated that the present value of these shares to her was $22 a share at that time.

Norris received cash dividends of 50 cents a share on December 30, 19x1. On December 31, 19x1, she estimated the present value of these shares at $24 a share. She sold the shares on that date at a price of $25 a share.

a. If Norris were to measure her income on a present-value basis and ignore income taxes, how much income would she say she had earned from this investment (1) on July 1, 19x1, and (2) between July 1, 19x1, and January 1, 19x2?
b. How, if at all, would your answer to part *a* change if Norris hadn't sold her stock on December 31, 19x1? Discuss the differences between this situation and the situation addressed in part *a* and the arguments for and against treating the two situations differently.

26. Effect of Timing of Cash Flows on Asset Value. Cole Hammerlowe, the famous author-composer of Broadway musicals in the 1940s, bequeathed the rights to all his literary and musical works to the Hammerlowe Foundation, a newly established charitable organization. Some of these rights were due to expire in a few years, but others would be valid for 30 years.

Hammerlowe's work had a small but loyal band of admirers, and a steady stream of royalty payments could be counted on for a number of years. In addition, the trustees of the foundation expected that Hammerlowe's works would have several years of renewed popularity as a new generation of theater critics rediscovered them, a phenomenon that had been observed for every other author-composer of Hammerlowe's stature in the past. Accordingly, the trustees prepared the following estimates of the cash flows the foundation would be likely to receive:

Year	Annual Cash Receipts
1–5	$ 50,000
6–10	200,000
11–15	100,000
16–20	50,000
21–30	20,000

The trustees expect to be able to invest funds that become available to them to yield an annual rate of return of 10 percent. The foundation is not subject to income taxes.

a. Compute the value of Hammerlowe's gift to the foundation.
b. The anticipated cash flows in this case average $70,000 a year for 30 years. Suppose that a long-established, respectable commercial publisher were to offer to pay the foundation $70,000 a year *forever* in exchange for the rights to Hammerlowe's works. Should the trustees accept this offer? Explain briefly.

27. Income Measured on a Present Value Basis. Wilkinson Associates was a U.S. firm of economic, business, and actuarial consultants. At the beginning of 19x5, Wilkinson expected its operations to generate cash flows amounting to $2.5 million each year for the next 25 years. The interest rate was 12 percent.

During 19x5, the cash flow from operations amounted to the expected $2.5 million, of which $1.5 million was withdrawn by the owners in the form of cash dividends. The remaining $1 million was reinvested in the business.

At year-end, the owners revised their expectations on the basis of increased demand for Wilkinson's services caused primarily by the firm's expansion into foreign countries. Cash flows were expected to be $3.5 million each year for 30 years, and the interest rate was increased to 14 percent in deference to worldwide inflation being greater than that of the United States.

In making calculations, assume that all cash flows occur at year-end and that interest is compounded annually.

a. What was the present value of Wilkinson Associates at the beginning of 19x5?
b. Assume that at the end of 19x5, Wilkinson's owners had withdrawn all of the year's cash flows and that they didn't revise their cash flow

expectations beyond 19x5. Calculate what the firm's 19x5 income would have been on a present value basis.

c.˙ In the light of Wilkinson's revised expectations beyond 19x5, what was the present value of the firm at the end of 19x5?

d. Given the revised expectations and the reinvestment of 40 percent of 19x5's cash flow from operations, what was Wilkinson's 19x5 income on a present value basis?

e. If Wilkinson's end-of-year revision had assumed that the $3.5 million annual cash flow would continue in perpetuity, what was the present value of the firm at the end of 19x5?

f. Reconcile your answers to parts c and e.

28. Reviewing a Proposed Interest Schedule. The United States Internal Revenue Service has a rule requiring that part of the amounts received in installment sales of property be treated as interest in the year in which they are received. If the interest rate specified in the installment sale contract is significantly lower than the current market rate of interest, the Internal Revenue Service will force the seller to classify some of the nominal selling price of the property as interest.

For example, suppose Sheila Clidas sells an investment on January 1, 19x5, under a contract that provides for the buyer to pay $28,000 for the investment in four equal installments of $7,000 each, plus interest, as follows:

Date	Payment for Investment	Payment for Interest	Total Payment
January 1, 19x6	$7,000	$2,000	$9,000
January 1, 19x7	7,000	1,700	8,700
January 1, 19x8	7,000	1,000	8,000
January 1, 19x9	7,000	800	7,800

The Internal Revenue Service determines that these interest payments are significantly smaller than they would be if currently available rates were applied. It further determines that the appropriate nominal annual rate of interest is 12 percent, compounded semiannually, and calculates the present value of the four payments as follows:

Date	Amount of Payment	Present-Value Multiplier (6%)	Present Value
January 1, 19x6	$ 9,000	0.8900	$ 8,010
January 1, 19x7	8,700	0.7921	6,891
January 1, 19x8	8,000	0.7050	5,640
January 1, 19x9	7,800	0.6274	4,894
Total	$33,500		$25,435

In other words, the Internal Revenue Service calculates the selling price as $25,435, not the nominal selling price of $28,000. The remaining $2,565 of the nominal selling price is to be classified as interest, spread equally over the four years at approximately $641 a year. Total interest therefore is as follows:

Date	Stated Interest	Additional Interest	Total Interest
January 1, 19x6	$2,000	$ 641	$2,641
January 1, 19x7	1,700	641	2,341
January 1, 19x8	1,000	641	1,641
January 1, 19x9	800	641	1,441
Total	$5,500	$2,564*	$8,064

* $1 rounding error.

One of Sheila's friends thinks she should argue this matter and calculate interest expense each year at one fourth of $8,064, or $2,016 a year, thereby reducing her taxes in the first two years. Another friend says neither of these methods is a correct application of the present-value concept.

Prepare an analysis and a brief report reflecting your recommendation on this issue. (Note: This is an exercise in determining what is "good accounting;" it is not an exercise in determining what the tax regulations require.)

(Derived from an illustration prepared by
Deloitte Haskins & Sells)

29. Calculating Income on a Present-Value Basis. The city of El Dorado has decided to sponsor an international exposition promoting the values of rural living. The exposition will operate for four years. The city will provide a site for the exposition in Bucolic Park, rent free.

Turning to experts, the city has asked the International Corporation for Expositions (ICE) to construct the buildings and operate the exposition. ICE has prepared the following estimates of operating cash receipts and cash disbursements:

Year	Receipts	Disbursements
1.......	$2,000,000	$1,300,000
2.......	3,000,000	1,500,000
3.......	2,000,000	800,000
4.......	1,350,000	350,000

Construction costs, all to be paid at the beginning of year 1, are estimated to be $4 million. An additional investment of $300,000 will be necessary at that time to provide a working cash fund; the need for this will continue throughout the four-year period. The exposition buildings will be sold to the city at the end of year 4 for $1 million.

ICE has enough confidence in the predictions to participate in the venture if it will earn a return of 10 percent before income taxes. If it decides to do so, it will form a subsidiary, the El Dorado Exposition Corporation. This subsidiary will issue common stock to ICE for $1,000 and will borrow the remaining $4,299,000 from ICE, giving noninterest-bearing notes as evidence of its indebtedness. The subsidiary will repay the notes as rapidly as possible, keeping only a cash balance of $300,000. ICE assumes in all its calculations that all cash receipts and disbursements take place at the end of the year.

The subsidiary will be liquidated at the end of year 4, and its remaining cash assets will be paid back to ICE at that time.

a. Assuming that ICE agrees to undertake this project and that all the forecasts are correct, calculate the subsidiary's income for each year if assets are measured by the present-value approach. Ignore income taxes.

b. If the historical-cost approach is used instead of present value, what will be the income for each year? Historical-cost depreciation will be the same for each of the four years. Ignore income taxes.

Part 2

Financial Accounting

Chapter 7

Revenue/Expense Recognition

One of the major precepts in financial economics is that income occurs whenever the present value of the owners' equity increases. Under generally accepted accounting principles, however, changes in value enter the income statement, for the most part, only as revenues and their related expenses are recognized. The income statement reports the difference between the sum of a set of current values (revenues) and the sum of another set of past values and current values (expenses).

For example, Exhibit 7–1 shows the amount invested in an inventory asset increasing gradually as costs are incurred to bring it to the point of revenue and expense recognition. At that point, the accounting measurement increases because the value of the asset—that is, the inventory or the cash or receivable exchanged for it—exceeds the cost incurred up to that point.

This chapter has two goals: (1) to explain the criteria accountants use in deciding when the value of marketable goods and services is measurable enough to justify the recognition of revenue, and (2) to see how the choice of a revenue-recognition point affects the amounts shown in the financial statements.

Criteria for Revenue Recognition

At least six distinct events can be found in the operating cycle of a manufacturing company:

1. Acquisition of resources.
2. Receipt of customer orders.
3. Production.
4. Delivery of goods or performance of services.

EXHIBIT 7–1
Accounting Measurement of Value Changes

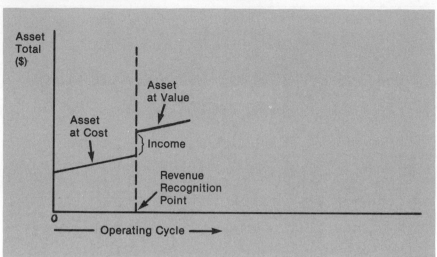

5. Collection of cash.
6. Completion of all contractual obligations.

In the illustrations we used in earlier chapters, revenues were always recognized at the *time of delivery,* and our task was to decide which costs were to be reported as the expenses of generating those revenues. The time of delivery isn't the only possible choice, however. Any of the six events in our list might conceivably be taken as the signal that revenues have been earned—that is, it is conceivable that each might be adopted under certain circumstances as the **revenue-recognition basis.** Our first problem, therefore, is to see what criteria accountants use in choosing among these six possibilities.

We should point out at the outset that *each* of these is a productive activity that adds value in some measure to the goods or merchandise purchased. On these grounds, a portion of the ultimate sale price ought to be recognized as revenue as each activity is performed. The difficulty is that the ultimate sale price is the *joint* product of *all* activities, and it is impossible to say with certainty how much is attributable to any one of them. *For this reason, accountants select one event as the signal for revenue and expense recognition and ignore the others.*

In choosing a basis for revenue and expense recognition, accountants follow a basic rule: the investor's interests call for recognizing revenue and expense just as soon as the value change it represents can be measured reliably. Investors' decisions presumably are influenced by the *rate* at which value changes take place; the sooner they learn about changes in this rate, the sooner they can act on this information.

Given this rule, accountants generally recognize revenue and expense at the *first* point in the operating cycle at which *all* the following **revenue-recognition criteria** are satisfied:

1. The principal revenue-producing service has been performed.
2. All costs that are necessary to create the revenue but have not yet been incurred either are negligible or can be predicted with reasonable accuracy.
3. The amount ultimately collectible in cash or its equivalent can be estimated with reasonable accuracy.

Revenues and their related expenses aren't recognized until these conditions are met because, before this time, no one can be sure that the value change has actually taken place in the amount indicated. The accountant wants to notify the public promptly, but only if the amounts reported are a reasonable measure of what has actually happened. In other words, there is a trade-off between promptness and reliability—the accountant's job is to locate the point beyond which more promptness can be had only by too great a sacrifice in reliability.

Keep in mind that companies consciously incur costs because they are necessary to generate revenues. When revenue recognition occurs in the same period in which the cost is incurred, the cost is recognized as an immediate expense. If, however, the revenues are expected to occur in a *future* period, expense recognition is deferred. In such cases, the costs are said to be *capitalized*—that is, they are recorded as assets (e.g., inventory, prepaid rent, and machinery).

Selecting the revenue-recognition basis therefore also determines whether costs are (1) expensed immediately or (2) capitalized and expensed subsequently. When revenues are recognized "late" in the operating cycle, more costs will be capitalized than when revenues are recognized relatively "early." The amount of income that will be reported will always be the same, however—only the timing is affected by the choice of revenue/expense-recognition basis.

The Delivery Basis   We'll look at the **delivery basis** first because it is used most frequently in practice. Specifically, we'll address four questions:

1. What is the delivery basis?
2. Why is the delivery basis used so widely?
3. What estimates have to be made when this basis is used?
4. How will assets, income, and expenses be measured?

The Nature of the Delivery Basis

The delivery basis probably should be called the *shipment basis.* When the delivery basis is used, revenues and their related expenses are usually recognized at the time merchandise is shipped to customers and invoices are prepared, even though actual delivery takes place a few days or weeks later. The time lag is usually short, however, and the distinction between shipment and delivery usually has no practical significance.

We might also have referred to this as the *sale basis* of revenue-and-expense recognition, the term most accountants use. We don't use this term because we find it ambiguous. The sales force "makes a sale" when a customer agrees to place a purchase order. This may be days, weeks, or even months before delivery takes place. Since accountants identify the time of delivery as the time of sale, we find it simpler to refer to this revenue-and-expense recognition basis as the delivery basis.

Reasons for the Use of the Delivery Basis

The delivery basis is widely used because, in most cases, it's the first point in the operating cycle at which all three revenue-recognition criteria are met:

1. The seller's economic role has been performed, for the most part, when the goods are delivered or the services are performed.
2. Few, if any, costs remain to be incurred in the future, and those that do remain can be predicted accurately—e.g., warranty costs.
3. While the amount that eventually will be collected from customers is unknown, it is usually predictable. Bad debts, customer discounts, and other future leakages from the stated price of the goods delivered are generally small and predictable.

A second reason for the prevalence of the delivery basis is that it permits the company to reduce its recordkeeping costs. Invoices have to be prepared to notify customers that payments are due. These invoices are usually prepared when the merchandise is shipped or when services are performed for customers. Using these invoices as the source to recognize revenues avoids the need to perform these same calculations at some other time. Although recognition of revenue at some other time might provide better information, the added cost of providing that information would probably outweigh the added benefits.

Estimating the Amount of Cash to be Collected

In any basis of revenue recognition, the key amounts to estimate are (1) the sum to be collected from the customer and the date it will be collected, and (2) the costs still to be incurred after the recognition point.

As to the first of these, the total amount of cash collected from customers is almost always less than the total invoice price, for one or more of the following reasons:

1. The company grants **cash discounts** to its customers for prompt payment.
2. The company grants **sales allowances** (price reductions) to customers who agree to accept merchandise not meeting their specifications.
3. The company cancels all or part of the amounts owed by customers who return merchandise they don't need or can't use (**sales returns**).
4. Customers fail to pay full amounts they owe the company (customer defaults, or bad debts).
5. The company accepts an asset other than cash or a short-term receivable in exchange for the merchandise.

Each of these needs to be estimated if the amounts are large enough to affect the readers' interpretation of the financial statements. Estimating the amounts of cash discounts, sales allowances, and sales returns is seldom difficult because these amounts are usually determined fairly soon after goods are delivered to customers. Estimating bad debts is more of a problem, but we gave that enough attention in Chapter 4 and needn't repeat that discussion here. Acceptance of assets other than cash poses some new problems, however, and we need to study these for a moment.

DEFINITION: NET REVENUE

Net revenue is the value of the resources received in exchange for goods and services, after appropriate deductions from the gross selling price to allow for discounts, returns, allowances, bad debts, and delays in the conversion of the resources received into cash.

Resources Other Than Cash or Short-Term Receivables. Acceptance of assets other than cash or short-term receivables may be a way of giving a customer a concealed discount, a way of settling an account that otherwise would be uncollectible, or sometimes a way of making a sale to a customer who is short of cash but rich in longer-term assets. Regardless of the reason, the company's problem is to determine the amount at which to record the asset it receives in exchange for its goods and services *and* the gain or loss on the exchange.

Long-Term Receivables. When the asset is a *long-term* receivable, the company is lending money to the customer. Part of the face value of the receivable, therefore, is interest on this loan. For example, the sale of merchandise for a $10,000, one-year promissory note when the appropriate lending rate is 10 percent, compounded annually, should lead to the recognition of $9,091 in revenues, the present value of the $10,000 future amount. The remaining $909 represents a year's interest on the $9,091 loan. (The $9,091 would appear on the balance sheet as a note receivable, or at the $10,000 face value of the note less $909 in unearned interest.)

Other Kinds of Resources Received.   In other cases, the company may exchange goods or services for some asset the customer owns, not for cash or the customer's promise to pay. The customer, for example, may transfer shares of stock in other companies, corporate bonds, equipment, or real estate; the problem is to determine the current value of the asset received. Value in such cases is measured either by the estimated market value of the asset given up or by the estimated market value of the asset received, whichever is more clearly evident. For example, if the company accepts 100 shares of actively traded stock in exchange for merchandise with a list price of $10,000, the revenue is measured by the market value of the stock at the time of the settlement, and not the hoped for $10,000. The stock's market value is likely to be more readily determinable than the market value of unsold inventories.

Effects of Accepting These Other Assets.   Establishing value in this way has two effects. First, if revenues are recognized in the usual way, the subsequent acceptance of a new asset in exchange for the previously recognized receivable is likely to result in a gain or a loss. If our company accepted stock worth $9,000 to settle a $10,000 account receivable, the loss would be $1,000.

Second, this estimate of *value* is accounted for as the *cost* of the asset received when it is used or sold later. Suppose the stock was worth $9,000 at the exchange but was sold later for $7,000. The $2,000 difference was a loss resulting from management's decision to hold onto the stock instead of selling it right away. After all, a decision not to sell an asset is economically equivalent to a decision to buy it. Any change in the value of an asset held for investment is a gain or loss on the act of investment—it doesn't matter how the asset was acquired in the first place.

Measuring Inventories, Receivables, and Income

When revenues are recognized at the time of delivery, the past, present, and future costs associated with those revenues should be recognized as expenses at the same time. For example, suppose Castle Company incurs costs of $85 for each unit of product it delivers to a customer,

EXHIBIT 7–2
Costs Incurred in a Manufacturer's Operating Cycle

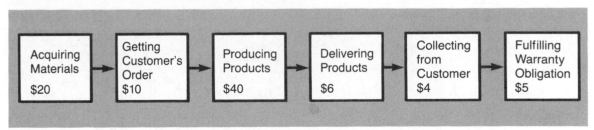

distributed over the operating cycle, as shown in Exhibit 7–2. It spends $20 to buy the materials for a unit of product, $10 a unit to a sales representative to secure an order from a customer, $40 to process the materials into a unit of finished product, $6 to deliver it to the customer, $4 a unit to collect the amount due from the customer, and $5 to provide service under the terms of the warranty attached to the product.

Now suppose the company sells each unit at an invoice price of $100. It offers no sales discounts, expects to receive payment within 30 days, has negligible sales returns and allowances, and expects bad debts to average 2 percent of the average invoice price. The *net* revenue from an average shipment of a unit of merchandise therefore is $100 − $2 = $98.

Since net revenue from a unit of product is $98 and the total cost associated with each unit is $85, the income is $98 − $85 = $13 a unit. According to generally accepted accounting principles, when the delivery basis is used, this entire $13 is recognized as income when Castle Company ships the merchandise to a customer. At that time, the asset ceases to be measured by its cost; instead, it is measured by the amount of cost incurred to date *plus* the amount of income it generates.

These relationships are represented in Exhibit 7–3. Each of the unshaded bars at the left represents the costs incurred to date at each of the first three stages in the operating cycle. The fourth bar has an unshaded portion (total cost incurred through the delivery stage) and a shaded portion (the income recognized at the time of delivery). The height of the entire bar represents the value of the asset, now classified as a receivable. The next bar to the right is slightly higher as more cost is incurred, increasing the height of the unshaded portion, but the height of the shaded portion remains the same, $13. All of the income is recognized at the delivery stage.

If the accounting is consistent with this diagram, none of the costs incurred prior to delivery—for materials, order getting, and production—will be expensed before delivery takes place. And there will be no effect on income later, when collection and warranty service costs are incurred. In other words, the expenses in the period of delivery will be those shown

EXHIBIT 7–3
Delivery Basis: Cumulative Total Cost and Income

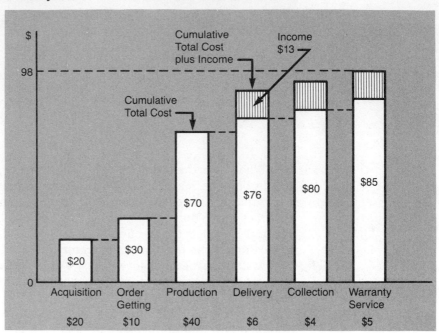

in Exhibit 7–4. The costs of the first four elements are known at the time of delivery; the costs of the other two are estimated.

Under this approach, undelivered finished goods would appear in the balance sheet as a cost of $70—$20 materials costs, $10 order-getting costs, and $40 production costs. The $10 order-getting costs might be capitalized separately from the costs of the physical inventory, similar in effect to prepaid expenses such as rent or insurance.

Delivery of a unit priced at $100 would then have the following effects:

Increase in receivables:
Gross amount..	$100	
Less: Anticipated customer defaults (bad debts)...........	2	
Net amount collectible................................	98	
Less: Anticipated collection costs.......................	4	
Net value of the receivable...........................		$94
Decrease in inventory and capitalized order-getting costs	70	
Decrease in cash (delivery costs)	6	
Increase in liability for warranty service....................	5	81
Increase in owners' equity (income)		$13

To be consistent with this approach, the amount receivable after the delivery is made should appear in the balance sheet at $94, the net

EXHIBIT 7–4
Expenses Associated with a $100 Order from an Average Customer

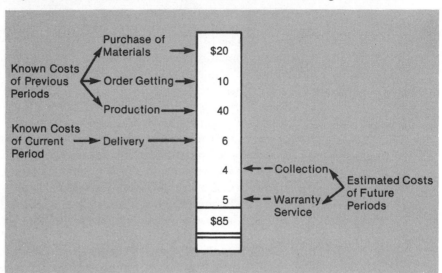

amount the company expects to realize at the time of collection. This could be recorded in a single account or the gross amount could be recorded in one account, with the anticipated discounts and collection costs entered in appropriately titled contra-asset accounts. The estimated warranty liability would be entered in a separate liability account, as explained in Chapter 4.

Delivery Basis: Pragmatic Criteria

Actual practice may depart from the income and asset measurement principles described in the preceding paragraphs. For example, accountants usually recognize order-getting costs and collection costs as expenses when they are incurred, not when delivery is made. Warranty costs, too, are sometimes expensed as they are incurred rather than when goods are delivered. Three factors account for these practices:

1. The amounts may be small enough to be classified as immaterial.
2. The amounts may be very difficult to attribute to individual customer orders or groups of orders.
3. Companies can reduce their clerical costs by adopting income tax definitions for financial reporting, and income tax regulations encourage or require expensing these items at the time of the actual expenditure.

Materiality is an important accounting concept that refers to whether the difference between two alternative accounting measurements or modes of presentation will affect the meaning readers of financial statements attribute to the amounts in the statements. A difference is immaterial if it is highly unlikely to change the interpretation of the statements. Immateriality is probably the main reason collection costs are expensed when they are incurred. It may also explain the failure to accrue warranty service liabilities in some cases.

The *difficulty of attributing costs* to individual orders applies particularly to order-getting costs. Management incurs costs, such as advertising and sales salaries, not to obtain a specific order, but in the hope and expectation of securing many orders. The company may spend millions of dollars and never receive an order from a customer. And when the orders do come in, management seldom knows whether they resulted from the current period's order-getting activities or from those of one or more previous periods. Lacking any clear basis for associating the current period's costs of order getting with specific current or future orders, accountants ordinarily treat them as expenses as they occur.

In the United States, *tax considerations* merely reinforce the first two reasons for expensing the costs of order getting, collection, and warranty fulfillment as they are incurred. If the costs are material in amount and readily identifiable with specific revenues, generally accepted accounting principles require that they be recognized as expenses when the related revenues are recognized, no matter what the tax regulations require or allow. Tax considerations, therefore, affect the financial accounting treatment only in borderline cases, when materiality or ease of association is in doubt.

Acquisition Basis

We'll point out in Part Three that management should base its decisions to acquire inventories and equipment on estimates of the difference between the present values of the cash flows they will generate and their present cost. For decision purposes, in other words, management should recognize revenues and expenses at the time resources are acquired.

The acquisition basis is never used for public financial reporting, however, because some (usually all) of the three revenue-recognition criteria haven't been met at that time. The company hasn't performed all its major value-creating functions, costs subsequent to acquisition are large and uncertain, and the amounts of cash to be received from customers are usually even more uncertain. This means that the income numbers measured under this basis would be too unreliable for use in financial accounting.

Sales Order Basis

Another possible point for revenue and expense recognition is the point at which the sales order is received. The order is a significant event in the operating cycle. Most companies that experience significant lags between the date of the order and the date of the shipment do keep track of the orders received so that the amount of orders on hand for future delivery (the backlog) can be reported periodically to management. In these circumstances, the performance of the sales force probably should be judged more on the basis of orders received than on goods shipped.

Order and backlog information may also be reported to creditors and stockholders to guide the appraisals of the company's future prospects, but revenues and receivables are never recognized in financial accounting on the basis of orders received during the period. The reason is simply that the criteria for revenue recognition are not met at the time the order is received—the goods have not yet been produced, the costs of producing them are not adequately predictable, and order cancellations are frequent and variable.

Production Basis

The third potential alternative to recognizing revenue at the time of delivery is the **production basis.** Under this method, revenue and expenses are recognized during or at the end of the production process, even though title to the goods still belongs to the seller. The production basis may be used only when the following conditions exist:

1. The costs to be incurred subsequent to production are either immaterial or highly predictable.
2. The amount of ultimate collection is reasonably certain, and collection costs are immaterial.
3. The timing of deliveries is more volatile than the timing of production.

As the method that views completion of production as tantamount to a sale, its application is most common in shipbuilding and other industries in which the production cycle is very long and production is initiated only on receipt of firm orders.

Measuring Inventories, Receivables, and Expenses

Applying the production basis to our previous example, Castle Company would recognize income of $13 at the time of production. Exhibit 7–5 identifies the bases on which the various components of expense would be recognized. This exhibit is like Exhibit 7–4, except that delivery costs have been moved from the *known* costs to the *estimated* costs associated with the order.

When the production basis is used, the amount at which the asset is measured is called its **net realizable value**—the amount the company expects to collect less the estimated costs of future periods. For Castle, the amount is $83: while the company expects to collect $98, it also expects to incur costs of $15 ($6 delivery, $4 collection and $5 warranty).

EXHIBIT 7–5
Expenses Associated with a $100 Order from an Average Customer:
Production Basis

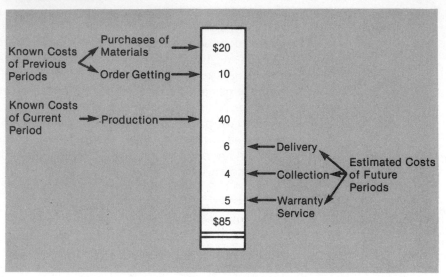

Notice what has happened. The company now has an $83 asset, even though it has incurred costs of only $70 ($20 materials, $10 order getting, and $40 production). This asset is classified as an *inventory*. Neither cash nor accounts receivable is affected until the goods are delivered. Since the merchandise is still owned by Castle, it is part of Castle's inventory. But since revenue has been recognized, the inventory is measured at its net realizable value rather than at its cost. The effect of production therefore is as shown in the following diagram:

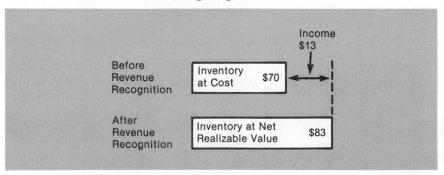

Journal entries to record production must record both revenues and expenses, as well as the changes in assets. The exact structure of the journal entries is less important than the effects on the assets, liabilities, and owners' equity, but we can use the following set of entries to reflect the sequence of events ending with production:

Purchase of Materials

Inventory (at cost)..	20	
Accounts Payable		20

Order Getting

Prepaid Costs	10	
Salaries Payable		10

Production

Inventory (at cost)...	40	
Cash (and other accounts)...............................		40
Cost of Goods Sold	60	
Inventory (at cost).......................................		60
Selling Expense	10	
Prepaid Costs		10
Inventory (at net realizable value)............................	83	
Bad Debts..	2	
Delivery Expense	6	
Collection Expense	4	
Warranty Expense	5	
Gross Revenues from Production..........................		100

The net effect of the last three entries is to recognize net revenues of $98 ($100 − $2), expenses of $85 ($60 + $10 + $6 + $4 + $5), income of $13 ($98 − $85), and an inventory increase of $13 ($83 − $70).

When the production basis is used in practice, provisions for delivery and collection costs are seldom made. Furthermore, order-getting costs might not be capitalized, and provisions for warranty liabilities might not be accrued. The reasons are the same as those we listed in discussing departures from the strict application of the delivery basis: (1) future costs are immaterial in amount, or (2) no clear basis can be found for attributing costs to individual production orders. The second of these reasons is particularly applicable to order-getting and collection costs, but it may apply to the others as well.

Advantages of the Production Basis

Using the production basis when the recognition criteria are met at the time of production serves investors by informing them more promptly of owners' equity increases or decreases arising from operations. This is particularly important whenever production precedes delivery by a substantial or widely varying time interval *and* production is the last major value-creating activity.

For example, consider a mining company that produces ore and sells it under a long-term contract at $12 a ton, the buyer to pay all delivery costs. During the first three quarters of 19x1, it produced and delivered

600,000 tons at a total cost of $6.3 million. It mined an additional 180,000 tons of ore during the final quarter of the year at a cost of $1.8 million, but a transportation strike prevented the delivery of this ore until 19x2. If the company used the production basis, it would recognize $360,000 more income than if it used the delivery basis, as the following table shows:

	Delivery Basis	Production Basis
Revenues:		
First three quarters		
(600,000 tons × $12)	$7,200,000	$7,200,000
Fourth quarter		
(180,000 tons × $12)	—	2,160,000
Total revenues	7,200,000	9,360,000
Expenses	6,300,000	8,100,000
Income before taxes	$ 900,000	$1,260,000

The production basis in this case is clearly more informative than the delivery basis. With a contract under which the customer takes all the company's production at an agreed-upon price, and with all costs known when production is completed, the act of production really completes the earning process, and investors should be informed of its success or failure at that time rather than later, when delivery takes place.

Percentage-of-Completion Accounting

The most widely used version of the production basis is the **percentage-of-completion method** of revenue-and-expense recognition. Percentage-of-completion accounting has four main features:

1. Costs are accumulated separately for each distinct work project, contract, or job order. For simplicity, we'll refer to each of these as a *job.*
2. The ratio of the amount of work done on each job to the total amount of work required by that job is estimated at the end of each period.
3. Revenue from each job is recognized in proportion to progress on the job, as measured by the ratio of work done to total work required.
4. Job costs are recognized as expenses as revenues are recognized.

An Illustration. Marsden-Brown, Inc., decided to adopt the production basis for recognizing revenues and expenses. Marsden-Brown is an engineering firm specializing in the design and installation of lighting systems. In mid-19x1, the firm obtained a contract to install the lighting for the Arkwright County Sports Arena, a job that was to take six months. The contract price was $200,000, and the estimated total cost was $160,000. Marsden-Brown was to bill the customer at the end of each quarter for 80 percent of the sales value of the work done in that quarter.

Work began on October 18, 19x1, and the actual costs charged to the job prior to December 31, 19x1, amounted to $80,000. Progress on the contract was reviewed at the end of the year, and the job was estimated to be 45 percent completed. Production-basis accounting therefore required recognizing revenue of $90,000 for 19x1 (45 percent of the $200,000 contract price). The customer was billed for progress payments of $72,000 (80 percent of $90,000).

In practice, the account structure to record this information would be relatively complex. In essence, however, Marsden-Brown's income statement showed a gross margin of $10,000:

Contract revenue	$90,000
Less: Cost of work performed	80,000
Gross margin on contract work performed	$10,000

The balance sheet showed:

Accounts receivable		$72,000
Inventory (market value of contract		
work performed to date)	$90,000	
Less: Progress billings	72,000	
Inventory (net)		18,000

The novel element here is the method used to measure the inventory. The inventory is measured *not at cost,* but at the value of the work done. Furthermore, since a portion of this value has already been billed to customers, only the unbilled portion is shown as inventory. The inventory, in other words, can be viewed as being tantamount to an unbilled receivable, not unlike the undelivered goods in the previous example.

We should also emphasize that the $72,000 amount *billed* in 19x1 had no effect on the amount of revenue recognized during 19x1. When the job was completed in 19x2, the revenue for that year was $110,000—that is, the full contract price ($200,000) minus the $90,000 that was recognized in 19x1.

Applicability of the Percentage-of-Completion Method. The percentage-of-completion method is most often used when the production cycle is long, the work is done under contracts with specific clients or customers, and adequate data on progress are available. The contracts provide a basis on which to estimate the amount of cash to be collected after all production work has been completed; if the progress percentage data are valid, they provide assurance that the work done to date will ultimately lead to the collection of cash. Since the cost of the work done to date is readily measurable, the three revenue-recognition criteria are satisfied at the time of production as long as valid progress percentage data are available.

Income Effects of the Percentage-of-Completion Method. Use of the percentage-of-completion method when the production cycle is long has two effects. First, it leads to earlier recognition of revenue and expense than the delivery basis would yield. Investors, therefore, will be informed more promptly of changes in the volume of activity or in the profit rate.

Second, this method is likely to report a smoother income stream in long-cycle operations than delivery-basis accounting would report. **Income smoothing** is said to occur when a company selects from among acceptable alternative accounting methods to achieve income results that are relatively stable (i.e., *smooth*) over time.

In our case, suppose Marsden-Brown completed four contracts in 19x1, eight contracts in 19x2, and two contracts in 19x3. Its reported income on a delivery basis might follow the path traced by the solid line in Exhibit 7–6. The work done was approximately constant over the three years,

EXHIBIT 7–6
Income Smoothing Effect of Production Basis

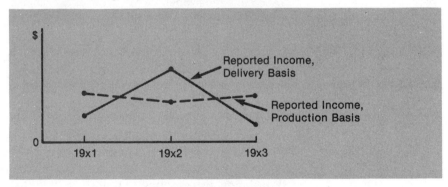

however, and revenue-and-expense recognition on a production (percentage-of-completion) basis might lead to the income pattern traced by the dashed line in the exhibit. Although the number of deliveries declined drastically in 19x3, production-basis income rose because the company was able to work more efficiently in 19x3 than in 19x2.

In addition to considering the effect of the percentage-of-completion method on reported earnings, justification for its use ultimately lies in the nature of the company's operations. For situations in which the method is appropriate, its use better reflects each period's actual activity. It would be wrong not to apply the percentage-of-completion method when in fact the circumstances warrant its use.

Estimating the Percentage of Completion. Estimating the percentage of completion isn't easy. Most authorities agree that it should be based on the amount of progress achieved rather than the amount of cost actually incurred, but how to measure progress is not at all clear. For example, should the purchase of materials to be used on the job be regarded as progress?

Probably the best solution is to decide in advance how much of the contract price is to be assigned to each phase of the contract, with most if not all of the weight assigned to labor and other services that are intended to add value to purchased materials. If the available evidence points to the probability of substantial cost overruns on remaining portions of the contract, however, the profit margin on the contract as a whole should be reestimated and a new allocation prepared. In practice, if the anticipated overrun is large enough to produce a loss on the contract, the entire amount of the anticipated loss will be reported immediately.

Collection Basis

In most situations, as we've already said, revenue is recognized at the time products or services are delivered to customers. We've also pointed out that the revenue-recognition criteria are sometimes met earlier, when goods are produced or the work is done. When this happens, revenues and expenses are recognized at the time of production.

Another set of circumstances is that either the amount of cash to be collected or the amount of cost yet to be incurred isn't readily predictable at the time of production or delivery. In this situation, revenue and expense recognition is deferred until cash or its equivalent is collected from the customer; this is called the **collection basis** of recognizing revenues and expenses.

Measuring Inventories, Receivables, and Expenses

A strict application of the collection basis requires capitalizing all the costs related to particular products and customer orders until the customers have actually paid for the goods. At the time of delivery, the inventory asset becomes a receivable, but it is still measured at cost until revenue is recognized at the time of collection. No allowance for customer defaults is made; instead, the costs of goods delivered to defaulting customers are written off when the defaults occur.

If the collection basis is applied to our earlier Castle Company example, $76 in costs will be capitalized as *inventory* prior to the time revenue is recognized, i.e., as the costs are incurred:

Materials	$20
Order getting	10
Production	40
Delivery	6
Total	$76

Neither expenses nor revenues are recognized until cash is received from the customers.

In our example, only $98 of the $100 invoice price was collected. When the cash was received, Castle Company recognized $98 of revenue and $85 of expenses, as follows:

Cash	98	
Bad Debts	2	
Sales Revenues (gross)		100
Cost of Goods Sold	60	
Order-Getting Expense	10	
Delivery Expense	6	
Collection Expense	4	
Warranty Expense[1]	5	
Inventory		76
Cash		4
Liability for Warranty Claims		5

In practice, the order-getting and delivery costs might not be capitalized, for the reasons we cited earlier.

Comparison with Production and Delivery Bases

If we assume that all costs except the warranty costs arise in cash transactions, we can construct the table in Exhibit 7–7. As this shows, although various assets and liabilities change at each stage in the operating cycle, only one change in owners' equity takes place, and this change is always $13. In the production basis, owners' equity changes at the time of production; in the delivery basis, owners' equity changes at the time of delivery; and in the collection basis, owners' equity changes at the time of collection.

Collection Basis versus Cash-Basis Accounting

We also want to keep in mind that all three methods are valid applications of accrual accounting. In each case, amounts are accrued or deferred to assure that expenses are recognized in the same period as the revenues they help generate. The collection basis of revenue and expense recognition therefore should not be confused with the so-called cash basis of accounting, the alternative to the accrual-basis system we are describing in this book. In cash-basis accounting, the expenses of a period are measured by the cash disbursements of that period; under the collection basis of revenue and expense recognition in accrual accounting, expenses may be recognized either before or after cash disbursements are made.

---

[1] We assume, for simplicity, that deliveries are made to dealers, some of whom default, but warranty service is provided to ultimate consumers who don't lose their warranty rights because the dealers default.

EXHIBIT 7–7
Comparison of Recognition Bases

	Production Basis		Delivery Basis		Collection Basis	
Time of Production	Inventory	+83	Inventory	+60	Inventory	+60
	Materials	−20	Cash	−40	Cash	−40
	Prepayment	−10	Materials	−20	Materials	−20
	Cash	−40				
	Revenue	*98*				
	Expense	*85*				
Time of Delivery	Receivables	+94	Receivables	+94	Receivables	+76
	Cash	− 6	Inventory	−60	Inventory	−60
	Warranty	+ 5	Prepayment	−10	Prepayment	−10
	Inventory	−83	Cash	− 6	Cash	− 6
			Warranty	+ 5		
			Revenue	*98*		
			Expense	*85*		
Time of Collection	Cash	+98	Cash	+98	Cash	+98
	Cash	− 4	Cash	− 4	Cash	− 4
	Receivables	−94	Receivables	−94	Receivables	−76
					Warranty	+ 5
					Revenue	*98*
					Expense	*85*

Use of the Collection Basis

The collection basis is used very sparingly. Very few types of receivables are so uncertain of collection that customer defaults can't be forecasted accurately enough to satisfy the revenue criteria earlier than the time of collection. The collection basis is now encountered mainly in small businesses that sell services rather than goods.

The best-known application of the collection basis is the **installment method,** used to account for certain types of installment sales. Under the installment method, revenues and expenses are identified at the time of delivery, but the resulting gross margin is deferred and recognized as cash collections occur. Land development companies, for example, use the installment method when they can't predict collections and future costs reliably enough at the time of delivery or production. This method shouldn't be used for most installment sales of merchandise, however, because customer defaults ordinarily can be predicted quite accurately.

To illustrate, assume Mason Company marketed parcels of land in resort areas, and 800 properties were sold in 19x1 for $20,000 each, a total of $16 million. Each buyer remitted $3,000 when the contract was signed, and was expected to pay the remainder in installments over five years; 30 percent of the $16 million was collected in 19x1. Given Mason's expectation that 20 percent of its installment sales will never be collected (and assuming away interest charges and the effect of repossessions), its 19x1 income based (*a*) on the installment method or (*b*) on the delivery basis was as shown in Exhibit 7–8. Under the installment method, since

EXHIBIT 7–8
Mason Company: Comparison of Installment Method with Delivery Basis

	Installment Method	Delivery Basis
Gross sales	$16,000,000	$16,000,000
Less: Bad debts.	3,200,000	3,200,000
Net sales.	12,800,000	12,800,000
Cost of goods sold	10,000,000	10,000,000
Gross margin.	2,800,000	2,800,000
Less: Deferred gross margin . .	$ 1,960,000*	
Realized gross margin	840,000	2,800,000
Less: Other expense.	800,000	800,000
Net income.	$ 40,000	$ 2,000,000

* 70% × $2,800,000.

only 30 percent of the sales were collected in 19x1, the *realized* gross margin was $840,000 (0.3 × $2,800,000). The remaining 70 percent ($1,960,000) was *deferred* to future years, to be recognized in proportion to actual collections.

Before leaving this topic, we should point out that collection doesn't always *follow* the delivery of goods and services. In many cases the two events coincide, and sometimes customers even pay cash *before* delivery is made. Magazine subscribers, for example, usually pay cash before the publisher begins producing and delivering the magazines covered by the subscriptions. In such cases, revenues are recognized as magazines are published and mailed to the subscribers. Revenues aren't recognized when cash is received because the first criterion of revenue recognition— completion of all significant revenue-producing activities—hasn't been met at that time. Instead, the receipt of cash gives rise to a liability.

Completed Obligations Basis

In most cases, the final stage in the operating cycle is the completion of all obligations to the purchasers of the company's products or services. For companies with warranty obligations that hadn't existed in earlier years, this stage is being reached later than it used to be, and the revenue-recognition criteria are becoming harder to meet before the obligations have been completed than they used to be. Consumer groups and government agencies in the United States are more active in demanding product reliability, and individual consumers are more preconditioned to demand service, even beyond the end of formal warranty periods. This means that income measured at earlier stages is somewhat less predictable than it used to be in like circumstances.

Even so, accountants never use the *completed obligations* basis. The main reason is that waiting for the last obligation to be liquidated would deprive investors of timely information and thereby presumably reduce the quality of their decisions. Fortunately, the costs of warranty service are seldom a large percentage of the selling price, and the inaccuracies in estimates of warranty liabilities are relatively small. In other words, we can still use other methods even though product warranty costs are larger than they used to be.

Impact on the Financial Statements

Only one revenue-recognition basis is appropriate in any given situation. The three recognition criteria we discussed earlier—performance of service, determination of costs, and probability of collection—must be used, and they will point to only one method in each situation. The financial statements of a production-basis company don't have quite the same meaning as the statements of a collection-basis business, however, and the reader should be aware of these differences.

We have already seen that one effect of the production basis may be to reduce or "smooth" the fluctuations in reported income because the rate of production is likely to be more stable than the rate of delivery or the collection rate. The basis selected has other effects, however, even if the delivery pattern is stable. These effects depend on four factors:

1. The volume of business done.
2. The size of the profit margin.
3. The length of the operating cycle.
4. The rate of growth.

The No-Growth Case

We'll illustrate the effects of these factors by using the same amounts we've been using until now. Net revenue was $98 and manufacturing costs were $60 ($20 materials and $40 production costs). To simplify the discussion, we'll assume the other $25 of costs ($10 order getting, $6 delivery, $4 collection, and $5 warranty) are expensed as they're incurred, which reflects what does often occur in practice. We'll also assume a stable volume of production, deliveries, and collections of 160 units a year. The interval from production to delivery is three months; delivery and collection are separated by the same interval.

Income Statement Effects. At a zero growth rate, the number of units sold in an average period equals the number of units delivered and also the number of units on which collections are made. In others words, each of the three revenue-recognition bases—production, delivery, and collection—will lead to the same total revenue and, therefore, the same net income. In this case, net revenue will be 160 × $98 = $15,680 a year, no matter which revenue-recognition basis is used. The gross margin will be 160 × ($98 − $60) = $6,080.

Balance Sheet Effects. The choice of the revenue-recognition basis will affect the balance sheet, even if business volume remains steady from period to period. Given our assumptions of three-month intervals between production and delivery and between delivery and collection, the company will always have three months of produced but undelivered production (inventory) and three months of receivables from products already delivered to customers. The inventory at any time, therefore, will be 3/12 of 160, or 40 units. The receivables will represent another 40 units. At a cost of $60 a unit, the inventory or receivable will amount to 40 × $60 = $2,400; at $98, the net realizable value of 40 units will add up to 40 × $98 = $3,920.

If these assumptions hold, the following amounts will appear in the balance sheets of production-basis, delivery-basis, and collection-basis companies:

	Production Basis	Delivery Basis	Collection Basis
Accounts receivable	$3,920	$3,920	$2,400
Inventory	3,920	2,400	2,400
Total	$7,840	$6,320	$4,800
Percentage of delivery-basis total	124.1%	100.0%	75.9%

Since income is the same in all three cases, the apparent rate of return on assets for the collection-basis company is higher than for the other two companies—because of its smaller asset base.

Changing the Assumptions. What happens if we change the assumptions on which these calculations were based? The first three factors—profit margin, volume, and cycle length—will determine the relative size of the differences between revenue-recognition bases:

1. Increasing the profit margin from $38 a unit ($98 − $60) to some larger amount will increase the balance sheet differences.
2. Increasing the physical volume of business done from 160 units to some larger quantity will increase the balance sheet differences.
3. Lengthening the interval between production and delivery will in-

crease the balance sheet differences between the production and delivery basis; lengthening the interval between delivery and collection
will increase the balance sheet differences between the delivery and
collection bases.

Conversely, decreasing the size of any one of these three variables—
profit margin, volume, or interval—will decrease the balance sheet differences between bases.

Changes in the profit margin or volume of business, incidentally, will
change the amount of income reported each year. Because there is no
growth from year to year, however, the sale value of the goods delivered
each year will be identical to the sale value of the goods produced and to
the amount collected. The amount of income therefore will be identical
for all three bases of revenue recognition.

The Impact of Growth

The illustration so far has reflected a no-growth assumption in which
production, deliveries, and collections are all at the same level. Suppose,
however, the business is growing by 32 units a year. Now we'll see differences in reported income as well as differences in balance sheet totals.
The reason: collections in one period arise from deliveries in an earlier
period, when volume was lower, and from production in a still earlier
period, when volume was lower yet.

The 32-unit annual growth in our revised example is achieved by
increasing production by two units each quarter. While the production of
160 units represented quarterly volumes of 37, 39, 41, and 43 units in
19x1, the quarterly production in the next year was 45, 47, 49 and 51
units. This means that production each quarter was eight units larger
than production in the comparable period a year earlier. Production
amounts for the two years are shown in the upper panel of Exhibit 7–9. If
revenues are recognized at the time of production, revenues and gross
margins for 19x2 will reflect the production of the four quarters of 19x2—
the top bar in the lower panel of the exhibit. If the delivery basis is used,
however, revenues and gross margins will be recognized with a one-
quarter lag.

The second bar in this panel is slightly smaller. Since production in the
fourth quarter of 19x1 was eight units less than production in the fourth
quarter of 19x2, delivery-basis revenues are eight units less than production-basis revenues in this growth situation. The bar at the bottom of the
lower panel is the smallest of all because the collection basis takes units
into revenue with a two-quarter lag—that is, it brings in two quarters of
19x1 production instead of only one.

These amounts translate into the following gross margin results for
19x2:

EXHIBIT 7–9
Revenue Recognized on Different Bases in 19x2

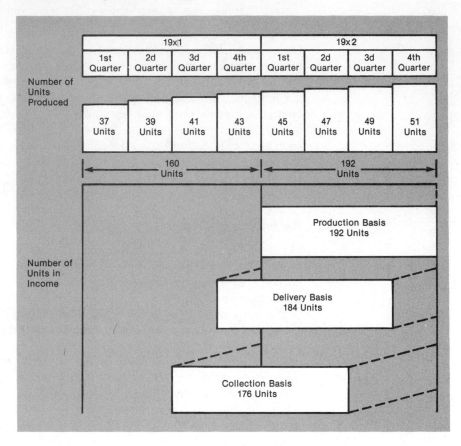

	Production Basis	**Delivery Basis**	**Collection Basis**
Revenues (at $98)..................	$18,816	$18,032	$17,248
Directly related expenses (at $60)	11,520	11,040	10,560
Gross margin (at $38)	$ 7,296	$ 6,992	$ 6,688
Percentage of delivery-basis margin	104.3%	100.0%	95.7%

Using the production basis increases both revenues and gross margins by 4.3 percent over those yielded by the delivery basis ($7,296/$6,992 − 1.0) and by 9.1 percent over those yielded by the collection basis ($7,296/$6,688 − 1.0).

The recognition basis also affects the asset amounts. Remember that both inventories and receivables are measured at cost under the collection basis; both are measured at value under the production basis. The comparison is:

	Production Basis	Delivery Basis	Collection Basis
Accounts receivable (49 units):			
At $98 value	$4,802	$4,802	
At $60 cost			$2,940
Inventory (51 units):			
At $98 value	4,998		
At $60 cost		3,060	3,060
Total	$9,800	$7,862	$6,000
Percentage of delivery-basis total	124.7%	100.0%	76.3%

The basis-to-basis differences are substantial, but the percentage differences are only slightly larger than they were in the no-growth case.

Summary

In most companies, revenues are recognized at the time goods are delivered or services are performed for outside customers or clients. This is known as the sale basis or delivery basis of revenue recognition. The justification for this method is that delivery is the first point in the operating cycle at which the income is both earned and quantifiable with sufficient accuracy. Later revenue recognition would delay the transmission of information unnecessarily.

Under the delivery basis, the reported revenue is the selling price of the goods or services delivered, less discounts, returns, allowances, and any anticipated bad debts arising from these transactions. If the goods or services are exchanged for an asset other than a short-term receivable, the revenue is measured by the current market value of the goods and services delivered, unless the market value of the asset received from the customer is more clearly evident.

The costs of producing the delivered goods or services are subtracted, when the delivery basis is used, as expenses of the period in which delivery is made, along with the delivery costs actually incurred during that period. Order-getting costs should be capitalized as incurred, if they are material and identifiable with the goods, and expensed as goods are delivered. Provision should also be made for estimated collection costs, if they are material. If the costs of fulfilling the company's warranty obligations to its customers are likely to be substantial, estimates of these amounts are recognized as expenses in the period when delivery is made.

In delivery-basis companies, inventories are measured at the cost of production (including the costs of raw materials). Receivables are measured at the amount billed less the estimated bad debts included in these amounts. A liability for warranty service is recognized if the future cost of discharging present warranty obligations is substantial.

The delivery basis is not always used, however. Revenues should be and are recognized prior to delivery if their contribution to income is both earned and accurately determinable earlier. They should be and are deferred to a later point if quantification is subject to too much uncertainty at the time of delivery. On these grounds, revenues are sometimes recognized as production takes place (production basis) or as cash is collected (collection basis). In each case, the expenses deducted from the revenues of a given period are the costs attributable to those revenues, to the extent that a ready basis can be found for linking costs with specific revenues. Until the point of revenue-and-expense recognition, the inventory or account receivable is measured at cost.

Key Terms

Cash discount	Percentage-of-completion
Collection basis	accounting
Delivery basis	Production basis
Income smoothing	Revenue-recognition criteria
Installment method	Revenue-recognition basis
Net realizable value	Sales allowance
Net revenue	Sales return

Independent Study Problems (Solutions in Appendix B)

1. Effect of Recognition Basis on Assets and Owners' Equity. Burfran Company has just been formed to manufacture a new product at a manufacturing cost of $12 a unit, which will be paid in cash at the time of production. It will cost $6 a unit to sell the product, and this amount will be paid at the time of shipment. The sale price is to be $25 a unit; all sales will be on credit. No collection costs are incurred.

The following results are expected during the first two years of the company's operations:

	Units Produced	Units Shipped	Cash Collected from Customers
First year	100,000	70,000	$1,500,000
Second year.....	80,000	90,000	1,875,000

a. State the effect on the various assets and owners' equity of producing one unit, shipping one unit, and collecting $25, if revenues and expenses are recognized at the time of production.

b. What total income will the company report each year if revenue and expense are recognized at the time cash is collected from the customer? (For this purpose, assume that general administrative expenses amount to $200,000 a year and that income taxes are zero.)

2. Production Basis versus Delivery Basis. Gilbert Company recognizes revenue at the time of production and classifies selling costs as expenses as they are incurred. You have the following information about Gilbert Company's operations for 19x1:

1. The company produced 100,000 units of product in 19x1 at a total production cost of $350,000. It sold and delivered 90,000 units at a price of $5 a unit.
2. Payments to factory employees and suppliers of raw materials and other goods and services for use in the factory (as described in item 1) totaled $330,000.
3. Factory depreciation (included in the production costs listed in item 1) amounted to $10,000.
4. Bad debts were estimated to be $.10 a unit.
5. Selling costs for the year, all paid in cash, totaled $80,000.
6. Administrative costs for the year, including collection costs, amounted to $50,000, all paid in cash.
7. Collections from customers totaled $420,000; write-offs of specific accounts as uncollectible totaled $8,500.
8. The company's liability under its product warranties was negligible.

a. Prepare an income statement for Gilbert Company for the year 19x1. (Ignore income taxes.)
b. The company had no inventories at the beginning of 19x1. At what amount was the finished goods inventory reported on the company's December 31, 19x1, balance sheet?
c. Recalculate net income on the assumption that the company recognizes revenue at the time of delivery.
d. What effect, if any, would changing to a delivery basis of revenue recognition have on the reported finished goods inventory amount?

3. Measuring Revenue When Collections Are Deferred. Harris Company recognizes revenues at the time goods are shipped to customers. Last month it shipped 1 million pounds of product X to Davis Company. The selling price of product X was $2 a pound, but because this was such a large order, Harris agreed to accept $1 million in cash immediately, with the other $1 million to be collected a year later. The applicable interest rate was 12 percent.

a. How much revenue arose last month from the Davis shipment?
b. How should the amount receivable from Davis have appeared on Harris's balance sheet as of the end of last month?

Exercises and Problems

4. Cash-Basis Accounting versus Recognition on Collection Basis.
Joan and Samuel Marx, doing business as Marx Enterprises, design and

make fine wooden furniture. They have always kept their records on a cash basis, meaning that they recognize revenues when customers pay their bills and measure expenses each year by the amounts of cash paid to employees, suppliers, and government agencies in that year.

The business has grown, and the Marx family has been advised to move from the cash basis to accrual accounting. Because the company sells mainly to customers whose credit ratings are difficult to establish, they have decided to recognize revenues on the collection basis once the changeover to accrual accounting is made.

a. What changes will have to be made immediately in the balance sheet of Marx Enterprises to reflect the changeover to accrual accounting?
b. In what respects will the income statement on the collection basis differ from a cash-basis income statement?

5. Measuring Revenue When Collections Are Deferred.   On January 1, 19x1, Arleigh Equipment Company sold and delivered 10 earth movers to Denby Contractors, Inc., at a list price of $20,000 each. To secure this order, Arleigh agreed to let Denby pay for this equipment on the following schedule:

Immediately	$ 50,000
One year later.	50,000
Two years later.	100,000

Arleigh recognizes revenues at the time of delivery. Denby made its payments on schedule. The applicable interest rate was 8 percent, compounded annually.

a. How much revenue did Arleigh Equipment Company report at the time of delivery?
b. How much additional revenue did Arleigh earn in 19x1 as a result of the Denby transaction? What is this additional revenue called?
c. What effect did this transaction have on Arleigh's income before taxes in *19x2?*

6. Deferred-Payment Revenues.   On January 2, 19x4, Taney Corporation sold merchandise that had cost Taney $29,000. The cash sale price was $36,000, but Taney agreed to accept an equivalent series of four equal semiannual payments beginning on June 30, 19x4, that would reflect interest compounded semiannually at a nominal annual interest rate of 12 percent.

a. What was the amount of each of the four payments?
b. What was the gross margin on the sale?
c. How much interest did Taney earn in 19x4 as a result of this sale?

7. Effects of Transactions; Different Recognition Bases. Quantify the effects on the assets, liabilities, and owners' equity of the events described in each of the following:

a. Company A recognizes revenue at the time of production. *Events:* The company produced goods at a cost of $10,000 and paid cash in this amount. The estimated selling price was $16,000, estimated selling costs were $4,000, and collection costs and uncollectible accounts were insignificant.

b. Company B recognizes revenue at the time of delivery. *Events:* Goods that had cost $10,000 in a previous period were sold on account for $16,000. Selling costs, paid in cash, were $4,000. Estimated collection costs were $500. Of the $16,000, $300 was expected to be uncollectible.

c. Company C recognizes revenue at the time of collection. *Events:* Goods that had cost $12,000 in a previous period were sold on account for $19,000. Selling costs, paid in cash, were $3,500. Estimated collection costs were $200. Of the $19,000, $1,500 was expected to be uncollectible.

8. Measuring Revenue. Herklion Company purchased a large quantity of used industrial equipment and shipped it to a foreign country for use in the government's industrialization program. Herklion paid $800,000 for the equipment and an additional $30,000 to transport it to the foreign country.

By the time the equipment arrived at its destination, the customer government had no foreign exchange to pay for it. Instead, it offered to give Herklion one of its own 15-percent $100 bonds for every $95 due on the shipment of equipment. At that time, these bonds had a market value in the United States of $91 for every $100 bond.

Herklion accepted the offer and received $1 million in bonds which it kept for two years and then sold at a price of $90 for every $100 bond. During this two-year period, the foreign government paid interest promptly and regularly on these bonds at the prescribed interest rate of 15 percent a year.

a. Did Herklion make a profit or a loss on the equipment transaction? When and how much?

b. How, if at all, would your answer to part *a* have differed if the bonds had been sold immediately at the $91 market price?

c. How, if at all, would your answer have differed if the bonds had been held until their maturity date and then collected in full?

9. Sale for Nonmonetary Proceeds. Henderson Company manufactures and sells furniture to retailers for resale and directly to large business and institutional customers. It recognizes sales revenues at the time it delivers furniture to customers. Last year, Henderson delivered several suites of office furniture to a law firm. The retail value of this furniture was $62,000, its ordinary wholesale price was $48,000, and the manufacturing cost had been $35,000.

In lieu of being paid in cash, Henderson accepted 800 shares of Data Tech common stock from the law firm. These shares had cost the law firm $44,000, but their current stock exchange price was $53,000. When Henderson sold the stock six weeks later, the cash proceeds were $51.75 a share.

Calculate the effects of these events on Henderson Company's net income (*a*) when the furniture was delivered, and (*b*) when the Data Tech stock was sold.

10. Delivery Basis.   A company recognizes revenue at the time it delivers merchandise to its customers. The beginning-of-year balance sheet showed gross accounts receivable of $20,000 and an allowance for uncollectibles of $1,000.

During the year, goods that had cost $100,000 were delivered to customers on account for $160,000. Selling and administrative costs amounting to $40,000 were paid in cash.

Collections on accounts receivable amounted to $155,000 during the year. A bill-collecting agency was paid $5,000 for its services in helping the company collect a portion of this, representing part of the beginning-of-year balance in accounts receivable. Collection costs of this kind ordinarily amount to 3 percent of credit sales, but collection costs are expensed only when they are incurred.

Accounts with a face value of $1,200 were written off as uncollectible during the year.

The company expected that 1 percent of its credit sales would eventually prove uncollectible and a year-end aging of accounts confirmed that estimate.

a. Prepare an income statement for the year, ignoring income taxes.
b. Show how the accounts receivable would be presented on the year-end balance sheet.
c. Is the company's method of accounting for collection costs consistent with the delivery basis of revenue recognition? Explain.

11. Choosing a Recognition Basis.   Sam Stephens operates a pig farm. Each year his sows give birth to piglets, which he raises for eventual sale to meat packers. Each year he buys feed for the pigs and pays a hired man to feed them. Some years when pig prices are high, he sells more pigs than are born; in other years, he sells fewer pigs than are born, resulting in an increase in the total number and weight of his herd. Sales are always for cash, and quotations of prices from hog auctions are published daily in the newspapers.

a. What basis of revenue and expense recognition would be most meaningful to Stephens in this case? Explain your reasoning.

b. Assume that feed and labor costs average $2 per pig per month. A pig born on July 1 weighs 80 pounds in December when hog prices are 30 cents a pound. It is sold the following March for $40. Using the method of revenue recognition you selected in part a, compute the cumulative effect of these transactions on the amounts shown as total assets and total owners' equity on the December 31 and March 31 balance sheets.

12. Percentage-of-Completion Basis: Discussion. Easton Company builds office buildings. It recognizes revenues at the time of production on a percentage-of-completion basis. It is now building the Ward Tower building at a total contract price of $60 million. The estimated cost of construction is $50 million.

The only expenditure Easton has made on this construction project so far is $5 million for construction materials, and these have now been delivered to the site.

a. How much revenue and expense should Easton recognize if the $5 million is classified as progress toward completion of this contract?

b. If you were a potential shareholder in Easton Company, interested in making a decision whether to buy some of the company's shares, would Easton's net income be a more useful information signal to you if the $5 million were classified as progress toward completion of this contract, or would you prefer that it be excluded from the calculation of this year's income? Explain your reasons.

13. Comparing Recognition Bases. Saranac Company produces a single product at a cost of $6 a unit, all of which is paid in cash when the unit is produced. Selling expenses of $3 a unit are paid at the time of delivery. The sale price is $10 a unit; all sales are on account. No bad debts are expected, and no costs are incurred at the time of collection.

During 19x1, the company produced 100,000 units, shipped 76,000 units, and collected $600,000 from customers. During 19x2, it produced 80,000 units, shipped 90,000 units, and collected $950,000 from customers.

a. Determine the net income that would be reported for each of these two years:
   1. If revenue and expense are recognized at the time of delivery.
   2. If revenue and expense are recognized at the time of production.
   3. If revenue and expense are recognized at the time of collection.

b. Would the asset total shown on the December 31, 19x2, balance sheet be affected by the choice among the three recognition bases used in part *a*? What would be the amount of any such difference?

14. Delivery Basis and Production Basis. A precious metal called *Mep* has far-reaching ramifications for strategic military purposes. As a result, legislation has been enacted that makes it illegal for any individual or business to own or trade even the slightest amount of Mep, except temporarily as a result of the extraction of this metal from ore.

Mining companies are required to deliver to the federal government all Mep they extract from the ores they mine; the government is required to pay $3 a gram for all Mep it receives. The mining companies are required to deliver Mep to the government as soon as possible after it is extracted. They are allowed to accumulate inventories of Mep until they have enough for an economical shipment to the government.

Stanley Mining Company had no inventory of Mep at the beginning of 19x1. It extracted 40,000 grams of this metal during the year and delivered 25,000 grams to the government in exchange for cash. The cost of extraction was $2 a gram and administrative expenses were $12,000 for the year as a whole.

Stanley's year-end balance sheet contained only the following six items:

Accounts payable	$187,000	Inventory	?
Capital stock	100,000	Plant assets...........	$180,000
Cash	90,000	Retained earnings	?

a. Prepare Stanley Mining Company's 19x1 income statement and December 31, 19x1, balance sheet, using first the delivery basis and then the production basis. Explain your treatment of administrative expenses.
b. Which basis of revenue and expense recognition should the company adopt? Why?

15. Revenue and Expense Recognition: Discussion Question. Body Shop Corporation operated 22 health spas in the New England states. Use of the company's facilities was restricted to people who bought Body Shop memberships. Each member was charged a $2,100 fee, payable in advance, that entitled the member to unlimited access for three years to any Body Shop facility in the six-state area. A study of the company's costs indicated that $900 was the cost of servicing each three-year enrollment.

From its inception, Body Shop Corporation recorded $2,100 as revenue when it was collected and recorded expenses as expenditures were made. When the company's new accountant pointed out the inconsistencies in this method, the president said she was prepared to record both the revenue and the expense when the $2,100 was collected. Although the accountant couldn't dispute that this method did in fact match revenues and expenses, he wondered about its propriety. The president countered by pointing out that her approach did reflect good accrual accounting, and that recognizing the $900 expense at the time of collection was analogous to the way manufacturers account for expected future warranty claims.

Identify the relative merits of both the existing method and the president's proposed approach, and select the method you believe would be most appropriate for Body Shop Corporation. Explain the reasons for your choice.

16. Recognition Exercise; Missing Numbers. Garden Company produced a single product, a uranium substitute called Liquo. Garden had been founded as a joint venture by six multinational companies that had in turn become Garden's sole customers. The six companies had a 25-year agreement with Garden that entitled them to buy all the Liquo produced, at a price to be recalculated every five years.

The price in effect from 19x1 through 19x5 was $50 a gallon. Administrative expenses totaling $190,000 in 19x4 were not causally related to production levels. Other Garden Company data for 19x4 were as follows:

Inventory, January 1.	120,000 gallons
Inventory, December 31.	350,000 gallons
Units produced.	1,840,000 gallons
Units delivered	? gallons
Accounts receivable, January 1	$ 5,800,000
Accounts receivable, December 31	$20,300,000
Production cost per gallon	?

Garden Company's accountant correctly calculated 19x4 net income to be $36,200,000 based on recognizing revenue when production was completed. The company's board of directors wants to evaluate this result in comparison with alternative approaches to income measurement.

a. Determine net income if revenues and expenses are recognized at the time of delivery.
b. Determine net income if revenues and expenses are recognized at the time of collection.

17. Percentage-of-Completion Accounting. Lark Construction Company was hired to build a stadium for $32 million. Work began late in 19x1, and the stadium was completed in 19x3. Lark had expected to earn $7 million in income before taxes on this project and did in fact earn this amount. Relevant data are:

Year	Amounts Billed	Cash Collected	Costs Incurred	Estimated Remaining Cost to Complete
19x1.....	$ 3,000,000	$ 1,900,000	$ 2,500,000	$22,500,000
19x2.....	22,500,000	14,100,000	17,500,000	5,000,000
19x3.....	6,500,000	14,400,000	5,000,000	—

Since most of Lark's previous construction jobs had been started and completed in the same calendar year, it had consistently recognized revenues and expenses when the jobs were completed. In the light of the company's experience with the stadium project, however, Lark's management decided to investigate the desirability of adopting the percentage-of-completion method.

a. Calculate the percentage of completion each year. Explain the basis for your calculation and the reason you chose it.
b. Calculate each year's income under both methods.
c. Given the amounts of cost, revenues, and expenses identified in your answers to parts *a* and *b*, discuss the ways contract-related amounts might be reported each year under each recognition method. Quantify your answer insofar as possible.

18. Installment Basis. Oliver Company sold merchandise on an installment-payment basis, beginning in 19x1. Its deliveries in 19x1 totaled $10 million and the cost of the goods delivered was $7 million. It collected $4.2 million in cash from these customers, consisting of $3.8 million for the merchandise and $400,000 for interest. Its expenses, other than the cost of goods sold, amounted to $700,000 in 19x1.

Oliver's management estimated that 5 percent of the sale price of delivered merchandise would eventually be uncollectible. Except for the uncollectible amount, the amounts not collected in 19x1 would be collected 60 percent in 19x2 and 40 percent in 19x3, plus accrued interest. The $400,000 in interest received in cash in 19x1 was the full amount of interest accured on all the installment contracts initiated in 19x1.

a. Using a format similar to that of Exhibit 7-8, calculate Oliver Company's net income for 19x1 using (1) the installment method, and (2) the delivery basis. Ignore income taxes.
b. Including interest and allowing for bad debts, the total amount Oliver expected to receive in exchange for goods delivered in 19x1 amounted to $11 million. Knowing this, what changes, if any, would you make in your answer to part *a*? Explain.

19. Different Revenue-Recognition Bases. Swazy Company secured a contract with the sate of Iowa for the construction of 15 miles of highway at a contract price of $1 million a mile. Payments were to be made as follows for each mile of construction:

1. 40 percent when concrete was poured.
2. 50 percent when all work on that mile was completed.
3. 10 percent when all 15 miles of highway were completed, inspected, and approved.

At the end of the first period of operation, five miles have been entirely completed and approved, concrete has been poured and approved on a second five-mile stretch, and preliminary grading has been done on the third five-mile stretch.

The job was originally estimated to cost $800,000 a mile. Costs to date have coincided with these original estimates and have totaled the following amounts: (1) $800,000 a mile on the completed stretch; (2) $640,000 a mile on the second stretch; and (3) $100,000 a mile on the third stretch. It is now estimated that each unfinished stretch will be completed at the costs originally estimated.

a. Determine revenue, expense, and income for the period to date if revenue is recognized at the time of production (percentage of completion).
b. Determine revenue, expense, and income if revenue is recognized at the time of delivery (completion).
c. Determine revenue, expense, and income if revenue is recognized at the time of cash receipts (collection).

20. Different Revenue-Recognition Bases. Aim Company, a farm corporation, produced the following in 19x1, its first year of operations:

	Selling Price per Bushel
9,000 bushels of wheat	$2.40
6,000 bushels of oats	1.40

During the year, it sold and delivered two thirds of the grain produced and collected three fourths of the selling price on the grain delivered; the balance of the selling price is to be collected in equal amounts during each of the two following years. You also have the following additional data for 19x1:

Depreciation on productive plant and equipment	$3,000
Other production costs (cash)	4,500
Administrative costs (cash)	3,600
Selling and delivery costs (incurred and paid at the time of delivery) per bushel	0.10

Aim Company's administrative costs are incurred exclusively to support its production activities.

a. What is income before taxes in 19x1 if revenues and expenses are recognized when production is completed?

b. What is income before taxes in 19x1 if revenues and expenses are recognized when goods are delivered?
c. What is income before taxes in 19x1 if revenues and expenses are recognized when cash is collected from customers?

(AIPCA adapted)

21. Effect of Recognition Basis on Income; Managerial Aspects. XYZ Manufacturing Company was in a declining industry. Each year its sales decreased, each year it reduced its inventories, and each year the accounts receivable balance decreased. Uncollectibles, fortunately, were insignificant.

In 19x1, the company delivered products to its customers with a total sales value of $1,050,000. It manufactured 10,000 units of product at a total manufacturing cost of $700,000, an average of $70 a unit. All manufacturing costs were paid for immediately in cash. The company's inventories of manufactured products, measured at their manufacturing cost, decreased in 19x1 by $35,000, to $210,000. The amounts due from customers decreased by $15,000, to $150,000. Selling and administrative costs totaled $200,000, none of them readily attributable to specific deliveries or collections.

Management expected deliveries to fall by 10 percent in 19x2. Selling and administrative costs would amount to $190,000; increasing them wouldn't increase deliveries enough to justify the expenditure. Production volume would also be reduced by 10 percent, but average manufacturing cost would remain at $70 a unit. The amount due from customers would be $15,000 less at the end of 19x2 than at the beginning. Selling prices were the same in 19x2 as in 19x1.

a. Calculate total revenue, gross margin, and income before taxes for 19x1: (1) on a production basis, (2) on a delivery basis, and (3) on a collection basis. You should assume that the ratio of manufacturing cost applicable to revenue was the same for all three bases. (Suggestion: start with the delivery basis and then redo the calculation on the other two bases.)
b. Make the same calculations for 19x2.
c. In these circumstances, would you suggest that reports to management reflect the production basis for revenue recognition even though the company uses the delivery basis for public financial reporting? Why might management even consider doing this—that is, what purpose would it be intended to serve? In particular, consider whether this practice would be likely to do a better job than other methods of achieving the purpose you have ascribed to it.

22. Effect of Recognition Basis. Naive Manufacturing Company produces a product at a cost of $7.50 a unit, all of which is paid at the time of production. It costs $2 a unit to sell the product, all of which is paid at the time the product is shipped to the customer. The sale price is $10 a unit. All sales are on account. Collection costs are 2 percent of the amount collected, all paid during the period of collection. No customer defaults are expected, and the income tax rate is zero.

During the first year of operation, the company expects to produce 20,000 units, ship 18,000 units, and collect $170,000 from its customers.

During the second year it expects to produce 30,000 units, ship 29,000 units, and collect $280,000 from its customers.

a. Suppose the company recognizes revenue and all related expenses at the time of production:
  1. State the effect on the various assets and owners' equity of producing one unit and incurring the related production costs.
  2. State the effect on the various assets and owners' equity of shipping one unit and incurring the related selling costs.
  3. State the effect on the various assets and owners' equity of collecting $10 and incurring the related collection costs.
  4. What net income will be reported for the first year?
  5. What net income will be reported for the second year?
b. Repeat the calculations called for in part a, but on the assumption that the company recognizes revenue and all related expenses at the time of shipment.
c. Repeat the calculations called for in part a, but on the assumption that the company recognizes revenue and all related expenses at the time of collection.
d. Companies that recognize revenue at the time of shipment ordinarily treat collection costs as an expense of the period of collection. Using this procedure, what is the net income for each year?
e. Companies that recognize revenue at the time of collection ordinarily treat selling costs as an expense of the period in which they are incurred. Using this procedure, what is the net income for each year?

(Prepared by Carl L. Nelson)

23. Usefulness as a Criterion in Choosing a Recognition Basis.[2]   Smith & Wells, Ltd., manufactures a variety of machined parts that it sells to customers in the automotive and transportation industries. About half the company's sales are of products listed in the company's regular catalog. The remainder of the annual sales is in custom items. Sales revenues for both types of products are recognized at the time the goods are shipped to the customers.

[2] Copyright 1967, 1985 by l'Institut pour l'Etude des Méthodes de Direction de l'Entreprise, (IMEDE), Lausanne, Switzerland. Reproduced by permission.

Deliveries of catalog items, except for very large orders, are made from warehouse inventories, that are allowed to fluctuate from month to month to help stabilize production levels.

Custom items, often designed to the customer's own specifications, are manufactured only upon receipt of a firm order. Cancellations of orders on which production operations have commenced are extremely rare, and Smith & Wells, Ltd., can always recover its costs on any such cancelled orders.

During 19x3 the company's sales force turned in a gratifying 20 percent increase in new orders over their 19x2 level, almost all the increase being for custom products. To meet this increased demand, the rate of

EXHIBIT

SMITH & WELLS, LTD.
Selected Financial Data for 19x1–x3
(in 000s)

	19x1	19x2	19x3
Net revenue from goods shipped:			
Catalog items	£xxx	£ 960	£ 970
Custom products	xxx	990	1,030
Total	xxx	1,950	2,000
Cost of goods shipped	xxx	1,170	1,240
Selling and administrative expenses	xxx	600	620
Net operating income before taxes and special charges	£xxx	£ 180	£ 140
New orders received, net of cancellations (at sale prices):			
Catalog items	£xxx	£ 980	£1,000
Custom products	xxx	1,020	1,400
Total	£xxx	£2,000	£2,400
Inventories on December 31 (at cost):			
Materials	£100	£ 100	£ 150
Work in process:			
Catalog items	45	50	50
Custom products	148	155	230
Finished goods (catalog items only)	470	500	480
Details of custom products work in process on December 31:			
Total contract sale prices	£480	£ 500	£ 625
Estimated total production cost	290	300	375
Production costs incurred to date	148	155	230
Percentage of work completed to date	50%	50%	60%
Orders on hand but not yet put into production on December 31, custom products (at contract sale prices)	£790	£ 800	£1,045

xxx—Data not available.

production in the company's factory was increased twice during the year, once in July and once again in October. Because the production cycle for custom items averages four to six months, however, the increase in the rate of production did not lead to any marked rise in revenue.

In mid-January 19x4, T. E. S. Evans, the managing director of Smith & Wells, Ltd., received a preliminary set of financial statements for 19x3 from his chief accountant, J. B. Burke. Excerpts from these statements are shown in the accompanying exhibit.

Evans understood that income was recognized at the time of delivery, but asked Burke whether something could be done to reflect the increase in customer orders in the income amounts. Burke replied that the company's auditors would never accept customer orders as evidence that revenue had been earned.

a. Could the revenue-recognition criteria be met for either product line under an *order basis* for revenue recognition? Under a *production basis?*

b. Reconstruct the income statements for 19x2 and 19x3 with revenues from custom products recognized at the time of production.

c. Do the income amounts you derived in answer to part *b* provide a better measure of management's operating performance than those stated at the top of the Exhibit? Would they meet Evans' objections to the existing reporting basis? Would you recommend a shift to the production basis?

Chapter 8

Inventory Measurement

Companies that recognize revenue on a production basis measure their inventories at the value of the net cash flows they will generate in the future, as we noted in Chapter 7. All other companies measure inventories at their historical cost or at their market value, whichever is lower. This chapter explains how these companies determine the historical cost of their inventories and the cost of goods sold. We'll also discuss how the market value of the inventories affects accountants' measurements, and the effect on financial statements of not using market values universally.

Historical-Costing Methods

When each item passing through a company's inventory is unique, cost measurement is relatively simple. As each item is received, its cost is identified as the cost of inventory. When it is sold, this cost becomes the cost of goods sold.

Interchangeable items can't be accounted for this easily, however. In this section, we'll identify the components of the costs of interchangeable items in any period (the *cost of goods available*) and describe three commonly used methods of distributing these costs:

1. First-in, first-out (FIFO) costing.
2. Last-in, first-out (LIFO) costing.
3. Average costing.

The Cost of Goods Available

The total number of physical units sold (or otherwise disposed of) during a period and the number of units in the ending inventory must equal the total number of units available for sale during the period. By the same token, the total of the costs of the goods sold and the costs of the ending inventory must equal the total costs of the goods available for sale during the period.

For example, suppose Alpha Company had two units in inventory at the beginning of 19x1, *bought* ten units and *sold* eight units during the year, and had four units on hand at the end of the year. Each of these units was acquired at a historical cost of $50. These amounts are shown in Exhibit 8–1. The numbers in the upper diagram refer to physical quantities; the amounts in the lower diagram refer to dollars of cost. Goods available for sale in any period come from two sources: inventory at the beginning of the period and the quantity acquired during the period—represented by the two blocks at the left of each diagram. The

EXHIBIT 8–1
Goods Acquired, Available, and Sold during a Period

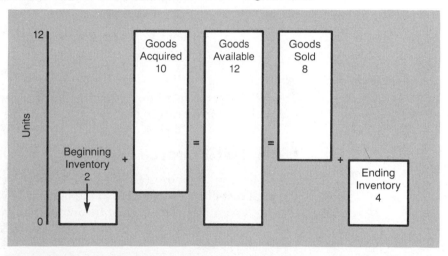

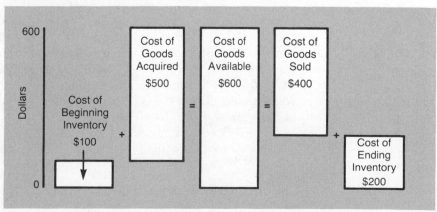

total of these two sources is the goods available, represented by the large block at the center: the *quantity* available in the upper diagram, the *cost* of the goods available in the lower diagram.

Two things can happen to the goods available for sale in any period: They will either be sold (or stolen, damaged, evaporated, or lost in other ways) or remain in inventory at the end of the period.[1] If an item isn't sold or lost, it will be in inventory at the end of the period. These two outcomes are represented by the two blocks at the right in each diagram of Exhibit 8–1. In the upper diagram, the two blocks represent the number of units sold and the number of units still on hand. In the lower diagram, these two blocks represent the *cost* of goods sold and the *cost* of the ending inventory. The cost of the goods available for sale thus becomes the cost of goods sold *and* the cost of the goods that remain in inventory at the end of the period.

From Exhibit 8–1, we see that the cost of goods sold in 19x1 was $400. If these goods were sold for $100 a unit, or a total of $800, the income statement would show the following:

Revenue from sale of goods	$800
Cost of goods sold	400
Gross margin	$400

The $200 cost assigned to the ending inventory will become the cost of the beginning inventory in the next period, and the cycle will be repeated.

First-In, First-Out (FIFO) Costing

The **first-in, first out (FIFO)** method assigns the oldest unit costs in the total cost of goods available to the items that were transferred out of the stockroom first. The ending inventory is therefore measured at the unit cost(s) of the purchase or purchases that were made closest to the end of the period.

19x2 Illustration. Suppose Alpha Company started operating in 19x1. All the goods acquired during 19x1 cost $50 each, and at year-end four units remained in inventory. The company's beginning inventory in *19x2* therefore had a cost of $200 (4 × $50). The company bought seven units in April 19x2 at a price of $60 each, and eight units in July at $75 each. It sold 12 units during the year, leaving seven units in inventory at the end of the year (4 + 7 + 8 − 12 = 7).

The FIFO costing method divides the cost of the goods available in 19x2 as shown in the upper panel of Exhibit 8–2. The first four units sold

---

[1] For inventories of materials destined for use in manufacturing, the words "goods issued" should be used in place of "goods sold."

EXHIBIT 8–2
Alpha Company: First-In, First-Out (FIFO) Costing

	19x2

Cost of Goods Available		**Costs Distributed**	
Beginning inventory: 4 × $50 ..	$ 200	Cost of goods sold:	
Purchases:		4 × $50	$ 200
7 × $60	420	7 × $60	420
8 × $75	600	1 × $75	75
Total purchases	1,020	Total cost of goods sold . . .	695
		Ending inventory: 7 × $75	525
Total cost available	$1,220	Total cost distributed	$1,220

	19x3

Cost of Goods Available		**Costs Distributed**	
Beginning inventory: 7 × $75 ..	$ 525	Cost of goods sold:	
Purchases: 13 × $85	1,105	7 × $75	$ 525
		7 × $85	595
		Total cost of goods sold . . .	1,120
		Ending inventory: 6 × $85	510
Total cost available	$1,630	Total cost distributed	$1,630

are assigned a unit cost of $50, the cost of the *first* four units that were available during the year ($200). The next seven units sold are assigned a unit cost of $60 each, the unit cost of the *next* seven units to become available during the year ($420). The twelfth unit sold is assigned a cost of $75 since that was the unit cost of the next batch of goods to be acquired. The FIFO cost of goods sold is the sum of these three amounts ($200 + $420 + $75 = $695).

The seven units in inventory at the end of the year are assigned the unit costs of the *last* seven units to enter the inventory during the year: 7 × $75 = $525. (The first-in, first-out method may also be viewed as the "last-in, still-here" method.) In fact, we could have started by determining the cost of the ending inventory, then subtracting this from the total cost of goods available to determine the FIFO cost of goods sold:

Beginning inventory	$ 200
Goods acquired ($420 + $600)	1,020
Cost of goods available	1,220
Less: Ending inventory.	525
Cost of goods sold	$ 695

19x3 Illustration.   The $525 FIFO cost of the December 31, 19x2, inventory is also the FIFO cost of the January 1, 19x3, inventory. Alpha Company bought 13 additional units in 19x3 at a cost of $85 each. It sold 14 units during the year and had six units in the inventory on December 31, 19x3 (7 + 13 − 14 = 6). FIFO costing in 19x3 would produce the results shown in the lower half of Exhibit 8–2. The cost of goods sold consists of the cost of the seven units in the beginning inventory ($525), plus the cost of the first seven units purchased during 19x3 (7 × $85 = $595). The six units in the ending inventory are assigned the costs of the last six units bought during 19x3 (6 × $85 = $510).

Last-In, First-Out (LIFO) Costing

The second method of dividing the total cost of goods available between the income statement (cost of goods sold) and the balance sheet (inventory on hand) is the **last-in, first-out** method, or **LIFO.** Under LIFO, unit costs enter the cost of goods sold in the reverse of the order in which they enter the cost of goods available. The unit cost of the last purchase during the year is the first to be assigned to the cost of goods sold, the unit cost of the next to last purchase is the next to be assigned to the cost of goods sold, and so on. The costs in the ending inventory are determined by starting with the earliest unit costs in the cost of goods available ("first-in, still-here") and moving to later and later unit costs until the inventory quantity has been fully accounted for.

19x2 Illustration.   As we pointed out earlier, Alpha Company was founded in 19x1. All its purchases in 19x1 were at a unit cost of $50, meaning that its December 31, 19x1, inventory of four units had a cost of $200, no matter which inventory method was used. The company bought 15 units in 19x2, seven of them in April at $60 each and the other eight in July at $75 each. The cost of goods available therefore was $1,220, as shown in the upper panel of Exhibit 8–3.

The LIFO distribution of these costs is shown in the right-hand section of the upper panel. As this shows, the company sold 12 units in 19x2. The *first* eight units sold are assigned the unit costs of the *last* eight units bought during the year (8 × $75 = $600). The cost of the other four units sold is measured at the unit cost of the *next most recent* purchase (4 × $60 = $240). The total of these two amounts is $840.

The LIFO cost of the ending inventory is measured by starting with the *oldest* unit cost and working forward. The cost assigned to the first four units in the ending inventory therefore is the cost of the four units in the beginning inventory, $50 each. This is known as the **LIFO base quantity,** or *initial layer.* The next oldest unit cost is the cost of the first lot purchased during the year, $60 a unit, and this is the unit cost assigned to the other three units in the ending inventory. The $180 cost of these

EXHIBIT 8–3
Alpha Company: Last-In, First-Out (LIFO) Costing

19x2

Cost of Goods Available		
Beginning inventory: 4 × $50 . .	$ 200	
Purchases:		
7 × $60	420	
8 × $75	600	
Total cost of goods available. . .	$1,220	

Costs Distributed		
Cost of goods sold:		
First eight units: 8 × $75	$ 600	
Next four units: 4 × $60	240	
Total cost of goods sold . . .	840	
Ending inventory:		
19x1 layer: 4 × $50	200	
19x2 layer: 3 × $60	180	
Total inventory	380	
Total cost distributed	$1,220	

19x3

Cost of Goods Available		
Beginning inventory:		
19x1 layer: 4 × $50	$ 200	
19x2 layer: 3 × $60	180	
Total inventory	380	
Purchases: 13 × $85	1,105	
Total cost of goods available. . .	$1,485	

Costs Distributed		
Cost of goods sold:		
First 13 units: 13 × $85	$1,105	
Next unit: 1 × $60	60	
Total cost of goods sold . . .	1,165	
Ending inventory:		
19x1 layer: 4 × $50	200	
19x2 layer: 2 × $60	120	
Total inventory	320	
Total cost distributed	$1,485	

three units (3 × $60) constitutes the 19x2 layer in the inventory. The total LIFO inventory therefore consists of two layers: the 19x1 layer of $200 and the 19x2 layer of $180, a total of $380. Once again, the total of the cost of goods sold and the cost of the ending inventory equals the cost of goods available, $1,220.

This illustration reflects the method known as **LIFO-periodic,** in that variations in inventory levels during the year are ignored. Thus, none of the costs of the beginning inventory appear in the cost of goods sold as long as the number of units in the year-end inventory is at least as large as the number of units on hand at the beginning of the year.

For example, suppose Alpha sold three units each quarter, while buying seven units in April at a cost of $60 each and eight units in July at $75 each. If inventory cost were measured on a **LIFO-perpetual** basis, it

EXHIBIT 8–4
Alpha Company: LIFO-Perpetual versus LIFO-Periodic Inventory, 19x2

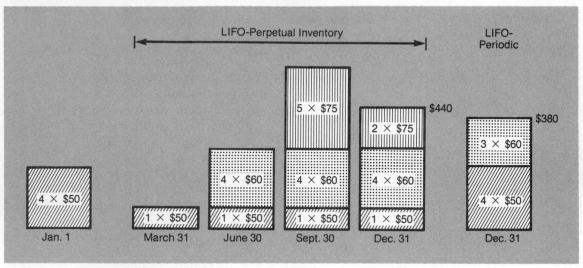

would follow the path traced in the first five blocks in Exhibit 8–4. Under LIFO-perpetual, the inventory dip in the first quarter would move some of the base quantity to the cost of goods sold. When inventory was rebuilt in the second quarter, the increment would be measured at the purchase cost of that period, $60. In Alpha's case, this would still be in inventory at the end of the year, together with two units at $75, the cost of the purchase in the third quarter. As a result, the LIFO-perpetual inventory at year-end would amount to $440 rather than the $380 shown in Exhibit 8–3 and represented by the right-hand block in Exhibit 8–4. The LIFO-perpetual cost of goods sold would be $780 (6 × $75 + 3 × $60 + 3 × $50), instead of the $840 shown in Exhibit 8–3.

LIFO-periodic ignores temporary dips and bulges in the inventory during the year, so that Alpha's year-end LIFO inventory consists of the four-unit base quantity at its 19x1 cost of $50 a unit, plus a new 19x3 layer of three units at $60. Under LIFO-periodic, even if the company was completely out of stock on March 31, 19x2, before the first purchase was made, the entire cost of goods sold would still reflect only 19x2 purchase prices. In practice, companies that use LIFO use LIFO-periodic, not LIFO-perpetual; we'll therefore use LIFO-periodic in this chapter.

19x3 Illustration.   Alpha Company entered 19x3 with the same inventory (seven units at a total LIFO cost of $380) it had at the end of 19x2. It bought 13 units in 19x3 at a cost of $85 a unit. The cost of goods available in 19x3 therefore was $1,485, as shown on the left of the lower panel of Exhibit 8–3. This differs from the total cost of goods available in 19x3 under FIFO because the LIFO cost of the beginning inventory was only $380 instead of the FIFO cost of $525.

The company sold 14 units in 19x3, leaving six units in inventory at year-end. The LIFO cost of goods sold is once again determined by working backward, starting with the most recent purchase. The cost assigned to the first 13 units sold in 19x3 is therefore 13 × $85 = $1,105. The cost of the other one unit sold comes from the beginning inventory. Since under LIFO the first costs to leave the inventory are the most recent costs to go into it, they must come first from the last-in layer, in this case the 19x2 layer: 1 × $60. This transfer from the beginning inventory is known as a **LIFO liquidation** because part of an inventory layer is being liquidated.

The six units in the ending inventory are measured at the six oldest unit costs in the beginning inventory. The oldest costs are those in the 19x1 layer (four units at $50); the remaining two units are measured at the unit costs of the 19x2 layer (2 × $60).

Measuring an Inventory Layer.   In this illustration, we determined the cost of the 19x2 inventory layer on what we might call a *strict* LIFO basis—that is, we started with the first purchases of the year and continued until we had accounted for the number of units added to the inventory in 19x2. While this method may be the conceptually preferred approach, in practice, accountants may use other alternatives, provided that they are applied consistently from year to year.

One of these alternatives is to measure the cost of each year's inventory layer at the *average* cost of the units purchased during the year. Alpha Company, for example, bought a total of 15 units in 19x2 at a total cost of $1,020 (Exhibit 8–2). The average cost of the 19x2 purchases therefore was $1,020/15 = $68. If Alpha had measured its 19x2 cost of goods sold and year-end inventory using this alternative, the year's purchase costs would have been distributed as follows:

Cost of goods sold: 12 units × $68	$ 816
Ending inventory:	
19x1 layer: 4 × $50	200
19x2 layer: 3 × $68	204
Total ending inventory	404
Total cost distributed	$1,220

This would have produced a 19x2 inventory layer $24 larger than the one the strict LIFO application produced—$204 versus the $180 in Exhibit 8–3. Its main advantage is convenience; management needn't keep track of the costs of individual purchases during the year, but can simply wait until the end of the year and calculate an average.

Once a layer has been placed in inventory, all units in that layer are usually measured at the same unit cost. This wasn't an issue in our illustration because the units in each layer were already measured at a single unit cost. In subsequent illustrations, however, we'll treat each layer as a homogeneous whole, with a uniform unit price and no within-the-layer layers even if different prices are paid during the year. For example, if a particular year's layer has a cost of $1,800, based on 100 units bought in January at $4 a unit and 200 units bought in March at $7 a unit, the layer will be viewed as consisting of 300 units at an average cost of $6.[2]

The LIFO Adjustment. Companies that use LIFO costing often also calculate what their financial statement results would have been had FIFO costing been used. Different cost of goods sold amounts obviously yield different amounts of pretax income, and the implications of the variations are discussed later in this chapter. The difference between the inventory-cost amounts that would appear in a balance sheet is a *cumulative* difference, however. It represents the cumulative effect of having used LIFO costing since the date it was adopted.

For Alpha Company, the amounts were as follows (from Exhibits 8–2 and 8–3):

	19x1	19x2	19x3
LIFO cost of goods sold	—	$840	$1,165
FIFO cost of goods sold	—	695	1,120
Difference	—	$145	$ 45
Year-end inventory, at FIFO cost	$200	$525	$ 510
Year-end inventory, at LIFO cost	200	380	320
Difference	—	$145	$ 190

The $145 difference in the end-of-19x2 inventory costs is equal to the amount of the difference in 19x2's cost of goods sold ($840 − $695). The end-of-19x3 inventory costs differ by $190, the sum of *both years'* cost of goods sold differences—19x3's $45 ($1,165 − $1,120) and 19x2's $145. The difference in year-end inventory amounts—$145 in 19x2 and $190 in 19x3—is sometimes called the **LIFO adjustment** (or the *LIFO reserve*). It measures the amount by which pretax retained earnings would have been higher had LIFO costing *not* been used.

---

[2] This differs from the alternative mentioned in the preceding paragraph, which would have calculated the total cost of the layer on the basis of all the unit costs experienced during the entire year.

STUDY REMINDER

FIFO (first-in, first-out) is an inventory costing method that lists the units available for sale in any year and their unit costs in the order in which these units become available. The cost of goods sold is determined by starting with the oldest unit cost on the list and working forward until the requisite number of units has been included. The cost of the ending inventory is determined by starting with the most recent unit costs and working backward.

LIFO (last-in, first-out) is an inventory costing method that lists the units available for sale in any year and their unit costs in reverse order. The cost of goods sold is determined by starting with the most recent unit cost and working backward until the requisite number of units has been included. The cost of the ending inventory is determined by starting with the oldest unit costs and working forward.

Average Costing

The third major method of determining the cost of goods sold and the cost of the ending inventory is known as **average costing.** Under average costing, a single average cost per unit is used to determine both the cost of goods sold during a period of time and the cost of the inventory on hand at the end of that period. This average may be recalculated every time a new purchase is made, once a month, or once a year.

Exhibit 8–5 illustrates the application of average costing under the

EXHIBIT 8–5
Alpha Company: Average Costing

	Units	Unit Cost	Total Cost	
Inventory, January 1, 19x2	4	$50	$ 200	
19x2 purchases:				
April	7	60	420	
July	8	75	600	
Available in 19x2	19		1,220 →	New average: $1,220/19 = $64.21
Goods sold in 19x2	12	64.21	771	
Inventory, December 31, 19x2	7	64.21	449	
19x3 purchases	13	85	1,105	
Available in 19x3	20		1,554 →	New average: $1,554/20 = $77.70
Goods sold in 19x3	14	77.70	1,088	
Inventory, December 31, 19x3	6	77.70	$ 466	

periodic inventory method, which means using a full year as the averaging period. This exhibit is based on the Alpha Company data we used in illustrating the FIFO and LIFO methods. The calculation consists of dividing the total cost of the goods available for sale by the number of units available. During 19x2, 19 units were available for sale at a total cost of $1,220. Dividing $1,220 by 19 units gives an average cost of about $64.21 a unit. The 12 units that were sold in 19x2 therefore have an average cost of $771 (12 × $64.21, rounded to the nearest dollar), and the seven units in the ending inventory appear in the balance sheet at $449 (7 × $64.21).

These amounts appear in the middle of the right-hand column in Exhibit 8–5. The remainder of the exhibit shows what happens when the procedure is repeated in 19x3. Notice that each unit in the 19x3 beginning inventory brings with it a cost of $64.21. Since these units are available in 19x3, their cost is included in the determination of 19x3's average unit cost. As the exhibit indicates, 19x3's average unit cost turns out to be $77.70—heavily influenced by the $85 unit cost incurred during the year but also by the $64.21 unit cost of the beginning inventory. Using $77.70, we can distribute the $1,554 cost of the goods available— $1,088 (14 × $77.70) to the goods sold and $466 (6 × $77.70) to the ending inventory.[3]

Consequences of the Choice of Costing Method

Although LIFO isn't an acceptable costing method in some countries, all three inventory costing methods described in the preceding section are equally acceptable for U.S. companies. Management is therefore free to choose among them, subject to the requirement that the method selected be used consistently, year after year. This being the case, we need to answer four questions:

1. Which method is most likely to maximize the company's net income?
2. Which method is most likely to minimize the company's income taxes and thereby maximize its net cash inflow?
3. Which method is most likely to have the greatest information value?
4. Which method is least subject to abuse?

---

[3] Average costing under the *perpetual inventory method* entails calculating a new average unit cost after each purchase, or a *moving average*. In our illustration, we would have to know the sequence in which purchases and sales occurred. If 19x2 had been a case of "bought 7, sold 6, bought 8, sold 6, " we'd make the following calculations:

After first purchase (4 × $50 + 7 × $60)/(4 + 7)	$ 56.36
After second purchase (5 × $56.36 + 8 × $75)/(5 + 8)	67.83
Cost of goods sold 6 × $56.36 + 6 × $67.83.	$ 745.14
Ending inventory 7 × $67.83.	474.81
Total costs distributed (with $.05 rounding effect)	$1,220.00

Because average costing and FIFO costing produce virtually identical income and cash-flow amounts in most practical situations, we'll limit our analysis to a comparison of FIFO and LIFO.

Income Effects

Other things being equal, management prefers to report higher income to the company's shareholders rather than smaller income. This preference may be due in part to executive compensation agreements that tie managerial bonuses and other rewards to the company's reported income. Another reason that higher income is more attractive than low income may be that the company's creditors have imposed restrictions on managerial actions if reported income (or retained earnings) falls below a specified level.

A third possible explanation of managers' preference for high rather than low income is that they may assume that large reported earnings can induce higher market prices for the company's shares. Although research in the past two decades suggests that this result is likely to occur only if larger positive cash flows will follow as well, many managers apparently believe that the market accepts earnings numbers at face value.

Management's decision on which method to adopt should be based on its estimate of the impact of this decision in most future periods rather than in one year only. Whether FIFO or LIFO is likely to maximize net income in most years depends mainly on whether acquisition prices are rising or falling. In general, FIFO leads to a higher net income than LIFO if prices are rising. The cost of goods sold amounts in our Alpha Company illustration were as follows:

	FIFO Cost of Goods Sold	LIFO Cost of Goods Sold	Difference
19x2	$ 695	$ 840	$145
19x3	1,120	1,165	45

With a smaller cost of goods sold in periods of rising prices, FIFO produces a larger gross margin and a greater net income.

Income considerations therefore favor the use of FIFO costing for any item that is subject to a generally rising price trend. But how does the choice affect income in any one year? The answer depends on a number of factors, mainly the following:

1. Whether prices this year are higher or lower than the FIFO unit cost of the beginning inventory.
2. Whether the physical inventory quantity at the end of the year is greater than, equal to, or less than the inventory on hand at the beginning of the year.

3. Special additional considerations when a liquidation takes place—that is, when the inventory quantity decreases during the year.

If the inventory quantity increases or remains constant, FIFO income will exceed LIFO income when acquisition prices are increasing, will equal LIFO income when prices are steady, and will be less than LIFO income when prices are falling. The reason is that LIFO never brings prior-year prices into the income statement if inventories increase or remain constant, whereas FIFO always brings these old prices into the cost of goods sold. If prices are rising, these old prices will be lower than LIFO costs; if prices are falling, the old prices will be higher than current LIFO costs.

The comparison is more complex for a year in which an inventory reduction takes place. The impact on income depends on (1) the size of the liquidation relative to the quantity of goods sold, and (2) whether the spread between current acquisition prices and the average price of the liquidated LIFO layers is greater than the increase in price from the preceding year.

Income Tax Effects

Although the effect of a company's operations on its cash position is its *net cash inflow,* the term that tends to be used in practice is simply *cash flow.* If cash flow were the only variable, management would be expected to choose the method that would maximize the company's cash flows. A large net cash flow gives management the ability to make the company grow, to pay its employees competitive salaries and wages, to declare cash dividends, and to reward the managers themselves. The more cash that can be generated, the faster the company can grow and the greater the prestige and monetary rewards the managers can reap for themselves.

The only direct effect of the choice of inventory method on cash flow is on the company's income taxes. A peculiarity of income taxation in the United States is that a company that elects to use LIFO for tax determination can't use FIFO or average costing for financial reporting. Although our concern, as always, is with the measurement of results and position for financial reporting, we must consider the tax effects because these are likely to have a strong influence on management's choice of inventory methods.

The impact of the FIFO/LIFO choice on taxable income is the same as its impact on the income before income taxes that is reported in the company's financial statements. If FIFO income is greater than LIFO, FIFO income taxes will be greater than LIFO's—and FIFO cash flow therefore will be smaller than LIFO's. Conversely, in a year in which LIFO income is greater than FIFO income would be, LIFO's cash flow will be less than FIFO's cash flow.

LIFO generally meets the cash-flow criterion better than FIFO because the prices of most products and commodities have been and continue to be on long-term upward trends. In addition, since most businesses are usually growing, the quantity of inventory that is bought and sold tends to be increasing as well. With a combination of rising prices and generally rising or steady inventory levels, LIFO produces a greater cost of goods sold, lower income taxes, and a greater cash flow than FIFO.

Notice that the tax advantage of LIFO in a period of rising prices is cumulative—and it isn't cancelled out when prices eventually stabilize. By placing more costs in the income statement and therefore on the income tax return, the company places fewer costs on the balance sheet. The difference in inventory cost therefore is the *cumulative* difference in taxable income. For example, the costs of Alpha Company's December 31, 19x3, inventory were as follows:

FIFO inventory cost (Exhibit 8–2)	$510
LIFO inventory cost (Exhibit 8–3)	320
Difference	$190

In other words, the use of LIFO would shield $190 of Alpha Company's cash flow from taxation in 19x2 and 19x3. And because the LIFO cost of the first two inventory layers would remain constant as long as the inventory never fell to a lower level, this tax advantage would persist as long as current prices remained above the 19x2 level.

In practice, management's inventory method decision is usually whether to switch to LIFO from FIFO or average costing, effective in the fiscal year that has just ended. The reason is that FIFO and average costing have been in use much longer than LIFO, and one of them is likely to have been adopted long ago in the company's history. Whenever prices move upward sharply and appear likely to continue rising for a number of years, the tax advantages of LIFO are likely to seem more important to management than its unfavorable income effects. In 1974 alone, a year of great price changes, 153 of a sample of 600 of the largest U.S. corporations changed the bulk of their inventories to LIFO. By 1984, 68 percent of the companies in this group had all or part of their inventories on LIFO.[4]

Although the decision to adopt LIFO isn't based on the situation in a single year, the switch tends to be made in a year in which LIFO will reduce taxable income. This means that the LIFO base quantity will be at a low unit cost relative to the year-end LIFO cost, and this low cost will carry forward into the future. Since inventory-method decisions are made after the end of the year but before the tax returns and financial statements for the year have been prepared, management has the data neces-

---

[4] See *Accounting Trends and Techniques,* 31st and 38th editions [New York: American Institute of Certified Public Accountants, 1977 (p. 111) and 1984 (p. 123)].

sary to make the LIFO/FIFO comparison for the year. If the long-term price trend is upward but prices fell during the year just ended, the switch to LIFO would likely be postponed.

Information Effects

Outsiders expect to use the data in company financial statements to predict the amount and timing of the company's future cash flows *and* the uncertainty surrounding them. The inventory costing method with the greatest information value therefore is the method that is the most likely to be useful to those who make these predictions.

Although it isn't entirely clear how this requirement can be implemented, we suggest it might mean that the preferable method is the one that comes closest to providing investors and other outsiders with the following:

1. The dollar cost assigned to the goods sold should help the investor identify the **sustainable gross margin**—that is, the profit the company can sustain on a continuing basis.
2. The dollar cost of the inventory on hand should bear a normal relationship to the amount to be realized from a future sale of that inventory.

Sustainable Gross Margin. *Sustainable gross margin* is the spread between products' selling prices and replacement costs. As the cost of buying goods increases, the selling price is likely to rise as well. If the selling price doesn't increase as fast as the unit cost rises, the company's ability to generate cash and pay dividends will be reduced. The company will also find it difficult to continue to replace the sold goods and to maintain its operating capacity at the previous level, let alone expand it. Investors in turn might reasonably conclude that the company is stagnating and losing its competitive edge.

Insights such as these can be obtained by examining income amounts that reflect a company's sustainable gross margin. Measures of net income that don't reflect the spread between selling price and replacement cost may convey erroneous and misleading impressions if they are used in these kinds of analyses. For example, suppose a retailer buys 10 units of merchandise from a wholesaler at $10 a unit and sells them to retail customers at a price of $15, a margin of $5 a unit. If the replacement cost had risen to $12 at the time of the sale, the sustainable gross margin will be only $3 a unit. Unless conditions change, the gross margin on the *next* sale of 10 units will be only $3 a unit, because the cost of goods sold will be $12, not $10, a unit.

Given this argument, the best inventory method is the method which produces a gross margin that best approximates the margin between the current selling price and the current acquisition cost of the items sold. In a period of stable or increasing inventory levels, the LIFO cost of goods sold is likely to be closer than FIFO to the current acquisition price.

For example, Exhibit 8–6 shows the relationship between FIFO income and sustainable income in a situation in which selling prices move

EXHIBIT 8–6
Sustainable Income versus FIFO Income

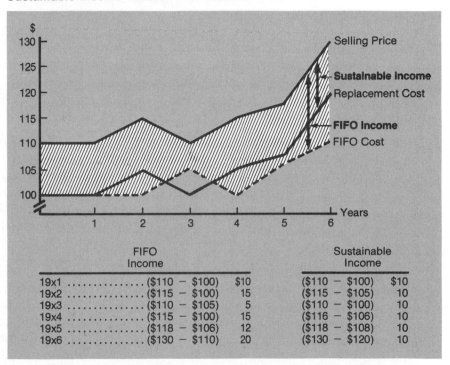

	FIFO Income			Sustainable Income	
19x1	($110 − $100)	$10		($110 − $100)	$10
19x2	($115 − $100)	15		($115 − $105)	10
19x3	($110 − $105)	5		($110 − $100)	10
19x4	($115 − $100)	15		($116 − $106)	10
19x5	($118 − $106)	12		($118 − $108)	10
19x6	($130 − $110)	20		($130 − $120)	10

in parallel with replacement prices and the company has a one-period inventory on hand at all times. The vertical distances in the shaded area in Exhibit 8–6 represent FIFO income, the difference between revenue and the FIFO historical cost of goods sold. This amount varies from period to period. It is greater when prices are rising and smaller when prices are falling. Sustainable income—the vertical distance between the selling price and replacement price lines—remains constant in this illustration.

The main disadvantage of LIFO is that the direction and size of the gap between LIFO gross margin and sustainable gross margin are difficult to determine when inventory liquidation takes place. The FIFO cost of goods sold can be closer to current acquisition cost than LIFO if a substantial inventory reduction takes place, bringing lower prior-year prices into the cost of goods sold. FIFO may also produce better approximations of sustainable gross margin if purchases are made during the year at prices that reflect unusual conditions. For example, if most purchases during the year are made at penalty prices during a strike in suppliers' plants, these will be reflected in their entirety in the LIFO cost of goods sold if the year-end inventory is at or below the beginning-of-year level. The FIFO cost of goods sold in that year may be closer to the normal replacement cost.

In short, LIFO may approximate the current replacement cost of goods sold better than FIFO, but not always. Furthermore, the amount and direction of the error are difficult to estimate without supplemental information.

Inventory Measurement.   In a strict sense, inventories are measured at their historical cost because this shows the amount of resources that have been used to acquire them. Many readers of balance sheets, however, interpret *cost* to be a surrogate for the *value* of companies' inventories. Although accountants disclaim any responsibility for this interpretation, many readers of financial statements would like to use the cost of companies' inventories as the basis for imputing the value of the merchandise on hand. This value, in turn, becomes an important number for investors seeking to predict the company's future cash flows. They reason that cost is a reasonable approximation of the amount that will remain from the ultimate selling price after deducting such factors as selling costs, interest on investment, bad debts, and normal merchandising profit.

This assumption, if it is valid at all, is valid only if the unit costs in the end-of-period inventory reflect current or near-current prices. Prices paid for inventory in the distant past have no relevance to how much can be recovered from their sale today. The only prices that come close to answering this question are those that could be obtained for the inventory sold in an orderly manner, less selling costs, bad debts, and interest on the investment in the inventory in the interim. Alternatively, under certain conditions, current replacement costs could serve as surrogates for the recoverable amounts.

FIFO does a better job of approximating the current replacement cost of inventories than LIFO does. The unit costs in a FIFO inventory are seldom more than a few months old; LIFO inventories, by contrast, may be measured at the unit costs of 10, 20, or even more years in the past.

Susceptibility to Abuse

Outside readers of financial statements need assurance that management has few opportunities to affect net income by taking actions that don't affect the company's wealth. FIFO passes this test better than LIFO.

For example, suppose a company is approaching the end of its fiscal year with fewer items in inventory than it had at the beginning of the year. If it takes no action, and if LIFO is used, some of the current year's cost of goods sold will be measured at prior-year prices. Management can prevent this by buying enough before the end of the year to bring the inventory up to the beginning-of-year level. Management therefore is in a position to affect net income by its year-end purchasing decisions. Under FIFO, these purchasing decisions will merely affect the cost of the ending inventory.

The Flow of Goods

The choice of inventory methods has nothing to do with the physical flow of goods into and out of inventory. Goods may be taken out of inventory in the same order they come in, in reverse order, or in random order. Any of the inventory methods we've described can be used for any of these physical-flow patterns.

The reason for this freedom of choice is that the various items in the inventory are assumed to be interchangeable. They may be physically interchangeable because they have the same physical properties (size, weight, etc.). More importantly, they are economically interchangeable because they fill similar consumer needs. In other words, the user will obtain the same satisfaction (or utility) no matter which interchangeable units are used.

When the units passing through inventory are interchangeable in one of these senses, any division of costs between the goods that are sold and the goods that remain in inventory is arbitrary. This arbitrariness can't be avoided by choosing one costing method rather than another, because all methods produce arbitrary distributions of the cost of goods available. Conceptually, the essential question is which method provides the most useful information. In practice, as we have just pointed out, the decision is likely to reflect management's perception of the company's best interests.

The Current-Cost Perspective

Since both FIFO and LIFO deal only with historical costs, neither method measures the gain or loss that occurs when the current cost of merchandise changes. Furthermore, neither method gives an up-to-date measure of inventories or a reliable measure of sustainable income. To overcome these shortcomings, some accountants suggest using a **current-cost** measurement system, in which inventories and the cost of goods sold are measured at their *current* costs instead of their *historical* costs. The current cost of a company's inventory on any date is the amount the company would have to spend to replace the merchandise at the prices prevailing on that date. The current cost of goods sold is their replacement cost on the date of the sale.

Holding Gains and Losses

A company that holds inventories when prices change will have holding gains and losses in addition to income from manufacturing or merchandising operations. A **holding gain** results from the holding of inventory at the time the price of the goods increases; a **holding loss** results from the holding of inventory at the time the price of the goods decreases.

We measure inventory holding gains and losses by the changes in the *purchase prices* of the items in inventory. The idea is that a purchase before the date of a price change is a substitute for a purchase after that date. By buying early, the company gets the benefit or incurs the penalty of buying at the old price.

To illustrate, remember that Alpha Company started operating late in 19x1. It acquired its first four units of merchandise in 19x1 at a cost of $50 each, and placed them in inventory for sale in 19x2. On December 31, Alpha's supplier announced an increase in the price to $60 a unit. Alpha's year-end current-cost balance sheet measured inventory at $240 (4 units × $60), and the holding gain for the year was calculated as follows:

Units in Inventory at Time of Price Change	×	Amount of Price Change	=	Holding Gain
4		+$10		$40

This holding gain was reported as income in Alpha's current-cost income statement for 19x1.

We can see from this brief illustration that the adoption of current costing as the basis for company financial statements would affect both income and inventory. In the remainder of this section, we'll see how these differences arise and what they mean.

The Current-Cost Income Statement

With respect to inventory, there are two differences between a current-cost income statement and a historical-cost income statement: the amount of cost of goods sold and the inclusion of a holding gain or loss. To illustrate these differences, we'll use the information contained in our earlier description of the FIFO and LIFO methods. The illustration began in our introduction to holding gains and losses—that is, when we calculated Alpha Company's 19x1 holding gain. The illustration now proceeds to the following year, and the pertinent information is summarized in the upper panel of Exhibit 8–7.

EXHIBIT 8–7
Alpha Company: Current-Costing, 19x2

	Units	Unit Cost
January 1, 19x2 inventory	4	$60
January 1–June 30:		
Purchases	+7	$60
Sales.	−6	
June 30, 19x2 inventory.	5	$75
July 1–December 31:		
Purchases	+8	$75
Sales.	−6	
December 31, 19x2 inventory	7	$85

Current cost of goods available		Current cost distributed	
Beginning inventory: 4 × $60	$ 240	Current cost of goods sold:	
Purchases:		January 1–June 30 6 × $60	$ 360
7 × $60	420	July 1–December 31 6 × $75 . . .	450
8 × $75	600	Total current cost	
Total purchases.	1,020	of goods sold.	810
Holding gain:		Ending inventory: 7 × $85	595
June 30 5 × $15	75		
December 31 7 × $10	70		
Total holding gain.	145		
Total current cost available.	$1,405	Total current cost distributed	$1,405

In 19x2, Alpha's beginning inventory had a current cost of $240 (4 × $60). During the first six months, the company bought seven units at a price of $60 each and sold six units. On June 30, Alpha's supplier increased the price to $75 a unit. During the second half of 19x2, eight units were purchased for $75 each and six units were sold; on December 31, the supplier raised the price to $85 a unit. The income statement effect of these events is illustrated in the lower panel of Exhibit 8–7.

The left side of the panel identifies the cost of the beginning inventory ($240), the actual cost of the 15 units purchased ($1,020), and the amount of Alpha's holding gain. The five units on hand when the price increased on June 30 resulted in a $75 holding gain, while the seven units on hand on December 31 gave Alpha a $70 holding gain. The difference between the $1,405 current cost of the goods available for sale and their $1,220 historical cost (4 × $50 in 19x1 + $1,020 in 19x2) − $185 − represents Alpha's *cumulative* holding gains ($40 in 19x1 and $145 in 19x2).

The right side of the panel shows how the $1,405 current cost of the goods available for sale was distributed in current-cost financial statements. The six units sold during the first six months had a sale-date current cost of $60 each, and the six units sold during the latter half of the year had a sale-date current cost of $75 each. The current cost of the goods sold—that is, their sale-date current cost—therefore totaled $810. The seven units on hand at year-end were measured at the $85 year-end current cost, or $595.

Current Cost versus FIFO Cost

Exhibit 8–8 presents the income effects for 19x2. The exhibit assumes a selling price of $100 for each of the 12 units sold, and it ignores income taxes and selling and administrative expenses. While Column 1 contains the current-cost amounts we derived in Exhibit 8–7, the FIFO-cost results in Column 2 are based on the calculations that were presented in Exhibit 8–2. The differences between current cost and FIFO cost appear in Column 3.

The gross margin difference exists because the FIFO-cost gross margin included $115 of holding gains that are *not* identified as such in FIFO-cost income statements. Not disclosing the nature of this favorable result misleads readers into concluding that the entire $505 gross margin was merchandising income rather than the actual $390. The $115 is called the **inventory profit:** it represents the portion of the historical-cost-based income that resulted from the company's purchases of inventory at prices that were lower than their sale-date replacement costs.

Column 1 reveals that the $115 inventory profit is *not* the amount of Alpha's 19x2 holding gain ($145). There are two reasons for this. First, the $115 *includes* the $40 holding gain that occurred in December 19x1; second, it *excludes* the holding gain experienced in 19x2 on the seven units that were still on hand at year-end. This distinction is explained by the middle panel of Exhibit 8–8.

The $40 holding gain Alpha experienced in 19x1 is said to have been **unrealized** as of the end of 19x1 because it hadn't yet been confirmed in a revenue transaction. Realization was contingent on what transpired by the time the four units were sold—that is, that there be no decline in

EXHIBIT 8–8
Alpha Company: Income Comparison with FIFO, 19x2

ALPHA COMPANY
Income Comparison: Current Cost versus FIFO Cost
For the Year Ended December 31, 19x2

	(1) Current Cost	*(2)* FIFO Cost	*(3)* Current Cost versus FIFO
Sales revenues (12 × $100)	$1,200	$1,200	
Cost of goods sold:			
(6 × $60) + (6 × $75)	810		
(4 × $50) + (7 × $60) + (1 × $75) .		695	$ 115
Gross margin	390	505	115
Holding gain (5 × $15) + (7 × $10) . .	145		(145)
Income	$ 535	$ 505	$ (30)

Calculation of Realized Holding Gain (Loss)

Unrealized holding gain, January 1: 4 × ($60 − $50)	$ 40
Add: Holding gain arising in 19x2: (5 × $15) + (7 × $10)	145
Total	185
Less: Unrealized holding gain, December 31: 7 × ($85 − $75) . . .	(70)
Holding gain realized in 19x2: $810 − $695	$115

Reconciliation

Holding gain realized in 19x2	$115
Increase in unrealized holding gain in 19x2: $70 − $40	30
Holding gain arising in 19x2	$145

prices below the end-of-19x1 $60 level. The $40 holding gain from 19x1, together with the new $145 holding gain that arose in 19x2, meant that there was a total of $185 of holding gains that would be **realized** once sale transactions occurred. Whereas FIFO-cost ending inventory reflected each of the seven units on hand at its $75 purchase price, their $85 current cost per unit resulted in an unrealized holding gain of $70 (7 × $10). As a result, only $115 of the $185 holding gain was realized in 19x2.

The *reconciliation* section of Exhibit 8–8 identifies the reason for the $30 difference between the $535 current-cost income and the $505

FIFO-cost income. Current-cost income contains the full $145 holding gain that Alpha experienced during the year. FIFO-cost income is affected by only the $115 realized portion of Alpha's current and past holding gains. In addition to the $30 measurement difference between the income amounts, there is also a disclosure difference. Whereas current cost distinguishes between the $390 merchandising income and the $145 holding gain, FIFO cost does not isolate the $115 realized holding gain (*inventory profit*) component of its $505 gross margin from the $390 merchandising income.

Current Cost versus LIFO Cost

Exhibit 8–9 presents the 19x2 differences between current-cost income and LIFO-cost income. Column 2's LIFO-cost results are based on the calculations that were presented in Exhibit 8–3, and the differences between current cost and LIFO cost appear in Column 3.

While the analysis we used to compare current cost and FIFO cost applies here as well, we are faced with a somewhat different outcome. Alpha Company's LIFO-cost income was smaller than current-cost income by $175 ($535 − $360). Column 3 reveals that $145 of this difference was due to the holding gains that arose in 19x2. The remaining $30 difference reflects the amount by which LIFO cost of goods sold ($840) exceeded the current cost of the goods sold ($810). This difference happened because the LIFO cost of goods sold included all of the last-in, high-cost units—unit costs that were greater than some of the actual current costs in effect when the sales occurred.

The lower panel of Exhibit 8–9 helps us understand why current-cost income provides a more substantive measure of income *and* better disclosure of the composition of income. From the LIFO-cost perspective, not only was none of the $185 cumulative holding gain realized in 19x2, the *unrealized* holding gain increased to $215. This is the expected LIFO result for a company that experiences increases in the quantity of units on hand while prices are rising. Using LIFO cost therefore results in (1) measuring the period's cost of goods sold at an amount that includes the unidentified $30 realized holding loss, and (2) understating the end-of-period inventory by the $215 unrealized holding gain.

Current Cost versus Historical Cost: 19x2 Summary

Our analysis of Alpha Company's 19x2 inventory transactions demonstrated that relative to current-cost income, both FIFO-cost and LIFO-cost results reflect the same types of income variations, albeit by different amounts. Exhibit 8–10 identifies the amounts by which FIFO-cost and LIFO-cost financial statements differed from those prepared on a current-cost basis.

EXHIBIT 8–9
Alpha Company: Income Comparison with LIFO, 19x2

ALPHA COMPANY
Income Comparison: Current Cost versus LIFO Cost
For the Year Ended December 31, 19x2

	(1) Current Cost	*(2)* LIFO Cost	*(3)* Current Cost versus LIFO
Sales revenues (12 × $100)	$1,200	$1,200	
Cost of goods sold:			
(6 × $60) + (6 × $75)	810		
(8 × $75) + (4 × $60)		840	$ (30)
Gross margin.	390	360	(30)
Holding gain (5 × $15) + (7 × $10) .	145		(145)
Income	$ 535	$ 360	$(175)

Calculation of Realized Holding Gain (Loss)

Unrealized holding gain, January 1: 4 × ($60 − $50)	$ 40
Add: Holding gain arising in 19x2: (5 × $15) + (7 × $10)	145
Total	185
Less: Unrealized holding gain, December 31:	
7 × $85 − (4 × $50 + 3 × $60)	(215)
Holding (loss) realized in 19x2: ($810 − $840)	$ (30)

Reconciliation

Holding (loss) realized in 19x2.	$ (30)
Increase in unrealized holding gain in 19x2: $215 − $40.	175
Holding gain arising in 19x2	$145

This exhibit demonstrates that both historical-cost methods' 19x2 income differed from current-cost income because the $145 holding gain that arose during the year was excluded from income. An additional distortion occurred because 19x2 income was affected by the holding gains or losses realized during the year, even though some of these gains had arisen in an earlier period. The conclusion we reach is that historical-cost income is misstated because the amount of inventory holding gain or loss that is included in FIFO- or LIFO-income—the *realized* holding gain

EXHIBIT 8–10
Alpha Company: Financial Statement Effects, 19x2

	FIFO	LIFO
Income:		
Exclusion of 19x2 holding gain	$ 145	$145
Inclusion of holding (gain) loss realized in 19x2 . .	(115)	30
Income understatement.	$ 30	$175
Retained earnings, December 31:		
19x1 income understatement	$ 40	$ 40
19x2 income understatement	30	175
Total understatement.	$ 70	$215
Inventory understatement, December 31:		
Exclusion of realized holding gain:		
$595 − $525	$ 70	
$595 − $380		$215

or loss—bears no necessary relationship to the amount of holding gain actually arising during the period.

Exhibit 8–10 also identifies the balance sheet effect of using FIFO cost or LIFO cost instead of current cost. The cumulative differences in income resulted in an understatement of year-end retained earnings. In addition, the inventory asset was understated by the same dollar amount for the very same reason: historical-cost methods don't account for unrealized holding gains—that is, for holding gains on merchandise still on hand.

Current Cost in Practice

Although current-cost measurements have strong theoretical support, United States companies do not prepare financial statements on a current-cost basis. This situation exists because generally accepted accounting principles in the United States call for financial statements based on companies' historical costs, and none of the standards-setting bodies has seen fit to endorse such a comprehensive departure from historical-cost accounting methods. During the past 50 years of standards-setting in the United States, there have been three piecemeal responses to current costing, however.

The first development was the introduction and popularization of LIFO costing. One of the incentives to use LIFO, and one way to justify the method conceptually, is its inclusion of relatively current unit-cost amounts in a period's cost of goods sold. This positive income effect, of course, generates an opposite effect on balance sheet measurements, and can distort reported income in periods when LIFO layers are liquidated.

A second response to the economic effect of current costs was the accounting profession's adoption of the lower-of-cost-or-market rule. The manner in which this rule is applied is discussed in the next section.

The third and most recent development involving current costs has been the FASB rule that certain large corporations must prepare current-cost supplements to their financial statements. The designated companies must calculate and disclose (1) the current cost of their year-end inventories, (2) the sale-date current cost of the goods sold during the period, and (3) the amount of holding gains or losses that arose during the period. The presumption is that even though the financial statements proper continue to reflect historical-cost data, the publication of selected current-cost information fosters more insightful understanding of a company's financial position and operating results.

The Lower-of-Cost-or-Market Rule

Although the purchase or manufacture of merchandise is recorded at its historical cost, the inventory asset is written down to *market value* if the market value of the end-of-period inventory is lower than its recorded cost. The write-down results in income statement recognition of a holding loss. The procedure through which the asset basis is reduced and the loss is recognized is called the **lower-of-cost-or-market rule.**

Illustration: FIFO Cost

To illustrate, suppose a company has an ending inventory of 10 units at a FIFO cost of $25 each. Just prior to year-end, the market value of this merchandise falls to $18 a unit. The inventory will be written down by $7 a unit ($25 − $18), a total of $70. Let's now assume that the income statement contains sales revenues of $800, cost of goods sold of $450, and other expenses of $220. The $70 write-down loss this year is recognized as a determinant of this year's income, with alternative disclosure formats as follows:

	Format A	Format B
Sales revenues	$800	$800
Cost of goods sold	450	520
Gross margin	350	280
Operating expenses	220	220
Inventory loss	70	—
Total	290	220
Income before income taxes	$ 60	$ 60

The conceptually preferred disclosure is Format A because it identifies the loss as an autonomous determinant of income. In practice, however, companies tend to use Format B because the amount of such a write-down is usually not significant enough to warrant independent disclosure. We'll therefore assume that the loss is included in a company's cost of goods sold.

In the company's balance sheet, the ending inventory will be reported as $180 (10 × $18). This is the amount of the asset's historical cost that the company will carry forward into the next year. Under FIFO, it will be the cost of the first 10 units sold in the next year. In other words, *the year-end inventory is still measured on a cost basis, even under the lower-of-cost-or-market rule;* current market value measures the proportion of the historical cost the company normally can expect to recover in the future—and the written-down sum is treated as a *cost* amount in all subsequent accounting.

Pros and Cons

The argument in favor of the lower-of-cost-or-market rule is that no asset should appear on a company's balance sheet in an amount greater than is likely to be recovered from the use or sale of that asset in the normal course of events. Unrecoverable amounts have no value and therefore aren't assets. The main objection to this rule is that it treats value increases and value decreases differently. If the market value of merchandise is greater than its cost, there is no recognition of the increased value on the balance sheet.

What we have, then, is an adjustment that is used in only one direction. This inconsistent approach is defended by accountants on the grounds of "conservatism." Even though the market-value data are as reliable and as relevant whether they are greater or less than cost-based amounts, accounting doesn't recognize value increases until they are realized in arm's-length transactions. The nature of decreases in value, on the other hand, demands measurement and disclosure as soon as the marketplace indicates the likelihood of an adverse outcome.

Generally accepted accounting principles in the United States require the use of the lower-of-cost-or-market rule, no matter which method is used to establish the cost of the ending inventory. LIFO-basis companies can't use the lower-of-cost-or-market rule for tax purposes in the U.S., however. If market value drops below year-end LIFO cost, the inventory must continue to be measured at LIFO cost for tax purposes. This seldom affects a company's cash flows, because LIFO unit costs are almost always much lower than current market values.

Definition of Market Value

Determining the **market value** of the inventory is a judgmental process for which the accounting profession has developed technical guidelines. We needn't concern ourselves with the details of these guidelines, except to say that market value is usually determined either by net realizable value or by current replacement cost. **Net realizable value** is the amount of cash an outside buyer will pay in an orderly transaction (i.e., not a forced sale), reduced by any costs that must still be incurred to make the inventory ready for sale, sell it, and collect the proceeds.

Current replacement cost is likely to be used if it is easier to determine than net realizable value and if there is no reason to suspect that net realizable value is lower than replacement cost. Net realizable value is the *maximum* amount accountants will use to measure an inventory's market value. It will be used when it is more readily measurable than current replacement cost.

Inventory Pooling

An important issue in the application of the lower-of-cost-or-market rule is whether inventory write-downs should be calculated for individual products or for groups of related products.

For example, suppose a company has two items in inventory—a unit of product X with a cost of $30 and a market value of $35, and a unit of product Y with a cost of $50 and a market value of $48. If the rule is applied product by product, product Y will be written down to $48, a $2 write-down. If the rule is applied to the two products as a group, however, no write-down will be made—because total market value ($35 + $48) exceeds total cost ($30 + $50).

As this illustration shows, product-by-product application of the rule will lead to more write-downs and lower reported inventories than application of the rule to pools. The main purpose of the lower-of-cost-or-market rule is to insure that reported inventory doesn't exceed its recoverable value, however; pooling is likely to achieve that.

Summary

When revenues are recognized at the time of delivery, inventories are measured for financial reporting purposes at their historical costs. When different units of product are interchangeable, the costs of the goods available in any year are distributed between the cost of goods sold and the cost of the ending inventory on the basis of a preselected sequence. The main inventory costing sequences are first-in, first-out (FIFO), last-in, first-out (LIFO), and average costing. Each method is equally acceptable in financial reporting by U.S. businesses.

In periods of rising prices, LIFO tends to produce a higher cost of goods sold and lower net income in most periods than either FIFO or average costing, because current acquisition costs constitute more of the LIFO cost of goods sold than of the FIFO or average-costing cost of goods sold. For the same reason, LIFO is likely to produce income statements that reflect the concept of the sustainable gross margin better than FIFO-based statements in most periods, but the closeness of fit varies and is difficult to determine without supplemental information.

Because LIFO produces a higher cost of goods sold in most periods when prices are rising, it also produces lower income taxes if it is used for income tax determination. LIFO inventory costs are usually a much poorer approximation than FIFO costs to the current acquisition costs of the goods in inventory. Finally, LIFO is more subject to abuse than FIFO because inventory reduction will bring prior years' purchase prices into the LIFO cost of goods sold, and management can control whether this reduction will take place and how large it will be.

Current costing is another method with which accountants can measure the cost of goods sold during a period and the cost of inventory on hand at the end of the period. While this method may not be used by U.S. companies in preparing financial statements for external users, an understanding of its nature allows the reader to appreciate the shortcomings of historical-cost methods. Holding gains and losses that arise during a period are measured and disclosed in a current-cost income statement. A historical-cost income statement not only fails to measure any such gains and losses, but it also conceals the presence in income of those past and present holding gains and losses that are realized in the current period. As a result, FIFO-cost income may contain so-called inventory profits on a recurring basis when purchase prices are rising, while LIFO-cost income is likely to be overstated when low unit-cost LIFO layers of earlier periods are liquidated because of a decline in units on hand at the end of the period.

In addition to using an inventory costing method consistently each year, accountants compare the derived cost of the period's ending inventory with its market value. When the indicated value is less than the recorded cost, the asset is written down and a loss is recorded, resulting in reduced income for the period. Such adjustments are made only when value is less than cost, not when value exceeds cost. In practice, because the LIFO cost of the inventory almost never exceeds market value, this lower-of-cost-or-market adjustment ordinarily comes into play in connection with inventories measured on a FIFO or average-costing basis.

Key Terms	Average costing	Holding gain/loss
	Current cost	Inventory profit
	First-in, first-out (FIFO)	Last-in, first-out (LIFO)

LIFO adjustment
LIFO inventory layer
LIFO liquidation
LIFO-periodic
LIFO-perpetual
Lower-of-cost-or-market rule

Market value
Net realizable value
Realized holding gain/loss
Replacement cost
Sustainable gross margin
Unrealized holding gain

Independent Study Problems (Solutions in Appendix B)

1. FIFO Cost; LIFO Cost. Higby Company had 10,000 pounds of product in inventory on January 1, 19x1, at a FIFO cost of $30,000. Management decided to switch to the LIFO method beginning in 19x1. Purchases and sales for the next eight years were as follows:

Year	Purchases	Sales (pounds)
19x1	60,000 × $3.10 = $186,000	55,000
19x2	70,000 × $3.50 = 245,000	68,000
19x3	90,000 × $3.75 = 337,500	80,000
19x4	70,000 × $3.80 = 266,000	72,000
19x5	80,000 × $4.00 = 320,000	75,000
19x6	70,000 × $4.25 = 297,500	80,000
19x7	100,000 × $4.40 = 440,000	85,000
19x8	95,000 × $4.50 = 427,500	95,000

a. Calculate the LIFO cost of goods sold for each year and the LIFO cost of the inventory at the end of each year.
b. Calculate the FIFO cost of goods sold for each year and the FIFO cost of the inventory at the end of each year.

2. FIFO and LIFO Exercise. New York Corporation made the following purchases during its first year of operation:

January 10, 19x7	1,000 units @ $3.00
March 20, 19x7	2,000 units @ 3.25
May 12, 19x7	2,500 units @ 3.30
November 10, 19x7	1,200 units @ 4.00
December 20, 19x7	1,800 units @ 4.05

The company sold 6,000 units during 19x7 at a price of $5 a unit. It had pretax operating expenses of $5,000 and was subject to income taxes at a rate of 25 percent.

a. Calculate the cost of goods sold, the cost of the ending inventory, and the gross margin, all on a FIFO basis.
b. Perform the same calculations, using LIFO costing.
c. Discuss the impact of the choice between the two inventory costing methods on the company's income and cash flows.

3. Lower-of-Cost-or-Market Rule.   Apex Corporation has four products in inventory at year-end:

Product	No. of Units	Cost/Unit	Market Price/Unit
A	10,000	$10	$ 8
B	20,000	15	16
C	30,000	20	23
D	40,000	10	8

a. Calculate the ending inventory by applying the lower-of-cost-or-market rule (1) item by item and (2) to the inventory as a whole.
b. Calculate the effect on the net income of using one version of the lower-of-cost-or-market rule instead of the other.
c. Which way of applying the lower-of-cost-or-market rule do you prefer? State your arguments.

4. LIFO: Effect of Inventory Liquidation and Replenishment.   Franklin Steel Warehouse Company adopted LIFO on January 1, 19x2, and its 15,000-ton inventory was costed at its FIFO cost of $125 a ton on that date, a total of $1,875,000.

Franklin bought 100,000 tons and sold 95,000 tons in 19x2. Prices varied during the year: (1) the purchase price of the first 20,000 units bought during the year was $128.75 a ton; (2) the average purchase price during the year was $130 a ton; and (3) the price of the last 20,000 tons bought during the year (and included in the $130-a-ton average) was $135 a ton.

Sales in 19x3 amounted to 105,000 tons, but purchases totaled only 90,000 tons at an average cost of $140 a ton. (The last 5,000 tons purchased during 19x3 also cost $140 a ton.) The inventory was down to 5,000 tons at the end of 19x3 because a steel strike had cut off supplies. The company expected to rebuild its inventories to 15,000 tons as soon as steel became available again in 19x4.

Franklin Steel Warehouse Company measures the annual increments to its LIFO inventory at the average of all purchase prices paid during the year, $130 a ton in 19x2 and $140 a ton in 19x3.

a. Provide the amounts necessary to complete the following table, showing inventories and cost of goods sold on both a FIFO and a LIFO basis:

	Inventory Cost			Cost of Goods Sold	
	FIFO	LIFO		FIFO	LIFO
January 1, 19x2	$1,875,000	$1,875,000			
			19x2	_____	_____
December 31, 19x2	_____	_____			
			19x3	_____	_____
December 31, 19x3	_____	_____			

b. Assuming that 15,000 tons is the normal inventory quantity and that the company intended to rebuild its inventories to this level as soon as possible, what was the effect of the "involuntary liquidation" of inventory on income before taxes for 19x3?

c. Assuming that inventories were increased to 15,000 tons by the end of 19x4, with 19x4 purchases at a cost of $145 a ton, what was the net effect of the 19x3 involuntary liquidation on LIFO inventory cost as of December 31, 19x4?

d. Assuming an income tax rate of 50 percent, calculate the effect of the choice between FIFO and LIFO on the company's cash flows in 19x2, 19x3, and 19x4. The company purchased 100,000 tons of steel in 19x4.

5. Comprehensive Problem: LIFO and FIFO; Holding Gains and Losses. Alpha Company (the illustrative company in this chapter) began the year 19x3 with seven units in inventory when the current replacement cost was $85 a unit. The costs of this inventory under the three main methods of inventory costing described in this chapter were as follows:

	FIFO Cost	LIFO Cost	Current Cost
7 units at $75	$525		
LIFO base quantity: 4 units at $50 . .		$200	
19x2 LIFO layer: 3 units at $60		180	
LIFO total		$380	
7 units at $85			$595

The company's transactions in 19x3 and other data were as follows:

	No. of Units	Amount per Unit
Inventory, January 1, 19x3	7	
January 1–September 30:		
Purchases	+13	$ 85 (cost)
Sales	− 9	100 (selling price)
Inventory, September 30, 19x3	11	
October 1–December 31:		
Sales	− 5	100 (selling price)
Inventory, December 31, 19x3	6	

On September 30, Alpha's supplier announced an increase in the price to $90 a unit. Alpha Company had no general and administrative expenses and no income tax expense in 19x3.

a. Calculate the amount of the inventory holding gain or loss that took place in 19x3. (Remember: The answer to this is *not* affected by the company's choice of inventory costing method.)

b. Calculate the FIFO cost of goods available, the FIFO cost of goods sold, the FIFO cost of the December 31, 19x3, inventory, and FIFO net income for 19x3.

c. Calculate the LIFO cost of goods available, the LIFO cost of goods sold, the LIFO cost of the December 31, 19x3, inventory, and LIFO net income for 19x3.

d. Calculate the current cost of goods available, the current cost of goods sold, the current cost of the December 31, 19x3, inventory, and current-cost net income for 19x3.

e. Assuming that Alpha Company used the FIFO method, calculate the unrealized holding gain at the beginning and end of 19x3 and the realized holding gain or loss (inventory profit or loss) for the year.

f. Assuming that Alpha Company used the LIFO method, calculate the unrealized holding gain at the beginning and end of 19x3 and the realized holding gain or loss for the year.

g. Ignoring the effects of income taxes, if any, which balance sheet amounts are affected by an unrealized holding gain? Are these amounts overstated or understated?

h. Explain the reasons for the difference between the realized holding gain under FIFO and the comparable amount under LIFO.

i. LIFO-cost income in 19x2 contained a $30 realized holding *loss*. Explain the reasons for any difference between this amount and the 19x3 amount in your answer to (f).

6. Calculating Inventory Holding Gains and Losses.   Company A had 50,000 units of merchandise in inventory on January 1, 19x1. The replacement cost of these units at that time was $2 a unit.

The company bought 40,000 units between January 1 and May 15, 19x1, at a cost of $2 each. It sold 55,000 units during this period at a price of $3 each.

On May 16, 19x1, Company A's supplier increased the wholesale price of this merchandise from $2.00 to $2.20. The company bought 60,000 units at this price between May 16 and the end of the year and sold 35,000 units at an average price of $3.10. Replacement cost remained at $2.20 a unit through the end of 19x1. The company's inventory on December 31, 19x1, amounted to 60,000 units.

a. Calculate the current cost of goods sold in 19x1 and the current cost of the inventory on December 31, 19x1.

b. Calculate the holding gain or loss for the year.

c. Calculate the current-cost margin for the year.

7. Company without Inventories.   Company B is in the same business as Company A (see problem 6) but carries no inventories. Between January 1 and May 15, 19x1, it bought 55,000 units of merchandise at a cost of $2 each; it sold 55,000 units during this period at a price of $3 each.

Between May 16 and December 31, 19x1, it bought 35,000 units at $2.20 a unit and sold 35,000 units at a price of $3.10 each.

a. Calculate the current cost of goods sold, the inventory holding gain or loss which arose during the year, and the current-cost margin for the year.
b. What conclusion can you draw from a comparison of Company B's performance with that of Company A?

8. Realized Inventory Holding Gains and Losses. Company A (see problem 6) uses the FIFO method to cost inventories and the merchandise it sells. On January 1, 19x1, the FIFO cost of its inventory was $1.95 a unit.

a. Calculate the FIFO cost of goods sold during 19x1 and the FIFO cost of the December 31, 19x1, inventory.
b. Calculate the unrealized inventory holding gain or loss on January 1 and on December 31, 19x1.
c. Calculate the amount of inventory holding gain or loss that was included in pretax income for 19x1. How would this amount be reported to the shareholders?

Exercises and Problems

9. LIFO Costing Exercise. A company had 60,000 units in inventory on January 1, 19x8, at the following LIFO cost:

	No. of Units	Unit Cost	Total Cost
Base quantity	30,000	$ 5	$150,000
19x1 layer	15,000	6	90,000
19x4 layer	10,000	8	80,000
19x6 layer	5,000	10	50,000
Total.............	60,000		$370,000

It made the following purchases and sales during 19x8 and 19x9:

January 1–June 30, 19x8	Sales, 40,000 units
July 1, 19x8....................	Purchase, 100,000 units @ $12
July 1–December 31, 19x8	Sales, 50,000 units
January 1–June 30, 19x9	Sales, 60,000 units
July 1, 19x9....................	Purchase, 100,000 units @ $13
July 1–December 31, 19x9	Sales, 70,000 units

Calculate the LIFO cost of goods sold and the LIFO cost of the ending inventory for each year—based on the *periodic* inventory method.

10. FIFO Costing Exercise. A company had 60,000 units in inventory on January 1, 19x8, at a FIFO cost of $11 a unit. It made the purchases and sales in 19x8 and 19x9 described in Problem 9. The market value of the company's inventories was determined to be $12.50 at the end of 19x8 and $12.40 at the end of 19x9.

a. Calculate the FIFO cost of goods sold and the FIFO cost of the ending inventory for each year.
b. Apply the lower-of-cost-or-market rule to determine the inventory and the cost of goods sold for each year.

11. Average Costing Exercise. A company had 60,000 units in inventory on January 1, 19x8, at an average cost of $10.90 a unit. It made the purchases and sales in 19x8 and 19x9 described in problem 9.

a. Calculate the cost of goods sold and the cost of the ending inventory for each year on an average costing basis, assuming a *periodic* inventory measurement system.
b. Repeat the calculations in (*a*), assuming a *perpetual* inventory measurement system—that is, average cost is recalculated after each purchase.
c. Using the market-value information contained in problem 10, apply the lower-of-cost-or-market rule to determine the inventory and the cost of goods sold for each year.
d. Comment on the numerical differences among your answers to parts (*a*), (*b*), and (*c*) and the answers to problems 9 and 10.

12. Current Costing.   Coastal Company had 10,000 pounds of product in inventory on January 1, 19x2. The replacement cost of that inventory on that date was $10 a pound. The following events took place during 19x2:

Jan. 30:   Supplier announced a price increase to $11 a pound.
Feb. 20:   Company sold 3,000 pounds at a price of $15 a pound.
May 15:   Supplier announced a price increase to $12 a pound.
June 6:   Company sold 4,000 pounds at a price of $15 a pound.
Sept. 15:   Company bought 5,000 pounds at a price of $12 a pound.
Dec. 10:   Supplier announced a price decrease to $11.50 a pound.

a. Calculate the cost of goods sold and the cost of the ending inventory on a current-cost basis.
b. Calculate the inventory holding gain or loss arising during the year.

13. Realized Inventory Holding Gains and Losses.   Coastal Company (see problem 12) used FIFO to account for its inventories and the cost of goods sold in 19x2. The FIFO inventory cost on January 1, 19x2, was $9.80 a pound. The market value of the year-end inventory was greater than its cost.

a. Calculate the FIFO cost of goods sold for 19x2.
b. Calculate the amount of the unrealized holding gain, if any, (1) at the beginning of 19x2, and (2) at the end of 19x2.

c. How much of the FIFO gross margin consisted of realized holding gains and losses?

14. Realized Inventory Holding Gains and Losses (LIFO). Suppose Coastal Company (see problem 12) used LIFO to cost its inventory and the cost of goods sold in 19x2. Coastal applies LIFO using the periodic inventory method. The LIFO cost of the January 1, 19x2, inventory was as follows:

Base quantity	6,000 pounds	$6.00	$36,000
19x0 layer	3,000 pounds	8.50	25,500
19x1 layer	1,000 pounds	9.50	9,500
Total.............	10,000 pounds		$71,000

a. Calculate the LIFO cost of goods sold for 19x2.
b. Calculate the amount of the unrealized holding gain, if any, (1) at the beginning of 19x2, and (2) at the end of 19x2.
c. How much of the LIFO gross margin consisted of realized holding gains and losses?

15. Calculating Inventory Holding Gains and Losses. Prescott Company started the year 19x8 with an inventory of 50,000 units of merchandise. The replacement cost of this merchandise was $2.00 a unit on January 1; it rose to $2.50 on March 22, to $2.80 on July 1, and to $3.00 on September 16. It remained at $3.00 to the end of the year.

The following purchases and sales were made during 19x8:

Period	Purchases	Sales
January 1–March 21.........	60,000 × $2.00	45,000 × $2.70
March 22–June 30	70,000 × 2.50	65,000 × 3.20
July 1–September 15	50,000 × 2.80	65,000 × 3.40
September 16–December 31..	40,000 × 3.00	60,000 × 3.50
Total	220,000	235,000

The company had 35,000 units in inventory at the end of 19x8.

a. Calculate the current cost of goods sold in 19x8 and the current cost of the inventory on December 31, 19x8.
b. Calculate the holding gain or loss for the year.
c. Calculate the current-cost margin for the year.

16. Realized Inventory Holding Gains and Losses. Prescott Company (see problem 15) used LIFO to account for its inventories and the cost of goods sold. Prescott applies LIFO using the periodic inventory method. The LIFO cost of its January 1, 19x8, inventories was:

Base quantity	30,000 units × $1.00	$30,000
19x2 layer	16,000 units × 1.40	22,400
19x5 layer	4,000 units × 1.60	6,400
Total.............	50,000 units	$58,800

a. Calculate the LIFO cost of goods sold during 19x8 and the LIFO cost of the December 31, 19x8, inventory.

b. Calculate the unrealized inventory holding gain or loss (1) on January 1, 19x8, and (2) on December 31, 19x8.

c. Calculate the amount of inventory holding gain or loss that was included in pretax income for 19x8. How would this amount be reported to the shareholders?

17. Supplying Missing Amounts. You have the following information from three companies for a recent year:

	Company A	Company B	Company C
Current cost, beginning inventory............	$100	E	$ 50
Current cost, ending inventory	110	$150	65
Current cost of goods sold	315	650	J
Historical cost, beginning inventory............	A	120	45
Historical cost, ending inventory...	65	110	K
Historical cost of goods sold......	320	F	285
Holding gain (loss) arising during the year................	B	20	L
Holding gain (loss) realized during the year................	C	G	(5)
Unrealized holding gain, beginning of year..............	40	80	M
Unrealized holding gain, end of year	D	H	Zero

a. Make the calculations necessary to supply the missing amounts.

b. Identify each company as a probable user of FIFO or a probable user of LIFO. Explain how you reached your conclusion in each case.

18. FIFO and LIFO Costs. Paragon Corporation was founded in January, 19x1. Its first three purchases of merchandise were (in chronological order) 900 units at $450 each, 1,600 units at $480, and 1,200 units at $530.

By early December, Paragon's management knew that 3,500 units would be sold by year-end at an average selling price of $840. Management decided to purchase an additional 400 units in December at a unit cost of $575. Paragon's supplier, anxious to increase 19x1 sales, offered a substantial quantity discount if Paragon would triple the size of its order. Under the terms of this offer, Paragon could buy 1,200 units at a unit cost of $535.

a. What effect, if any, would the December purchase decision have had on Paragon's FIFO-based financial statements in 19x1?

b. What effect, if any, would the December purchase decision have had on Paragon's LIFO-based financial statements in 19x1, if units in each year's LIFO inventory layer are entered in the order in which they are bought?

19. Meaning of Published Replacement Cost Data. The balance sheet in Crown, Inc.'s annual report described the company's inventories as follows:

Inventories—substantially all stated at cost on "last-in, first-
out" basis with current replacement cost approximately
$28,100,000 in excess of stated cost $53,334,933

A year earlier, the corresponding inventory cost was $56,047,919, and the current replacement cost was approximately $24,200,000 in excess of stated cost.

What information about the financial position and operations of the company is provided by the amounts of the excess of replacement cost over stated cost?

20. FIFO Cost and Lower-of-Cost-or-Market. Percy, Inc.'s inventory purchases in 19x2 were as follows:

Date	Quantity	Unit Cost
January 18	3,500	$14
May 12	4,200	28
October 3	2,700	37
December 20	1,100	34

Percy uses the FIFO cost method and applies the lower-of-cost-or-market rule each year-end.

The merchandise on hand on January 1 had been written down to $15 a unit. During the year, 10,900 units were sold at an average selling price of $41. At year-end, Percy's inventory consisted of 1,400 units whose market value was $32 a unit. Operating expenses (other than the cost of goods sold and write-down loss) were $114,900.

a. What was the amount of the loss from writing down the year-end inventory to its market value?
b. Prepare Percy, Inc.'s income statement for 19x2. Ignore income taxes.

21. FIFO Cost and Lower-of-Cost-or-Market. Riley Corporation had 850 units of merchandise on hand on December 31, 19x3; all were reflected in inventory at that date's $22 market value. During 19x4, Riley had the following transactions:

March 18..........	Bought	1,750	@	?
July 9.............	Sold	1,630	@	$56
August 3..........	Bought	?	@	$31
October 5	Sold	1,510	@	$58
November 30	Bought	300	@	$34

Riley used the perpetual system of inventory recordkeeping and recorded FIFO-based cost of goods sold of $38,200 on July 9 and $40,990 on October 5. When Riley discovered that the market value of all 1,200 units on hand at December 31 was less than their recorded costs, it recorded a $3,300 write-down loss. Operating expenses (other than the cost of goods sold and write-down loss) were $74,230.

a. At what amount should inventory be recorded in Riley Corporation's December 31, 19x4, balance sheet?
b. Prepare Riley Corporation's 19x4 income statement. Ignore income taxes.

22. LIFO Layers. Blackwell Corporation's December 31, 19x4, LIFO-based inventory consisted of 5,000 units at $48 each, bought in 19x2, and 15,000 units at $45 each, bought in 19x1 when the company was founded. During 19x5, 45,000 units were sold. Purchases in 19x5 occurred in April (15,000 units at $59 each), in August (13,000 at $60.50), and in December (at $62 each). Annual increments to inventory, if any, were added in the order in which units were bought during the year of the increment.

a. If Blackwell had wanted to avoid a LIFO liquidation, how many units should it have purchased in December?
b. What would have been the effect on the year-end inventory and on 19x5 income before taxes if Blackwell had purchased 6,000 *fewer* units than indicated in your answer to *a*?
c. What would have been the effect on the year-end inventory and on 19x5 income before taxes if Blackwell had purchased 6,000 *more* units than indicated in your answer to *a*?
d. By what amounts would your answers to parts *a*, *b*, and *c* be different if the units bought in December had had a unit cost of $60 (instead of $62)?

23. LIFO Liquidation. Cox Associates accounts for its inventories on a LIFO basis. It experienced LIFO liquidations in 19x4 and 19x6:

	Units	Unit Cost	Ending Inventory	Replacement Cost at End of Year
December 31, 19x1	400 ×	$ 8 =	$3,200	$ 9.50
December 31, 19x2:				
Beginning inventory	400 ×	8 = 3,200		
Purchase, 19x2	300 ×	10 = 3,000	6,200	12.00
December 31, 19x3:				
Beginning inventory	700	= 6,200		
Purchase, 19x3	200 ×	13 = 2,600	8,800	14.50
December 31, 19x4	675 ×	? =	?	16.00
December 31, 19x5:				
Beginning inventory	675 ×	? = ?		
Purchase, 19x5	320 ×	15 = 4,800	?	19.00
December 31, 19x6	350 ×	? =	?	20.00

The company could have avoided these liquidations by making the necessary purchases at the prices prevailing in December of those years. These were equal in each case to the replacement cost at year-end, shown in the right-hand column of the table.

a. What was the effect of each year's LIFO liquidation on Cox Associates' income before taxes?

b. What was the effect of the spread between the LIFO cost and the current cost of the inventory on each year's financial statements?

24. LIFO Liquidation: Effect of Managerial Decision. On November 1, 19x7, Bristol Bearing Company suffered a strike by its production personnel. This strike was expected to continue into 19x8. To meet customer demand, Bristol's management faced the prospect of having to sell more bearings during the year than the company had been able to produce.

Bristol's LIFO-based beginning-of-year inventory consisted of the following:

Base quantity	16,000 units at $ 7.00	$112,000
19x3 layer	12,000 units at $ 8.50	102,000
19x5 layer	4,000 units at $ 9.25	37,000
19x6 layer	28,000 units at $10.40	291,200
Total		$542,200

During the first ten months of 19x7, Bristol sold 152,000 units at $25 each and produced 165,000 new units, the first 90,000 at a cost of $11.50 each and then 75,000 units at $12 each. Any units sold during November and December would also be priced at $25 a unit.

At a meeting of Bristol's top management on November 1, the sales director proposed meeting customer demand until 10,000 units were still on hand, while the company's controller argued that 25,000 units should remain unsold at the end of the year. The production manager advocated maintaining the same inventory level that existed at the beginning of the year, and the head of purchasing presented the case for suspending sales immediately.

a. Calculate Bristol's gross margin under each of the four proposals.
b. Assuming that without the strike Bristol Bearing Company could have produced up to an additional 63,000 units in 19x7 at a cost of $12 each, calculate the impact of any LIFO liquidation on each proposal's gross margin outcome.
c. Do the calculations in parts *a* and *b* provide an adequate basis for management's choice among these four proposals? What additional information would you find useful?

25. Inventory Profits, Holding Gains.   Royce Corporation was founded late in 19x1. It bought inventory before year-end and therefore was able to engage in merchandise transactions throughout 19x2. Listed below are the events that related to Royce's inventory transactions.

December 29, 19x1	Buy 15,000 @ $2.00
January 6, 19x2	Replacement cost = $2.15
January 7–August 11	Sell 6,000 @ $7.00
August 12	Replacement cost = $2.20
August 13–December 29	Sell 4,000 @ $8.50
September 20	Buy 12,000 @ $2.20
December 30, 19x2	Replacement cost = $2.30

During 19x2, Royce's other expenses totaled $20,000, and income taxes should be ignored.

a. Using FIFO cost, calculate the 19x2 net income and the inventory amount that will appear in the December 31, 19x2, balance sheet.
b. Prepare the same accounting measurements using the current-cost approach.
c. Calculate the amount of inventory profit or loss contained in the FIFO-cost net income included in your answer to part *a*.
d. Reconcile the amount of inventory profit contained in your answer to part *c* with the holding gain appearing in your answer to part *b*.

26. Realized/Unrealized Holding Gains. Royce Corporation (see problem 25) experienced the following events in 19x3 (the year after the events described in problem 25):

January 2–April 9	Sell 9,000 @ $9.00
April 10	Replacement cost = $2.38
July 9	Buy 24,000 @ $2.38
April 11–December 29	Sell 11,000 @ $10.00
December 30	Replacement cost = $2.45

During 19x3, Royce's other expenses totaled $55,000; income taxes should be ignored.

a. Using FIFO cost, calculate the 19x3 net income and the inventory amount that will appear in the December 31, 19x3, balance sheet.
b. Prepare the same accounting measurements using the current-cost approach.
c. Calculate the amounts of the realized and unrealized portions of the holding gain or loss in 19x3, and reconcile these amounts with the unrealized inventory holding gains as of January 1 and December 31, 19x3.

27. Change from FIFO to LIFO; Recommendation to Management. Weeks Woolen Company had always used the FIFO method of inventory costing. For the years 19x7 and 19x8, its reported income or loss before deducting income taxes was as follows:

19x7	$234,690 profit
19x8	60,140 loss

Early in 19x9, the company's management was considering shifting to the LIFO basis. Investigation revealed that the inventory amounts for the three years were or would have been as follows:

	Pounds	FIFO Amount	LIFO Amount
December 31, 19x6.	500,000	$225,000	$225,000
December 31, 19x7.	475,000	403,000	210,000
December 31, 19x8.	513,000	338,000	235,000

The cost of goods purchased amounted to $400,000 in 19x7 and $350,000 in 19x8. The inventory had a market value of 90 cents a pound on December 31, 19x7, and 66 cents a pound on December 31, 19x8.

a. Calculate the income before taxes that Weeks Woolen Company would have reported each year if it had adopted the LIFO method of inventory costing as of January 1, 19x7.
b. Would adoption of LIFO as of that date have led to more informative income statements for the two years? Explain your reasoning.

c. By the beginning of 19x9, management no longer had the option of adopting LIFO as of January 1, 19x7, but it could adopt it as of January 1, 19x8. Write a brief report to management, recommending for or against adoption of LIFO as of that date, giving reasons for your recommendation.

28. LIFO Costing; Inventory Recordkeeping. Monumental Company uses FIFO for inventory recordkeeping in its perpetual inventory system and LIFO for external financial reporting. The inventory accounts showed the following balances on January 1, 19x1:

> Inventories (50,000 units)......... $50,000 dr.
> LIFO Inventory Adjustment .... 20,000 cr.

The balance in the LIFO Inventory Adjustment account measured the difference between LIFO and FIFO inventory costs on that date. In other words, the LIFO cost of the January 1 inventory was $30,000.

Purchases and sales during the year were as follows:

Quarter	Purchases	Sales
1	50,000 units × $1.10	45,000 units
2	40,000 × 1.15	50,000
3	60,000 × 1.12	55,000
4	70,000 × 1.25	60,000

Annual increments to the LIFO inventory were measured at the prices paid for the first units purchased during the year.

a. Calculate the FIFO cost of goods sold for each quarter and for the year as a whole.

b. Calculate the LIFO cost of goods sold for the year.

c. Set up a T-account to represent the Inventories account, enter the opening balance, record the purchases and cost of goods sold as the company would record them each quarter on a FIFO basis, and calculate the ending balance in this account.

d. Prepare the entry that should be made to adjust the balance in the LIFO Inventory Adjustment account at the end of the year.

e. Management told the shareholders that "inventory losses" in the fourth quarter erased most of the net income reported on the interim financial statements for the first three quarters of the year, despite record fourth-quarter sales. Explain what happened.

29. Effect of Inventory Method on Income. Barrow Company uses FIFO for inventory recordkeeping in its perpetual inventory system and periodic LIFO for external financial reporting. The company had an inventory of 15,000 pounds of product on January 1, 19x9. This was shown on the balance sheet in the following way:

Inventory, at FIFO cost		$30,000
Less: Adjustment to reduce inventory to a LIFO basis		15,200
Inventory, at LIFO cost.		$14,800

The supporting data showed the following:

Base quantity.	8,000 lbs. × $0.80	$ 6,400
19x0 layer.	4,000 lbs. × $1.00	4,000
19x3 layer.	2,000 lbs. × $1.40	2,800
19x6 layer.	1,000 lbs. × $1.60	1,600
Total inventory, at LIFO cost		$14,800

The company bought 25,000 pounds of material during 19x9 and sold 29,000 pounds. Each unit purchased cost $2.50, and the purchase price remained constant at this level throughout the year. On December 31, 19x9, however, the company's supplier announced that the price of the material had been raised to $3, effective immediately.

a. Calculate the December 31, 19x9, inventory on a LIFO basis.
b. Suppose Barrow had always used FIFO instead of LIFO. By what amount would FIFO income before taxes in 19x9 have differed from the LIFO income Barrow actually reported in that year?
c. What was the total effect of Barrow Company's use of LIFO on income before taxes in all years since the adoption of LIFO, taken together?

30. Relationship of Inventory Growth to Effects of Inventory Method. Chesapeake Company started in business on January 1, 19x0, by purchasing 10,000 units of merchandise at a cost of $10 each. Sales amounted to 50,000 units in 19x0, and the company had 10,000 units in inventory at the end of 19x0.

The purchase price of the merchandise increased by $1 a unit on January 1 of each year for the next four years. For example, all purchases in 19x0 were made at a price of $10, all purchases in 19x1 cost $11, and all purchases in 19x4 cost $14. The income tax rate was 40 percent for the entire five-year period, and the company had taxable income each year.

a. Calculate the cost of the ending inventory for each of the five years on the assumption that the inventory quantity remained at its 19x0 level: (1) on a FIFO basis, and (2) on a LIFO basis.
b. Repeat the calculations called for in part a on the assumption that year-end inventory quantities increased by 2,000 units each year, beginning in 19x1.
c. Repeat the calculations for the situation described in part b, except that the year-end inventory quantity fell to 4,000 units in 19x3 and then returned to 18,000 units at the end of 19x4.

d. Given these calculations, describe briefly how growth influences the effects of the inventory costing method choice on income and cash flow.

31. Using LIFO to Keep Holding Gains off the Income Statement. Ethereal Spirits Company is a wholesale distributor of wines and liquors. It measures all its inventories on a LIFO basis. Increments to the LIFO inventories in any year are measured at the prices paid for the first units purchased during the year.

One of Ethereal's products is Sonoma Mountain Red, produced and bottled by the Carson Brothers Winery in California. Ethereal's inventory of this product on January 1, 19x9, was as follows:

	No. of Gallons	LIFO Cost Per Unit	LIFO Cost Total
Base quantity	1,000	$1.50	$1,500
19x2 layer	200	2.00	400
19x7 layer	100	2.20	220
Total	1,300		$2,120

The price charged by Carson Brothers was $2.50 a gallon on January 1, 19x9, and remained at that level until October 15, 19x9, when it was increased to $2.75. Ethereal's purchases and sales during 19x9 were as follows:

	Gallons Purchased	Gallons Sold
Prior to October 15	8,000	6,000
From October 15 to December 31	3,000	4,000
Total	11,000	10,000

a. Calculate the current cost of goods sold in 19x9 and the current cost of the December 31, 19x9, inventory.
b. Calculate the LIFO cost of goods sold for 19x9 and the LIFO cost of the December 31, 19x9, inventory.
c. Calculate the total inventory holding gain or loss arising during 19x9, including both the realized and the unrealized components.
d. Using data from this problem, comment on the proposition that LIFO keeps inventory holding gains and losses out of the income statement as long as the number of units purchased in any year equals or exceeds the number of units sold.

32. Effect of Inventory Method on Managerial Decision. "We'd be foolish to buy now," Helen Hunt, Carthage Company's purchasing agent, said. "The price can't be any higher next spring than it is now, and I expect it to be much lower. We can make $7,000 by keeping our inventory down to 80,000 pounds until the new crop comes in next year."

"You forget," replied Dave Jones, the company's controller, "that if we don't replace these inventories before the end of the year, we'll lose our favorable LIFO base. Not only that, but if you aim at an 80,000-pound inventory, you'll be buying in uneconomically small lots. You'll probably have to pay premiums on rush orders, too."

Carthage Company is a large wholesale distributor of food products. One product is made from citrus fruits. The annual price is determined largely by the size of the winter crop in Florida. A very severe winter in 19x6–19x7 caused heavy damage to the Florida citrus crop. The purchase price went up to 32 cents a pound in January 19x7 and remained at this level throughout the year.

In 19x1, the company had adopted the LIFO method of inventory costing for all its products, both for tax purposes and for financial reporting. The balances in the company's inventory accounts on January 1, 19x1, became the costs of the LIFO base quantities.

Separate accounts were established at that time for the materials cost and processing cost components of the LIFO inventories. The company's inventories of its citrus-based product on January 1, 19x1, contained materials with a purchase weight of 100,000 pounds, at an inventory cost of 20 cents a pound, a total of $20,000. Increments to inventories in subsequent years were at the prices paid for the first purchases during the year cumulating to the incremental quantity.

The following table shows purchases and inventory data for the materials content of this product for the years 19x1 through 19x7:

Year	Beginning-of-Year Inventory (Pounds)	Purchases (Pounds)	Price Paid for First Purchases (Per Pound)	Total Cost of Materials Purchased
19x1	100,000	300,000	$0.20	$ 60,000
19x2	100,000	335,000	0.22	73,700
19x3	110,000	400,000	0.23	92,000
19x4	150,000	400,000	0.24	96,000
19x5	180,000	295,000	0.30	88,500
19x6	130,000	430,000	0.26	111,800
19x7	200,000	300,000*	0.32	96,000*

* Through October.

Because of the high purchase prices, Hunt deliberately bought less citrus fruit in 19x7 than the company was using. As a result, the inventory had dropped to 80,000 pounds by the end of October 19x7, the quantity referred to in the conversation quoted earlier. Her recommendation was to maintain inventories of this product at this level until the new crop was processed in the spring of 19x8.

Jones opposed this and recommended that inventories be rebuilt to 200,000 pounds by the end of 19x7, at a purchase price of about 32 cents a pound. He estimated that if this were not done, the lower inventory levels would increase purchasing and handling costs by $2,000 in 19x7 and $400 in 19x8.

Both executives agreed that an inventory of 200,000 pounds of this product was an optimum inventory level. If her proposal was accepted, Hunt planned to rebuild inventories to this level as soon as the 19x8 crop was processed. An average crop in 19x8 would lead to a price of about 26 cents a pound.

At this point, Peter Brooks, the production superintendent, offered a countersuggestion. "Why not go part-way? Build up to 130,000 pounds now, and go the rest of the way to 200,000 pounds when the new crop comes in next year? That way we could cut the purchase-and-handling penalty to about $1,000 in 19x7 and $200 in 19x8."

The income tax in both years was 40 percent of taxable income.

a. Calculate the materials cost component of the cost of goods sold and the materials cost component of the end-of-year inventory of this product for each year, 19x1–19x6.
b. By how much would 19x7 reported income before taxes have increased or decreased if Helen Hunt's proposal had been accepted?
c. Assuming that all purchases, penalties, and income taxes are paid for immediately in cash, and that all of the estimates were correct, which of the three alternatives would have led to the largest cash balance after inventories were replenished in 19x8?
d. Should Helen Hunt's proposal have been accepted? Would your conclusion be different if Carthage Company's inventory had been on FIFO? How, if at all, does the inventory costing method influence decisions of this kind?

Chapter 9

Plant Assets

A business enterprise incurs costs to create income—either by generating revenues in excess of cost or by reducing other costs. These income effects may be expected to occur either in the current period or in one or more future periods. The cost of any resource that has been consumed to obtain the current period's revenues is an expense. By contrast, the cost of any resource that will be used to obtain revenues or reduce operating costs in future accounting periods is an asset. When an expenditure qualifies to be recorded as an asset, it is said to be *capitalized.*

These distinctions aren't always easy to apply in practice, and accountants therefore have to exercise judgment. Our objective in this chapter is to examine the factors that affect capitalization decisions and to learn how accountants then determine when capitalized costs become expenses in future periods.

Capitalizable Costs

An expenditure to acquire an asset is often accompanied by one or more **ancillary expenditures,** more or less related to the acquisition. Our task in this section is to study how accountants decide whether to capitalize these costs.

Basic Principle

The basic principle is that the cost of an asset consists of all outlays necessary to render the asset suitable for its intended use. For example, Dixon Company acquired a machine at a total cost of $61,800, incurred as follows:

```
                        TERMINOLOGY REMINDER
Cost:              The amount of resources sacrificed to obtain
                   something or achieve some objective.
Expense:           The cost of resources given up to obtain revenues
                   of the current period.
Expenditure:       Any use of resources. Companies make expendi-
                   tures when they acquire a machine, when they use
                   a machine, or when they use their employees' ser-
                   vices. Some expenditures lead to expenses of the
                   current period, others do not.
Capitalized costs: Expenditures of the current period which are ex-
                   pected to generate revenues in future periods.
                   Such costs are costs of assets until the period in
                   which revenues occur, at which time they become
                   expenses.
```

Vendor price, net of discount...........	$53,500
Freight..............................	1,800
Concrete foundation for machine	2,200
Installation	3,000
Test runs (three weeks)...............	1,300
Total...........................	$61,800

All these costs were necessary to enable Dixon Company to begin using the machine commercially. Even though company employees built the foundation, installed the machine, and conducted the test runs, the costs of these activities were just as much part of the machine as the price charged by the vendor for the machine itself.

The same principle applies to real property—land and buildings. The cost of land therefore includes not only the contract price but also brokers' commissions and legal fees. The cost of a building includes the contract price or construction costs, architects' charges, building permit fees, and costs incurred in the preparation of plans, specifications, blueprints, etc.

Joint Acquisition Cost

Two or more assets are sometimes acquired at a single purchase price, known as their *joint cost*. The joint cost is usually allocated on the basis of the relative market values of the purchased assets. For example, Dixon Company bought a building and its site for a lump sum of $8 million. Consultation with an independent appraiser provided the following estimated market values: land $3 million and building $9 million. Since the sum ($12 million) exceeds the cost actually incurred ($8 million), allocation is effected on the basis of the assets' relative market values:

	Market Value	Percentage	Allocated Cost
Land	$ 3 million	25%	$2 million
Building	9 million	75%	6 million
Total	$12 million		$8 million

Since the relative values are 25 percent land and 75 percent building, 25 percent of the $8 million cost is allocated to the land ($2 million) and 75 percent is assigned to the building ($6 million). This approach is based on the assumption that the separate prices of the individual assets would have borne the same relationship to market value as in the joint acquisition.

Cost of Unwanted Assets. A company may sometimes buy a group of assets to obtain one of them. For example, Eagle, Inc., bought land for $5 million *and* an old loft building on the land for $2 million, intending to raze the building and erect a new one. In this case, the entire purchase price ($7 million) clearly relates to the land. What distinguishes this situation from the previous case is that we don't have two joint products, because only the land is desired. Were Eagle then to expend $200,000 to demolish the old building, this too would be treated as a cost of the land because it's a cost incurred to place the land in a condition to be used as the site of the new structure.

Noncash Acquisitions

When a company acquires an asset for consideration other than cash or the promise of cash, this is called a *nonmonetary transaction*. The basic rule when the assets exchanged are dissimilar is to record the acquired asset at the current value of the asset(s) exchanged for it. For example, if a company acquires a machine in exchange for government bonds which had cost $4,000 and whose current market value is $5,000, it will record the machine's cost as $5,000 and recognize a $1,000 gain.

When *similar* assets are exchanged, however, the asset acquired is usually recorded at the same amount as the asset given up. For example, Garden Company exchanges land in a distant location for property adjacent to one of its factories, with both parties agreeing that each tract is worth $95,000. Garden Company bought the distant land some years ago at a total cost of $80,000. Because the assets are similar, the new property is recorded at $80,000, the cost basis of the land given up. The accounting rationale is that because trading similar assets does not signify culmination of the earning process, a ($15,000) gain shouldn't be recorded. The earning process is concluded only when dissimilar assets are traded.

The accounting treatment is different if the current value of each property is *less* than its cost basis. If the market value of each property in

Garden Company's exchange in $70,000 (rather than the earlier $95,000), trading land that had cost $80,000 indicates that a $10,000 loss had already occurred. In the light of accountants' preference for reporting losses sooner rather than later, the $10,000 indicated loss is recognized and the newly acquired land is recorded at its $70,000 market value. These two cases are summarized in the upper portion of Exhibit 9–1.

EXHIBIT 9–1
Exchanging Similar Assets

	Old Basis of Old Asset	Fair Value	Indicated Gain (Loss)	Reported Gain (Loss)	Basis for New Asset
No cash exchanged:					
Case 1.............	$80,000	$95,000	$ 15,000	—	$80,000
Case 2............	$80,000	$70,000	$(10,000)	$(10,000)	$70,000
Some cash paid:					
Case 1					
Truck............	$ 6,000	$ 7,000	$ 1,000		
Cash	2,500	2,500			
Total	$ 8,500	$ 9,500		—	$ 8,500
Case 2					
Truck............	$ 6,000	$ 5,700	$ (300)		
Cash	2,500	2,500			
Total	$ 8,500	$ 8,200		$ (300)	$ 8,200

These rules for the exchange of similar assets apply even when some cash is included in the exchange. For instance, Circle Corporation acquired a new delivery truck by giving up an old truck and cash. The cost of the old truck, less accumulated depreciation, was $6,000, its market value was $7,000, and cash paid was $2,500. The new truck was recorded at $8,500, the sum of the cash ($2,500) and the undepreciated portion of the old truck ($6,000). If the market value of the old truck had been $5,700, the indicated loss of $300 ($6,000 − $5,700) would have been recorded, and the new truck would have been recorded at $8,200 ($2,500 + $5,700). These two exchange transactions are summarized in the lower portion of Exhibit 9–1.

Interest Cost

If a great deal of time is required to construct a plant asset and bring it to the condition necessary for its intended use, the related interest cost incurred during that period is treated by U.S. companies as a cost of the asset.[1] The amount of interest that is capitalized is the sum that would have been avoided if expenditures for the asset hadn't been made.

Interest capitalization raises a number of issues which can be dealt with effectively only in an advanced text. The basic principle, however, is that interest on interest-bearing debt outstanding during the period of construction is just as much a cost of bringing a plant asset to the condition necessary for its intended use as are the costs of bricks and bricklayers' services.

Ancillary Expenditures: Pragmatic Criteria

In practice, the facts are often less clear-cut than a textbook description may make them appear. Although the Financial Accounting Standards Board is making an effort to reduce freedom of choice on accounting questions, companies still have a good deal of latitude in applying the general measurement principles stated above. In exercising their judgment, companies' managers and accountants are influenced by pragmatic considerations, most of which generally lead to *earlier* expense recognition than the principles themselves would suggest.

Recordkeeping Convenience

Among the least impressive but by no means least important of these influences is recordkeeping convenience. Work in connection with an asset already in place frequently has a mixture of objectives: making improvements in the asset, extending its *useful life,* and doing normal maintenance. Separating the costs of achieving each of these objectives from the costs of achieving the others is difficult and often requires decisions that can only be characterized as arbitrary. Treating all such expenditures as expenses makes life a good deal simpler.

Much the same reasoning is often used to justify expensing the cost of hand tools and other high-volume, low-unit-cost items that will be used for more than a year. Although the total cost of these items may be millions of dollars a year in large corporations, they are usually expensed to avoid the cost of maintaining detailed property records. This also relieves accountants of the need to make a large number of accounting judgments. A limit of, say, $500 is established: the costs of all items costing less than this are expensed automatically, no matter how long they are expected to last.

---

[1] The same capitalization treatment also applies in the United States to assets produced for lease or sale in lengthy production processes—such as ships or real estate developments. Interest arising during the process of maturing inventories intended for sale (e.g., timber or whiskey) isn't capitalized as part of the cost of these inventories, even though the economic causes of the interest cost are essentially the same.

Tax Advantage

Another reason to expense costs that might otherwise be capitalized is the tax advantage that would result. So long as a company has current taxable income, increasing the amount of current expense will reduce current tax payments. Although treating a cost as an immediate expense rather than deferring it to future periods generally will inflate future taxable income, this is a deterrent only when the tax rate is expected to increase. Dollars saved this year are unquestionably worth more than dollars that may be saved in some future year, both because money has a time value and because the purchasing power of dollars is likely to be less in the future than it is today.

Since taxable income is not necessarily the same as accounting income, a cost may be capitalized for financial reporting while being expensed for tax purposes. The taxpayer may be better able to make a case for current tax deductibility of borderline items, however, by expensing them for both purposes.

Accounting Conservatism

When a legitimate question exists as to whether to capitalize or expense a cost, even though the decision will have no impact on tax treatment, accountants tend to expense the cost because it is the conservative thing to do. Although the cost of training cashiers to operate sophisticated cash registers could justifiably be capitalized and then expensed over several future periods, accountants are likely to treat the training cost as an expense as soon as it is incurred.

Income Control

All three factors just discussed introduce a bias toward expensing costs that might, on theoretical grounds, be capitalized. The fourth factor, income control, can work in either direction.

Managers of companies have an understandable interest in influencing the amount that is reported as net income. Net income, often expressed in terms of earnings per share, is widely regarded as a primary index of corporate performance. If earnings exceed the level anticipated by the securities market, the price per share is likely to increase; if income turns out to be disappointing, the market price is likely to decrease.

Reported income is also widely regarded as a measure of managerial skill. Even if managers' compensation isn't tied directly to the company's earnings, managers who are able to generate income levels that in turn cause the market price of the stock to rise are likely to be rewarded. Management might be expected, therefore, to select a capitalize-or-expense strategy—for costs on the borderline between asset and expense—

that will most likely help achieve a specified bias in the pattern of reported income. This strategy may be to maximize net income (by capitalizing all borderline costs) or to smooth net income (by expensing more in high-income years than in low-income years).

Consistency and Disclosure

Probably the most serious problem posed by the application of these pragmatic criteria is that they give management a great deal of power to affect reported income. To limit management's ability to distort net income, the accounting profession requires companies to be *consistent* from year to year in their treatment of specific types of cost. This requirement is based on the belief that a bias consistently followed impairs the usefulness of information less seriously than a bias that depends on what management wants investors to believe.

A company is said to be consistent if it adopts a set of accounting policies and applies them each year. For example, if a company's policy is to expense employee training costs as they occur, it must expense them every year, not just in years in which expensing meets management's income objectives.

Assuring total consistency in practice is very difficult, probably impossible, to achieve. Management can alter the way it views transactions from year to year even without deliberately attempting to do so. The costs of materials processed in test runs of new equipment might be classified as production costs in some years and as training costs in others.

The consistency doctrine doesn't lock a company into a single set of accounting practices forever. Conditions change, and companies change the ways they account for some of their assets, liabilities, and owners' equity from time to time. For example, partly because a particular amount is not material (that is, not large enough to be significant), a company may decide to expense the cost of alterations to equipment and find this accounting practice to be satisfactory for a number of years. Sooner or later, however, it may come to a year in which the cost is large because of a large-scale plant modernization effort. Under these circumstances, the company's accountants may well insist that this cost should be capitalized and expensed over the expected remaining life of the equipment. This departure from consistent reporting is justified by the materiality of the amount. The company, however, must disclose in its financial statements the nature and dollar-amount effect of this change.

Post-Acquisition Expenditures

Although a company may spend a significant amount of money to buy a plant asset, it frequently expends additional funds to preserve and improve the asset during its operating life. This raises the question of whether such expenditures should be capitalized (i.e., added to the asset) or treated as expenses of the period in which the costs are incurred.

Betterments versus Maintenance

When a plant asset is first acquired, the criterion is whether the expenditure is necessary to render the asset suitable for its intended use, the ultimate purpose being to generate revenues in the future. When dealing with a post-acquisition expenditure, however, the question is: did the expenditure *expand* or did it *maintain* the previously anticipated service capacity of the asset? Accountants treat this as a problem of distinguishing between a **betterment,** effecting some form of progressive change, and **maintenance,** preventing or retarding retrogressive change. Costs of betterments are capitalized; maintenance costs are expensed immediately.

Although the distinction between maintenance and betterments requires the exercise of judgment, it is conceptually quite clear. A capitalizable betterment is any cost incurred to increase the lifetime productive capacity by increasing the output rate, extending the economic life past the length that was estimated at the time of acquisition, or reducing operating costs to less than their originally anticipated level. Maintenance, in contrast, is designed to conserve previously established capacity. At the time of acquisition, each asset has an expected lifetime capacity reflecting an intended maintenance policy. Any cost incurred to carry out that maintenance policy therefore is incurred to obtain the service initially expected of the asset and thus is a maintenance cost.

Maintenance versus Replacement

A second important distinction is between maintenance expenditures and replacement expenditures. The question is whether an expenditure that is made to replace one or more components of a plant asset should be treated as maintenance (a current expense) or as replacement cost (capitalized as an asset cost).

The answer depends on whether the plant asset was originally identified as a single asset or as a set of related assets. Replacement of an *entire* asset requires removing that asset from the accounting records and capitalizing the cost of the replacement. The cost of replacing *part* of an asset, however, is usually treated as a maintenance cost, unless it is expected to increase the asset's service potential or extend its useful life beyond the amounts anticipated at the time the asset was acquired. For example, although most people would regard an entire airplane as a single asset, an airline may capitalize the costs of the airframe, engines, and interior fittings as three separate assets.

As a second example, suppose a company has installed a conveyor system to transport materials, work in process, and finished products between work stations in its two-story factory. Every five years the company has to replace the treads which form the load-carrying surface of the conveyor system. If the conveyor is the unit of account and its estimated useful life is based on the assumption that the treads will be replaced periodically, then subsequent expenditures for replacement treads will be treated as maintenance costs and will be expensed immediately. If the treads are capitalized separately at the outset, however, then the cost of the original treads must be removed from the accounting records when they're replaced. The cost of replacement treads then must be capitalized in their place.

Let's suppose the conveyor is expected to last for 20 years, with treads costing $8,000 to be replaced every five years. If the cost of the first set of treads is capitalized as part of of the cost of the conveyor, it will be depreciated over 20 years at an average of $400 a year. The sum of depreciation and maintenance expenses therefore will be $400 each year, except in years 6, 11, and 16, when replacements take place. In those three years, the depreciation and maintenance expenses will total $8,400. This cost pattern is indicated by the solid line in Exhibit 9–2. The dashed

EXHIBIT 9–2
Effect of Separate Capitalization on Reported Annual Cost

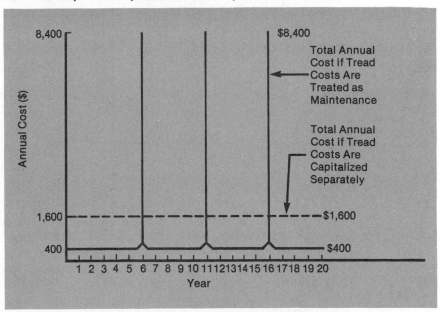

line in the exhibit depicts the annual cost if the treads are capitalized separately. In that case, the cost of each set of treads will be depreciated over five years at an average of $1,600 a year ($8,000/5), thereby smoothing the annual cost.

If the unit of account is made small enough, even a routine lubrication can be treated as a replacement with no room left for the concept of maintenance. Although this conclusion would appear to be extreme, it does point out that separate capitalization is likely to have a slight smoothing effect on year-to-year movements in operating costs.

Major Overhauls

A similar question arises in connection with expenditures made for major overhauls of existing assets. If the overhaul is made to *restore* the service potential that was anticipated at acquisition, the cost of the overhaul is treated as a maintenance cost. If the overhaul *extends* an asset's remaining lifetime service potential beyond the amount originally anticipated, the cost to achieve this extension is capitalized.

To illustrate, suppose Elastic, Inc., bought a tractor trailer for $90,000 with the expectation that it would provide five years of service. The company planned to record depreciation expense of $18,000 ($90,000/5) each year for five years. At the beginning of the fourth year, a new transmission had to be installed at a cost of $5,000. If, as a result of this development, Elastic expects the useful life of the truck now to be seven years, the cost of the new transmission will be capitalized.[2] If the truck is still expected to last only five years, the expenditure will be treated as an immediate expense.

Accounting for Depreciation

Capitalization occurs only for expenditures that are expected to provide future benefits. Annual charges for depreciation represent the accountants' effort to assign capitalized costs to the periods in which the anticipated benefits are expected to materialize.

Depreciation and Economic Value

The use of an asset's services is expected to result in future net cash flows to the company in excess of the net cash flows that would have been generated in the absence of that asset. These excess cash flows are known as the *incremental cash flows* attributable to the asset. As we saw in Chapter 6, the present value of these incremental cash flows measures the value of the asset to the company. Since management won't buy an asset that isn't expected to be worth its cost, we can assume that the present value of these cash flows is expected to be at least equal to the asset's cost at the time it is acquired.

---

[2] The $5,000 would probably be recorded as a reduction of Accumulated Depreciation rather than as an addition to the asset's original cost. In other words, rather than have the asset's $41,000 book value be based on $95,000 − $54,000, Elastic's balance sheet would reflect the amounts as $90,000 − $49,000.

This means that two amounts can be identified or estimated for every asset starting its life in a company: (1) its economic value, based on its estimated incremental cash flows, and (2) its acquisition cost. Each of these could be a starting point to calculate depreciation.

One possibility is to base depreciation on the change in value that occurs each year. As the asset's services are used during a given year, the incremental cash flows attributable to it and arising in that year are realized. This leaves fewer services available for the future and fewer cash flows; the asset's value therefore will be less at the end of the year than it was at the beginning (unless some of the estimates change). An economist would use *this* decline as the estimated depreciation for the year—that is, **economic depreciation.**

Accountants don't record economic depreciation, in part because they start with a different total amount to be depreciated. They base annual depreciation charges on the asset's original cost instead of on its value. In other words, they use *cost* to represent the asset's total lifetime service potential; depreciation in any year is the cost of the asset's services used up during the year.

Depreciable Cost

In a conventional accounting system in which expenses are measured by the historical cost of the resources used to generate current revenue, the total cost applicable to a depreciable asset's usable service potential is the difference between the asset's original cost and its end-of-life resale or salvage value. This difference is known as the **depreciable cost:**

$$\text{Depreciable Cost} = \text{Original Cost} - \text{Estimated End-of-Life Salvage Value}$$

An asset's anticipated salvage value is treated as the cost of services the company doesn't expect to use but plans to sell to someone else. In practice, salvage is often assumed to be zero, in which case the original cost becomes the depreciable cost. By contrast, *book value* is the term accountants use to refer to an asset's cost less its accumulated depreciation.

Useful Life

To determine the schedule of depreciation charges, management estimates the length of the period during which each asset is likely to be used. The usefulness of an asset is likely to be affected both by physical deterioration and by functional obsolescence. *Physical deterioration* arises through asset use, the passage of time, and accidental damage, the result being a decline in the quantity of the asset's output or a rise in its unit cost. *Obsolescence* results from shifts in market demand (e.g., the shift from cloth diapers to throwaways) or from changes in technology that cause an existing asset to be less efficient than a new unit. At some point, it pays to abandon the existing asset to be able to reap the benefits of a successor model.

TERMINOLOGY REMINDER

Depreciable cost is original cost less expected salvage value.
Book value is original cost less accumulated depreciation.

Depreciation Patterns

In our illustrations in earlier chapters, we assigned the same amount of depreciation to each year of an asset's useful life. Depreciation isn't always calculated that way in practice, nor should it be. In principle, each year's depreciation should be proportional to the year's anticipated percentage of the amount of benefit the company expects to reap from the asset during its useful life. To eliminate the possibility of year-by-year manipulation of the depreciation charge, the formula governing the amount of depreciation to be recognized each year is established when the asset is first placed in service. In the next few pages we'll describe several depreciation methods or formulas, each of which will approximate some assets' lifetime benefit patterns:

1. Straight-line depreciation.
2. Accelerated depreciation (two formulas).
3. Production unit depreciation.
4. Implicit-interest depreciation.

Straight-Line Depreciation.   In **straight-line depreciation,** the depreciation amount is the same each year, no matter how lightly or heavily the asset is used. If a new machine costing $36,000 is expected to last 12 years with an estimated $1,500 end-of-life salvage value, the amount of straight-line depreciation each year will be:

$$\frac{\$36,000 - \$1,500}{12} = \$2,875$$

For convenience, the straight-line method is usually expressed as a **depreciation rate,** equal to the reciprocal of the expected years of useful life—in our example, $1/12 = 8.33$ percent. This rate is then multiplied each year by the depreciable cost (original cost less estimated end-of-life salvage value). In practice, a salvage value of zero is almost always used except for assets with well-established resale markets, such as automobiles and trucks.

Accelerated Depreciation.   As the term implies, the **accelerated depreciation** approach produces annual depreciation amounts that are larger than the straight-line result in the earlier years and smaller in the later years. This approach therefore may also be called a *diminishing-charge* approach. Two formulas that may be used to implement this approach are the **sum-of-the-years'-digits** and the **double-rate, declining-balance** methods.

Sum-of-the-Years'-Digits Depreciation.   The first step in the sum-of-the-years'-digits method is to number each year of the asset's estimated useful life, starting with 1 for the first year, 2 for the second, and so on. The next step is to add these digits to get their sum. In our example, in which the asset is expected to last 12 years, the sum of the digits is $1 + 2 + \ldots + 12 = 78$. Using n to signify the number of years, the formula to derive this sum is as follows:

$$\text{Sum} = \frac{n(n + 1)}{2}$$

In this case, since $n = 12$, the sum is $(12 \times 13)/2 = 78$.

The third step is to assign the 12 numbers to the years in reverse order. Thus, the number 12 is assigned to year 1, the number 11 to year 2, and so on. The fourth step is to calculate a *separate* depreciation rate for each year. This is done by dividing each year's assigned number (12, 11, . . .) by the sum of the digits (78). The depreciation rates are 12/78 for the first year, 11/78 for the second, and so on, down to 1/78 for the 12th year.

The final step is to multiply these rates by the depreciable cost to determine the annual depreciation amounts. The sum of these amounts will reduce the asset's book value to its expected salvage value at the end of its estimated life. In our example, depreciable cost is $36,000 - $1,500 = $34,500, and the first year's depreciation is 12/78 $\times$ $34,500 = $5,308. This amount appears on the first line in the second column of Exhibit 9–3. The rest of this column lists the depreciation amounts for the subsequent years, computed in this way. Book value at the end of 12 years is $1,500, the amount that had been estimated at the outset to be the expected salvage value.

Double-Rate, Declining-Balance Depreciation.   Double-rate, declining-balance depreciation is calculated by using a *fixed rate* to determine

EXHIBIT 9–3
Comparison of Depreciation Schedules

Year	Sum of the Years' Digits Beginning Book Value	Annual Charge	Double Rate, Declining Balance Beginning Book Value	Annual Charge	Straight Line Beginning Book Value	Annual Charge
1	$36,000	$ 5,308	$36,000	$ 6,000	$36,000	$ 2,875
2	30,692	4,865	30,000	5,000	33,125	2,875
3	25,827	4,423	25,000	4,167	30,250	2,875
4	21,404	3,981	20,833	3,472	27,375	2,875
5	17,423	3,538	17,361	2,894	24,500	2,875
6	13,885	3,096	14,467	2,411	21,625	2,875
7	10,789	2,654	12,056	2,009	18,750	2,875
8	8,135	2,212	10,047	1,674	15,875	2,875
9	5,924	1,769	8,373	1,395	13,000	2,875
10	4,155	1,327	6,978	1,163	2,875	2,875
11	2,828	885	5,815	969	7,250	2,875
12	1,943	442	4,846	807	4,375	2,875
13	1,500	—	4,039	2,539	1,500	—
Total		$34,500		$34,500		$34,500

each period's depreciation. The fixed rate is applied to the asset's book value, which declines each year. The amount of depreciation recorded each period therefore is smaller than that of the previous period.

The fixed depreciation rate in this formula is double the straight-line rate, and salvage value is ignored when using this method. Since the straight-line rate for an asset with an estimated 12-year life is 8.33 percent a year, the double rate is 16.67 percent a year. The depreciation amounts generated by this method are shown in the fourth column of Exhibit 9–3. For year 1, depreciation is $0.167 \times \$36,000$, or $6,000; depreciation in year 2 is $0.167 \times \$30,000$, or $5,000.

As we consider the depreciation amounts for the last years of the machine's useful life, we observe that the asset's book value didn't reach the amount of the estimated salvage value by the end of year 12. Instead, the book value stands at $4,039, or $2,539 more than the estimated salvage value. If the asset were in fact sold in year 13 for the $1,500 that had been estimated, a $2,539 loss would be recorded in year 13. Because this outcome results in an income statement charge that would not have occurred under the two other popular methods, it is common for companies that use this method to modify its application by switching to straight-line depreciation in the last years of the asset's life.[3]

---

[3] The switchover occurs in the year in which the depreciation is less than it would be if the remaining depreciable cost had been subjected to straight-line depreciation thenceforth.

(*cont.*)

Comparing the Results. Both the sum-of-the-years'-digits and the double-rate, declining-balance methods produce depreciation amounts greater in the early years of an asset's life and smaller in the later years than straight-line depreciation.

To make these relationships stand out as clearly as possible, study the diagrams in Exhibit 9–4. The upper graph depicts annual depreciation amounts for an asset that costs $100,000 and for which management expects no salvage value at the end of its five-year useful life. The lower graph presents the book-value amounts that would appear in the compa-

EXHIBIT 9–4
Graphic Comparisons of Annual Depreciation and Book Value

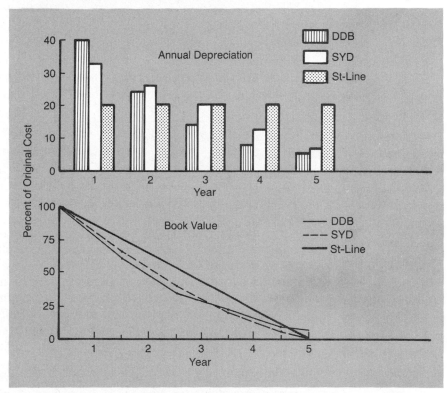

In our illustration, this happens in year 8, when the remaining depreciable cost is $10,047 − $1,500 = $8,547, and the asset still has five years of life left. The comparison for that year is:

Straight-line depreciation of remaining depreciable cost: $8,547/5 = $1,709.

Double-rate, declining-balance depreciation: $0.167 \times \$10,047 = \$1,674$.

Depreciation for years 8 through 12 would be $1,709. This would bring the book value down to $1,500 at the end of year 12.

ny's balance sheet each year under each depreciation method. The link between the two graphs is: the higher the annual depreciation charges, the lower the end-of-period book value.

Production-Unit Depreciation. While the three depreciation methods discussed so far are all based on the passage of time, depreciation is calculated for some assets on the basis of production units. The **production-unit depreciation** approach uses the following formula:

$$\text{Depreciation per Unit} = \frac{\text{Original Cost} - \text{Estimated Salvage Value}}{\text{Units of Lifetime Production Capacity}}$$

Each year's depreciation is equal to the number of units of output (e.g., pounds, liters, miles, or usage hours) multiplied by the *production-unit depreciation rate.* For a machine that costs $36,000, has a $1,500 estimated salvage value, and is expected to provide 20,000 hours of service in its lifetime, the production-unit depreciation rate is:

$$\frac{\$36,000 - \$1,500}{20,000 \text{ hours}} = \$1.725 \text{ an hour}$$

If the machine is used for 4,200 hours during the first year, production-unit depreciation for that year will be $7,245.

Production-unit depreciation is rarely used for ordinary commercial or industrial assets because useful life is more likely to be determined by rising costs or obsolescence—due to the passage of time—than by the number of units produced or hours of use. The method is used widely, however, to account for the *depletion* of such natural resources as oil and gas reserves and mineral deposits and the depreciation of the costs of the wells, mines, and other assets used to extract these resources. For example, if a company buys an oil field for $25 million with an estimated reserve of 20 million barrels, the depletion cost per barrel is $1.25 ($25 million/20 million). If 4 million barrels of oil are removed during the first year, a depletion expense of $5 million (4 million barrels × $1.25) will be recorded in that year.

Implicit-Interest Depreciation. None of the four depreciation methods we described recognizes explicitly the reasons why companies acquire plant assets. Companies buy assets because they expect them to generate net cash inflows at various times in the future. For an acquisition to be profitable, these future cash flows must be large enough to recover the cost of the asset *and* to provide an adequate rate of return each year on the amount the company invested in the asset.

A fifth method, **implicit-interest depreciation,** produces a cost-based depreciation schedule that reflects the relationship between the original cost of the asset and the future cash flows it is expected to generate. This method may show level annual charges, decreasing charges, or even increasing charges, depending on the anticipated time pattern of the cash flows.

The implicit-interest method derives each year's depreciation expense by comparing the year's anticipated cash flow with income based on the asset's expected rate of return. For example, since management expected a machine that cost $36,000 to yield a 15 percent rate of return each year, income in the first year should be $5,400 (0.15 × $36,000). If the first year's anticipated cash flow is $8,275, depreciation expense for the year would be $2,875 ($8,275 − $5,400).

The book value of this asset is $33,125 at the end of the first year ($36,000 − $2,875). Income in the second year therefore must be $4,969 (15 percent of $33,125) if the 15 percent rate of return is to be maintained. Depreciation in the second year is the difference between $4,969 and the anticipated cash flow that year.

If the anticipated cash flow is *constant* from year to year, implicit-interest depreciation will be small at first and then rise more and more rapidly as the asset ages. This outcome arises because a smaller percentage of each succeeding year's cash flow will represent income. The reason is that the book value on which the fixed rate of return is calculated gets smaller and smaller as the asset ages.

If the anticipated cash flow decreases slowly enough each year, the annual depreciation charge may still increase from year to year. The charge may be constant from year to year if the decrease in cash flow is sharper—because the decrease in the annual income requirement will be offset by the decrease in the annual cash flow. How much sharper the cash flow must decline to achieve this result depends on the starting level, the length of life, and the rate of return or interest rate. And at some faster rate of decline in the cash flows, the implicit-interest method will produce depreciation amounts that resemble those generated by one of the accelerated depreciation methods.

The appendix at the end of this chapter illustrates the implicit-interest method with numerical examples. Based on this introductory discussion alone, however, we can make an important observation: even though the implicit-interest method isn't used explicitly in practice, each method used in practice is consistent with a particular pattern of future cash flows. Use of an accelerated method implies the most sharply decreasing set of cash flows, and straight-line depreciation implies gradually decreasing cash flows.

Choosing a Depreciation Method

From the standpoint of investors and other external users of a company's financial statements, the best accounting method is the one that best helps them predict the company's cash flows, the timing of those flows, and the uncertainty surrounding them. Implicit-interest depreciation (or another method that produces roughly similar depreciation schedules) probably meets this criterion better than other methods because it produces income numbers closer to the sustainable rate of return on the company's assets.

In practice, the anticipated time patterns of the future cash flows are ordinarily difficult to verify. In most cases, therefore, the company's independent public accountants have little basis for disputing management's choice of a depreciation method. The result is that management may choose a depreciation method to achieve a desired pattern of year-to-year movements in net income.

The income effect of the choice of depreciation method depends on the rate of growth. If a company isn't growing but has a stable mix of assets of different ages, the total depreciation will be the same, no matter which method is selected. Some assets will be in their early years, others in the middle, and some in their final years. Book value amounts, however, will be smaller when an accelerated method is used than under straight-line depreciation, thus yielding a higher reported rate of return because of the smaller asset denominator of the rate-of-return fraction.

A growing company, in contrast, will have proportionally more young assets that will be generating depreciation amounts that are higher under accelerated methods than under straight-line depreciation. Book value amounts will be smaller, as in the no-growth company. The effect of the choice on the rate of return will depend on the relationship between the percentage difference in income and the percentage difference in the investment denominator.

Most large, publicly owned corporations in the United States use straight-line depreciation for investor reporting. This may reflect management's judgment that benefits are associated with greater reported income. Alternatively, it may mean that management's choice is based on information considerations, and management believes that straight-line depreciation approximates the anticipated time pattern of future cash flows better than accelerated methods.

Tax Depreciation versus Financial Depreciation

The depreciation method chosen for use in public financial reporting in the United States has no bearing on how a company reports depreciation expense on its federal income tax returns. Tax considerations therefore don't affect the choice of depreciation methods.

Large, publicly owned corporations in the United States have generally used some form of accelerated depreciation in determining taxable income since accelerated methods became permissible decades ago. Accelerated depreciation is more attractive than straight-line depreciation for income tax purposes because it shifts tax deductions to earlier years, thereby reducing taxable income and income taxes in those years. Reducing income taxes increases companies' cash flows in the early years of assets' lives, thereby giving these cash flows greater present values than if they came later.

The separation of tax depreciation from depreciation for financial reporting was made virtually absolute in 1981, when the U.S. Congress adopted for tax purposes a new system known as the accelerated cost recovery system (ACRS) for assets placed in service after 1980. In fact, the break with financial accounting was so great that the law establishing this system didn't use the term *depreciation* to describe the annual tax deductions—the term *cost recovery* was used throughout the law. When useful life is much longer than the amortization period prescribed for tax reporting, the latter cannot be used for financial reporting. We'll examine the implications of these differences in Chapter 10.

Revisions of Depreciation Schedules

Depreciation schedules adopted at the time assets are acquired may turn out to be incorrect. Two situations require changes in depreciation schedules. In the first, it becomes inescapably clear that the economic value of the asset's remaining service potential has fallen materially below its book value. This requires a **write-down** of the asset.

For example, suppose an asset costing $10,000 has been depreciated on a straight-line basis for three years at $1,000 a year. It has been used mainly to manufacture a product the company has withdrawn from the market, and it will be used only intermittently in the future, probably for another seven years. Suppose in this use it is worth $2,800 or 40 percent of its present book value. The entry to recognize this fact is:

```
Loss from Write-Down of Equipment.....................  4,200
     Accumulated Depreciation...........................           4,200
```

The write-down debit has an immediate, one-time effect on income; the increase in Accumulated Depreciation reduces the amount of the asset's cost that has yet to be depreciated.

Once a write-down has taken place, the remaining portion of the depreciation schedule has to be redrawn to amortize the remaining depreciable cost over the remaining life. With seven years to go, an adjusted book value of $2,800, and zero estimated salvage value, this machine would have annual straight-line depreciation charges of $2,800/7 = $400 for the remaining seven years of its life.

A second situation in which a revision in the original depreciation schedule is necessary arises when evidence is found that a useful-life estimate is seriously wrong. An error in an estimate of useful life results in an overstatement or understatement of depreciation during the years before the error is discovered.

In the interests of greater accounting accuracy, the accountant ought to correct the depreciation charges for prior years and calculate future depreciation as it would have been calculated originally if the estimates had been made accurately. Current practice in the United States, however, is to make no corrections of prior-year depreciation, mainly on the grounds that these changes would reduce public confidence in the statements and might confuse readers. Instead, the remaining depreciation amount is spread over the remaining years of useful life reflected in the new estimate.

For example, suppose an asset's book value is $150,000 and the remaining life estimate has been shortened from five years to three, with no salvage value. Under straight-line depreciation, the annual depreciation charge would be raised from $30,000 to $50,000 a year. The accumulated depreciation from prior years would not be changed to reflect the new estimate.

Intangible Assets

Companies sometimes buy intangible assets, consisting of valuable rights such as patents, trademarks, copyrights, and franchises. The costs of intangible assets must be amortized systematically—that is, recognized as expenses—during their anticipated useful lives. When the period of usefulness can be predicted easily, the cost is amortized during this period. When no such basis can be found, current practice in the United States is to amortize the cost over an arbitrarily chosen period, not to exceed 40 years. The argument for setting an upper limit of this sort is that all intangibles lose their value at some time, meaning that their cost should be deducted from the revenues of the years in which the assets are expected to be productive.

Expenditures for sales promotion and for the research and development of new products are expensed immediately by U.S. companies and therefore aren't subject to amortization. Even though they are usually incurred to generate benefits in future periods, the amounts and duration of these benefits are so difficult to estimate that no attempt is made to recognize the creation and use of the intangible assets arising from these expenditures.

Since amortization of the costs of intangibles takes the same form as depreciation of plant assets, we won't illustrate it separately here.

**Current-Cost
Accounting**

Throughout our discussion of accounting for plant assets, the focal point has been the historical-cost basis of accounting. We have pointed out that an economic value orientation might enable investors to discern more effectively the potential cash-flow impact of plant assets, but we've noted that practical difficulties preclude any widespread adoption of this approach.

An alternative avenue that accountants could use is the current-cost basis that was described in our discussion of inventory accounting. Current-cost accounting measures assets at their current cost and it includes in income the effect of changes in the assets' current cost.

Current Costs and Plant Assets

Current-cost measurements of plant assets in a period of generally rising prices result in the following:

1. The current cost of most plant assets is likely to be greater than the historical cost.
2. Higher depreciation expense causes current-cost operating income to be lower than historical-cost operating income.
3. Current-cost income will include holding gains on plant assets.

To see how current-cost measurements are applied to plant assets, we'll assume Gray Company bought a machine in January 19x1 for $20,000. Gray expected the machine to last 20 years, and it was depreciated at a straight-line rate of $1,000 a year.

The manufacturer of this machine went out of business in 19x3, but other companies continued to make roughly comparable machines. Because specific replacement prices aren't available, we have to approximate them by constructing a series of **index numbers.** Unlike the *consumer price index,* which most people are familiar with and which measures the average price change of a broad range of goods and services, other indexes are prepared specifically to gauge the price changes of narrow classes of assets relative to a selected *base-period* level.

To simplify our calculations, we'll assume that replacement prices change each year on December 31 and then remain steady for 12 months. Our price indexes for this type of equipment were as follows:

$$
\begin{array}{ll}
\text{January 1, 19x1} \ldots\ldots\ldots & 120 \\
\text{January 1, 19x9} \ldots\ldots\ldots & 180 \\
\text{December 31, 19x9} \ldots\ldots & 204
\end{array}
$$

The first two numbers tell us that machinery prices were 120 percent of the base-period level at the beginning of 19x1 and 180 percent of the base-period level at the beginning of 19x9 and throughout that year (due to our simplifying assumption that prices don't change during the year). By dividing these two numbers, we find that the prices prevailing at the beginning of 19x9 were 180/120 = 150 percent of the prices prevailing at the beginning of 19x1, when the machine was acquired. The comparable ratio on December 31, 19x9, was 170 percent (204/120).

These ratios are used in Exhibit 9–5 to determine the current cost of Gray Company's machine in 19x9. At beginning-of-year prices, the ma-

EXHIBIT 9–5
Gray Company: Calculation of Current Cost of Machine, 19x9

	Historical Cost	Multiplier	Current Cost
January 1, 19x9:			
Machine	$20,000	150%	$30,000
Accumulated depreciation (8/20)	8,000	150	12,000
Undepreciated cost	$12,000	150	$18,000
Depreciation, 19x9	$ 1,000	150	$ 1,500
December 31, 19x9:			
Machine	$20,000	170	$34,000
Accumulated depreciation (9/20)	9,000	170	15,300
Undepreciated cost	$11,000	170	$18,700

chine had an undepreciated current cost of $18,000 at the beginning of 19x9 (the third line in the right-hand column). Current-cost depreciation for the year was $1,500, reducing undepreciated current cost to $16,500 just before the year-end price increase. The price increase then pushed the current cost of the machine up to $18,700 (the bottom line of the exhibit). The holding gain therefore was $2,200 ($18,700 − $16,500). The realized holding gain for the year was only $500, however—the difference between the $1,000 historical-cost depreciation and the $1,500 current-cost depreciation.

Exhibit 9–6 compares Gray Company's historical-cost and current-cost income statements. We start by assuming a $9,000 income before depreciation (any other number would do as well) and no income taxes. The

EXHIBIT 9–6
Gray Company: Income Calculated on Historical-Cost and Current-Cost, 19x9

	Historical-Cost Basis	Current-Cost Basis
Income before depreciation	$9,000	$9,000
Depreciation	1,000	1,500
Operating income...............	8,000	7,500
Holding gain	—	2,200
Net income	$8,000	$9,700

first column shows the conventional historical-cost amounts; the second column shows the current-cost income statement, reflecting both the operating income and the holding gain for the year. Net income is different by $1,700 ($9,700 − $8,000). The historical-cost income statement classifies the $500 realized holding gain as an *undisclosed* component of operating income; current-cost income excludes this amount (because it actually arose in previous years) but reports the entire 19x9 holding gain on a separate line.

Exhibit 9–7 identifies the holding-gain aspects of our analysis. At the beginning of 19x9, there was an unrealized holding gain of $6,000—the

EXHIBIT 9–7
Gray Company: Holding Gains, 19x9

Unrealized holding gain, January 1: $18,000 − $12,000. . . . . $6,000
Add: Holding gain arising in 19x9: $18,700 − ($18,000 − $1,500) . .   2,200

   Total   8,200
Less: Unrealized holding gain, December 31: $18,700 − $11,000 . .   7,700
Holding gain realized in 19x9: $1,500 − $1,000 . . . . $ 500

difference between the asset's undepreciated current cost and its book value (undepreciated historical cost). The increase in replacement cost in 19x9 resulted in a $2,200 holding gain—measured and disclosed only in the current-cost income statement. At year-end, the asset had an unrealized holding gain of $7,700—the difference between the two undepreciated-cost amounts. During the year, the realized gain was $500, the difference between the two methods' depreciation expense.

The $500 realized holding gain caused the historical-cost operating income to be $500 higher than the current-cost operating income—without disclosing the nature of this difference. The two methods' net income amounts differ by $1,700, the difference between current-cost income's inclusion of the $2,200 holding gain that arose in 19x9 and historical-cost income's inclusion of the $500 holding gain that was realized in 19x9.

Large corporations in the United States are required to provide supplemental disclosures relating to the effects of changes in replacement costs, as they relate to selected financial statement items. Among the designated items, two disclosures deal specifically with plant assets: The current cost of plant, property, and equipment must be disclosed as well as depreciation expense based on the assets' current costs. A full current-cost income statement is not prepared, however.

Summary

The use of *historical cost* to measure assets when they're acquired raises a number of difficult questions. Some result from uncertainty—for example, will the expenditures lead to a commensurate future benefit? Others are definitional—for example, did the expenditure increase the company's total productive capacity or merely prevent it from deteriorating? All such questions require the exercise of accounting judgment. The basic accounting approach calls for capitalizing all costs that are incurred in anticipation of benefits beyond the current accounting period. An apparent exception is maintenance costs, but here the future benefit was already assumed in the decision to capitalize the costs of the asset to which the maintenance relates.

The measurement of depreciation expense is intended to allocate the original cost of assets to the future periods that will benefit from them. Accountants measure depreciation by estimating the amount of each asset's service potential that is consumed each period. This means that there be a determination of both the asset's useful life and the salvage value once its life has ended. In addition, it is necessary to identify the time pattern of depreciation; the most popular approaches are straight-line (uniform annual amounts) and accelerated methods (smaller amounts in each succeeding year).

The criteria for determining the amount of cost to be capitalized and the ensuing depreciation schedule are difficult to apply precisely. As a result, management has some discretion over the amounts to capitalize and the time pattern of depreciation charges. Once an accounting policy on these matters has been adopted, however, it must be implemented consistently each period.

When the current cost of a plant asset increases, the company experiences a holding gain. Such gains are said to be realized as the asset is used. In the case of depreciable assets, the difference between current-cost depreciation expense and the historical-cost amount is the measure of the realized gain. Although current-cost accounting is not used by U.S. companies, large corporations do include piecemeal disclosures as supplements to their published financial statements.

Appendix: Implicit-Interest Depreciation

Implicit-interest depreciation is calculated in such a way that the income attributable to an asset each year will be a constant percentage of the beginning-of-year book value, if all cash-flow forecasts turn out to be correct. For example, suppose Bolton Company buys a machine for $6,000. Management expects the machine to generate incremental cash flows of $1,503 at the end of each of the next five years. The machine is expected to come to the end of its life five years from now, at which time it will have no salvage value. These cash flows are equivalent to an annual rate of return of 8 percent during the asset's life.[4]

---

[4] We'll explain this calculation in Chapter 21, but what we've done is find the rate of interest at which the present value of the future cash flows is equal to the machine's $6,000 cost. The present-value multiplier for five periods at 8 percent is 3.9927; except for a rounding error, $1,503 × 3.9927 = $6,000.

EXHIBIT 9–8
Implicit-Interest Depreciation: Level Cash-Flow Stream

(1) Year	(2) Book Value (= Present Value), Beginning -of-Year [line above: (2) − (5)]	(3) Anticipated Cash Flow	(4) Income (2) × 8%	(5) Implicit-Interest Depreciation (3) − (4)
1	$6,000	$1,503	$480	$1,023
2	4,977	1,503	398	1,105
3	3,872	1,503	310	1,193
4	2,679	1,503	214	1,289
5	1,390	1,503	111	1,392

Column (5) in Exhibit 9–8 shows a depreciation schedule calculated to enable the company to report an 8 percent rate of return on the asset's book value each year, if the cash flows are as predicted. For example, income for the first year must be $6,000 × 0.08 = $480 if the asset is to earn 8 percent on the asset's $6,000 beginning book value. This $480, referred to as *implicit interest*, is the first amount in column (4) of the exhibit. This leaves $1,023 of the $1,503 cash flow to cover amortization of the asset's cost, and this amount is entered in the first line of column (5).

Depreciation of $1,023 in the first year reduces the asset's book value from $6,000 to $4,977 at the beginning of the second year. An 8 percent return on this amount would be $398, the amount shown in the second line of column (4). If Bolton Company reports this income in the second year, its reported rate of return on book value will be just 8 percent:

Rate of Return   = $398/$4,977   =   8 percent

Depreciation for the second year therefore must be $1,503 − $398 = $1,105, the amount shown in the second line of column (5). Repeating this process for the other three years produces the amounts shown in the last three lines of column (5). The $2 difference between the depreciation charge for the fifth year and the asset's book value at the beginning of the year is a rounding error and has no significance.

Each book value amount in column (2) equals the present value of the machine's anticipated future cash flows, discounted at 8 percent. For example, the book value at the beginning of the second year is the present value of four annual receipts of $1,503 each. [$1,503 times 3.3121, the four-year multiplier in Table 2 of Appendix A, equals $4,978, which differs from the amount in column (2) by a $1 rounding error only.] Similarly, the present value of three annual $1,503 receipts is $3,872, the book value at the beginning of the third year, and so on.

Alternatively, we could have derived the depreciation schedule in column (5) by computing the present values of the machine in succeeding years [as in column (2)] and subtracting. Depreciation for the first year thus is $6,000 − $4,977 = $1,023.

To summarize, if Bolton Company calculates present value at the interest rate that is implicit in the acquisition decision—that is, if acquisition cost equals present value at the time of acquisition—then the periodic cash flows produced by an asset are exactly equal to economic depreciation plus interest.

Key Terms		
	Accelerated (diminishing-charge) depreciation	Implicit-interest depreciation
	Ancillary expenditure	Index number
	Betterment	Maintenance
	Depletion	Obsolescence
	Depreciable cost	Production-unit depreciation
	Depreciation rate	Straight-line depreciation
	Double-rate, declining-balance depreciation	Sum-of-the-years'-digits depreciation
	Economic depreciation	Useful life
		Write-downs

Independent Study Problems (Solutions in Appendix B)

1. Depreciation Exercises. Fast Buck, Inc., has just bought a sophisticated copying machine for $30,000. It is expected to last five years and has an estimated salvage value of $1,500. The annual cash flow from ownership and use of this machine is expected to be $7,668, and this will produce a rate of return on investment of 10 percent. Calculate depreciation for each of the five years by:

a. The straight-line method.
b. The double-rate, declining-balance method.
c. The sum-of-the-years'-digits method.
d. The implicit-interest method.

2. Ancillary Expenditures. An automobile manufacturer bought six heavy stamping machines at a price of $16,250 each. When they were delivered, the purchaser paid freight charges of $4,200 and handling fees of $1,200. Four employees, each earning $10 an hour, worked three 40-hour weeks setting up and testing the machines. Special wiring and other materials applicable to the new machines cost $600.

How much of these costs should be capitalized as costs of these machines?

3. Major Overhaul. In January 19x4, Abercrombie Mills, Inc., bought and placed in service a new paper machine costing $50,000. Its estimated useful life was 20 years, with no major overhauls planned for that period. Depreciation was to be calculated on a straight-line basis, with a zero estimated salvage value.

In December 19x7, certain improvements were added to this machine at a cost of $6,000. Twelve years later, in the fall of 19x19, the machine was thoroughly overhauled and rebuilt at a cost of $12,000. It was estimated that the overhaul would extend the machine's useful life by five years, or until the end of 19x28. Depreciation charges for 19x19 were unaffected by the overhaul.

a. Calculate the machine's book value at the end of 19x7, after depreciation for the year was recorded but before the improvements were accounted for.
b. Prepare the journal entry required to record the improvements added in December 19x7.
c. Calculate depreciation for 19x8 on a straight-line basis.
d. Calculate depreciation for 19x20 on a straight-line basis.

4. Choosing a Depreciation Method. Book publishers spend substantial sums to edit textbook manuscripts and to prepare the photographic plates from which the books themselves are printed. Textbook A is expected to remain in print for about five years. Up-to-date competing textbooks will be published each year by other publishing companies. The longer a textbook has been in print, the more out of date it is likely to be, making it more and more difficult to compete with the newer textbooks on the market.

a. What depreciation method should be adopted for textbook A?
b. What effects would your choice have on the publisher's financial statements?

5. Equipment Holding Gains and Losses. Weston Company had the following equipment in its factory on January 1, 19x9:

Year of Purchase	Original Cost	Accumulated Depreciation, January 1	Depreciation for 19x9
19x0	$150,000	$90,000	$10,000
19x2	45,000	21,000	3,000
19x5	60,000	16,000	4,000

The replacement cost index for equipment of this kind traced the following path:

Year	Index
19x0	100
19x2	110
19x5	150
19x9:	
Beginning of year	180
Average for year	190
End of year............	200

No equipment was purchased or retired during 19x9.

a. Calculate the unrealized equipment holding gain or loss as of January 1, 19x9.
b. Calculate depreciation for 19x9 on a current-cost basis.
c. Calculate the realized equipment holding gain or loss for 19x9. Where and in what manner would this be reported to investors?
d. Calculate the unrealized equipment holding gain or loss as of December 31, 19x9.
e. Calculate the total equipment holding gain or loss arising during the year 19x9 (including both the realized and unrealized portions).

Exercises and Problems

6. Consistency versus Uniformity. A financial executive recently stated that the only important requirement for a capitalization policy is consistency; in others words, the details of the policy are unimportant so long as it is applied consistently from year to year. Can you identify any possible adverse effects of allowing management to choose its own capitalization policy and apply it consistently? If so, are they likely to be important?

7. Joint Acquisition Costs. Coyle Construction Company paid $61,000 for a house and lot. The house was then torn down at an additional cost of $2,000 so that Coyle could begin to construct a gasoline service station on the site. At the time of the acquisition, an appraisal of the property placed the value of the land at $48,000 and the value of the house at $19,000.

What asset(s) did Coyle acquire? Calculate the cost of each asset you identified.

8. Replacement-Cost Depreciation: Discussion Question. Miller Enterprises, Inc., is incorporated in a country in which corporations aren't required to base their financial statements on U.S. generally accepted accounting principles. In view of the steadily rising costs of equipment and building construction in that country, Miller's controller has suggested basing depreciation each year on replacement cost. Depreciation each year would be reflected in a journal entry of the following form:

```
Depreciation. . . . . . . . . . . . . . . . . . . . . . . . . . . . . . . . . . . . . . . . . . . . . . . . . . .   X
     Accumulated Depreciation . . . . . . . . . . . . . . . . . . . . . . . . . . . . . . . .      Y
     Reserve for Replacement . . . . . . . . . . . . . . . . . . . . . . . . . . . . . . . . .      Z
```

in which X is the depreciation charge based on replacement cost and Y is the depreciation charge based on acquisition cost.

a. What effect would the proposed method have on net income during a period of rising equipment costs? Would this effect continue after equipment costs stopped rising? Explain.

b. If the controller's proposal were accepted, how would you interpret the "reserve for replacement"? Would it appear on the income statement for the year or would it go directly to the year-end balance sheet? In which section of that financial statement should it appear? State your reasons.

c. If a machine is replaced at the end of its anticipated useful life by an identical machine with a higher replacement cost, will the reserve for replacement equal the difference between the original cost of the first machine and the cost of its replacement? Explain.

9. Depreciation Exercises. Regent, Inc., bought a machine for $26,000 on January 2, 19x5. Management expects to use the machine for 10 years, at the end of which time it will have a $1,000 salvage value. Answer the following four mutually exclusive questions:

a. If Regent uses straight-line depreciation, what is the book value of the machine on December 31, 19x8?

b. If Regent uses double-rate, declining-balance depreciation, what is depreciation expense for 19x7?

c. If Regent uses sum-of-the-years'-digits depreciation, what is the Accumulated Depreciation balance on December 31, 19x6?

d. If Regent uses straight-line depreciation and sells the machine on April 1, 19x9, for an amount of cash that results in neither a gain nor a loss, what is the amount of cash Regent will receive?

10. Plant Asset and Depreciation Exercises. Gardner, Inc., manufactures industrial tools. Listed below is information relating to three of Gardner's plant assets that were bought on January 1, 19x1. Each of the six questions that follow should be analyzed *independently*. In other words, they represent six unrelated mini-problems that happen to be based on a common set of data.

Machine	Original Cost	Estimated Useful Life	Expected End-of-Life Salvage Value
A	$19,000	6 years	$6,400
B	32,000	8 years	2,000
C	13,000	5 years	4,000

a. By what amount would machine A's depreciation in 19x4 based on the sum-of-the-years'-digits differ from straight-line depreciation?

b. If double-rate, declining-balance depreciation was used, what is the amount of the gain or the loss that would have been recorded when machine B was sold for $15,400 on January 1, 19x4?

c. If machine C was depreciated using sum-of-the-years'-digits depreciation, what is the amount of cash proceeds that would have had to be received upon the machine's sale on April 1, 19x3, so that there would have been neither a gain nor a loss?

d. Assume that the three machines' original-cost amounts were their market values on January 1, 19x1. As an incentive for Gardner to buy the three machines at once, their previous owner had sold them to Gardner on January 1, 19x1, for a lump-sum price of $48,000. What was the cost that would have been assigned to machine A?

e. Machine D was purchased on January 2, 19x5. Although its list price was $13,200, Gardner obtained it by paying $6,700 cash and surrendering machine C to the seller. If machine C had been depreciated on a straight-line basis, what was the cost of machine D?

f. On January 1, 19x7, Gardner bought a balance-tie mechanism for $2,400 to improve the quality of machine B's output. Although the new mechanism was guaranteed to last three years, it would not be transferable to another machine when machine B's useful life ended. If machine B was depreciated on a straight-line basis, what was the book value of machine B (including the balance-tie mechanism) on December 31, 19x7?

11. Capitalization: One Asset or Two? A machine that had cost $21,000 is expected to be useful for 12 years, with no end-of-life salvage.

A major component of this machine is a heavy-duty air compressor that must be replaced every four years. Replacement compressors cost $6,000 each.

Straight-line depreciation is appropriate both for the machine and for the compressor.

a. Determine for each of the next 12 years the effect on net income of capitalizing the compressor and the other components of the machine as separate assets instead of as a single asset.

b. Which of these two alternatives do you prefer? Give your reasons.

12. Exercise: Different Depreciation Methods. Shakey Corporation bought a building on January 1, 19x1, together with title to the land on which the building was located. The building and land cost $1 million, and the land was appraised at $300,000. The building was assumed to have a 35-year useful life, with zero net salvage value.

Calculate depreciation for the second year (19x2) by:

a. The straight-line depreciation method.
b. The sum-of-the-years'-digits depreciation method.

13. Exercise: Different Depreciation Methods. King Company has just bought four assets for which you have the following data:

Asset	Cost	Life	Salvage	Method
Truck........	$ 11,000	200,000 miles	$ 1,000	Production unit
Machine	300,000	12 years	25,000	Double rate, declining balance
Typewriter....	660	3 years	—	Sum-of-the-years'-digits
Furniture.....	3,500	8 years	500	Straight line

The truck was driven 50,000 miles the first year and 40,000 miles the second year.

Calculate the depreciation for each asset for each of the first two years.

14. Exchanging Assets. Hayden Corporation bought a new computer whose list price was $30,000. In exchange, Hayden paid cash and gave the supplier an old computer whose book value was $14,000.

a. What was the cost of the new computer if Hayden paid cash amounting to $17,000?
b. What was the cost of the new computer if Hayden paid cash amounting to $13,500?
c. How, if at all, would you change your answers to parts *a* and *b* if you were told that the old computer had a market value of $15,000 at the time of the exchange? Explain your answer.
d. Suppose Hayden determined that the market value of the old computer was $20,000, and it exchanged the computer for two used forklift trucks that had a combined book value of $16,200 and a combined appraised value of $18,700 at that time. What was the total cost of the two trucks? Why did you choose this amount?

15. Depreciation Calculations; Trade-In. Sanders, Inc., bought a machine for $52,000 on January 2, 19x3. Management estimated that the machine would be used for eight years, and that it would then be sold for $4,000.

a. If the machine was depreciated using the straight-line method and it was sold on April 1, 19x5, for $44,000, what was the amount of the gain or loss?
b. If the machine was depreciated using the sum-of-the-years'-digits method, what was its book value on December 31, 19x7?
c. If the machine was depreciated using the double-rate, declining-balance method, what was the balance in Accumulated Depreciation on December 31, 19x5?

d. Assume that your answer to part *c* had been $31,000, that the machine was traded for a new machine on January 2, 19x6, that the new machine's cash sale price was $65,000, and that Sanders received a $25,000 trade-in allowance for its old machine. What cost should Sanders assign to the new machine? Why?

16. Calculating Depreciation Schedules; Justifying the Choice. Fox Coons, Inc., bought a dump truck for $10,450. This truck was delivered on January 2, 19x1, and was placed in service immediately hauling salt for the local highway department. The company's past experience led management to believe the costs of maintaining and operating the truck would increase as it grew older, but the truck would be used about the same number of weeks each year and carry about the same number of loads.

Management decided to depreciate this truck by the sum-of-the-years'-digits method, based on a six-year life and a $1,000 estimated end-of-life salvage value.

a. Prepare a depreciation schedule for this truck.
b. Recalculate the depreciation schedule by the double-rate, declining-balance method.
c. Do the company's estimates justify the use of one of these accelerated methods instead of straight-line depreciation?

17. Choosing a Depreciation Method. A company has just bought a new electric typewriter for $750. The manufacturer of the typewriter will provide service on this typewriter for eight years at an annual cost of $100. With this service contract, the typewriter will be inoperative, awaiting service, for approximately five days each year.

After eight years, the manufacturer will provide service only on a time-and-parts basis. This arrangement is likely to be so expensive that the company will sell the typewriter at the end of eight years. In the past, used electric typewriters have been sold to employees for about 20 percent of their original cost.

a. Which depreciation method would you recommend for this typewriter? Give your reasons.
b. Calculate the annual depreciation charge for each of the next eight years.

18. Betterment or Maintenance. Bay Shore Company built an office building 10 years ago. It rented space to several tenants, but its major tenant, Gallagher Coal Company, gradually took more and more space so that, by last year, it occupied the entire 10-story building.

A year ago, Gallagher notified Bay Shore that it would not renew its lease on the building unless Bay Shore made extensive alterations to the building to make it suitable for use as the company's headquarters. Since other tenants were unlikely to use as much space as Gallagher or to pay the rentals Gallagher was paying, Bay Shore decided to make the changes.

The alterations cost $1.4 million. Bay Shore's management estimated the present value of the future cash flows from the renovated building to be $3.2 million.

Before the renovation took place, the book value of the building was $1.6 million: cost of $2.4 million, less accumulated depreciation of $800,000. The land on which the building was located had cost $400,000. An appraiser estimated that the land and the renovated building had a market value of $3 million but that finding a buyer might take a year or more.

How should the renovation expenditure be accounted for? List the alternatives you considered and your reasons for choosing the one you are recommending.

19. Noncash Acquisition. Griffin Company bought a 10-acre plot of land from Gargoyles, Ltd., issuing 20,000 shares of its own capital stock in exchange for this land. The land was to be the site of Griffin's new corporate headquarters.

Gargoyles had bought this land 15 years earlier for $20,000 and had used it as the site of a drive-in theater. The land was near the intersection of an interstate highway and the local arterial highway, making it very attractive for potential users.

Gargoyles' balance sheet listed the land at $20,000; the theater installations had been destroyed in a storm six months earlier and the company had written the costs off completely. Although the assessed valuation for tax purposes was $100,000, an appraiser estimated that the land was worth twice that amount.

Griffin's stock was traded actively on the New York Stock Exchange at prices ranging from $24 to $26 at the time of the acquisition.

List the alternative bases on which Griffin might have capitalized this property, choose the basis you would have recommended, calculate the capitalized amount, and state the reasons for your choice.

20. Ancillary Expenditures; Joint Costs. To obtain a new factory site, the Mosk Manufacturing Company purchased a 12-acre tract of waste-land, paying $13,000 to the former owners. Costs of searching titles and drawing and recording deeds amounted to $300. Grading cost $2,800. As only six acres were required for its own factory, it considered two offers for six acres: (1) $12,000 for the north half and (2) $8,000 for the south half. It accepted the offer of $8,000 for the south half and received a certified check in payment.

a. At what amount should the remaining land be carried on the next balance sheet?

b. What gain or loss, if any, should be reported on the income statement for the current period?

21. Cost Determination: The Compound-Interest Dimension. In each of the following independent cases, interest is compounded annually.

a. Blanket, Inc., bought a new word processor on January 2, 19x1. Blanket was required to remit five $13,000 payments each January 1, beginning on January 1, 19x3. If Blanket's payments reflected a 15 percent interest rate, what was the cost of the word processor on January 2, 19x1?

b. On January 3, 19x3, Durwood Company bought a tract of real estate that it may use for plant expansion in the future. Durwood paid $200,000 cash immediately, transferred to the seller 4,000 shares of Universal Corporation stock whose $90-a-share market value was 50 percent higher than Durwood's cost, and agreed to remit three annual $100,000 payments beginning in January 19x4. Had Durwood borrowed the money from a bank to be able to pay the $750,000 cash selling price immediately, Durwood would have incurred a 12 percent interest rate. At what amount should Durwood record its purchase of the land?

c. By incurring $300,000 in drilling costs, Cooper, Ltd., discovered an oil-bearing formation under the parking lot of its industrial park corporate headquarters. A petroleum engineering consultant estimated that the net cash receipts from exploiting this oil reserve would probably be $3 million during each of the first two years and $2 million in each of the following three years. Assuming 14 percent interest and each year's receipts occurring at the end of the year, what was the present value of the oil reserve on the discovery date? At what amount would the company report the oil reserve on its discovery-date balance sheet?

22. Implicit-Interest Depreciation. On January 1, 19x1, Lubberdink Company purchased a machine for $56,910. The machine was expected to produce cash savings at the rate of $15,000 a year for five years and to have a salvage value of $5,000 at the end of that time.

a. Calculate annual depreciation using the straight-line method. For each year, compute the ratio of the machine's earnings after depreciation to its beginning-of-year book value.

b. Recalculate annual depreciation using the implicit-interest method such that the annual rate of return on the machine's January 1 book value is 12 percent each year.

c. Is the rate of 12 percent appropriate to use in this case? Could the implicit-interest method have been applied with a rate such as 15 percent? Support your conclusion with appropriate calculations.

d. Calculate economic depreciation as the difference between successive present values, using the same interest rate (12 percent).

23. Depreciable Assets; Missing Amounts. For each of the six independent cases (I–VI) in the accompanying table, determine the missing amounts.

	I	II	III	IV	V	VI
					Double Rate, Declining	
			Sum-of-the-			
	Straight Line		**Years'-Digits**		**Balance**	
Year number	4	5	3	3	2	3
Original cost	$14,000	$17,300	G	$39,000	$50,000	P
Estimated salvage value	2,000	D	$ 1,400	I	4,000	$ 5,000
Book value, January 1	A	E	9,400	J	L	33,750
Depreciable life (years)	B	7	5	4	10	8
Depreciation expense	C	2,200	H	6,000	M	Q
Accumulated depreciation, January 1	4,500	F	12,000	K	N	26,250

24. Plant Asset Transactions. Barkley, Ltd., engaged in the following transactions in 19x8:

1. On January 3, it traded a used delivery truck for a new vehicle that had a list price of $12,000. The used truck had cost $9,000 and had a book value of $3,200 on January 3. Barkley received a $4,000 trade-in allowance and therefore paid $8,000 cash. Barkley expected to use the new truck for four years.

2. On January 4, it sold for $16,500 office equipment that had cost $72,000, 75 percent of which had been depreciated.

3. On March 1, the company bought a parcel of land and the building on that land. Barkley paid $1.2 million cash. The appraised value of the land at that time was three times the appraised value of the building. On March 10, the structure was razed at a cost of $10,000, paid in cash. By the end of November, a new building had been constructed at a cost of $1,440,000 cash; it began functioning as a warehouse on December 2, and it had an expected useful life of 30 years.

4. The company paid $24,000 cash on April 1 to buy the exclusive right to use the trademark of a defunct business. Management believed the value of this trademark would last forever and that it was likely to increase in value by $5,000 each year under Barkley's management.

5. It paid $45,000 cash at a bankruptcy auction on May 1 for a "package" consisting of a factory machine, a photocopier, and a delivery truck. An appraiser was engaged to estimate their market values and expected remaining useful lives, and this was the result:

Machinery..........	$37,500	5 years
Office equipment.....	30,000	8 years
Delivery truck........	7,500	2 years

a. Prepare entries in general-journal form to record the transactions. The company uses a separate account for each class of plant asset.

b. Record the necessary year-end adjusting entry or entries. Barkley uses straight-line depreciation on a monthly basis and assumed zero salvage value.

25. Ancillary Expenditures; Trade-In Value.   In January 19x1, a storekeeper bought a used delivery truck for $2,000. Before putting the vehicle into service, $280 was spent for painting and decorating the body and $520 for a complete engine overhaul. Four new tires were bought and mounted for $200. The storekeeper expected to keep the truck in service for three years, at the end of which time it would have a trade-in value of $600.

Gasoline, oil, and similar items were charged to expense as procured. In January 19x2, a new battery ($40) and miscellaneous repairs ($180) were purchased. Straight-line depreciation was used.

Four new tires were bought for $220 in January 19x3, and the body was repainted at a cost of $350. Miscellaneous repairs were made at a cost of $300. Management still expected to trade in the truck at the end of 19x3.

In January 19x4, the storekeeper traded the old truck for a new truck with a list price of $6,800, giving the dealer $5,940 in cash and receiving an $860 trade-in allowance on the old truck.

a. Which of the outlays made in 19x1 should be capitalized?

b. Which of the outlays made in 19x2 and 19x3 should be capitalized?

c. Calculate depreciation on a straight-line basis for each year, 19x1 through 19x3. (A full year's depreciation should be taken in each year.)

d. Indicate how the replacement of the old truck by a new one would be accounted for in 19x4.

26. Betterment, Overhaul, and Retirement.   A barge with an estimated life of 20 years and no end-of-life salvage value was bought in January 19x1 for $200,000. Straight-line depreciation was used.

The barge proved too small to be profitable, and five years after it was bought the company lengthened it at a cost of $30,000, paid in cash.

At the end of 15 years, the barge was thoroughly overhauled and reconditioned at a cost of $40,000, paid in cash. This action was expected to extend the life of the barge to 10 years from the date of the reconditioning (that is, to 25 years from the original acquisition date).

Early in its 22d year, the barge struck a rock and sank in a heavy storm. The company collected $15,000 from the insurance company.

a. Determine the book value of the barge at the end of five years.
b. Should the cost of lengthening the barge have been capitalized or expensed? State your reasons.
c. Calculate depreciation for the sixth year.
d. Should the cost of reconditioning the barge have been capitalized or expensed? State your reasons.
e. Calculate depreciation for the 16th year.
f. Determine the book value of the barge at the end of 21 years.
g. Calculate the gain or loss resulting from the sinking of the barge and the collection of the insurance.

27. Discussion Question: Stating and Applying an Accounting Principle. The general ledger of Enter-tane, Inc., a corporation engaged in the development and production of television programs for commercial sponsorship, contains the following accounts before amortization at the end of the current year:

Account	Balance (debit)
Sealing Wax and Kings	$51,000
The Messenger	36,000
The Desperado	17,500
Shin Bone	8,000
Studio Rearrangement	5,000

An examination of contracts and records has revealed the following information:

1. The balances in the first two accounts represent the total cost of completed programs that were televised during the accounting period just ended. Under the terms of an existing contract, Sealing Wax and Kings will be rerun during the next accounting period at a fee equal to 50 percent of the fee for the first televising of the program. The contract for the first run produced $300,000 of revenue. The contract with the sponsors of The Messenger provides that they may, at their option, rerun the program during the next season at a fee of 75 percent of the fee on the first televising of the program.
2. The balance in The Desperado account is the cost of a new program that has just been completed and is being considered by several companies for commercial sponsorship.
3. The balance in the Shin Bone account represents the cost of a partially completed program for a projected series that has been abandoned.
4. The balance of the Studio Rearrangement account consists of payments made to a firm of engineers that prepared a report recommending a more efficient utilization of existing studio space and equipment.

a. State the general principle or principles by which accountants are guided in deciding how much of the balances in the first four accounts should be shown as assets on the company's year-end balance sheet.

b. Applying this principle or principles, how would you report each of these first four accounts in the year-end financial statements? Explain.

c. In what way, if at all, does the Studio Rearrangement account differ from the first four? How would you report this account in the company's financial statements for the period?

28. Small Tools; Effect of Capitalization Policy. Asobat, Inc., commenced business operations at the beginning of year 1. At that time its accountants decided, with the approval of management and the company's independent auditors, to expense immediately the costs of all small tools and other long-life items that cost less than $50 apiece. The company's purchases of these items during the first 11 years of operations, together with its reported net income, were as follows:

Year	Purchases	Net Income (Loss) before Taxes
1	$20,000	$(21,000)
2	2,000	400
3	0	5,400
4	6,000	6,600
5	4,000	6,600
6	10,400	1,800
7	11,200	4,200
8	5,600	16,600
9	4,400	21,800
10	7,680	20,920
11	11,280	21,720

Having noticed how large these purchases have been in comparison with net income, the controller asked an assistant to look into the matter. The assistant's inquiry has turned up the following additional information:

1. Purchases seem to have been amply justified by legitimate operating needs.
2. Twenty percent of the items purchased were discarded after four years' use, another 60 percent were discarded after five years' use, and the remaining 20 percent were disposed of at the end of six years.
3. The scrap value of the discarded items was negligible.
4. The company's new computer could be used to calculate annual depreciation charges on these items at a very low cost.

a. Calculate straight-line depreciation, year by year, on the items purchased in the first 11 years of Asobat's existence. Assume that all purchases were made at the beginning of the year and all retirements took place at the end of the year, after the annual depreciation charge was calculated. Depreciation on all items should be based on a five-year life.

b. Restate income before taxes for each of these years as it would have been reported if these expenditures had been capitalized and depreciated on the basis described in part *a*.

c. What conclusions, if any, about Asobat's capitalization policy do these calculations seem to point to?

29. Capitalizable Costs. Universal Airlines discovered that the recruiting and training costs for its flight attendants were affecting only certain years' income statements. This was due to the company's tendency to hire new personnel only once every three years. The entire cost of its flight-attendant school as well as the hiring fees were expensed when the expenditures occurred.

During 19x5, Universal interviewed 400 candidates and accepted 245. Of these, 180 began and completed the six-week training course. One hundred of these began working on September 1, and 50 others started on December 1. The following costs were incurred:

January:	Advertising (outside agencies)	$185,000
March:	Processing (internal staff)	74,500
April:	Interviewing (75% internal, 25% external) . .	69,800
June/July:	Training school:	
	Instructors' salaries	165,000
	Trainees' salaries	324,000
	Facilities rental/housing	242,600
	Support materials	212,600

Salaries for trainees were $300 a week each, including the training period and their first four weeks online, when they were the fourth members of standard three-person crews. Universal estimated that fringe benefits added 20 percent to trainees' salary costs and 25 percent to experienced employees' payroll costs. Based on past experience, the company expected 120 of the new employees to work more than one month: 75 percent to average two years, and 25 percent to average seven years of service before leaving the airline.

How should Universal Airlines account for the cost of hiring and training its flight attendant class of 19x5?

30. Current-Cost Measurements; Holding Gains. Brown Company's only depreciable asset was a machine the company had bought for $30,000 on January 1, 19x2. Brown Company established a straight-line depreciation schedule for this machine based on a 15-year life and zero end-of-life salvage value. Purchase prices for this kind of equipment change on December 31 each year and remain constant until the next December 31. Price indexes for this machine were as follows:

> January 1, 19x2 125
> January 1, 19x8 175
> December 31, 19x8 200

a. Calculate (1) accumulated historical-cost depreciation as of January 1, 19x8, (2) accumulated historical-cost depreciation as of December 31, 19x8, and (3) historical-cost depreciation expense for 19x8.

b. Calculate (1) the current cost of the machine as of January 1, 19x8, and December 31, 19x8, (2) accumulated depreciation of the machine on a current-cost basis as of January 1, 19x8, and December 31, 19x8, and (3) depreciation expense for 19x8 on a current-cost basis.

c. Assuming income before depreciation of $12,000 in 19x8 and a zero income tax rate, calculate net income (1) on a historical-cost basis, and (2) on a current-cost basis.

d. Calculate the realized holding gain for 19x8.

e. Comment on the significance of your answers to parts c and d.

31. Capitalizable Costs; Analogy to Manufacturing. Casey Wilson, chief accountant for the Mudville Mice major league baseball team, proposed that the cost of developing future superstars be treated as the cost of a plant asset. To illustrate, Wilson cited the team's experience with its outstanding shortstop, Charlie Hustle.

When Hustle had been given a $300,000 bonus to sign a contract with the Mice, it was treated as the cost of raw material. For the first three years of his Mice career, Hustle earned salaries of $45,000, $55,000, and $60,000 while performing for affiliated minor league teams. These amounts were paid by the Mice, and the $160,000 total was the cost of labor. The $170,000 salary paid to a special instructional coach those three years represented an additional developmental cost. Wilson also wanted to capitalize the $180,000 subsidy Mudville paid the teams to assure that Hustle stayed in the best hotels on road trips and that he always flew first class rather than travel by trains and buses with his teammates.

Hustle's first year with the Mice team itself was a disappointment because he wasn't competent enough to be a regular performer, despite drawing a $90,000 salary. His second year was a disaster because a spring training injury limited his playing time to the last 15 percent of the season. Hustle's salary was $100,000 that year. Wilson wanted to capitalize these salary costs on the grounds that they were the equivalent of manufacturing costs.

In Charlie Hustle's third year, he had a magnificent season, even earning designation as a league all-star. Casey Wilson estimated that this was the first of the 10 years during which Hustle's superstar performance would result in significantly increased paid attendance at Mice games as well as higher television advertising revenues and other revenue-producing benefits for the Mudville Mice baseball club.

Evaluate Casey Wilson's proposal in terms of its implications for the Mice organization's measurement of its annual income and balance sheet assets.

32. Self-Manufactured Equipment: Determining the Capitalizable Amount. Beckman Company late in 19x1 requested bids from several equipment manufacturers on the construction of a unique piece of special-purpose equipment to be used in the Beckman factory to replace an outmoded piece of equipment then in use. Several bids were received, the lowest in the amount of $55,000. The management of the Beckman Company felt that this was excessive. Instead, the machine was manufactured in the company's own machine shop which was then operating at substantially less than full capacity.

The machine was built during the early months of 19x2 and was placed in service on July 1, 19x2. The machine was capitalized at $55,000, comprising the following elements:

Raw materials used in construction of new machine	$ 8,000
Direct labor used in construction of new machine	20,000
Amount paid to Ace Machinery Service Company for installation of new machine	1,000
Cost of dismantling old machine	800
Cost of direct labor for trial runs	1,500
Cost of materials for trial runs	500
Costs of special tooling for use in operating the machine	6,000
Savings in construction costs	17,700
Less: Cash proceeds from sale of old machine	(500)
Total cost of machine	$55,000

The following additional information is available:

1. Factory costs other than labor and materials averaged 80 percent of direct labor cost. This percentage was used to assign these other costs to products made in the factory for sale to outside customers.
2. Freight charges on the materials used in construction of the machine amounted to $250. This amount was debited to an expense account.
3. The replaced equipment had an original cost of $25,000 and accumulated depreciation of $21,000 at the time it was dismantled and sold.
4. The new machine had an anticipated useful life of 15 years; the special tooling would be useful for three years.
5. Savings in construction costs were calculated on the basis of the difference between the lowest outside bid and the net costs charged to the job during construction. These savings were credited to the account Gain on Construction of Equipment.

6. Products produced during the trial runs were scrapped; scrap value was negligible.

a. At what amount should the new machine have been capitalized in the equipment account on July 1, 19x2? Show the details.
b. Explain how you would have accounted for each of the cost elements in the above list that you would not have capitalized as part of the cost of this piece of equipment.

33. Ancillary Expenditures.

Realty Corporation owns a large number of buildings that it rents to commercial and residential tenants. In January 19x1, it bought a building for conversion into quarters suitable for use by a trade association. The building was in an advanced state of disrepair but was structurally sound except for the top (fourth) floor. This floor had been vacated two years earlier on the order of a city building inspector.

The purchase price of this property was $300,000 for the building and $500,000 for the land. Extensive remodeling and interior decorating were begun immediately to adapt the building to its intended use. The following outlays were made during the period January through June, 19x1:

1. Interior painting and decorating	$ 40,000
2. Structural alterations including replacement of plumbing fixtures at a cost of $50,000 and landscaping at $20,000	130,000
3. Replacement and renewal of electrical wiring	20,000
4. Removal of fourth story	50,000
5. Payment of hospital and medical expenses of passerby injured by falling brick	5,000
6. Architect's fees, building permits, and so forth	30,000
Total	$275,000

In addition, property taxes accrued for the period January 1 through June 30 amounted to $15,000.

Late in June, the company was notified that it was being sued for $1 million for the personal injuries and mental anguish suffered by the passerby who was hit by the falling brick (item 5 above). The suit was scheduled for trial in February 19x2. At the time the remodeling work was done, Realty Corporation had elected to be its own insurer in matters pertaining to public liability, and therefore it was not insured for either the medical expenses or the amount of any payment that might result from the lawsuit. The premium that an insurance company would have charged for liability coverage during the period of remodeling was $3,200.

The building was ready for occupancy on July 1, 19x1, and a 10-year lease, running from July 1, 19x1, was signed with the tenant.

Indicate how these facts should have been reflected in the company's accounts as of July 1, 19x1. How much should have been capitalized and under what account titles? How much should have been charged to expense for the first half of 19x1? Give reasons for your treatment of each item.

34. Choosing a Depreciation Method.[5] Alexander Cargo Service carries freight from a coastal seaport in the United States to several inland locations. By the beginning of 1982, the company had three small cargo vessels capable of operating in the small river that flowed into the port.

A fourth ship was purchased for $550,000 and placed in service on July 1, 1982. The public accountant who audited the company's financial statements pointed out that the company's first three ships were being depreciated on a straight-line basis over a 20-year period. Although a shorter life was prescribed by the taxing authorities in 1982, the auditor argued that this wasn't a relevant consideration in choosing a depreciation rate for financial reporting.

Mr. Alexander couldn't agree that the estimated life of this new vessel would be as long as 20 years. He had seen so many changes in the transportation pattern in his area just since he started in business that he felt a 10-year life would be much more likely. From experience that he had had in buying and selling secondhand ships, he also concluded that he could sell the ship for at least $50,000 at the end of 10 years even if economic conditions did not permit its use for containerized service locally after that time.

By the time the ship went into service on July 1, 1982, it was clear to Alexander that his original estimates were sound, at least for the first few years of the new ship's life. Contracts had been signed with several shippers. Bookings for space on the new vessel continued near capacity throughout the first six months of its operation. Alexander felt that he might gradually lose some of this business from year to year as the pattern of local cargo operations changed, but he saw no reason why he could not continue to operate the vessel for at least 10 years before the volume of business declined so far that he would find it necessary to take the new vessel out of service and sell it.

Sales revenues of Alexander Cargo Service amounted to $5 million in 1982 and were expected to reach $6 million in 1983. Income before taxes and before deducting depreciation on the new ship amounted to $250,000 in 1982 and was expected to total $500,000 in 1983. The book value of all assets other than this new vessel totaled $1,250,000 and was expected to remain constant at this level. The income tax rate was 40 percent of taxable income.

The company had sometimes used the tax basis in the past for capitalizing and depreciating costs when this seemed to fit the facts of the case.

---

[5] Abstracted from an original case, copyright 1967, 1983 by l'Institut pour l'Etude des Méthodes de Direction de l'Entreprise (IMEDE), Lausanne, Switzerland. Published by permission.

At other times, it had felt justified in using some basis other than the tax basis. For its financial statements, however, Alexander Cargo Service used only straight-line depreciation or the double-rate, declining-balance method, with the choice depending on the circumstances.

a. Which depreciation method should have been used for this new ship in the company's financial statements? Explain your reasoning.
b. Using this method, calculate depreciation for 1982. (Only one-half year's depreciation should be charged for the year.)
c. How important was the decision called for in part a? Support your answer by citing numbers from this problem.

Chapter 10

Liabilities and Related Items

A company's financial structure has great significance to management and outsiders alike. The amount and composition of the liabilities can have a great influence on the profitability of the shareholders' investment and on the risks of investment in the company. This chapter will examine the problems encountered in measuring various kinds of liabilities. Because liability measurement is inseparable from asset measurement in some cases and from expense measurement in others, our examination will cover some of these related topics too. The discussion falls under four major headings:

1. Long-term borrowing.
2. Interperiod income tax allocations.
3. Pension plans.
4. Leases in lessees' financial statements.

Long-Term Borrowing

Most large corporations obtain at least part of their funds through long-term borrowing. This kind of debt financing permits shareholders to benefit from the use of relatively low-cost funds to finance high-yield operations. It also allows the company to grow larger than it could if it had to rely on shareholder capital alone. These benefits are obtained at some sacrifice, however. Increasing long-term borrowing relative to the shareholders' equity also increases the risks the shareholders assume. This happens because the residual earnings that accrue to shareholders become more uncertain as the fixed payments required by the long-term debt increase.

Kinds of Borrowing

As we begin to examine the nature of long-term borrowing, let's first recall the nature of the types of loans we encountered in earlier chapters. In Chapter 4, we discussed short-term borrowings—generally, time intervals from 60 days to 18 months. In such cases, the borrower usually makes one payment at maturity consisting of *both* the sum borrowed and the accrued interest.

In Chapter 6, we discussed the use of intermediate-term loans—typically of two to eight years duration. It was in the context of these loans that we encountered repayment through a series of annuity payments. Each equal-amount payment consists of (1) interest on the loan balance for that compounding interval, and (2) a partial reduction of the loan balance.

In the case of long-term borrowings—normally longer than 10 years—the loan agreement is often effected through the issuance of bonds. The typical bond calls for the borrower (1) to pay a large fixed sum at the end of the loan period, and (2) to make interest payments at regular intervals during the entire life of the bond.

In this section, we'll examine the nature of bonds and how accountants measure and disclose their issuance, their interest cost, and their retirement. We'll be especially alert to the fact that in practice the amount recorded as a bond's interest cost may differ from the amount the borrower pays periodically to the lender. Let's also note that although the two parties to a bond agreement are the borrower and the lender, the borrower is usually called the issuer and the lender is referred to as the *bondholder* (or the investor).

The Nature of Bonds

Corporations often borrow money for long periods from single lenders such as insurance companies. In other cases, they meet their needs by borrowing from many lenders at the same time, each one lending a relatively small percentage of the total. Under these circumstances, a single long-term loan contract is signed by the borrower and a representative of the lenders. The contract is known as an *indenture,* and the lenders' representative is the *trustee.*

Each of the lenders in one of these long-term contractual arrangements receives one or more documents known as bond certificates or *bonds.* These certificates specify the amounts to be paid to the owners of the bonds and the times at which the payments are to be made. The final payment to the bondholder, the amount to be paid on the maturity date (the date on which the contract expires if all its provisions have been met), is called the **face value** (or maturity value) of the bond. Interim interest payments are customarily made semiannually, but they are normally expressed as an annual percentage of the face value. This percentage is called the **coupon rate** (or face rate) of interest. Thus, a $1,000, twelve percent, 20-year bond represents an agreement to pay $1,000 at the end of 20 years *plus* $60 (one half of 12 percent of $1,000) at the end of each half-year for 20 years. Exhibit 10–1 illustrates the lifetime pattern of cash payments to the holder of one of these bonds.

EXHIBIT 10–1
Cash Payments Required for a 20-Year, 12 Percent, $1,000 Bond

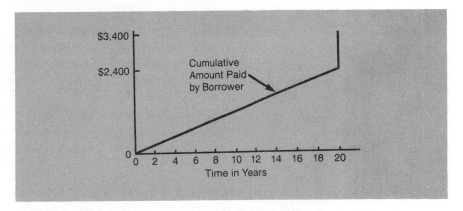

Bond Values

The value of bonds to investors depends on the **yield to maturity** they could earn on other bonds of comparable risk that are available in the market. *Yield to maturity* is the rate of interest investors can earn if they buy bonds at a given price, collect the specified interest payments on schedule, and collect the face value from the borrower on the maturity date.

For example, suppose other comparable bonds now yield 14 percent if held to maturity. If bonds are offered with a coupon rate of 12 percent, investors have to figure out how much to pay for these bonds so that they will yield 14 percent, the yield investors can get elsewhere. They do this by calculating the present values of the cash flows they will receive.

Calculating Present Value. Investors who buy the 12 percent bonds when they are issued become entitled to two kinds of payments for each $1,000 bond they hold: (1) a stream of 40 semiannual payments of $60 each, and (2) a payment of $1,000 at the end of 40 periods, 20 years from the issue date. The present values of these cash flows can be determined by multiplying them by multipliers taken from Tables 1 and 2 in Appendix A.

Because interest is paid twice a year, the usual technique is to use *semiannual* compounding. A quoted bond yield of 14 percent means that investors can earn 7 percent on their investment every six months.[1] This means using the present-value multipliers in the 7 percent columns of the two tables for 40 six-month periods. The calculations are:

Period	Amount	Multiplier	Present Value
1 to 40....	$60 a period	13.3317	$799.90
40........	$1,000	0.0668	66.80
Total....			$866.70

The value of this 12 percent bond on the issue date therefore is $866.70 to an investor whose comparable alternative is an investment yielding 7 percent every six months. The $133.30 difference between this amount and the $1,000 maturity value brings the yield on the bond up from 12 percent to 14 percent. This difference is referred to as a **discount.**

In other words, the issuer prints bonds with a 12 percent coupon rate. When the bonds are issued, the yield rate is 14 percent, and investors are understandably unwilling to pay the full $1,000 to buy the bonds. They will pay only that amount that will result in the semiannual $60 interest payment giving them a 7 percent return on the amount invested. They therefore seek to buy the bond at a $133.30 discount.

From the point of view of the issuer, it must incur a semiannual interest cost of 7 percent, not just the 6 percent represented by the $60 interest payment. While the remaining portion of the 7 percent interest must also be paid, it isn't paid during the periods when the interest accrues. Instead, payment is deferred until the bond matures—to be repaid as a result of the issuer paying the bondholder the higher face value of the bond rather than the lower amount of proceeds that were received when the bonds were issued.

Use of Bond-Value Tables.   If investors had to go through the previous calculations every time they considered buying or selling a bond, much time would be wasted unnecessarily. To avoid this, special tables have been prepared for the financial community, based on the kind of calculations just illustrated. A partial set of such tables is included in Appendix A (Tables 3 through 9). The present value of a 20-year, 12 percent bond in a market in which the prevailing yield is 14 percent may be found in Table 6 (the table for a coupon rate of 12 percent) by locating the column

---

[1] The effective *annual* yield is more than twice the six-months' rate because the bondholders can earn interest of 7 percent in the second half of the year on the 7 percent interest they earned in the first half. If investors can always reinvest the interest they receive at the same rate, the effective annual yield is $(1.07)^2 - 1 = 14.49$ percent. We'll conform to common practice, however, and quote annual yields at twice the six-month rate—in this illustration, 14 percent.

for bonds with 20 years to maturity and the row for the 14 percent yield rate. The multiplier is 86.67, which means that the market price will be $866.70 for each $1,000 of face value—the same amount we obtained using Tables 1 and 2.

Changes in Bond Prices as Maturity Approaches. The market value of the bond won't remain $866.70 forever, of course. The day it matures it will be worth $1,000, because that's how much the company will pay the bondholder at that time. The lowest line in Exhibit 10–2 shows how the

EXHIBIT 10–2
Market Value of a 12 Percent, $1,000 Bond for 20 Years with Different Market Yield Rates

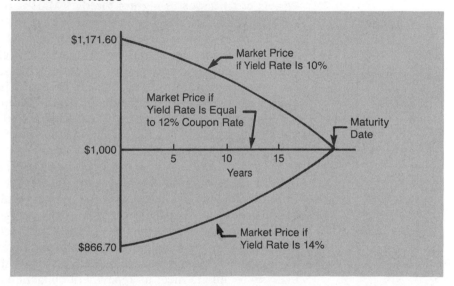

market value of a 12 percent bond will change as it approaches the maturity date, other things being equal. For example, if the bond is still outstanding five years after it is issued (15 years before maturity) and the market yield rate is still 14 percent at that time, Table 6 indicates the bond will have a value of $875.90. The price will be $894.10 at the end of 10 years and $929.80 after 15 years.

The horizontal line in the middle of the diagram shows the market price of a bond for which the market yield always equals the coupon rate. In such cases, the present value of the future stream of payments is always $1,000, and buying a bond for $1,000 will always bring a yield equal to the coupon rate, in this case 12 percent ($120/$1,000 = 12 percent every year).

Finally, the top line in Exhibit 10–2 shows how market prices will move if the bond is issued at a **premium**—that is, at a price higher than its face value. A 20-year, 12 percent bond issued in a 10 percent market should sell for $1,171.60. (The 10 percent row of the 20-year column in Table 6 shows a value of $117.16 for every $100 in face value.) This premium arises because the company is paying $120 a year, or $20 more than the market expects to receive on $1,000 invested in bonds at 10 percent. The $171.60 is the price the market pays for this extra $20 a year. As the bond approaches maturity, of course, the investor has fewer and fewer of these $20 extra payments to look forward to, and the market price will fall. At the maturity date, the market price will equal the face value.

Effects of Changes in Market Yields. Market prices change for other reasons, of course. The market's perception of the risk of owning a particular company's bonds may change, or market yields generally may change. For example, suppose market conditions changed five years after our 12 percent bond was issued, so that newly issued bonds of comparable risk were being sold to yield only 10 percent. The $120 annual interest payments would then command a premium. From Table 6 we find that a 12 percent bond with 15 years to maturity in a 10 percent market would command a price of $1,153.70 rather than the $875.90 it brought just before the market changed.

The market-price path on this bond is traced by the line in Exhibit 10–3. After rising gradually for five years, the market price jumped dramatically as market yields fell. Assuming market yields remained at 10 percent for the next 15 years, this bond's market price would decline gradually until it reached face value at maturity. In practice, the path would be much more irregular as market yields moved up and down, but it would always be moving toward face value at maturity if the company seemed likely to be able to meet its repayment obligation at that time.

Measuring Bond Liability and Interest Expense

The major accounting problem in connection with bonds is to measure the issuing corporation's liability and annual interest expense. We'll examine three situations:

1. The bonds are sold at their face value.
2. The bonds are sold at a discount.
3. The bonds are sold at a premium.

Bonds Sold at Face Value. Bond accounting is relatively simple when bonds are sold at their face value. The initial liability is the amount received from the lenders, and it remains at that level until the maturity

EXHIBIT 10–3
Market Value of a 12 Percent, $1,000 Bond with Yield of 14 Percent for 5 Years and 10 Percent for the Remaining 15 Years

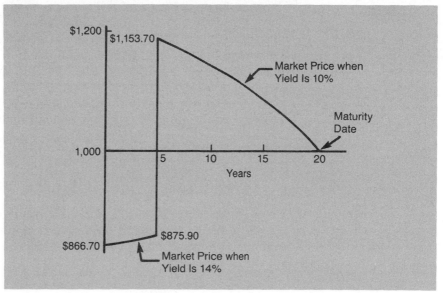

date. The entry to record the sale of $1 million, 14 percent bonds at their face value would be:

Cash..	1,000,000	
Bonds Payable.............................		1,000,000

The entry to record the payment at maturity would be:

Bonds Payable	1,000,000	
Cash		1,000,000

In this case, the payment of face value at maturity cancels out the amount originally received from the lenders, and the only payments to the bondholders for the use of their money are the $140,000 interest payments made each year. In other words, interest expense each year is equal to the annual interest payment.

Bonds Sold at a Discount.   The accounting problem isn't quite as simple when bonds are sold at a discount or at a premium. For example, suppose Reading Company decided late in 19x1 to issue $1 million of 14 percent, 20-year mortgage bonds. (Mortgage bonds are bonds secured by mortgages on specified company properties, usually land and buildings, meaning that if the company fails to pay the amounts it has promised to pay when they are due, the bondholders can have the property sold and collect the amounts due them from the proceeds of the sale.)

By the time the bonds were issued on January 1, 19x2, the market rate of interest had gone up to 16 percent. The bonds therefore had to be sold at a discount. The total amount received from the sale was $880,800. The investors needed the $119,200 discount from face value to compensate them for accepting annual interest payments of $140,000 (coupon rate times face value) instead of the $160,000 (market rate times face value) they could have obtained by investing $1 million somewhere else.

The general rule in accounting for liabilities and owners' equities is to record for each source of funds *the amount the investor has invested in the corporation.* Accordingly, the company's accountants might have recorded the issue of the bonds on Reading Company's books as follows:

```
Cash...........................................  880,800
    Bonds Payable................................            880,800
```

Although this entry is correct, the more usual practice is to record the face value of the bonds and the discount or premium in two separate accounts, as follows:

```
Cash ...........................................  880,800
Discount on Bonds .............................  119,200
    Bonds Payable ...............................          1,000,000
```

Some accountants consider this treatment more informative because it discloses the final lump-sum payment the borrower is obliged to make (the face value). This provides investors with additional information regarding the magnitude and timing of major cash outflows. The same information could be disclosed in footnotes to the financial statements, of course, but the general practice is to put the face value in the balance sheet itself.

The form of the journal entry doesn't affect the amount of the liability, which should have appeared on the January 1, 19x2, balance sheet as follows:

```
Bonds payable................  $1,000,000
Less: Discount on bonds .......      119,200
    Liability to bondholders ......  $  880,800
```

If Reading Company's bonds were to remain outstanding until the maturity date, the bondholders would receive the $1 million face value plus $2.8 million in coupon interest payments ($70,000 every six months for 20 years). The difference between this lifetime total of $3.8 million and the $880,800 proceeds of the issue ($3,800,000 − $880,800 = $2,919,200) represents the price paid by the corporation for the use of the bondholders' money—its interest expense. The $119,200 discount is as much a component of interest expense as the semiannual payment—

after all, the company's alternative was to sell the bonds at a higher coupon rate and higher semiannual payments.

The accounting problem is to decide how much of the $2,919,200 lifetime interest to record as expense each period. The preferred method of doing this is known as the *effective-interest method.*[2] This method calculates each period's interest expense by applying the yield rate of interest to the liability outstanding during the period. In doing this, we use the yield rate that was in effect when the bond was issued—that is, we don't consider subsequent fluctuations in the yield rate. The amount of liability outstanding does change each period, however, because with each successive period the liability to bondholders gets closer to the face value that will be repaid at maturity.

The yield on Reading Company's bonds was 16 percent. As we mentioned earlier, this means a return on the bondholders' investment of 8 percent every six months. Each six-month period's interest expense is calculated by multiplying 8 percent by the amount of the liability at the beginning of the period. The first six months' interest expense was $0.08 \times \$880,800 = \$70,464$.

This interest expense decreased the owners' equity by $70,464 and increased the liability to the bondholders by the same amount, from $880,800 to $951,264. A portion of the liability ($70,000) was current; the remainder ($881,264) was a long-term liability. In other words, the long-term liability increased by $464 during the first six-month period. This portion of the interest was to be paid when the bond became due at maturity:

Interest payable currently $70,000	+	Interest payable at end of 20 years $464	=	Interest expense $70,464

The entry to record interest expense for the first six months and the cash payment at the end of that period was:

```
Interest Expense.....................................   70,464
    Cash .............................................            70,000
    Discount on Bonds.................................               464
```

The credit to Discount on Bonds recorded the increase in the long-term liability during the first six months.

---

[2] Other methods of amortization such as straight-line are allowed only if the results obtained are not materially different from those obtained under the effective-interest method.

The bonds were reported on the company's June 30, 19x2, balance sheet as follows:

Bonds payable................	$1,000,000
Less: Discount on bonds	118,736
Liability to bondholders	$ 881,264

As indicated in Exhibit 10–4, the interest expense during the second six-month period was 8 percent of the liability at the beginning of that

EXHIBIT 10–4
Calculating Interest Expense and Liability to Bondholders

	(1) Interest Expense 0.08 × (4)*	(2) Coupon Interest 0.07 × $1 million	(3) Discount Amortization (1) − (2)	(4) Liability to Bondholders (4)* + (3)
January 1, 19x2.........				$ 880,800
June 30, 19x2	$ 70,464	$ 70,000	$ 464	881,264
December 31, 19x2......	70,501	70,000	501	881,765
June 30, 19x3	70,541	70,000	541	882,306
.	.	.	.	.
.	.	.	.	.
December 31, 19x20.....	.	.	.	982,168
June 30, 19x21	78,573	70,000	8,573	990,741
December 31, 19x21.....	79,259	70,000	9,259	1,000,000
Total	$2,919,200	$2,800,000	$119,200	

* *Beginning-of-period* Liability to Bondholders.

period, $881,264. Interest expense was thus $70,501, of which $70,000 was payable currently and $501 was payable at the bonds' maturity date. Interest expense was slightly greater during the second six months because the liability was greater during this period ($881,264 instead of $880,800), and it continued to increase as the liability increased. Eventually, the interest during the final six-month period (in year 20) will be 8 percent of $990,741, or $79,259.

Calculating interest expense and the accrual of the amount not paid currently (by a credit to Discount on Bonds) for the other 38 six-month periods produces the liability amounts diagrammed in Exhibit 10–5. The nearer the company comes to the maturity date, the closer the liability comes to the face value of the bonds.

Bonds Sold at a Premium. The effective-interest method is also used when bonds are sold for more than their face value—that is, at a premium. For example, Craft Company sold $1 million in 20-year, 14 per-

EXHIBIT 10–5
Liability to Holders of $1 Million in 20-Year, 14 Percent Bonds Yielding 16 Percent to Maturity

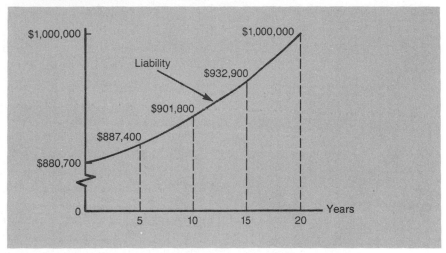

cent debentures in 19x6. (Debentures are unsecured bonds—that is, they are secured only by the company's ability to generate cash flows, not by special claims against specific pieces of property.) The market yields on other bonds comparable in risk and maturity were 12 percent at that time. Craft's bonds, therefore, sold at a premium price of $1,150,500 (see the 12 percent row of the 20-year-column of Table 7 in Appendix A). The balance sheet should have shown the following liability at that time:

Bonds payable...............	$1,000,000
Add: Premium on bonds	150,500
Liability to bondholders......	$1,150,500

Using the effective-interest method, the company calculated interest expense for the first six months as follows:

$$\$1,150,500 \times 12\% \times \tfrac{1}{2} = \$69,030$$

This was $970 less than the $70,000 of cash paid to the bondholders at the end of the first six months. This $970 represented a payment of a portion of the $1,150,500 the company had borrowed six months earlier:

Cash Payment	=	Interest Expense	+	Payment of Liability
$70,000		$69,030		$970

This company had used a separate account to record the initial premium on the issuance of the bonds. The entry to recognize the interest accrual and the payment of cash at the end of the first six months was:

```
Interest Expense.....................................   69,030
Premium on Bonds ...................................      970
   Cash ...........................................            70,000
```

The debit to Premium on Bonds decreased the liability by that amount, and a balance sheet prepared immediately after this payment showed the following liability:

```
Bonds payable....................  $1,000,000
Add: Premium on bonds sold .......     149,530
   Liability to bondholders ..........  $1,149,530
```

Notice what all this amounts to. In purchasing the bonds, the lenders paid $150,500 for the privilege of receiving $140,000 a year instead of the $120,000 they could have gotten from investing $1 million elsewhere at 12 percent. That $150,500 will be repaid to them gradually during the 20 years the bonds will be outstanding. As a result, the liability at maturity will be only $1 million, the face value of the bonds.

CALCULATION OF INTEREST AND LIABILITY

1. Identify the liability at the beginning of the period.
2. Determine the per-period yield-to-maturity rate when the bonds were first issued.
3. Multiply this yield rate by the beginning-of-period liability—this is the interest expense for the period.
4a. If the interest expense is greater than the payment, add the excess to the beginning-of-period liability to determine the liability at the end of the period.
4b. If the payment is greater than the interest expense, subtract the excess from the beginning-of-period liability to determine the liability at the end of the period.

Retirement and Refunding of Long-Term Debt

When a corporation buys its bonds back from the bondholders, the bonds are said to be **retired.** Bonds are sometimes retired at maturity, but other arrangements are also common. For one thing, bond issues are often very large, and it may be more convenient to retire them gradually rather than all at once. Furthermore, a company may not need all the borrowed funds continuously until the maturity date, or it may have an opportunity to obtain substitute financing on more favorable terms prior to that date. In principle, long-term debt will be retired whenever the company can maximize the net present value of future cash flows by doing so. Most bond issues, therefore, provide the issuing corporation with opportunities to retire some or all bonds before they mature.

Debt retirement is sometimes a one-way street—that is, the company pays cash and thereby reduces both its total assets and its total liabilities. In other cases, the company merely replaces one bond issue with another. We'll look briefly at each of these situations.

Debt Retirement by Conversion. Some bonds are **convertible** into shares of common stock. This means the bondholders have the right to exchange their bonds for a specified number of shares of common stock. Convertible bonds give the bondholders an opportunity to share in the benefits if the company is able to use their funds profitably. For this reason, convertible bonds are easier to sell than nonconvertible bonds carrying the same coupon rate. In some cases, the conversion price (the number of common shares obtainable for each bond) is so favorable that everyone expects all the bonds to be converted within a very few years. Such issues are really indirect means of selling common stock.

Debt Retirement by Serial Redemption. A second possibility is to provide for the gradual retirement of the bonds by making the issue subject to serial redemption—that is, by staggering the due dates of the component securities. Thus, an issue of $100 million of serial bonds may provide for $10 million to mature each year for 10 years, the first maturity coming 11 years after the date of original issue. Serial bonds are usually offered at a range of prices, set to provide higher yields for the longer maturities. Accountants treat each series as a separate issue, using the measurement method we described earlier.

Debt Retirement by Sinking Fund. A third device for orderly debt retirement is the **sinking fund.** Each year the corporation sets aside a certain amount of cash for the sinking fund, and this is then used to purchase company bonds. The trustees of the sinking fund will either buy bonds in the market *or* require the holders of certain bonds chosen at random to sell them to the sinking fund at specified prices. Bonds the trustees can force bondholders to sell to the company are said to be **callable** for sinking-fund purposes.

Debt Retirement by Direct Buy-Back. Companies may also take advantage of changes in market conditions and ample cash balances to purchase their own bonds in the open market and retire them. For example, on January 2, 19x4, Dawson Company issued $1 million of 20-year, eight percent bonds with cash proceeds reflecting an 8.5 percent yield to maturity. By January 19x9 (five years later), market yields had gone up to 10 percent, and the market price of Dawson's bonds on January 2, 19x9, was $846,300—as indicated by the 84.63 in the 15-year column, 10 percent row of Table 4 in Appendix A.

Suppose the company bought $100,000 of its bonds at this price, paying $84,630 for them. The book value of these bonds, reflecting the 8.5 percent yield to maturity five years earlier, can be found by looking at the 8.5 row in the 15-year column of Table 4. The multiplier is 95.81, which means the book value of the liability is $95,810, and the unamortized discount on bonds is $4,190 ($100,000 − $95,810).

The $11,180 difference between the liability ($95,810) and the amount paid ($84,630) would be reported in the income statement for 19x9 as an extraordinary item. The entry to record the purchase and retirement would be:

Bonds Payable	100,000	
Discount on Bonds		4,190
Cash		84,630
Gain on Bond Retirement		11,180

Market prices, it should be emphasized, have no effect on the company's records until the company engages in some market transaction. The company continues to amortize bond discount (or bond premium) on the basis of the *original* yield rate because this represents the cost of the financing.

Bond Refunding. For most large corporations, debt is a more or less permanent component of the capital structure. Far from wishing to reduce its indebtedness, the corporation seeks to maintain or increase it. When one bond issue matures, it is succeeded by another. Replacing one bond issue with another is known as **refunding.**

Refunding is relatively easy when the bonds are callable. Some bonds are callable for sinking-fund purposes only, but others can be called for other purposes as well. Callability allows the corporation to refund prior to maturity if conditions seem right. The borrowing corporation can take advantage of declines in money rates by calling the old higher-yield bonds, replacing them with bonds at the new lower rates.

To protect the bondholder, the bond contract usually specifies that an amount greater than the face value of the bond will be paid in the event of premature retirement. This *call price* normally varies with the age of the debt, approaching the face value at maturity or at some earlier date.

To illustrate, let's modify the example we used to illustrate bond retirements. Dawson Company issued $1 million of 20-year, 8 percent bonds on January 2, 19x4, when the market yield was 8.5 percent. Now suppose that five years later the bond market was *more* favorable to borrowers, and an insurance company offered Dawson a $1,070,000 loan at 7 percent interest for 15 years. The proceeds would be used to pay off the entire $1 million, 8 percent bond issue at its call price of $107 for each $100 of face value.

This refunding would have two effects:

1. A reduction in the interest payments each year, from $80,000 (0.08 × $1,000,000) to $74,900 (0.07 × $1,070,000), a saving of $5,100 a year for 15 years.
2. A $70,000 increase in the face value to be paid at the end of 15 years.

Management found this offer attractive because the present value of the $5,100 series of annual cash savings was greater than the present value of the $70,000 increase in the face value.[3]

Paradoxically, however, the company's income statement in the year the refunding took place would include a reported *loss* of $111,900. The reported gain or loss is the difference between the bond's *book value* and the amount of cash paid to effect the retirement. Dawson's loss would have been recorded with the following entry:

Bonds Payable	1,000,000	
Loss on Bond Retirement	111,900	
Discount on Bonds		41,900
Cash		1,070,000

Table 4 in Appendix A indicates a bond-value multiplier of 95.81 for 8 percent bonds reflecting an 8.5 percent yield rate 15 years from maturity. The $958,100 book value is retired with a $1 million reduction in the face value and a $41,900 reduction in the discount.

The reason for this apparent inconsistency—reporting a loss on a transaction that benefited the company—is that the loss actually took place earlier, when the market rate of interest dropped from 8.5 to 7 percent. This loss went unrecorded as long as the company continued to pay the higher rate of interest implicit in the earlier borrowing. Retiring the old debt was an exchange transaction that forced the company to recognize the loss that had already taken place.

Interperiod Income Tax Allocations

Taxable income, as we have indicated, may differ substantially from the amounts shown in income statements that are prepared for outside investors. Some of these differences are permanent—that is, they lead either to tax reductions the company will never have to pay back under any circumstances, or to added taxes the company will never be able to

---

[3] These cash flows should be adjusted to reflect the effects of this transaction on the company's income taxes, a technique we'll describe in Chapter 21. If we ignore income taxes and calculate the pretax cash flows at 10 percent, compounded annually—a rate we assume Dawson Company can earn on the cash savings as they materialize—the present value of the annual saving is $5,100 × 7.6061 = $38,791. The present value of the $70,000 payment is $70,000 × 0.2394 = $16,758.

recover. Others arise because of timing differences—that is, revenues or expenses appear on both the tax return and the income statement but in different periods. In this section, we'll see how these differences affect the company's financial statements.

Product-Warranty Expense

Some timing differences arise because expenses are included in financial reporting *before* they are allowable as tax deductions. Product-warranty expenses fall in this category in the United States. Expenses and liabilities for product-warranty claims are accrued when the related revenues are recognized; warranty expense for income tax purposes is based on expenditures actually made under terms of the warranty, and these come after the revenues are recognized.

The accepted treatment in such cases is to calculate income tax *expense* on the basis of the financial reporting amounts. For example, Revere Company started selling a line of products in 19x1 with a one-year repair warranty. Sales of these products in 19x1 totaled $1 million, and income before warranty expense and income taxes was $195,000. The income tax rate in 19x1 was 40 percent.

The estimated warranty costs arising from the year's sales amounted to $50,000. This amount was reflected in the following entry:

Warranty Expense	50,000	
Liability for Product Warranty		50,000

Only $20,000 of warranty-related expenditures were actually made in 19x1, however, leaving a $30,000 liability at the end of the year:

Liability under Product Warranty

Expenditures	20,000	Accrual	50,000
		Bal. 30,000	

For financial reporting, the appropriate warranty expense is $50,000. Only $20,000 was deductible from revenues in calculating taxable income, however. Taxable income, in other words, was $195,000 − $20,000 = $175,000. At the 40 percent tax rate, the current tax liability was $175,000 × 0.4 = $70,000. If this amount had been reported as the income tax expense for the year, the income statement would have shown the following:

Income before warranty expense and income tax	$195,000
Warranty expense	50,000
Income before taxes	145,000
Income tax expense	70,000
Net income	$ 75,000

The apparent income tax rate in this amount is $70,000/$145,000 = 48 percent, a rate we know is too high. If the $50,000 warranty expense had been allowed as a 19x1 tax deduction, taxable income would have been only $195,000 − $50,000 = $145,000, and the tax for the year would have been $58,000 rather than $70,000.

Accountants recognize the $12,000 difference between these two tax amounts as a prepayment, using **Deferred Income Taxes** as a *prepaid taxes* asset account. The entry to record income taxes for the year was:

Income Tax Expense	58,000	
Deferred Income Taxes	12,000	
Income Taxes Payable		70,000

In other words, the company deferred reporting $12,000 of its current income tax payments as income tax expense until some later period.

The situation was reversed in 19x2. The amount accrued for warranty expense in that year was $65,000, but the amounts expended totaled $75,000. This meant that taxable income was $10,000 less than pretax reported income. At a 40 percent tax rate, $4,000 was transferred *from* the Deferred Income Taxes account. The tax return for 19x2 showed a tax of $80,000, and the entry was:

Income Tax Expense	84,000	
Deferred Income Taxes		4,000
Income Taxes Payable		80,000

Income tax expense for the year was $4,000 more than the tax return showed because warranty expense was $10,000 less than the amount allowed for tax purposes. Part of 19x2's tax obligation ($4,000) had been "prepaid" in 19x1.

These two entries illustrate the process known as **interperiod income tax allocation,** the assignment of income tax expense to the periods in which the related revenues are reported rather than to the periods in which current income tax liabilities are accrued. When this is done, the income tax expense is said to be **normalized.**

The case for allocating income taxes to the periods in which the related pretax income is reported is that it is *these* revenues and expenses which create the tax liability. Congress may decide that these taxes are to be paid earlier or later, but how much is to be paid depends on the profitability of the company's operations. Normalizing the tax is intended to provide a net income amount that is representative of this underlying profitability. If warranty expense is shown at $50,000 but taxes are calculated on the basis of $20,000, the net income amount will be a poor approximation to the company's continuing earning power.

Depreciation

Interperiod income tax allocations arising from warranty expenses and similar items are relatively insignificant for most companies in the

United States. In the typical case, however, substantial amounts of cost appear as income tax deductions *before* they appear as expenses in the income statement. Most of these arise from differences between the amounts of depreciation reported on the companies' financial statements and the amounts shown on their income tax returns. The reason is that the depreciation amounts used for federal income tax purposes provide depreciation charges that are higher in assets' earlier years than the depreciation amounts that are used for financial reporting.

Creating the Deferral. Let's assume that Brubeck Corporation started business on January 1, 19x1. It bought equipment costing $300,000 and placed it in a rented building. Brubeck used an accelerated depreciation method for federal income tax purposes, and calculated $45,000 tax depreciation for 19x1. For financial reporting, however, Brubeck calculated depreciation on a straight-line basis with a 10-year estimated life and zero estimated end-of-life salvage value—that is, $30,000 a year.

Income before depreciation and income taxes was $100,000 in 19x1, and the tax rate was 40 percent. The tax calculation for 19x1 was as follows:

Income before depreciation and taxes.........	$100,000
Tax depreciation............................	45,000
Taxable income.............................	$ 55,000
Tax at 40 percent	$ 22,000

Using interperiod income tax allocation, however, the income statement showed the following:

Income before depreciation and taxes.........	$100,000
Depreciation expense (0.10 × $300,000)	30,000
Income before taxes........................	70,000
Income tax expense (0.40 × $70,000)..........	28,000
Net income................................	$ 42,000

In other words, income tax allocation led the company to report $6,000 ($28,000 − $22,000) *more* income tax expense in 19x1 than it was currently obligated to pay. An appropriate entry to record the income tax expense for 19x1 under these assumptions would be as follows:

Income Tax Expense	28,000	
Current Taxes Payable		22,000
Deferred Income Taxes............................		6,000

The debit to Income Tax Expense records a decrease in the owners' equity in that amount, while the two credit entries record increases in the company's current and long-term liabilities.

The explanation of this treatment is that the due date for payment of $6,000 of the current income tax expense was postponed, not canceled.

By postponing the collection of taxes, the government increased the amount of the company's cash flow it could retain and use during the first part of the assets' lives. The government hoped this would encourage businesses to buy more equipment and stimulate the economy. Payment of these taxes was only deferred, however; it wasn't avoided. As the assets aged, annual tax depreciation would drop below the straight-line amount, and the company would have to start paying these deferred amounts. As a result, Brubeck had to recognize a $6,000 deferred-tax liability as of the end of 19x1.

Reducing the Deferral. Reduction of the liability starts as soon as tax depreciation falls below financial depreciation. For Brubeck Corporation, tax depreciation exceeded financial depreciation every year for five years. At the end of that time, 100 percent of the $300,000 original cost had been depreciated for tax purposes. In 19x6, therefore, tax depreciation was zero, while straight-line financial depreciation was once again reported as $30,000.

Brubeck's income before depreciation and taxes in 19x6 once again was $100,000. With no tax depreciation to shield any of that, taxable income that year was also $100,000, and the tax currently due for payment that year (at a 40 percent tax rate) was $40,000. Income tax *expense*, however, continued to be calculated on the basis of the $70,000 income before taxes reported in the company's income statement, and amounted to $28,000:

Income before depreciation and taxes.........	$100,000
Depreciation expense (0.10 × $300,000)	30,000
Income before taxes........................	70,000
Income tax expense (0.40 × $70,000)..........	28,000
Net income................................	$ 42,000

This means that $12,000 of the deferred income tax had to be reclassified as a current tax liability, as in the following entry:

Income Tax Expense	28,000	
Deferred Income Taxes	12,000	
Current Taxes Payable		40,000

Lifetime Pattern. The basis for this process of tax deferral and eventual payment is illustrated in Exhibit 10–6. This compares the tax depreciation on Brubeck Corporation's $300,000 equipment purchase with straight-line depreciation. In this case, tax depreciation rose to a high in the second year and then leveled off for three more years before falling to zero in the sixth year.

As a result, tax depreciation exceeded straight-line depreciation for the first five years, reducing taxable income in those years. In each of the next five years, however, tax depreciation was zero, meaning that taxable

EXHIBIT 10–6
Depreciation Expense versus Tax Depreciation for Assets Costing
$300,000 with 10-Year Life and 5-Year Tax Life

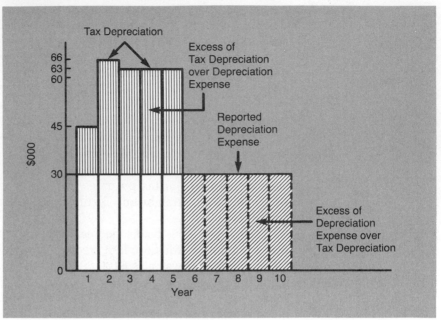

income was $30,000 more than it would have been with straight-line depreciation. The total of the vertically-shaded areas in the first five blocks of Exhibit 10–6 is just equal to the total of the diagonally-shaded areas in the other five blocks. In other words, if these had been the company's only depreciating assets, the amount of the company's deferred income tax liability would have been exactly zero.

Pros and Cons.   Under this treatment, the deferred portion of the tax is classified as a liability. Many accountants and financial analysts aren't convinced it is really a liability, however. Their argument is that these taxes may never have to be paid, and, if paid, the amounts may be different from the amounts accrued. The liability will never decrease as long as the cumulative difference in tax timing doesn't decrease. And the deferred amounts won't be paid in their entirety unless the corporation is liquidated. Liquidation is highly unlikely, and if it does take place, the deferred taxes may be erased by tax-deductible losses arising in the liquidation process.

The fact remains, however, that the deferral results from a privilege granted to taxpayers by the taxing authorities. The taxing authorities can always rescind or reduce this privilege for assets acquired in the future. If this happens, or if the company ceases to grow and allows its depreciable assets to age, current taxable income will exceed current income before taxes—and taxes will exceed tax expense. The deferral can even lead to tax obligations at the time of liquidation even if the assets are sold at a reported loss. Treating deferred taxes as a liability is an effective way of recognizing these facts.

The Investment Tax Credit

The tax laws of many countries provide for complete forgiveness of a portion of income taxes if the taxpayer satisfies specific requirements. A typical provision of this sort is the so-called *investment tax credit,* which has been available to taxpayers in the United States at various times.

For example, Trilby Company's equipment purchases in 19x1 amounted to $1 million. The investment tax credit was 10 percent of $1 million, or $100,000, and this amount was deducted in full from the amount of taxes to be paid the first year.

The accounting question is whether the entire tax credit should flow through the current income statement or be spread over the estimated life of the depreciable assets. In the **flow-through method,** income tax expense is reduced initially by the full amount of the investment tax credit.

Exhibit 10–7 illustrates the differences between the flow-through and deferral methods. Trilby Company expected to use the equipment for five

EXHIBIT 10–7
Investment Tax Credit

	19x1		19x2	
	Flow-Through	Deferral	Flow-Through	Deferral
Income statement:				
Income before income tax	$450,000	$450,000	$500,000	$500,000
Income tax expense (40 percent)..	180,000	180,000	200,000	200,000
Less: Investment tax credit	100,000	20,000	—	20,000
Total........................	80,000	160,000	200,000	180,000
Net income	$370,000	$290,000	$300,000	$320,000
Balance sheet, end of year:				
Deferred investment tax credit	—	$ 80,000	—	$ 60,000
Retained earnings	$370,000	290,000	$670,000	610,000

years, its income before taxes was $450,000 in 19x1, and its income was subject to a 40 percent tax rate. Columns 1 and 3 show the results of applying the flow-through method in 19x1 and 19x2; columns 2 and 4 show the effects of the deferral method.

As the third line of column 1 shows, under flow-through the entire investment credit would have been reported as an increase in net income in 19x1. The **deferral method,** in contrast, would have brought only one fifth of the $100,000 investment credit, or $20,000, into net income in that year. This is shown in the third line of column 2. The other $80,000 appears in the year-end balance sheet, to be included in income during the next four years.

Columns 3 and 4 display the financial statement differences in 19x2. Trilby's pretax income was $500,000, and it acquired no additional assets that would qualify for an investment credit in that year. The third line of column 3 shows that there would be no carryover effect under the flow-through method. Column 4, however, shows that another fifth of the 19x1 investment credit, $20,000, would be added to income in 19x2 under the deferral method, and the balance sheet deferred amount would be reduced by that sum, down to $60,000 at the end of 19x2.

The case for the flow-through method is that since the investment credit is simply a tax reduction that leaves income before taxes unchanged, income after taxes in the current period should be increased by the full amount of the tax credit. Advocates of the deferral method, on the other hand, argue that the tax credit is conditional on the purchase and use of equipment, and that it therefore represents a reduction in the cost of the equipment. Recognition of the benefit offered by the credit should be deferred because it is the counterpart of the asset's cost being depreciated over its expected useful life. Deferral therefore is a better application of accrual accounting.

The main difficulty with the deferral method is in classifying the deferred tax credit in the balance sheet. Since the deferral method is predicated on the assumption that the credit represents a reduction in the asset's cost, it should be classified as a contra account to the asset itself. Similarly, in calculating depreciation each year, a portion of the investment credit should be offset against the depreciation charges that are based on the purchase price of the equipment.

Most companies that use deferral treat the credit either as a liability or as a deferred credit, listed in the limbo between the liabilities and owners' equity. This is a way of dodging the issue. It cannot be owners' equity, because this would imply that it reflects a benefit already earned, an assumption that is totally inconsistent with the logic of the deferral method. It can be regarded as a liability, but only if it is assumed to compensate the company for incurring higher operating costs in the future than it would have incurred if it had not purchased the equipment in the first place. The difficulty of verifying this assumption lends further support to our case for listing the deferred investment credit as a reduction of the asset's cost.

Liabilities under Pension Plans

Some of the more complex questions in the recognition and measurement of liabilities have arisen in connection with employee pension plans. Legislation in the 1970s solved some of the accounting issues, but others linger on. In this section, we'll study three topics:

1. Common attributes of pension plans.
2. Accounting for current-service benefits.
3. Accounting for past-service benefits.

Attributes of Pension Plans

The number of variations in pension plans is virtually limitless, but the most important variations come in a few key elements. The diagram in Exhibit 10–8 identifies four of these elements. First, the plan may be

EXHIBIT 10–8
Attributes of Pension Plans

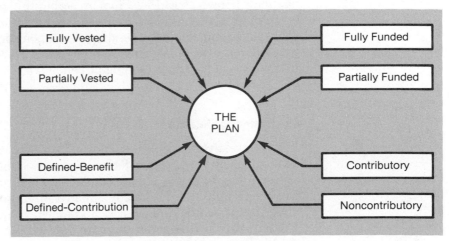

fully vesting or *partially vesting.* Under a fully vesting plan, the employees' rights to retirement benefits accrue periodically and can't be revoked or withdrawn by the employer. If the employees' rights are partially vested, they may lose some of their retirement benefits if they leave the company prior to retirement.

Second, the plan may be *fully funded* or *partially funded.* In a fully funded plan, enough cash has been set aside to meet the expected future costs of all retirement benefits earned to date, assuming that these segregated funds are invested at a rate of interest assumed or specified in the plan. In a partially funded plan, the employees rely in part on the employer's future solvency; some of the cash isn't set aside until payments actually have to be made.

Some plans are *defined-contribution* plans, meaning that the company fulfills its obligations by making specified payments to the pension fund; the employees' pensions then depend on the amounts contributed on their behalf and how effectively these funds are invested by the fund administrators.

Other plans are *defined-benefit* plans, in which the employees' pensions are determined by a formula, usually based on the employees' length of service and average salary during some part of this period. In such cases the company's obligation is to set aside enough funds at some time to pay the amounts required.

Plans in either of these categories may be *contributory*, meaning that employees pay part of the cost of the plan; others have the employer bear all the costs.

Most pension plans in the United States today must meet the requirements of the Employee Retirement Income Security Act of 1974, more popularly known as ERISA. From an accounting point of view, this very complex legislation is important because it requires rapid vesting of pension rights, immediate full funding of the pension benefits under plans covered by the act and arising from services performed after the act went into effect, and gradual funding of benefits arising from service before that time.

Illustration: Defined-Benefit Plan

Let's take a very simple case. Carter Company adopted a fully vested, defined-benefit pension plan for its employees as of January 1, 19x4. The company had 10 employees on that date, each 60 years old. Each of them had been with Carter for exactly three years. Annual retirement benefits under the plan would amount to 50 percent of the employee's average annual salary in the three years immediately prior to retirement and would continue until the employee's death. Each of Carter's employees was expected to retire on December 31, 19x8, on an annual pension of $10,000, payable at the *end* of each year after retirement. Based on actuarial tables, payments were expected to occur through December 31, 19x18, exactly 10 years after retirement.

The company agreed to fund the cost of **current-service benefits** each year by paying an insurance company, beginning on December 31, 19x4, an amount equal to the present value of the pension payments attributable to that year. It would also make 15 equal annual payments to this insurance company, starting on December 31, 19x4, to pay for the employees' **past-service benefits.** Carter Company agreed to the insurance company's proposal to calculate interest on amounts paid to it at 10 percent compounded annually. This same interest rate would have been available in 19x1 through 19x3.

Exhibit 10–9 shows the four sets of time periods relevant to this pension plan. The first box represents the eight years each employee was

EXHIBIT 10–9
Carter Company: Periods Reflected in Pension Plan

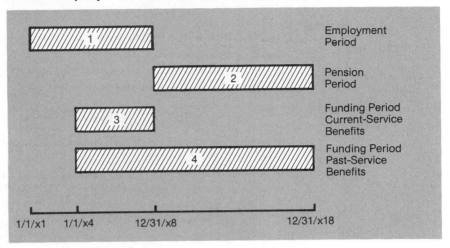

expected to work for the company, the second box stands for the 10 years each employee was expected to receive pension benefits, the third box shows the timing of the payments to fund the costs of current-period benefits, and the bottom box shows the timing of the payments to fund the costs of past-service benefits.

Current-Service Benefits

One issue is the size of the required annual payment to cover current-service benefits. In defined-benefit plans, the pension expense in any year arising out of the services provided by employees in that year is referred to as the cost of *current-service benefits*. It is measured by the present value of the portion of future pension payments attributable to services performed in the current year, using the average rate of interest the assets in the fund are expected to achieve.

In Carter Company's plan, all the pension benefits (box 2 in Exhibit 10–9) derived from the pensioners' years of active service (box 1). If Carter had begun funding the pensions in 19x1 with equal annual payments, by December 31, 19x8, it would have built up a fund equal to the present value on that date of the ten pension payments. To determine the annual cost of current-service benefits, therefore, we need to perform two operations:

1. Determine the present value on December 31, 19x8, of the 10 pension payments.
2. Calculate the eight-year annuity that will accumulate to this present value.

Present Value of the Pension Series. The December 31, 19x8, present value of the 10 pension payments is determined easily enough, by applying the multiplier in the 10-year row of the 10 percent column in Table 2 of Appendix A to the annual pension payment:

$$\text{Present value }_{19x8} = 6.1446 \times \$10,000 \times 10 \text{ employees}$$
$$= 614,460.$$

The Equivalent Annuity. Our next task is to calculate the size of the annuity necessary to produce a fund of $614,460 on December 31, 19x8. The way to do this, using only the interest tables in Appendix A, is to calculate the present value of the $614,460 as of January 1, 19x1, and determine the eight-year annuity that would buy. The reason this would work is that the present value of $614,460 is an amount that would pay for the pension series on that date; any annuity with the same present value would also pay for that same pension series.

The present value of the pension series as of January 1, 19x1, can be calculated by multiplying $614,460 by the multiplier from the 8-year row in the 10 percent column of Table 1 of Appendix A (0.4665):

$$\text{Present value }_{1/1/x1} = 0.4665 \times \$614,460 = \$286,645.59$$

We know that the present value of an annuity is equal to the multiplier times the annual amount, and this is equivalent to:

$$\text{Annual sum} = \text{Present value/Multiplier}$$

The multiplier for an eight-year annuity (from Table 2 in Appendix A) is 5.3349. The annual sum therefore is:

$$\text{Annual sum} = \$286,645.59/5.3349 = \$53,730.27 \text{ a year}$$

In other words, if Carter had begun funding the pension at the end of 19x1 with annual payments of $53,730.27, the balance in the fund would have stood at $614,460 on December 31, 19x8, the day the employees retired. Exhibit 10–10 demonstrates this the long way, by showing how much each of the eight payments would have built up to by that date. The first $53,730.27 payment would have seven years to earn interest, so it

EXHIBIT 10–10
Building a Pension Fund

Payment Date	Amount of Payment	Multiplier	Fund Balance on December 31, 19x8
December 31, 19x1	$53,730.27	$(1.1)^7 = 1.9487$	$104,704.18
December 31, 19x2	53,730.27	$(1.1)^6 = 1.7716$	95,188.55
December 31, 19x3	53,730.27	$(1.1)^5 = 1.6105$	86,532.60
December 31, 19x4	53,730.27	$(1.1)^4 = 1.4641$	78,666.49
December 31, 19x5	53,730.27	$(1.1)^3 = 1.3310$	71,514.99
December 31, 19x6	53,730.27	$(1.1)^2 = 1.2100$	65,013.63
December 31, 19x7	53,730.27	$(1.1)^1 = 1.1000$	59,103.30
December 31, 19x8	53,730.27	$(1.1)^0 = 1.0000$	53,730.27
Total			$614,454.01

would contribute $104,704.18, the amount in the right-hand column, to the retirement-date fund. The second payment would build up to $95,188.55 by the retirement date, and so on. The sum of the these future amounts is $614,454.01, which differs from the $614,460 we calculated earlier only by a $5.99 rounding error.

This means that the cost of the pension attributable to each of the working years was $53,730.27, and this therefore was the cost of current-service benefits attributable to the year 19x4.

Pension Liability

The next question is how much pension liability had accrued as of January 1, 19x4, as a result of work performed before that date. We can determine this by calculating how large the fund would have amounted to on that date if funding payments had been made from the beginning:

Payment Date	Amount of Payment	Multiplier	Fund Balance on December 31, 19x3
December 31, 19x1	$53,730.27	$(1.1)^2 = 1.2100$	$ 65,013.63
December 31, 19x2	53,730.27	$(1.1)^1 = 1.1000$	59,103.30
December 31, 19x3	53,730.27	$(1.1)^0 = 1.0000$	53,730.27
Total			$177,847.20

This was Carter Company's pension liability as of January 1, 19x4, the date the pension plan went into effect.

Expense Attributable to Past-Service Benefits

Total expense in 19x4 therefore had to include the $53,730.27 cost of current-service benefits, plus something to amortize the $177,847.20 unfunded cost of past-service benefits. This can't be a simple matter of dividing $177,847.20 by the number of years in the amortization period, however. Like most other liabilities, the pension liability is assumed to accrue interest until it is paid off.

The amount that will be amortized each year for 15 years (19x4 through 19x18) therefore must include both (1) the December 31, 19x3, $177,847.20 and (2) the interest that accrues on that amount beyond 19x3. This means we need to determine the annuity amount payable at the end of each year for 15 years whose present value is $177,847.20. We turn to Table 2 in Appendix A: for 10 percent interest and a 15-year annuity, the multiplier is 7.6061. This tells us that the annual total of the amortization and interest costs of past-service benefits is $23,382.18 ($177,847.20 divided by 7.6061). This total can be broken down into its components for the first year, as follows:

Total annual amortization and interest	$23,382.18
Interest: $177,847.20 × 0.10	17,784.72
Reduction of liability	$ 5,597.46

In the absence of an interest rate change, the interest component will be smaller in the second year, because the interest rate will be applied to a smaller total liability: $177,847.20 − $5,597.46 = $172,249.74.

Total Pension Expense and End-of-Year Liability

Given the assumptions and the calculations in the preceding paragraphs, Carter Company's total pension expense for 19x4 would have been as follows:

Current-service benefit.	$53,730.27
Past-service benefits.	23,382.18
Total expense.	$77,112.45

The liability at the end of 19x4, after the payment to the insurance company, would have been as follows:

Liability, January 1, 19x4.	$177,847.20
Add: Interest on the liability at 10%. . . .	17,784.72
Current-service benefit expense. .	53,730.27
Less: Payment to trustee	(77,112.45)
Liability, December 31, 19x4.	$172,249.74

This of course is the same number we calculated earlier—the liability at the beginning of the period, minus the first year's amortization.

Under generally accepted accounting principles, this liability would *not* appear in Carter's balance sheet. Liabilities arising in connection with operating costs or expenses are recognized only when the operating costs or expenses are recognized. The argument for deferring the recognition of past-service costs is that the company has granted pension rights for past service in the expectation that the company will reap commensurate future benefits—that future production costs will be reduced through lower employee turnover, greater company loyalty, and so forth. A counterargument is that the employees have earned their pensions by their past services and, once the vesting date has been reached, can retain these pension rights even if they leave the company.

Most companies with unfunded pension obligations are now accruing their past-service costs gradually, over periods of 30 years or so. The unaccrued amount is reported in a footnote.

We don't pretend that these calculations are simple, and this may give a hint as to just how complicated the calculations for a defined-benefit plan can be. Notice all the assumptions we had to make:

1. The length of past service of each employee covered by the plan.
2. The length of time before each employee would retire.
3. Each employee's salary level during the period prior to retirement (this amount determines the annual pension payment).
4. The length of time during which each employee would receive a pension.
5. The applicable rate of interest.

For each of these, we made a far simpler assumption than would be possible in practice. Furthermore, we made no mention of the fact that these assumptions are likely to change from year to year. As a result, the unfunded portion of the cost of past-service benefits can increase even if funding proceeds on schedule, or can decrease by a greater amount than the amount funded in the current year.

Leases in Lessees' Financial Statements

In the past, accountants regarded leases as unfulfilled agreements to buy the use of property. The signing of a lease wasn't regarded as a transaction; the only recognized transaction was the *use* of the property by the lessee, the payment of rent, or the prepayment of rent. Leases are now very common means of acquiring the use of land, buildings, and equipment, however, and these leases often run for many years. As a result, accountants have had to develop a new approach to lease accounting. In this final section, we'll examine some common characteristics of long-term leases and describe situations in which lessees are required to recognize leases in their balance sheets.

Lease Characteristics

Many leases serve the same purposes as purchases of property financed by long-term borrowing and have many similar characteristics. For example, to serve its southeastern market, Trevett Company has decided to build a new manufacturing plant in a small town about 50 miles from Atlanta, Georgia. The cost of the land and buildings is $10 million, and it is estimated that the facility will be used for 30 to 40 years. The company doesn't have the liquid assets needed to finance the investment. Its financial position is strong, but a firm of investment bankers has advised Trevett against trying to float a bond issue until additional ownership capital has been obtained. Trevett's present owners are unwilling to invest additional funds and are equally unwilling to endanger their operating control by broadening the ownership base to include new outside owners.

With the conventional avenues to new financing closed off, Trevett has decided to enter into a sale-leaseback agreement with the Globe-Wide Insurance Company. This agreement provides that Trevett will have the plant built to its own specifications, after which the insurance company will buy the land and building at Trevett's cost ($10 million) and lease it back to Trevett on a 30-year lease. Trevett will pay Globe-Wide $947,780 at the beginning of each year for 30 years and will also pay property taxes, insurance, maintenance, and all other operating costs. All Globe-Wide will do each year is collect the rent. At the end of the initial 30-year lease term, Trevett can either vacate the property or buy it by meeting the best offer received by Globe-Wide at that time.

A sale-leaseback of this type differs from a purchase financed by borrowing in that the lease entitles Trevett to the use of the property for a specified period of time, but it doesn't convey any title to the rights to any residual values at the end of the lease period. If conventional debt financing had been available at an effective interest rate of 8 percent, and if the estimated market value of the property at the end of 30 years is $3 million, the two alternatives might be described as follows:

1. *Purchase* (financed by borrowing): Pay $800,000 a year (8 percent of $10 million) for 30 years, the interest portion of the loan, and $10 million, the amount borrowed, at the end of the 30 years.
2. *Sale-leaseback:* Pay $947,780 a year for 30 years, starting immediately at the beginning of the first year (the leasing charge per year), and $3 million at the end of the 30 years, the sale price of the property at that time, if the continued use of the property is desired.

In other words, the choice of lease financing requires Trevett to pay $147,780 more each year than if it had borrowed the money in a more conventional manner. If it leases, however, it will have to pay out $7 million less ($10 million minus $3 million) 30 years from now.

The effective cost of each of these methods of financing can be calculated from an analysis of the anticipated cash flows. In this case, the cost of conventional borrowing is 8 percent before taxes and 4 percent after taxes at a 50 percent tax rate. The cost of lease financing is 10 percent before taxes and considerably more than 5 percent after taxes, depending on the tax depreciation method used.[4]

The popularity of leasing stems from its adaptability to a wide variety of specific circumstances and its availability when conventional borrowing is either not feasible or impossible. In addition, leasing is often a considerably cheaper source of funds than additional ownership investment, when used within limits, an advantage it shares with long-term bonds.

Lease Capitalization

The concern here is not with the desirability of lease financing, difficult though it is to keep away from that topic. The main interest is the representation of the lease in the company's financial statements. If the plant were financed by conventional borrowing, Trevett's balance sheet would report increases in plant assets *and* in long-term debt. Investors considering the purchase of the company's stock would note the greater risk caused by the increased debt. Furthermore, they would also include the $10 million cost of the plant in its asset base in calculating return on investment.

The lease imposes no less a debt burden than long-term borrowing. If anything, the burden is heavier because the fixed annual payments include the amortization of the amount borrowed as well as the interest on the loan. Given this, a strong argument can be made to disclose the lessee's rights to use the property and the corresponding liability for future rental payments in the asset and liability sections of the company's balance sheets.

Balance sheet recognition of this sort is known as **lease capitalization.** Leases can be capitalized in much the same manner as any other asset and liability—at the present value of the future obligatory payments under the lease, using an appropriate rate of interest. If the lease payments were capitalized at an interest rate of 10 percent, compounded annually, their present value would be $9,828,100[5], and an appropriate entry would be:

Leased Property	9,828,100	
Lease Liability		9,828,100

---

[4] At these rates, the present value of the future cash flows under leasing is $10 million. The method of deriving these rates will be discussed in Chapter 21.

[5] $9,828,100 is $947,780 × 10.3696, the 10.3696 being the sum of the present value of the first payment, 1.0000, and the 9.3696 present-value multiplier for 10 percent and n = 29 (calculated from the formula at the top of page 968).

Once leases have been capitalized, both the asset and the liability must be amortized. For example, suppose Trevett decided to depreciate the asset's cost by the straight-line method. The annual depreciation would be $9,828,100/30 = $327,603. Interest expense, calculated by the effective-interest method, would be $888,032, calculated as follows:

Initial liability	$9,828,100
First rental payment (paid immediately)	947,780
Principal, first year.	$8,880,320
Interest (10 percent of $8,880,320).	$ 888,032

Total expense therefore would be $327,603 + $888,032 = $1,215,635, considerably greater than the annual rental of $947,780. In the later years of the lease, annual expense would be less than if the lease were regarded as a simple rental agreement.

Lessees must capitalize leases if they meet *any one* of the following four criteria:

1. The lease transfers ownership of the property to the lessee by the end of the lease term.
2. The lease contains a bargain (less than fair value) purchase option for the lessee.
3. The lease term is equal to 75 percent or more of the estimated economic life of the leased property.
4. The present value at the beginning of the lease term of the minimum lease payments equals 90 percent or more of the net fair value of the leased property at that time.

Summary

In this chapter, consideration has turned from the forms capital takes once it has been injected into the enterprise to an examination of some problems in accounting for the funds invested by the company's creditors. In the first part of the chapter we outlined a consistent procedure whereby any long-term liability can be capitalized, and illustrated the application of this method to the liability associated with long-term bonds.

We followed this with a discussion of interperiod tax allocation, a practice that is made necessary by differences between the tax and accounting bases for reporting revenues, expenses, gains, and losses. Although these allocations occasionally lead to the recognition of assets, in most cases taxes are deferred and a liability is shown in the balance sheet.

The chapter also examined three topics that have been major issues in contemporary financial reporting: the investment tax credit, pension plans, and long-term leases. Although the accounting profession has identified acceptable and preferred methods of resolving these issues, differences of opinion exist among accountants and readers of financial statements. In all such cases, the reporting company must identify which method it has used.

Key Terms

Bond discount	Flow-through method
Bond premium	Income tax allocation
Callable bonds	Investment tax credit
Convertible bonds	Lease capitalization
Coupon rate	Normalization of tax expense
Current-service benefits	Past-service benefits
Debt retirement	Refunding
Deferral method	Sinking fund
Deferred taxes	Yield to maturity
Face value	

Independent Study Problems (Solutions in Appendix B)

1. Accounting for Long-Term Bonds.   Mountain Electric Company sells a million-dollar issue of 12 percent bonds on a 14 percent basis, payable semiannually.

a. What does this mean?
b. Is the price $1,150,500 or $866,700? Why?
c. What is the term of this issue?
d. Calculate interest expense for the first six months. What entry should be made to record the accrual of interest and the payment of the first semiannual coupon?
e. What entry should be made to record the second coupon payment?
f. How should this bond issue be shown on the balance sheet one year after it is issued and all interest for the first year has been paid?

2. Income Tax Allocation.   Winston Corporation's income before depreciation and taxes in 19x3 was $6 million. Its depreciation for tax purposes was $1.25 million, and the depreciation for financial statement purposes was $850,000.

a. Derive the corporation's income after taxes, assuming a 50 percent tax rate.
b. Present journal entries to account for the year's depreciation and accrual of the income tax liability for the year.

3. Lease Accounting.   Butler Company has leased a truck from Truck Lessors, Inc., for $4,000 a year, payable at the beginning of each year for five years. Butler Company is responsible for all taxes, insurance, and maintenance on this truck, and the lease is to be accounted for as a means of borrowing money at 12 percent.

a. Show how this lease would be reflected on Butler's balance sheet prepared immediately after it was signed and the first payment was made.
b. Calculate the amount of expense that would be reported in the income statement for the first year of the lease, assuming that depreciation was straight-line with zero salvage value.
c. Calculate the book value of the asset and of the liability at the beginning of the second year, immediately after the second lease payment.

4. Self-Amortizing Loan. Bell Company borrows $100,000 with the understanding that it will pay the interest and repay the loan in five equal annual payments, the first payment to be a year from the date the money is borrowed.

a. If the interest rate is 14 percent, what will be the amount of each annual payment?
b. Present a schedule showing the interest and loan-reduction components of each of the five payments, assuming a 14 percent interest rate.
c. Prepare journal entries to record the loan and the payment at the end of the first year.

5. Pension Accounting: Defined Benefit Plan. A small company has only one employee, Leroy Williams. Williams started to work for the company 30 years ago, when he was 33 years old. The company established a pension plan at the beginning of this year, when Williams was 63 years old. According to this plan, Williams will receive a pension payment each year equal to $100 times the number of years he has worked for the company by the time he retires. This pension will be given to him every year until his death, the first payment being made one year after the date of his retirement.

The company will amortize and fund the past-service costs during the next two years, and Williams will retire at the end of that time, when he is 65 years old. Williams, being in poor health, is expected to live only three years after his retirement. He will receive the payment due him on the day of his death, however.

Each year the company will also fund an amount equal to the current-service cost. The interest rate to be used in these calculations is 8 percent.

a. Calculate the past-service costs at the present time, when Williams is 63 years old.
b. Calculate the annual amortization amount for the past-service costs.
c. Calculate this year's pension expense.

Exercises and Problems

6. Calculating Bond Value. What is the maximum price you would pay for a $1,000, 10 percent bond maturing eight years hence if you required a return of at least 6 percent every six months, compounded semiannually? (Don't use the bond-value tables except to check your answer.)

7. Calculating Liability and Interest. Howell Company borrowed $2 million. It repaid the loan, with interest, by making 10 annual payments of $311,638 each at year-end.

a. What was the interest rate on the loan? (Assume annual compounding.)
b. What was the interest expense for the first year? Prepare a journal entry to record the accrual of the first year's interest and the payment to the lender.
c. What was Howell's liability at the end of the first year, after making the first payment?
d. What was interest expense for the second year?

8. Bonds Issued at a Discount. Harlequin, Ltd., issued $250,000 face-value, 15-year bonds on July 1, 19x4, at a $31,025 discount. Each December 31 and June 30, the company mailed $15,000 cash interest to its bondholders.

a. What was Harlequin's interest expense in 19x4 and 19x5?
b. What was Harlequin's liability to bondholders as of December 31, 19x4, and December 31, 19x5?

9. Bonds Issued at a Premium. On July 1, 19x2, Hayden Company issued bonds that would mature in 10 years. Interest was payable each December 31 and June 30. The following entries were recorded correctly by Hayden's accountant:

June 30, 19x2:

Cash.....................................	21,964,000	
Bonds Payable..........................		20,000,000
Premium on Bonds......................		1,964,000

December 31, 19x2:

Interest Expense............................	1,757,120	
Premium on Bonds...........................	42,880	
Cash		1,800,000

a. What was the coupon rate of interest?
b. What was the yield-to-maturity rate of interest?
c. What was the liability to bondholders in the December 31, 19x2, balance sheet?

d. What was the interest expense for the six months ended June 30, 19x3?

e. What was the interest expense for the six months ended June 30, 19x12?

10. Bonds Issued at a Premium. On January 1, 19x1, Babcock, Ltd., issued bonds with $1 million face value when the market yield to maturity was 13 percent. Annual cash interest was $160,000 payable in two installments on June 30 and December 31; the bonds were scheduled to mature on December 31, 19x10.

a. Fill in the missing amounts in the following table.

	Interest Expense	Coupon Interest	Premium Amortization	Liability to Bondholders
January 1, 19x1.......				A
June 30, 19x1	B	C	D	E
December 31, 19x1....	F	G	H	J
...				
December 31, 19x5....				K
June 30, 19x6	L	M	N	P

b. Why did the amounts *B*, *F*, and *L* decrease while the amounts *D*, *H*, and *N* increased?

c. What was the total amount of interest expense that Babcock incurred during the 10-year life of the bonds?

11. Self-Amortizing Loan; Calculating Number of Payments. A company borrowed $20,000 from a bank at an interest rate of 12 percent, compounded annually. It promised to pay the bank $4,000 at the end of each year until the loan was paid off. The final payment would be the amount of the last repayment of principal plus the final year's interest on this amount. This final payment, therefore, would be less than $4,000.

a. How many years will it take to pay off the loan?

b. What will be the amount of the final payment?

(Prepared by Carl L. Nelson)

12. Zero-Coupon Bonds. The management of Waldorf Enterprises wanted to issue bonds to raise funds that would facilitate major renovations and expansion. Waldorf's management didn't want the pressure of making semiannual cash interest payments, however. Consultation with a knowledgeable investment banker indicated that the market would still be receptive to Waldorf's zero percent coupon bonds. Waldorf's implicit interest cost reflected a yield to maturity of 9 percent per semiannual compounding period (i.e., an 18 percent nominal rate per year).

   a. What would be the proceeds if Waldorf issued $25 million face-value bonds that would mature in 10 years?

   b. Disappointed with the answer to part *a*, management reversed itself and decided to establish a face value that would produce proceeds of $15 million. What was the face value of the bonds?

   c. What was Waldorf's interest expense for the first year that the bonds issued in part *b* were outstanding?

   d. What was Waldorf's interest expense during the final year that the bonds were outstanding?

   e. What was Waldorf's total interest expense during the 10-year life of the bonds?

   f. Suppose Waldorf had instead issued 10-year $15 million face-value bonds. The bonds contained an annual coupon rate of 18 percent payable semiannually and were issued with neither a premium nor a discount. What would the 10-year interest cost have been? Show how this amount can be reconciled with your answer to part *e*.

13. Bond Accounting.   Boswell Corporation issued $10 million in 16 percent, two-year bonds on January 1, 19x5. These bonds were sold to yield 9 percent per half-year. The $800,000 payments were made on each July 1 and January 1; the face value was paid on January 1, 19x7.

   a. How much cash did the company receive?

   b. How did the sale affect the Boswell's assets, liabilities, and owners' equity?

   c. How did the bonds appear on the balance sheet at the time they were sold?

   d. How did the liability appear on the December 31, 19x5, balance sheet?

(Prepared by Carl L. Nelson)

14. Notes Payable: Alternative Repayment Plans.   Technocracy, Inc., had an opportunity to borrow $300,000 for four years at 12 percent annual interest compounded semiannually.

   a. If the loan were to be repaid in eight equal semiannual payments beginning six months from today, what would be the amount of each payment?

   b. If the loan were to be repaid with one $250,000 payment four years from today and seven equal semiannual payments beginning six months from today, what would be the amount of each of the seven equal payments?

   c. If the loan were to be repaid with eight semiannual payments including seven $18,000 payments beginning six months from today, what would be the amount of the eighth payment to be paid four years from today?

d. Given the different repayment plans identified in parts *a*, *b*, and *c*, what is the highest amount of interest expense that Technocracy would record for the first six-month period?

e. Given the different repayment plans identified in parts *a*, *b*, and *c*, what is the highest amount of interest expense that Technocracy would record over the entire four-year loan period?

15. Bonds Payable; Missing Amounts. Each of the four columns in the following table refers to an independent case. All the data represent amounts in effect on January 1, the day the bonds were issued. The last item in the table, however, relates to the interest expense for the first six months of the first year. Since all the interest rates reflect semiannual payments and semiannual compounding, use the bond-value tables in Appendix A when filling in the missing amounts.

	I	II	III	IV
Bonds payable, face value....	$10,000	$200,000	G	K
Market price	A	D	$58,032	L
Yield to maturity............	12%	E	H	11%
Coupon interest rate	8%	12%	16%	12%
Life of bond (years)	20	15	J	M
Bond discount (premium)	B	$ (7,080)	$ 1,968	$(7,272)
Interest expense,				
January 1–June 30, year 1..	C	F	$ 4,933	$ 5,900

16. Interperiod Tax Allocation; Discussion Question. A member of the U.S. Congress complained that several large government contractors had paid no federal income taxes, or virtually none, for 10 years. During the same period, these companies reported billions of dollars in income and income tax expenses of many hundreds of millions of dollars.

The reason for this phenomenon was that these companies measured revenues and expenses for tax purposes by the "completed contract method." Under this method, revenues and expenses on even very long contracts are deferred until the entire contract is completed.

Discuss this apparent inconsistency. Is it likely to be self-correcting, in time? If not, should it be corrected? What alternatives for correcting it can you identify? Which of these do you prefer, and why?

17. Bond Market Changes; Debt Retirement. On July 1, 19x1, Sunset Company issued $10 million of 20-year, 12 percent bonds at their face value, with interest to be paid semiannually, on June 30 and December 31 each year.

In 19x6, interest rates rose sharply, and by July 1, 19x6, the market value of Sunset's bonds fell to $82.28 for each $100 of face value.

a. If Sunset's management decided *not* to buy the bonds back from the bondholders at the market price on July 1, 19x6, did the decline in market value give Sunset a gain or loss? If so, how much? Explain.

b. Would Sunset report a gain or loss in its income statement for 19x6 if the company did buy the bonds at their market price? If so, how much? Explain.

c. If Sunset didn't buy the bonds, what was the amount of the company's interest expense in the second half of 19x6?

d. Sunset didn't buy the bonds in 19x6. Interest rates fell in the next three years, and the market value of Sunset's bonds rose on July 1, 19x9, to $94 for each $100 of face value. If Sunset still didn't buy the bonds, did the increase in market value give Sunset a gain or loss? If so, how much? Explain.

e. Sunset eventually bought the bonds at $94 on July 1, 19x9. Did the company report a gain or loss in its income statement for 19x9? If so, how much? Explain.

18. Interperiod Tax Allocation. Before 19x3, Morley Software Company had no differences between taxable income and accounting income before taxes. In that year, the company adopted an accelerated method of tax depreciation for newly acquired plant assets. It also began providing purchasers of its software packages with the right to have their program disks updated, free of charge, whenever new versions of these programs were published within 12 months of the purchase date.

Based on other software producers' experience and on its own software development plans, Morley's management believed that the cost of updating program disks would amount to one percent of sales. Sales in 19x3 totaled $13 million, all of which was subject to the new updating commitment. $14,000 was spent in 19x3 to update some of Morley's "Databed" program disks, which came out in a new version in November 19x3. Sales in 19x4 amounted to $17 million, and $102,000 was spent to update customers' disks. The amounts of expense that appeared in Morley's income statement were based on management's estimates of disk-updating costs, but only the amounts actually spent were deductible in the calculation of taxable income.

Tax depreciation on plant assets bought in 19x3 and 19x4 amounted to $500,000 in 19x3 and $900,000 in 19x4. Depreciation expense reported in Morley's income statement totaled $400,000 in 19x3 and $600,000 in 19x4. No investment credits were available in either year. Other expenses were $10 million in 19x3 and $12 million in 19x4.

The effective tax rate was 45 percent in both years.

a. Calculate the difference between income tax expense in 19x3 and the amount of income tax payable on 19x3 taxable income.

b. Calculate the accumulated interperiod tax differences in the December 31, 19x3 and December 31, 19x4 balance sheets, and indicate for each year whether it would be included with the assets or with the liabilities.

19. Investment Tax Credit.   In 19x1, Andrew Corporation purchased equipment with a 10-year estimated life, entitling it to a $35,000 investment credit. This investment tax credit did not reduce the amount subject to depreciation for tax purposes. Its income before taxes and before reflecting the investment credit was $370,000. The income tax rate was 40 percent.

a. Calculate net income for 19x1 if the investment credit was accounted for on a flow-through basis.
b. Make the same calculations, using the deferral method of accounting for the investment credit.
c. Is the difference between your answers to parts *a* and *b* large enough to be regarded as significant?

20. Income Tax Allocation.   Pelican Corporation purchased a machine for $10,296, delivered and installed. The service life of the machine was estimated to be eight years, at the end of which time it was estimated that the machine would have no salvage value. The machine was put into service the first day of the fiscal year, and it was Pelican's only depreciable asset.

Pelican used the straight-line method of depreciation in its financial statements. For tax purposes, Pelican used a government-mandated depreciation method known as the accelerated cost recovery system (ACRS). Pelican had no other differences between the amounts reported in its tax return and the amounts appearing in its income statement. The tax depreciation rates, year-by-year for five years, were as follows: 15 percent, 22 percent, 21 percent, 21 percent, and 21 percent. There would be no tax depreciation during the last three years of the machine's expected service life.

Pelican's accounting income before taxes was $6,000 for the first year in which the machine was used. The amount of income taxes currently due as a result of Pelican's operations for that year was $2,297.04. The income tax rate was 40 percent.

a. Calculate the amount of accounting income *before* recording depreciation and income taxes.
b. Calculate the net income (after income taxes) that Pelican reported for the year.
c. What was the amount of *deferred* income taxes for the year?
d. Assuming that this machine was Pelican's only asset and that the tax

rate did not change, calculate the deferred-income-taxes balance at the end of each year of the asset's life.

(Adapted from a problem prepared by Charles W. Bastable)

21. Capitalized Leases; Missing Amounts. Determine the missing amounts in each of the following five independent cases:

	I	II	III	IV	V
Present value of lease payments.............	$80,000	$7,828	F	H	K
Depreciation expense, 19x1.................	A	C	$1,688	$ 9,326	$5,000
Lease life (years).........	10	5	10	I	12
Annual payment..........	$11,836	$2,000	$4,000	$15,000	L
Interest expense, 19x1.....	B	D	$2,558	J	M
Depreciable life (years)....	10	5	G	7	13
Interest rate.............	10%	E	12%	15%	8%

The leases begin on January 1, 19x1, and the first lease payment is remitted at that time. The company depreciates its assets on a straight-line basis and assumes zero salvage value.

22. Liability Transactions.   Ralston Company's December 31, 19x4, balance sheet included the following amounts:

Cash...........	$ 10,000	Accounts payable........	$ 24,000
Inventory	15,000	Capital stock............	1,000
Land...........	125,000	Retained earnings	125,000
Total	$150,000	Total................	$150,000

The company's independent auditors discovered that the following four transactions that occurred during the first week of January 19x4 had never been recorded:

1. The company bought a truck for $21,000 cash. Although it would be used for five years, for tax purposes it was depreciated over three years, as follows: 25 percent, 38 percent, and 37 percent.
2. Ralston bought a machine for $60,000 cash. Although this machine probably would be used for eight years, for tax purposes it was depreciated only through 19x8, year by year as follows: 15 percent, 22 percent, 21 percent, 21 percent, and 21 percent.
3. As a result of these two purchases, Ralston applied an investment tax credit of $8,100 against its 19x4 federal income tax obligations— $2,100 for the truck and $6,000 for the machine. No part of either of these amounts was deducted from original cost to determine the amounts subject to depreciation, either for tax purposes or for the company's income statement.
4. Ralston issued a 12 percent, 10-year, $200,000 bond on January 2,

19x4, priced to yield a 13.5 percent return to investors. Interest was to be paid semiannually on June 30 and December 31 of each year.

For both financial reporting and tax reporting, Ralston's income before depreciation, interest, and income tax was $125,000. Ralston expected zero salvage value for its plant assets. For financial reporting, Ralston used straight-line depreciation and applied the flow-through method of recognizing investment tax credits. Ralston's tax rate was 40 percent, and the tax payment for 19x4 was to be made in January 19x5.

a. Prepare Ralston's 19x4 income statement.
b. Prepare journal entries to record the additional transactions, the year-end adjustments, and income tax expense for 19x4.
c. Prepare Ralston's balance sheet as of December 31, 19x4.

23. Investment Credit; Depreciation Differences. Lambert Corporation purchased equipment on January 1, 19x0, at a cost of $10 million. A portion of this expenditure was for elements that made the company eligible for an investment credit of $400,000. For tax purposes, the company was allowed to depreciate the full cost of the equipment over five years at the following annual rates: 15 percent, 22 percent, 21 percent, 21 percent, and 21 percent.

Management estimated that the equipment would be useful for 20 years, with negligible end-of-life salvage value, and that straight-line depreciation would be appropriate for public financial reporting. The equipment was Lambert Corporation's only depreciable asset, and the company's income before depreciation and income taxes was $3 million each year. The income tax rate was 40 percent, and the investment credit was to be accounted for by the deferral method.

a. Derive Lambert's net income in 19x3 and 19x9, as reported to the stockholders.
b. Calculate the amounts of deferred income taxes and deferred tax credit at the close of 19x0, 19x2, 19x6, and 19x9.

24. Lease Accounting. On January 1, 19x0, Green Company entered into a noncancelable lease agreement under which Blatt Company would have the use of one of Green's machines for 10 years. This machine was carried on Green's accounting records at $2 million. Payments under the lease agreement, which extended to December 31, 19x9, amounted to $355,080 a year for 10 years, with the first payment due in January 19x0, when the lease agreement came into effect. Although the form of the agreement was a lease, for accounting purposes this transaction was treated as a sale by Green and as a purchase by Blatt.

The lease agreement stipulated that the cost of the machine to Blatt was $2.4 million and that the interest rate implicit in the agreement was

10 percent. This was considered fair and adequate compensation to Green for the use of its funds. Blatt expected the machine to have a 10-year life, no salvage value, and a straight-line benefit pattern.

a. Ignoring income taxes, what were Blatt's expenses from this lease in the years ended December 31, 19x0 and 19x1?
b. How much income before income taxes did Green derive from this lease for the years ended December 31, 19x0 and 19x1?

(AICPA adapted)

25. Lease Accounting. Crystal Company needed an additional machine and determined that it could acquire the use of a particular machine two different ways:

1. It could buy the machine for $92,442, paying $10,000 in cash on the date of purchase and promising to pay the remainder and 8 percent interest in 14 equal payments of $10,000 a year, starting one year after the date of purchase. Depreciation would be by the straight-line method over the machine's anticipated useful life of 15 years, with no estimated salvage value.
2. It could lease the machine for 10 years, paying rent of $10,000 at the beginning of each year. The machine was expected to have a market value of $43,121 at the end of the 10 years. The lease contained no purchase or renewal options, and if the company wanted to continue using the machine after the end of 10 years, it would have to negotiate a new lease.

a. Would the balance sheet at the date of acquisition be any different if the asset were purchased rather than leased? If so, how?
b. Calculate income before taxes for the first year under each of these two financing methods, assuming that income before taxes, interest, and depreciation or rent on this machine was $50,000.

26. Pension Costs. Crosby Company adopted a pension plan for its four employees on January 1, 19x8. These employees had worked for the company for seven years (since January 1, 19x1) and were expected to work for four more years, retiring on January 1, 19x12. At that time, the plan would terminate as the pension fund trustee purchased retirement annuity contracts for the retiring employees, and a new plan would be drawn for the replacement employees. Payments to the pension fund trustee were to be made annually, beginning on January 1, 19x9, and continuing to January 1, 19x12, so that the pensions would be fully funded by the latter date.

An actuarial consultant concluded that a reasonable prediction was that each of the four employees would live exactly 10 years after retirement, i.e., to January 1, 19x22. Each employee would be paid $10,000 every year during the retirement period, the first payment to be made on the retirement date. Management selected an annual interest rate of 10 percent to determine the value of its obligations under this plan, with interest compounded annually.

a. The assumptions in this question have been greatly simplified to make the calculations manageable. Identify these assumptions and indicate how they might differ in a more realistic illustration.
b. Assuming that each year of employment was equally responsible for the ultimate series of pension payments, calculate the pension cost applicable to each year from 19x1 to 19x11.
c. Calculate the amount of the unfunded pension liability as of January 1, 19x8.
d. Assuming that Crosby Company decided to amortize the cost of past-service benefits equally over four years, beginning in 19x9, and that the actuarial assumptions remained unchanged, calculate the company's pension expense for the year 19x8.

27. Pension Liabilities.   Walter Company has a defined-benefit pension plan for its employees. On January 1, 19x1, its estimated unfunded past service liability was $19,090,000, determined as follows:

Present value of accumulated plan benefits	$49,090,000
Net assets held by pension plan trustee	30,000,000
Unfunded past service benefits	$19,090,000

The net assets—i.e., assets less liabilities—held by the pension fund trustee were measured at their current market values. The present value of accumulated plan benefits was calculated on the basis of an assumed interest rate of 8 percent and assumed pension payments to pensioners of $5 million a year for 20 years, beginning in 19x1. Each payment was to be made on December 31.

Pension expense was $5,531,000 in 19x1, including $3,240,000 for current-service benefits, $1,527,000 interest on the unfunded balance at the beginning of the year, and $417,000 for amortization of unfunded past-service benefits. Payments equal to 19x1 pension expense were made to the pension fund trustee on December 31, 19x1. The trustee, in turn, made all required payments to the company's pensioners, totaling $4.9 million, and the market value of the net assets held by the trustee was $34 million on December 31, 19x1.

At the end of 19x1, the company announced that it had revised its actuarial assumptions to reflect an assumed interest rate of 10 percent and assumed pension payments of $5.2 million a year for 22 years, starting in 19x2. Walter's balance sheet on that date showed total assets of $200 million and total liabilities of $50 million. These totals did *not* include the pension fund assets and liabilities.

a. Calculate the unfunded past-service pension benefits as of December 31, 19x1 (to the nearest thousand dollars).

b. Identify, insofar as possible, the reasons for the change in the unfunded past-service pension benefits between the beginning and end of 19x1.

c. Comment on the significance of Walter Company's omission of its unfunded past-service pension benefits from its balance sheet.

d. What disclosures would be included in the footnotes to Walter's financial statements?

28. Bond Accounting; Refunding. Only July 1, 19x2, ABC Corporation sold a $1 million issue of 6 percent, 10-year bonds to an insurance company at a price to yield 8 percent. Interest was payable semiannually, on June 30 and December 31 of each year.

The company paid interest regularly for five years. In 19x7, the need for additional debt capital prompted ABC's management to try to borrow an additional $1 million. The insurance company refused to lend more money to ABC, but ABC's management found a pension trust that was willing to take a $2 million, 10-year issue of 10 percent bonds to yield 9 percent if ABC would pay off its debt to the insurance company. Interest again would be payable semiannually on June 30 and December 31 of each year.

ABC Corporation accepted the pension trust's offer and issued the new 10 percent bonds on June 30, 19x7. Concurrently, it used part of the proceeds from the new 10 percent bond issue to retire the old 6 percent bonds.

a. Calculate the issue price of the 6 percent bond issue on July 1, 19x2.

b. Prepare an entry in general journal form to record the issuance of the bonds on July 1, 19x2. Indicate how the bonds would be reported on the balance sheet as of that date.

c. Prepare an entry in general journal form to record the accrual of interest expense and the interest payment on December 31, 19x2. Indicate how the bonds would be reported on the balance sheet as of that date.

d. Calculate the amount ABC Corporation should have shown as its liability for the 6 percent bonds on a balance sheet as of June 30, 19x7, just after the interest payment but before the bonds were redeemed from the insurance company.

e. Calculate the issue price of the 10 percent bond issue on June 30, 19x7.

f. Prepare an entry in general journal form to record the issuance of the 10 percent bonds on June 30, 19x7. Indicate how the bonds would be reported on the balance sheet as of that date.

g. Calculate the gain or loss, if any, from the retirement of the 6 percent bonds on June 30, 19x7, and prepare a journal entry in general journal form to record the retirement, consistent with each of the following independent assumptions:

1. The retirement of the 6 percent bonds was effected by the use of the "call" provision, which entitled ABC to require the insurance company to surrender the bonds at their "call price" of $102 for each $100 of face value.
2. The retirement of the 6 percent bonds was effected by their purchase in the open market at a price to yield 9 percent.

h. Prepare the general journal entry to record the accrual of interest expense and the interest payment on December 31, 19x7. Indicate how the bonds would be reported on the balance sheet as of that date.

(Restructured by Hugo Nurnberg)

29. Pension Liabilities: Discussion Question. Global Tire Company is a manufacturer of automobile and truck tires, chemicals, rubber goods, and plastic products. Its sales revenues in 19x2 exceeded $2.5 billion, and its net income was almost $35 million. Accruals for employees' pay and benefits amounted to $877 million in 19x2. Retained earnings at the end of 19x2 amounted to $472 million, and the owners' equity totaled $644 million.

One footnote to the financial statements for 19x2 read as follows:

> The company and certain subsidiaries have trusteed retirement plans covering the great majority of their employees. In general, the plans provide for normal retirement at age 65. The domestic plans permit early unreduced retirement at age 55 with 30 years of service. Accounting for the plans is on an accrual basis. Most plans are funded by payments to independent trustees of amounts, computed by independent actuaries, sufficient to provide for current service costs and the amortization of past-service costs over periods not exceeding 30 years.

> The total cost for all plans (before reduction for income tax) was $82,209,000 in 19x2 and $79,362,000 in 19x1.

> At January 2, 19x2, the date of the most recent actuarial valuation, the actuarially computed value of vested benefits of domestic plans, determined in the manner specified by the Pension Benefit Guaranty Corporation (PBGC), exceeded the pension funds by $515 million; amounts related to foreign subsidiaries are not significant. The decrease of $45 million from that reported in 19x1 results from more favorable actuarial assumptions under the PBGC method.

Five years earlier, the company reported that the actuarially computed value of vested pension benefits for employees in the United States exceeded the pension funds and balance sheet accruals by $395 million.

In replying to a question from a securities analyst in 19x2, the company's financial vice president made the following statement:

> We began funding [the unfunded vested amount] 16 years ago, and 4 years ago we went to a 30-year program, which now has 25 more years to go. We are very much aware that this represents a substantial obligation for Global, but it must be put into perspective. This is not a current liability. It is a projection of the future pension payments we will pay to retired employees, extending from the present through approximately the next 50 years.

a. Since the company began funding its unfunded vested benefits six years ago, what explanation can you offer for the substantial increase in the unfunded amount in the intervening six years?

b. The company's treatment of its "past-service obligation" was in accord with generally accepted accounting principles. Should those principles be modified to require companies such as Global to recognize the past-service obligation more quickly? State the arguments you considered on both sides of this question.

c. Suppose the Financial Accounting Standards Board had issued a new standard in 19x3 requiring Global to recognize a major portion of the $515 million unfunded past-service obligation in 19x3. If you had been empowered to decide how this change was to be implemented, would you have established the pension liability by a deduction from revenues on the 19x3 income statement or by some other means? State the reasons for your choice.

Chapter 11

The Owners' Equity

The concluding balance sheet category—owners' equity—has two main subdivisions: *contributed capital* and *retained earnings*. Previous chapters focused on changes in retained earnings—the earning of income and the declaration of cash dividends. The purpose of this chapter is to examine events and circumstances that affect either the contributed capital component alone or both contributed capital and retained earnings simultaneously. This discussion falls under four major headings:

1. Classes of capital stock.
2. Issuance of additional shares.
3. Treasury stock.
4. Contingencies.

Classes of Capital Stock

Each state in the United States has a general incorporation law. Anyone meeting the requirements of this law is entitled to draw up a set of articles of incorporation and receive a corporate charter from the state. The owners of the corporation then receive shares of capital stock in exchange for the resources they contribute to the corporation. Many companies have only one class of capital stock; others have two or even more. Although the detailed provisions vary from stock issue to stock issue, stocks can be classified generally into two categories: *common stock* and *preferred stock.*

Common Stock

When a corporation has only one class of capital stock, it is usually called **common stock.** Each share of common stock represents a proportionate share of all the ownership rights in the corporation. Owners of the common stock (and sometimes others with specified voting rights) elect a board of directors to appoint and oversee the company's officers.

The articles of incorporation specify the number of shares of common stock the corporation is authorized to issue and the **par value** of each share. In some cases, the articles will specify that the shares are no-par shares, in which case either the articles or the directors may designate a portion of the issue price as the *stated value* of the stock. For most corporations, the number of shares issued is smaller than the number of shares authorized in the articles of incorporation.

Par value had its origin in the concept of legal capital. The amount designated as the legal capital is intended to establish a minimum limit on the owners' equity. In concept, this provides a cushion or margin of protection for the creditors. The economic significance of par or stated value today is minimal, however. The issue price of shares of common stock in the United States is frequently a large multiple of the par or stated value, and the total par value of a company's shares is likely to be only a small fraction of the total of its liabilities. The creditors' protection comes from the amount and continuity of the company's cash flows rather than from the designation of part of the owners' equity as par value or legal capital.

The excess of the issuance price over the par or stated value is reported in the balance sheet under some heading such as **additional paid-in capital.** The entry to record the issue of 100,000 shares of $1 par common stock in exchange for $1 million in cash might be the following:

```
Cash ..............................................  1,000,000
        Common Stock...............................            100,000
        Additional Paid-In Capital ......................            900,000
```

At any time after the stock is issued and after earnings have been recorded, the owners' equity structure will be as reflected in Exhibit 11–1. In this diagram, the left half of the circle represents contributed capital and the right half represents retained earnings. The circle is divided down the middle to emphasize this two-way split; contributed capital isn't necessarily half the total.

Preferred Stock

Some corporations have one or more classes of capital stock in addition to the common stock. These other classes of stock are usually called **preferred** or *preference stock.* Exhibit 11–2 shows the shareowners' equity of a corporation with two classes of preferred stock. Three of the wedges of this diagram represent the par or stated values of the three classes of stock; the remainder of the contributed capital is shown as a single wedge, containing the amounts originating in the issuance of *all*

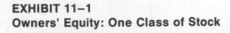

EXHIBIT 11–1
Owners' Equity: One Class of Stock

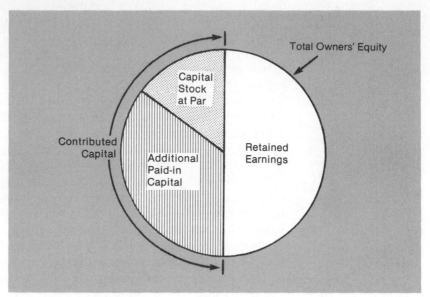

classes of stock. The amounts attributable to the preferred shares aren't reported separately on the balance sheet, although they could be.

The rights of each class of shares are specified in the articles of incorporation and by-laws, but each share of a given class has the same rights as any other share of that class. Thus, an owner of 1,000 shares of $5 preferred stock receives twice as much dividend money as a holder of 500 shares of this stock.

Shares of preferred stock usually entitle their owners to dividends of a fixed amount that must be paid before any dividends can be paid on the common stock. The owners of preferred ordinarily also have precedence over the common stockholders in any liquidation of assets, up to a specified maximum amount per share. They usually do not have voting rights, however.

The dividend priority on the preferred shares is usually *cumulative,* meaning that no dividends can be paid to the common shareholders until all current and back dividends have been paid on the preferred. In most cases, shares of preferred stock are also **callable** at a specified price. This means that the company has the right to repurchase the stock if certain conditions are met, even if the owners of the stock don't wish to sell it. All these characteristics of preferred stock limit the risks of its owners, but at the same time they limit the owners' return on the amounts they have invested in the stock.

EXHIBIT 11–2
Owners' Equity: Several Classes of Stock

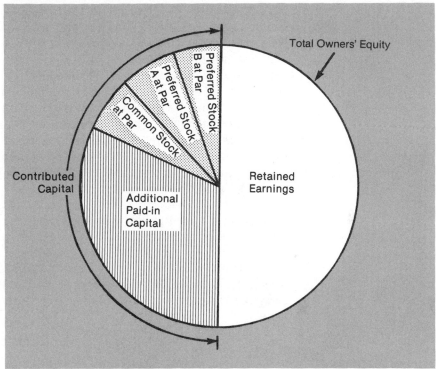

A preferred stock differs from a bond in that the stockholders have no legal right to insist on payment of their dividends on specified dates; dividend distributions are decided by the directors. Furthermore, the stock usually has no maturity date. A corporation may omit or pass the dividend on the preferred indefinitely, although some preferred stocks provide for the transfer of corporate control to the preferred shareholders when the dividends have reached a specified amount in arrears. Thus, preferred stock lies somewhere between bonds and common stock on the risk-return spectrum: It typically offers higher risk and a higher return than bonds, but lower risk and a lower return than common stock.

Many preferred stocks are **convertible** into a predetermined number of shares of common stock. The sale of preferred stock and bonds with the conversion privilege or with detachable options to buy common stock is sometimes an indirect way of selling common stock. Noteworthy features of such securities and the accounting problems they raise will be discussed later in this chapter.

Book Value

The book value of common stock is the common stockholders' equity in the corporation. If only common stock is outstanding, book value and owners' equity are identical. When preferred shares are outstanding, the book value of the common stockholders is limited to that portion of the total owners' equity not attributable to the preferred shareowners.

Book value per share can be calculated to measure the equity in the corporation of the holder of a single share of common stock. It is calculated by dividing the total book value of the common stock by the number of shares outstanding. When a company's shares are traded publicly, the market price per share invariably differs from the book value. This is understandable since market value is a measure of the market's future expectations, while book value reflects only those amounts already recorded for assets and liabilities.

Book value may take on slightly more importance when a company's shares aren't traded publicly. In such cases, no market price exists because there is no market; book value per share may be used in these circumstances to estimate the fair value of the shares. It must be remembered, however, that book value is only a starting point for this estimate, because it is based on measurements of past transactions, not on the company's future prospects, and these are the determinant of fair market value.

Issuing Additional Common Shares

The initial source of corporate financing is the sale or issuance of capital stock. Without an adequate base of ownership capital, the corporation would be unable to obtain debt financing and would even experience difficulties in obtaining short-term trade credit. Most of this initial ownership capital usually comes from the issuance of common stock. Common stock may also be issued later on, usually in connection with one of the following:

1. Straight cash sales.
2. Stock dividends.
3. Stock splits.
4. Securities conversions.
5. Exercise of stock options.
6. Acquisitions of other companies.

We'll discuss the first five of these now, leaving the issuance of shares of stock in exchange for the stock or assets of other companies to Chapter 12.

Cash Sales of Additional Shares

Small numbers of shares of capital stock are often sold to employees as part of company employee-savings plans. The most significant kind of straight cash sales, however, are sales of additional shares either to the company's current shareowners or to new outside investors. The company is likely to do this because it needs more funds to finance its growth than the company's ongoing operations are able to generate.

Registration Requirements.   Large corporations wishing to raise capital in this way in the United States must register each new issue with the Securities and Exchange Commission and make a detailed prospectus available to any potential purchaser of the shares.[1] The task of the SEC is to insure that the information provided in the registration statement is complete and credible. SEC approval of a registration statement does not constitute or even imply an endorsement of the shares as a sound investment opportunity.

Preemptive Rights.   The common shareowners in some companies have the right to purchase any additional shares of common stock the company may offer for sale. Rights of this kind are known as **preemptive rights.** For example, if a company with 1 million shares of common stock outstanding wants to raise capital by selling 100,000 additional shares of stock, each current shareowner will have the right to buy one share of the new issue for every 10 shares he or she now owns.

All new issues aren't offered through rights. The owners of many companies don't have this privilege; in other cases, the shareowners may vote to waive their preemptive rights, leaving the company free to offer the shares to the general public. These are known as *public offerings,* as opposed to rights offerings.

Dilution of the Market Value of the Equity.   When shares of stock are offered to the general public, the existing shareowners are very interested in the price at which these shares are offered. For example, suppose Drake Corporation has 100,000 shares of common stock outstanding with a market value of $30 a share. If the company sells an additional 100,000 shares at $20 a share, it's reasonable to expect that all the shares will trade at $25 a share. If this happens, the market value of the old shareholders' holdings will fall from $3 million to $2.5 million, while the new shareowners will have paid $2 million for stock worth $2.5 million ($25 × 100,000 shares).

This transfer of part of the old shareowners' equity to the new shareowners is known as **dilution of the equity.** As illustrated in Exhibit 11–3, the old shareowners give $5 of the value of their stock to the new shareowners to induce them to invest their money in the corporation. The

---

[1] In 1982, the SEC began approving registration statements covering not only immediate issues of shares but subsequent issues as well, provided that the issuer amended the registration statement whenever significant new information became available. This is known as *shelf registration.*

EXHIBIT 11–3
Dilution of the Equity

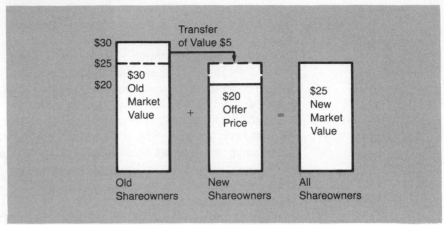

dilution is measured by the difference between the market price before the offer was made and the market price after the new shares were issued, adjusted for other influences on the stock's price.

Offering the new shares at a price lower than the current market price is intended to make the new issue attractive to potential buyers. The reason the existing shareowners may be willing to make this offer has to be that *they expect little or no dilution to take place* because they are convinced that management can invest the new capital so effectively that the price of a share of stock will rise within a reasonable time to the level it would have reached without the new capital or even higher. For example, if the old shareholders had expected the stock to increase in price to $36 within two years and if it actually does reach that level as a result of management's ability to invest the new $2 million profitably, the long-term dilution of the equity is zero. In fact, the dilution may even be negative if prices rise faster than they would have without the infusion of new capital into the company. This approach to dilution is illustrated in Exhibit 11–4.

It is difficult to anticipate accurately how new investments will work out, let alone document these expectations. To avoid challenges by dissident stockholders, the board of directors generally tries to set the offer price in a public offering very close to the market price prevailing at the time of the offer.

Dilution of Earnings. The funds obtained from the sale of additional shares are unlikely to generate enough income in the short run to keep net income per share unchanged. If the shares are issued to enable the company to retire debt, for example, interest expense will fall and total

EXHIBIT 11–4
Elimination of Dilution by Effective Investment

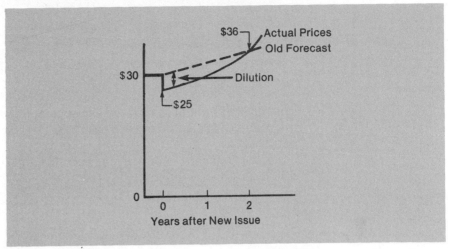

net income will rise. The percentage increase in the number of shares outstanding will probably be larger than the percentage increase in net income, however, and earnings per share will fall. (Net income is often referred to as *earnings* and net income per share as *earnings per share.*)

This reduction in earnings per share is referred to as **dilution of the earnings** due to the stock issue. This doesn't mean that the stock issue was unwise; if future earnings per share are higher than they would have been without the new issue, the financing will have been worthwhile.

Stock Dividends

Corporations sometimes increase the number of shares of common stock outstanding without increasing the company's assets. One way to accomplish this is to issue what is known as a **stock dividend.** A stock dividend consists of the distribution of additional shares of stock to the existing stockholders in proportion to their holdings and without any payment of cash or other property by the stockholders.

For example, Space Age Corporation was very successful during its early years of operations, and retained earnings had reached $715,000 by the end of 19x6. The need for funds to finance the company's growth was equally strong, however, and the company therefore had no money to pay dividends. In this situation, the directors declared a 10 percent stock dividend when the market price was $60 per share. With 55,000 shares outstanding, the Space Age 10 percent dividend consisted of 5,500 shares ($10 par value per share), one for every 10 outstanding.

This transaction was recorded as if (1) the corporation had declared a cash dividend equal to the market price of the 5,500 shares, and (2) the stockholders had immediately purchased the 5,500 shares at this market price. Because the market price of the stock at the time of the stock dividend was $60, the journal entry was:

Retained Earnings (5,500 × $60) 330,000
    Common Stock ($5,500 × $10)   55,000
    Additional Paid-In Capital ($5,500 × $50).   275,000

The "dividend" reduced retained earnings, and the "stock sale" increased the contributed capital, in each case by the market price imputed to the new shares.

The total owners' equity before and after the stock dividend—shown schematically in Exhibit 11–5—was unaffected by the stock dividend. It was merely divided into a larger number of shares, each representing a smaller portion of the company than formerly. The book value per share amounts were as follows:

	Before Stock Dividend	After Stock Dividend
Common stock (par value)	$10.00	$10.00
Additional paid-in capital	17.00	20.00
Retained earnings	13.00	6.36
Total.	$40.00	$36.36

These results were obtained by dividing the amounts in Exhibit 11–5 by 55,000 and 60,500, the numbers of shares outstanding before and after the stock dividend.

EXHIBIT 11–5
Effect of a Stock Dividend

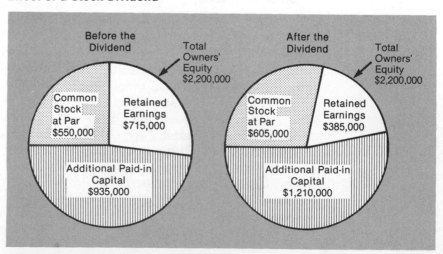

It should be evident that the stock dividend in substance is a paper transaction. After the dividend, each stockholder had 11 shares which conveyed the same rights as the 10 shares owned previously. After the dividend, 11 shares had the same $400 equity interest (11 × $36.36) the owner's 10 shares had had previously.

Although the stock dividend does not give the stockholder any new asset, the market in the stock might become slightly more active than formerly because of the increase in the number of shares outstanding. Many companies also follow the practice of paying the same cash dividend per share after the stock dividend that they had been paying previously, which means increased dividend income for the shareowners.

Furthermore, the market often interprets the declaration of a stock dividend as a prediction of continued company growth. Once dividends have been increased, large corporations show a great resistance to reducing them, except under the most extreme conditions. To a large extent, directors avoid dividend cuts by increasing dividends only when they are confident of their ability to maintain them in the future. Maintaining a constant dividend per share, therefore, is likely to increase the total market value of the company's stock because the dividends are assumed to convey the directors' positive assessment of the company's long-run earning and dividend-paying potential. In other words, although 11 shares should sell for what 10 shares would have brought previously (10 × $60 = $600), in fact, they may sell for more (for example, 11 × $56 = $616). This effect won't persist, however, if the expected cash flows don't materialize.

Stock Splits

A **stock split** is similar to a stock dividend in that each stockholder is given additional shares in proportion to the number already owned. The main difference is in the *number* of shares distributed. When an increase of more than about 20 or 25 percent in the number of shares outstanding is to be achieved, the mechanism of the stock split is usually used. The par value is usually reduced to accompany a stock split, whereas it remains unchanged in a stock dividend.

For example, the market price of Space Age Corporation had risen to $90 by the end of 19x9, and the board of directors decided to declare a two-for-one stock split and to reduce the par value of the stock from $10 to $5. Since the par value per share was reduced in proportion to the change in the number of shares outstanding, the total par value remained unchanged. Furthermore, no transfer was made from Retained Earnings because, in substance, stock splits are merely restatements of the existing contributed capital.

The owners' equity section of the balance sheet and book value per share before and after the stock split are shown in Exhibit 11–6. The total

EXHIBIT 11–6

SPACE AGE CORPORATION
Owners' Equity and Book Value per Share
As of December 31, 19x9

	Before Stock Split		After Stock Split	
	Total	Per Share	Total	Per Share
Common stock (par value)	$ 605,000	$10	$ 605,000	$ 5
Additional paid-in capital	1,210,000	20	1,210,000	10
Retained earnings	1,089,000	18	1,089,000	9
Total owners' equity..........	$2,904,000		$2,904,000	
Book value per share		$48		$24

owners' equity remained unchanged at $2,904,000, but the book value per share dropped from $48 to $24.

Stock splits, like stock dividends, may be signals to the financial markets about the company's future cash flows. For instance, it may be that the market uses the announcement of a split to reevaluate the stream of expected cash flows from the shares. If the consensus is that future dividends will increase, the market price per share is likely to decline less than proportionally to the increase in the number of shares. The price may also be affected by the increase in the number of shares available for trading, thereby making them slightly more marketable. Except for the effects of these two factors, a proportionate change in market price can be expected.

Securities Conversions

Corporations often attach conversion privileges to shares of their preferred stock or to their bonds. They do this either to make the securities more attractive to potential investors or to use these senior securities (that is, senior to the common stock) as an indirect way of selling common stock to the public. To see how this works, we'll examine a simple issue of convertible preferred stock in some depth and then deal very briefly with convertible debt.

Convertible Preferred Stock. The convertibility of shares of preferred stock enables their owners to increase the market value of their investment in a company if the market value of the company's common stock goes up. They can do this by exchanging their preferred shares for common shares when the dividend and market price on the common shares have risen above the dividend and market price of the equivalent number of preferred shares.

For example, in 19x1, Taylor, Inc., issued 1,000 shares of convertible preferred stock at an issue price of $100 a share. The annual dividend on the preferred was $5, and each share was convertible into five shares of common stock at the discretion of the holder. The cash dividend on Taylor's common stock was 75 cents a share, and the market price of the common shares was $18 a share.

Given these amounts, the preferred stockholders had no incentive to exercise their conversion option. By converting one share of preferred into five shares of common, they would have lost $1.25 in dividends and $10 in market value:

	Dividends	Market Value
1 preferred share........	$5.00	$100
5 common shares	3.75	90
Difference...........	$1.25	$ 10

This doesn't mean the conversion option was valueless, however. If earnings and dividends on the common stock continued to rise in the years ahead, the market price of the common would probably rise, too. If that happened, conversion could become very desirable. For example, the cash dividend on the common rose to $1.60 a share in 19x6. The market price of a common share at that time was $40. Conversion of the preferred shares would then give the preferred shareholders $8 in dividends instead of $5, and a market value of $200 (five shares at $40 each).

If all 1,000 shares of preferred stock were then converted into 5,000 shares of $1 par common stock, Taylor's accountants would make the following entry:

Preferred Stock.....................................	100,000	
Common Stock		5,000
Additional Paid-In Capital.........................		95,000

The debit to Preferred Stock shows that this form of owners' equity was eliminated by the conversion.[2] The credit to Common Stock is the par value of the 5,000 new common shares, and the $95,000 credit to Additional Paid-In Capital shows that the new common shareowners contributed this amount in excess of the par value of their common shares when they originally invested $100,000 in Taylor's preferred shares.

---

[2] When the preferred was originally issued, the $100 issue price might have been greater than the par value. For example, if the par value had been $2, Additional Paid-In Capital would have been increased by $98 a share at that time ($100 − $2). This means that in the record of the conversion into common shares, only $2,000 would have been debited to the Preferred Stock account. A possible entry would have been as follows:

Preferred Stock (1,000 × $2)	2,000	
Additional Paid-In Capital—Preferred (1,000 × $98)	98,000	
Common Stock (5,000 × $1).......................		5,000
Additional Paid-In Capital—Common (5,000 × $19)......		95,000

In other words, the conversion privilege clearly has value if the price of the common is expected to rise. In practice, most holders of the preferred stock are likely to convert even before the benefits of conversion are as great as in this example. Moreover, the market price of the preferred shares will probably increase in response to the higher value of the common stock.

Issuing convertible securities also involves a cost to the common shareholders. To retire the 1,000 shares of preferred in 19x6, Taylor, Inc., had to issue 5,000 shares of common, worth $40 a share, or $200,000. If the preferred had been callable at $100, however, Taylor could have retired the entire issue with the payment of $100,000 in cash. This $100,000 could have been obtained by issuing only 2,500 shares of common stock at $40 a share. The conversion privilege, in other words, does carry with it a potential dilution of the common equity.

TERMINOLOGY

A stock is *callable* if the terms on which it was issued permit the company to force the owners to sell their shares to the company at a specified price.

Performance Shares and Stock Options

Shares of stock may be issued as compensation to key employees (performance shares) in recognition of their contribution to the company's success. The number of performance shares to be issued is determined by the shareholders; the awards themselves are generally made by a committee set up for this purpose.

Shares may also be issued to individuals who exercise **stock options** they have received or bought from the company. Some stock options are given to major lenders as part of their inducement to lend money to the company. The U.S. government, for example, guaranteed loans to the Chrysler Corporation of up to $1.5 billion to enable it to survive a crisis and rebuild for the future. In return, Chrysler gave the government options to buy 14.4 million shares of new common stock at a price of $13 a share. The shares were trading at about $5 a share at the time. Chrysler's efforts to rebuild were successful, and the market price rose at one point to $35 a share. At that point, the government auctioned the options and Chrysler won with a bid of $311 million, roughly the difference between the $13 option price and the $35 peak market price.

The most highly publicized stock options are *executive stock options*, awarded to key corporate executives as part of their compensation. In most option plans, executives are given options to buy at a later date specified numbers of shares at a fixed price, usually the market price at the time the options are granted. If the market price goes up, the executives can exercise some or all of their options and benefit from the price increase.

Shares issued pursuant to a stock option plan differ from performance shares in that the executives must pay for the shares they choose to buy. The reason for giving stock options to executives is to increase their incentives to perform effectively so that the price of the company's stock will rise. In other words, the executives can't benefit from the options unless the stockholders also benefit.

Because the company receives no direct payment when stock options are *granted* to employees, no changes in the owners' equity are recognized. The potential dilution must be recognized in the financial statements, however. This is accomplished in part by disclosing in a footnote such information as the number of options outstanding and the option price and by calculating earnings per share on the assumption that all outstanding options have been exercised in full. We'll describe the earnings per share calculation in the next section.

Earnings per Share

One of the most widely quoted financial ratios is **earnings per share.** In principle, this is the ratio of the net income for a year to the number of shares of common stock outstanding during that year. The calculation may not be that simple, however. Calculations of earnings per share that ignore potential conversions of convertible securities, the granting of performance shares, or the exercise of stock options could mislead investors. We'll examine two of these adjustments, for convertible preferred stock and for convertible debt.

Convertible Preferred.   Taylor, Inc., had 20,000 shares of common stock outstanding in 19x5 and net income of $65,000. The total preferred dividend was $1,000 \times \$5 = \$5,000$, and the earnings available to the common shareowners therefore was $\$65,000 - \$5,000 = \$60,000$. If the potential dilution were ignored, earnings per common share would be calculated as follows:

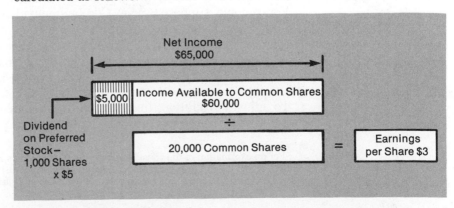

The conversion of all the preferred, however, would raise the number of common shares outstanding to 25,000 and would make the entire $65,000 net income available to the common shareholders. Earnings per share calculated on this basis would be:

$$\frac{\text{Adjusted income available}}{\text{Adjusted number of shares}} = \frac{\$65,000}{25,000} = \$2.60 \text{ a share}$$

Accountants in the United States are required to consider the potential dilutive effects of outstanding convertible preferred stocks when they calculate earnings per share. Two earnings per share amounts are calculated and published: fully diluted earnings per share, reflecting *all* existing potential dilutions, and primary earnings per share, reflecting potential dilutions only if they are so large as to lead to a reasonable presumption that they have already occurred. In other words, primary earnings per share may reflect not just the number of common shares already outstanding, but some dilutive effects as well.[3]

Convertible Debt. Bonds, too, can be issued with a conversion feature, as we saw in Chapter 10. When bonds are convertible into shares of common stock, their dilutive effect is considered in the calculation of earnings per share. Like convertible preferred, convertible bonds affect fully diluted earnings per share, and in some cases are also considered in the determination of primary earnings per share.

There is one important difference between convertible preferred and convertible bonds. In the adjustment for convertible preferred, the full amount of the preferred dividend is restored to the numerator—in our example, adding back $5,000 to what would have been a $60,000 numerator showing earnings available for the common stock. In the adjustment for convertible bonds, in contrast, less than the full amount of the bond interest is added back to net income because interest is tax deductible.

For example, suppose Bradley Corporation had only common stock and $100,000 in 10 percent convertible bonds outstanding, and its taxable income was subject to a 40 percent tax rate. Net income was $48,000, 20,000 common shares were outstanding, and unadjusted earnings per share was $2.40. These amounts are given in the left column of Exhibit 11–7.

To adjust for dilution, the accountant must calculate the net income Bradley would have reported if the debt had been converted into common

---

[3] For an explanation of the considerations which require this kind of adjustment, see Jon A. Booker and Bill D. Jarnagin, *Financial Accounting Standards: Explanation and Analysis,* 7th ed. (Chicago: Commerce Clearing House, Inc., 1985), chap. 9.

EXHIBIT 11–7
Earnings per Share with Convertible Bonds Outstanding

	Bonds Outstanding	Bonds Converted
Income before interest and income tax	$90,000	$90,000
Interest (0.10 × $100,000)	10,000	—
Income before taxes	80,000	90,000
Income tax (40 percent)	32,000	36,000
Net income	$48,000	$54,000
Shares outstanding	20,000	25,000
Earnings per share	$2.40	$2.16

stock. Without debt, the company would not have had to pay interest at 10 percent on the $100,000 debt, or $10,000. This was tax deductible, meaning that the aftertax interest cost was $(1.0 - 0.4 = 0.6) \times \$10,000$, or $6,000. Without debt, therefore, the company would have reported net income of $54,000 ($48,000 + $6,000), as the right column of Exhibit 11–7 shows.

The $100,000 debt was convertible into 5,000 shares of common stock. Conversion therefore would have increased the number of shares outstanding to 25,000. The revised earnings per share is $54,000/25,000 = $2.16.

Treasury Stock

Corporations from time to time repurchase shares of their own stock. These repurchased shares are called **treasury stock.**

Objectives of Treasury-Stock Purchases

Share repurchase may have a number of objectives. Some reacquired shares may be used for distribution to executives in bonus or stock option plans. Others may be used for distribution to shareholders as stock dividends, to employees in stock-purchase plans, or to the company's pension funds for long-term investment. Share repurchasing eliminates the necessity to issue new shares for these purposes and thus helps the company avoid the costs and additional reporting requirements associated with new issues.

Share repurchase may also be viewed as a more profitable use of the company's funds than the available alternatives. If the company has more cash than it can invest profitably internally, stock repurchase may prevent a dilution in earnings per share, particularly when market prices seem unjustifiably low.

The negative aspects of these transactions should not be overlooked, however. For one thing, the purchase and sale of treasury stock in any volume can generate short-term movements in the market price of the stock, which might be interpreted as the use of the corporation's funds by "insiders" to influence the price of the stock to their advantage. Similar objections can be raised to the use of the corporation's funds to purchase stock to prevent voting control from being concentrated in unfriendly hands.

A third drawback is that the purchase of treasury stock reduces the company's assets and equities. Treasury stock, in other words, represents a reduction of the stockholders' total investment in the enterprise and may impair the company's ability to discharge its obligations to its creditors. This would hurt not only the creditors but the shareholders and employees as well.

Reporting Treasury Stock at Cost

The usual method of accounting for treasury stock is to include it in the balance sheet as a separate amount, measured at the price paid to acquire it—as a negative element of owners' equity.

For example, suppose Space Age Corporation repurchased for $46,000 a total of 1,000 shares of its common stock on December 31, 19x9. This transaction was recorded by the following entry:

```
Treasury Stock ......................................   46,000
        Cash ...........................................            46,000
```

Treasury stock is not an asset. Shares of stock represent portions of the owners' equity in the company. When the shares are repurchased, the assets are reduced and so is the owners' equity. To treat treasury stock as an asset would imply that the company has ownership rights in itself, and this is impossible. Treasury shares can't be voted, nor do they participate in cash dividends or carry any other perquisites of ownership. The purchase of treasury shares represents a partial, usually temporary liquidation of the enterprise and therefore is a reduction in both total assets and total owners' equity. Thus, the cost of the shares is deducted from the owners' equity and is not included among the assets.

Resale of treasury stock at prices different from their acquisition cost is not reported as a gain or loss in the company's income statement. The company cannot make or lose money by buying and selling a portion of itself, although the equity of the surviving shareholders can be increased or decreased by such actions. The accepted accounting treatment is to add positive differences to the additional paid-in capital and, with some exceptions, to subtract negative differences from retained earnings.

An Illustration

The December 31, 19x9, owners' equity and book value per share of Space Age Corporation are shown on a *before* and *after* basis in Exhibit 11–8. The treasury shares were purchased for $46 a share ($46,000/1,000).

EXHIBIT 11–8

SPACE AGE CORPORATION
Owners' Equity and Book Value per Share
As of December 31, 19x9

	Before Repurchase	After Repurchase
Common stock (par value)	$ 605,000	$ 605,000
Additional paid-in capital	1,210,000	1,210,000
Retained earnings	1,089,000	1,089,000
Total		2,904,000
Less: Treasury stock		(46,000)
Total owners' equity	$2,904,000	$2,858,000
Book value per share:		
$2,904,000/121,000	$24.00	
$2,858,000/120,000		$23.82

Notice that the owners of the 1,000 purchased shares received more than the prepurchase book value of $24 a share. This means that the book value of the remaining 120,000 shares declined—to $23.82 ($2,858,000/120,000). If Space Age Corporation subsequently sold its treasury shares for $50 a share, Additional Paid-In Capital would increase by $4,000 [1,000 shares × ($50 − $46)]. Book value per share would increase as well—to $24.03 ($2,908,000/121,000 shares)—because the $50 sale price exceeded the $23.82 presale book value.[4]

Retained Earnings

Companies usually prepare a statement of changes in retained earnings. In most cases, this includes only the beginning and ending balances, the net income of the period, and dividends declared during the

---

[4] If the shares were sold instead for $40, owners' equity would decline by $6,000 [1,000 × ($46 − $40)]. Book value *per share* would increase, however, because the $40 sale price still was greater than the $23.82 presale book value. The new book value per share would be $23.95, based on ($2,858,000 + $40,000)/121,000 shares. The total effect of the purchase and resale of the treasury shares would be to reduce book value per share from $24.00 to $23.95.

period. This may take the form of a separate financial statement, as part of a combined statement of earnings and retained earnings, or as one column in a table showing changes in all of the owners' equity categories on the balance sheet. Exhibit 11–9 represents an example of a statement of this sort, from the 1983 annual report of General Dynamics Corporation.

EXHIBIT 11–9

GENERAL DYNAMICS CORPORATION
Consolidated Statement of Common Shareholders' Equity
(dollars in millions)

	Common Stock		Retained Earnings	Treasury Stock	
	Shares	Amount		Shares	Amount
Balance, 31 December 1982	55,442,100	$82.9	$1,111.7	952,739	$ 19.6
Net earnings			286.6		
Cash dividends.....................			(52.2)		
Stock options exercised		(3.9)		(433,334)	(15.0)
Conversions of preferred stock		(.3)	(29.7)	(1,228,110)	(57.0)
Shares acquired, at cost				3,524,132	190.2
Shares issued under Incentive Compensation Plan		1.4		(94,144)	(1.9)
Balance, 31 December 1983	55,442,100	$80.1	$1,316.4	2,721,283	$135.9

Although some people think that dividends are paid out of retained earnings, this of course isn't the case. Dividends are paid with assets, usually cash.[5] All the retained earnings in the world won't buy a lollipop at the local supermarket. It is generally true, however, that dividends won't be declared unless the Retained Earnings account has a positive balance. The laws of incorporation in most states in the United States limit the amount of assets that can be distributed to stockholders as dividends. In many of these states, the maximum is the amount of the company's retained earnings. Even though a company's retained earnings balance may represent the upper limit, however, its board of directors usually uses lower self-imposed limits when making dividend decisions.

Contingencies

Businesses operate in an environment of uncertainty. A previously successful company may suffer serious reverses from events it wasn't

---

[5] Stock dividends *aren't* distributions of assets or of anything valuable; they are distributions of additional certificates of stock which don't increase any stockholder's relative equity in the corporation.

able to foresee. To provide for these, management may wish to make deductions from revenues in good years to reflect the possibility that unforeseen events in the future may impair the values of the company's resources.

For example, suppose most of a company's facilities are in an area that is subject to the possibility of earthquakes. Management has decided that outside insurance against earthquake damage is too expensive. Instead, it has decided to show in its financial statements that its investment in plant, equipment, and inventories is subject to the risk of loss due to earthquakes. It has done this by setting up a **reserve for contingencies,** a subdivision of the owners' equity calling attention to the *possibility* that a present condition or commitment will lead to a future event that will reduce the company's assets or increase its liabilities. The company's owners' equity, including this subdivision, is shown schematically in Exhibit 11–10. Both unshaded segments of this diagram are parts of the retained earnings.

EXHIBIT 11–10
Owners' Equity, Including Contingency Reserve

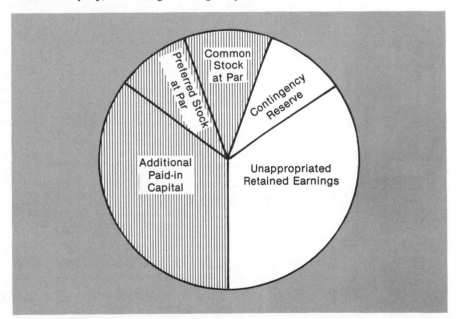

We face two difficulties in attempting to reflect the contingency of an earthquake in the financial statements. First, the probability that an earthquake will occur and that this earthquake will be strong enough to cause damage (that is, will impair the value of assets or give rise to new liabilities) can't be assessed reliably because adequate statistics are unavailable. Earthquakes just don't happen in ways that are predictable enough to support the necessary accounting measurements. Second, the amount of the possible loss can't be estimated accurately enough. An earthquake, if it happens, may destroy all of the company, part of it, or none of it.

For these reasons, the accounting profession in the United States has taken the position that contingency reserves can't be set up by deductions from revenues in the income statement. Revenue deductions (expense charges) are permitted only if it is deemed probable that a loss has *already* occurred and that it can be estimated accurately enough. In such cases, the affected assets are written down or a liability (provision for loss) is established.

If contingency reserves are set up, therefore, they are carved out of retained earnings by an entry of the following form:

```
Retained Earnings ......................................... xxxx
     Reserve for Contingencies............................          xxxx
```

This reduces the amount of retained earnings on the balance sheet and creates a new item, shown on a separate line. Because the meaning of the amount on the separate line is seldom clear, many companies prefer to omit any mention of contingencies from the balance sheet, leaving that discussion entirely to the footnotes. Others may present a contingencies category on the balance sheet, but without a dollar amount.

We should point out that the creation of a contingency reserve has no effect on the way actual losses are accounted for. If losses of the predicted type actually materialize, they are deducted from current revenues on the income statement, just as any other losses are. They are *not* charged against the contingency reserve. The balance in the contingency reserve itself may remain unchanged or may be transferred back to the unappropriated portion of retained earnings. In no case is any of the reserve transferred to the income statement.

Summary   All corporations have common stock. Some also have one or more classes of preferred stock, with a prior but limited right to dividends. The amounts invested directly in the corporation (contributed capital) are divided into two parts, the par (or stated) values of the shares and the amounts paid in excess of par.

The initial issuance of common stock provides the base for the company's capital structure. Additional shares are issued from time to time, and the proceeds from these issues are also divided between par value and additional paid-in capital. These additional shares may be issued to the general public, used to acquire the stock of other companies, issued to investors who choose to exchange convertible securities for them, given to executives as rewards for meritorious service, or turned over to employees or others who exercise stock options they hold. Shares held for conversions and options are included with the number of shares outstanding in certain calculations of earnings per share.

The line between contributed capital and retained earnings is clouded by stock dividends, which require the transfer of amounts from retained earnings to the contributed capital section. Stock dividends and stock splits are generally regarded as signals that the company intends to increase the total cash dividend payment, and the market price of the shares is likely to move higher. It will stay at this higher level, however, only if the cash dividend actually does increase as anticipated.

Corporations in the United States occasionally use funds to repurchase some of their own outstanding shares. These shares are known as treasury stock. They are shown at cost on the balance sheet, deducted from the total of contributed capital and retained earnings to determine the net owners' equity. Sometimes part of the retained earnings is earmarked as a "contingency reserve," but this is never allowed to affect the income statement.

Key Terms	Additional paid-in capital	Par value
	Book value per share	Preemptive rights
	Callable stock	Preferred stock
	Common stock	Reserve for contingencies
	Convertible securities	Stock dividend
	Dilution of earnings	Stock option
	Dilution of the equity	Stock split
	Earnings per share	Treasury stock

Independent Study Problems (Solutions in Appendix B)

1. Issuance of Common Stock for Cash; Dilution. Angel Rings, Inc., had the following owners' equity on January 1, 19x1:

Common stock, $1 par (authorized, 1 million shares)..	$ 800,000
Additional paid-in capital	300,000
Retained earnings	500,000
Total..	$1,600,000

On January 2, 19x1, the shareowners were given the opportunity to purchase 160,000 new shares of common stock at a price of $4 a share when the market price of the stock was $5 a share. One hundred sixty thousand shares were issued on February 18, 19x1.

Net income for the year ended December 31, 19x1, was $441,600. A cash dividend of 20 cents a share was declared on December 15, 19x1, and paid on January 15, 19x2.

a. Prepare the owners' equity section of the company's balance sheet on December 31, 19x1.

b. Did the issuance of the new shares lead to a dilution of the equity? State the reasons for your answer, including any calculations you find necessary.

2. Stock Dividend. Ambrose Company's board of directors declared and distributed a stock dividend of one share of common stock for each 20 shares outstanding. Prior to the stock dividend, 20,000 shares were outstanding with a par value of $10 a share. The company recorded the stock dividend at the shares' market value of $30 a share.

State the effect of this transaction on the amounts shown on Ambrose's balance sheet.

3. Treasury Stock. On January 1, 19x1, Barrister Company had 100,000 shares of $5 par common stock outstanding. On January 4, 19x1, the company purchased 100 shares of this stock in the market at a price of $30 a share and placed these shares in the treasury. On March 2, 19x1, Barrister declared a cash dividend on the outstanding shares of common stock at the rate of 30 cents a share; this dividend was distributed on April 5, 19x1. On May 15, 19x1, the company sold its treasury stock at a price of $40 a share.

State the effects of each of these transactions on Barrister's assets, liabilities, and owners' equity. Be careful to specify which portions of the owners' equity were affected.

4. Dilution: Calculating Earnings per Share. Denver Corporation in 19x1 had a net income of $312,000. It had 100,000 shares of common stock outstanding and 10,000 shares of $5 convertible preferred stock. Each share of preferred was convertible into two shares of common.

a. Calculate primary earnings per common share, ignoring the convertibility of the preferred stock.

b. Calculate the fully diluted earnings per common share.

Exercises and Problems

5. Issuance of Stock for Cash; Book Value. On January 8, 19x1, Alpine Company started operations by issuing 100,000 shares of common stock, $10 par, at a price of $15 a share. No additional shares of stock were issued between that date and December 31, 19x4. Retained earnings of the company as of December 31, 19x4, totaled $2 million.

a. How did the issuance of the stock affect the various components of the owners' equity?

b. What was the book value per share of common stock on December 31, 19x4?

6. Purchase of Treasury Stock. On January 2, 19x5, Alpine Company (see problem 5) repurchased 1,000 shares of its stock at the market price of $28 a share. This stock was held as treasury stock.

a. How should this treasury stock have been listed on Alpine's June 30, 19x5, balance sheet?
b. Did the purchase of this treasury stock increase, decrease, or leave unchanged the book value per share of stock issued and outstanding?
c. Should a gain or loss be shown in the 19x5 income statement as a result of the repurchase of the stock? Why?

7. Sale of Treasury Stock. On July 1, 19x5, Alpine Company (see problem 6) resold its treasury stock at a price of $34 a share.

a. How did the sale of the treasury stock affect the various components of the owners' equity?
b. Should a gain or loss be shown on the 19x5 income statement as a result of the resale of stock? Why?

8. Additional Paid-In Capital. During 19x6, Avondale, Inc., had the following four transactions. It issued 100,000 shares of $3-par common stock for $1.8 million, and then declared a 6 percent stock dividend when its shares' market value was $27 a share. Avondale then bought 10,000 treasury shares for $38 a share and resold 70 percent of those shares for $44 a share.

What was the amount of Additional Paid-In Capital in Avondale, Inc.'s December 31, 19x6, balance sheet?

9. Book Value per Share; Treasury Stock. Bolton Corporation's balance sheet showed the following owners' equity section on December 31:

$5 par value common stock (5,559,500 shares issued)	$27,797,500
Additional paid-in capital	10,960,500
Retained earnings	55,389,500
Treasury stock (9,500 shares)	(153,500)
Total owners' equity	$93,994,000

The market price of the stock on December 31 was $25 per share.

a. What was the book value per share of the common stock issued and outstanding at the end of the year?
b. Give three alternative explanations for how the "Additional paid-in capital" might have been accumulated. (One phrase or sentence for each will be adequate.)

10. Stock Dividend. Assume Bolton Corporation in problem 9 declared a 10 percent stock dividend to the owners of the shares outstanding on December 31. The treasury shares didn't participate in this distribution.

a. How would this transaction affect the various components of the owners' equity?

b. What would be the new book value per share?

c. What would be the new book value (on Bolton's books) of the shares owned by an investor who had owned 10 shares of stock prior to the stock dividend?

11. Stock Split.   Assume that instead of a stock dividend, Bolton Corporation in problem 9 declared a two-for-one stock split (two new shares exchanged for each old one) and changed the par value to $3 a share.

a. How would this transaction affect the various components of the owners' equity?

b. What would be the new book value per share?

c. What would be the new book value (on the corporation's books) of the shares owned by an investor who had owned 10 shares of stock prior to the stock split?

12. Elements of Owners' Equity.   David Dillon, president of Dillon Company, bought a new personal computer. He used a program which he thought would calculate the company's net income, but it only generated the following data for 19x3:

Cost of treasury shares bought July 2, 19x3	$ 19,000
Total liabilities, December 31, 19x3	138,000
Common stock issued, March 14, 19x3	40,000
Declaration of cash dividend, December 10, 19x3	18,000
Owners' equity, January 1, 19x3	280,000
Total assets, December 31, 19x3	$495,000

Although Dillon was disappointed that the amount of net income was not identified, he was astonished to observe that all six amounts were in fact accurate.

Prepare a schedule to calculate Dillon Company's 19x3 net income.

13. Book Value per Share: Missing Amounts.   Determine the one missing amount in each of the following three independent cases.

	I	II	III
Cash dividend per share	$ 2.25	$ 4.00	C
Common stock, January 1	$ 5,000	B	$ 2,000
Book value per share, December 31 . .	A	$ 5.60	$ 25
Additional paid-in capital, January 1 . .	$16,000	$ 9,000	$118,000
Shares outstanding, January 1	2,500	10,000	8,000
Retained earnings, January 1	$ 9,000	$22,000	$ 56,000
Earnings per share	$ 3.50	$ 6.00	$ 16

14. Calculating Earnings per Share.   Massena Corporation in 19x1 had a net income of $4,416,000. It had 1 million shares of common stock outstanding and 100,000 shares of $6 convertible preferred. Each share of preferred was convertible into 1.7 shares of common stock.

The company also had $5 million in 9 percent bonds payable, convertible into common shares at a ratio of 18 shares of common for every $1,000 in bonds. The effective tax rate in 19x1 was 40 percent.

a. Calculate primary earnings per common share, ignoring the convertibility of the bonds and the preferred stock.
b. Calculate the fully diluted earnings per common share.

15. Earnings per Share: Missing Amounts. Determine the missing amounts in each of the three independent cases that appear in the table. Each preferred share is convertible into four common shares, and each $1,000 bond is convertible into 15 common shares. Conversion is assumed only for purposes of calculating fully diluted earnings per share, and the company's income tax rate is 40 percent.

	I	II	III
Common shares...................	20,000	6,000	5,000
$9 preferred shares	5,000	3,000	E
12 percent bonds.................	$200,000	$90,000	F
Net income......................	$225,000	C	$57,600
Earnings per share:			
Primary	A	D	$7.20
Fully diluted	B	$2.71	$4.32

16. Owners' Equity: Book Value per Share. Cousins Corporation had 28 stockholders all of whom were cousins. The corporation's common stock wasn't traded publicly and individual shares therefore had no market value. Company policy stated that new shares were to be issued for cash equal to 125 percent of the existing book value per share, and stockholders who sold shares to the corporation would receive cash equal to 110 percent of the existing book value per share. During 19x3, book value per share increased from $60 to $80.

Cousins Corporation's owners' equity on January 1, 19x3, consisted of the following amounts:

Common stock ($5 par).........	$ 125,000
Additional paid-in capital	720,000
Retained earnings	655,000
Total.....................	$1,500,000

During March, 5,000 shares were sold to qualifying investors for cash. In mid-July, Cousins Corporation bought 4,000 treasury shares. On November 1, $923,100 was received from existing stockholders in exchange for previously unissued shares. Net income of $516,900, earned during 19x3, was recorded on December 31.

Prepare the owners' equity section that would appear in Cousins Corporation's December 31, 19x3, balance sheet.

17. Owners' Equity Transactions. The January 1, 19x2, balance sheet of Globe Corporation contained an owners' equity section which appeared as follows:

Common stock ($2 par value)	$ 300,000
Additional paid-in capital	1,450,000
Retained earnings	975,000
Less: Treasury stock (average cost, $7) . .	(280,000)
Total	$2,445,000

The directors decided to increase the number of shares outstanding by 11,000 shares on January 2, 19x2, when the market price per share was $16. They wanted to evaluate three different ways of achieving their objective: issue 11,000 new shares, sell 11,000 treasury shares, or declare a 10 percent stock dividend on the 110,000 shares currently outstanding.

What would be the effect of each of the three approaches on (*a*) Globe's 19x2 earnings per share, and (*b*) Globe's December 31, 19x2, owners' equity—if 19x2 income turned out to be $484,000 and the July 19x2 cash dividend were to be $3 a share?

18. Issuance of Common Shares for Cash; Dilution. The owners' equity in Beehive Industries was as follows on January 1, 19x1:

Common stock (no par) stated value,	
$5 a share (authorized 2 million shares;	
outstanding, 1.8 million shares)	$ 9,000,000
Additional paid-in capital	6,300,000
Retained earnings	4,500,000
Total	$19,800,000

The company's shareholders voted in April 19x1 to increase the authorized number of shares of common stock from 2 million to 5 million. In September 19x1, the company gave its common shareholders rights to purchase 450,000 new shares of common stock at a price of $15 a share. All rights were exercised, and the new shares were issued on October 1, 19x1. The market price of Beehive Industries' common stock just prior to the offering was $20 a share.

The company's net income for the year ended December 31, 19x1, was $956,250. Cash dividends of 10 cents a share were declared and paid in May and in November 19x1.

a. Present the owners' equity section of Beehive's balance sheet as of December 31, 19x1.

b. Did the issuance of these shares result in a dilution of the equity? Present calculations to support your conclusion.

c. If the earnings per share amount is to be used as an approximation of future earnings per share, should the denominator of the ratio in 19x1 be 1,800,000 shares, 1,912,500 shares, 2,250,000 shares, or some other number? Give the reasons for your choice and any assumptions you had to make.

19. Effects of Owners' Equity Transactions. The composition of the owners' equity section of Grant Corporation's balance sheet was as follows:

Common stock ($10 par)........	$ 50,000
Additional paid-in capital	110,000
Retained earnings	90,000
Owners' equity	$250,000

The following seven events then occurred in sequence:

a. Issued 2,000 new common shares for $65,000.
b. Effected a four-for-one stock split; new par value, $2.50.
c. Declared and paid a $2 cash dividend per share.
d. Net income was $175,750.
e. Declared and distributed a 15 percent stock dividend when the market value was $10 a share.
f. Bought 2,200 treasury shares for $35,200.
g. Bought 1,500 additional treasury shares for $16,500.

Set up a matrix consisting of seven rows (*a* through *g*), one for each of the seven events listed above, and four columns (1 through 4), one for each of the following four items:

1. Shares outstanding.
2. Retained earnings.
3. Owners' equity.
4. Book value per share.

Show how each of the seven events affected each of the four items, by placing the appropriate letter in each of the 28 (7 × 4) cells, as follows: *I* = increase, *D* = decrease, *N* = no effect.

20. Owners' Equity Transactions and Balances.   Commonwealth Corporation was founded in January 19x1. Its accountants were so busy measuring assets and liabilities in 19x1 and revenues and expenses in 19x2 that they neglected to measure properly the component parts of the owners' equity at the end of both 19x1 and 19x2. It is now the beginning of 19x3, and you have been given the assignment of preparing the owners' equity section of each year-end balance sheet.

The only demonstrably correct amounts the accountants were able to provide were:

December 31, 19x1:
  Total owners' equity.............. $700,000
December 31, 19x2:
  Common stock issued, $2 par value
    (includes treasury shares) $138,000
  19x2 net income.................. $562,000

Commonwealth's president thought it was no coincidence that the $700,000 end-of-19x1 owners' equity was equal to the sum of 19x2's net income and its year-end common-stock account balance.

During 19x1, the only events affecting owners' equity were (1) the one-time sale of common stock whose proceeds were equal to 2½ times the shares' par value, and (2) the earning of income. There were neither dividends nor treasury stock transactions.

During 19x2, the following events occurred:

1. During February, when Commonwealth's stock had a fair market value of $26 a share, a 15 percent stock dividend was declared and distributed.
2. During April, Commonwealth bought 3,000 of its outstanding shares for $30 a share.
3. During July, a cash dividend of $4 a share was declared and paid.
4. During November, Commonwealth sold 2,000 of its treasury shares for $36 a share.

Prepare the owners' equity section that would appear in Commonwealth Corporation's December 31, 19x1, and December 31, 19x2, balance sheets.

21. Executive Stock Options. The stockholders of Topper Corporation voted approval of an executive stock option plan at the annual stockholders' meeting on May 14, 19x0. The vote authorized the board of directors to grant purchase options to key executives up to a maximum of 30,000 shares of the company's previously unissued stock.

The first options were granted on September 10, 19x0. Various executives were given rights to purchase a total of 12,000 shares at $22 a share, the market price of the stock at the close of trading on that date. These options would lapse within five years if they were not exercised.

On June 1, 19x2, officers were given three-year options to buy an additional 15,000 shares at $28 a share, the market price on that date.

Options on 8,000 shares at $22 a share were exercised in November 19x3. The company's stock was then selling at $36 a share.

In 19x4, the stockholders approved the addition of another 20,000 shares to the stock option plan. In September of that year, three-year options were granted on 6,000 shares at $43 a share, the market price at that time.

Options on 4,000 shares at $22 a share and 3,000 shares at $28 a share were exercised in 19x4. The stock was selling at $40 a share at the time.

a. Prepare a footnote to be appended to the 19x0 financial statements, giving adequate disclosure of the stock option plan. The company's fiscal year ends on December 31 each year.

b. Prepare a footnote on the stock option plan for the 19x4 financial statements. Explain your reasons for disclosing each item you have included. Why is it important to disclose this information?

c. Did the exercise of the options in 19x3 and 19x4 constitute dilution of the equity? Explain.

d. What was the effect of all the above transactions on the owners' equity in Topper Corporation?

Chapter 12

Investments and Combinations

Investments are company-owned bonds, notes, and stock of other corporations and bonds and notes of government bodies. Sometimes the investment in another company's stock may be the result of a *business combination;* in such cases, *consolidated financial statements* are usually prepared to report the combined results of the two companies.

In this chapter, we'll study different kinds of investments in securities, the accounting measurements that apply, and the financial reporting practices that come into play. We'll cover the topics in the following order:

1. Investments in short-term debt instruments.
2. Long-term investments in bonds.
3. Noncontrolling investments in stocks.
4. Business combinations.
5. Consolidated financial statements.

Investments in Short-Term Debt Instruments

Corporations often invest in the bonds issued by other corporations or by government units. They may also hold short-term government notes, bank certificates of deposit, or commercial paper (promissory notes of corporations with the highest credit ratings). Financial corporations (banks, in particular) also hold the promissory notes of other corporations and of individual borrowers.

Most bonds, government notes, and commercial paper are **marketable** in the sense that brokers, dealers, and other intermediaries stand ready to buy them at some price or to locate others who are willing to buy. Many of these mature within a few months or even within a few days. These short-term instruments have a large place in the portfolios of financial corporations such as banks and mutual funds; nonfinancial corporations also buy and hold them for short periods to earn interest, instead of holding cash temporarily in excess of current operating needs.

Securities of this type usually either will be or can be sold on short notice at prices not significantly lower than current prices. They are reported as current assets and are ordinarily measured at cost plus accrued interest. Interest on these notes and bonds is recognized as it accrues unless the amounts are too small to be material.

Long-Term Investments in Bonds

Bonds or notes purchased as long-term investments are measured at their amortized cost. **Amortized cost** means (1) the purchase cost *less* the amortized portion of the investment premium, or (2) the purchase cost *plus* the amortized portion of the investment discount. For example, suppose Granite Corporation bought $10,000 of XYZ Corporation's 8 percent bonds on July 1, 19x1, five years before their maturity date. The price paid was $9,604, and interest was to be received semiannually, on January 1 and July 1 each year. In other words, Granite bought the bonds at a $396 discount ($10,000 − $9,604). The accounting entry to record this purchase was:

Investments	9,604	
Cash		9,604

This recorded the decrease in the company's Cash asset and the increase in its Investment asset.

The Nature of Bonds

We pointed out in Chapter 10 that the price paid by the bondholder reflects the purchase of the right to receive two types of payments— periodic interest based on the coupon interest rate *and* the face value of the bond at maturity. The purchase price will differ from the bond's face value when the market yield rate to maturity isn't the same as the coupon rate. Granite's purchase of the XYZ bonds at a discount indicates that the yield rate was greater than the coupon rate.

When studying this subject from the vantage point of the issuer of the bonds, we learned two important lessons. First, each period's interest expense is calculated by applying the yield rate to the actual debt outstanding during the period. Second, the premium or discount is amortized each period by the dollar-amount difference between the recorded interest expense and the coupon interest transferred from the issuer to the bondholder (the interest *payment*).

Calculating Interest Revenue

These same rules apply as well to the bondholder, who in our case is Granite Corporation. To be able to proceed, we need to determine the percentage yield to maturity implicit in the $9,604 price. We do this by turning to Table 4 in Appendix A. Going down the column showing market prices for five years to maturity, we find that when 8 percent bonds with a face value of $100 have a market price of $96.04, the effective market yield to maturity is 9.0 percent (the ninth row in the table).

In other words, bonds with the risk and maturity characteristics of the XYZ bonds were priced on July 1, 19x1, at levels that would earn investors half of 9 percent, or 4.5 percent, every six months. Granite's interest revenue in the first six months therefore was 4½ percent of $9,604, or $432. Granite was to receive only $400 in cash, however. The $32 difference between these two amounts was the interest it earned currently, but would collect only at maturity; recall that $10,000 will be received at maturity, not the $9,604 that had been invested. The accounting entry to accrue the interest on December 31, 19x1, was:

```
Interest Receivable......................................  400
    Investment............................................       32
    Interest Revenue......................................      432
```

This showed owners' equity going up by $432, the Interest Receivable asset going up by $400, and the Investment asset going up by $32. Receipt of $400 from XYZ Corporation the next day (January 1, 19x2)

EXHIBIT 12–1
Calculating Interest Revenue on a Bond Investment

	(1) **Interest Revenue** 0.045 × *(4)***	*(2)* **Coupon Interest** 0.04 × $10,000	*(3)* **Discount Amortization** *(1)* − *(2)*	*(4)* **Investment in Bonds** *(4)** + *(3)*
July 1, 19x1				$ 9,604
December 31, 19x1	$ 432	$ 400	$ 32	9,636
June 30, 19x2.	434	400	34	9,670
December 31, 19x2	435	400	35	9,705
.	.	.	.	.
.	.	.	.	.
June 30, 19x5.				9,906
December 31, 19x5	446	400	46	9,952
June 30, 19x6.	448	400	48	10,000
Total	$4,396	$4,000	$396	

* *Beginning-of-period* Investment in Bonds.

converted the interest receivable into cash; the investment was reported in the December 31, 19x1, balance sheet at $9,636 ($9,604 + $32). This pattern continued in later periods as both interest and the investment asset increased until the bonds matured, as illustrated in Exhibit 12–1.

CALCULATING INTEREST AND INVESTMENT BALANCE FOR BONDS WITH SEMIANNUAL INTEREST PAYMENTS

1. Calculate the percentage yield to maturity at the time of purchase.
2. Multiply the investment balance at the beginning of the period by half this yield percentage—this is interest revenue for six months.
3. Calculate the difference between interest revenue and the semiannual interest payment—this difference represents an addition to, or partial payment of, the amount of the investment balance.
4. Add or subtract this difference to or from the investment balance at the beginning of the period—this is the investment balance at the end of the period.

Gains and Losses on Sales of Notes and Bonds

If a company buys bonds or notes and holds them to maturity, the entire difference between the purchase price and the maturity value is interest revenue—$396 in the Granite example. If the securities are sold prior to maturity, however, part of the difference between the purchase price and the selling price may be a gain or a loss.

For example, suppose Granite changed its mind about making the XYZ bonds a *long-term* investment and sold them on January 1, 19x2, at a price of $9,700. The investment in the bonds at that time was $9,636, as we just saw, so the company recognized a $64 *gain* on the sale ($9,700 − $9,636).

Effect of Changes in Interest Rates

Measuring investments in bonds at their amortized cost may lead to serious misstatements of the investments. Suppose a sharply restrictive national monetary policy drove interest rates up sharply in the six months after Granite bought its XYZ bonds. The effective market interest rate on January 1, 19x2, for bonds of comparable risk and 4½ years to maturity was 8 percent each six-month period. Discounting the future cash flows for nine six-month periods at 8 percent a period gives the following present values:

Periods after January 1, 19x2	Cash Flow	Present Value Multiplier at 8%	Present Value
1 to 9	+$400 a period	6.2469	+$2,499
9	+$10,000	0.5002	+ 5,002
Total			+$7,501

This table tells us that investors on January 1, 19x2, were willing to pay no more than $7,501 for these bonds, the amount they would have to pay to get the same cash-flow stream from another source in the current market. Granite reported its investment in the bonds at their amortized cost of $9,636, however, staying with the original amortization schedule based on the yield to maturity in effect on July 1, 19x1.

Accountants measure bond investments at their amortized cost on the grounds that the company intends to hold the bonds to maturity, at which time market value and unamortized cost will come together at the maturity value.[1] The economic fact, however, is that the owners of fixed-payment securities lose part of their wealth when interest rates rise. Under conventional accounting practice, this loss is not reported in the income statement because it is an **unrealized loss.** If the intercompany investments in long-term bonds were measured at market value, the loss would be reported as a negative component of current income.

Noncontrolling Investments in Shares of Stock

Investments in stocks that constitute 50 percent or less of the voting rights of their corporations are mostly of three types:

1. Short-term investments of temporarily idle cash.
2. Long-term investments that *don't* give their owners significant influence on the investees' actions.
3. Long-term investments that *do* give their owners significant influence on the investees' actions.

Short-Term Investments

Companies sometimes use their temporarily idle cash to invest in the shares of stock issued by other corporations. The investor company earns a return on its investment (1) when it receives dividends and (2) through capital appreciation. Although capital appreciation occurs as the market price of the shares increases, accounting recognizes such gains only when the shares are sold. When the market price of shares declines, however, accountants in the United States use the lower-of-cost-of-market rule to record the effect of the decrease in the value of the investment.

---

[1] Mutual investment funds are an exception to this rule; they measure and report the market value of their portfolios on a daily basis.

Long-Term Noninfluential Investments in Stocks

Any ownership of less than 50 percent of the voting shares of a corporation is a **minority interest** in that corporation. If the number of shares is small enough relative to the total, the investor won't be able to influence the operating and financial policies of the investee significantly. The only question is: how small is small enough? The rule of thumb in the United States is that ownership of less than 20 percent of the voting stock leads to a presumption that the investor lacks the ability to have significant influence on the investee. This presumption will carry the day unless there is evidence that the investor is able to exert influence on the investee.

The reasons for making this distinction is that accountants use different methods to account for investments, depending on whether the investor is able to exert at least a significant amount of influence. For stock investments classified as not significant (generally, those with less than 20 percent of the voting rights), the investment is measured at the lower of the original cost or its current market price. Income is measured by the investor's share in cash dividends declared by the investee, plus or minus any gains or losses on sales of investments. (Unlike unrealized losses on the current portfolio, unrealized losses are direct adjustments to retained earnings and don't affect net income.)

The reason for this treatment is that since the investor doesn't own enough shares to influence the investee's board of directors, it has no way of increasing the dividend or of making sure the rest of the cash flows from the investee's operations are invested profitably to generate a larger stream of cash flows in the future.

Long-Term Influential Investments in Stocks

The policy of recognizing only dividends as income can be criticized on the grounds that the shareholders benefit eventually from the asset growth indicated by the current earnings, because the investment will produce additional future cash flows. The accounting method reflecting this reasoning is known as the **equity method.** It is used for influential investments—that is, those that give the investor a significant influence over the operating and financial policies of the investee. This is generally presumed to be the case if the investor owns 20 percent or more of the voting rights in the company.

Equity in Income and Dividends.   To illustrate this method, let's suppose National Company bought 30,000 shares of Local Company's stock on January 2, 19x1, at a price of $30 a share. The entry was:

Investments...	900,000	
Cash		900,000

The $900,000 National paid was equal to 30 percent of Local's $3 million reported owners' equity.

Local's earnings per share were $3.25, and cash dividends totaled $1.50 a share during 19x1. With 100,000 shares outstanding, Local's total net income therefore was $325,000, and its total dividend was $150,000. These amounts are shown in the box at the bottom of Exhibit 12–2. The volume of the *entire box* represents the net income; the vol-

EXHIBIT 12–2
National's Share of Local's Earnings and Dividends

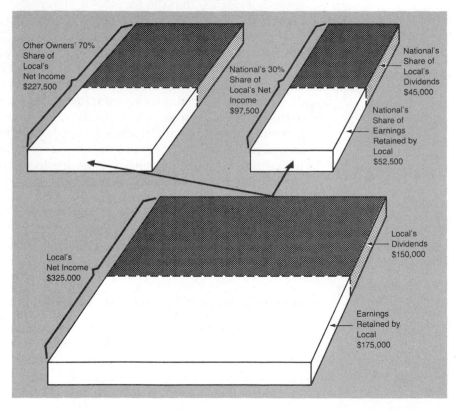

ume of the *shaded section* stands for the dividends. National's share in Local's earnings was 30,000 × $3.25 = $97,500, or 30 percent of the total. This is represented by the volume of the box in the upper right-hand portion of the exhibit. National's share of the dividends paid by Local was 30,000 × $1.50 = $45,000, represented by the shaded segment of this smaller box.

As a result of its 30 percent ownership share, National's income statement contains 30 percent, or $97,500, of Local's net income. National's year-end balance sheet reflects asset increases totaling the same amount. Cash increased by the $45,000 that was realized as a result of the dividends declared and paid by Local during the year; the remaining, yet-to-be-realized $52,500 equity in Local's net income appears as an increase in National's Investment asset. National records these facts by an entry or entries with the following effects:

```
Cash.............................................  45,000
Investments......................................  52,500
    Revenue from Investments......................          97,500
```

Under the equity method, in other words, the Investment asset is measured by the original cost *plus* the investor's yet-to-be-realized share in the investee's post-investment earnings.

Differences between Cost and Equity Methods. The differences between the cost and equity methods are diagrammed in Exhibit 12–3. The

EXHIBIT 12–3
Income and Investment under the Cost and Equity Methods

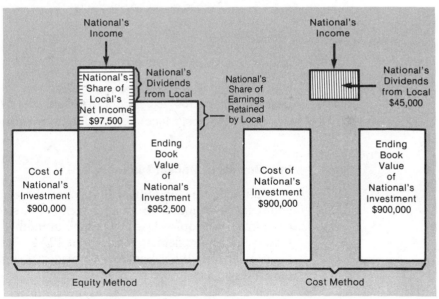

three blocks at the right illustrate the cost method. National would include in its income statement only its $45,000 share in Local's dividends. It would measure the investment at its $900,000 cost unless its market value declined to less than that amount.

The three blocks at the left illustrate the equity method. National's income statement now includes National's full $97,500 share in Local's net income. Some of this amount (the cash dividend) serves to increase National's cash flow; the rest (National's share of the earnings retained by Local) is added to its investment, represented by the second unshaded block in the exhibit. This block would appear as the block at the left in a similar diagram drawn for 19x2.

Excess Investment Cost. In the first part of this illustration, we assumed that National's cost of its investment in Local was equal to its share of Local's common stockholders' equity as Local reported it. More often, the purchase price exceeds the underlying owners' equity. When this happens, the excess is amortized systematically as the investor records its share of the investee's net income or loss; the maximum amortization period in the United States is 40 years.

In our example, if Local's owners' equity had been $2.6 million instead of $3 million when National acquired its 30 percent interest for $900,000, National's cost would have exceeded its underlying equity by $120,000:

Investment cost	$900,000
Underlying equity: 30% × $2,600,000	780,000
Excess of cost over equity	$120,000

One fortieth of that amount, or $3,000, would have been deducted from income. National's equity in Local's earnings therefore would have been reported as $94,500, not $97,500:

Equity in Local's income: 30% × $325,000	$97,500
Less: Amortization of excess of investment cost over equity	3,000
Equity in Local's income, as reported by National	$94,500

Investments In Stocks: Summary

Accountants in the United States use three different methods to account for investments in another company's stock—cost, lower-of-cost-or-market, and equity. Use of a particular method depends on a variety of factors, which are depicted in Exhibit 12–4. The boxes in the left of the diagram identify the factors to be considered, and the financial reporting outcomes appear in the right of the exhibit.

Business Combinations

A company's ownership of more than 50 percent of the voting stock of another company gives it a controlling interest in that company. Since a controlling interest is often obtained through a *business combination,* we have to see what business combinations are and how accountants account for them before we can discuss how companies report investments they classify as controlling interests.

EXHIBIT 12–4
Classification of Investments in Stock

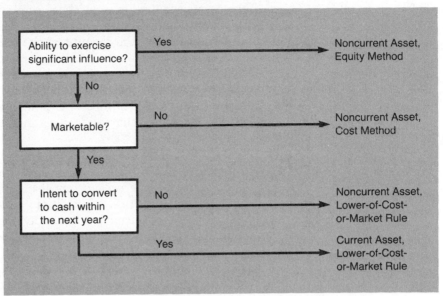

Nature of a Business Combination

A **business combination** occurs when two companies enter into a transaction that results in one group of common stockholders having equity in the assets and liabilities of both companies. The combining companies are called the **combinor** and the **combinee,** and the resulting company is called the **combined enterprise.** Combinations are effected when the combinor gives cash, securities, or both to the combinee's stockholders in exchange for their shares.

In some combinations, the combined enterprise is operated as one legal entity, while in others the combined enterprise functions as two legal entities—that is, as two separate corporations. We'll begin in this section by considering business combinations in which the combined enterprise operates as a single legal entity. We'll consider the two-entity case in the following section.

The Purchase Method

Two accounting methods are used to record business combinations: the **purchase method** and the **pooling-of-interests method.** The two methods are *not* alternatives to each other in the sense that a company might select *either* LIFO *or* FIFO as a basis for determining the cost of its ending inventory. The circumstances surrounding a particular combination dictate which method must be used.

The purchase method reflects the belief that the combinor has *purchased the assets and assumed the liabilities* of the combinee. The total cost of the assets acquired in a purchase combination is dictated by the purchase price paid to effect the combination. When cash is given to the combinee's stockholders, the amount of the purchase price is self-evident. It consists of the amount of cash paid plus the value of the combinee's liabilities assumed as part of the deal. When securities are given in exchange for the combinee's stock, *their* current value is likely to define the amount of the purchase price of the net assets, unless the market value of the combinee's shares received in exchange is more readily determinable.

The Accounting Problem.   The accounting problem is that by buying the stock the combinor buys a *package* consisting of the combinee's assets and liabilities. The total price is known or can be estimated reasonably accurately; the amounts paid for the individual assets are unknown. These relationships can be diagrammed as follows:

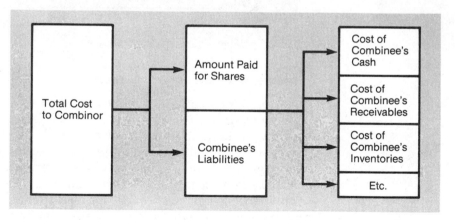

To record the purchase, in other words, the accountants have to estimate how much of the total purchase price has been paid for each of the combinee's assets. The presumption is that the purchaser must have paid what each asset was worth—that is, its **fair market value.** Fair market value in this context is defined as the amount the company would have had to pay to buy each of the acquired assets in an arm's length transaction.

The combinor, of course, knows the book values of the combinee's assets. Unfortunately, these book values aren't always a good measure of their fair market value. This means that some other estimation basis ordinarily must be found. Sometimes quoted market prices can be used; at other times the services of professional appraisers must be sought. Appraisers develop their measures of **appraised value** from their knowl-

> ### TERMINOLOGY REMINDER: BOOK VALUE AND NET ASSETS
>
> *Owners' equity* by definition is the excess of assets over liabilities. Assets and liabilities are not measured by their current market values. Instead, they are expressed at the historical exchange prices entered in the company's accounting records—i.e., its "books." Hence, the expression *book value* refers to the excess of recorded assets over recorded liabilities—namely, the recorded owners' equity.
>
> Similarly, individual assets and liabilities can be said to appear in a balance sheet at their *book values*—e.g., the cost of a depreciable asset, less its accumulated depreciation, is said to be the measure of the asset's book value.
>
> *Net assets* is another term denoting the excess of assets over liabilities. The total of all the company's assets can be referred to as its *gross* assets; *net* assets then signifies the portion of the gross asset total not offset by obligations to creditors.

edge of market transactions in other assets or from data on the costs of replacing the assets currently.

Illustration. To demonstrate, let's suppose Worthy Company paid $220,000 cash to acquire all the common shares of Able, Inc. Able had liabilities of $60,000 at that time, and this seemed to be a reasonable measure of their fair market value. The cost of the assets acquired therefore totaled $280,000. Able's combination-date balance sheet showed the following amounts:

Cash	$ 40,000	Liabilities	$ 60,000
Inventory	90,000	Common stock	50,000
Machinery	80,000	Retained earnings	100,000
Total	$210,000	Total	$210,000

The book value of the common equity therefore was $50,000 + $100,000 = $150,000, and that was $70,000 less than Worthy paid for the stock.

With the help of an independent appraisal firm, Worthy's management determined that the fair market value of the inventory was $110,000, and the fair market value of the machinery was $115,000. This information begins to explain why Worthy was willing to pay $70,000 more than the book value of Able's owners' equity: $20,000 ($110,000 − $90,000) was attributable to undervalued inventory, and $35,000 ($115,000 − $80,000) was associated with undervalued machinery.

Purchased Goodwill. These two amounts ($20,000 and $35,000) explain $55,000 of the $70,000 excess of the purchase price over Able's book value. The remaining $15,000 might have arisen because the present value of the liabilities was lower than their recorded amounts, but Worthy's management had already established that $60,000 was a good measure of the fair market value of Able's liabilities.

The only other possibility is that the $15,000 measured the cost of an asset or assets that didn't appear in Able's balance sheet. These are the company's intangible assets. If the appraisers can't identify specific intangible assets, such as a favorable patent or a favorable property lease, the unrecorded intangible assets are likely to be identified as **goodwill,** or more accurately as *excess of cost over net assets acquired.*[2]

The price paid to effect a business combination may include a payment for goodwill—in other words, goodwill is not an unexpected arithmetic residual. The combinor will have applied its rate-of-return criterion to the combinee's average annual cash flow—approximated by (1) its anticipated annual income, plus (2) the anticipated annual depreciation expense, less (3) the anticipated average capital expenditures each year for plant.

For example, assume that Able's average amounts for the past five years had been as follows:

Net income	$42,000
Add: Depreciation.	12,000
Less: Capital expenditures	(18,000)
Cash flow.	$36,000

If the minimum rate of return that Worthy would accept was 15 percent, it would be willing to pay as much as $36,000/0.15 = $240,000 to acquire Able. Since the fair market value of the net assets totaled $205,000, Worthy would have been willing to pay as much as $35,000 ($240,000 − $205,000) for Able's unrecorded goodwill.

The Accounting Treatment. The nature of the purchase method can be demonstrated by considering the accounting entry Worthy recorded when it acquired Able's assets and assumed its liabilities:

Cash.	40,000	
Inventory	110,000	
Machinery	115,000	
Goodwill	15,000	
Liabilities		60,000
Cash		220,000

In our example, the actual cost of the assets acquired was $280,000 (the $220,000 cash payment plus $60,000 in liabilities taken over).

---

[2] "Negative goodwill" is *not* recorded when the purchase price is *less* than the estimated current value. Instead, the estimates of the current values of various tangible assets are reduced, or the estimated value of one or more liabilities is increased.

It should be noted that when the purchase method is used, the recorded current-value amounts become the combined enterprise's costs. For inventories, these costs will flow fairly quickly into the cost of goods sold if FIFO is used; they are likely to remain more or less permanently in the inventory balance if LIFO is used. Depreciation is also measured on the new fair market value basis (now treated as the assets' cost), and the newly recorded goodwill is subject to amortization.

In conclusion, the purchase method reflects the assumption that the combinor *purchases* the combinee's assets and liabilities. As is the case in all other types of purchases, a new basis of accountability arises, with the result that some assets and liabilities will be recorded at amounts that differ from the amounts that had previously appeared in the combinee's financial statements.

The Pooling-of-Interests Method

The alternative to the purchase method is the pooling-of-interests method. Under this method, the combinor measures the assets and liabilities of the combinee at their book values. The method is used when the combinor acquires the assets and liabilities of the combinee by exchanging its shares for the shares of the combinee, with no significant payment of cash or other assets.

The Basis for Poolings.   The theory underlying the pooling-of-interests method is based on the following proposition: instead of the combinee's stockholders *selling* their shares for cash, they *exchange* their stock for shares in the combined enterprise. The transaction is significantly different from a purchase. In a purchase for cash, only the combinor's stockholders are the stockholders of the combined enterprise; in a pooling, both companies' stockholders continue as stockholders of the combined enterprise. As a result, the combined enterprise in a pooling of interests is simply a continuation of the two previous businesses.

This conclusion has three important implications. First, since the combinor hasn't purchased anything, all the combinee's assets and liabilities continue to be measured at the combinee's (book value) amounts. Second, goodwill is *not* recognized despite its undoubtedly having been a factor in determining the number of combinor shares that are given to the combinee's stockholders in exchange for their shares.

Third, the precombination earnings of both the combinor and the combinee are viewed as being the earnings of the combined enterprise. This means that the retained earnings of both the combinor and the combinee carry over to the combined enterprise. It also means that all the combination-year earnings of both companies are included in the net income and earnings per share of the combined enterprise, even the portion that was earned before the combination.

Illustration. To demonstrate the nature of the pooling-of-interests method, let's use the same information we used to illustrate the purchase method in the preceding section, except that Worthy Company (the combinor) gave Able's stockholders shares of its voting common stock instead of cash. Again, Able's balance sheet on the merger date showed the following amounts:

Cash	$ 40,000	Liabilities	$ 60,000
Inventory	90,000	Common stock	50,000
Machinery	80,000	Retained earnings	100,000
Total	$210,000	Total	$210,000

The shares Worthy issued in exchange for Able's shares had a par value of $14,000. If Worthy Company had dissolved Able, Inc., immediately after the exchange of shares and treated Able's assets and liabilities as its own from then on, Worthy would have added $210,000 to its assets, $60,000 to its liabilities, $50,000 to its paid-in capital ($14,000 in par value and $36,000 in additional paid-in capital), and $100,000 to its retained earnings. A summary entry in general journal form would have been as follows:

Cash	40,000	
Inventory	90,000	
Machinery	80,000	
Liabilities		60,000
Common Stock		14,000
Additional Paid-In Capital.		36,000
Retained Earnings.		100,000

Notice that the assets, liabilities, and retained earnings in this entry are at the same amounts that had appeared in Able's (the combinee's) financial statements. The only difference is that Able's $50,000 contributed capital is divided into two parts.[3]

Applicability of Pooling. The pooling-of-interests method may be used only when the underlying circumstances indicate that the stockholders of the combinor and the combinee have truly pooled their interests—by becoming stockholders in the combined enterprise.[4] To foster uniform attainment of this objective, the accounting profession in the United States uses a series of 12 conditions that a combination must meet to

---

[3] In practice, many more individual accounts would be affected. At a minimum, the original cost of the machinery and its accumulated depreciation would be recorded separately, and separate liability accounts would be used to record accounts payable, wages payable, etc. The entry here has been kept simple to show the basic effects of the event.

[4] Many stock-for-stock combinations in the United States may also qualify as *tax-free* exchanges, thereby making the combinations more attractive to stockholders of prospective combinees. The criteria used by the taxing authorities differ from those used by the accounting profession in deciding whether a given combination can be classified as a pooling of interests.

qualify for treatment as a pooling of interests. For our purposes, the one most pervasive condition is that voting common stock must be exchanged for substantially all the combinee's voting common stock; *substantially all* means at least 90 percent. The 90 percent provision permits cash or other consideration to be exchanged for the remaining shares, or those shares may continue as a minority interest.

In summary, under the pooling-of-interests method, the combination is viewed as a *non*transaction. As opposed to the combinor purchasing the combinee's assets and liabilities through the acquisition of its outstanding stock, the pooling-of-interests method reflects the two companies' stockholders pooling their interests to become stockholders of one company. Since the combinor is not engaged in a purchase, the current values of the combinee's assets aren't recorded and goodwill isn't recognized.

Consolidated Financial Statements

In many business combinations, the combinee will continue to operate as a legal entity even though all its common stock is owned by the combinor. In these cases, the combinor is called the **parent company** and the combinee is called the **subsidiary company.** In this section, we'll describe how the parent company records a purchase-method combination with its subsidiary, how the parent accounts for its investment as the subsidiary reports earnings and declares dividends, and how most parent companies disclose the combined-enterprise relationship in their public financial reporting.

Recording a Purchase-Method Combination: Two Entities

To record the investment in its subsidiary, the parent company sets up an Investment in Subsidiary asset account with an initial balance equal to the purchase price of the shares it acquires. For example, suppose Worthy paid cash of $220,000 to acquire all the common shares of Able, Inc., as in the previous illustration, and Able's combination-date balance sheet again showed the following amounts:

Cash	$ 40,000	Liabilities	$ 60,000
Inventory	90,000	Common stock	50,000
Machinery	80,000	Retained earnings.	100,000
Total	$210,000	Total	$210,000

Once again, the fair market value of the inventory was $110,000, the fair market value of the machinery was $115,000, and the purchase price exceeded the fair market value of the net tangible assets by $15,000.

None of these amounts entered Worthy's books. It recorded its investment as follows:

Investment in Subsidiary   220,000
   Cash   220,000

This accounting entry is similar to that of any other cash investment in corporate stock.

Able, Inc., made no entry to record Worthy's purchase of its shares, because it continued to operate as a legal entity. Corporations make no accounting entries when their shares are traded from one shareholder to another.

Post-Investment Purchase Accounting: Two Entities

A parent and its subsidiary maintain separate accounting records, similar to those they would have if the intercorporate investment didn't exist. The parent applies the equity method just as a company does when it has an influential but noncontrolling interest in another company. That is, it reports as part of its own income its equity in the subsidiary's net income, less an amortization of a portion of the excess of investment cost over the fair market value of the subsidiary's net tangible assets.

Parent companies seldom present their own financial statements to their shareholders. Instead, they usually prepare **consolidated financial statements.** Consolidation is based on the premise that the parent and its subsidiaries constitute a single economic entity. Consolidated financial statements therefore contain the same information that would have been presented had the parent and its subsidiary been operating as one legal entity.

A first approximation to consolidated financial statements can be made by adding the comparable accounts of a parent and its subsidiaries to get combined totals. The consolidated cash balance, for example, is the sum of the cash held by the parent and the cash held by the subsidiaries. The combined totals can't always be used without adjustment, however, because some amounts are likely to reflect **intercompany transactions.** We'll illustrate three major kinds of adjustments, known as **eliminations,** designed to deal with some of these transactions:

1. Intercompany receivables and payables.
2. Intercompany sales.
3. The intercompany investment that created the parent-subsidiary relationship.

Intercompany Receivables and Payables.   If a subsidiary owes money to the parent, the parent's balance sheet will show a receivable and the subsidiary's will show a liability. Including these amounts in consolidated receivables and liabilities would overstate both amounts; the consolidated statements would no longer show the financial position of the combined enterprise as a single economic entity facing the outside world.

For example, suppose Worthy and Able had the following accounts receivable and accounts payable at the end of a certain year:

	Worthy	Able	Combined
Accounts receivable	$100,000	$70,000	$170,000
Accounts payable	80,000	60,000	140,000

Able owed Worthy $25,000 at the end of the year for merchandise Worthy shipped to Able during the year. This means that only $35,000 ($60,000 − $25,000) of Able's accounts payable and $75,000 ($100,000 − $25,000) of Worthy's accounts receivable represented relationships with suppliers or customers outside the combined enterprise. From the point of view of the combined enterprise, the combined totals in the table therefore reflect double counting. We can avoid this by preparing an eliminating entry, as follows:

Accounts Payable..................................	25,000	
Accounts Receivable............................		25,000

This entry *isn't* recorded in either company's journal or ledger because it doesn't correct an error in either company's accounts. Instead, it is entered in a special consolidation worksheet that is prepared solely to facilitate the consolidation process. If a columnar worksheet is used, the receivables and payables lines will appear as follows:

	Worthy	Able	Eliminations	Consolidated
Accounts receivable ..	$100,000	$70,000	$(25,000)	$145,000
Accounts payable	80,000	60,000	(25,000)	115,000

The amounts in the right-hand column then can be placed in the consolidated balance sheet because they represent amounts owed by and to parties outside the combined enterprise.

Intercompany Sales. Transactions between a parent company and its subsidiaries also affect their income statements. For example, the two companies' records showed the following amounts:

	Worthy	Able	Combined
Sales revenues...........	$700,000	$400,000	$1,100,000
Cost of goods sold	450,000	250,000	700,000
Gross profit...........	$250,000	$150,000	$ 400,000

The amounts in Worthy's column reflect Worthy's sales of merchandise to outsiders *and* its sales to Able. Worthy's sales to Able had a total price of $52,000 and Worthy's cost of goods sold on these items was $40,000. Able sold all these goods during the same year to outside customers at a $65,000 price, which yielded Able a profit margin of 20 percent of sales ($13,000).

If we look only at the results of the two companies' dealings in *these* goods, we see the following:

	Worthy	Able	Combined
Sales revenues............	$52,000	$65,000	$117,000
Cost of goods sold	40,000	52,000	92,000
Gross profit............	$12,000	$13,000	$ 25,000

The $25,000 combined gross profit is correct; merchandise costing the combined enterprise $40,000 was sold to outsiders for $65,000. Combined sales revenues and cost of goods sold, however, are both overstated by $52,000. The revenues of the *combined* enterprise should include only the $65,000 Able got by selling the goods to the public; the consolidated cost of goods sold should include only the $40,000 cost to Worthy.

Thus, $52,000 has to be removed both from the sales total and from the total cost of goods sold before the combined enterprise can prepare *its* income statement. This can be accomplished by another eliminating entry in the consolidation worksheet:

Sales Revenues...................................... 52,000
   Cost of Goods Sold..............................   52,000

These two lines on the worksheet now show the following:

	Worthy	Able	Eliminations	Consolidated
Sales revenues	$700,000	$400,000	$(52,000)	$1,048,000
Cost of goods sold....	450,000	250,000	(52,000)	648,000

The *consolidated* gross profit is identical to the *combined* gross profit in this case because Able's ending inventory included none of the amounts it paid Worthy for the merchandise. The elimination is somewhat different when a portion of intercompany sales is *not resold* to outside customers by year-end. Suppose Able resold only 75 percent of the merchandise at a price of $47,000. For these goods alone, the two companies' records would show the following at the end of the year:

	Worthy	Able	Combined
Sales revenues	$52,000	$47,000	$99,000
Cost of goods sold	40,000	39,000	79,000
Gross profit	$12,000	$ 8,000	$20,000
Inventory (25 percent of purchases)......	—	$13,000	$13,000

It should be clear that the *consolidated* income statement should show (1) sales revenues of only $47,000 from these transactions and (2) a cost of goods sold of $30,000 (75 percent of Worthy's $40,000 cost). The consolidated balance sheet should report the goods remaining on hand at the end of the year at *their cost to Worthy,* $10,000 (25 percent of $40,000).

The corrections can be made by the following eliminating entry in the worksheet:

Sales Revenues....................................	52,000	
Cost of Goods Sold.............................		49,000
Inventory.......................................		3,000

This entry reduces the combined gross profit arising from these transactions by $3,000, because part of the merchandise wasn't sold to outsiders before the end of the year. The consolidated enterprise, in other words, still hadn't earned 25 percent of the $12,000 profit that Worthy had recognized on its sales to Able. These calculations are summarized in Exhibit 12–5.

EXHIBIT 12–5
Elimination of Effects of Intercompany Sales

	Combined Balances	Consolidated Balances	Amounts Eliminated
Sales revenues:			
$52,000 + $47,000	$99,000		
Sold by Able		$47,000	
Intercompany sale			$52,000
Cost of goods sold:			
$40,000 + (0.75 × $52,000)..............	79,000		
0.75 × $40,000		30,000	
(0.75 × $52,000) + (0.25 × $40,000)			49,000
Inventory:			
0.25 × $52,000	13,000		
0.25 × $40,000		10,000	
0.25 × ($52,000 − $40,000)..............			3,000

Intercompany Investment in Stock. The third and final elimination we'll examine deals with the parent company's investment in the subsidiary's stock. Again, our main task is to eliminate double counting. For example, just after Worthy bought Able's shares, the two companies' balance sheets showed the amounts listed in Exhibit 12–6. (For simplicity, we've omitted the classification of Worthy's paid-in capital into its par-value and excess-over-par-value components.)

Unfortunately, the combined amounts in the right-hand column reflect double counting. Worthy's $220,000 Investment asset represented its 100 percent share of Able's book value (assets minus liabilities). We would overstate the assets of the combined enterprise if we included both this amount *and* Able's assets of $210,000 and liabilities of $60,000 in the consolidated totals. For the combined enterprise, the $220,000 investment was simply the company's investment in itself, and that was no

EXHIBIT 12–6
Worthy Company and Able Company: Acquisition-Date Balance Sheet Amounts

	Worthy	Able	Combined
Assets			
Cash	$ 60,000	$ 40,000	$100,000
Inventory	70,000	90,000	160,000
Machinery	100,000	80,000	180,000
Investment in subsidiary (Able)	220,000	—	220,000
Total assets..........................	$450,000	$210,000	$660,000
Liabilities and Owners' Equity			
Liabilities	$200,000	$ 60,000	$260,000
Owner's equity:			
Common stock...........................	80,000	50,000	130,000
Retained earnings	170,000	100,000	270,000
Total liabilities and owners' equity	$450,000	$210,000	$660,000

asset at all. We know, therefore, that the company had to remove $220,000 from the combined asset total.

It would also be wrong to include in the owners' equity section of the consolidated balance sheet the *subsidiary's* owners' equity when the parent is the one and only stockholder. In fact, the owners of the parent company's shares of stock are the only owners of the combined enterprise. They are the only ones who have claims to the owners' equity in the combined enterprise. Able's $150,000 owners' equity ($50,000 common stock and $100,000 retained earnings) therefore had to be removed from the combined owners' equity amounts before a consolidated balance sheet can be prepared.

In other words, to prepare a consolidated balance sheet, Worthy had to eliminate the $220,000, $100,000, and $50,000 balances. As a first effort to do this, it recorded the following entry in the worksheet:

Common Stock....................................	50,000	
Retained Earnings	100,000	
Excess..	70,000	
Investment in Subsidiary		220,000

The $70,000 *excess* is the excess of the investment cost ($220,000) over the book value of the owners' equity acquired ($150,000). We discovered earlier that Worthy paid most of this additional amount because the market value of Able's inventory exceeded its book value by $20,000 ($110,000 − $90,000) and the market value of Able's machinery exceeded its book value by $35,000 ($115,000 − $80,000). The remaining $15,000 of the excess was attributed to unrecorded goodwill. In the light of this information, the eliminating entry in the worksheet could be restated as follows:

Common Stock	50,000	
Retained Earnings	100,000	
Inventory	20,000	
Machinery	35,000	
Goodwill	15,000	
Investment in Subsidiary		220,000

As a result of this eliminating entry, Able's inventories, machinery, and goodwill entered the consolidated balance sheet at the same amounts that would have appeared if the combined enterprise had elected to operate as one legal entity.

It is also worth noting that when purchase-method accounting is used, none of the subsidiary's precombination retained earnings is included in consolidated retained earnings. Consolidated retained earnings therefore includes the parent's retained earnings plus the parent's share of the earnings retained by the subsidiary from the date of the combination onward.

Minority Interest

When the parent company owns *less than 100 percent* of its subsidiary's stock, accountants still prefer to prepare fully consolidated financial statements in most cases. As Exhibit 12–7 shows, the consolidated balance sheet includes all the parent's and all the subsidiary's net assets (i.e., all their assets and all their liabilities); the consolidated income

EXHIBIT 12–7
Minority Interest in Consolidated Net Assets and Net Income

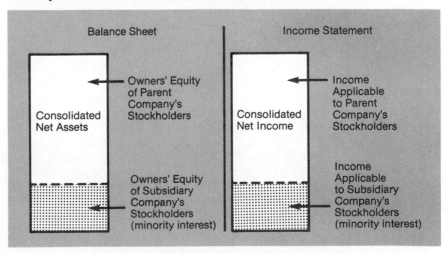

statement includes all the parent's and all the subsidiary's income. The minority stockholders' equity in the consolidated assets is based on the book value of the *subsidiary* company's net assets, multiplied by the percentage of subsidiary stock they own. Similarly, their interest in consolidated net income is based on their proportionate share of the *subsidiary's* net income.

An Illustration

To illustrate, let's assume that Worthy paid $180,000 to acquire 80 percent of Able's stock. Neither Worthy nor Able had any amounts receivable from or payable to the other on the acquisition date. The current fair value of Able's owners' equity (and net assets), including inventories and machinery measured at the amounts that equivalent assets could have been bought for in the market on that date, totaled $205,000, as follows:

Cash.	$ 40,000
Inventory	110,000
Machinery	115,000
Total assets	265,000
Less: Liabilities	60,000
Net assets, at fair value	$205,000

Able's owners' equity, as reported on *its own* balance sheet, was $150,000, and Worthy's 80 percent share of this total was $120,000, or $60,000 less than the $180,000 Worthy paid.

The distribution of this $60,000 is shown in the right column in Exhibit 12–8. The left column contains the amounts we derived in the 100 percent example in the previous section. Remember from our earlier discussion that Able's inventories and machinery were reported on its

EXHIBIT 12–8
Worthy Company: Calculation of Purchased Goodwill

	100 Percent	80 Percent
Equity in Able, Inc.'s reported owners' equity:		
Common stock	$ 50,000	$ 40,000
Retained earnings	100,000	80,000
Total	150,000	120,000
Worthy Company's investment cost	220,000	180,000
Excess of cost over reported owners' equity	70,000	60,000
Portion of excess attributable to undervaluation of:		
Inventory	20,000	16,000
Machinery	35,000	28,000
Total	55,000	44,000
Portion of excess attributable to goodwill	$ 15,000	$ 16,000

own statements at amounts $20,000 and $35,000 less than Worthy would have had to pay to buy equivalent assets in the open market. Its 80 percent share of these amounts is $16,000 and $28,000, as shown in the lower portion of Exhibit 12–8. The other $16,000 of the $60,000 premium over book value is the price Worthy paid for its share of Able's goodwill.

In other words, in preparing consolidated financial statements, Worthy had to make three adjustments:

1. Add the book values of Able's assets and liabilities to its own assets and liabilities, item by item, *plus* the amounts paid for unrecorded inventory and machinery values and for goodwill.
2. Remove its Investment in Subsidiary asset from the balance sheet.
3. Set up 20 percent of Able's recorded owners' equity as a separate balance sheet item, labeled **minority interest.**

The resulting inventory and machinery figures are peculiar. They include Worthy's own assets at historical cost and Able's assets at a hybrid amount: 80 percent of Able's assets is at Worthy's cost (based on current market value) and the other 20 percent is at Able's cost. This hybrid measurement is inevitable as long as accountants adhere to historical-cost accounting. The addition of $16,000 to the inventory and $28,000 to the machinery and the recognition of $16,000 in goodwill arise because Worthy paid these amounts as part of the purchase price of Able's shares. The remaining portions of the current values of these assets don't appear because the combined enterprise didn't pay for them.

The Acquisition-Date Balance Sheet

The three adjustments Worthy had to make were made by a single elimination entry in the consolidated acquisition-date worksheet:

Common Stock (50,000 × 0.8)	40,000	
Retained Earnings (100,000 × 0.8)	80,000	
Inventory (20,000 × 0.8)	16,000	
Machinery (35,000 × 0.8)	28,000	
Goodwill	16,000	
Investment in Subsidiary		180,000

This entry (1) increased the reported cost of Able's inventory and machinery assets by 80 percent of the excess of fair market value over historical cost, (2) recorded the amount Worthy paid for goodwill, and (3) removed Worthy's Investment in Subsidiary asset from the consolidated balance sheet. These are the amounts identified by the numeral (1) in the third column in Exhibit 12–9. In effect, what Worthy did in the worksheet was to *substitute* Able's assets and liabilities ($210,000 and $60,000) for its own Investment in Subsidiary asset ($180,000), adjusting the former to Worthy's share of their fair market value.

EXHIBIT 12–9
Worthy Company and Subsidiary: Acquisition-Date Consolidated Balance Sheet

	Worthy	Able	Eliminations*		Consolidated
Assets					
Cash	$100,000	$ 40,000			$140,000
Inventory	70,000	90,000	(1)	16,000	176,000
Machinery	100,000	80,000	(1)	28,000	208,000
Investment in subsidiary	180,000	—	(1)	(180,000)	—
Goodwill	—	—	(1)	16,000	16,000
Total assets	$450,000	$210,000			$540,000
Liabilities and Owners' Equity					
Liabilities	$200,000	$ 60,000			$260,000
Minority interest	—	—	(2)	30,000	30,000
Owners' equity:					
Common stock	80,000	50,000	(1)	(40,000)	80,000
			(2)	(10,000)	
Retained earnings	170,000	100,000	(1)	(80,000)	170,000
			(2)	(20,000)	
Total liabilities and owners' equity	$450,000	$210,000			$540,000

* Parentheses signify a decrease.

After entry (1) was made, however, 20 percent ($30,000) of Able's reported owners' equity ($10,000 listed on the common stock line and $20,000 opposite retained earnings) remained *un*eliminated. This was the 20 percent equity of Able's minority stockholders. It was eliminated, or rather assembled as a single number, by the following entry:

Common Stock	10,000	
Retained Earnings	20,000	
Minority Interest		30,000

This entry is identified by the numeral (2) in the third column in Exhibit 12–9. Once it was made, Worthy could develop the consolidated balance sheet amounts in the right-hand column of this exhibit.

Notice that the amount of the minority interest wasn't affected by the fact that the parent paid more for Able's assets than their cost to Able. The minority interest was based on the cost of the assets to Able, not on their current fair market value. Notice also that the minority interest is listed between the liabilities and the equity of Worthy's stockholders in the combined enterprise. The subsidiary's minority stockholders aren't creditors, so the minority interest can't be classified as a liability. They aren't shareholders in Worthy's other activities either, so they can't be thought of as Worthy's shareholders. Instead, their equity in the combined enterprise is a peculiar kind of owners' equity; they have contributed to and can participate in the performance of only a portion of the combined enterprise, not the entire entity.

Minority Interest in the Income Statement

The minority stockholders' equity in the subsidiary's net income has to be deducted from consolidated net income, as we demonstrated in Exhibit 12–7. The bottom portion of Able's income statement for the year following the acquisition therefore might show the following:

Consolidated net income	$54,400
Less: Income applicable to minority stockholders in Able, Inc.........................	11,000
Earnings available to common shareholders	$43,400

A brief illustration of this calculation is contained in the appendix to this chapter.

Consolidation Policy   Nonfinancial corporations in the United States sometimes don't consolidate all of their wholly owned subsidiaries. These nonconsolidated subsidiaries fall largely into two categories: (1) consumer finance companies and commercial insurance companies, and (2) foreign subsidiaries.

Finance and insurance subsidiaries are usually excluded on the grounds that their operations are so different from those of the parent that to include them would produce distorted statements. For example, General Motors Acceptance Corporation (GMAC) finances consumer purchases of General Motors automobiles and other products. GMAC assets are almost exclusively the promissory notes of the purchasers of General Motors products, and GMAC finances these assets predominantly by borrowing. Consolidated statements for General Motors and GMAC therefore would show a much higher ratio of debt to equity than is typical for a manufacturing company.

Although a consolidated balance sheet would show a more complete picture of the overall financial position of General Motors, the accounting profession doesn't require consolidation in this case. Instead, General Motors presents separate financial statements for GMAC in its annual report, along with the consolidated statements for the parent company and the rest of its subsidiaries.

Most companies with foreign operations do consolidate the results of operations and the resources of their foreign subsidiaries with those of the parent for external financial reporting. Some foreign subsidiaries are excluded from the consolidation, however, on the grounds that their operations are highly regulated, expropriation is a near possibility, or the repatriation of dividends is prohibited or severely restricted.

The exclusion of foreign subsidiaries from the consolidation should be justified by the circumstances of each individual case. Even when one or more subsidiaries are excluded, however, a U.S. parent does use the equity method to account for its investments in any subsidiaries which aren't included in the consolidation. This means that net income isn't affected by the subsidiary's decision to declare dividends or to use earnings to build up the subsidiary's assets. Possible variations in the ratio of the subsidiary's dividends to its earnings make dividends a very poor measure of the subsidiary's contribution to the parent company's well-being.

Summary

Nonfinancial corporations often hold government and commercial securities to earn a return on temporarily idle funds. Securities held for this purpose ordinarily earn relatively modest yields but are highly liquid. Most of these temporary investments are in notes, bonds, or other credit instruments with relatively early maturities, and these are measured at their cost.

A company's primary motive for owning other corporations' stock as a longer-term investment is to produce income; short-term marketability is seldom a consideration. When these investments are too small to give their owners any significant influence over the companies they represent, they are stated at the lower of cost or market. When the investments are large enough to give their owners some influence but not control, they are reported on an equity basis—that is, the investor reports as investment revenue the proportionate share of the investee's earnings, not just the dividends received. The investment is measured at cost plus the investor's equity in the increase in the investee's retained earnings since the investment was made.

When an investment constitutes a majority of the voting power in the other corporation, the holder is referred to as a parent company. The parent company's financial statements incorporate the parent's investments in its subsidiaries and its equity in their earnings. Most parent companies in the United States present consolidated financial statements, reflecting the consolidated results and year-end position of parent and subsidiary combined. This means the assets, liabilities, revenues, and expenses of the subsidiary are combined with those of the parent.

Preparation of consolidated financial statements is a demanding technical process, and we have made no effort to explain it in depth. Our purpose has been to foster an appreciation of the significance of the relationships between investor and investee, between parent and subsidiary. The appendix to this chapter is designed for those who wish to obtain a general view of the measurement of consolidated post-combination income in a purchase-method combination.

Appendix: Post-Combination Accounting

Preparing consolidated statements for periods subsequent to the business combination date is a difficult task, particularly when the combination is treated as a purchase. To illustrate the process and identify some of the calculations that must be made, we'll follow the Worthy-Able business combination through its first year of operation as a combined enterprise. We'll assume that Worthy paid $180,000 in cash to Able's stockholders on January 1, 19x1, in exchange for 80 percent of their shares.

The Combination-Date Position

Worthy decided not to attempt to buy the shares of Able's minority stockholders, and the two companies continued to operate as separate legal entities. Worthy therefore recorded the $180,000 purchase price as an asset, Investment in Subsidiary. The amounts on Worthy's combination-date balance sheet (January 1, 19x1) were the amounts in the right-hand column of the consolidation worksheet in Exhibit 12–9.

Post-Combination Information

To prepare consolidated statements for 19x1, Worthy's accountants had to decide how much of the $60,000 Worthy paid in excess of its equity in Able's book value was to be treated as a determinant of consolidated net income in 19x1 and how much was to appear in the year-end consolidated balance sheet. They also had to determine how much of the two companies' reported income, assets, and liabilities was to appear in the consolidated financial statements. To illustrate this process, let's assume that the two companies' preliminary financial statements contained the amounts shown in the first two columns of Exhibit 12–10. The entries in the *eliminations* columns are based on the following additional information:

1. Able's net income in 19x1 amounted to $55,000; Able declared no dividends to its shareholders during the year.
2. Worthy sold merchandise to Able for $30,000 during the year. This was 20 percent above Worthy's cost. At year-end, 60 percent of the $30,000 was still included in Able's inventory.
3. As of December 31, 19x1, there was a $6,000 intercompany debt.
4. Worthy determined that depreciation expense based on the January 1, 19x1, market value of Able's machinery was $2,500 *greater* than historical-cost depreciation of this asset.
5. Worthy decided to amortize the goodwill created by the business combination over 40 years on a straight-line basis.
6. Able's inventory was measured partly on a FIFO basis and partly on LIFO. Its December 31 inventory included items that still carried the

EXHIBIT 12–10
Consolidated Statement Worksheet—First Year after Acquisition Date

	Worthy	Able	Eliminations Debt		Eliminations Credit		Consolidated
Cash........................	100,000	80,000					180,000
Receivables.................	90,000	60,000			(2)	6,000	144,000
Inventory	47,000	25,000	(3)	4,800	(1)	3,000	73,800
Machinery (net)..............	115,000	70,000	(3)	26,000			211,000
Investment in subsidiary	180,000				(3)	180,000	
Goodwill.....................			(3)	15,600			15,600
Liabilities	266,000	30,000	(2)	6,000			290,000
Minority interest					(4)	41,000	41,000
Common stock	80,000	50,000	(3)	40,000			80,000
			(4)	10,000			
Retained earnings, January 1	170,000	100,000	(3)	80,000			170,000
			(4)	20,000			
Income statement:							
Sales revenues............	372,000	185,000	(1)	30,000			527,000
Cost of goods sold	200,000	90,000	(3)	11,200	(1)	27,000	274,200
Other expenses	156,000	40,000	(3)	2,400			198,400
Minority interest...........			(4)	11,000			11,000
Net income	16,000	55,000					43,400
Retained earnings, December 31	186,000	155,000					213,400

costs they had borne on January 1. The costs of these items constituted 30 percent of the total cost of Able's January 1 inventory.

7. Worthy had made no entries in its books to record its equity in Able's
earnings.

The Elimination Entries

Worthy's first task was to remove intercompany sales and intercompany profits from the financial statements. Worthy's sales revenues included **$30,000** of sales to Able rather than to outside customers (item 2
in the list above). From item 2 we also find that Worthy's sales revenues
were 120 percent of its cost of goods sold for these items. Worthy's cost of
goods sold on these sales therefore amounted to $25,000 ($30,000/1.2).

From item 2 we also find that Able sold 40 percent of these goods to its
outside customers in 19x1. This means that it recognized $12,000 (0.4 ×
$30,000) as part of its cost of goods sold, even though the cost to the
combined enterprise was only $10,000 ($12,000/1.2). In other words, the
total of the two companies' cost of goods sold amounts had to be reduced
by **$27,000** [$25,000 + ($12,000 − $10,000)].

The remaining 60 percent of the goods Able bought from Worthy were still in Able's inventory at the end of 19x1, recorded at Able's cost of $18,000 (0.6 × $30,000). The cost to the combined enterprise, however, was only $15,000 ($18,000/1.2). The difference, **$3,000,** was an intercompany profit the combined enterprise hadn't earned by the end of 19x1. The eliminating entry, reflecting all these calculations, was:

(1)

Sales Revenues.	30,000	
Cost of Goods Sold.		27,000
Inventory.		3,000

(In practice, these amounts would be entered only in the consolidation worksheet, not in either company's ledger.)

Worksheet entry (2) eliminated the intercompany debt that was outstanding on December 31, 19x1 (item 3):

(2)

Liabilities.	6,000	
Receivables		6,000

The accountants' next chore was to eliminate the $180,000 cost of Worthy's investment in Able. Worthy's $180,000 purchase cost had to be removed in the consolidation process because it represented Able's assets (positive) and liabilities (negative) at the time of the combination, and it was already included in the consolidated amounts. Also, 80 percent of Able's $150,000 combination-date owners' equity ($120,000) had to be removed because it didn't represent equity of owners of the combined enterprise. In the absence of any amortization of the three components of the $60,000 difference between these two amounts, the eliminating entry on December 31, 19x1, would have been the same as the entry used in Exhibit 12–9 to eliminate the intercompany investment:

Common Stock (0.8 × $50,000)	40,000	
Retained Earnings (0.8 × $100,000)	80,000	
Inventory (0.8 × $20,000).	16,000	
Machinery (0.8 × $35,000).	28,000	
Goodwill	16,000	
Investment in Subsidiary		180,000

In fact, however, portions of the three asset amounts identified in the original consolidation were applicable to 19x1 revenues. From item 6 we find that 70 percent of the January 1, 19x1, inventory cost was included in the cost of goods sold in 19x1. This means that 70 percent of the $16,000 combination-date inventory write-up (0.7 × $16,000 = $11,200) had to be transferred to expense in 19x1.

From item 4 we find that depreciation of the fair market value of combination-date machinery exceeded historical cost depreciation by $2,500. Worthy's consolidated statements reflected only its 80 percent ownership share in this amount, so the transfer to depreciation expense in 19x1 was $0.8 \times \$2,500 = \$2,000$.

Finally, item 5 tells us that the $16,000 goodwill was to be amortized in 40 equal installments of $400 each. The remaining portions of these three assets were applicable to the year-end assets, as follows:

	January 1 Asset		19x1 Expense		December 31 Asset
Inventory	$16,000	=	$11,200	+	$ 4,800
Machinery	28,000	=	2,000	+	26,000
Goodwill	16,000	=	400	+	15,600
Total	$60,000	=	$13,600	+	$46,400

The elimination of the $180,000 initial investment therefore was made in worksheet entry (3):

(3)

Common Stock (0.8 × $50,000)	40,000	
Retained Earnings (0.8 × $100,000).	80,000	
Inventory (0.3 × $16,000).	4,800	
Machinery [0.8 × ($35,000 − $2,500)]	26,000	
Goodwill (39/40 × $16,000).	15,600	
Cost of Goods Sold (0.7 × $16,000).	11,200	
Other Expenses [(0.8 × $2,500) + ($16,000/40)].	2,400	
Investment in Subsidiary		180,000

The final entry in the consolidation worksheet recognized the equity interests of Able's minority stockholders:

(4)

Common Stock (0.2 × $50,000)	10,000	
Retained Earnings (0.2 × $100,000).	20,000	
Income Statement (0.2 × $55,000).	11,000	
Minority Interest (0.2 × $205,000)		41,000

The debits to Common Stock and Retained Earnings removed the final 20 percent of the owners' equity shown in Able's books *at the time of the combination.* The other two amounts in entry (4) identify the minority shareholders' interest in consolidated net income in 19x1 and in the consolidated net assets as of December 31, 19x1.

Recording the Parent Company's Equity in Income

Worthy had to make an entry *in its own books* as of the end of 19x1 as well as worksheet entry (3). Because it used the equity method to account for its ownership of Able's stock, it had to increase the investment asset by its equity in the increment to Able's retained earnings, less its share of the amortization of any portion of the purchase cost of the investment. This amounted to $27,400, calculated as follows:

80 percent of Able's $55,000 net income............	$44,000
Additional depreciation (0.8 × $2,500)..............	− 2,000
Additional cost of goods sold (0.7 × $16,000)	− 11,200
Amortization of goodwill ($16,000/40)..............	− 400
Yet-to-be-earned intercompany profit [0.6 × 0.2($30,000/1.2)]	− 3,000
Equity in Able's income........................	$27,400

The entry to bring Worthy's investment asset up to date as of the end of 19x1 was:

Investment in Subsidiary.............................	27,400	
Revenue from Investments.........................		27,400

The ending investment balance on Worthy's own balance sheet therefore was $207,400 ($180,000 + $27,400). The $27,400 increment was included in Worthy Company's corporate net income.

Key Terms

Amortized cost	Fair market value
Appraised value	Goodwill
Business combinations	Intercompany transactions
Combined enterprise	Minority interest
Combinee	Parent company
Combinor	Pooling-of-interests method
Consolidated financial statements	Purchase method
Eliminations	Subsidiary company
Equity method	Unrealized loss

Independent Study Problems (Solutions in Appendix B)

1. Equity Method. Cantara Company on January 1, 19x1, bought 2,500 shares of the common stock of Denby Corporation. These shares constituted 25 percent of Denby's outstanding common shares. Cantara paid $30 a share for this stock.

Denby reported net income of $30,000 in 19x1 and declared cash dividends of $1.60 a share on its common stock.

a. How much investment income should Cantara report in 19x1 from its investment in Denby?

b. At what amount should Cantara report its investment in Denby on its December 31, 19x1, balance sheet?

2. Goodwill; Minority Interest. On December 31, 19x1, Pilot Company paid $92,000 in cash for an 80 percent interest in Essex Company. The Essex balance sheet on that date showed the following balances in the owners' equity:

Common stock	$ 40,000
Additional paid-in capital	20,000
Retained earnings	50,000
Total	$110,000

The appraised value of Essex's tangible assets was equal to their book value on the date of acquisition.

a. What was the amount of the goodwill on the date of the purchase?
b. What was the amount of the minority interest on this date?

3. Long-Term Investment in Bonds.   On January 1, 19x8, Durant Corporation bought 100 of Russell Company's 12 percent debenture bonds. Although the bonds' maturity value on December 31, 19x22, would be $100,000, Durant's investment cost was $87,590. Interest was compounded semiannually, and interest payments were received each June 30 and December 31.

An unanticipated need for cash caused Durant to sell the bonds on January 1, 19x13, when the yield rate was 15 percent.

a. Calculate the anticipated yield to maturity on these bonds at the time of purchase.
b. Prepare an entry in general journal form to record Durant's purchase of the bonds in 19x8.
c. Calculate Durant's income from these bonds in 19x8.
d. How much did Durant receive for the bonds on January 1, 19x13? How much gain or loss did it realize on the sale?
e. Prepare an entry in general journal form to record Durant's sale of the bonds in 19x13.

4. Goodwill.   The book value of Bolton Company's net assets (owners' equity) was $100,000. The current appraised value was $125,000.

Net income before extraordinary items averaged $15,000 a year for the last five years, and capital expenditures each year equaled the annual depreciation of $22,000. Present forecasts are that net income and capital expenditures will continue at these levels indefinitely.

a. Calculate the amount of goodwill, assuming the normal rate of return in this industry is 10 percent.
b. Barth Corporation bought all of Bolton's common stock for $145,000. How much goodwill should Barth recognize in its balance sheet?

5. Intercompany Transactions.   Alcon Corporation owned 100 percent of the shares of Nonon Company. In 19x1 the two companies had the following income:

	Alcon	Nonon
Sales revenues	$ 5,000,000	$1,000,000
Dividend income (from Nonon)	50,000	—
Cost of goods sold	(3,000,000)	(700,000)
Other expenses	(1,500,000)	(200,000)
Net income	$ 550,000	$ 100,000

You have the following additional information:

1. The price Alcon paid for Nonon's shares was equal to the book value of Nonon's net assets at the time the shares were bought.
2. Nonon sold merchandise to Alcon for $250,000 during 19x1. This merchandise had cost Nonon $180,000.
3. Alcon's inventory on December 31, 19x1, included $100,000 of merchandise bought from Nonon. Nonon's cost of this merchandise was $70,000.
4. On December 31, 19x1, Alcon owed Nonon $35,000 for merchandise purchases. This amount was included in Alcon's accounts payable and in Nonon's accounts receivable.
5. Income tax effects of intercompany transactions can be ignored.
6. Alcon didn't use the equity method since it knew consolidated statements would be prepared at year-end.

a. Prepare appropriate elimination entries to reflect this information.
b. Prepare a consolidated income statement for Alcon Corporation and its subsidiary for the year 19x1.

6. Calculating Consolidated Income, Retained Earnings, and Minority Interest. Company X purchased an 80 percent interest in Company Y on January 1, 19x2. The price was $80,000, paid in cash, and the purchase was recorded in the Investments account of Company X. The appraised value of Y's tangible assets was equal to their book value at the time the stock was bought.

The directors of Company Y declared cash dividends in the amount of $10,000 during 19x2.

Company X published no financial statements on a parent-company-only basis; it recorded its investments at cost in its own accounts. Upon receiving Company Y's dividends, it debited Cash and credit Dividend Income. Company X's unconsolidated reported earnings for 19x2 amounted to $55,000, including dividend income. No other transactions between Company X and Company Y took place during the year.

Company X declared cash dividends of $30,000 during 19x2.

The owners' equity section of the beginning and ending balance sheets of the two corporations showed the following:

	Company X		Company Y	
	1/1/x2	12/31/x2	1/1/x2	12/31/x2
Common stock............	$100,000	$100,000	$ 30,000	$ 30,000
Additional paid-in capital	20,000	20,000	10,000	10,000
Retained earnings	375,000	400,000	60,000	65,000
Total.	$495,000	$520,000	$100,000	$105,000

Goodwill, if any, was to be amortized in 20 equal annual installments.

a. Calculate Company X's unconsolidated net income, based on the equity method.

b. What would Company X have reported as its investment in Company Y on an unconsolidated balance sheet as of December 31, 19x2, if it had used the equity method?

c. Calculate consolidated net income for 19x2.

d. At what amount would the minority interest be reported in the December 31, 19x2, consolidated balance sheet?

Exercises and Problems

7. Pooling versus Purchase: Discussion Question.   Company P has just acquired all the assets of Company Q by an exchange of stock. Company Q has achieved a notable rate of growth in recent years, both in sales and in earnings, and its stock has been selling at market prices considerably in excess of its book value. The financial statements of Company P are footnoted to indicate that this acquisition was treated as a pooling of interests.

In what ways would next year's reported net income and the end-of-year balance sheet have differed if the acquisition had been treated as a purchase rather than as a pooling of interests?

8. Appraised Value versus Book Value.   Park Wells Company purchased all the tangible and intangible assets of the Crawford Corporation, giving in exchange government bonds that were purchased two years earlier for $1 million. The market price of these bonds was $960,000 on the day Park Wells purchased the Crawford assets.

On the date of the purchase by Park Wells, Crawford's books showed current assets of $300,000 and plant and equipment with a book value of $200,000. No other assets or liabilities were listed on Crawford Corporation's books.

An appraiser hired by Park Wells estimated that the replacement value of the current assets on the purchase date was $360,000. The replacement cost of the plant and equipment, less an allowance for depreciation, was $540,000.

a. Should Park Wells Company recognize $1 million, $960,000, or some other amount as the total cost of the Crawford assets?

b. How should this total amount be allocated among the various assets acquired? Prepare a journal entry reflecting your allocation and give reasons for your choice.

9. Goodwill; Appraised Values. The book value of Young Company's tangible assets was $750,000, and its liabilities amounted to $250,000. The tangible assets had a total appraised value of $800,000; the liabilities were appraised at $250,000. The historical-cost balance sheet had no intangible assets.

Young's net income has been $72,000 a year for the last five years. Annual expenditures on plant and equipment have equaled the depreciation each year, $20,000.

a. Calculate the present value of the owners' equity in Young Company on the assumption that shareholders expect to receive a rate of return of 12 percent on investments in this industry and that income and expenditures for plant and equipment will continue at their current levels forever.
b. Calculate the value of Young's goodwill.
c. Post, Inc. has offered to buy Young's assets, giving in exchange $650,000 in cash and also accepting responsibility for Young's liabilities. How much has Post offered to pay for Young's goodwill?
d. If Young rejects Post's offer, how much goodwill will appear on Young balance sheet immediately after the rejection? Explain.

10. Stock Investments. On January 2, 19x6, Madison Corporation bought 32,000 of Unitech Company's 80,000 shares of common stock for $4 a share. Madison was thereby able to exercise significant influence over Unitech. On January 10, 19x6, Madison used $13,500 of temporarily idle cash to buy 1,500 of Nash, Inc.'s 50,000 shares of common stock.

Pertinent information regarding Unitech and Nash was as follows:

	Unitech		Nash	
	19x6	19x7	19x6	19x7
Earnings per share......................	$0.40	$1.10	$1.00	$1.15
Dividends (declared and paid) per share.....	—	0.25	0.30	—
December 31 market price per share........	3.50	4.25	9.50	8.00

What were the effects of these two investments on Madison Corporation's income in 19x6 and 19x7?

11. Parent-Subsidiary, Intercompany Inventory Profit. World, Inc., is a wholly owned subsidiary of Universal Corporation. During 19x2, Universal sold merchandise to World for $109,200; the goods had cost Universal $84,000 to manufacture. By year-end, 75 percent of the merchandise had been resold for $150,000.

The two companies' individual financial statements contained the following data:

	Universal	World
Sales	$850,000	$418,000
Cost of goods sold	490,000	304,000
Gross margin	$360,000	$114,000
Ending inventory	$ 79,000	$ 36,500

Prepare a schedule that identifies the comparable amounts that should appear in the companies' consolidated financial statements for 19x2.

12. Equity Method. On January 2, 19x2, Carson Corporation bought 300 shares of the outstanding common stock of Baldwin, Inc., for $275,000 in cash. Baldwin's owners' equity consisted of 1,000, $5 par-value shares, additional paid-in capital of $285,000, and retained earnings of $410,000. Carson paid an amount in excess of book value because Baldwin had an unrecorded goodwill asset that Carson believed would last for 10 more years.

Baldwin declared and paid a $12,000 cash dividend in July 19x2 and reported net income of $50,000 for the year.

a. How much equity in Baldwin, Inc.'s income should be recognized in Carson Corporation's 19x2 income statement?
b. At what amount should the investment in Baldwin, Inc., be reported in Carson Corporation's December 31, 19x2, balance sheet?

13. Long-Term Investment in Bonds. On July 1, 19x1, Redwood, Inc., bought 400 debenture bonds that had been issued six months earlier by Saxony Company. The bonds' maturity value on December 31, 19x20, would be $400,000. Their coupon interest rate was 10 percent, and interest was paid each June 30 and December 31.

The bonds had been issued on January 1, 19x1, to yield 9 percent, but by the time Redwood bought them, it was able to achieve a yield to maturity of 10.5 percent.

Redwood held the bonds until January 1, 19x6, when it sold them to Maxwell, Inc. It recorded a $30,800 gain on the sale to Maxwell.

a. What was the cost of the July 1, 19x1 investment?
b. What was the interest earned in 19x1?
c. What would Redwood's interest income have been in 19x1 if it had bought the bonds on January 1, 19x1, at Saxony's issue price?
d. What annual yield would Maxwell earn if it held the bonds to maturity?

14. Business Combination, Minority Interest. On January 1, 19x1, Royal Company bought 900 of Yankee, Inc.'s 1,000 outstanding shares of common stock for $162,000. At that time, Yankee's balance sheet showed its outstanding shares at a par value of $10 a share. Yankee's additional paid-in capital amounted to $90,000 and its retained earnings were $80,000. Royal's retained earnings on January 1, 19x1 were $99,000.

The following events occurred during 19x1:

	Royal	Yankee
Operating income	$40,000	$30,000
Dividends declared and paid	3,000	7,000
Cash loan by Royal to Yankee in July, 19x1, $12,000; this amount was still outstanding on December 31, 19x1		

a. What was Royal Company's unconsolidated 19x1 net income?
b. What was Royal Company's *Investment in Yankee* account balance as of December 31, 19x1?
c. What was consolidated net income for 19x1?
d. What was the minority interest as of December 31, 19x1?

15. Purchase or Pooling? Two companies had the following balance sheets on December 31, 19x1:

	Company X	Company Y
Assets		
Current assets	$ 5,500	$1,000
Plant and equipment, net.................	7,000	1,700
Total assets	$12,500	$2,700
Liabilities and Owners' Equity		
Current liabilities.......................	$ 2,500	$ 500
Common stock ($5 par)	2,000	250
Additional paid-in capital	3,000	750
Retained earnings.......................	5,000	1,200
Total liabilities and owners' equity	$12,500	$2,700

These balance sheets included $200 that Company Y owed Company X for goods Company Y purchased during 19x1 and sold to its customers.

These two companies merged on January 1, 19x2, Company X issuing 100 shares of its common stock in exchange for all the common shares of Company Y. The fair value of a share of Company X's stock at that time was $30.

In 19x2, Company X reported unconsolidated net income of $1,000, including $100 in cash dividends from Company Y. Company X paid $400 in cash dividends to its shareholders. Company Y reported unconsolidated net income of $180. No intercompany sales were made during the year, and the $200 beginning-of-year intercompany debt was paid by Company Y during the year.

The appraised value of Company Y's tangible assets was equal to their book value on the date of the merger. As a matter of policy, X's directors insist that any purchased goodwill will be amortized in 20 equal annual installments.

a. Should the merger have been accounted for as a purchase or as a pooling of interests? Explain why.
b. Prepare a consolidated balance sheet immediately after the merger.
c. Calculate consolidated net income for the year 19x2.
d. Prepare the owners' equity section of the consolidated balance sheet as of December 31, 19x2.
e. How would your answers to parts *b* and *c* have differed if you had answered part *a* differently?

16. Measurement Basis: Minority Investment. The market price of the common stock of Epstein Drugs had ranged from $23 to $35 a share during 19x1 and 19x2. Its price in January 19x3 was $32. At that point, Harlow Enterprises offered to buy any or all of the common shares of Epstein Drugs at $40 a share. Epstein's management advised its shareholders to reject this offer, saying the company was worth more than $40 a share, but 350,000 shares were sold to Harlow at that price. Epstein had 1 million shares outstanding at that time.

At the time Harlow made these purchases, Epstein's shareowners' equity was as follows:

Common stock, $5 par	$ 5,000,000
Additional paid-in capital	8,000,000
Retained earnings	4,000,000
Total	$17,000,000

During 19x3, Epstein had net income of $5 a share and distributed cash dividends of $3 a share.

a. Calculate Harlow's investment income in 19x3 from its ownership of Epstein shares. Harlow amortizes goodwill in 40 equal annual installments.
b. At what amount should Harlow report its investment in Epstein on its December 31, 19x3, balance sheet?
c. An investment analyst commented that consolidated financial statements for Harlow would have been more meaningful than the statements it actually issued. How would consolidated statements differ from nonconsolidated statements? State your reasons for agreeing or disagreeing with the analyst.

17. Consolidated Sales and Cost of Goods Sold. On March 1, 19x1, Company P sold merchandise to its wholly owned subsidiary for $120. Company P had bought this merchandise on February 1, 19x1, for $80. The subsidiary paid Company P on April 5, 19x1, and sold the merchandise on account to an outside customer for $150 on December 15, 19x1.

 a. How were these transactions reflected in the unconsolidated income statements for Company P and its subsidiary for the year ended December 31, 19x1?

 b. How should these transactions be reflected in the companies' consolidated income statement for the year? Prepare a worksheet elimination entry to produce this result.

 c. How would your answers to parts *a* and *b* have differed if the merchandise had remained in the subsidiary's inventory on December 31, 19x1?

18. Acquisition-Date Consolidated Balance Sheet. On January 3, Prince Company bought 1,600 of the 2,000 outstanding $2.50 par, common shares of Wright, Ltd. Immediately after recording the investment, Prince's balance sheet was as follows:

	Unconsolidated	**Consolidated**
Assets		
Cash	$180,000	$280,000
Inventory	350,000	640,000
Investment in Wright.	160,000	
Goodwill.		14,000
Total	$690,000	$934,000
Liabilities and Owners' Equity		
Payables.	$440,000	$650,000
Minority interest		34,000
Common stock	20,000	20,000
Retained earnings.	230,000	230,000
Total	$690,000	$934,000

Prepare Wright, Ltd.'s balance sheet as of January 3.

19. Consolidated Net Income, Minority Interest, Retained Earnings. Homer Company bought 8,000 shares of the common stock of Cicero Corporation on December 31, 19x3. The purchase price was $12 a share, paid in cash. These shares constituted 80 percent of Cicero Corporation's outstanding common stock. Cicero's balance sheet on that date showed the following owners' equity:

Common stock.	$ 60,000
Additional paid-in capital	25,000
Retained earnings	35,000
Total.	$120,000

The appraised value of Cicero's assets was equal to their book value on the date of the acquisition.

 In 19x4, Cicero Corporation had net income of $30,000 and paid $20,000 in dividends to its stockholders. Homer Company's net income for the year amounted to $50,000, including dividends from Cicero but before the year-end adjustment was made in Homer's accounts to bring them in line with the equity method. Neither company included any intercompany profit in the inventory it reported at the end of the year.

a. What was the consolidated net income for 19x4, after providing for minority interests?

b. At what amount would minority interest be shown on the December 31, 19x4, consolidated balance sheet?

c. How much of Cicero's retained earnings would be shown in consolidated retained earnings as of December 31, 19x4?

20. Business Combination: Alternative Methods. Company A and Company B were completely independent. Neither had invested in the other; neither had ever bought goods or services form the other. These two companies merged at the beginning of this year. Immediately before the merger, their balance sheets showed the following:

	Company A	Company B
Assets		
Cash	$290	$ 30
Other current assets	90	60
Property and equipment (net)	120	60
Total	$500	$150
Liabilities and Owners' Equity		
Liabilities	$100	$ 50
Common stock.....................	50	15
Additional paid-in capital	150	45
Retained earnings.................	200	40
Total	$500	$150

The amounts shown for common stock were the total par values of the shares.

a. Assume Company A purchased all the outstanding common stock of Company B for $160 cash and operated B as a subsidiary. The appraised value of the property and equipment was equal to its book value. What would A's consolidated balance sheet show immediately after the acquisition?

b. Assume Company A acquired all the outstanding stock of Company B, issuing in exchange its own stock with a market value of $160 (par $40). The merger of the two companies was treated as a pooling of interests. After the merger, B ceased to exist as a legal entity. What would appear on A's post-combination balance sheet?

c. For the year preceding the merger, net income was $50 for Company A and $11 for Company B (after depreciation of $6). Assuming the same operating revenues and expenses for the year after the merger except as they may be affected by the accounting method, what net income would be reported under each of the two circumstances described above? (Where appropriate, assume that company policy calls for goodwill to be written off on a straight-line basis over a five-year period.)

d. Compare the results under the two sets of circumstances. Which is more attractive to a management that is interested in putting its best foot forward?

21. Business Combination, Minority Interest. On January 1, 19x4, Paxton Company bought 90 percent of Nicely Corporation's common stock by paying $325,000 cash to Nicely stockholders. The two companies' January 1, 19x4, pre-combination balance sheets showed the following:

	Paxton	**Nicely**
Assets		
Cash	$ 500,000	$ 80,000
Receivables	440,000	150,000
Land	60,000	170,000
Total	$1,000,000	$400,000
Liabilities and Owners' Equity		
Payables.	$ 300,000	$100,000
Common stock	400,000	100,000
Retained earnings.	300,000	200,000
Total	$1,000,000	$400,000

It was determined that the market value of Nicely's land was $350,000. The two companies then began operating as parent and subsidiary.

On December 31, 19x4, Nicely informed all its stockholders that it had a net income of $20,000 during 19x4 ($82,000 sales − $62,000 expenses), and that on December 24 its board of directors had declared an $8,000 cash dividend payable on January 30, 19x5, to stockholders of record as of December 31, 19x4.

During 19x4, Paxton's sales revenues were $175,000, its cost of goods sold and other expenses totaled $150,000, it declared a $13,000 cash dividend, and there were no sales between Paxton and Nicely.

a. Prepare Paxton's post-combination unconsolidated balance sheet as of January 1, 19x4.

b. Prepare the companies' consolidated balance sheet as of January 1, 19x4.

c. What was Paxton's unconsolidated income for 19x4?

d. What was the consolidated net income for 19x4?

22. Business Combination, Journal Entries. Larsen Corporation has identified the following five scenarios through which it might acquire a controlling or significant interest in Garcia, Ltd.:

1. Larsen pays $202,000 cash to buy 100 percent of Garcia's outstanding shares, and the combined enterprise is operated as one legal entity.
2. Larsen pays $202,000 cash to buy 100 percent of Garcia's outstanding shares, and the combined enterprise is operated as a parent and subsidiary.
3. Larsen pays $135,000 cash to buy 70 percent of Garcia's outstanding shares, and thereby creates a parent-subsidiary relationship.
4. Larsen pays $81,000 cash to buy 40 percent of Garcia's outstanding shares.
5. Larsen exchanges 4,800 of its $1 par-value common shares for all Garcia's outstanding shares. The market values per share were: Larsen $5.00 and Garcia $2.40. The combined enterprise is operated as one legal entity.

The transaction would occur on January 1, 19x4, when Garcia's balance sheet is expected to appear as follows:

Assets

Cash	$ 40,000
Inventory	80,000
Machinery	180,000
Total	$300,000

Liabilities and Owners' Equity

Payables	$140,000
Common stock ($2 par)	20,000
Additional paid-in capital	90,000
Retained earnings	50,000
Total	$300,000

The market value of the inventory is expected to be $90,000, and the market value of the machinery is expected to be $200,000.

Prepare a journal entry Larsen would find appropriate under each of the five scenarios.

23. Post-Combination Earnings. Larsen Corporation (see problem 22) acquired stock of Garcia, Ltd., on January 1, 19x4. Three of the five scenarios described in problem 22—scenarios 2, 3, and 4—resulted in Garcia continuing to operate as a legal entity. The estimates in problem 22 proved to be correct.

The following information relates to the two companies' operations in 19x4:

	Larsen	Garcia
Sales revenues	$350,000	$190,000
Expenses:		
Cost of goods sold	140,000	70,000
Depreciation.	20,000	18,000
Other expenses	100,000	42,000
Total expenses	260,000	130,000
Net income.	$ 90,000	$ 60,000

Dividends declared and paid were $15,000 by Larsen and $10,000 by Garcia. Garcia didn't buy or sell machinery during 19x4, and 20 percent of its January 1 inventory remained unsold at year-end. Larsen amortized goodwill over 10 years on a straight-line basis.

a. For scenarios 2, 3, and 4 identified in problem 22, what was Larsen Corporation's net income in 19x4?

b. For scenarios 2 and 3, prepare the 19x4 consolidated income statement.

c. For scenarios 1 and 5, prepare Larsen's 19x4 income statement.

24. Business Combination. On November 30, 19x3, Fair Deal Corporation exchanged 10,000 shares of its $5 par common stock for a 100 percent ownership in Strate & Shute, Inc. At that time, Fair Deal stock was selling at a market price of $40 per share; Strate & Shute was a family-owned corporation and there was no market in its shares. The acquisition was treated as a pooling of interests.

Balance sheets drawn up for the two corporations as of November 30, 19x3, just before the acquisition transaction was consummated, showed the following (in summary form):

	Fair Deal	Strate & Shute
Assets		
Assets	$1,000,000	$250,000
Owners' Equity		
Common stock.	$ 200,000	$100,000
Additional paid-in capital	300,000	70,000
Retained earnings	500,000	80,000
Total owners' equity.	$1,000,000	$250,000

Earnings for the two companies for 19x3 were:

	Fair Deal	Strate & Shute
January 1–November 30	$120,000	$40,000
December 1–December 31	20,000	5,000
Total	$140,000	$45,000

There were no intercompany sales during the year. No dividends were declared by either company during the year. A set of consolidated financial statements was prepared at the end of 19x3.

a. At was amounts would goodwill and retained earnings appear on the consolidated balance sheet at December 31, 19x3?
b. Calculate consolidated net income for the year. (Goodwill, if any, is to be amortized in equal amounts for 20 years.)
c. How would your answers to parts a and b have differed if the Strate & Shute stock had been acquired in exchange for $394,000 in cash?

25. Business Combination.   Below are the balance sheets of Single and Multiple Corporations as of December 31, 19x3:

	Multiple	Single
Assets		
Assets.	$3,400,000	$156,000
Liabilities and Owners' Equity		
Liabilities	$ 650,000	$ 50,000
Capital stock, 32,000 shares		32,000
Capital stock, 800,000 shares	800,000	
Additional paid-in capital.	600,000	17,000
Retained earnings.	1,350,000	57,000
Total	$3,400,000	$156,000

The appraised value of Single's tangible assets was equal to their book value at that time.

At the start of 19x4, Multiple paid $190,000 in cash for the 32,000 shares of Single. The two companies then began operating as parent and subsidiary.

The two companies' unconsolidated income statements for 19x4, drawn up before the end-of-year adjustments were made to reflect the equity method, were as follows:

	Multiple	Single
Sales	$10,000,000	$800,000
Expenses	8,700,000	700,000
Operating income	1,300,000	100,000
Dividend from Single	40,000	
Income before taxes	$ 1,340,000	$100,000

No intercompany sales took place during 19x4, and consolidated income before taxes was taxed at a rate of 50 percent.

a. Would the merger have been accounted for as a purchase or as a pooling of interests? Why?
b. Prepare the combination-date consolidated balance sheet.
c. Present a consolidated income statement for 19x4. Goodwill, if any, was to be amortized equally over seven years.
d. How, if at all, would your answers to the questions above have differed if the shares of Single had been obtained in exchange for 20,000 shares of Multiple's stock, valued at $9.50 a share?

26. Advantages of Consolidated Statements. Indico, Inc., has its headquarters in a country in which corporations are not required to follow U.S. generally accepted accounting principles in preparing their financial statements. Indico has one subsidiary, Dilex, Inc. Indico established Dilex in 19x1 by buying 100,000 shares of its $1 par common stock for $500,000. No other shares were issued, either then or later.

The income statements of the two companies for the year 19x7 were as follows:

	Indico	Dilex
Sales revenue	$150,000	$600,000
Dividend income (from Dilex)	40,000	—
Total revenue	190,000	600,000
Cost of goods sold	85,000	420,000
Selling and administrative expenses	45,000	53,000
Interest expense	—	22,000
Income tax expense	10,000	30,000
Net income	$ 50,000	$ 75,000

Dilex's sales revenues included $50,000 in sales to Indico; the cost of goods sold attributable to these sales was $35,000.

The two companies' balance sheets as of December 31, 19x7, contained the following information:

	Indico	Dilex
Assets		
Current assets:		
Cash	$ 10,000	$ 25,000
Accounts receivable	20,000	170,000
Inventories	30,000	205,000
Total current assets	60,000	400,000
Investment in subsidiary	500,000	—
Plant and equipment (net)	140,000	670,000
Total assets	$700,000	$1,070,000

	Indico	Dilex
Liabilities		
Current liabilities:		
Accounts payable	$ 5,000	$ 35,000
Taxes payable	5,000	10,000
Total current liabilities	10,000	45,000
Bonds payable	—	275,000
Total liabilities	$ 10,000	$ 320,000
Owners' Equity		
Common stock	$200,000	$ 100,000
Additional paid-in capital	100,000	400,000
Retained earnings	390,000	250,000
Total owners' equity	$690,000	$ 750,000

On December 31, Indico owed Dilex $2,000 for purchases of merchandise, and this amount was included in the accounts payable. Indico's inventory included merchandise purchased from Dilex at a price of $3,000. Dilex's cost of this merchandise was $1,800.

a. Prepare a set of 19x7 consolidated financial statements for Indico and its subsidiary.
b. Indico has never published either consolidated financial statements or the separate financial statements of Dilex. A group of Indico's shareholders have asked management to publish consolidated statements for 19x7. The company's treasurer has opposed this but has suggested meeting the shareowners' needs by shifting to the equity method in the parent company's statements. Evaluate this suggestion, indicating the benefits, if any, consolidated statements would give the shareholders and whether the equity method would be an adequate substitute for consolidation. Use numbers from the problem to support your arguments.

Chapter 13

Flows of Funds

A business's operating performance is usually measured by its earnings, based on accrual accounting and the application of suitable revenue-recognition criteria. The results of this measurement process are communicated through the income statement, which sets forth the enterprise's revenues, expenses, gains, and losses. Unfortunately, the income statement doesn't show the effects of all the events which affected the company's liquidity—its ability to meet its cash obligations on time—nor does it reflect all the flows of resources into or out of the company during the period.

To overcome these deficiencies, a second performance-related statement is prepared—the **statement of changes in financial position,** or *funds statement*. The term *funds* denotes cash or any other form of liquid resources. To most people, *funds* is used interchangeably with *cash;* in corporate finance, *funds* is occasionally used to denote all of an enterprise's financial resources. *Funds* therefore is a term that should be used only when there is a common understanding of the context in which it is being used.

In this chapter, we'll discuss the flows of *cash*, both because it is the simplest way to measure funds and because it is now the focus of the funds statements published by most U.S. companies.[1]

---

[1] In practice, most companies that adopt the cash definition actually combine cash and short-term marketable securities—that is, investments of temporarily idle cash in commercial paper, bonds, notes, and stocks.

Cash Flow from Operations

For a majority of companies, the most important single source of cash is the ongoing operations of the business itself. Although operations do generate income, **cash flow from operations** isn't the same as net income. Net income summarizes the effects of the company's operations on the owners' equity. To measure income, the company's accountants subtract one set of resource *outflows* (expenses) measured at their *cost,* from another set of resource *inflows* (revenues) measured at their *value* to the company. While cash flow from operations looks at the same set of resource flows, it measures them by their effects on cash rather than by their effects on the owners' equity.

To determine cash flow from operations, therefore, we need to examine each of the resource flows in the income statement to see how that resource flow has affected the company's cash position.

Cash Flow: A First Approximation

Peabody, Inc., is a retail merchandising company. Its income statement for 19x2 is shown in Exhibit 13–1. The first step in calculating cash

EXHIBIT 13–1

PEABODY, INC.
Income Statement
For the Year Ended December 31, 19x2

Sales revenue		$400,000
Gain from the sale of investments		3,000
Total		403,000
Expenses:		
Cost of goods sold	$240,000	
Depreciation	11,000	
Salaries	55,500	
Interest	7,000	
Loss on sale of machinery	1,000	
Miscellaneous expenses	20,500	
Income taxes	26,000	361,000
Net income		$ 42,000

flow from operations is to remove from this income statement all revenues and expenses that clearly don't measure inflows or outflows of cash. Peabody's 19x2 income statement listed three of these:

1. Depreciation.
2. A loss on the sale of machinery.
3. A gain on the sale of investments.

Depreciation is simply the amortization of expenditures made in previous periods—it doesn't measure current cash flows. Similarly, the loss on the sale of machinery measures the portion of a reduction in a noncash asset that isn't matched by an inflow of other assets, presumably cash. The cash inflow from the sale of machinery will appear elsewhere in the funds statement; the loss itself is neither a cash inflow nor a cash outflow.

Conversely, the gain on the sale of investments does represent a cash flow, but it doesn't arise from the company's ordinary commercial operations—it should be shown elsewhere in the funds statement as part of the total cash proceeds from the sale of investments, one of the company's sources of cash during the period.

Exhibit 13–2 shows how Peabody's income statement for 19x2 can be adjusted to remove these three elements, thereby producing a first approximation to the amount of cash provided by operations.

EXHIBIT 13–2

PEABODY, INC.
Preliminary Estimation of Cash Flow from Operations
For the Year Ended December 31, 19x2

	Income	Cash Flow (First Approximation)
Sales revenue....................	$400,000	$400,000
Gain from sale of investments	3,000	—
Total.........................	403,000	400,000
Expenses:		
Cost of goods sold..............	240,000	240,000
Depreciation	11,000	—
Salaries	55,500	55,500
Interest.......................	7,000	7,000
Loss on sale of machinery.........	1,000	—
Miscellaneous expenses	20,500	20,500
Income taxes...................	26,000	26,000
Net income/cash flow	$ 42,000	$ 51,000

Another way of making this adjustment, exactly equivalent to the first, is to start with net income, add the depreciation and the loss on the sale of machinery, and subtract the gain on the sale of investments:

Net income	$42,000
Add: Depreciation..............	11,000
Loss on sale of machinery ...	1,000
Less: Gain on sale of investments..	(3,000)
Cash flow from operations	$51,000

What's the logic of this procedure? It implies that net income is the starting point, a preliminary estimate of the amount of cash flow from operations. Depreciation and the loss on the sale of machinery would never have been subtracted from revenues, however, if the purpose had been to measure cash flow from operations. Since they were deducted in the calculation of net income, we have to add them back to the net income number. Similarly, we wouldn't have added the gain on the sale of investments to revenues if what we'd wanted was a cash flow estimate—that being the case, we have to subtract it now.

Cash Flow: Adjusting for Balance Sheet Changes

Some version of this first approximation is used in practice very often. The financial press, for example, often refers to the sum of net income and depreciation as the company's cash flow. It doesn't really measure cash flow, however, because some of the other revenues and expenses in the income statement don't measure inflows and outflows of cash. To remove the noncash components from these revenues and expenses, we need to examine a number of changes in balance sheet amounts, shown in Exhibit 13–3.

Peabody's cash flow from operations in 19x2 had only six components:

1. Collections from customers.
2. Payments to suppliers of merchandise.
3. Payments to employees.
4. Interest payments.
5. Tax payments.
6. Payments to suppliers of other services.

Both the income statement and the balance sheets have been condensed to allow us to concentrate on these six components of Peabody's cash flow stream. In practice, either a larger or a smaller number of components might be identified; we have chosen these six because they demonstrate the most important aspects of the relationships among the (1) income statement, (2) the balance sheet, and (3) the flow of cash from operations.

Cash Collected from Customers

The first component of cash flow from operations is the amount of cash collected from customers. The amount collected may be either greater or less than current revenues, for the following reason: cash for some revenue amounts is collected during the same period, some cash won't be collected until a future period, and some amounts recognized as revenues in previous periods will be collected this period.

The amount of cash collected from operations in a period can be determined from an examination of the period's revenues and the beginning and ending accounts receivable balances. For Peabody, the cash collected from customers in 19x2 was:

Sales revenue	$400,000
Add: Accounts receivable, January 1	+ 70,000
Less: Accounts receivable, December 31	− 85,000
Cash collected from customers	$385,000

Payments to Suppliers of Merchandise

Payments to outside suppliers of merchandise constitute the second component of the cash flow stream. The amount of cash paid to suppliers in a period can be determined by using an approach similar to that which

EXHIBIT 13–3

PEABODY, INC.
Comparative Balance Sheets
January 1 and December 31, 19x2

	January 1	December 31
Assets		
Current assets:		
Cash	$ 20,000	$ 17,000
Accounts receivable	70,000	85,000
Inventories	90,000	95,000
Total current assets...................	180,000	197,000
Investments	10,000	—
Plant assets:		
Machinery	290,000	310,000
Accumulated depreciation.................	(90,000)	(75,000)
Total plant assets	200,000	235,000
Total assets........................	$390,000	$432,000
Liabilities and Owners' Equity		
Current liabilities:		
Accounts payable	$ 79,000	$ 69,000
Salaries payable	1,300	1,000
Taxes payable	9,700	12,000
Total current liabilities	90,000	82,000
Noncurrent liabilities:		
Bonds payable...........................	90,000	80,000
Deferred income taxes	15,000	20,000
Total noncurrent liabilities	105,000	100,000
Owners' equity:		
Common stock	20,000	30,000
Additional paid-in capital.................	80,000	120,000
Retained earnings........................	95,000	100,000
Total owners' equity	195,000	250,000
Total liabilities and owners' equity	$390,000	$432,000

enabled us to calculate the period's cash collections. In this case, we use the period's amount of goods purchased and the beginning and ending accounts payable balances. The trouble is we don't know the amount purchased. To determine that, we first have to examine the period's cost of goods sold and the beginning and ending inventory balances.

From Exhibit 13–1, we find that the cost of goods sold was $240,000; from Exhibit 13–3, we can see that the inventory went from $90,000 at the beginning of 19x2 to $95,000 at the end. Peabody's purchases therefore must have been $245,000, determined as follows:

Cost of goods sold.........................	$240,000
Add: Inventory, December 31	+ 95,000
Less: Inventory, January 1....................	− 90,000
Purchase of merchandise	$245,000

This is $5,000 greater than the total of the cost of goods sold, because $5,000 of the year's purchases were made to increase the company's inventory.

Now we can go back to calculate the amount of payments to suppliers:

Purchases of merchandise	$245,000
Add: Accounts payable, January 1.............	+ 79,000
Less: Accounts payable, December 31	− 69,000
Cash payments to suppliers	$255,000

Because accounts payable went down by $10,000 during the year ($79,000 − $69,000), the total amount paid to suppliers was $10,000 more than the total cost of the period's purchases.

This calculation is based on two fundamental assumptions: (1) all accounts payable arose from the purchases of merchandise, and (2) no purchases of these items were financed by any source other than current accounts payable.[2]

Payments to Employees

The amounts paid to employees can be determined by considering the period's salaries expense and the beginning and ending salaries payable balances, as follows:

---

[2] For example, if some suppliers accepted Peabody's promissory notes in exchange for their goods or services, the amount actually paid was smaller than the amount we just determined. On the other hand, if some of the year-end accounts payable arose from the purchase of furniture and equipment, then the amount we just calculated understates the amounts paid to suppliers of merchandise and other currently consumed goods or services. Lacking further information on the composition of accounts and notes payable, we have to estimate what that composition was. In most cases, it is reasonable to make the assumptions that we've made in our analysis here.

Salaries expense	$55,500
Add: Salaries payable, January 1	+ 1,300
Less: Salaries payable, December 31	− 1,000
Salary payments to employees	$55,800

Since the salary liability at the end of the period was less than the liability at the beginning, the amount paid was greater than the expense for the period.[3]

Interest Payments

Although interest is usually classified as a nonoperating expense, we include the payment of interest in the definition of cash flow from operations because we want this to be the cash flow counterpart of net income.

The calculation reflects the same approach that is used for salaries—namely, we consider the period's interest expense and the beginning and ending interest payable balances:

Interest expense	$7,000
Add: Interest payable, January 1	0
Less: Interest payable, December 31	0
Interest payments to creditors	$7,000

Since Peabody had no interest payable either at the beginning or at the end of the year, its 19x2 interest payments were equal to its interest expense for the year, $7,000.

When a company has bonds outstanding, the amortization of a discount or a premium is a noncash component of the period's interest expense. In calculating cash flow from operations, accountants therefore also add to net income the amount of discount amortized and subtract the amount of premium amortized.

Tax Payments

The next component of cash flow from operations is the amount of taxes paid. In principle, the calculation of the amounts paid in taxes follows the same approach that is used for salary payments and interest payments. To perform the tax payment calculation, however, accountants examine both the current liability, taxes payable, *and* the noncurrent liability, deferred income taxes. Peabody's calculation for 19x2 was as follows:

---

[3] In practice, not all salary payments go to the employees themselves, because part of each employee's salary is withheld for various kinds of taxes, insurance, and other deductions. Since these amounts are cash payments on the employees' behalf, however, it does no harm to include them as part of the payments *to employees*.

Income tax expense......................		$26,000
Add: Taxes payable, January 1.............	+$ 9,700	
Less: Taxes payable, December 31.........	− 12,000	
Adjustment...........................		− 2,300
Add: Deferred income taxes, January 1.....	+ 15,000	
Less: Deferred income taxes, December 31..	− 20,000	
Adjustment...........................		− 5,000
Tax payments.......................		$18,700

The amount paid was less than the tax expense because both of these tax liabilities increased during the year.

Other Payments

Peabody's income statement (Exhibit 13–1) also contained miscellaneous expenses of $20,500—representing expenses such as rent, insurance, advertising, and utilities. To determine whether the cash actually paid was a different amount would require examining the appropriate balance sheet items. We would treat changes in an asset such as prepaid insurance and a liability such as accruals payable similar to the approach we used to determine the other cash flow amounts. Since Peabody's balance sheets don't contain such items, we can assume that the entire $20,500 was paid in cash in 19x2.

Cash Flow from Operations

We've now calculated all the components of cash flow from operations. These components are summarized in Exhibit 13–4. The numbers in the left-hand column are from the income statement; those at the right determine the cash flow from operations.

Once again, the logic is that the noncash amounts never should have been added or deducted if the purpose of the income statement had been to present a statement of cash flows. If net income is to be used as a first approximation to the amount of funds provided by operations, then the noncash amounts must be subtracted or added back.

Disclosing Cash Flow from Operations

Until this point we've limited our analysis to the question of how accountants *measure* cash flow from operations. A related issue is how accountants *disclose* the cash flow information. For financial reporting purposes, U.S. accountants use a *reconciliation* approach. Rather than

EXHIBIT 13–4

PEABODY, INC.
Adjusting Income Statement to Determine
Cash Flow from Operations
For the Year Ended December 31, 19x2

	Income Statement	Noncash Components	Cash Flow from Operations
Sales revenues...............	$400,000	−$15,000	$385,000
Gain from sale of investments ..	3,000	− 3,000	—
Total...................	403,000	− 18,000	385,000
Expenses:			
Cost of goods sold..........	240,000	+ 15,000	255,000
Depreciation	11,000	− 11,000	—
Salaries	55,500	+ 300	55,800
Interest..................	7,000	—	7,000
Loss on sale of machinery ...	1,000	− 1,000	—
Miscellaneous..............	20,500	—	20,500
Income taxes..............	26,000	− 7,300	18,700
Total...................	361,000	− 4,000	357,000
Net income/Cash flow.........	$ 42,000	−$14,000	$ 28,000

present the cash flow amounts that appear in the right-hand column in Exhibit 13–4, accountants identify the *adjustments* that convert the net income amount into cash flow from operations. This disclosure appears at the very beginning of the comprehensive **funds flow** statement that each company prepares in conjunction with its balance sheet and income statement.

The manner in which Peabody, Inc., discloses its cash flow from operations appears in Exhibit 13–5. Since each of the eight adjustments to net income has already been discussed, we'll only summarize how accountants determine whether each amount is an **add-back** or **subtract-from adjustment** of net income. Exhibit 13–6 lists the **income adjustments** that accountants make most often; Peabody's accountants, however, identified only five types of adjustments—numbers 1, 2, 3, 5, and 6.

Cash Flow Reporting in Practice

Some published statements of changes in financial position present the changes in the components of working capital in a different fashion. Instead of adjusting the components of the income statement to a cash flow basis, as in Exhibit 13–4, or instead of adding and subtracting these elements from net income, as in Exhibit 13–5, they go partway toward

EXHIBIT 13–5

PEABODY, INC.:
Cash Flow from Operations

Net income		$42,000
Add: Depreciation......................	$11,000	
Deferred taxes	5,000	
Loss on sale of machinery	1,000	
Increase in taxes payable	2,300	
Total		+ 19,300
Less: Gain on sale of investments	3,000	
Increase in receivables	15,000	
Increase in inventories.............	5,000	
Decrease in accounts payable	10,000	
Decrease in salaries payable........	300	
Total		− 33,300
Cash flow from operations		$28,000

EXHIBIT 13–6
Adjustments to Derive Cash Flow from Operations

	Adjust by	
Income Element	**Adding**	**Subtracting**
1. Changes in current assets		
Increases.........................		x
Decreases........................	x	
2. Changes in current liabilities		
Increases.........................	x	
Decreases........................		x
3. Depreciation of plant assets	x	
4. Amortization of intangible assets	x	
5. Deferred income taxes	x*	
6. Sale of noncurrent asset		
Gain.............................		x
Loss.............................	x	
7. Undistributed affiliate earnings†		x
8. Early extinguishment of debt		
Gain.............................		x
Loss.............................	x	
9. Interest expense		
Premium amortized.................		x
Discount amortized	x	

* Subtract if the amount of the deferral is negative.
† The equity method—as explained in Chapter 12—requires a qualifying investor in stock to recognize as income its share of the investee's income. Since the investor's cash is unaffected until dividends are received, a subtract-from adjustment to income is necessary to the extent that cash wasn't received during the period.

that solution. They add back such items as depreciation, deferred income taxes, and capital losses and subtract capital gains, but show the changes in accounts receivable, inventories, accounts payable, and other working capital items separately at the bottom of the statement or even in a supplementary schedule. Under this approach, funds flow from operations is measured as the effect of operations on working capital.

Other Receipts and Disbursements of Cash

The measurement of a company's cash flow from operations during a period accounts for some but not all of the company's cash flows during the period. To identify the other cash flows, we need to account for the changes in all of the balance sheet items except cash.

To explain why this is so, we need to start with a slightly modified version of the accounting equation:

$$\text{Cash} + \text{Other assets} = \text{Liabilities} + \text{Owners' equity}$$

Since the accounting equation must remain balanced at all times, we know that the sum of the *changes* in the items on the left of this equation must equal the sum of the *changes* in the items on the right. The equation in this form is:

$$\Delta\ \text{Cash} + \Delta\ \text{Other assets} = \Delta\ \text{Liabilities} + \Delta\ \text{Owners' equity}$$

Finally, we can transpose, as follows:

$$\Delta\ \text{Cash} = \Delta\ \text{Liabilities} + \Delta\ \text{Owners' Equity} - \Delta\ \text{Other assets}$$

Balance Sheet Changes

This equation can be applied to the changes in the balance sheet amounts in Exhibit 13–3 to prepare the rudimentary funds statement shown in Exhibit 13–7. This is simply a list of balance sheet changes, with (*a*) all the increases in liabilities and owners' equity and decreases in assets shown as *sources* of cash, and (*b*) all decreases in liabilities and owners' equity and increases in assets shown as *uses* of cash—the difference being the $3,000 change in the cash balance from $20,000 on January 1, 19x2, to $17,000 on December 31, 19x2.

Exhibit 13–7 is only a starting point for our analysis. In measuring the cash flow from operations, we've already accounted for many of the balance sheet changes listed in this exhibit. Exhibit 13–8 compares the changes in all the balance sheet items (from Exhibit 13–3) with the changes we accounted for in our calculation of cash flow from opera-

EXHIBIT 13–7

PEABODY, INC.
Statement of Balance Sheet Changes
From January 1, 19x2 to December 31, 19x2

Sources of cash:

Increase in retained earnings		$ 5,000
Increase in deferred income taxes		5,000
Increase in capital stock		10,000
Increase in additional paid-in capital		40,000
Increase in taxes payable		2,300
Decrease in investments		10,000
Total sources of cash		72,300

Uses of cash:

Increase in plant assets	$35,000	
Increase in accounts receivable	15,000	
Increase in inventories	5,000	
Decrease in salaries payable	300	
Decrease in accounts payable	10,000	
Decrease in bonds payable	10,000	
Total uses of cash		75,300
Decrease in cash balance		$ 3,000

tions.[4] The ten items in column (2) other than the change in cash itself are the adjustments we made to convert the $42,000 net income (shown on the last line) to the $28,000 cash flow from operations (shown on the top line).

---

[4] An equivalent alternative to the increase/decrease format in Exhibit 13–8 on p. 493 is to identify all of the amounts in terms of debits and (credits), as follows:

	(1)	(2)	(3)
Cash	$ (3,000)	$ 28,000	$(31,000)
Accounts receivable	15,000	15,000	—
Inventories	5,000	5,000	—
Machinery	20,000	(1,000)	21,000
Accumulated depreciation . .	15,000	(11,000)	26,000
Investments	(10,000)	3,000	(13,000)
Accounts payable	10,000	10,000	—
Salaries payable	300	300	—
Taxes payable	(2,300)	(2,300)	—
Bonds payable	10,000	—	10,000
Deferred income taxes	(5,000)	(5,000)	—
Common stock	(10,000)	—	(10,000)
Additional paid-in capital . . .	(40,000)	—	(40,000)
Retained earnings	(5,000)	(42,000)	37,000
Total	$ —	$ —	$ —

As always, the sum of the debits equals the sum of the credits, so the net sum at the bottom of each column is zero.

EXHIBIT 13–8

PEABODY, INC.
Changes in Balance Sheet Amounts
For the Year Ended December 31, 19x2

	(1) Net Changes During 19x2 (Exhibit 13–3)		(2) Changes Reflected in Cash Flow from Operations		(3) Changes Still to be Analyzed (1) − (2)
Cash	−$ 3,000	(*)	+$28,000		−$31,000
Accounts receivable	+ 15,000	(1)	+ 15,000		—
Inventories	+ 5,000	(2)	+ 5,000		—
Machinery	+ 20,000	(3)	− 1,000		+ 21,000
Accumulated depreciation . .	− 15,000	(4)	+ 11,000		− 26,000
Investments	− 10,000	(5)	+ 3,000		− 13,000
Accounts payable	− 10,000	(6)	− 10,000		—
Salaries payable	− 300	(7)	− 300		—
Taxes payable	+ 2,300	(8)	+ 2,300		—
Bonds payable.	− 10,000		—		− 10,000
Deferred income taxes	+ 5,000	(9)	+ 5,000		—
Common stock	+ 10,000		—		+ 10,000
Additional paid-in capital . . .	+ 40,000		—		+ 40,000
Retained earnings.	+ 5,000	(10)	+ 42,000		− 37,000

(*) The $28,000 increase in cash is the net result of changes (1) through (10).

For example, the $15,000 increase in accounts receivable was a determinant of net income but not of cash flow. Adjusting net income by this amount meant that this change was fully accounted for in the calculation of the cash flow from operations and needn't be considered in the remainder of the analysis. Similarly, $11,000 of the change in accumulated depreciation was accounted for in cash flow from operations by the depreciation charge, leaving a $26,000 decrease to be explained in other ways.

Our task in this section is to account for the remaining changes (column 3 in the exhibit), specifically the changes in the following:

1. Machinery and accumulated depreciation.
2. Investments.
3. Bonds payable.
4. Common stock and additional paid-in capital.
5. Retained earnings.

Changes in Machinery

The changes in Peabody's machinery and accumulated depreciation, as shown in Exhibit 13-3, were as follows:

	January 1	December 31	Increase (Decrease)
Machinery..................	$290,000	$310,000	$20,000
Accumulated depreciation.....	(90,000)	(75,000)	(15,000)

Machinery *increased* by $20,000 during the year, while Accumulated Depreciation *decreased* by $15,000. If depreciation expense had been the only change in Accumulated Depreciation during 19x2, the balance would have increased by $11,000. Something must have happened to reduce its balance by $26,000 (January 1's $90,000 plus the $11,000 depreciation expense versus December 31's $75,000).

We know that accountants reduce Accumulated Depreciation when a depreciable asset is sold, and that presumably explains the $26,000 decrease. But this in turn raises another question—namely, what was the original cost of the sold machinery?

Peabody's accountants knew that during 19x2 the company (1) had expended $50,000 to acquire new machinery, and (2) had sold for $3,000 machinery that had cost $30,000. This information in turn enabled them to explain the year's changes in both accounts *and* to derive the effect of these changes on Peabody's cash flow.

The $50,000 expenditure to buy the new machinery was a **use of cash,** as there was no indication that a liability was created or that shares of stock were issued for that purpose. The $3,000 received from the sale of the old machinery was a **source of cash.**

The $26,000 reduction in Accumulated Depreciation and the $1,000 loss on the sale can be understood by analyzing the entry that recorded the sale:

Cash...	3,000	
Accumulated Depreciation	26,000	
Loss on Sale of Machinery	1,000	
Machinery..		30,000

The book value of the machinery sold was $4,000—the original cost of $30,000 less accumulated depreciation of $26,000. The $1,000 loss was due to the $3,000 cash proceeds being $1,000 less than the $4,000 book value.

As a result of this analysis, the accountants recognized three amounts in their summary of cash flows: (1) the $3,000 proceeds as a source of cash, (2) the $50,000 cost of the new machinery as a use of cash, and (3) the $1,000 loss on the sale as an add-back adjustment to income. The add-back is necessary because although the $1,000 was a legitimate negative determinant of net income, it wasn't a negative determinant of cash flow from operations.

Changes in Investments

The change in Peabody's investment asset, as shown in the balance sheets in Exhibit 13–3, was $10,000:

	January 1	December 31	(Decrease)
Investments.....	$10,000	$ —	$(10,000)

Lacking any further information, we'd have to assume that this decrease was the proceeds from the sale of Peabody's investments during the year. We know from the income statement, however, that Peabody realized a $3,000 gain on the sale of this asset. The proceeds of the sale therefore must have been $10,000 + $3,000 = $13,000. This was a source of cash in 19x2.

Notice what we have done. Instead of entering the $10,000 change in the *sources* section of the funds statement, we've entered *two* numbers: (1) the $13,000 proceeds and (2) the $3,000 gain we subtracted in calculating cash flow from operations. The net effect on total sources is still $10,000, but our two numbers increase the information content of the statement by showing more clearly where the $10,000 came from.

Changes in Bonds Payable

We've spent a good deal of time analyzing the relationships between changes in noncurrent assets and changes in cash. Most other relationships are simpler than these and can be disposed of more quickly. To begin with, Peabody's balance sheets (Exhibit 13–3) provide the following information on bonds payable:

	January 1	December 31	(Decrease)
Bonds payable ..	$90,000	$80,000	$(10,000)

Although we try to look for *gross* changes rather than *net* changes, in this case we have no additional information to indicate that there had been any transactions other than the early extinguishment of a portion of Peabody's bonds. Even at this point, however, we cannot assume that the use of cash was necessarily $10,000. We turn to the income statement (Exhibit 13–1) to determine if there had been a gain or a loss on the early extinguishment. Since Peabody reported *no* gain or loss in the income statement for 19x1, we can reasonably conclude that $10,000 was the amount of cash used to retire bonds that year.

If a gain or a loss does occur, the amount of the retirement *payment*— not the face value of the bond—is identified as the cash flow effect. In addition, a loss is added back to net income in the measurement of cash flow from operations, just as we added Peabody's loss on the sale of machinery. Again, the reason is that although a loss is a legitimate deduction from revenue in the calculation of net income, it doesn't measure a current outflow of cash. Since it has been deducted from revenue in the income calculation, it must be added back to net income in the calculation of cash flow from operations.

Changes in Common Stock and Additional Paid-in Capital

In the course of preparing Peabody's financial statements for 19x2, the accountants prepared a schedule of changes in owners' equity. This appears in Exhibit 13–9. One change in owners' equity, the issuance of

EXHIBIT 13–9

PEABODY, INC.
Schedule of Changes in Owners' Equity
For the Year Ended December 31, 19x2

	Common Stock (par)	Additional Paid-in Capital	Retained Earnings
Balance, January 1	$20,000	$ 80,000	$ 95,000
Net income	—	—	42,000
Stock dividends	3,500	16,500	(20,000)
Cash dividends	—	—	(17,000)
Shares issued for cash	6,500	23,500	—
Balance, December 31	$30,000	$120,000	$100,000

new shares in exchange for $30,000 cash, was clearly a source of cash. This accounted for $6,500 of the $10,000 increase in common stock and $23,500 of the $40,000 increase in additional paid-in capital.

The remainder of the increases in these two owners' equity items came from the issuance of stock dividends. This had *no* effect on Peabody's cash, however. The stock dividend was recorded by a simple transfer from one owners' equity account (Retained Earnings) to two others (Common Stock and Additional Paid-in Capital). In entry form, this transfer was as follows:

Retained Earnings	20,000	
Common Stock		3,500
Additional Paid-in Capital		16,500

Changes in Retained Earnings

The net change in Peabody's retained earnings in 19x2 was a $5,000 increase. We have already accounted for two transactions affecting retained earnings:

Net income	$42,000	increase
Stock dividend	20,000	decrease
Difference	$22,000	increase

Exhibit 13–9 lists only one other change in retained earnings, the $17,000 cash dividend. This was obviously a $17,000 use of cash, and the $5,000 net change in retained earnings is therefore completely accounted for.

The Statement of Changes in Financial Position

All of these analyses are summarized in the **statement of changes in financial position** in Exhibit 13–10. This title points out the interrela-

EXHIBIT 13–10

PEABODY, INC.
Statement of Changes in Financial Position
For the Year Ended December 31, 19x2

Sources of Cash:		
Operations:		
Net income	$ 42,000	
Add: Depreciation	11,000	
Deferred taxes	5,000	
Loss on sale of machinery	1,000	
Increase in taxes payable	2,300	
Less: Gain on sale of investments	(3,000)	
Increase in receivables	(15,000)	
Increase in inventories	(5,000)	
Decrease in accounts payable	(10,000)	
Decrease in salaries payable	(300)	
Cash flow from operations	28,000	
Sale of common stock	30,000	
Sale of machinery	3,000	
Sale of investments	13,000	
Total sources of cash		$74,000
Uses of cash:		
Purchases of machinery	50,000	
Cash dividends	17,000	
Retirement of debt	10,000	
Total uses of cash		77,000
Decrease in cash		$ 3,000

tionship of funds flow analysis with the balance sheet. A balance sheet is a statement of financial position because it depicts financial position as of a point in time—assets, liabilities, and owners' equity. Since funds flow analysis revolves around changes between a period's beginning and ending balance sheets, it's understandable that it be presented as the statement of changes in financial position.

The upper half of the exhibit identifies the sources of cash, the lower half presents the uses of cash, and the $3,000 decrease in cash appears as a residual.

The All-Resources Concept. The objective of the statement of changes in financial position is to report the effects of all changes in financial position, not just those that affect cash. The statement therefore includes significant transactions involving flows of noncash resources even if cash itself is not affected. Statements prepared on this basis are said to reflect the **all-resources concept.** To recognize changes in *all* resources, these transactions are disclosed as *both* sources *and* uses of cash. Three examples follow:

Example A.   Issue a promissory note to acquire land at a cost of $12,000.

> Source of cash:
>   Issue note $12,000
> Use of cash:
>   Purchase land. $12,000

Example B.   Acquire a $250,000 building for $50,000 cash and a $200,000 mortgage note.

> Source of cash:
>   Issue mortgage note $200,000
> Use of cash:
>   Purchase building $250,000

Example C.   Issue 400 shares of stock in exchange for 50 of the company's outstanding convertible debenture bonds with $50,000 book value and $50,000 face value.

> Source of cash:
>   Issue common stock $50,000
> Use of cash:
>   Retire debentures. $50,000

In each example, each side of the transaction has a significant effect on the company's financial position. By applying the all-resources concept, we can produce funds flow statements that more fully reflect these significant effects.

> ### STATEMENT PREPARATION TECHNIQUE
>
> The technique that we suggest entails analyzing the change in each balance sheet amount—other than *cash* itself. The amount of each change is obtained by comparing the year-end balance sheet with the year-earlier balance sheet. The very first step, however, is to enter in the funds flow statement the period's net income—as the starting point to determine cash flow from operations.
>
> The first balance sheet changes to analyze are the accounts receivable, inventories, and operations-related payables, e.g., accounts payable, salaries payable, and taxes payable. (The treatment of notes payable and dividends payable is covered by the description in the paragraph below.) Increases and decreases are adjustments to income, as we showed in Exhibit 13–6 earlier.
>
> Next, we proceed to analyze the remaining balance sheet amounts. For each amount, we ask the following question: If the nature of the change indicates an effect on cash, what was the amount of the source of cash, the use of cash, or the adjustment to income?
>
> In performing these analyses, we are also mindful of the all-resources concept—treating as a source and as a use the effects of any noncash transaction that had a significant effect on two or more components of financial position (e.g., issue a note to buy land).

Using Funds Flow Analysis

The purpose of the statement of changes in financial position is to offer insights not otherwise available from either an income statement or a balance sheet. It is useful mainly because it throws light on management's investing and financing practices. The uses a company makes of its funds have a considerable influence on its future profitability and on the risks investors in the company are exposed to. Knowledge of how management gets the funds to finance these activities is important for the same reason.

Sources of Funds

The sources of business funds can be grouped into four main categories:

1. Current operations.
2. Borrowing.
3. Issuance of additional shares of the company's capital stock.
4. Sale of assets not originally acquired for resale.

Funds from current operations have four important advantages: (1) they come from a continuing source, the result of a myriad of individual actions and decisions, not the result of intermittent activity; (2) their source is the one most completely under management's control; (3) they provide a base that is essential if management wishes to raise additional funds by borrowing or by issuing additional shares of stock; and (4) they expose the company to no additional risks of the kind generally associated with borrowing.

Funds from the issuance of additional shares of capital stock also expose the company to no additional risks and provide part of the equity base for borrowing. Companies issue new shares primarily in connection with mergers or acquisitions of other companies, or from the conversion of convertible bonds or preferred stock. Public sales of new shares are relatively rare, partly because the costs of floating new issues can't be justified unless large sums are required.

Borrowing also has advantages. Investors in bonds may accept lower yields than investors in the company's common stock require. Furthermore, the company can deduct interest as an expense on its income tax returns, further reducing the cost of debt. Borrowing also gives the company access to the funds controlled by certain types of investors who don't participate in equity markets.

Borrowing increases the riskiness of investments in the company, however. Interest or the face value may fall due for payment just when the company finds itself temporarily short of cash. The company may have to curtail its other activities to make these payments or, in extreme cases, may fail to make the payments, causing it to fall into bankruptcy or receivership.

Given these factors, investors need to appraise the relative amounts of funds the company obtains from borrowing and from other sources. Is the company using enough debt to profit from the advantages of borrowing? Is it using too much debt, increasing the riskiness of investments in the company to too high a level? The amount that constitutes "enough" or "too much" depends on the industry, the company's existing financial structure, the state of financial markets, the company's own dynamics, and the investor's preferences.

Analysts ordinarily expect funds from operations to cover a major portion of most companies' needs for funds in most periods. In some periods, however, internally generated funds (i.e., cash flow from operations) may be relatively small or even negative. For a development-stage company, for example, or an established enterprise heavily engaged in research and product development, current operations are likely to generate small amounts of funds relative to management's needs.

Uses of Funds

The manner in which a company uses funds can also be revealing. The relative amounts of funds that are used to decrease the company's debt, pay cash dividends, and expand its productive capacity can disclose a great deal about its managerial priorities. Parties with specialized interests—creditors seeking to be paid and stockholders interested in cash dividends, for example—want to assess the company's past patterns of funds use.

Another key comparison the funds statement permits is the relationship between the company's purchases of plant assets and the amount of cash flow from operations. The more of its expenditures it can finance internally, the less exposed it is to weaknesses and disruptions in the financial markets.

The Funds Flow Perspective

Some readers of financial statements could become so enamored of funds flow analysis that they might conclude it is a valid *substitute* for profitability analysis. The fallacy lies in their failure to appreciate that these two types of analysis are complementary. One is concerned with profitability, the other with changes in financial structure and liquidity. One matches each period's revenues and expenses to document growth or decline in the long run; the other summarizes each period's events in terms of their short-run effects. Both statements are essential to a proper understanding of the results of the current period's activities; neither serves all purposes by itself.

Summary

The objective of the income statement is to summarize the economic productivity of the company's resources during the period. A statement of changes in financial position, in contrast, is designed to show how the company obtained and used financial resources during the period. The relationships between the structure of the resources provided and the amounts devoted to such uses as dividends, property additions, and debt retirement are important information for the evaluation of the company's financial management and for future planning by management. This statement also provides information on the business's ability to meet its short-term needs for cash.

This chapter has tried to explain what funds flows are and has presented a simple method that can be used to develop funds statements from income statement and balance sheet information. The method itself is less important, however, than the relationships between the funds statement and the other financial statements with which it is coupled.

**Appendix:
Worksheet Analysis**

The analysis in this chapter was conducted informally. In practice, an organized approach is generally necessary to prevent errors and to discover information that might otherwise go unnoticed. The procedure we'll describe consists of four steps:

1. Enter the balance sheet amounts or changes in a worksheet consisting of a set of T-accounts, one for each balance sheet element.
2. Set up three additional analytical T-accounts: Cash Flow from Operations, Other Sources of Cash, and Uses of Cash.
3. Using the income statement and any other available information, construct a set of entries the company could have made to produce the balance sheet changes that actually occurred, and enter these in the worksheet.
4. Transcribe the amounts in the three analytical T-accounts and put them in a statement format.

Exhibit 13–11 is the worksheet showing Peabody's balance sheet changes for 19x2, before the insertion of the explanatory entries reflecting our analyses of these changes. Although any sequence is acceptable, we prefer to concentrate on one balance sheet account or one pair of related balance sheet accounts at a time until its change has been completely accounted for. In view of that, we'll make our explanatory entries in the following order:

1. Changes in owners' equity.
2. Adjustments of net income to reflect changes in noncash elements of working capital.
3. Changes in plant assets.
4. Changes in other assets and liabilities.

Changes in Owners' Equity

1. Net income:

Cash Flow from Operations	42,000	
Retained Earnings		42,000

This entry shows that net income increased the balance in Retained Earnings and provided $42,000 in cash, other things being equal. The debit to the Cash Flow from Operations analytical account actually represents a debit to Cash; we use the separate account to enable us to assemble the amounts that, taken together, will give us the amount of cash flow from operations.

2. Cash dividends:

Retained Earnings	17,000	
Uses of Cash		17,000

This shows that the declaration and payment of cash dividends reduced the balance in Retained Earnings and required the disbursement of cash. (We know the entire amount was paid in cash because the balance sheet included no Dividends Payable amount.) The credit to Uses of Cash actually represents a credit to Cash; again, we use a separate analytical

EXHIBIT 13–11

PEABODY, INC.
T-Account Worksheet for Funds Statement Preparation
For the Year Ended December 31, 19x2

Accounts Receivable				Accounts Payable	
Net change	15,000			Net change	10,000

Inventories				Salaries Payable	
Net change	5,000			Net change	300

Investments				Taxes Payable	
		Net change	10,000	Net change	2,300

Machinery				Bonds Payable	
Net change	20,000			Net change	10,000

Accumulated Depreciation				Deferred Income Taxes	
Net change	15,000			Net change	5,000

Cash				Common Stock	
		Net change	3,000	Net change	10,000

Cash Flow from Operations				Additional Paid-in Capital	
				Net change	40,000

Other Sources of Cash				Retained Earnings	
				Net change	5,000

		Uses of Cash	

account to help us assemble data for use in preparing the funds statement.

3. Stock dividend:

Retained Earnings	20,000	
Common Stock		3,500
Additional Paid-in Capital...........................		16,500

This shows the effects of the stock dividend. None of the three analytical accounts is affected because the stock dividend neither provided nor used cash, nor did it constitute a flow of resources into or out of the company.

4. Issue of common stock:

Other Sources of Cash	30,000	
Common Stock		6,500
Additional Paid-in Capital...........................		23,500

This shows the amount of cash provided by the sale of new shares of the company's common stock. Together with entry 3, it accounts for the entire change in common stock and additional paid-in capital. These elements play no further role in the analysis.

Changes in Noncash Components of Working Capital

5. Increase in Accounts Receivable:

Accounts Receivable	15,000	
Cash Flow from Operations..........................		15,000

Since we know that Accounts Receivable increased by $15,000, we know that revenues exceeded collections by $15,000. This entry shows that cash flow from operations was $15,000 less than net income, other things being equal.

6. Increase in Inventories:

Inventories...	5,000	
Cash Flow from Operations..........................		5,000

The $5,000 increase in the inventory shows that, other things being equal, Peabody paid out $5,000 more cash than the cost of the goods it sold during the year. Taken by itself, this means that cash flow from operations was $5,000 less than net income.

7. Decrease in Accounts Payable:

Accounts Payable.....................................	10,000	
Cash Flow from Operations..........................		10,000

The $10,000 decrease in Accounts Payable is another indicator that $10,000 of the cash flow Peabody's net income provided was drawn off to pay suppliers $10,000 more than the amounts arising from Peabody's purchases during the year. This means that $10,000 must therefore be subtracted from net income.

8. Decrease in Salaries Payable:

Salaries Payable...	300	
Cash Flow from Operations................................		300

This shows that payments to employees exceeded the amounts shown as salaries expense by $300. Once again, this has to be subtracted from net income in the calculation of cash flow from operations.

9. Increase in Taxes Payable:

Cash Flow from Operations	2,300	
Taxes Payable		2,300

This adjustment to net income has the opposite effect to those of the four that preceded it. The company paid $2,300 less income tax in 19x2 than it accrued as currently payable and included in the determination of income that year. When an expense amount overstates the associated cash outflow, net income understates the amount of cash flow from operations. This entry corrects that understatement.

Changes in Plant Assets

10. Depreciation:

Cash Flow from Operations	11,000	
Accumulated Depreciation..........................		11,000

The debit to Cash Flow from Operations recognizes the need to add the year's depreciation expense back to net income for funds statement purposes.

11. Purchases of machinery:

Machinery	50,000	
Uses of Cash		50,000

This shows the effect on cash and on the machinery asset of the company's purchases of machinery during the year.

12. Sale of machinery:

Other Sources of Cash	3,000	
Cash Flow from Operations	1,000	
Accumulated Depreciation	26,000	
Machinery..		30,000

The debit to Other Sources of Cash identifies the proceeds from the sale of machinery, while the $1,000 debit to Cash Flow from Operations places the loss on the sale in a position to be added to net income. The debit to Accumulated Depreciation and the credit to Machinery remove the record of the machinery from the balance sheet.

Changes in Other Assets and Liabilities

13. Sale of investments:

Other Sources of Cash	13,000	
Cash Flow from Operations........................		3,000
Investments		10,000

The $13,000 debit to Other Sources of Cash shows the amount of cash received from the sale of investments during the year. The credit to Investments records the decrease in the balance of that account as a result of the transaction, while the credit to Cash Flow from Operations removes the gain from the net income, so that it won't be counted both there and in the proceeds from the sale under other sources of cash.

14. Retirement of bonds:

Bonds Payable	10,000	
Uses of Cash		10,000

This identifies the use of cash to retire outstanding bonds payable during the year.

15. Deferral of income taxes:

Cash Flow from Operations	5,000	
Deferred Income Taxes..............................		5,000

The debit to Cash Flow from Operations is our final addition to net income to identify the amount of cash provided by operations. The credit to Deferred Income Taxes brings the balance in this T-account up to the amount shown on the year-end balance sheet.

The Completed Worksheet

Exhibit 13–12 shows the T-account worksheet with all the analytical entries posted to the T-accounts. The entries in the balance sheet T-accounts other than cash itself account for all the changes in those elements. No entry has been made in the Cash T-account, because the entries we would have made there were made in the three analytical T-accounts. The algebraic sum of the balances in those three accounts is equal to the $3,000 net change in the cash balance:

Debit balances:	
Cash flow from operations	$28,000
Other sources of cash	46,000
Total	74,000
Credit balance: Uses of cash	77,000
Net change in cash (credit)	$ (3,000)

EXHIBIT 13–12

PEABODY, INC.
Completed Funds Statement Worksheet
For the Year Ended December 31, 19x2

Accounts Receivable		
Net change	15,000	
(5)	15,000	

Accounts Payable		
Net change	10,000	
(7)	10,000	

Inventories		
Net change	5,000	
(6)	5,000	

Salaries Payable		
Net change	300	
(8)	300	

Investments		
	Net change	10,000
	(13)	10,000

Taxes Payable		
	Net change	2,300
	(9)	2,300

Machinery			
Net change	20,000		
(11)	50,000	(12)	30,000

Bonds Payable		
Net change	10,000	
(14)	10,000	

Accumulated Depreciation			
Net change	15,000		
(12)	26,000	(10)	11,000

Deferred Income Taxes		
	Net change	5,000
	(15)	5,000

Cash		
	Net change	3,000

Common Stock		
	Net change	10,000
	(3)	3,500
	(4)	6,500

Cash Flow from Operations

(1)	Income	42,000	(5)	Receivables	15,000
(9)	Taxes	2,300	(6)	Inventories	5,000
(10)	Depreciation	11,000	(7)	Payables	10,000
(12)	Loss on		(8)	Salaries	300
	sale of		(13)	Gain on	
	machinery	1,000		invest-	
(15)	Deferred			ments	3,000
	income				
	taxes	5,000			

Bal. 28,000

Additional Paid-in Capital		
	Net change	40,000
	(3)	16,500
	(4)	23,500

Retained Earnings

			Net change	5,000
(2)		17,000	(1)	42,000
(3)		20,000		

Other Sources of Cash

(4)	Sale of	
	stock	30,000
(12)	Sale of	
	machinery	3,000
(13)	Sale of	
	invest-	
	ments	13,000

Bal. 46,000

Uses of Cash

(2)	Dividends	17,000
(11)	Machinery	
	purchases	50,000
(14)	Debt	
	retirement	10,000

Bal. 77,000

Since all other balance sheet changes have been accounted for, our work is complete. The only step remaining is to assemble the amounts shown in the three analytical accounts in a form suitable for funds statement presentation.

Key Terms	Add-back adjustment	Sources of cash
	All-resources concept	Statement of changes in financial position
	Cash flow from operations	
	Funds flow	Subtract-from adjustment
	Income adjustments	Uses of cash

Independent Study Problems (Solutions in Appendix B)

1. Analysis of Plant and Equipment Changes.   Below are certain balances from Placque Corporation's financial statements:

	19x2	19x3
Balance Sheet		
Plant and equipment............	$8,500	$8,900
Accumulated depreciation	3,300	3,600
Income Statement		
Depreciation expense		$ 900
Loss on retirements.............		400

A note to the financial statements reports that property with an original cost of $1,300 and accumulated depreciation of $600 was sold during 19x3 for $300.

a. List the transactions that affected the plant and equipment and accumulated depreciation during the year.
b. Indicate how, if at all, each of these would be shown on a statement of changes in financial position.

2. Preparing a Funds Flow Statement Without an Income Statement. The following amounts (in $000) have been taken from Anderson Company's balance sheets for the beginning and end of the year 19x1:

	Beginning	Ending
Cash.	$ 14,739	$ 19,239
Accounts receivable.	18,585	35,916
Inventory	23,422	21,936
Long-term marketable securities, at cost . . .	—	1,005
Plant assets.	31,414	49,096
Accumulated depreciation.	(13,237)	(18,421)
Total assets	$ 74,923	$108,771
Accounts payable.	$ 23,312	$ 20,844
Accruals payable	8,733	13,029
Current taxes payable	10,491	15,025
Long-term bonds payable	—	7,000
Deferred income taxes.	4,362	4,899
Total liabilities.	46,898	60,797
Preferred stock ($100 par value per share). .	1,347	1,123
Common stock ($1 par value per share)	4,317	4,492
Additional paid-in capital.	7,179	19,014
Retained earnings	15,182	23,345
Total owners' equity	28,025	47,974
Total liabilities and owners' equity . . .	$ 74,923	$108,771

Additional information on transactions during 19x1:

1. Net income for the year, $8,243,000.
2. Preferred dividends declared and paid, $80,000.
3. Preferred stock repurchased and retired, 2,240 shares; the purchase price exceeded the par value by $37,000, and this excess was charged correctly to additional paid-in capital.
4. Common stock issued, 175,000 shares.
5. Depreciation (on income statement), $5,501,000.
6. Cost of property, plant, and equipment acquired, $18,082,000.

Prepare a statement of changes in financial position for the year.

3. Cash Flow from Operations. Andy, Inc.'s 19x6 income statement was as follows:

Revenue from sales....................		$325,400	
Less: Bad debts.......................		4,100	
Net sales.........................			$321,300
Equity in Wilson Corporation's earnings ..			12,000
Total revenues..................			333,300
Expenses:			
Cost of goods sold...................		178,600	
Salaries...........................		68,800	
Depreciation.......................		14,900	
Insurance		1,000	
Research and development		2,500	
Patent amortization..................		1,800	
Interest		21,300	
Income tax:			
Current...........................	$13,200		
Deferred..........................	3,100	16,300	
Total expenses			305,200
Net income..........................			$ 28,100

You have the following additional information:

1. Seventy percent of gross revenues from sales were on account.
2. All the $184,000 merchandise purchases were on account.
3. Salaries payable totaled $3,200 at year-end.
4. Amortization of premium on bonds payable was $2,700.
5. No dividends were received from other corporations.
6. Andy declared cash dividends of $8,000.
7. Changes in current assets and current liabilities were as follows:

	Increase (Decrease)
Cash..................................	$ 1,000
Marketable securities.....................	3,200
Accounts receivable.....................	(14,300)
Allowance for uncollectibles..............	(3,800)
Inventory	5,400
Prepaid insurance......................	1,400
Accounts payable (for merchandise)	11,300
Salaries payable	(4,100)
Dividends payable......................	(6,000)

Prepare a schedule that calculates the amount of cash flow from operations.

4. Components of Funds Flow Statement. Gamma Corporation had $179,000 of cash on May 1, 19x2. The ten transactions listed below occurred during May, and you are to determine which amounts should appear in Gamma's May 19x2 statement of changes in financial position.

For each item, identify both the dollar amount and its location—that is, whether it would appear as a positive or a negative adjustment to net income in the measurement of cash flow from operations, as some other source of cash, or as a use of cash.

1. Declared and paid a $7,000 cash dividend.
2. Sold for $24,000 cash land that had cost $27,000 two years earlier.
3. Sold for cash 2,000 shares of $2 par stock for $5 a share.
4. Bought machinery for $6,500 in exchange for a note due in eight months.
5. Bought a computer, giving in exchange $10,000 cash plus real estate that had cost $7,000 in an earlier period.
6. Equipment depreciation for May, $2,200.
7. Issued for cash $250,000 face-value bonds at a 6 percent premium.
8. Bought treasury stock for $4,000 and resold the stock four days later for $4,500.
9. Paid a lawyer $2,400 for services performed, billed, and recorded correctly in 19x1.
10. Borrowed $20,000 on May 1 at an 18 percent rate of interest, loan and interest to be repaid on August 1, 19x2.

Exercises and Problems

5. Changes in Plant and Equipment. Granada Corporation's income statement for 19x1 showed depreciation of $150,000 and a $42,000 loss on the sale of equipment. The amount of accumulated depreciation increased by $37,000 between the beginning and the end of the year, and the original cost of the company's plant and equipment went from $1 million at the beginning of the year to $2 million on December 31, 19x1. The original cost of the equipment retired during the year amounted to $175,000.

Which amounts arising from changes in plant and equipment would appear on the funds flow statement for the year? Where would they appear and in what amounts?

6. Changes in Plant and Equipment. A note to the financial statements of Solo Corporation revealed the following:

	Plant and Equipment	Accumulated Depreciation
Beginning balance	$ 650,000	$ 200,000
Additions	210,000	45,000
Retirements	(140,000)	(110,000)
Ending balance	$ 720,000	$ 135,000

One item on the company's income statement for the year was a gain on the sale of equipment, $15,000.

Which of these items would appear on the statement of changes in financial position for the year, and how would they be shown?

7. Interpretation: Funds Flow versus Income Flow. Arkville Transit Company operates a network of bus lines in a small city. The company can abandon a bus route only with the approval of the city government, which also regulates the fares it charges bus riders. Last year, Arkville Transit reported a small operating loss, and earnings are unlikely to improve in the near future. The following income statement for last year is likely to be typical of those to be prepared for the next few years:

Fares and other revenues		$1,000,000
Expenses:		
Salaries and wages	$650,000	
Fuel and lubricants	170,000	
Depreciation	100,000	
Tires and batteries	20,000	
Repair parts	30,000	
Other expenses	40,000	
Total expenses		1,010,000
Net income (Loss)		$ (10,000)

The company's balance sheet showed the following amounts at the beginning and end of last year:

	Beginning of Year	End of Year
Assets		
Current assets:		
Cash	$ 100,000	$ 90,000
Receivables	50,000	40,000
Inventories	150,000	160,000
Total current assets	300,000	290,000
Plant and equipment (net)	940,000	920,000
Total assets	$1,240,000	$1,210,000
Liabilities and Owners' Equity		
Current liabilities:		
Accounts payable	$ 66,000	$ 147,000
Salaries payable	4,000	3,000
Total current liabilities	70,000	150,000
Bonds payable	100,000	—
Common stock	260,000	260,000
Retained earnings	810,000	800,000
Total liabilities and owners' equity	$1,240,000	$1,210,000

John Bergson bought an 80 percent interest in this company late last year for $200,000. When shown the income statement above, he replied, "Good! That's just what I'd hoped for."

Bergson is a professional investor, not given to letting sentiment or emotion affect his investment decisions. Furthermore, he has little time to devote to active participation in the management of the companies he invests in.

a. How did he probably justify his decision to invest in Arkville Transit Company?

b. What plans does he probably have for his investment in Arkville Transit? How do these plans differ from the actions of the previous owners? Do you think he is likely to achieve his objectives? Support your answers with numbers from the problem.

8. Statement Format: Discussion Question. Borst Corporation's annual report for 19x1 presented its funds statement in the following format:

Sources of funds:		
Cash flow from operations		$417
Sale of treasury stock		14
Sale of land.		48
Short-term borrowing		100
Total sources of funds.		579
Uses of funds:		
Purchases of investments.	$ 75	
Purchases of plant and equipment	280	
Retirement of long-term bonds	200	
Cash dividends.	240	
Total uses of funds.		795
Decrease in cash and marketable securities		$216

Jean Daniels, a member of the company's board of directors, asked why the decrease in cash and marketable securities wasn't shown as one of the sources of funds, so that total sources and total uses were shown to be equal. "After all," she said, "we used the money to help meet our needs for funds this year. We had to find sources totaling $795, and if we hadn't had the cash we'd have been in tough shape."

"I don't agree," replied Andy Grady, Borst's director of public relations. "The purpose of this statement is to help people like me understand what has happened to our cash balance. Burying this change in the sources, or in the uses when the cash balance goes up, just wouldn't show that. I think it would be confusing."

Take a position in this dispute and explain the reasons for your conclusions.

9. Income and Cash Flows. Stratton Corporation's accounting records were in a state of disarray. Management was satisfied that the seven amounts that follow were correct. It was disconcerting, however, that the absence of three key amounts would prevent timely and accurate issuance of Stratton's 19x4 financial statements.

Accounts receivable:
January 1	$11,400
December 31	A
Collections of receivables	47,300
Cost of goods sold	B
Gross margin	29,400

Merchandise inventory:
January 1	17,500
December 31	18,900
Purchases of merchandise	63,600

Sales:
Cash sales	39,500
Credit sales	C

Calculate the amounts designated by A, B, and C.

10. Converting Income Statement to Cash Flow Statement. Lazarus Company's annual report showed the following income statement for the year 19x2:

Sales		$50
Cost of goods sold	$30	
Depreciation	2	
Other expenses	10	42
Net income		$ 8

The balance sheets at the beginning and end of the year showed the following:

	Beginning		End			Beginning	End
Cash		$ 4		$ 5	Accounts Payable	$ 5	$ 3
Accounts receivable		8		10	Capital Stock	11	14
Merchandise inventory . . .		6		7	Retained Earnings	15	22
Plant and equipment:							
Original cost	$20		$26				
Accum. depreciation . . .	(7)	13	(9)	17	Total liabilities and		
Total assets		$31		$39	owners' equity	$31	$39

All accounts payable arose out of the purchase of merchandise or the purchase of other goods and services for immediate consumption. All accounts receivable arose out of sales of merchandise to customers.

a. How much cash was received from customers in 19x2?

b. What was the total cost of goods purchased in 19x2?

c. How much cash was paid to suppliers, employees, and others during the year for goods or current services?

d. How much cash was provided by the company's operations during the year?

e. Calculate and list the company's other sources and uses of cash during this year.

11. Funds Flow Components. Digitonic Corporation earned $42,000 net income during 19x4, and its directors declared and paid a cash dividend in November. Machinery was sold for $58,000, and a $12,000 loss on the sale was recorded. Machinery purchases totaled $165,000 including a July purchase for which a $40,000 promissory note was issued. Bonds were retired at their face value, and the issuance of new common shares produced an infusion of cash.

Digitonic's comparative balance sheets were as follows (in thousands):

	December 31	
	19x3	19x4
Cash	$ 42	$ 52
Receivables	111	98
Inventory.............................	155	162
Machinery............................	630	675
Accumulated depreciation	(105)	(95)
Total assets	$ 833	$892
Accounts payable	$ 143	$119
Long-term notes payable	75	100
Deferred income taxes	40	46
Bonds payable.........................	160	120
Common stock	20	28
Additional paid-in capital................	260	322
Retained earnings......................	135	157
Total liabilities and owners' equity	$ 833	$892

a. What was Digitonic's depreciation expense in 19x4?

b. What was the amount of cash flow from operations?

c. What was the amount of cash proceeds from the issuance of new shares of stock?

d. What was the amount of the cash dividend declared and paid?

e. By what amount would you expect the total sources of cash to differ from the total uses of cash?

12. Cash Flow from Operations: Alternative Formats. Sanford Corporation's accountant prepared the following schedule to convert 19x4 net income to cash flow from operations (all amounts in thousands).

	Accrual	Adjustment	Cash Flow
Sales	$946		
Change in accounts receivable		$ (22)	
Collections from customers			$924
Cost of goods sold	364		
Change in inventory		48	
Change in accounts payable		(27)	
Payments to suppliers			343
Depreciation expense	44	44	—
Salaries expense	275		
Change in salaries payable		34	
Salary payments			241
Rent expense	58		
Change in prepaid rent		(8)	
Rent payments			66
Income tax expense	190		
Change in taxes payable		(12)	
Change in deferred income taxes		58	
Tax payments			144
Net income	$ 15		
Net adjustment		$115	
Cash flow from operations			$130

Although Sanford's chief financial officer favored this format for communicating within the company, he didn't want competitors to have access to the components of cash flow.

a. Prepare the presentation in which adjustments are made directly to net income rather than to the determinants of net income.

b. Explain whether the alternative achieves the chief financial officer's objective.

13. Cash Flow from Operations: Alternative Formats. Dudley Corporation's 19x6 income statement was as follows:

Sales revenues		$2,564,700
Less: Cost of goods sold	$742,500	
Salaries expense	268,600	
Depreciation expense	114,200	
Advertising expense	221,500	
Interest expense	156,000	
Tax expense	347,400	1,850,200
Net income		$ 714,500

During 19x6, accounts receivable increased by $28,600 and accounts payable to suppliers increased by $19,800. Current taxes payable fell by

$2,700 while deferred taxes payable increased by $5,800. Cash interest payments amounted to $147,500 while payments to Dudley's advertising agency exceeded advertising expense by $12,300. Salaries payable at year-end exceeded the year-earlier balance by $8,800, and the cost of Dudley's ending inventory was $16,600 less than the cost of the goods on hand at the beginning of the year.

a. Calculate the cash flow from operations as it would be calculated using *net income* as the starting point.
b. Calculate the cash flow from operations by transforming each income determinant into its cash counterpart.

14. Using Fund Flows to Derive Cash Balance.   Eagan, Inc.'s treasurer prepared the following schedule for 19x5 (all amounts in thousands):

Acquisition of treasury stock	$ 200
Cash, January 1	8,000
Payments on long-term borrowings	500
Proceeds from long-term borrowings	1,500
Payments for machinery	2,800
Total	$13,000

Cash dividends declared and paid	$ 900
Exchange of mortgage note for real estate	3,000
Increase in accounts payable	3,000
Net income	2,000
Reduction in accounts receivable	4,000
Sales of stock to company employees	100
Total	$13,000

Eagan's president recognized that many of the amounts contained in the report customarily appear in statements of changes in financial position. Despite the fact that the two *total* amounts were in balance, the president found it disconcerting that the report disclosed neither the end-of-year cash balance nor the amount of the change in the cash balance during 19x5.

Calculate the two amounts that the president was unable to discern.

15. Preparing a Funds Flow Statement Without an Income Statement.
General Ferry Corporation reported the following beginning and ending balance sheets in 19x3:

	January 1, 19x3		December 31, 19x3	
Assets				
Current assets:				
Cash.....................................		$ 15		$ 10
Accounts receivable.....................		10		15
Inventory...............................		40		60
Total current assets		65		85
Plant and equipment.....↓..................	$100		$113	
Less: Accumulated depreciation	40	60	45	68
Total assets		$125		$153
Liabilities and Owners' Equity				
Current liabilities:				
Accounts payable.........................		$ 10		$ 12
Bank loan payable		20		40
Total current liabilities..................		30		52
Deferred income taxes		5		7
Owners' equity:				
Common stock ($1 par)....................	$ 25		$ 29	
Additional paid-in capital	15		20	
Retained earnings	50	90	45	94
Total liabilities and owners' equity		$125		$153

Additional information:
1. Net income for the year (including $1 gain on sale of plant and equipment), $5.
2. Cash dividends declared and paid during the year, $10.
3. Depreciation on plant and equipment during the year, $8.
4. Plant and equipment acquired during the year:
   For cash, $10.
   For four new shares of common stock, $9.

Prepare a statement of changes in financial position.

16. Sources and Uses of Funds.
Summit Company had the following transactions during 19x5:

1. Bought equipment for $150,000. Paid 10 percent cash and signed a three-year note for the balance.
2. Used temporarily idle cash to buy government securities for $14,000.
3. Issued 10,000, $2 par value preferred shares for $10.50 a share.
4. Reclassified a $50,000 note payable as a current liability, in recognition of its November 30, 19x6, maturity date.

5. On December 31, 19x5, issued a $1 million, 20-year, 12 percent bond for $880,000.
6. Declared a $12,000 cash dividend payable on January 20, 19x6.
7. Bought 1,200 treasury shares for $22 a share.
8. Sold real estate for $40,000, yielding a $15,000 gain.
9. Bondholders converted 220 of the company's $1,000 debenture bonds. These bonds had a net-of-unamortized-discount balance of $196,000. In exchange, Summit issued 8,800 common shares.
10. Sold the government securities (item 2) for $15,000.
11. Sold the treasury shares (item 7) for $25,000.

For each of these items, determine the amounts, if any, that would be shown as (1) sources of cash, (2) uses of cash, or (3) adjustments to net income in the calculation of cash flow from operations.

17. Preparing a Funds Flow Statement Given an Income Statement. Hartwell Stores operates a chain of retail hardware stores. Its income statement for 19x5 showed the following:

Gross sales		$120
Less: Bad debts	$ 2	
Cost of goods sold	80	
Wages and salaries	15	
Depreciation	5	
Income tax expense	4	
Miscellaneous operating expense	8	114
Net income		$ 6

The following amounts were taken from the company's balance sheets at the beginning and end of 19x5:

	January 1	December 31
Assets		
Cash	$10	$16
Accounts receivable (net)	20	23
Inventory (at cost)	15	19
Plant and equipment (net)	30	35
Total assets	$75	$93
Liabilities and Owners' Equity		
Accounts payable	$11	$17
Bonds payable (long-term)	22	21
Deferred income taxes	3	4
Common stock	25	39
Retained earnings	14	12
Total liabilities and owners' equity	$75	$93

You have the following additional information:

1. The company declared and paid $3 in cash dividends to its shareholders in 19x5.
2. A stock dividend of $5 was declared and distributed.
3. Equipment with an original cost of $7 and accumulated depreciation of $6 was sold. There was neither a gain nor a loss on this transaction.
4. All accounts payable arose from the purchase of merchandise.

Prepare a statement of changes in financial position for 19x5.

18. Preparing a Funds Flow Statement Given an Income Statement.

You have the following information about the financial affairs of Carter Company:

CARTER COMPANY
Balance Sheets
As of December 31, 19x2 and December 31, 19x3

	19x2		19x3	
Assets				
Current assets:				
Cash		$ 2		$ 1
Accounts receivable		3		4
Inventories		5		6
Total current assets		10		11
Land, plant, and equipment, cost	$20		$29	
Less: Accumulated depreciation	8	12	9	20
Total assets		$22		$31
Liabilities and Owners' Equity				
Current liabilities:				
Accounts payable		$ 4		$ 3
Taxes payable		1		2
Notes payable		—		2
Total current liabilities		5		7
Bonds payable		—		5
Deferred taxes		3		4
Total liabilities		8		16
Owners' equity:				
Common stock	$ 4		$ 5	
Additional paid-in capital	2		4	
Retained earnings	8		6	
Total owners' equity		14		15
Total liabilities and owners' equity		$22		$31

CARTER COMPANY
Income Statement
For the Year Ended December 31, 19x3

Sales revenues		$51
Operating expenses:		
Cost of goods sold	$25	
Depreciation	4	
Other	15	44
Operating income		7
Gain on sale of equipment		2
Income before taxes		9
Income tax expense		4
Net income		$ 5

Additional information:

1. Land purchased during the year in exchange for bonds, $5.
2. Cash dividends declared and paid, $4.
3. Stock dividends, capitalized at $3.
4. Original cost of plant and equipment retired and sold during the year, $7.

Prepare a statement of changes in financial position.

19. Preparing and Interpreting a Funds Flow Statement Without an Income Statement. Traydown Corporation's financial position went from bad to worse during 19x8, although net income showed a satisfactory increase over that of prior years. Despite the company's negotiation of a $100,000 bank loan early in 19x8, the cash balance decreased to a dangerous point by the end of the year. The balance sheets showed the following:

TRAYDOWN CORPORATION
Comparative Balance Sheets
As of December 31, 19x7 and December 31, 19x8
(in thousands)

	19x7	19x8
Assets		
Current assets:		
Cash	$ 50	$ 30
Receivables	200	220
Inventories	150	200
Total current assets	400	450
Buildings and fixtures	300	280
Less: Accumulated depreciation	(90)	(70)
Total buildings and fixtures	210	210
Total assets	$610	$660

Liabilities and Owners' Equity

Current liabilities:		
Accounts and wages payable..............	$200	$180
Bank loan payable........................	50	150
Total current liabilities	250	330
Mortgage payable.........................	70	55
Deferred income taxes.....................	20	23
Long-term note payable...................	10	12
Total liabilities	350	420
Owners' equity:		
Common stock (par)....................	140	130
Retained earnings......................	120	110
Total owners' equity.................	260	240
Total liabilities and owners' equity....	$610	$660

Notes (all amounts in thousands):

1. Net income for 19x8 was $29.
2. Total sales were approximately the same in 19x8 as in 19x7.
3. A building with an original cost of $52 and accumulated depreciation of $30 was sold for $56, cash.
4. Depreciation for the year was $10.
5. Cash dividends paid were $23.
6. One stockholder sold her common stock back to the company for $26, cash. The par value of this stock was $10, and the remaining $16 of the repurchase price was charged to retained earnings.

a. Prepare a statement of changes in financial position.
b. Prepare a brief report, addressed to the loan officers of the company's bank, commenting on any items in your statement you think would help them reach a decision on renewing or increasing the bank's loan to the company. They have a statement of forecasted cash flows for 19x9 but feel that the 19x8 funds flow statement can provide additional information the forecast does not give.

20. Preparing a Funds Flow Statement Without an Income Statement.

Argus Company's annual report showed the following balance sheets for the beginning and end of its most recent fiscal year:

		Beginning		End		Change
Assets						
Current assets:						
Cash		$ 10		$ 20		+$10
Accounts receivable		30		51		+ 21
Inventory		50		45		− 5
Total current assets		90		116		+ 26
Investments in other corporations		80		50		− 30
Plant assets	$220		$228		+$ 8	
Less: Accumulated depreciation	120		124		+ 4	
Total plant assets		100		104		+ 4
Total assets		$270		$270		—
Liabilities and Owners' Equity						
Current liabilities:						
Accounts payable		$ 40		$ 35		−$ 5
Dividends payable		—		2		+ 2
Total current liabilities		40		37		− 3
Bonds payable		40		—		− 40
Deferred income taxes		20		23		+ 3
Total liabilities		100		60		− 40
Owners' equity:						
Common stock (par)	$ 25		$ 30		+$ 5	
Additional paid-in capital	65		90		+ 25	
Retained earnings	80		90		+ 10	
Total owners' equity		170		210		+ 40
Total liabilities and owners' equity		$270		$270		—

You have the following additional information:

1. Net income for the year, $30.
2. Cash dividends declared during the year, $8.
3. Stock dividends declared during the year (par value $2), $12.
4. Depreciation on fixed assets for the year, $17.
5. Purchases of fixed assets during the year:
   For cash, $21.
   In exchange for stock (par value $3), $18.
6. Cash proceeds from sale of fixed assets during the year, $2.
7. Cash proceeds from sale of investments during the year, $42; no investments were purchased during the year, and all investments are shown on the balance sheet at cost.
8. All accounts payable were to vendors of merchandise bought for resale.

9. Argus Company called and retired all its bonds payable, five years before their maturity date.

a. Prepare a statement of changes in financial position.

b. The year in question was a year of severe inflation. Judging from the funds flow statement and from information in the problem, do you think the actions taken by management were appropriate in an inflationary situation?

21. Preparing a Funds Flow Statement: Without an Income Statement.

The net changes in the balance sheet of Manor Company for the year 19x1 are shown below:

	Debit	Credit
Cash	$ 11,400	
Accounts receivable		$ 4,100
Inventory.....................	47,600	
Investments		25,000
Land	3,200	
Buildings	35,000	
Machinery....................	6,000	
Office equipment..............		1,500
Accumulated depreciation:		
Buildings....................		2,000
Machinery....................		900
Office equipment.............	600	
Accounts payable		13,800
Salaries payable...............		3,700
Bonds payable.................		40,000
Discount on bonds	2,000	
Preferred stock	10,000	
Common stock.................		12,400
Additional paid-in capital		5,400
Retained earnings.............		7,000
Total....................	$115,800	$115,800

Additional information:

1. Cash dividends of $18,000 were declared in November 19x1 and paid in December 19x1. A 2 percent stock dividend on the common stock was issued March 31, 19x1, when the market value was $12.50 per share.
2. The investments were sold for $27,500.
3. A building that had cost $45,000 and had a book value of $40,500 was sold for $50,000.
4. The following entry was made to record an exchange of an old machine for a new one:

Machinery...	13,000	
Accumulated Depreciation—Machinery	5,000	
Machinery...		7,000
Cash		11,000

5. A fully depreciated office machine that cost $1,500 was written off.
6. Preferred stock of $10,000 par value was redeemed for $10,200.
7. The company sold 1,000 shares of its common stock (par value $10) on June 15, 19x1, for $15 a share. There were 13,240 shares outstanding on December 31, 19x1.

Prepare a statement of changes in financial position for the year 19x1.

(AICPA adapted)

22. Cash Flows in Growth Company. John Q. Wixon, sole owner and chief executive of Wixon Widget Company, operated a very simple business. He made widgets at a cost of 80 cents each and sold them for $1. He had no other expenses, and Wixon Widget Company's income therefore amounted to 20 cents for each widget he sold.

All production costs were paid in cash; suppliers in this industry were unwilling to provide credit to their customers. Mr. Wixon tried to keep his inventory at the end of each month equal to the number of units sold during that month. Inventory *turnover* therefore was 12 times a year when sales were constant; this was better than any of Mr. Wixon's competitors had been able to achieve.

All sales were made on 30-day credit—that is, customers were required to pay cash one month after receiving their widgets. These terms were strictly enforced, even though Mr. Wixon's competitors granted more liberal terms.

Wixon Widget Company had no liabilities on January 1, 19x1. It had the following assets on that date:

Cash	$1,075
Accounts receivable	1,000
Inventory	800

During January, Mr. Wixon produced 1,000 widgets, sold 1,000 widgets, and collected $1,000 in cash from his customers. The company's net income for January was $200 and its assets on January 31, 19x1, were:

Cash	$1,275
Accounts receivable	1,000
Inventory	800

In February, sales increased to 1,500 widgets (500 widgets more than in January). The company produced 2,000 widgets during the month and collected $1,000 from customers. Net income was $300.

Mr. Wixon sold 2,000 widgets in March, produced 2,500 widgets, and collected $1,500. The company's net income jumped to $400.

Sales continued to increase in April and seemed likely to continue to increase by 500 units a month indefinitely. In fact, the sales picture looked so good that Mr. Wixon went on vacation on April 20. On May 1, he received a telegram from home: "Return immediately. We're overdrawn at the bank." Returning to the office, he found that production, sales, and collections had gone according to plan but that the company's bank account was overdrawn by $225. Extremely puzzled, he rushed to the bank, asking for a loan and an explanation of what had gone wrong.

a. Prepare a table showing revenues, expenses, and net income for each month, January through December, assuming no further action is taken.

b. Prepare a table showing cash receipts, cash disbursements, and net cash flow for each month.

c. Prepare a list of the company's assets as of the end of each month. (The company had no liabilities at the beginning of the year. If the results indicate that cash disbursements will reduce the cash balance to less than zero, show the deficiency as a negative amount on the *Cash* line rather than as a liability. Ignore interest costs on any such amounts.)

d. Using the amounts in the tables above, prepare an answer to Mr. Wixon's question. What were the factors that determined the size of the monthly cash flows?

e. What actions could Mr. Wixon take to solve the problem that had arisen? (Suggestion: examine the effects on cash flows of actions that might be taken to influence each of the factors that you have identified as a determinant of cash flow.)

23. Preparing and Interpreting a Funds Flow Statement, Given an Income Statement. Apex Company's financial statements for 19x2 showed the following (all amounts are in thousands):

APEX COMPANY
Balance Sheets
As of December 31, 19x1 and December 31, 19x2

	19x1	19x2
Assets		
Current assets:		
Cash	$ 2,250	$ 1,783
Accounts receivable, net	1,064	1,382
Inventories	936	1,179
Total current assets	4,250	4,344
Long-term assets:		
Land	198	273
Buildings, machinery, and equipment	6,750	6,700
Less: Accumulated depreciation	(2,000)	(2,270)
Investments in subsidiaries	3,002	3,018
Goodwill	100	90
Total assets	$12,300	$12,155

	19x1	19x2
Liabilities and Owners' Equity		
Current liabilities:		
Accounts payable	$ 2,350	$ 1,080
Taxes payable	650	550
Total current liabilities	3,000	1,630
Long-term liabilities:		
Bonds payable	—	1,000
Bond premium	—	72
Liability for pensions	150	150
Deferred income taxes	90	110
Total liabilities	3,240	2,962
Owners' equity:		
Common stock, at par	1,500	1,510
Additional paid-in capital	1,910	2,000
Appropriation for contingencies	300	400
Retained earnings	5,350	5,283
Total liabilities and owners' equity	$12,300	$12,155

APEX COMPANY
Income Statement
For the Year Ended December 31, 19x2

Sales		$ 9,880
Income from unconsolidated subsidiaries		206
Gain on sale of land		15
Total		10,101
Expenses:		
Cost of goods sold	$7,414	
Selling and administrative expenses	1,843	
Amortization of goodwill	10	
Bond interest expense	97	
Income taxes	354	
Total expenses		9,718
Net income		$ 383

Additional information:

1. All the company's subsidiaries were in the United States. Income on investments in unconsolidated subsidiaries was recognized on an equity basis.
2. Expenses for the year included depreciation in the amount of $496,000.
3. The only dividend declared during the year on Apex common stock was the cash dividend declared during November and paid in December.
4. Buildings, equipment, and machinery purchased in 19x2 cost $246,000.

5. Apex Company issued stock during the year in exchange for land. No other common stock transactions occurred during the year.
6. Bonds were issued on January 2, 19x2, with a 10 percent coupon rate.

a. Prepare a statement of changes in financial position for the year.
b. What does this funds flow statement tell you about management's financial policies and practices?

24. Using Funds Flows Statements to Explain Changes in Financial Status. Mastik Company was incorporated in 19x1 by two young electronics engineers, Frank Orsini and Rosemary Newman, to manufacture and market a new electronic relay they had developed. The initial share capital consisted of 10,000 shares, divided equally between the two founders. Each founder paid the company $10,000 in cash for those shares. An additional block of 2,000 shares was issued in 19x3 to a friend of the founders in exchange for $5 a share, paid in cash.

The company's first product was highly successful, and in 19x3 operations were transferred to a larger building which the company leased for five years. Purchase of additional equipment at that time was financed by a five-year loan from an equipment finance company. This same company also granted loans for equipment purchased in subsequent years.

Mastik's sales continued to grow at a rapid rate as new products and services were introduced. Net income grew even faster, as shown in the following table:

	19x4	19x5	19x6
Sales	$194,000	$318,000	$390,000
Expenses:			
Wages and salaries	87,000	178,000	191,000
Materials and supplies	58,000	75,000	94,000
Rent	12,000	12,000	12,000
Depreciation	5,000	7,000	8,000
Other operating expenses (including interest)	20,000	22,000	31,000
Income taxes	4,000	8,000	18,000
Total expenses	186,000	302,000	354,000
Net income	$ 8,000	$ 16,000	$ 36,000

In March 19x7, Mastik's commercial bank notified management that the company's bank balance had fallen to less than the minimum required by the bank. The bank was unwilling to extend additional credit unless the company was able to broaden its ownership base and attract more stockholder capital. The company's balance sheets for the previous four years were as follows:

	19x3	19x4	19x5	19x6
Assets				
Current assets:				
Cash....................................	$18,000	$ 21,000	$ 15,000	$ 8,000
Accounts receivable.....................	20,000	29,000	48,000	74,000
Inventories.............................	11,000	15,000	30,000	55,000
Prepayments............................	2,000	3,000	4,000	5,000
Total current assets	51,000	68,000	97,000	142,000
Plant assets:				
Machinery and equipment................	50,000	60,000	65,000	82,000
Less: Accumulated depreciation..........	(6,000)	(11,000)	(18,000)	(26,000)
Net plant assets......................	44,000	49,000	47,000	56,000
Total assets......................	$95,000	$117,000	$144,000	$198,000
Liabilities and Owners' Equity				
Current liabilities:				
Accounts payable........................	$ 3,000	$ 6,000	$ 10,000	$ 14,000
Wages and taxes payable	4,000	5,000	9,000	20,000
Notes payable to bank...................	2,000	7,000	12,000	20,000
Total current liabilities	9,000	18,000	31,000	54,000
Equipment loan payable..................	30,000	35,000	30,000	25,000
Notes payable to stockholders.............	4,000	4,000	7,000	12,000
Total liabilities	43,000	57,000	68,000	91,000
Owners' equity:				
Common stock..........................	30,000	30,000	30,000	30,000
Retained earnings	22,000	30,000	46,000	77,000
Total owners' equity	52,000	60,000	76,000	107,000
Total liabilities and owners' equity ..	$95,000	$117,000	$144,000	$198,000

Orsini and Newman were stunned by this news. They didn't understand how they had gotten into such a difficult position, since they had never reported a loss, even in their first year of operations, their customers were all good credit risks, and finished goods were always shipped soon after completion.

Prepare a report for Orsini and Newman, explaining what had happened.

Chapter 14

Values, Prices, and Exchange Rates

Throughout the first 13 chapters, our coverage of financial accounting revolved around the historical-cost basis of accounting—because that is the only generally accepted way to practice accounting and prepare financial statements in the United States. Cost-based financial statements don't reflect the current values of the assets, liabilities and owners' equity, however, and this may reduce their usefulness. In this chapter, we'll examine three major factors that often may impair the utility of cost-based financial statements:

1. Differences between historical cost and the present value of future cash flows.
2. Changes in general price levels.
3. Fluctuations in foreign currency exchange rates.

Present-Value Financial Statements

Assets are the economic resources that will benefit the enterprise in the future. An individual asset's *value* is defined by the future benefits the company expects to receive from it. The fact that the asset cost a particular amount in the past has no effect on the benefits it is expected to provide in the future:

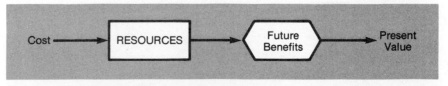

It is this phenomenon that suggests the importance of preparing financial statements on a value basis rather than on a cost basis. An understanding of the **present-value basis of accounting** will enable us to obtain at least two benefits: (1) it provides a conceptual framework we can use to prepare present-value financial statements, if we wish; and (2) it points out the likely departures of cost-based statements from the underlying values for which they are surrogates.

Requirements of Value-Based Measurement

Adoption of a value orientation places two obligations on the accountant: (1) estimating the amount of the future benefits, and (2) adjusting for the time lag between now and when the benefits will occur. Since the benefits are future benefits, their value to the company *now* is some amount less than their future value. The time-value-of-money concept—which was described in detail in Chapter 6—uses an appropriate interest rate to calculate the present value of future amounts. The compound-interest tables appearing in Appendix A—Tables 1 and 2—enable the accountant to make these calculations with relative ease, once the estimates of future cash flows have been prepared.

Present Value of a Going Concern

Most individual assets are likely to generate cash flows for a few years at most. The company as a whole—that is, the company as a *going concern*—is likely to have a much longer life, replacing assets with other assets to maintain its overall cash-flow stream. We therefore introduce the concept of *net cash flow*, which in any year consists of the following:

Net cash flow	=	Cash receipts from use of assets	+	Cash receipts from sale of discarded assets	−	Cash outlays to pay for purchased assets

The question is how to calculate the present value of a series of company-wide cash flows defined in this way.

To begin with, let's assume that Star Company's cash flow will be $1 million each year for 20 years, after which the company will be worthless. Let's also assume that the appropriate interest rate for this company is 15 percent, compounded annually.[1] From Table 2 in Appendix A, we find that the present-value multiplier for a 20-year annuity at 15 percent is 6.2593. The present value of the company under these assumptions therefore is $1 million × 6.2593 = $6,259,300.

---

[1] We determine this by estimating the interest rate the company has to pay to obtain funds from investors. This rate is determined primarily by forces outside the company, in the financial markets. We'll explore the meaning of this rate more thoroughly in Chapter 21.

The Cash Flow/Present Value Ratio. In a sense, the $1 million annual net cash inflow is the reward Star Company gets for keeping its resources invested in their present uses, much as a bank pays interest to its depositors to reward them for letting the bank use their money for a time. With no new deposits or withdrawals, depositors can calculate the bank's effective annual interest rate by dividing the amount of interest added to their account balances in a year by the amount they had on deposit at the beginning of the year:

$$\text{Effective interest rate} = \frac{\text{Interest added}}{\text{Beginning balance}}$$

We can make the same calculation for an assumed investment of $6,259,300, invested to obtain $1 million a year for 20 years:

$$\frac{\$1,000,000}{\$6,259,300} = 16 \text{ percent}$$

This *doesn't* mean that the business is earning 16 percent on the present value of its investments, however. Unlike a savings bank deposit, the investment here will be worthless at the end of 20 years, when the cash-flow stream finally dries up. Part of each annual cash flow therefore can be regarded as recovery of part of the initial present value. The part that's left after we deduct this recovered amount is the amount we can call interest. The *real* interest therefore must be less than 16 percent. In fact, the interest rate is 15 percent, because the denominator of the fraction is $6,259,300, the present value of the future cash flows *at 15 percent. By definition,* this is the amount someone could spend to obtain the rights to the future net cash inflow of $1 million a year and earn a full 15 percent interest each year on the amount invested.

If we add more years to the cash-flow stream, we'll increase the present value—but we'll also decrease the amount of the initial present value we have to deduct from each year's cash flow to determine the amount available for interest. This will bring the ratio of annual cash flow to present value closer to the interest rate used in the present value calculation.

For example, using the multiplier for a 30-year annuity in Table 2 of Appendix A, we find that the present value of a 30-year annuity of $1 million a year is $6,566,000. The ratio of the annual net cash flow to the present value is now only 15.23 percent:

$$\frac{\$1,000,000}{\$6,566,000} = 15.23 \text{ percent}$$

This is much closer to 15 percent than the ratio at a 20-year life because the initial value can be spread over an extra 10 years. If the life of the annuity is 50 years, the present value is $6,660,500, and the ratio is 15.01

percent—virtually identical to the 15 percent interest rate on which the present value amount is based. Since the recovery of the initial value can be spread over 50 years, it has only an insignificant effect on the ratio.

The relationship between the life of the business and its value if cash flows are steady is diagrammed in Exhibit 14–1. Value reaches its limit at $1,000,000/0.15 = $6,666,667. This limit is the present value of a *perpetual annuity,* an annuity that goes on forever. A business that produces

EXHIBIT 14–1
Relationship between Life of a Business and Present Value (Based on Cash Flows of $1 Million a Year and a 15 Percent Interest Rate)

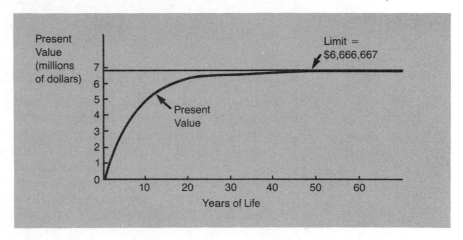

a steady flow of cash in perpetuity will have a cash flow/present value ratio equal to the interest rate. An investment of $6,666,667 in Star Company will earn 15 percent interest if the cash flow goes on forever. This happens because none of the annuity has to be used to pay off any of the original investment.

Determinants of Value. Star Company's value may be either greater or less than $6,666,667, for any or all of four reasons:

1. The annual cash flow is greater or less than $1 million.
2. The annual cash flow is growing or shrinking from year to year.
3. The life of the business is limited.
4. The appropriate interest rate is greater or less than 15 percent.

Anyone who wants to estimate Star Company's value as a going concern must estimate each of these determinants of value.

A Balance Sheet Based on Present Value

A balance sheet prepared on the present-value basis should list each asset and each liability at its present value. The present values of some assets and liabilities are fairly easy to determine. The present value of cash, for example, is equal to the amount of cash the company has on hand. Current accounts receivable are reported on conventional balance sheets at the amounts the company expects to collect in the very near future; these amounts are generally close enough to the receivables' present value to be used in value-based balance sheets. For instance, Star Company had cash of $350,000 and accounts receivable of $1 million on January 1, 19x1. These amounts appeared in its value-based balance sheet without change:

	Cost-Based Balance Sheet	Value-Based Balance Sheet
Cash	$ 350,000	$ 350,000
Receivables	1,500,000	1,500,000

Similarly, current accounts payable and other short-term, noninterest-bearing liabilities are listed in conventional balance sheets at the amounts to be paid to creditors in the very near future; again, these amounts are generally close enough to the payables' present value to be used in value-based balance sheets. Star Company had $300,000 in current taxes payable and $750,000 in current accounts payable on January 1, 19x1. These amounts also appeared in its value-based balance sheet.

Unfortunately, the amounts shown on conventional balance sheets for inventories and plant assets are much less likely to approximate their present values. For one thing, their conventional measurement reflects costs incurred at various times in the past, and these are unlikely to approximate current values. Just as important, the future cash flows associated with individual plant assets are ordinarily inseparable from the present value of the business as a whole. As a result, to prepare a balance sheet on a present-value basis we must find some other measure that will approximate the present value of the inventories and plant assets.

Appraised Value. The method we use is to measure each identifiable asset at its appraised value, if a good approximation to present value isn't available from another source. The appraised value of an asset is an expert's informed estimate of the amount the company would have to pay to acquire a comparable asset in an arm's-length market transaction under current conditions.[2] Star Company's inventories on January 1, 19x1, for example, had a cost of $1.6 million, while their appraised value amounted to $2.1 million. The company's plant assets had a book value of

---

[2] Appraisals can also measure the estimated *selling* prices of the company's assets. We don't use appraisals of this sort in these calculations because our calculations assume that the company is a *going concern*, one that will continue to use its assets rather than sell them.

$2.9 million, but the appraised value totaled $3.8 million. These amounts are shown in the upper portions of the two balance sheets in Exhibit 14–2. The first column shows the amounts appearing in a conventional cost-based balance sheet; the second column shows the amounts that appeared in a balance sheet based on the present-value concept.

EXHIBIT 14–2

STAR COMPANY
Balance Sheets on Conventional and Present-Value Bases
As of January 1, 19x1

	Conventional Basis	Present-Value Basis
Assets		
Current assets:		
Cash	$ 350,000	$ 350,000
Receivables.	1,500,000	1,500,000
Inventories	1,600,000	2,100,000
Total current assets	3,450,000	3,950,000
Plant and equipment.	2,900,000	3,800,000
Total tangible assets	6,350,000	7,750,000
Goodwill	—	209,000
Total assets	$6,350,000	$7,959,000
Liabilities and Owners' Equity		
Current liabilities:		
Taxes payable.	$ 300,000	$ 300,000
Accounts payable.	750,000	750,000
Current liabilities	1,050,000	1,050,000
Bonds payable	800,000	650,000
Total liabilities.	1,850,000	1,700,000
Owners' equity:		
Capital stock.	2,000,000	2,000,000
Retained earnings	2,500,000	4,259,000
Total owners' equity.	4,500,000	6,259,000
Total liabilities and owners' equity . .	$6,350,000	$7,959,000

The amounts shown in conventional balance sheets for long-term liabilities, such as bonds payable, are also unlikely to measure their present values. Star Company's long-term bonds payable, for example, amounted to $800,000 on January 1, 19x1, but they entered the value-based balance sheet at only $650,000. The reason for this $150,000 difference is that bonds are fixed-dollar obligations, with fixed interest payments due each year for a number of years. Star Company's bonds were issued when interest rates were 6 percent, but the market rate of interest for comparable securities was 15 percent on January 1, 19x1. Since investors could get 15 percent interest on their money elsewhere, they were unwilling to pay as much for these bonds ($800,000) as they had been willing to pay when the bonds were first issued. Instead, they forced the market price of the bonds down until it equaled the present value of the company's future payments to the bondholders, based on a yield-to-maturity rate of 15 percent. In other words, long-term bonds appear in a value-based balance sheet at the amount the company could obtain from a creditor in the current market for the cash payments the company is now obligated to make, and this amount depends on current interest rates, not the rates that prevailed when the bonds were issued.[3]

Intangible Assets. Only one asset appears in the second column of Exhibit 14–2 but not in the first. This is the asset identified as *goodwill*, and it represents the value of the company's intangible assets. An intangible asset is any attribute that enables a business to generate more net income than the business's tangible assets would normally be expected to generate.

A company's intangible assets sometimes have specific names. For example, the company's high earning power may be clearly ascribable to the ownership of a well-known trademark or a particularly valuable patent. In such cases, it may be possible to estimate the present value of one or more specific intangible assets; any such amounts can be listed separately on a value-based balance sheet.

Most of the time, however, high earning power is the *joint* result of many factors, such as superior product design, marketing and managerial skills, and a reputation for providing prompt, careful attention to customers' needs. In these cases, we generally use a single term, *goodwill,* to describe the entire package of intangible assets. Goodwill is the set of attributes that gives an ongoing business enterprise a total value in excess of the amounts ascribed specifically to other assets.

Conceptually, the way to measure goodwill is to estimate the present value of the company as a going concern and then subtract the present value of the cash flows the company would have if it had no intangible assets:

| Present value of intangible assets | = | Present value of future cash flows from all assets (going-concern value) | − | Present value of future cash flows from net tangible assets |

---

[3] The application of the present-value concept in the measurement of corporate bond liabilities was discussed in detail in Chapter 10.

As a practical matter, the values used in this calculation will be a mixture of present values and appraised values, as we explained earlier.

Star Company had no specific intangible assets for which separate estimates of present value could be derived. Instead, its January 1, 19x1, value-based balance sheet listed a single intangible asset, goodwill, in the amount of $209,000. This was derived from the values we calculated for Star's individual tangible assets and liabilities as follows (to the nearest thousand dollars):

Present value of the going concern		$6,259,000
Value of the net tangible assets (from Exhibit 14–2):		
Total tangible assets	$7,750,000	
Total liabilities	1,700,000	6,050,000
Value of the intangible assets		$ 209,000

The owners' equity in a balance sheet based on the concept of present value is the company's *going-concern value.* For Star Company, this was $6,259,000 on January 1, 19x1. This differed from the $4.5 million book value of the owners' equity by $1,759,000; all but $209,000 of this difference was accounted for by differences in the measures of the inventories, plant assets, and bonds payable. The division of the owners' equity into two components is arbitrary; we have chosen to concentrate all the adjustments in the retained earnings amount.

Notice that we haven't calculated goodwill by comparing the company's total present value with the total book value of its tangible assets. Book values of tangible assets reflect transactions that took place in the past, when conditions were very different from those of today. The fact that a company bought land 50 years ago for $1 an acre is irrelevant; if it buys the land as part of a package today, it is paying current prices for the land, not the prices of 50 years ago.

Companies list intangible assets in their cost-based balance sheets *only* if they bought them from outsiders. A company that buys a patent, trademark, or copyright, for example, would list it as an asset, measured at its cost. Even goodwill may be listed if the company has bought it—that is, if it has bought an ongoing business at a price greater than the current appraised value of its net tangible assets.[4]

Most intangible assets are developed internally, not bought. The typical company builds goodwill gradually by patient and skillful development of its organization, product lines, and markets. The accountants classify the costs of the activities that produce this result as expenses as they take place, however. No portion of the current marketing cost, for example, is treated as the cost of acquiring an intangible asset. As a result, intangible assets acquired in this way don't appear in conventional balance sheets.

---

[4] Accounting for purchased goodwill was discussed in detail in Chapter 12.

Income Measured on a Present-Value Basis

If we take a value approach to the measurement of business income, we can define income as the increase in the value of the owners' personal assets resulting from their ownership of the business during a specified period of time.[5] The owners' equity in the business is one of their personal assets; cash in their possession is another. Income measured on this basis therefore has two components: (1) the amounts distributed to the owners during the period, thereby increasing their cash assets; and (2) the difference between the present value of their equity in the business at the beginning of the period and the present value at the end of the period.

For example, suppose Star Company began the year 19x1 with an expectation of a 20-year annuity of net cash inflows amounting to $1 million a year. The interest rate was 15 percent. During the year, the net cash inflow amounted to $1 million, as anticipated, of which $800,000 was distributed to the owners as cash dividends. The other $200,000 was reinvested by the company in plant assets and working capital to provide for future growth. At the end of the year, the new expectation was that the future net cash inflow would be $1,050,000 a year for 25 years; the interest rate was 14 percent. (A possible explanation is that the company is in the oil-producing business and operations this year reveal a richer and longer-lasting underground oil deposit in the company's drilling area; a reduction in the rate of inflation has been accompanied by a reduction in the interest rate.)

The income calculated under these circumstances is diagrammed in Exhibit 14–3. Block A at the left shows the present value of the 20-year annuity at the beginning of the year, $6,259,300, as calculated earlier in this chapter. Block B shows the present value of the $1,050,000 25-year annuity at the end of the year: $1,050,000 × 6.8729 = $7,216,545. The 6.8729 present-value multiplier comes from the 25-year row of the 14 percent column in Table 2 of Appendix A. The difference between these two present values is $957,245 and is shown in the lower portion of block C. *Economic income* for the period, represented by block D, was the sum of this increase in present value and the dividends of $800,000 that were distributed during the year, a total of $1,757,245.

This income is the result of three factors: (1) the size of the expected annual cash flow has *increased* from $1 million to $1.05 million, (2) the length of the annuity has been *extended* from 20 to 25 years, and (3) the interest rate has *decreased* from 15 percent to 14 percent. Notice what would have happened if the original expectations had remained constant, and if the business had distributed the entire $1 million cash flow as

---

[5] Background for this discussion can be found in J. R. Hicks, *Value and Capital* (London: Oxford University Press, 1939), p. 172; and in Robert K. Jaedicke and Robert T. Sprouse, *Accounting Flows: Income, Funds, and Cash* (Englewood Cliffs, N.J.: Prentice-Hall, 1965), chap. ii.

EXHIBIT 14–3
Income on a Present Value Basis

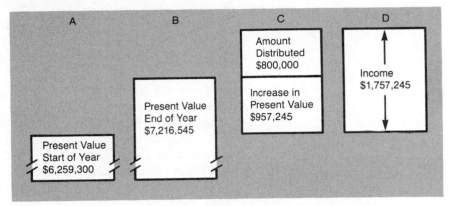

dividends. The business would have had a 19-year annuity remaining at the end of the year, and the change in present value would have been a $61,100 decrease:

Present value, January 1, 19x1: $1,000,000 × 6.2593 . . . . $6,259,300
Present value, December 31, 19x1: $1,000,000 × 6.1982   6,198,200

    Decrease in present value . . . . $ 61,100

Net income for the year on a present-value basis therefore would have been $1,000,000 − $61,100 = $938,900. Not surprisingly, this is 15 percent of the initial present value, $6,259,300, showing that the owners did earn exactly the rate of interest specified at the beginning of the year.

This calculation can be incorporated into an income statement. The right-hand column of Exhibit 14–4 shows how an income statement

EXHIBIT 14–4

STAR COMPANY
Income Statements on Conventional and Present-Value Bases
For the Year Ended December 31, 19x1

	Conventional Basis	Present-Value Basis
Sales revenues.	$10,000,000	$10,000,000
Cost of goods sold	6,000,000	6,300,000
Gross margin	4,000,000	3,700,000
Operating expenses	(1,900,000)	(2,100,000)
Income tax expense	(900,000)	(900,000)
Income before value adjustment	1,200,000	700,000
Value adjustment.	—	1,057,245
Net income	$ 1,200,000	$ 1,757,245

based on present value might look. The $1,757,245 net income is the amount we derived in Exhibit 14–3; the depreciation and cost of goods sold amounts are based on appraised values. The final item in the income statement—*value adjustment*—is a residual, reflecting changes in value not reflected in the revenues and expenses. It is determined by subtracting the income before the value adjustment from the estimated net income on a present value basis.

The conventional net income in the first column of Exhibit 14–4 is $1,200,000, not the $1 million net cash inflow on which Exhibit 14–3 was based. The reason is that during the year the company paid more cash to *purchase* inventories, plant, and equipment than it expensed for the *use* of these kinds of assets. As we pointed out earlier, the annual cash flow used in present-value calculations includes *both* the proceeds from discarded plant assets *and* the cash paid to acquire new plant assets during the year. During and after an inflationary period and during periods of growth, cash flow calculated on this basis is likely to be less than net income. During and after inflation, replacement prices generally exceed the original costs of the equipment on which current depreciation charges are based. And in a period of growth, purchases of plant assets ordinarily include both purchases for replacement and purchases for expansion.

Inapplicability of Present Value for Periodic Financial Reporting

In the light of the relevance of present value to managerial and investor decisions, why isn't it the primary basis of routine financial reporting on the position and performance of business enterprises? Two major objections may have become apparent in our explanation of how the concept might be applied:

1. The cash-flow estimates in most situations can't be verified satisfactorily.
2. The appropriate interest rate isn't known with certainty.

The amount, timing, and duration of the future cash flows of a business are highly uncertain, to say the least. Accountants can verify management's past estimates of future cash flows to some extent, but their ability to verify current estimates is much more limited. Present value-based financial statements therefore would summarize management's estimates, relatively unrestrained by objective tests applied by outsiders. The most accountants could do would be to review the assumptions on which management based its estimates, using available information on economic conditions and the political climate. The credibility of statements prepared on a present-value basis probably would be quite low.

The second obstacle to financial reporting on a present-value basis is that estimates of the appropriate rate at which to calculate the present value of the estimated future cash flows are far from precise. Errors in the rate can have significant effects on estimates of present value and on income amounts based on these estimates. For example, we found that the present value of a 20-year, $1 million annuity at 15 percent interest is $6,259,300. If we vary the interest rate just one percentage point, to 14 percent or 16 percent, we change the present value by more than $300,000—to $6,623,100 or $5,928,800 (based on the present-value multipliers in Table 2 of Appendix A). Reducing the interest rate to 10 percent increases the present value to $8,513,600; increasing the rate to 20 percent reduces the present value to $4,870,000.

The choice of the interest rate would also affect the relevance of the statements to individual investors. Some investors may wish to capitalize future cash flows at 15 percent, some may wish to use 12 percent, and others may prefer to adjust for perceived differences in future cash flows by calculating the present value of different portions of the cash-flow stream at different interest rates. No matter which rate or set of rates is chosen, it won't meet everyone's needs.

As a result of these difficulties, present value has been ruled out as the basis for routine financial reporting. It is a powerful and useful concept, however, as evidenced by its use in accounting for bond liabilities, investments, pensions, and long-term lease agreements. Furthermore, it plays a central role in management's decisions to acquire or dispose of long-term assets, as we'll see in some detail in Chapter 21.

Purchasing-Power Changes

As we've just seen, historical-cost financial statements may reflect the underlying economic facts very poorly because they aren't based on the cash flows and interest rates that determine the economic value of a going concern. They may also be defective for another reason: they ignore changes in the purchasing power of the measuring unit. We'll examine this phenomenon in this section.

Attributes and Measuring Units

All measurement systems take two factors into consideration: the attribute to be measured and the measuring unit. In conventional financial statements, two attributes are measured—most monetary assets (mainly cash and receivables) are measured at their values to the company, and nonmonetary assets are generally measured at their historical cost. In discussing value-based financial statements, we learned that alternative attributes—market value, appraised value, or replacement cost—might be used as the measured attributes for individual assets. We introduced the same idea in Chapters 8 and 9, when we examined the implications of differences between the historical costs and the current replacement costs of inventories and plant assets.

We chose one measuring unit to measure all of these attributes, **nominal dollars**—that is, the dollars associated with any one resource were regarded as fully additive to or subtractive from the dollars associated with any other resource, without further adjustment.

> ### TERMINOLOGY
>
> **Purchasing-power changes** are changes in the average level of resource prices throughout the economy or a particular segment of it. An increase in the price level (**inflation**) reduces the purchasing power of a nominal dollar; a decrease in the price level (deflation) increases the purchasing power of a nominal dollar.

An alternative to nominal dollars is a constant-dollar measuring unit. **Constant-dollar** accounting recognizes that changes in the **general price level** cause the value—that is, the purchasing power—of one period's dollars to differ from the value of the dollars that measure other periods' transactions. Rather than counting the number of dollars, this approach counts units of constant purchasing power.

Exhibit 14–5 depicts the attribute and measuring unit dimensions of accounting measurement—using current cost (rather than present

EXHIBIT 14–5
Dimensions of Accounting Measurement

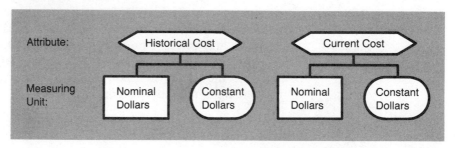

value) as the attribute alternative to historical cost. In the remainder of this section, we'll examine the implications of a constant-dollar measuring unit.

Constant-Dollar Measurements

Both historical-cost and current-cost financial statements can be expressed in constant dollars. To use constant dollars, accountants must restate each dollar amount, by the use of index numbers, in dollars that have the purchasing power of those on a selected date. The date accountants generally use is the end of the *current* year.

For example, suppose Wheaton Company bought land for $10,000 in 19x3 when the **consumer price index** (CPI) was 120. The year 19x8 has just ended, and the CPI has risen to 180. To restate the nominal-dollar historical cost of the land in constant dollars of December 19x8 purchasing power, we need merely multiply it by the ratio of the CPI index numbers on the two dates:

$$\text{Historical cost in constant dollars} = \text{Historical cost} \times \text{Relative index}$$
$$= \$10,000 \times \frac{180}{120} = \$15,000$$

Holding Gains and Losses—Nominal versus Real

Proponents of a constant-dollar measuring unit believe that inflation-induced holding gains aren't real and therefore should be excluded from reported gains relating to inventory and plant assets. One way of accomplishing that is to restate each historical-cost or current-cost number with an index number reflecting changes in the general price level. Holding gains then would appear only if the current costs of the company's non-monetary assets rose more rapidly than the general price level; holding losses would appear if current costs fell, held steady, or rose less rapidly than the general price level.

> **TERMINOLOGY REMINDER: HOLDING GAINS AND LOSSES**
>
> A holding gain (loss) occurs when the current cost of an owned asset, such as inventory or plant, increases (decreases) prior to the time it is sold or exchanged for another asset. Contrast this with the merchandising income (loss) on the sale of inventory—the difference between the current cost (which may be the input price in the whole-sale market) and the sale price (the output price in the retail market).

To illustrate, let's assume that the current cost of Wheaton Company's land was estimated to be $19,000. In other words, although the general price level increased by 50 percent (180/120 − 1.0), the current cost of the land increased even more, by 90 percent [($19,000 − $10,000)/$10,000]. Historical-cost/nominal-dollar accounting reports the $10,000 cost of the asset and no gain during the five-year period. Historical-cost/constant-dollar accounting reports the land at $15,000 ($10,000 × 180/120). No gain is recognized, however, because all we've done is change the measuring unit. Changing the measuring unit doesn't make an owner better or worse off than before, just as measuring weight in kilograms instead of in pounds doesn't signify an instantaneous loss of weight (70 kilograms is the same as 154 pounds, not 84 units less).

Current-cost accounting takes us in a different direction. Current-cost/nominal-dollar accounting (1) reports the land at its $19,000 current cost, and (2) recognizes the $9,000 increase as a holding gain. Current-cost/constant-dollar accounting, in contrast, responds both to specific price changes and to general price changes. While the land is written up to its $19,000 current cost, the entire $9,000 increase is *not* recognized as the holding gain. Instead, the holding gain is $4,000—the difference between the $19,000 current cost and the $15,000 constant-dollar equivalent of the $10,000 historical cost.

While the current-cost/nominal-dollar holding gain measures the nominal increase in the asset's cost and therefore recognizes the **nominal holding gain,** current-cost/constant-dollar accounting (1) isolates the $5,000 general price level component of the $9,000 nominal gain, and (2) recognizes only the **real holding gain** of $4,000. In other words, the company's purchasing power actually increased because it held land instead of assets whose nominal-value changes paralleled the increase in the general price level index.

Exhibit 14–6 diagrams this holding-gain difference by using data for the following year (19x9) when the year-end CPI was 198 and the current cost of the land was $23,000. While both current-cost methods measure the land at $23,000, the *nominal* holding gain is $4,000 ($23,000 − $19,000) and the *real* holding gain is $2,100 [$23,000 − ($19,000 × 198/180)]. The $1,900 difference ($4,000 − $2,100) is the effect of inflation.

Calculating Purchasing-Power Gains and Losses

Constant-dollar measurements also perform another function: determination of gains or losses resulting from the company's **net monetary position** (total monetary assets minus total monetary liabilities). Accountants calculate the purchasing-power gain or loss for a period by restating in end-of-period constant dollars (1) the beginning-of-period monetary balances, and (2) the monetary transactions that occurred during the period. They then compare the adjusted total with the actual net monetary position at the end of the period.

To illustrate, we'll assume that Walsh Company had the following monetary balances at the beginning and end of 19x3:

	January 1	December 31
Monetary assets	$120,000	$170,000
Monetary liabilities	80,000	105,000
Net monetary position	$ 40,000	$ 65,000

EXHIBIT 14–6
Nominal and Real Holding Gains

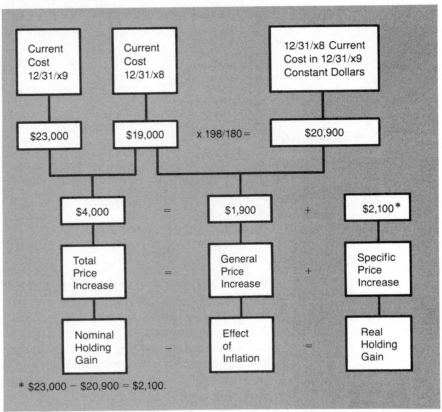

Walsh first adjusted its January 1, 19x3, net monetary position to end-of-year constant dollars. The consumer price index (CPI) was as follows in 19x3:

Date or Period	CPI
January 19x3	100
Average, 19x3	107
December 19x3	114

Exhibit 14–7 illustrates how Walsh's accountants adjusted the net monetary assets on January 1, 19x3, to end-of-year constant dollars, multiplying $40,000 × 114/100 = $45,600. In other words, the company would have needed $45,600 at the end of 19x3 to buy the same package of goods and services $40,000 would have commanded in January of that year. If Walsh hadn't engaged in any monetary transactions during the year, it would have had the same net monetary assets ($40,000) on hand

EXHIBIT 14–7

Walsh Company
Calculating Purchasing-Power Loss, 19x3

	(1) Nominal Dollars	(2) Multiplier	(3) Constant Dollars (1) × (2)	(4) Purchasing-Power Gain/ (Loss) (3) − (1)
Net monetary position, January 1	$40,000	114/100	$45,600	$(5,600)
Net monetary transactions, 19x3	+ 25,000	114/107	26,636	(1,636)
Total			72,236	
Net monetary position, December 31	65,000		65,000	
Purchasing-power loss, 19x3				$(7,236)

at year-end as it had on January 1—but this amount would have been $5,600 ($45,600 − $40,000) less than would have been needed to buy the goods and services $40,000 could have bought in January.

Walsh's next task was to restate the year's monetary transactions in dollars of year-end purchasing power. Since the net effect of these transactions accounted for the full increase in the company's net monetary position from $40,000 at the beginning of 19x3 to $65,000 at the end of the year, the amount was $25,000.

Sales, collections, purchases, and payments occurred relatively evenly throughout the year. Walsh's accountants decided to simplify the analysis by assuming that all of 19x3's monetary transactions took place continually throughout the year; hence, the appropriate multiplier is based on the year-average CPI 114/107 = 106.54. The restatement of the company's monetary transactions in 19x3 is shown in the second line of Exhibit 14–7.

The calculation of the purchasing-power loss in 19x3—expressed in year-end constant dollars—comes from the numbers in column 3 of the exhibit. Restating both the beginning-of-year $40,000 net monetary assets and the $25,000 increase yields $72,236 as the constant-dollar purchasing power the company should have had at the end of 19x3 had it not been affected adversely by the year's inflation. Since the actual purchasing power on hand at year-end was $65,000, a $7,236 loss in purchasing power ($72,236 − $65,000) occurred during the year.

Column 4 of the exhibit explains this result from a somewhat different perspective. The first amount—$5,600—represents the loss in purchasing power that Walsh would have experienced had its January 1 net monetary asset position remained unchanged throughout the entire year. This purchasing-power loss was aggravated by the $25,000 increase in net monetary assets that occurred during the year. That increase in its own right resulted in an additional $1,636 loss in purchasing power by year-end. The total effect of the general price level increase therefore was the $7,236 loss in purchasing power during the year.

Financial Reporting Requirements

The Financial Accounting Standards Board requires large U.S. companies to supplement their basic financial statements with disclosures relating to changing prices. The requirements apply to publicly held corporations that have either inventory and gross plant assets in excess of $125 million or total assets greater than $1 billion. Approximately 1,500 companies therefore publish changing-prices information each year in their annual reports to stockholders. The specific items that are disclosed are as follows:

1. Income from continuing operations, with cost of goods sold and depreciation expense measured on a current-cost/constant-dollar basis.
2. Purchasing-power gain or loss.
3. Inventory and plant assets at their current cost.
4. Holding gain or loss—nominal, real, and the inflation effect.
5. Five-year comparison of selected historical-cost and current-cost data—including sales, cash dividends, and year-end market price per share.

Although different forms of these disclosures have been operational since the mid-1970s, there has been no consensus as to how the information ought to be used or the extent to which it has been used. The FASB does believe, however, that these supplemental measurements do provide sufficient benefits to justify the cost of compiling the information.

Foreign Currency Translation

Limitations on the ability of financial statements to convey information in current-value terms are compounded when the company owns properties in countries with currencies (e.g., francs, pounds) other than the currency in which the statements are expressed (e.g., U.S. dollars). In this final section, we'll examine some of the problems accountants encounter in this situation.

The Translation Process

A subsidiary of a U.S. company records all its transactions in the currency units of the country in which it is domiciled. When the U.S. parent company prepares its financial statements, however, it has to **translate** the subsidiary's amounts into an equivalent number of U.S. dollars. To make these translations, the company's accountants use a **foreign currency exchange rate**—the dollar price of a unit of foreign currency.

When financial statements are prepared, the exchange rate that is used depends on (1) the circumstances and (2) the nature of the amount to be measured. One candidate is the historical rate that existed when the transaction occurred; another possibility is the current rate in effect at the end of the period (i.e., on the balance sheet date).

We'll first study how accountants measure the effect of foreign currency transactions of U.S. companies themselves. We'll then look at the case of these companies' foreign subsidiaries whose own financial statements have been measured in a foreign currency.

Foreign Currency Transactions

The historical-cost basis of accounting requires that once *nonmonetary* assets such as inventory and plant are recorded, the amounts can be superseded only by subsequent transactions. This means that inventory and plant assets bought in a transaction expressed in foreign currency and recorded in dollars are *not* adjusted when exchange rates fluctuate subsequently.

However, when accountants translate *monetary* assets and liabilities—cash, receivables, and payables—they do make adjustments. They adjust each dollar amount so that it will reflect the *current* exchange rate. Depending on the direction of the fluctuation, a gain or loss occurs and is recognized *immediately*—not when the cash is used or the debt is paid. The gain or loss represents the positive or negative effect of having been exposed to the exchange rate fluctuation.

Let's assume that on December 15, 19x1, Allied, Inc., purchased inventory on account in a foreign country whose currency was the *hub*—designated by the symbol, *H*. The purchase price was H10,000, and Allied paid this amount on January 12, 19x2. The exchange rates between dollars and hubs were as follows:

$$
\begin{array}{ll}
\text{December 15, 19x1} \ldots\ldots\ldots & \$1.30/H \\
\text{December 31, 19x1} \ldots\ldots\ldots & \$1.45/H \\
\text{January 12, 19x2} \ldots\ldots\ldots\ldots & \$1.39/H
\end{array}
$$

On December 15, Allied recorded the purchase of inventory and the increase in its accounts payable at $13,000 each (H10,000 × $1.30). The $0.15 increase in the rate during December ($1.45/H − $1.30/H) caused Allied's accountants to make the following year-end adjustment:

Foreign Currency Exchange Loss	1,500	
Accounts Payable		1,500

Since payables are measured using the current rate, Allied's dollar-denominated liability was increased by $1,500. And since more dollars would have to be expended on December 31 to meet the H10,000 debt than had been the case on December 15, Allied recorded the loss as a determinant of 19x1 income.

When Allied paid the amount due in 19x2, its accountants recorded the payment as follows:

Accounts Payable..................................	14,500	
Cash...		13,900
Foreign Currency Exchange Gain...................		600

Accounts Payable was reduced by the $14,500 that had measured the debt previously (December 15's $13,000 plus December 31's $1,500). Cash was decreased by the $13,900 paid to liquidate the debt (H10,000 × $1.39). The $600 gain was the result of the decline in the exchange rate during 19x2—H10,000 × ($1.45 − $1.39).

The inventory asset was not adjusted, however: it continued to be measured in dollars at its $1.30/H historical rate. This nonadjustment approach applies to plant assets as well because both inventory and plant are nonmonetary assets. As nonmonetary assets, they are measured at their historical cost, which means using historical exchange rates. Only monetary items—accounts payable in Allied's case—are adjusted to reflect the current exchange rate because only cash, receivables and payables cause companies to benefit or suffer from fluctuations in exchange rates.

The Functional Currency

To determine which exchange rate to use in translating foreign currency amounts—the historical rate, the current rate, or some combination—the accountants have to decide which currency (the dollar or the foreign currency) is the **functional currency**. A company's functional currency is the currency of the primary economic environment in which it operates. Normally this is the environment in which the company primarily generates and expends cash. For example, although U.S. residents vacationing in a foreign country engage in transactions using only the local currency, they view all such transactions in terms of their dollar equivalent—because the dollar is their functional currency. Exchange rate fluctuations that occur while holding foreign currency cash, receivables, or payables therefore yield gains and losses.

By contrast, companies that operate relatively autonomous foreign subsidiaries generally view the foreign currency as the functional currency. Consider the case of the foreign subsidiary that purchased inventory by borrowing local currency it will repay with the foreign currency proceeds from local sales. Since dollars won't be used to repay the debt, the parent doesn't perceive itself as benefiting or suffering when the exchange rate fluctuates.

Translation with the Foreign Currency as the Functional Currency

The typical U.S. parent company treats its subsidiary's local currency as the functional currency, for the reason outlined in the preceding paragraph. When such a parent acquires its controlling interest in a foreign subsidiary, the then-current rate is used to translate all the amounts contained in the acquisition-date balance sheet—assets, liabilities, and owners' equity. The parent also translates the subsidiary's assets and liabilities in its subsequent balance sheets by using the new current rate. Owners' equity amounts, however, continue to be restated on the basis of the historical rate.

The dollar-amount effect of foreign currency fluctuations is called the **cumulative translation adjustment** (CTA). It is measured by calculating the difference in owners' equity resulting from differences between the current rate and the historical rate. The change in the CTA each period reflects the effect of that period's exchange rate fluctuation. Since each balance sheet discloses the *cumulative* translation adjustment, the dollar effect of the period's exchange rate fluctuation can be determined only by comparing the end-of-period CTA with the CTA reported at the end of the preceding period.

When the foreign currency is the functional currency, the change in the CTA is *not* a determinant of income, on the grounds that it reflects only the effect of measuring foreign assets and liabilities at a different exchange rate. According to this view, no gain or loss can occur simply because a different measuring unit (i.e., exchange rate) was used to translate the subsidiary's assets and liabilities. Instead, the change in the cumulative translation adjustment is treated as an adjustment to a separate component of the owners' equity.

Foreign Currency Translation: An Illustration

On December 31, 19x2, Worthy Company acquired all the voting common stock of a foreign company, Able, Inc., whose financial statements were measured in *hubs*—designated by the symbol, *H*. Column 1 of Exhibit 14–8 contains Able's acquisition-date balance sheet amounts expressed in hubs. Column 2 presents these balance sheet amounts translated into dollars using the $1.50/H current exchange rate for all eight amounts.

Column 3 reflects the dollar amounts that would be disclosed in the next day's balance sheet, prepared in response to a sudden increase in the exchange rate from $1.50/H to $1.80/H. In the January 1 balance sheet, only the assets and liabilities are translated using the $1.80/H current rate. The owners' equity amounts (H10,000 and H70,000) continue to be restated using the $1.50/H historical rate, and a $24,000 cumulative translation adjustment emerges as a result. The $24,000 CTA

EXHIBIT 14–8

Worthy Company
Foreign Currency Translation

	(1) Amounts in Hubs	*(2)* $1.50/H	*(3)* $1.80/H
		Translated Amounts	
Cash	H 20,000	$ 30,000	$ 36,000
Receivables	30,000	45,000	54,000
Inventory	40,000	60,000	72,000
Plant	110,000	165,000	198,000
Total	H200,000	$300,000	$360,000
Accounts payable	H 20,000	$ 30,000	$ 36,000
Bonds payable	100,000	150,000	180,000
Common stock	10,000	15,000	15,000
Retained earnings	70,000	105,000	105,000
Cumulative translation adjustment			24,000
Total	H200,000	$300,000	$360,000

reflects the dollar effect of the exchange rate increase: (H10,000 + H70,000) × ($1.80 − $1.50) = $24,000.

Exhibit 14–9 presents Able, Inc.'s balance sheet one year later, that is, as of December 31, 19x3. In addition to changes in its assets and liabilities, Able's retained earnings increased because of the H40,000 net income earned during the year. The exchange rate increased during 19x3 from $1.80/H to $2.00/H, with an average exchange rate of $1.90/H.

EXHIBIT 14–9

Worthy Company
Foreign Currency Translation with Income

	(1) Hubs	*(2)* $2.00/H
Cash	H 30,000	$ 60,000
Receivables	50,000	100,000
Inventory	70,000	140,000
Plant	100,000	200,000
Total	H250,000	$500,000
Accounts payable	H 40,000	$ 80,000
Bonds payable	90,000	180,000
Common stock	10,000	15,000
Retained earnings	110,000	181,000*
Cumulative translation adjustment		44,000
Total	H250,000	$500,000

* H70,000 × $1.50 + H40,000 × $1.90 = $181,000.

Column 2 in the exhibit reflects (1) assets and liabilities translated using the $2.00/H current rate, and (2) owners' equity restated using historical rates.

The historical rate for common stock and beginning-of-period retained earnings is $1.50/H. The historical rate for the H40,000 increase in retained earnings reflects the fact that income was earned throughout the year: its historical rate therefore is the $1.90/H average rate for the year. The $181,000 year-end retained earnings in turn is based on H70,000 × $1.50 + H40,000 × $1.90.

The cumulative translation adjustment increased during 19x3 from $24,000 to $44,000. The $20,000 increase measures the effect of the increase in the exchange rate during the year, as follows:

Cumulative translation adjustment, January 2, 19x3............................			$24,000
Owners' equity, January 2, 19x3	H80,000		
Change in exchange rate: $2.00/H − $1.80/H	× $.20	$16,000	
Net income, 19x3........................	H40,000		
Change in exchange rate: $2.00/H − $1.90/H	× $.10	4,000	20,000
Cumulative exchange adjustment, December 31, 19x3.....................			$44,000

The CTA disclosure reflects the assumption that Worthy did *not* benefit from the $0.50/H increase in the exchange rate ($2.00/H − $1.50/H) that occurred since it became Able's parent company. Although the owners' equity did increase by $120,000 ($15,000 + $181,000 + $44,000 on December 31, 19x3, versus $15,000 + $105,000 on December 31, 19x2), $44,000 of the increase was simply the result of using a different measurement unit (i.e., exchange rate).

The CTA included in a consolidated balance sheet is cumulative—that is, it covers the entire period from when the parent-subsidiary relationship began. The CTA can be either a positive or a negative component of owners' equity. A *positive* CTA signifies that the foreign currency (in which foreign subsidiaries measure their assets and liabilities) has strengthened relative to the currency of the parent company's country— viz, the exchange rate movement from $1.50/H to $1.80/H to $2.00/H in our illustration. A *negative* CTA depicts the case of the foreign currency having weakened relative to the parent company's currency. The interperiod increase or decrease in a positive or a negative CTA reflects the relative strengths of the two currencies during that period.

Summary

The value of business assets depends on the amount and timing of the cash flows they can produce in the future *and* on the rate of interest the owners expect to earn from these future cash flows. A conventional business balance sheet doesn't pretend to measure the value of the business, nor does a conventional income statement measure all the changes in value arising during the period. A balance sheet reflecting values would require accountants to approximate the present value of each company's assets and liabilities, including any intangible assets the company may have. An income statement based on present value would show the change in the company's present value from the beginning of the period to the end, plus the amount of dividends distributed during the period.

Some of these present values can be estimated directly, such as those for receivables and payables; for others, such as inventories and plant assets, present values would have to be approximated by appraisals. Accountants don't develop these estimates for their regular financial statements because they would require the use of judgment that couldn't be verified satisfactorily by objective tests.

Current-cost financial statements reflect only changes in specific prices, not the effect of changes in the general price level. A portion of holding gains and losses measured for nonmonetary assets under current-cost accounting may not be *real* if the general price level changed concurrently with changes in the prices of the company's specific assets. Furthermore, current-cost accounting ignores changes in the purchasing power of the company's net monetary position. Neither current costs nor general price-level adjustments are acceptable in the United States as the primary basis for financial reporting. Large corporations, however, are required to disclose the effects of changing prices on their income and resources.

The basic financial statements do have special measurement rules relating to foreign currency transactions. Parent companies that translate the assets and liabilities appearing in subsidiaries' foreign currency balance sheets record the effects of exchange rate fluctuations as direct adjustments to their owners' equity. But when U.S. companies themselves hold foreign currency cash, receivables, and payables, exchange rate fluctuations do result in immediate gain or loss recognition.

Key Terms

Constant dollars	Net monetary position
Consumer price index	Nominal dollars
Cumulative translation adjustment	Nominal holding gain/loss
Foreign currency exchange rate	Present-value basis of accounting
Functional currency	Purchasing-power gain/loss
General price level	Real holding gain/loss
Inflation	Translation

Independent Study Problems (Solutions in Appendix B)

1. Holding Gains and Losses: Nominal and Real. Wheaton Company bought land in January 19x8 for $10,000 when the consumer price index was 120. The following information was available:

	December 31			
	19x8	**19x9**	**19x10**	**19x11**
Current cost of the land	$19,000	$23,000	$27,000	$30,000
Consumer price index.........	180	198	225	270

The effects of specific price increases and general price increases in 19x8 and 19x9 were discussed in conjunction with Exhibit 14–6.

a. Calculate the nominal holding gain or loss for 19x10 *and* the real holding gain or loss in dollars of end-of-year purchasing power.

b. Calculate the nominal holding gain or loss for 19x11 *and* the real holding gain or loss in dollars of end-of-year purchasing power.

2. Purchasing-Power Gain or Loss. Gregory Company presented the following historical-cost/nominal-dollar balance sheets in its annual financial report for 19x9:

	December 31, 19x8	December 31, 19x9
Assets		
Current assets:		
Cash	$ 10	$ 15
Accounts receivable	20	40
Inventory.............................	30	35
Total current assets..................	60	90
Plant and equipment....................	200	220
Less: Accumulated depreciation	(80)	(83)
Total assets	$180	$227
Liabilities and Owners' Equity		
Current liabilities:		
Accounts payable	$ 5	$ 7
Notes payable........................	10	30
Total current liabilities...............	15	37
Bonds payable........................	10	10
Total liabilities.....................	25	47
Common stock	100	100
Retained earnings.....................	55	80
Total liabilities and owners' equity..	$180	$227

The general price level index traced the following path during the year:

December 19x8	180
Average, 19x9............	190
December 19x9	200

All purchases, collections, and payments can be assumed to have taken place evenly throughout the year.

 a. Calculate the company's monetary position on January 1 and on December 31.

 b. Calculate Gregory's purchasing-power gain or loss from its holdings of net monetary assets during the year, expressed in dollars with December 19x9, purchasing power. Carry your calculations to two decimal places.

3. Present-Value Financial Statements. Valentine Company's conventional-basis balance sheet showed the following on January 1, 19x1:

VALENTINE COMPANY
Conventional-Basis Balance Sheet
As of January 1, 19x1

Assets

Current assets:	
Cash.....................................	$ 100,000
Accounts receivable.........................	300,000
Inventories.................................	200,000
Total current assets	600,000
Plant and equipment (net)	800,000
Total assets	$1,400,000

Liabilities and Owners' Equity

Current liabilities:	
Accounts payable...........................	$ 80,000
Notes payable..............................	70,000
Total current liabilities....................	150,000
Bonds payable	350,000
Total liabilities..........................	500,000
Owners' equity:	
Common stock.............................	650,000
Retained earnings	250,000
Total owners' equity.....................	900,000
Total liabilities and owners' equity	$1,400,000

The appraised values of the cash, accounts receivable, accounts payable, and current notes payable on that date were equal to their balance sheet amounts. The inventories were appraised at 250 percent of their balance sheet amount, however, and net plant assets were appraised at $1,200,000. The company's bonds were trading on the market at a discount of 20 percent.

At the beginning of 19x1, Valentine's management estimated that with proper maintenance of the company's assets and customer base, the company's operations would generate cash inflows for its owners of $250,000 a year for 10 years and have a cash value of $1,500,000 at the end of that time. The interest rate was 10 percent.

The company's conventional-basis income statement for 19x1 showed the following:

VALENTINE COMPANY
Conventional-Basis Income Statement
For the Year Ended December 31, 19x1

Sales revenues.		$2,000,000
Cost of goods sold		1,400,000
Gross margin		600,000
Depreciation.	$ 60,000	
Other operating expenses	230,000	
Interest expense	10,000	
Income tax expense	100,000	400,000
Net income		$ 200,000

The current-cost of goods sold was $1,550,000, and depreciation on a current-cost basis was $80,000. All other income statement items would be shown in a value-based income statement at their conventional-basis amounts.

The net cash flow from operations, after taxes and interest, was greater than expected, and $90,000 was distributed to the owners as cash dividends. Valentine's management estimated at the end of 19x1 that future net cash inflows would amount to $260,000 a year for the next 10 years, leaving the owners an equity with a cash value of $1,600,000 at the end of that time. The interest rate remained 10 percent.

a. Prepare a value-based balance sheet for Valentine Company as of January 1, 19x1. For this purpose, assume that all cash flows occur at year-end and that interest is compounded annually.

b. Calculate the company's 19x1 income on a present-value basis and prepare a value-based income statement for the year.

4. Foreign Currency Transactions. During September 19x5, Roeder Corporation agreed to buy 600 lots of merchandise directly from a manufacturer in the country of Gotham, in which the currency was the apple, symbolized by *A*. As agreed, delivery and billing occurred on October 20, 19x5: 600 lots at a unit cost of A780.

Roeder paid A117,000 on October 30, 19x5, and the balance on January 8, 19x6. All of the merchandise was sold to U.S. customers: 60 percent on December 15, 19x5, and 40 percent on January 8, 19x6.

Pertinent exchange rates were as follows:

October 20, 19x5	$8.50/A
October 30, 19x5	$8.20/A
December 15, 19x5	$8.30/A
December 31, 19x5	$8.75/A
January 8, 19x6	$8.55/A

a. In Roeder's 19x5 income statement, what were the amounts of (1) cost of goods sold and (2) exchange gains/losses?

b. In Roeder's 19x6 income statement, what were the amounts of (1) cost of goods sold and (2) exchange gains/losses?

Exercises and Problems

5. Calculating the Value of a Business. In October 19x1, Ralph Sargent was presented with the opportunity to purchase Sports Galleria, a merchandise boutique for sports enthusiasts. Ralph envisioned the enterprise with a net cash flow of $100,000 after taxes each year for 10 years. Given his existing investment portfolio, Ralph was determined to earn a 12 percent return compounded annually.

Because Ralph's bid wasn't high enough, the business was sold to a different investor. Two years later, in December 19x3, the owner offered Ralph the chance to buy the business. Ralph studied the situation and estimated that annual aftertax net cash flow would likely be $175,000 each year for the next 15 years. Ralph's minimum rate of return had fallen to 10 percent.

Ralph's bid was accepted, and he purchased Sports Galleria for cash. By the end of 19x4, Ralph concluded that with his hands-on management of the business, there was no reason that each year's aftertax net cash flow wouldn't be at least $300,000, and that this performance level would likely continue indefinitely. Ralph revised his rate-of-return criterion to 13 percent as well.

Actual financial data were as follows:

	Net Assets, December 31	Aftertax Net Cash Flow
19x1	—	—
19x2	$600,000	$150,000
19x3	850,000	170,000
19x4	940,000	280,000

a. What was the highest amount that Ralph should have bid in October 19x1, given his estimates at that time?

b. What was the highest amount that Ralph should have bid in December 19x3, given his estimates at that time?

c. What was lowest amount that Ralph should demand from a prospective buyer of Sports Galleria in January 19x5?

6. Value of Shares of Stock. Carrington Corporation has been in operation for three years. It markets a new kind of plastic foam for sale to industrial customers. The company has reported a net loss each year since it was founded, but sales are now increasing, and management expects to report a small net income this year.

To finance the company's growth and broaden its ownership base, the owner-managers have decided to "go public" and have offered to sell shares of the company's common stock at $10 a share. Book value per share is now $4.

You have $25,000 you wish to invest in a growth situation of this sort, and you are willing to buy this stock if you think it will yield an annual return of 12 percent before taxes.

You forecast that Carrington Corporation will report net income and pay dividends as follows:

Years from Now	Net Income per Share	Dividends per Share
1	$0.10	—
2	0.75	$0.50
3	1.00	0.50
4	1.25	0.50
5	1.50	0.50
6	1.75	0.50
7	2.00	1.00
8	2.00	1.00
9	2.00	1.00
10	2.00	1.00

(For simplicity, you should assume that dividends will be paid once each year, at the end of the year.)

You believe that the market price of this stock 10 years from now will probably be about $16 a share.

What is this stock worth to you? Show the calculations that support your answer. Ignore income taxes.

7. Purchasing-Power Gains and Losses. Vara Company presented the following information on assets and liabilities in its 19x1 annual report:

	January 1	December 31
Cash	$ 20	$ 19
Accounts receivable	40	50
Inventory (LIFO)	50	55
Plant and equipment (net)	100	110
Accounts payable	10	8
Notes payable	20	24

Transactions during the year had the effect of increasing the company's net monetary position by $7 in nominal dollars.

The general price level index at the end of the year was 150. It was 125 at the beginning of the year and 140, on the average, during the year.

a. Calculate Vara Company's net monetary position on January 1 and on December 31, 19x1.

b. Calculate the purchasing-power gain or loss in 19x1 on the company's holdings of net monetary assets.

8. Purchasing-Power Gain or Loss. As of January 1, 19x6, the monetary assets of Monarch, Ltd., were $11,000; its monetary liabilities were $6,000.

Sales of merchandise during the year amounted to $60,000, and land that had cost $20,000 in 19x3 was sold for $36,000. Inventory costing $12,000 was bought during the year, and $26,000 of Monarch's operating expenses had immediate effects on the company's net monetary position.

Monarch bought a computer in February for $19,000 cash and purchased machinery in March for $40,000 which was paid in October. During June, Monarch sold treasury shares of common stock for $30,000, in July it paid off $4,000 of its long-term notes with $4,000 cash, and in November it expended $38,000 to retire shares of preferred stock.

The following consumer price index numbers related to 19x6:

	Consumer Price Index
December 19x5	110
December 19x6	132
19x6 average	120

Using the end-of-year purchasing power as the constant dollar, calculate the gain or loss in purchasing power resulting from Monarch's net monetary position during 19x6.

9. Purchasing-Power Gain and Loss. The following information is available for Companies A and B (in thousands):

	Company A		Company B	
	Jan. 1	Dec. 31	Jan. 1	Dec. 31
Cash	$150	$170	$ 60	$ 70
Accounts receivable	180	200	40	40
Inventory.	110	90	320	275
Total	$440	$460	$420	$385
Accounts payable	$ 30	$ 40	$ 20	$ 30
Bonds payable	200	200	160	130
Owners' equity.	210	220	240	225
Total	$440	$460	$420	$385

The general price level index was 100 as of January 1 and 116 as of December 31. The December 31 index was 108 percent of the average of the index during the year. Monetary-flow transactions occurred uniformly during the year.

a. What was the nominal-dollar increase or decrease in each company's net monetary position during the year?

b. What was the purchasing-power gain or loss experienced by each company from its holdings of net monetary assets?

c. Explain how and why the year's inflation affected the two companies differently.

10. Holding Gains during Inflation.   In 19x1, when the consumer price index (CPI) was 120, Parker Enterprises paid $1.4 million for real estate on which it planned to construct a world-class family amusement park. Although Parker was unable to begin construction by the end of 19x4, its management was pleased with the knowledge that the value of the land had increased to $2.5 million. The CPI was then 192. Newly enacted zoning ordinances prevented pursuing the project, and Parker therefore sold the property in December 19x6 to an industrial-park developer for $3.5 million, when the CPI was 288.

Although holding gains and losses aren't determinants of historical-cost income, Parker's top management was interested in determining these amounts for the board of directors' information.

a. What was the holding gain or loss between 19x1 and 19x4 in nominal dollars? What was the holding gain or loss in December 19x4 constant dollars?

b. What was the holding gain or loss between 19x4 and 19x6 in nominal dollars? What was the holding gain or loss in December 19x6 constant dollars?

c. What was the holding gain or loss between 19x1 and 19x6 in nominal dollars? What was the holding gain or loss in December 19x6 constant dollars? Is the answer to part *c* consistent with the answers to parts *a* and *b*?

11. Holding Gains/Losses, Nominal and Real.   Webster, Inc., a manufacturing company, bought a parcel of land for $400,000 cash in 19x1. Although its original intention had been to build a plant on the property, Webster's president began to doubt in 19x4 that construction would be undertaken, mainly because inflation had caused construction costs to rise dramatically. The company had determined, however, that the market value of the land had also risen dramatically during the first three years of ownership, as follows:

	Increase	
	Absolute	**Percent**
19x1 cost, $400,000		
19x2 market, $468,000	$ 68,000	17.0%
19x3 market, $550,000	82,000	17.5
19x4 market, $616,000	66,000	12.0
	$216,000	54.0

Although impressed by the 54 percent *increase* in value, the president was reminded that the just-published consumer price index for 19x4 indicated an identical 54 percent *decrease* in the purchasing power of the dollar between 19x1 and 19x4. Since the president's immediate reaction was that there was something sinister about this coincidence, the accountants assembled the following CPI numbers from published sources: 19x1 = 100, 19x2 = 110, 19x3 = 132, 19x4 = 154.

Prepare a schedule that identifies the real holding gains or losses experienced by Webster, Inc., during each of the three years it owned the land.

12. Cumulative Translation Adjustment. On December 29, Multionics, Inc., purchased 100 percent of Polar Corporation's common stock for $210,000 cash. This amount was the dollar equivalent of Polar's H300,000 owners' equity, H being the symbol of the currency in the foreign country in which Polar was located.

a. Calculate the cumulative translation adjustment that would be disclosed in Multionics, Inc.'s December 31 balance sheet if the exchange rate had become $0.90/H.
b. Calculate the December 31 exchange rate if you had known instead that the cumulative translation adjustment had been "negative $15,000."

13. Foreign Currency Financial Statements. Chesterton Industries operated a wholly owned subsidiary in a foreign country where the currency, symbolized by Z, was treated by Chesterton as the functional currency. Highlights of the subsidiary's 19x7 financial results were as follows:

	January 1		December 31	
	Z	$	Z	$
Assets.........................	300	720	430	
Liabilities	180	432	230	
Owners' equity	120	288	200	
Exchange rate...................		2.40/Z		2.10/Z
Net income			80	180
Cumulative translation adjustment..		60 cr.		

a. Calculate the assets, liabilities, and owners' equity amounts that would appear in the subsidiary's December 31 dollar-based balance sheet.
b. Calculate the amount of the cumulative translation adjustment that would be disclosed in the December 31 dollar-based balance sheet.

14. Foreign Currency Balance Sheet. During 19x5, Arleigh, Inc., contemplated purchasing 100 percent of the common stock of a foreign corporation. Although top management was impressed by the $100,000 increase in the dollar-based owners' equity total each year for the past three years, you are asked to (1) calculate the four missing amounts (A, B, C, and D) and (2) explain the significance, if any, of the changes in the amount of the cumulative translation adjustment.

	December 31—in Thousands			
	19x1	**19x2**	**19x3**	**19x4**
Monetary assets	$520	$510	$710	$620
Monetary liabilities	310	350	360	450
Nonmonetary assets	380	490	C	840
Nonmonetary liabilities	A	200	250	360
Owners' equity:				
Account balances	290	350	580	700
Cumulative translation adjustment . .	60	B	(30)	D

15. Foreign Currency Transactions. Synergonics, Ltd., sold made-to-order electronic components to the government of Tolesia whose currency was the *tol,* symbolized by *T.* The agreement identified October 1, 19x1, as the date of sale, a sale price of $600,000 to be remitted in tols. The terms of payment were as follows: 10 percent cash tols to be received upon delivery, 30 percent cash tols to be collected four months later, and 60 percent in Tolesian industrial diamonds to be transferred to Synergonics upon delivery of the electronic components.

Pertinent exchange rates were as follows:

October 1, 19x1	$4.00/T
December 31, 19x1	$3.25/T
February 1, 19x2	$3.75/T
August 7, 19x2	$3.00/T
November 15, 19x2	$3.40/T

On October 1, 19x1, Synergonics received T15,000 cash and industrial diamonds with a market value of T90,000. In 19x2, Synergonics received T45,000 cash on February 1, and $300,000 cash when the diamonds were sold on August 7. On November 1, 19x2, Synergonics sold its holdings of tols for $204,000.

a. At what dollar amount should the cash, accounts receivable, and diamonds assets be measured in Synergonics's December 31, 19x1, balance sheet?

b. What was Synergonics's foreign currency exchange gain or loss in 19x1 and in 19x2?

16. Interpreting Published Information. The 1984 annual report of Polaroid Corporation reported the following comparative information for fiscal years 1980–1984:

	Net Sales	Net Earnings	Cash Dividends per Share
1980	$1,450.8 million	$85.4 million	$1.00
1981	1,419.6	31.1	1.00
1982	1,293.9	23.5	1.00
1983	1,254.5	49.7	1.00
1984	1,271.5	25.7	1.00

A pension fund portfolio manager observed that it was remarkable that Polaroid's dividend rate remained constant despite the 12 percent decline in net sales and the 70 percent decline in net earnings. An economist acquaintance suggested that the data be evaluated in the light of each year's average consumer price index (CPI).

1980	246.8
1981	272.4
1982	289.1
1983	298.4
1984	311.1

Perform the calculations suggested by the economist, using 1984 constant dollars, and determine whether the constant dividend rate was appropriate in the light of the inflation that affected Polaroid and its stockholders.

17. Interpreting Published Information. The observations regarding Polaroid Corporation's five-year comparative data (problem 16) were presented to a securities analyst. Her reaction was to point to the following table that appeared on page 36 of Polaroid's 1984 annual report:

FIVE-YEAR COMPARISON OF OTHER SELECTED DATA ADJUSTED FOR THE EFFECTS OF CHANGING PRICES
(Average 1984 dollars in millions, except per share data)

	1984	1983	1982	1981	1980
Net sales	$1,271.5	$1,308.0	$1,392.0	$1,622.0	$1,828.0
Current cost information					
Net earnings/(loss)	$ 12.9	$ 39.1	$ (27.3)	$ 14.5	$ 40.8
Earnings/(loss) per share	$ .42	$ 1.26	$ (.86)	$ .44	$ 1.25
Changes in specific prices in excess of (less than) general inflation*	$ (26.0)	$ (8.3)	$ 40.9	$ (37.7)	$ (118.5)
Net assets at year-end*	$1,019.0	$1,074.0	$1,109.0	$1,229.0	$1,340.0
Other information					
Loss from decline in purchasing power of net monetary assets	$ (10.5)	$ (9.8)	$ (9.0)	$ (20.3)	$ (24.9)
Cash dividends per share	$ 1.00	$ 1.04	$ 1.07	$ 1.14	$ 1.26
Stock price per share at year-end	$ 27¾	$ 35	$ 26⅞	$ 22⅞	$ 30⅛
Average consumer price index (1967 = 100)	311.1	298.4	289.1	272.4	246.8

* At December 31, 1984, current cost of inventory was $348.0 million and current cost of property, plant, and equipment net of accumulated depreciation was $420.0 million. The effect of the increase in general inflation on inventory and net property, plant, and equipment held during 1984 amounted to $30.0 million. The increase in the specific prices of these assets amounted to $4.0 million, or $26.0 million less than the increase in general inflation.

a. Does the information contained in Polaroid's table confirm, complement, or contradict the observations made by the portfolio manager and the economist?
b. Did Polaroid experience a holding gain or a holding loss as a result of owning inventory and plant assets during 1984?
c. Identify any additional insights provided by Polaroid's table.

18. Interpreting Published Information. The 1984 annual report of Foxboro Company included the following historical-cost information:

Income statement:

Net sales	$515,856,000
Cost of sales	$313,015,000
Income before taxes	$ 972,000
Taxes on income	(3,300,000)
Net income	$ 4,272,000

Balance sheet:

Inventories	$176,400,000
Property, plant, and equipment, at cost	198,078,000
Accumulated depreciation	91,820,000

The annual report contained the following information about the negative amount of income taxes:

During 1984 and 1983, the Company developed a negative tax provision, even though earning pretax income in both years. This dichotomy resulted from the Company's ability to benefit from loss carrybacks in certain high-tax jurisdictions, while at the same time earning pretax income in other low-tax jurisdictions. It also reflects the effects of special income tax credits.

The information in the box at the top of page 565 was presented in Foxboro's 1984 annual report as a supplement to its basic financial statements.

a. What was Foxboro's nominal and real holding gain or loss during 1984?
b. What was the unrealized nominal holding gain as of December 31, 1984?
c. What was the amount of the holding gain that was realized in 1984?
d. During 1984, the consumer price index increased from 289.4 to 311.1. What conclusion can be reached regarding Foxboro's net monetary assets/liabilities during the year?

The following table summarizes the adjustment to reflect the company's income on a current cost basis (all dollar figures are thousands of dollars).

Income before taxes, as reported in the Consolidated Statement of Income	$ 972
Adjustments to restate costs for the effects of inflation (current costs):	
Cost of sales, including $3,034 of depreciation	(3,841)
Other depreciation and amortization of facilities........	(1,753)
	(4,622)
Taxes on income, as reported in the Consolidated Statement of Income	(3,300)
Net loss adjusted for specific inflation...................	$(1,322)
Loss from decline in purchasing power of net amounts due the company..	$ 2,418
Increase in specific prices (current costs) of inventories and property, plant, and equipment held during the year .	$ 6,533
Effect of increase in the general price level	9,583
Excess of increase in the general price level over increase in specific prices......................................	$ 3,050

The aggregate amount of depreciation expense for the year ended December 31, 1984, on a current cost basis, was $25,329. At December 31, 1984, the current costs of inventories and property, plant, and equipment (net of accumulated depreciation) were $216,473 and $177,623, respectively.

No adjustments have been made to taxes on income in the above information since adjustments to restate costs for the effects of inflation are not deductible for income tax purposes.

19. Replacement-Cost Depreciation: Discussion Question. Miller Enterprises, Inc., is incorporated in a country in which corporations aren't required to base their financial statements on generally accepted accounting principles. In view of the steadily rising costs of equipment and building construction in that country, Miller's controller has suggested basing depreciation each year on replacement cost. Depreciation each year would be reflected in a journal entry of the following form:

Depreciation...	X	
Accumulated Depreciation		Y
Reserve for Replacement		Z

in which X is the depreciation charge based on replacement cost and Y is the depreciation charge based on acquisition cost.

a. What effect would the proposed method have on net income during a period of rising equipment costs? Would this effect continue after equipment costs stopped rising? Explain.

b. If the controller's proposal was accepted, how would you interpret the "reserve for replacement"? Would it appear on the income statement for the year or would it go directly to the year-end balance sheet? In which section of the statement should it appear? State your reasons.

c. If a machine is replaced at the end of its anticipated useful life by an identical machine with a higher replacement cost, will the reserve for replacement equal the difference between the original cost of the first machine and the cost of its replacement? Explain.

20. Financial Statements on a Present-Value Basis. Vista Realty Company raised $25 million by issuing shares of its capital stock to a small group of wealthy investors. It then built the Vista Hotel at a cost of $16 million on land acquired at a cost of $9 million. Construction was completed on January 1, 19x1, and the company leased the hotel on that date to an operator who agreed to pay Vista 40 percent of the hotel's revenues, with payment to be made in cash at the end of each year for 25 years. The operator also agreed to pay all the hotel's operating expenses, including property taxes. Vista Realty had no other assets and no liabilities on January 1, 19x1.

Vista Realty's management estimated that the hotel would gross an annual revenue of $10 million. The hotel would probably close its doors at the end of 25 years, and the land and building would be sold at that time for an estimated $9 million.

In its conventional income statements, Vista Realty depreciated the cost of the building by $640,000 a year.

Because the Vista Hotel was built under a special economic incentive program, Vista Realty was exempt from income taxes for 25 years on its income from ownership of the hotel. One provision of this arrangement was that the company would obtain an appraisal of the land and building each year. No appraisal was necessary on January 1, 19x1, because both the land and building had been obtained in recent market transactions.

The Vista Hotel had revenues of $8 million in its first year, and the operator made the first year's rental payment on schedule. Vista Realty had no expenses other than depreciation and paid no dividends to its shareholders in 19x1.

Toward the end of 19x1, the local government began building a domed stadium and related facilities for conventions, professional sports, and so forth. Vista Realty's management believed this would increase annual hotel revenue to about $12 million a year, starting in 19x3. The revenue projection for 19x2 remained at $10 million.

The annual appraisal of the land and building on December 31, 19x1, gave the land an appraised value of $11 million and the building an appraised value of $15.8 million, after deducting accumulated depreciation.

a. Calculate the present value of Vista Realty Company as of January 1, 19x1, at an interest rate of 15 percent, compounded annually.

b. Prepare a value-based balance sheet as of January 1, 19x1, reflecting your answer to part *a*.

c. Calculate the present value of Vista Realty Company as of December 31, 19x1, at an interest rate of 15 percent, compounded annually.

d. Calculate Vista Realty's 19x1 income on a present value basis. Did the company earn 15 percent on its owners' investment in 19x1?

e. Prepare a balance sheet as of December 31, 19x1, reflecting your answers to parts *c* and *d*. Explain the meaning of any change in goodwill.

f. Amanda Jones, a wealthy investor, had an opportunity to buy a 10 percent interest in Vista Realty Company on December 31, 19x1. Assuming she accepted management's estimates, calculate the maximum price she should have been willing to pay for this stock if she required a 12 percent return on her investment.

Chapter 15

Financial-Statement Analysis

Corporate financial statements summarize part of the company's history. Their main purpose, however, is to help managers and investors make decisions that will affect the company's future. The study of financial statements for this purpose is known as financial-statement analysis. The purpose of this chapter is to explain what financial-statement analysis is and what it is expected to accomplish. We'll also introduce some of the devices financial analysts use. The chapter has four parts:

1. The basic tools of financial analysis.
2. Measures of profitability.
3. Measures of debt-paying ability and risk.
4. Measures of efficiency.

The Basic Tools of Financial-Statement Analysis

To appreciate the nature of financial-statement analysis, we need to recognize that a number in isolation is meaningless. To be told, for example, that Grant Company earned $60 million this year conveys no substantive information. We don't know whether this was good or bad, desirable or undesirable, worthy of replication or not. What we need is a frame of reference in the form of a benchmark so that the $60 million net income can be evaluated in an appropriate context.

Performance Benchmarks

Readers of financial statements generally use three main kinds of performance benchmarks. The most common is performance in one or more prior periods. Thus, if we're told that Grant's net income was $75 million last year, we can conclude that this year's $60 million net income represented a 20 percent reduction.

A second commonly used benchmark is the income earned by comparable companies or average industry income. Learning that a competitor, Nickel, Inc., earned only $40 million enables us to calculate that Grant's earnings were 50 percent larger than Nickel's.

Additional insight can be obtained by using both benchmarks simultaneously. Assuming Nickel earned $30 million last year, we can display all four income amounts—two companies, two years—as follows:

	Net Income ($ millions)		Percentage Increase (Decrease)
	19x1	19x2	
Grant Company.	$75	$60	(20%)
Nickel, Inc.	30	40	33
Percentage advantage	150%	50%	

Although Grant's income was 50 percent larger than Nickel's in 19x2, it had been 150 percent larger than Nickel's in 19x1. The concurrent use of two benchmarks enables us to see that even though Grant's income continued to exceed Nickel's earnings, Grant's relative position was declining.

The third benchmark with which to analyze financial results is the anticipated outcome. The notion of anticipated outcome is not as well defined as the other two benchmarks. Within the company itself, budgeted amounts would serve this function, and this will be discussed further in Chapter 20. External parties, however, find it much more difficult to identify an anticipated outcome. Although some companies provide their bankers with projected financial statements, and some corporation presidents announce publicly the income their company expects to earn during the coming year, analysts and investors usually have to determine for themselves the amount of income they expect companies to earn.

However definitive or official the expectation, users of financial statements do evaluate results against the amounts that had been anticipated or hoped for. To give this benchmark an added dimension, it should be used in conjunction with the other two guides. In our example, the 20 percent decline in Grant's income is seen in an altogether different light if earnings had been expected to decrease by 35 percent than if they had been expected to increase by 10 percent.

The Role of Ratios

The basic building block in financial-statement analysis is the *ratio,* a percentage or decimal relationship of one number with another. Ratios are an important means by which benchmarks are used to analyze financial statements; the three different ways to use ratios are as follows:

1. *Structural analysis* entails examining the relationship between two financial-statement items or groups of items in the same period, such as relating the amount of cash on hand to total current liabilities.
2. *Time-series analysis* involves comparing individual financial-statement ratios of the same company in different time periods.
3. *Cross-sectional analysis* refers to comparing the company's financial-statement items with those of other companies in the same industry or with some market-wide measure or measures.

The advantage of ratios is that they bring the numbers being expressed as ratios down to a common scale. A company may be twice as large as it was 10 years ago, for example, so comparing total expenses in the two periods won't be as useful as comparing the expense/revenue *ratios* in the two periods.

Stating relationships on a common scale doesn't necessarily make them perfectly comparable, however. A high ratio may be appropriate for a company in one industry but not for a company in another industry or for a company at a different stage in its development or for a much larger or smaller company.

Both time-series analysis and cross-sectional analysis may be distorted by inflation or unusual business conditions. Time-series comparisons tend to be distorted by inflation to a larger extent than cross-sectional comparisons because all observations in a cross-sectional analysis are made in the same time period, with the same general price level. The analyst's problem is to decide how serious these distortions are and how to adjust for them.

For these reasons, we can't prescribe an ideal value for any ratio. The ideal varies with the circumstances the individual company finds itself in. Our objective will be to provide some insight into whether high ratios are likely to signal strengths or weaknesses in different circumstances. Before proceeding to learn about those ratios that tend to be used most frequently, we need to be aware of what accountants call the *comparability* quality of financial statements.

Accounting Comparability

To be in a position to compare different sets of financial statements, the analyst needs to determine that they are comparable. This applies to all three benchmarks—a company's interperiod comparisons, between-company and industry comparisons, and a company's actual-versus-projected results. While comparability refers to organizational, economic, and environmental considerations, there is also the need to be concerned with *accounting comparability.*

Determinants of Income. One aspect of accounting comparability is that the components of net income be comparable. The reason this can be an issue is that a company may sometimes engage in a unique transaction that affects only one period's income. Analysts who are unaware of the presence of this once-only determinant of income would unknowingly treat it as one of the company's regular determinants of income. Three such special situations can affect income, and in each case, the nature, amount, tax effect, and per-share effect are disclosed.

The first special situation is an **extraordinary item.** This refers to a gain or loss that both is unusual in nature *and* occurs infrequently. Examples include losses resulting from an earthquake, an expropriation, or a violation of a newly enacted law or regulation. A loss sustained by a manufacturer upon selling a warehouse is not extraordinary; even though it's infrequent, in general it's not unusual for an owner to sell a warehouse. A weather-induced crop loss by a hurricane-belt farmer is not extraordinary; despite its being unusual for farmers in general, hurricanes are not infrequent for this particular company.

The second situation that accountants identify separately in an income statement is the effect of **discontinued operations**—namely, the case of a company that divests itself of a major line of business. Accountants isolate both (1) the income (or loss) resulting from its revenues and expenses, and (2) the gain (or loss) resulting from its sale or abandonment.

The third amount that accountants disclose separately is the cumulative effect of a **change in an accounting principle.** This refers to a company that adopts a different accounting method to record transactions from the method that had been used previously; an example would be switching from sum-of-the-years'-digits depreciation to the straight-line method. When this happens, the cumulative effect of the change on income is included in the income statement in the period in which the change is first introduced.[1]

A company that experiences any of these special situations displays the disclosure in the lower portion of its income statement. To illustrate, we'll assume that Samuels Company earned income before taxes of $216,000 and incurred income tax expense of $51,000—yielding net income of $165,000. Because its income contained all three of the special situations we've been describing, the income statement contained in Exhibit 15–1

---

[1] Accountants generally don't restate prior years' earnings; the only exceptions are (1) a mathematical mistake, (2) the misapplication of an accounting principle, and (3) the failure to use information that was known when the financial statements had originally been prepared.

EXHIBIT 15–1
Samuels Company: Special Income Statement Disclosures

Pretax income from continuing operations.........		$174,000
Income tax expense		(44,000)
Income from continuing operations..............		130,000
Discontinued operations:		
Income from discontinued operations (less applicable taxes of $7,000)	$23,000	
Loss on disposal of discontinued operations (less applicable taxes of $3,000)..................	(11,000)	12,000
Income before extraordinary items...............		142,000
Loss from uninsured earthquake damage (less applicable taxes of $2,000).................		(9,000)
Income before effect of accounting changes		133,000
Cumulative effect of a change in an accounting principle (less applicable taxes of $5,000)		32,000
Net income....................................		$165,000

identifies neither the $216,000 pretax income nor the $51,000 tax expense. Instead each of the disclosed components is expressed on a net-of-tax basis; the $165,000 net income that emerges at the very end is of course the difference between $216,000 and $51,000.[2]

This form of segmentation helps readers of financial statements predict future income and cash flows. The effects of extraordinary events and accounting changes, if unsegregated, would obscure period-to-period movements in income from ordinary operations—and it is income from ordinary operations that will be the principal source of cash flows in the future.

Segregation of the income contribution of discontinued operations is important for much the same reason. Since these operations have been discontinued, they will neither contribute to nor siphon off income and cash flows in the future. By reporting this component of net income separately, the company gives the statement reader a clearer picture both of the reason for discontinuing the operation and of the income and cash-flow stream that will remain in the future.

---

[2] The amounts can be reconciled with the following schedule:

	Pretax	Tax	Aftertax
Continuing operations............	$174,000	$(44,000)	$130,000
Discontinued operations:			
Income from operations.........	30,000	(7,000)	23,000
Disposal	(14,000)	3,000	(11,000)
Extraordinary loss	(11,000)	2,000	(9,000)
Accounting change	37,000	(5,000)	32,000
Net income	$216,000	$(51,000)	$165,000

Disclosure of Accounting Policies.   While identifying special components of income improves comparability when applying any of the benchmarks, intercompany comparability poses an additional challenge. Since there are no uniform accounting methods in the sense that all companies use identical procedures, each company must disclose which one method it has adopted from among the various acceptable alternatives. This would encompass situations such as (1) identifying the inventory costing method it has selected (e.g., FIFO versus LIFO), (2) revealing the number of years over which intangible assets are amortized, and (3) disclosing that it is recognizing revenue earlier than the point of delivery on the basis of its unique industry situation (e.g., recording revenue from mining silver as it is extracted). These disclosures are generally presented as the opening section of the notes accompanying the financial statements.

Measures of Profitability

Whether or not the company's income statement is segmented in the ways described in the preceding section, informed readers of financial statements are likely to calculate a number of ratios to help them evaluate the company's strengths and weaknesses. We'll use the financial statements of a hypothetical business, Grant Company, to illustrate the role of ratios in this process. Exhibit 15–2 presents Grant's balance sheets as of the end of 19x1 and 19x2. Exhibit 15–3 shows the company's income statement for 19x2, and Exhibit 15–4 is Grant's statement of changes in retained earnings for 19x2. We'll introduce the company's funds flow statement later in the chapter.

The first set of ratios are designed to throw light on the company's profitability. Investors become and remain stockholders in a company because they believe that dividends and capital gains (increases in the market price of the stock) will compare favorably with the amounts they can earn on alternative investments of comparable risk. The most important determinant of future dividends and capital gains is the corporation's future earnings, and the first source of data for use in forecasting future earnings is the corporation's past-earnings record.

Three ratios used widely as measures of the company's past-earnings record are:

1. Earnings per share of common stock.
2. Return on common equity.
3. Return on assets.

We'll discuss each of these in turn and then describe a way of breaking the return-on-assets ratio down into two component ratios, the asset-turnover ratio and the profit-margin ratio. We'll also discuss the concept of the quality of earnings and the dividend-payout ratio.

EXHIBIT 15–2

GRANT COMPANY
Balance Sheets
As of December 31, 19x1 and 19x2

	19x1	19x2
Assets		
Current assets:		
Cash	$ 4,300	$ 2,600
Receivables	17,100	19,800
Inventories	28,700	35,900
Total current assets	50,100	58,300
Plant assets	44,800	50,500
Less: Accumulated depreciation	(18,100)	(19,400)
Net plant assets	26,700	31,100
Total assets	$76,800	$89,400
Liabilities and Owners' Equity		
Current liabilities:		
Accounts payable	$ 4,800	$ 6,600
Notes payable	6,200	15,500
Taxes payable	2,200	2,100
Total current liabilities	13,200	24,200
Long-term debt	17,400	11,700
Total liabilities	30,600	35,900
Owners' equity:		
8 percent preferred stock, par value $10 (700 shares)	7,000	7,000
Common stock, par value $5 (2,000 shares in 19x2, 1,800 shares in 19x1)	9,000	10,000
Additional paid-in capital	9,900	12,600
Retained earnings	20,300	23,900
Total owners' equity	46,200	53,500
Total liabilities and owners' equity	$76,800	$89,400

Earnings per Common Share

The most widely used measure of financial performance is the aftertax earnings per common share, usually referred to as **earnings per share.** As we saw in Chapter 11, dividends the holders of preferred stock are entitled to must be subtracted from net income to get earnings applicable to the common stock. The 19x2 calculation for Grant Company is:

$$\frac{\text{Net income} - \text{Preferred dividends}}{\text{Number of common shares}} = \frac{\$6,460 - \$560}{2,000}$$
$$= \$2.95 \text{ per share}$$

EXHIBIT 15–3

GRANT COMPANY
Income Statement
For the Year Ended December 31, 19x2

Sales revenue		$105,460
Expenses:		
Cost of goods sold	$57,700	
Depreciation.	2,500	
Research and development	4,630	
Selling and administration	27,470	92,300
Income before interest and taxes		13,160
Interest expense		2,500
Income before taxes		10,660
Income taxes		4,200
Net income.		$ 6,460

EXHIBIT 15–4

GRANT COMPANY
Statement of Changes in Retained Earnings
For the Year Ended December 31, 19x2

Retained earnings, January 1, 19x2		$20,300
Add: Net income, 19x2		6,460
Total		26,760
Less: Dividends on preferred stock	$ 560	
Dividends on common stock	2,300	
Total dividends		2,860
Retained earnings, December 31, 19x2		$23,900

Earnings per share amounts are used to compare one year's earnings with those of prior years. They are also combined with other data, such as market price per share, to reveal relationships the analyst wishes to examine. The relationship between a company's earnings per share and a market index of earnings (total earnings of a large sample of corporations) can be particularly useful in predicting the company's future earnings.

Both the numerator and the denominator of this ratio need to be studied carefully. The dilution adjustments we discussed in Chapter 11 are made routinely and we needn't dwell on them here. What we need to concentrate on is the earnings numerator. For one thing, analysts distinguish between earnings from ordinary, continuing operations and earnings from operations about to be discontinued, and from the effects of extraordinary events. In fact, even ordinary operating earnings have to be examined carefully because many items that are unusual or nonrecurring but do not meet the accounting profession's test to be *extraordinary* are included in ordinary income. The total amount of income or loss from these sources is likely to fluctuate more widely than the normal determinants of income. The analyst should be alert to identify the underlying movements in earnings from these fluctuations.

Quality of Earnings

Analysts also study the company's financial statements to appraise what they refer to as the **quality of earnings.** *Quality* has many dimensions, one of which refers to the company's accounting policies. Companies using FIFO for inventories, straight-line depreciation, the flow-through method of accounting for the investment tax credit, and pooling-of-interests accounting for business combinations are likely to report greater earnings than comparable companies using LIFO, accelerated depreciation, investment-credit deferral, and the purchase method of accounting for business combinations.

Quality also depends on the nature of the company's products and markets. It is important to know whether the bulk of current earnings comes from growing business segments or from declining segments, from domestic markets or foreign markets, from a few large customers or many small ones, and so on. The publication of segment-income data, including a geographic breakdown, provides analysts with the raw material to analyze these aspects of quality. Exhibit 15–5 contains an excerpt of the 1984 segment disclosures of The Gillette Company.

A third aspect of earnings quality is the extent to which current earnings are affected by current expenditures on research and development or promotional marketing activities. Sales revenues from these activities won't be recognized until some time in the future, but their costs show up among the current year's expenses. Similarly, if equipment-replacement prices have been rising rapidly, current depreciation charges are likely to be much lower than they will be in the future when the present equipment is replaced. In fact, a good deal of our discussion in earlier chapters was designed to provide the foundation for an analysis of the quality of earnings.

Return on Common Equity

The absolute amount of income isn't an adequate measure of profitability because it doesn't indicate how much had to be invested to achieve it. One way to put earnings and investment amounts together is to calculate the rate of **return on common equity**—that is, the ratio of net income available to common shareholders to the book value of the common shareholders' equity in the company. For Grant, the book value of the common equity was the total of the par value of the common stock,

EXHIBIT 15-5
The Gillette Company: Segment Disclosures for the Year Ended December 31, 1984

Financial Information by Business Segment

(Millions of dollars)

1984	Blades & Razors	Toiletries & Cosmetics	Writing Instruments & Office Products	Braun Products	Other	Total of Segments	Corporate	Total
Net sales...........	$767.8	$697.0	$275.3	$394.3	$154.2	$2,288.6	$ —	$2,288.6
Profit from operations....	255.9	56.6	11.3	43.8	5.9	373.5	(21.2)	352.3
Identifiable assets......	481.7	343.3	257.8	280.3	344.8	1,707.9	316.5	2,024.4
Capital expenditures....	53.3	20.0	11.4	19.1	8.6	112.4	6.7	119.1
Depreciation.......	25.3	10.5	12.0	16.1	6.7	70.6	4.5	75.1

Financial Information by Geographic Area

(Millions of dollars)

1984	Europe	Latin America	Other	Total Foreign Excluding Canada	United States & Canada	Total for Geographic Areas	Corporate	Total
Net sales...........	$724.4	$255.4	$206.4	$1,186.2	$1,102.4	$2,288.6	$ —	$2,288.6
Profit from operations....	90.1	60.5	39.6	190.2	183.3	373.5	(21.2)	352.3
Identifiable assets......	578.1	245.4	96.2	919.7	788.2	1,707.9	316.5	2,024.4

In calculating profit from operations for individual business segments, substantial expenses incurred at the operating level which are common to more than one segment are allocated on a net sales basis. Certain corporate expenses of an operational nature are also allocated to business segments and geographic areas.

All intercompany transactions have been eliminated, and transfers of finished goods between geographic areas are not significant. Area profit from operations of Canadian subsidiaries amounted to approximately 11%, 9% and 6% of the total for the United States and Canada for 1984, 1983 and 1982, respectively. Net sales of deodorants/antiperspirants averaged approximately 10% of total net sales for the three-year period. Assets in the Corporate column include cash, short-term investments, and oil and gas investments.

additional paid-in capital, and retained earnings, adding up to $46,500 at the end of 19x2.[3] The rate of return on common equity therefore was as follows:

$$\frac{\text{Net income} - \text{Preferred dividends}}{\text{Common equity}} = \frac{\$6,460 - \$560}{\$46,500} = 12.7 \text{ percent}$$

In trying to decide whether this represents good or bad performance, a number of questions must be answered. For example, how does this amount compare with the return of other companies in the industry and in industry in general? Is this company's rate of return holding steady, going up, or declining? How wide are the year-to-year fluctuations in rate of return?

The rate of return on common equity can also be calculated in another way, with the market value of the common shares as the denominator of the ratio. After all, book value represents investment decisions investors made in the past. The current question is: how large a return is the company making on the amounts investors are *now* willing to invest in this company?

This ratio is calculated routinely but in inverted form—that is, one of the most widely quoted ratios in the financial press is the **price/earnings ratio,** usually referred to simply as the *P/E ratio.* For example, if Grant's common stock was being traded on the market at a price of $29.50 a share at the end of 19x2, the P/E ratio was $29.50/$2.95 = 10. This is simply the reciprocal of the earnings/market value ratio: $2.95/ $29.50 = 10 percent.

Return on Assets

An alternative to measuring return on common equity is to calculate **return on assets.** This measure relates income to *total* assets, not just to that portion of the assets contributed by the common shareholders. Because the return-on-assets denominator includes the equity of preferred shareholders and creditors, the income in the numerator has to be adjusted by the methods described in the next paragraph.

As we saw earlier, the numerator of the return-on-common-equity ratio is adjusted by *subtracting* the preferred dividends. In the calculation of the return-on-assets ratio, however, the numerator is adjusted by *adding*

---

[3] Earnings may be related to the investment at the beginning of the year, the investment at the end of the year, or an average of the two. We have used year-end investment because it is generally the most convenient.

the aftertax interest expense. For Grant Company in 19x2, the adjustment is as follows:

$$\frac{\text{Net income} + \text{Aftertax interest}}{\text{Total assets}} = \frac{\$6,460 + \$1,500}{\$89,400} = 8.9 \text{ percent}$$

The purpose of the $1,500 add-back to the numerator is to achieve consistency with the denominator, for the following reason. Whereas stockholders view interest as a *determinant* of income, stockholders and creditors together view interest as a distribution of income. If we assume a 40 percent marginal tax rate,[4] including the $2,500 interest as a deductible expense in Grant's tax return resulted in a $1,000 reduction in the company's tax expense. The aftertax effect therefore was $1,500 [$2,500 − $1,000, or (1.0 − 0.4) × $2,500].

The appendix to this chapter discusses return on common equity, return on assets, and the effect of **financial leverage**—the phenomenon of investing borrowed funds to earn a return that is greater than the interest cost incurred to effect the borrowing. The discussion focuses on the difference between Grant's 8.9 percent return on assets and its 12.7 percent return on common equity.

Percentage-of-Sales Ratios

The rate of return on assets is the product of two factors: (1) the rate of asset turnover, and (2) the profit margin. This relationship can be stated in the form of an equation:

$$\text{Return on assets} = \text{Asset turnover} \times \text{Profit margin}$$
$$= \frac{\text{Sales}}{\text{Assets}} \times \frac{\text{Income}}{\text{Sales}}$$

We'll discuss **profit-margin ratios** here, leaving asset-turnover ratios for the final section of this chapter.

---

[4] Grant's income tax expense was calculated at the rate of 30 percent of the first $640 of income before taxes and 40 percent of all amounts in excess of $640. Since the $2,500 interest deduction reduced income before taxes from $13,160 to $10,660, its impact on taxes must be measured by the tax rate applicable to a reduction in that portion of the income range, 40 percent. (These rates and the dollar limit for the lower rate are purely illustrative; in practice, both the rates and the limit will differ, depending on the location of the company's operations and the revenue needs of the taxing authorities.)

The profit-margin ratio and other percentage-of-sales ratios are widely used in profitability analysis, mainly to identify trends or intercompany differences. In calculating the overall profit-margin ratio, we need to use the same income amount that we use in the return-on-investment comparisons. If return on investment is calculated as a return on assets, as in our present example, then the income amount should be *before interest but after taxes.*

Grant's adjusted income after taxes was $7,960—based on (1) $13,160 income before interest and taxes, less (2) the $5,200 income tax expense in the absence of interest ($4,200 + 0.4 × $2,500). Its profit margin for 19x2 was:

$$\frac{\text{Adjusted net income}}{\text{Sales revenue}} = \frac{\$7,960}{\$105,460} = 7.5 \text{ percent}$$

If return on investment is measured by the rate of return on common equity, the numerator would be the amount of income available to the common stockholders—net income minus preferred dividends.

The overall profit-margin ratio is usually supplemented by various subordinated ratios, such as the **operating ratio** (the ratio of operating expenses to operating revenues), the *gross-margin ratio* (the ratio of the total gross margin to gross revenues), and the *research-and-development ratio* (the ratio of research and development expenses to gross revenues). These ratios are useful both in intercompany comparisons and in analyzing trends in the company's own performance. A rising operating ratio, for example, may be a signal of operating difficulties; an operating ratio higher than competitors' ratios may be a signal of competitive weakness. Alternatively, a high and rising operating ratio may signal a shift by the company to an aggressive marketing strategy, in which low profit margins are accompanied by large increases in sales volume, now or in the future.

This dual interpretation reinforces a point we made earlier. The ratio is only an analytical tool. A high ratio may be a good sign or a bad sign, and the analyst can decide which it is only by placing it in the context of other ratios and other available information.

The Payout Ratio and the Rate of Growth

Potential purchasers of a company's stock are buying not only dividends at the current rate but also prospects of future growth (or decline). This growth is provided, in large part, by the reinvestment of funds provided by operations. An index of the company's commitment to growth is the **payout ratio.** For Grant in 19x2, this ratio was:

$$\text{Payout ratio} \quad = \quad \frac{\text{Dividends per share}}{\text{Earnings per share}} \quad = \quad \frac{\$1.15^*}{\$2.95} \quad = \quad 39 \text{ percent}$$

* $2,300 (Exhibit 15–4)/2,000 (Exhibit 15–2).

The payout ratio is often used with two related ratios: (1) the *price/earnings ratio* which was discussed earlier, and (2) the *dividend yield ratio*. With the current period's cash dividend as the *sole* measure of an investor's return, the yield ratio is the rate of return relative to the current market price per share. The following illustration assumes the market price of a common share of Grant Company was $29.50:

Dividend yield ratio		Price/earnings ratio		Payout ratio
$\dfrac{\text{Dividends per share}}{\text{Market price per share}}$	$\times$	$\dfrac{\text{Market price per share}}{\text{Earnings per share}}$	$=$	$\dfrac{\text{Dividends per share}}{\text{Earnings per share}}$
$\dfrac{\$1.15}{\$29.50}$		$\dfrac{\$29.50}{\$2.95}$		$\dfrac{\$1.15}{\$2.95}$
3.9%		10		39%

Investors are interested in both dividend yield and capital appreciation. The price/earnings ratio indicates the market's current disposition toward the company's stock, and it may also offer some clues about future capital appreciation.

Grant paid dividends equal to 39 percent of its earnings (its payout ratio); the 61 percent that was retained is called its **retention ratio.** The retention ratio, together with the **return on common equity** we discussed earlier, enables the analyst to address the question of how effectively the company can use the funds it retains and reinvests in the business. The resulting measure is called the **sustainable-growth ratio:**

$$\begin{aligned} \text{Sustainable-growth ratio} \quad &= \quad \text{Return on equity} \quad \times \quad \text{Retention ratio} \\ &= \quad 12.7\% \quad \times \quad 0.61 \quad = \quad 7.75 \text{ percent} \end{aligned}$$

This result reflects the $3,600 increase in retained earnings divided by the $46,500 common stockholders' equity. This shows us that in 19x2 the book value of Grant's owners' equity was growing at a rate of 7.75 percent a year; if all other relationships were steady, earnings presumably were growing at the same rate.[5] The higher the return on equity and the higher the retention rate, the higher the rate of growth in earnings the company can sustain.

Market-Value Ratio

The rate of return on equity is likely to be reflected in the *market value ratio:*

$$\text{Market-value ratio} = \frac{\text{Market price per share}}{\text{Book value per share}} = \frac{\$29.50}{\$23.25} * = 1.27$$

* $46,500/2,000 shares

Problems of asset measurement aside, companies with higher rates of return on equity will have higher stock prices relative to the current book value of the stock than comparable companies (with similar risk characteristics) having lower return-on-equity ratios, as long as the market believes the company can continue to generate these returns on the funds reinvested in the business. Earnings retention means the stockholders are exchanging current cash dividends in the expectation of receiving greater cash dividends or increased market prices in the future. If the company can't use the cash profitably, the return on equity will fall, the growth rate will drop, and the market-value ratio will decline.

The size of the market-value ratio depends on investors' appraisals of the ability of book values to measure the present value of the company's future cash flows. Grant's market-value ratio ($29.50/$23.25 = 1.27) could reflect a relatively low asset-measurement profile—LIFO inventory measurement, for example. Alternatively, it could mean that the company's assets would likely yield a higher rate of return than investors considered normal.

Measures of Debt-Paying Ability and Risk

Both lenders and investors in stocks are interested not only in profitability but also in the risks associated with investments in individual companies. Lenders think of risk as the uncertainty about whether they will receive the amounts due them and on time; equity investors see it as the degree of uncertainty surrounding their estimates of the rate of re-

---

[5] This statement isn't strictly accurate because we are using the end-of-year balance sheet amounts in the return-on-equity ratio. If we had used the *average* owners' equity for the year, the sustainable-growth ratio would have been slightly higher.

turn on their investments. Financial-statement analysis includes three techniques for evaluating risk:

1. Analysis of the asset-liability structure.
2. Funds-flow analysis.
3. Coverage analysis.

TERMINOLOGY

Solvency refers to the mix of an enterprise's assets and liabilities. For instance, a company is said to be insolvent if it doesn't have enough assets to meet all of its debt obligations. By contrast, **liquidity** generally refers to a company's ability to meet its short-term cash obligations.

Analysis of the Asset-Liability Structure

One kind of analysis of the sources and uses of funds is a study of the *structure* of the company's assets and of its liabilities and owners' equity.

Debt Structure. The order in which the sources of funds are listed in the balance sheet corresponds to two important characteristics: the interest cost of obtaining the funds and the risk they bring with them. Current accounts payable and wages payable are attractive sources of funds because they have no explicit interest cost. Current notes payable do have explicit interest costs, but the rates of interest on these notes are likely to be lower than on longer-term debt, at least in times of interest-rate stability. Despite these attractive features, current liabilities aren't unmixed blessings. Their main drawback is that they must be paid in a relatively short time. The *risk* cost is therefore high because payment may fall due just when the company finds itself temporarily short of cash.

Long-term debt, in contrast, typically carries a higher interest rate in periods of financial-market stability. Its advantage is that it poses less immediate threat to the company's solvency—that is, the ability to pay its debts when they come due. For instance, a company ordinarily can pick a convenient time to refinance long-term debt before it falls due, thereby minimizing the likelihood that it will fall due when the company lacks ready cash.

Finally, funds obtained from shareholders through the sale of stock or retention of earnings carry no risk of insolvency. The company has no contractual obligation to make payments on specified dates, even to the preferred shareholders. In return for removing this risk from the corporation, the stockholders expect a higher yield on their investment than that earned by the company's creditors. This desired yield can and should be considered a *cost* of stockholder capital.

The relative importance of debt in the capital structure is measured by several different ratios, of which we'll consider only three. The first of these, the **long-term-debt ratio,** is obtained by dividing the book value of the long-term debt by the book value of the owners' equity. For Grant at the end of 19x2 this ratio was:

$$\frac{\text{Long-term debt}}{\text{Total owners' equity}} = \frac{\$11,700}{\$7,000 + \$46,500} = 21.9 \text{ percent}$$

The long-term-debt ratio is used as a measure of risk. Because only near-term debt retirement and interest requirements constitute immediate threats to the company's solvency, however, this ratio applies more to long-term than to short-term risks.

A more inclusive ratio is the **debt/equity ratio,** the ratio of total liabilities to total owners' equity:

$$\frac{\text{Total liabilities}}{\text{Total owners' equity}} = \frac{\$35,900}{\$53,500} = 67.1 \text{ percent}$$

(A variant of this ratio is the ratio of total liabilities to total assets; both give essentially the same information.)

The debt/equity ratio is a more inclusive measure of risk than the long-term-debt ratio, but it still doesn't give much information on near-term risks. In 19x2, for example, Grant Company increased its short-term debt and decreased its long-term debt. As a result, the debt/equity ratio remained almost constant, but the ratio of current liabilities to total liabilities increased from 43.1 percent at the end of 19x1 ($13,200/$30,600) to 67.4 percent a year later ($24,200/$35,900). Other things being equal, this represented an increase in risk.

The main difficulty in interpreting these ratios is that they can be affected significantly by the company's asset-measurement policies. The choices of inventory method, depreciation method, and similar matters affect the asset-liability structure ratios just as they affect the profitability ratios.

One way to get around this difficulty is to use market values instead of book values to measure the liabilities and owners' equity that enter into the calculation of the asset-liability structure ratios. The advantage of market values is that they provide a more up-to-date measure of the debt burden. Market values of debt represent the present value of future debt-service payments under current market conditions. For example, if the market rate of interest is 12 percent, a company with $1 million of 8 percent debt incurred when the market yield was 8 percent has a smaller debt burden than a company with a $1 million issue of 12 percent bonds of the same maturity but issued when the market yield was 12 percent. Each will appear on the balance sheet as a $1 million liability, but the market value of the 8 percent issue will be much smaller, reflecting its smaller burden to the company.

Asset Structure. The way the company's funds have been used is also significant. Current assets are more liquid than plant and equipment, for example—that is, they can be made available more quickly to meet unexpected cash needs. Investments in current assets may also be highly profitable if they enable the company to increase total revenues or reduce total operating costs. Beyond some point, however, additional investments in current assets add less than enough to income to provide an adequate rate of return on the additional investment; idle cash balances, for example, earn nothing.

With these relationships in mind, the analyst can use asset-structure ratios to see how management is using the company's funds. For instance, two of Grant's asset-structure ratios for 19x2 reflected a clear decline in the company's liquidity:

	19x1	19x2
Cash/assets	5.6%	2.9%
Cash and receivables/assets	27.9	25.1

This was a *favorable* change if it resulted from a reduction in the amount of idle assets, an *unfavorable* change if it resulted from the company's inability to generate enough cash to meet its needs.

Working-Capital Ratios. Whether a company is liquid enough depends on its ability to meet short-term demands for cash. Analysts frequently use two balance sheet ratios to throw light on this question: the *current ratio* and the *quick ratio*.

TERMINOLOGY REMINDER

Liquidity refers to a company's ability to meet its short-term cash obligations. One commonly used measure of business liquidity is the company's *working capital,* defined as the excess of total current assets over total current liabilities. *Current assets* are those assets that management reasonably expects to convert to cash within one operating cycle, usually a year, and *current liabilities* are those obligations that will require an outlay of cash within a year.

The **current ratio** is the ratio of total current assets to total current liabilities. Looking back at Exhibit 15–2, we see that Grant Company's current ratio at the end of 19x2 was:

$$\frac{\text{Current assets}}{\text{Current liabilities}} = \frac{\$58,300}{\$24,200} = 2.41$$

Since the comparable ratio at the beginning of the year was $50,100/$13,200 = 3.80, the company's activities during the year obviously caused a substantial weakening in its liquidity position.

A high current ratio isn't an unmixed blessing. It shows that the company is financing a large proportion of its current assets from long-term sources—long-term debt and owners' equity. This provides a cushion or margin of safety against possible short-term downswings in the company's business. This reduces financial risk but it is also costly. As we pointed out earlier, short-term credit is likely to be cheaper than long-term credit, and a high current ratio means the company is either unable or unwilling to use this cheaper credit as extensively as a company with a low ratio.

One shortcoming of the current ratio is that it can be controlled by management. We'll illustrate this by using Grant Company's working-capital data as of December 31, 19x1 and 19x2—as they appeared in Exhibit 15–2:

	December 31	
	19x1	**19x2**
Current assets.	$50,100	$58,300
Current liabilities	13,200	24,200
Working capital	$36,900	$34,100
Current ratio	3.80	2.41

While the working capital fell by $2,800 ($36,900 − $34,100), or 7.6 percent, the current ratio decreased by almost five times that much, 36.6 percent [(3.80 − 2.41)/3.80].

Management may prefer that analysts not be confronted with this downward movement. Since $12,500 of Grant's current liabilities were scheduled to be paid early the following month anyway, management could have ordered these payments to be made during the third week of December. As a result, both current assets and current liabilities would have been reduced by $12,500, bringing the current ratio up to 3.91 ($45,800/$11,700). Although the absolute decrease in working capital would have remained $2,800, the increase in the current ratio from 3.80 to 3.91 would have implied that Grant was relatively more liquid on December 31 than it had been one year earlier.

A second defect of the current ratio is that its level depends on the method used to measure inventories. Other things being equal, a company using FIFO or average costing will have a higher current ratio after purchase prices have been rising than a company measuring inventories on a LIFO basis. Fortunately, inventory-replacement-cost data are now available for many companies, and these data give the analyst the raw materials to make adjustments to eliminate this source of noncomparability.

A third shortcoming of the current ratio is that it conveys no information on the *composition* of the current assets. Clearly, a dollar of cash or even of accounts receivable is more readily available to meet obligations than a dollar of most kinds of inventory. A measure designed to overcome this defect is the **quick ratio** (or *acid-test ratio*). This is the ratio of the "quick" assets—cash, short-term marketable securities, and short-term receivables to current liabilities. This ratio for Grant was as follows at the end of 19x2:

$$\frac{\text{Quick assets}}{\text{Current liabilities}} = \frac{\$2,600 + \$19,800}{\$24,200} = 0.93$$

This represented a sharp decline from the previous year's value of ($4,300 + $17,100)/$13,200 = 1.62, reflecting the large increase in inventory and current notes payable. This shift might be regarded as a cause for some concern.

Funds Flow Analysis

The main defect of all the balance sheet ratios is that they represent static relationships. Very few companies have enough cash or liquid assets at the beginning of the year to cover all the payments they will have to make during the year. Nor should they, because this would tie up the company's funds unnecessarily. Instead, they rely on the cash coming in during the year to cover most of their cash obligations.

For this reason, the best guarantee that a company will be able to pay its bills when they come due is an ample *cash flow from operations*—that is, the excess of cash receipts from operations over cash disbursements required by operations. Whether Grant's current ratio of 2.41 or its quick ratio of 0.93 represented an adequate margin of safety depended on (1) the variability of the cash-flow stream, (2) the ability to renew or replace its existing short-term obligations with other short-term obligations, and (3) the ability to reduce the amount of its current assets without impairing its operating performance.

Management uses a cash budget to determine whether the anticipated cash flow from operations is likely to be adequate to meet the company's needs for cash during the coming period, and we'll discuss cash budgets in Chapter 20. Outside investors have no access to the cash budget, however, and must try to approximate it by other means. The handiest tool for this purpose is the statement of changes in financial position, the funds flow statement.

Grant's funds flow statement for 19x2, prepared by the methods described in Chapter 13, is presented in Exhibit 15–6. Although the com-

EXHIBIT 15–6

GRANT COMPANY
Statement of Changes in Financial Position
For the Year Ended December 31, 19x2

Sources of cash:		
Operations:		
Net income	$ 6,460	
Add: Depreciation	2,500	
Increase in accounts payable	1,800	
Less: Increase in accounts receivable ..	(2,700)	
Increase in inventories..........	(7,200)	
Decrease in taxes payable.......	(100)	
Cash flow from operations..........		$ 760
Sale of common stock.................		3,700
Sale of plant assets		500
Increase in notes payable		9,300
Total sources of cash		14,260
Uses of cash:		
Retirement of long-term debt	5,700	
Cash dividends.......................	2,860	
Purchase of plant assets...............	7,400	
Total uses of cash..............		15,960
Decrease in cash		$ 1,700

pany's net income was $6,460, its cash flow from operations was significantly lower—$760. If this continued at the same level in 19x3, it wouldn't be big enough to cover dividends and plant and equipment expenditures at the 19x2 level. The analyst would have to estimate (1) how large the company's capital expenditures would be in 19x3 and (2) whether other sources of funds would be available in 19x3 to meet those needs. On the other hand, some changes in the current assets and current liabilities are temporary, and, in the absence of growth, increases in one period will be offset by decreases in the next period. If the company's growth rate is rapid, however, the analyst will have to make explicit forecasts of the effect of this growth on the company's cash flows.

Coverage Ratios

Although funds flow statements are probably the most valuable single basis for judging debt-paying ability, **coverage ratios** are also widely used for this purpose. Like the funds statement, a coverage ratio deals with *dynamics,* measuring a relationship between two sets of *flows.* The basic coverage ratio is the **times-charges-earned ratio,** the ratio of (1) income before interest and taxes to (2) interest and preferred dividend requirements. On this basis, Grant's ratio for 19x2 was:

$$\frac{\text{Income before interest and taxes}}{\text{Interest} + \text{Preferred dividends}} = \frac{\$13,160}{\$3,060} = 4.3$$

In other words, the company's earnings could shrink to 23 percent (1.0/4.3) of their 19x2 size and still be adequate to cover the interest and preferred dividend requirements.[6]

The times-charges-earned ratio is obviously incomplete. Interest and preferred-dividend payments aren't the only payments the company is committed to make on a continuing basis. A company's fixed obligations also include such items as property taxes, rentals, scheduled retirements of maturing debt, and even management salaries and other operating costs that wouldn't shrink quickly in the face of a reduction in the company's operating volume. A better ratio therefore is a ratio of the cash flow available to cover fixed-cash payments of all kinds. This is the **fixed charges ratio:**

$$\text{Fixed-charges ratio} = \frac{\text{Cash flow before fixed charges}}{\text{Total fixed charges}}$$

To calculate the (numerator) amount of cash flow available, we must identify the fixed costs we had subtracted in calculating the cash flow from operations and add them back. The (denominator) total fixed charges consist of both the fixed operating cash payments and other fixed cash payments (such as interest and preferred dividends):

$$\frac{\text{Cash flow from operations} + \text{Fixed operating cash payments}}{\text{Fixed operating cash payments} + \text{Other fixed cash payments}}$$

---

[6] Preferred dividends are not deductible from revenues in calculating taxable income. Therefore, the amount entered in the coverage ratio formula ought to be the *pretax* amounts necessary to provide for preferred dividends. This added refinement can be left for more advanced texts on the grounds that it will be important only if the coverage ratio is very low.

Outsiders don't have full access to the amounts entering into the calculation of this ratio, but they have enough information to approximate it. We'll return to this idea in Chapter 17 in which we discuss a technique known as break-even analysis.

No matter which coverage ratio is used, however, it has to be examined in conjunction with some measure of volatility—that is, the amplitude of fluctuations in annual earnings or operating cash flows before taxes and interest. Presumably, the higher the earnings volatility, the higher the coverage ratio should be.

Measures of Efficiency

As we pointed out earlier, a company's profitability depends on the profit margin on sales *and* on the amount of assets required to support a given sales volume. The main danger in focusing profitability analysis on revenue-based income or expense ratios is that they don't measure economic efficiency in any absolute sense. Businesses such as grocery chains and meat-packing companies operate with exceptionally narrow margins on sales and rely on a large sales volume to cover operating expenses and yield a satisfactory return on investment. Others, such as high-fashion clothing shops and yacht manufacturers, take the opposite tack and operate with low volume and high markups.

The solution to this problem is to supplement the profit-margin ratios with asset-turnover ratios. We'll take a brief look at three of these:

1. Total-asset turnover.
2. Receivables turnover, or collection period.
3. Inventory turnover.

Total-Asset Turnover

The principal turnover ratio is the ratio of total sales to total assets. Using year-end total assets as the base, this ratio for Grant in 19x2 was:

$$\frac{\text{Sales revenue}}{\text{Total assets}} = \frac{\$105,460}{\$89,400} = 1.18$$

In other words, $1 of assets was required to support every $1.18 of sales.

Once again, the main use of this kind of ratio is to identify ways in which the company is departing from its own previous operating pattern or from that of its competitors. Turnover and percentage-of-sales ratios must be examined together, in parallel—the significance of a change in one can be appraised only if movements in the other are known.

The main shortcoming of these ratios is that they are sensitive to variations in asset-measurement and revenue-recognition practices.

We've said enough about these in general to make repetition here unnecessary, but if all the accounting policy differences between two companies run in the same direction—that is, one company's policies all lead to higher asset figures than the other's—the asset-turnover ratios may be very difficult to compare.

The significance of total-asset turnover lies in the following relationship. A company invests in assets to produce sales revenue, and sales revenue in turn generates income. All told, a company invests in assets to be able to earn income. This relationship can be depicted as follows, using Grant's 19x2 data:

$$\underset{\substack{\text{Asset} \\ \text{turnover}}}{\underbrace{\frac{\text{Sales revenue}}{\text{Total assets}}}} \times \underset{\substack{\text{Profit} \\ \text{margin}}}{\underbrace{\frac{\text{Adjusted income}}{\text{Sales revenue}}}} = \underset{\substack{\text{Return} \\ \text{on assets}}}{\underbrace{\frac{\text{Adjusted income}}{\text{Total assets}}}}$$

$$\frac{\$105{,}460}{\$89{,}400} \qquad \frac{\$7{,}960}{\$105{,}460} \qquad \frac{\$7{,}960}{\$89{,}400}$$

$$1.18 \qquad\qquad 7.55\% \qquad\qquad 8.9\%$$

Although the three ratios are calculated individually, it is readily apparent that having computed any two of these ratios, the third can be determined very easily. The significant implication, however, is that to maximize return on assets, a company must try to maximize its asset turnover while holding its profit margin constant or maximize its profit margin while holding its asset turnover constant.

Receivables Turnover and the Collection Period

The efficiency of individual kinds of assets may be easier to appraise than overall efficiency. Again, we use turnover ratios to measure efficiency. For example, the **receivables-turnover ratio** is usually calculated as the ratio of annual sales revenues to accounts receivable on some date. Based on 19x2 year-end receivables balances, this ratio for Grant was:

$$\frac{\text{Sales revenues}}{\text{Receivables}} = \frac{\$105{,}460}{\$19{,}800} = 5.3$$

This ratio implies that the company's receivables "turned over" or went through the cycle of collection and regeneration 5.3 times during the year.

A related and perhaps more easily understood statistic is the **collection period**—the number of days' sales in accounts receivable. On the basis of a 360-day year, $292.94 is the average daily sales ($105,460 ÷ 360). Dividing the accounts receivable balance by this amount produces $19,800 ÷ $292.94 = 68, the number of days' sales in accounts receivable. This can also be calculated by dividing the number of days by the receivables-turnover ratio: 360/5.3 = 68 days.

These ratios are regarded as indicators of (1) the liquidity of the receivables, (2) the quality of the receivables, and (3) management's credit-granting policies. A low turnover ratio—that is, a long collection period—means that in the normal course of business, receivables are turned into cash somewhat slowly. A collection period that is long relative to the normal credit period in the industry indicates either that the company is using a liberal credit policy to stimulate sales or that the receivables are of low quality, with many customers failing to pay their bills on time. If Grant's terms of sale call for payment within 30 days, for example, its 68-day collection period would be regarded as quite long.

Neither ratio is very precise. The year-end receivables may be lower than their average for the year; sales revenues may include revenues from *cash* sales. An aging of the receivables would give a much better indication of the quality of those receivables; a weighted average of the collection times during the year would be more indicative of the collection period. This means that once again the emphasis must be less on the absolute size of the ratio than on trends and intercompany comparisons.

A high turnover of receivables may not always be the most efficient policy for a company. It may be the consequence of a tight credit policy and a vigorous collection program that unduly restricts the volume of sales. A loosening of credit standards will often increase receivables by a larger percentage than the increase in sales, but the increase in profit may be considerably higher than the company's desired rate of return on the added investment.

Inventory Turnover

Another ratio similar in purpose to the receivables-turnover ratio is the **inventory-turnover ratio.** Inventory and revenue accounting data are not precisely comparable: The former are on a cost basis, while the latter represent selling prices. Strictly speaking, therefore, the number of days' inventory on hand can be calculated only if the cost of goods sold is known, in which case the ratio is cost of goods sold per day divided by inventory. The same purpose can be served by a sales/inventory ratio, however, and inventory turnover is often calculated on this basis.

Fortunately, we have Grant's cost of goods sold for 19x2. Based on the year-end inventory, the 19x2 inventory-turnover ratio for Grant was:

$$\frac{\text{Cost of goods sold}}{\text{Inventories}} = \frac{\$57,700}{\$35,900} = 1.61$$

The number of days' inventory on hand therefore was 360/1.61 = 224 days.

A low ratio is indicative of slow-moving inventory, and a ratio that is falling or lower than competitors' or both is a sign of potential danger. On the other hand, a company may deliberately carry large inventories to reduce the loss of sales caused by inadequate stocks and to avail itself of economies of large purchase or production lots. Nevertheless, a falling ratio is presumptive evidence of a decline in liquidity, high carrying costs, and potential future losses from obsolescence.

Inventory-turnover ratios are subject to the same defects as receivables-turnover ratios. They say little about the quality of the year-end inventory mix, nor do they reflect seasonal variations in sales and inventories. Probably even more important, however, are the effects of the company's inventory-measurement methods. During and after a period of generally rising prices, for example, LIFO inventories will have higher turnover ratios than FIFO inventories. When replacement-cost data are available, they can be substituted for the historical-cost amounts to make the ratios more comparable over time and among companies.

Summary

Outside financial analysts use the data in corporate financial statements to help them predict corporations' future earnings (profitability analysis) and debt-paying ability (solvency analysis). Various ratios are calculated for these purposes. Other ratios indicating the efficiency of asset utilization are related both to profitability analysis and to solvency analysis. A representative set of ratios in each of these three categories is listed in Exhibit 15–7.

The validity of these kinds of analysis is conditioned not only by the comparability of past and future but also by the quality of the underlying data. The measurement methods used in preparing company financial statements have great effects on the ratios discussed in this chapter, and these effects must be considered when the ratios are interpreted.

While financial statements provide data and information in absolute-number terms, ratios enable analysts to obtain insights in relative terms as well. Although ratios have therefore become the most popular means of analyzing financial statements, their role is in fact limited to *identifying* critical aspects of a company's financial results and nothing more. Ratios deal with the issues of *what* and *how*; they do not address the overriding question of *why*. Ratios direct the analyst to the areas that may

EXHIBIT 15–7
Selected Financial Ratios

Profitability

Profit-margin ratio
$$\frac{\text{Net income}}{\text{Total revenue}}$$

Earnings per
common share
$$\frac{\text{Net income} - \text{Preferred dividends}}{\text{Number of common shares outstanding}}$$

Return on
common equity
$$\frac{\text{Net income} - \text{Preferred dividends}}{\text{Common equity}}$$

Return on assets
$$\frac{\text{Adjusted net income}}{\text{Total assets}} \quad \text{or} \quad \left(\frac{\text{Sales}}{\text{Assets}} \times \frac{\text{Income}}{\text{Sales}}\right)$$

Payout ratio
$$\frac{\text{Common dividends}}{\text{Income applicable to common shareholders}}$$

Price/earnings ratio
$$\frac{\text{Market price per common share}}{\text{Earnings per common share}}$$

Debt-Paying Ability and Risk

Current ratio
$$\frac{\text{Current assets}}{\text{Current liabilities}}$$

Quick ratio
$$\frac{\text{Cash} + \text{Marketable securities} + \text{Receivables}}{\text{Current liabilities}}$$

Debt/equity ratio
$$\frac{\text{Total liabilities}}{\text{Total owners' equity}}$$

Long-term-debt ratio
$$\frac{\text{Long-term debt}}{\text{Total owners' equity}}$$

Times-charges
earned
$$\frac{\text{Net income before interest} + \text{Taxes}}{\text{Interest} + \text{Preferred dividends}}$$

Fixed-charges ratio
$$\frac{\text{Cash flow before fixed charges}}{\text{Total fixed charges}}$$

Efficiency

Accounts-receivable
turnover
$$\frac{\text{Sales revenues}}{\text{Receivables}}$$

Inventory turnover
$$\frac{\text{Cost of goods sold}}{\text{Inventories}}$$

Total-asset turnover
$$\frac{\text{Sales revenues}}{\text{Total assets}}$$

require investigation; they do not themselves offer answers. Ratios point out symptoms, sometimes even a series of symptoms; they say nothing about underlying causes.

Appendix: Financial Leverage

A corporation's return on its common equity is a consequence of two factors: (1) its return on assets, and (2) the extent to which financial leverage is used by the company. *Financial leverage* occurs when the return earned on investing borrowed funds is greater than the interest cost incurred to effect the borrowing (e.g., borrowing at 12 percent interest to invest in real estate that provides an 18 percent return).

Return on assets is measured by the ratio of earnings *before interest* to total assets. The percentage of total assets that is supplied by creditors and preferred shareholders represents the leverage used by the company.[7]

Pretax Analysis

The leverage effect can be seen most easily in an analysis of pretax amounts. For example, Grant Company had $89,400 in assets and $13,160 in income before interest and taxes in 19x2 (from Exhibits 15–2 and 15–3). Its pretax rate of return on assets was:

$$\frac{\text{Income before interest and taxes}}{\text{Total assets}} = \frac{\$13,160}{\$89,400} = 14.7 \text{ percent}$$

The reason for using both earnings *before* interest and dividends as the numerator in this ratio is that the denominator represents *all* assets, not just those supplied by the shareholders. To be comparable, the earnings amount should measure earnings before distributions to both creditors (interest) and shareholders (dividends).

By using leverage, the company was able to earn a much higher return on its common equity than it earned on its total assets. If the income tax rate had been zero, the earnings available to the common stockholder would have been $13,160 less the $2,500 interest expense and the $560 dividends on the preferred stock, or $10,100:

---

[7] Leverage can also be measured by the ratio of *long-term* debt and preferred stock to the book value of the common stock, or as the ratio of *interest-bearing* debt and preferred stock to common equity. Our measure, which uses total liabilities in the numerator and total assets in the denominator, is appropriate when the comparison is to be made between return on total assets and return on the common shareholders' equity in those assets, as it is here.

Income before interest and income taxes $13,160	−	Interest expense $2,500	−	Preferred dividends $560	=	Pretax leveraged income $10,100

The book value of the common stockholders' equity was $46,500 ($10,000 + $12,600 + $23,900).[8] The pretax rate of return on common equity therefore was:

$$\frac{\text{Pretax income on common equity}}{\text{Common stockholders' equity}} = \frac{\$10,100}{\$46,500} = 21.7 \text{ percent}$$

The leverage effect in this case is illustrated in Exhibit 15–8. This was *successful* leverage because each of these costs—the 7 percent average interest cost of debt ($2,500 interest/$35,900 total liabilities) and the 8 percent cost of preferred stock—taken alone was *less* than the overall

EXHIBIT 15–8
Grant Company: Pretax Effect of Financial Leverage

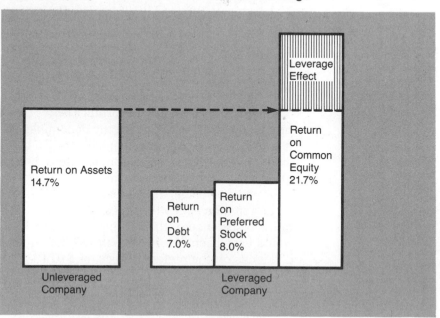

---

[8] The year-end amounts (from Exhibit 15–2) for common stock par value, additional paid-in capital, and retained earnings.

earnings rate on total assets (14.7 percent). The common shareholders, in other words, gained the full 14.7 percent on their own investment plus more than half the return on the assets financed by creditors and preferred stockholders. To get this additional return, the common stockholders had to assume the greater *risk* (uncertainty of the rate of return on their investment) arising from the increased fixed burden of debt service. (*Debt service* is the total of the payments for interest and the amount borrowed in any period.)

Three technical aspects of this analysis are worth noting. First, some liabilities, such as accounts payable and accrued taxes payable, lead to *no* recognized interest expense. The presence of these liabilities in the mix *reduces* the average interest cost of the company's debts to less than the interest rate on those liabilities that do give rise to recognized interest expense.

Second, year-end liability balances may be a very poor approximation to the *average* amount of liabilities outstanding during the year, which may have been much larger or much smaller than the year-end amounts. These variations within the year make leverage analysis much less precise than it appears to be.

Finally, both interest and preferred-dividend rates are the historical rates in effect when the debt was incurred and the preferred stock was issued. They don't necessarily represent the current costs of those kinds of capital. Grant's pretax costs of *new* borrowing in 19x2 may have been much higher than the historical rates reflected in this analysis. For current leveraging decisions, management has to compare *current* borrowing rates with the anticipated returns on additional investments in assets.

Aftertax Analysis

The *aftertax* analysis is likely to be even more dramatic than the pretax analysis because tax deductibility reduces the nominal aftertax cost of debt. The analysis is in three steps:

1. Calculate the aftertax rate of return on common equity for the actual capital structure.
2. Recalculate the aftertax rate of return on equity on the assumption that common stock was the company's sole source of capital.
3. Compare these two rates; the difference between them is the leverage effect.

The first of these steps is simple. We subtract the dividends on any preferred stock outstanding from net income and divide the difference by the common shareholders' equity. Since dividends are not tax deductible, the aftertax rate of return on equity is the same 12.7 percent we calculated in the preceding section.

To make the second calculation, we have to find out what tax rate is applicable to the portion of "earnings before interest and taxes" that interest deductibility has shielded from income taxation. The correct tax rate for this adjustment is the marginal tax rate—that is, the rate on the next *i* dollars of taxable income.

In the absence of debt financing, Grant's taxable income in 19x2 would have been $2,500 greater, and the income taxes would have been increased by 40 percent of $2,500, or $1,000, if we assume a 40 percent marginal tax rate.[9] Income taxes therefore would have been $4,200 + $1,000 = $5,200, and aftertax income would have been $13,160 − $5,200 = $7,960. The aftertax return on assets therefore was:

$$\frac{\text{Adjusted after tax income}}{\text{Total assets}} = \frac{\$7,960}{\$89,400} = 8.9 \text{ percent}$$

This is the return Grant would have earned on the common equity if no debt or preferred financing had been used.

The aftertax leverage effect is illustrated in Exhibit 15–9 showing that the use of debt and preferred stock raised Grant's return on its common

EXHIBIT 15–9
Grant Company: Aftertax Effect of Financial Leverage

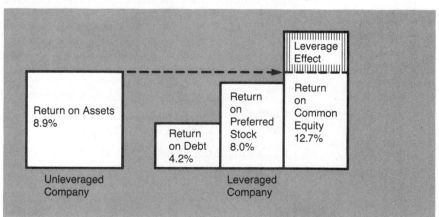

[9] Grant's income tax expense was calculated at the rate of 30 percent of the first $640 of income before taxes and 40 percent of all amounts in excess of $640. Since the $2,500 interest deduction reduced income before taxes from $13,160 to $10,660, its impact on taxes must be measured by the tax rate applicable to a reduction in that portion of the income range, 40 percent. (These rates and the dollar limit for the lower rate are purely illustrative; in practice, both the rates and the limit will differ, depending on the location of the company's operations and the revenue needs of the taxing authorities).

equity from 8.9 percent to 12.7 percent. The aftertax cost of debt was only 4.2 percent (60 percent of 7 percent) because the interest was deductible from taxable income.

The same calculations can be performed with market values substituted for book values in the denominator.

Successful versus Unsuccessful Leverage

Leverage works both ways, of course. If the overall return on assets is *lower* than the rates of return on debt and preferred stock, the rate of return on the common equity will be lower than the return on assets and may even be negative. The rate of return on the common equity will be equal to the rate of return on assets when the rate of return on assets (ROA) equals the average rate of return required by lenders and preferred stockholders. We can express this in an equation:

$$\text{ROA} = \frac{r_p P + r_d D}{P + D}$$

where P is the amount of preferred equity, D is the amount of debt, r_p is the dividend rate on the preferred, and r_d is the aftertax interest expense rate on the debt.

In Grant's case, with preferred stock of $7,000, debt of $35,900, an 8 percent preferred stock dividend rate, and a 4.2 percent average aftertax cost of debt, the average aftertax rate of return on assets has to be only 4.82 percent for the return on common equity to be equal to the return on assets:

$$\text{ROA} = \frac{0.08 \times \$7,000 + 0.042 \times \$35,900}{\$7,000 + \$35,900} = 4.82 \text{ percent}$$

If return on assets is higher than that, leverage will be successful; if return on assets is lower, leverage will be unsuccessful.

The relationship between return on assets and return on equity is diagramed in Exhibit 15–10. The line of the relationship is shown as a straight line. This won't always be true, partly because different tax rates are likely to apply to different portions of the taxable income and partly because the tax status of losses depends on the company's tax history. The basic relationship holds, however: the success or failure of leverage depends on the relationship between the return on assets and the aftertax book rate of return on senior securities.

The possibility of unsuccessful leverage adds to the risks of investment in the company, and the market will adjust the prices it is willing to pay for the company's stocks and bonds to reflect this risk. In simple terms,

EXHIBIT 15–10
Effect of Variations in Return on Assets on Leveraging Success

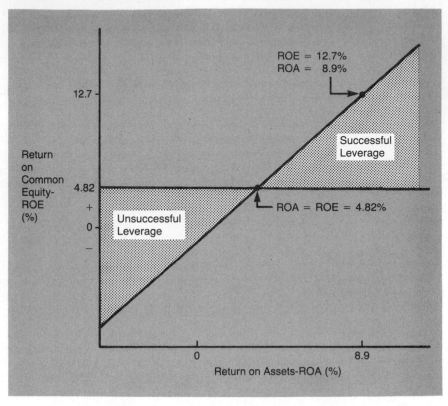

the common stock will have a lower price/earnings ratio than that of a comparable company with no leverage.

Key Terms

Change in an accounting principle	Operating ratio
Collection period	Payout ratio
Coverage ratios	Price/earnings ratio
Current ratio	Profit-margin ratio
Debt/equity ratio	Quality of earnings
Discontinued operations	Quick ratio
Earnings per share	Receivables turnover
Extraordinary items	Retention ratio
Financial leverage	Return on assets
Fixed-charges ratio	Return on common equity
Inventory turnover	Solvency
Liquidity	Sustainable-growth ratio
Long-term-debt ratio	Times-charges-earned ratio
Market-value ratio	

Independent Study Problems (Solutions In Appendix B)

1. Calculating Return on Equity. Barnes Company had net income after taxes of $106 million for 19x4, $111.3 million for 19x5, and $109.1 million for 19x6. Preferred dividends were $10 million in each year. The owners' equity section of the company's balance sheets during this period showed the following:

	12/31/x3	12/31/x4	12/31/x5	12/31/x6
Preferred stock..........	$ 170,000,000	$ 170,000,000	$ 170,000,000	$ 170,000,000
Common stock, $1 par	50,000,000	50,000,000	52,000,000	52,000,000
Additional paid-in capital	200,000,000	200,000,000	238,000,000	238,000,000
Retained earnings	580,000,000	626,000,000	677,300,000	724,400,000
Total..............	$1,000,000,000	$1,046,000,000	$1,137,300,000	$1,184,400,000

a. Calculate the earnings per common share in 19x4, 19x5, and 19x6, basing your calculations on the number of shares outstanding at the end of the year.

b. Calculate the book value per common share at each balance sheet date.

c. Calculate the return on common equity for 19x4, 19x5, and 19x6. In each case, base your calculations on average common equity for the year.

2. Effect of Transactions on Ratios. A company has just sold one of its buildings at a price equal to its book value and has used the proceeds from the sale to retire long-term bonds payable. The price paid to retire the bonds was equal to the amount at which they were shown on the balance sheet. Upon selling the building, the company entered into a lease with the new owner.

a. If the new lease is treated as an operating lease, not requiring lease capitalization, how will this series of transactions affect:
  1. The debt/equity ratio?
  2. The current ratio?
  3. The asset-turnover ratio?

b. If the new lease is treated as a repurchase of the property (requiring lease capitalization), how will this series of transactions affect these three ratios?

3. Effect of Leverage. The following data have been taken from the financial statements of a manufacturing company:

Total assets....................	$100,000
Interest expense...............	$ 2,000
Tax rate......................	45%
Return on common equity	7.2%
Debt/equity ratio	0.25

The company had no preferred stock outstanding.

a. Calculate the overall rate of profitability (return on assets).

b. Did the company use leverage successfully?

4. Components of Income.   Cosmo Corporation's 19x7 income statement appeared as follows:

Net sales	$14,275,300
Effect of change in timing of	
revenue recognition	525,000
Gain on sale of all retail outlets	850,000
Cost of goods sold.....................	(3,866,700)
Selling and administrative expenses	(4,791,400)
Loss on uninsured flood damage..........	(2,400,000)
Income tax expense	(1,377,660)
Net income	$ 3,214,540

Cosmo was a longtime apparel manufacturer whose effort to operate retail outlets had proved to be unprofitable after a three-year experimental period. Although the sale of the 14 stores itself yielded a gain, ownership of these stores until they closed in April 19x7 had the following effect on Cosmo's 19x7 income:

Net sales	$ 424,300
Cost of goods sold.......................	(117,600)
Selling and administrative expenses	(336,700)
Income taxes............................	9,000
Net (loss)	$ (21,000)

Prepare Cosmo's income statement in a manner that isolates *income from continuing operations* from the other determinants of income. Cosmo's income tax rate was 30 percent.

Exercises and Problems

5. Effects of Transactions on Selected Ratios.   Casey Company has a current ratio of 3.0, a quick ratio of 1.5, a receivables turnover of 6.1, and an inventory turnover of 4.5. How will each of the transactions listed here affect these ratios?

a. Purchase of merchandise for cash.

b. Purchase of merchandise on credit.

c. Sale of a short-term marketable security at cost (that is, at zero gain or loss).

d. Sale of merchandise at a profit for cash.

6. Using Ratios: Missing Amounts. In each of the three independent cases in the table, determine the missing amounts.

	I	II	III
Owners' equity (all "common")	$104,000	F	K
Total-asset turnover	A	6.5	L
Return on common equity	0.25	0.3	M
Return on assets	B	G	0.35
Profit-margin ratio	0.05	H	N
Debt/equity ratio.	0.6	I	0.37
Sales	C	J	$600,000
Total assets.	D	$120,000	P
Net income	E	$ 24,000	$ 90,000

7. Using Ratios to Calculate Unknowns. For each of the following three independent cases, use the data provided to determine the unknown quantity:

a. What is the cash balance?

Profit-margin ratio	8%	Number of current	
Accounts receivables		assets.	3
turnover.	10	Current ratio.	2.5
Gross margin/sales ratio. . . .	22%	Net income	$40,000
Inventory turnover	13	Current liabilities	$50,000

b. What is the profit-margin ratio?

Book value per share	$1.50	Owners' equity	$75,000
Earnings per share	$0.40	Total liabilities	$50,000
Total-asset turnover.	8		

c. What is the total of the liabilities?

Total-asset turnover.	12	Dividend yield ratio	5%
Price/earnings ratio.	8	Debt/equity ratio	0.4
Profit-margin ratio	2%	Cash dividends.	$24,000

8. Using Ratios to Determine Balance Sheet Amounts. The December 31, 19x5, balance sheet of Ratio, Inc., is presented with some omissions. The items listed are the only items in the balance sheet. Amounts indicated by question marks can be calculated from the additional information given.

Assets

Cash	$ 25,000
Accounts receivable (net).	?
Inventory	?
Plant and equipment (net)	294,000
Total assets	$432,000

Liabilities and Owners' Equity

Accounts payable (trade)	$?
Income taxes payable (current)	25,000
Long-term debt	?
Common stock	300,000
Retained earnings	?
Total liabilities and owners' equity	$?

Additional information:

Current ratio (at year-end)	1.5 to 1
Total liabilities divided by total owners' equity (at year-end)	0.8
Inventory turnover:	
Based on sales and ending inventory	15 times
Based on cost of goods sold and ending inventory ..	10.5 times
Gross margin for 19x5	$315,000

a. Calculate Ratio's trade accounts payable on December 31, 19x5.

b. Calculate retained earnings on December 31, 19x5.

c. Determine the cost of Ratio's inventory on December 31, 19x5.

(AICPA adapted)

9. Leverage Exercise. Company X and Company Y were identical in all respects except for their capital structure. Company X obtained $1 million in assets from the issuance of 100,000 shares of common stock. It had no debt. Company Y obtained $500,000 in assets by issuing 20-year, 8 percent bonds at their face value; it obtained another $500,000 by issuing 50,000 shares of common stock. Each company had $1 million in sales revenue and earnings before interest and income taxes (EBIT) of $150,000. The income tax rate was 50 percent.

a. Calculate earnings per share for each company. Did Company Y use leverage successfully?

b. How would your answer change if each company had sales of $350,000 and EBIT of $60,000?

10. Effects of Transactions on Ratios. A company's current ratio was in excess of 1.0, the times-charges-earned ratio was 3.0, and the ratio of earnings before interest and income taxes to net sales was 0.15. Net income was positive. Each of the following transactions occurred independently of the others:

1. Issued common stock in exchange for cash.
2. Sold building for cash at a price in excess of book value.
3. Declared and paid cash dividend on common stock.
4. Paid cash to retire long-term debt.
5. Paid accounts payable 30 days after receipt of merchandise.

6. Issued a long-term note payable in exchange for land.
7. Sold goods costing $10,000 on current account for $15,000.
8. Issued common stock in exchange for outstanding convertible preferred stock.
9. Issued common stock in exchange for outstanding convertible bonds.

For each of these transactions, *taken by itself* (all other things unchanged), state whether each of the following ratios will increase, decrease, or remain the same:

a. Current ratio.
b. Times-charges-earned ratio.
c. Debt/assets ratio.
d. Net income/sales ratio.

11. Leverage Exercise.   Doud Company has a return on common equity of 12 percent, based on net income of $12,000 (after income taxes). Its debt/owners' equity ratio is 50 percent and the income tax rate is 40 percent. Interest expense is $4,600 a year.

a. Calculate total assets.
b. Calculate earnings before interest and income taxes (EBIT).
c. Calculate the before-tax rate of return on total assets.
d. Calculate the aftertax rate of return on total assets.
e. Is this company using leverage successfully? Explain.

12. Trend Analysis: Interpretation of Ratios.   Analysis of a company's financial statements reveals the following information for three consecutive years:

	19x1	19x2	19x3
Return on common equity	8.1%	9.7%	10.5%
Current ratio	2.5:1	2.7:1	2.6:1
Earnings per share	$1.62	$2.04	$2.31
Times charges earned	10.0	4.2	3.9
Debt/equity ratio	1:5	2:3	9:11

The tax rate was 50 percent in each of these years, and 50,000 shares of common stock were outstanding throughout the entire three-year period.

a. Did the company's basic profitability increase during this period? Support your position with amounts developed from the information supplied.
b. Did the shareowners' risk increase? Cite data to support your position.

13. Effects of Transactions on Ratios.   An analyst is interested in the effects of various events on the following four measures of a company's performance or position:

1. Working capital, $40,000.
2. Current ratio, 3:1.
3. Total debt/equity ratio, 0.6.
4. Return on common equity, 25 percent.

Determine the effect of each of the 10 events listed below on each of the four measures:

a. Declared a $10,000 cash dividend.
b. Declared and distributed a 12 percent common stock dividend to common stockholders: $8 market value, $1 par value per share.
c. Adjustment to record $6,500 estimated bad debts.
d. Adjustment to record $9,000 expected future warranty claims.
e. Paid the $10,000 cash dividend.
f. Wrote off $4,100 receivables as uncollectible.
g. Paid $5,600 to satisfy warranty claims.
h. Used flow-through method to record investment tax credit.
i. Changed from FIFO to LIFO prior to a period of increasing prices.
j. Changed revenue recognition from point of delivery to completion of production.

Use a matrix consisting of 10 rows (a through j) and four columns (1 through 4). In each of the 40 cells, place the appropriate letter as follows: I = increase, D = decrease, N = no effect.

14. Income Statement Disclosures.   The year 19x4 was one that Troy Company had aptly characterized as a year of transition. Although Troy's $18.5 million sales exceeded 19x3's sales, its net income was a disappointing $648,000. The company president was concerned that the earnings press release that would be issued in January 19x5 explain as succinctly as possible the seemingly dismal story of the poor 19x4 profit. He requested a summary report and was given the following condensed income statement.

TROY COMPANY
Income Statement
For the Year Ended December 31, 19x4

Revenue from sales		$18,500,000
Expenses and losses:		
Normal expenses	$12,910,000	
Pollution penalty.	800,000	
Revenue-recognition switch	1,800,000	
Inventory write-down	550,000	
Business abandonment	1,360,000	17,420,000
Income before taxes		1,080,000
Income taxes.		432,000
Net income		$ 648,000

The president was somewhat taken aback by what the report did not reveal. He discovered, for instance, that the business segment that had been sold represented $4.1 million of Troy's sales and was responsible for $3,860,000 of the company's expenses. The pollution penalty related to fines and restitution costs resulting from a fluke case of water and air pollution of a variety that neither had happened previously nor was likely to ever happen again in an era of EPA and OSHA monitoring and enforcement.

The company's income had been adversely affected by two other matters whose timing was somewhat controllable by the management. Top management had decided that as of January 1, 19x4, all revenues would be recognized when merchandise was delivered. The cumulative accounting effect relates to those sales that had previously been recorded when production was completed that hadn't been delivered as of December 31, 19x3. The $550,000 inventory write-down pertained to an overstock of obsolete and spoiled raw materials and finished products that probably could have been written off a year or two earlier.

Prepare Troy Company's 19x4 income statement in accordance with the accounting profession's prescribed disclosure rules. The tax rate was 40 percent.

15. Intercompany Comparisons of Profitability.   Companies A, B, and C are three of the largest merchandising companies in the United States. We have the following data on these companies for a recent year (in thousands):

	Company A	Company B	Company C
Rank (by sales) among merchandising firms..	26	11	2
Sales revenues	$627,349	$1,293,765	$5,458,824
Assets.	120,363	274,603	884,001
Shareholders' equity . . .	43,554	163,317	627,366
Net income	11,477	8,327	55,897
Interest expense	3,994	5,342	13,088

a. Calculate income as a percentage of sales, asset turnover, return on assets, return on equity, and debt/asset ratio for each company. Assume a 50 percent income tax rate.

b. For return on common equity, Company A ranked first, Company B ranked 46th, and Company C ranked 39th among the merchandising companies on the list. Basing your analysis on the financial-statement data alone, prepare an explanation of the difference between the relative sales ranking and the relative return on common equity ranking.

16. Effect of Financing Method.   A company needs approximately $1 million in new capital to finance its expansion program. Management is undecided whether to obtain the needed funds from the sale of bonds or from the sale of additional shares of common stock. You have the following information:

1. Number of shares of stock now outstanding: 300,000.
2. Current annual earnings after taxes: $1.2 million ($4 a share).
3. Anticipated increase in earnings (before interest and income taxes) from investment of additional capital: $400,000.
4. The proposed bond issue would consist of 20-year, 14 percent bonds with a face value of $1 million, to be sold to an insurance company at their face value.
5. The proposed stock issue would consist of 40,000 shares of common stock, to be sold at a price of $25 a share.
6. The effective income tax rate is 40 percent.
7. The company now has no long-term debt.

a. Calculate the anticipated earnings per share under each method of financing.
b. How great an effect is this decision likely to have on the riskiness of investments in the company's common stock?

17. Quality of Earnings: Effect of Inventory Method. Alpha Company and Omega Company are both engaged in the smelting and refining of copper. The year 19x8 was a poor year for the copper industry in general, with rates of return on assets clustering mainly between 1 and 2 percent. The following data were taken from the balance sheets of these two companies as of the beginning and end of that year:

	December 31, 19x7	December 31, 19x8
Alpha Company inventories (LIFO)	$ 32,825,000	$ 26,450,000
Omega Company inventories (FIFO, lower of cost or market)	77,140,000	63,750,000
Alpha Company total assets	128,448,000	119,856,000
Omega Company total assets	312,660,000	285,918,000

Neither company had any interest-bearing debt at any time during 19x8.

Alpha adopted LIFO 15 years before 19x8, when copper prices were about half the level they had reached at the beginning of 19x8. Its inventories had grown about 10 percent in that period.

The market prices of copper and copper ores were the same on December 31, 19x8, as they had been on January 1, 19x8.

The income statements for the two companies for the year ended December 31, 19x8, were as follows:

	Alpha	Omega
Sales	$95,000,000	$215,000,000
Cost of goods sold	74,300,000	180,000,000
Depreciation	3,700,000	9,000,000
Other expenses	9,000,000	20,000,000
Total expenses	87,000,000	209,000,000
Income before taxes	8,000,000	6,000,000
Income taxes	4,000,000	3,000,000
Net income	$ 4,000,000	$ 3,000,000

a. Using the average of the beginning-of-year and end-of-year amounts as the base, calculate each company's return on assets in 19x8.

b. Which of these companies appears to have been more profitable in 19x8? Support your answer with amounts insofar as you can, and indicate how the differences in the companies' inventory methods influenced your conclusion.

c. How would your answer to part *b* have differed if the prices of copper and copper ores had been 10 percent lower throughout 19x8 than at the end of 19x8?

18. Evaluating Receivables and Credit Policy. Delta Company and Gamma Company sell similar lines of products. The manager of Delta Company has collected the following statistics:

	Delta	Gamma
Sales, 19x3	$7,000,000	$5,000,000
Estimated bad debts, 19x3	35,000	50,000
Income before interest and taxes, 19x3	600,000	500,000
Total assets, December 31, 19x3	4,800,000	4,000,000
Accounts receivable, December 31, 19x3	800,000	750,000

The manager wants answers to the following questions. You are expected to answer the questions if possible. If the information provided is not adequate for a satisfactory answer, state the additional information you need and explain how you would use it to answer the question.

a. Which company has the more liberal credit policy?

b. Which company has the more liquid receivables?

c. By how much will Delta's accounts receivable increase during 19x4?

d. Which company is managing its accounts receivable more profitably?

19. Manipulation of Financial Ratios. On December 15, 19x1, the controller of Redwood, Inc., gave the president a copy of an estimated year-end balance sheet for the company, containing the following amounts:

Assets

Cash	$ 300,000
Accounts receivable	120,000
Inventories	180,000
Plant and equipment (net)	900,000
Total assets	$1,500,000

Liabilities and Owners' Equity

Accounts payable	$ 300,000
Long-term debt	100,000
Common stock	800,000
Retained earnings	300,000
Total liabilities and owners' equity	$1,500,000

The president was concerned that the *quick ratio* was so low, and asked the controller to suggest some way of improving this ratio in the two weeks remaining before the end of the year.

a. Calculate the quick ratio.
b. Which suggestion probably would be the easiest to implement? Would carrying out this suggestion impose any costs on the company?
c. What action might analysts take that would either neutralize this kind of year-end "window dressing" or make it unnecessary?

20. Inadequacy of Position Ratios. At the beginning of 19x2, Davis Company's current ratio was 3.25, the quick ratio was 1.25, and the ratio of long-term debt to the common shareholders' equity was 0.3. The return on equity in 19x1 was 15 percent. All these ratios were well within the range regarded by financial analysts as satisfactory for this industry.

Davis Company had begun a plant-expansion program in 19x1. To finance the completion of that program in 19x2 and 19x3, the company negotiated an additional long-term loan of $7 million early in 19x2. Market conditions deteriorated during 19x2, however. Sales volume fell from $25 million in 19x1 to $20 million in 19x2, while net income fell from $3 million to $400,000. Davis's cash position deteriorated even more severely, and in December 19x2 it was unable to make its scheduled payments to its creditors.

Davis's income statement for 19x2 and condensed balance sheets for the beginning and end of the year were as follows:

DAVIS COMPANY
Statement of Income
For the Year Ended December 31, 19x2
($ millions)

Sales revenue		$20.0
Expenses:		
Cost of goods sold*	$13.7	
Selling and administrative expense	4.1	
Interest expense	1.5	
Income tax expense	0.3	19.6
Net income		$ 0.4

* Schedule of cost of goods sold:		
Materials inventory, January 1	$ 2.7	
Purchases of materials	10.8	
Cost of materials available	13.5	
Materials inventory, December 31	4.9	
Cost of materials used	8.6	
Factory labor	5.9	
Factory depreciation	0.5	
Other factory costs	2.3	
Total costs of production	17.3	
Less: Cost of added finished goods inventory	3.6	
Cost of goods sold	$13.7	

DAVIS COMPANY
Condensed Balance Sheets
As of December 31, 19x1 and 19x2
($ millions)

	19x1	19x2		19x1	19x2
Cash	$ 1.0	$ 0.2	Accounts payable . . .	$ 1.0	$ 4.7
Accounts			Notes payable	3.0	3.0
receivable	4.0	6.3	Taxes payable	—	0.3
Inventory	8.0	13.8	Interest payable	—	0.4
Net plant and			Long-term debt	6.0	13.0
equipment	17.0	20.5	Common stock	5.5	5.5
			Additional paid-in		
			capital	2.5	2.5
			Retained earnings . .	12.0	11.4
			Total liabilities		
			and owners'		
Total assets	$30.0	$40.8	equity	$30.0	$40.8

a. Calculate the current ratio, quick ratio, and long-term-debt/equity ratio at the end of 19x2.

b. Prepare an analysis to explain what led to Davis's inability to pay its creditors on schedule in 19x2.

c. Comment on the usefulness of position ratios such as the quick ratio as indicators of short-term bill-paying ability.

21. Comparison of Two Companies. Here are the income statements and balance sheets of Franklin Company and Morgan Company, taken from their annual reports for the year ended December 31, 19x1:

Income Statement
For the Year 19x1

	Franklin Company	Morgan Company
Sales	$8,000,000	$7,000,000
Cost of goods sold	6,000,000	4,700,000
Selling, general, and administrative expenses	1,200,000	1,900,000
Interest on debt	—	70,000
Income before taxes	800,000	330,000
Income taxes	390,000	160,000
Net income	$ 410,000	$ 170,000
Dividends declared	$ 100,000	$ 70,000

Condensed Balance Sheets
As of December 31, 19x1

	Franklin Company	Morgan Company
Assets		
Cash	$ 300,000	$ 300,000
Accounts receivable	800,000	650,000
Inventory	1,300,000	850,000
Net plant and equipment	2,100,000	1,500,000
Total assets	$4,500,000	$3,300,000
Liabilities and Owners' Equity		
Accounts payable	$ 710,000	$ 400,000
Taxes payable	390,000	160,000
Long-term debt	—	1,400,000
Common stock	2,200,000	800,000
Retained earnings	1,200,000	540,000
Total liabilities and owners' equity	$4,500,000	$3,300,000

On the basis of the available information, which do you consider to be (1) more liquid? (2) more solvent? (3) more profitable? Explain your conclusions.

22. Effect of Accounting Methods. Dalton Company two years ago established two subsidiary corporations to develop two new markets. The two companies started with identical sets of assets and no liabilities. Dalton distributed the stock of these two companies to its shareholders, and, thereafter, they operated independently of each other and of Dalton.

One of these companies, Littler, Inc., elected to use the LIFO inventory method, the deferral method of accounting for the investment credit, and accelerated depreciation. The other company, Bigler Enterprises, used FIFO, the flow-through method, and straight-line depreciation. The income tax rate was 50 percent, and tax depreciation was 15 percent in the first year and 22 percent in the second year.

The balance sheets of the two companies at the end of last year, their second year of operation, contained the following information:

	Littler	Bigler
Assets		
Current assets:		
Cash	$ 4,100	$ 3,200
Accounts receivable	7,000	7,000
Inventory	10,000	12,000
Total current assets	21,100	22,200
Plant and equipment	20,000	20,000
Less: Accumulated depreciation	(7,200)	(4,000)
Total assets	$33,900	$38,200
Liabilities and Owners' Equity		
Current liabilities:		
Accounts payable	$ 2,500	$ 2,500
Taxes payable	1,000	1,100
Total current liabilities	3,500	3,600
Long-term debt	10,000	10,000
Deferred income taxes	100	1,700
Deferred investment tax credits	1,600	—
Total liabilities	15,200	15,300
Common stock	5,000	5,000
Additional paid-in capital	10,000	10,000
Retained earnings	3,700	7,900
Total liabilities and owners' equity	$33,900	$38,200

The two companies' income statements for last year showed the following:

	Littler	Bigler
Sales revenues	$75,000	$75,000
Cost of goods sold	51,000	50,000
Gross margin	24,000	25,000
Selling and administrative expenses*	10,000	8,800
Interest expense	1,000	1,000
Income tax expense	6,300	7,600
Net income	$ 6,700	$ 7,600

* Includes depreciation.

The two companies have had identical sales volumes and have paid identical amounts as dividends each year. Inventory replacement costs have been rising at a rate of about 10 percent a year. Neither company made any capital expenditures last year.

Prepare an analysis comparing the profitability of these two companies, taking into consideration the differences in their accounting policies insofar as you are able.

(Suggested by Charles W. Bastable)

23. Intercompany Comparisons: Profitability Analysis. Anderson, Ltd., and Zoysia, Inc., are incorporated and operate in a country in which generally accepted accounting principles are followed but the income tax rate is only 25 percent. The two companies offer the same general line of products to the same potential customers.

The following data were taken from the 19x1 financial statements of these two companies:

	Anderson	Zoysia
Cash	$ 8,000	$ 24,000
Accounts receivable	17,000	19,200
Inventories	27,200	29,568
Prepaid expenses	2,000	4,000
Property and equipment	100,000	220,000
Accumulated depreciation	(62,400)	(57,152)
Total	$ 91,800	$ 239,616
Current liabilities	$ 20,000	$ 40,000
Long-term debt—6 percent	40,000	—
Long-term debt—9 percent	—	20,000
Owners' equity	31,800	179,616
Total	$ 91,800	$ 239,616
Sales	$ 204,000	$ 460,800
Cost of goods sold	(163,200)	(354,816)
Other expenses	(22,440)	(46,080)
Interest	(2,400)	(1,800)
Income taxes	(3,990)	(14,526)
Net income	$ 11,970	$ 43,578

Anderson's long-term debt was obtained about 10 years earlier. Its low interest rate constituted a subsidy from a state economic development agency. Zoysia's long-term debt also arose about 10 years before 19x1, but it was a straight financial-market transaction, with no government subsidy.

All sales in both companies are on account and there are only minor seasonal variations in sales.

a. Compare the current debt-paying ability of the two companies. To what extent can the inventories be looked upon as a means of paying debts due in 30 days? In 60 days?

b. Compare the profitability of the two companies. What factors account for the difference?

c. Compare the long-term debt-paying ability of the two companies.

Part 3

Managerial Accounting

Chapter 16

Basic Decision Concepts

With this chapter, we begin our examination of **managerial accounting,** the body of knowledge underlying the information and analytical skills accountants use in helping management plan and control the company's activities.

Managerial accounting differs from financial accounting in several ways. First, it serves *management,* while financial accounting serves investors and others outside the company. Second, managerial accounting focuses on particular activities, responsibilities, programs, and revenue segments, while financial accounting deals primarily with the company as a whole. Third, management ordinarily is free to tell the accountants which aspects of performance to measure, and the accountants are free to decide how to measure these, whereas financial accounting must conform to measurement standards issued or adopted by some outside authority.

Managerial accounting has two sides. On one side, it provides management with information to use in reviewing the success or failure of the company's operations and the performance of managers at all levels. This is the **control** side of managerial accounting: management's efforts to prevent undesirable departures from planned results, keep track of what is happening, interpret this information, and take action in response to it. Control is such an important aspect of managerial accounting that a company's chief accounting officer usually bears the title of *controller.*

The second side of managerial accounting is the **planning** side, providing information and analytical skills to help management decide how to use the company's resources. In this chapter, we'll study one element of the planning side and some of the basic concepts underlying management's use of accounting data. Before we do that, however, we need to explain something about the planning processes themselves.

Planning Processes

Managerial planning takes many forms, from the very broad to the very specific. Five different kinds of planning can be identified, each appropriate to a particular planning context:

1. **Strategic planning**—establishing the basic directions top management wants the organization to take.
2. **Long-range periodic planning**—translating the strategic plan into preliminary action proposals and making rough estimates of the resources required to carry them out.
3. **Short-range periodic planning (budgeting)**—developing a coordinated program to govern the use of all the organization's resources in a single short period, usually the first year of the long-range plan.
4. **Project and situation planning**—making final decisions to use specific portions of the organization's resources in specific ways.
5. **Scheduling**—determining in detail what needs to be done to carry out the planned program, establishing timetables for the performance of these tasks, and seeing to it that people, materials, facilities, and funds are available in the necessary quantities at the necessary times and places to carry out the plan.

The diagram in Exhibit 16–1 traces the relationships among these processes. The progression moves from the top of the chart toward the bottom, from the general to the specific, from the tentative to the firm commitment.

EXHIBIT 16–1
Managerial Planning Processes

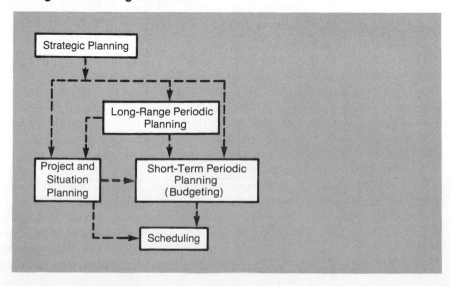

EXHIBIT 16–2
Elements of a Decision

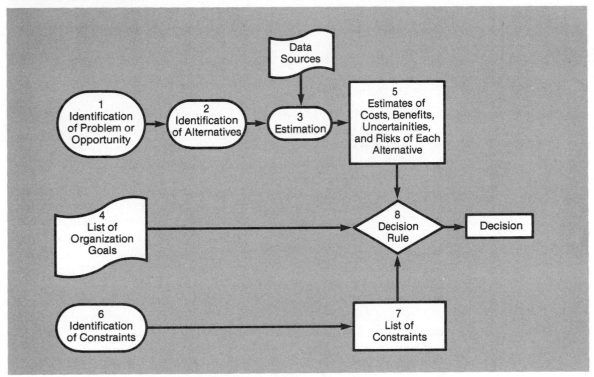

In this chapter, we'll introduce a number of decision-related concepts and principles in the context of project and situation planning, deferring the discussion of periodic planning to Chapter 20. Although we also need to be aware of the three other types of planning, they deal with techniques and processes that are beyond the scope of this book.

Most project and situation planning decisions are likely to include the elements appearing in Exhibit 16–2. The wavy ribbon segments in this diagram represent *external inputs* to the decision, the ovals identify *processes,* and the rectangular blocks identify the *results* of these processes.

For example, suppose the marketing vice president of Eclectic Software, Inc., has discovered that many of the company's health-care industry customers are dissatisfied with commercially available word processing packages. This is the opportunity represented by oval number 1 at the top left of the diagram in Exhibit 16–2. At this point, the vice president would likely request that an analysis be prepared. Some of these analyses can be performed by accounting staff personnel working alone; other analyses will require the use of nonaccounting staff.

The next step is to proceed to oval number 2, identification of alternatives. Without alternatives, no decision needs to be made. In the simplest situations, only two alternatives need be considered: act or don't act, accept a proposal or reject it. In other situations, management may be able to identify three, four, or even more plausible actions that management might take. In our example, Eclectic Software's marketing vice president and the company's controller have agreed that three alternatives are worth considering:

1. Contract with an independent consulting firm to develop a software package to Eclectic's specifications.
2. Increase the size of Eclectic's work force to enable the company to develop the package internally.
3. Forgo the opportunity entirely.

Oval number 3 in the diagram is the preparation of estimates of costs, benefits, and risks of each alternative. Before this can be done, the analysts must make sure they understand the organization's goals, represented by block number 4. The reason is that decisions are intended to lead to actions that will foster the organization's progress toward its goals. Eclectic Software's primary goal is to generate profits for its shareholders, whereas a not-for-profit organization has a service goal or goals (care for sick people, improve the environment, increase human knowledge, and so forth).

The estimates emerging from this process (block number 5 in Exhibit 16–2) must be considered against the background of oval number 6, the constraints on management's freedom of action with regard to the decision at hand. Constraints might arise, for instance, because materials or labor are in short supply, or because environmental pollution must be kept below specified levels. Some constraints apply to all decisions (e.g., a flat prohibition against trade in certain markets); others are particular to the specific decision situation (e.g., only 1,400 service-hours are available this month).

The list of these constraints is represented by block number 7 in the exhibit. For Eclectic Software, the main constraints on the software development decision are time and cash. The marketing vice president believes that the new package must be ready for test marketing within 12 months if the company is to have a competitive edge in this particular market. And the controller has established that no more than $500,000 will be available to finance the project within the next six months.

The final step is to choose and apply a method of comparing the alternatives with one another. This is known as a **decision rule** and is represented by the diamond-shaped block (number 8) in Exhibit 16–2, where all the other elements in the decision come together. Eclectic Software's decision rule for this decision is: select the alternative that appears to be most likely to maximize the present value of the company's future *cash flows* without violating any of the constraints.

In the next section, we'll describe the concepts underlying a relatively uncomplicated decision rule that can be applied to short-term, capacity-utilization decisions when the outcome of each alternative can be predicted with certainty.

Basic Concepts for Resource-Allocation Decisions

Decisions, in the final analysis, hinge on management's perceptions of the costs, benefits, and risks associated with each alternative it has been able to identify. Our objective in this section is to explain how the principal costs and benefits of business activity should be measured for decision-making purposes.

Cash Flows

While financial accounting measures costs and benefits on an accrual basis, managerial decision making defines both costs and benefits in terms of **cash flows.** *Benefits* consist of cash receipts (or reductions in cash outlays); *costs* consist of cash outlays (or reductions in cash receipts).

The reason for this emphasis on cash flows is that in most circumstances cash is the only resource management can use to obtain productive goods and services and to reward the enterprise's owners. If the company has no cash and can't get any, it won't be able to meet its payroll or pay its suppliers, no matter how many receivables or how much equipment it has. On the other hand, if cash *is* coming in, it can be used to buy materials and pay employees. Noncash resource outflows, such as depreciation on existing equipment, reduce net income, but they don't reduce management's ability to meet its immediate obligations.

The Incremental Principle

Each possible course of action available to management will produce future cash flows—positive, negative, or both. While management's choice of one course of action brings with it the cash flows associated with that action, it may also prevent the company from experiencing the cash flows associated with other possible actions. In other words, the *effect* of a decision consists of the *differences* between (1) the cash flows associated with the chosen course of action and (2) the cash flows associated with a rejected alternative.

This idea is illustrated in Exhibit 16–3. The proposed action and the alternative action are depicted in the boxes on the left and in the center of the exhibit. The difference between these two actions, identified by the smaller rectangle on the far right, is called the *incremental cash flow*. It is this incremental cash flow which is the focal point of the **incremental principle,** which states that decisions should be based on perceived differences among the alternatives being considered.

EXHIBIT 16–3
Cash Flows Attributable to a Proposed Action

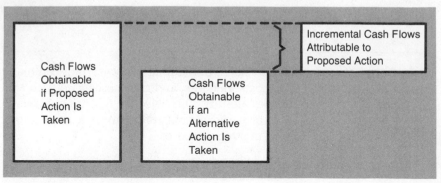

An incremental cash flow—the difference between the cash flow associated with one course of action and the cash flow associated with an alternative—can be either positive or negative. When the proposed course of action calls for a larger cash inflow or a smaller cash outflow than the alternative course of action, we have a positive incremental cash flow, which is sometimes called an *incremental cash receipt.* When the proposed course of action is expected to produce a smaller cash inflow or a larger cash outflow than the alternative course of action, we have a negative incremental cash flow, and this is sometimes called an **incremental cost.**

A particular proposed course of action often has several incremental cash flows associated with it—incremental cash receipts *and* incremental costs. When all of these positive and negative incremental cash flows are offset against each other, they yield the incremental net cash inflow; when incremental cash receipts are less than incremental costs, the proposal is said to have an incremental net cash outflow.

TERMINOLOGY

Incremental net cash flow in any period is the difference between the algebraic sum of the cash flows associated with a proposed course of action in the period and the algebraic sum of the cash flows in that period associated with an alternative course of action.

Time Horizon of the Decision

Some decisions affect the cash flows of only one period. We refer to these as tactical decisions, and the incremental net cash flow can be stated as a single amount—the algebraic difference between the alternatives' net cash flows in the affected period. Single-period estimates of incremental net cash flows can also be used if the direction of the incremental net cash flow appears likely to be the same in *each* future period, or if the cash flows of future periods seem likely to be unaffected by the decision.

Other decisions affect the company's future cash flows in such a way that choosing one alternative instead of another is likely to result in an incremental net cash inflow in one or more periods *and* an incremental net cash outflow in one or more other periods. We refer to these as investment decisions. For these decisions, both the *timing* and the *amounts* of the cash flows are important. Rather than try to deal with both dimensions of costs and benefits at once, we'll limit our discussion in this chapter to tactical decisions. We'll return to investment decisions in Chapter 21.

Opportunity Cost

We defined incremental cost as a negative incremental cash flow. The incremental costs associated with a proposal therefore must include any cash inflows that will be lost if that proposal is accepted. Any such portions of the incremental cost are called the **opportunity cost** of the resources the proposal would divert from another use. It is the value of a forgone opportunity.

For example, Van Horn Company manufactures and sells lawnmowers. It has a stockpile of 10,000 reels, designed originally for use in manually operated mowers. The marketing manager has proposed that these reels be used in a low-priced power mower for a special promotion by a regional chain of hardware stores. No cash outlay need be made to obtain these reels—the company already owns them—but the reels nevertheless do have an incremental cost (an opportunity cost) because Lawntex Company, one of two remaining manufacturers of manually operated mowers, has offered to buy them for $10 each. The opportunity cost therefore becomes Van Horne's incremental cost of the reels: $100,000 ($10 × 10,000).

(1) **Cash Flow if Proposal Is Accepted**	*(2)* **Cash Flow if Proposal Is Rejected**	*(3)* **Incremental Cash Flow *(1) − (2)***
0	+$100,000	−$100,000

Opportunity cost is a component of incremental cost because *an action that eliminates a cash inflow is equivalent to an action that produces a cash outflow.*

Sunk Cost

In our discussion of opportunity cost, we made no mention of the amounts Van Horn paid previously to obtain the reels. The reason is that management's present decision on the use of the reels cannot affect the cash outlay that was made to obtain them in the first place.

The original cost of the reels is an example of a **sunk cost,** defined as any cash outflow that will be unaffected by the decision to be made. Cash outlays that haven't yet been made may also be sunk costs, if the decision won't affect them. For example, Van Horn Company will pay the plant manager's salary each month whether the marketing manager's proposal is accepted or rejected. This negative portion of the company's net cash inflow will be the same no matter which of these two alternatives is selected. The plant manager's salary therefore is a sunk cost with respect to the marketing manager's proposal and need not be included in the analysis.

Time Lags

Time lags between payments for resources and collections from customers can affect management's decisions because they deprive the company of the use of cash during the lags. If the lags are long enough, the decision should be treated as an investment decision and the analysis should be based on the methods we'll outline in Chapter 21. If the time lags are relatively short, however, they generally can be ignored in incremental analysis for tactical decisions. In such cases, incremental cash receipts are assumed to be equal to incremental revenues, and incremental cash outlays are assumed to be equal to the incremental costs of the resources consumed. **Incremental profit** therefore will approximate the effect of the decision on the company's income before taxes.

TERMINOLOGY REMINDER

Incremental cost is any difference between the cash outflow associated with one course of action and the cash outflow associated with an alternative course of action.

Opportunity cost is any net cash inflow that will be lost if the course of action under consideration is pursued.

Sunk cost is any cash outflow, past or future, that is not affected by the decision to pursue the course of action under consideration. Sunk costs are *not* a component of that course of action's incremental cost.

**Short-Term
Cost-Volume
Relationships**

Many resource-allocation decisions focus on management's efforts to use existing capacity profitably. Increasing or decreasing the amount of capacity takes time and, in the meantime, management must try to do its best with what it has.

The question in a decision of this kind is whether to increase or decrease the rate of output of a particular product or service within existing capacity limits. For this purpose, management needs to estimate how costs will change when the rate of output increases or decreases.

Variable Costs

Some costs go up or down in total almost automatically in response to small changes in operating volume. Operating volume, or level of activity, is the rate at which resources are used (pounds of materials per hour) or at which goods or services are produced (meals served per week). Any cost that must be increased in total if the company is to achieve a small increase in the level of activity is a **variable cost.**

The diagrams in Exhibit 16–4 represent the behavior of a cost element—operating supplies, in this case—that is *proportionally* variable

**EXHIBIT 16–4
Proportionally Variable Cost**

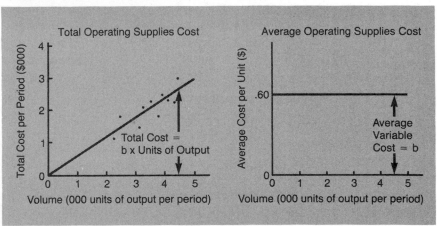

with volume. Each dot in the left-hand diagram stands for the cost and volume recorded in one specific month in the past, adjusted for changes in the prices the company paid to obtain these supplies. The line which seems to fit the pattern of the relationship described by the dots indicates the cost of the operating supplies this company might be expected to use at each level of activity, on the average, if future conditions are like those of the past.

The line fitted to the observations plotted in Exhibit 16–4 is described by the equation:

$$C = bV$$

in which C = total cost per month, V = the volume of activity, measured by units of output, and b = the rate of variable cost per unit of output. In this case, average variable cost is constant (and equal to b) per unit of output throughout the entire volume range, as shown in the right-hand diagram in exhibit 16–4.

TERMINOLOGY REMINDER

Variable cost is any cost that must be increased in total if the company is to achieve a small increase in the level of activity.

Fixed Costs: Providing Capacity

Costs that don't change in total as a necessary result of small changes in volume are known as **fixed costs.** Some of these are incurred to enable the company to respond to the customer orders it receives. We call these **capacity costs,** the costs of the resources management uses to provide or maintain current operating capacity. The horizontal line in the left-hand panel of Exhibit 16–5, for example, represents the relationship

EXHIBIT 16–5
Fixed Cost

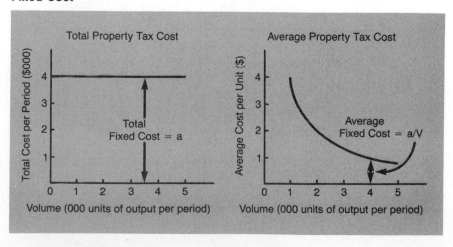

between the total cost of property taxes each month and the volume of activity. The line of relationship is given by the formula:

$$C = a$$

in which a represents the total cost of property taxes each month. Since the total property tax cost doesn't vary as a result of output changes, the cost per unit of output decreases as the rate of output per period increases. At any output (V), the average cost is a/V. This is shown in the right-hand panel of Exhibit 16–5.

Stepped Costs.   Some capacity costs are affected by variations in volume—but in large steps rather than gradually. These are called **stepped costs.** For example, the left-hand diagram in Exhibit 16–6 shows the estimated total cost of supervisory time in one of Van Horn's factory departments. In this case, the basic supervisory force can handle any level of volume up to 2,500 units of output a month. For sustained operations above this level, additional supervisory time must be provided, and the total cost increases as a result. The effects of this kind of cost behavior on average cost are shown in the right-hand diagram in Exhibit 16–6.

EXHIBIT 16–6
Stepped Fixed Cost

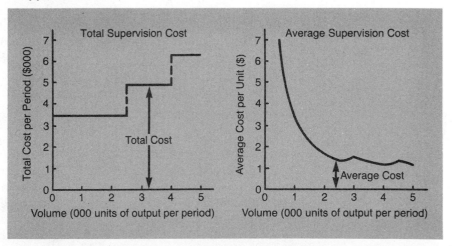

Whether stepped costs are classified as fixed or variable costs depends on the width of the steps. In our illustration, only three broad steps were identified, and supervision costs therefore are likely to be classified as fixed. If volume is likely to fluctuate between 2,500 and 4,000 units a month, for example, supervisory costs are expected to remain constant at $4,900 a month. In contrast, if the total cost of another cost element moves up a step each time volume increases by 500 units, management probably will think of that element as a variable cost.

TERMINOLOGY REMINDER

Fixed costs are costs that don't change in total as a necessary result of small changes in volume.

Capacity costs are costs of the resources management uses to provide or maintain current operating capacity—e.g., property taxes.

Stepped costs are capacity costs that are affected by variations in volume, but in large steps rather than continuously—e.g., supervisory time.

Incremental Fixed Costs.   While it is self-evident that variable costs are incremental costs in connection with any decision affecting the total level of activity, whether fixed costs are or are not incremental costs may not be immediately apparent. As we proceed to answer this question, let's keep in mind that variable cost and incremental cost are *not* synonymous terms.

Consider, for example, an entrepreneur about to establish a new business. All costs are incremental costs: some will be fixed and some will be variable. Once the business is established, however, the fixed costs of providing capacity become sunk costs with respect to decisions as to the use of that capacity. They are no longer incremental costs with respect to those decisions. We therefore observe that fixed costs are either sunk costs or incremental costs, depending on whether their being incurred is affected by the decision to pursue a particular course of action.

Semivariable Costs

Some costs are partly fixed and partly variable—that is, they are *semivariable costs*. Exhibit 16–7 displays the cost-volume relationship of one of these costs. The diagram at the left shows that power consumption increases as volume rises, but not in proportion to the change in volume. The explanation is that some uses of power—lighting, for example— don't respond to variations in volume. This kind of cost can be described by an equation that combines elements from the two equations cited earlier:

$$C = a + bV$$

in which both a and b are positive. Dividing both sides by V, we get:

$$\text{Average cost} = \frac{C}{V} = \frac{a}{V} + b$$

EXHIBIT 16–7
Semivariable Cost

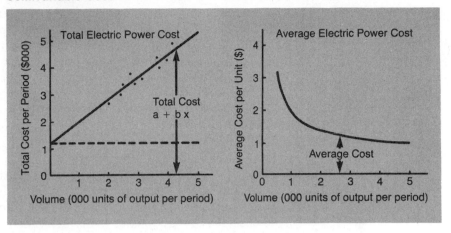

As output (*V*) increases, *a/V* decreases and so does average cost per unit (*C/V*).

Fixed Costs: Programmed Activities

In addition to fixed costs that are capacity costs—that is, costs incurred to provide or maintain current operating capacity—every business organization has a second group of fixed costs, the costs of programmed activities or **programmed costs,** undertaken at management's initiative to meet objectives other than demands for service imposed on the business from outside. Programmed activities determine the company's scope and direction. Some of them are innovative, designed to enable the company to change the way it operates—by developing new products, acquiring other companies, improving operating methods, and so forth. Others are promotional, intended to stimulate demand for the company's goods and services; most selling activities fall in this category.

The costs of programmed activities are generally agreed upon at the beginning of each planning period. They may be changed during the period, but any such changes are not *necessitated* by changes in volume. In other words, they are discretionary fixed costs. Because these costs don't respond to changes in volume, average programmed cost per unit will be low if volume turns out to be high and high if volume is low.

Estimating Cost Variability

Estimating the rate at which costs vary with volume isn't easy. For one thing, it isn't always clear how volume should be measured. If a department produces only one kind of product or service, volume can be measured by the number of units produced. In the more typical multiproduct situation, however, the units produced are so dissimilar that physical output totals are meaningless—one automobile plus one bicycle doesn't add up to two of anything. The usual solution is to use some measure of input, such as the number of labor-hours or machine-hours.

Having chosen a measure of volume, we still have to develop a method of estimating the rate at which costs change in response to changes in volume. Most analysts prefer to use the statistical method known as **least squares regression analysis.** This approach uses a set of equations to position a line of relationship on a diagram such as the left-hand diagram in Exhibit 16–7. This line, known as a regression line, is drawn in such a way that the sum of the squares of the vertical distances between the line and the dots in the diagram is minimized.[1]

An introductory accounting text is not the place to describe the problems of regression analysis or to discuss various ways of responding to these problems. Even so, we must call attention to the danger that the mathematical precision of the regression equation will be taken to mean that this equation is a foolproof forecasting formula. This may not be true. For one thing, the estimates are subject to error ranges, and these errors may be very large. Second, a number of restrictive assumptions must be valid if the regression line is to be useful. For example, since costs may really be determined by some variable other than volume, the regression line would reflect the correlation between this variable and volume fluctuations, rather than a *causal* relationship between volume and cost.

Circumstances often justify the use of estimation methods that are less rigorous than least-squares analysis. One of these methods is to rely on the judgment of experienced personnel. This approach, known as the inspection-of-accounts method, requires someone to classify each kind of cost as wholly fixed, wholly variable, or a mixture of the two. The analyst then estimates the monthly amount for each fixed-cost element and the average unit cost for each proportionally variable element.

The inspection-of-accounts method is less scientific than regression analysis, but it can be used when historical data are inadequate for some reason. It should also be used to check the results of regression analysis.

Summary

Accounting serves the information needs of management, first by providing data management can use in *planning* the company's future activities, and second by providing information on the results of operations, useful in judging performance and *controlling* those operations. These

---

[1] The calculation of a linear regression line by the least-squares method is outlined in the appendix to this chapter.

contributions are the product of managerial accounting, the subject of the remaining chapters in this book.

This first chapter has identified various contexts in which managerial planning takes place, and has examined a number of basic analytical concepts, all in the context of short-term project and situation planning decisions.

The basic approach to quantitative analysis for management decisions is to estimate the incremental cash flows, the *differences* between the anticipated results of a proposed course of action and the anticipated results of the action the company would take if the proposal were rejected. This is known as incremental analysis.

In applying incremental analysis to various decision situations, the accountant or other analyst must have a clear understanding of concepts such as opportunity cost, sunk cost, incremental cost, fixed cost, capacity cost, and variable cost. We have defined these terms in this chapter and have shown in an introductory way how these concepts can be applied in managerial decision making.

Appendix: The Least-Squares Method

The process of fitting a line to approximate the relationship between a dependent variable (cost) and one or more independent variables (volume, average lot size) is known as regression analysis. The formula describing the relationship is known as a *regression equation*. With only one independent variable, the process is known as simple regression; with two or more independent variables, the analysis becomes one of multiple regression.

In this appendix, we'll describe the calculations required by simple regression to fit a straight line to a set of data points by the method of least squares. The equation for a straight line is

$$y = a + bx$$

where

y = the dependent variable (total cost)
a = a constant (total fixed cost)
x = the independent variable (volume)
b = the variation (variable cost per unit) of the dependent variable for a unit variation in the independent variable

These relationships are represented graphically in Exhibit 16–8. By moving one unit of x to the right, the total cost increases by b; this is the slope of the regression line. The constant, a, is the y-intercept. The object of regression analysis is to estimate the values of a and b.

The first step is to record a number of paired values of x and y. Each pair of values (one for x and one for y) represents a single observation.

EXHIBIT 16–8
Equation for a Straight Line

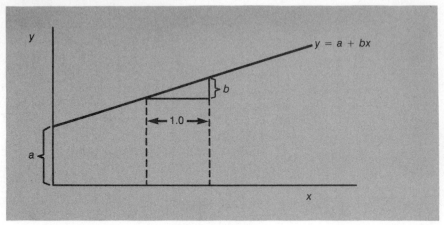

Enough observations must be made to allow the analyst to conclude that the resulting regression equation and the values of a and b are reliable enough to be used. Furthermore, these observations should cover all portions of the likely range of the independent variable. And if conditions (input prices, technology, or methods) change during the period in which the observations are made, observations made before the change should be either adjusted (e.g., by a price index) or discarded.

The objective of simple linear regression analysis based on the least squares method is illustrated in Exhibit 16–9. Each observed value of y is labeled y_o, and this value is plotted as a point in the exhibit. [A fully correct label would be (y_o, x_o) but since our interest is in the values of y,

EXHIBIT 16–9
A Least-Squares Regression Line

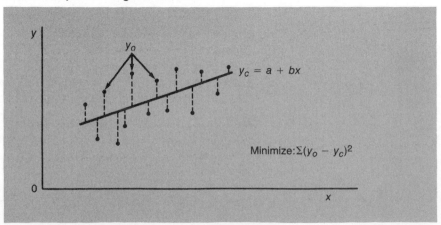

we've used the simpler notation.] The symbol y_c stands for the value of y calculated from the regression equation for any given value of x. As the expression in the lower right of the diagram shows, the objective of least-squares regression analysis is to find the line that minimizes the sum of the squares of the differences $(y_o - y_c)$ between y_o and y_c for each y_o.

The regression equation for a straight line that has this property and represents the relationship between y and x can be found by calculating the sums required by the following two equations, known as the normal equations, and solving for a and b:

$$\Sigma y = an + b\Sigma x$$
$$\Sigma xy = a\Sigma x + b\Sigma x^2$$

in which n = the number of observations of x and y.

To make these normal equations easier to work with, we can translate them into the following form:

$$a = \frac{\Sigma y}{n} - \frac{b\Sigma x}{n} \tag{1}$$

$$b = \frac{n\Sigma xy - \Sigma x\Sigma y}{n\Sigma x^2 - (\Sigma x)^2} \tag{2}$$

To illustrate the method without unnecessary arithmetic, let's suppose we have six cost/volume observations from which we wish to estimate the relationship between cost and volume. The observation and the computational quantities required by the two normal equations are as follows:

Volume x	Cost y	xy	x^2
3	5	15	9
4	6	24	16
5	6	30	25
6	9	54	36
7	9	63	49
8	10	80	64
$\Sigma =$ 33	45	266	199

With six observations, $n = 6$.

Substituting these amounts in the normal equations, we get the following:

$$a = \frac{45}{6} - \left(\frac{33}{6}\right)b \tag{1}$$

$$b = \frac{6 \times 266 - 33 \times 45}{6 \times 199 - (33)^2} \tag{2}$$

Solving equation (2), we find that b equals $111/105 = 1.057$. Putting this in equation (1) yields a value of $a = 7.500 - 5.814 = 1.686$. The regression line therefore is described by the following equation:

$$y = \$1.686 + \$1.057x$$

We can use this formula to predict the cost that will be incurred at any volume in the normal volume range. At a volume of 3, for example, cost should be $\$1.686 + 3 \times \$1.057 = \$4.857$. This is $0.143 less than the amount observed at that volume. Repeating this calculation for each of the other observed volumes, we get the following comparison:

Volume x	Observed Cost y_o	Calculated Cost y_c	Deviation $(y_o - y_c)$	Deviation² $(y_o - y_c)^2$
3	$ 5	$ 4.857	+$0.143	$0.0204
4	6	5.914	+ 0.086	0.0074
5	6	6.971	− 0.971	0.9428
6	9	8.028	+ 0.972	0.9448
7	9	9.085	− 0.085	0.0072
8	10	10.142	− 0.142	0.0202
$\Sigma =$				1.9428

If we were to alter either a or b, the sum of the squared deviations would be greater than 1.9428.

Before management uses a regression equation, it needs to know how closely it has fit the observed facts in the past and then whether it is likely to continue to describe the relationship in the future. This requires the calculation of various measures of reliability. One such measure is the coefficient of determination (r^2):

$$r^2 = 1 - \frac{\Sigma(y_o - y_c)^2}{\Sigma(y - \bar{y})^2}$$

($\bar{y}$ is the mean of the observed values of y.)

The general term for the degree of association between variables is *correlation*. If all the observations fall on the regression line, $\Sigma(y_o - y_c)^2$ will be 0, and r^2 will be equal to 1. This is known as perfect correlation. On the other hand, if the deviations from the predicted values are as great as the deviations from the mean, then $\Sigma(y_o - y_c)^2/\Sigma(y_o - \bar{y})^2$ will equal 1, and r^2 will equal 0. This is known as no correlation or zero correlation. In our simple illustration, r^2 is 0.91, meaning that by introducing variations in volume as a possible way of predicting variations in cost, we accounted for 91 percent of the variation of the squared deviations from the mean.[2]

Key Terms

Capacity cost
Cash flow
Decision rule
Fixed cost
Incremental cost
Incremental principle
Incremental profit
Least-squares method
Long-range planning
Managerial accounting
Opportunity cost

Planning
Programmed cost
Project and situation planning
Regression analysis
Scheduling
Short-range planning
Stepped cost
Strategic planning
Sunk cost
Variable cost

Independent Study Problems (Solutions in Appendix B)

1. Cost-Volume Relationships. Johnson Company has prepared the following estimates of average total factory cost at different volumes:

Weekly Volume (Units)	Average Cost per Unit
1	$11.00
2	6.00
3	4.33
4	3.50
5	3.00
6	2.67
7	2.43
8	2.25
9	2.22
10	2.30

a. Calculate average variable cost at each volume. (For this purpose, assume that total fixed cost is the same at all volumes.)

b. Calculate average fixed cost at each volume.

c. Assuming the company is now operating at a weekly volume of nine units, calculate the cost relevant to a decision to increase the rate of operations to 10 units a week.

---

[2] For a more complete discussion of regression analysis and measures of reliability, see Wayne E. Leininger, *Quantitative Methods in Accounting* (New York: D. Van Nostrand, 1980), pp. 95–123; for a more advanced treatment, see Edmond Valinvaud, *Statistical Methods of Econometrics*, 2d rev. ed. (New York: American Elsevier, 1970), chaps. 3–10.

2. Opportunity Cost. Nancy Smith bought 100 shares in Hydrophonics, Ltd., on January 15, 19x1, paying $15 a share. She bought an additional 100 shares on March 18, 19x4, paying $20 a share. The market price of this stock fell rapidly in 19x5, reaching a low of $6 a share. Early in 19x6, the market price had recovered to $8 a share. At that point General Enterprises, Inc., offered to buy all shares tendered to it at a price of $10 a share.

What cost should Smith use in evaluating this offer?

3. Identifying Incremental Costs. Marmon, Inc., owns two delivery trucks. The costs of owning and operating these trucks are as follows:

	Truck A	Truck B
Yearly fixed costs:		
Garage space	$ 800	$ 800
Depreciation	2,400	2,000
Registration and insurance	1,500	1,500
Maintenance	500	500
Variable costs:		
Drivers' wages and benefits	$15 an hour	$15 an hour
Gasoline and oil	0.20 a mile	0.22 a mile
Maintenance	0.08 a mile	0.10 a mile

Marmon normally operates truck A 1,800 hours a year; truck B is used only 650 hours. On the average, trucks in service cover 15 miles in an hour. The company rents garage space for its trucks in a nearby garage. The garaging contract for either truck can be canceled on one month's notice. Maintenance is provided by a local truck-repair shop.

Marmon has just purchased merchandise in a liquidation sale and must pick this merchandise up next week. Unfortunately, truck A is now fully scheduled for regular deliveries all next week. Truck B isn't scheduled for use next week, but it can't be used to pick up the new merchandise because it is too wide for the loading platform where the merchandise is located. Truck B could be used for truck A's regular deliveries, thereby releasing truck A to pick up the merchandise, but Marmon's management is concerned that that would be too costly.

Management estimates that the merchandise-moving job will take one full week. If truck A were used to move the merchandise, it would travel 400 miles and use 40 hours of a driver's time. Truck B, if used in the regular delivery service while truck A was on this special assignment, would operate 40 hours and cover 600 miles. The additional truck driver would be hired for the week on a contract basis at the regular wage-and-benefits cost of $15 an hour.

As an alternative, an independent trucking company has offered to pick up and deliver the purchased merchandise to Marmon's warehouse for $780.

a. Should Marmon use truck A to pick up this merchandise, or should it use the independent trucker? Show your calculations and indicate how you treated each cost element. (You may assume a year of 50 weeks.)

b. Because truck B is used so little, management is considering scrapping it and using an independent trucker to make the deliveries it is now used for. Assuming truck B has no significant scrap value, what is the highest annual amount Marmon could afford to pay an independent trucker each year instead of using truck B? Show your calculations. (Ignore income taxes.)

Exercises and Problems

4. Identifying a Cost Concept: Discussion Question. "I see no difference between the decision to buy something I don't own and a decision not to sell that item if I already own it. The economic effect is the same."

Identify the cost concept implicit in this statement. Do you agree with it? Cite an example of its truth or falsehood. (You need not quantify your example.)

5. Forms of Planning: Discussion Question. "I can't see why you refer to a decision to buy a car as a form of planning. I can't think of anything I do that is less poorly planned."

Defend the classification of this decision as a form of planning. What definition of planning does the speaker appear to use?

6. Cost Concepts: Discussion Question. Mutual investment funds own bonds, notes, and shares of stock issued by other companies and government agencies. Investors who provide money to such a mutual fund thereby become shareholders of the fund.

An *open-end* mutual fund stands ready on any business day to sell additional shares in the fund at the average current market value of the fund's net assets on that day. It also stands ready to buy, at that price, any shares any shareholder in the fund wishes to sell. *Net assets* is the mutual fund equivalent of a manufacturer's owners' equity per share except that the investment portfolio is measured at its current market value.

A shareholder in one of these mutual investment funds recently wrote one of its directors, asking the following question: "Every three months the fund issues a report, listing the current market value of the securities in the fund but not listing the amounts the fund paid to obtain these securities. Why don't you list these cost amounts?"

What reply should the director make? Use in your answer at least one of the cost concepts described in this chapter.

7. Sunk Cost; Opportunity Cost. Nora Mann bought 100 shares of ABC Company's $5 par common stock on June 14, 19x1, at a cost of $23 a share. On April 22, 19x3, she considered selling those shares at the then-current market price of $44 a share. On that same date, Robert Budd offered to give her 400 shares of preferred stock in a company he was forming, in exchange for her ABC shares. The new preferred shares had a par value of $10 a share.

Identify and measure (a) an opportunity cost, and (b) a sunk cost from Nora Mann's point of view on April 22, 19x3. Explain for each why the amount you have identified fits the definition of an opportunity cost or a sunk cost.

8. Effect of Special Order. Relay Corporation manufactures batons. Relay can manufacture 300,000 batons a year at a total variable cost of $750,000 and a total fixed cost of $450,000. Relay's prediction is that 240,000 batons will be sold at the regular price of $5 each. In addition, a special order has been placed by a customer for 60,000 batons at a 40 percent discount off the regular price.

By what amount will income before income taxes be increased or decreased as a result of this special order?

(AICPA adapted)

9. Make or Buy Decision. Buck Company manufactures Part No. 1700 for use in its production cycle. The costs per unit for 5,000 units of Part No. 1700 are as follows:

Variable materials costs	$ 2
Variable labor costs.	12
Other variable costs.	5
Fixed costs	7
Total cost	$26

Hollow Company has offered to sell Buck 5,000 units of Part No. 1700 for $27 a unit. If Buck accepts this offer, some of the facilities presently used to manufacture Part No. 1700 can be used in the manufacture of Part No. 1211, thereby reducing the company's cost of manufacturing Part No. 1211 by $40,000. In addition, if the company stops making Part No. 1700, it can reduce its total fixed factory cost by $15,000.

What is the incremental profit or loss to be obtained by accepting Hollow's offer?

(AICPA adapted)

10. Cost-Volume Relationship. From the following estimates of total cost at different hourly volumes, calculate for each volume of activity: (a) average total cost, (b) average fixed cost, (c) average variable cost, and (d) the incremental cost of producing the final unit. Assume that total fixed cost is the same at all volumes.

Units	Cost
0	$100
1	200
2	250
3	290
4	330
5	370
6	410
7	450
8	500
9	570
10	670

11. Exercises in Incremental Analysis.

a. Light Company has 2,000 obsolete light fixtures that are carried in inventory at a manufacturing cost of $30,000. If the fixtures are re-worked for $10,000, they can be sold for $18,000. Alternatively, the fixtures can be sold for $3,000 to a jobber in a distant city. In a decision model used to analyze the reworking proposal, what is the opportunity cost?

b. Woody Company, which manufactures sneakers, has enough idle capacity to accept a special order of 20,000 pairs of sneakers at $6 a pair. The normal selling price is $10 a pair. Variable manufacturing costs are $4.50 a pair, and fixed manufacturing costs are $1.50 a pair. Woody will incur no incremental selling expenses as a result of the special order, nor will total fixed manufacturing costs be affected. What will be the effect on income before taxes if the special order can be accepted without affecting other sales?

c. Argus Company, a manufacturer of lamps, budgeted sales of 400,000 lamps at $20 a unit for the year 19x0. Variable manufacturing costs were budgeted at $8 a unit, and fixed manufacturing costs were budgeted at $5 a unit. A special offer to buy 40,000 lamps for $11.50 each was received by Argus in April 19x0. Argus had enough plant capacity to manufacture the additional quantity of lamps; the production would have to be done by the regular work force on an overtime basis, however, at an estimated additional cost of $1.50 per lamp. Argus would incur no incremental selling expenses as a result of the special order. What would be the effect on income before taxes if the special order could be accepted without affecting normal sales?

d. Cardinal Company needs 20,000 units of a certain part to use in its production cycle. The following information is available on costs per unit:

Cost to Cardinal to make the part:

Materials (variable)	$ 4
Labor (variable)	16
Other variable..................	8
Fixed	10
Total.......................	$38

Cost to Cardinal if it buys the part
from Oriole Company $36

If Cardinal buys the part from Oriole instead of making it, Cardinal will not be able to use the released facilities in another manufacturing activity. Sixty percent of the fixed costs will continue if Cardinal buys the part from Oriole. In deciding whether to make or buy the part, what estimate of the incremental cost of making the part would you use?

e. Motor Company manufactures 10,000 units of part CRX-16 for use in its production annually. The following costs are reported:

Materials (variable)	$ 20,000
Labor (variable)	55,000
Other variable	45,000
Fixed	70,000
Total	$190,000

Valve Company has offered to sell Motor 10,000 units of part CRX-16 for $18 a unit. If Motor accepts the offer, some of the facilities presently used to manufacture part CRX-16 can be rented to a third party at an annual rental of $15,000. Additionally, $4 a unit of the other fixed costs will be eliminated. Should Motor accept Valve's offer, and why?

(AICPA adapted)

12. Opportunity Cost; Sunk Cost. Jack Marshall, a corporate personnel director, decided to hire Cornelia Wright to become his company's resident actuary, a specialist position that had opened up because of the untimely death of a valued employee.

When Marshall asked Wright the amount of salary she was earning at her then-current position, Wright stated that it was $55,000, quickly adding that from her point of view that was a sunk cost. Wright then asked what salary had been paid to the deceased employee. Marshall replied that it had been $72,000 but that that was irrelevant because it was a historical cost.

Wright then asked what the cost would be if the position weren't filled and the work were performed instead on a fee basis by outside consultants. Marshall answered that the fees would probably total $80,000 a year, but the company would also avoid the cost of fringe benefits, which was about 30 percent of each employee's salary. Wright proceeded to indicate that a recently published industry survey reported that this type of position on average carried an annual salary of $65,000.

Which costs were relevant to each party's decision?

13. Identifying Sunk Costs. Meredith Machine Company entered into a contract to manufacture certain specially designed processing equipment for a foreign buyer. When the equipment was completed and in the testing stage, currency controls which nullified all import contracts were instituted by the government to which the purchaser was subject. The manufacturing costs incurred by Meredith Company up to that time amounted to $700,000. The scrap value of the equipment was estimated to be approximately $80,000.

No purchaser could be found for the equipment in its existing form, but one company was interested if certain major modifications were made. This company offered $500,000; the estimated cost of modification to fit the revised specifications was $200,000.

What action should Meredith Company have taken? To what extent was the decision affected by the manufacturing cost the company had already incurred?

14. Analyzing Costs. John Robinson lives 28 miles from his place of work. He drives his automobile to and from work five days a week, 50 weeks a year. All told, he drives this car 10,000 miles a year. He estimates his expenses as follows:

Gasoline	$0.08 a mile
Parking	$3 a day
Depreciation	$200 a month
Maintenance and repairs	$500 a year
Insurance	$750 a year

A fellow worker has asked John to give him a ride to and from work each day. Even though this would add seven miles each morning and each afternoon, the travel time would be the same as it had been because John would then drive on a toll road that charges a 75 cent toll in each direction.

If John is determined not to make a profit from doing his co-worker a favor but doesn't want to lose money, what amount should he charge each week? Show your calculations.

15. Drawing a Regression Line. The following table shows departmental output and total departmental labor cost for each of the past 12 months:

	Output (no. of units)	Labor Cost
January	35	$27,600
February	63	20,700
March	132	28,200
April	150	33,000
May	125	30,400
June	111	25,500
July	116	24,300
August	98	23,200
September	135	24,000
October	120	27,300
November	114	20,700
December	140	30,000

a. Plot these data on a sheet of graph paper and draw a straight line which seems to fit the observations most closely. Fit this line visually; do not use the least-squares method described in the appendix to this chapter.

b. Derive the mathematical equation that describes the line you drew in answer to part *a*.

c. Use the least-squares method described in the appendix to this chapter to derive another mathematical equation to describe the apparent relationship between total labor cost and output in this case.

d. Compare the equations in your answers to parts *b* and *c*. How similar are they? Why aren't they identical?

16. Identifying Incremental Costs. Stratford Company has four large presses of approximately the same capacity. Each was run at close to its full capacity during 19x8. Each machine is depreciated separately; a declining-charge method is used. Data for each press are:

	No. 1	No. 2	No. 3	No. 4
Date acquired	1/1/x0	1/1/x4	1/1/x6	1/1/x7
Cost	$100,000	$120,000	$145,000	$175,000
Operating costs, 19x8:				
Labor	$ 11,000	$ 10,500	$ 10,000	$ 9,500
Maintenance	3,800	2,400	2,000	1,000
Repairs	600	1,200	800	500
Depreciation	3,500	5,400	7,800	10,800
Total	$ 18,900	$ 19,500	$ 20,600	$ 21,800

It is expected that activity in 19x9 will be substantially lower than in 19x8. As a result, one machine is to be put on standby. It has been proposed that No. 4 should be that machine on the grounds that it has the highest operating cost. A standby machine would require neither maintenance nor repairs.

Do you agree with this proposal? Explain, citing amounts from the problem.

17. Multiple Alternatives.   Archway Corporation decided to modernize its operations by introducing computerized controls. The 19x4 budget included authorization to incur added costs of $300,000 to retrain foremen and division supervisors. After 75 percent of the retraining cost had been incurred, top management realized that one third of these employees wouldn't be needed after all. If that group were to be fired immediately, Archway would incur a severance-pay cost of $100,000, payable immediately.

Alternatively, these employees could be retrained for internal auditing positions at an added cost of $90,000, an amount that was 40 percent less than the cost of training newly hired personnel. Archway's chief accountant pointed out that because of seniority, hiring new people to serve as internal auditors would cost Archway $45,000 less in salaries each year for the next four years than would have to be paid to the retrained foremen and supervisors. She therefore proposed letting all the foremen and supervisors complete the original retraining program and then pay placement-agency fees of approximately $60,000 to relocate these employees in other companies.

a. Identify the three available alternatives and show who would be performing the internal audit functions under each.
b. Identify the costs that Archway's management should consider in arriving at a decision as to which course of action to pursue. Ignore differences among the alternatives in the timing of these costs.
c. What additional information should management have before choosing a course of action?

18. Incremental and Sunk Costs.   Merkle Publications, a publisher of college textbooks and instructional software products, gave David Talbert a $50,000 cash grant a year ago to develop a new instructional software program for use in small-business accounting courses. It also paid $90,000 to rent, equip, and staff a laboratory for one year for Talbert's use on this project.

Merkle's contract with Talbert provided that if his product was accepted for publication, Merkle would pay him a royalty of $5 for each of the first 20,000 packages sold and $7.50 for each package sold in excess of that number.

Talbert has just delivered a program that Merkle's technical experts regard as acceptable. If Merkle decides to publish this program, the company will have to spend $40,000 to prepare the instruction manual and tutorial program, $30,000 to prepare master disks, and $10,000 to design the box and binder to contain the diskettes and manual. Merkle would also spend $200,000 to introduce the package to accounting faculty members and $10 to manufacture each disk package it sold. The selling price would be $25 a package.

Since no comparable package is now on the market, Merkle believes it reasonable to forecast sales of 50,000 disks the first year. Because the market is so dynamic, however, Merkle's management believes it would be unwise to count on any significant volume of sales after the first year. Even if the product proved popular, substantial rewriting probably would be necessary to keep its marketing edge for another year.

The state tax office has just notified Merkle that it must pay a 15 percent, onetime surcharge tax on the $50,000 advance it gave to Talbert last year. This tax will be paid next month. No surcharge would be imposed on any other costs the company might incur in the future.

Should Merkle Publications complete the development of the new product and offer it for sale in the market? Prepare an analysis to support your recommendation.

19. Using Materials on Hand.   Jones Company has 2,000 yards of a plastic material on hand; 1,000 yards were purchased two months ago for $2.00 a yard, and 1,000 yards were purchased last month for $2.20 a yard. This material deteriorates in storage, and the present inventories will become worthless if the company doesn't use or sell them during the next six weeks.

Some of the inventory of the plastic material could be used to make product A. Each unit of product A would require one yard of the material plus $3 in other incremental costs. A maximum of 500 units of product A could be sold in the next six weeks at a price of $5.25 each.

Jones Company's management is also thinking of manufacturing product B. Each unit of B would require one yard of the material plus $4 in other incremental costs.

Jones Company could sell any quantity of the plastic material, without further processing, for $1.80 a yard. It could also buy additional quantities of the material for $2.40 a yard.

a. A customer has offered to buy 1,500 units of product B in the next six weeks if the price is right and if Jones agrees to sell no product B to anyone else during that period. What unit cost would you compare to the offer price in evaluating the desirability of accepting this order?
b. How would your answer to part *a* differ if the offer was for 2,000 units, with each unit to bear the same price? If the offer was for 2,500 units?
c. How would your answers to parts *a* and *b* differ if the customer were willing to pay a different price for each successive batch of 500 units to

be delivered in the next six weeks? In other words, calculate a unit cost for the first 1,500 units, a separate unit cost for the next 500 units, and another separate unit cost for the final 500 units.

d. Suppose the customer in part *a* has offered to buy 2,000 units at a price of $6 a unit. The customer will not accept any units unless Jones supplies the full 2,000 units ordered. Should Jones accept this order and produce and sell 500 units of product A as well?

(From a problem by Alfred Oxenfeldt)

Chapter 17

Applications of Decision Concepts

The basic concepts we identified in Chapter 16 can be applied in a wide variety of decision contexts. The purpose of this chapter is to illustrate their usefulness in the context of several short-term project or situation decisions. The chapter has two main parts:

1. Using cost variability data to estimate incremental cost.
2. Cost-volume-profit analysis in short-term decision making.

TERMINOLOGY REMINDER

Incremental cost is any difference between the cash outflow associated with one course of action and the cash outflow associated with an alternative course of action.

Using Cost-Variability Data to Estimate Incremental Cost

Estimates of short-term relationships between costs and volume are useful in a wide range of decision situations. A study of two such situations will help illustrate this point: (1) pricing additional business, and (2) discontinuing a product. Examination of these problems will also show that all the relevant considerations can't always be quantified, so that accounting data alone don't determine what the decision should be.

Pricing Additional Business

Most companies do most of their business with customers who buy the products and services that are the company's regular stock in trade. Opportunities sometimes arise, however, to fill special orders for products

646

that aren't part of the regular line. For example, the purchasing agent of Wilde, Inc., which operates a chain of automotive and hardware stores, asked Van Horn Company's sales manager whether Van Horn would be interested in manufacturing 2,000 power mowers to be sold by Wilde under its own brand name, Wilcut. Van Horn could have this order at a price of $48 a unit. Production capacity was easily adequate to handle this order, and the marketing manager saw no reason why sales of Wilcut mowers would affect sales of Van Horn's regular mowers. Van Horn's controller proceeded to estimate the cost of filling this special order.

Full-Costing. Under **full costing,** the cost of output is calculated on the basis of all costs—i.e., both incremental and sunk costs. Starting with existing cost estimates for Van Horn's Zephyr mower, which was very similar to the Wilcut mower, the controller estimated that the Wilcut mowers would have to be sold to Wilde at a price of $55.80 if they were to generate a normal profit margin. The calculation was as follows:

Manufacturing cost:	
Materials..........................	$25.80
Labor.............................	7.00
Other.............................	9.35
Total manufacturing cost	42.15
Selling expense.....................	1.45
Administrative expense.	2.90
Total cost......................	46.50
Desired profit margin (20 percent)	9.30
Target price..................	$55.80

Incremental Costing. Under **incremental costing,** the cost of output is calculated on the basis of incremental costs only, both fixed and variable. The estimates of incremental costs and cash flows for the Wilcut mowers were as follows:

	Per Unit	Total	
Incremental sales revenues	$48.00		$96,000
Incremental costs:			
Incremental variable costs:			
Variable materials................	25.80	$51,600	
Variable labor...................	7.00	14,000	
Other variable factory costs	5.00	10,000	
Variable administrative costs	0.20	400	
Incremental variable costs........	38.00	76,000	
Incremental fixed factory costs		2,000	
Total incremental costs			78,000
Incremental net cash receipts			$18,000

In this analysis, the manufacturing vice president accepted the original estimates of labor and materials costs as fully incremental costs because they represented employee salaries and materials-purchase costs that would not be incurred if the proposal were rejected. For example, some factory employees scheduled to be placed on a reduced workweek if the Wilcut order was refused would be given full-time work if it was accepted, thereby increasing the factory's total labor cost. Labor efficiency would be about the same in either case, so incremental labor cost would be about $7 a unit, as shown in the table.

The variable portions of other factory costs also were fully incremental, and these were estimated at $5 a unit. Fixed factory costs were mostly sunk, however, and the manufacturing vice president excluded these from the analysis. The idea was to include only those fixed factory costs likely to be added to the total by acceptance of the order. The only likely increment here seemed to be a slight increase in supervisory costs, adding up to about $2,000 for the contract as a whole.

The selling and administrative expenses in the original estimates were based on average cost/revenue ratios for the company as a whole. The only selling and administrative costs to be affected by the acceptance of this order were clerical costs in the accounting department, which seemed likely to go up by about 20 cents for each additional unit manufactured and sold. This increment is listed on the fourth line of the table of incremental variable costs.

Nonquantitative Considerations.   These estimates are all presented as definite amounts, with no allowances for uncertainty or errors of estimation. We noted in Exhibit 16–2 that decision making calls for estimates of the uncertainties and risks associated with each potential course of action. In this case, the proposal didn't appear likely to expose the company to any special risks, but the estimates of cash flows were far from certain. The main uncertainties centered on the accuracy of the manufacturing vice president's assumption that Wilcut sales wouldn't affect revenues from Van Horn's other models. The president, for example, was afraid that the company's regular customers, mostly small independent dealers, would regard this as unfair to them and might shift to competitors' lines. The controller suggested that the low price might lead competitors to retaliate by price cutting on models that competed directly with Van Horn's own branded models. Another worry was that if the sales force were encouraged to cut the price this time, it would want to do so again and again. This would undermine the company's entire pricing structure.

The sales manager had a different perspective, pointing out that Van Horn had been losing market share in recent years by not participating in the rapidly growing portion of total mower sales handled by mail-order houses and other large retail distributors. This initial order would give the company valuable experience in dealing in this market and might lay the groundwork for a substantial penetration of the market in the future.

How this argument was resolved is unimportant here, but it does illustrate two things. First, a purely quantitative analysis is unlikely to resolve the issues in decision making involving major policy questions. Second, the arguments summarized represent the typical range of managerial reactions to the use of incremental-cost data. How the issues are resolved in any case will depend on management's considered judgment on the validity of the arguments raised in this illustration.[1]

Dropping an Unprofitable Product

Van Horn's management also faced another problem. Its top-of-the-line Estate power mower, with a volume of about 5,000 units a year, was selling at a price that was $4.10 less than the average cost assigned to it. Van Horn's president asked the controller to prepare an estimate of the financial impact of discontinuing sales of the Estate mower.

The controller's first step was to ask the sales manager whether withdrawal of the Estate mower would affect the company's sales of any of its other mowers. The sale manager reported that if this item were dropped, many buyers would switch to the company's Suburban mower, a somewhat less expensive model with many of the same features as the Estate mower. Sales of the Suburban mower seemed likely to increase by about 3,000 units a year if the Estate mower were dropped. None of the company's other models would be affected.

The controller's next step was to prepare estimates of the incremental cost of manufacturing and selling these two mowers. Since for this decision all variable costs were incremental, the controller proceeded at first to consider only the variable costs; the resulting estimates were as follows:

	Estate	Suburban
Variable factory costs:		
Materials	$32.00	$27.50
Labor	12.00	7.50
Other	6.00	5.00
Total	50.00	40.00
Variable selling cost..............	3.50	3.00
Variable administrative cost	0.20	0.20
Total variable cost..........	$53.70	$43.20

---

[1] Although managers often rely on their own judgment to resolve issues arising from the uncertainties surrounding their estimates of incremental costs and benefits, formal techniques of varying levels of complexity and sophistication are widely available and highly useful for dealing with many of these issues. See, for example, D. Warner North, "A Tutorial Introduction to Decision Theory," in *Accounting for Managerial Decision Making,* 2d ed., ed. Don T. DeCoster, Kavasseri V. Ramanathan, and Gary L. Sundem (Los Angeles: Melville Publishing Co., 1978), pp. 15–36; or Robert S. Kaplan, *Advanced Management Accounting* (Englewood Cliffs, N.J.: Prentice-Hall, 1982), pp. 181–204.

Variable selling costs in this table represented the commissions the company's sales force received on all sales of the regular lines of mowers.

Finally, the controller tried to estimate how dropping the Estate mowers would affect the fixed factory costs. This effect was not measured by average fixed cost at the existing volume, but had to be estimated from an item-by-item analysis. After careful study, the manufacturing vice president reported that $27,000 of the factory's fixed costs, which were fixed as long as *any* Estate mowers were manufactured, could be eliminated if *none* were produced. Production of an additional 3,000 Suburban mowers a year wouldn't lead to any increases in fixed factory costs.

The analysis of this proposal is summarized in Exhibit 17–1. The estimates in column (2), taken alone, indicate that the company would

EXHIBIT 17–1
Van Horn Company: Incremental Net Cash Flow from Proposal to Discontinue Sales of Estate Mowers

	Cash-Flow Effects of Forgone Sales of Estate Mowers		Cash-Flow Effects of Additional Sales of Suburban Mowers		(5) Incremental Effects on Net Cash Flow
	(1) Per Unit	*(2)* Total	*(3)* Per Unit	*(4)* Total	*(2) + (4)*
Effect on receipts	−$70.00	−$350,000	+$60.00	+$180,000	−$170,000
Effect on costs:					
Variable costs	− 53.70	− 268,500	+ 43.20	+ 129,600	− 138,900
Fixed factory costs		− 27,000		—	− 27,000
Total effect on costs		− 295,500		+ 129,600	− 165,900
Effect on cash flow.		−$ 54,500		+$ 50,400	−$ 4,100

lose $54,500 in net cash receipts if it discontinued production and sales of the Estate mower. Column (4), however, shows that $50,400 of this loss would be offset by the increased net cash receipts from increased sales of the Suburban mower.

The net effect of the discontinuation proposal is shown in column (5). It indicates that withdrawing the Estate mower would reduce net cash receipts by about $4,100 a year. The company therefore probably should continue to manufacture and sell Estate mowers for now. Their incremental contribution to the company's net cash flow is so small, however, that management might prefer to spend its time developing markets for other products—unless it could find ways to improve the cash flows from the Estate mower business.

The Use of Averages

Average labor and materials costs were used in both these illustrations, but only as a means of estimating the total labor and materials costs associated with each alternative. The average of the other factory costs and the averages of selling and administrative expenses didn't enter the analysis because these costs weren't expected to be proportionally variable with volume. We use averages only when they are valid predictors of totals—that is, when total cost appears likely to vary proportionally with variations in volume.

A simple example should demonstrate this point. Suppose Van Horn's service department now serves 2,000 customers at an average cost of $10 a month. It has an opportunity to pick up an additional 500 customers without affecting the volume of business it does with its present customers or the prices they pay. While the additional volume will increase *total* cost, it will reduce the department's *average* cost to $9.75 a month per customer. Since the new customers will pay only $9 a month for service, serving these potential new customers appears to be a losing business.

A careful analysis, however, shows that the new business will be marginally profitable if the present estimates are valid. The correct comparison is as follows:

		Incremental Total	Incremental per Customer
Incremental receipts: 500 × $9		$4,500	$9.00
Incremental cost:			
Cost to service 2,500 customers:			
2,500 × $9.75	$24,375		
Cost to service 2,000 customers:			
2,000 × $10	20,000		
Total incremental cost		4,375	8.75
Incremental profit		$ 125	$0.25

The reason the incremental analysis shows an incremental profit instead of a loss is that some of the department's costs won't rise proportionally with volume. The incremental cost for the additional customers will average $4,375/500 = $8.75 a customer, and this is less than the incremental receipts of $9. If the cost increment weren't less than $10, the average wouldn't fall. The revised average will always be between the original average and the increment.

Identifying the Increment

The incremental receipts attributed to proposals to expand total volume may not be the receipts actually collected from the new customers. The analytical rule is to compare the total receipts if the expansion proposal is accepted with the total receipts obtainable without expansion. We'll explain with an illustration.

Suppose Van Horn's service department's present business is to service four different 500-customer groups who are now paying $15, $12, $10.50, and $8.50 a month, respectively. If we make the simplifying assumption that all the customers are alike except for the prices they pay, then the department will be able to increase its net cash receipts without expanding its total volume. How? By servicing the new group of customers at a price of $9 a month *instead of* servicing the *least* profitable group of its present customers—those paying only $8.50 a month—the department can increase its pretax net cash inflow by $250, a month [500 × ($9.00 − $8.50)]. It can do this without increasing its physical volume or increasing its total costs. This being the case, the expansion decision has to hinge on whether the $8.50 price is high enough to cover the incremental costs of expansion—and in this case we know it falls $0.25 short of the incremental costs, which average $8.75 a customer.

Exhibit 17–2 shows this comparison graphically. Group A customers contribute $6.25 *more* than incremental cost; group D customers contrib-

EXHIBIT 17–2
Identifying Incremental Receipts

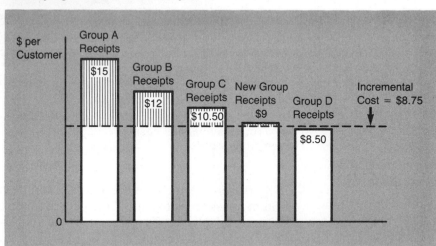

ute $0.25 *less* than incremental cost. The 2,000 most profitable customers are the 1,500 in the first three existing groups, plus the 500 in the new group. All these can be served without increasing total volume and without incurring incremental costs of $8.75 a customer. The only reason for incurring the incremental costs necessary to expand volume is to enable the company to serve customer group D, and this is clearly unprofitable. Van Horn presumably should either charge more for its services to customers in this group or discontinue service to them unless management believes these customers will move into one of the other groups later on.

The conclusion from all this is that when resources are interchangeable, the same incremental cost figure applies to *each* portion of total volume, not just to the volume provided by potential new customers. Each group of customers—current and prospective—can be regarded as the incremental group.

Different Costs for Different Purposes

The illustrations in this chapter demonstrate the following important point: *Each decision calls for its own definition of incremental cost.* For decisions that affect only a small percentage of total volume for short periods of time, only short-term variable costs are likely to be incremental. For decisions that affect a large amount of volume, affect volume for a long time, or call for major differences in the amount of marketing, production, development, or administrative effort, incremental cost will include fixed costs as well as variable costs.

For example, if Van Horn is considering discontinuing the service business entirely, the average incremental cost may be closer to $9.75 than to $8.75 because many fixed costs are incremental with respect to that decision. The cost of servicing *one* more customer, however, may very well be less than $8.75 because that customer's work may fit easily into an idle period in the daily schedule. Incremental cost may even be close to zero for a decision to make one additional service call.

Cost-Volume-Profit Analysis

The outcomes of few decisions can be predicted with certainty. One major uncertainty is the operating volume management will be able to achieve. One technique management uses to help judge the sensitivity of results to errors in forecasting operating volume is known as **cost-volume-profit analysis.** In this section, we'll describe this technique and point out some of its limitations.

Basic Calculations

The objective of cost-volume-profit analysis is to identify three quantities: (1) the rate at which income varies in response to variations in sales, (2) the break-even sales volume, and (3) the spread between anticipated volume and break-even volume.

Break-Even.   We'll explain the meaning of **break-even analysis** by using an example. Van Horn's mower division's estimated pretax income for next year is $600,000, based on estimated sales of 50,000 mowers. Management needs to know how sensitive its income estimate is to errors in the forecasts of the division's sales. Failure to reach the planned sales levels would decrease both net income and the cash flow from operations, thus jeopardizing the company's ability to pay cash dividends and finance its other discretionary outlays.

Van Horn's accountants have made the following estimates of revenues and expenses:

Sales revenues: 50,000 × $75		$3,750,000
Expenses:		
Variable: 50,000 × $45	$2,250,000	
Fixed	900,000	
Total expense		3,150,000
Mower division income before tax		$ 600,000

These estimates can be stated algebraically. Total revenue, R, at volume V is:

$$R = \$75V \qquad (1)$$

in which V stands for the number of mowers sold.

Total divisional cost, C, at volume V is:

$$C = \$900,000 + \$45V \qquad (2)$$

The division will break even at the volume at which $R = C$. This volume can be identified by equating the right-hand sides of equations (1) and (2) and solving for V:

$$\$75V = \$900,000 + \$45V$$
$$V = 30,000 \text{ mowers}$$

This is known as the break-even volume or **break-even point.**

Contribution Margin.   Implicit in our analysis to this point has been the notion that while some of a company's expenses are fixed, its revenues and some of its expenses do vary as volume varies. It follows, therefore, that the amount by which each unit's revenue exceeds each unit's variable expense contributes to the company's ability to pay its fixed expenses. This excess is called **contribution margin.** At the break-even point, the total contribution margin is exactly the amount needed by the company to meet its fixed expenses. For levels beyond the break-even point, the total contribution margin enables the company both to meet its fixed expenses and to earn income.

Break-even calculations can be simplified if variable cost per unit can be assumed to be constant as total volume changes. In that case, we can use the contribution margin estimates on a per-unit basis. In other words, instead of identifying separately the revenue per unit (to the left of the equal sign) and the variable cost per unit (to the right), it is often more efficient to express these sums as a single amount—the **contribution margin per unit.** In our Van Horn example, the revenue per unit was $75 and the variable cost was equal to 60 percent of revenue, or $45 a unit. This means the contribution margin was $30 a unit ($75 − $45).

The break-even point can be located by finding out how many mowers must be sold to produce a *total* contribution margin equal to the anticipated fixed costs. This is obtained by dividing total fixed cost by the contribution margin per unit:

$$\text{Break-even volume} \quad = \quad \frac{\$900,000}{\$30} \quad = \quad 30,000 \text{ mowers}$$

In monetary terms, the division's break-even point is reached when it has revenues of $2,250,000 (30,000 × $75).

Margin of Safety. A companion to the break-even volume is the **margin of safety,** the difference between the break-even volume and the actual or anticipated volume of activity. The division's budgeted volume for the year was 50,000 mowers. The estimated margin of safety therefore was:

$$\text{Margin of safety} \quad = \quad 50,000 \quad - \quad 30,000 \quad = \quad 20,000 \text{ mowers}$$

In other words, the division will cover its total costs even if volume turns out to be 20,000 mowers fewer than management is anticipating.

Break-Even and Profit-Volume Charts

This same analysis is presented graphically in Exhibit 17–3 in a diagram we call a break-even chart or profit-volume chart. These charts can be constructed in various ways, but in this case total revenue and total variable cost are represented by straight lines rising from the origin. The vertical spread between these two lines at any volume measures the total contribution margin at that volume. Total fixed cost is entered in the

EXHIBIT 17–3
Van Horn Company, Mower Division: Profit-Volume Chart

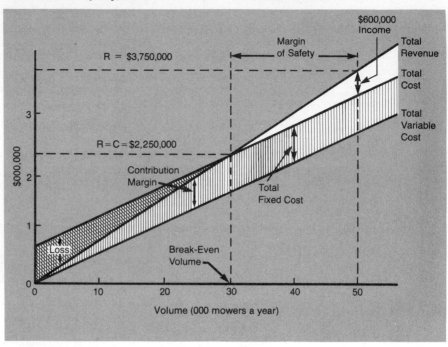

chart by drawing the total-cost line parallel to the total-variable-cost line, but $900,000 higher in this case.

A glance at the chart in Exhibit 17–3 reveals four key estimates:

1. If fixed costs are at planned levels and no sales are made, the division will lose $900,000 because the fixed costs won't be covered.
2. As volume increases from zero, the contribution margin from sales will cover more and more of the fixed costs until at a 30,000-mower sales volume the division will just break even.
3. At the anticipated sales volume of 50,000 mowers in 19x3, the division will earn $600,000 income (represented by the vertical distance between the total-revenue and total-cost lines at that volume), and the margin of safety will be 20,000 mowers.
4. If volume exceeds or falls short of the planned level, income is likely to increase or decrease by $30 times the excess or shortfall in the number of mowers sold.

What does all this mean? First, if we take the margin of safety as a measure of risk, the mower division's operations next year appear to be relatively unrisky. Volume would have to fall 20,000 units short of the planned level, a 40 percent drop, to fall to the break-even level. A drop of this magnitude is highly unusual.

Second, efforts designed to expand sales volume can be evaluated by comparing the costs of those efforts with the anticipated volume effect, multiplied by $30. For example, a proposal to spend an extra $150,000 advertising the mower line can be justified only if management can reasonably expect the advertising to increase sales by more than 5,000 units ($150,000/$30).

Third, estimates of income sensitivity may affect management's spending and financing plans. If the uncertainty surrounding the income estimate produces a wide range within which income may vary, management is likely to make fewer firm commitments to maintain or increase capital expenditures or dividend payments unless flexible financing arrangements can be made in advance.

Sensitivity of Incremental Cash Flow

In addition to its use in analyzing income effects, cost-volume-profit analysis can be incorporated in incremental cash flow analysis to throw extra light on the risks and opportunities surrounding a proposed use of resources.

For example, recall that in one of our earlier illustrations, Van Horn's mower division was considering an offer by Wilde, Inc., to buy 2,000 Wilcut mowers. Let's change this illustration by assuming that the offer is to purchase 1,000 to 3,000 mowers, the exact quantity depending on Wilde's success in marketing this product. Furthermore, let's assume that the increment in fixed costs in this new situation is $12,000 instead of the $2,000 we assumed earlier.

With these revisions we now have the following estimates of the increments:

Incremental contribution margin per unit:		
Incremental revenue	$	48
Incremental variable cost		38
Incremental contribution margin	$	10
Incremental fixed cost...................		$12,000

At a 2,000-mower volume, incremental cash flow would be $10 × 2,000 − $12,000 = $8,000.

The estimates of the increments also fit smoothly into our break-even formula:

$$\text{Break-even volume} = \frac{\$12,000}{\$10} = 1,200 \text{ mowers.}$$

At an anticipated volume of 2,000 mowers, the margin of safety is 800 mowers (2,000 − 1,200); the break-even volume is a mere 200 mowers higher than the guaranteed minimum volume (1,200 − 1,000). Furthermore, if volume turns out to reach to 3,000-mower upper limit, incremental cash flow will be $10 × 3,000 − $12,000 = $18,000, substantially greater than the $8,000 Van Horn would earn at a 2,000-mower volume. This additional information should help management evaluate the risks and opportunities this offer provides.

Probability-Adjusted Profit Charts

Answers to break-even questions—either income or cash flow—really call for another kind of information we haven't introduced yet, estimates of the *probabilities* of various possible volumes. The break-even point is of no significance whatsoever if the probability of approaching it is zero.

Exhibit 17–4 shows how a set of probability estimates might be merged with the income variability numbers we've been working with—by using

EXHIBIT 17–4
Van Horn Company, Mower Division: Probability-Adjusted Profit Chart

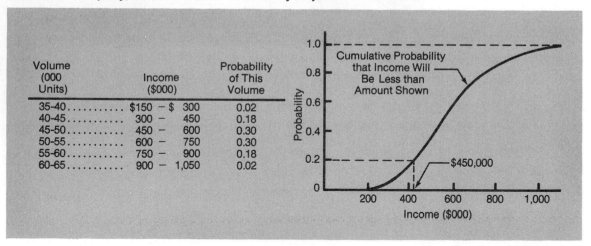

Volume (000 Units)	Income ($000)	Probability of This Volume
35-40	$150 − $ 300	0.02
40-45	300 − 450	0.18
45-50	450 − 600	0.30
50-55	600 − 750	0.30
55-60	750 − 900	0.18
60-65	900 − 1,050	0.02

a **probability-adjusted profit chart.** The table at the left shows that the probability of mower income smaller than $450,000 is about 20 percent. The same set of relationships is shown graphically at the right. The height of the line at any income level represents the probability that income will be no lower than that level. This particular line rises very sharply at first because the probability of low volume is very small. The line then flattens out as the probability of even larger income declines. Van Horn's management has to decide whether a 20 percent probability of falling short of $450,000 is small enough to justify making firm dividend commitments.

Multiproduct Operations

The careful reader must be wondering why we haven't mentioned that Van Horn makes and sells *several* kinds of mowers, not just one. Earlier in this chapter, we noted that it makes Estate mowers, Suburban mowers, Zephyr mowers, and Wilcut mowers, and it may well have several others. We overlooked this variety deliberately, to keep the introductory discussion as simple as possible. In fact, of course, multiproduct operations are more common than single-product operations.

Multiproduct operations introduce three major kinds of difficulties into cost-volume-profit analysis:

1. The contribution margin is likely to differ from product to product.
2. A common physical measuring unit may be hard to find.
3. Some costs are incurred to support two or more products as a group and are not uniquely traceable to any one product.

We'll discuss the first two of these in this section and the next, deferring the third to Chapter 19.

Product Mix: Differing Contribution Margins. The break-even volume and average contribution margin in a multiproduct company can be heavily influenced by the **product mix**—the percentages of total sales accounted for by the company's various products or services. To illustrate this, let's simplify our Van Horn mower example slightly, and assume it has only two kinds of mowers, with the following sales volumes and contribution margins:

	Estate	Wizard
Estimated sales volume (units)....	25,000	25,000
Contribution margin per unit:		
Revenue.....................	$61.60	$88.40
Variable cost	53.70	36.30
Contribution margin per unit..	$ 7.90	$52.10

At the estimated product mix, the average contribution margin is $30, calculated from the following estimates:

	Number of Units	Contribution Margin per Unit	Total Contribution Margin
Estate mower........	25,000	$ 7.90	$ 197,500
Wizard mower	25,000	52.10	1,302,500
Total	50,000		$1,500,000

The average contribution margin is $1,500,000/50,000 = $30 a unit. As we've already seen, the estimated break-even volume at this product mix is 30,000 units ($900,000 total fixed cost divided by $30).

Suppose the mower market changes, however, so that 35,000 Estate mowers and 15,000 Wizard mowers can be sold. The total volume is still 50,000 mowers, but the average contribution margin has fallen to $21.16 ($1,058,000/50,000):

	Number of Units	Contribution Margin per Unit	Total Contribution Margin
Estate mower..........	35,000	$ 7.90	$ 276,500
Wizard mower	15,000	52.10	781,500
Total	50,000		$1,058,000

The break-even volume is now 42,533 mowers:

$$\text{Break-even} = \frac{\text{Total fixed cost}}{\text{Average contribution margin}} = \frac{\$900,000}{\$21.16} = 42,533.$$

The change in product mix therefore reduces the margin of safety to 7,467 mowers (50,000 − 42,533), a much less comfortable margin than the previous 20,000-mower margin was—$1,058,000 contribution margin less $900,000 fixed cost yields $158,000 income instead of $600,000 ($1.5 million − $900,000). Income is also less sensitive to volume changes, as additional sales bring in only $21.16, on the average, instead of $30.

Product mix, in other words, can be a highly important determinant of income. Management may find it useful to analyze the sensitivity of its income in two directions—sensitivity to volume and sensitivity to mix. The result will be a two-way matrix of income estimates rather than a simple schedule. The amounts in the cells of the following partial matrix are estimates of the pretax income at each of nine volume/mix combinations:

	Estimated Income before Taxes when Wizard Mower Sales Account for		
	40% of Total	50% of Total	60% of Total
Volume (number of mowers):			
40,000	$123,200	$300,000	$ 476,800
50,000	379,000	600,000	821,000
60,000	634,800	900,000	1,165,200
Average contribution margin per mower..............	$25.58	$30.00	$34.42
Break-even volume (number of mowers)	35,184	30,000	26,148

Management's willingness to make discretionary outlays will be greater if it anticipates that Wizard sales will be a high percentage of the total than if that percentage is low.

Composite Measures of Volume. When a company sells products that have substantially different physical characteristics, or when it offers both physical products and personal services, measuring overall volume in physical units is impossible. In our Van Horn Company examples, we used the *number of mowers* as the common unit of volume, even though the various mower models differed in many ways. We completely ignored Van Horn's service business—it operates a number of repair centers in which it services customers' mowers—because we wanted to use a physical measure of volume in our initial illustrations.

Once we introduce this additional variety into the product line, the only feasible measure of overall volume is revenue dollars. For example, suppose the mower division's plans call for service revenues of $450,000, with variable costs of $186,000 and fixed costs of $150,000. An aggregate income function can be put together as follows:

	Mower Sales	Service	Total	Percent
Revenues	$3,750,000	$450,000	$4,200,000	100%
Variable costs	2,250,000	186,000	2,436,000	58
Contribution margin . . .	1,500,000	264,000	1,764,000	42
Fixed costs	900,000	150,000	1,050,000	25
Division income.	$ 600,000	$114,000	$ 714,000	17%

These relationships can be expressed in a simple formula:

$$\text{Income before tax} = \text{Average contribution margin} \times \text{Sales revenue} - \text{Fixed cost}$$
$$= 0.42\,R - \$1,050,000$$

The break-even volume then can be calculated in the usual way:

$$\text{Break-even volume} = \frac{\text{Total fixed cost}}{\text{Average contribution margin}} = \frac{\$1,050,000}{0.42}$$
$$= 2,500,000 \text{ revenue dollars}$$

A break-even or profit-volume chart can be drawn with dollars of revenue on the horizontal axis, as we had placed the number of mowers earlier.

Company-Wide Cost-Volume-Profit Analysis

All of our discussion of cost-volume-profit analysis so far has focused on individual revenue segments—a product line, a marketing proposal, or a division. Cost-volume-profit analysis can also be applied to the company as a whole, to gain insight into the risks and opportunities arising from possible volume fluctuations.

For this type of analysis, volume almost always must be measured by revenue dollars, and income is likely to be measured on an aftertax basis. Tax structures vary so much from country to country and from time to time that we hesitate to use a specific tax structure in our illustration. In the United States, for example, the first $25,000 of corporate taxable income is taxed at a lower rate than taxable income in excess of that amount. Some income is subject to state taxation; some expenditures are given special tax treatment.

An introductory text is no place to try to deal with these institutional variations. We'll make the highly simplified assumption that all income is subject to tax at a uniform 40 percent rate, and that losses result in tax refunds at the same rate because the company is permitted to offset those losses against income on which it has paid taxes in previous years.[2]

Given these assumptions, the analysis is straightforward. Let's suppose that when all of Van Horn's divisions and administrative offices are combined—that is, not just the mower division but the company as a whole—variable costs average 65 percent of revenues and estimated fixed costs total $2.5 million. The pretax contribution margin is 35 percent of total revenue (100 percent less 65 percent). At a 40 percent tax rate, the company's net income can be estimated from the following formula:

$$\text{Net income} = (1.0 - 0.4)(0.35R - \$2,500,000)$$
$$= 0.21R - \$1,500,000$$

Setting this equal to zero (break-even income) and solving for R gives us an estimated break-even volume of 7,142,857 revenue dollars:

$$R = \$1,500,000/0.21 = \$7,142,857.$$

Van Horn isn't in business to break even, however. Its objective is to earn an aftertax rate of return of 10 percent on its assets. Suppose it has assets totaling $10 million. Its income objective won't be met unless it earns net income of at least 10 percent of $10 million, or $1 million.

We can introduce this income target into the cost-volume-profit analysis very easily. The $1 million is much like an aftertax fixed cost and can be placed in the equation as follows:

$$\text{Excess income} = 0.21R - \$1,500,000 - \$1,000,000$$

---

[2] Differences between taxable income and accounting income before taxes that are due to differences in the *timing* of tax *payments*—e.g., the effects of different depreciation assumptions for tax and reporting purposes—don't affect the income analysis because income tax *expense* is calculated on the basis of accounting income before tax, as we saw in Chapter 10.

We can find the volume at which Van Horn's operations will just meet its income target by solving this equation at zero excess income:

$$R = (\$1,500,000 + \$1,000,000)/0.21 = \$11,904,762.$$

If Van Horn expects revenues to total, say, $11 million, it will earn net income, but fall short of its income objective by $190,000 (0.21 × $904,762).[3]

This analysis is diagrammed in Exhibit 17–5. The diagram has been deliberately drawn offscale to emphasize the spreads between the lines. This chart shows two break-even points, one at a sales volume of $3,846,153 (the zero-income volume) and the other at $6,410,256 (the target volume). Actual volume falls somewhere between the two. Van

EXHIBIT 17–5
Van Horn Company: Profit Chart Incorporating Fixed Income Target

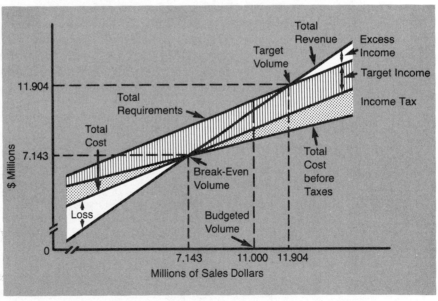

---

[3] It may be helpful to see this analysis presented in conventional income statement format:

	Target Volume	Actual Volume
Total revenue.................	$11,904,762	$11,000,000
Variable expenses (0.65)........	− 7,738,095	− 7,150,000
Fixed expenses.................	− 2,500,000	− 2,500,000
Pretax income	1,666,667	1,350,000
Income tax (0.40)..............	666,667	540,000
Net income....................	$ 1,000,000	$ 810,000

Horn can try to meet its income target by (1) increasing volume, (2) increasing the average contribution margin, or (3) reducing fixed costs. Before settling for the estimated results reflected in Exhibit 17–5, management should decide whether any actions it might take in any of these directions would be both effective and consistent with the company's long-term goals.

Assumptions and Limitations

Cost-volume-profit analysis is useful in conjunction with incremental analysis, but care must be exercised to insure that it isn't misused or misinterpreted. First, the revenues and costs in a typical analysis are unlikely to be exactly equal to operating cash receipts and disbursements. Management may wish to construct cash-based charts if short-term cash flows are the focus of attention.

Second, the cost and revenue functions may not be represented accurately by linear equations or straight lines running all the way across the break-even chart. This may not be as serious a criticism as it may seem, however. The reason we draw straight lines isn't because we think management believes the relationships are linear from zero volume to capacity; instead, the straight lines reflect an assumption that the charts are to be used to describe cost and revenue behavior within a limited portion of this total range, as in Exhibit 17–6. This limited portion of the range is

EXHIBIT 17–6
Customary Range of Volume

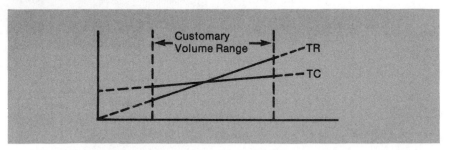

known as the **customary range.** Within this range, the responses of costs and revenues to changes in physical volume are likely to be linear or very close to linear. The portions of the lines extending outside the customary range aren't used. Extending the lines beyond the customary range, as in Exhibit 17–6, is useful because it allows us to describe the relationships between these limits in simple linear equations.

If volume moves toward the edge or outside the customary range and appears likely to stay there, management may change its evaluation of those activities that are at least partly discretionary. As a result, the actual break-even volume is likely to be lower than the break-even volume on the chart. Similarly, the profit spread at high volumes is likely to be narrower than the chart implies, as cost control seems less urgent and fringe activities seem more attractive in that more benevolent climate.

Third, despite the introduction of an independent variable (volume) that can take any of a large number of values, cost-volume-profit analysis is essentially static. It illustrates the profit *normally* associated with *steady* operation at various operating volumes within the customary range, given a specified marketing and administrative plan. It shows what will happen to the profit margin if volume turns out to be different from the level anticipated when the marketing and administrative plan was proposed *and* if management adjusts the scope of its activities promptly and efficiently every time volume changes.

As this implies, cost-volume-profit analysis ignores a number of dynamic forces. One is that when volume moves rapidly from one level to another, costs may respond either faster or more slowly than the chart indicates. Another is that management may choose deliberately not to adjust its cost structure to a new volume if the change appears likely to be temporary. For example, it will accept the costs of idle time or overtime premiums rather than contract or expand the work force for temporary valleys and peaks in demand.

Finally, the profit chart reflects a given set of marketing and administrative plans. If management doesn't like what it sees, it can draw up a new set of plans. These then can be reflected in a new chart showing the new level of fixed costs, the new relationship between variable costs and revenues, and the new estimated break-even point. This is how break-even analysis is supposed to be used; one chart isn't expected to include all the options open to management.

Summary

Incremental analysis is a powerful concept, but one which is by no means easily applied in all cases. In simple situations, for example, a product's variable cost may be a good estimate of the cost of increasing product output, but revenue effects may be extremely difficult to forecast. In other cases, many fixed costs will also be affected, particularly if large amounts of business are affected by the decision.

This chapter has illustrated the application of the concepts of incremental analysis to decisions to accept additional orders or to drop unprofitable products from the company's line. In doing this, we've distinguished clearly between the *incremental* cost of a product or service and the *average* cost of providing goods or services generally. We've also shown that the average can be used in incremental analysis only in certain carefully specified decision problems. Average variable cost often can be used, however, in measures of contribution margin to help management approximate the likely effects on profits of changes in the level of activity.

Finally, we've explained how estimates of cost and income variability, when incorporated in a technique known as cost-volume-profit analysis or break-even analysis, can be used to help evaluate the risks and opportunities inherent in a variety of decision situations.

Key Terms

Break-even analysis
Break-even point
Contribution margin
Contribution margin per unit
Cost-volume-profit analysis
Customary range

Full costing
Incremental costing
Margin of safety
Probability-adjusted profit chart
Product mix
Profit chart

Independent Study Problems (Solutions in Appendix B)

1. Minimum Feasible Volume; Fixed and Variable Costs. Larkin Company operates an assembly line to manufacture cannister vacuum cleaners. It could set up a second line in currently idle space, if volume were big enough to justify it. The second line would require the following monthly costs at a production volume of 2,000 vacuum cleaners a month:

Supervisors	$ 2,300
Inspector	1,800
Assemblers (6 workers)	10,000
Power.	2,500
Total	$16,600

In addition, materials and parts cost $30 for each vacuum cleaner made. The vacuum cleaners are sold to wholesalers for $40 each.

a. What is the minimum monthly volume to justify starting the second line if all of the costs of the assembly line are fixed?
b. What is the minimum monthly volume to justify starting the second line if supervision and inspection costs are fixed and the costs of assemblers and power are proportionally variable with volume?
c. What generalization can you draw from this exercise as to the impact of the variations in the relative proportions of fixed and variable costs? (Suggestion: consider how your answer to part *a* or *b* would change if you found that *all* production costs were proportionally variable with volume.)

2. Using Average Costs in Decisions. The manager of a department in a social welfare agency has proposed the inauguration of a new social service, requiring the addition of 15 social workers to the department's payroll. The costs of other departments in the agency would not be affected by the addition of this new service, except as noted below.

The director of the agency agrees that the social service would fill an important need and that providing it would be consistent with the agency's charter. She can make $200,000 available to finance this service by discontinuing one of the services now being provided by one of the agency's other departments, but will do so only if the new service can be provided for $200,000 or less.

The department head has developed the following estimates of the department's requirements:

	If Service Is	
	Provided	Not Provided
Total number of social workers	25	10
Average cost of operations per social worker . .	$14,000	$15,500

Calculate incremental cost. Should the proposal be approved?

3. Choosing a Product Mix. Harley Company produces three products—A, B, and C—in a single set of production facilities. Fixed costs are distributed among the three products by means of a formula, but they will not change in total, no matter how many units of the three products are produced.

Harley Company's management has assembled the following estimates for each of the three products for next month:

	A	B	C
Total production cost per unit (including average fixed cost)	$ 4	$ 5	$11
Variable production cost per unit	2	4	6
Selling price per unit.	4	6	10
Maximum possible sales at this price (number of units)	25	40	12
Hours to make one unit	2	1	5

The company's peak capacity is 100 hours a month. Selling and administrative costs are entirely fixed, and total $70 a month.

How much of each product would you advise the company to produce next month? Why?

4. Profit-Volume Diagrams. Cranby Company manufactures and sells a single product. You have the following data:

Fixed costs	$32,000 a month
Variable costs.	$3 a unit
Selling price	$5 a unit
Anticipated sales	20,000 units

a. Construct a profit-volume chart.

b. Calculate the break-even point, the margin of safety, and the anticipated income before taxes at the anticipated sales volume.

c. The company is considering increasing the selling price to $5.50. At this price it expects to sell 18,000 units.

1. Recalculate the break-even point, the margin of safety, and the anticipated income before taxes.
2. Redraw the profit-volume chart, showing both the old and the new profit spreads.
3. How many units would have to be sold at the new price to produce a 10 percent increase in total income before taxes?

d. The sales manager has offered a counterproposal. The price would be reduced to $4.60, and an additional $4,000 a month would be spent on advertising.
   1. Recalculate the break-even point.
   2. How many units would have to be sold at the new price to produce a 10 percent increase in total income before taxes?

5. Use of Contribution-Margin Ratios.   Carillo Company sells two products, A and B, with contribution-margin ratios of 40 and 30 percent and selling prices of $5 and $2.50 a unit. Fixed costs amount to $72,000 a month. Monthly sales average 30,000 units of product A and 40,000 units of product B.

a. If the company spends an additional $9,700 on sales promotion, sales of product A can be increased to 40,000 units a month. Sales of product B will fall to 32,000 units a month if this is done, however, as some customers shift from one product to the other. Should this proposal be accepted?

b. As an alternative to the proposal in part *a*, management is considering redesigning product A and reducing the price of product B to give both products more market appeal. The variable cost of product A would be increased by 10 cents a unit; the price of product B would be reduced by 10 cents a unit. Unit sales of each product would increase by 5,000 units a month. What action would you recommend?

6. Proposed Price Reduction.   The manager of the university print shop is trying to decide whether to meet the prices and delivery-time performance of local commercial printing shops on small printing jobs. The commercial shops quote prices that are 10 percent lower than the university shop's prices and also offer faster delivery at no extra charge. Until now, university departments have been required to use the university shop for this sort of work, but a mounting volume of complaints has led the university controller to authorize the use of off-campus shops. The university shop will continue to do large-volume jobs and confidential work, such as examinations and research reports. The university shop would require the same amount of equipment it now has, even if it were to let small jobs go outside.

At its present operating volume of 2,000 labor-hours a month, the operating costs of the university print shop are:

Paper stock	Varies with nature of work
Labor	$8 a labor-hour
Other processing costs	$6 a labor-hour

All labor is regarded as wholly variable with volume; other processing costs include $8,000 of fixed costs, the remainder being wholly and proportionally variable with volume and volume being measured in terms of labor-hours.

Approximately 600 labor-hours a month are now being spent on the work affected by the decision. Materials cost on this work is approximately $6,000 a month, and the amount now being charged by the university shop to other university departments for this work is $15,000 a month.

The shop manager is convinced the shop will lose the work unless it meets both the competitive price and the competitive delivery time. To permit faster deliveries, an additional 80 hours of labor a month would be required in excess of the 600 labor-hours now devoted to this work. Fixed costs would not be affected by this choice between those two alternatives.

Which alternative should the manager choose? Show your calculations.

Exercises and Problems

7. Cost Indivisibilities; Discussion Question. "I don't see how you can classify labor costs as incremental costs of small production orders. Our workers work a 40-hour week, with no overtime. We only increase or decrease the size of the work force if we expect overall production volume to be maintained at a higher or lower level for a substantial period of time. Taking on one more job calling for a few hours of labor is feasible only if our workers will have some idle time if we don't accept that order. That means the incremental cost of labor is zero."

The speaker works for a company that produces a wide variety of products, mostly in small batches, using various combinations of a common set of equipment. What reply would you make?

8. Effect of Eliminating a Division. Hayden Enterprises operates wholesale and institutional sales divisions in company-owned facilities. Operating results for 19x7 were as follows:

	Wholesale	Institutional	Total
Sales revenues.	$420,700	$242,000	$662,700
Variable costs	190,300	173,500	363,800
Divisional fixed costs	85,600	54,600	140,200
Branch fixed costs	44,200	36,400	80,600
Home office fixed costs	17,000	8,500	25,500
Income (loss) before taxes.	$ 83,600	$ (31,000)	$ 52,600

Since the institutional sales division has been reporting losses for four consecutive years, Hayden's president wants to eliminate the division. He has been cautioned, however, that only the division's own variable and fixed costs will be eliminated if the division ceases to exist. The president has now requested that you calculate the amount of income before taxes Hayden would have earned in 19x7 if the institutional sales division had already been eliminated.

9. Profit-Volume Exercises. Each of the following exercises is independent of the others.

Exercise A. Oliver Company plans to market a new product. Based on its market studies, Oliver estimates it can sell 5,500 units in 19x1. The selling price will be $2 a unit. Variable costs are estimated to be 40 percent of the selling price. Fixed costs are estimated to be $6,000.

a. Calculate the break-even point (in units).
b. Calculate the margin of safety.

Exercise B. Breiden Company sells rodaks for $6 a unit. Variable costs are $2 a unit. Fixed costs are $37,500.

a. How many rodaks must be sold if the company is to realize income before income taxes of 15 percent of sales revenue?
b. How many rodaks must be sold if the company is to realize income before taxes of $10,000?

Exercise C. At a break-even point of 400 units sold, the variable costs were $400 and the fixed costs were $200. How much will the 401st unit sold contribute to income before income taxes?

(AICPA adapted)

10. Profit-Volume Exercise. Elkton, Inc.'s controller reported to top management that in 19x3 the company would probably earn $1 million from sales of its duplex paint brushes. This estimate was based on an expected selling price of $10 a unit, $6 million of variable costs, and $3 million of fixed costs.

Elkton's vice president of marketing proposed that the company increase the selling price by 15 percent and invest $1 million in a mass media promotion campaign. The marketing staff cited marketing research which found that by creating a new image for the product, the promotion campaign would increase physical sales volume by 10 percent despite the price increase. The recommendations were accepted.

a. How much income would Elkton earn if the indicated increased volume did materialize?

b. How many units would have to be sold under the new marketing plan to attain the $1 million income the controller had predicted under the former plan?
c. How many units would have to be sold to break even under the new marketing plan?

11. Profit-Volume Exercises. Each of the following exercises is independent of the others:

Exercise A. Label Corporation's product A has sales of $300,000, variable costs of $240,000, and fixed costs of $40,000.

a. Assuming the cost relationship is linear, calculate the break-even dollar sales volume.
b. How much income before taxes would product A generate if its sales volume increased by 20 percent?

Exercise B. Dallas Corporation wishes to market a new product for $1.50 a unit. Fixed costs to manufacture and market this product are $100,000 if volume is less than 500,000 units and $140,000 if volume is 500,000 units or more. The contribution margin is 20 percent. How many units must be sold to realize income before taxes of $100,000 from this product?

Exercise C. Freedom, Inc., has projected the following annual costs based on 40,000 units of production and sales:

	Total Annual Costs	Variable Portion's Percent of Total Annual Costs
Material........................	$400,000	100%
Labor..........................	360,000	75
Other manufacturing............	300,000	40
Selling and administrative	200,000	25

a. Calculate Freedom's unit selling price that will yield income before taxes of 10 percent of sales revenues if sales are 40,000 units.
b. Assume management selects a selling price of $30 a unit. Calculate Freedom's dollar sales that will yield a projected 10 percent margin on sales, assuming the above variable/fixed cost relationships are valid.

(AICPA adapted)

12. Covering Minimum Return on Investment Requirements. Degas Company sells products with an average pretax contribution margin of 35 percent of sales. Fixed costs amount to $500,000 a year, and the income tax rate is a uniform 40 percent of all gains and losses.

To support its production and marketing activities, the company must maintain assets of $700,000 plus an amount equal to 10 percent of sales.

The company's management wishes to maintain a rate of return on assets of at least 12 percent after taxes.

a. Calculate the minimum dollar sales volume at which the company can generate its desired rate of return on assets.
b. What is the company's net income at this volume? What is the margin of safety?

13. Break-Even Exercises. Answer each of the following independent questions.

a. Thomas Company sells products P, Q, and R. Thomas sells three units of P for each unit of R, and two units of Q for each unit of P. The contribution margins are $1.00 per unit of P, $1.50 per unit of Q, and $3.00 per unit of R. If fixed costs are $600,000, how many units of P would Thomas sell at the break-even point?
b. Felder Company is a medium-sized manufacturer of lamps. During 19x9, a new line called Twilight was made available to Felder's customers. The break-even point for sales of Twilight was $400,000 with a contribution margin of 40 percent. If income before taxes was $200,000, what were the revenues from sales?
c. Rawlings, Ltd., had break-even sales of $1 million and variable costs of $3.50 a unit. Rawlings wants to sell an additional 50,000 units at the same selling price to generate income before taxes equal to 10 percent of the new revenue generated by the additional sales. If Rawlings expects the contribution margin to remain at 30 percent of sales revenues, what is the maximum amount of additional fixed costs that could be incurred?

(AICPA adapted)

14. Break-Even Exercise: Multiproduct Company. Danvers Corporation has two products, for which you have the following data:

	Product A	Product B
Sales volume (units).........	200,000	300,000
Selling price per unit	$2	$3
Contribution-margin/Sales ...	30%	40%
Fixed costs	$150,000	$260,000

a. Calculate the break-even dollar sales volume for each product. State any assumptions you had to make.
b. Calculate the break-even dollar sales volume for the company as a whole. State any assumptions you had to make.
c. Compare the break-even point you calculated in part b with the sum of the break-even points you calculated in part a. Explain why these two amounts are or aren't identical.

15. Effect of Changes on Break-Even Point. During 19x1, Arapahoe Company sold 300,000 units of product and had net income (after taxes) of $60,000. The contribution margin was $1 a unit before taxes, and the selling price was $2.50. Fixed costs were $200,000, and the income tax rate was 40 percent.

For 19x2, variable costs went up 10 cents a units, fixed costs went up $22,000, and income taxes increased to a rate of 50 percent.

a. What was the break-even sales volume for 19x1, in dollars?
b. What will be the break-even sales dollars for 19x2 if the selling price is not changed?
c. How many units will have to be sold to earn net income of $60,000 in 19x2 if the selling price is not changed?
d. By how much will the selling price have to be increased if the break-even point, in units, is to be the same in 19x2 as in 19x1?
e. At what selling price would the company continue to earn $60,000 net income after taxes on sales of 300,000 units?

16. Average Costs; Minimum Price. A factory's costs can be estimated accurately from the following schedule of average cost per hour:

Hours	Cost
4,000	$6.25
4,500	6.11
5,000	6.00
5,500	5.91

The company has a chance to bid on a new job that would add 500 hours a month for two months to the factory's volume. Qualified workers for this job can be obtained without difficulty or loss of efficiency. The job would have no effect on nonfactory costs.

Without this job, the factory would operate at a monthly volume of 4,000 hours. When built, the plant was expected to operate 5,000 hours a month, on the average.

What is the minimum price the company could afford to quote for this job without being worse off?

17. Make or Buy. The Blade Division of Dana Company produces hardened steel blades. One third of the Blade Division's output (10,000 blades) is sold to the Lawn Products Division of Dana; the remainder is sold to outside customers. The Blade Division's estimated sales and cost data for the coming year are as follows:

	Lawn Products	Outsiders
Sales revenues	$15,000	$40,000
Variable cost of goods sold	(10,000)	(20,000)
Fixed cost of goods sold.	(3,000)	(6,000)
Gross margin.	$ 2,000	$14,000

The Lawn Products Division now has an opportunity to buy 10,000 blades of identical quality from an outside supplier on a continuing basis at a delivered cost of $1.25. The Blade Division cannot sell any additional products to outside customers, and average fixed cost in the Blade Division will increase from its present 30 cents to a new level of 40 cents a blade if Lawn Products buys its blades from the outside supplier.

By how much will Dana Company's income before tax increase or decrease if Lawn Products buys the blades from the outside supplier?

(AICPA adapted)

18. Taking on Additional Business. Precision Printing Company is considering an opportunity to print a new monthly magazine for an organization of professional social workers. The organization isn't wealthy, and it can't pay more than $1 a copy to have its new magazine printed, or $10,000 a month for the anticipated press run of 10,000 copies a month. Precision would like to help out, but only if it can recover its costs plus a margin of 5 percent of cost to allow for contingencies. If the contingencies don't materialize, the company will make a small profit.

The total cost of labor, paper stock, and ink would vary in direct proportion to the number of copies printed. Precision's other costs, which average $4.00 a labor-hour at the company's current operating volume of 8,000 labor-hours a month, would fall to an average of $3.90 a labor-hour as the new magazine would increase the company's volume to 8,500 labor-hours a month. Management has drawn up the following profit estimate for the new magazine:

Revenue per hour		$20.00
Costs per hour:		
Labor	$12.00	
Paper stock and ink	5.00	
Miscellaneous	3.90	20.90
Profit/(loss) per hour		$ (0.90)

The print shop supervisor says the miscellaneous costs are sunk costs and should be ignored. Since the anticipated margin over the costs of labor, paper stock, and ink amounts to $3 an hour, the job should be taken on.

Prepare an analysis and make a recommendation. If your analysis indicates the proposal should be rejected, prepare a response to be made to the social workers' representative.

19. Pricing Additional Business. Harley Company operates a contracting business. Its supervisors and administrative personnel are paid monthly salaries. Salaries of administrative personnel, including employee benefits, amount to $11,850 a month; supervisors work a total of 250 hours a month at salaries amounting to $3,150, again including the costs of employee benefits. The company's other employees are paid only for the hours they work, and this amount varies from week to week.

Costs other than materials and employees' salaries and wages amount to $6,000 a month plus 10 cents for each hour worked by the hourly paid employees. In an average month, the hourly paid employees work 2,000 hours, earn $20,000, and use materials costing $30,000. The company's managerial and physical capacity is large enough to handle a total volume of business amounting to 2,500 hours of work by the hourly paid employees.

Harley has an opportunity to enter a bid on a contracting job at Burns Products, Inc. The work would be done next month and would require materials costing $4,800 and 300 hours of work by hourly paid employees at wages and benefits totaling $11 an hour. The company's supervisors would spend 50 hours supervising work on this contract.

If Harley doesn't win this contract, it will use 1,500 hours of hourly paid employees' time next month, at wages and benefits of $10 an hour. Total materials costs will amount to $22,500 on that work, and revenues will amount to $58,000.

a. Calculate Harley Company's anticipated income before taxes if it fails to win the Burns Products contract.
b. Calculate Harley Company's anticipated average cost per hour of hourly paid employees' time (1) if it wins the Burns Products contract, and (2) if it fails to win the contract.
c. What is the minimum price Harley could bid on the Burns Products contract without losing money as a result of entering into this contract? Show your calculations.
d. Comment on the relevance of your answers to parts *a* and *b* to your answer to part *c*, explaining either how you were able to use those answers or why you didn't use them.

20. Simple Pricing Model. Middleton Enterprises, Inc., owns a baseball stadium with a seating capacity of 5,000. The fixed costs of operating this stadium are $45,000 a year, and variable costs are 50 cents per spectator per game. These variable costs actually increase in steps, with an increase of 500 spectators requiring a $250 increase in costs, but management sees no harm in converting this $250 increment into an average.

One hundred games are played each year, and the average attendance is 1,000 spectators a game. Fixed costs, therefore, average 45 cents per spectator per game. The stadium is adequate for all games except a special series of five exhibition games with major-league teams. For each of these five games, the estimated demand is as follows:

If the Price Is—	Then Estimated Attendance Is—
$6.00.................	2,000
5.50.................	6,000
5.00.................	9,000
4.50.................	11,000
4.00.................	16,000
3.00.................	20,000

The company can rent a nearby stadium (25,000 capacity) for a fee of $4,000 for each game plus 10 percent of gross receipts. In addition, the company would still have the variable costs of 50 cents per spectator per game.

Assuming that the price charged will be one of the six alternatives above, prepare a table that will indicate the admission price that will be most profitable for the company and also whether the larger stadium should be rented. Show all calculations.

21. Discontinuing a Product.   Dignan Company manufactures and sells more than 200 products to industrial customers. Management is now reviewing one of these, product T. Although this product seemed highly promising when it was introduced two years ago, competitive developments have cut into its market, and the marketing manager says no one will be buying it three years from now. You have been given the following estimates:

	This Year	Next Year	Year after Next
Sales..................	$1,000,000	$ 600,000	$ 200,000
Costs:			
Variable factory........	500,000	300,000	100,000
Fixed factory	250,000	150,000	50,000
Development	200,000	200,000	200,000
Selling	150,000	120,000	60,000
Total cost	1,100,000	770,000	410,000
Product margin..........	$ (100,000)	$(170,000)	$(210,000)

Further investigation reveals that:

1. The charges for fixed factory costs in the table are based on averages. When production of this product is discontinued, $70,000 in fixed factory costs will be eliminated each year.
2. The company spent $1 million to acquire the rights to this product. This amount is being amortized over a five-year period at $200,000 a year, and $600,000 remains unamortized today.
3. Selling costs are all traceable to this product and consist of items such as sales-force salaries and travel expenses.
4. Investment in working capital to support this product is negligible.

Prepare an analysis to help management decide whether to discontinue manufacturing and selling product T right now or keep it in the line for one, two, or three years.

22. Make or Buy; Maximum Purchase Price; Long Term versus Short Term. Grandview Corporation has been manufacturing a chemical compound known as corolite. Its entire output of this compound, about 100,000 gallons a year, has been used in the production of several of the company's finished products.

Grandview uses 10,000 gallons of corolite a year in the manufacture of blivets in a separate factory. A gallon of corolite is used for each dozen blivets manufactured. You have the following cost estimates:

	Corolite	Blivets
Annual volume..........	100,000 gal.	10,000 doz.
Materials..............	$4/gal.	$2/doz.*
Labor	8/gal.	5/doz.
Other variable	6/gal.	3/doz.
Fixed................	5/gal.	4/doz.
Total cost	$23/gal.	$14/doz.*

* Plus 1 gallon of corolite per dozen.

Boxboro Corporation has just developed a substitute for corolite, known as formulane, and has offered to sell 10,000 gallons of this product to Grandview for use in the manufacture of blivets during the coming year. The price would be $20.50 a gallon. Formulane has one advantage over corolite: it can be used directly in the manufacture of blivets without further processing in the blivets plant. Management estimates this would reduce the labor cost of manufacturing blivets by $1 a dozen, or 20 percent of the total labor cost of this product in the blivets factory.

The manager of the blivets factory has asked top management to approve the purchase of 10,000 gallons of formulane from Boxboro, on the basis of the following cost comparison:

Purchase price of formulane	$20.50
Reduction in processing time:	
20 percent of ($5 + $3 + $4).......	2.40
Net cost of formulane...........	18.10
Cost of corolite...................	23.00
Net saving..................	$ 4.90

The manager of the corolite plant has objected, saying the corolite plant's fixed costs would go on anyway; therefore, the net cost of formulane to Grandview would be $18.10 + $5.00 = 23.10.

Total fixed costs in the blivets plant wouldn't change if formulane were to be substituted for corolite. "Other variable" costs in each factory vary in proportion to changes in labor cost.

a. Should Grandview buy formulane from Boxboro? Summarize the amounts on which your answer is based and show how you calculated them.

b. Calculate the maximum price Grandview could afford to pay Boxboro for an order of 10,000 gallons of formulane.

c. Suppose Grandview was considering discontinuing the manufacture of corolite entirely, using formulane obtained from Boxboro in all products now based on corolite. Formulane has the same advantages over corolite in all these products as in the manufacture of blivets. Would the maximum purchase price of formulane probably be greater, less, or equal to the maximum purchase price you calculated in your answer to part b? Explain.

23. Closing a Factory.   Arcadia Corporation has its home office in Ohio and leases factory buildings in Texas, Montana, and Maine, all of which produce the same product. The operations of the Maine factory have been unprofitable for a number of years. The lease on the Maine building will expire at the end of this year, and Arcadia's management has decided to cease operations there rather than renew the lease. This factory's machinery and equipment will be sold. Arcadia expects the proceeds from the sale of these assets will exceed their book value by an amount just adequate to cover all termination costs.

Prior to the decision to close the Maine plant, Arcadia's management had prepared the following projection of operating results for the next year:

	Total	Texas	Montana	Maine
Sales revenue	$4,300,000	$2,200,000	$1,400,000	$700,000
Fixed costs:				
Factory	1,100,000	560,000	280,000	260,000
Selling and administrative	350,000	210,000	110,000	30,000
Variable costs	1,450,000	665,000	425,000	360,000
Home office costs	500,000	225,000	175,000	100,000
Total operating expense	3,400,000	1,660,000	990,000	750,000
Operating income (loss) before taxes	$ 900,000	$ 540,000	$ 410,000	$ (50,000)

Home-office costs are divided among the factories in proportion to their labor costs and will remain $500,000 in total even after the Maine factory is closed.

Arcadia would like to continue serving the customers now being served by the Maine factory, if it can do so economically. Accordingly, management is considering the following alternatives, all based on the assumption that the selling price remains $25 a unit:

Alternative 1. Close the Maine factory and expand the operations of the Montana factory by using space presently idle there. This move would result in the following changes in operations at the Montana factory:

a. Sales revenue would increase by 50 percent.
b. Factory fixed costs would increase by 20 percent.
c. Selling and administrative fixed costs would increase by 10 percent.
d. Average variable costs would be $8 a unit.

Alternative 2. Close the Maine factory and enter into a long-term contract with an independent manufacturer to serve the area's customers. This manufacturer would pay Arcadia a royalty of $4 a unit based on an estimate of 30,000 units being sold.

Alternative 3. Close the Maine factory and discontinue serving its present customers.

Prepare an analysis to help management decide which of these three alternatives is the most desirable for Arcadia.

(AICPA adapted; restructured by Hugo Nurnberg)

24. Special Order. Anchor Company manufactures several different styles of jewelry cases. Management estimates that during the third quarter of 19x6 the company will be operating at 80 percent of maximum capacity. Because the company desires a higher utilization of plant capacity, the company will consider accepting a special order.

Anchor has received special-order inquiries from two companies. The first order is from JCP, Inc., which would like to market a jewelry case similar to one of Anchor's cases. The JCP jewelry case would be marketed under JCP's own label. JCP, Inc., has offered Anchor $5.75 per jewelry case for 20,000 cases to be shipped by the end of the quarter. The cost data for the Anchor jewelry case, which is similar to the specifications of the JCP special order, are as follows:

Regular selling price per unit	$9.00
Cost per unit:	
Materials	$2.50
Labor: 0.5 hours × $6	3.00
Other: 0.25 machine-hours × $4	1.00
Total	$6.50

According to the specifications provided by JCP, Inc., the special-order case requires materials that are less expensive than those in Anchor's regular case. Consequently, the materials would cost only $2.25 a case. Management has estimated that the remaining costs, labor time, and machine time would be the same as on the Anchor jewelry case.

The second special order was submitted by the Krage Company for 7,500 jewelry cases at $7.50 a case. These cases would be marketed under the Krage label and would have to be shipped by the end of the quarter. The Krage jewelry case is different from any jewelry case in the Anchor line, however. The estimated unit costs of this case are as follows:

Materials	$3.25
Labor: 0.5 hours × $6	3.00
Other: 0.5 machine-hours × $4	2.00
Total	$8.25

In addition, Anchor would have to buy a $2,500 special device to manufacture these cases and would have to spend an additional $1,500 to install and adjust this device for use on this product. The device would be discarded once the special order was completed.

Anchor's cost estimates include provisions for costs other than materials and labor at their estimated average of $4 a machine-hour. Factory fixed costs are expected to amount to $18,000 a month ($216,000 for the year), and the factory's maximum capacity under normal conditions is 90,000 machine-hours a year or 7,500 machine-hours a month.

Anchor will have the entire third quarter to work on the special order, if it decides to accept one of them. Production of its regular products will increase in the fourth quarter, leaving no capacity available for filling a special order. Management doesn't expect any repeat sales to be generated by either special order, and company policy precludes Anchor from subcontracting any portion of an order that isn't expected to generate repeat sales.

Should Anchor Company accept either special order? Justify your answer and show your calculations.

(CMA adapted)

Chapter 18

Process Costing

Decision analyses of the kinds described in Chapters 16 and 17 often begin with data on the company's operating costs, drawn from the company's records. These data are also used (1) to distinguish between the cost of goods sold and the cost of the ending inventory for financial reporting and tax purposes, (2) to help management judge the effectiveness and efficiency of current operations, and (3) in some cases to establish the amounts customers or others should be charged for the company's goods or services.

Our main purpose in this chapter and the next is to describe the key elements of the systems accountants use to classify and record costs for these purposes. These systems are the central focus of the branch of accounting known as **cost accounting.**[1] We'll also examine some of the problems of deriving estimates of incremental cost from cost accounting records. The chapter has four parts:

1. A discussion of the three major ways operating costs can be classified.
2. A description of the use of the technique known as *process costing* to measure the full costs of certain kinds of activities.
3. Modification of the process costing technique to allow it to measure the short-term variable costs of these activities.
4. A brief discussion of the impact of inflation on the relevance of operating cost data to managerial decisions.

---

[1] Cost accounting encompasses the methods and techniques relating to costs incurred in operations. Its findings are used to effect measurements for both financial accounting and managerial accounting.

**The Three
Dimensions of
Operating Costs**

Operating costs can be accumulated on three bases—their nature, their purpose, and where they were incurred. The *nature* of a cost refers to the kind of resources it represents—for example, whether it is wages, materials, depreciation, or something else. The *purpose* of a cost relates to such questions as whether it was incurred to help produce product A, product B, or product C. Finally, the question of *where* a cost is incurred requires the identification of the organization unit—for example, whether it was incurred by production department X, by assembly department Y, or by quality control department Z.

Any given cost can be classified in all three of these ways. For example, the wage cost relating to a worker in assembly department Y who was working on product A can be recorded as the cost of wages, as part of the cost of operating assembly department Y, and as part of the cost of producing product A.

These three dimensions are displayed graphically in Exhibit 18–1 for a three-element, three-product, three-department organization. Each cell

EXHIBIT 18–1
The Three Dimensions of Operating Costs

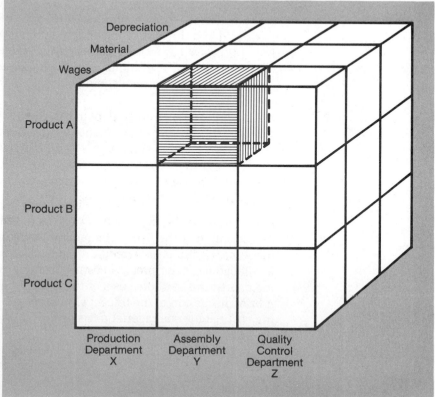

in this diagram corresponds to a unique combination of nature, purpose, and location. The wage cost we just described would fit into the shaded cell in the center of the diagram.

Although costs can be accumulated in any or all of these three dimensions, each organization needs to use those dimensions that are most useful to its accounting information needs. One aspect of managerial accounting requires that costs be accumulated in a manner that is responsive to managers' decision-making responsibility—that is, identifying the costs of each of the activities that are the purposes for which the costs are incurred. While cost accounting may be used in this vein to identify the costs of individual order-getting, service, and support activities, our concern in this chapter and the next is with end-product activities—providing services to outside customers or producing finished products.

The end-product activities in factories result in the production of identifiable quantities of individual products. The process of measuring the costs of these activities is known as product costing; the total cost assigned to a particular product is known as **product cost.** Product cost can be calculated in four different ways, as in the following table:

Method	Basis	
Process costing	Full-cost basis	Variable-cost basis
Job order costing	Full-cost basis	Variable-cost basis

Product cost measured on a variable-cost basis—**variable costing**—includes only short-term variable production costs. Fixed production costs and all of the costs of other activities—mainly marketing, administration, and research and development—are not recognized as costs of products. By contrast, product cost measured on a full-cost basis—**full costing**—includes *all* production costs, both fixed and variable. In some cases, it may also include marketing, administration, and research and development costs, but we won't go that far in this chapter.

In the next section, we'll see how product cost can be determined on a full-cost basis by the technique known as **process costing.** Following that, we'll examine the use of process costing to measure product cost on a variable-cost basis. Job order costing, the other method identified in the table, will be discussed in Chapter 19.

Process Costing; Full-Cost Basis

Product costing can be designed to measure or estimate the *total* cost of specified sets of product units, the *average* cost of the units in each set, or both. In process costing, the **costing entity**—the set of products for which costs are accumulated—is the output of goods or services produced in a production center in a specified period of time.

TERMINOLOGY

A **production center** is a specific set of facilities in which end-product activities take place—the production of goods or services for inventory or delivery to customers.

Once this total cost has been determined, the cost of each unit in the set, referred to as *unit cost,* is determined in process costing by dividing the total by the number of units in the set. If costing is on a full-cost basis, each unit produced is assigned a proportionate share of *all* the costs of operating the production center in that period. The calculation is:

$$\text{Average unit cost} \;=\; \frac{\text{Total production costs for the period}}{\text{Total units of product manufactured}}$$

Measuring the Output of a Production Center

To calculate average unit cost, we must measure both the costs of operating the production center and the number of units produced. We'll discuss the second of these first, because if we can't count the production center's output, we can't use process costing.

Why is this true? Notice that costs in process costing are divided by a *single* divisor (units, pounds, bottles filled, etc.). This means that all units of output must be *homogeneous*—that is, they must be measurable in the *same* units so that we can add them together. In other words, process costing can be used in any production process which turns out a single kinds of product (e.g., cement or flour) or performs a single operation (e.g., filling bottles of uniform size) for long periods at a time.

We'll illustrate the use of process costing by examining the operations of Apex Company's factory, which manufactures industrial coatings and pesticides. This factory has only two production centers—the coatings department and the pesticides department. The unit-cost divisor in the coatings department is the number of *gallons* of coatings manufactured; unit cost in the coatings department is *cost per gallon.* The unit-cost divisor in the pesticides department is the number of *pounds* manufactured; unit cost in the pesticides department therefore is *cost per pound.* Output in May 19x1 amounted to 100,000 gallons of coatings and 300,000 pounds of pesticides.

Determining Product Cost: Direct Product Costs

Product cost in process costing consists of two broad classes of costs: (1) the **direct costs** of the production centers in which the product is manufactured and (2) the **indirect costs** assigned to these production centers.

The distinction between these two classes of costs is based on the concept of **traceability.** The term *direct* in cost accounting means *readily traceable* to a specified costing entity (e.g., a department); the term *indirect* means *not readily traceable* to the costing entity in question. A cost is said to be traceable to a cost center if it is incurred entirely to support the activities of that cost center or of cost centers subordinate to it. A cost may be fully traceable (direct) to one costing entity (e.g., a department) but not traceable (indirect) to another (e.g., a specific product). For example, the factory manager's salary is traceable only to the factory as a whole, while the salary of the manager of the coatings department is traceable both to the factory and to the coatings department. In using these terms, therefore, accountants must specify the costing entity they are applying them to; otherwise, the meaning isn't clear.

In full-costing systems, all the direct costs of a production center (department) are direct costs of the products passing through that production center, and all are assigned to those products. The direct costs of the two production centers in Apex Company's factory in May 19x1 are shown in the upper portion of Exhibit 18–2, along with the costs that are direct to the factory management support center but indirect to the production centers.

Physical production data and labor-hour statistics for the two produc-

EXHIBIT 18–2
Apex Company: Factory Operating Costs for the Month Ended May 31, 19x1

	Service Center (Factory Management)	Production Centers	
		Coatings Department	Pesticides Department
Materials............................	—	$150,000	$ 50,000
Processing labor.....................	—	30,000	30,000
Other labor.........................	$35,000	5,000	10,000
Supplies...........................	1,000	6,000	10,000
Depreciation........................	2,000	4,000	15,000
Other direct departmental costs	7,000	25,000	20,000
Total direct departmental cost.......	$45,000	$220,000	$135,000
Product output.......................		100,000 gallons	300,000 pounds
Processing labor-hours................		10,000 hours	5,000 hours
Average direct product cost:			
Coatings: $220,000/100,000		$2.20 a gallon	
Pesticides: $135,000/300,000			$0.45 a pound

tion centers are shown in the lower part of the exhibit. The bottom line shows that each unit of product in each production center is assigned the average of the direct costs in that production center—$2.20 a gallon in coatings and $0.45 a pound in pesticides.

Determining Product Costs: Indirect Product Costs

The direct costs of Apex's factory management cost center aren't traceable to either the coatings department or the pesticides department. Instead, they are incurred to support the operations of *both* production centers.

TERMINOLOGY

A **cost center** is any department or other unit of the organization or any portion of such a unit for which management chooses to accumulate operating costs.

Factory management is an example of a **service center;** a service center is an organizational unit that provides services or support to other units in the organization. Both *production centers* and *service centers* are cost centers. The direct costs of a service center—factory management, in our example—are **indirect costs** with respect to the operations of the two production centers. Although these costs aren't readily traceable to individual production centers, they are just as necessary to produce coatings and pesticides as the direct costs of operating the coatings and pesticides departments. Because product cost is to include all the costs required to manufacture these products—as it is when product cost is prepared on a full-cost basis—some means must be found to assign a portion of these indirect costs to each unit of each product.[2]

Apex assigns the cost of the overall management of the factory to individual products by a technique called **apportionment**—effected by using an *apportionment rate.* An apportionment rate is the ratio of a given set of costs to the total of some feature of *all* the products these costs relate to. For factory management costs, the apportionment rate Apex uses is the ratio of total factory management cost to total processing labor-hours in the two production centers combined:

---

[2] The costs of Apex's nonfactory cost centers aren't assigned to individual products and don't enter this illustration. In general, the causal relationships between production and administrative costs above the factory level are extremely remote and difficult to identify. Costs in these categories are seldom assigned to individual products except in some situations in which the price the customer pays is tied by formula to cost.

$$\text{Apportionment rate} = \frac{\text{Total factory management cost}}{\text{Total processing labor-hours}} = \frac{\$45,000}{15,000} = \$3 \text{ an hour}$$

Since the coatings department used 10,000 processing labor-hours in May, it was assigned $30,000 (10,000 hours × $3) in factory management costs; the pesticides department was assigned the remaining $15,000 (5,000 hours × $3).

Apex uses total processing labor-hours to distribute factory management costs because this is a measurable characteristic of each product and because total factory management cost appears to vary in the long run with the number of processing labor-hours. In the long view, therefore, the production of a gallon of coatings requiring 1/10 of a labor-hour (10,000 hours/100,000 gallons) can be said to cause the company to spend 1/10 × $3 = $0.30 of the company's factory management costs.

The full-costing calculations for Apex's two products in May 19x1 are summarized as follows:

	Coatings	Pesticides
Production costs:		
Direct costs	$220,000	$135,000
Indirect costs.	30,000	15,000
Total	$250,000	$150,000
Production output	100,000 gallons	300,000 pounds
Unit cost	$2.50 a gallon	$0.50 a pound

Apportionment of factory management costs therefore raised the average cost of a gallon of coatings by $0.30 (from $2.20 to $2.50) and the cost of pesticides by $0.05 a pound (from $0.45 to $0.50). The $0.05 is based on $3 × 5,000 hours/300,000 pounds.

Apportionment versus Allocation of Indirect Costs

We assumed Apex Company was able to use a single apportionment rate to assign factory management costs to individual products because this appeared to approximate the long-term relationship between production volume and total factory management cost. This simple solution would be unsatisfactory if some elements of factory management cost were determined by one product characteristic (e.g., processing labor) while other elements were determined by one or more different product characteristics (e.g., weight of raw materials). To obtain more accurate product costs in these situations, the accountant may decide to use two or more apportionment rates, one for each major group of cost elements.

The costing problem is even more complex if various elements of factory management cost are affected by the production center in which production takes place. For example, an hour of processing labor in the pesticides department may require more factory management support than a labor-hour in the coatings department. This could happen if pesticides hours required more machine maintenance or scheduling services from factory management. In other words, the level of Apex's indirect costs is determined by characteristics of the production centers (number of maintenance hours used) rather than by some characteristic that is common to all the end products (number of processing labor-hours). In such cases, an hour in one department can be said to cause more factory management cost than an hour in another department.

Instead of continuing to use the relatively uncomplicated single apportionment rate, the accountant would now use a two-stage process called interdepartmental **allocation.** In the first stage, indirect costs are allocated—i.e., reassigned—to the various production centers; in the second stage, the costs allocated to each production center are combined with the production center's direct costs. The resulting sum becomes the numerator of the product costing rate in that production center. This costing rate is then used to apportion both the direct costs and the indirect costs to the units of product produced during the period, as shown in the diagram in Exhibit 18–3.

Although we'll examine interdepartmental allocations in depth in the next chapter, we can illustrate the procedure using the Apex example. If Apex had determined that 80 percent of the factory management support cost was allocable to the pesticides department, we'd have the following result:

	Coatings	Pesticides
Production costs:		
Direct costs	$220,000	$135,000
Indirect costs:		
0.2 × $45,000	9,000	
0.8 × $45,000		36,000
Total	$229,000	$171,000
Production output	100,000 gallons	300,000 pounds
Unit cost	$2.29 a gallon	$0.57 a pound

Comparison with the apportionment-only result indicates that the coatings department has a $0.21 lower unit cost ($2.50 − $2.29), and the pesticides department's unit cost increases by $0.07 ($0.57 − $0.50).

Process Costing in Multiproduct Operations

The costs of any set of goods or services requiring production activities in more than one production center is the sum of the costs assigned to that set in each production center it passes through. If a factory produces more than one kind of end product, it still may be able to use process

EXHIBIT 18–3
Using Allocations in Process Costing

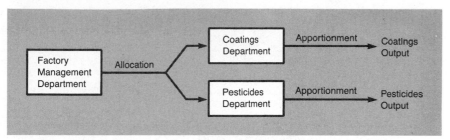

costing if a common measure of output can be found for each of its production centers.

For example, ABC Company's factory has three production centers (departments A, B, and C) and two products (X and Y). Each production center has a single kind of output. The costs of materials, labor, and other resources used by these three production centers are listed in the following table, along with each department's output:

Department	Total Cost	Output	Production Volume
A.........	$200,000	Concentrate	100,000 pounds
B........	100,000	Product X	40,000 gallons
C........	310,000	Product Y	50,000 boxes
Total	$610,000		

Department A produces a concentrate which it transfers to departments B and C. As the table shows, its output is 100,000 pounds of concentrate, at an average cost of $2 a pound ($200,000/100,000). These amounts are shown in the block at the left center of Exhibit 18–4. Department A transfers 30,000 pounds of concentrate and $60,000 of its costs (30,000 × $2) to department B; the other 70,000 pounds (and $140,000 of costs) go to department C.

The total cost of department B is $160,000 ($100,000 of its own costs and $60,000 transferred from department A). Its finished output, 40,000 gallons of product X, has a unit cost of $4 a gallon ($160,000/40,000), as shown in the block in the upper right-hand corner of the exhibit. Department C has total costs of $450,000 ($310,000 plus $140,000 from department A) and its output, product Y, therefore has a unit cost of $9 a box ($450,000/50,000). All $610,000 of the factory's costs are now assigned to finished products:

Department B: 40,000 gallons of product X × $4 .... $160,000
Department C: 50,000 boxes of product Y × $9   450,000
Total. $610,000

EXHIBIT 18–4
Calculating Departmental Unit Cost

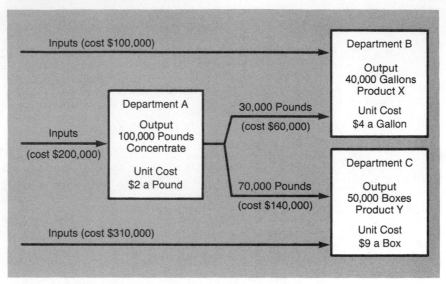

Process Costing: Variable-Costing Basis

Full-cost data, no matter how carefully constructed and no matter how useful for their intended purposes, don't identify the short-run variable costs that are affected by variations in the use of operating capacity. To provide unit costs that are more useful and to introduce more flexibility into cost data generally, some companies calculate product cost on a *variable-costing* basis (sometimes called direct costing).

Calculating Variable Product Cost

Variable costing isolates the variable components of manufacturing costs in product cost records *and* subsequently in internal profit performance reports. *Under variable costing, unit cost is defined as the estimated increase in total variable cost that results from the production of an additional unit of the product.* Fixed manufacturing costs are excluded from product cost completely because they are unaffected by the volume of units produced.

For example, management estimates that the coatings department's costs will amount to $50,000 a month plus $2 for each gallon produced. Some of the department's costs are proportionally variable with volume—e.g., materials costs at $1.50 a gallon. One cost element—depreciation—is entirely fixed. The others include both fixed and variable components. The biggest of these, factory management costs, consists of a fixed component ($25,000) *and* a variable component ($0.05 a gallon). In this case, the variable portion of factory management cost varies in proportion to the number of processing labor-hours. Since the amount of processing labor time is proportional to the number of gallons produced, however, variable factory management costs can be said to vary with gallonage. The department's cost estimates are summarized in the following table:

	Fixed Cost per Month	Variable Cost per Gallon
Materials......................	—	$1.50
Processing labor................	—	0.30
Other labor....................	$ 4,000	0.01
Supplies......................	2,000	0.04
Depreciation...................	4,000	—
Other direct costs..............	15,000	0.10
Factory management costs.......	25,000	0.05
Total......................	$50,000	$2.00

Variable Costing for Easier Cost Estimation

The cost amounts in this chapter represent the coatings department's anticipated experience in a time when operations are at the volume level for which the facilities were designed, 100,000 gallons a month. We refer to this as **normal volume.** We'll now assume the department has a good deal of idle capacity because it is processing only 80,000 gallons a month. In the light of this low volume, management has made some reductions in its fixed-cost structure, mainly a $500 a month reduction in equipment rentals below the normal amount.

Apex's management is considering a proposal to market coatings in a new geographic area, with an estimated sales volume of 10,000 gallons a month in the first year. The question is whether this is profitable for the company in the short run.

This 10,000-gallon increment is clearly within existing capacity limits. Relying on its variable costing data, management estimates that the increment in total variable cost will be $20,000 a month (10,000 gallons × $2). Although management sees no reason why the variability on this incremental volume would depart from the normal $2 rate, departmental equipment rental costs would have to go back up to their normal level, an increase of $500 a month over their present level.

Apex's entry into the new market would be through a regional distributor. Apex would charge the distributor $2.70 a gallon, and the distributor would pay all freight, taxes, and regional marketing costs. Apex's selling and administrative expenses would be likely to increase by about $1,000 a month, the salary of one additional clerk in the accounting department. The first year's monthly incremental income before income taxes therefore is estimated to be as follows:

	Per Unit		Total
Sales revenues	$2.70		$27,000
Less: Variable costs	2.00		20,000
Contribution margin	0.70		7,000
Less: Incremental fixed			
manufacturing costs . .		$ 500	
Incremental fixed			
administrative costs . .		1,000	1,500
Incremental income			$ 5,500

Variable Costing: The Advantages

Variable costing contributes two insights to management. First, by identifying the variable costs of producing a gallon of coatings, variable costing gives management a basis on which to estimate the increment in the variable component of total cost. Second, by *not* including fixed costs in factory unit cost, variable costing calls attention to fixed costs by reporting them as separate totals for the period. With fixed costs highlighted in this way, management presumably would avoid the temptation to assume that the increment in fixed cost would be zero or that it could be approximated by multiplying the change in volume by the average fixed cost per gallon at normal volume.

Variable costing also gives management a clearer view of the impact on income of errors in its forecasts of sales volume. For example, suppose management decides to enter the new market this year, thereby increasing the fixed factory costs of the coatings department by $500 a month and selling and administrative expenses by $1,000. With the information made available by variable costing, management can quite easily prepare the following estimates of income sensitivity:

	Incremental Gallons per Month		
	5,000	10,000	15,000
Sales revenues ($2.70)	$13,500	$27,000	$40,500
Less: Variable costs ($2.00)	10,000	20,000	30,000
Contribution margin ($0.70)	3,500	7,000	10,500
Less: Incremental fixed costs	1,500	1,500	1,500
Incremental income	$ 2,000	$ 5,500	$ 9,000

Management is likely to be reassured by this indication that the new market will generate an incremental income even if the incremental volume turns out to be only half the forecasted amount.

Variable Costing: The Negative Side

A full evaluation of variable costing requires more background than we have been able to provide in this brief description. We must caution, however, that variable costing isn't the answer to all problems in all situations.

First, product costs derived by variable costing imply that variable costs are linearly proportional to variations in operating volume in the short run. If this assumption isn't valid, variable costing may produce misleading estimates of product cost.

Second, product costs based on variable costing can be misinterpreted, just as full-costing product costs can be misinterpreted. If management is led to believe that variable costs are the *only* costs to be affected by volume-determining actions, it will overlook any changes in fixed costs that are likely to take place in the short run.

Third, many decisions have a time horizon that extends beyond the short run—that is, the immediate period. Apex's management, for example, should determine whether its venture into the new market is (1) strictly a short-term expedient to soak up idle capacity this year, or (2) a foray into a promising market for ongoing penetration in the future. If the venture is to succeed on an ongoing basis, revenues from the new market must be large enough to cover all the costs attributable to it—and these will include many costs that won't change in the short run, as long as operating capacity remains unchanged. At least some of the coatings department's fixed costs could be eliminated in time if the company decided to reduce its capacity rather than use it to supply all its existing customers as well as those in the new market.

By the same token, a company planning to introduce a new product needs to know how much cost the product will cause, on the average, at a volume appropriate to the capacity of the facilities it requires. At least some of these costs will be fixed in the short run.

Impact of Inflation   So far we've been assuming that unit costs are likely to be the same from period to period as long as volume remains unchanged. One factor that may interfere with this happy assumption is the impact of systematic changes in the level of input prices—generally associated today with periods of persistent price inflation.

Inflation's impact is uneven, as we pointed out in Chapter 14. Some input prices may remain unchanged or even decrease, even though prices generally are mounting rapidly. Furthermore, product costs determined by processing actual transactions data will reflect various combinations of past and current input prices. The depreciation-cost component, for example, will reflect prices of many previous periods, while operating costs reflect current wage rates.

Systems for measuring unit costs can respond to inflation in two ways. First, product costs emerging from the routine processing of current transactions can be calculated to reflect the current-costing approach we outlined at various points in our coverage of financial accounting—that is, each resource input can be measured at an estimate of its current replacement cost rather than its historical cost. The main purpose of this change is to keep management abreast of the current impact of resource price changes—to identify the profit spreads we referred to in Chapter 8 as the sustainable gross margin. In some countries, product costs calculated in this fashion can also be applied to the inventories and cost of goods sold reported in company financial statements, but in the United States they now are presented by large companies as supplementary financial information only.

Second, estimates of future unit costs should be based on estimates of future trends in input prices and production efficiency during the period affected by the decision. For a decision applicable to the next six months only, adjustments may not be large. For decisions on extended construction contracts, however, adjustments in at least some input costs are likely to be substantial. Again, the adjustments should be made input by input, not on the basis of the consumer price index. What matters is what will happen to the prices of resources the company actually uses, not the prices of a general resource package.

Summary

Accounting systems typically classify operating costs by their nature, by their purpose, and by the company location in which they are used. Classification by purpose is the focus of this chapter—it is used in financial accounting, in managerial decision making, and sometimes in calculating the amounts due from customers or reimbursement agencies. It is also the most difficult, because activity costs ordinarily must include costs that can't be traced unequivocally to specific activities.

This chapter has described two different bases of measuring the costs of goods or services in operations in which the output of individual production centers is essentially homogeneous—that is, in process-costing situations. The full-costing basis provides unit cost data for use in financial accounting and in certain kinds of managerial decisions with a long-term focus. Variable costing—in which product cost is limited to the variable costs of production—provides unit cost data that are useful in short-term utilization-of-capacity decisions.

Historical product cost data of these kinds may need to be adjusted for managerial use because input prices are changing (e.g., in inflationary periods), because the company has installed new facilities incorporating more modern technology, or because management and the work force have learned how to use the existing facilities more efficiently. Without a historical record of product cost, however, management would find it much more difficult to estimate future product costs.

Appendix: Calculating Equivalent Production

Calculations of unit costs in process costing are straightforward when the number of units completed by a production center reflects all the work done in that center during the period. In some cases, however, the amount of work in process at any time is quite large, and this amount can change from period to period. This creates a slightly different measurement problem.

For example, suppose the coatings department had 50,000 gallons of work in process at the beginning of June, completed work on 100,000 gallons, and had 80,000 gallons in process on June 30. Its direct costs for the month totaled $241,500. Not all of these costs were assignable to the 100,000 completed units, however—some of them were incurred to increase the amount of work in process by 30,000 gallons:

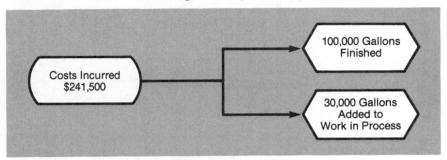

Equivalent Production

At first glance, it might seem that coatings output in June was 130,000 gallons: 100,000 finished gallons plus the 30,000-gallon increase in the amount of work in process. This ignores the fact that the gallons in process on any date are only *partially* processed. Some costs still have to be incurred to finish them. The accountants' task, therefore, is to estimate how many finished gallons could have been finished with the inputs the company used to add to the work in process—that is, how many *equivalent units* were added to (or subtracted from) the work in process.

Management estimated that the work in process in the coatings department on June 1 was half-processed. This means that the 50,000 partially completed gallons in the beginning inventory were equivalent to only 25,000 completed gallons. If the 80,000 gallons in process on June 30 were also half-processed, they were equivalent to 40,000 finished gallons. **Equivalent production** for the month of June therefore was as follows:[3]

Gallons finished		100,000
Equivalent gallons added to work in process:		
Ending inventory in process	40,000	
Beginning inventory in process.	(25,000)	15,000
Equivalent production (gallons)		115,000

---

[3] Separate calculations may have to be made for different cost elements if some costs are more completely committed to the work in process than others—for example, if all materials required to complete the units are already in process but the labor is only half done. We'll leave this complication to more advanced texts, such as Gordon Shillinglaw, *Managerial Cost Accounting,* 5th ed. (Homewood, Ill.: Richard D. Irwin, 1982), chap. 14.

Unit cost for June therefore was $2.10 a gallon:

$$\text{Average cost} = \frac{\$241,500}{115,000 \text{ equivalent gallons}} = \$2.10 \text{ a gallon}$$

The derivation of equivalent production is illustrated in a slightly different way in Exhibit 18–5. The upper half of the diagram shows the

EXHIBIT 18–5
Equivalent Production

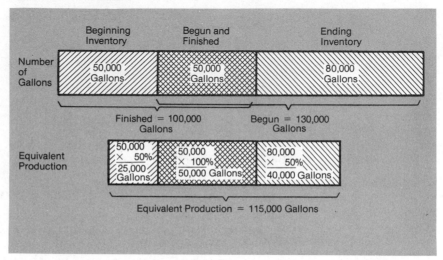

number of physical units in the beginning inventory, those begun and finished during the month, and those begun but not yet finished by the end of the month. The gallonage in each of these blocks is then translated in the lower half of the diagram into the number of equivalent finished units.

Inventory Costing

Unit cost calculated on the basis of equivalent production is an important indicator of the production center's current efficiency. It may not be used to measure the amount of cost to be transferred from the work in process to the finished goods inventory for financial accounting purposes, however. To calculate that amount, the accountants must first decide whether departmental inventories are to be measured by FIFO, LIFO, or average costing.

A common method of recording cost transfers for interim reporting purposes is the *moving average method.*[4] Under this method, all costs available for distribution are divided proportionally among the equivalent units available to receive them. The coatings department's June 1 inventory had a cost of $54,600, representing $2.184 an equivalent gallon, carried forward from the preceding month. This means that the costs to be distributed in June were:

Costs in process, June 1	$ 54,600
Costs incurred in June	241,500
Total cost to be distributed in June.	$296,100

These costs had to be divided between the 100,000 gallons finished and the 40,000 equivalent gallons in the ending inventory, a total of 140,000 equivalent gallons. The moving average cost for the month therefore was:

$$\text{Moving average cost} = \frac{\$296,100}{140,000 \text{ gallons}} = \$2.115 \text{ a gallon}$$

The cost distribution for June, based on a $2.115 average, is shown in Exhibit 18–6. Each equivalent unit is assigned the same unit cost, $2.115; as a result, all of the costs are distributed.

EXHIBIT 18–6
Cost Distribution

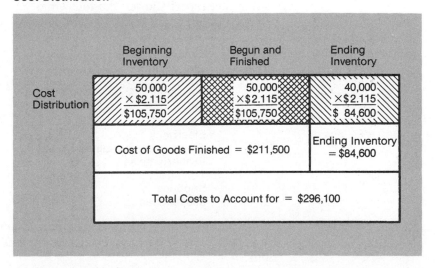

---

[4] Even if the moving average method is used to record transfers monthly, the work in process can be restated on a FIFO or LIFO basis for external financial reporting by means of a year-end adjustment.

Key Terms

Allocation	Indirect cost
Apportionment	Normal volume
Cost accounting	Process costing
Cost center	Product cost
Costing entity	Production center
Direct cost	Service center
Equivalent production	Traceability
Full costing	Variable costing

Independent Study Problems (Solutions in Appendix B)

1. Chart of Cost Accounts. Zebra Company has 84 employees: 56 in manufacturing, 18 in marketing and sales, and 10 in administrative positions. Its manufacturing employees occupy three quarters of the space in a single-story building in a suburban industrial park; the remainder of the space is divided equally between administrative staff and the marketing division, which includes the finished goods storage area.

Part of the factory area is used to assemble low-price vacuum cleaners from purchased parts; most of the rest is used to cut, stamp, bend, and assemble sheet metal into air-conditioning ducts. The remainder of the factory area is used for parts storage, the factory manager's office, and a small maintenance shop.

Zebra Company's cost account structure is very simple. Last month's operating cost report showed the following:

Salaries	$ 55,000
Wages	82,000
Materials	157,000
Depreciation	22,000
Freight	23,000
Insurance	8,000
Heat	6,000
Telephone	4,000
Electricity	5,000
Travel and entertainment	9,000
Property taxes	18,000
Postage	3,000
Supplies	7,000
Miscellaneous	15,000

a. What changes would you suggest making in the chart of cost accounts? Be as specific as you can and state the reasons for your recommendations.

b. Offer at least one plausible explanation of Zebra's previous lack of interest in making the changes you are recommending.

2. Unit Costs: Multiple Departments. Flax Company manufactures two products, PDX and QYK. The company's factory has only four production centers (departments), each performing a single operation on each product. Both products are processed first in production department A. PDX is then finished in production department B, while QYK goes to production department C and then to production department D for finishing.

The costs and production volumes of Flax Company's production departments in a normal month are as follows:

Department	Variable Costs	Fixed Costs	Output (Units)
A........	$30,000	$10,000	50,000
B........	20,000	5,000	12,500
C........	24,000	15,000	37,500
D........	15,000	12,000	37,500
Total	$89,000	$42,000	

a. Calculate the unit cost of each of the company's two products on a full-costing basis.
b. Recalculate unit costs on a variable-costing basis.
c. Why are the relative variable costs of these two products so different from their relative full costs?

3. Unit Costs: Apportionment.   Flax Company's accountants (see problem 2) have just discovered that the costs supplied in problem 2 are only the *direct* costs of the four production departments. The costs of the factory's service centers amount to $27,500 a month. Although service-center costs are fixed costs, major expansions or contractions of production departments' capacity are likely to call for proportional changes in service-center capacity.

An analysis indicates that the work done in the service centers parallels the amount of labor time required by the work of the production departments. A unit of product QYK requires 50 percent more labor time than a unit of product PDX.

a. Apportion the total cost of the service centers to the two products in proportion to total labor time, and calculate the average full cost of each product.
b. At the unit cost you calculated in answer to part *a*, QYK has a very narrow profit margin. The sales manager suggests that apportioning service-center costs in proportion to the number of units of output would distribute these costs more fairly. Perform the calculations necessary to carry out this suggestion.
c. Should the sales manager's proposal be implemented? What does "more fairly" mean in this context? Explain your reasoning.

4. Equivalent Production.   Haskins Company assembles electronic watches of a single design. Component materials are issued to production as the assembly operations progress, roughly in proportion to the amount of labor required in the assembly process.

On April 1, Haskins had 4,000 half-assembled watches in process, at a moving-average inventory cost of $8.60 an equivalent watch. In April, Haskins' assembly department incurred costs totaling $76,500 and transferred 10,000 completed watches to the packing department. Two thousand watches were in process at the close of business on June 30, but they were only one-quarter assembled.

a. Calculate equivalent production for the month of April.
b. Calculate the average unit cost of the *work done* (equivalent production) in April.
c. Using the moving average method, calculate the amount of cost to be assigned to the watches transferred in April (1) to the packing department, and (2) to the work in process on April 30.

Exercises and Problems

5. Discussion Question. University Hospital's main operating room is the scene of many operations, ranging from simple diagnostic procedures requiring the assistance of one nurse to complex microsurgery requiring a large team of surgeons, nurses, and other professional staff. The costs of all operating personnel except surgeons and the costs of all equipment and supplies used in the operating room are charged to the operating room cost center in the hospital's accounts.

Each operating room patient is charged the estimated average cost of the operating room per operating room hour, multiplied by the number of hours (or fraction) the patient spends there. In that way, patients requiring more operating room time are charged more than those who are in the operating room only briefly.

Is this a good example of an appropriate process-costing situation? Explain.

6. Unit Cost: Full Costing. Troy Company makes inexpensive plastic pens. Its factory has three production centers, each responsible for one process: molding, filling, and packing. It has two service centers: administration and maintenance. The direct factory costs of these five cost centers last month were as follows:

	Administration	Maintenance	Molding	Filling	Packing
Materials	—	$ 600	$ 5,000	$10,000	$ 4,000
Salaries and wages	$ 7,500	3,200	7,000	6,000	8,000
Depreciation	100	700	2,500	1,000	100
Rent	12,000	—	—	—	—
Power	1,200	—	—	—	—
Other	4,200	500	1,500	2,000	900
Total	$25,000	$5,000	$16,000	$19,000	$13,000

The factory produced 500,000 pens last month.

Determine the unit cost in each of the three production centers and develop a combined apportionment rate for the two service centers last month.

7. Unit Cost: Variable Costing. Materials costs in Troy Company's factory (see problem 6) are proportionally variable with volume in all four cost centers that have materials costs. Salaries and wages are 20 percent fixed and 80 percent variable with volume in the three production centers, and 100 percent fixed in the two service centers. Depreciation and rent are entirely fixed in all cost centers. Power costs are 65 percent fixed and 35 percent variable. "Other" costs are 90 percent fixed and 10 percent variable in factory administration and 50 percent fixed and 50 percent variable in each of the other four cost centers.

a. Calculate unit cost on a variable-costing basis.
b. What reasons might management have for preferring this unit cost calculation to the calculation you made in answer to problem 6? What disadvantages does it have?

8. Allocation and Apportionment. Troy Company's managers (see problems 6 and 7) have found that most of the company's competitors buy molded pen casings in bulk from manufacturers of molded plastic products rather than do their own molding. You have the following additional information about Troy Company's factory:

1. The $12,000 monthly rental cost is for the use of the factory building. The five cost centers occupy the following percentages of the space in this building: administration, 20 percent; maintenance, 5 percent; molding, 35 percent; filling, 15 percent; packing, 25 percent.
2. A consulting engineer has estimated that 50 percent of the power consumption is for interior lighting in the building, 5 percent is used by equipment in the factory's administrative offices, 10 percent is used in maintenance, 20 percent is used in molding, and 15 percent is used in the filling operation.
3. Sixty percent of the time of maintenance personnel is spent in the molding department; virtually all the remaining 40 percent is spent in the filling department.
4. No other relationship has been established between administrative and maintenance costs and characteristics of the three production centers.

a. Allocate the cost of rent and power among the five cost centers in the proportions indicated.
b. Allocate the cost of maintenance (including its share of rent and power costs) to the molding and filling departments.
c. Calculate the average unit cost for last month, in four parts: molding, filling, packing, and administration. Each of these four parts should

include the costs you allocated to these four cost centers in answer to
parts *a* and *b*.

d. How, if at all, would the unit costs you calculated in answer to part *c*
bear on management's interest in competitors' use of independent
molding companies? What factors limit their usefulness in this connection?

9. Apportionment versus Allocation.   The president of Troy Company
(see problem 8) believes that a more accurate product cost can be derived
if, after the allocations in problem 8, parts *a* and *b* have been made, the
remaining costs of factory administration are allocated to the three production centers in proportion to their relative percentages of the total of
all other costs, including the costs allocated to them in answer to parts *a*
and *b*.

a. Perform this allocation and calculate the unit cost for last month, with
three components: molding, filling, and packing.
b. Calculate the differences between the unit costs you developed in
answer to part *a* and those you calculated in answer to problem 8,
part *c*.
c. What does the president mean by "more accurate" unit costs? Why
might this added accuracy be important? Are the unit costs produced
by the final allocation called for in part *a* more accurate than those you
developed in answer to problem 8, part *c*? Explain.

10. Equivalent Production.   Omega Company assembles coffee grinders. Materials are issued to the assembly department in proportion
to the amount of labor expended—thus, a grinder that has had half the
labor operations required by a completed unit also incorporates half of the
materials a finished unit requires.

A materials shortage in June caused the inventory of work in process to
fall to 10,000 grinders, 80 percent complete, at a moving average cost of
$48,000. Production resumed its normal pace in July. Assembly depart-
ment costs incurred in July totaled $84,500, and 15,000 grinders were
completed and turned over to the shipping department. An additional
12,000 half-assembled grinders were in process in the assembly department at the close of business on July 31.

a. Calculate equivalent production for the month of July.
b. Calculate the amount of cost to be assigned to (1) the work in process
in assembly on July 31, and (2) the goods transferred to shipping
during the month.

11. Equivalent Production.   Mavis Enterprises mixes paints in a series
of continuous operations. Labor and materials are applied to units in
process at identical rates. This assures that the ratio of materials costs to

other costs is the same for units in process as it is for completed units. Costs are assigned to finished goods on the basis of the moving average method. Given the following information, calculate the missing numbers:

Costs incurred during the month.............	A
Unit cost of equivalent production...........	$14.20
Cost of work in process:	
Beginning of month......................	$32,500
End of month	B
Cost of units finished during the month.......	$146,300
Equivalent production (units)................	9,000
Units finished during the month.............	C
Units in process:	
Beginning of month......................	D
End of month	3,000
Portion completed, work in process:	
Beginning of month......................	1/2
End of month	1/3

12. Classification of Costs. Stan Brown is the manager of one of Griffin Company's five processing departments. Stan has an excellent understanding of the technical intricacies of his department's work tasks and he is quite adept as a motivator of people.

As a conscientious manager, however, Stan is disturbed by his inability to fathom the managerial significance of cost data. Stan knows that some costs vary with volume while others don't. He also recognizes that some costs are incurred exclusively by his department while others are shared. For starters, Stan wants to know if these different dimensions of cost can be considered concurrently.

Stan didn't pursue the matter until he was somewhat taken aback to learn that last month his department incurred costs of more than $100,000 for the first time during his seven months on the job. The nature and amounts of the costs were as follows:

Materials used.................	$ 11,200
Home-office support............	16,200
Stan Brown's salary	2,400
Janitorial services	2,300
Quality control inspection	1,800
Processing labor...............	59,400
Building depreciation...........	4,100
Machinery depreciation	8,600
Heat, light, and power	1,700
Fire insurance	1,900
Total	$109,600

Machinery depreciation is the depreciation cost of the machines in Stan's department. Depreciation is calculated on the basis of the machines' useful lives, and the cost of fire insurance is assigned on the basis of the original cost of each department's machines.

Stan's department is charged for janitorial services in proportion to the department's share of the floor space in the factory. The charge for quality control inspection is based on a predetermined fee for each unit completed and transferred to another processing department. Factory heat, light, and power costs are accumulated initially in factorywide accounts and are then reassigned to departments each month on the basis of the number of worker-hours recorded in each department. Finally, although Stan doesn't know how the charge for home-office support is determined, he has noticed that it increases by $100 each month, no matter what happens to volume.

a. Prepare a two-by-two table, classifying the department's costs as (1) variable or fixed, and (2) direct or indirect.

b. How can Stan use your answer to part *a* in interpreting the unit cost of operations in his department?

13. Average Full Cost. Dandy Panda Company manufactures toys. Its factory has four production centers—stuffed animals, dolls, figurines, and packaging—and three service centers—administration, scheduling, and maintenance. It has the following factory costs and output per month:

	Variable Costs	Fixed Costs	Output (Units)
Stuffed animals	$21,000	$ 3,000	5,000
Dolls	12,000	3,000	1,000
Figurines.	13,000	5,000	2,000
Packaging.	8,000	1,000	8,000
Administration	—	10,000	
Scheduling	—	6,000	
Maintenance.	4,000	2,000	
Total	$58,000	$30,000	

Packaging operations are essentially the same for each product, so the output of the packaging center consists of the sum of the outputs of the other three production centers.

a. Calculate the average direct cost of each of the company's products.

b. Apportion all service-center costs to products on the basis of their direct production costs and calculate average full cost on that basis.

c. Apportion all service-center costs to products on the basis of the number of units of output and calculate average full cost on that basis.

d. How would you choose between your answer to part *b* and your answer to part *c*? In other words, under what circumstances would you recommend that management use the unit costs in part *b* in preference to the unit costs in part *c*?

14. Average Variable Cost. Dandy Panda Company (see problem 13) has an opportunity to accept a special order for 1,000 figurines, to be manufactured and delivered to the customer at the rate of 500 units a month. You have the following information in addition to the data in problem 13:

1. Variable maintenance department costs vary in response to variations in the number of maintenance hours used.
2. The maintenance costs in problem 13 cover 250 hours of maintenance service. The figurines department uses 120 of those hours, and this usage is proportionally variable with figurine output.
3. The packaging department uses 10 maintenance service hours, and this usage is completely fixed.
4. Acceptance of the special order for figurines would require a 10 percent increase in the fixed costs of the figurines production center in each of the two months in which production would take place.
5. Acceptance of the figurines order would have no effect on the fixed costs of any cost center except those of the figurines production center.
6. Acceptance of the figurines order would have no effect on the company's other business.

a. Calculate the average unit cost of figurines on a variable-costing basis.
b. If the offer price of the special order is $10 a unit and the sales force would receive a 3 percent commission on the sale, should Dandy Panda accept the order? Show your calculations.

15. Chart of Cost Accounts; Unit Cost. Marina Corporation bottles soft drinks. It had the following operating costs in June:

1. Employees' salaries and wages: factory management, $3,500; bottling crews, $5,000; factory maintenance staff, $1,500; sales force, $5,700; executive office, $4,500.
2. Rent: factory building, $3,200; executive offices, $1,800; sales offices, $2,500; executive office equipment, $200.
3. Materials used: sugar, $2,500; flavorings, $1,000; carbon dioxide, $300.
4. Depreciation: factory equipment, $2,100; executive office equipment, $100; sales force vehicles, $500.
5. Electricity: factory, $800; executive offices, $150; sales offices, $200.
6. Telephone: factory, $100; executive offices, $400; sales offices, $600.
7. Water: factory, $400; executive offices, $50; sales offices, $100.
8. Supplies used: factory, $600; executive offices, $800; sales offices, $400.

Marina Corporation had 1,000 cases of soft drinks in inventory at the start of business on June 1. It bottled 10,000 cases in June and had 1,500 cases in inventory at the close of business on June 30. Inventories of work in process were negligible at the end of each working day.

a. Establish a two-dimensional chart of cost accounts for Marina Corporation—by organization unit (the *where* aspect) and by the *nature* of the expenditure—and use these accounts to classify the company's costs in June.

b. Should Marina Company add an activity dimension (i.e., the *purpose* aspect) to its chart of cost accounts? State your reasons.

c. Calculate the average cost of manufacturing a case of soft drinks in June.

d. Calculate the cost of goods sold on a FIFO basis. The FIFO cost of the June 1 inventory of soft drinks was $2,000.

16. Multiple Products. Larkin Company's factory has four production centers and an administrative service center. It manufactures five different products, but each production center performs an identical set of operations on each product it processes. Production costs in a typical month are as follows:

	Variable Costs	Fixed Costs	Output (Units)
Production A	$20,000	$ 4,000	16,000
Production B	10,000	5,000	10,000
Production C	25,000	8,000	16,000
Production D	12,000	8,000	16,000
Administration	—	20,000	
Total	$67,000	$45,000	

Production in a typical month is as follows:

Product	Output (Units)	Production Centers Used
X	5,000	A, B, D
XL	8,000	A, C, D
Y	2,000	B, C
YL	3,000	A, B, C
Z	3,000	C, D

a. Calculate the average direct cost in each production center.

b. Calculate the average full cost of each product, using an apportionment rate based on units of output to apportion administrative costs.

c. Calculate the cost of each product on a variable-costing basis.

d. Larkin Company is considering adding a new product, YM, to its line. YM would be identical to Y, except that it would be processed further in production center D. Monthly volume probably would average 1,000 units, and production capacity is now available to manufacture this volume. Prepare a brief report summarizing the estimated cost implications of the proposal to add this new product.

17. Cost Classification Systems. Ace Maintenance Company provides routine equipment maintenance service and performs equipment repairs for a large number of industrial users in the New York metropolitan area. The company will service or repair almost any factory equipment and has built a reputation for prompt, efficient service.

Ace Maintenance was founded 10 years ago by Paul Mace, a highly gifted salesman and administrator. Mace is still president of the company, doing most of the direct selling himself. His vice president, Don Dynant, is responsible for hiring all service personnel and for the day-to-day operation of the service end of the business.

The company's operating cost accounts for a typical month show the following balances:

	Executive Office	Accounting	Operations
Salaries and wages	$10,000	$3,000	$26,000
Overtime premiums	—	—	1,100
Materials and supplies	500	450	1,000
Repair parts	—	—	14,000
Utilities	1,200	—	—
Payroll taxes	300	120	1,200
Pension plan.	700	150	1,300
Travel.	100	—	2,100
Advertising	200	—	—
Insurance	800	—	—
Taxes.	900	—	—
Rent.	2,500	—	—
Miscellaneous.	400	30	600
Total.	$17,600	$3,750	$47,300

A large industrial service company has offered to buy Mace's interest in the business. Mace would retire and his place would be taken by a president and a salaried sales manager.

a. The company's chart of accounts has three departmental codes (one each for the executive office, accounting, and operations) and the 13 object-of-expenditure classifications listed in the table. In what ways, if any, will the chart of accounts have to be changed to meet the needs of the new owners and the new manager? Give reasons for your suggestions.

b. What problems would you be likely to encounter in trying to carry out your suggestions?

18. Full Costing; Implications for Production Decisions. Segal Corporation owns and operates two factories. Factory A manufactures an industrial material that it sells both to Segal's factory B and to outside customers. Factory costs and volumes are now at the following levels:

	Factory A	Factory B
Costs:		
Variable:		
From factory A	—	$ 80,000
Other	$150,000	100,000
Fixed	50,000	40,000
Total costs	$200,000	$220,000
Volume (units)	100,000	20,000

Factory A charges factory B its average full cost of production for each unit of the industrial material it transfers to factory B. Each unit of factory B's output requires two units of material from factory A. The costs assigned to these units are included in factory B's variable costs in the table.

Segal's management is considering increasing factory B's output by 20 percent. This additional output would then be processed further in a new factory. The costs of processing these units in the new factory would be as follows:

> Variable processing costs .... $3 a unit
> Fixed processing costs.......... $8,000 a month

Factory A has ample capacity to supply factory B and factory B has ample capacity to supply the new factory's requirements of factory B's output, with no increase in fixed costs either in factory A or in factory B.

a. Calculate the average unit cost of the new product if Segal Corporation transfers material from factory B to the new factory, and if it uses the same method of transferring costs from factory B to the new factory as it uses to transfer industrial materials from factory A to factory B.
b. Calculate the average incremental manufacturing cost attributable to the decision to establish the new factory and use it to process a portion of factory B's output.
c. Prepare a brief explanation of any difference between your answers to parts *a* and *b*. If your two answers are identical, explain why.

19. Average Full Cost; Departmental Inventories. Edgeware Company's factory manufactures a single product which passes through four production departments in succession, starting with department A. To allow for possible irregularities in delivery schedules, each department except department A usually maintains a small inventory of the output of the immediately preceding department. The cumulative cost of work completed by one department is transferred to the next department; the cumulative cost of transfers from department D is credited to department D and charged to the finished goods inventory. Each department's costs are accounted for on a FIFO basis.

You have the following information for the month of May:

Department	Direct Costs	Units Started and Completed	Unprocessed Units in Beginning Inventory	Unprocessed Units in Ending Inventory
A	$60,000	100,000	0	0
B	22,000	100,000	10,000	10,000
C	27,000	90,000	0	10,000
D	15,000	100,000	10,000	0
Service	24,000			

None of the production departments had done any of its work on the units in its inventory at the beginning or at the end of the month.

a. Calculate the average direct cost in each department in May.
b. Calculate the average full cost of producing a unit of finished product in May. Service costs are apportioned only to units finished by department D during the month.
c. The beginning inventory in department B had a FIFO cost of $.50 a unit. How much cost was transferred from department B to department C in May? What was the average of those costs?
d. The average cost you calculated in answer to part *c* should be slightly different from the average cost you calculated in answer to part *a*. Why did that difference arise? Assuming that the difference is significantly large in some months, for what purpose or purposes would you use the unit cost in your answer to part *a* in preference to the unit cost in your answer to part *c*? Why?
e. What additional costing problems would have to be solved if the beginning and ending inventories in any department were partly processed by that department?

20. Allocation and Apportionment of Costs. Computeronics Corporation is engaged in two types of service: preparation of business payrolls by computer for various outside customers, and word processing of documents and briefs for law firms. In addition to maintaining a task-oriented production department for each of these services, Computeronics has a marketing group and a staff of technicians responsible for equipment repairs and preventive maintenance.

Although Computeronics has been profitable during its four-year corporate life, it recently began to encounter intense competition. Top management decided it needed to know more about its costs. It soon discovered that no information was available on either the source or the distribution of the company's costs. Costs therefore were carefully tabulated on a departmental basis for the first time. The table identifies the direct costs incurred by each of the company's departments in October.

	Materials, Parts, and Supplies	Salaries, Wages, and Benefits	Other Expenses
Top management	$ 4,100	$ 67,700	$ 12,200
Marketing group—department A	6,300	39,800	13,900
Technical staff—department B.	23,800	69,400	26,800
Word processing—department C.	29,500	216,000	54,500
Payroll preparation—department D	53,300	162,000	24,700
Total	$117,000	$554,900	$132,100

In addition, Computeronics had $80,000 of costs that weren't incurred for the exclusive benefit of any one department. These costs were primarily for rent, insurance, and utilities.

Top management decided to assign costs as follows:

Rent, insurance, and utilities: equally to departments A, B, C, and D.

Marketing: 30 percent to C and 70 percent to D.

Technical staff: to C and D proportional to their salaries, wages, and benefits costs.

Top management: to A, B, C, and D proportional to their direct costs.

Word-processing customers were charged $1.20 a page, and 750,560 pages were processed and billed in October. Payroll-preparation cost $1.75 per employee-week, of which 230,500 were processed and billed in October.

a. Using management's cost-assignment methods, calculate the unit cost in Computeronics Corporation's payroll-preparation department and in its word-processing department.

b. Did top management's method of assigning costs yield valid results? Justify your conclusion on this point, including a statement of what you think the word *valid* means in this context.

21. Variable Costing; Full Costing. Plymouth Corporation converted its department 23 to the manufacture of a new product. Production of this product was begun in November, and the department incurred the following costs that month:

	Fixed Cost	Variable Cost per Unit
Materials.		$ 0.90
Processing labor		12.40
Other labor.	$ 8,000	
Supplies		0.20
Depreciation.	24,000	
Other costs.	28,000	0.30
Total	$60,000	$13.80

During November, 8,000 units were completed; 6,000 units were sold for $23 a unit.

The general manager of department 23 proudly informed top management that $10,200 had been earned. This conclusion was challenged by a cost analyst at Plymouth's headquarters on the basis of the following calculation:

Sales revenue (6,000 × $23)		$138,000
Variable expenses (6,000 × $13.80)	$82,800	
Fixed expenses.	60,000	142,800
Net loss		$ 4,800

a. Which measure of department 23's November performance is valid? State reasons and implications.

b. Assume that Plymouth uses FIFO costing and that in December 15,000 units were completed and 14,000 units were sold (again, at $23 a unit). Calculate income or loss (1) as the general manager would calculate it, and (2) as the cost analyst would calculate it. Ignore income taxes.

c. What are the relative merits of the two income-calculation methods you used in answer to part b?

Chapter 19

Job Order Costing

The second major system of measuring the costs of products or services—in addition to process costing—is **job order costing.** In job order costing, the costing entity is the specific product, service contract, batch of products, or other distinctly identifiable segment of the company's total output.

The objective of this chapter is to explain how companies determine the costs of individual job orders—first on a full-cost basis, then on a variable-cost basis. Although job order costing is used in many kinds of businesses—including advertising agencies, research laboratories, and small service companies—we'll illustrate its use in manufacturing where it is most firmly established. We'll end the chapter with a brief examination of the use of full-cost data in product pricing and other decisions.

TERMINOLOGY

A **costing entity** is any activity or organizational grouping for which costs are to be measured or estimated.

A **direct cost** is a cost that can be traced in its entirety to a single, specified costing entity. An **indirect cost** is one that can be traced only to groups of two or more costing entities.

Job Order Costing: Full-Cost Basis

Job order costing is used only when work is performed on a batch or job order basis—that is, when the goods or services the company produces can be identified with specific projects, contracts, customers, or production batches while the work is going on. Whereas process costing is used for the continuous production of homogeneous output, job order costing relates to the production of nonsimilar batches of different products. In most cases, individual production centers (departments) work on many jobs concurrently or in rapid succession (e.g., advertising copy, job printing, and furniture manufacture).

The Job Cost Sheet

Production in a job order operation begins when someone in authority issues a production order or project authorization—the *job order*. This specifies the work to be done; it may also specify the resources to be used.

An identifying name or number is assigned to the job, and a **job cost sheet** is prepared, calling for information such as the information provided in Exhibit 19–1. This sheet (which may actually be a file in a

EXHIBIT 19–1
Job Cost Sheet

LION CORPORATION
Job Cost Sheet

Job No. ___111___   Quantity ___320___

Description ___Flister blidgets, large___   Date ___5/7/x1___

Direct Materials			Direct Labor		Factory Overhead	
Quantity	Item	Cost	Hours	Cost	Department	Cost
340	Frames #22A	$510	30	$360	C	$450
688	Brackets #31X	344				
		854				

computer's memory) is used to accumulate the costs of the job. As the exhibit shows, these costs fall into three categories: direct materials, direct labor, and factory overhead. We'll define each of these categories in this section and explain how accountants decide how much cost in each category to enter on a specific job's cost sheet.

Direct Materials Costs

In job order costing, as in process costing, we start by identifying the costs we can trace readily to the costing entity, in this case the individual job. These are the *direct costs* of the job. The costs of materials that are traced to a job therefore are the **direct materials** costs of that job.

Direct materials may include materials to be cut, mixed, formed, or processed, such as sheet steel, cloth, plastic powders, and pulpwood—these are generally called *raw materials*. Direct materials may also include purchased or manufactured component parts or subassemblies, such as microprocessors, disk drives, and electric motors.

Direct materials data are likely to be entered on materials requisitions, which instruct storeroom personnel to deliver these materials—that is, *issue* them—to the production people who will use them on jobs. The costs of these materials are then transferred from the materials inventory records to the job cost sheets.

For example, Lion Corporation makes disk drive units and other peripheral equipment for sale to computer manufacturers and consumers. Materials costing $854 were issued to production supervisors in Lion's factory for use on Job No. 111. These were classified as direct-materials costs of that job and entered in the job cost sheet in Exhibit 19–1. The accounting entry to record the issuance of these materials was:

```
Work in Process Inventory ................................... 854
        Materials Inventory ......................................        854
```

This entry recorded the change in the status of the inventory but didn't change the total of the company's assets. Similar entries were made to record all other direct-materials costs in May; the total was $133,000.

Both accounts in the entry above are **control accounts.** A control account is used to reduce the amount of detail in a ledger: The balance in a control account must equal the total of the balances in the detailed records it controls. The debit of $854 to Work in Process Inventory was necessary because $854 was entered on a job cost sheet. Otherwise, the balance in the Work in Process inventory account wouldn't have equaled the total of the costs on the job cost sheets. By the same token, the $854 credit to Materials Inventory showed that this amount was removed from one part or another of the detailed materials inventory record. (Referring back to the first three columns of Exhibit 19–1, we find that $510 was removed from the materials inventory record for Frames #22A, and $344 was removed from the record for Brackets #31X.)

This relationship between the Work in Process Inventory account and the job cost sheets is illustrated in Exhibit 19–2. This shows the balance in the Work in Process Inventory account and the cost totals of all the job orders in process on May 8, 19x1. For simplicity, we're assuming that the work in process inventory on this date consisted of only four jobs—Nos. 101, 104, 109, and 111.

As we said earlier, three kinds of costs are entered on the typical factory job cost sheet: direct materials and two categories of costs we haven't explained yet—direct labor and factory overhead. It should be apparent,

EXHIBIT 19–2
Relationship between Work in Process Inventory Account and Job Order Cost Sheets, May 8, 19x1

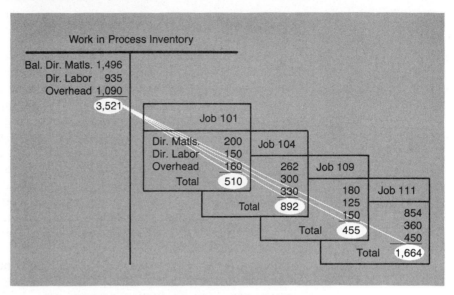

however, that since direct-labor and factory overhead costs are entered on the job cost sheets, along with direct-materials costs, the control account balance must reflect these amounts, too.

Direct-Labor Costs

The costs of the time employees spend working on individual job orders are known as **direct-labor** costs. Lion Corporation uses time tickets to record the time factory employees work on specific jobs. Each employee fills in a time ticket each time he or she works on a job. This ticket identifies the employee, the job, and the times the employee began and finished working on that job. Someone in the accounting department then calculates the direct-labor time and locates the employee's hourly wage rate in the personnel records. The dollar amount is then entered on the job cost sheet.

The direct-labor costs of Lion Corporation's job No. 111 amounted to $360 (30 hours × $12 an hour), and this was entered on the job cost sheet for that job (see Exhibit 19–1). The same amount was charged to the Work in Process Inventory account by the following entry:

```
Work in Process Inventory ................................   360
        Wages Payable .........................................       360
```

Similar entries were made to record all other direct-labor costs in May: the total was $122,000.

Factory Overhead Costs: Indirect Materials

Manufacturing costs that aren't readily traceable to specific jobs are generally known as **factory overhead** costs. Some of these are indirect materials or supplies, materials issued to production centers not for use on specific jobs but to enable the centers to operate effectively. Examples are lubricants for power equipment and cleaning compounds.

Indirect materials costs, like other factory overhead costs, are just as necessary in the production of finished products as direct materials and direct labor. They can't be recorded on the job cost sheets, however, because they can't be traced readily to individual jobs. This also means they can't be recorded in the Work in Process Inventory account when they are incurred, because doing so would destroy the equality of the balance in this control account and the sum of the balances in the job cost sheets.

Instead, Lion Corporation records the costs of indirect materials in operating-cost accounts for the departments they are issued to. Lion's factory has three production departments—A, B, and C—and the accountants made the following summary entry to record the issuance of factory indirect materials in May 19x1:

Indirect Materials—Department A	3,200	
Indirect Materials—Department B	7,500	
Indirect Materials—Department C	900	
Materials Inventory		11,600

This entry established departmental responsibility for the use of these materials but did not assign these costs to individual job orders. We'll return in a moment to the method Lion Corporation did use to assign these costs to individual job orders.

Factory Overhead: Indirect Labor

Employees in each department in Lion Corporation's factory spend at least some of their time on tasks that aren't readily traceable to specific jobs. All this work falls into the general category of *indirect labor*—cleaning floors, maintaining equipment, and waiting while equipment is repaired are three examples. Since this time isn't readily traceable to individual jobs, the costs of indirect labor time can't be entered on the job cost sheets or in the Work in Process Inventory control account. Instead, Lion Corporation records them in departmental operating-cost accounts. The entry for May 19x1 was:

Indirect Labor—Department A	5,200	
Indirect Labor—Department B	14,100	
Indirect Labor—Department C	6,500	
Wages Payable		25,800

Once again, the debits to the departmental accounts established departmental responsibility for the use of these resources.

Other Factory Overhead

Lion Corporation's factory operations incurred many other overhead costs in May—electric power, depreciation, and property taxes are only three examples. The totals of these other overhead costs of the three production departments in May were as follows:

Department A	$ 38,400
Department B	49,600
Department C	21,700
Total	$109,700

The entries to record these costs as they were incurred took the same general form as the entries recording indirect materials and indirect labor, but with the credits going to accounts such as Accumulated Depreciation and Accounts Payable.

Production Department Costs: A Preliminary Recapitulation

Lion Corporation's factory had materials inventories costing $231,000 on May 1, 19x1. It bought materials on credit for $125,000 during the month of May and issued direct materials costing $133,000 and indirect materials costing $11,600 during the month. Its Materials Inventory account showed the following at the end of the month:

Materials Inventory

Bal. 5/1	231,000	Direct materials	133,000
Purchases	125,000	Indirect materials	11,600
	356,000		144,600
Bal. 5/31	211,400		

The costs of materials issued during the month were as follows:

Work in process (direct materials)	$133,000
Department A (indirect materials)........	3,200
Department B (indirect materials)........	7,500
Department C (indirect materials)........	900
Total	$144,600

The factory's three production departments incurred labor costs of $147,800 in May, and these were distributed as follows:

Work in process (direct labor)............	$122,000
Department A (indirect labor)............	5,200
Department B (indirect labor)............	14,100
Department C (indirect labor)............	6,500
Total	$147,800

Combining indirect materials and indirect labor costs with the other overhead costs charged to the three production departments in May gives us the following overhead cost totals:

	Department A	Department B	Department C	Total
Indirect materials.........	$ 3,200	$ 7,500	$ 900	$11,600
Indirect labor.............	5,200	14,100	6,500	25,800
Other overhead	38,400	49,600	21,700	109,700
Total overhead	$46,800	$71,200	$29,100	$147,100

Our next chore is to find out how the company decided how much of these costs to assign to each job the factory worked on in May.

Overhead Rates

When product costs are determined on a full-cost basis, the cost of each product must include an appropriate share of all production costs, including factory overhead costs. By their very nature, overhead costs *can't* be traced readily to specific job orders. Instead, they are assigned to jobs by means of averages known as **overhead rates**.

Averages are always relationships between two quantities. In this case, the accountants try to relate overhead cost to some other quantity that represents the amount of production in the factory. Sometimes the accountants can measure the overall amount of production by the number of units manufactured—numbers of memory chips, gallons of antifreeze, etc. Lion Corporation can't do this, however, because its factory makes many different products. Because a disk drive doesn't require the same amount of resources as a print wheel or a dust cover, the company's accountants can't add the numbers of units of each of these to get a total that makes any sense.

In fact, this is precisely why Lion uses job order costing. If the units of all of its products had the same relationship to operating costs, it could use process costing, which is much simpler.

In situations such as this, *accountants usually look for some other quantity they can measure for each job*—the number of direct labor-hours used, the amount of direct-labor cost, or the amount of raw material used, to mention just three possibilities. For example, an overhead rate with the number of direct labor-hours as the denominator is calculated as follows:

$$\text{Overhead rate} \quad = \quad \frac{\text{Total overhead cost}}{\text{Total volume (direct labor-hours)}}$$

Ideally, we'd like to find a measure of volume that is most closely correlated with long-term changes in the overhead cost. If we can't find the one measure that does this better than others, we'll probably choose the one that's easiest to measure.

Predetermined Overhead Rates

Overhead rates measuring the actual average overhead cost in each period are often used in costing government contracts; *predetermined* rates are more common elsewhere, however. A predetermined overhead rate is based on estimates of (1) overhead cost and (2) production volume, (3) under a specified set of conditions. These estimates are made before the beginning of the period, usually the company's fiscal year, and the resulting rates are generally used without change throughout the period, no matter what the actual experience is.

If the rates are to reflect the estimated average overhead cost in a *normal*—i.e., typical—month, they'll be calculated as follows:

$$\text{Overhead rate} \quad = \quad \frac{\text{Estimated overhead costs in a normal month}}{\text{Estimated total volume in a normal month}}$$

Lion Corporation made several preliminary calculation of overhead rates prior to the beginning of 19x1. The first of these was a factorywide rate based on estimates of the overhead costs the factory would incur if it operated steadily at the volume it was designed for—that is, its **normal volume.** Normal volume is smaller than maximum volume, because facilities are generally designed with enough capacity to handle most of the probable peak demand; the expected average therefore is bound to be smaller than the expected peak.

Lion's management estimated that the amount of overhead costs in most departments was determined primarily by the amount of direct-labor time. This first tentative overhead rate therefore had the number of direct labor-hours as its denominator. A total of 16,000 factory direct labor-hours would be used if all departments were at normal volume, and factory overhead at that volume was expected to be $148,000 a month. An overhead rate based on these estimates would have been $9.25 an hour:

$$\text{Overhead rate} = \frac{\$148,000}{16,000} = \$9.25 \text{ an hour}$$

Using this rate, the company would have assigned $185 in factory overhead cost to a job that used 20 direct labor-hours (20 × **$9.25**).

Departmental Overhead Rates

Lion's management didn't use the factorywide overhead rate for two reasons. First, the ratio of overhead cost to the number of direct labor-hours differed substantially from department to department. Second, the factory's three production departments' respective shares in the amount of work done were likely to vary from job to job. Some jobs required only assembly work, done in department B with little overhead cost; other jobs required a good deal of machining, performed in departments A and C which had heavy overhead costs. Using a single overhead rate, therefore, would have overstated the costs of some jobs and understated the costs attributable to others.

To accommodate job-to-job differences in the use of various factory departments, Lion's management decided to use departmental overhead rates.[1] Exhibit 19–3 identifies the estimated overhead costs at normal volume in each of the company's three production departments in 19x1. Management decided to use the number of machine-hours as the denominator of the overhead rate in department A because most of its overhead costs were more closely related to the amount of machine time than to the amount of labor time. Overhead costs in departments B and C were largely labor-related, and the number of direct labor-hours seemed to be an appropriate denominator for the overhead rates in these departments.

The impact of management's decision to departmentalize the overhead rates can be seen by examining the overhead costs assignable to two of Lion Corporation's products, X and Y. Each unit of these products required 20 hours of direct labor. Product X was produced entirely in department B; product Y was manufactured in department C. The effect of departmentalizing the overhead rate is shown in the following table:

	Factorywide Rate	**Departmental Rates**
Product X.........	20 × $9.25 = $185	20 × $ 7 = $140
Product Y.........	20 × $9.25 = 185	20 × $15 = 300

---

[1] In practice, a composite rate may be used for several production departments that appear to have roughly similar overhead cost patterns. In other cases, a single department may be subdivided for product-costing purposes into two or more overhead cost centers, each with its own overhead rate. We'll refer to all of these as *departmental rates.*

EXHIBIT 19–3
Lion Corporation: Budgeted Monthly Factory Overhead Costs at Normal Volume for the Year 19x1

| | Department | | | |
	A	B	C	Total
Indirect labor	$ 6,000	$15,000	$ 7,000	$ 28,000
Indirect materials	3,000	7,000	1,000	11,000
Power	4,000	2,000	4,000	10,000
Depreciation	7,000	4,000	5,000	16,000
Building services	10,000	16,000	4,000	30,000
Equipment maintenance	9,000	6,000	3,000	18,000
Factory management	8,000	12,000	4,000	24,000
Other	1,000	8,000	2,000	11,000
Total	$48,000	$70,000	$30,000	$148,000
Direct labor-hours		10,000	2,000	
Machine-hours	8,000			
Overhead rate per machine-hour	$6			
Overhead rate per direct labor-hour		$7	$15	

With a single rate, both products appear to be equally costly; with departmental overhead rates, it can be seen that product Y was responsible for more than twice as much of the overhead cost because it used more costly resources. This is a significant difference.

Assigning Overhead Costs to Job Orders

The process of assigning factory overhead costs to individual job orders is commonly called the **absorption of overhead.** Every time work is performed on a job order, some overhead is assigned to it—i.e., *absorbed* by it. For example, job No. 111 in Lion Corporation's factory used 30 hours of direct labor in department C. With a departmental overhead rate of $15 an hour, $450 of department C's overhead was assigned to this job.

The amounts absorbed were recorded on individual job cost sheets for the job orders on which the work was done. The same amounts were assigned to the Work in Process Inventory account. Lion Corporation's entry to record the assignment of factory overhead costs to job No. 111 in May was as follows:

```
Work in Process Inventory ..................................   450
    Factory Overhead Absorbed—Department C...............         450
```

Factory Overhead Absorbed—Department C was an offsetting account to the department's various overhead accounts. The credit to this account represents the assignment of $450 of these costs to the work in process inventory.

Cost of Jobs Finished and Sold

We pointed out in Chapter 5 that when production is completed, the costs assigned to the completed products are transferred from the work in process inventory to the finished goods inventory. The job cost sheets provide the basis for this transfer.

For example, work on job No. 111 was completed in June and the assignment of costs to this job was completed when $450 of overhead cost was entered on the job cost sheet. The entries described so far produced the amounts we showed in Exhibit 19–1 and now summarize in Exhibit 19–4. Completion of this job called for an entry such as the following:

Finished Goods Inventory 1,664
    Work in Process Inventory   1,664

This entry recorded this job's change in status from an in-process asset to a finished goods asset.

EXHIBIT 19–4
Elements of Job Order Cost

Job Order Cost Sheet Job No. 111	
Direct materials	$ 854
Direct labor	360
Factory overhead	450
Total	$1,664

Direct materials: the costs of materials that can be traced readily to individual job orders.

Direct labor: the costs of the time employees spend working directly on individual job orders.

Factory overhead: all factory costs not readily traceable to individual job orders; assigned to jobs by means of averages known as *overhead rates.*

Once costs have entered the Finished Goods Inventory account, they make their way to the Cost of Goods Sold account by the same route as any other cost of salable merchandise—that is, on a FIFO, LIFO, or average-costing basis. Job No. 111 consisted of 320 units of finished products, so the average unit cost was $5.20 ($1,664/320). When sales occurred, the transfer to Cost of Goods Sold of the costs of, say, 300 units from job No. 111, the entry was as follows (300 × $5.20 = $1,560):

Cost of Goods Sold 1,560
    Finished Goods Inventory   1,560

Overhead Under- or Overabsorbed

The total amount of overhead absorbed in any period is the sum of the amounts assigned to individual job orders during the period. This amount can also be determined by applying the following formula:

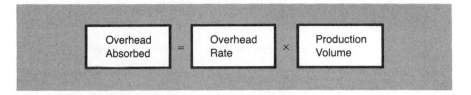

For example, Lion Corporation used 1,800 hours of direct labor in department C in June 19x1. The total amount of overhead absorbed by production in that department in June therefore was $27,000 (1,800 × $15). The company's system, in other words, identified $27,000 as the overhead cost of creating new inventory assets during the month.

When predetermined overhead rates are used, the total cost recorded as having been absorbed in any period is likely to differ from the actual amount of overhead incurred in that period. For example, the actual overhead costs in department C in June 19x1 were as follows:

Indirect labor..................	$ 6,500
Indirect materials	900
Power.......................	4,100
Depreciation	5,000
Other direct overhead	1,800
Building services	3,200
Equipment maintenance	3,600
Factory management	4,000
Total.....................	$29,100

Only $27,000 of this total was absorbed by production; the remaining $2,100 is known as **underabsorbed overhead.** (If the amount absorbed exceeds the actual overhead cost, the excess is labeled **overabsorbed.**)

We'll examine the reasons for under- or overabsorption of overhead in Chapter 24. In practice, the under- or overabsorbed overhead is generally included in the income statement for the period in which it arises. Some portion of it may be placed in an interim-period balance sheet if management expects it to be offset later in the year, but this practice isn't extended to annual reporting.

The practice of deducting underabsorbed overhead from current revenues reflects the idea that a wasted cost is a *loss*—a cost that doesn't produce a benefit. Only costs that can be assigned to products produce benefits—all others are wasted. The overhead rate identifies the amount of overhead cost that is necessary to support a unit of volume (e.g., a direct labor-hour) under normal conditions. If more is spent or if the volume doesn't materialize—that is, if some of the overhead costs are not absorbed—those costs will be wasted. Since losses are reported in the income statement when they are identified, unabsorbed overhead costs should be treated as a loss of the current period. A predetermined overhead rate, in other words, is the *preferred* basis for product costing, not a poor substitute for a historical rate that is adopted for reasons of convenience.

REMINDER: COST DISTRIBUTION

The factory costs to be accounted for in any period are (1) the costs of the beginning inventories, (2) the costs of materials purchased, and (3) the factory operating costs of that period. These costs are accounted for by assigning them (4) to the ending inventories, (5) to the cost of goods sold, or (6) to the over(under)absorbed overhead. This requirement is illustrated in the following diagram, using a simple set of hypothetical costs:

Beginning Inventory: Raw Materials Work in Process Finished Goods	$40	Cost of Goods Sold	$75
Materials Purchased	$30	Underabsorbed Overhead	$10
Labor and Other Resources Used in the Factory	$50	Ending Inventory: Raw Materials Work in Process Finished Goods	$35

Costs to Account for $120   Costs Accounted for $120

The over(under) absorbed overhead is either assigned in its entirety to the cost of goods sold or divided between the cost of goods sold and the ending inventory.

Cost Classification Problems

Some factory costs are classified as overhead even though they are or appear to be traceable to individual job orders. Some of these are classified as overhead because the cost and effort required to trace them to individual jobs are prohibitive—for example, the costs of the glue and upholstery nails used in making furniture. Others are classified as overhead because other costs incurred for the same object-of-expenditure and for similar purposes aren't traceable to individual jobs.

For example, some jobs require work to be performed on customers' premises. The costs of employees' travel to and from the customers' places of business can be classified as direct costs of specific jobs if the travel is always exclusively for a single customer. Most travel time is likely to be shared by several customers, however, and the costs of this travel are classified as overhead. If the averaging procedure includes multicustomer travel costs as overhead, then classifying single-customer travel time and cost as a direct cost would constitute double counting. The result: single-customer travel time costs in these situations are also classified as overhead.

A slightly different problem arises in connection with **overtime premiums**. Factory employees are paid more than their regular (straight-time) wage rates for hours they work in excess of some specified number. The difference between the straight-time wage rate and the special rate is the overtime premium. If the straight-time wage rate is $10 an hour, the employee ordinarily will be paid $15 (time and a half) for overtime work. The overtime premium is $5 an hour.

Overtime premiums almost always should be classified as overhead—that is, the cost of an overtime hour spent on a specific job order should be distributed as follows:

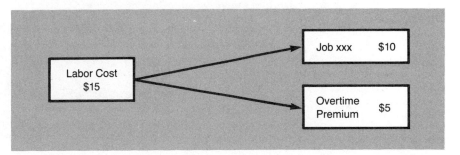

The reason for this is that the job that management schedules for the overtime period is no more responsible for the overtime premium than another job that management had put on the production schedule earlier in the day. This is true even if the job processed in the overtime period has been accepted as a rush order—it could just as well have been processed earlier in the day, with some other job moved to the premium period. Overtime results from the *total* demand on the production facilities, and *all* production shares in the responsibility for the overtime. This isn't to say that management shouldn't charge the rush-order customer a high price for fast service—that's a question of pricing strategy or tactics, not a costing question.

**Interdepartmental
Cost Allocations**

Some costs of operating a factory aren't specifically traceable to the production departments in which the products are actually manufactured. Depreciation on the factory building and the plant manager's salary are two examples; the cost of production scheduling is another. Lion Corporation's predetermined overhead rates included provisions for these costs. In this section, we'll explain briefly how the company did this.

Service and Support Centers

Costs that aren't readily traceable to factory production centers are traceable to other cost centers in the factory—namely, to those that provide service or support to the production centers. The plant manager's salary, for example, can be traced to the factory's administrative office; the wages of the equipment maintenance crew are traceable to the equipment maintenance department.

For simplicity, we'll refer to all service and support centers as *service centers*, regardless of the kind of service or support they provide. The relationships between these service centers and the production centers are diagrammed in Exhibit 19–5. To keep this exhibit relatively simple,

**EXHIBIT 19–5
Product Flows versus Service Flows**

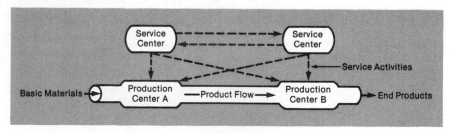

we've diagrammed it to show only two service centers and two production centers, even though Lion Corporation has three production centers and three service centers. As the diagram shows, service centers ordinarily provide their services to the production centers *and* sometimes to each other as well. In general, they don't work directly on job orders; jobs don't often pass through them on their way to completion.

Interdepartmental Allocations

Lion Corporation uses the service flows represented by the dashed lines in Exhibit 19–5 to assign the costs of its three factory service centers to its production centers, using a process known as **allocation**. The direct costs of the service centers thereby become indirect costs of the production centers. These indirect costs are then included in the numerators of the three departmental overhead rates. The amounts shown in Exhibit 19–3 as building services, equipment maintenance, and factory management costs were all allocated amounts. In total, these allocations accounted for almost half the factory's overhead costs at normal volume; in department A, allocated building service, equipment maintenance, and factory management costs accounted for $27,000, more than half of the department's $48,000 total estimated overhead cost at normal volume.

TERMINOLOGY REMINDER

A *direct cost* is a cost that is traceable to a specified costing entity. Unless otherwise specified or evident from the context, indirect materials and indirect labor aren't traceable to specific end products. Indirect labor and indirect materials costs are traceable to other costing entities, however, such as specific cost centers.

Indirect labor, for example, may be indirect with respect to jobs but direct with respect to a particular production center—because it is traceable in its entirety to that production center (e.g., salaries of departmental supervisors). In such cases, indirect labor is a component of the direct departmental overhead of the production center—that is, all overhead costs that are traceable to that specific production center.

The allocations in this case were made *before the year began,* so that management could include them in the predetermined overhead rates. Management estimated that if the factory operated at its normal volume in 19x1, the costs of the three service centers would be as follows:

	Building Services	Equipment Maintenance	Factory Management
Indirect labor*	$ 6,000	$13,000	$15,000
Indirect materials*	1,000	1,500	1,000
Power	2,200	500	300
Depreciation	15,000	1,000	500
Property taxes	8,000	—	—
Other direct overhead	1,800	1,000	4,200
Total	$34,000	$17,000	$21,000

* In practice, the labor and materials costs in service departments are likely to bear titles other than indirect labor and indirect materials. These titles are used here to keep the exhibits compact.

Lion Corporation's Allocations

The accountants' task was to find a way to allocate these costs among the three production departments so that the allocations would most closely approximate the amounts of service department cost attributable to the operations of each production department.

They decided to proceed sequentially, starting with the building services department's costs, on the grounds that building services used far less of the sevices of the other two service departments than it provided to them.[2] They allocated building services costs in proportion to the amount of floor space the other departments occupied, as follows:

Department	(1) Floor Space Occupied (sq. ft.)	(2) Cost Allocated (1) × $0.40*
Equipment maintenance	2,500	$ 1,000
Factory management	7,500	3,000
Production A	25,000	10,000
Production B	40,000	16,000
Production C	10,000	4,000
Total	85,000	$34,000

* $34,000/85,000 = $0.40.

The allocation rate of $0.40 a square foot was the ratio of estimated building services costs ($34,000) to the amount of floor space occupied by the other five cost centers (85,000 square feet). This allocation reflected an assumption that the cost of providing building services was determined by the amount of floor space the factory required.

In the second allocation, Lion's accountants distributed the estimated monthly costs of equipment maintenance to the three production centers, where all the maintenance services were likely to be performed. Estimated usage of maintenance services and the resulting cost allocations were as follows:

Production Department	(1) Equipment Maintenance Hours Used	(2) Cost Allocated (1) × $15*
A.................	600	$ 9,000
B................	400	6,000
C................	200	3,000
Total...........	1,200	$18,000

* $18,000/1,200 = $15.

The total estimated maintenance cost at normal volume in 19x1 amounted to $18,000, including $1,000 as the equipment maintenance department's share of building services costs. The assumptions here are

---

[2] Service departments often provide services to each other. In such cases, allocations can be determined by iteration, or as the solution to a set of simultaneous equations.

(1) that the usage of maintenance services is the *cause* of maintenance costs, and (2) that these costs are roughly proportional in the long run to the amount of usage.

Lion Corporation's final allocation was the allocation of factory management costs—scheduling, recordkeeping, and overall factory administration. Here the accountants faced a new problem. In allocating building services costs they had a reasonable measure of the amount of building *capacity* each department required, and in allocating equipment maintenance costs they had a good measure of service *usage*. For factory management, however, no measure of capacity or usage could be found that represented satisfactorily the factors that cause factory management costs to be incurred. Factory management costs were necessary to the operation of the three production centers, however, and therefore had to be included in overhead rates to reflect the full cost of the factory's output.

The accountants decided to distribute these costs in proportion to the amounts of direct labor and overhead costs that the three departments were expected to incur during the year. They reasoned that factory management costs were incurred to support the activities of the other departments, and activity in this case could best be measured by *total cost added* (all departmental costs except direct materials costs). Direct materials costs were excluded because few of Lion Corporation's factory management activities were devoted to the management of materials.

The total cost in all departments combined was expected to amount to $300,000 in 19x1, as shown in column (5) of Exhibit 19–6. Factory management costs were expected to total $24,000 ($21,000 + $3,000 in allocated building services costs). The allocation rate therefore was 8 percent of the total cost added ($24,000/$300,000). The allocations based on this rate are shown in column (6) of Exhibit 19–6.

The three sets of allocations Lion's accountants made in developing its

EXHIBIT 19–6
Lion Corporation: Allocation of Factory Management Costs

Production Department	(1) Direct Labor	(2) Direct Overhead	(3) Building Services	(4) Maintenance	(5) Total Cost Added (1) + (2) + (3) + (4)	(6) Allocated Costs of Factory Management 8%* × (5)
			Allocations			
A........	$ 60,000	$21,000	$10,000	$ 9,000	$100,000	$ 8,000
B........	92,000	36,000	16,000	6,000	150,000	12,000
C........	24,000	19,000	4,000	3,000	50,000	4,000
Total ...	$176,000	$76,000	$30,000	$18,000	$300,000	$24,000

* $24,000/$300,000 = 8 percent.

factory overhead rates in 19x1 are summarized in the lower portion of Exhibit 19–7. The end result is that all the costs associated with operations at normal volume were assigned to the three production departments. The amounts in the three right-hand columns are those we presented earlier in Exhibit 19–3.

EXHIBIT 19–7
Lion Corporation: Estimated Factory Overhead Cost Allocation for 19x1

	Building Services	Equipment Maintenance	Factory Management	Production Department A	B	C
Indirect labor............	$ 6,000	$13,000	$15,000	$ 6,000	$15,000	$ 7,000
Indirect materials........	1,000	1,500	1,000	3,000	7,000	1,000
Power.................	2,200	500	300	4,000	2,000	4,000
Depreciation	15,000	1,000	500	7,000	4,000	5,000
Property taxes...........	8,000	—	—	—	—	—
Other direct overhead	1,800	1,000	4,200	1,000	8,000	2,000
Total direct overhead ...	34,000	17,000	21,000	21,000	36,000	19,000
Building services	(34,000)	1,000	3,000	10,000	16,000	4,000
Equipment maintenance ..		(18,000)	—	9,000	6,000	3,000
Factory management.....			(24,000)	8,000	12,000	4,000
Total				$48,000	$70,000	$30,000

Full-Cost Assumptions

Management may find full-cost data useful in establishing long-term pricing targets or in deciding whether certain products deserve to be kept in the line for the indefinite future. Eventually, the price of each product must cover the full cost attributable to it or be withdrawn from the market, because all these costs are incremental with respect to a decision to market the product on a continuing basis.

Using average full-cost estimates in this way is valid if three major assumptions hold true:

1. The amount of indirect costs apportioned to a product is a reasonable approximation to the amount caused by this product—that is, this amount of cost could be eliminated eventually if the product were discontinued.
2. The unit prices of resource inputs are at the levels anticipated during the period covered by the decision management needs to make.
3. Departmental volume is at the level at which the facilities were designed to operate—that is, fixed costs are spread over the volume they were intended to support.

The first of these assumptions is violated if the apportionments or allocations don't really measure the indirect costs caused by the product.

The second assumption is most likely to be violated in periods of rapid price changes—mostly during inflation. The second and third assumptions may be violated if the cost calculation is based on the historical costs of only one period: If volume in that period is abnormally high or low, the average fixed cost will be lower or higher than management has reason to expect. This error can be avoided by performing the calculation on estimated data rather than on actual historical data.

Even so, full cost is likely to approximate long-term incremental cost better than short-run average variable cost. This suggests that management may wish to calculate product cost on at least two bases: (1) a variable-costing basis for use in decisions with short time horizons, and (2) a more comprehensive basis for financial accounting and long-term decisions. These latter unit costs are likely to be closer to full cost than to variable cost.

Job Order Costing: Variable-Cost Basis

We pointed out in Chapter 16 that decisions with short time horizons require estimates of the short-term variability of operating costs in response to variations in operating volume. In Chapter 18 we showed how accountants can measure product costs to meet this need. We referred to systems designed to accomplish this as variable-costing systems.

Variable costing differs from full costing in job order costing only in the treatment of factory overhead. Direct-labor and direct-materials costs are typically assumed to be proportionally variable with volume, and therefore are assigned to product units in the manner described earlier in this chapter. The variable-costing difference is that factory overhead is included in product cost by means of overhead rates that cover only the variable components of the various overhead cost elements.

For example, suppose an analysis of the overhead costs in Lion Corporation's department C provided the estimates shown in Exhibit 19–8. In

EXHIBIT 19–8
Lion Corporation, Department C: Estimates of Fixed and Variable Overhead Costs

	Fixed Cost per Month	Variable Cost per Direct Labor-Hour
Indirect labor	$ 4,000	$1.50
Indirect materials	200	0.40
Power	—	2.00
Depreciation	5,000	—
Other direct departmental overheads	1,600	0.20
Building services	4,000	—
Equipment maintenance	1,200	0.90
Factory management	4,000	—
Total	$20,000	$5.00

this case, the overhead rate would be $5 a direct labor-hour. Job No. 111, requiring 30 direct labor-hours in this department, would be charged $150 (30 hours × $5 an hour) for variable overhead. No charge would be made for any portion of the $20,000 in fixed costs.

Developing the Overhead Rate

Four of the cost elements in Exhibit 19–8 were semivariable. Indirect labor, for example, has a normal monthly expenditure of $4,000 plus increments of $1.50 a direct labor-hour in response to the use of the department's facilities. By further subdividing the chart of accounts, Lion's accountants could do a better job of separating the fixed component of actual indirect labor from the variable component. Supervision, for example, is ordinarily fixed within fairly wide volume ranges, and a separate object-of-expenditure account could be (and probably would be) established to accumulate these costs.

Product inspection and quality control labor, on the other hand, may contain both a fixed component and a variable component, and the accountant may be unable to label any particular hour of this kind of indirect labor as part of the fixed component or of the variable component. Fortunately, this is no barrier to variable costing. Since the overhead rate is predetermined, the only requirement is that a *rate of variability* be estimated for each cost element.

Allocations in Variable Costing

Allocations of building services and factory management costs were treated as completely fixed in department C. They therefore didn't enter into product cost under variable costing. Equipment maintenance costs, on the other hand, contained both a fixed component and a variable component. The problem was to estimate the response of costs in the equipment maintenance department to variations in the volume of activity in production department C.

For example, suppose an analysis of the costs of the equipment maintenance department indicated that at the department's normal volume of 1,200 maintenance hours, (1) fixed costs were expected to be $6,000 a month and (2) variable costs were expected to total $10 a maintenance hour. Further investigation showed that department C's consumption of equipment maintenance services was expected to amount to 20 hours a month plus 9 maintenance hours for every 100 direct labor-hours in department C. If the accountants measured each of these hours at equipment maintenance's variable cost of $10 a maintenance hour, they would get the following:

Department C's fixed usage: 20 hours × $10 . . . $200 a month
Department C's variable usage:
    (9 hours × $10)/100 . . . . $0.90 a direct labor-hour

In other words, although the equipment maintenance department's variable cost of providing an hour of service is $10, none of this should have been treated as a variable cost of the departments using the services unless their service *usage* was also variable.[3]

Absorption and Underabsorption of Factory Overhead

Use of variable costing in department C would lead to the absorption of only $9,000 of variable factory overhead in June 19x1 (1,800 direct labor-hours × $5 an hour). The accounting entry to record this absorption would have been:

```
Work in Process Inventory .............................  9,000
     Variable Overhead Cost Absorbed—Department C .......          9,000
```

But remember that the department was actually charged overhead costs totaling $29,100 in June.[4] The amount of overhead unassigned to products (unabsorbed) therefore would have been $20,100. This amount would have been due partly to variations in the rate of spending, as it was in our full-costing example, but most of it would have been the result of our deliberate decision to exclude fixed costs from the overhead rates.

Exclusion of fixed costs from inventory in this manner is unacceptable for external financial reporting in the United States. Under generally accepted accounting principles, some procedure must be adopted to assign an appropriate portion of the year's fixed costs to the goods in inventory at the end of each year (FIFO) or to the inventory addition, if any (LIFO). One way to handle this is to segment the full-cost overhead rate, with one segment covering variable overhead costs and another segment covering fixed overheads. In this way, both the short-term variability information and the inventory costing data will be available at the same time.

Adjusting Full-Cost Data to Identify Short-Term Variable Cost

When product cost includes overhead at full-cost rates, it can't be used directly to approximate short-term variable cost. If the accountants have prepared estimates of the size of the fixed-cost component of each over-

---

[3] The average fixed cost of providing equipment maintenance services was $5 an hour ($6,000 divided by 1,200 maintenance hours). The $1,200 estimated fixed costs of equipment maintenance in department C, as shown in Exhibit 19–8, has two components: (1) $300 for its fixed *usage* of 20 hours times the sum of the fixed and variable costs of maintenance services ($5 + $10), and (2) the $900 in the fixed costs of equipment maintenance assignable to department C's expected usage of equipment maintenance services at normal volume ($5 × 9/100 × 2,000). This allocation didn't enter into the product-costing rates in variable costing.

[4] Adoption of variable costing might affect the methods used to distribute the fixed costs of service departments. Discussion of any changes of that sort doesn't bear on the issue we're examining here, however, and we'll defer any further mention of those changes to Chapter 23.

head rate, however, they can make the necessary adjustments to convert full-cost data to a variable-cost basis.

For example, the full-cost overhead rate for Lion Corporation's factory department C was $15 a direct labor-hour in 19x1 (from Exhibit 19–3) at a normal volume of 2,000 direct labor-hours a month. From Exhibit 19–8 we find that the variable-cost component of this rate was $5, or one third of the total. Suppose department C was scheduled to operate at a volume of 1,500 direct labor-hours in November 19x1. The company had an opportunity to fill an order that could be completed in 200 direct labor-hours in November. In the normal full-costing routine, this order would be assigned 200 × $15 = $3,000. To calculate incremental variable cost, however, the accountants had to isolate the fixed-cost component, as follows:

Full-cost absorption	$3,000
Less: Absorbed fixed cost (200 × $5)	1,000
Incremental variable cost	$2,000

Notice that this calculation uses the average fixed cost at *normal* volume, not the average at the volume budgeted for the current period. The reason is that the number to be adjusted—the amount of cost absorbed—is based on the full-cost overhead rate, also reflecting normal volume. The adjustment has to be consistent with that.

Summary

The second major method of measuring the costs of products or services is job order costing, which is used when the focus of production is the individual batch, project, contract, or assignment. Three categories of costs are assigned to specific job orders: direct materials, direct labor, and factory overhead. Direct materials and direct labor are traced uniquely to individual jobs; factory overhead is assigned to jobs by means of averages known as overhead rates.

Except in special cost-reimbursement situations, overhead rates are usually predetermined. Once the amount of materials, labor, or machine time used on a job is known, the overhead cost of the job can be calculated, even if actual overhead costs are still unknown at that time. Overhead rates are also likely to be departmentalized—that is, each department or production center is given its own rate, used for assigning overhead costs to the work it does. This requires the allocation of the costs of service departments to the various production departments.

Job order costing can be based on either full cost or variable cost. Under full costing, the objective is to estimate the cost attributable to the product in the long run. Under variable costing, the accountant tries to approximate the effect on total cost of short-run variations in the volume of production.

Management can use job order costing to improve the quality of its cost estimates and to obtain useful information on the company's success in meeting product cost-performance standards. Job order costing systems are expensive, however, and management needs to decide whether the added benefits are great enough to justify the added costs.

Full-cost data may be useful in allowing management to identify the amount of revenue the product has to generate in the long run to justify its place in the product line. In some cases, it may be useful in identifying target prices, which can be used as the basis for setting prices to be quoted to customers. If management needs estimates of incremental variable cost, however, and if the only product cost data are full-cost data, the accountants will have to estimate the percentage of fixed costs in the full-cost overhead rates, so these can be removed from full cost to get estimates of variable costs.

Key Terms	Allocations	Job cost sheet
	Control account	Job order costing
	Direct costs	Normal volume
	Direct labor	Overhead absorbed
	Direct materials	Overhead rate
	Factory overhead	Overtime premium
	Indirect costs	Under-/overabsorbed overhead

Independent Study Problems (Solutions in Appendix B)

1. Job Cost and Overhead Variance.   Chailly, Inc., uses a job order costing system in its factory with a predetermined overhead rate based on direct labor-hours. You are given the following information:

1. Job No. 423 was started on March 3 and finished on March 28.
2. Other data:

	Job No. 423	All Jobs (in March)	Estimated Annual Amount at Normal Volume
Direct labor-hours	60	10,000	100,000
Direct-labor cost...........	$400	$ 60,000	$ 350,000
Direct-materials cost	$800	$150,000	$1,300,000

3. Factory overhead budgeted for the entire year was $900,000; actual overhead for the month of March was $106,000.

a. Calculate the cost of job No. 423.
b. Calculate the amount of overhead over- or underabsorbed in March.

2. Job Order Costing: Predetermined Overhead Rate. Webber Corporation has a job order costing system and a plantwide predetermined overhead rate of $4 a direct labor-hour. You have the following data:

1. Inventory balances on December 1:

Materials	$10,000
Work in process	15,000
Finished goods	20,000

2. Data recorded during December:

Materials purchased..................	$16,000
Direct materials issued...............	18,000
Direct labor, 5,000 hours.............	48,000
Manufacturing overhead (actual)	17,000
Cost of goods finished...............	80,000

3. Finished goods inventory on December 31: $23,000.

a. Calculate the cost of the materials inventory and the cost of the work in process inventory on December 31.
b. What was the cost of goods sold during December?
c. What was the over- or underabsorbed overhead in December?

3. Departmental Overhead Rates. Robertson Company has been using a single overhead rate for its entire factory. An alternative has been proposed: departmental overhead rates. You are given the following information:

1. Three products (A, B, C) are produced in three departments (1, 2, 3).
2. Labor-hours required for a unit of each product are:

	Department			
	1	**2**	**3**	**Total**
Product A	2	1	1	4
Product B	0	2	2	4
Product C	2	3	3	8

3. Products produced in a normal year: A—40,000 units; B—40,000 units; and C—10,000 units.
4. Overhead incurred in a normal year: department 1—$400,000; department 2—$300,000; and department 3—$100,000.

Should the company use a plantwide overhead rate or department overhead rates? Why? (In either case, the overhead rate or rates would be based on direct labor-hours.)

4. Interdepartmental Allocations. A factory has two production departments (Able and Baker) and four service departments (building, office, storeroom, and maintenance). The company uses predetermined departmental overhead rates for product costing on a full-costing basis.

To develop these overhead costing rates, the company allocates normal service department costs to the two production departments sequentially, using the following statistics for operations at normal volume:

	Direct Labor-Hours	Total Labor-Hours	Percentage of Floor Space	Maintenance Hours	Percentage of Requisitions	Direct Overhead Costs
Building......	—	500	—	—	—	$ 5,000
Office........	—	600	15	10	—	6,370
Storeroom....	—	300	10	—	—	2,260
Maintenance..	—	500	5	—	5	6,000
Able.........	5,000	5,600	40	150	35	2,770
Baker........	2,000	2,500	30	250	60	3,100
Total.......						$25,500

a. Prepare a table to develop departmental full-cost overhead rates for Able and Baker, based on direct labor-hours. You should distribute the service department costs in the following sequence and on the following bases:

Building...........	Percentage of floor space
Office.............	Total labor-hours
Storeroom.........	Percentage of requisitions
Maintenance.......	Maintenance hours

b. Calculate the amount of overhead assigned to the following two jobs, using the allocated rates you developed in answer to part a:

	Job 123	**Job 321**
Direct labor-hours—Able........	5	2
Direct labor-hours—Baker.......	2	5

5. Variable Costing. Xavier Company manufactures many products. Each product passes through two production departments, which have the following cost structures:

	Department A	**Department B**
Normal monthly volume (base for overhead rate)	5,000 direct labor-hours	10,000 pounds of materials
Monthly fixed costs at normal volume	$10,000	$40,000
Monthly variable costs at normal volume..	15,000	20,000

Two job orders that went through the factory last month had the following results:

	Job 1 (Product X)		Job 2 (Product Y)	
	Quantity	Cost	Quantity	Cost
Direct inputs:				
Direct materials	480 lbs.	$2,400	1,500 lbs.	$4,800
Direct labor:				
Department A	180 hrs.	1,620	100 hrs.	900
Department B	60 hrs.	420	40 hrs.	280
Output................	600 units		1,000 units	

a. Calculate the unit cost of each of these jobs on a full-costing basis.

b. Recalculate unit costs on a variable-costing basis.

c. Why are the relative variable costs of these two products so different from their relative full costs?

Exercises and Problems

6. Overhead Cost Absorption: Discussion Question. Andy Murphy, a new staff accountant with Normal Enterprises, has suggested that full-cost absorption in any period be carried out in such a way that the total amount absorbed will be equal to total budgeted fixed cost, plus budgeted variable cost per unit, times the number of units produced.

Discuss the feasibility of adopting this proposal in a cost accounting system that incorporates predetermined full-cost overhead rates.

7. Job Order Costs. Alpha Company's factory uses job order costing. You have the following information about the factory's operations last week:

1. Direct labor and direct materials used:

Job Order	Direct Materials	Direct Labor-Hours
878	$ 250	46
882	412	32
891	346	18
905	1,215	81
906	811	20
910	1,440	62
912	196	10
Total	$4,670	269

2. The direct-labor wage rate was $8 an hour.

3. Actual factory overhead costs for the week totaled $1,545. They were applied to jobs at a rate of $5 a direct labor-hour.

4. Jobs completed: Nos. 878, 882, 905.

5. The factory had no work in process at the beginning of the week.

a. Prepare a summary table that will show all the costs assigned to each job.

b. Calculate the cost of the work in process at the end of the week.

c. Calculate the amount of overhead over- or underabsorbed last week.

8. Manufacturing Transactions. Goodhue Chemical Company buys chemicals in bulk and packages them for sale to local customers. The company's activities last month included the following:

1. Ordered from a supplier 30 55-gallon drums of chemicals. The price of the chemicals was $60 a drum, plus a $5 returnable deposit on the drum. In addition, Goodhue was responsible for paying freight and delivery charges on these chemicals.
2. Received 27 of the drums ordered in item 1.
3. Paid freight charges of $108 for delivery of the 27 drums.
4. Returned two drums of chemicals to the supplier for full credit as defective merchandise; the supplier agreed to pay the return freight charges on these two drums and also to reimburse Goodhue for freight costs on the original shipment of these drums.
5. Paid the bill due to the supplier after deducting the amount paid for incoming freight charges on the two defective drums.
6. Paid 12 months' property taxes on the factory building, $8,700.
7. Bought 5,500 empty quart tins on credit at a total cost of $475, delivered and labeled.
8. Paid each of five temporary employees $5 an hour; each of these employees worked 16 hours filling the tins with chemicals and putting them on the shelves.
9. Paid the factory janitor's regularly monthly salary, $1,100, for 170 hours' work sweeping floors, moving materials, etc.
10. Received utility bills for telephone and electric service in the factory last month, $850.
11. Returned 25 empty drums to the supplier for credit against the next purchase.
12. Applied factory overhead costs to the tin-filling job at the predetermined full-cost rate of $2 a direct labor-hour.
13. Sold 4,400 tins of chemicals on account at a price of 80 cents each.

a. Calculate the cost of the tin-filling job in total and per tin, with separate amounts for direct materials, direct labor, and factory overhead.

b. For each cost described above that you didn't assign to the tin-filling job, explain why you excluded it.

c. Calculate the cost of goods sold and the gross margin on sales of tinned chemicals from this batch last month.

9. Factory Overhead.   Answer each of these three unrelated questions.

a. Empire Corporation budgeted overhead at $374,000 for November for department G based on a budgeted volume of 110,000 direct labor-hours. The overhead costs were assigned to job orders by means of a predetermined overhead rate per direct labor-hour based on budgeted overhead cost at budgeted volume. Actual overhead was $374,000 and actual direct labor-hours were 114,000. What was the over- or underabsorbed overhead for November?

b. Ingleside Shoe Company applied factory overhead by means of a predetermined overhead rate based on direct-labor cost, reflecting normal overhead cost at normal volume. Data for 19x2 were as follows:

Normal direct-labor cost	$180,000
Underabsorbed overhead	2,000
Actual direct-labor cost	190,000
Normal overhead cost	270,000

It was discovered subsequently that both when establishing the overhead rate and when calculating actual overhead, $45,000 of indirect labor had been treated as sales salaries expense. What was the correct over- or underabsorbed overhead for 19x2?

c. Erie, Inc., wanted to determine the fixed portion of its factory electricity costs. Although one of the vice presidents had stated that electricity costs varied with direct labor-hours, no one had been able to estimate the fixed and variable elements of factory electricity cost. The data in the following table are representative of the company's experience:

Month	Direct Labor-Hours	Electricity Cost
July	23,000	$4,360
August	26,000	4,710

What was the fixed portion of Erie, Inc.'s factory electricity cost?

10. Calculating Variable Product Cost. Danforth Company has three production departments, each with its own full-cost overhead rate:

Department A	$2 per pound of materials
Department B	$3 per machine-hour
Department C	$4 per direct labor-hour

Overhead costs are assigned to products by means of predetermined departmental overhead rates based on normal volume. You are told that at normal volume variable costs account for 40 percent of the overhead cost in department A, 30 percent of the overhead cost in department B, and 60 percent of the overhead cost in department C.

A job lot of 1,000 units of product X was manufactured in April. This job used 2,000 pounds of materials (in department A), 400 machine-hours in department B, and 200 direct labor-hours in department C.

a. Calculate the overhead cost of this job lot on a full-costing basis.

b. Calculate the overhead cost of this job lot on a variable-costing basis.

c. What do you do with the costs that are included in part *a* but excluded in part *b*?

11. Fill in the Blanks.   Dowbar Company manufactures candlesticks on a job order basis, using a predetermined plantwide overhead rate based on normal volume. You have the following data for three recent years:

	19x1	19x2	19x3
Overhead rate per direct labor-hour	A	D	$ 3.20
Actual direct labor-hours.	B	9,000	8,000
Normal direct labor-hours.	8,000	8,500	G
Overhead absorbed	$30,000	$27,900	H
Actual overhead	29,000	E	27,000
Overhead over(under)absorbed	C	(600)	I
Overhead cost at normal direct labor-hours. .	24,000	F	28,800

Make the necessary calculations and supply the missing amounts in this table.

12. Effect of Predetermined Overhead Rate.   Bates Company has been using a relatively small percentage of its capacity for the past year and this is likely to persist. You have the following data:

1. Estimated factory overhead cost at normal volume (10,000 direct labor-hours a month), $40,000.
2. Estimated factory overhead cost at estimated actual volume (8,000 direct labor-hours a month), $36,000.
3. Actual factory overhead cost at actual volume for April (7,500 direct labor-hours), $37,000.

a. Calculate a predetermined overhead rate on the basis of normal volume.
b. Calculate the amount of overhead under- or overabsorbed during April.
c. Would the amount of overhead under- or overabsorbed have been increased or reduced if the overhead rate had been based on estimated actual volume? Would you have preferred this alternative? Explain.

13. Classifying Labor Costs.   A factory department has four direct production workers. They work an eight-hour day plus occasional overtime. The pay for overtime hours is 150 percent of the regular-time rate.

Three jobs (Nos. 125, 127, and 129) were in process when the employees reported for work on the morning on July 6. Operations were begun during the day on four new jobs (Nos. 126, 128, 130, and 131). Work was completed on Jobs 125, 126, 127, and 130. The following time tickets were filed for the day's work:

Employee	Hourly Wage Rate	Job. No.	Hours
Abt, J.	$4.00	127	1
		126	5
		Lubrication	1
		128	1
Davis, P.	6.00	125	1
		127	2
		130	2
		Training	3
		Clean-up	1
Rogers, L.	5.00	128	4
		Sweeping	1
		130	3
		128	2
Thomas, G.	7.00	129	1
		Maintenance	2
		129	1
		131	4
		130	2

These time tickets are listed in the sequence in which the work was performed.

Prior direct-labor costs on jobs in process at the beginning of the day were as follows: Job 125, $28; Job 127, $73; Job 129, $48. Completed jobs were transferred to the finished goods storeroom.

a. Calculate the total labor cost for the day. How much should be entered on each of the job order cost sheets? How much would you classify as overhead cost?

b. Indicate any alternative(s) you considered and rejected in answering part a and give reasons for your choice(s).

c. Calculate the direct-labor cost of the goods finished.

d. Calculate the direct-labor cost of the work in process at the end of the day.

14. Effect of Overtime Premiums. Collins Company uses a predetermined full-cost overhead rate based on normal volume. This rate includes no provision for overtime premiums, on the grounds that the use of overtime results from inefficient management. Its estimated overhead costs at a normal volume of 20,000 direct labor-hours a month are $50,000 in fixed overhead costs and $20,000 in proportionally variable overhead costs.

Actual volume in May amounted to 22,000 direct labor-hours, and actual overhead costs were as follows:

Fixed.	$49,500
Proportionally variable	22,440
Overtime premiums.	2,200
Total.	$74,140

   a. Calculate the amount of cost absorbed in May.

   b. Treating overtime premiums as overhead costs, calculate (1) average overhead cost, and (2) the amount of overhead under- or overabsorbed in May.

   c. Do the facts indicate that the use of overtime in May represcnted inefficiency? What additional information would help you answer that question?

15. Calculating Over(Under)Absorbed Overhead. Grace Manufacturing Company uses a job order costing system with a predetermined factorywide overhead rate based on normal volume. The factory's normal operating volume is 100,000 pounds of direct material a month, and its estimated overhead cost at that volume is $93,000 a month.

   a. Calculate the amount of under- or overabsorbed overhead in months in which the following data were recorded (production volume was equal to sales volume in each case):
     1. Volume, 90,000 pounds; overhead cost, $90,000.
     2. Volume, 110,000 pounds; overhead cost, $99,000.
     3. Volume, 80,000 pounds; overhead cost, $86,000.
     4. Volume, 100,000 pounds; overhead cost, $95,000.

   b. Calculate the amount of factory overhead cost Grace would charge against revenues in each of these four months.

   c. Grace Manufacturing estimates that half its estimated overhead cost at normal volume will vary in direct proportion to variations in volume above and below the normal level. If a predetermined overhead rate based on variable costing were used, how much overhead cost would be absorbed in each of the four situations described in part *a*? How much overhead cost would be charged against revenues in each situation?

16. Distributing Manufacturing Costs. Eagleby Company uses a job order costing system with a predetermined factorywide overhead rate based on normal volume. The overhead rate in 19x1 was $2.50 a direct labor-hour. Over(under)absorbed overhead is included in full each month as a component of the cost of goods sold.

   On May 1 and May 31, 19x1, the company had the following inventories:

	May 1	May 31
Raw materials	$20,000	$17,000
Work in process	13,000	15,000
Finished goods	32,000	32,500

You have the following information about the factory's transactions during May 19x1:

1. Raw materials purchased: $8,000.
2. Direct labor used: 5,000 hours, $45,000.
3. Factory overhead cost: $14,000.
4. Indirect materials used: None.

a. Calculate the cost of direct materials used during May.
b. Prepare a schedule showing (1) the costs to be accounted for during May, and (2) the amounts of these costs to be assigned to each inventory category and to the cost of goods sold.
c. How much of the cost of goods sold represented over(under)absorbed overhead?

17. Single versus Multiple Overhead Rates. Franklin Company's factory has a drill press department with six style A, three style B, and two style C machines. These machines have the following characteristics:

	Machine Style A	Machine Style B	Machine Style C
Cost—each machine..................	$4,000	$6,000	$9,000
Space occupied—each machine (sq. ft)..	20	50	60
Horsepower-hours per month—each machine.........................	850	1,600	3,000
Hourly wage rate, machine operators....	$11.00	$13.20	$15.60
Operating hours per month at normal volume—each machine.............	184	160	150

A machine operator operates only one machine at a time; the number of direct labor-hours is, therefore, equal to the number of machine-hours.

The normal overhead costs of the drill press department for one month are as follows:

Depreciation, taxes, and insurance—buildings	$1,820
Depreciation, taxes, and insurance—machinery	1,200
Heat and light...................................	520
Power...	1,590
Miscellaneous...................................	660
Total......................................	$5,790

a. Calculate a full-cost overhead rate applicable to all the machines in this department, expressed as a rate per machine-hour.
b. Allocate the departmental overhead costs among the three machine styles and calculate a separate full-cost overhead rate for each machine style, expressed as a rate per machine-hour. (Miscellaneous costs are to be divided equally among the 11 machines in the department.)
c. Job No. 2051 was run on one of the style C machines and required 15 hours of machine-time. Compare the amount of overhead costs that would be assigned to this job under the two different costing systems implicit in parts a and b. How would you choose between the two?

18. Costing Individual Jobs. Broxbo Manufacturing Company uses a job order costing system in its factory. Factory overhead costs are assigned to jobs by means of a predetermined full-cost overhead rate based on direct labor-hours and reflecting average anticipated overhead cost in a normal month. On July 1, the cost of the work in process was $2,700, made up as follows:

Job No.	Direct Materials	Direct Labor	Overhead
101	$ 620	$640	$340
102	730	250	120
Total	$1,350	$890	$460

Finished goods on this same date amounted to $4,000, representing the cost of Job No. 100.

During July, direct materials cost, direct labor cost, and direct labor-hours were:

Job No.	Direct Material Cost	Direct Labor Cost	Direct Labor-Hours
101	$ 100	$ 860	200
102	200	1,900	300
103	1,500	780	150
104	2,000	820	200
105	3,000	245	50
Total	$6,800	$4,605	900

In a normal month, the factory is expected to operate at a volume of 1,000 direct labor-hours, and factory overhead is expected to amount to $3,000. Actual factory overhead cost for July was $2,950.

Job Nos. 101, 102, and 103 were completed during July and were placed in the finished goods storeroom.

Job Nos. 100, 101, and 102 were delivered to customers during July at a billed price of $15,000.

a. Calculate the total cost assigned to each job order.
b. What was the total gross margin on job Nos. 100, 101, and 102?
c. What was the amount of the over- or underabsorbed overhead for the month?
d. For what purposes might management wish to use the information summarized in your answers above? Is this information well suited to these purposes?

19. Calculating Interdepartmental Allocations. Minkin Enterprises, Inc., operates a factory with two production departments, a service department, and a factory office. All factory overhead costs except the costs of building ownership and operation are assigned initially to the departments to which they are traceable. The costs of building ownership and operation are accumulated in a separate set of accounts.

In developing predetermined, full-cost, departmental overhead rates, Minkin Enterprises first distributes the estimated building ownership and operation costs among the four factory departments in proportion to the amount of floor space each occupies. The estimated costs of the factory office, including its share of building ownership and operation costs, are then reassigned to the other three factory departments in proportion to the number of employees in each department. Finally, the estimated costs of the factory service department are divided between the two production departments in proportion to the amount of service each is expected to require.

Estimated overhead costs and statistics for next year are as follows:

	Production No. 1	Production No. 2	Factory Service	Factory Office	Building Ownership and Operation
Traceable overhead costs per month	$10,925	$6,550	$5,975	$3,150	$7,000
Floor space (sq. ft.)	9,000	7,000	3,000	1,000	—
Number of employees	35	60	5	3	2
Service-hours used per month	400	200	—	—	—
Machine-hours per month.................	5,000	—	—	—	—
Direct labor-hours per month	—	9,000	—	—	—

a. Using the company's method, allocate the estimated costs.
b. Calculate predetermined overhead rates for the two production departments: No. 1, based on machine-hours; No. 2, based on direct labor-hours.

20. Calculating Inventory Costs; Proposed Allocation of Underabsorbed Overhead. On November 30, a fire destroyed the plant and factory offices of Swadburg Company. The following data survived the fire:

1. From the balance sheet at November 1, you find the beginning inventories: materials, $5,000; work in progress, $15,000; finished goods, $27,500.
2. The full-cost factory overhead rate in use during November was 80 cents per dollar of direct-material cost.
3. Total sales for the month amounted to $60,000. The gross profit margin constituted 25 percent of selling price.
4. Purchases of materials during November amounted to $30,000.

5. The payroll records show wages accrued during November as $25,000, of which $3,000 was for indirect labor.
6. The charges to factory overhead accounts totaled $18,000. Of this, $2,000 was for indirect materials and $3,000 was for indirect labor.
7. The cost of goods finished during November was $52,000.
8. Underabsorbed overhead amounted to $400. This amount was not deducted in the computation of the gross profit margin (item 3 above).

a. Calculate the amount of cost that had been assigned to the inventories of raw materials, work in process, and finished goods that were on hand at the time of the fire on November 30.
b. Swadburg Company's management has claimed that a portion of the underabsorbed overhead should be assigned to the inventory, thereby increasing the amount due from the insurance company. The insurance company has denied this claim, and you have been called upon to arbitrate the dispute. What answer would you give? What arguments would you advance to support it?

21. Analyzing Effects of Transactions; Clerical Errors. Sandrex Company uses a job order cost accounting system. Direct-labor costs are charged daily to Work in Process and credited to Wages Payable on the basis of time tickets. Direct-materials costs are charged to Work in Process and credited to Materials Inventory. Factory overhead costs are charged initially to a Factory Overhead account. Overhead costs are charged to the Work in Process account by means of a predetermined full-cost overhead rate of $2 a direct labor-hour. The costs of goods finished are transferred from Work in Process to a Finished Goods account at the time each job is completed. A perpetual inventory system is used for both materials and finished goods.

Following are some of the events that took place in 19x1:

1. Goods manufactured in 19x0 at a cost of $8,000 were sold on credit for $14,000. The job cost sheets for these goods showed a total of $2,000 for materials, $3,000 for direct labor, and $3,000 for overhead.
2. Factory overhead was charged to a job on which 480 direct labor-hours were recorded during 19x1. The job was still unfinished at the end of the year.
3. It was discovered prior to the end of 19x1 that an error in analyzing a batch of time cards resulted in treating 500 hours of direct labor at $5 an hour as indirect labor (that is, the charge was made to Factory Overhead). The job on which this labor was used was finished but not sold in 19x1.
4. Materials costing $5,000 and supplies costing $500 were issued from the factory storeroom. Of the materials, $1,000 was for use in constructing new display cases in the company's salesrooms. The display cases were completed and placed in use during 19x1. The remaining

materials were issued to the factory for specific job orders which were still in process at the end of 19x1. Of the supplies, $100 was for the immediate use of the sales office, and the remainder was for general factory use.

5. Prior to the end of 19x1, it was discovered that $1,000 of direct materials had been charged to the wrong job. At the time this error was discovered, both jobs had been completed but not yet sold.

6. Prior to the end of the year, it was discovered that an error had been made in adding up the direct labor-hours on a certain job order which had been completed and the products sold during 19x1. The dollar amount of direct labor was added correctly, but the hours were overstated by 100.

7. At the end of 19x1, factory wages earned but still unpaid amounted to $3,000 for direct labor (at $10 an hour) and $1,000 for indirect labor. Time tickets for these amounts of labor had not yet been processed. Employer's payroll taxes on these wages were 9 percent. This company treats all payroll taxes as overhead. The direct labor was expended on jobs that were still in process at the end of 19x1.

Indicate how discovery of these facts would affect the cost assigned to the work in process inventory at the end of the year, the cost of the finished goods inventory, or the cost of goods sold. Each event should be regarded as independent of the others.

22. Discussion Question: Interdepartmental Cost Allocation.   A company's own power-generating department provides electric power to four factory departments. Two of these are production centers (A and B) and two are service centers (X and Y). Power consumption isn't measured; instead, it is assumed to vary in proportion to the number of horsepower-hours used by the equipment in the four user departments. The cost of operating the power-generating department is expected to be $4,000 a month plus 40 cents per horsepower-hour. The amount of fixed cost is determined mainly by the amount of power-generating capacity the power department has and will increase or decrease roughly in proportion to the capacity provided.

The estimated volume of activity in each of the four power-using departments, as measured by the number of horsepower-hours, is as follows:

	Production Centers		Service Centers		
	A	B	X	Y	Total
Horsepower-hours needed at capacity production.........	10,000	20,000	12,000	8,000	50,000
Horsepower-hours used in an average month.............	8,000	13,000	7,000	6,000	34,000

You have been asked to help management develop predetermined departmental overhead rates for each of the two production centers. The rates are to be full-cost rates, each representing the average cost attributable in the long run to the activities of the production center in question.

What dollar amount of estimated power-department cost should be assigned to each production center and each service center for this purpose? Give reasons for your answer, including your reasons for allocating or not allocating power-department costs to the two service centers.

23. Overhead Rates under Variable Costing. The management of Leininger Company has decided to use variable costing for cost-estimating purposes. Full-cost amounts will be entered on the job order cost sheets and in the financial accounts. The estimated overhead costs of factory department 77 at a normal volume of 4,000 direct labor-hours a month are as follows:

Supervision	$ 4,000
Indirect labor	6,000
Fringe benefits	8,400
Supplies	1,200
Power	1,000
Depreciation	800
Miscellaneous	600
Total	$22,000

You have the following additional information:

1. Supervision costs remain at $4,000 a month for any volume between 3,000 and 5,000 direct labor-hours. If volume drops below 3,000 hours, supervision can be cut to $2,800; if volume exceeds 5,000 hours, supervision costs will go up to $5,000 a month.
2. One third of indirect-labor costs at normal volume are fixed; two thirds are proportional to the number of direct labor-hours.
3. Fringe benefits amount to 20 percent of labor cost, including direct labor, supervision, and indirect labor. Direct labor wage rates average $8 an hour.
4. Supplies and power costs should be proportional to the number of direct labor-hours.
5. Depreciation and miscellaneous overhead costs are entirely fixed.
6. The volume of activity ordinarily fluctuates between 3,200 and 4,600 direct labor-hours.

Calculate overhead rates for this department, both for variable costing and for full costing.

24. Interpreting Job Cost Data. Dan Roman is a contractor specializing in small house-remodeling jobs. Most of his employees are specialists who work for other contractors as well, so the size of his payroll rises and falls with fluctuations in the amount of work to be done. Higher wage rates are paid to the more highly skilled workers, but the average rate in the construction industry in Roman's area is about $11 an hour and Roman uses this rate in preparing estimates of job order costs.

Roman recently installed a job order costing system and now has the following labor cost data:

Job Number	Estimated Labor-Hours	Estimated Labor Cost	Actual Labor-Hours	Actual Labor Cost
47	600	$6,600	650	$ 8,125
48	400	4,400	380	4,520
50	900	9,900	1,000	13,100
51	200	2,200	210	2,400
52	500	5,500	460	5,290
54	700	7,700	750	9,150
55	800	8,800	820	9,840

During the period covered by these amounts, Roman submitted bids on 18 jobs. Other contractors underbid him on 11 of these; he was the low bidder on the seven jobs shown. Roman's profit margin was considerably lower than that of most of his competitors during this period.

a. What advice can you give Roman on the basis of these amounts? Do they help explain his low profit margin? Is there anything he can do about it?

b. What further data would you probably find in Roman's job cost sheets that would throw more light on these questions?

c. Would charging overhead costs to individual job orders provide Roman with useful information?

25. Product Cost under Variable Costing. Gaddis Corporation owns and operates two factories. One manufactures component parts, either for sale to outside customers or for use in the company's other factory.

Each factory uses a job order costing system with a factorywide predetermined overhead rate based on estimated overhead costs at normal volume, determined as follows:

	Factory A	Factory B
Overhead cost at normal volume:		
Variable	$10,000	$ 8,000
Fixed	50,000	12,000
Total	$60,000	$20,000
Normal monthly volume	20,000 machine-hours	10,000 direct labor-hours
Overhead rate	$3 per machine-hour	$2 per direct labor-hour

Management is considering the possibility of using factory B to manufacture a new product, product X. Monthly volume would amount to 5,000 units, which would require 1,000 direct labor-hours in factory B at a direct labor wage rate of $8 an hour, add $25,000 to factory B's direct-materials costs, and increase factory B's fixed overhead by $500 a month. Factory B's variable overhead costs would vary in proportion to the number of direct labor-hours used.

All the direct materials for product X would be component parts manufactured in factory A. Their costs would be:

Direct materials.......	$11,000
Direct labor	8,000
Factory overhead	6,000
Total	$25,000

Fixed overhead costs in factory A would be unaffected by the manufacture of the parts necessary to make product X.

Gaddis Corporation's marketing vice president asked the controller for cost estimates to be used in an analysis of the sensitivity of the company's income to errors in the forecasts of sales volume for product X. The controller provided these estimates from the data supplied here. When asked why the company didn't use variable costing to determine product costs on a regular basis, the controller replied that prices had to cover fixed costs too. Besides, full-cost data could be adjusted to a variable-costing basis any time management needed estimates of variable cost.

a. Calculate the unit cost of product X on a variable-costing basis.
b. Comment on the controller's argument, including an analysis of the differences between your answer to part *a* and the cost of product B on a full-costing basis.

26. Departmental Overhead Rates; Allocations.   Sender Company has four product departments (machine No. 1, machine No. 2, assembly, and painting) and three service departments (storage, maintenance, and office) but uses a plantwide overhead rate based on direct labor-hours. At normal volume, 100,600 direct labor-hours would be used and factory overhead costs would be as follows:

Indirect labor and supervision:

Machine No. 1	$33,000
Machine No. 2	22,000
Assembly	11,000
Painting	7,000
Storage..	44,000
Maintenance..	32,700

Indirect materials and supplies:

Machine No. 1	2,200
Machine No. 2	1,100
Assembly	3,300
Painting	3,400
Maintenance.	2,800

Other:

Rent of factory.	96,000
Depreciation of machinery and equipment	44,000
Insurance and taxes on machinery and equipment	2,400
Compensation insurance at $2 per $100 of labor payroll.	19,494
Power	66,000
Factory office salaries.	52,800
General superintendence	55,000
Miscellaneous office costs	21,620
Heat and light	72,000
Miscellaneous storage charges (insurance and so forth).	3,686

You have the following additional information about the various departments:

Department	Area (sq. ft.)	Cost of Machinery and Equipment	Raw Materials Used	Horse-power Rating	Direct Labor-Hours	Direct-Labor Payroll	Number of Employees
Machine No. 1	65,000	$220,000	$520,000	2,000	48,000	$440,000	100
Machine No. 2	55,000	110,000	180,000	1,000	17,600	220,000	60
Assembly.	44,000	55,000		100	24,000	110,000	30
Painting.	32,000	22,000	90,000	200	11,000	55,000	15
Storage	22,000	11,000					14
Office.	11,000	5,500					11
Maintenance.	11,000	16,500					10
Total.	240,000	$440,000	$790,000	3,300	100,600	$825,000	240

a. Calculate a plantwide overhead rate on a full-cost basis.

b. Calculate departmental overhead rates based on full costing. For this purpose you will need to distribute some of the general overhead costs among the seven departments and then allocate the costs of the service departments among the four production departments. You should allocate office and general superintendence costs on the basis of direct labor-hours, maintenance on the basis of machinery and equipment cost, and storage costs on the basis of materials (direct and indirect) used.

c. How would the use of these departmental overhead rates instead of the plantwide rate affect the cost assigned to a job order requiring 100 direct labor-hours in machine No. 1, 200 direct labor-hours in machine No. 2, 20 hours in assembly, and 10 hours in painting?

d. Someone has questioned the allocation you made in answer to part *b,* saying that the allocation bases appear to be arbitrary. Formulate a reply, including a statement of what each overhead rate ought to mean and comparing the rates you have developed against that standard. You may either agree or disagree with the critic of your allocations, but if you agree you should indicate how you would change the procedure. *No calculations are required by this question.*

Chapter 20

Budgetary Planning

Many of the project and situation decisions we discussed in Chapters 16 and 17 are made as part of short-term periodic (usually one year) operating and financial planning, otherwise known as **budgeting.** The purpose of this chapter is to show why and how management uses budgeting as a key planning tool. The chapter has three parts:

1. A discussion of the form and purposes of budgeting and the annual budgetary plan.
2. A step-by-step illustration of the budgetary planning process.
3. An overview of accounting's role in budgetary planning.

Budgetary Planning: Form and Purpose

The short-term operating and financial plan, or **budget,** identifies the resources the organization has decided to use during a period. It shows where the organization plans to get these resources, where and how it plans to use them, and what it expects to accomplish during this period. The budget also assembles the project and situation decisions that have already been made, incorporates a preliminary forecast of those still to be made and implemented during the period, and presents the results as an integrated, coordinated plan for the period.

The best way to understand budgeting is to follow the steps an organization takes in developing a budget. Before we get into an example, however, we need to look briefly at four questions:

1. What are the various components of the budget?
2. How does the budget relate to the structure of the organization?
3. What are the goals budgeting is expected to attain?
4. What criteria should be applied in budgeting?

754

Components of the Budget

We usually classify the parts of the budget into two groups, *operating budgets* and *financial budgets*. **Operating budgets** list the amounts of goods and services the organization plans to consume during the operating period and the benefits it expects these activities to produce. In most organizations, the resources consumed are generally represented by dollar costs as well as by physical quantities; in a profit-oriented company, benefits are represented by revenues. **Financial budgets,** on the other hand, show how much money the organization plans to spend during the period and where it plans to get the funds to finance these expenditures.

Each block in Exhibit 20–1 represents one or more components of the overall budget of a manufacturing company. For convenience, we'll refer to each component as a budget, although we find it useful to remember that these are all part of a single budgetary plan.

The Organizational Dimension

The budget also has an organizational dimension. All but the smallest organizations are subdivided, with different people responsible for the operation of the various subdivisions. In small organizations, one layer of

EXHIBIT 20–1
Budget Components

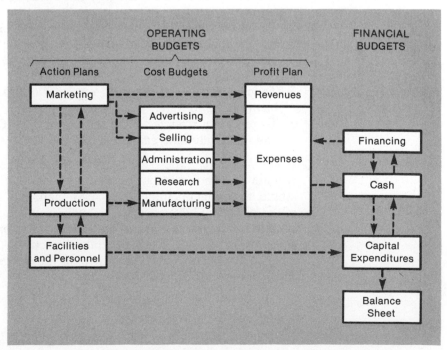

subdivisions is enough—one *department* for purchasing, another for production, another for selling, and so forth. In larger organizations, the departments will be subdivisions of larger units, each one a subdivision of the whole. A sales *division,* for example, may include a dozen or more branch offices. And if the branches are numerous, they are likely to be grouped into regions, each with a regional manager reporting to the division manager.

The organizational dimension of the budget doesn't appear in Exhibit 20–1. Each division, each department has its own portion of the overall plan. Departmental budgets are narrow in scope, dealing with only one or two elements. Divisional budgets are more comprehensive—divisions with both sales and production operations even have their own profit plans and may have divisional balance sheets and partial financing plans. Overall financing remains a head-office responsibility, however, and most organizations control cash mainly in the head office.

The Goals of Budgeting

The annual budgetary planning process has at least six major objectives:

1. To force managers to *analyze* the company's activities critically and creatively.
2. To direct some of the management's attention from the present to the *future.*
3. To enable management to *anticipate* problems or opportunities in time to deal with them effectively.
4. To reinforce managers' *motivation* to work to achieve the organization's goals and objectives.
5. To give managers an ongoing *reminder* of the courses of action they have agreed to.
6. To provide a *reference point* for control reporting—that is, to be the basis for evaluating actual results.

The first four of these are benefits of the budgeting *process.* The final two items are advantages of the budget documents themselves. For example, the budget is intended to serve managers as a constant reminder of the plan they have adopted. As such, it provides a blueprint they can consult from time to time as they work to implement the plan. In this sense, it serves as a set of general instructions to the department and division managers, reflecting the actions they have agreed to take and the results they have agreed to strive for.

Decision Criteria in Budgeting

Budgeting, like other forms of planning, is a process focusing on a set of decisions. For this purpose, each manager typically submits proposals to higher management. Higher management then decides whether to approve these proposals as they stand, modify them in some way, or return them to the originators for revision and resubmission.

Higher management needs to examine individual proposals from four points of view: (1) Do the anticipated *benefits* of proposed expenditures justify the costs? (2) Are the estimates *realistic*? (3) Is the proposal *consistent* with the company's strategic plans and with the proposals of other parts of the organization? and (4) Is it *feasible* in the light of the company's financial, marketing, and production capacities?

The budgeting process is more iterative than this description is likely to imply—that is, tentative budgets are proposed, discussed, and revised again and again as they move upward toward final approval. The process is a progressive dialogue; an executive seldom receives a budget proposal from a subordinate without having discussed vital aspects of it ahead of time. Through vertical and horizontal communication within the management group, these plans are adjusted and readjusted until they become integrated and realizable objectives consistent with the organization's overall policies.

Yet another function of some portions of the budget is to define *spending limits*. For example, budgeted advertising expenditures may be the maximum amount the advertising manager can spend. Budgeting is in its essence a planning process, however, not a limiting process. The budgeting procedure should allow for changes in the amount or pattern of the budgeted expenditures as conditions change and as management gains more knowledge of its resources and opportunities.

Preparing the Annual Budget

The development of a formal budgetary plan requires careful examination of the interrelationships among its various components. Although the complexity of this process cannot be conveyed effectively in a few pages, a simple example may at least identify the issues. Since a manufacturing illustration would be too complex for our purposes at this point, let's see how the management of a small publishing house, Darwin Books, Inc., developed its annual budget for 19x3.

The Organization

Activities at Darwin Books fall broadly into three major categories: manuscript procurement, production, and sales. *Production*, in this case, consists mainly of editing manuscripts, preparing them for typesetting, proofreading, and designing book covers and dust jackets. All printing and binding of books is done on contract by outside printers.

The company has two main product lines—textbooks for college and university use and textbooks for secondary schools. This split provides the basis for the company's organization chart, portions of which are

EXHIBIT 20–2
Darwin Books, Inc.: Partial Organization Chart

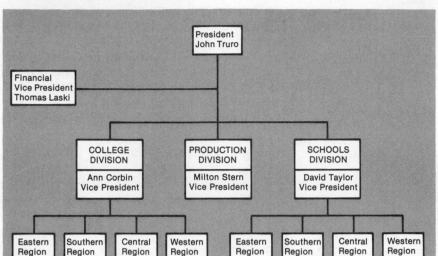

shown in Exhibit 20–2. The vice president who serves as division manager of a textbook division is responsible for both manuscript procurement and sales. Each division has a force of field representatives, organized into four regional groups, each headed by a regional manager with
the title of field editor. The financial vice president is in charge of all
financial activities, including coordination of the annual budget.

The Marketing Plan

Darwin's fiscal year begins July 1. Early in March 19x2, John Truro,
the company's president, asked each textbook division manager to submit
a tentative **marketing plan** for the 19x3 fiscal year (July 1, 19x2–June
30, 19x3), showing the size and composition of the field organization, the
promotional pattern to be followed, and anticipated revenues and expenses.

Ann Corbin, manager of the college division, started by preparing an
up-to-date list of the book titles that were then available or were scheduled for introduction during the next fiscal year. She gave copies of this
list to her field editors and asked each of them to spell out in detail a
promotional program for the coming year, estimate its cost, and predict
the resulting sales volume. Dave Taylor, the schools division manager,
followed a similar procedure.

Both division managers reviewed the projected sales and the underlying marketing plans with their field editors. Corbin, for example, com-

pared the proposed expense/sales ratio for each region with the ratio thus far in 19x2 and with the ratios in other regions. She compared the proposed increase in selling expense in each region with the projected increase in sales volume. She encouraged her western region field editor to hire an additional field representative to work actively in locating new manuscripts for textbooks in computer science, and her comments and suggestions led to changes in each of the regional plans.

At one point, she turned down a proposal of the southern region field editor to expand the field staff to increase the number of contacts with junior colleges in the area. Darwin Books had few titles that were appropriate for use in the junior college market. Corbin felt that any promotional effort in that market should be concentrated on only a few departments and only in the larger junior colleges. This would not require an increase in the size of the field sales force.

After working with the field editors, the two division managers presented the tentative sales and expense budgets summarized in Exhibit 20–3 to Tom Laski, the financial vice president. Laski questioned Dave

EXHIBIT 20–3

DARWIN BOOKS, INC.
Tentative Divisional Sales and Expense Budgets
For the Year Ending June 30, 19x3

	College Division	Schools Division
Sales revenues	$4,200,000	$2,700,000
Less: Returns	180,000	20,000
Net sales	$4,020,000	$2,680,000
Marketing and administration:		
Division office salaries	$ 100,000	$ 85,000
Field salaries	400,000	300,000
Travel and entertainment	130,000	80,000
Advertising	50,000	50,000
Miscellaneous	40,000	50,000
Total marketing and administrative expenses	$ 720,000	$ 565,000

Taylor, the schools division manager, on the slow growth in sales in his division and the high ratio of marketing expenses to sales. Taylor blamed both of these on the lack of any large-volume titles on the list. Darwin Books was a relative newcomer in the schools market, with a line of innovative texts, but none of these had broken through with sales to the large school districts that accounted for the bulk of textbook purchases.

After further analysis of his proposal, Taylor agreed that the proposed budget for miscellaneous marketing and administrative expenses could be reduced by $20,000 and the travel and entertainment budget could be reduced by $10,000 without reducing forecasted sales revenues. These changes reduced the tentative divisional budget for marketing and administrative expenses to $535,000. Laski endorsed these changes but pointed out that Truro would want to discuss the schools division's future with Taylor at the final budget review session in June.

EXHIBIT 20–4

DARWIN BOOKS, INC.
Tentative Profit Plan
For the Year Ending June 30, 19x3

	College Division	Schools Division	Total
Net sales....................	$4,020,000	$2,680,000	$6,700,000
Divisional expenses:			
Printing and binding...........	2,400,000	1,700,000	4,100,000
Copy editing.................	120,000	80,000	200,000
Authors' royalties.............	480,000	250,000	730,000
Marketing and administration ...	720,000	535,000	1,255,000
Total divisional expenses	3,720,000	2,565,000	6,285,000
Divisional profit................	$ 300,000	$ 115,000	415,000
General administrative expenses...			300,000
Income before income taxes			115,000
Income taxes			50,000
Net income....................			$ 65,000

EXHIBIT 20–5

DARWIN BOOKS, INC.
Tentative Cash Budget
For the Year Ending June 30, 19x3

Cash receipts:		
Customers.......................		$6,500,000
Other sources		100,000
Total cash receipts		6,600,000
Cash disbursements:		
Salaries	$1,350,000	
Printing	4,500,000	
Other suppliers...................	210,000	
Authors' royalties	700,000	
Taxes	50,000	
Dividends.......................	40,000	
Furniture and equipment purchases ..	100,000	
Total cash disbursements		6,950,000
Cash deficit......................		$ 350,000

The Production Plan

At this point, Laski asked the textbook division managers to meet in his office with Milt Stern, the production manager. The textbook division managers gave Stern the **production plans** for their divisions—the proposed schedules for new books and new editions and their estimates of sales for each title on the active list. They reviewed inventory levels and identified titles that should be allowed to go out of print as soon as present stocks were exhausted.

Stern complained that the manuscript-preparation schedules were too heavily concentrated in the autumn months. Although many of his copy editors were part-time employees, some tasks had to be done by full-time personnel, and they simply couldn't handle the projected peak load. Darwin Books had solved this problem occasionally in the past by delaying publication dates for several books, but this time it seemed more sensible to authorize an increase in the size of Stern's full-time staff.

Tentative Profit Plan and Cash Budget

After his meeting with the division vice presidents, Laski assembled the available data into a tentative **profit plan** for the coming year. This plan is summarized in Exhibit 20–4.

Laski also received proposals for such items as dividends and purchases of furniture and equipment, and then prepared the tentative **cash budget** summarized in Exhibit 20–5. Some disbursements on this list can be classified as discretionary outlays, meaning that most and maybe all of the marketing and production goals embodied in the current operating plan could be achieved even if the expenditures leading to these disbursements weren't made. Dividends, research and development outlays, and most disbursements for the purchase of furniture and equipment are discretionary in this sense; some manufacturing overhead costs, advertising and selling expenses, and general administrative expenses may also be discretionary, at least in the short run.

Responses to the Tentative Plans

As the table shows, Darwin's expected cash receipts were $350,000 *less* than anticipated disbursements. This left management with several options to investigate, mainly the following:

1. Reduce existing cash balances.
2. Defer payments to suppliers.
3. Press customers for faster payment.
4. Curtail discretionary spending plans.
5. Borrow.
6. Revise marketing plans.
7. Reduce dividends.

Although these choices are top management's responsibility, the financial executives are usually expected to analyze the alternatives and make recommendations. In practice, they are likely to work closely with the division managers and other senior operating managers, so that the final budget will reflect the consensus of top management before it is presented to the board of directors for approval.

The main problem at this point is to find adequate criteria to guide management's choices among these alternatives. In this case, management felt that any reduction in the dividend would have had an unacceptable effect on the market price of the company's stock. This alternative, therefore, was regarded as a last resort.

TERMINOLOGY

An *expenditure* is any use of resources—such as acquiring an asset, using an asset, or using an employee's services.

A *capital expenditure* or capital outlay is any use of resources to acquire an asset that will benefit the organization for an extended period of time—usually associated with the purchase of plant assets.

An *operating expenditure* is any use of resources in pursuit of the organization's objectives for the current operating period.

A *disbursement* is an immediate outlay of cash.

Note that an expenditure (capital or operating) may or may not result in a disbursement in the same fiscal period in which the expenditure is made.

Analysis of Alternatives. Reductions in the proposed amount of capital expenditures often can produce a marked improvement in the company's short-term cash position. Furthermore, the fact that an expenditure is proposed doesn't necessarily mean it is desirable. Many proposals fail to pass muster when subjected to the kinds of tests we'll describe in Chapter 21. Other proposals may meet these tests but still have to be rejected or postponed because a temporary shortage of funds prevents the company from making all the desirable capital expenditures and other discretionary outlays that have been proposed.

Laski's review of the capital-expenditure proposals at Darwin Books led him to recommend deleting proposals requiring outlays of $45,000 in fiscal 19x3. Proposals accounting for the remaining $55,000 in requested capital outlays appeared likely to meet Darwin's capital-expenditure tests or other criteria management was likely to apply, so Laski left them in the tentative budget for the moment.

Reducing the tentative budget for disbursements for furniture and equipment by $45,000 reduced the estimated cash deficit from $350,000 to $305,000, still a substantial gap. One way to reduce a deficit of this size is to reduce the company's bank balances or to liquidate any holdings of short-term marketable securities. In this case, Laski's analysis indicated that reduction of the cash balance would jeopardize the company's ability to meet its payrolls and other obligations on time, and Darwin Books had no marketable securities to liquidate. Its credit rating was very good, however, and Laski was able to get a commitment for a $200,000 line of credit from a local bank, at 10 percent interest. By projecting the time at which the borrowed funds would be needed, Laski estimated that the borrowing against the line of credit would increase interest payments by $15,000 and decrease tax payments in 19x3 by $6,000. The additional borrowing, therefore, would reduce the cash gap by $191,000 ($200,000 − $15,000 + $6,000).

With a remaining cash deficit of $114,000 ($350,000 − $45,000 − $191,000), Laski knew that more drastic measures would be necessary. As a start, he asked both the company's credit manager and the purchasing agent whether they could help solve 19x3's anticipated cash-flow problem by pressing customers for prompt payment of their bills or by deferring some supplier payments to the following year. (Previous consultations with the division managers had convinced him that significant further reductions in discretionary divisional outlays wouldn't be feasible.)

Laski approached these possibilities with a great deal of caution. Unless a company's collection efforts have been lax, faster collections from customers ordinarily can be achieved only at the cost of lost sales because of a more restrictive credit policy. If the profit contribution from sales exceeds the benefits from faster collections, a tighter credit policy would be self-defeating. In this case, since Darwin's customers were generally prompt in their payments, neither Laski nor the credit manager saw much chance of help from this source in 19x3.

Slower payments to suppliers also had to be approached very carefully. A reputation as a slow payer can weaken a company's credit rating and increase its purchasing costs. In this case, however, the purchasing agent agreed that payments to the company's printers could be reduced by $100,000 in 19x3 without adverse effects. Darwin had always paid its printers before the end of the normal credit period, and slowing the rate of payment would only be using a privilege already available to the company. In most cases, the printers would hardly notice this change in Darwin's practice.

Final Resolution. The slowdown in payments to the printers, together with the paring of the capital budget and the additional borrowing, left an estimated cash deficit of only $14,000 for 19x3. To close this gap, Laski decided to recommend reducing the budget for capital expenditures by an additional $14,000. Few of the capital-expenditure proposals remaining after the initial $45,000 reduction were ready for final approval, and a

$14,000 reduction in the capital budget would require a more thorough scrutiny of the proposals as they came up for final approval during the year. The poorest of these proposals—including some that would help department heads meet their personal objectives without benefiting the company—would likely be rejected when they came up for approval later on.

The changes Laski suggested to prevent the cash deficit inherent in the initial budget proposal can be summarized as follows:

Reductions in proposed capital outlays:
Unacceptable proposals........................	$ 45,000	
Low-priority proposals	14,000	
Total reductions in proposed capital outlays....		$ 59,000
Deferral of payments to suppliers.................		100,000
Additional borrowing	200,000	
Less: Aftertax cost of additional borrowing ($15,000 − $6,000).........................	9,000	
Net effect of additional borrowing		191,000
Total reduction in cash deficit		$350,000

Both the tentative profit plan and the tentative cash budget were modified to reflect these changes. The board of directors reviewed and approved the revised plans but indicated their dissatisfaction with the profit level being achieved. Truro was asked to work with his division managers on ways to improve profit performance, with particular attention to the schools division. A full-fledged review of the schools division was scheduled for an autumn board meeting.

Budgeting as a Decision-Making Process

Budget approval is top management's signal that the methods selected and the ends to be achieved are acceptable. When top management receives a proposed profit plan, it can (1) accept it, (2) send it back for revision, or (3) take steps to terminate the operation. In practice, some question is almost always raised about the adequacy of the plan, thus ruling out immediate acceptance. Termination, on the other hand, is unlikely to be ordered unless such a decision had been considered before and deferred to give the division manager an opportunity to come up with a viable alternative.

The result is a response pattern such as that schematized in Exhibit 20–6. Management's rejection of an initial proposal, represented by the *No* arrow under the top diamond, ordinarily starts the process again, as lower management seeks ways to improve the anticipated results. This is shown by the arrows looping back into the block at the upper left-hand corner of the exhibit.

EXHIBIT 20–6
System Responses to Proposed Profit Plan

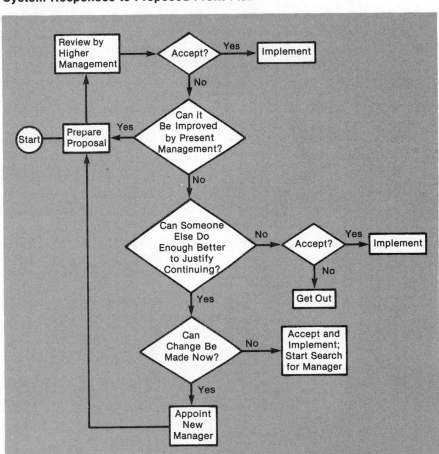

Notice that three of the blocks at the right of the diagram represent decisions to accept and implement the budget. These decisions reflect top management's conclusion that existing management can't be expected to surpass the performance levels embodied in the proposals being accepted. This is important because one purpose of the budget, as we mentioned earlier, is to serve as a standard against which the performance of division and department managers can be evaluated. Top management's approval of a budget, therefore, carries with it a commitment to recognize the budgeted performance levels as satisfactory if actual conditions are as anticipated. If top management is unwilling to make this commitment, the proposal should be routed back into the loop for another revision and review.

Meeting the budget constraints in this illustration was a good deal easier than it usually is in practice. Internal politics, personal idiosyncracies, and genuine disagreements as to the feasibility and effectiveness of various parts of the plan often make budgeting a painful and time-consuming process. We don't wish to ignore these factors, but we see no reason to dwell on them at length. Our objective has been to make it quite clear that budgeting is a creative, decision-oriented process. It may also be the most important single phase in the management control process, in that much of what the organization will do is decided at this time.

The Capital Budget

At the time of annual budget preparation, division managers or department heads are asked to submit tentative lists of the capital expenditure proposals they expect to make during the coming year—major projects individually and in detail, minor projects grouped in meaningful categories. Preliminary estimates of the anticipated benefits of major projects and groups of minor projects are ordinarily submitted along with the preliminary requests for budget inclusion. These lists are combined with schedules of planned expenditures on projects that already will have been approved and begun before the beginning of the fiscal year.

TERMINOLOGY

An *appropriation* is a formal authorization to make an expenditure. A *sponsor* is the division or department that requests an appropriation to effect a particular course of action.

For Darwin Books, the 19x3 **capital budget** took the form of the schedule in Exhibit 20–7. (For simplicity, we've assumed that expenditures in 19x3 will equal disbursements in that year.) Darwin's projects are relatively simple, with little carryover from year to year. In this case, the company planned to spend $13,000 in 19x3 on projects approved and started in previous years, plus another $28,000 on new projects. Future outlays necessary to complete projects were expected to amount to another $1,500.

Appropriation Requests

Budget inclusion seldom serves as the final authorization to undertake a capital-expenditure project. Most budgeting systems require submission of a written appropriation request for each proposal at the time the sponsor is ready to begin committing funds to it. The main purpose is to give the sponsor more time to plan as well as to consider events that have occurred since the budget was prepared. It also gives the company more

EXHIBIT 20–7

DARWIN BOOKS, INC.
Capital Budget
For the Year Ending June 30, 19x3

	Expenditures		
	Previous Years	19x3	Future Years
Prior-year approvals:			
Office addition	$45,000	$ 5,000	
Telephone system	2,000	8,000	
Subtotal	$47,000	13,000	
Current-year approvals:			
Forklift trucks.		12,000	
Furniture and equipment:			
College division		3,000	
Schools division.		4,000	$ 500
Production division		2,000	
Administrative offices		7,000	1,000
Subtotal		28,000	$1,500
Total current expenditures.		$41,000	

flexibility in that all of its resources aren't fully committed at the start of the year. If an emergency or an extraordinarily profitable opportunity arises during the year, projects can be initiated at once without upsetting the overall budget. It will be necessary to delay or cancel other projects only if additional investment funds can't be obtained from other sources on short notice.

Each appropriation request must show the reasons the sponsor believes it should be undertaken. For many projects, this includes a detailed estimate of future cash flows, from either reduced costs or expansion of capacity. For others, the justification is more qualitative: the sponsor asserts that the benefits will be substantial even though they are now unmeasurable. Good capital budget administration should encourage efforts to estimate both costs and benefits.

Approval Authority

In large companies, final approval authority for small projects is usually delegated to managers at lower levels. Department heads may approve individual projects smaller than, say, $10,000; division managers may have authority to approve projects up to some higher amount, such as $100,000; and the president may be able to approve projects up to amounts as large as $500,000 or even more, with the limit depending on the size of the company. Final decisions on very large projects, however, are almost always made or ratified by the board of directors.

Delegated approval authority is generally limited and subject to review. Lower-level managers are still expected to apply company profitability standards to proposals within their **authority limits,** and they are usually subject to limits on the total amounts they can approve. These latter limits are embodied in lump-sum budget provisions for groups of small proposals in each responsibility center.

Adjustable Budget

Budgets similar to the one Darwin Books adopted for 19x3 are really valid only if all of management's predictions about the environment *and* about the company's own cost-volume and volume-cost relationships are valid. Since this assumption is never precisely true, we might reasonably ask two questions:

1. Does the adopted budget (the *fixed budget*) serve any purpose when the premises on which it was based prove to have been incorrect?
2. What can be done to recognize uncertainties in the budget?

Role of the Fixed Budget

As we pointed out earlier, most of the purposes of budgeting are achieved by the *process* of preparing the budget rather than by the budget itself. Even as we accept that argument, however, the question remains whether the objectives we have ascribed to the resulting budget documents can be achieved when the conditions on which they were predicated don't materialize.

It should be clear that when conditions either change or don't develop as predicted, the fixed budget can no longer serve as a guide to current actions. To the extent that the budget is intended to remind management of the decisions it has made, as a means of keeping day-by-day actions on the chosen path, it is obsolete as soon as those original decisions no longer appear to be valid.

The other major purpose of the budget documents still can be achieved, however, even when actual conditions and relationships depart from those embodied in the budget. This purpose is to provide a benchmark from which departures can be measured and analyzed. If the budget were changed every time a forecast of an important economic variable was changed, measured departures of actual results from budgeted results would give management no information on the effects of these changes.

In other words, the fixed budget enables management to examine the implications of *all* departures from the assumed conditions, not just those that reflect management's over- or underachievement under actual operating conditions. A financing plan based on a cash flow of $10 million a month is just as out of date in an $8 million month that results from a downturn in the economy as in an $8 million month that is the result of managerial ineffectiveness. Adjustments of some kind totaling $2 million will have to be made in either case.

Probabilistic Budgets

Even so, this doesn't mean that the fixed budget is the only one management might prepare. In fact, the fixed budget itself could be a weighted average of several possible budgets, each appropriate to a particular set of economic conditions. The weights attached to each of these alternative budgets would be the estimated probability that its set of economic conditions will in fact prevail. A fixed budget prepared on this basis is called a **probability-adjusted budget.**

The major barrier to the use of probability-adjusted budgets is the lack of objective data on which the probabilities can be based. This objection can be raised to almost any managerial tool that requires the use of probability estimates, however. If management recognizes the validity of the concept, it should be willing to make an effort to develop alternative scenarios and assign probabilities to them. *Any fixed budget reflects a set of weighted probabilities; if they are not assigned explicitly, they will be assigned implicitly as management applies its judgment to conflicting signals about what the future will bring.*

Flexible Budgets

A probability-adjusted budget is still a fixed budget, but the alternative budgets on which it is based could be used in still another way. Each could reflect a conditional plan of action, to be called into service if its predicated economic conditions do materialize. A set of conditional or alternative budgets of this sort is known as a **flexible budget.**[1]

The main advantage of a flexible budget is that it may enable management to respond more quickly and more effectively to changes in the economic environment. The reason is that it requires management to consider in advance how it would respond to various economic conditions, rather than improvise in a hurry as conditions change.

Flexible operating and financial budgets also serve a second purpose. By projecting the impact of a variety of possible combinations of environmental conditions and rates of effectiveness of managerial programs, management can assess in advance the potential risks and rewards of its proposed actions. These "what if" projections are the heart of various commercially available spreadsheet programs such as Visicalc © and

---

[1] This same term is used in a narrower sense in Chapters 23 and 24 to apply to alternative sets of cost budgets, each one applicable to a specific level of activity. Flexibility can also be built into the marketing plan, however, or any other component of the overall budgetary plan if management believes that the ensuing benefits are likely to justify the effort of doing so.

Lotus 1-2-3 ©. These programs enable management or its analytical staff to vary any variable that can be identified as a significant determinant of the rate of success or failure of management's actions to see how these variations affect income and cash flow.

For any planned action, this kind of analysis of the variables can reveal that some possible plans are more likely than others to place the company in a high-risk situation. It may also reveal how rich a set of rewards these more risky plans can generate if conditions and the rate of effectiveness are favorable. In short, the preparation of alternative budget scenarios of this sort not only can provide a basis later on for adapting actions as conditions change, but it also can enrich the decision process by laying bare the implications of alternative courses of action long before any action is taken.

Alternative Scenarios: An Illustration

These alternative budget scenarios can be drawn up for a division, a product line, or the organization as a whole. To illustrate the process in the simplest possible way, let's see how Darwin Books analyzed a proposal to expand its activities. Assume that Darwin was approached by the American Institute of Actuaries to become the exclusive distributor of its professional handbook for one year. Darwin would pay the institute a $350,000 fee, and it would be committed to expending $50,000 to promote the product during the year. Darwin also would incur three other incremental costs: a $3 sales commission on each book sold, 12 percent interest to compensate the company's creditors and shareholders for advancing the $350,000 fee, and delivery charges consisting of a flat fee of $10,000 plus $1 a book. The institute stipulated that the selling price be $50 a book.

Darwin's management decided that it would be unrealistic to evaluate this proposal solely on the basis of the institute's assertion that the most likely outcome would be the sale of 12,000 books. Instead, Darwin decided to consider alternative results as well. Exhibit 20–8 illustrates how Darwin identified the probable effects on pretax income of volumes of 8,000, 10,000, 12,000, and 14,000 books.

If 12,000 books would in fact be sold, Darwin would earn pretax income of $100,000. If more books were sold, income would be greater; conversely, lower volume would result in lower income or a loss.

Probabilities and Expected Value

Using alternative budgets provides an additional before-the-fact benefit as well. Management can estimate what it believes will be the probability that each outcome will occur. By applying these probability factors to the various possible outcomes, management can project the effect of uncertainty on its decision. For example, let's assume Darwin's management

EXHIBIT 20–8
Darwin Books, Inc.: Flexible Budget

Volume (number of books) . . .	8,000	10,000	12,000	14,000
Revenues.	$400,000	$500,000	$600,000	$700,000
Costs:				
Marketing license	350,000	350,000	350,000	350,000
Advertising.	50,000	50,000	50,000	50,000
Commissions.	24,000	30,000	36,000	42,000
Delivery	18,000	20,000	22,000	24,000
Interest.	42,000	42,000	42,000	42,000
Total	484,000	492,000	500,000	508,000
Pretax income (loss)	$(84,000)	$ 8,000	$100,000	$192,000

determined that the probability of selling 12,000 books was only 40 percent, and that probability factors were assigned as follows:

Volume	Pretax Income/(Loss) [Exhibit 20–8]	Probability
8,000	$(84,000)	0.20
10,000	8,000	0.30
12,000	100,000	0.40
14,000	192,000	0.10

Before responding to these estimates, management first had to choose the **decision rule** it deemed appropriate in this situation. It decided to base its decision on the **expected value** of the results associated with the proposal. The expected value of any course of action is the probability-weighted average of the possible outcomes. For the handbook proposal, the expected value was as follows:

Volume	*(1)* Pretax Income/(Loss) [Exhibit 20–8]	*(2)* Probability	*(3)* Contribution to Probability-Weighted Income/(Loss) [(1) × (2)]
8,000	$(84,000)	0.20	$(16,800)
10,000	8,000	0.30	2,400
12,000	100,000	0.40	40,000
14,000	192,000	0.10	19,200
Expected value.			$ 44,800

Another decision rule Darwin's management could have adopted was to minimize the potential loss. For example, suppose one alternative has an expected value of $100,000 but could lead to a loss of $50,000 if conditions were unfavorable; another has an expected value of $125,000 but a potential loss of $75,000. A loss-minimization rule would lead to the selection of the first of these alternatives, despite its lower expected value. This rule would have led Darwin to reject the handbook proposal, because accepting it would have exposed the company to the possibility of an $84,000 loss. Management decided that this approach was far too cautious.

The Budget as Benchmark

Given these estimates, it appeared that, on the average, the company would gain $44,800 from marketing the institute's handbook. Given that prediction, Darwin accepted the proposal and initiated the $50,000 marketing plan. The results were disappointing. Only 10,000 books were sold, and Darwin's pretax income was $15,000, not the budgeted $100,000 that was based on the anticipated sale of 12,000 books. Reference to Darwin's flexible budget, however, indicated that the $15,000 actual income was greater than the $8,000 income budgeted for the 10,000-book volume. Item-by-item analysis yielded the following:

	Actual	Volume-Adjusted Budget	Difference
Marketing license............	$350,000	$350,000	$ 0
Advertising	53,000	50,000	(3,000)
Commissions	30,000	30,000	0
Delivery	13,500	20,000	6,500
Interest....................	38,500	42,000	3,500
Net favorable effect			$7,000

The *higher* advertising cost was the result of a conscious decision by management to use a particular type of promotional campaign. Delivery costs were *lower* because Darwin was able to engage a different carrier whose only fee was $1.35 a book. The interest amount was *lower* because a review of Darwin's rate-of-return experience indicated that 11 percent was the proper rate of compensation rather than the 12 percent that had been assumed initially.

This illustration of a flexible budget demonstrates the potential of budgetary planning. It enables top management to measure in advance the likely effects of various outcomes. As important, the flexible budget provides a meaningful basis for comparing actual results with the budgeted amounts appropriate to the experienced level of volume. We'll learn more about the analytical benefits of flexible budgeting in Chapter 23.

The Role of Accounting

Budgetary planning is a management process and a responsibility of the organization's operating managers. Accounting and other staff personnel don't make the plans. They do have several important roles to play, however, and a few words about each of these should be useful to round out our discussion of budgetary planning:

1. They provide data for use in preparing estimates.
2. They analyze and interpret these data.
3. They design and operate the budgeting procedures.
4. They consolidate and review the budgetary proposals originating in various parts of the organization.

Data Collection

The estimates managers use in making budgeting decisions reflect their forecasts of the future consequences of those decisions. To make those estimates, however, managers usually draw very heavily on records of what happened in the past. The future may be very different from the past, but it is likely to be closer to the past than to estimates drawn at random. In other words, managers are more comfortable adjusting past amounts than starting fresh, with no underlying data at all.

One function of the accounting system, therefore, is to provide a record of the costs and benefits of the company's various activities in considerable detail. Ideally, these data should enable management to identify the sensitivity of costs, expenses, revenues, and cash flows to various kinds of managerial actions. For example, the management of our illustrative company, Darwin Books, would like to know how sales and expenses in the college division responded in the past to increases in advertising and field-selling effort. It probably would also like to know what would happen to net income if revenues were to fall, say, 10 percent short of their forecasted levels.

Data Analysis

Accounting's contribution doesn't end with data collection. The accounting numbers need to be interpreted; adjusted to allow for changes in company-specific, industry-specific, and economy-wide conditions; and recombined in various ways. Since accountants know more about their own numbers than anyone else, it is understandable that they do a good deal of this analytical work.

Budget Administration

The headquarters financial staffs, often including others as well as accountants, play two other roles in the budgeting process. The first of these is that they are responsible for designing and securing support for the procedural aspects of periodic planning, mainly the questions of what is to be budgeted, when, and by whom. This is ordinarily done by the budget staff, working closely with operating executives. The final version is likely to be summarized in a budget manual, spelling out deadlines for various budget components, assigning responsibilities for budget preparation, prescribing forms, and describing the overall budget pattern.

Consolidation and Review

The final role of accountants and others on the central financial staff is in the review and coordination phase of budgeting. Although the operating managers have the main responsibility for developing operating and financial plans, the central financial staff is responsible for putting the pieces together.

Even if budget proposals have been reviewed carefully and critically all the way up the line within a given segment of the organization, the corporate financial staff members often have the authority to subject these proposals to their own tests of feasibility and profitability. They are free to seek clarification or to question whether other alternatives have been investigated; in some cases, they even have the power to ask individual managers to revise their proposals.

We must emphasize, however, that in taking any action of this sort, the controller, budget director, or other financial executive is acting as the agent of the chief executive. Planning is a managerial function first, a technical operation second.

Summary

Periodic planning, or budgeting, is not simply a matter of forecasting what the future may offer. It is a creative process in which managers at all levels are expected to evaluate and compare different possible courses of action, selecting those that seem most likely to meet company goals. Budgeting, in other words, is a decision-making process.

In this chapter we've begun describing the complexity and dynamics of the budgeting process without getting bogged down in complicated numerical examples. In our illustration, budget preparation was initiated by top management, but the major effort took place at the divisional level. The division managers developed their marketing plans and translated them into production requirements and profit estimates. These plans were reviewed, revised, and consolidated before being presented to top management for final approval. The end result was a profit plan, cash budget, and capital budget that were both feasible and acceptable to top management.

Budgeting takes place in the face of uncertainty. Management may prepare alternative budgets, each corresponding to a possible set of environmental conditions. If management believes these outcomes have different probabilities, it may decide to weight each outcome by its probability to determine the expected value of the outcome. Management may also use these alternative budgets as flexible budgets, providing back-up plans in case actual conditions differ from those underlying the primary budget.

Accounting and other financial personnel have vital roles to play in the budgetary process. They provide, interpret, and analyze data; design and administer the budgeting procedures; review the proposals submitted by managers in various parts of the organization; and consolidate the final proposals into a feasible, workable plan.

Key Terms

Authorization limit	Financial budgets
Budget	Flexible budget
Budgeting	Marketing plan
Capital budget	Operating budgets
Cash budget	Probability-adjusted budget
Decision rule	Production plan
Expected value	Profit plan

Independent Study Problems (Solutions in Appendix B)

1. Developing a Profit Plan and Cash Budget; Feasibility Test. Darnell Company is organized in three divisions, each with a division manager, a small office staff, and its own sales force. The various divisions sell different kinds of products and deal with different groups of customers.

The company's budget director has received the following proposals and estimates for next year from the division managers:

	Division A	Division B	Division C
Divisional marketing costs amounting to	$ 150	$ 500	$ 300
Will produce revenues of	1,000	3,000	2,100
And cost of goods sold of	650	1,650	1,260
Administrative expenses to support these activities will total	150	300	200
Accounts receivable will increase by	10	200	50
Inventories will exceed this year's ending balances by	50	100	50
Accounts payable will increase by.	15	50	80

The expenses of the company's central management are tentatively budgeted at $400 for the year, to be paid in cash. Cash purchases of equipment amounting to $130 and cash dividends of $350 are also proposed. Of the equipment purchases, $60 is to replace existing equipment and $70 is for expansion. The expansion proposals, which management has approved in principle, will have no effect on next year's income statement.

Depreciation is included in the administrative expense figures above as follows: central management, $10; division A, $5; division B, $15; division C, $20.

a. Prepare a tentative profit plan and cash budget for next year, on the assumption that all these proposals are approved.

b. The company will start next year with a cash balance of $290 and an unused line of bank credit of $100. The minimum cash balance is 5 percent of sales. Is the tentative plan feasible?

2. Tentative Cash Budget. The management of Cranmore Manufacturing Company at the beginning of 19x2 anticipated (1) a decrease in sales as compared with 19x1 because of production time lost in converting to new products, and (2) a considerably smaller profit margin due to higher material and labor costs. The controller was asked to prepare a cash budget based on estimated 19x2 sales of $2.4 million (a decrease of $300,000) and, in particular, to forecast the cash position at the close of 19x2.

The treasurer's forecast of certain balance sheet and other items was as follows:

Accounts receivable (net)	$ 35,000 decrease
Accounts payable	20,000 decrease
Inventories	17,000 increase
Additions to plant (gross)	125,000
Additions to retained earnings appropriated for contingencies	25,000
Income for 19x2 (after depreciation but before income taxes)	95,000
Depreciation expense, 19x2	48,000
Income taxes for 19x2 (payable in 19x3)	45,000
Dividend payments (at 19x1 rates)	30,000

The cash balance on January 1, 19x2, was $54,000, and the tax liability on that date, arising from 19x1 taxable income, amounted to $93,000. The company had no bank loans outstanding.

a. Assuming that any balance sheet items not listed above would be unchanged, prepare a schedule of forecasted cash receipts and cash disbursements for 19x2, and determine the expected cash balance as of December 31, 19x2.

b. What action would you expect management to take when it sees the cash flow estimates for the year?

Exercises and Problems

3. Cash Budgeting Exercises. Make the calculations required in each of the following exercises:

Exercise A. Walsh, Inc., is preparing its cash budget for the month of November. The following information is available concerning its inventories:

Inventories at beginning of November	$180,000
Estimated cost of goods sold in November	900,000
Estimated inventories at end of November..........	160,000
Estimated payments in November for purchases prior to November	210,000
Estimated payments in November for purchases in November	80%

What are the estimated cash disbursements for inventories in November?

Exercise B. Fresh Company is preparing its cash budget for the month of May. The following information is available concerning its accounts receivable:

Estimated credit sales in May	$200,000
Actual credit sales in April....................	150,000
Estimated collections in May:	
For credit sales in May......................	20%
For credit sales in April	70%
For credit sales prior to April.................	$ 12,000
Estimated write-offs in May for uncollectible accounts from credit sales...................	8,000
Estimated provision for bad debts in May for credit sales in May	7,000

Calculate the estimated cash receipts from accounts receivable collections in May.

Exercise C. Serven Corporation has estimated its activity for June 19x1. Selected data from these estimates are as follows:

Gross sales revenue	$700,000
Gross margin (based on gross sales)	30%
Increase in trade accounts receivable during month (at invoice prices, before write-offs of uncollectible accounts)...........	$ 20,000
Change in accounts payable during month.......	0
Increase in inventory during month	10,000

Total selling, general, and administrative expense (SG&A) is $71,000 a month plus 15 percent of gross sales.

Serven Corporation classifies deductions for uncollectible accounts as variable selling expenses instead of as a determinant of net sales. The variable SG&A percentage in the preceding paragraph includes a provision for uncollectible accounts amounting to 1 percent of gross sales.

Depreciation expense of $40,000 a month is included in fixed SG&A.

On the basis of the above data, what are the estimated cash disbursements for operations in June?

Exercise D. Davis Company has budgeted its activity for April. Selected data from estimated amounts are as follows:

Net income	$120,000
Increase in gross amount of trade accounts receivable during month after write-off of uncollectibles............	35,000
Uncollectible accounts written off during month	25,000
Depreciation expense	65,000
Provision for income taxes during month......	80,000
Income taxes paid during month.............	0
Provision for bad debts during month.........	45,000

On the basis of the above data, calculate Davis's budgeted cash increase for the month.

(AICPA adapted)

4. Expected Value and Decision Rules. Chandler Company is trying to decide how much to produce. Unsold units must be destroyed. Each unit costs $2 and sells for $3. The probabilities of various sales volumes are:

Units Sold	Probability
10	0.1
11	0.2
12	0.3
13	0.2
14	0.15
15	0.05

a. What level of production would maximize the expected value of the outcome in this case?

b. How much should be produced if the company decides to maximize the *possible* gain? Minimize the *possible* loss?

5. Expected Value Exercise. Duguid Company is considering a proposal to introduce a new product, XPL. An outside marketing consultant has prepared the following probability distribution describing the relative likelihood of monthly sales volume levels and related income (loss) for XPL:

Monthly Sales Volume	Probability	Income (Loss)
3,000	0.10	$(35,000)
6,000	0.20	5,000
9,000	0.40	30,000
12,000	0.20	50,000
15,000	0.10	70,000

Calculate the expected value of the added monthly income before taxes if Duguid decides to market XPL.

(AICPA adapted)

6. Calculating Expected Value; Bidding on a Special Order. Yvette Barclay, the sales manager of Franglais Company, has been asked to submit a price quotation for 100,000 units of a product used by a customer. The incremental cost of filling the order, if it can be obtained, is $90,000. Three possible prices are being considered: $1, $1.25, and $1.50.

Barclay is not certain how busy competitors' factories are, but in the light of their bids on recent jobs, she thinks that the chance of their operating at a rate as high as 80 percent of capacity or higher is only 20 percent. Similarly, she believes that the probability that competitors are operating at 60 percent of capacity or less is 30 percent.

She estimates that if competitors' operating rates are 80 percent or higher, she can secure the order at any bid up to and including $1.50. If competitors are operating between 61 and 79 percent of capacity, a price of $1.25 or less will secure the order, but if competitors' operating rates are 60 percent or less, it will take a bid of $1 to land the order.

Assuming that the decision rule is to maximize the expected value of the monetary return, which bid should be submitted?

7. Product-Line Budgeting. Hammersmith, Ltd., has three regional factories, each of which manufactures all the company's products. The sales force is also organized geographically in 10 regional divisions, and each sales representative has a geographic territory in which he or she is the company's sole representative.

In the past, the annual budgeting process started with the development of tentative sales and marketing plans by the regional sales managers. These were then used to estimate the requirements for production and for administrative support. After review and revision, the final budget was structured along organizational lines.

Hammersmith's management became convinced in the early 1980s that this approach was preventing the development of coherent, aggressive marketing plans for individual products. Four product managers were appointed, each one responsible for setting objectives and developing marketing programs for one of the company's four main product groups. The regional manufacturing and sales organizations remained; the product managers were planners and coordinators without direct-line authority over factory or sales personnel.

In line with this change, top management decided that all future budgets would be drawn up on a product-line basis. Each product manager would draw up a proposed marketing and production plan for his or her line, working closely with the head-office sales and production staffs.

What problems do you foresee in the new system? How would you try to anticipate them and minimize their importance?

8. Budgeting: Benefits and Implementation Problems. "This budget is a big nuisance," said Hiram Baumgartner, president of Colleyford, Inc., the U.S. subsidiary of a large European manufacturer of electrical and electronic products. "I have to spend most of my time on it for the better part of a month, and I don't know how many hours my controller puts in on it. As far as I'm concerned, it's just another report I have to make."

Colleyford operated one small electronics factory in upstate New York but otherwise imported all its needs from parent-company factories in Europe and Japan. It operated primarily in the northeastern United States and on the West Coast and had fairly large product-distribution warehouses in New York and San Francisco.

For budgeting purposes, Colleyford used the parent company's product-classification scheme. It marketed products in six of the parent's product categories:

1. Lighting products.
2. Electronic tubes and transistors.
3. Components for computers and industrial communications equipment.
4. Radios, television receivers, and phonographs.
5. Industrial equipment and parts.
6. Service and repair.

Some products were marketed through wholesalers, while others were sold directly to industrial consumers by the company's own sales force. Colleyford had a sales force of approximately 40 men and women. Although some of them tended to concentrate on one or two product groups, they all handled all the company's lines.

Baumgartner was allowed to manufacture any product his plant was equipped to produce. The types and amounts of this production were included in the budget that he submitted to headquarters each November. The parent-company headquarters then informed him which factories would supply his remaining requirements. The prices charged for these intergroup transfers were established by the head office in advance of budget preparation.

Two or three staff executives from the parent company's headquarters ordinarily spent a week or so at the Colleyford offices while the budget was being prepared and were also in frequent communication by telephone. They offered their advice and suggestions and raised questions about parts of the budget proposal as it was in process. Baumgartner usually presented his budget to the parent company in person at the end of November; and the final budget received from headquarters in December was ordinarily almost identical to the one Baumgartner submitted.

a. What benefits might Baumgartner reap from the company's system of budgetary planning? Comment on possible reasons for his attitude toward the budget and offer suggestions as to what might be done to give him a more favorable view of the budgetary process.

b. Discuss the problems of data classification in Colleyford, Inc. What kinds of data should the profit plan include, and how should these data be subdivided and classified?

9. Budgeting Decisions: Identifying Criteria and Data Required. A consulting firm has a professional staff of 10, giving it a capacity to provide 1,500 hours of consulting service in an average month. Commitments to and from the company's present clients will require the firm to provide them with approximately 1,000 hours of service in each of the next six months, yielding revenues of approximately $40,000 a month and project-related expenses of $10,000 a month. Salaries of the professional staff amount to $25,000 a month; rent, and other office expenses average $8,000 a month.

The firm would like to submit bids for four additional consulting projects to be completed during the next six months. The staff have been working closely on these with the prospective clients and are quite convinced that the firm will be given the assignments if it can promise completion within the six-month period. The estimates for these four projects are as follows:

	Project A	Project B	Project C	Project D
Hours per month	125	250	375	450
Consulting fees to be charged to the client each month	$5,000	$6,000	$16,500	$22,500
Unreimbursed project expenses per month (other than salaries of professional staff, rent, and other office expenses)	$ 100	$ 500	$ 7,500	$ 9,000

a. What should the firm do? Show your calculations.
b. What criterion or criteria did you use in reaching your conclusions?
c. What other kinds of information about these projects would you, as the budget officer, find useful and perhaps essential in the development of a budget for the next six months?

10. Budgeting Cash Receipts and Cash Disbursements. Alumabilt, Inc., is making an effort to manage its cash more effectively and profitably. It therefore is developing a forecast of two critical components of March 19x3 cash receipts and cash disbursements.

Sales in March are expected to be $3.2 million: 90 percent cash sales and 10 percent credit sales. Accounts receivable as of March 1 are $300,000: one quarter represents January credit sales, the remainder represents February sales. Pre-19x3 receivables either have been collected or were written off as uncollectible.

Alumabilt believes that its past experience with collecting accounts receivable is likely to continue as follows:

In the month of sale	20%
In the first month after the month of sale	50%
In the second month after the month of sale	25%
Written off as uncollectible at the end of the second month after the month of sale	5%

Alumabilt has also prepared the following information relating to inventory payments during March 19x3:

Cost of Inventory on hand, March 1	$180,000
Estimated cost of goods sold for March	900,000
Estimated cost of inventory on hand, March 31	160,000
Estimated payments in March for pre-March purchases	210,000
Percentage of March purchases expected to be paid in March	80%

a. What are the expected cash receipts for March 19x3?

b. What are the expected cash disbursements for inventory for March 19x3?

(AICPA adapted)

11. Cash Budgeting. Analysis of alternative marketing plans led Ross Company's management to adopt a tentative profit plan and capital budget for 19x2 calling for the following:

	Projected for 19x2	Increase (Decrease) Over 19x1
Profit plan:		
Sales revenues	$1,000,000	$100,000
Cost of goods sold	550,000*	50,000
Marketing expense	200,000	30,000
Administrative expense	100,000	5,000
Interest expense	75,000	(5,000)
Tax expense	30,000	6,000
Cash dividends to shareholders	80,000	10,000
Debt retirement	50,000	50,000
Capital budget	120,000	55,000

* Includes $40,000 depreciation

Ross's controller made the following estimates of the determinants of cash flow:

Collections from customers:	19x2 sales revenues, less 10 percent of increase over 19x1
Payments for production:	19x2 production costs, less depreciation and less 10 percent of increase over 19x1
Production costs:*	19x2 cost of goods sold, plus 5 percent of increase in cost of goods sold over 19x1

Payments for marketing:	19x2 marketing expense, less 5 percent of increase over 19x1
Interest payments:	$75,000
Payments for administration:	19x2 administrative expense
Tax payments:	$20,000
Dividend payments:	$80,000
Debt retirement payments:	$50,000
Payments for capital expenditures:	$115,000

* Production costs totaled $542,500 in 19x1

Proposed capital expenditures consist of eight major proposals and a $20,000 general allowance for minor replacements and other expenditures that will seem appropriate during the year. The debt retirement is to "clean up the balance sheet," now that no call premium has to be paid. The debt still has five years to maturity.

a. Prepare a tentative cash budget for Ross Company for 19x2.
b. Ross Company's treasurer determined that no more than $100,000 in cash could be obtained in 19x2 from sources other than cash flow from operations. Describe the actions management might take in response to that information.

12. Flexible Profit and Cash Budgets. Grant Fabrics, Inc., manufactures synthetic fabrics. Its profit plan for the coming year is as follows:

Sales revenues	$14,000,000
Cost of goods sold	10,000,000
Gross margin	4,000,000
Marketing expense	1,800,000
Administrative expense	800,000
Income before taxes	1,400,000
Income tax expense	550,000
Net income	$ 850,000

The operating cash flow associated with this plan is $1.3 million, and the cash budget for the year contains the following:

Sources of cash:		
Operating cash flows		$1,300,000
Borrowing		1,000,000
Total sources of cash		2,300,000
Uses of cash:		
Capital expenditures	$1,800,000	
Dividends	900,000	
Total uses of cash		2,700,000
Decrease in cash balance		$ 400,000

Management is concerned about the probable consequences of a shortfall in sales volume because the company has used almost all of its borrowing capacity. Management estimates that the cost of goods sold will increase or decrease by 60 percent of any increase or decrease in sales revenues. (All production cost variances are included in the cost of goods sold.) Marketing expenses increase or decrease by 3 percent of any increase or decrease in sales revenues. Income tax expense will increase or decrease by 40 percent of the change in pretax income. Finally, operating cash flow will increase or decrease by 20 percent of any change in sales revenues.

a. Estimate the probable impact on net income and on operating cash flow of a 10 percent reduction in sales revenues.

b. What kinds of flexibility can management build into its budget in response to this information?

13. Revising a Budget Proposal; Criteria. Division A is a marketing division of LMN Company. It acquires the products it sells from LMN's central manufacturing division. It has just presented its capital and operating budget proposals for next year to LMN's central budget office for review and consolidation with the proposals submitted by the company's five other operating divisions and by the company's central-office departments. Division A's proposed operating budget for next year contains the following:

	Product X		Product Y		Product Z		Total	
	This Year	Next Year	This Year	Next Year	This Year	Next Year	This Year	Next Year
Revenues	$130	$140	$ 50	$ 55	—	$ 30	$180	$225
Variable expense.	65	70	35	40	—	25	100	135
Contribution margin	65	70	15	15	—	5	80	90
Fixed expenses	20	22	8	9	—	11	28	42
Profit contribution.	45	48	7	6	—	(6)	52	48
General expenses							20	25
Income before taxes . . .							$ 32	$ 23

Budgeted sales revenues in each line represent realistic estimates of the amounts achievable next year, given the division's proposed marketing plan. No additional revenues can be realized without additional marketing expenditures, and the division's management has concluded that additional marketing expenditures next year would not bring in enough additional revenues to justify the expenditures. All marketing expenditures are classified in the table above as "fixed expenses" and make up virtually the entire amount of fixed expenses.

Products X and Y are long-established products in the company's line which still appear to have some years of slow growth ahead of them. Product Z is a new product that the division's management believes can reach a sales volume of $150 and a contribution margin ratio of 40 percent within five years, with fixed expenses leveling off at no more than $25 a year at that volume.

Implementation of LMN's strategic plans for its other divisions next year will leave only enough manufacturing capacity to support total *variable expense* of $115 for division A. Accordingly, division A's management has been told to submit a revised budget that will conform to this constraint.

If it can't get enough manufacturing capacity to meet the needs of its proposed level of sales, division A can curtail its marketing plans for its three products, but marketing requirements are such that if the *revenues* for any product are reduced to less than a specified level, that product would have to be withdrawn from the market entirely. These specified minimum revenue levels are $100, $44, and $30, respectively, for the three products.

If budgeted revenues for any product are reduced to the specified minimum level, division A will submit a revised fixed expense budget of $20, $8, or $11 for product X, Y, or Z, respectively. Complete withdrawal of any product from the market would enable the division to eliminate that product's fixed expenses in their entirety. At any other production level for any product, budgeted fixed expense would be at the level listed in the originally proposed budget.

Division A's proposed general expenses would be unaffected by any of these changes.

a. Prepare a revised operating budget proposal that you, as manager of division A, would submit to top management. Explain and defend any decisions you had to make in developing this revised proposal.

b. LMN's chief executive officer is convinced that division A's general expenses are too high and is considering three alternative proposals for reducing them: (a) imposing a maximum dollar amount to be spent; (b) imposing a 9 percent maximum ratio of general expenses to sales revenues; or (c) requiring the management of division A to submit a detailed general expense proposal subdivided according to the kinds of functions to be performed, with a justification for each portion of the proposed level of spending for each function. Under either of the first two alternatives, the division manager would decide which general-expense activities would take place. Under the third alternative, the chief executive officer and head office staff would make the final decisions on how much would be spent and for what purposes. Discuss the strengths and weaknesses of these three alternatives and describe the approach you would recommend.

14. Budgeting Decisions: Ranking Competing Proposals. You have just been appointed budget director of a manufacturing company, responsible for reviewing and coordinating the budget proposals submitted by the company's operating executives. On your first day on the job, you are given the following summaries of budget proposals for each of the company's three products:

	Product A	Product B	Product C
Sales revenues	$240,000	$120,000	$40,000
Expenses:			
Manufacturing cost of the goods sold	120,000	72,000	28,000
Sales salaries.	32,000	12,000	4,000
Travel and entertainment	48,000	16,000	4,800
Advertising	20,000	4,000	2,400
Total expenses	220,000	104,000	39,200
Product profit margin	$ 20,000	$ 16,000	$ 800

All three products are sold by the same sales force. The advertising costs in each of the budget proposals are specific to the particular product line, however; that is, each advertising amount in the table is the amount the company proposes spending to advertise that particular product.

The three products are manufactured in the same factory, but each product has its own production line in the factory. The finishing operation on each product must be performed on highly sophisticated equipment, however, and this equipment is so expensive that separate installations for each product line would be uneconomical. For this reason, the factory has only one finishing department, which performs the finishing operations on all the company's products.

The manufacturing cost of goods sold amounts in the budget proposals summarized above were made up as follows:

	Product A	Product B	Product C
Direct materials	$ 16,000	$10,000	$ 4,500
Direct labor:			
Finishing department	8,000	12,800	2,000
Other departments	28,000	10,000	6,000
Overhead:			
Finishing department	12,000	19,200	3,000
Other departments	56,000	20,000	12,500
Total cost of goods sold	$120,000	$72,000	$28,000

The finishing department has a total practical capacity of 2,500 hours a month. The budget proposals summarized above call for the following amount of time in the finishing department:

Product A . . . . . . 1,000 hours
Product B . . . . . . 1,600 hours
Product C . . . . . .   250 hours

Finishing work can also be performed by independent local firms at a cost of $25 an hour.

a. Outline the steps you would take in reviewing the proposed budgets for the three product lines. Illustrate each step, using amounts supplied here, and indicate how you would decide how much finishing work should be performed by outside contractors.

b. What additional classifications of these costs would help you in making the budgeting decisions your review procedures would require? Explain how these classifications would help.

15. Budgeting Decisions: Profitability and Feasibility. The president of Ethelred, Inc., has a commitment from the company's bank for a loan of $100,000 if the company needs it during the coming year. No other outside source of cash will be available during the year.

Ethelred provides bookkeeping services to local business firms and other organizations and has been growing rapidly in recent years. Its experience has been that accounts receivable increase as its sales volume increases. A $10 increase in annual sales volume will require a $1 increase in accounts receivable.

If the company continues its present operations, maintaining its sales force at current levels, total sales volume will increase next year by $100,000 and reported income will be:

Sales	$1,100,000
Expenses (including $10,000 depreciation)	980,000
Net income	$ 120,000

The company's present facilities will be adequate to handle this sales volume, requiring capital expenditures of only $12,000 for routine replacement of furniture and equipment.

The company's president would like to add another sales representative to contact a new group of potential customers. Additional data-processing equipment would have to be rented to handle any business the new sales representative brought in. These changes would increase Ethelred's annual operating expenses by the following amounts:

Sales representative's salary and expenses	$22,000
Equipment rental	30,000
Other expenses	60,000 + 10% of added sales

The president believes that the additional sales volume from this market would amount to $50,000 in the first year, but it might amount to nothing at all. If the operation proved successful, revenues in later years would be substantially higher.

Ethelred's shareholders have received cash dividends of $50,000 in each of the last three years, and the board of directors has tentatively decided to increase the dividend next year to $60,000 if the cash flow is adequate. It also wishes to contribute $20,000 to the local art museum as a community service.

a. Are these proposals feasible? Prepare a tentative profit plan and a tentative cash budget to support your answer. You may assume that all expenses other than depreciation and all equipment expenditures must be accompanied by immediate cash payments.

b. What action should the president take? If you conclude that you lack enough information on which to base a recommendation, identify the issues which still need to be resolved before a recommendation can be made.

16. Revising a Proposed Budget.   Noting substantial increases in the proposed levels of marketing and administrative costs over those of the current year, Darnell Company's budget director asked the company's three division managers for additional information to be used in reviewing the divisional budget proposals summarized in problem 1. It wasn't clear how much of the increases were due to changes in prices and how much resulted from changes in the amount or structure of marketing effort.

To supplement the forecasted results for the proposed marketing plans, the budget director asked each division manager for estimates of the following:

1. This year's results.
2. The results to be expected next year if this year's marketing program were to be continued unchanged.
3. The results to be expected next year if marketing and administrative expenses were to be kept at this year's levels (an "austerity budget").

With the help of personnel from the central market-research and controller's departments, the division managers supplied the following additional data:

	Division A	Division B	Division C
Expected results this year from this year's program:			
Sales	$800	$2,000	$2,000
Cost of goods sold	496	1,200	1,200
Marketing expenses	120	380	280
Administrative expenses	110	200	190
Accounts receivable, year-end	40	350	330
Inventories, year-end	195	320	360
Accounts payable, year-end	60	120	550
Expected results next year if this year's program were to be repeated:			
Sales	840	2,400	2,000
Cost of goods sold	546	1,392	1,260
Marketing expenses	125	400	300
Administrative expenses	120	220	200
Accounts receivable, year-end	42	400	330
Inventories, year-end	215	368	360
Accounts payable, year-end	64	141	550

	Division A	Division B	Division C
Expected results under austerity budget:			
Sales	820	2,100	1,900
Cost of goods sold	533	1,218	1,197
Marketing expenses	120	380	280
Administrative expenses	110	200	190
Accounts receivable, year-end	41	360	314
Inventories, year-end	205	324	332
Accounts payable, year-end	62	124	517

Central administrative expenses for the current year are expected to total $380, cash purchases of equipment will amount to $120, and cash dividends of $300 will be paid. Depreciation expenses included in the administrative expenses are: central management, $10; division A, $5; division B, $15; division C, $20.

a. Calculate expected net income for the current year.

b. Prepare a profit plan on the assumption that current marketing programs will be continued next year. (Central administrative expenses would be at their proposed level, $400.)

c. Prepare an austerity budget profit plan on the assumption that marketing and administrative expenses next year are held to this year's level. (Under an austerity budget, central administrative expenses would amount to $395.)

d. Assuming that these estimates are sound, and basing your recommendations solely on the amounts given in these two problems, what action should Darnell's management take on the budget proposals?

Chapter 21

The Capital-Expenditure Decision

The relatively short-term decisions described in Chapters 16 and 17 were shown to be based on estimates of their effects on the organization's cash flows in a single time period no longer than a year. That approach is inadequate when management is faced with an *investment* decision. An **investment problem** is a situation requiring management to decide whether to expend cash in one or more time periods to obtain cash inflows in *another* time period or periods.

One of the most important types of investment problems is the capital-expenditure decision, in which an initial cash outlay—**the capital expenditure**—is made in the expectation that it will produce cash receipts in a later year or years. Typical examples are proposals to build, acquire, replace, or expand long-lived productive assets.

The approval process for capital expenditures typically has two major phases. In the first phase, general approval is given to the *overall* level of capital spending during the coming year, including *preliminary* approval of specific major proposals that will be submitted in detail later on. This is done as part of the annual budgetary process. For example, the capital budget adopted by Darwin Books, Inc., in Chapter 20 constituted both final approval for the *level* of capital spending incorporated in that budget and *preliminary* approval for major proposals.

In the second phase, management makes its final decision on each specific proposal. This occurs when the sponsor of the proposal is ready to begin committing funds to expenditure by placing orders, letting contracts, etc. The purpose of this chapter is to see how management can decide whether specific capital-expenditure proposals are good enough both to be included in the capital budget and to get final approval when the time comes for the expenditures to be made.

The Net Present Value Approach

The most widely recommended method of evaluating proposals to make capital expenditures is to calculate for each proposal the **net present value** of the anticipated cash flows. This method requires using an interest rate representing the company's minimum acceptable rate of return on investment. The focal point of the net present value method is the time-value-of-money concept which was explained in detail in Chapter 6. The long-term nature of capital-expenditure decisions understandably demands that all cash flow amounts—both positive and negative—be expressed in a common dimension. Since the capital-expenditure decision is made now, the dimension we use is the cash flow's present value.

> ### TERMINOLOGY REMINDER
>
> The present value of a future sum of cash is the amount that must be invested now at the specified rate of compound interest to grow to an amount equal to the future sum at the specified future date.

The Procedure

Implementing the net present value approach entails treating all estimates as equivalent to amounts that can be predicted with certainty. The analysis in this form consists of four steps:

1. Identify the proposal and at least one alternative to accepting it.
2. Estimate the cash flows, year by year, that would result if the proposal were accepted; make a similar set of estimates for each alternative being considered. Enter these estimates in a table known as a *timetable,* in which each row identifies a period or point in time and each column lists a series of cash flows associated with a particular alternative.
3. Determine, by using appropriate present-value calculations, the *net* present value of the estimated cash flows associated with each alternative. The net present value of an alternative is the algebraic sum of the present values of the estimated cash inflows (receipts) and estimated cash outflows (outlays) associated with that alternative.
4. Choose the alternative with the highest net present value.

An Illustration

The best way to explain the net present value method is through an illustration. In the next few paragraphs, we'll see how Barclay Company can evaluate a proposal to spend $34,000 to buy new labor-saving equipment. We'll call this *proposal A.*

Step 1: Identify the Alternatives. To evaluate proposal A, management has to identify at least one alternative to accepting it. If it has no alternative, it has no decision to make. In this case, management has decided to introduce only one alternative: *reject proposal A.*

Step 2: Estimate the Cash Flows. One way to proceed would be to estimate the cash flows for the entire company under each alternative. This might be necessary for truly major capital-expenditure proposals that would affect the basic nature and structure of the company's operations. A simpler approach, adequate for most capital-expenditure decisions, is to select one alternative as a benchmark and measure the cash flows of each other alternative as differences from that benchmark. In this case, management has selected "reject proposal A" as the benchmark alternative. The estimated cash flows from accepting proposal A relative to this benchmark are shown in the following table:

Years from Now	Cash Flow
0	−$34,000
1	+ 10,000
2	+ 10,000
3	+ 10,000
4	+ 10,000
5	+ 10,000
Total	+$16,000

In this table, cash receipts are identified by + signs; the cash outlay is identified by a − sign. Since the five anticipated annual cash inflows (receipts) in this case are identical, we can also show them in the timetable as a five-year annuity of $10,000 a year.

Step 3: Estimate the Net Present Value of Each Alternative. The prices investors pay for Barclay Company's stocks and bonds establish the rate of return they demand as their reward for investing in the company. This demanded rate is known as the **cost of capital** and is discussed more fully in the appendix to this chapter.

Barclay estimates that *its* cost of capital is 10 percent: its management therefore insists that the capital expenditures it makes promise a rate of return of 10 percent or more as well. To test an expenditure's ability to earn this much, Barclay's management determines the estimated present value of the expected cash flows at an interest rate of 10 percent, compounded annually. The present-value multiplier for a five-year annuity at 10 percent (from Table 2 of Appendix A) is 3.7908, and the present value of the anticipated cash flows associated with this proposal is as follows:

Years from Now	Cash Flow	Present Value at 10 Percent	
		Multiplier	Amount
0	−$34,000	1.0000	−$34,000
1 to 5	+ 10,000 a year	3.7908	+ 37,908
Net present value			+$ 3,908

Step 4: Choose the Best Alternative. Barclay Company has recognized only one alternative to accepting proposal A: *reject proposal A* and continue present operations unchanged. The cash flows in the tables above represent the *differences* between the results with proposal A and the results with this benchmark alternative. The estimated net present value in the table above therefore is an *incremental* net present value, the *difference* between the net present value of proposal A and the net present value of the benchmark alternative. The difference between the net present values is positive in this case, meaning that the cash flows proposal A is expected to generate will be more than enough (1) to recover the $34,000 initial outlay *and* (2) to provide a 10 percent rate of return on the company's investment. The *excess* cash flows have a present value of $3,908. Since the company finds 10 percent an acceptable rate of return, it should accept proposal A.

Multiple Alternatives

The procedure we've just described can be applied to proposals with several alternatives as well. This is particularly important, because for major capital-expenditure proposals management should insist that a real effort be made to identify one or more alternative proposals that might fill the same needs in different ways. Once this has been done, management should select the proposal with the highest positive net present value; if none of the proposals has a positive net value, all should be rejected.

For example, we saw that proposal A has an estimated net present value of $3,908. Let's now assume, however, that management could accept either proposal B or proposal C. The cash flows and multipliers for proposals B and C are shown in Exhibit 21–1. Proposal B offers a *higher* net present value than proposal A; the net present value of proposal C is lower than that of either of the other two. Proposal B therefore should be chosen.

Reasons for the Net Present Value Approach

Net present value is used as the measure of the desirability of a capital-expenditure proposal mainly for two reasons:

1. It provides a means of testing whether the estimated cash inflows are adequate to (*a*) cover the cost of capital, *and* (*b*) recover the outlays required by the proposal.
2. It takes into account differences in the *timing* of the cash flows associated with individual proposals.

EXHIBIT 21–1
Present Value of Multiple Alternatives

	(1)	*(2)*	*(3)*	*(4)*	*(5)*
		Proposal B		**Proposal C**	
Years from Now	**Present Value Multiplier at 10 Percent***	**Cash Flow**	**Present Value *(1) × (2)***	**Cash Flow**	**Present Value *(4) × (1)***
0	1.0000	−$56,000	−$56,000	−$45,000	−$45,000
1	0.9091	+ 16,000	+ 14,546	+ 15,000	+ 13,636
2	0.8264	+ 16,000	+ 13,222	+ 15,000	+ 12,396
3	0.7513	+ 16,000	+ 12,021	+ 15,000	+ 11,270
4	0.6830	+ 16,000	+ 10,928	+ 10,000	+ 6,830
5	0.6209	+ 16,000	+ 9,934	+ 5,000	+ 3,105
Net present value.			+$ 4,651		+$ 2,237

* From Table 1, Appendix A.

Capital Recovery.   *Net* present value is the present value of the cash flows that aren't needed to recover the initial outlay or cover the cost of capital. To illustrate, let's go back to proposal A, for which the initial outlays are expected to be $34,000. The first year's interest on $34,000 at 10 percent amounts to $3,400. Since $10,000 in cash is received, the remaining $6,600 can be treated as a partial recovery of the original investment. This leaves an unrecovered balance of $27,400 at the end of the first year. These calculations are summarized in the first line of Exhibit 21–2.

The $27,400 unrecovered investment at the end of year 1 is also the unrecovered investment at the beginning of year 2, and this is shown in column (2) in the second line in the exhibit. Interest on that amount in the second year is $2,740, leaving $7,260 of the second year's cash receipts to be treated as the recovery of another portion of the initial outlay. This brings the unrecovered portion of the outlay down to $20,140, shown on the second line in column (4).

Continuing these calculations for three more years completes the table. As this shows, by the end of the fifth year, the entire investment has been recovered, despite annual interest payments at a 10 percent rate, and the company still has $6,294 left over. In other words, Barclay could have

EXHIBIT 21–2
Capital Recovery under Proposal A

Year	(1) Unrecovered Investment, Beginning of Year	(2) Interest at 10 Percent [0.1 × (1)]	(3) Amortization of Investment [$10,000 − (2)]	(4) Unrecovered Investment, End of Year (1) − (3)
1......	$34,000	$3,400	$6,600	$27,400
2......	27,400	2,740	7,260	20,140
3......	20,140	2,014	7,986	12,154
4......	12,154	1,215	8,785	3,369
5......	3,369	337	9,663	(6,294)

paid *more* than 10 percent interest from the cash inflows stemming from this investment.

This capital recovery pattern is shown diagramatically in Exhibit 21–3. The company starts at the left with a $34,000 unrecovered outlay, shown as the point from which the curved line leaves the vertical axis. As time passes, the amount unrecovered gradually diminishes and the curve gets closer and closer to the horizontal zero line. Sometime in the fifth year, the last dollar of capital is recovered and the curved line crosses the zero line. Beyond that point, with all capital already recovered, the project generates *excess* cash flows amounting to $6,294. This is the future value, five years later, of the $3,908 present value we calculated earlier for proposal A, compounded annually at 10 percent [$3,908 ÷ (Table 1, $r = 0.10$, $n = 5$) 0.6209 = $6,294].

EXHIBIT 21–3
The Investment-Recovery Pattern

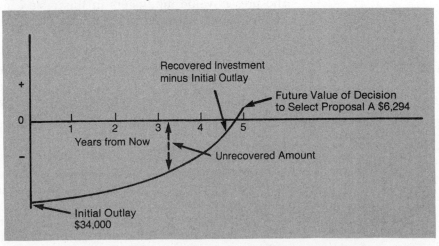

Timing Differences. A second important feature of net present value is that it takes into account the *timing* of the anticipated cash flows. For example, suppose Barclay Company can invest in any or all of the following proposals:

Years from Now	Net Cash Receipts (+) or Outlays (−)		
	Proposal X	Proposal Y	Proposal Z
0...................	−$13,000	−$13,000	−$13,000
1...................	+ 1,000	+ 5,000	+ 9,000
2...................	+ 5,000	+ 5,000	+ 5,000
3...................	+ 9,000	+ 5,000	+ 1,000
Net cash flow	+$ 2,000	+$ 2,000	+$ 2,000

These three proposals have identical lifetime net cash flows—$2,000—but they are far from equally desirable. Proposal Z is the best because cash is received earlier under this proposal than under either of the others. Proposal X is the worst of the three.

These differences can be quantified with present-value calculations. Assuming a 10 percent interest rate, the net present values of these proposals are:

Years from Now	Present-Value Multipliers	Proposal X	Proposal Y	Proposal Z
0........	1.0000	−$13,000	−$13,000	−$13,000
1........	0.9091	+ 909	+ 4,545	+ 8,182
2........	0.8264	+ 4,132	+ 4,132	+ 4,132
3........	0.7513	+ 6,762	+ 3,757	+ 751
Net present value		−$ 1,197	−$ 566	+$ 65

The present-value multipliers in this table came from the 10 percent column in Table 1 in Appendix A.

In this case, proposals X and Y promise a return on investment of less than 10 percent; only proposal Z promises a return in excess of 10 percent. Therefore, only proposal Z should be accepted. The net present value measure, in other words, permits management to compare proposals that differ in the timing of their cash flows.

Internal Rate of Return

Use of the net present value approach can take on a somewhat different format. Rather than express the method's findings in terms of an absolute dollar amount, some managers prefer to evaluate company activities by the rate of return the activities produce. For this reason, some companies use the **internal rate of return** to measure the incremental value of a capital-expenditure proposal. The internal rate of return is the rate of interest at which the incremental net present value of a proposal is zero. Calculating the internal rate of return is a three-step, trial-and-error process:

1. Calculate the present values of all cash flows at a trial rate.
2. Calculate the present values of all cash flows at a second trial rate.
3. Interpolate.

Step 1: Use of First Trial Rate. We have already performed this step for Barclay's proposal A. The net present value of the cash flows at 10 percent is $3,908. This indicates that the rate of return is *greater* than 10 percent, but it doesn't show how much greater.

Step 2: Use of Second Trial Rate. Since we now know that the internal rate of return is higher than 10 percent, a reasonable second trial rate is 15 percent. The multipliers and present values at this rate are as follows:

Years from Now	Cash Flow	Present Value at 15 Percent Multiplier	Amount
0	−$34,000	1.0000	−$34,000
1–5	+ 10,000 a year	3.3522	+ 33,522
Net present value.........................			−$ 478

The present value of the cash receipts at the 15 percent interest rate is only $33,522, or $478 less than the initial outlay required by proposal A. In other words, at a 15 percent rate, net present value is *negative*. This means that the cash inflows aren't big enough to produce a rate of return as high as 15 percent.

Step 3: Interpolation. The internal rate of return from proposal A *is greater than 10 percent* because the cash inflows are expected to be more than adequate to cover a 10 percent cost of capital; the estimated net present value is positive at 10 percent. The internal rate of return *is less than 15 percent* because the cash inflows are expected to be less than adequate to cover a 15 percent cost of capital; the estimated net present value is negative at 15 percent.

The *correct* rate therefore is somewhere between 10 and 15 percent. To locate it precisely, we could determine the present value of the cash flows at various interest rates between 10 and 15 percent until we found the rate at which proposal A's estimated net present value was zero. In general, however, an approximation obtained by interpolating between two points on a graph, as in Exhibit 21–4, will be close enough.

EXHIBIT 21-4
Interpolating to Approximate the Internal Rate of Return

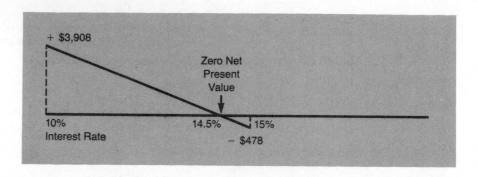

We can make this same calculation algebraically, using as our focal point $4,386, the total distance between +$3,908 and −$478:

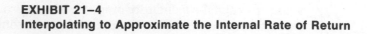

$$\text{Approximate rate} = 10\% + \frac{\$3,908}{\$3,908 + \$478} \times (15\% - 10\%) = 14.5\%$$

Estimating Cash Flows

Any subdivision of the cash flows associated with a capital-expenditure proposal is partly arbitrary. All that matters is the *amount* and *timing* of the cash flows; whether some are called capital outlays while others are called maintenance expenses is relevant only insofar as the classification coincides with the classification scheme used by the taxing authorities to determine the tax effects of the outlays. Even so, we find it convenient to distinguish four components of the cash-flow stream:

1. The initial outlay.
2. Subsequent investment outlays.
3. Operating cash flows.
4. End-of-life residual values.

The Initial Outlay

The initial outlay consists of all the cash outflows that must take place *before* significant operating cash receipts or cash cost savings begin to flow in. It contains some or all of the following:

1. Cash outlays for plant and equipment.
2. Opportunity costs of existing facilities to be incorporated in the proposal.

3. Outlays for working capital.
4. Disposal values of facilities to be displaced by the proposal.
5. Immediate income tax effects.

Plant and Equipment.   For most proposals, the major outlays are for the acquisition and installation of physical facilities. For example, a proposal to modernize a portion of Barclay Company's factory is expected to require the following outlays before the investment begins to bring in cash receipts:

Equipment	$80,000
Installation	10,000
Training and test runs	7,000
Total	$97,000

If these outlays are spread over a period longer than a few months, accuracy will be served if they are split up and entered into the cash-flow timetable at the amounts associated with each time period. In this case, however, Barclay's management estimates that they'll all take place within a very short time, which we'll refer to as the **zero date** for present-value calculations.

Existing Facilities Used.   One of Barclay's present machines, now idle, will be put back in service only if the modernization proposal is approved. No cash needs to be paid for this machine since the company already owns it. Even so, it does belong since in the timetable of cash flows. By accepting the proposal, management will make this machine unavailable for any other use. This proposal therefore should be charged for the machine's value in its best other use—that is, its opportunity cost.

TERMINOLOGY REMINDER

Opportunity cost is the value of the opportunity the company must forgo if it wishes to divert a resource for use in a proposed course of action.

In this case, Barclay's management has decided that the machine will be sold if it isn't needed for the modernization proposal. The estimated sale price is $12,000. This is part of the investment outlay because, in accepting the proposal, the company is depriving itself of $12,000 in cash:

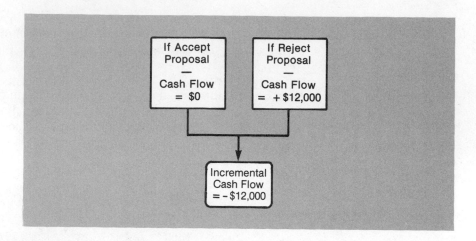

A cash receipt forgone is always equivalent to a cash outlay. By contrast, since the book value of the equipment measures neither current nor future cash flows, it is ignored.

Working Capital. Capital-expenditure proposals often require outlays for resources other than land, buildings, and equipment. Cash outlays for product development, working capital, or market research are just as much a part of the investment required by a capital-expenditure proposal as are outlays for plant assets.

The only additional outlays required by our illustrative modernization proposal are for working capital. To use the new equipment effectively, management will have to increase inventories by $5,000. Suppliers will finance only $3,000 of this amount. In addition, management will have to immobilize $1,000 of its cash balances to support the additional activity the proposal will generate. Putting these estimates together, we get an estimated working-capital requirement of $3,000, all to be provided at the time the equipment is put in place:

Cash	$ 1,000
Inventory.	5,000
Accounts payable	(3,000)
Working capital	$ 3,000

The proposal also calls for a further increase in working capital, as additional receivables are created by the first year's operations. Although it is often convenient to include this increase as part of the initial outlay, we'll handle it as part of the *operating* cash flow because it actually arises when sales revenues exceed collections from customers in the period of sales expansion.

Displaced Facilities. The cash flows we've mentioned so far haven't included one additional determinant of the initial outlay. If the proposal is accepted, Barclay will be able to dispose of a machine serving a standby purpose. This machine has a tax basis (book value for tax purposes) of only $1,000, but once again opportunity cost, *not* book value, is the right measure of the cash flow. Opportunity cost is measured by the machine's scrap value, $6,000. The displaced machine, in other words, can finance $6,000 of the gross pretax outlays the proposal will require.

This may become clearer if we recognize that we're really comparing two alternatives in our cash-flow estimates:

A Accept the Proposal and Dispose of Existing Standby Equipment +$6,000	**B** Reject the Proposal and Keep the Standby Equipment +$0

The only way to get the $6,000 cash inflow is to accept this proposal. It therefore becomes a cash *inflow* attributable to the proposal and must be included in the analysis.

Tax Effects of the Initial Outlay

Income taxes are cash flows. Like other cash flows, their amount and timing can affect the present value of capital-expenditure proposals.

Each country has its own rules of taxation, and individual states, provinces, and local government bodies may also tax the organization's income. These rules are often extremely complex; they also change frequently. For these reasons, we can only illustrate how some kinds of tax provisions can affect the cash flows, if they happen to be applicable.

Tax rates also vary and different tax rates may apply to different portions of the taxable income stream. To simplify the presentation, we'll assume that a tax rate of 40 percent is applied to all amounts that enter into the calculation of taxable income. We'll also assume that the company has taxable income from other sources to offset any losses the proposal generates for tax purposes. Losses therefore are also subject to the 40 percent tax rate.[1]

---

[1] The principle here is that since a loss is included as a negative determinant of a company's taxable income, the tax will be reduced as a result. Accordingly, the cash-flow effect of a loss is measured by its pretax cash flow, less the tax rate applied to the loss as determined for tax purposes. If the taxable loss is equal to the pretax cash outflow, and if the income tax rate is 40 percent, the aftertax effect of a pretax loss is 60 percent of its gross amount.

Our initial outlay has four separate kinds of tax effects: a tax credit, a tax deduction, a tax-deductible loss, and a taxable gain. (A tax credit is a direct reduction in the amount of tax due; a tax deduction is a reduction in the amount of taxable income on which the tax due is based.)

Tax Credit.   Many governments offer tax credits to induce businesses to invest in facilities or to increase their inventories, thereby creating jobs and stimulating the economy. In our illustration, the $80,000 outlay for new equipment is eligible for a 10 percent tax credit. This will reduce the tax by $8,000, and this amount should be deducted in calculating the initial outlay because Barclay's investment effectively is $72,000 ($80,000 − $8,000).

Tax Deduction.   Both the purchase price and the installation cost of the new equipment will be capitalized initially and depreciated for tax purposes over a period of years. The $7,000 in training and test-run costs, however, will be fully deductible for tax purposes right away. At a 40 percent tax rate, this will reduce current taxes by $2,800. The aftertax outlay for these items therefore is $7,000 − $2,800 = $4,200.

Tax-Deductible Loss.   We have already seen that accepting the proposal will deprive the company of the $12,000 cash flow from selling an idle machine. It will also deprive the company of the right to enter the loss from the sale of the machine on the current income tax return. The loss for tax purposes is the difference between the proceeds from the sale and the book value for tax purposes (the tax basis), which in this case happens to be $20,000:

Sale value	$12,000
Tax basis	20,000
Tax-deductible loss	$ 8,000

Since the sale of this machine would reduce taxable income, it would also reduce taxes. Using the machine will deprive the company of this reduction. It thus becomes another incremental cash outflow arising from the proposed expenditure. At a tax rate of 40 percent, the tax effect is $3,200. The aftertax cash inflow is:

Sale value forgone		$12,000
Tax basis	$20,000	
Sale value	12,000	
Tax-deductible loss	8,000	
Tax rate	×40%	
Tax increase due to loss deferred		3,200
Aftertax cash outflow		$15,200

Taxable Gain. The final element in the initial outlay calculation, the sale of the displaced machine, also has a tax effect. The market value of this machine is $6,000 and the tax basis is $1,000, so the taxable gain is $5,000. Although we had earlier treated this displacement as a $6,000 cash inflow, we now recognize that a portion of it will not benefit Barclay because of the income tax effect. The cash flows are:

Market value	+$6,000
Tax on the gain: 40% × $5,000	− 2,000
Aftertax cash flow	+$4,000

The Aftertax Investment Outlay. All these tax-effect amounts are summarized in Exhibit 21–5. In this case the net difference between the

EXHIBIT 21–5
Calculation of Incremental Aftertax Initial Outlay

Item	Incremental Outlay before Tax	Tax Effect	Incremental Outlay after Tax
Equipment, installed...........	$ 90,000	$(8,000)	$ 82,000
Working capital...............	3,000	0	3,000
Training and test runs	7,000	(2,800)	4,200
Surplus equipment used	12,000	3,200	15,200
Equipment displaced	(6,000)	2,000	(4,000)
Total	$(106,000)	$(5,600)	$(100,400)

Alternative format:

Item	If Accept Proposal	If Reject Proposal	Incremental Cash Flow
Equipment, installed...........	−$82,000	0	−$ 82,000
Working capital...............	− 3,000	0	− 3,000
Training and test runs	− 4,200	0	− 4,200
Surplus equipment used	0	+$15,200	− 15,200
Equipment displaced	+ 4,000	0	+ 4,000
Net Outlay	−$85,200	+$15,200	−$100,400

pretax and aftertax amounts is relatively small, less than 6 percent; in other cases it can be much greater. In the exhibit's alternative format, minus signs identify cash outlays and plus signs identify cash receipts. The alternative form of display has the advantage of showing the alternatives clearly, but it obscures the tax adjustment.

Subsequent Investment Outlays

Management can often predict special outlays that will have to be made in later time periods to keep the investment alive. These, too, may be for equipment or for additional working capital. Each also has to be examined for its tax implications.

Subsequent investment outlays of this sort are no different in concept from the initial outlay and need no further discussion here. The only subsequent investment outlay Barclay's management anticipates for the plant modernization proposal is $20,000 to replace equipment at the end of the fifth year. This, too, will be eligible for a 10 percent investment credit ($2,000), thereby reducing the aftertax cash outlay to $18,000.

Operating Cash Flows

The incremental operating cash flow facing Barclay is expected to come from increased sales volume *and* from reduced operating costs. Once again, we'll present the cash flows under our two alternatives in two columns, with an incremental column at the right:

Years from Zero Date	If Accept Proposal	If Reject Proposal	Incremental Cash Flow
n	*X*	*Y*	*X − Y*

In this case, however, management has much less confidence in its ability to forecast the *absolute results* under each alternative than in its ability to forecast the differences *between* them. Although costs and therefore expenses are expected to increase from year to year, the gap between the two alternatives is expected to remain roughly constant at $9,000 a year in increased revenues and $16,000 in reduced operating expenses (other than depreciation and income taxes), a total of $25,000.

Translating Income into Cash Flow.   The $25,000 increment we just described is an *increase in operating income* before depreciation and income taxes. What we want, of course, is the increment in *cash flow*. The reasons our focal point is *predepreciation* and *pretax* are that (1) accounting depreciation has no effect on cash flow since cash flow is affected only when the depreciable asset is paid for or sold, and (2) the tax effect of tax depreciation will be discussed separately in the next section.

In this illustration we have only one adjustment to make to convert predepreciation operating income into the pretax cash flow—to reflect a $2,000, onetime increase in accounts receivable during the first year of operations. In other words, the first year's net incremental cash flow before taxes will be $2,000 less than incremental operating income, because the incremental collections from customers will be $2,000 less than the first year's increase in sales revenues. The first year's pretax operating cash flows therefore are expected to be as follows:

Increase in collections: $9,000 − $2,000........	$ 7,000
Decrease in disbursements...................	16,000
Incremental pretax cash inflow, first year	$23,000

Adjusting for Income Taxes.   The next step in the analysis is to calculate the effect of the estimated increments in operating income on the company's income taxes. In this calculation, we start with the pretax cash flows. In doing so, however, we recognize that the spread between taxable income (based on the revenues and expenses shown on the company's income tax return) is likely to differ significantly from the amount of the pretax cash flow.

One reason for the difference between the taxable income and pretax cash flow is the effect of accrual accounting on taxable income, such as in the treatment of product warranty costs. Another difference exists because of government attempts to influence taxpayer behavior by disallowing certain kinds of cash outflows as deductible expenses in calculating taxable income (e.g., court fines and penalties in some taxing jurisdictions) or by accelerating or decelerating the recognition of certain kinds of revenues or expenses.

The only significant differences between pretax cash flows and incremental taxable income in our illustration are (1) the first-year increase in receivables we just described and (2) incremental tax depreciation. Depreciation charges *aren't* cash flows; however, they do enter into the calculation of taxable income and therefore do affect the aftertax cash flow.

We'll assume that tax depreciation on the new facilities required by the proposal is on an accelerated basis somewhat similar to the accelerated cost recovery system (ACRS) used in the United States in the early 1980s. The tax life on the new equipment and on the subsequent investment outlay 5 years after the zero date is 5 years, even though the original facilities are expected to last 10 years. The applicable tax depreciation schedule for this equipment (in percentages of original cost) is as follows:

Year	Percentage
1.............	15
2.............	22
3.............	21
4.............	21
5.............	21

The existing equipment being incorporated in the project, with a present tax basis of $20,000, is depreciated for tax purposes at a straight-line amount of $5,000 a year. The standby equipment replaced by the proposal has a tax basis of $1,000, which is now depreciated by the straight-line method at $500 a year.

Depreciation calculated on these bases is summarized in Exhibit 21–6. Our reason for deducting tax depreciation on the displaced equipment

EXHIBIT 21–6
Calculation of Incremental Tax Depreciation

	(1)	(2)	(3)	(4)	(5)
	Tax Depreciation if Proposal Is Accepted			**Tax Depreciation if Proposal Is Rejected**	**Incremental Tax Depreciation (3) − (4)**
Year	**New Equipment**	**Present Equipment**	**Total**		
1	$ 13,500*	$ 5,000	$ 18,500	$ 500	$ 18,000
2	19,800*	5,000	24,800	500	24,300
3	18,900*	5,000	23,900	—	23,900
4	18,900*	5,000	23,900	—	23,900
5	18,900*	—	18,900	—	18,900
6	3,000†	—	3,000	—	3,000
7	4,400†	—	4,400	—	4,400
8	4,200†	—	4,200	—	4,200
9	4,200†	—	4,200	—	4,200
10	4,200†	—	4,200	—	4,200
Total	$110,000	$20,000	$130,000	$1,000	$129,000

* Depreciation of $90,000 cost of new equipment.
† Depreciation of $20,000 original cost of equipment purchased by subsequent outlay.

may be easier to understand if it is recognized as a simple time shift. If the proposal is accepted, the equipment will be replaced and $1,000 will be deducted immediately in the calculation of taxable income. We incorporated this $1,000 deduction in our calculation of the tax effect of the initial outlay. If the proposal is rejected, on the other hand, the equipment will be retained and Barclay Company will deduct the $1,000 on its tax returns during the next two years.

Aftertax Operating Cash Flows.   Given the before-tax cash flows and the tax depreciation amounts, we can now calculate taxable income, income tax effects, and aftertax cash flows. Exhibit 21–7 summarizes the operating cash-flow calculations. The amounts in column (1) show the estimated effect of the proposal on the company's tax returns, except for tax depreciation. The next three columns are used to calculate the income tax effect. Column (5) shows the estimated pretax cash flows, in this case identical to the amounts in column (1) except for the $2,000 increment in accounts receivable in the first year. The incremental cash

EXHIBIT 21–7
Calculation of Aftertax Operating Cash Flows

Year	(1) Incremental Income before Depreciation and Income Tax	(2) Incremental Tax Depreciation (Exhibit 21–6)	(3) Incremental Taxable Income (1) – (2)	(4) Incremental Income Tax 40% × (3)	(5) Incremental Cash Flow before Income Tax	(6) Incremental Cash Flow (5) – (4)
1........	$ 25,000	$ 18,000	$ 7,000	$ 2,800	$ 23,000	+$ 20,200
2........	25,000	24,300	700	280	25,000	+ 24,720
3........	25,000	23,900	1,100	440	25,000	+ 24,560
4........	25,000	23,900	1,100	440	25,000	+ 24,560
5........	25,000	18,900	6,100	2,440	25,000	+ 22,560
6........	25,000	3,000	22,000	8,800	25,000	+ 16,200
7........	25,000	4,400	20,600	8,240	25,000	+ 16,760
8........	25,000	4,200	20,800	8,320	25,000	+ 16,680
9........	25,000	4,200	20,800	8,320	25,000	+ 16,680
10........	25,000	4,200	20,800	8,320	25,000	+ 16,680
Total	$250,000	$129,000	$121,000	$48,400	$248,000	+$199,600

flow is then found by subtracting the incremental tax in column (4) from the pretax cash flow.

Notice how the rapid depreciation schedules provided by the taxing authority have turned a level annual pretax cash flow into an irregular stream that is much larger in the first five years than in the final five years of this proposal's estimated useful life. This makes the proposal more valuable than if only the straight-line method were available, because the present value of near-term cash flows is greater than the present value of distant cash flows.

End-of-Life Residual Value

The final cash flow associated with a capital-expenditure proposal is the cash value of the facilities and working capital remaining when the project's life comes to an end. This value is usually referred to as the **end-of-life residual value** (or, less elegantly, salvage value). Residual values are quite important for short-lived investments, less so for projects with long lives. To find out whether residual values are important, we should always prepare rough estimates except for extremely long-lived projects.

Pretax Residual Values.   Management expects the plant modernization expenditures to be productive for about 10 years, for the reasons we'll describe in the section headed "Economic Life." At the end of that time, the company can renovate the facilities once again or liquidate them. If it liquidates them, Barclay can reasonably expect to recover most of its investment in working capital, together with the residual value of the remaining equipment. Removal costs and severance pay for employees who will leave the company's employ if the operation is terminated are deducted from these amounts as well.

Barclay's management anticipates only the pretax incremental residual values shown in Exhibit 21–8. This shows that the company expects to

EXHIBIT 21–8
Calculation of Incremental Pretax Residual Value

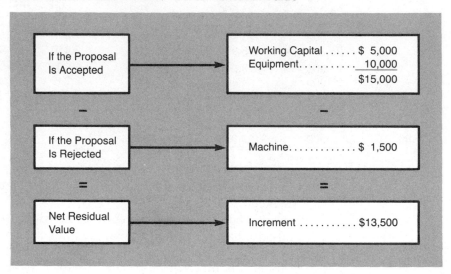

be able to recover $10,000 from the sale of equipment *and* $5,000 from the liquidation of the incremental working capital required by the proposal, a total of $15,000. The incremental residual value is $1,500 less than $15,000, however. If the proposal is rejected, the company will keep its standby machine instead of selling it now. The estimated sale value of that machine 10 years from now is $1,500, and this must be deducted in calculating the pretax incremental residual value.

Notice how we are handling the old standby machine in this analysis. The anticipated cash flows associated with this machine are as follows:

Years from Now	If Proposal Is Accepted	If Proposal Is Rejected	Incremental Cash Flow
0	+$6,000	—	+$6,000
10	—	+$1,500	− 1,500

Our approach is to enter the $6,000 as a negative determinant of the initial outlay (see Exhibit 21–5) and the $1,500 forgone residual value 10 years from now as a negative determinant of the net residual value. The effect is to subtract a total of $4,500 ($6,000 − $1,500) from the lifetime cash inflows arising from this proposed investment.

Tax Effect on Residual Value. The calculation of the end-of-life residual value is summarized in Exhibit 21–9. As the first line shows, no tax

EXHIBIT 21–9
Calculation of End-of-Life Residual Value

	Incremental Pretax Cash Flow	Incremental Income Tax	Incremental Aftertax Cash Flow
Working capital	$ 5,000	—	$ 5,000
Equipment	10,000	$4,000	6,000
Total	15,000	4,000	11,000
Less: Standby equipment.	1,500	600	900
Net residual value.	$13,500	$3,400	$10,100

adjustment applies to the recovery value of the working capital. The reason is that the $5,000 estimated liquidation value of the incremental working capital ($1,000 in cash, $2,000 in receivables, $5,000 in inventories, less $3,000 in trade payables) is just equal to its tax basis, and no taxable gain or loss will arise.

The equipment, however, will have a zero tax basis at the end of 10 years. Both the initial equipment and the equipment acquired by the subsequent outlay will be fully depreciated, and the standby equipment that will be retained if the proposal is rejected will also be fully depreciated if it is held for 10 more years. The entire cash flow from the sale of the equipment therefore is exposed to income taxes. The incremental residual value associated with this capital-expenditure proposal therefore is $10,100, the amount shown in the lower right-hand corner of Exhibit 21–9.

Calculating Net Present Value

Once the cash flows have been estimated, calculating net present value is relatively simple. The first step is to enter the cash flows in a timetable, as in the first three columns of Exhibit 21–10. The first column shows the initial outlay, the renovation outlay five years later, and the end-of-life residual value. These are added to the operating cash flows [column (2)] to get the total cash-flow amounts in column (3).

The second step is to calculate the minimum acceptable rate of return. For Barclay Company, this is 10 percent after taxes. This amount was established independently—based on the company's cost of capital. The

EXHIBIT 21–10
Timetable: Calculation of Net Present Value

Years from Now	(1) Investment Cash Flow after Taxes	(2) Operating Cash Flow after Taxes‡	(3) Total Cash Flow after Taxes (1) + (2)	(4) Present Value at 10% Multiplier*	(5) Present Value at 10% Amount (3) × (4)
0	−$100,400†		−$100,400	1.0000	−$100,400
1		+$20,200	+ 20,200	0.9091	+ 18,364
2		+ 24,720	+ 24,720	0.8264	+ 20,429
3		+ 24,560	+ 24,560	0.7513	+ 18,452
4		+ 24,560	+ 24,560	0.6830	+ 16,774
5	− 18,000	+ 22,560	+ 4,560	0.6209	+ 2,831
6		+ 16,200	+ 16,200	0.5645	+ 9,145
7		+ 16,760	+ 16,760	0.5132	+ 8,601
8		+ 16,680	+ 16,680	0.4665	+ 7,781
9		+ 16,680	+ 16,680	0.4241	+ 7,074
10	+ 10,100§	+ 16,680	+ 26,780	0.3855	+ 10,324

Net present value	+$ 19,375

* From Appendix A, Table 1.
† From Exhibit 21–5.
‡ From Exhibit 21–7.
§ From Exhibit 21–9.

calculation of the cost of capital is discussed in the appendix to this chapter.

The third step is to take present-value multipliers from present-value tables and apply these to the cash flows. The result of this step is shown in the right-hand column of the exhibit. These calculations show that the net present value of the modernization proposal is $19,375, the total of the amounts in the right-hand column. This means that, if the estimates are correct, the future operating cash receipts will (1) pay back the amounts invested ($100,400 and $18,000), (2) pay interest on these amounts at an annual rate of 10 percent after taxes, and (3) have enough left over to increase the company's value now by $19,375. Other things being equal, the proposal should be accepted.

If Barclay's management wants to analyze this capital-expenditure proposal using the internal rate of return perspective, the calculations will be relatively straightforward. Since the net present value at 10 percent is positive, the internal rate of return is *greater* than 10 percent. If we select 15 percent as the second trial rate, we must use Table 1 multipliers (for $r = 0.15, n = 1 . . . 10$) to calculate the present value of each year's cash flow. Using the format of Exhibit 21–10—columns (3), (4) and (5)—the 15 percent interest rate produces a $1,567 negative net present value. The approximate internal rate of return is that calculated by interpolation:

$$\text{Approximate rate} = 10\% + \frac{\$19,375}{\$19,375 + \$1,567} \times (15\% - 10\%) = 14.6\%$$

Economic Life

Cash flows in the preceding example were estimated for a 10-year period. This period was selected because management estimated that the investment had an economic life of 10 years. The **economic life** of an investment is the length of time before the combination of assets, people, and purposes it embodies will have to be reconstituted or disbanded.

In practice, the economic life of an investment is often defined to coincide with the economic life of one or more of the major tangible assets acquired at the time the investment is made. These assets may be replaced at the end of this period, either because the costs of owning and operating them are high relative to the costs of owning and operating replacement assets then available, or because the replacement assets can produce a greater quantity or variety of output. Alternatively, economic life may come to an end because the revenues from the products or services provided can no longer cover the costs of providing them, including a return on the investment. In such cases, the assets will be sold or diverted to other uses.

Some Recurring Questions

The illustrations in this chapter have given implicit answers to a number of potentially troublesome analytical questions. We need to examine several of these before we move on to other material:

1. Why did we ignore the unamortized costs of existing facilities or programs, except in connection with tax calculations?
2. Why did we make no provision for annual depreciation charges on newly acquired facilities?
3. How do internal cost allocations and absorptions enter into the estimates of incremental cash flows?
4. Why don't we include in the cash-flow stream estimates of the cash flows from long-term borrowing, interest payments, and debt-retirement transactions?
5. How should we provide for the impact of inflation?

Unamortized Costs

Management often finds it difficult to ignore amounts spent in the past to provide equipment or to develop new products. Suppose, for example, an automobile company has spent $2 billion to design, test, tool, and market a new automobile model. Sales have been disappointing, and management is considering discontinuing the model. Only $1.5 billion of the development and marketing costs have been amortized, however, leaving $500 million in tooling costs to be written off now if the company decides to drop the model from the line.

The $500 million in unamortized costs is irrelevant to the decision to discontinue the model—it is not a cash flow. In other words, it is a sunk cost—not an incremental cost. Even so, it may influence the decision:

1. Money is always spent to create value. Belief that a value has been created is slow to die, and managers are often reluctant to terminate an old project. ("It's a shame to write off all that money. If we just put in another $500 million, the model is sure to take hold.")
2. Managers often think of costs as amounts to be recovered. If not recovered as originally intended, they have to be charged against something else. ("We can't accept that proposal. It won't cover amortization of the costs of tooling we already have.") Result: Proposals that don't bring in enough cash to cover depreciation of past outlays as well as future cash outlays may be turned down.

These are two examples of the **sunk-cost fallacy,** the notion that costs not yet amortized are somehow relevant to decision making. One of these makes it harder to get rid of old projects; the other makes it harder to adopt new ones. The relevant concept in both cases is *opportunity cost:* What is the present salvage value of the investment, and by how much will that salvage value decline if the investment is not liquidated now? The amounts invested in the past are sunk costs; neither these amounts nor amortizations of them are relevant to today's decisions.

Depreciation on New Facilities

Annual depreciation charges on the equipment required by Barclay's plant modernization proposal were *not* reflected in the $25,000 annual cash flow. Depreciation charges don't measure current cash outlays. This doesn't mean that present-value calculations overlook depreciation, however. Accountants do recognize depreciation in *financial accounting* by recognizing it systematically over the assets' estimated lives. They reflect it in present-value analysis by entering *two* amounts in the cash-flow timetable—the initial outlay *and* the end-of-life residual value—at the times these cash flows take place.

For example, on an investment proposal calling for an outlay of $100,400 now and an estimated residual value of $10,100 in 10 years, the lifetime depreciation amounts to $90,300. This enters the timetable in the following way:

Time	Cash Flow
0	−$100,400
10	+ 10,100
Total	−$ 90,300

Entering depreciation again in the form of annual deductions from cash receipts would be double counting.

Allocations and Cost Absorption

The overhead rates and interdepartmental cost allocation rates used in product costing are likely to be poor approximations to the incremental costs accompanying changes in departmental volume or changes in the way the department operates. A company, for instance, may apply factory overhead to products by means of a predetermined overhead rate of $2 a direct labor-dollar. It is very unlikely, however, that the company will save $2 in overhead for every dollar of direct labor it saves. In fact, most labor-saving investments actually *increase* total company overhead rather than the other way around.

Interdepartmental cost allocations can be misleading in a similar way. In our example, plant modernizations will decrease the amount of floor space required by the operations affected by the proposal. This will reduce the amount of building occupancy costs allocated to these operations. The opportunity cost of the space saved may be zero, however, because the company has no way of using it or renting it out. If this is so, the cash-flow estimates must ignore this apparent difference in costs.

The Treatment of Interest

Timetables for capital-expenditure proposals show neither borrowings as cash inflows nor interest charges and debt extinguishments as cash outflows. The reason is that the capital-expenditure decision controls the investment of *all* the long-term funds available to the company, not just the funds invested by the shareowners. Since the present-value calculation implicitly provides for the rewards both the long-term lenders and the shareowners require, these rewards don't have to be deducted a second time.

For Barclay Company's proposal A, the initial cash outlay is $34,000, the estimated future cash receipts amount to $10,000 a year for five years, and the present value of the future cash receipts is $37,908. The left block in Exhibit 21–11 shows that the sum of the net cash flows in the five-year period is +$16,000; the right block shows that the net present value is only +$3,908. The $12,092 difference between these two amounts represents interest at 10 percent on the investment for the full life of the proposed expenditure.

The explanation is that the amounts in the left block represent the present values of the cash flows at a *zero* rate of interest. The amounts in the right column are smaller because interest at 10 percent has been subtracted. This being the case, charging interest explicitly against the cash flows generated by a proposal would be double counting.

EXHIBIT 21–11
Calculation of Implicit Interest

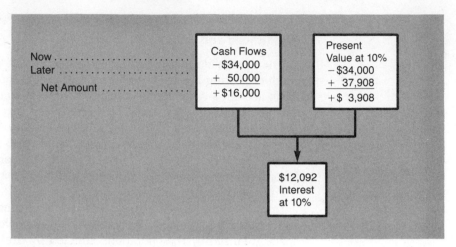

Adjusting for Inflation

Inflation affects both the *cost of capital* and the *cash flows* emanating from capital expenditures. The aftertax cost of debt capital in the United States, for example, rose from less than 3 percent in the mid-1950s to more than 9 percent in the early 1980s, as investors sought to compensate themselves for the declining purchasing power of the money they would be receiving in return for the use of their funds. Inflation also affected the cash flows during this period. Equipment that was originally expected to produce labor savings at labor costs of $5 an hour turned out to yield savings of $10 an hour as wage rates and employee benefits rose.

Management should build its expectations of future prices and wage rates into its cash-flow forecasts. As the cost of capital goes up, with its built-in adjustment for inflation, the apparent desirability of capital-expenditure proposals will fall unless the cash-flow estimates are adjusted accordingly. Some proposals will benefit, as their cash-flow rates advance more rapidly than the rate of inflation; others will suffer, as the markets in which they operate fail to provide benefits matching the rate of inflationary change. This means that multiplying currently anticipated cash flows by some general-purpose index of the overall inflation rate won't work. Management has to be willing to distinguish between (1) proposals that will benefit from inflation or resist its inroads and (2) others that will suffer.

Disinvestment Decisions

All the investment problems we've looked at so far have been proposals to tie up company funds in plant, equipment, and working capital. A similar kind of problem arises when someone proposes to sell a factory, withdraw from a market area, or discontinue selling a product—thereby converting the amounts invested in those activities into ready cash. These are **disinvestment decisions.**

For example, Barclay sells one of its products to other companies which process it on equipment that is no longer being manufactured. Sales have been declining for some time, as customers have been replacing their old equipment with machines that don't use Barclay's product. Management now forecasts that sales will continue for the next five years, but at steadily declining amounts. If Barclay discontinues marketing the product now, it can sell the trade name and liquidate working capital, making about $500,000 in cash available for other uses almost immediately. This amount is shown in column (1) of Exhibit 21–12. If Barclay continues to

EXHIBIT 21–12
Net Present Value of Disinvestment Decision

Years from Now	(1) Cash Flows from Dropping the Product	(2) Cash Flows from Keeping the Product	(3) Incremental Cash Flows (2) − (1)	(4) Present Value at 10% Multiplier	(5) Present Value at 10% Amount
0.........	+$500,000		−$500,000	1.0000	−$500,000
1.........	0	+$250,000	+ 250,000	0.9091	+ 227,275
2.........	0	+ 200,000	+ 200,000	0.8264	+ 165,280
3.........	0	+ 150,000	+ 150,000	0.7513	+ 112,695
4.........	0	+ 100,000	+ 100,000	0.6830	+ 68,300
5.........	0	+ 50,000	+ 50,000	0.6209	+ 31,045

Net present value.	+$104,595

market the product for the next five years, however, management expects the product to generate the cash-flow stream shown in column (2). (All these cash flows are aftertax cash flows.)

This problem is in substance no different from any of the other problems we have been looking at. To see why this is true, let's turn the problem around. Instead of thinking of this as a proposal to sell the rights to manufacture and market the product, we can think of it as a proposal to keep it in the line. To do that, the company must forgo an immediate cash inflow of $500,000. Doing that is just like investing $500,000 to keep the product flowing. If we look at it that way, we can subtract column *(1)* from column *(2)* instead of the other way around, and get the incremental cash flows shown in column *(3)*.

Given that the minimum acceptable rate of return is the 10 percent we assumed earlier and that we assume that cash flows are concentrated at the end of each year, the present value of keeping this product in the line is $104,595, as shown at the bottom of column (5). This suggests that Barclay Company should continue to produce the product rather than accept the outside offer to buy the rights to manufacture and market it. Management can review the situation next year if another offer can be generated at that time—and so on each year until the calculation produces a *negative* net present value, which would suggest a decision to disinvest.

Other Measures of Investment Value

Two significantly simpler measures than *net present value* and *internal rate of return* are sometimes used in the evaluation of capital-expenditure proposals: (1) payback period and (2) average return on investment.

Payback Period

The **payback period** is the time that will elapse before net cash receipts will cumulate to an amount equal to the initial outlay. The shorter the payback period, the better the project, or so it is assumed.

If the amounts of the annual cash flows are *uneven* from year to year, the payback period is calculated by adding cash flows until their total equals the initial outlay. Otherwise it can be calculated by applying the following formula:

$$\text{Payback period (years)} = \frac{\text{Investment outlay}}{\text{Average annual cash receipts}}$$

For example, if the installed cost of a piece of equipment is $50,000 and it will produce cash operating savings of $10,000 a year, it has a payback period of five years:

$$\frac{\text{Investment}}{\text{Annual cash receipts}} = \frac{\$50,000}{\$10,000} = 5 \text{ years}$$

The main defect of *payback period* is that it ignores the estimated useful life of the proposed facilities. If the facilities in our example will have to be replaced five years from now, the project will have achieved no net earnings for the company. The company will have invested $50,000 to earn a zero rate of return. Or, if a large portion of the investment outlay is for working capital with a high end-of-life recovery value, the project may be more desirable than another with a lower payback period but no end-of-life residual value.

Average Return on Investment

A second method is to compute for each proposal the expected **average return on investment.** This may be defined in many ways, perhaps most commonly by the following formula:

$$\text{Average return} = \frac{\text{Average cash receipts} - \text{Average annual depreciation}}{\text{Average lifetime investment}}$$

The average lifetime investment amount is affected by the method used to calculate depreciation. The use of straight-line depreciation for financial accounting purposes presumes that investment declines in a linear fashion as facilities age. The *average* investment under this assumption is halfway between (1) the amount of the initial outlay and (2) the residual investment at the end of the project's life measured by the recoverable value of the facilities and working capital at that time.

For example, the project for which payback period was computed earlier required an initial outlay of $50,000 and had no end-of-life residual value. Average investment was thus $25,000. Assuming that the life of this project was expected to be 10 years, average annual depreciation was $5,000, and the average before-tax return on investment was 20 percent:

$$\frac{\text{Average net earnings}}{\text{Average investment}} = \frac{\$10,000 - \$5,000}{\$25,000} = 20 \text{ percent}$$

This method does consider the expected life of the facilities, and it does consider the amount of end-of-life residual. It fails, however, to allow for differences in the *timing* of outlays and receipts. By this method, a project in which no cash receipts appear until the 10th year will appear to be just as profitable as a project in which most of the cash receipts are received in the first few years of the project's life—as long as the average is the same.

Summary

Many of management's resource-allocation problems can be classified as *investment* decisions. Decision models for investment problems must provide a mechanism for comparing incremental cash outflows in one or more time periods with the incremental cash inflows in another time period or periods.

The measure that does this most satisfactorily is the *net present value,* in which all anticipated incremental cash flows are expressed at their present-value equivalents at an interest rate based on the company's cost of capital. Other things being equal, the alternative with the greatest positive net present value should be selected; proposals with negative net present values should be rejected. A related technique is the calculation of each proposal's internal rate of return, which is then compared directly with the cost of capital.

In calculating either net present value or the internal rate of return, the analyst has to estimate the economic life of the investment, the amount and timing of the investment outlays, the amount and timing of the operating cash flows, and the end-of-life residual value attributable to the proposal. All these estimates should reflect incremental cash flows, *not* accounting allocations made for other purposes. Sunk costs should be ignored. The incremental amounts should be measured from a benchmark that will be acceptable to the company, which means that opportunity costs should be taken into account as well.

Appendix: The Cost of Capital

The managers of a business must be careful to make investments that will produce an adequate rate of return. The money they have to invest comes from the company's stockholders and lenders, and these investors expect to be rewarded for letting the company use their money.

Cost of Debt Capital

The cost of *debt* capital is the rate of interest that equates (1) the present value of the future stream of interest payments (after allowing for income tax effects) *and* maturity-date repayment of face value with (2) the current net proceeds from sale of the debt instruments.

For example, assume that bonds with a coupon rate of 9 percent and a 20-year maturity can be sold at their face value. After providing for the tax deductibility of interest at a tax rate of 40 percent, the aftertax cost of this debt offering is 5.4 percent.

The cost of debt capital at any time is a combination of (1) the interest rate the company would have to pay if the lenders incurred no risk by lending to the company, and (2) a premium to compensate the lenders for the perceived risks of lending to this particular company. The risk-free interest rate—the first component of the cost of debt capital—also consists of two parts: the *real* cost of money and a premium reflecting the rate of inflation the market expects the economy to experience.

Cost of Equity Capital

The cost of *equity* capital can be defined as the rate of interest stockholders apply to the expected future receipts from stock ownership to determine the price they are willing to pay.[2] To determine this rate, we

---

[2] Although stockholders don't earn *interest* on their investment, they do expect to earn a return. Their required *rate* of return can be expressed in terms of an equivalent rate of interest, sometimes called the *implicit* interest rate.

need data on the market price of the stock and the stockholders' future expectations. The latter information being unavailable, the analyst typically falls back on a study of past relationships between market prices, dividends, and capital appreciation.

As a simple illustration of the concept, if a stock is selling for $50 per share and the company's earnings are stable at $5 a share, this is some evidence that the marginal stockholders in the company are willing to pay $10 for each dollar of earnings. To attract additional funds into the company, therefore, management must be able to communicate an expectation that these funds will also earn a return of at least 10 percent on investments, and perhaps more.

The cost of equity capital includes risk-free and risk-premium components, similar in concept to these two components of the cost of debt capital. The size of the risk-free component depends on market forces in general, rather than on the characteristics of individual companies, and it includes a provision for the rate of inflation equity investors are anticipating.

The size of the risk premium depends on the perceived risks of investing in that company relative to the risks of investing in the market generally. The so-called capital-asset pricing model links the size of the risk premium to the contribution the stock makes to the variability of a diversified portfolio. Companies whose stock prices are very sensitive to movements in the stock market will have high risk premiums, and vice versa.

Weighted Average Cost of Capital

Most companies use *both* debt capital and equity capital. Public utility companies have a high proportion of debt, mining companies relatively little. A company's *average* cost of capital will depend not only on the costs of the two kinds of capital but also on the proportions in which they are to be used.

What this means is that a company's minimum acceptable rate of return on its capital expenditures should be based on a weighted average of the costs of both debt and equity capital. The weights should represent the relative role each has in the company's financing plans:

	Aftertax Capital Cost	Weight	Weighted Cost
Debt	5.4%	40%	2.16%
Equity	12.0	60	7.20
Total			9.36%

If the company's capital expenditures do not yield a rate of return at least as great as the cost of capital, they will dilute the company's earnings and likely impair its ability to secure additional funds on a balanced basis in the future.

Allowances for Risk

Management may decide not to subject all capital expenditure proposals to the same minimum acceptable rate of return (called the **hurdle rate**). The reason is that some expenditures are riskier than others: the riskier the expenditure, the higher the hurdle rate it must surmount.

How large the risk adjustment should be is a difficult question, requiring more space than we can offer here. What we can say is that each company's capital ventures constitute a portfolio of capital expenditures with different degrees of risk. Its external investors, in turn, adjust the terms on which they are willing to invest to the riskiness of the company's portfolio. The overall riskiness of the portfolio, and therefore the company's cost of capital, depends on the mix of ventures in the portfolio. Making high-risk expenditures increases the riskiness of the portfolio and raises the overall cost of capital. Proposals to make high-risk expenditures therefore should meet the higher hurdle rates with which other capital investments with the same perceived riskiness have to contend.

For example, nuclear power projects in the United States are now perceived to be highly risky. The cost of capital to a public utility company with a large commitment to nuclear power is higher than the cost of capital to an otherwise comparable utility that relies exclusively on other sources of energy. For this reason, any proposal to invest in nuclear facilities should have a higher hurdle rate than a proposal to replace steam turbines with turbines of a more efficient design.

This concept can be applied as well to different classes of expenditures (e.g., equipment replacement versus new-product development) and to different divisions of the company (e.g., food service and pesticides). When this is done, the proposals subjected to the higher hurdle rates will have to indicate greater anticipated yields than those subject to lower hurdle rates.

Key Terms

Average return on investment	Internal rate of return
Capital expenditure	Investment problem
Cost of capital	Net present value
Disinvestment decision	Payback period
Economic life	Sunk-cost fallacy
End-of-life residual value	Zero date
Hurdle rate	

Independent Study Problems (Solutions in Appendix B)

1. Calculating Present Value and Internal Rate of Return. Calculate net present value at 10 percent, compounded annually, and the internal rate of return for each of the following capital-expenditure proposals. You should assume that the initial outlay is made immediately and each subsequent cash flow takes place at the end of the year in which it arises. All cash flows have been adjusted to reflect the impact of income taxes.

a. Initial outlay.............. $10,000
   Annual cash receipts .... $ 1,750
   Estimated life.............. 10 years
   End-of-life residual value..... None

b. Initial outlay.............. $10,000
   Annual cash receipts:
      First five years .... $ 2,000
      Second five years .... $ 1,500
   Estimated life.............. 10 years
   End-of life residual value..... None

c. Initial outlay.............. $10,000
   Annual cash receipts:
      First five years .... $ 1,500
      Second five years .... $ 2,000
   Estimated life.............. 10 years
   End-of-life residual value..... None

d. Initial outlay.............. $10,000
   Annual cash receipts .... $ 1,350
   Estimated life.............. 10 years
   End-of-life residual value..... $ 4,000

e. Initial outlay.............. $10,000
   Annual cash receipts .... $ 1,750
   Estimated life.............. 15 years
   End-of-life residual value..... None

2. Calculating Payback Period and Average Return on Investment. For each capital-expenditure proposal described in problem 1, calculate the payback period and the average return on investment, using average lifetime investment as the denominator.

3. Estimating Cash Flows: Make or Buy Decision. Arnold Machine Company has been having a neighboring company perform certain operations on a part used in its product at a cost of 50 cents per piece. The annual production of this part is expected to average 6,000 pieces.

Arnold Machine Company can perform this operation itself by bringing two machines into operation: a spare lathe that has a net tax basis of $2,000 and a new machine that can be purchased at a price of $7,000. The new machine is expected to last seven years. The old machine has a remaining physical life of at least 10 years and could be sold now for approximately $1,500. The final salvage value of both machines is considered negligible. In performing the operation itself, Arnold will incur incremental costs for direct labor, power, supplies, and so forth, of 20 cents per piece.

The old machine is being depreciated for tax purposes at a straight-line amount of $500 a year. The cost of the new machine would be depreciated for income tax purposes in five annual installments of 15, 22, 21, 21, and 21 percent of its original cost, respectively. The income tax rate is 40 percent.

a. Arrange the pretax cash flows in a timetable.
b. Calculate the aftertax cash flows and arrange them in a timetable.

4. Estimating Aftertax Cash Flows. Under a proposal just submitted by the production manager of Romano Company, proposed new facilities will cost $100,000, half of which will be capitalized for tax purposes. The rest will be expensed immediately. A government investment incentive device known as an investment credit allows the company an immediate tax rebate of 10 percent of the capitalized portion of the outlay. Tax depreciation will be based on the amount capitalized.

The proposal will also require a $10,000 increase in working capital.

Cash operating savings are expected to amount to $20,000 a year for 10 years. The new facilities would be depreciated for income tax purposes in five annual installments of 15, 22, 21, 21, and 21 percent of capitalized cost, respectively. The income tax rate is 40 percent.

a. Calculate the aftertax initial cash outlay for this proposal.
b. Calculate the aftertax cash savings for each of the first two years of the life of the facilities.

5. Calculating Present Value and Internal Rate of Return. The expected life of a proposed facility is 10 years, the installed cost will be $65,000, and the expected end-of-life salvage value is zero. The new facilities will replace facilities now in use that have a tax basis (book value) of $32,000 and a market value of $10,000.

A staff analyst has prepared the following estimates of the annual pretax savings from this proposal:

	At Present	After New Installation	Savings
Labor	$32,500	$23,000	$ 9,500
Materials wastage	6,200	1,000	5,200
Depreciation (10% of cost)	4,000	6,500	(2,500)
Supplies, repairs, and power	11,600	6,400	5,200
General factory management (5% of labor)	1,625	1,150	475
Insurance and miscellaneous	1,900	2,000	(100)
Total	$57,825	$40,050	$17,775

All these costs except general factory management are direct costs of the facilities. General factory management consists of the costs of building depreciation, the plant manager's salary, and similar items. In a year of normal volume, these average 5 percent of facilities labor costs.

The new facilities, if acquired, will be depreciated for income tax purposes in five annual installments of 15, 22, 21, 21, and 21 percent of capitalized cost, respectively. No investment credit is available, but $15,000 of the new facility's installed cost can be expensed immediately for tax purposes. The facilities to be replaced are now being depreciated for tax purposes by the straight-line method down to an end-of-life salvage value of zero.

The income tax rate is 40 percent, and all savings are assumed to take place at the end of each year. The tax rate applies to all taxable income, including gains and losses on the sale of equipment.

a. Prepare a timetable of the estimated incremental cash flows associated with this proposal.

b. Calculate the estimated incremental aftertax present value of this proposal at 12 percent, compounded annually. If 12 percent is the aftertax minimum rate of return, should this proposal be accepted?

Exercises and Problems

6. Present Value Exercises. Prepare a timetable of cash flows for each of the following independent proposals, calculate the net present value, and indicate whether the outlay should be made. You may decide to accept some, all, or none of these proposals. The minimum acceptable rate of return is 10 percent. All cash flows have been adjusted to reflect the impact of income taxes.

a. Immediate outlay, $100; cash to be received at one-year intervals for 10 years, the first to be received exactly one year after the immediate outlay, $15 a year.

b. Immediate outlay, $67; cash receipts, $20 a year for five years, starting one year after the immediate outlay.

c. Immediate outlay, $100; cash receipts $15 a year for five years, starting one year after the immediate outlay, plus one additional receipt of $75 10 years after the immediate outlay.

d. Immediate outlay, $67; cash receipts: $35 one year later, $30 two years later, $20 three years later, $10 four years later, and $5 five years later.

e. Immediate outlay, $67; cash receipts: $5 one year later, $10 two years later, $20 three years later, $30 four years later, and $35 five years later.

7. Mutually Exclusive Proposals. The company can accept only one of the proposals described in problem 6. Which one would you recommend? Why would you recommend it?

8. Internal Rate of Return. Calculate the internal rate of return for each of the exercises in problem 6. Do these calculations point to the same recommendations you made in answer in problems 6 and 7? Does this seem reasonable?

9. Payback Period and Average Return on Investment. Calculate the payback period and the average return on average investment for each of the situations described in problem 6. Assume straight-line depreciation for purposes of calculating average investment. How satisfactory is each of these measures as a device for ranking investment proposals? In your analysis of this question, you should use net present value and the internal rate of return as comparison standards.

10. Present Value Exercises. Heslin, Inc., invested in a machine with a useful life of five years and no salvage value. The annual cash inflow from operations, net of income taxes, was $1,000. Heslin used a minimum acceptable rate of return of 12 percent.

a. Assuming this investment just satisfied the company's minimum rate of return on investment, what was the amount of the original investment?

b. Assuming the amount of the original investment was $3,500, what was the net present value, rounded to the nearest dollar?

(AICPA adapted)

11. Net Present Value: Three Exercises. Answer each of the following three independent questions.

a. Thomson Company is planning to invest $80,000 on January 1, 19x1, in a three-year project. The aftertax cash inflow will be $30,000 in 19x1 and $36,000 in 19x2. Assuming the internal rate of return is 10 percent and each cash inflow occurs at year-end, what will the aftertax cash inflow be in 19x3?

b. On January 1, 19x4, Jackson Corporation purchased for $520,000 a new machine with a useful life of seven years and no salvage value. The machine is expected to produce an aftertax cash flow of $120,000 at each year-end. If Jackson's minimum internal rate of return on this kind of expenditure is 14 percent, what was the net present value of the machine on January 1, 19x4?

c. Victoria, Inc., invested in a four-year project that would yield a 12 percent annual rate of return. The aftertax cash inflow that was expected at the end of each of the four years was $4,000, $4,400, $4,800, and $5,500. If the positive net present value was $3,492, what was the amount of the original investment?

(AICPA adapted)

12. Value of Tax Benefits. Freedom Corporation acquired a truck at a cost of $50,000. The estimated life was four years, but for income tax purposes the truck was depreciated over three years as follows: 25 percent, 38 percent and 37 percent of original cost. The estimated salvage value was zero, the relevant interest rate was 8 percent after taxes, and the income tax rate was 40 percent.

What was the present value of the tax benefits resulting from using the three-year tax depreciation (instead of four-year, straight-line depreciation) for tax purposes?

(AICPA adapted)

13. Discussion Question: Effect of Past Purchase Price. David and Zelda are co-owners of 1,000 shares of the common stock of Arlington Farms, Inc., an industrial conglomerate. They bought these shares five years ago at a price of $46 a share. The market price of a share of Arlington Farms common stock is now $12.50.

Zelda thinks the stock should be sold now because the company's future seems dim. David agrees with Zelda's forecast but thinks the stock should be kept because selling it now would prevent them from recovering their investment. David and Zelda live in a country in which losses on the sale of securities lead to income tax reductions only if the taxpayer has similar taxable capital gains on sales of other securities. For this reason, their tax advisor thinks they should keep their Arlington Farms stock until they have enough offsetting capital gains.

What position do you take in this argument? What flaws do you find in the position(s) you rejected?

14. Amortization Schedule. A machine costs $29,906 payable immediately in cash. Use of this machine is expected to reduce cash outflows by $10,000 a year for five years. The controller has calculated that the internal rate of return from the purchase of this machine would be 20 percent. Cash flows take place at one-year intervals and interest is compounded annually.

Without using the interest tables, prepare a schedule showing the amount of each annual cash flow that can be regarded as a recovery of part of the $29,906 investment in the machine and the amount to be regarded as a return on investment (to the nearest dollar).

15. Indifference Point. Ander Company can invest $4,980 in a piece of equipment with a three-year life. The minimum desired rate of return is 10 percent after taxes and the annual expected cash savings amount to $2,500 (net of taxes) and will be received at year-end. What is the amount by which the annual cash flows could change before the company would be indifferent to acquiring the equipment?

(CMA adapted)

16. Pretax versus Aftertax Analysis. You have the following estimates relating to a proposal to buy and install new equipment:

1. The company's cost of capital is 10 percent after taxes; this is assumed to be equivalent to 20 percent before taxes.
2. Initial investment outlays amount to $80,000, of which $30,000 can be expensed immediately for income tax purposes.
3. The capitalized portion of the initial outlay is subject to special tax treatment. Half of the capitalized cost can be written off in equal annual installments during the first five years. The other half is subject to tax depreciation at the straight-line rate of 6 percent a year, including the first five years.
4. The investment is expected to produce net cash receipts (before taxes) for 15 years: $16,500 a year for the first five years, $11,500 a year for the next five years, and $6,500 a year for the third five years.
5. It is expected that the new equipment will be retired and sold at the end of 15 years and that salvage value will be $5,000.
6. All income taxes are to be calculated on the basis of a 50 percent tax rate. The company has taxable income from other sources against which to offset any tax losses from this project.
7. The initial outlay and its related tax effects should be assumed to take place immediately; annual cash flows from operations should be assumed to take place at the end of the year.

Analyze this proposal on both before-tax and aftertax bases. How, if at all, would your recommendation to management be different if you used the before-tax basis instead of the aftertax basis?

17. Tax Shield. It is sometimes useful to separate the aftertax cash flows into two parts: (1) the pretax cash flows, less the income taxes that would accrue to these cash flows in the absence of depreciation and other items on the tax return not representing current cash flows; and (2) the effects of these other items on income taxes. This second component is known as the *tax shield*.

a. Make this separation for the proposal described in problem 16 and calculate the present value of each of these two components.
b. Recalculate your answer to a to reflect the following assumptions: (1) the entire initial outlay is capitalized for tax purposes; (2) depreciation for income tax purposes is spread over five annual installments of 15, 22, 21, 21, and 21 percent of the initial outlay; the (3) the income tax rate is 50 percent. Note the difference between your answers to parts a and b.
c. Recalculate your answer to part b at a 40 percent income tax rate, all other assumptions remaining the same. Note the difference between this answer and your answer to part b.

18. Disinvestment Proposal: Estimating Cash Flows.   J. T. Long, owner of the Long Office Building, was recently approached by a buyer for that property. The offer consisted of $200,000 in cash immediately plus $50,000 at the end of each of the next five years—a total of $450,000.

Long had bought the land and built the building 15 years earlier. The land had cost $40,000; the building had cost $600,000. Annual depreciation for tax purposes had been charged at a straight-line rate of $20,000 a year.

The appraised value of the land at the time of the offer was $100,000. The remaining useful life of the building at that time seemed to be about 10 years. At the end of that time, the land and building probably could be sold to a developer for $150,000. The amount of working capital required to support the operation of this building was negligible and seemed likely to remain so.

Long expected future income to be about $30,000 a year for the remaining life, calculated as follows:

Yearly revenues from office rental...		$79,000
Yearly expenses:		
Taxes	$ 4,000	
Repairs......................	12,000	
Depreciation	20,000	
Heat and miscellaneous.........	13,000	49,000
Total income		$30,000

The cash flows from ownership of the property each year would become available to Long at the end of the year.

a. Prepare a timetable of the pretax cash flows associated with this proposal.
b. Disinvestment decisions of this sort should take into consideration the tax consequences of the different alternatives. Which of the cash flows you identified in part *a* would have to be adjusted, and what information would you need to make these adjustments?

19. Sensitivity of Rate of Return.   The initial investment outlay is $40,000, of which $30,000 will be capitalized for tax purposes. The remaining $10,000 of the initial outlay will be expensed immediately for tax purposes. Before-tax operating cash receipts will be $12,000 a year for five years; these amounts will be received at the end of each year. Estimated end-of-life salvage value is zero.

The $30,000 capitalized portion of the initial outlay is to acquire a vehicle which will be depreciated for income tax purposes in three annual installments of 25, 38, and 37 percent of original cost, respectively. The income tax rate is 40 percent of taxable income. Taxes are paid or tax credits are received immediately, as soon as the taxable or tax-deductible transaction takes place.

a. What is the estimated present value of this proposal at an annual aftertax interest rate of 8 percent?

b. What is the aftertax internal rate of return?

c. What would be the internal rate of return if end-of-life salvage were $5,000 but annual depreciation for tax purposes continued to be based on zero salvage?

d. What would be the rate of return on investment if economic life were six years, with zero salvage value, and all other estimates were as listed above?

e. Calculate the rate of return if economic life were five years, salvage value were zero, and the required equipment were depreciated for income tax purposes over five years as follows: 15, 22, 21, 21, and 21 percent of the capitalized cost.

f. Prepare a short commentary on the relationships indicated by your answers to the preceding parts of this question.

20. Cost-Reducing Investment. An investment in equipment would reduce factory labor costs by $15,000 a year for 10 years. Factory overhead costs are assigned to products by means of a predetermined overhead rate of 75 percent of direct-labor cost. Forty percent of factory overhead costs at normal volume are proportionally variable with volume. Maintenance and energy requirements of the new machine would increase fixed factory overhead costs by $2,000 a year.

The equipment would cost $72,000 and would be depreciated for income tax purposes in five annual installments of 15, 22, 21, 21, and 21 percent of original cost, respectively. The company expects the equipment to have no residual value at the end of 10 years.

The company has a minimum acceptable aftertax return on investment of 10 percent. The income tax rate is 40 percent. All operating and tax cash flows are assumed to occur at year-end, except for the initial outlay for the equipment.

a. Prepare a timetable of estimated cash flows for this proposal.

b. Calculate estimated net present value. Should the investment be made?

21. Investment in New Facilities: Relevant Benchmark. Artling Corporation manufactures four products in four identical processing operations. The only differences among the four products are in the raw materials used. The facilities are completely interchangeable, although newer machines have higher depreciation and generally lower operating costs than older machines. Processing costs (that is, all costs other than materials costs) are determined by the machines used, not by the product being manufactured.

The company is now considering a proposal to acquire a fifth set of processing facilities to manufacture a new, higher grade of product, using a more expensive raw material that has just come on the market. All machines, new as well as old, would still be completely interchangeable, but the new machine would probably be used to make the new product.

The following table shows the selling prices of the five products and all the costs per pound that would be incurred in the factory to operate the machines:

Product/Machine	Selling Price	Materials Cost	Depreciation	Other Factory Costs	Gross Margin
A/1	$0.70	$0.15	$0.08	$0.31	$0.16
B/2	0.76	0.20	0.08	0.30	0.18
C/3	0.83	0.25	0.09	0.28	0.21
D/4	0.91	0.30	0.09	0.29	0.23
E*/5*	1.00	0.35	0.10	0.29	0.26

* Proposed.

Depreciation cost per pound is an average straight-line rate based on estimated annual production of 100,000 pounds of each product and an estimated life of 10 years. Estimated salvage value of the production equipment is zero; in fact, once the facilities are installed, their only market value is their scrap value, which is negligible.

In support of the proposal to add the fifth product (product E) and corresponding facilities (machine 5), Artling Company's sales manager has pointed out that this would increase the company's gross margin by $26,000 ($0.26 a pound on an added sales volume of 100,000 pounds annually). Incremental variable selling and administrative costs amounting to 5 percent of sales would reduce this by $5,000, but this would still leave $21,000 to provide a handsome rate of return on investment.

Calculate the incremental annual cash flow that you would use in deciding whether the proposed investment is adequately profitable. State your reasoning. Ignore income taxes.

22. Make or Buy Decision. Griffa Machine Company has been purchasing from a neighboring company a part used in one of its products. The purchase price of this part is 95 cents each, and the expected average annual production is 6,000 parts.

The methods department of Griffa Machine Company has submitted a proposal to manufacture this part in the company's own plant. To do this, the company would have to purchase a new machine at a price of $10,800. It would also use a lathe now owned by the company but not in current use. This lathe has an estimated market value now of $1,000, but its book value is $2,000. Depreciation for tax purposes on the old lathe is at a straight-line rate of $400 a year. The cost of the new machine would be depreciated for income tax purposes in five annual installments of 15, 22, 21, 21, and 21 percent of its original cost, respectively. Griffa's management believes that both machines would be usable for 10 years if the proposal were accepted, and the final salvage value of both machines is assumed to be negligible.

The incremental costs of operating the two machines, other than depreciation costs, would be as follows:

	Unit Cost
Direct labor, 0.05 hour at $8 an hour	$0.40
Direct materials	0.10
Power, supplies, and so forth	0.05

All other factory costs would be unaffected by the decision to manufacture this part. The company uses an overhead rate of $3 per direct labor-hour to absorb factory overhead costs.

Assuming an income tax rate of 40 percent and a minimum acceptable rate of return on investment of 12 percent after taxes, should this proposal be accepted?

23. Unprofitable Operations; Relevant Benchmark. National Company bought Summit Corporation five years ago. Summit is a franchiser of restaurants operating under the name Omar's Tent. The franchise business has been depressed for the past two years, so that Summit has had a $10,000 operating cash deficit each year. This seems likely to continue unless something is done.

Gerald Avakian, Summit's founder and former owner, has offered to buy the company back for $125,000 any time National wants to sell in the next 10 years. National paid him $3 million for Summit's stock five years ago, however, and none of this has been amortized. Unfortunately, National's tax position is such that if it sells Summit back to Mr. Avakian it will receive no tax credit on the loss incurred in the sale.

National's management is now considering three proposals it has received from Summit. The three proposals are mutually exclusive—acceptance of one means rejection of the others. In each case, Summit's management expects the proposed new facilities to be economically productive for 10 years and to have no salvage value at the end of that time. Operating cash flows may be assumed to occur at the end of the year.

1. *Proposal A.* Invest $100,000 in a new dough-making facility to supply the franchisees with bread dough to be baked on the premises. Management estimates this would bring an additional cash inflow of $40,000 a year, after taxes.
2. *Proposal B.* Invest $400,000 in a new baking and packaging facility to supply franchisees with frozen bread to be served in the restaurants and to be sold there in packages under the brand name Omar's Loaf. This would bring in additional aftertax cash flows of $50,000 in the

first year, rising to $75,000 in the second year and $100,000 in each year after the second.

3. *Proposal C.* Invest $300,000 in a new baking facility to supply suitably located franchisees with freshly baked bread daily. This would produce additional annual cash inflows of $70,000, after taxes.

National Company has a minimum acceptable rate of return on investment of 12 percent, after taxes. Assuming that all the cash flow estimates are valid (and occur at year-end), what action should National's management take? Present the calculations supporting your recommendation, including a calculation of the incremental rate of return on your recommended action over the next best alternative.

24. Maximum Purchase Price. Company Z has contracted to supply a government agency with 50,000 units of a product each year for the next five years. A certain component of this product can be either manufactured by Company Z or purchased from the X Corporation, which has indicated a willingness to enter into a subcontract for 50,000 units of the component each year for five years if the price offered is satisfactory. These alternative methods of procurement are regarded as equally dependable.

If Company Z decides to manufacture the component, it expects the following to occur:

1. A special-purpose machine costing $110,000 will have to be purchased. No other equipment will be required.
2. The cost of the new machine will be depreciated for income tax purposes in five annual installments of 15, 22, 21, 21, and 21 percent of its original cost, respectively. Management doesn't expect the machine to be useful beyond the five-year contract period.
3. No investment credit is available.
4. Estimated salvage value at the end of five years is $10,000.
5. The manufacturing operation will require 1,000 feet of productive floor space. This space is available in a building owned by Company Z and will not be needed for any other purpose in the foreseeable future. The costs of maintaining this building (including repairs, utilities, taxes, and depreciation) amount to $2 per square foot of productive floor space per year.
6. Variable manufacturing costs—materials, direct labor, and so forth—are estimated to be 50 cents a unit.
7. Fixed factory costs other than those mentioned in items 1 through 4—such as supervision—are estimated at $20,000 a year.
8. Income taxes are calculated at the rate of 40 percent of taxable income or taxable savings.
9. The policy of Company Z is to subcontract if and only if the costs saved by manufacturing instead of subcontracting provide less than a 10 percent annual return on investment. For this purpose, return on

investment is defined as the relationship between cost saving, after provision for income taxes, and the capital investment that will have to be made to permit Company Z to manufacture the component in its own plant.

What is the maximum price per unit Company Z should be willing to offer the X Corporation? Make explicit any assumptions you believe to be necessary in solving the problem.

25. Adjusting for Inflation. Nelson Company plans to introduce a new product, requiring immediate outlays of $200,000 for equipment and $100,000 for working capital. The product will sell at a price of $18 a unit the first two years. The price will increase to $20 in the third year and then increase another $1 each year for the next five years to reach a final plateau at $25 a unit in the eighth year. Operating cash outlays for manufacturing costs will be as follows:

	First Year	Annual Rate of Increase
Direct materials	$5 a unit	10%
Direct labor.	2 a unit	5
Variable overhead	1 a unit	8
Fixed overhead.	$50,000	4

The additional equipment required by this new product will be depreciated for income tax purposes in five annual installments of 15, 22, 21, 21, and 21 percent of original cost, respectively.

No investment tax credits are available for this equipment purchase, and the company expects it to have a zero net residual value at the end of the product's life cycle, which management expects will be at the end of 10 years. Management intends to depreciate the $200,000 equipment cost for financial reporting at a straight-line amount of $20,000 a year for 10 years. Working capital investments can be recovered without gain or loss at the end of the product's life.

Sales and production volume are expected to reach 10,000 units the first year, 20,000 the second year, and 25,000 in the third year, continuing at that level through the eighth year, then decline to 20,000 in the ninth year and 15,000 units in the 10th year as substitute products take over.

To achieve these volumes, marketing expenditures will be $90,000 the first year and $60,000 the second year, rising each year thereafter by 5 percent of the previous year's expenditure until the 10th year. Marketing outlays in the 10th year will be cut to half the level they would otherwise reach in that year, as the product is gradually phased out.

The income tax rate is expected to be 40 percent for the entire period, and the required rate of return is 15 percent after taxes. It should be assumed that each year's operating cash flows are received at year-end and that income taxes on the year's taxable income are also paid at year-end. Annual compounding is appropriate. Nelson Company expects to have ample taxable income from other sources to enable it to capture the tax benefits of any operating loss the new product will incur in any year.

a. Prepare a timetable for cash flows for this proposal.
b. Should Nelson Company's management accept it and introduce the new product? Show calculations to support your recommendation.

26. Expansion Proposal. The management of Taunton Cotton Company is considering the acquisition of new spinning machinery, partially to replace certain less efficient equipment and partially to increase total productive capacity. Market surveys indicate that the anticipated increase in productive capacity can be disposed of only by additional sales effort coupled with a price reduction. Pertinent data are as indicated:

Cost of new equipment, including freight and installation $55,000
Cost of removal of equipment replaced, rearrangement and revamping, and so forth, to be charged to expense for tax purposes. 25,000
Net book value (tax basis) of equipment replaced (original cost: $40,000). 8,000
Amount to be realized from sale of equipment replaced. 5,000
Expected salvage value, new equipment (end of 10 years) 0

Annual processing costs:

	Present		Proposed	
	Dollars	**Per Pound**	**Dollars**	**Per Pound**
Labor.	$120,000	$0.0600	$135,000	$0.0540
Supplies, repairs, and power . . .	80,000	0.0400	93,000	0.0372
Taxes, insurance, and miscellaneous.	20,000	0.0100	22,000	0.0088
Depreciation (10% of cost, straight-line)	4,000	0.0020	5,500	0.0022
Total.	$224,000	$0.1120	$255,500	$0.1022

Annual production:
Present. . . . . 2 million pounds
Proposed . . . . 2.5 million pounds
Estimated manufacturing margin per pound (estimated selling price minus estimated material cost):
Present. . . . . $ 0.150
Proposed (allowing for reduction of ½¢ in selling price). 0.145
Estimated additional selling and administrative expenses:
Commissions. . . . . $ 5,000
Branch office sales expense (including advertising) . 11,000
Billing and miscellaneous administrative 1,500
Total $17,500

Depreciation for tax purposes on present equipment has been by the straight-line method at 10 percent of cost. The new equipment would be depreciated for income tax purposes in five annual installments of 15, 22, 21, 21, and 21 percent of original cost, respectively.

The income tax rate is 40 percent.

a. Prepare a timetable of the estimated pretax cash flows, and make the necessary adjustments for the effects of income taxation.

b. Would you recommend the expenditure if a 12 percent return after taxes is required?

27. Multiple Alternatives: Cash Flows from Income Data. David Adams burst into the office of his supervisor, the works manager, to announce that a new machine that had just come out should be bought to replace the one used in the manufacture of product W. To support his argument, he presented the following comparative income statements for product W:

	Using the Present Machine	Using the New Machine
Sales revenues	$200,000	$200,000
Expenses:		
Factory direct materials	50,000	50,000
Factory direct labor	40,000	30,000
Machinery depreciation	5,000	10,000
Other factory overhead		
(200 percent of direct labor)	80,000	60,000
Selling and administrative expenses		
(15 percent of sales)	30,000	30,000
Total expenses	205,000	180,000
Income (loss) before taxes	(5,000)	20,000
Less: Income taxes	2,000	8,000
Net income (loss)	$ (3,000)	$ 12,000

"The cost of the present machine is a sunk cost," Adams said. "The new machine will cost us $110,000, and since it will increase our net income by $15,000 a year, it will bring us a good deal more than the 10 percent annual aftertax return on investment we want."

Upon investigation, you discover the following additional information:

1. If the present machine isn't disposed of now, it can be used for the next 10 years in the manufacture of product W. The price of product W and the cash flows required to operate either machine are expected to rise slightly from year to year, but these increases are expected to offset each other. Estimates can be based on the data in 3 below.

2. All the company's requirements of product W are manufactured in a single plant, along with a number of other products. Product W is now being assigned 25 percent of the total factory overhead cost other than

equipment depreciation. Factory overhead other than equipment depreciation can be predicted from the following formula:

$$\$240,000 + 0.5 \times \text{Direct labor cost}$$

Installation of the new machine would add $500 a year in electric power costs over and above the amounts indicated by this formula.

3. Machine data:

	Present Machine	New Machine
Expected life......................	Not applicable	10 years
Original cost......................	$55,000	$110,000
Tax depreciation to date............	27,000	0
Present trade-in value	10,000	Not applicable
Expected trade-in value after 7 years....................	5,000	35,000
Expected trade-in value after 10 years...................	0	10,000
Capacity in units per year...........	60,000	80,000
Expected output (units per year)	50,000	50,000

4. Tax depreciation on the old machine has been calculated with the sum-of-the-years'-digits method, based on a 10-year life and zero salvage. The new machine would be depreciated for income tax purposes in five annual installments of 15, 22, 21, 21, and 21 percent of its original cost, respectively.

5. Gains and losses on the sale of equipment would be taxed at the regular tax rate, and no "investment credit" is available. Depreciation for internal financial reporting is calculated on a straight-line basis.

6. If production of product W were discontinued, the present machine could be disposed of. None of the present fixed factory overhead costs other than equipment depreciation would be affected by the discontinuation of product W, nor would there by any saving in selling and administrative expenses. Working capital of $10,000 would be released for use elsewhere, however.

a. Identify the major alternatives the company should consider.

b. Present and support a recommendation as to the desirability of continuing the manufacture of product W and purchasing the new machine, indicating the anticipated consequences of each alternative you identified in answer to part *a.*

28. Expansion Proposal; Cash-Flow Estimates.[3]   Walter Weber, general manager of Sovad Company, looked across his desk at Karl Huber, the

---

[3] Copyright 1968, 1985 by l'Institut pour l'Étude des Méthodes de Direction de l'Entreprise (IMEDE), Lausanne, Switzerland. Reprinted by permission. Amounts have been restated in dollars.

company's sales manager. Mr. Huber had just suggested that Sovad increase its capacity to manufacture automatic timing devices.

"All right," said Mr. Weber, "let's see if the profits from the increased sales will give us a big enough return on investment. As soon as you're ready, give John Berner (the company's controller) your estimates of sales and what you'll need for advertising and sales promotion. He can work with purchasing and manufacturing to get the rest of the data he needs. I'll ask him to give me a recommendation on your proposal sometime next week."

Sovad was a manufacturer of industrial controls and precision instruments, with headquarters and manufacturing facilities in Winterthur, Switzerland. Its manufacturing operations in 1984 were conducted entirely in Winterthur, but more than half of its 1984 sales were made in other countries.

First introduced in 1981, the company's automatic timers had been well received by Sovad's customers both at home and abroad. By 1984, Sovad was selling all it could manufacture. Mr. Huber was convinced that he could expand his sales in Switzerland by large amounts if adequate factory capacity could be provided.

Before going to Mr. Weber with his suggestion, Mr. Huber had discussed the idea of expansion with Franz Gluck, the company's director of manufacturing. "Our Winterthur factory is already crowded," Mr. Gluck told him. "The authorities won't give us a building permit to expand it, but I know of some vacant space that we can rent in Zurich for $50,000 a year. We could put all the timer operations in there." Zurich is only 15 miles from Winterthur, and Mr. Gluck was confident that he could supervise manufacturing operations in both places without difficulty.

Working with Mr. Gluck, Mr. Huber prepared the preliminary estimates shown in Table 1. As he gave this exhibit to Mr. Berner, Mr. Huber remarked that an eight-month payback period was hard to beat. He hoped that Mr. Berner wouldn't take too long to pass the proposal on to Mr. Weber for approval.

In the course of his examination of these estimates, Mr. Berner discovered two things. First, the sales and expense estimates in Table 1 were not expected to be achieved until the third year of the new factory's operation. Second, they represented the *total* sales and expenses of the timers. Since the company was already selling 100,000 timers a year, Mr. Berner didn't believe that the profit on these units should be used to justify the opening of the new factory. As he put it, "The data we need are differential or incremental amounts, the differences between having the new factory and not having it." Mr. Huber estimated that he would be able to sell 300,000 timers a year after a two-year introductory period. His detailed estimates of annual sales and marketing expenses are summarized in Table 2.

TABLE 1
Zurich Timer Factory: Preliminary Profitability Estimate

Sales (300,000 units at $5)		$1,500,000
Out-of-pocket expenses:		
Factory labor and materials		
(300,000 at $2.84)	$852,000	
Rent	50,000	
Other factory costs (not including		
depreciation)	70,000	
Marketing expenses	160,000	
Total expenses		1,132,000
Profit contribution		$ 368,000
Equipment outlays:		
New equipment to be purchased	$250,000	
Old equipment, to be moved from Winterthur . . .	0	
Cost of moving old equipment from Winterthur		
and installing it at Zurich.	5,000	
Total equipment outlays.		$ 255,000

$$\text{Payback period} = \frac{\$255,000}{\$368,000} = 0.69 \text{ years} = 8.3 \text{ months}$$

TABLE 2
Zurich Timer Factory: Estimated Annual Timer Sales and Marketing Expenses

	Annual Sales		Annual Marketing Costs
	Units	Value	
If all timers are made in Zurich:			
Year 1	200,000	$1,000,000	$260,000
Year 2	250,000	1,250,000	260,000
Year 3 and after.	300,000	1,500,000	160,000
If timers are not made in Zurich	100,000	500,000	60,000

Mr. Berner knew that these volumes of sales would require sizable investments in working capital that Mr. Huber had omitted from Table 1. On the basis of the company's past experience, he estimated that the cumulative balance of working capital required at the beginning of each year would be as follows:

If all timers are made in Zurich:	
Year 1	$700,000
Year 2	750,000
Year 3	800,000
If timers are not made in Zurich	300,000

When questioned about the manufacturing cost estimates in Table 1, Mr. Gluck gave Mr. Berner the estimates shown in Table 3. Mr. Gluck explained that if the Zurich factory were opened, all automatic-timer production would be shifted to Zurich. If the expansion proposal were to be rejected, however, the cost of producing 100,000 timers a year at Winterthur would be $3.10 a unit plus $20,000 a year. All of these costs could be eliminated if operations were transferred to Zurich.

TABLE 3
Zurich Timer Factory: Estimated Factory Costs

	Variable Costs per Units	Fixed Costs per Year		
		Rental	Depreciation	Other
Year 1	$2.96	$50,000	$25,000	$70,000
Year 2	2.88	50,000	25,000	70,000
Year 3 and after . .	2.84	50,000	25,000	70,000

Mr. Berner also questioned Mr. Gluck about the equipment that would be moved from Winterthur to Zurich. "That's the old test equipment we're now replacing here in Winterthur," he replied. "It's perfectly adequate for the timers, and it saves us from buying new equipment for the new location. It's fully depreciated on our books, but it's in perfect condition and I see no reason why it wouldn't last for years.

"If we don't open in Zurich, we'll sell this old equipment locally for about $10,000. If we keep it, our only cost will be about $5,000 to get it from Winterthur to Zurich. We can subtract this $5,000 from the taxable income from our other operations right away, even before we start operating at Zurich."

For purposes of analysis, Mr. Berner and Mr. Huber agreed that the new Zurich plant should be able to operate for at least 10 years and that the company's investment in working capital would be a reasonable measure of the value of the Zurich assets at the end of that time.

In evaluating capital expenditure proposals, Mr. Berner used an income tax rate of 30 percent of ordinary taxable income. Gains on the sale of equipment were also taxed at a 30 percent rate. Depreciation for tax purposes on the new equipment to be purchased for the Zurich plant would be $50,000 a year for five years.

a. Prepare a timetable of the before-tax cash flows attributable to this expansion proposal.
b. Restate the cash flows on an aftertax basis. If Sovad's minimum acceptable aftertax rate of return was 14 percent, should the company have opened the Zurich factory? Show your calculations.

Chapter 22

Profit Reporting for Control

The preceding five chapters focused on the contribution of managerial accounting to management's *planning* processes. The other function of managerial accounting is to help management effect its control responsibilities. **Control** consists of management's efforts (1) to prevent unwanted departures from planned results and (2) to take action in response to signals that the plan is no longer appropriate or isn't being executed properly.

The objective of this chapter is to examine one important aspect of accounting's contribution to the control process—namely, how management uses accounting measurements of income and assets to control major segments of the business. We'll begin by looking at the control process in general terms.

The Control Process
Control begins with the formulation of a business plan. This process enables management to control the ways the organization's limited resources are used. Next, using the plan as a blueprint, management monitors results by directing, supervising, and observing operations. Finally, management exerts control by responding to deviations from planned results and reacting to other signals from the external environment.

Once the plan has been adopted, management uses three broad types of control:

1. Yes/no controls.
2. Steering controls.
3. Scorecard controls.

Each of these controls is described below, and the relationships among them are diagramed in Exhibit 22–1.

EXHIBIT 22–1
Types of Controls

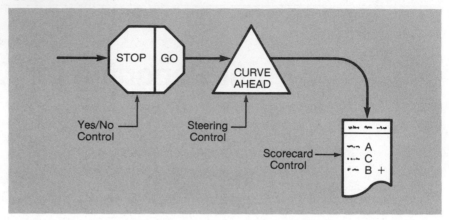

Yes/No Controls

Yes/no controls are rules that must be consulted before certain kinds of actions are taken. These rules identify the conditions that must be met if the manager is to proceed to effect a particular course of action. A good example is the "open to buy" allowance for department store buyers. These allowances are reduced when the buyers place orders and are ordinarily reinstated in time for the next buying season. By looking at the current open balances, the buyers know whether they are free to buy the quantities they have in mind.

Steering Controls

Steering controls provide signals intended either to reassure management that the present course is satisfactory or to indicate the need for some kind of action. The most useful steering controls are forecasts of what will happen if management continues to follow its present plan compared with some measure of what management wants to achieve. In practice, few steering controls fit this specification because adequate data usually aren't available. Instead, steering controls generally spotlight differences between actual results and planned (or satisfactory) results.

There are two kinds of active responses to steering controls. A **corrective response** leaves the objective alone but tries to change the methods being used to achieve it. An **adaptive response** is an action by management to redefine the objective and develop a new plan to achieve it.

Management's decision to make a corrective response assumes three things: (1) the original plan is still valid, (2) the cause of the poor performance is occurring within the organization, and (3) the manager can do something to rectify it. An adaptive response, on the other hand, presumes that the cause is outside the organization. Either the assumptions underlying the plan were wrong or the external environment has changed in unexpected ways. Since the manager isn't able to change outside conditions, the only course of action is to see how best to adapt to the emerging situation. This means a new decision, or *replanning*.

Scorecard Controls

A company's top executives can't control everything themselves. They must delegate part of their authority to managers and supervisors at lower levels in the organization who then become responsible for using resources effectively and efficiently. *Effectiveness* refers to getting the job done as it was supposed to be done—achieving the *ends; efficiency* relates to maintaining an acceptable balance between costs and benefits—using the right *means.*

Top-level and even middle-level managers are seldom able to be intimately familiar with the operations they've delegated to their subordinates. Instead, they rely on **scorecard controls** to keep informed on progress toward achieving the organization's goals. Scorecard controls are summary reports on the performance (1) of various activities or organization segments and (2) of the managers responsible for them.

Management uses scorecard reports for three reasons:

1. To evaluate the effectiveness and efficiency of individual managers and groups in the organization; this is called **managerial evaluation.**
2. To foster *motivation* to work toward achieving the goals behind the agreed-upon plan.
3. To identify activities that seem to be either particularly good or particularly bad uses of the organization's resources so that top management can consider putting additional resources in or taking some out; this is called **economic evaluation.**

Scorecard controls bear very much the same relationship to planning that steering controls do. These relationships are diagrammed in Exhibit 22–2 beginning in the upper left corner. Planning produces a plan which then becomes a set of instructions to be implemented. The results of these actions are then compared with the plan and are interpreted to determine what kinds of response are appropriate. A corrective response requires a change in the way the plan is carried out, while an adaptive response requires replanning. Each of these leads back to an earlier phase of the process and the loop is completed.

Both scorecard controls and steering controls use data that report what has happened. Since both use the kind of information known as **feedback,** both can be referred to as control by feedback response. The main

EXHIBIT 22–2
Planning and Control Loops

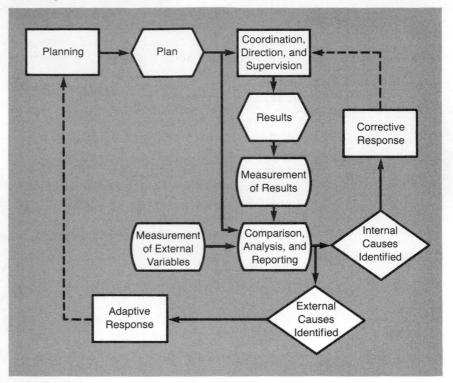

differences are that (1) steering controls typically come earlier and more often, and (2) the response, if any, comes sooner. Their similarity, however, becomes even more pronounced once we realize that scorecard reports on segments and activities at lower levels in the organization serve as steering-control signals for top management action.

| **Profit Reporting: The Organizational Setting** | The final two chapters of this book discuss the specific-issue reports that managerial accountants prepare for lower-level managers. In this chapter, we'll look at the comprehensive feedback reports that detail for top management the profit performance of relatively broad-based segments of a company's business. |

Profit-performance reports can be issued for any segment of the company's business. A business segment is any portion of the business for which both revenues and expenses can be identified. Companies in which the managers reporting to the chief executive officer are responsible for generating profits in specific business segments are generally referred to as **decentralized** companies. Their major operating divisions are known as **profit centers.** In this section, we'll see how these and other kinds of organization units fit into the decentralized company.

Profit Centers

The profit center is intended to function much like an independent business. It has four main characteristics:

1. It has a defined profit objective.
2. Its management has authority to make decisions affecting the major determinants of profit.
3. Its management is expected to use profit-oriented decision rules.
4. Its management is accountable to higher management for the amount of profit generated.

The result is that the typical profit center is a division selling a limited number of product lines or serving a specific geographic area. It encompasses both the means of providing goods or services and the means of marketing them.

Top management is likely to (1) make all the major decisions on financing and capital expenditures, (2) require that divisions conform to overall company policies, and (3) stipulate that each division's activities be coordinated with those of other divisions. Although other restrictions are also common, a true profit center should have at least three kinds of authority, within the limits established by company policy:

1. Freedom to choose its customers.
2. Freedom to choose the sources of supply for most of the materials and other goods and services it buys.
3. Authority to decide how many people to use in pursuing its profit goals and how to use them.

Why Companies Decentralize

Companies decentralize because they want their division managers to act, within limits, as though they were administering independent companies. They expect this kind of behavior to yield benefits such as the following:

1. Decisions will be made more quickly, with less red tape.
2. Decisions will be of higher quality, because the decentralized manager can devote more time to individual decisions and bring more specialized knowledge to bear on these decisions than top management could.
3. Division managers will recognize that specific parts of the company's income are the result of their own efforts, and this recognition will reinforce their motivation to strive for greater profits.

4. Top management will have more time to concentrate on strategic planning and other higher-level activities.
5. More people will gain experience in making profit-based decisions, and this will increase the number of experienced candidates for senior managerial positions.

Decentralization can also produce harmful effects. First, subordinate managers may make mistakes that managers with more experience might be able to avoid. Second, some actions that increase one division's profits may hurt other divisions and the entire company as well; this is called *suboptimization*. Third, decentralized companies are likely to have more staff personnel, both because more managers need staff assistance and because top management needs staff to help provide central guidance and oversight of decentralized operations. Finally, the quest for short-term profits may cause division managers to underemphasize nonfinancial objectives or to shortchange the future.

A company shouldn't decentralize unless it is confident it can keep the harmful effects at levels commensurate with the value of the benefits to be reaped.

Service Centers

Many organization units in decentralized companies are classified as service centers. A service center is a unit providing services or support to other units in the organization. The relationships between service centers and profit centers are illustrated in Exhibit 22–3. These service centers have three common characteristics:

1. The volume of production, service, or support they provide is determined elsewhere in the company.

Exhibit 22–3
Relationships between Service Centers and Profit Centers

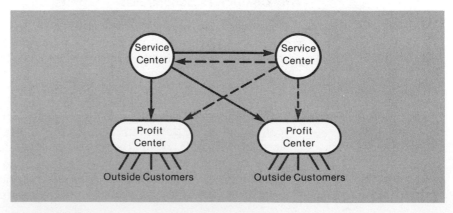

2. Their managers are evaluated on the basis of cost, quality, effectiveness, and other internal performance criteria—not on a profit basis.
3. The activities they perform are evaluated either jointly with other activities or on the basis of benefit criteria other than profit (e.g., amount of cost saved or public goodwill created).

Service centers in corporate headquarters help top management analyze the strategic plans and implementation proposals submitted by the division managers. They also advise and assist the division managers on technical matters, supplementing the efforts of the divisions' own staff analysts. In addition, corporate service centers may administer the controls top management has established to set limits within which the division managers are free to exercise their authority. And they help top management review and evaluate the performance of individual divisions and their managers. In a sense, dealing with central staff is the price division managers pay for the authority they've been given.

Profit Standards for Managerial Evaluation

In evaluating divisional performance either for managerial evaluation or for economic evaluation, management needs to select performance standards that are appropriate for the reports' intended purposes.

Standards used in evaluating division managers' profit performance need to be tested against two major criteria:

1. Current *attainability* by competent division managers.
2. Consistency with the degree of profit *controllability*.

Attainability

Attainability is a highly qualitative characteristic. In this context, it refers to levels of performance the division managers themselves believe they can reach. The attainability criterion is important because standards that are unattainable will be perceived as unfair by the division managers. This means that they won't *internalize* these standards—that is, they won't accept them as goals worthy of their efforts.

The attainable level of performance must be determined division by division. Profit differences can be created by variations in the age or condition of production facilities; by differences in local wage structures, transportation costs, or raw materials prices; by differences in the types of products handled or customers served; or by differences in the degree of competition faced in the marketplace. This means that the standard must be adapted to each division's situation each period—otherwise, it may not be attainable.

Controllability

Profit standards for use in managerial evaluation must also satisfy the controllability criterion, which specifies that the manager being evaluated must have authority to influence the variables which may create differences between actual performance and the performance standard. The controllability criterion is important because divisional profit reports are intended to reinforce the division manager's *motivation* to pursue goals that are consistent with the company's overall profit goals. *Profit variances*—differences between reported profits and the managerial performance standard—won't have that effect if they result from forces the manager can't control.

The Profit Plan

The performance standard that comes closest to satisfying both the attainability and the controllability criteria is the current profit plan, adjusted for the effects of unforeseen changes in the economic environment. As we pointed out in Chapter 20, most profit plans are established jointly by profit-responsible executives, their subordinates, and their immediate superiors. Once established, the profit plan becomes a commitment—by the profit center manager to strive to carry it out and by higher management to accept the achievement of planned results as satisfactory managerial performance. If superiors are unwilling to make this commitment, they should reject the plan and either demand a new one or find a new manager for the profit center.

Two safeguards are essential if this standard is to be used in managerial evaluation. First, top management has to carry out a rigorous, critical review of all budget proposals, usually with strong central-staff participation (i.e., by a corporate service center). Second, management has to include improvement targets in the budgeting process. Low profit levels may be acceptable for a while, particularly in declining industries with heavy investments in plant assets, but eventually the division must either improve or close up shop. Recognizing this, top management should judge division managers' performance at least as much by the quality of their budget proposals as by their current profit performance.

Failure to produce the results anticipated in the annual plan doesn't necessarily imply managerial failure. Many noncontrollable factors may have influenced the results. For this reason, most internal profit reports include analyses or commentaries on the differences between actual and budgeted performance. The commentaries, in calling attention to unusual events that affected income favorably or unfavorably, may indicate whether these effects are expected to continue and what actions management is taking to cope with, or to capitalize on, the situation.

Qualitative commentaries on profit variances are often supported and supplemented by quantitative breakdowns of the aggregate profit variance in each segment of the business. The variance can be subdivided to identify the effects of any influences management thinks are likely to be significant.[1]

Profit Standards for Economic Evaluation

For economic evaluation, the question is no longer whether current division management is doing a good job, but whether the division's activities are generating enough income to justify the amount of funds invested in it. In other words, is the division generating an adequate rate of return on investment?

To answer this question, management should compare the return the division is getting with a standard based on the cost of capital, applied uniformly to all divisions in a given risk category. For economic evaluation, differences in the market environment don't justify the use of different return-on-investment standards for different divisions, as they do in managerial evaluation; top management's only concern is whether invested capital produces more than it costs.

The profit plan does play a role in economic evaluation, particularly for divisions conducting development-stage business. Major capital investment or promotional programs usually are accompanied by low short-term profits. Major increases in spending in independent research and development programs are likely to have the same effect, (1) because the benefits of the activity won't come until later periods, and (2) because the expenditures themselves are treated as expenses as they are made.

The approach that is used in these situations is to draw up long-range plans, detailing the anticipated results year by year during the period it takes the expenditures to produce their results. As long as current performance is consistent with this timetable, the division deserves a favorable economic evaluation, even though the current rate of return on investment is lower than the cost of capital.

The long-range plan has to be revised each year, as additional expenditures are made and new information becomes available. This updating also gives management a chance to see whether the promises of future rewards still appear likely to be fulfilled. If the promised rewards seem to remain just as distant year after year, top management will have to consider whether the long-range plans are more the product of wishful thinking than of realistic analysis.

Measuring Divisional Profit

For economic evaluation, divisional profit should reflect *all* the revenues, expenses, gains, and losses attributable to each division and its

---

[1] For one analytical scheme, see Gordon Shillinglaw, *Managerial Cost Accounting,* 5th ed. (Homewood, Ill.: Richard D. Irwin, 1982), Chap. 27.

activities, together with an estimate of the resources committed to the support of those activities. For managerial evaluation, divisional profit should be measured in such a way that the differences between reported profit and the profit plan result from actions and events over which division management has some influence.

Given these two criteria—for economic evaluation and for managerial evaluation—let's examine four possible measures of divisional profit performance:

1. Profit contribution.
2. Net income.
3. Return on investment.
4. Residual income.

Profit Contribution

Exhibit 22–4 shows a monthly income statement for the college division of Darwin Books, Inc., a publisher of textbooks. Five of the division's expense classes are traceable expenses—that is, they are incurred solely and exclusively to carry out the division's activities. Two of these—printing-and-binding and authors' royalties—are wholly variable with sales volume. Subtracting these from net sales revenues determines the division's contribution margin.

> ### TERMINOLOGY REMINDER
>
> *Contribution margin* is the difference between the total revenues of a segment and the variable costs occasioned by those revenues.

The other three classes of traceable expenses—copy editing, advertising and selling, and administration—are fixed, in that they don't change in response to changes in divisional volume. Subtracting these traceable fixed expenses from the contribution margin identifies the division's **profit contribution,** the amount the division's operations contribute to help the company cover the fixed costs that aren't traceable to any one division and provide income for the shareowners.

Darwin's divisional income statements also include an allocation of the fixed expenses that are incurred in the company's head office and can't be traced to any one division. From the division's point of view, these are indirect (nontraceable) expenses. These allocations are deducted from profit contribution to determine the division's income before income taxes. **Divisional net income** is then determined by calculating the amount of income tax applicable to the division's income, and subtracting it from the division's pretax income.

EXHIBIT 22–4
Darwin Books, Inc., College Division: Profit Contribution Report for the Month Ended June 30, 19x3

	Current Month			Year to Date		
	Actual	**Budget**	**Over/ (Under) Budget**	**Actual**	**Budget**	**Over/ (Under) Budget**
Net sales	$320,000	$300,000	$20,000	$4,250,000	$4,020,000	$230,000
Variable expenses:						
Printing and binding	192,000	180,000	12,000	2,580,000	2,400,000	180,000
Authors' royalties	42,000	39,000	3,000	485,000	480,000	5,000
Total variable expenses	234,000	219,000	15,000	3,065,000	2,880,000	185,000
Contribution margin	86,000	81,000	5,000	1,185,000	1,140,000	45,000
Traceable fixed expenses:						
Copy editing	11,000	10,000	1,000	118,000	120,000	(2,000)
Advertising and selling	48,000	50,000	(2,000)	567,000	580,000	(13,000)
Administration	10,000	9,000	1,000	143,000	140,000	3,000
Total traceable fixed expenses	69,000	69,000	—	828,000	840,000	(12,000)
Profit contribution	17,000	12,000	5,000	357,000	300,000	57,000
Indirect fixed expenses:						
Head office charges	14,000	10,000	4,000	287,000	260,000	27,000
Income before taxes.......	3,000	2,000	1,000	70,000	40,000	30,000
Income tax..............	1,200	800	400	28,000	16,000	12,000
Net income.............	$ 1,800	$ 1,200	$ 600	$ 42,000	$ 24,000	$ 18,000

The first three columns in this exhibit show that the college division exceeded its sales budget by $20,000 in June while its profit contribution was $5,000 better than the amount budgeted for the month. This advantage was largely eaten up by the allocation of head office costs, so that the division's net income beat the budget by only $600. We'll discuss the role of allocations at the bottom of Exhibit 22–4 in the next section.

One advantage of the profit-contribution format is that it emphasizes the sensitivity of profit to variations in the use of the capacity established by the structure of fixed costs. A 10 percent increase in the college division's sales volume, for example, presumably would increase the contribution margin by 10 percent (from $86,000 to $94,600) but would leave the fixed costs unchanged.

Profit contribution fails to satisfy either the economic evaluation criterion or the managerial evaluation criterion, however. It is unsatisfactory for economic evaluation (1) because it overlooks centrally administered costs attributable to the division, and (2) because it doesn't reflect divisional investment at all. It does come closer to meeting the needs of managerial evaluation, because it is likely to encompass most of the income statement elements the division manager can influence (and only those elements). Its drawback is that it ignores the investments under the division manager's control. A division may be able to increase its profit contribution by increasing its investments in inventories and receivables. Unless the profit-performance measure reflects these investments, it will provide a misleading impression of managerial performance. The manager will get credit for the benefits of the investment without being evaluated for the costs of the investment.

Net Income

Under the profit-contribution approach, company fixed costs that can't be traced to individual divisions or other revenue segments—that is, indirect fixed costs—aren't distributed among the segments. *Company net income consists of the profit contributions of the various revenue segments (divisions) less the total of the indirect fixed costs.* To move from profit contribution to net income for individual segments, as we did at the bottom of Exhibit 22–4, we have to find some way of allocating indirect fixed costs.

An ideal solution would be to allocate to each segment the fixed costs the company could eliminate if it were to withdraw from that segment. To try to approximate this, we might subdivide the indirect fixed costs into groups, each of which has its own set of determinants, and then allocate the costs in each group to the segments in proportion to the segments' shares of these determinants. The cost of office space in a company's headquarters, for example, might be divided among the company's divisions in proportion to the amount of space each of them occupies in the headquarters buildings.

Although this approach is promising, it can't succeed completely. Many indirect fixed costs just can't be identified clearly with determinants that can also be identified with individual segments. The salaries of the company's principal executive officers are a case in point. As a result, some or all of the indirect fixed costs are typically allocated arbitrarily, in proportion to some broad measure of segmental activity such as sales volume or the number of employees. Company income taxes are then allocated among the segments in proportion to the determinants of taxable income.

Darwin Books, for example, had $25,000 in headquarters fixed costs (indirect with respect to the activities of the individual divisions) in June 19x3. Darwin's accountants allocated $14,000 of this amount to the college division, against a budgeted allocation of $10,000. This left $3,000 ($17,000 − $14,000) income before taxes in June, against $2,000 in the original budget ($12,000 − $10,000). Darwin used a 40 percent income tax rate in its monthly profit reports, leaving the *divisional net income* amounts shown on the bottom line of Exhibit 22–4.

Divisional net income is a better economic-evaluation measure than profit contribution if the allocations of headquarters expenses fairly approximate the amount of headquarters expenses attributable to the division's activities. Unfortunately, most allocations of nontraceable fixed costs are arbitrary. How much of the president's salary should be charged to the college division is a question of metaphysics, not of scientific measurement. General percentage allocations are the worst because they make no pretense of measuring the amount of fixed cost the company could avoid by discarding the segment. The larger these allocations are, the less reliance management can place on net income. Even if the allocation problem could be solved, divisional net income alone wouldn't meet the needs of economic evaluation because it doesn't reflect the amount of investment attributable to each division's activities.

Divisional net income also fails the managerial evaluation test because it contains allocations of headquarters expenses the division manager can't control and because it doesn't reflect controllable investments. The controllability consideration can be met if headquarters allocations are entirely predetermined, yielding no differences from the budgeted amounts; reflecting divisional investments takes us away from the net income concept altogether, into return-on-investment or residual-income reporting.

Return on Investment (ROI)

We've already said that the standard for economic evaluation is expressed as a rate of return on investment, linked to the cost of capital. We shouldn't be surprised, therefore, to find that **return on investment** (usually abbreviated ROI) is the most widely used measure of divisional profit performance.[2] The ratio is:

$$\text{Return on investment} = \frac{\text{Net income}}{\text{Investment}}$$

The rate of return should always be measured on an *annual* basis. Seasonal variations are difficult to allow for, and the effort seldom is worthwhile. Darwin Books' college division generated net income of $1,800 in June 19x3 (as shown in Exhibit 22–4) and $42,000 in the year

---

[2] See James S. Reece and William R. Cool, "Measuring Investment Center Performance," *Harvard Business Review*, May–June 1978, p. 29.

as a whole. The company's net investment in the college division (mainly in inventories and receivables) averaged $800,000 in fiscal 19x3. The reported rate of return on investment in 19x3 therefore was:

$$\text{Return on investment} = \frac{\$42,000}{\$800,000} = 5.25 \text{ percent}$$

Measurement of a division's return on investment is intended to be used in two ways:

1. To direct top management's attention to segments that persistently earn less than the target return on investment.
2. To show how viable the segment is likely to be on a continuing basis—that is, are the revenues covering all the costs attributable to them? If not, the future is bleak, no matter how favorable the current cash-flow relationships.

A division with a persistently low return on investment is an obvious candidate for disposal. Conversely, as long as the reported return on investment is at a level management considers satisfactory, management probably won't find it necessary to consider disposing of the division. The measure is imperfect, however. The use of reported return on investment to measure divisional profit performance introduces all the measurement problems we identified in discussing net income-based measurements plus the additional problems of measuring divisional investment and annualizing both income and investment.

In any case, the disposal decision should be based, not on the amounts shown in the historical return-on-investment reports, but on estimates of cash flows, using the techniques outlined in Chapter 21. This analysis requires a comparison of (1) the present value of the cash flows from continued operation with (2) the cash flows to be generated by withdrawing from the segment immediately.

The cash flows from immediate withdrawal come from the aftertax liquidation value of the facilities and working capital attributable to the segment, less any liquidation costs (employee severance pay and so on), also adjusted for the tax effects. The cash flows from continued operation are the net receipts the company would lose if it were to drop out of the market now.

Before moving on, we should note one hidden danger in return-on-investment reporting. Faced with persistently low return-on-investment ratios in some of its operations, management may find it extremely difficult to remember that the failure of these segments to meet minimum profitability standards is a suitable topic for economic evaluation, not managerial appraisal. No manager should be rewarded for being placed in charge of a profitable operation or stigmatized for being assigned to activities that are inherently unprofitable.

Residual Income

A variant of return on investment is **residual income,** defined as divisional net income less an investment carrying charge, determined by multiplying divisional investment by an interest rate based on the cost of capital. The interest rate should be an aftertax rate if income taxes have been deducted in calculating divisional income; for monthly reporting, it should be divided by 12.

For example, suppose Darwin Books had an aftertax cost of capital of 10 percent, approximately 0.8 percent a month. Budgeted investment for the month of June 19x3 was $750,000; actual investment was $800,000. Taking the divisional income amounts from Exhibit 22–4 and ignoring seasonal factors, we have the following:

	Actual	Budget	Over/ (Under) Budget
Net income	$ 1,800	$ 1,200	$600
Investment carrying charge (0.8% of investment)	6,400	6,000	400
Residual income/(loss)	$(4,600)	$(4,800)	$200

Residual income's main advantage over return on investment is that it places budget-versus-actual differences (variances) on equivalent scales. For example, having $50,000 more inventory than the budget calls for can be said to cost the company $400 a month (0.8 percent × $50,000). If this much extra inventory were to increase divisional income by $1,000 a month after taxes, it certainly would be worth having.

Even so, residual income shares most of the defects of return on investment. It reflects allocations of indirect fixed costs and centrally administered assets, allocations that may be partly arbitrary, and it includes noncontrollable variances in expenses and investments. Users should understand these limitations when interpreting residual income amounts.

Adjusting for Inflation

The amounts reported for investments in assets, depreciation, and the cost of goods sold on most divisional profit-performance statements are based on measures of historical cost. Most depreciable assets in use today were acquired when prices were lower than they are now, however. A similar time lag affects some cost of goods sold amounts, particularly when inventories are measured on a FIFO basis. As a result, reported expenses are likely to *understate* the current cost of the resources used to obtain current revenues.

Similar problems surround the measurement of the inventory and plant asset components of the divisional investment base at their historical costs. Historical cost is likely to understate the investment currently required by the division's activities.

One solution to these problems is to measure assets, depreciation, and the cost of goods sold at their replacement costs. Most companies in the United States have shied away from doing this, perceiving the cost of measuring replacement prices to be far greater than the benefits to be derived. With income overstating the margin over current cost and with the investment base understating current investment requirements, however, historical-cost reporting may cover up deteriorating profit situations until price levels stabilize and asset replacement at higher prices begins to be felt in a lower return on investment. As inflation persists and large companies develop replacement-cost estimates for external financial reporting, the internal use of these estimates in divisional performance reporting is likely to increase.

Achieving Long-Term Goals

One danger of profit-based decentralization is that the managers of profit centers may sacrifice *the company*'s long-term interests to increase *their divisions*' short-term profits. Two ways of counteracting this tendency can be tried: (1) establishing additional criteria for evaluating the performance of division managers, and (2) establishing centrally administered constraints and guidelines.

Multiple Performance Criteria

Current income reports can never capture the full effect of current actions. Decisions made now may pay off or have disastrous consequences a year, a decade, or a generation hence. Some decisions affect nonfinancial indexes before they have visible effects on reported income, however; market share, absenteeism, product defects, and productivity are among the many nonfinancial indexes top management may wish to monitor.

One way to insure that managers do let these variables affect their decisions is to require them to set both profit and nonprofit objectives and include both in their proposed operating plans. These proposed objectives will be reviewed by top management or by the headquarters staff; after revision, they too will become standards against which future performance can be measured.

The development of multiple performance criteria may help division managers adopt the company's goals as their own—because more dimensions of their activities can be encompassed in the evaluation of managerial performance. Top management faces two problems in using multiple performance criteria, however. First, some goals are difficult to quantify. As a result, management is likely to measure performance by comparing actual inputs with planned inputs, rather than by measuring divisional outputs. Second, the goals may be inconsistent with each other. Expenditures designed to enhance management development may reduce the rate of growth; increases in market share may occur only at the expense of current profitability.

The presence of inconsistent goals forces division managers to determine the amount of effort to devote to the pursuit of each goal. Division managers are likely to learn to identify top management's implicit priorities by watching the responses to their successes and failures in meeting the various objectives. If top management wants the divisions to pursue nonprofit objectives, therefore, it must be prepared to react both when they are met and when they are missed.

Centrally Administered Constraints and Guidelines

Many large decentralized companies try to protect their long-term interests by imposing centrally administered constraints and guidelines on their division managers. These may take the form of minimum-performance objectives, one in each performance dimension. These minima limit the managers' freedom to sacrifice progress toward one objective to achieve greater progress toward another.

Another possibility is to give central staff groups authority to review and reject portions of proposed divisional plans, and to audit compliance with centrally established standards. Internal control systems are subjected to this kind of review, for example. Similarly, a central maintenance staff might have the authority to make sure that divisional maintenance expenditures will be adequate to keep plant and equipment from accumulating "deferred maintenance" obligations.

These arrangements reduce the autonomy of the division managers, leading to some violation of the profit-center concept. The profit-center structure is only a means to an end, however, and top management is free to modify it if the benefits of these modifications seem likely to exceed the costs.

Interdivisional Transfer Pricing

Profit centers and other organization units for which profit-performance measures must be prepared often buy from and sell to one another. The prices at which these interdivisional transactions are recorded are known as **transfer prices.** These prices can affect the amount of profit each division reports. In this final section, we'll review the criteria for transfer pricing and three of the many methods available for pricing interdivisional transfers.

Criteria for Transfer Pricing

The first criterion to be observed in setting transfer prices is that *the transfer price should lead division management to make the same decisions headquarters management would make it if had the time to study the problems and apply all the data available to the managers of both divisions.* The second criterion is that *division managers should be able to regard the transfer prices as fair.* If managers doubt the fairness of the transfer prices, they may be less motivated to achieve profits for their divisions and the company as a whole.

Neither of these two criteria makes any reference to the effects of transfer prices on taxes or other fiscal variables. If fiscal considerations require the use of transfer prices that fail to meet the two managerially oriented criteria we've identified, management may try to find economical ways of maintaining two parallel transfer-pricing systems.

Dictated Prices Equal to Full Cost

Under this pricing method, the pricing authority (higher management or one of the two divisions) establishes a price, which is then used to record transfers. The implicit assumption is that a transfer price set in this way measures the supplying division's long-run incremental cost of supplying the intermediate product on a continuing basis.

Even if a particular set of full-cost-based prices approximates long-run incremental cost, it will fail to provide a sound guide to current resource-utilization decisions, as required by our first criterion. As long as a supplying division is operating below capacity—that is, in the portion of the volume range in which average cost exceeds the cost of a one-unit increase in volume—transfer prices based on full cost will overstate the supplying division's economic sacrifice and suboptimization may result.

The situation will be just the reverse if the supplying division is pressing its capacity limits. At full capacity, the market value of the intermediate product is likely to be higher than average full cost. If the transfer price is based on full cost, the buying division will receive a signal that understates the sacrifice the company makes in making the intermediate product available to the buying division. A forced transfer at this price may be suboptimal and will be perceived as unfair by the supplying division manager.

Dictated Prices Equal to Marginal Cost

Under this pricing method, the division supplying the goods to be transferred quotes a schedule of prices equal to its estimated marginal costs of production. **Marginal cost** at any volume is the increase in total cost that is necessary to increase total volume by a single unit. The division wishing to use the goods decides how many units it wishes to buy, given the quoted price schedule.

When the supplying division is operating below capacity, marginal cost measures the sacrifice the supplying division (and therefore the company) makes by supplying the product. When the supplying division is operating at capacity, however, it is likely to be able to use its capacity to produce and sell products at prices exceeding marginal cost. The division's sacrifice therefore is measured by opportunity cost—the current market value of the amount of capacity the transferred product uses up. The buying division shouldn't be allowed to use the transferred product unless it can afford to pay this opportunity cost. Most commonly used estimates of marginal cost understate opportunity cost in this situation and therefore fail to meet the first transfer-pricing criterion: congruence with top management's decision rules.

Marginal-cost transfer prices are also likely to seem unfair to one division manager or the other—or both. For one thing, the use of marginal cost implies that neither division can influence the price. Division managers therefore have no control over this variable. This abrogation of authority is likely to weaken the managers' perception of the fairness of the system. Furthermore, if volume is low enough so that marginal cost is lower than average full cost, most of the profit contribution of internally transferred goods will be lodged in the internal buying division. The supplying division manager therefore may find it more difficult to justify capital-expenditure proposals. If the system is seen to discriminate against the supplying division in this way, this may reduce its manager's commitment to the system's objectives.

Market-Based Negotiated Prices

In negotiated transfer pricing, the two divisions negotiate the amounts to be transferred and the prices to be paid. Negotiated systems are based on the notion that the division managers, with intimate knowledge of their own markets and opportunities, are in the best position to decide whether internal transfers should take place. Part of the division manager's job is to be aware of market conditions affecting the division's operations. Each division manager is expected to make many decisions in which estimates of opportunity cost are crucial. The internal transfer decision is simply one of many.

A simple situation of this kind is illustrated in Exhibit 22–5. This shows a supplying division with average total costs of $17 and some outside customers paying enough to yield $18 a unit after marketing costs are deducted. The shaded area in the block representing the supplying division is the amount of capacity now devoted to filling outside customers' orders; the rest is idle.

The buying division has an opportunity to buy the product from an outside supplier for $15 and has offered to pay this amount to the supplying division. The situation can be summarized quickly:

1. The buying division won't pay more than $15.
2. It appears that the company will be better off if the transfer takes place (cost will be the $13 incremental cost, not $15).
3. The supplying division will be $2 better off ($15 − $13) if it fills the order than if it lets the capacity stand idle.

EXHIBIT 22–5
Market Influences on Transfer-Pricing Negotiations

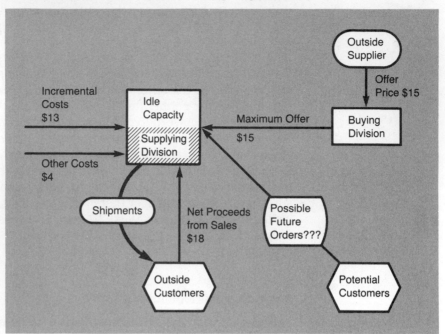

In these circumstances it would seem that the two division managers have a mutual interest in reaching agreement on a transfer price. They will fail to agree only if the supplying division's manager estimates that the potential customers in the lower right-hand corner of the diagram are likely to come in with higher-priced orders that will fill the division's capacity.

Division managers are paid to exercise their judgment in situations like this. They are expected to be right often enough to justify giving them the authority to make these decisions. The presumption is that the managers will negotiate an agreement if interdivisional transfers seem to be in the company's best interests, because both managers will benefit if this is the case.

Negotiation should also contribute to the participants' sense of the fairness of the system, if the conditions necessary to negotiation are present. Without negotiation, internal transfers are either take-it-or-leave-it decisions or command decisions made by higher management. In either case, the division managers' freedom of action is reduced, and this reduces their accountability for profit. Negotiation restores the managers' freedom of action and thereby increases their accountability for profits.

Negotiation will work, however, only if four conditions are met:

1. There must be some form of outside market for the intermediate product.
2. Any available market information should be communicated to both parties to the negotiation.
3. Both parties must have freedom to deal outside.
4. Top management must indicate its support of the principle of negotiation.

Negotiation can be time-consuming and divisive, even when the four conditions are met. If these problems are serious enough, top management may decide to fall back on another transfer-pricing method, relying on other devices to offset the weaknesses of any such method.[3]

Summary

Planning needs to be reinforced by control activities. Managerial accounting provides scorecard control information, primarily for use in managerial and economic evaluation of individual managers and activities. These control reports emphasize the differences between actual results and appropriate performance standards for individual segments of the company's activities.

The major organization segments in decentralized companies are known as profit centers, designed to operate, within limits, much as independent businesses. The performance of a profit center is appraised primarily on the basis of comparisons of actual profit or return on investment with an appropriate performance standard. The appropriate performance standard for economic evaluation is the cost of capital; the relevant standard for managerial evaluation is the current profit plan, adjusted for any changes in economic conditions that were not anticipated in the plan.

The profit performance of a profit center may be measured by its profit contribution, its net income, its return on investment, or its residual income. Only return on investment and residual income encompass all the variables attributable to the profit center or controllable by its managers. Unfortunately, each of these measures also includes allocations of centrally administered assets and headquarters expenses, and these allocations may be neither attributable to the division's activities nor controllable by the division's management.

When a profit center transfers part of its output to or receives goods or services from another part of the company, the transfer is recorded by a transfer price. This price can be set by negotiation between the parties to

---

[3] For a more complete discussion of transfer pricing and a review of other methods, see Shillinglaw, *Managerial Cost Accounting*, Chap. 26.

the transfer if outside markets exist and other conditions are met; otherwise, some system abrogating a portion of the divisions' autonomy must be used.

Profit decentralization is designed to provide the motivation and flexibility to improve the company's profitability. A danger is that managers may sacrifice the company's long-term interests to increase the divisions' short-term profits. The use of multiple performance objectives and centrally administered constraints and guidelines should help counteract any such tendencies.

Key Terms

Adaptive response	Profit center
Control	Profit contribution
Corrective response	Profit variance
Decentralization	Residual income
Divisional net income	Return on investment (ROI)
Economic evaluation	Scorecard controls
Feedback	Steering controls
Managerial evaluation	Transfer price
Marginal cost	Yes/no controls

Independent Study Problems (Solutions in Appendix B)

1. Scorecard and Steering Controls. Prairie Airways, Inc., provides scheduled passenger airline service connecting Chicago with 14 other airports in the Midwest. It operates 18 flights each weekday and 10 flights each Saturday and Sunday. Each flight either originates or terminates in Chicago; some are nonstop but most take two or more stops on the way to or from Chicago.

Prairie Airways has a small staff of ground personnel at each airport it serves. Routine maintenance of its aircraft is performed on contract in Chicago by a major airline.

What kinds of steering control and scorecard control information do you think Prairie's management should have?

2. Managerial Evaluation: Residual Income. The investment in division A consists of $200,000 in traceable working capital, $400,000 in traceable plant and equipment, and $100,000 in centrally administered assets, allocated to the division at a rate of one sixth of traceable investment. The budgeted amounts for these three totals were $150,000, $420,000, and $95,000.

Division A's net income for the year is $63,000, after deducting $30,000 in traceable depreciation, $40,000 in head-office charges (allocated to the division at the rate of 5 percent of sales), and income taxes at

50 percent. The budgeted amounts were $70,000, $32,000, $45,000, and 50 percent.

The company estimates that its minimum acceptable rate of return is 12 percent, after taxes.

a. Calculate budgeted and actual return on investment.
b. Calculate budgeted and actual residual income.
c. Discuss the division manager's performance. Explain why the information provided by your answer to part *a*, your answer to part *b*, or some other calculation is relevant to managerial evaluation.
d. What action should management take in response to your evaluation of this division's activities, based on the amounts supplied here?

3. Transfer Pricing; Negotiation. Ballou Corporation, a diversified manufacturing company, has seven main product divisions, each with its own manufacturing facilities and selling most of its output to outside customers. One of these divisions, the Hull Division, manufactures and sells a broad range of industrial chemicals.

Hull Division supplies product X to outside customers and also to the Hingham Division, another of Ballou's seven product divisions. Hingham Division uses product X as a raw material in the manufacture of several products. Hull charges Hingham $1.80 a pound for product X, 10 percent less than it charges outside customers.

Hingham has been happy with this arrangement for several years, but an outside supplier has just offered to supply a perfectly satisfactory substitute for product X at a firm contract price of $1.60 a pound, delivered to the Hingham factory. The Hingham Division manager has proposed that the interdivisional transfer price of product X be reduced to $1.60 to meet the competing offer; otherwise, the contract will go outside.

You are the assistant controller in the Hingham Division. Your division manager has just given you a copy of Hull Division's estimated monthly income statement for product X (in $thousands):

Sales—outside (100,000 pounds at $2)...............		$200
Sales—Hingham (50,000 pounds at $1.80)............		90
Total sales..................................		290
Product-traceable costs:		
Variable manufacturing costs ($0.90 per pound).....	$135	
Sales commissions—outside sales	10	
Depreciation......................................	20	
Other traceable fixed costs......................	40	205
Product profit contribution		85
Share of divisional fixed costs.....................		60
Income before taxes		$ 25

The fixed costs traceable to product X wouldn't be reduced if the production volume were reduced by a third. The divisional fixed costs, allocated among the division's products at a flat 40 cents a pound, are even stickier. These costs would continue even if Hull Division stopped making product X entirely.

a. Draft a short memorandum, outlining the points Hingham's manager should make in trying to convince Hull's manager to reduce the transfer price.
b. Is negotiation the right way to determine a transfer price in this situation?

Exercises and Problems

4. Steering and Scorecard Controls. The manager of a chain of motion-picture theaters relies on written reports to keep informed about the operations of the individual theaters. Films are booked for a week at a time, with an unlimited renewal option. Runs of six to eight weeks are not uncommon, but many films are replaced at the end of one week. The film shown at one theater may also be shown at one or more others in the chain, but a separate booking decision is made at each theater each week.

Each theater has a manager responsible for maintaining and operating the theater. Employees are hired by the local manager, but salaries must be approved by the chain manager. The chain manager selects the films to be shown, makes all the booking decisions, hires the theater managers, and controls all advertising and sales promotion activities.

a. What reports is the chain manager likely to find useful? Indicate how each of these reports would be used and whether you regard it as a steering control or a scorecard control.
b. What would you report to the individual theater managers, and how frequently would you report it? Indicate how the manager would use this information and whether it would be steering control or scorecard control information.
c. To what extent should the theater managers be held responsible for income from sales of refreshments? How would you evaluate their performance?

5. Planning and Control Information; Role of Accounting. Helen and Hilda Haldi, former Olympic downhill skiers, were hired by Haddon Hill Associates to manage the Haddon Hill ski area. Their facilities included restaurants, shops, ski lifts, snowmaking and grooming equipment, and five downhill ski runs. They also ran a full instruction program for children and adults.

The Haldi sisters were expected to decide when to open or close individual lifts, slopes, restaurants, and other customer service facilities. They hired and supervised the work of a controller and the heads of Haddon Hill's three operating departments: the restaurant manager, the chief ski instructor, and the maintenance manager. The chief instructor was in charge of all customer service activities except the restaurants, lifts, and ski runs. The maintenance manager was responsible for all maintenance of physical plant and equipment and for the operation of lifts and ski runs. The chief instructor also organized and supervised the ski patrol and first-aid operations.

The department heads determined how many employees they would need in their departments each day, following guidelines the Haldi sisters had established at the beginning of the season. Each department head was expected to control costs, maintain the quality of the services provided, hire and fire employees, and maintain effective employee relations. The restaurant manager and chief instructor were also expected to produce revenues in excess of the costs of operating their departments.

a. Outline the kinds of information the Haldi sisters probably received when they were planning for this year's skiing season and state how they probably used it. In what format (that is, what kinds of items and how much detail) did they probably express their financial plan for the year?

b. What kinds of financial information would management probably require during the skiing season? How often would this information be reported and to whom? What kinds of actions would you expect management to take in response to this information?

c. What part would you expect the controller (chief accounting officer) of the Haddon Hill ski area to play in the planning and control process?

6. Preparing a Profit-Contribution Statement. Morgan Wicker Company markets three products. You have the following information (in $thousands):

	Product A	Product B	Product C
Contribution margin (percentage of sales)	40%	30%	45%
Sales revenues	$10,000	$8,000	$6,000
Fixed expenses*	2,000	2,300	3,100

* Includes allocations of nontraceable fixed costs at the rate of 10 percent of sales revenues.

a. Prepare a profit-contribution statement, with a separate column for each product and one column for the company as a whole.

b. Comment briefly on the profitability of each product.

7. Preparing a Profit Contribution Statement. The following income report was prepared for product A last month:

Sales revenues		$400,000
Cost of goods sold		250,000
Gross margin		150,000
Marketing expenses	$80,000	
Administrative expenses	30,000	110,000
Income before taxes		$ 40,000

Product A is manufactured in a factory that makes many other products as well. The cost of goods sold last month consisted of direct materials, $50,000; direct labor, $80,000; and factory overhead, $120,000. Fixed costs account for 85 percent of factory overhead costs.

Sixty percent of product A's marketing expenses last month, including sales commissions amounting to 3 percent of sales, were fully traceable to that product; the remainder consisted of head office and branch expenses, allocated to product A on the basis of sales volume.

Product A's administrative expenses last month represented that product's share of head office administrative costs, allocated on the basis of sales revenues.

All marketing and administrative expenses except sales commissions were fixed costs.

Prepare a profit contribution statement for product A, in good form.

8. Calculating and Interpreting Residual Income and Return on Investment. Thompson Enterprises regards 10 percent after taxes as the minimum acceptable rate of return on capital expenditures. You have the following data for the Digby division for the last three years:

	19x1		19x2		19x3	
	Actual	**Budget**	**Actual**	**Budget**	**Actual**	**Budget**
Net income	$ 500	$ 480	$ 700	$ 650	$1,000	$ 950
Net investment	2,500	2,500	4,000	3,800	6,400	6,300

a. Calculate budgeted and actual residual income and return on investment for each year.

b. Assuming that allocations haven't distorted the division's results materially, what do these data tell you about managerial performance and investment performance in this division?

9. Allocating Indirect Fixed Costs. Localio Products Company has three divisions operating as profit centers and three central administrative departments operating as service centers. You have the following information on the three profit centers:

	Western Division	Central Division	Eastern Division	Total
Sales revenues	$2,000,000	$5,000,000	$3,000,000	$10,000,000
Profit contribution	300,000	1,200,000	1,100,000	2,600,000
Investment................	1,500,000	4,000,000	3,500,000	9,000,000
Number of employees	1,250	2,500	1,250	5,000

The operating costs of the three administrative departments were:

Accounting	$300,000
Marketing	250,000
Executive offices	360,000

The income tax rate is 40 percent.

a. Calculate the return on investment in each division, allocating the costs of the three administrative departments on the following bases: accounting, number of employees; marketing, sales revenues; executive offices, investment.

b. Do these allocations give you a better basis for managerial evaluation or economic evaluation than you would have in their absence? As part of your answer, identify the criterion you believe should underlie allocations for each of these purposes.

10. Discussion Question: Identifying Profit Centers. Carnegie Improvements, Inc., buys parcels of land and builds condominium housing developments on them. Once a parcel of land has been bought, a manager is appointed to supervise construction and marketing operations at that development and to manage the commercial and recreational facilities in the development until it is completed and all facilities are sold.

Building plans for each development are drawn up by the headquarters design department. Most building materials are selected and bought by a central purchasing department, and the terms of sale of condominium units are established by Carnegie's central management. Central management also establishes the selling-price schedule, although the local manager is authorized to reduce individual offering prices by as much as 10 percent if this seems necessary to get condominium units sold.

a. What problems would have to be solved before income or return on investment could be calculated for a condominium development?

b. Should the individual developments be classified as profit centers? Indicate the elements in this situation affecting your answer.

11. Departmental Evaluation. Lawrence & Company, an old-line investment banking firm, has hired three highly regarded recent business-school graduates to join its professional staff at annual salaries of $40,000 each. Each of the firm's seven operating departments is interested in having at least one of the new hires become a full-time member of its staff.

As a means of determining which departments will receive the new employees, the chairman of the board has proposed having three auctions, one for each new employee. In each auction, the department bidding the most money would win the auctioned employee. Although no money would change hands, the amount of each winning bid would become part of the victor's investment base in return-on-investment calculations. The new employee's salary would become an expense of the winning department. Each auction would occur after the winner of the previous auction was announced.

a. Would this system be consistent with the company's system of evaluating its departments and their managers on the basis of their reported return on investment? Explain.

b. What are the likely costs and benefits of this approach—to the firm, to the victorious departments, and to the new employees themselves?

12. Steering Controls and Scorecard Controls.   Mabel Corson is managing director of Perigrinations, Inc., a multi-office travel service company. Head-office personnel assemble special travel packages (e.g., seven days and six nights in the Caribbean with an all-inclusive price covering round-trip airfare, ground transportation, meals and lodging), administer the companywide advertising program, and provide information and counsel to the company's local offices.

Each local office is headed by a manager who is responsible for local sales promotion and for providing local customers with information, travel advice, and reservation services. The local office is expected to promote the travel packages Perigrinations has assembled and receives the standard commission on all such sales. Each local office is also allowed to sell packages assembled by other packagers.

Ms. Corson's head-office staff negotiates the office rental and the manager's salary for each local office; all other local office costs are the responsibility of the local manager. The local offices earn fees only from their reservations services, including their sales of travel packages. The percentage commissions from sales of travel packages are higher than those on other kinds of reservation services, so local managers are expected to promote these actively.

Ms. Corson expects each local manager to operate independently and profitably, without head-office interference. She and other head-office personnel are available whenever a local manager requests advice or information; otherwise she tends to leave each local office pretty much alone.

a. Describe the steering control information you would like to have if you were a local manager.

b. Describe the scorecard control information Ms. Corson would probably find useful. To what extent, if any, would this also be steering control information?

c. In what ways would a report summarizing local office profit performance differ, depending on whether the report was to be used for economic evaluation or for managerial evaluation? Why would those differences arise?

13. Usefulness of Profit-Contribution Reports.   Epsom Company's plastics division is the company's largest division, both in sales volume and in profit contribution. The plastics division's marketing vice president received the following report on operations in the division's 10 sales districts in October (in $ thousands):

District	Sales Amount	Sales Over/(Under) Budget	Profit Contribution Amount	Profit Contribution Over/(Under) Budget
Boston	$ 220	$ (10)	$ 59	$ 4
New York	380	(20)	110	1
Pittsburgh	170	(30)	24	(16)
Atlanta	340	20	91	6
Chicago	210	(40)	46	(9)
New Orleans	140	(10)	18	(6)
Denver	90	(30)	10	—
Dallas	120	—	21	11
Los Angeles	290	(10)	66	6
Seattle	130	(30)	25	(15)
Total	$2,090	$(160)	$470	$(18)

Each sales district is headed by a district manager who is responsible for selling the division's products to customers in the district. The district managers report to the marketing vice president, who also has a small central staff. All products are manufactured in the plastics division's factories under the general direction and supervision of the division's manufacturing vice president.

Divisional expenses (marketing, manufacturing, and administration) other than those reflected in the district profit contributions averaged 12 percent of sales in October. This percentage included both direct and indirect divisional expenses.

a. Give at least one example of a direct divisional expense and one example of an indirect divisional expense that isn't reflected in the district profit-contribution amounts, and explain why it isn't reflected there.

b. How would you expect the marketing vice president to use the sales district profit-contribution report? What significant facts does the October report reveal, and how would you expect the marketing vice president to respond to it?

c. How well does the $470,000 total of the district profit contributions measure managerial performance and economic performance in the plastics division? What additional amounts would you incorporate in the report if it is to be used for these purposes?

14. Comparison of Two Divisions. BIG Industries, Inc., is a decentralized, multidivision company. The following data summarize the operations of two of BIG's divisions (Able and Baker) in 19x1:

	Able Division		Baker Division	
	Actual	**Budget**	**Actual**	**Budget**
Net sales	$110	$100	$280	$300
Cost of goods sold*	44	40	150	150
Selling and administrative expense	30	30	80	80
Income before taxes	$ 36	$ 30	$ 50	$ 70
* Including depreciation	10	10	12	12

The following amounts were taken from the two divisions' balance sheets of December 31, 19x1:

	Able Division		Baker Division	
	Actual	**Budget**	**Actual**	**Budget**
Current assets	$150	$140	$100	$105
Fixed assets (cost)	220	218	275	275
Accumulated depreciation	176	177	25	25
Current liabilities	50	45	50	55

During 19x1, the market conditions facing each division were about what had been expected when the 19x1 budgets were drawn up. The company estimated that its pretax cost of capital in 19x1 was about 20 percent.

a. Which division is in the more profitable business? Cite numbers to support your conclusions and defend the measures you have chosen.

b. Which division manager is doing the better job of running the division? Again cite numbers to support your conclusions and defend the measures you have chosen.

(Prepared by Michael Ginzberg)

15. Monitoring Sales Department Profit Performance. "I don't understand it. My sales were 10 percent higher than the budget, but I still didn't make the budgeted income!" lamented Cathy Goldman, manager of the housewares department in Clancy's, an independent department store. The report covering the housewares department's profit performance in the month of August showed the following results:

	Actual	**Budget**	**Variance**
Sales	$132,000	$120,000	$12,000
Expenses:			
Cost of goods sold	93,400	84,000	9,400
Salaries and wages	2,470	2,400	70
Employee benefits and taxes	1,235	960	275
Billing and accounting	4,445	3,600	845
Warehousing and receiving	3,045	2,000	1,045
Occupancy	13,875	13,750	125
General overhead	6,400	5,800	600
Total expense	124,870	112,510	12,360
Income before taxes	$ 7,130	$ 7,490	$ (360)

Each department manager has responsibility for staffing the department, selecting and ordering merchandise, setting prices, and deciding how the floor space allotted to the department is used. As a result, Clancy's management believes the department managers should be responsible for the income their departments generate.

Salaries and wages include the salaries and wages of all departmental personnel. Employee benefits and taxes were budgeted this year at a rate of 40 percent of salaries and wages, but a change in the employee benefit plan agreed upon after the budget was prepared resulted in an increase in the percentage charge to 50 percent.

Billing and accounting costs are charged to each department as its share of the accounting department's expenses. The budgeted amount was based on the assumption that 75 percent of the department's sales would be credit sales, and that the costs of running the accounting department would be 4 percent of total credit sales. Housewares' credit sales for August did indeed amount to 75 percent of its total sales.

The warehousing and receiving charge is based on the average number of cubic feet of storage space occupied by the department's products in Clancy's warehouse. Housewares' products were budgeted to occupy 8,000 cubic feet in the warehouse but actually occupied 8,700 cubic feet in August.

The occupancy charge includes building depreciation, heat, light, maintenance, and property taxes, allocated on the basis of the number of square feet of floor space occupied by the department. Housewares occupied 11,000 square feet of floor space in August, the amount budgeted at the beginning of the year.

General overhead is an allocation of the costs of Clancy's central administrative costs. These costs are allocated to departments monthly on the basis of their gross sales revenues.

a. Recast the housewares department's income report for August in a profit contribution format, showing both the department's profit contribution and its income before taxes.

b. To what extent did the $360 unfavorable variance in departmental income reflect Ms. Goldman's failure to achieve a satisfactory income level from her department's operations in August? Quantify your answer insofar as you can do so from the information provided, and comment on the likely cause or causes of each variance component.

c. To what extent would you use the information in the departmental income statement provided above to evaluate the department's economic performance in August? What additional information or adjustments would you ask for to help you use this information for that purpose?

(Adapted from a problem by Michael Ginzberg)

16. Evaluating Managerial Performance. Harry Keeler was the president of Anorak, Inc., a manufacturer of consumer goods. The income statements for the company's two divisions indicated that division A was highly profitable, while division B was a break-even operation at best.

Keeler was due to retire soon, and the board of directors was examining the credentials of the two division managers. Both had been with the company for many years and had enviable performance records in other positions before being named to head their respective divisions.

Both division managers seemed to have organizational ability, and employee morale in both divisions was extremely good. Both were well liked by the board members and seemed capable of representing the company effectively in dealings with outsiders.

The main difference between the two seemed to be that the manager of division A was able to generate profits, while the manager of division B could not. The following divisional income statements were prepared for the month of September:

	Division A		Division B	
	Actual	Budget	Actual	Budget
Sales revenues	$1,000,000	$1,050,000	$500,000	$490,000
Costs of goods sold	600,000	630,000	400,000	395,000
Gross margin	400,000	420,000	100,000	95,000
Operating expenses:				
Marketing and selling	100,000	95,000	50,000	50,000
Divisional administration	50,000	48,000	40,000	45,000
Head-office expense	42,000	41,000	21,000	19,000
Income taxes	85,000	94,000	(5,000)	(8,000)
Total operating expenses	277,000	278,000	106,000	106,000
Net income (loss)	$ 123,000	$ 142,000	$(6,000)	$(11,000)

The following assets and liabilities were traced or assigned to these divisions at the end of September:

	Division A		Division B	
	Actual	Budget	Actual	Budget
Directly traceable:				
Accounts receivable	$1,200,000	$1,200,000	$ 500,000	$ 520,000
Inventories	1,100,000	1,100,000	800,000	860,000
Plant and equipment	700,000	700,000	300,000	300,000
Accounts payable	(900,000)	(900,000)	(600,000)	(580,000)
Net traceable assets	2,100,000	2,100,000	1,000,000	1,100,000
Allocated (percentage of sales):				
Cash	400,000	389,000	200,000	181,000
Headquarters buildings, furniture, and equipment	300,000	307,000	150,000	143,000
Net assets	$2,800,000	$2,796,000	$1,350,000	$1,424,000

Additional information:

1. Each division is operated as a profit center. Each division manufactures all its products in its own factories and sells them through its own sales force.
2. The income statement comparisons for the year to date revealed similar relationships to those in the statements for September.
3. The company used a minimum aftertax rate of return on investment of 12 percent in evaluating new capital-expenditure proposals.
4. Head-office expenses were allocated to product lines in proportion to actual sales.
5. Market conditions for the products sold by both divisions were very close to those forecast at the beginning of the year.
6. The market for division B's products appeared unlikely to show any major improvement for some time. Barring a radical change in the market or the introduction of a major new product, industry sales were likely to remain at or near their current levels for some time.
7. The market for division A's products had been growing dramatically for several years, but the industry's growth had abated during this year, as anticipated.

Do these statements indicate that the manager of division A had a clearly superior profit performance in September? Prepare a summary report, showing, insofar as you can, the relative profit performance of the two managers, with your interpretation of the amounts you are assigning to each.

17. Supplementing Divisional Profit Information. Monica Davis, a member of the board of directors of Anorak, Inc. (see problem 16) asked the company's controller for more information to help evaluate the qualifications of the two division managers. The controller provided the following data for the nine months in the year to date (19x4) and for the first nine months of 19x1, when both managers were fairly new to their present positions (no budget data were available for these items):

	Division A		Division B	
	19x1	**19x4**	**19x1**	**19x4**
Sales revenues..........................	$7,200,000	$8,950,000	$3,950,000	$4,300,000
Research and development expense (included in divisional administration expense)	245,000	305,000	140,000	110,000
Product-warranty expense (included in marketing and selling expense)	210,000	195,000	45,000	90,000
Training and management development expenses (included in divisional administration expense)	36,000	42,000	26,000	27,000
Market share.............................	10%	10%	8%	6%
Number of customers served	106	193	85	12
Employee turnover (percentage of work force)	8%	7%	5%	10%
Absenteeism (percentage of hours worked)	5%	4%	5%	8%

a. Use this information to throw additional light on the performance of Anorak's two division managers.

b. To what extent would comparisons of these statistics with budgeted amounts have helped you answer part *a*? Explain the role of budgeted data of this sort.

c. What conclusions can you draw from your analysis of the additional data in this problem as to the adequacy or relevance of divisional profit information to the evaluation of managerial performance?

18. Transfer Pricing. Caplow Company is a multidivision company, and its division managers have been given full profit responsibility and complete autonomy to accept or reject transfers to or from other divisions. Division A's factories manufacture a large number of products and most of these are sold to outside customers by division A's own sales force.

One of division A's products, accounting for about 10 percent of the division's sales, is a subassembly. Most of these subassemblies are sold at a price of $700 each to outside customers, in competition with roughly similar products marketed by other companies. Some of division A's subassemblies are now being sold to division B, however, for use in a final product (one subassembly per unit), which it sells outside at a price of $1,200 a unit. Division A charges division B $700 a unit for the subassembly, the same price it charges outside customers. Variable costs of the subassembly are $520 a unit in division A; division B's variable costs of the final product (excluding subassembly costs) are $600 a unit. Total fixed costs in the two divisions are unaffected by the volume of business represented by this subassembly or the final product made from it. Although other manufacturers make subassemblies of roughly similar design, they have features which prevent their use in division B's final product—that is, suitable subassemblies aren't available from any outside supplier.

Division B's manager feels that division A should transfer the subassembly at a price lower than market because division B is unable to make a profit if it has to pay the market price.

a. Calculate division B's profit contribution from the sale of a unit of the final product if transfers are made at the $700 price; also calculate the total profit contribution to the company of the sale of a unit of the final product.

b. Assume division A can sell all its production in the open market at a price of $700 a unit. Should division A transfer goods to division B? If so, at what price?

c. Assume division A can produce 1,000 units a month but can sell only 500 units in the open market at $700 each. A 20 percent price reduction would be necessary to sell full capacity. Division B could sell as many as 1,000 units of the final product at the $1,200 price. Should transfers be made? If so, how many units should be transferred and at what price? Submit a schedule showing comparisons of profit contribution under three different alternatives to support your decision.

d. Is negotiation between division A and division B likely to be an appropriate way to establish an economically sound transfer price in this situation? Explain why or why not.

(SMAC adapted)

19. Transfer Pricing; Selecting a Source of Supply. Gunnco Corporation has several divisions operating as profit centers. Two are the Ajax and Defco divisions. Each division sells most of its output to customers outside the Gunnco group.

Divisional residual income is used in the periodic evaluations of the performance of the divisions and of the division managers. Residual income for each division is calculated by deducting interest at a pretax annual rate of 18 percent on Gunnco's net investment in the division.

The Ajax division is now operating at capacity, meaning that it could expand its total production and sales volume in the near term only at a very high cost. Defco, on the other hand, is now operating at only 50 percent of its capacity, with many of its production employees either on unpaid furlough or on a short workweek. The division's administrative and clerical staffs have not been cut, with the result that a good deal of administrative capacity is idle.

Defco's manager is actively seeking profitable ways to utilize the division's idle capacity. A commercial airplane manufacturer has offered to buy 1,000 brake units from Defco, to be delivered during the next 12 months at a price of $52.50 each. Defco could meet this delivery schedule without difficulty. Defco's management sees this order as an opportunity to penetrate a new market that holds promise of substantial future growth, and is anxious to meet the price, if at all possible. Defco's estimated cost of the brake unit is as follows:

Purchased parts—outside vendors	$22.50
Ajax electrical fitting No. 1726	5.00
Other variable costs	14.00
Fixed overhead and administration	8.00
Total cost per unit	$49.50

Defco's total fixed overhead and administrative costs are unlikely to increase as a result of the brake unit order, but Defco's management believes any business it takes on should cover its fair share of the division's costs.

Defco's management estimates that $5,000 in additional working capital would be required to support the brake unit business.

The Ajax fitting required for this brake unit would be supplied by the Ajax division. This fitting is now being produced and sold to Ajax's outside customers at a price of $7.50 each, and approximately 10,000 of these fittings are likely to be sold this year at that price. Ajax's variable cost of producing fitting No. 1726 is $4.25 each. Estimated fixed cost is $1.25 a unit.

Other transfers to Defco now account for about 5 percent of Ajax's total volume; the transfer prices negotiated for these are generally the prices Ajax charges its outside customers for the same products. These prices aren't in dispute.

Defco could obtain roughly similar fittings from outside suppliers for about $7.50, the same price Ajax charges. If it had to pay this much, however, Defco's profit margin on the brake unit would virtually disappear. Since Defco's marketing people see no possibility of getting a higher price for the brake units, Defco's manager has asked the Ajax manager to supply these fittings at a price of $5 each.

a. As the Ajax division controller, would you recommend that Ajax supply fitting No. 1726 to Defco at the $5 price? Cite amounts and explain your reasoning in two or three well-chosen sentences. (Ignore income taxes.)

b. Suppose Ajax refuses to sell at any price less than $7.50. As the Defco division controller, would you recommend paying this price? Again cite amounts and explain your reasoning.

c. As the Gunnco corporate controller, would you recommend that top management classify this item as one for which the transfer price should be set by top management? Give a brief explanation of your reasoning.

(CMA adapted)

20. Divisional Performance, Inflation Impact. Argus Corporation is a diversified company operating four divisions, each competing in a different market: lumber, chemicals, rail equipment, and consumer retail stores. In each of the past five years (19x1–19x5), the consumer retail division has generated a higher ratio of contribution margin to sales, profit contribution to sales, and return on investment than any other division.

Argus isn't large enough to be required to prepare and disclose FASB-mandated information about the effects of changing prices (see Chapter 14). The corporate controller, however, believes that the consumer retail division may be the one Argus segment most directly and significantly affected by economywide inflation. The controller suggests that management take changes in the consumer price index (CPI) into consideration when it evaluates the profit performance of this one division.

The following data have been extracted from the consumer retail division's annual submissions for the past five years (in $ millions), together with the average consumer price index (1967 = 100.0):

	19x1	19x2	19x3	19x4	19x5
Sales revenue	$ 20	$ 25	$ 37	$ 49	$ 60
Identifiable net assets	6.0	6.6	7.5	8.2	8.5
Contribution margin	2.0	3.75	4.0	4.75	5.0
Profit contribution	1.5	1.8	2.3	2.2	2.7
Average CPI.	181.5	195.4	217.4	246.8	272.3

a. Using the consumer price index, restate the historical amounts in constant dollars of 19x5 purchasing power. (See Chapter 14 for a brief description of this technique.)

b. What conclusions can you draw from these adjusted data about the impact of inflation on the consumer retail division's reported results? How meaningful are the adjustments you have made? What additional information would you find helpful?

21. Effect of Return-on-Investment Measures on Decisions.[4] Percy Jones, managing director of Orkney Biscuit Company, Ltd., is trying to decide whether to expand the company by adding an entirely new and different product line. The proposal seems likely to be profitable, and adequate funds can be obtained from outside investors to finance the new venture.

Orkney Biscuit has long been regarded as a well-managed company. It has succeeded in keeping its present product lines up to date and has maintained a small but profitable position in a highly competitive industry.

---

[4] Copyright 1968 by l'Institut pour l'Etude des Méthodes de Direction de l'Entreprise (IMEDE), Lausanne, Switzerland. Published by permission.

The amount of capital used by the company in support of its present operations is approximately $4 million, and it is expected to remain at this level whether the proposal for the new product line is accepted or rejected. Net income from these existing operations now amounts to about $400,000 a year, and Jones's best forecast of the future is that this will continue to be the income from present operations, regardless of whether the new product line is introduced or rejected.

Introduction of the new product line would require an immediate investment of $400,000 in equipment and $250,000 in additional working capital. A further $100,000 in working capital would be required a year later.

Sales of the new product line would be relatively low during the first year but would increase steadily until the sixth year. After that, changing tastes and increased competition would probably begin to reduce annual sales. After eight years, the product line would probably be withdrawn from the market. At that time, the company would sell the equipment for its scrap value and liquidate the working capital. The cash value of the equipment and working capital at that time would be about $350,000.

The low initial sales volume, combined with heavy promotional outlays, would lead to heavy losses in the first two years, and no net income would be reported until the fourth year. The profit forecasts for the new product line are summarized in Exhibit 1.

Using these amounts, Jones has prepared the cash-flow analysis summarized in Exhibit 2. Investment cash flow, shown in the first column, is added to the operating cash flows in column (2) [from Exhibit 1, column (1)]. The total is then adjusted for income taxes and discounted to find its

EXHIBIT 1
Orkney Biscuit Company, Ltd.: Income Forecast for New Product Line

Year	(1) Forecasted Incremental Cash Flow from Operations	(2) Depreciation on New Equipment	(3) Forecasted Incremental Income before Tax (1) − (2)	(4) Income Tax at 40%*	(5) Forecasted Incremental Net Income after Tax (3) − (4)
1	−$ 350,000	$50,000	−$400,000	−$160,000	−$240,000
2	− 100,000	50,000	− 150,000	− 60,000	− 90,000
3	0	50,000	− 50,000	− 20,000	− 30,000
4	+ 200,000	50,000	+ 150,000	60,000	90,000
5	+ 500,000	50,000	+ 450,000	180,000	270,000
6	+ 1,000,000	50,000	+ 950,000	380,000	570,000
7	+ 900,000	50,000	+ 850,000	340,000	510,000
8	+ 650,000	50,000	+ 600,000	240,000	360,000

* When income before taxes is negative, the company is entitled to a tax refund at 40 percent, either from taxes paid in previous years or from taxes currently due on other company operations.

EXHIBIT 2
Orkney Biscuit Company, Ltd.*: Present Value of New Product Proposal (in $ thousands)

Year	(1)† Investment Cash Flows	(2) Operating Cash Flows	(3) Total Cash Flow before Tax (1) + (2)	(4)‡ Tax Depreciation	(5)§ Taxable Income (2) − (4)	(6) Income Tax 40% of (5)	(7) Cash Flow after Tax (3) − (6)	(8)‖ Present Value Factor at 10%	(9) Present Value at 10% (7) × (8)
1	−650	− 350	−1,000	50	− 400	−160	− 840	0.9516	−799
2	−100	− 100	− 200	50	− 150	− 60	− 140	0.8611	−121
3	0	0	0	50	− 50	− 20	+ 20	0.7791	+ 16
4	0	+ 200	+ 200	50	+ 150	60	+ 140	0.7050	+ 99
5	0	+ 500	+ 500	50	+ 450	180	+ 320	0.6379	+204
6	0	+1,000	+1,000	50	+ 950	380	+ 620	0.5772	+358
7	0	+ 900	+ 900	50	+ 850	340	+ 560	0.5223	+292
8	+350	+ 650	+1,000	50	+ 600	240	+ 760	0.4726	+359
Total.....	−400	+2,800	+2,400	400	+2,400	960	+1,440		+408

* *IMPORTANT NOTE*: This exhibit is provided for later reference. It need not be reviewed prior to an analysis of the questions raised at the end of the problem.

† The first year's outlay consists of $400,000 for equipment and $250,000 for working capital. An additional working-capital outlay of $100,000 is required in the second year. Working-capital outlays are completely recovered in the eighth year.

‡ One eighth of the equipment costs are recorded each year as depreciation. Orkney Biscuit Company operates in a country that requires the use of straight-line depreciation for tax purposes.

§ When taxable income is negative, the company is entitled to a tax refund at 40 percent, either from taxes paid in prior years or from taxes currently due on other company operations.

‖ These present-value multipliers are based on the assumption that each year's cash flow is spread uniformly throughout the year. They differ slightly, therefore, from those in Appendix A.

present value at a 10 percent rate. These present values are shown in the right-hand column of Exhibit 2.

As Exhibit 2 shows, the present value of the anticipated cash receipts from the new product line exceeds the present value of the anticipated cash outlays by $408,000.

Jones seldom has an opportunity to invest funds as profitably as this, and he would like to approve this investment proposal. He is concerned by its effect on Orkney Biscuit's reported rate of return on investment, however. His accountants have given him the following figures (in $000):

Year	Total Investment, Start of Year	Net Income after Tax	Reported Return on Investment
1	$4,000	$160	4.0%
2	4,600	310	6.7
3	4,650	370	8.0
4	4,600	490	10.7
5	4,550	670	14.7
6	4,500	970	21.6
7	4,450	910	20.4
8	4,400	760	17.3

The accountants explain that they have obtained the forecasted net income by adding the forecasted aftertax net income for the new product line [Exhibit 1, column (5)] to $400,000, the forecasted net income on the company's other product lines. They have obtained the total investment figures by adding $4 million to the investment outlays on equipment and working capital [Exhibit 2, column (1), cumulated] and subtracting depreciation on the new equipment [Exhibit 2, column (4), cumulated].

a. To what extent, if any, would the low anticipated rate of return on investment in the first three years be likely to affect the decision to launch the new product line if Orkney Biscuit is a private company, owned entirely by Jones?

b. How would your answer differ if you found that the Orkney Biscuit Company is a publicly owned company, with shares owned by a large number of small investors, and Jones is purely a salaried administrator?

c. How would your answer differ if the Orkney Biscuit Company were a wholly owned profit center of a much larger company and Jones expects to be a candidate to succeed one of the parent company's top executives who will retire from the company about two years from now?

Chapter 23

Departmental Cost Control

Periodic profit reports are used primarily by division managers and members of top management with profit responsibility. By contrast, most other control reports are more limited in scope, focusing on narrower sets of responsibilities in responsibility centers below the top-management level.

Some control reports focus on *effectiveness*—that is, success in meeting output objectives. Reports on product deliveries or progress toward project completion are effectiveness reports. Other reports monitor *compliance*—success in observing rules and constraints on behavior. Reports on accident rates, employee absenteeism, and polluting emissions fall into this category. Finally, some reports focus on *efficiency*—success in minimizing the cost per unit of goods or services produced.

> ### TERMINOLOGY
>
> A *responsibility center* is an organization segment headed by a single manager, obligated to carry out a specified function or group of functions, and answerable to higher authority for its performance of these functions.

The purpose of this chapter is to examine the methods accountants use to measure and report on the efficiency of operations in certain kinds of responsibility centers. We'll begin, however, with a short review of the reasons for control reporting.

**Management by
Exception**

Managers need performance reports for either or both of two reasons. First, they may rely on reports to provide them with signals that identify emerging problems or opportunities; this is called *steering-control information.* Second, higher-level managers may need information to evaluate their subordinates or the activities they are responsible for; this is *scorecard information,* as we used that term in Chapter 22.

In both cases, management's interest focuses on the *deviations* of actual performance from some specified performance level. This emphasis on deviations is known as **management by exception,** the notion that management should devote its scarce time only to operations in which results depart significantly from the performance standards. Operations in which results are close to the performance standard are presumed to be performing satisfactorily.

Causes of deviations and desirable responses are often readily apparent to the managers who are closest to the operations in question. In some cases, however, determining causes is costly and not always successful. Management has to estimate whether the benefit from any eventual response is likely to exceed both the costs of identifying the causes of deviations from performance standards and the costs of dealing with these causes. Although decision models are available to guide managers in making these comparisons of costs with benefits, in most cases the decisions will be based on management's judgment. This, too, is part of the practice of *management by exception.*

**Cost-Control
Reporting; Process
Production**

Cost-control standards can be developed for **responsive activities**—activities that are carried out to fill orders for goods or services or to provide goods for later delivery to customers—because meaningful cause-and-effect relationships can be established between the outputs of these activities and their costs.

Cost-Control Standards

One possible approach to cost-control reporting is to compare actual costs with performance standards for individual tasks—for example, assembling components to produce one personal computer on March 13. This approach may be appropriate if management needs these detailed comparisons for steering control information. Most cost reports are used as scorecard reports, however, reflecting the assumption that management has other, more efficient ways of providing first-level steering-control information on a timely basis.

When this is the case, control reporting on an individual-task basis is likely to be too fragmented to serve management's needs. Of much more importance are the *cumulative* effects of the activities of the many people in individual responsibility centers *in a particular period.* This calls for the cost standards that are identified in individual departments' **flexible budgets.**[1]

Flexible Budgets

A flexible budget for a responsibility center consists of a number of alternative cost budgets, each identifying the amounts of resources that *should have been necessary* to enable the center to produce a specified amount of output during a specified length of time. The applicable performance standard in any period is the specific budget for the level of output the responsibility center actually achieved in that period.

The flexible budget ordinarily can be embodied in a series of formulas—one for each cost element, covering all feasible volumes. Exhibit 23–1 shows the 19x1 flexible budget for Apex Company's factory coatings department.

EXHIBIT 23–1
Apex Company, Coatings Department: Flexible
Budget for the Year 19x1

	Fixed per Month	Variable per Gallon
Materials..................	—	$1.50
Processing labor	—	0.30
Support labor...............	$ 1,000	0.01
Supplies	2,000	0.04
Other controllable costs......	15,000	0.10
Supervision	3,000	—
Depreciation...............	4,000	—
Factory management	25,000	0.05
Total	$50,000	$2.00

The cost elements in Exhibit 23–1 fall into three categories: (1) *proportionally variable* (materials and processing labor); (2) *fixed* (supervision and depreciation); and (3) *partly fixed, partly variable* (support labor, supplies, other controllable costs, and factory management). For a cost in the first category, the cost-control performance standard in any period is

---

[1] The term *flexible budget* is ordinarily associated with departmental overhead costs in job order production or with process production costs that aren't expected to vary proportionally with volume. Because these are merely special cases of a much broader set of relationships, we prefer to use the term pedagogically to describe the cost standards in all responsibility centers engaged in responsive activities.

ordinarily obtained by multiplying the number of units of output by the **standard cost** of a single unit:

$$
\begin{array}{ccc}
\text{Cost control} & & \text{Quantity} & & \text{Standard cost} \\
\text{performance} & = & \text{of} & \times & \text{per unit} \\
\text{standard} & & \text{output} & & \text{of output}
\end{array}
$$

For each proportionally variable input element such as processing labor in the coatings department, the standard cost of a unit of product is the **standard quantity** of input management estimates should be necessary to manufacture a unit of that product, multiplied by the **standard price** of a unit of that input—the price the company expects to have to pay to obtain an input unit during the current planning period.

$$
\begin{array}{ccc}
\text{Standard cost} & & \text{Standard quantity} & & \text{Standard price} \\
\text{per unit} & = & \text{of input per} & \times & \text{per unit} \\
\text{of output} & & \text{unit of output} & & \text{of input}
\end{array}
$$

For example, the standard processing labor cost of a gallon of coatings in Apex Company's coatings department is 0.03 labor-hour at a standard wage rate of $10 an hour, or $0.30 a gallon. This is the amount shown in the second line of the right-hand column in Exhibit 23–1. The cost-control performance standard for processing labor in any month in 19x1 is obtained by multiplying the number of gallons of output in that month by $0.30. For a month in which volume is 110,000 gallons, the cost-control performance standard is $33,000 (110,000 × $0.30).

The flexible budget for support labor is slightly more complicated, because it contains both fixed and variable components. The budget for support labor is:

$$
\text{Budgeted support labor cost} \quad = \quad \$1{,}000 \quad + \quad \$0.01 \quad \times \quad \text{Gallons}
$$

In a 110,000-gallon month, the cost-control performance standard for this cost element is $2,100 ($1,000 + $0.01 × 110,000).

Finally, the flexible budget for costs that are entirely fixed is identical at all volumes. Supervisory salaries in the coatings department, for example, are budgeted at $3,000 a month, no matter how much output is achieved. This constitutes the cost-control performance standard for this cost element at *each* level of volume.

In all three of these cases, the budgeted relationship is linear—that is, the flexible budget for any month can be determined by (1) multiplying the budgeted variable cost per unit, if any, by the number of units produced, and (2) adding the budgeted fixed costs, if any. These three elements are all represented by straight lines in the three diagrams in the top half of Exhibit 23–2.

EXHIBIT 23–2
Cost Variability Patterns

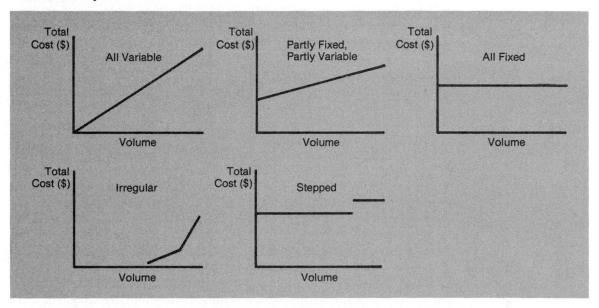

In the top left-hand diagram, budgeted fixed cost is zero and the budget is drawn as a straight line, sloping upward from the origin. In the top right-hand diagram in the exhibit, the budgeted variable cost is zero, so the budget is drawn as a horizontal straight line. The diagram in the center of the upper panel shows a cost element with a mixture of fixed and variable components. Again we have a straight line, but this time it slopes upward from a point higher than zero on the cost scale at zero volume.

A straight-line formula may not always be appropriate, however. The diagram at the lower left of Exhibit 23–2, for example, might fit the budgeted behavior of the coatings department's overtime premium. Budgeted overtime premium could be zero for all volumes up to 90,000 gallons, 6 cents a gallon for the next 30,000 gallons, and 15 cents a gallon for all gallons in excess of 120,000. The diagram at the lower center, in contrast, might describe the budget for the costs of supervision: $3,000 a month for all volumes up to 120,000 gallons; $4,500 a month when volume exceeds that level. In such cases, the flexible budget should conform to the anticipated cost behavior—that is, it shouldn't be distorted to conform to a straight-line formula.

Cost-Control Reports

The effectiveness of department managers in controlling costs is ordinarily reflected in cost reports that are prepared and issued at regular intervals. Some cost reports are issued daily, some weekly, and some at longer intervals. A month is the typical reporting interval for a company's main departmental cost summaries, although these are likely to be supplemented by daily or weekly reports on particular items, such as inspection rejects, scrap, and overtime.

The monthly cost summaries consist of *comparisons* of the actual costs incurred during the month with budget standards appropriate to the volume actually achieved during the month—that is, the amounts derived from the flexible budget for the month's actual volume.

The differences between the costs actually charged to a responsibility center and the flexible budget standards at actual volume are the **spending variances** for that center. If the actual cost exceeds the flexible budget, the spending variance is called *unfavorable;* if cost is less than the budget, the spending variance is *favorable.*[2]

For example, the report in Exhibit 23–3 was issued to the head of the coatings department, covering this department's operations in the month of June 19x1. During this month, the department produced 110,000 gallons of product. This volume, applied to the budget formulas of Exhibit 23–1, provides the flexible budget standards shown in the second column of Exhibit 23–3.[3]

Notice that this report covers only five of the eight cost elements listed in Exhibit 23–1. The reason is that Apex Company classifies each department's costs into two categories: (1) costs the department manager can influence or control directly, called *controllable costs,* and (2) costs that are controlled by decisions made by managers outside the department, called *noncontrollable costs.* The monthly departmental cost reports list only the costs that are partly or completely controllable by department personnel.

This practice reflects the principle known as the **controllability crite-**

---

[2] The term *spending variance* is ordinarily associated with variances in factory overhead costs in job order production. We have found it more effective in the classroom to apply the term to *all* variances of actual costs from cost-control performance standards.

[3]
$$
\begin{array}{lrl}
110,000 \times \$1.50 & = & \$165,000 \\
110,000 \times \$0.30 & = & 33,000 \\
110,000 \times \$0.01 + \$\ 1,000 & = & 2,100 \\
110,000 \times \$0.04 + \$\ 2,000 & = & 6,400 \\
110,000 \times \$0.10 + \$15,000 & = & 26,000
\end{array}
$$

EXHIBIT 23–3
Apex Company, Coatings Department: Cost-Performance Report for the Month of June 19x1

	Actual	Budget	(Under) or Over
Materials	$168,200	$165,000	$3,200
Processing labor	32,550	33,000	(450)
Support labor	2,450	2,100	350
Supplies	8,200	6,400	1,800
Other controllable costs	25,800	26,000	(200)
Total controllable costs	$237,200	$232,500	$4,700

rion—namely, that managers should be held responsible only for those variances that *they* are expected to influence or control. The costs of supervision, depreciation, and factory management in the coatings department therefore are excluded from the monthly cost report because they are controlled by decisions made outside the department. The amount and cost of supervision are the plant manager's responsibility, not the department manager's. Similarly, the amount of depreciation is determined by purchasing and disposal decisions made by top management. And the costs of factory management are controlled by the plant manager and by the company's vice president for manufacturing.

Usage Variances

Two kinds of events lead to spending variances—usage variances and price variances. **Usage variances** are those that lead the company to use either more or fewer units of input than the performance standard calls for.

> **TERMINOLOGY**
>
> A *usage variance* is the difference between actual input quantities and the quantities prescribed by the flexible budget for the output actually achieved.

Measures of Efficiency.   Usage variances are indexes of physical efficiency. They show the relationship between the quantities of resources used and the quantities of the outputs derived from them. Given enough data, we can always measure the usage variances in physical units.

For example, the production standards in the coatings department reflect the assumption that three hours of processing labor, when combined with other inputs, will yield 100 gallons of coatings. In other words, it is assumed that processing labor, if properly controlled, will vary in proportion to production volume. In June 19x1, the department produced 110,000 gallons of coatings from 3,100 hours of processing labor and other inputs.

Management might choose to measure efficiency by calculating the *ratio* of input to output (or output to input) during each period. In this case, the coatings department would show the following:

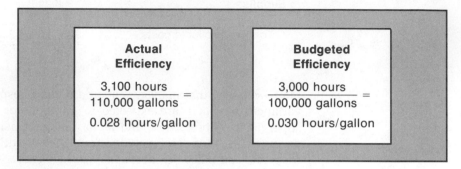

Most accounting systems are set up to measure efficiency in a different way, as a *difference* between actual and budgeted performance. The output of 110,000 gallons of coatings can also be stated in terms of their budgeted input content of 3,300 hours of processing labor (110,000 × 3 ÷ 100). If we measure output in this way, we can calculate the usage variance in hours, as follows:

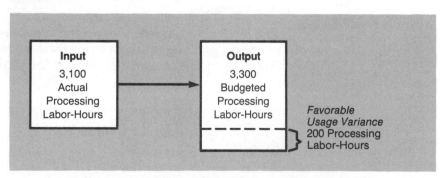

In other words, both input and output are now measured in the same units (processing labor-hours). The usage variance is the difference between the actual input quantity (3,100 hours) and the budgeted input quantity *for the work that was done* (3,300 hours). In this example, the department used 200 fewer hours of labor than the budget called for and the usage variance was *favorable*.

TECHNICAL NOTE

The budget used in the calculation of the usage variance is the budget for the *actual* volume of output (110,000 gallons or 3,300 budgeted hours). It is *not* the budget for the number of hours actually used or the budget for the budgeted volume of output.

Dollar Usage Variances. Although usage variances represent physical quantities, they are usually measured in monetary units (e.g., dollars). To get these dollar amounts, the accountant multiplies the physical quantities by *standard* input prices.

The standard wage rate in the coatings department in 19x1 was $10 an hour, and the usage variance in processing labor can be calculated in dollars as follows:

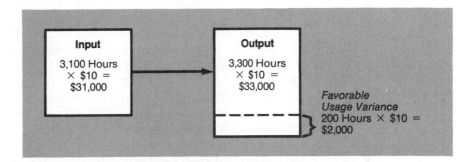

Usage variances are measured at standard prices rather than at actual prices (1) because standard prices are clerically simpler to use, and (2) because they make it easier to compare the usage variances from month to month. If the usage variance in processing labor in July 19x1 is $1,500—favorable—we know that the entire change is due to physical changes and is unaffected by changes in the average wage rate from one month to the next.

Price Variances

The second class of events that lead to spending variances—other than those leading to usage variances—are events that affect the prices the company pays for the resources it uses (including the wage rates it pays its employees). We call these **price variances** or, in the case of labor costs, **rate variances.**

> **TERMINOLOGY**
>
> A *price variance* or rate variance is a difference between an actual price and the price embodied in the flexible budget, multiplied by a specified quantity of resource inputs.

We calculate price variances by multiplying the *actual* input quantity by the difference between the actual input price and the budgeted input price. For example, processing-labor employees in the coatings department earned an average of $10.50 an hour in June 19x1, $0.50 more than the budgeted wage rate of $10. Since the department used 3,100 hours of this kind of labor, it paid $1,550 (3,100 × $0.50) more than if it had paid the budgeted wage rate. This was a labor rate variance.

Components of the Spending Variance

Our analysis of the spending variance in processing-labor costs in the coatings department is shown schematically in Exhibit 23–4. To isolate the price effect, we restated the actual input quantity (labor-hours) at the budgeted input price, in this case the budgeted wage rate of $10 an hour. This amount is shown in the center block of the upper part of Exhibit 23–4. The difference between this amount and the actual processing labor cost—the amount in the block at the left—is identified as the labor rate variance, $1,550 in this case and unfavorable.

The labor usage component, in contrast, was highly favorable, in that the department used 200 fewer hours than the amount budgeted for the output the department actually achieved. At the budgeted wage rate of $10 an hour, the accountants reported a $2,000 favorable usage variance in processing labor. The algebraic sum of these two components was $450—favorable—and this was the spending variance shown at the bottom of Exhibit 23–4.

Since wage rates may not be controllable by a department, top management can keep the price component out of the reported spending variance by simply using budgeted prices in the charges to departments for their use of resources. In such cases, the department head sees as the department's *actual* costs the product of actual input quantities and budgeted input prices. If this isn't done, any significant input price components of the spending variances should be separated in the performance-evaluation process.

Control Reporting: Job Order Production

The basic cost-reporting concepts in job order production centers are identical to those in process production, but determining departmental output is more complex. To illustrate, we've chosen a small factory in a

EXHIBIT 23–4
Apex Company, Coatings Department: Price and Usage Components of the Spending Variance in Processing Labor Costs

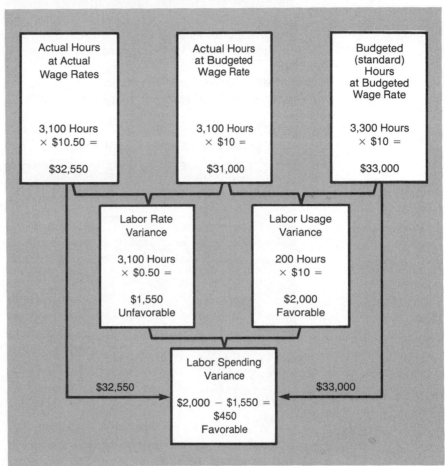

company we'll call Lion Corporation. This factory has three production departments (machining, stamping, and finishing) and three service and support centers (building services, equipment maintenance, and factory management). Most of its production is of products it has manufactured before or products made by methods it has used before.

TERMINOLOGY REMINDER

A *production center* is a specific set of facilities in which end-product activities take place—the production of goods or services for inventory or delivery to customers.

Standard Costs

Each production center in job order production performs a variety of operations on an even larger variety of products or production orders. A set of *standard costs* is developed for each of these products, specifying the inputs each product requires, multiplied by the *standard prices* of these inputs. These standard costs are assembled in a standard cost file.

For example, Lion Corporation's standard cost file contains the **standard cost sheet** shown in Exhibit 23–5. This lists the standard costs of a

EXHIBIT 23–5
Lion Corporation: Standard Cost Sheet

LION CORPORATION							
Standard Cost Sheet						Quantity 1,000	
Description Door Front No. 6948					Standard cost per unit $1.585		

		Direct Labor			Overhead	
Operation	Department	Hours	Rate	Amount	Rate	Amount
Cut	Machining	4.5	$14.00	$ 63.00	$12.00	$ 54.00
Drill	Machining	16.0	13.00	208.00	12.00	192.00
Stamp	Stamping	7.5	11.20	84.00	7.00	52.50
Buff	Finishing	18.5	12.00	222.00	15.00	277.50
Total				$577.00		$576.00

Direct Materials				Summary	
Item	Quantity	Price	Amount		
Steel sheet	3,600	$0.12	$432.00	Direct materials	$ 432.00
				Direct labor	577.00
				Overhead	576.00
				Total	$1,585.00

manufactured part identified as Door Front No. 6948. The columns in the center list the labor operations to be performed, the departments in which the work is done, the standard direct-labor times, the standard hourly wage rates, and the standard direct-labor cost. The two columns at the right show the departmental standard overhead rates (per direct labor-hour in each department) and the standard overhead cost (obtained by multiplying the rate times the number of standard direct labor-hours). Standard direct-materials costs are calculated in the panel at the lower left.

All components of standard product cost are brought together in the summary at the lower right. The standard unit cost shown in the upper right-hand corner of the standard cost sheet is obtained by dividing the $1,585 standard cost by 1,000, the number of units in a standard-sized batch of this product.

Standard Direct-Labor Cost of the Actual Output

The main difference between (1) cost-performance measurements for direct labor and materials costs in job order costing, and (2) similar measurements in process production is that a department's output in job order production in any period is likely to consist of many products, not just one. For example, suppose the finishing department in Lion Corporation's factory produced the following products in July 19x1:

	Standard Direct Labor-Hours per Thousand Units	Thousands of Units Produced	Total Standard Direct Labor-Hours
Door Front No. 6848	18.5	10	185
Panel No. 8207	24.0	20	480
Base No. 1991	37.5	32	1,200
Total			1,865

The standard wage rate in the finishing department was $12 an hour. Standard direct-labor cost for the period therefore was $22,380 (1,865 × $12). We can calculate the same total by multiplying the number of units of each product by its standard direct-labor cost per unit and adding the results, as in Exhibit 23–6.

EXHIBIT 23–6
Lion Corporation: Standard Direct-Labor Cost of Units Completed by Finishing Department

	Standard Direct Labor-Hours per Thousand Units	Standard Direct Cost per Thousand Units (at $12 an hour)	Thousands of Units Produced	Total Standard Direct-Labor Cost
Door Front No. 6948	18.5	$222	10	$ 2,220
Panel No. 8207	24.0	288	20	5,760
Base No. 1991	37.5	450	32	14,400
Total				$22,380

The output calculation is slightly more complicated if a department has work in process either at the beginning of the period or at the end. For example, the amounts in Exhibit 23–6 referred to units *completed* by the finishing department and transferred out of the department during the month. In addition, the company had one batch of 2,000 door fronts in process at the start of operations on July 1, 19x1, and half of the finishing department's work had been done on this batch in June. The standard direct-labor cost of the work *already done* on these units was calculated as follows:

1. Two thousand half-processed units were equivalent to 1,000 fully processed units (2,000 × ½ = 1,000).
2. One thousand fully processed units required 18.5 standard direct labor-hours.
3. At $12 a standard direct labor-hour, the July 1 inventory had a standard direct-labor cost of $222 (18.5 × $12).

In addition to the units completed in July, the company had a batch of 4,000 door fronts in process on July 31, 19x1, 75 percent completed. The standard direct-labor cost of the work done on these units in July was calculated in the same way as the standard cost of the beginning inventory:

1. Four thousand partially processed units were equivalent to 3,000 fully processed units (4,000 × 0.75 = 3,000).
2. Three thousand fully processed units required 55.5 standard direct labor-hours (18.5 × 3).
3. At $12 a standard direct labor-hour, the July 31 inventory had a standard direct-labor cost of $666 (55.5 × $12).

We can now see that the finishing department actually accomplished *more* in July with its direct labor than we had given it credit for in Exhibit 23–6. It not only finished goods with a standard direct-labor cost of $22,380, but it also increased the standard direct-labor cost of the work in process by $444:

	Standard Hours	Standard Cost
Standard direct labor in process, July 31	55.5	$666
Standard direct labor in process, July 1	18.5	222
Increase in standard direct-labor cost in process . . .	37.0	$444

This means that the standard direct-labor cost of all the work the finishing department did in July 19x1 was as follows:

	Standard Hours	Standard Cost
Standard direct labor cost of units completed (Exhibit 23–6)	1,865	$22,380
Increase in standard direct-labor cost in process	37	444
Total standard direct-labor cost, July 19x1	1,902	$22,824

These amounts are presented schematically in Exhibit 23–7. Blocks 1 and 2 represent the standard hours and standard direct-labor costs to be accounted for in July, including some standard hours and standard costs of the uncompleted work in the July 1 work in process inventory. Blocks 4 and 5 show how many standard hours and how much standard direct-labor cost went out of the department in July and how much remained in

EXHIBIT 23–7
Lion Corporation: Output, Product Completion, and Work in Process in Finishing Department

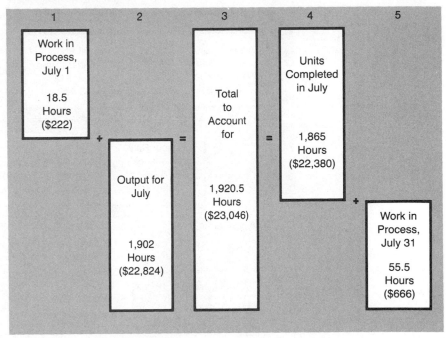

process at the end of the month. Since the ending standard direct-labor cost in process (block 5) is larger than the beginning work in process (block 1), the *total* amount of direct-labor work done (the output) was greater than the number of units completed during the period—$22,824 (block 2) versus $22,380 (block 4).

Spending Variances in Direct-Labor Costs

The spending variance for direct labor in job order production is calculated in exactly the same way as the spending variance for any proportionally variable cost element in process production. It is the difference between (1) the performance standard (standard direct-labor cost of the actual output for the period), and (2) the actual cost of direct labor.

Suppose the finishing department used 1,950 hours of direct labor in July 19x1 at an actual direct-labor cost of $23,985. Actual cost was determined by multiplying each worker's direct-labor time by that worker's straight-time wage rate (including a provision for fringe benefits but excluding overtime premiums). Exhibit 23–8 summarizes the calculation

EXHIBIT 23–8
Lion Corporation: Analysis of Direct-Labor Spending Variance, Finishing Department

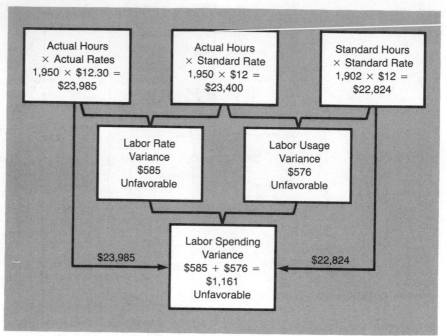

of the spending variance and its subdivision into price and usage components, using the same scheme as earlier.

Spending Variance in Direct-Materials Costs

The calculation for direct materials is similar in concept, except that (1) the price variance is usually calculated at the *time of purchase*, while the usage variance is determined at the *time of use*, and (2) the price variance therefore isn't departmentalized.

For example, suppose Lion Corporation bought 100,000 pounds of steel sheet in July 19x1 at 13 cents a pound. The standard price was 12 cents a pound. Its only other purchase in July was 30,000 pounds of finishing material at 27 cents a pound, against a standard price of 25 cents. The $1,600 total unfavorable price variance was calculated as follows:

	Actual Cost	Standard Cost	Price Variance
Steel sheet	100,000 × $0.13 = $13,000	100,000 × $0.12 = $12,000	$1,000 unf.
Finishing materials. . . .	30,000 × $0.27 = 8,100	30,000 × $0.25 = 7,500	600 unf.
Total	$21,100	$19,500	$1,600 unf.

The materials price variances were identified when the materials were purchased, mainly because management wanted to know the effects of changing prices immediately, rather than at some future time when the materials were used in production.

The materials purchased in July were placed in the materials storeroom and were recorded in inventory at their standard prices. The summary entry to record purchases in July was:

Raw Materials Inventory	19,500	
Materials Price Variance	1,600	
Accounts Payable		21,100

The $1,600 materials price variance was shown in the monthly variance report, where it signaled the need to revise the forecasts of cash flows and net income.

During July, the materials storeroom issued 90,000 pounds of steel sheet to the machining department and 25,000 pounds of finishing material to the finishing department. These quantities measured those departments' *actual* direct materials usage during the month. *Standard* direct materials usage was determined by the same process we described earlier for standard direct-labor usage:

1. Measure the standard direct-materials cost of all units completed during the period.
2. Measure the standard direct-materials cost of the work in process (*a*) at the beginning of the period, and (*b*) at the end of the period.[4]
3. Add (*a*) the standard direct-materials cost of the units completed to (*b*) the standard direct-materials cost of the work in process at the end of the period, and subtract (*c*) the standard direct-materials cost of the work in process at the beginning of the period.

Calculated in this way, *standard quantity* of steel sheet in the machining department in July (based on its actual output that month) amounted to 85,000 pounds; standard quantity of finishing material in the finishing department was 26,000 pounds. Both these quantities and the quantities actually issued in July were multiplied by their standard prices, yielding the following totals:

	Materials Issued	Standard Materials Cost	Usage Variance
Machining department	90,000 × $0.12 = $10,800	85,000 × $0.12 = $10,200	$600 unf.
Finishing department	25,000 × $0.25 = 6,250	26,000 × $0.25 = 6,500	250 fav.
Total	$17,050	$16,700	$350 unf.

---

[4] The standard direct-materials costs and the standard direct-labor costs of the units in process on any date needn't have identical percentages of the standard costs of fully completed units. The work in process, for example, may incorporate *all* the direct materials required to finish those units, yet be only half-processed insofar as direct labor is concerned. In other words, separate calculations of the degree of completion are made for each group of cost elements.

In other words, the machining department used more materials than the standards allowed, resulting in a $600 *unfavorable* direct-materials usage variance. The finishing department, on the other hand, had a $250 *favorable* direct-materials usage variance, calculated in the same fashion. The month's transactions in sheet steel and finishing materials therefore had the effects diagramed in Exhibit 23–9. In sum, the $21,100 actual

EXHIBIT 23–9
Lion Corporation: Materials Spending Variance and Inventory Change, July 19x1

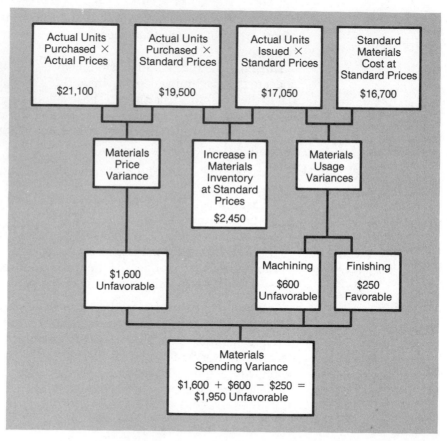

purchase cost exceeded the $16,700 standard direct-materials cost of the work done in the two departments by $4,400—a $2,450 addition to the materials inventory, $1,600 in unfavorable price variances, and a $350 *net* unfavorable usage variance. The diagram in this exhibit is entirely analogous to the labor spending variance diagramed in Exhibit 23–8, with two modifications: (1) it covers *all* materials purchased and used, not just those of one department; and (2) it includes one more element, the change in the materials inventory. This second difference makes it inappropriate, strictly speaking, to add the price and usage variances together to get a spending variance because the quantity used and the quantity bought are unequal. Putting the two components together is convenient, however, and we'll continue the practice.

Flexible Budgets for Overhead Costs

In job order production, factory costs other than the direct-labor and direct-materials costs of specific job orders are called *overhead costs*. Many of these costs don't vary proportionally with production. This means we can't derive the performance standard simply by multiplying total output by standard overhead cost per unit.

The flexible budget for Lion Corporation's finishing department is shown in Exhibit 23–10. The first six lines in this table contain the

EXHIBIT 23–10
Lion Corporation, Finishing Department: Flexible Budget for the Year 19x1

	Fixed per Month	Variable per Standard Direct Labor-Hour
Indirect labor............................	$ 1,000	$1.50
Overtime premium	—	—
Supplies...................................	—	2.00
Other direct department overhead......	1,600	0.20
Equipment maintenance	300	1.35
Supervision	3,000	—
Depreciation	5,000	—
Building services	4,000	—
Factory management	4,000	—
Total	$18,900	$5.05

flexible budget factors for overhead costs that are traceable to this department; the final three lines contain the flexible budget factors for the monthly allocations to the finishing department of portions of the costs of operating Lion Corporation's three indirect service and support centers.

The variable-cost components of the flexible budget formulas in Exhibit 23–10 are applied to *standard direct labor-hours* rather than to *physical units* of output. The reason is that we can't measure overall output in job order production by the number of physical units. We do have a composite measure of output, however—standard direct labor-hours in this case—in which each unit of output is *weighted* in proportion to the number of standard direct labor-hours it requires.

Whether standard direct labor-hours is an appropriate measure of volume for use in calculating a particular department's overhead cost performance standards depends on (1) whether the need for overhead cost is generated by the amount of output or by the amount of one or more direct inputs, and (2) whether overhead costs correlate better with total standard direct labor-hours than with some other measure of output (e.g., standard machine-hours).

Because Lion Corporation's management determined that the incidence of indirect labor and other overhead costs in the finishing department was more closely related to *standard* direct labor-hours than to *actual* direct labor-hours, the flexible budget standards were calculated on the basis of standard direct labor-hours (1,902 in July). The flexible budget for indirect labor in July therefore was $3,853 ($1,000 + $1.50 × 1,902).

Overhead Spending Variances

The amounts to be compared with a department's flexible budget for overhead costs in any period are the costs of overhead resources actually charged to the department during the period. Most of these will be fully traceable to the department, but some are likely to be *allocations* of costs incurred in service and support departments elsewhere in the company. Allocations are reported as controllable costs only when a department has the power to influence the costs of the service or support departments in question.

For example, department X is a direct user of the company's computer center, and the head of this department is the one who decides how much and what kinds of computer services to use. Charging department X for computer services should induce the department head to be economical in the use of these services, using them when and only when the benefits justify the costs. Charges for services of this sort should be made at prices agreed upon in advance, because the users can control only the *amount* of service usage (e.g., the number and complexity of the jobs it submits to the computer center), not the cost of performing them.

A report summarizing the finishing department's overhead costs for July 19x1 is shown in Exhibit 23–11. (Lion Corporation reports variances in direct labor and direct materials in another report.) As this exhibit shows, Lion Corporation makes three allocations to the finishing department each month—for equipment maintenance, building services, and factory management. The second and third of these are allocated at amounts equal to the amounts budgeted, and are shown in Exhibit 23–11 "below the line"—that is, in the section reserved for overhead costs not controllable at the departmental level.

EXHIBIT 23–11
Lion Corporation, Finishing Department: Overhead Cost Report for the Month Ended July 31, 19x1

	Actual Overhead	Flexible Budget at 1,902 Standard Direct Labor-Hours	Over/ (Under) Budget
Controllable:			
Indirect labor..................	$ 4,210	$ 3,853	$ 357
Overtime premium	360	—	360
Supplies......................	3,792	3,804	(12)
Other direct overhead	2,635	1,980	655
Equipment maintenance	2,700	2,868	(168)
Total controllable	13,697	12,505	1,192
Noncontrollable:			
Supervision...................	3,050	3,000	50
Depreciation	5,010	5,000	10
Building services	4,000	4,000	—
Factory management	4,000	4,000	—
Total	$29,757	$28,505*	$1,252

* Check figure based on column totals in Exhibit 23–10: $18,900 + $5.05 × 1,902 = $28,505.

The other allocation—of the costs of equipment maintenance service—is shown "above the line" as a controllable cost. Although Lion's management recognizes that the amount of maintenance required depends to some extent on the quality of the services the equipment maintenance department provides, top management is convinced that the managers of the three production centers have a great deal of influence over this quantity. The production center managers can exert their influence by supervising their employees properly, by insuring that routine maintenance is done on schedule, and by having department employees themselves make simple repairs and adjustments on the spot (as part of indirect labor) rather than calling in the equipment maintenance department. Responsibility for maintenance control, in other words, is *shared* by the equipment maintenance department and the production center managers, and spending variances in this cost appear in both sets of performance reports.

Summary

Feedback reports to managers of responsibility centers may focus on effectiveness, efficiency, or compliance. Cost control reports are usually intended to monitor the efficiency of responsibility centers, mainly for scorecard purposes. They are used as an input to *management by excep-*

tion, helping management focus its attention on activities that seem to need it the most.

Cost-control standards in responsibility centers engaged in responsive activities are reflected in flexible budgets, which adjust the performance standard to the actual volume of activity. For cost elements that are expected to vary proportionally with volume, the appropriate control standard is standard unit cost, multiplied by the number of units of output achieved in that period. For fixed costs and other costs that don't vary proportionally with volume, standard product cost isn't an appropriate standard. Instead, the flexible budget must provide separately for the fixed and variable components of cost.

Deviations of actual costs from the relevant cost-control standards are known as spending variances. These spending variances can be subdivided into price variance and usage variance components. The amounts to be reported to the manager of a responsibility center should include price variances only if that manager has responsibility for decisions that affect resource prices. In any case, the periodic cost-performance reports to the managers of responsibility centers should focus on the controllable elements of cost, placing noncontrollable variances "below the line" or excluding them from the reports submitted at this level.

Costs allocated to a responsibility center may be classified as controllable if the manager is responsible for controlling the amount of service used and if the allocation rates are predetermined. Otherwise the allocation should be either classified as noncontrollable or omitted from the reports entirely.

Key Terms

Controllability criterion
Cost-control standard
Flexible budget
Management by exception
Price (rate) variance
Responsive activity

Spending variance
Standard cost
Standard cost sheet
Standard price
Standard quantity
Usage variance

Independent Study Problems (Solutions in Appendix B)

1. Calculating and Analyzing Labor Cost Variances. You have the following information about the operations of department Y in a job order factory during the month of March:

	Product A	Product B
Units finished	5,000	10,000
Units in process:		
March 1	1,000	1,000
March 31	600	1,200
Standard direct-labor cost per unit	$2	$1

Products in process on any date are presumed to be half-processed by department Y's labor force.

Direct-labor cost in department Y amounted to $23,500 in March. The standard cost of this amount of labor totaled $22,000.

a. Calculate the total direct-labor cost variance (spending variance).
b. Analyze this variance in as much detail as you can and clearly label each component you have identified.
c. Calculate the standard direct-labor cost of the inventory in process at the end of the month.

2. Calculating and Analyzing Materials Cost Variances. Hillman Company manufactures a single product known as Quik-Tite. Material A is the only raw material used in the manufacture of Quik-Tite. Transactions in material A for the month of June are as follows:

	Standard	Actual
Units of Quik-Tite produced		61,000
Pounds of material A required to produce one unit of Quik-Tite	1.6 pounds	1.5 pounds
Cost of material A purchased during June	$2.00/pound	$2.05/pound
Inventory of material A on June 1..................		4,000 pounds
Amount of material A purchased during June		95,000 pounds

Calculate and analyze the material A spending variance for the month.

3. Cost-Performance Reporting: Overhead Costs. Riptide Company's factory manufactures on a job order basis, using department flexible budgets for cost reporting. The fiscal year is divided into 13 "months" of four weeks each. Department T has a normal production volume of 4,000 direct labor-hours a month and the following flexible budget for department overhead costs. This budget is valid for volumes between 3,000 and 4,500 direct labor-hours a month:

	Fixed per Month	Variable per Direct Labor-Hour
Nonproductive time, machine operators......	—	$0.25
Other indirect labor	$2,000	0.50
Operating supplies	—	0.15
Depreciation	2,000	—
Rent	700	—
Total	$4,700	$0.90

Actual costs and volumes in two successive months were as follows:

	Month 4	Month 5
Direct labor-hours	4,000	3,000
Nonproductive time	$ 800	$1,200
Other indirect labor	3,700	3,600
Operating supplies	650	430
Depreciation	2,100	2,150
Rent	770	730

a. Calculate the flexible budgets and prepare a cost-performance report for each of these months. This report should include each of the five overhead cost elements, arranged in any way you find appropriate.

b. Comment on the various items in these reports, indicating which items are likely to be of greatest significance in evaluating the cost-control performance of the department supervisor.

c. Looking only at those items for which cost performance was poorer in month 5 than in month 4, what would be your reaction to the statement that the manager of this department had been lax in enforcing cost control during month 5? What remedial action would you suggest, if any?

Exercises and Problems

4. Discussion Question: Applicability of Flexible Budgets. "I don't care what you say! Flexible budgets are used for overhead costs—for direct materials and direct labor you have to use standard costs for control reporting." Is this statement true? Does it make a difference whether it is applied to process production or to job order production?

5. Discussion Question: Communicating with Managers. "What do you mean, I'm over my budget?" said Bob Dietz, shop supervisor. "It says right here in the annual budget that my monthly indirect labor allowance is $3,300. I didn't make up the budget; you did. I only spent $3,200, so where do you get off telling me I'm $200 over? Maybe it's those birds up in the accounting department, fouling me up again."

a. As Dietz's boss, how would you explain the situation to him? Was he right? Should he have had an allowance of $3,300?

b. If Dietz's attitude is typical of the shop supervisors, what do you think should be done to strengthen the factory's overhead cost-control system?

6. Efficiency, Effectiveness and Compliance. Price Trade School trains young people to be plumbers and electricians. Admission to the school is limited to candidates who have (1) graduated from high school and (2) passed an admissions test. Each student proceeds at his or her own pace after the first week. The tuition fee and the program structure are based on the assumption that the average admitted student will complete the course satisfactorily by the end of 18 weeks; completion is signified when the student passes a proficiency examination.

Three outcomes are possible: (1) the student passes a proficiency examination before the end of 26 weeks; (2) the student withdraws from the program before the end of 26 weeks; or (3) the student is unable to pass the proficiency examination before the end of 26 weeks and is dismissed from the school at that time.

Suggest at least one measure to reflect each of (a) *efficiency* of the program, (b) *effectiveness* of the courses; and (c) *compliance* by school personnel.

7. Supplying Missing Information. You have the following data on Goodman Company's direct-labor costs:

Standard direct labor-hours	15,000
Actual direct labor-hours	14,500
Direct-labor usage variance—favorable	$ 4,000
Direct-labor rate variance—favorable	$ 5,800
Total direct-labor payroll.	$110,200

a. What was Goodman's actual direct-labor rate?
b. What was Goodman's standard direct-labor rate?

(AICPA adapted)

8. Calculating Department Output. Department X completed work on 4,300 units of product A and 2,700 units of product B in June. The standard direct-material and standard direct-labor costs of these two products were as follows:

	Product A	Product B
Standard direct-materials cost per unit	$5	$ 2
Standard direct-labor cost per unit.	6	10

The standard costs of the amounts of these two products in process in department X at the beginning and end of June were as follows:

	Product A	Product B
June 1:		
Standard direct-materials cost	$5,000	$1,000
Standard direct-labor cost.	3,000	2,500
June 30:		
Standard direct-materials cost	4,000	1,200
Standard direct-labor cost.	3,200	3,500

Calculate department X's output for the month, as measured by its standard direct-materials cost and by its standard direct-labor cost.

9. Efficiency, Effectiveness, and Cost Control Performance. The manager of Doan Corporation's refining department is responsible for meeting output objectives and for controlling departmental operating costs. You have the following information about this department for the month of March:

Budget = 100,000 pounds at budgeted cost of $10,000 + $0.15 × number of pounds, in which $0.15 = 0.01 prime units/pound × $15/prime unit

Actual = 90,000 pounds at actual cost of $24,570, including 950 prime units at $13,900 cost

A *prime unit* consists of one unit of direct materials and one unit of direct labor. No price variances arose in fixed costs in March.

For this department, calculate measures of (*a*) efficiency, (*b*) effectiveness, and (*c*) control performance.

10. Sequential Standard Costing Exercises. Follow the instructions given for each of the following three exercises. Do these exercises in the sequence in which they are presented.

Exercise A. Tapscott Enterprises, Inc., reports direct materials and direct labor usage variances to factory department heads each month. One department worked on only two products in January. Its standard inputs and actual outputs were as follows:

	Standard Direct-Material Quantity per Unit (Pounds)	Standard Direct Labor-Hours per Unit	Units of Product Manufactured during January
Product A.........	6	4	2,000
Product B.........	10	2	3,000

The following quantities of direct materials and direct labor were used in January: direct materials, 44,000 pounds; direct labor, 13,500 hours.

a. Calculate direct-materials and direct-labor usage variances for the month in terms of pounds of materials and hours of labor. Indicate whether each variance is favorable or unfavorable.
b. The standard materials price is $3 a pound. The standard wage rate is $10 an hour.
   1. Calculate the standard unit cost for each product in dollars.
   2. Restate your usage variances (from part *a*) in monetary terms.

Exercise B. Preston Pans, Ltd., manufactures cookware. All its factory operations are performed in a single department. The department's facilities were used during February to manufacture the following three products:

	Standard Direct-Materials Quantity (Pounds per Unit)		Standard Direct Labor-Hours per Unit	Units of Product Manufactured
	Material X	Material Y		
Product A..........	1	3	1	1,000
Product B..........	2	1	1	3,000
Product C..........	3	4	6	2,000

You have the following additional information:

1. Standard materials prices: material X, $2 a pound; material Y, $5 a pound.
2. Standard wage rate: $10 an hour.
3. Direct materials purchased during February:
     Material X: 10,000 pounds, $21,000.
     Material Y: 15,000 pounds, $77,000.
4. Direct material used during February:
     Material X: 12,600 pounds.
     Material Y: 15,000 pounds.
5. Direct labor used during February: 16,800 hours, $160,000.

a. Calculate direct-labor and direct-materials variances, in dollars.
b. Indicate to whom each of these variances should be reported.

Exercise C. Block Houses, Inc., manufactures prefabricated housing modules. The following information was collected for one department for the month of March.

1. Inventory of work in process, March 1 (at standard cost):
     Direct materials, $28,000.
     Direct labor, $16,000.
2. Direct materials with a standard cost of $22,000 were received in the department from the storeroom during the month.
3. Direct-labor cost for the month was $8,000 at actual wage rates and $7,500 at standard wage rates.
4. The standard cost of products finished and transferred out of the department during the month was as follows:
     Standard direct-materials cost: $21,200.
     Standard direct-labor cost: $7,800.
5. Inventory of work in process, March 31 (at standard cost):
     Direct materials, $24,000
     Direct labor, $15,000.

a. Calculate the standard direct-labor and standard direct-materials costs of the work done during the month.
b. Calculate the direct-labor and direct-materials spending variances for the month, and subdivide them as you deem appropriate.

c. Comment on the department head's cost-control performance during the month.

11. Calculating and Analyzing Labor Variances. You have the following information for a factory department for the month of September:

1.

	Product X	Product Y
Units finished......................	2,000	1,500
Units in process:		
September 1......................	1,000	500
September 30.....................	2,000	800
Standard direct-labor cost per unit		
(at $10 an hour)	$20	$30

2. Half the required department direct labor had been performed on each unit in process on the indicated dates.
3. Actual direct-labor cost, month of September: 9,500 hours, $100,000.

a. Calculate the standard direct-labor cost of the work done in this department during September.
b. Calculate and analyze the direct-labor spending variance.
c. Which portion of the spending variance is likely to be subject to the department head's control?

12. Materials Variances; Implications of LIFO. Playco, Inc., had materials inventories on January 1, 19x1, with a standard cost of $219,000. Materials price variances are identified and isolated at the time of purchase. The standard materials cost of the work in process on January 1, 19x1, was $87,000. The following transactions took place in January:

1. Materials purchased: actual cost, $112,000; standard cost, $105,000.
2. Materials issued and used: standard cost, $97,000.
3. Standard materials cost of goods finished: $102,000.

The standard materials cost of the work in process on January 31, 19x1, was $85,500.

a. Account for the difference between (1) the actual materials cost of goods purchased in January, and (2) the standard materials cost of the factory's output during the month, in as much detail as you can. What was the materials spending variance for the month?
b. You are told the company's materials inventory is measured on a LIFO basis for public financial reporting and that the January 1, 19x2, LIFO cost of the materials inventory was $119,000. Comment briefly on the implications of this fact for (1) company record-keeping and (2) the measurement of variances.
c. Management is concerned that materials usage variances don't reflect current purchase prices. Furthermore, measuring and reporting materials price variances at the time of purchase implies that the company

earns income or suffers losses by buying materials as well as by selling its products. Finally, management is also concerned that year-end LIFO adjustments may affect the income statement in ways inconsistent with the treatment of the variances. Discuss the issues underlying these concerns and indicate how you would respond to management.

13. Allocations in Control Reporting.   The closures department's flexible budget provides for the use of 100 service department hours each month plus 1 service department hour for every 30 direct-labor hours in the closures department. Closures' budget calls for a charge of $20 for every service department hour used. Closures is to be charged each month for usage of service department services at the service department's actual average cost of providing those services.

Last month, closures used 2,700 direct labor-hours and 180 service department hours and was charged $4,050 for usage of service department services.

a. Calculate the closures department's flexible budget for service department charges last month and determine the spending variance in this item. (Note: the flexible budget formula was established *before* last month's data became known.)

b. Analyze this spending variance insofar as you can. What explanations can you advance?

14. Supplying Missing Data.   You have the following information on direct labor and materials costs in two factory departments in the month of March.

	Department X	Department Y
Actual wage rate	$8.30 an hour	$9.00 an hour
Standard wage rate.	A	$9.20 an hour
Actual labor quantity used	9,200 hours	E
Standard labor quantity required by work done	9,600 hours	4,600 hours
Labor rate variance.	$2,760 unfav.	F
Labor usage variance	B	$1,840 unfav.
Actual materials quantity used.	10,000 pounds	G
Standard materials quantity required by work done. . . .	C	31,000 gallons
Standard materials cost of work finished and		
transferred out of department	$17,500	H
Standard price of materials	$2 a pound	$5 a gallon
Historical cost of materials.	$1.90 a pound	$4.90 a gallon
Materials usage variance	D	$5,000 fav.
Materials in process, March 1, at standard cost	$12,500	$25,000
Materials in process, March 31, at standard cost	$14,000	$23,200

Supply the information missing from this table.

15. Overhead Performance Report. The monthly flexible budget standards for the assembly department of Boyce Furniture Company for various quantities of direct labor-hours are shown in the following table:

	Direct Labor-Hours				
	10,000	10,500	11,000	11,500	12,000
Supervision	$ 1,800	$ 1,800	$ 1,800	$ 1,800	$ 1,800
Indirect labor	7,000	7,350	7,700	8,050	8,400
Supplies	4,000	4,200	4,400	4,600	4,800
Power, fuel, and water	1,000	1,050	1,100	1,150	1,200
Depreciation	2,000	2,000	2,000	2,000	2,000
Space occupancy	3,000	3,000	3,000	3,000	3,000
General plant overhead	2,800	2,800	2,800	2,800	2,800
Total	$21,600	$22,200	$22,800	$23,400	$24,000

Actual charges to the department for the month of March were as follows:

Supervision	$ 1,900
Indirect labor	7,700
Supplies	4,020
Power, fuel, and water	930
Depreciation	1,950
Space occupancy	3,000
General plant overhead	3,000
Total	$22,500

The actual volume of production during March totaled 10,500 direct labor-hours.

a. How much of the budgeted overhead cost would you classify as fixed? What is the average budgeted variable cost per direct labor-hour?

b. Prepare a department overhead cost report for the month.

c. Comment on the possible causes of each of the variances shown on the report.

16. Validity of Flexible Budgeting. Production in Blach Company's factory is on a job order basis. Each factory department has a monthly overhead cost budget, agreed upon at the beginning of the year, and a set of flexible budget formulas for overhead costs used for monthly performance reporting. The formulas for the finishing department are:

Supervision	$1,200 a month
Indirect labor	$800 a month + $1 per direct labor-hour
Overtime premium	$0.50 for each direct labor-hour in excess of 2,400 direct labor-hours a month
Supplies	$0.40 a direct labor-hour
Power	$200 a month + $0.15 a direct labor-hour
Depreciation	$500 a month
Other overhead	$0.10 a direct labor-hour

Normal volume in this department is 3,000 direct labor-hours a month, but this is a bad year and this year's budget anticipates volume to average only 2,700 hours a month. Volume in May was 2,500 direct labor-hours. The actual overhead costs for the month were as follows:

Supervision..............	$1,260
Indirect labor	3,340
Overtime premium........	140
Supplies	860
Power	600
Depreciation............	500
Other..................	300
Total................	$7,000

a. Prepare an overhead cost-performance report for the month of May, using the flexible budget.

b. The company's president isn't sure that flexible budgeting is a good idea because it may make department heads look good even though their average overhead cost keeps going up. The president prefers to compare average actual overhead cost with average planned overhead cost at planned volume. Make the calculations necessary for a report on this basis and draft a reply to the president's argument.

17. Significance of Spending Variances. Some indirect labor in Balch Company (see problem 16) is performed by regular bench operators who normally perform direct-labor operations. Management is reluctant to lay these operators off for short periods of time. Instead, some of the indirect labor work, such as cleaning and adjusting machines, is deferred until the production schedule is light.

The manager of the finishing department thinks this should be built into the flexible budget, with a larger indirect labor budget when volume is low, and vice versa. This would eliminate erratic fluctuations in the indirect labor spending variances. The plant controller disagrees, arguing that production creates the need for indirect labor services, even though these services may not be performed when production takes place.

Prepare a brief report on this issue, stating your position and indicating how management should interpret and use the spending variances arising under the solution you are recommending.

18. Process Production: Department Performance Report. Apex Company's coatings department operated at a volume of 80,000 gallons in August 19x1. The department's costs that month were as follows:

Materials	$127,400
Processing labor	26,250
Support labor	2,050
Supplies.	4,200
Other controllable costs	24,800
Supervision	3,300
Depreciation	3,900
Factory management	29,000
Total	$220,900

a. Using the flexible budget set forth in Exhibit 23–1 at the beginning of this chapter, prepare a cost-performance report for the month of August. Unlike the cost-performance report in Exhibit 23–3, your report should include all costs charged to the department in August.

b. The flexible budget for materials in 19x1 reflected a standard materials price of $1.20 a pound, a standard wage rate of $10 an hour for processing labor, and a standard wage rate of $8 an hour for support labor. The coatings department used 98,000 pounds of materials, 2,500 hours of processing labor, and 250 hours of support labor in August. Use this additional information to help management evaluate cost-control performance in the coatings department in August.

19. Preparing a Control Report. Neptune Company operates a small factory that makes only one product. Four production operations are necessary, one in each of the factory's four departments. The company's engineers have determined that these operations should require the following labor-hour allowances under normal conditions:

	Labor-Hours per Unit of Product			
	Operation No. 1	**Operation No. 2**	**Operation No. 3**	**Operation No. 4**
Operators	1.0	3.0	1.5	0.5
Helpers	0.5	2.5	2.0	0.1
Handlers	0.2	0.5	1.0	0.3

Operators are paid $12 an hour, helpers $8 an hour, and handlers $6 an hour.

During August, the factory's operations were:

	Operation No. 1	**Operation No. 2**	**Operation No. 3**	**Operation No. 4**
Units produced.	2,000	1,800	2,100	2,000
Labor-hours:				
Operators.	1,100	5,200	3,400	980
Helpers.	550	4,600	4,600	190
Handlers	210	1,000	2,200	610

a. Prepare a report for management, summarizing labor operations for the month in terms of both hours and dollars, and write a brief paragraph commenting on the effectiveness of labor control during the month.

b. What advantages, if any, do you see in including dollar amounts in this report? Explain.

20. Physical Unit Comparisons. Art Dangerfield had been department supervisor for 30 years. "All I want are a few key figures," he said. "The rest of the accounting numbers are rubbish. I want to know my scrap percentage [pounds of scrap divided by pounds of materials] and the materials yield [pounds of product divided by pounds of materials]. If scrap is less than 5 percent and the materials yield is better than 80 percent, I've got it made."

The department processes a number of different materials, and a certain amount of waste is inherent in the process. Some materials are lost in the process itself, and some take the form of recoverable scrap. Dangerfield retired last month and his longtime assistant, Dorothy Hellman, was promoted to take his place. The first report she saw contained the following statistics:

Scrap	3%
Materials yield	84%
Materials usage variance (percent of standard)	10% unfavorable

"Art's formula doesn't seem to be working," she observed, "I'm well within his limits, but how did that usage variance get so big?" She asked the plant controller to look into the matter.

The controller analyzed the materials requisitions and production records and came up with the following data:

	Standard Price (per Pound)	Standard Usage (in Pounds)	Quantity Used (in Pounds)
Material A	$ 0.10	4,000	3,700
Material B	1.00	600	630
Material C	10.00	400	450
Total		5,000	4,780

The percentage statistics were correct: the output weighed 4,015 pounds, 84 percent of the weight of the materials used, and 143 pounds of scrap were recovered.

a. Analyze the controller's data and provide an explanation for Hellman.
b. Does your analysis indicate that the standards should be changed? What other suggestions would you make?

21. Report Format; Interpreting Variances. The following report on direct-materials and direct-labor costs was prepared for a factory for the month of July:

	Direct Materials	Direct Labor
Materials inventory, July 1.................	$10,000	$ —
Work in process inventory, July 1	4,000	4,500
Materials purchased during July	24,000	—
Labor used during July	—	45,000
Total cost to be accounted for	$38,000	$49,500
Materials inventory, July 31..............	8,000	—
Work in process inventory, July 31	3,000	3,750
Goods completed during July............	29,000	44,700
Total cost accounted for	40,000	48,450
Variance.........................	$ 2,000	$ (1,050)

Additional data were as follows:

Materials purchased during July:	
At actual cost	$24,000
At standard cost	26,400
Direct materials used during July (at standard cost)..............	28,400
Direct labor used during July:	
At actual cost	45,000
At standard cost	45,250
Indirect materials used during July	None

a. Calculate the price and usage variances for direct materials and for direct labor.

b. Suggest ways of improving the format of the report on direct-labor and direct-materials variances that the accounting staff presents to the factory manager each month. What purpose would this report serve?

22. Determining and Reporting Direct-Labor and Direct-Materials Variances. Tufwun Products Company manufactures a limited line of machined products in its Albany factory. You have the following information on direct-labor and direct-materials costs in the milling department in September:

1. Direct labor in the department is divided into three pay grades, as follows:

Grade	Standard Wage Rate per Hour
101	$ 7
102	8
105	10

2. Wages actually earned by employees differ from these standard rates due to seniority provisions. Actual hours worked and actual gross pay during the month were as follows:

Grade	Hours	Gross Wages
101	1,250	$ 9,050
102	1,500	12,150
105	1,520	15,100
Total	4,270	$36,300

3. Production and product cost standards for the month:

	Standard Direct-Materials Cost per Unit	Standard Milling Department Direct Labor per Unit			Standard Direct-Labor Cost	Units Produced, September
Product		101 Hours	102 Hours	105 Hours		
A	$ 6	0.5	1.0	—	$11.50	400
B	12	1.0	0.5	1.5	26.00	800
C	15	0.5	1.0	0.5	16.50	600

4. Direct-materials costs charged to the department, at standard prices, $22,800.
5. The department had no unfinished work in process either at the beginning or at the end of the month.

a. Analyze the milling department's direct-labor and direct-materials cost variances in September and prepare a summary for the factory manager's use in evaluating the department head's effectiveness in controlling these costs.

b. If you identified any variance that wouldn't enter into the evaluation of the department head's performance, indicate who might be interested in it and for what purpose.

c. Under what circumstances would the department head need more information than this system provides? What kinds of additional information would be required, and what would have to be done to provide it?

23. Analyzing, Reporting, and Interpreting Overhead Variances. Tumbler Company uses a system of department flexible budgets to provide overhead cost-control information for its factory department managers. The monthly flexible budget for overhead costs in the machining department is as follows:

	Volume (Machine-Hours)				
	10,000	12,000	14,000	16,000	18,000
Supervision	$ 1,900	$ 1,900	$ 1,900	$ 2,200	$ 2,200
Indirect labor.	2,000	2,200	2,400	2,600	2,800
Supplies.	600	600	700	800	900
Payroll taxes	1,210	1,430	1,660	1,930	2,210
Overtime premiums	50	70	220	400	1,000
Depreciation	800	800	800	800	800
Floor-space charges.	3,000	3,000	3,000	3,000	3,000
Engineering services	600	650	700	750	800
Total	$10,060	$10,650	$11,380	$12,480	$13,710

During May, this department operated 16,000 machine-hours and was charged the following amounts:

Supervision	$ 2,500
Indirect labor.	2,710
Supplies.	720
Payroll taxes	2,000
Overtime premiums	900
Depreciation	850
Floor-space charges.	2,700
Engineering services	820
Total	$13,200

The following additional information is available:

1. The department supervision account is ordinarily charged for the straight-time wages earned by assistant supervisors. Although these assistant supervisors are paid on an hourly basis, they usually work a full workweek. When the department head deems it necessary, a senior machinist is given additional supervisory duties, and a proportional part of that person's wages is charged to the supervision account.

2. The plant manager assigned a quality-control supervisor to this department for three days in May to assist the department manager in the production of a long run of parts with very tight specifications. The department supervision account was charged $330 for the supervisor's services during this period.

3. The indirect labor account is charged for the wages of department materials handlers and helpers and also for the nonproductive time of machine operators. During May, machine operators were idle for approximately 40 hours because of machine breakdowns and delays in receiving work from other departments. The account was charged $420 for this idle time. The indirect labor budget amount includes an allowance for such costs in the amount of 1 cent per machine-hour.

4. Departments are charged for payroll taxes on all department wages, both direct and indirect. Payroll taxes are charged to the departments at a predetermined rate per labor-dollar. This rate is not changed during the year.

5. Overtime work in each department is scheduled monthly by the production scheduling department on the basis of scheduled production for the month. The department manager's primary responsibility is to meet the production schedule, using whatever overtime is necessary to accomplish this objective.

6. The depreciation charge is calculated monthly on the basis of the original cost of the equipment located in the department as of the first day of the month.

7. Floor-space charges are calculated monthly by multiplying the number of square feet of floor space occupied by each department by the average cost of building depreciation, insurance, utilities, and janitorial and maintenance services for that month.

8. Engineering services are provided to production departments by the factory engineering department. These services consist primarily of methods studies prepared at the request of the plant manager or on the initiative of the chief engineer. The charge for these services is based on a predetermined rate per engineering-hour.

a. Calculate and list the overhead spending variances in May, *ignoring* the "additional information" provided.

b. Using all the information available to you, determine the amounts you would report to the department manager and indicate why you believe the manager would find these amounts relevant. State your reason(s) for excluding any portion of any overhead spending variance.

c. Do the spending variances in May seem to warrant any action by the department manager? By anyone else? Explain.

Chapter 24

Cost-Control Reporting

Flexible budgets for responsive activities are only part of the overall cost reporting structure in complex organizations. In this final chapter, we'll consider three additional aspects of cost reporting systems:

1. Reporting overhead spending variances and reconciling them with unabsorbed overhead.
2. Control reporting for discretionary overhead costs.
3. Reflecting behavioral factors in system design.

We'll finish the chapter with a number of observations on cost control in service businesses.

Factory Overhead Cost Variances

In any factory costing system that uses predetermined overhead rates on a full-costing basis, some of the costs incurred to operate the factory are assigned to each individual product unit. These amounts are referred to as absorbed overhead. The difference between the actual overhead cost in any period and the total amount of overhead absorbed in that period is known as the **total overhead variance.**

When we encountered this phenomenon in Chapter 19, the total overhead variance was called the over- or underabsorbed overhead. Our concern there was limited to whether the entire variance should appear as an immediate determinant of income. Our objective in this section is to explain how the overhead spending variances we identified in Chapter 23 relate to the total overhead variance and how the remaining portion of the total can be interpreted.

Total Overhead Variance

In introducing job order costing in Chapter 19, we used a predetermined overhead rate with direct labor-hours as the denominator. The amount of overhead absorbed (charged to products) was determined by multiplying the rate by the actual number of direct labor-hours used. In a *standard costing* system, the procedure is the same but the amount of overhead absorbed is the predetermined overhead rate times the number of *standard* direct labor-hours, machine-hours, or other product characteristic that serves as the denominator of the overhead rate, not the *actual* number used.

Morley Company, a small manufacturer in job order production, uses the number of standard direct labor-hours each product requires to measure the volume of output for purposes of overhead absorption in its machining department—that is, the amount of overhead required by any product is assumed to be proportional to the number of standard direct labor-hours it requires in machining. Total output therefore is measured by making the following calculation for each product, and adding across all products manufactured in the period:

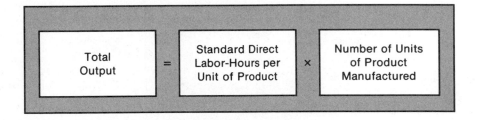

A product requiring two standard direct labor-hours in machining therefore causes twice as much machining department overhead cost to be included in the cost of the total output as a product requiring one standard direct labor-hour.

Morley Company's machining department's predetermined overhead rate in 19x1 was derived as follows:

- The monthly *flexible budget* for overhead costs was summarized in the following formula:

  Budgeted overhead = $27,500 + $4 × Standard direct labor-hours

- *Normal volume* was 2,500 standard direct labor-hours a month.
- The *standard overhead rate* therefore was ($27,500 + $4 × 2,500) divided by 2,500 hours = $15 a standard direct labor-hour.

Morley's machining department experienced the following in September 19x1:

1. Actual overhead costs incurred by the machining department totaled $35,910.
2. The department's output required 2,300 standard direct labor-hours, calculated as shown in Exhibit 24–1. In this case, 2,200 standard hours were required by the units finished, and 100 standard hours were required to increase the work in process from 400 standard hours on September 1 to 500 standard hours on September 30.
3. The total flexible budget for overhead costs for the month's actual output (2,300 standard direct labor-hours) was $27,500 + $4 × 2,300 = $36,700.
4. The amount of overhead absorbed was $34,500 (2,300 standard direct labor-hours × $15). The amount absorbed is called the *standard overhead cost* for the month. This amount was assigned to products manufactured in September and therefore became an inventory cost that eventually would be transferred to the cost of goods sold.

EXHIBIT 24–1
Machining Department: Standard Direct Labor-Hours of Output in the Month of September 19x1

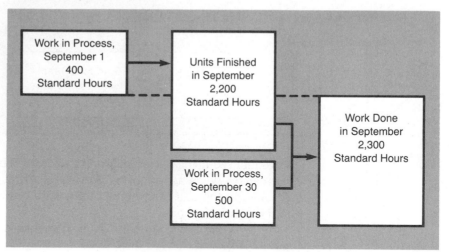

These numbers are assembled in Exhibit 24–2. This shows how the actual overhead for the period ($35,910) was split into two components. Of the total, $34,500 was spent to produce output with a standard overhead cost of $34,500—this was the amount of absorbed overhead in September 19x1. The rest of the overhead cost ($1,410) wasn't assigned to any of the machining department's output—instead, it was classified as an unfavorable cost variance, representing resources used without yielding any productive output.

EXHIBIT 24–2
Machining Department: Derivation of Total Overhead Variance

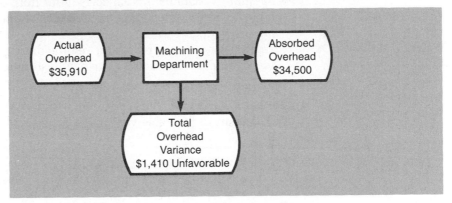

Reasons for an Overhead Variance

We know from Chapter 23 that a spending variance in overhead costs in job order production represents the difference between the actual overhead cost and the overhead-cost flexible budget for the actual volume of activity in the period. For Morley Company, we can calculate the September **overhead spending variance** as follows, using items 1 and 3 in the data supplied at the beginning of this section:

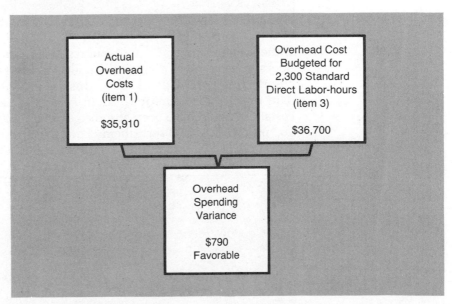

This is only part of the overhead variance, however. The total overhead variance, also referred to as the amount of overhead over- or underabsorbed, arises mainly as a result of two forces:

1. *Spending* variations: Actual costs differ from the amounts that would normally be expected at the production volume actually achieved during the period.
2. *Volume* variations: Production volume during the period differs from the volume used in setting the overhead rate.

We know that the *total* overhead cost variance this month was $1,410 and was *unfavorable*. This means that there was some other influence producing an unfavorable variance of $2,200:

Total variance.	$1,410	unfavorable
Spending variance.	790	favorable
Variance from other influences	$2,200	unfavorable

The other influence in this case was Morley's overall *production volume,* which amounted to 2,300 standard direct labor-hours in September instead of the 2,500-hour *normal* volume. Morley expected total fixed overhead cost to amount to $27,500 in an average month, and this fixed overhead cost accounted for $11 of the department's $15 predetermined overhead rate for 19x1:

$$\frac{\text{Total fixed cost}}{\text{Normal volume}} = \frac{\$27,500}{2,500 \text{ standard direct labor-hours}} = \$11 \text{ an hour}$$

If the actual volume of output had resulted in the use of 2,500 standard hours in September, then all the budgeted fixed costs would have been absorbed, as Exhibit 24–3 shows. Instead, actual volume was 200 standard direct labor-hours fewer than *normal.* This means that the fixed costs that would have been absorbed by these 200 hours had no place to go, no product to absorb them. Low volume therefore accounted for $200 \times \$11 = \$2,200$ of the unabsorbed overhead.

TERMINOLOGY

Normal volume is the production level management expects to achieve in a set of production facilities, on the average, when the facilities are operated as they were designed to do. It serves as the denominator for the overhead rate.

Normal overhead cost is the budgeted amount of overhead cost at *normal* volume.

Standard overhead cost is the amount of overhead cost absorbed at the *actual* volume of output achieved in a specific period of time.

EXHIBIT 24–3
Overhead Volume Variance

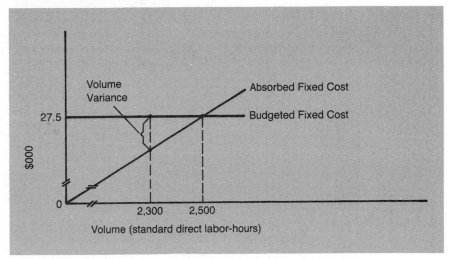

We call this the **overhead volume variance.** If the overhead rate had been recalculated at the actual volume (2,300 standard hours), the fixed-cost component would have been $11.956 an hour ($27,500/2,300). The $2,200 unfavorable volume variance therefore represents the additional $0.956 that each of the 2,300 standard hours would have had to absorb to make up for the 200-hour shortfall in volume (2,300 × $0.956 = $2,200).

Interpreting the Volume Variance

The volume variance must be interpreted carefully. It doesn't mean that costs were $2,200 more than expected because volume was lower than normal. It merely says that no production was available to absorb $2,200 of the costs that were expected to occur. Expressed differently, $2,200 was spent to provide production capacity the company didn't use.

Department heads don't establish their own production schedules. The volume of activity is determined outside the factory, on the basis of the number of customer orders in hand or anticipated. This being so, volume variances therefore aren't controllable by the department head or even by the plant manager. They should be reported to plant managers only to help them explain the total overhead variance to higher management, and they shouldn't be reported to the department managers at all.

Summarizing the Variances

The overall variance computation can be summarized in the following manner:

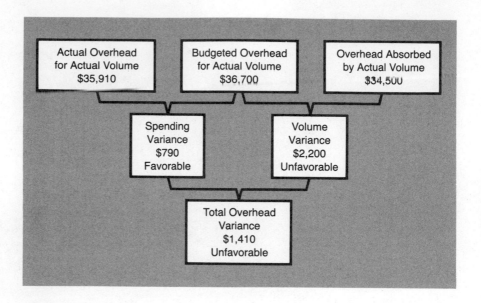

Exhibit 24–4 presents this same information in graphic form. This is similar to Exhibit 24–3 except that it includes the variable overhead costs as well as the fixed overhead. The amount of overhead absorbed is shown by the height of the straight line rising from the lower left-hand corner of the chart. The amount budgeted is shown by the height of the other line. Because some of the department's costs are fixed, this line has a gentler slope than the Absorbed Overhead line. Variable costs in this case are proportional to volume—$4 in budgeted variable costs for each standard direct labor-hour—and thus the flexible budget is shown as a straight line.

The amounts budgeted and absorbed at this month's volume of 2,300 standard hours are shown as large dots on these two lines. The actual amount spent is shown by another dot. By measuring the vertical distances between dots, we are able to identify the total variance and its two component parts.

Volume variances at volumes in excess of normal volume, such as *b* in Exhibit 24–4, represent *over*absorption and are identified as favorable. Volume variances at volumes lower than normal, such as *a* in the exhibit, represent underutilization of capacity and are referred to as unfavorable.

The overhead variance can be analyzed in many ways, depending on the behavioral patterns the company is able to identify and on the methods used to accumulate and distribute costs. The appendix to this chapter illustrates two variations on the analysis described in this section.

EXHIBIT 24–4
Reconciliation of Overhead Cost Variances

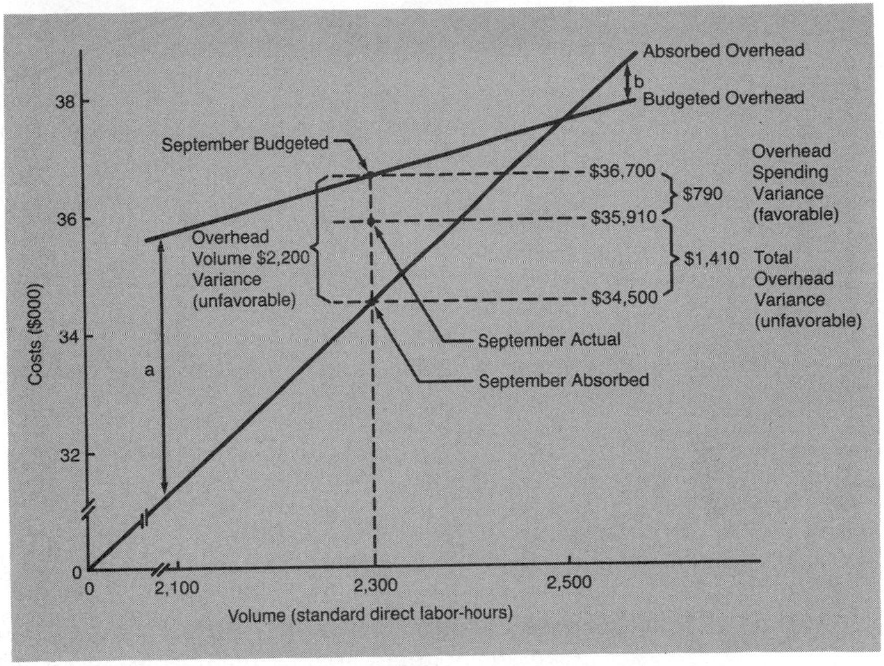

Management's Interest in Overhead Volume Variances

Responsibility for factory overhead volume variances lies with those who are responsible for generating volume. In most cases, marketing management, not manufacturing management, has this responsibility. Information on volume variances can be useful as a partial determinant of the profit-generating ability of marketing managers and marketing activities. It also lets higher management know how much fixed overhead cost will be deducted directly from revenues because production is too low to absorb it.

Assigning the responsibility for manufacturing volume variances to marketing management is a simple process if all the factory's output goes to a single revenue segment. For example, Fortune Company produced and sold 100,000 units of its only product in June at a selling price of $20 each. Its factory has fixed costs of $320,000 a month and variable costs of $8 a unit. Normal production volume was 80,000 units a month, so that the standard product cost was $12 a unit ($320,000/80,000 + $8). The standard cost of goods sold in June therefore amounted to $1.2 million (100,000 × $12). Since production volume in June was equal to sales volume (100,000 units) and exceeded normal production volume (80,000 units), the overhead volume variance was as follows:

Factory costs absorbed by production: 100,000 × $12........ $1,200,000
Budgeted factory costs at actual volume: $320,000 +
   100,000 × $8... 1,120,000
Overhead volume variance (favorable)................... $ 80,000

Because total fixed cost is the same at normal volume as at actual volume, the $80,000 favorable volume variance is equal to the product of standard fixed cost ($4 a unit) and the difference between actual and budgeted volume, 20,000 units (100,000 − 80,000).

Fortune Company's gross margin can be calculated on both full-costing and variable-costing bases:

	Full Costing	Variable Costing
Sales revenues	$2,000,000	$2,000,000
Cost of goods sold:		
Standard cost	1,200,000	800,000
Overhead volume variance	(80,000)	—
Budgeted fixed cost	—	320,000
Total cost of goods sold	1,120,000	1,120,000
Gross margin	$ 880,000	$ 880,000

This indicates that by adjusting the cost of goods sold to reflect the favorable volume variance, the full-costing company allows management to reap the full credit for above-normal sales volume, as it would under variable costing.

Suppose, however, Fortune Company had *two* marketing divisions, each selling 50,000 units of product manufactured in a single factory. Rather than split the volume variance equally between the two divisions (in proportion to unit sales), we need to determine how much of the variance each division was responsible for. In this case, we find that division A was budgeted to sell only 30,000 units, while division B was budgeted to sell the 50,000 units it actually sold. It is clear, therefore, that the entire volume variance should go to division A. In general, allocation of the volume variance becomes more and more difficult as the number of revenue segments served by a given factory increases.

In concluding our discussion of the overhead volume variance, we need to make only two final comments. First, overhead volume variances arise as a result of the volume of *production*. If production volume differs from sales volume, assigning the overhead volume variance to marketing management may distort the measure of the marketing group's profit performance in the current period. The overhead volume variance (from production) may even be favorable when *sales* volume is *below* its normal level, and vice versa.

Second, the argument for assigning volume variances to marketing management *shouldn't be extended to factory spending variances.* Marketing management is responsible for sales volume and sales mix, not for factory production costs. Only when marketing management's actions lead to changes in factory costs should it be accountable for portions of the factory spending variances. Design modifications or marketing-required changes in production schedules, for example, might justify distribution of some factory spending variances, but the controllability criterion will be violated unless the amounts to be distributed are established when the changes are authorized by marketing management.

Discretionary Overhead Costs	Most overhead costs of factory production centers are supportive overhead—that is, they are necessary to service the volume of orders that have entered the system. Another large group of overhead costs is **discretionary overhead,** incurred to secure some future benefit or to meet some independent objective set by management. In this category, we have such costs as product advertising, research, contributions to charitable organizations, and management consultants' fees. In this section, we'll examine how management can use accounting information in (1) planning discretionary activities and (2) responding to subsequent events.

Planning Criteria

Discretionary costs are fixed costs—by definition, since only costs that vary in response to volume changes are variable costs. This being the case, most decisions that determine the level of discretionary costs are made when the budget is established. People are hired, commitments are made, and orders are placed on the strength of budget authorizations.

This means that a crucial control process for discretionary overhead is budget review and approval. The basic criterion underlying these decisions is the cost-benefit criterion: Do the anticipated benefits justify the cost? For major self-standing activities, such as new-product-development projects, approval often comes in two stages, as diagrammed in Exhibit 24–5. The project is reviewed initially as part of the regular budgetary planning process. If it passes muster at that time, it is incorporated into the budget. Much can happen between the date the budget is approved and the date the first commitment of resources is made, however. Management is likely to avail itself of any additional information generated during this period before making the final decision to go ahead with the project or put it on the shelf.

Feedback Reporting: Marketing Activities

Feedback reporting is no less important than budgetary planning in the control of discretionary overhead costs. First, although these are fixed

EXHIBIT 24–5
Two-Stage Approval Process for Product-Development Projects

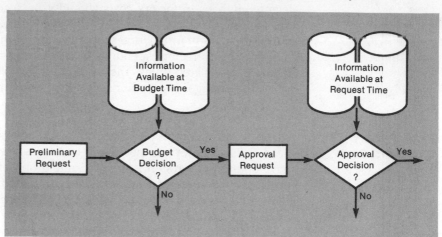

costs, they do change in response to the decisions management makes about the activities they support—that is, they can be incremental. Reporting the costs and benefits from these activities calls management's attention to situations that may call for replanning. Second, even without any change in management's plans, actual expenditures may deviate from the fixed budgets. Feedback reports call such deviations to management's attention.

Discretionary (or programmed) activities are of many types, each calling for its own reporting structure. Marketing expenditures are generally reviewed as part of profit-monitoring processes similar to those discussed in Chapter 22. For marketing activities, mere comparisons of actual expenses with budgeted expenses have little analytical value. What does matter is whether revenues and contribution margins have responded to marketing expenditures as management anticipated they would when the profit plan was adopted. The analysis therefore focuses on deviations from planned profit performance—the profit variances—and on how they arose.

Feedback Reporting: Product-Development Activities

Many discretionary activities consist of self-standing activities, such as company-initiated efforts to design and introduce new products that seem likely to be commercially successful—usually referred to as product-development projects. The usual focus of feedback reporting and control here is the individual project, clearly identifiable from start to completion and large enough to warrant specific management attention.

The same techniques can be applied to individual job orders that are large enough and important enough to warrant this kind of attention—major construction projects are a case in point.

The key to feedback reporting in connection with product-development projects and other project-centered activities is to break the overall project objectives down into identifiable, timed subobjectives. Costs can then be accumulated for each subobjective, and the reports can compare these costs with the amounts management had planned to incur to achieve each subobjective.

The breakdown of a simple project might take the form illustrated in Exhibit 24–6. This shows a project that was started on March 1 and

EXHIBIT 24–6
Project Milestones and Budget Allowances

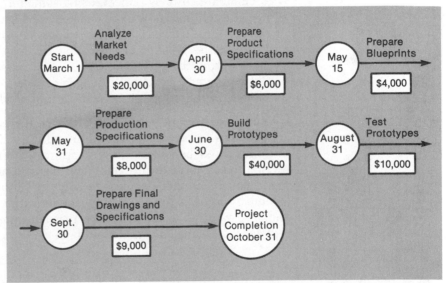

scheduled for completion on October 31 of the same year. Each circle in this diagram represents a significant milestone along the road to the completion of the project. The arrows between milestones represent activities, each with its own budgeted cost. Most of the activities, in turn, can be further subdivided into subactivities and intermediate milestones if management wants this additional detail.

In this case, the analysis stage proceeded as planned and was completed on April 30 at a cost of $19,500. Snags were encountered in the development of product specifications, however, and this activity wasn't completed until May 31, at a cost of $12,000. A cumulative report for the months of March, April, and May should show the following comparison:

	Actual Cost	Budgeted Cost	Over/(Under) Budget
Analysis................	$19,500	$20,000	$ (500)
Product specifications....	12,000	6,000	6,000
Total to date	$31,500	$26,000	$5,500

This is an activity-centered report, showing clearly that the company spent $5,500 more to do the work than it had planned, a signal of a serious cost overrun on this project.

To implement this approach, management has to divide the overall project into activities, each with its own budget estimate. Reports then can be issued either when key milestones are reached or at the end of each month or quarter. These reports require the following:

1. Accumulate costs by project, using some form of job order costing.
2. Record each milestone as it is passed, and estimate any progress that has been made toward the next milestone as of the date of the report.
3. Estimate the amount of cost budgeted for the amount of progress made during the period.
4. Compare actual costs with budgeted costs for the progress that has been achieved, explaining major variances whenever possible.

Reports of this kind focus exclusively on the past. Because discretionary activities can always be discontinued if the anticipated costs exceed the anticipated benefits, a strong case can be made for incorporating revised forecasts of future costs and completion dates in the reports. Management can then decide whether to continue the project—based on a comparison of estimated *future* benefits with estimated *future* costs—and, if so, whether to increase or decrease the rate of spending to advance or defer the estimated completion date.

Cost-Control Reporting in Service Businesses

Manufacturing operations account for a smaller and smaller percentage of economic activity in the United States every year, as service industries become proportionally more important. The cost-control reporting techniques developed for a factory structure can be adapted to these new nonfactory environments, sometimes with little modification, sometimes in highly modified form. We'll illustrate how this can be done with a brief examination of cost-control reporting in two different service businesses.

Health Care: Hospital Services

Health care institutions differ from manufacturing enterprises not only because their "product" is intangible but because many of the payments are made by third parties—insurance companies and federal, state, and local governments. Some health care institutions are funded entirely by government agencies, such as the U.S. Veterans Administration. Financial arrangements with these third parties determine the institutions' revenues and may be used to motivate management to control costs. In general, however, they have little effect on cost-control reporting.

For example, a number of states have adopted a so-called DRG (Diagnosis-Related Group) reimbursement plan for hospitals, under which each hospital is paid a set fee for each procedure, a set fee per day of hospital care, a set fee for each service by a physician, and a prescribed number of hospital days and physicians' services for each procedure. If a hospital is able to provide its services at less than these amounts, it can add the savings to the funds it has available for other purposes, such as the operation of walk-in clinics or preventive-medicine programs in lower-income urban areas. If a hospital can't meet those cost limits, it will have to subsidize the services from other sources.

Hospitals are organized in much the same way as manufacturing companies, with a set of mission centers (analogous to production centers) such as medical-surgical, maternity, intensive care, and mental hygiene; and service centers such as food service, laundry, and security. Most costs in most cost centers are fixed, with some short-term adaptability to fluctuations in the rate of utilization.

The main cost-control problem is to measure the volume of activity. Patient-days is a common measure in a medical-surgical nursing station; the number of X rays is used in the X-ray department, and so on. Once the volume measure has been chosen, the process of establishing and applying the flexible budget is no different from the analogous process in *process* production (a medical-surgical nursing station) or in *job order* production (an operating room).

Although most hospital costs are fixed in the short run, many of them can be adjusted to accommodate major shifts in volume. The nursery, for example, may have a normal complement of eight registered nurses, three nurses' aides, and three orderlies, on the assumption that 20 babies will be under care, on the average. If the average drops to 12 babies, the nursery can function with only six registered nurses, two nurses' aides, and two and a half orderlies (sharing orderlies' services with another department). This is part of the *stepped* cost function diagrammed in Exhibit 24–7. The straight line in the exhibit is our old acquaintance, the cost-absorbed line. It represents the number of patient-days in the nursery, multiplied by the average cost per patient-day. The spread between the two lines measures the volume variance; when the volume variance becomes large and appears likely to remain that way, management will respond by reducing or increasing the size of the staff at this nursing station.

Advertising: Account Management

Advertising agencies serve their clients by participating in the design of advertising strategy, developing and producing advertising copy, and

EXHIBIT 24–7
Nursing Station: Unabsorbed Costs

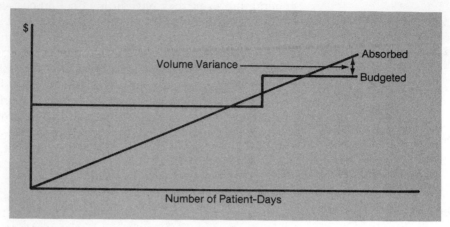

selecting the media through which the clients' advertising messages will be presented. In return, the agencies receive commissions equal in most cases to a fixed percentage of the fees charged by the various media.

The advertising business has several fundamental characteristics:

1. It is highly labor-intensive.
2. It is client-centered.
3. Its "product line" is nonstandardized and is constantly changing.
4. The people who develop and produce advertising copy, artwork, and special effects tend to be highly creative and individualistic.

These factors indicate that the primary focus of profit control and cost control is the individual client account—a brand of detergent, a line of personal computers, and so on. It also means that many of the advertising agency personnel who incur costs may lack both guidance and motivation to control the amount of costs incurred.

Exhibit 24–8 shows the report Kern and Ball, Inc., a large international advertising agency, prepared for one client account, Pop Nuts, for the month of March 19x1. The first two columns show the amounts spent and the amounts budgeted for this account for the first three months of 19x1. Column 3 shows the original budget for this account for the entire year, while column 4 shows the latest estimate of the results of this account for the entire year.

Several points should be noted in this report. First, this is a *seasonal* account, with 40 percent of the billings and 59.5 percent of the direct costs budgeted for the first three months of the year. Second, these same statistics show that the budget anticipates a lag between the time expenditures are made and the time gross income is realized. The result is a

EXHIBIT 24–8
Kern and Ball, Inc.: Pop Nuts Account: Financial Report, Month of March 19x1

	(1) Actual to Date	*(2)* Original Budget to Date	*(3)* Original Budget This Year	*(4)* Revised Budget This Year
Gross billings.............	$350,000	$400,000	$1,000,000	$1,000,000
Gross income	$ 52,500	$ 60,000	$ 150,000	$ 150,000
Direct expenses:				
Salaries:				
Contact................	8,500	8,000	16,000	17,000
Media.................	2,000	500	2,500	5,000
Copy	21,000	22,000	26,000	26,000
Art	19,500	16,500	25,000	28,000
Production	9,000	7,500	20,500	24,500
Total direct salaries	60,000	54,500	90,000	100,500
Travel	2,500	1,200	3,000	4,500
Entertainment	1,900	800	2,000	3,800
Materials.................	2,700	2,400	4,500	5,000
Other....................	500	300	500	1,000
Total direct expense....	67,600	59,200	100,000	114,800
Indirect expenses:				
Services	1,000	1,100	2,000	2,000
Production	4,900	3,600	13,000	15,000
General & administrative	5,300	6,000	15,000	15,000
Total expense	78,800	69,900	130,000	146,800
Pretax income/(loss)..........	$ (26,300)	$ (9,900)	$ 20,000	$ 3,200

budgeted loss of $9,900 in the first three months, even though this account was originally budgeted to produce $20,000 in pretax income for the year as a whole.

Third, Kern and Ball's system requires monthly revisions of the income budget on each account. In this case, management can see that only $3,200 of the originally budgeted income is likely to materialize. Finally, the agency's accountants use a net income format rather than profit contribution reporting. Actual general and administrative expenses are allocated to client accounts on the basis of their percentage shares of total agency billings. The anticipated profit contribution of this account therefore probably will be about $15,000 greater than the budgeted pretax income.

What can Kern and Ball's management do in response to a report of this kind? The first task is to find out why the substantial cost overruns are taking place. Are they due to unexpected client demands, to unforeseen difficulties, or to overenthusiastic creative people who want to turn out a luxury product when the account billings aren't big enough to support more than a modest product design?

When the cause of the variation appears to lie with the client, the account executive ordinarily must try to convince the client that the size of the advertising campaign doesn't justify such a costly production schedule. In extreme cases, the agency may even decide to resign from the account once the current campaign is completed, if it appears that the client's expectations will continue to outstrip the amount of the billings. If the cause is internal, however, the account executive needs to work with the creative staff to install a sense of cost consciousness and to devise ways of maintaining the profitability of the account without stifling the creative spirit of copy, art, and production personnel.

Control of indirect costs in Kern and Ball is no different in principle from the control of comparable costs in other kinds of businesses. Control of service usage—e.g., from the computer center or the photo shop—is the responsibility of the executives in charge of the various client accounts, and allocations based on predetermined charging rates or transfer prices provide the appropriate control signals. Responsibility for controlling the costs of providing the services is departmentally focused, however—that is, it rests, as always, with the service center managers, working with the guidance of the planning budget and the flexible budget. For general and administrative expenses, the most important control action is the approval of the planning budget itself. Subsequent variance reports are likely to be used primarily to reassure management that the spending plans are being followed.

Behavioral Issues in Cost-Control Systems

Cost standards designed for use in connection with a company's efforts to control its costs are only one element in a much broader system. Other elements include the leadership styles of managers at the various organizational levels and the structure of rewards and penalties for good and bad performance. In other words, the way standards are used may even be as important as the level at which they are set or the means by which they are derived. In this section, we'll summarize very briefly some of the behavioral issues that must be resolved if standards are to be used effectively.

Identifying Cost Responsibility

Assigning costs to organizational units whose managers are responsible for controlling them is not as easy as we may have implied. A cardinal rule of management is that department heads shouldn't be held responsible for personnel not under their supervision or for material or services they haven't requisitioned. For example, if workers and material under the supervision of Jones are used to provide a service used by Smith,

Smith can't be held responsible for the cost of providing the service. Smith may be held responsible for the use of the service, but the primary point for control of cost is Jones.

One problem is that actual authority/responsibility relationships typically depart in significant respects from those embodied in the formal organization structure. This can't be blamed on management incompetence in establishing the organization structure. Organization charts are a gross oversimplification of reality. Even the plant manager has more than one boss, and to represent all the connections between a staff worker or a department manager and other personnel in a company, one would have to draw lines upward, laterally, and at various angles.

In the light of these considerations, it is therefore especially important for all levels of management to recognize that (1) department managers aren't *solely* responsible for the costs assigned to them, and (2) they aren't *without* responsibility for these costs. Once these points are recognized, it should be easier to see that budgetary control systems should be used more to identify problem areas and effective actions than to assign absolute credit or absolute blame.

Budgets as Operational Objectives

The reporting systems that we've been describing in these three final chapters are based on the assumption that managers at all levels will strive to reach or surpass budgeted performance levels. In other words, it is assumed that other elements in the managerial system, not the budgets or standards themselves, will be effective in motivating managers. This doesn't happen automatically: individual motivation is determined by the needs of the employees themselves and their perception that performance (e.g., achieving budgeted performance) will lead to the satisfaction of these needs.[1]

The diagram in Exhibit 24–9 attempts to show the relationships between the needs of the individuals in the organization and other factors influencing their behavior. Managerial leadership is one of the other influences—the right-hand oval in the diagram—that determines whether the goals of the individual coincide with those of the organization. If leadership does bring this about, we say that **goal congruence** has been achieved—that is, the managers accept or *internalize* the organization's goals as their own because they believe that achieving the organization's goals will satisfy their needs better than not achieving

---

[1] See Edward E. Lawler III, *Motivation in Work Organizations* (Monterey, Calif.: Brooks/Cole, 1973). The relationships between control systems and individual needs are summarized in an excellent book by Edward E. Lawler III and John Grant Rhode, *Information and Control in Organizations* (Pacific Palisades, Calif.: Goodyear Publishing Co., 1976), especially chap. 2.

EXHIBIT 24–9
Influences on Personal Aspiration Levels

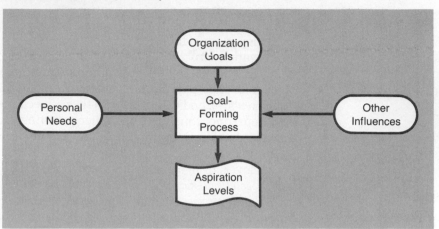

them. Goals that individuals have internalized are known as **aspiration levels,** the performance levels they undertake to reach.

Several factors affect the probability that individuals will internalize budgeted goals as their aspiration levels. One of these is past experience—success or failure in reaching budgeted goals in previous periods. Another is the priority they assign to their own needs for personal achievement. A third is the likelihood that meeting the budget will provide this sense of achievement. Still another is their perception of how difficult achieving the budgeted goals is likely to be under expected conditions.[2]

Goal congruence is the most critical behavioral problem management faces in the budgetary process. The prospect of promotion, incentive pay schemes, participation in setting the budget, and other means are used to bring about goal congruence. Aspiration levels differ among individuals, however. Some value the "good life" and the approval of their subordinates more than organizational success. Policies that achieve goal congruence for one individual may not succeed for another. Changes in operating conditions or in a person's thinking as time goes by may influence his or her aspiration level. This makes it difficult to use aspiration levels as the basis for performance standards.

---

[2] For a more extended discussion of the factors which influence performance, see L. W. Porter, E. E. Lawler, and J. R. Hackman, *Behavior in Organizations* (New York: McGraw-Hill, 1975).

Participation

One way to get subordinate managers to internalize performance standards is to have them participate in setting the standards. **Participation** means that decisions are, to some extent, joint decisions of managers and their supervisors. It doesn't mean that both must be in full agreement on every decision, but the subordinates must be convinced that they are being given a fair shake.

Participation doesn't automatically insure the internalization of performance standards. The gap between the individual's goals and those of the organization may be too great to be bridged. Furthermore, conditions may be such that a more authoritarian managerial style will be more effective in raising the aspiration levels of subordinates. Even so, participation may be very useful. First, it can be used to strengthen the bonds among members of the group by providing more effective communication. Second, it can increase the visibility of the progress that each member of the group is making toward internalization of organizational goals. The first of these increases the *desire* of individuals to share the goals of others in the group; the second increases their *ability* to do this.[3]

Attainability

One assumption underlying most responsibility-oriented accounting systems is that performance standards should be set at levels described as "tight but attainable" or "reasonably attainable." The argument for this assumption is that as long as performance standards don't exceed amounts that are reasonably attainable, managers will internalize them. If standards are set tighter than this, managers and their subordinates will regard them as unrealistic and will not be motivated by them.

The main issue isn't how to establish the performance level that is tight but attainable. The main problem is to design a package of techniques to motivate employees to perform better than they would in the absence of the standards. This shouldn't be confused with management by pressure. Some managers exert pressure on their subordinates to strive to meet standards that are difficult or even impossible to meet. This tactic is likely to backfire. Grievances mount and the relationships between managers and their subordinates deteriorate. Lower-level supervisors may unite with their subordinates against their superiors, creating problems which then become reasons for the failure to meet standards. Alternatively, managers and supervisors may seek ways to beat the system—for example, by falsifying records or by performing in such a way that variances will arise elsewhere or in later periods.

---

[3] For a further examination of these and related issues, see Lawler and Rhode, *Information and Control in Organizations.*

In short, standards that are too tight to be internalized are unlikely to be effective motivators for long.

Summary

Standard overhead costs don't provide performance standards for cost control, but they facilitate inventory record-keeping and they identify excess costs that will be likely to depress reported income. Variances between actual overhead cost and standard overhead cost in each period can be subdivided into components with the aid of data from the flexible budget. In most cases, there is (1) an overhead spending variance, which is the difference between actual overhead cost and the flexible budget for overhead cost in the current period, and (2) a volume variance, which reflects variations from the capacity utilization on which the overhead rates were predicated. Further subdivisions of the total overhead variance can be made to reflect other factors influencing the overhead cost.

Costs of discretionary activities require different kinds of control information. Marketing costs are monitored largely in the context of internal profit reporting. The costs of product-development projects and other project-oriented activities can be monitored, but the focus of control is the individual project rather than the individual responsibility center. Again, the comparison is between actual cost and the budgeted cost of the output or progress actually achieved by the project.

The same general principles can be applied to service businesses, such as health care institutions and advertising agencies. Cost control in health care institutions tends to have a departmental focus and the reporting structure is very similar to the reporting structure for overhead costs in manufacturing divisions. Cost control in advertising agencies tends to be client-account centered, and the appropriate reporting techniques are roughly similar to those used for research and development projects and other independent-program activities.

In all cases, management should consider the behavioral consequences of its performance standards. Although standards are only part of the overall system designed to achieve goal congruence in the organization, they should be set in such a way and at such levels as to improve the chances of achieving goal congruence. Participation by subordinates in the standard-setting process is widely believed to be a useful means toward this end.

**Appendix:
Variations in
Overhead Variance
Analysis**

The overhead variance can be analyzed in many ways, depending on the behavioral patterns the company is able to identify and on the methods used to accumulate and distribute costs. This appendix illustrates two variations on the analysis described in the first section of this chapter.

Three-Variance Analysis of Variances from Standard Overhead Cost

When standard overhead costs are used, the total overhead cost variance is the difference between actual overhead cost and the standard overhead cost of the work done. This difference can be divided into two parts—a spending variance and a volume variance—only if the overhead costs are budgeted to vary with *output*. That was the case in the illustration in this chapter, because total overhead cost was budgeted to vary with the number of *standard* direct-labor hours, a measure of output.

If overhead costs vary with *actual inputs*, however, the two-variance approach is no longer appropriate. In those situations, three variances can be identifed, and the spending variances are calculated by comparing actual costs with the flexible budget appropriate to the number of inputs actually used:

Spending Variance if Overhead Costs Vary with Actual Inputs: The Difference between Actual Costs and Budgeted Costs Appropriate for Actual Input Quantities	**Spending Variance if Overhead Costs Vary with Standard Inputs:** The Difference between Actual Costs and Budgeted Costs Appropriate for Standard Input Quantities

The difference between the total budget at the actual input level and the total budget at the standard input level then becomes a third variance, attributable to the company's efficiency in using these inputs.

For example, suppose management finds that variations in the machining department's overhead costs appear to be influenced by variations in the *actual* number of direct labor-hours used instead of by variations in output, as measured by the number of *standard* direct labor-hours. The flexible budget formula is:

$$\text{Total overhead cost} = \$27{,}500 + \$4 \times \text{Actual direct labor-hours}$$

This means that every time the department wastes (or saves) a direct labor-hour, it will be likely to waste (or ought to save) $4 in overhead costs. In September, the department wasted 20 direct labor-hours—it used 2,320 direct labor-hours instead of the 2,300 standard hours required by the work done during the month, given the actual volume of output. Inefficiency in labor usage, in other words, increased the budgeted overhead cost by $20 \times \$4 = \$80$. We call this the labor efficiency component of the overhead cost variance or, more simply, the **labor**

efficiency variance. It measures the estimated effect on the overhead cost of efficiency or inefficiency in the use of direct-labor inputs.

This new variance fits into the total overhead variance in the manner shown in Exhibit 24–10. The volume variance is the same as in the two-

EXHIBIT 24–10
Reconciling the Overhead Cost Variance: Three-Variance System

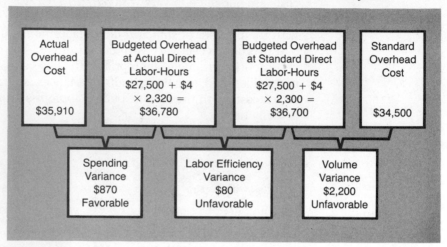

variance system, but the spending variance is different. The difference lies in the new third variance, the labor efficiency variance. The sum of the spending and labor efficiency variances is equal to the spending variance in a two-variance system.

The significance of the three-variance system is that it sheds additional light on the $790 favorable spending variance we calculated earlier. It reveals that the spending variance was really $870, but that labor inefficiency deprived the department of $80 of that favorable variance. This additional disclosure enables the company to measure the full effect of using 20 more labor-hours than the 2,300 standard hours.

Overhead Variance Analysis in the Absence of Standard Costing

Rather than use *standard* overhead costs for product costing, many companies use predetermined full-cost overhead rates, as we illustrated in Chapter 19. In these cases, the denominator of the overhead rate is likely to be the estimated number of *actual* input units that production in a *normal* period will require. When this is done, companies will be able to caclulate only two variances—a spending variance and a volume variance. The spending variance will be the same as in the three-variance system (a favorable $870 in our example), but the volume variance will be different and the labor efficiency variance can't be calculated at all.

For example, if a direct-labor-hour denominator is used, the overhead rate will be as follows:

$$\text{Predetermined overhead rate} = \frac{\text{Estimated overhead cost}}{\text{Estimated actual direct labor-hours}}$$

The amount of overhead absorbed then becomes (1) the predetermined rate, multiplied by (2) the number of direct input units (direct labor-hours in our illustration) actually used during the period. This amount is shown in the box in the upper right-hand corner of Exhibit 24–11.

EXHIBIT 24–11
Calculation of Overhead Variances without Standard Costing

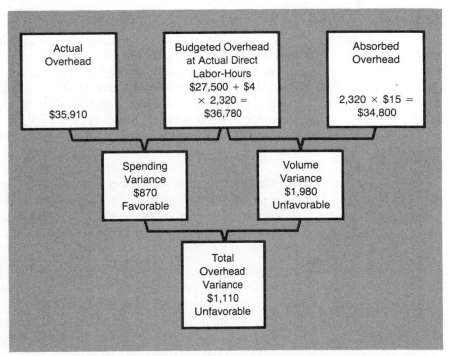

The flexible budget under these conditions is also likely to use the number of actual direct inputs as the measure of overall volume. Morley Company's machining department, for example, might have the following flexible budget:

> Budgeted overhead = $27,500 + $4 × Actual direct labor-hours

Without standard costing, the amount of overhead absorbed by production in September would be $34,800 (2,320 actual hours × $15 predetermined rate). The flexible budget for the month would be $36,780 ($27,500 + $4 × 2,320). The overhead variances would be those shown in the lower part of Exhibit 24–11.

Key Terms

Aspiration level   Overhead spending variance
Discretionary overhead   Overhead volume variance
Goal congruence   Participation
Overhead labor efficiency variance   Total overhead variance

Independent Study Problems (Solutions in Appendix B)

1. Overhead Variances without Standard Costing. Ajax Company uses predetermined departmental overhead rates in its factory but doesn't have a standard costing system. The factory's shaping department has an overhead cost budget of $10,000 a month plus $2.50 a direct labor-hour. The department's overhead rate is $4.50 a direct labor-hour. Actual overhead cost in May amounted to $19,900 on a departmental volume of 4,200 direct labor-hours.

Calculate the total overhead variance for the month and subdivide it into its components.

2. Calculating and Analyzing Factory Overhead Variances. Cotton Company uses a standard costing system and develops volume and spending variances in its overhead costs. You are given the following information for one of the company's factory departments for the month of May:

1. Overhead costs are expected to vary with output rather than with actual direct labor-hours. The overhead budget was $4,680 a month plus $1.15 per standard direct labor-hour.
2. The normal level of production was 9,000 standard direct labor-hours.
3. The standard overhead cost of the work in process inventory at the beginning of May was $6,680.
4. The standard direct-labor content of the products completed and transferred out of the department during the month was 10,500 hours.
5. The standard direct-labor content of the work in process was 4,000 hours at the start of the month and 3,600 hours at the end.
6. The department worked 10,800 direct labor-hours during the month.

7. The actual overhead cost for the month was $17,400.

a. Calculate the standard overhead cost of the work done in this department during the month.
b. What was the standard overhead cost of the work in process at the end of the month?
c. Develop the department's overhead spending and volume variances for the month.

3. Three-Variance Method (See Chapter Appendix). After further analysis, Cotton Company's management (problem 2) has concluded that variable overhead costs in this department vary at the rate of $1.15 for each actual direct labor-hour. All other facts are as stated in problem 2.

a. Prepare an analysis of the total overhead variance in this department, using the three-variance method.
b. Why is the three-variance method appropriate here, whereas the two-variance method was appropriate under the conditions stated in problem 2?

4. Overhead Variance Exercise. Darnley Company makes piston rings. A standard costing system is in use in its factory. From the following partial information for the grinding department, make the necessary calculations to supply the missing numbers:

1. Overhead volume variance, December: $1,500 unfavorable.
2. Standard machine-hours, December: 4,500.
3. Total overhead cost variance, December: $1,300 unfavorable.
4. Standard overhead cost, December: $22,500.
5. Standard machine-hours per month, at normal volume: 5,000.
6. Predetermined overhead rate per standard machine-hour: *A*.
7. Actual total overhead cost, December: *B*.
8. Overhead spending variance, December: *C*.
9. Budgeted overhead cost, December: *D*.
10. Budgeted fixed overhead cost per month: *E*.
11. Budgeted variable overhead cost per standard machine hour: *F*.
12. Budgeted total overhead cost, normal month: *G*.

5. Performance Reporting: Discretionary Overheads. A research plan called for the expenditure of $48,000, to be spread evenly over a six-month period. At the end of two months, $16,200 had been spent, the project was one-quarter complete, and management estimated that the project would be completed successfully seven months after it was begun, at a total cost of $60,000.

a. Present a brief financial report to the project manager's immediate superior, highlighting the financial performance of the project team.

b. What responses might management take in this situation? What criteria might it use in choosing among these? What data might it reasonably ask for to aid in this choice?

---

6. Calculating Department Volume. A standard costing system is
used. The department's overhead cost budget is based on standard direct
labor-hours. Normal volume for the department is 20,000 standard direct
labor-hours a month, and the overhead rate is $3 a standard direct labor-
hour. Overhead cost fluctuations correlate more closely with product output than with direct-labor input.

During the month, 21,300 actual direct labor-hours were used. The
department finished and transferred to other departments products with
a standard overhead cost of $69,000. The standard overhead cost of work
in process in this department was $16,200 on the first of the month and
$18,000 at the end of the month.

Calculate the number of hours on which the flexible budget allowances
for the month should be based.

7. Variance Calculation Exercise. Overhead costs in one of Bastian
Corporation's factory departments are expected to total $8,000 a month
plus $1.40 per standard direct labor-hour. The normal level of output is
11,000 standard direct labor-hours a month.

During the month of June, the actual overhead costs were $22,100,
and the actual level of activity was 9,300 standard direct labor-hours.

a. Calculate the standard overhead rate for this department.
b. Calculate the volume and spending variances for the month.

8. Overhead Costing: Terminology Exercise. You have the following
information for a factory department for the month of April 19x1:

Standard overhead cost, $33,600.

Normal overhead cost, $42,000.

Budgeted overhead cost, $39,600.

Actual overhead cost, $40,500.

a. Calculate the total overhead cost variance for the month.
b. Calculate the overhead spending variance and the overhead volume
variance for this month.
c. For each data item you *didn't* use in your answers to parts *a* and *b*, explain
why it is developed and why you didn't use it.

9. Variance Exercise. Alden Company has a standard costing system
and uses a two-way analysis of overhead variances. Selected data for
February are as follows:

Budgeted fixed factory overhead costs . . . . $ 64,000
Actual factory overhead costs incurred $230,000
Budgeted variable factory overhead rate per direct
   labor-hour . . . . $ 5
Standard direct labor-hours for actual production   31,000
Actual direct labor-hours   33,000

a. Calculate the overhead spending variance for February.

b. (See chapter appendix.) If Alden Company didn't have a standard costing system, but used a predetermined full-cost overhead rate based on a normal monthly volume of 32,000 direct labor-hours, what would be the amount of its total overhead variance?

(AICPA adapted)

10. Variance Calculation Exercise; Reporting to Management. A standard costing system is in use, and standard factory overhead cost is $2 per standard direct labor-hour. Overhead costs vary with the number of standard direct labor-hours, according to the following formula:

Costs = $11,000 per month + $0.90 per standard direct labor-hour

Actual overhead costs for October totaled $22,140, and 11,200 direct labor-hours were recorded. Product standard costs and actual production volumes for October were:

Product	Standard Overhead Cost per Unit	Units Produced, October
A	$ 5	100
B	6	500
C	10	1,000
D	3	1,200
E	2	2,000

a. Calculate the total overhead variance, an overhead spending variance, and an overhead volume variance for the month. Indicate in each case whether the variance is favorable or unfavorable.

b. How, if at all, should the volume variance be reported to management? To what management level would you report it?

11. Supplying Missing Information: Two-Variance Analysis. Manchester Tool Works has a standard costing system. Variable factory overhead costs in each department vary with department output, measured by the number of standard direct labor-hours. You have the following data for two departments for the month of June:

	Department S	Department T
Standard overhead rate per standard direct labor hour	A	$4.50
Actual direct labor-hours	1,900	4,500
Standard direct labor-hours (June)	1,800	F
Standard direct labor-hours at normal volume	B	4,000
Budgeted fixed cost	$5,000	G
Budgeted variable overhead cost for each standard direct labor-hour	$1	$2.50
Actual overhead cost	$6,700	$20,300
Standard overhead cost	C	$21,600
Overhead spending variance	D	H
Overhead volume variance	E	I
Total overhead variance	$400 unfavorable	J

Make the necessary calculations and supply the information missing from this table.

12. Supplying Missing Information: Three-Variance Analysis (*See Chapter Appendix*). Dorset, Inc., has a factory with 15 production departments. A standard costing system is in use. The following data apply to two factory departments during the month of May:

	Department A	Department B
Standard overhead rate per standard direct labor-hour	A	$8
Actual direct labor-hours (May)	2,200	G
Standard direct labor-hours (May)	2,000	5,500
Normal volume (standard direct labor-hours)	2,500	H
Budgeted fixed overhead cost	$10,000	$25,000
Budgeted variable overhead cost for each actual direct labor-hour	$2	$3
Total overhead variance	$3,000 unfavorable	I
Overhead spending variance	B	J
Overhead labor efficiency variance	C	$900 favorable
Overhead volume variance	D	K
Actual overhead cost	E	$42,000
Standard overhead cost of actual work done	F	L

Make the necessary calculations and supply the information missing from this table.

13. Effect of Variances on Income. A company has made the following estimates of the percentages of expenses to sales revenues, based on a normal sales volume of $10 million:

Variable manufacturing	45%
Fixed manufacturing...................	30
Selling and administrative (all fixed)	15
Total expenses.....................	90%

The cost of goods sold and the cost of units in inventory are measured at predetermined unit costs based on normal production volume. The company has units in inventory with a sale value of more than $1 million. The unit cost of manufacturing these units was identical to expected average manufacturing cost this year at normal volume. All factory cost variances are reported immediately in the income statement as they arise.

a. What effect would a $1 million increase in sales, unaccompanied by an increase in production, have on income before taxes?

b. What effect would increasing production by a quantity of goods with a sales value of $1 million have on income before taxes if that increase were unaccompanied by an increase in sales?

14. Interpreting Changes in Average Overhead Cost. Dearborn Company manufactures product X in standard batches of 100 units. A standard cost system is in use. The standard costs for a batch are as follows:

Direct materials—60 pounds at $0.45 a pound	$ 27.00
Direct labor—12 hours at $8.60 an hour	103.20
Overhead—12 hours at $6.10 an hour	73.20
Total standard cost per batch	$203.40

Dearborn's normal monthly output is 2,400 batches (240,000 units). Factory fixed costs are budgeted at $89,280 a month.

Dearborn Company's management is worried by the size of factory overhead costs, which make up more than a third of the standard costs of product X. Accordingly, when the actual average overhead cost for April fell to $6.05 per actual direct labor-hour, management felt somewhat encouraged.

Actual production in April amounted to 2,100 batches. Actual overhead cost totaled $166,375. Variable overhead costs vary with the number of standard direct labor-hours.

a. Should Dearborn's management be encouraged by the reduction in average overhead cost? Prepare an analysis of the overhead variance that will help you come to a conclusion on this point.

b. List the departures from normal conditions that affected average cost per direct labor-hour in April, and indicate which of them probably increased average cost and which of them probably decreased average cost. You need not quantify the effects.

c. Would average overhead cost per direct labor-hour be a useful index of production efficiency for the factory manager? For the president? Comment.

15. Labor and Overhead Variance Exercise. The data here relate to the month of April 19x1 for Marilyn, Inc., which uses a standard costing system:

Actual total direct-labor cost	$130,200
Actual direct labor-hours used	14,000
Standard direct labor-hours allowed for good output	15,000
Direct-labor rate variance—unfavorable.	$ 4,200
Actual total overhead cost	$ 32,000
Budgeted fixed overhead costs.	$ 9,000
Normal volume in standard direct labor-hours	12,000
Total predetermined overhead rate per	
standard direct labor-hour	$2.25

Variable overhead costs are expected to vary with department output, measured by the number of standard direct labor-hours.

a. Calculate the direct-labor usage variance for the month and indicate whether it was favorable or unfavorable.
b. Calculate the overhead spending variance for the month and indicate whether it was favorable or unfavorable.
c. Calculate the overhead volume variance and indicate whether it was favorable or unfavorable.

(AICPA adapted)

16. Cost Reporting: Product Marketing. "Marty, you've got to get your expense-to-sales ratio down," Clare David said. "Yours and Fran's are the highest in the company and we just can't support that kind of spending much longer. We'll okay your budget for this year, but we expect you to do everything you can to cut costs."

Marty Johnson and Fran Wilkes were regional sales managers for Fabrications, Ltd.; Clare David was marketing vice president. The budgets Clare approved and the actual results the two managers achieved were as follows:

	Marty	**Fran**
Budget:		
Sales	$1,000,000	$1,500,000
Standard cost of goods sold.	650,000	1,050,000
Regional marketing expenses.	200,000	285,000
Actual:		
Sales	800,000	1,400,000
Standard cost of goods sold.	530,000	980,000
Regional marketing expenses.	140,000	252,000

Economic conditions in the two regions were very similar to the conditions on which the budgets were based.

Which manager appears to have done a better job of complying with the marketing vice president's directive? Which manager has controlled costs better? Show your calculations and explain the criteria you used to reach your conclusions on these points.

17. Standard Costing: Service Organization. In an effort to control costs, Hilltop College has just established a "standard instructional cost per student" for each course in the college's catalog. A variance is then calculated each term for each course offered that term.

No standards have been developed for the costs of teaching materials and supplies, and the costs of these items are not assigned to individual courses.

The standard cost per student for Basket Weaving 476 is $90. In the spring term, 30 students enrolled in this course. The actual cost assigned to the course that term was $5,500, representing one sixth of the annual salary and fringe benefits of the instructor, Professor J. B. Braithwaite, chairman pro tem of the Basket Weaving Department, plus the cost of 100 hours spent by a graduate student writing multiple-choice examination questions and grading student term papers.

The college's controller made the following analysis of the variance for this course:

Standard cost, actual enrollment: 30 × $90 . . . . $2,700 ⎫ Enrollment variance
                                                                ⎬ = $1,800 unfavorable
Standard cost, planned enrollment: 50 × $90 . . . . .   4,500 ⎭

                                                               ⎫ Salary variance
                                                               ⎬ = $1,000 unfavorable
Actual cost. . . . .   5,500 ⎭

                                                               Total variance
                                                               = $2,800 unfavorable

The controller calculated that $800 of the salary variance arose because Braithwaite's salary per course was $800 more than the average salary of the members of the basket weaving faculty. The remainder arose because Braithwaite used more graduate-student time than was planned for this course.

a. How do the purposes of this system differ from the purposes ascribed in this chapter to factory standard costing systems? To what extent are they the same? In answering this, you should try to identify the actions management might take in response to information the system provides. Distinguish between the actions management might take in response to information contained in the standards themselves and actions it might take in response to variance information.

b. Does this system appear to be a good way to achieve the purposes you identified in part *a*? In answering this, try to identify any problems that might arise in implementing this system and indicate whether they can be solved without great difficulty.

18. Cost Control: Health Clinic. Marlin Health Care, Inc., operates a family-practice medical service. Its fees are fixed at $20 for an office visit, $40 for a house call, and $150 for a thorough physical examination. Fees for medicines and laboratory tests are not included in those rates. Marlin also offers other services, such as routine eye examinations and blood tests, at regularly posted fees.

Each doctor on Marlin's staff is expected to perform the required services in a professional way, but without unnecessary expenditure of time. A doctor assigned to office visits is expected to see four patients an hour, on the average. Physical examinations are expected to consume 20 minutes of a doctor's time, plus the time spent by the nurses and technicians who administer the required tests. A doctor on house-call duty is expected to see two patients an hour, on the average.

In October of last year, Marlin's five doctors recorded the following services:

Doctor	Hours	Number of House Calls	Number of Office Visits	Number of Physical Exams
Jones.........	150	20	480	33
Edwards	140	64	396	21
Rogers........	155	98	452	12
DiSilva........	130	56	412	36
Saunders......	148	36	420	48
Total........	723	274	2,160	150

a. Prepare a report for Marlin's management committee, reflecting the cost-control performance of each doctor and for the medical staff as a whole.
b. Discuss the implications of the report you have prepared. How would you expect management to use it? What effects would you expect this system to have?

19. Department Performance Report. Argus Company's research division has approximately 80 employees, organized as shown in the table on the next page.

Research proposals are prepared initially in the project planning and control section (PPC). Once a project is approved, an engineer on the PPC staff is assigned to direct that project, evaluate progress, and attempt to keep it on schedule. Line authority over the research staff is vested in the three section chiefs, however.

The project coordinators receive cost and progress reports on their

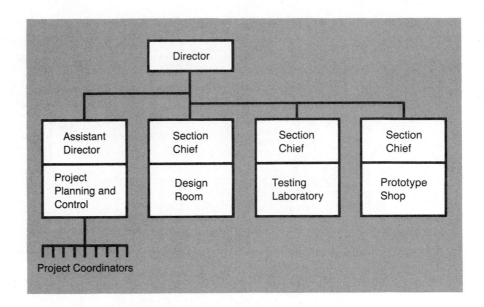

projects every month. In addition, each section chief receives a summary report on cost perfomance in that section. This is a two-page report, with an overall department summary on the first page and an element-by-element comparison on the second. The first-page summary for the testing laboratory for last October showed the following information:

	Actual	**Budget**	**Variance**
Project 246	$ 4,650	$ 4,700	$ 50
Project 289	3,300	1,300	(2,000)
Project 294	3,530	5,200	1,670
Total	$11,480	$11,200	$ (280)

The budget numbers in this summary were the expenditures planned for last October when these three projects were first approved.

a. What useful information, if any, would this report give to the section chief in charge of the tesing laboratory?

b. What changes would you make in this report to make it more useful to management?

20. Project Performance Report: Follow-Up Decisions. Broadway Contractors, Inc., has a contract to remodel one of the university laboratories. The contract price is $160,000, based on an estimated cost of $130,000. The contract calls for completion of the job in 12 weeks, with a penalty of $10,000 for each week of delay beyond the end of that period. The original plan for this project showed the following sequence of activities:

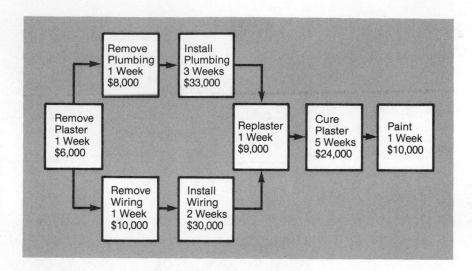

Removal of the old plumbing and removal of the old wiring were scheduled to take place simultaneously, to be followed immediately by the installation of the new plumbing and the new wiring. The job was started on the scheduled date, and the following work was done during the first three weeks:

Activity	% Completed	Cost
Remove plaster	100%	$ 6,200
Remove plumbing	100	16,000
Remove wiring	100	9,200
Install wiring..............	50	15,000

Management now estimates that installation of the new plumbing will take four weeks and will cost $40,000. All other cost and time estimates are unchanged. The project can be speeded up, but only at a cost. The estimated costs of various methods of speeding the project are:

	Additional Expenditures Required	
	To Save One Week	To Save Two Weeks
Install plumbing	$ 8,000	$19,000
Cure plaster................	10,500	18,500

a. Prepare a summary report that will show management the past performance, present status, and future prospects for this contract.

b. Should the company spend additional money to speed up one or more activities? If so, which one(s) and by how many weeks? State your reasons.

21. Discretionary Overhead Costs. The report shown here was prepared for Project No. 16321 at the end of the project's second month. It was issued on May 5, 19x1, to Gretchen Hill, project engineer in the research division, and to Hill's immediate superior.

RESEARCH DIVISION
PROJECT SPENDING REPORT

Project No.: 16321   Period: March–April 19x1
Project Title: Sandfly Attachment   Supervisor: G. Hill
Start Date: 3/6/x1   Scheduled Completion: 11/30/x1

	Actual	Budget	Under/(Over)
Professional salaries	$2,170	$1,000	$(1,170)
Technical salaries	1,130	450	(680)
Laboratory services	15	—	(15)
Drafting services	95	100	5
Purchased materials	350	—	(350)
Purchased equipment	3,100	3,000	(100)
Total	$6,860	$4,550	$(2,310)

Additional information:

1. The budget data in the report show the amounts the company had planned to spend to achieve the amount of progress it had planned to make during March and April.
2. The work done on this project in March and April consisted of synthesis and analysis (half the work on this phase was done in March and the remainder was finished in April) and preparation of design specifications (the first 20 percent of this work was done in April).
3. Budgeted costs of the first two project phases were as follows:

	Synthesis and Analysis	Design Specification
Professional salaries	$2,000	$ 300
Technical salaries	900	500
Laboratory services	—	100
Drafting services	200	50
Purchased materials	450	250
Purchased equipment	3,000	—
Total	$6,550	$1,200

4. Expenditures for all project inputs except purchased parts and equipment were budgeted to take place in steady flows while the phase was being carried out. The equipment purchase in the synthesis and analysis phase was scheduled to take place during the first half of that phase. Materials purchases were budgeted to take place in the second

half of the synthesis and analysis phase and uniformly throughout the specifications design phase.

5. The original budget called for the completion of half the synthesis and analysis phase during the first two months (March and April). No work on any other phase was scheduled for that period.

6. Shortly after work started on the project, Hill found that staff technicians had enough unscheduled time in March and April to allow her to accelerate the work on the synthesis and analysis phase and complete it during April, with time left over to begin work on the design specification phase.

7. When asked for a projection, Hill said that early completion of the synthesis and analysis phase would probably enable her to complete the entire project one month ahead of schedule, but she saw no reason to revise the original cost budget for the portions of the project that still lay ahead on April 30.

a. Prepare a revised cost-performance report for Project No. 16321 for the months of March and April 19x1, reflecting performance standards appropriate to the work done in April.

b. What information would you add to the report to give it a useful "future orientation"?

22. Allocating Variances: Interpreting Profit Contribution. Georgia Ellis was the marketing manager for her company's cosmetic products. She reported to Denise Thompson, the company's marketing vice president. Ellis supervised a field sales force engaged exclusively in marketing the cosmetics line. Factory operations, however, were within the jurisdiction of the manufacturing vice president. Many steps in the production process for the cosmetics products were performed on a job order basis by the personnel of factory departments also engaged in the manufacture of other company products.

Ellis received the following income statement for the cosmetics line for the month of August (in thousands):

	July Actual	August Actual	August Budget	August Variance
Sales	$1,000	$1,300	$1,200	$100
Standard cost of goods sold	600	800	720	(80)
Gross margin	400	500	480	20
Direct marketing expense.	150	155	150	(5)
Marketing margin	250	345	330	15
Favorable/(unfavorable) factory variances:				
Overhead volume variance	10	(50)	—	(50)
Overhead spending variance	5	(6)	—	(6)
Direct cost variances.	(12)	(54)	—	(54)
Profit contribution.	$ 253	$ 235	$ 330	$ (95)

Inventories of cosmetics products remained constant and at budgeted levels throughout July and August.

Thompson called Ellis into her office shortly after this report was issued and told her that in view of her poor performance in August, a scheduled promotion to the title of assistant vice president would be postponed. "We'll see how you do in September and October," she was told.

a. You are a consultant on retainer for this company and you happened to overhear this conversation. Draft a statement, outlining your evaluation of Ellis's performance. If you would like to have additional information, say what you would like to have, but you must give a tentative answer to this question before the additional information becomes available.

b. List changes, if any, that you would propose in the company's reporting system and give your reasons.

23. Setting a Standard Performance Level.   Alton Company is expanding its punch press department. It is about to purchase three new punch presses from Equipment Manufacturers, Inc. Equipment Manufacturers' engineers report that their mechanical studies indicate that for Alton's intended use, the output rate for one press should be 1,000 pieces an hour.

Alton has similar presses now in operation. Production from these presses averaged 600 pieces an hour last month, based on the following record of performance:

Worker	Hourly Output
L. Jones.	750
J. Green.	750
R. Smith	600
H. Brown	500
R. Alters.	550
G. Hoag	450
Total.	3,600
Average	600

Alton's management also plans to institute a standard cost accounting system in the near future. The company's engineers are supporting a standard based on 1,000 pieces an hour, the accounting department is arguing for 750 pieces an hour, and the production department supervisor is arguing for 600 pieces an hour.

a. What arguments would the various proponents be likely to use to support their recommendations?

b. Which alternative best reconciles the needs of cost control and the motivation of improved performance? Explain why you made that choice.

(CMA adapted)

24. Performance Standards for Motivation.   Ray Carlson, president of Scientific Equipment Manufacturing Company, wants to introduce standard costing into his company's factory. As a result of his participation in a two-week management development course at a nearby university, Carlson is convinced that some kind of standard costing system is just what he needs to strengthen his control over factory cost. The factory now has a simple job order costing system, and no one has ever attempted to establish standard costs.

Scientific Equipment makes and sells a line of highly technical equipment for industrial users. The company is in a small midwestern city with a population of 80,000. Quality, or the supplier's ability to meet exacting technical specifications, is a major consideration for most of the company's customers when deciding where to place an order.

Production is organized on a job order basis, and orders are typically manufactured to customer specifications. Most orders can be filled by producing items of standard design and specifications, or items that require only minor modifications of the standard designs. Jobs requiring major redesign and nonstandardized production techniques amount to 30 percent of the total. The cost estimates Carlson uses in developing price bids for this kind of nonstandardized business have been close to the actual costs of filling the orders in most cases, or at least close enough to satisfy Carlson.

Scientific Equipment is a small company with about 75 employees. The two largest segments of the work force are 30 machine operators and 20 assemblers. The machine operators are all men. Their jobs require considerable skill and experience. The assemblers, on the other hand, are all women. Their jobs are relatively routine but require a good deal of concentration to avoid costly assembly defects. The employees generally lunch together in a nearby cafeteria. Many of the men socialize off the job, and so do several of the women.

Carlson is considering engaging a consulting firm to develop and install a standard costing system. A letter from the managing partner of the consulting firm contained the following key paragraphs:

> In order to motivate people to their maximum productivity, standards must be based upon the company's best workers and what they can achieve. If the standard were lower, the high performers could meet it too easily and it wouldn't offer sufficient motivation for the low performers. I'd set the standard at the level of performance of the top 10 to 15 percent of your employees. This would establish a high aspiration level for your people and, therefore, motivate their best efforts.
>
> I also suggest that superior performance be well rewarded. This means that employees who exceed standard should receive a substantial bonus, while those who do not exceed standard should receive no bonus.

Since Carlson doesn't feel qualified to evaluate this kind of statement, he has contacted the faculty member who conducted the sessions on standard costing at the local university (you), asking what you think of the philosophy underlying the proposed system.

a. Prepare a reply to Carlson. Should he engage the consultant?
b. If you agree with the consultant's basic approach, outline how you would implement it at Scientific Equipment Manufacturing Company. If you disagree with the consultant, state the basic principles underlying an alternative system and outline how you would go about developing a standard costing system for this company.

(Prepared by Eric Flamholtz)

25. Separate Standards for Motivation and for Control.   Harden Company was experiencing increased production costs. The primary area of concern identified by management was direct labor. The company was considering adopting a standard cost system to help control labor and other costs. Useful historical data were not available because detailed production records had not been maintained.

Harden Company retained Finch & Associates, an engineering consulting firm, to establish labor standards. After a complete study of the work process, the engineers recommended a labor standard of 1 unit of production every 30 minutes, or 16 units a day for each worker. Finch further advised that Harden's wage rates were below the prevailing rate of $12 an hour.

Harden's production vice president thought this labor standard was too tight and the employees would be unable to attain it. From his experience with the labor force, he believed a labor standard of 40 minutes a unit or 12 units a day for each worker would be more reasonable.

Nan Jones, Harden's president, believed the standard should be set at a high level to motivate the workers, but she also recognized the standard should be set at a level to provide adequate information for control and reasonable cost comparisons. After much discussion, management decided to use a dual standard. The labor standard recommended by the engineering firm—known as the *engineering standard,* 1 unit every 30 minutes—would be used in the plant as a motivation device, while a labor standard of 40 minutes a unit— the *reporting standard*—would be used in reporting. Management also concluded that the workers would not be informed of the cost standard used for reporting purposes. The production vice president conducted several sessions prior to implementation in the plant informing the workers of the new standard cost system and answering questions. The new standards were not related to incentive pay but were introduced at the time wages were increased to $12 an hour.

The new standard cost system was implemented on January 1. At the end of six months of operation, the following statistics on labor performance were presented to top management:

	Jan.	Feb.	Mar.	Apr.	May	June
Production (units)	5,100	5,000	4,700	4,500	4,300	4,400
Direct labor hours	3,000	2,900	2,900	3,000	3,000	3,100
Labor usage variance from engineering standard	$5,400U	$4,800U	$6,600U	$9,000U	$10,200U	$10,800U
Labor usage variance from reporting standard	$4,800F	$5,200F	$2,800F	$ 0	$ 1,600U	$ 2,000U

Raw material quality, labor mix, and plant facilities and conditions did not change to any great extent during the six-month period.

a. Discuss the impact of different types of standards on motivation, and specifically discuss the effect on motivation in Harden Company's plant of adopting the labor standard recommended by the engineering firm.

b. Evaluate Harden Company's decision to use dual standards in its standard cost system.

(CMA adapted)

Appendixes

Appendix A

Compound Interest and Bond Tables

The tables in this appendix contain the **multipliers** (*conversion factors*) necessary to convert cash flow of one or more periods into their equivalent values at some other time. The underlying concept is explained in Chapter 6; only the mechanical details on how the numbers in the tables should be used are explained here. If more extensive tables or specialized tables are needed, they can be found in readily available financial handbooks or derived from simple computer programs.

Table 1: Present Value of $1

Each number in Table 1 is a *multiplier*—depicting the present value on a given *reference date* of $1 to be paid or received n periods later. To obtain the present value of any sum:

1. Select a date to serve as a reference date.
2. Determine the number of periods, n, between the reference date and the date on which the cash is to be paid or received.
3. Determine the interest rate, r, at which to calculate the present value.
4. Find the multiplier in Table 1 corresponding to these values of n and r.
5. Multiply the cash sum by this multiplier.

For example, to find the present value of $10,000 to be received five years from now, at a compound annual rate of 10 percent, multiply $10,000 by the number 0.6209 from the five-year row in the 10 percent column of Table 1. This says that $6,209 invested now at 10 percent will grow to $10,000 in five years if the interest is left on deposit and reinvested each year at 10 percent interest.

Once again, if compounding is to be semiannual, the multiplier should be taken from the column for a semiannual interest rate equal to $r/2$ and the row for a number of periods equal to $2n$. If quarterly compounding is used, use $r/4$ and $4n$ (for example, $2\frac{1}{2}$ percent for 40 periods to show present value compounded quarterly at $2\frac{1}{2}$ percent a quarter for 10 years.[1]

Extending Table 1

Table 1 can be extended easily to provide multipliers for any number of periods. The procedure consists of three steps:

1. Select the column for the desired interest rate.
2. From this column select any two or more multipliers for which the number of periods adds up to the number of periods, n, for which a multiplier is needed.
3. Multiply these multipliers.

For example, the present value of a dollar 35 years in the future at 10 percent compounded annually can be calculated in many ways. Three of these are:

Multiplier for ($n =$ 5) $\times$ multiplier for ($n = 30$) = 0.6209 $\times$ 0.0573 = 0.0356
Multiplier for ($n =$ 10) $\times$ multiplier for ($n = 25$) = 0.3855 $\times$ 0.0923 = 0.0356
Multiplier for ($n =$ 15) $\times$ multiplier for ($n = 20$) = 0.2394 $\times$ 0.1486 = 0.0356

Why does this work? Suppose the company expects to receive $1 35 years from now. Multiplying it by the multiplier for $n = 30$ brings it to its present value *at a point five years from now*, $0.0573. That amount is not the present value today, however. It is the future value five years from now. The present value today of any sum five years in the future can be calculated by using the multiplier for five years—in other words, by multiplying $0.0573 by 0.6209.

Table 2: Present Value of an Annuity of $1 per Period

The present value of a series of cash flows can be determined by using the multipliers in Table 1. For example, a series of three payments of $10,000 each, the first one a year from now, the second a year later, and the third a year after that, has a present value at 10 percent, compounded annually, as follows:

---

[1] Quarterly compounding at $2\frac{1}{2}$ percent a quarter is equivalent to an annual rate of $(1.025)^4 - 1 = 10.3813$ percent. The quarterly compounding rate equivalent to a 10 percent annual compounding rate is ($\sqrt[4]{1.10} - 1$), or approximately 2.41 percent each quarter. If this amount of precision is important, specially constructed quarterly tables, calculators, or computer programs should be used.

Years after Reference Date	Cash Flow	Multiplier at 10% (Table 1)	Present Value at 10%
1	$10,000	0.9091	$ 9,091
2	10,000	0.8264	8,264
3	10,000	0.7513	7,513
Total			$24,868

Doing this for a large number of periods would be time-consuming. Table 2 therefore is used whenever the cash flows in a series are identical each period; this is called an *annuity*. The multiplier in Table 2 for a three-year annuity at 10 percent is 2.4869. Multiplying this by the annual cash flow, $10,000, produces a present value of $24,869, identical to the amount we derived above except for an insignificant rounding error. *Each multiplier in Table 2 is merely the sum of the multipliers in Table 1* for periods 1 through *n*.

Converting Table 2 to Earlier Equivalents

The multipliers in Table 2 are used to calculate the present value of a series of cash payments on a reference date that is exactly one period prior to the date of the first payment. To find the present value at a still earlier reference date, the present value of the annuity is multiplied by the multiplier from Table 1 for the number of additional years desired.

For example, the present value at 10 percent of a 10-year, $10,000 annuity is:

$$\$10,000 \times 6.1446 = \$61,446$$

Suppose, however, that the first payment in this annuity is five years from now and that we want to know its present value *today*. The $61,446 amount is the present value *one year before the first payment is made*, or *four* years from now:

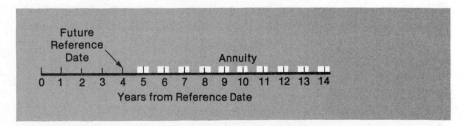

The present value today, therefore, can be obtained by multiplying $61,446 by the four-year multiplier from Table 1:

$$\$61,446 \times 0.6830 = \$41,968$$

The same present value can be derived in a different way. A 10-year annuity starting five years from now is the same as a 14-year annuity minus the first four payments. The multiplier in Table 2 for 14 years at 10 percent is 7.3667, and the multiplier for four years is 3.1699. The derived multiplier therefore is:

$$7.3667 - 3.1699 = 4.1968$$

Multiplying this by the $10,000 annual cash flow produces a present value of $41,968, the same present value amount we calculated earlier.

Converting Table 2 for Annuities in Advance

Each multiplier in Table 2 applies to an annuity *in arrears*—that is, the cash flow each period takes place at the *end* of the period, the first cash flow occurring one period after the reference date.

With a minor adjustment, Table 2 can also be used to find the present value of an annuity *in advance*—that is, one in which the first payment or receipt of cash takes place on the reference date, with subsequent cash flows occurring at one-period intervals thereafter.

The relationship between an annuity in advance and an annuity in arrears is diagrammed in Figure A–1. Looking at the two annuities in this diagram from January 1 of Year 1, we can see that the only difference between a four-year annuity in advance and a three-year annuity in arrears is a single payment or receipt at the reference date.

FIGURE A–1
Annuities in Arrears and in Advance

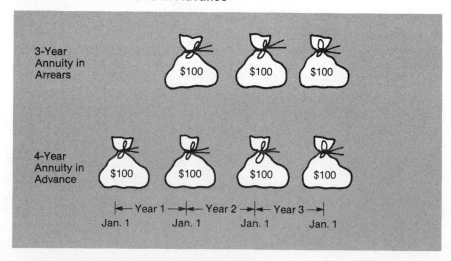

A four-year annuity in advance therefore is simply a three-year annuity in arrears plus one cash flow immediately. For $10,000 a year at 10 percent, the calculation is:

$10,000 + ($10,000 × 2.4869) = $34,869

(immediate cash flow)   (annual cash flow, three years)   (Table 2, 10 percent, three years)   (present value, four-year annuity in advance)

The same result could have been achieved by adding 1.0000 to the three-year multiplier from Table 2 and multiplying the sum (3.4869) by the annual cash flow. The general rule is: to convert a multiplier for the present value of an annuity in arrears to a multiplier for an annuity in advance, *take the multiplier for an interval one period shorter and add 1.0000.*

Finding Equivalent Annuities

It is sometimes useful to calculate an annuity that is equivalent to a given present sum. For example, how large a 10-year annuity could be bought with a $100,000 investment today given a 10 percent market rate of interest? Since the present sum *and* the interest rate are known, this becomes a basic arithmetic operation. The formula for the present value of an annuity can be expressed as:

$$\text{Present value} = \text{Table 2 multiplier} \times \text{Annual cash flow}$$

Restating this equation, we find:

$$\text{Annual cash flow} = \frac{\text{Present value}}{\text{Table 2 multiplier}}$$

The 10-year annuity in arrears that is equivalent at 10 percent interest to a present sum of $100,000 is:

$$\text{Annual cash flow} = \frac{\$100,000}{6.1446} = \$16,274$$

In other words, someone who is willing to pay $100,000 to buy a 10-year annuity in a 10 percent market can expect to receive $16,274 at the end of each year for 10 years.

Future Values

Present-value tables can also be used to calculate *future values*. To determine the future value of an amount on hand today, the present-value multiplier is used as a *divisor* instead of as a multiplier. For example, a company may want to know the value in seven years of $10,000 invested today at 13 percent interest compounded annually. Reference to Table 1 ($r = 0.13$, $n = 7$) indicates a present-value multiplier of 0.4251. Dividing the $10,000 present value by 0.4251 yields a future value of $23,524.

In a similar vein, present-value multipliers can also be used to determine the amount that annuity payments will grow to at some future time. For instance, a company may invest $10,000 at the end of each year for 12 years, the first payment to be invested one year from today. The value of this annuity 12 years from today assuming 11 percent interest compounded annually would be calculated as follows:

Amount of each annuity payment	$ 10,000
Present-value multiplier: Table 2, $r = 0.11$, $n = 12$	× 6.4924
Present value today	64,924
Present-value multiplier: Table 1, $r = 0.11$, $n = 12$	÷ 0.2858
Future value 12 years from today	$227,166

In practice, future-value compound interest tables are available to effect such calculations. Inasmuch as future-value calculations are not used by accountants with any regularity, future-value tables aren't included in this book.

Tables 3 to 9: Present Value of a $100 Bond

Tables 3 to 9 give the present values—at various yield rates—of bonds bearing coupon rates ranging from 6 percent to 18 percent, for terms that vary from six months to 30 years. These tables are applicable to bonds on which interest is paid semiannually.[2]

To find the present value of a bond when the *yield to maturity* is known, turn to the table with the appropriate coupon rate (for example, Table 4 for an 8 percent coupon) and find the column corresponding to the number of years to maturity (for example, 10 years). Finally, find the row identified by the known yield to maturity at the left (say, 9.5 percent) and read the present value from the appropriate column in that row (90.45). This indicates than an 8 percent coupon bond with a face value of $100 has a present value of $90.45 in a 9.5 percent market. To find the present value of any other face amount, multiply the face value by 1/100 of the multiplier shown in the table. For example, if 10-year bonds with an 8 percent coupon rate and $3,500,000 total face amount are issued in a 9.5 percent market, the proceeds will be $3,165,750 ($3,500,000 × 0.9045).

---

[2] The concepts and accounting measurement standards relating to bond interest are discussed in detail in Chapter 10.

These tables can also be used to find the yield to maturity when the market value and number of years to maturity are known. To find the yield to maturity of a fixed-payment bond, turn to the table for the bond's coupon rate, find the column for the number of years until the bond matures, and go down to the row on which the quoted market price is located. The yield is the number at the left end of this row. To pursue our example, let's assume that when five years remain until maturity, the market value of each $100, 8 percent bond is $86.97. Reference to the same 8 percent coupon table indicates that the yield to maturity is now 11.5 percent.

TABLE 1
Present Value of $1

$$P = F_n(1 + r)^{-n}$$

Periods	5%	6%	7%	8%	9%	10%	11%	12%
1	0.9524	0.9434	0.9346	0.9259	0.9174	0.9091	0.9009	0.8929
2	0.9070	0.8900	0.8734	0.8573	0.8417	0.8264	0.8116	0.7972
3	0.8638	0.8396	0.8163	0.7938	0.7722	0.7513	0.7312	0.7118
4	0.8227	0.7921	0.7629	0.7350	0.7084	0.6830	0.6587	0.6355
5	0.7835	0.7473	0.7130	0.6806	0.6499	0.6209	0.5935	0.5674
6	0.7462	0.7050	0.6663	0.6302	0.5963	0.5645	0.5346	0.5066
7	0.7107	0.6651	0.6227	0.5835	0.5470	0.5132	0.4817	0.4524
8	0.6768	0.6274	0.5820	0.5403	0.5019	0.4665	0.4339	0.4039
9	0.6446	0.5919	0.5439	0.5002	0.4604	0.4241	0.3909	0.3606
10	0.6139	0.5584	0.5083	0.4632	0.4224	0.3855	0.3522	0.3220
11	0.5847	0.5268	0.4751	0.4289	0.3875	0.3505	0.3173	0.2875
12	0.5568	0.4970	0.4440	0.3971	0.3555	0.3186	0.2858	0.2567
13	0.5303	0.4688	0.4150	0.3677	0.3262	0.2897	0.2575	0.2292
14	0.5051	0.4423	0.3878	0.3405	0.2992	0.2633	0.2320	0.2046
15	0.4810	0.4173	0.3624	0.3153	0.2745	0.2394	0.2090	0.1827
16	0.4581	0.3936	0.3387	0.2919	0.2519	0.2176	0.1883	0.1631
17	0.4363	0.3714	0.3166	0.2703	0.2311	0.1978	0.1696	0.1456
18	0.4155	0.3503	0.2959	0.2502	0.2120	0.1799	0.1528	0.1300
19	0.3957	0.3305	0.2765	0.2317	0.1945	0.1635	0.1377	0.1161
20	0.3769	0.3118	0.2584	0.2145	0.1784	0.1486	0.1240	0.1037
21	0.3589	0.2942	0.2415	0.1987	0.1637	0.1351	0.1117	0.0926
22	0.3418	0.2775	0.2257	0.1839	0.1502	0.1228	0.1007	0.0826
23	0.3256	0.2618	0.2109	0.1703	0.1378	0.1117	0.0907	0.0738
24	0.3101	0.2470	0.1971	0.1577	0.1264	0.1015	0.0817	0.0659
25	0.2935	0.2330	0.1842	0.1460	0.1160	0.0923	0.0736	0.0588
30	0.2314	0.1741	0.1314	0.0994	0.0754	0.0573	0.0437	0.0334
40	0.1420	0.0972	0.0668	0.0460	0.0318	0.0221	0.0154	0.0108
50	0.0872	0.0543	0.0339	0.0213	0.0134	0.0085	0.0054	0.0035

Periods	13%	14%	15%	16%	17%	18%	19%	20%	25%
1	0.8850	0.8772	0.8696	0.8621	0.8547	0.8475	0.8403	0.8333	0.8000
2	0.7831	0.7695	0.7561	0.7432	0.7305	0.7182	0.7062	0.6944	0.6400
3	0.6931	0.6750	0.6575	0.6407	0.6244	0.6086	0.5934	0.5787	0.5120
4	0.6133	0.5921	0.5718	0.5523	0.5337	0.5158	0.4987	0.4823	0.4096
5	0.5428	0.5194	0.4972	0.4761	0.4561	0.4371	0.4190	0.4019	0.3277
6	0.4803	0.4556	0.4323	0.4104	0.3898	0.3704	0.3521	0.3349	0.2621
7	0.4251	0.3996	0.3759	0.3538	0.3332	0.3139	0.2959	0.2791	0.2097
8	0.3762	0.3506	0.3269	0.3050	0.2848	0.2660	0.2487	0.2326	0.1678
9	0.3329	0.3075	0.2843	0.2630	0.2434	0.2255	0.2090	0.1938	0.1342
10	0.2946	0.2697	0.2472	0.2267	0.2080	0.1911	0.1756	0.1615	0.1074
11	0.2607	0.2366	0.2149	0.1954	0.1778	0.1619	0.1476	0.1346	0.0859
12	0.2307	0.2076	0.1869	0.1685	0.1520	0.1372	0.1240	0.1122	0.0678
13	0.2042	0.1821	0.1625	0.1452	0.1299	0.1163	0.1042	0.0935	0.0550
14	0.1807	0.1597	0.1413	0.1252	0.1110	0.0985	0.0876	0.0779	0.0440
15	0.1599	0.1401	0.1229	0.1079	0.0949	0.0835	0.0736	0.0649	0.0352
16	0.1415	0.1229	0.1069	0.0930	0.0811	0.0708	0.0618	0.0541	0.0281
17	0.1252	0.1078	0.0929	0.0802	0.0693	0.0600	0.0520	0.0451	0.0225
18	0.1108	0.0946	0.0808	0.0691	0.0592	0.0508	0.0437	0.0376	0.0180
19	0.0981	0.0829	0.0703	0.0596	0.0506	0.0431	0.0367	0.0313	0.0144
20	0.0868	0.0728	0.0611	0.0514	0.0433	0.0365	0.0308	0.0261	0.0115
21	0.0768	0.0638	0.0531	0.0443	0.0370	0.0309	0.0259	0.0217	0.0092
22	0.0680	0.0560	0.0462	0.0382	0.0316	0.0262	0.0218	0.0181	0.0074
23	0.0601	0.0491	0.0402	0.0329	0.0270	0.0222	0.0183	0.0151	0.0059
24	0.0532	0.0431	0.0349	0.0284	0.0231	0.0188	0.0154	0.0126	0.0047
25	0.0471	0.0378	0.0304	0.0245	0.0197	0.0160	0.0129	0.0105	0.0038
30	0.0256	0.0196	0.0151	0.0116	0.0090	0.0070	0.0054	0.0042	0.0012
40	0.0075	0.0053	0.0037	0.0026	0.0019	0.0013	0.0010	0.0007	0.0001
50	0.0022	0.0014	0.0009	0.0006	0.0004	0.0003	0.0002	0.0001	—

TABLE 2
Present Value of Annuity of $1 in Arrears

$$P_A = A \left[\frac{1 - (1 + r)^{-n}}{r} \right]$$

Periods	5%	6%	7%	8%	9%	10%	11%	12%
1	0.9524	0.9434	0.9346	0.9259	0.9174	0.9091	0.9009	0.8929
2	1.8594	1.8334	1.8080	1.7833	1.7591	1.7355	1.7125	1.6901
3	2.7232	2.6730	2.6243	2.5771	2.5313	2.4869	2.4437	2.4018
4	3.5460	3.4651	3.3872	3.3121	3.2397	3.1699	3.1024	3.0373
5	4.3295	4.2124	4.1002	3.9927	3.8897	3.7908	3.6959	3.6048
6	5.0757	4.9173	4.7665	4.6229	4.4859	4.3553	4.2305	4.1114
7	5.7864	5.5824	5.3893	5.2064	5.0330	4.8684	4.7122	4.5638
8	6.4632	6.2098	5.9713	5.7466	5.5348	5.3349	5.1461	4.9676
9	7.1078	6.8017	6.5152	6.2469	5.9952	5.7590	5.5370	5.3282
10	7.7217	7.3601	7.0236	6.7101	6.4177	6.1446	5.8892	5.6502
11	8.3064	7.8869	7.4987	7.1390	6.8052	6.4951	6.2065	5.9377
12	8.8633	8.3838	7.9427	7.5361	7.1607	6.8137	6.4924	6.1944
13	9.3936	8.8527	8.3577	7.9038	7.4869	7.1034	6.7439	6.4236
14	9.8986	9.2950	8.7455	8.2442	7.7861	7.3667	6.9819	6.6282
15	10.3797	9.7122	9.1079	8.5595	8.0607	7.6061	7.1909	6.8109
16	10.8378	10.1059	9.4466	8.8514	8.3126	7.8237	7.3792	6.9740
17	11.2741	10.4773	9.7632	9.1216	8.5436	8.0216	7.5488	7.1196
18	11.6896	10.8276	10.0591	9.3719	8.7556	8.2014	7.7016	7.2497
19	12.0853	11.1581	10.3356	9.6036	8.9501	8.3649	7.8393	7.3658
20	12.4622	11.4699	10.5940	9.8181	9.1285	8.5136	7.9633	7.4694
21	12.8212	11.7640	10.8355	10.0168	9.2922	8.6487	8.0751	7.5620
22	13.1630	12.0416	11.0612	10.2007	9.4424	8.7715	8.1757	7.6446
23	13.4886	12.3034	11.2722	10.3711	9.5802	8.8832	8.2664	7.7184
24	13.7986	12.5504	11.4693	10.5288	9.7066	8.9847	8.3481	7.7843
25	14.0939	12.7834	11.6536	10.6748	9.8226	9.0770	8.4217	7.8431
30	15.3725	13.7648	12.4090	11.2578	10.2737	9.4269	8.6938	8.0552
40	17.1591	15.0463	13.3317	11.9246	10.7570	9.7791	8.9511	8.2438
50	18.2559	15.7619	13.8007	12.2335	10.9617	9.9148	9.0417	8.3045

Note: To convert this table to values of an annuity in advance, take one less period and add 1.0000.

Periods	13%	14%	15%	16%	17%	18%	19%	20%	25%
1	0.8850	0.8772	0.8696	0.8621	0.8547	0.8475	0.8403	0.8333	0.8000
2	1.6681	1.6467	1.6257	1.6052	1.5852	1.5656	1.5465	1.5278	1.4400
3	2.3612	2.3216	2.2832	2.2459	2.2096	2.1743	2.1399	2.1065	1.9520
4	2.9745	2.9137	2.8550	2.7982	2.7432	2.6901	2.6386	2.5887	2.3616
5	3.5172	3.4331	3.3522	3.2743	3.1993	3.1272	3.0576	2.9906	2.6893
6	3.9975	3.8887	3.7845	3.6847	3.5892	3.4976	3.4098	3.3255	2.9514
7	4.4226	4.2883	4.1604	4.0386	3.9224	3.8115	3.7057	3.6046	3.1611
8	4.7988	4.6389	4.4873	4.3436	4.2072	4.0776	3.9544	3.8372	3.3289
9	5.1317	4.9464	4.7716	4.6065	4.4506	4.3030	4.1633	4.0310	3.4631
10	5.4262	5.2161	5.0188	4.8332	4.6586	4.4941	4.3389	4.1925	3.5705
11	5.6869	5.4527	5.2337	5.0286	4.8364	4.6560	4.4865	4.3271	3.6564
12	5.9176	5.6603	5.4206	5.1971	4.9884	4.7932	4.6105	4.4392	3.7251
13	6.1218	5.8424	5.5831	5.3423	5.1183	4.9095	4.7147	4.5327	3.7801
14	6.3025	6.0021	5.7245	5.4675	5.2293	5.0081	4.8023	4.6106	3.8241
15	6.4624	6.1422	5.8474	5.5755	5.3242	5.0916	4.8759	4.6755	3.8593
16	6.6039	6.2651	5.9542	5.6685	5.4053	5.1624	4.9377	4.7296	3.8874
17	6.7291	6.3729	6.0472	5.7487	5.4746	5.2223	4.9897	4.7746	3.9099
18	6.8399	6.4674	6.1280	5.8178	5.5339	5.2732	5.0333	4.8122	3.9279
19	6.9380	6.5504	6.1982	5.8775	5.5845	5.3162	5.0700	4.8435	3.9424
20	7.0248	6.6231	6.2593	5.9288	5.6278	5.3527	5.1009	4.8696	3.9539
21	7.1016	6.6870	6.3125	5.9731	5.6648	5.3837	5.1268	4.8913	3.9631
22	7.1695	6.7429	6.3587	6.0113	5.6964	5.4099	5.1486	4.9094	3.9705
23	7.2297	6.7921	6.3988	6.0442	5.7234	5.4321	5.1668	4.9245	3.9764
24	7.2829	6.8351	6.4338	6.0726	5.7465	5.4509	5.1822	4.9371	3.9811
25	7.3300	6.8729	6.4641	6.0971	5.7662	5.4669	5.1951	4.9476	3.9849
30	7.4957	7.0027	6.5660	6.1772	5.8294	5.5168	5.2347	4.9789	3.9950
40	7.6344	7.1050	6.6418	6.2335	5.8713	5.5482	5.2582	4.9966	3.9995
50	7.6752	7.1327	6.6605	6.2463	5.8801	5.5541	5.2623	4.9995	3.9999

TABLE 3
Bond Values: Coupon Rate of 6 Percent (Semiannual Interest Payments; Semiannual Compounding)

Annual Yield (%)	Years to Maturity							
	½	1	5	10	15	19½	20	30
5.0	100.49	100.96	104.38	107.79	110.47	112.37	112.55	115.45
5.5	100.24	100.48	102.16	103.81	105.06	105.94	106.02	107.31
6.0	100.00	100.00	100.00	100.00	100.00	100.00	100.00	100.00
6.5	99.76	99.52	97.89	96.37	95.25	94.52	94.45	93.44
7.0	99.52	99.05	95.84	92.89	90.80	89.45	89.32	87.53
7.5	99.28	98.58	93.84	89.58	86.63	84.76	84.59	82.20
8.0	99.04	98.11	91.89	86.41	82.71	80.42	80.21	77.38
8.5	98.80	97.65	89.99	83.38	79.03	76.39	76.15	73.01
9.0	98.56	97.19	88.13	80.49	75.57	72.66	72.40	69.04
9.5	98.33	96.73	86.32	77.72	72.31	69.19	68.91	65.43
10.0	98.10	96.28	84.56	75.08	69.26	65.97	65.68	62.14
10.5	97.86	95.83	82.84	72.54	66.38	62.97	62.68	59.13
11.0	97.63	95.38	81.16	70.12	63.67	60.18	59.88	56.38
11.5	97.40	94.94	79.52	67.81	61.11	57.58	57.28	53.84
12.0	97.17	94.50	77.92	65.59	58.71	55.15	54.86	51.52
12.5	96.94	94.06	76.36	63.47	56.44	52.89	52.60	49.37
13.0	96.71	93.63	74.84	61.44	54.29	50.77	50.49	47.38
13.5	96.49	93.20	73.35	59.49	52.27	48.79	48.52	45.55
14.0	96.26	92.77	71.91	57.62	50.36	46.94	46.67	43.84
14.5	96.04	92.34	70.49	55.84	48.56	45.20	44.95	42.26
15.0	95.81	91.92	69.11	54.12	46.85	43.57	43.33	40.78
15.5	95.59	91.50	67.76	52.48	45.24	42.04	41.80	39.41
16.0	95.37	91.08	66.45	50.91	43.71	40.61	40.38	38.12
16.5	95.15	90.67	65.17	49.40	42.26	39.28	39.03	36.91
17.0	94.93	90.26	63.91	47.95	40.89	37.98	37.77	35.78
17.5	94.71	89.85	62.69	46.56	39.59	36.78	36.58	34.71
18.0	94.50	89.45	61.49	45.23	38.36	35.65	35.46	33.71
18.5	94.28	89.04	60.33	43.95	37.19	34.58	34.40	32.77
19.0	94.06	88.64	59.19	42.72	36.07	33.57	33.39	31.87
19.5	93.85	88.25	58.07	41.54	35.02	32.61	32.44	31.03
20.0	93.64	87.85	56.99	40.41	34.01	31.70	31.55	30.23

TABLE 4
Bond Values: Coupon Rate of 8 Percent (Semiannual Interest Payments; Semiannual Compounding)

Annual Yield (%)	Years to Maturity							
	½	1	5	10	15	19½	20	30
5.0	101.46	102.89	113.13	123.38	131.40	137.10	137.65	146.36
5.5	101.22	102.40	110.80	119.03	125.31	129.68	130.10	136.53
6.0	100.97	101.91	108.53	114.88	119.60	122.81	123.11	127.68
6.5	100.73	101.43	106.32	110.90	114.24	116.45	116.66	119.69
7.0	100.48	100.95	104.16	107.11	109.10	110.55	110.68	112.47
7.5	100.24	100.47	102.05	103.47	104.46	105.08	105.14	105.93
8.0	100.00	100.00	100.00	100.00	100.00	100.00	100.00	100.00
8.5	99.76	99.53	98.00	96.68	95.81	95.28	95.23	94.60
9.0	99.52	99.06	96.04	93.50	91.86	90.89	90.80	89.68
9.5	99.28	98.60	94.14	90.45	88.13	86.79	86.68	85.19
10.0	99.05	98.14	92.28	87.54	84.63	82.98	82.84	81.07
10.5	98.81	97.68	90.46	84.75	81.32	79.43	79.27	77.30
11.0	98.58	97.23	88.69	82.07	78.20	76.11	75.93	73.83
11.5	98.35	96.78	86.97	79.51	75.25	73.00	72.82	70.63
12.0	98.11	96.33	85.28	77.06	72.47	70.10	69.91	67.68
12.5	97.88	95.89	83.63	74.71	69.84	67.38	67.19	64.95
13.0	97.65	95.45	82.03	72.45	67.35	64.84	64.64	62.42
13.5	97.42	95.01	80.46	70.29	65.00	62.45	62.25	60.07
14.0	97.20	94.58	78.93	68.22	62.77	60.21	60.00	57.88
14.5	96.97	94.14	77.43	66.23	60.66	58.10	57.90	55.84
15.0	96.74	93.72	75.98	64.32	58.66	56.11	55.92	53.94
15.5	96.52	93.29	74.55	62.49	56.77	54.25	54.06	52.16
16.0	96.30	92.87	76.16	60.73	54.97	52.49	52.30	50.49
16.5	96.07	92.45	71.80	59.04	53.26	50.83	50.65	48.93
17.0	95.85	92.03	70.47	57.41	51.64	49.26	49.08	47.46
17.5	95.63	91.62	69.18	55.86	50.10	47.77	47.61	46.07
18.0	95.41	91.20	67.91	54.36	48.63	46.37	46.21	44.76
18.5	95.19	90.80	66.67	52.92	47.24	45.04	44.89	43.52
19.0	94.98	90.39	65.47	51.53	45.91	43.79	43.64	42.36
19.5	94.76	89.99	64.29	50.20	44.64	42.59	42.45	41.25
20.0	94.55	89.59	63.13	48.92	43.44	41.46	41.33	40.20

TABLE 5
Bond Values: Coupon Rate of 10 Percent (Semiannual Interest Payments; Semiannual Compounding)

Annual Yield (%)	Years to Maturity							
	½	1	5	10	15	19½	20	30
5.0	102.44	104.82	121.88	138.97	152.33	161.83	162.76	177.27
5.5	102.19	104.32	119.44	134.26	145.56	153.42	154.18	165.75
6.0	101.94	103.83	117.06	129.75	139.20	145.62	146.23	155.35
6.5	101.69	103.34	114.74	125.44	133.22	138.38	138.86	145.94
7.0	101.45	102.85	112.47	121.32	127.59	131.65	132.03	137.42
7.5	101.20	102.37	110.27	117.37	122.29	125.40	125.69	129.67
8.0	100.96	101.89	108.11	113.59	117.29	119.58	119.79	122.62
8.5	100.72	101.41	106.01	109.97	112.58	114.17	114.31	116.19
9.0	100.48	100.94	103.96	106.50	108.14	109.11	109.20	110.32
9.5	100.24	100.47	101.95	103.18	103.96	104.40	104.44	104.94
10.0	100.00	100.00	100.00	100.00	100.00	100.00	100.00	100.00
10.5	99.76	99.54	98.09	96.95	96.26	95.89	95.85	95.46
11.0	99.53	99.08	96.23	94.02	92.73	92.04	91.98	91.28
11.5	99.29	98.62	94.41	91.22	89.39	88.43	88.35	87.41
12.0	99.06	98.17	92.64	88.53	86.24	85.05	84.95	83.84
12.5	98.82	97.72	90.91	85.95	83.24	81.88	81.77	80.53
13.0	98.59	97.27	89.22	83.47	80.41	78.90	78.78	77.45
13.5	98.36	96.82	87.57	81.09	77.73	76.10	75.98	74.59
14.0	98.13	96.38	85.95	78.81	75.18	73.47	73.34	71.92
14.5	97.90	95.95	84.38	76.62	72.77	70.99	70.85	69.43
15.0	97.67	95.51	82.84	74.51	70.47	68.65	68.51	67.10
15.5	97.45	95.08	81.34	72.49	68.30	66.45	66.31	64.92
16.0	97.22	94.65	79.87	70.55	66.23	64.36	64.23	62.87
16.5	97.00	94.22	78.44	68.68	64.26	62.40	62.26	60.94
17.0	96.77	93.80	77.04	66.88	62.39	60.53	60.40	59.13
17.5	96.55	93.38	75.67	65.15	60.60	58.77	58.64	57.42
18.0	96.33	92.96	74.33	63.49	58.91	57.10	56.97	55.81
18.5	96.11	92.55	73.02	61.89	57.29	55.51	55.39	54.28
19.0	95.89	92.14	71.75	60.34	55.74	54.01	53.89	52.84
19.5	95.67	91.73	70.50	58.86	54.27	52.58	52.46	51.47
20.0	95.45	91.32	69.28	57.43	52.87	51.21	51.10	50.16

TABLE 6
Bond Values: Coupon Rate of 12 Percent (Semiannual Interest Payments; Semiannual Compounding)

Annual Yield (%)	Years to Maturity							
	½	1	5	10	15	19½	20	30
5.0	103.41	106.75	130.63	154.56	173.26	186.56	187.86	208.18
5.5	103.16	106.24	128.08	149.49	165.81	177.16	178.25	194.97
6.0	102.91	105.74	125.59	144.63	158.80	168.42	169.34	183.03
6.5	102.66	105.24	123.16	139.98	152.20	160.31	161.07	172.20
7.0	102.42	104.75	120.79	135.53	145.98	152.76	153.39	162.36
7.5	102.17	104.26	118.48	131.27	140.12	145.72	146.24	153.41
8.0	101.92	103.77	116.22	127.18	134.58	139.17	139.59	145.25
8.5	101.68	103.29	114.02	123.27	129.36	133.05	133.39	137.79
9.0	101.44	102.81	111.87	119.51	124.43	127.34	127.60	130.96
9.5	101.19	102.33	109.77	115.91	119.78	122.01	122.20	124.69
10.0	100.95	101.86	107.72	112.46	115.37	117.02	117.16	118.93
10.5	100.71	101.39	105.72	109.15	111.21	112.34	112.44	113.62
11.0	100.47	100.92	103.77	105.98	107.27	107.96	108.02	108.72
11.5	100.24	100.46	101.86	102.93	103.54	103.86	103.88	104.20
12.0	100.00	100.00	100.00	100.00	100.00	100.00	100.00	100.00
12.5	99.76	99.54	98.18	97.19	96.65	96.38	96.35	96.11
13.0	99.53	99.09	96.41	94.49	93.47	92.97	92.93	92.48
13.5	99.30	98.64	94.67	91.90	90.45	89.76	89.70	89.11
14.0	99.07	98.19	92.98	89.41	87.59	86.74	86.67	85.96
14.5	98.83	97.75	91.32	87.01	84.87	83.88	83.81	83.02
15.0	98.60	97.31	89.70	84.71	82.28	81.19	81.11	80.26
15.5	98.38	96.87	88.12	82.49	79.82	78.65	78.56	77.68
16.0	98.15	96.43	86.58	80.36	77.48	76.24	76.15	75.25
16.5	97.92	96.00	85.07	78.31	75.26	73.97	73.87	72.96
17.0	97.70	95.57	83.60	76.34	73.13	71.81	71.71	70.81
17.5	97.47	95.15	82.16	74.44	71.11	69.76	69.67	68.78
18.0	97.25	94.72	80.75	72.61	69.18	67.82	67.73	66.86
18.5	97.03	94.30	79.37	70.85	67.34	65.98	65.89	65.04
19.0	96.80	93.88	78.02	69.16	65.58	64.23	64.13	63.32
19.5	96.58	93.47	76.71	67.52	63.90	62.56	62.47	61.68
20.0	96.36	93.06	75.42	65.95	62.29	60.97	60.88	60.13

TABLE 7
Bond Values: Coupon Rate of 14 Percent (Semiannual Interest Payments; Semiannual Compounding)

Annual Yield (%)	½	1	5	10	15	19½	20	30
5.0	104.39	108.67	139.38	170.15	194.19	211.29	212.96	239.09
5.5	104.14	108.16	136.72	164.72	186.06	200.90	202.33	224.20
6.0	103.88	107.65	134.12	159.51	178.40	191.23	192.46	210.70
6.5	103.63	107.15	131.58	154.52	171.18	182.24	183.28	198.45
7.0	103.38	106.65	129.11	149.74	164.37	173.86	174.74	187.31
7.5	103.13	106.15	126.69	145.16	157.95	166.05	166.79	177.15
8.0	102.88	105.66	124.33	140.77	151.88	158.75	159.38	167.87
8.5	102.64	105.17	122.03	136.56	146.14	151.94	152.46	159.38
9.0	102.39	104.68	119.78	132.52	140.72	145.57	146.00	151.60
9.5	102.15	104.20	117.59	128.64	135.60	139.62	139.97	144.44
10.0	101.90	103.72	115.44	124.92	130.74	134.03	134.32	137.86
10.5	101.66	103.24	113.35	121.35	126.15	128.80	129.03	131.79
11.0	101.42	102.77	111.31	117.93	121.80	123.89	124.07	126.17
11.5	101.18	102.30	109.31	114.63	117.68	119.28	119.42	120.98
12.0	100.94	101.83	107.37	111.47	113.76	114.95	115.05	116.16
12.5	100.71	101.37	105.46	108.43	110.05	110.87	110.94	111.68
13.0	100.47	100.91	103.59	105.51	106.53	107.03	107.07	107.52
13.5	100.23	100.45	101.78	102.70	103.18	103.41	103.43	103.63
14.0	100.00	100.00	100.00	100.00	100.00	100.00	100.00	100.00
14.5	99.77	99.55	98.26	97.40	96.97	96.78	96.76	96.60
15.0	99.53	99.10	96.57	94.90	94.09	93.73	93.70	93.42
15.5	99.30	98.66	94.91	92.50	91.35	90.85	90.81	90.43
16.0	99.07	98.22	93.29	90.18	88.74	88.12	88.08	87.62
16.5	98.85	97.78	91.71	87.95	86.25	85.54	85.48	84.98
17.0	98.62	97.34	90.16	85.80	83.88	83.09	83.03	82.49
17.5	98.39	96.91	88.64	83.74	81.61	80.76	80.70	80.13
18.0	98.17	96.48	87.16	81.74	79.45	78.55	78.49	77.90
18.5	97.94	96.06	85.72	79.82	77.39	76.45	76.38	75.80
19.0	97.72	95.63	84.30	77.97	75.41	74.45	74.38	73.80
19.5	97.49	95.21	82.92	76.18	73.53	72.54	72.48	71.90
20.0	97.27	94.79	81.57	74.46	71.72	70.73	70.66	70.10

TABLE 8
Bond Values: Coupon Rate of 16 Percent (Semiannual Interest Payments; Semiannual Compounding)

Annual Yield (%)	Years to Maturity							
	½	1	5	10	15	19½	20	30
5.0	105.37	110.60	148.14	185.74	215.12	236.02	238.07	270.00
5.5	105.11	110.08	145.36	179.94	206.31	224.64	226.41	253.42
6.0	104.85	109.57	142.65	174.39	198.00	214.04	215.57	238.38
6.5	104.60	109.06	140.01	169.06	190.16	204.17	205.49	224.70
7.0	104.35	108.55	137.42	163.96	182.76	194.96	196.10	212.25
7.5	104.10	108.04	134.90	159.06	175.77	186.37	187.34	200.89
8.0	103.85	107.54	132.44	154.36	169.17	178.34	179.17	190.49
8.5	103.60	107.05	130.04	149.85	162.92	170.83	171.54	180.97
9.0	103.35	106.55	127.69	145.53	157.01	163.80	164.41	172.23
9.5	103.10	106.06	125.40	141.37	151.42	157.22	157.73	164.19
10.0	102.86	105.58	123.17	137.39	146.12	151.05	151.48	156.79
10.5	102.61	105.10	120.98	133.56	141.10	145.26	145.62	149.95
11.0	102.37	104.62	118.84	129.88	136.33	139.82	140.12	143.62
11.5	102.13	104.14	116.76	126.34	131.82	134.71	134.95	137.76
12.0	101.89	103.67	114.72	122.94	127.53	129.90	130.09	132.32
12.5	101.65	103.20	112.73	119.67	123.46	125.37	125.52	127.26
13.0	101.41	102.73	110.78	116.53	119.59	121.10	121.22	122.55
13.5	101.17	102.27	108.88	113.50	115.91	117.07	117.16	118.15
14.0	100.93	101.81	107.02	110.59	112.41	113.26	113.33	114.04
14.5	100.70	101.35	105.21	107.79	109.08	109.67	109.72	110.19
15.0	100.47	100.90	103.43	105.10	105.91	106.27	106.30	106.58
15.5	100.23	100.45	101.70	102.50	102.88	103.05	103.06	103.19
16.0	100.00	100.00	100.00	100.00	100.00	100.00	100.00	100.00
16.5	99.77	99.56	98.34	97.59	97.25	97.11	97.10	97.00
17.0	99.54	99.11	96.72	95.27	94.63	94.36	94.34	94.16
17.5	99.31	98.68	95.13	93.03	92.12	91.75	91.73	91.48
18.0	99.08	98.24	93.58	90.87	89.73	89.27	89.24	88.95
18.5	98.86	97.81	92.07	88.79	87.44	86.92	86.88	86.55
19.0	98.63	97.38	90.58	86.78	85.25	84.67	84.63	84.28
19.5	98.41	96.95	89.13	84.84	83.15	82.53	82.49	82.12
20.0	98.18	96.53	87.71	82.97	81.15	80.49	80.44	80.07

TABLE 9
Bond Values: Coupon Rate of 18 Percent (Semiannual Interest Payments; Semiannual Compounding)

Annual Yield (%)	Years to Maturity							
	½	1	5	10	15	19½	20	30
5.0	106.34	112.53	156.89	201.33	236.05	260.75	263.17	300.91
5.5	106.08	112.00	154.00	195.17	226.56	248.38	250.49	282.64
6.0	105.83	111.48	151.18	189.26	217.60	236.85	238.69	266.05
6.5	105.57	110.96	148.48	183.60	209.15	226.10	227.70	250.96
7.0	105.31	110.45	145.74	178.17	201.16	216.06	217.45	237.20
7.5	105.06	109.94	143.12	172.96	193.60	206.69	207.89	224.62
8.0	104.81	109.43	140.55	167.95	186.46	197.92	198.96	213.12
8.5	104.56	108.93	138.05	163.15	179.70	189.72	190.62	202.57
9.0	104.31	108.43	135.61	158.54	173.30	182.03	182.81	192.87
9.5	104.06	107.93	133.22	154.11	167.24	174.83	175.49	183.95
10.0	103.81	107.44	130.89	149.85	161.49	168.07	168.64	175.72
10.5	103.56	106.95	128.61	145.76	156.04	161.72	162.20	168.11
11.0	103.32	106.46	126.38	141.83	150.87	155.75	156.16	161.07
11.5	103.07	105.98	124.21	138.05	145.96	150.13	150.48	154.55
12.0	102.83	105.50	122.08	134.41	141.29	144.85	145.14	148.48
12.5	102.59	105.02	120.00	130.91	136.86	139.86	140.11	142.84
13.0	102.35	104.55	117.97	127.55	132.65	135.16	135.36	137.58
13.5	102.11	104.08	115.99	124.31	128.64	130.72	130.89	132.67
14.0	101.87	103.62	114.05	121.19	124.82	126.53	126.66	128.08
14.5	101.63	103.15	112.15	118.18	121.18	122.56	122.67	123.78
15.0	101.40	102.69	110.30	115.29	117.72	118.81	118.89	119.74
15.5	101.16	102.24	108.48	112.50	114.41	115.25	115.31	115.95
16.0	100.93	101.78	106.71	109.82	111.26	111.88	111.92	112.38
16.5	100.69	101.33	104.98	107.23	108.25	108.68	108.71	109.01
17.0	100.46	100.89	103.28	104.73	105.37	105.64	105.66	105.84
17.5	100.23	100.44	101.62	102.32	102.63	102.75	102.76	102.84
18.0	100.00	100.00	100.00	100.00	100.00	100.00	100.00	100.00
18.5	99.77	99.56	98.41	97.76	97.49	97.38	97.38	97.31
19.0	99.54	99.13	96.86	95.59	95.08	94.89	94.88	94.76
19.5	99.32	98.69	95.34	93.50	92.78	92.51	92.49	92.34
20.0	99.09	98.26	93.86	91.49	90.57	90.24	90.22	90.03

Appendix B

Solutions to Independent Study Problems

Chapter 1

1. *a.* The $14,860 retained earnings is the amount entered in the balance sheet in part *b* to achieve equality between *total assets* and *total liabilities and owners' equity.*

b.

BOLTER COMPANY
Balance Sheet
As of December 31, 19x1

Assets

Current assets:

Cash....................................	$ 6,600	
Accounts receivable.....................	8,120	
Inventory..............................	11,200	
Total current assets..................		$ 25,920

Plant assets:

Land...................................	18,000	
Buildings..............................	65,760	
Equipment.............................	4,450	
Total plant assets.....................		88,210
Total assets......................		$114,130

Liabilities and Owners' Equity

Current liabilities:

Accounts payable.......................	$13,300	
Notes payable..........................	9,000	
Wages payable.........................	1,770	
Total current liabilities.................		$ 24,070

Long-term liability:

Bonds payable.........................		40,200
Total liabilities......................		64,270

Owners' equity:

Capital stock...........................	35,000	
Retained earnings......................	14,860	
Total owners' equity..................		49,860
Total liabilities and owners' equity....		$114,130

2. *a.*

	December 31, 19x1	December 31, 19x2
Total assets...........	$846,000	$798,000
Total liabilities.........	237,000	169,000
Owners' equity	609,000	629,000
Capital stock..........	400,000	400,000
Retained earnings..	$209,000	$229,000

b. Retained earnings:

December 31, 19x2	$229,000
December 31, 19x1	209,000
Increase.............	20,000
Dividends	45,000
Net income.............	$ 65,000

Net income increases retained earnings; dividends decrease retained earnings. For a net increase of $20,000 in retained earnings while dividends of $45,000 were distributed, net income must have been $65,000.

3.

MORGAN CORPORATION
Income Statement
For the Year Ended December 31, 19x4

Sales revenues		$521,600
Cost of goods sold...............		326,700
Gross margin.....................		194,900
Operating expenses:		
Salaries and wages expense	$82,400	
Advertising expense	14,500	
Rent expense..................	12,600	
Supplies expense	4,100	
Total operating expense.......		113,600
Income before income taxes.......		81,300
Income tax expense		37,500
Net income		$43,800

Chapter 2

1. *a.* The way to solve this problem is to calculate the owners' equity at the beginning of the year, adjust it for the year's transactions other than income transactions, and then subtract this adjusted balance from the owners' equity at the end of the year, calculated by subtracting the year-end liabilities from the year-end assets:

	Assets	− Liabilities =	Capital Stock	Retained + Earnings
January 1	$120,000	$64,000	$20,000	$36,000
New stock			+ 6,000	
Dividends				− 24,000
Adjusted balance . .				12,000
December 31	140,000	68,000	26,000	46,000
Income				$34,000

b. Capital stock: 2,100 shares $26,000
    Retained earnings   46,000
    Total owners' equity $72,000

2. 1. Collections from customers = $100 + $500 − $80 = $520.
   2. Purchases on account = $250 + $40 − $50 = $240.
   3. Ending balance = $20 + $300 − $295 = $25.
   4. Beginning balance = $90 + $265 − $240 = $115.
   5. Rent expense = $45 + $130 − $60 = $115.

3. *a.* 1. Asset, Merchandise, increased by $1 million; Liability, Accounts Payable, increased by $1 million.
   2. Asset, Accounts Receivable, increased by $1.5 million; Owners' Equity increased by this amount. (Note: We know that the owners' equity didn't increase by this amount once all expenses were taken into consideration. This amount is a first approximation, to be corrected by additional information.)
   3. Liability, Wages Payable, increased by $300,000; Owners' Equity decreased by this amount. (Note: This is one of the expenses offsetting the gross increase in owners' equity identified in item 2.)
   4. Liability, Accounts Payable, increased by $100,000; Owners' Equity decreased by this amount. (This is another expense, offsetting the gross increase in owners' equity identified in item 2.)
   5. Asset, Cash, decreased by $1,050,000; Liability, Accounts Payable, decreased by the same amount.
   6. Asset, Cash, decreased by $280,000; Liability, Wages Payable, decreased by this amount.
   7. Asset, Cash, increased by $1.6 million; Asset, Accounts Receivable, decreased by this amount.
   8. Asset, Equipment, increased by $40,000; Asset, Cash, decreased by $25,000; Liability, Accounts Payable, increased by $15,000.
   9. Asset, Merchandise, decreased by $940,000; Owners' Equity decreased by this same amount, the cost of the goods that were sold.

10. Asset, Equipment, decreased by $18,000; Owners' Equity decreased by the same amount.

11. Liability, Dividends Payable, increased by $10,000; Owners' Equity decreased by this amount.

12. Asset, Cash, decreased by $7,500; Liability, Dividends Payable, decreased by this amount.

b.

A STORE
Income Statement
For the Year Ended December 31, 19x1

Sales revenue............		$1,500,000
Expenses:		
Cost of goods sold......	$940,000	
Wages	300,000	
Depreciation	18,000	
Other	100,000	1,358,000
Net income		$ 142,000

4. *a.* 1. Assuming that the equipment is equally useful in each of the 12 years, the annual depreciation should be $4,200/12 = $350. Since the furniture was purchased on July 1, only one-half year's depreciation, or $175, should be recorded in 19x3.

2. The timing of the payments is irrelevant. The sales representative worked three months in 19x3, and expense is $3 \times \$1,500 = \$4,500$.

3. The cost of goods sold is $220,000, and this is an expense, deductible from the revenues recognized in 19x3.

4. No expense. The payment merely canceled a liability that was assumed in 19x2.

5. Rent expense = three months' rentals = $\frac{3}{6} \times \$22,500 = \$11,250$.

b. 1. *July 1:* Asset, Furniture, increased by $4,200; Liability, Accounts Payable, increased by the same amount. *October 1:* Liability, Accounts Payable, decreased by $4,200; Asset, Cash, decreased by the same amount. *December 31:* Owners' Equity decreased by $175; Asset, Furniture, decreased by the same amount.

2. *October 1:* No effect. *November 15:* Asset, Cash, decreased by $1,500; Owners' Equity decreased by the same amount. *December 15:* Same as November 15. *December 31:* Owners' Equity decreased by $1,500; Liability, Salaries Payable, increased by the same amount.

3. Asset, Accounts Receivable, increased by $300,000; Asset, Inventory, decreased by $220,000; Owners' Equity increased by $80,000.

4. Asset, Cash, decreased by $24,000; Liability, Accounts Payable, decreased by the same amount.
5. Asset, Cash, decreased by $22,500; Asset, Prepaid Rent, increased by $18,750 (5/6 × $22,500); Owners' Equity decreased by $3,750 (1/6 × $22,500). *December 31:* Owners' Equity decreased by $11,250; Asset, Prepaid Rent, decreased by the same amount.

5. *a* and *b*.

Assets: Liabilities: Owners' equity:

Cash	
Bal. 1/1	12,510
(2)	+296,000
(7b)	− 44,400
(8)	−248,850
(10)	+ 60,000
Bal. 12/31	75,260

Accounts Payable	
Bal. 1/1	35,180
(3)	+246,300
(4)	+ 3,800
(5)	+ 15,000
(6)	+ 21,000
(8)	−248,850
Bal. 12/31	72,430

Capital Stock	
Bal. 1/1	50,000
(10)	+60,000
Bal. 12/31	110,000

Accounts Receivable	
Bal. 1/1	23,060
(1)	+301,000
(2)	−296,000
Bal. 12/31	28,060

Salaries Payable	
Bal. 1/1	1,400
(7a)	+ 43,000
(7b)	− 44,400
Bal. 12/31	0

Retained Earnings	
Bal. 1/1	35,210
(11)	−25,000
Bal. 12/31	10,210

Merchandise Inventory	
Bal. 1/1	67,200
(1)	−181,000
(3)	+246,300
Bal. 12/31	132,500

Dividends Payable	
(1)	+25,000

Income	
Bal. 1/1	—
(1)	+301,000
(1)	−181,000
(5)	− 15,000
(6)	− 21,000
(7)	− 43,000
(9)	− 4,800
Bal. 12/31	36,200

Equipment	
Bal. 1/1	19,020
(4)	+ 3,800
(9)	− 4,800
Bal. 12/31	18,020

c.

HANDYMAN TOOL SHOP, INC.
Income Statement
For the Year Ended December 31, 19x2

Sales revenues		$301,000
Cost of goods sold		181,000
Gross margin		120,000
Operating expenses:		
Salaries	$43,000	
Rent	15,000	
Depreciation	4,800	
Other	21,000	83,800
Net income		$ 36,200

HANDYMAN TOOL SHOP, INC.
Balance Sheet
December 31, 19x2

Assets

Current assets:		
Cash		$ 75,260
Accounts receivable		28,060
Merchandise inventory		132,500
Total current assets		235,820
Plant assets:		
Equipment		18,020
Total assets		$253,840

Liabilities and Owners' Equity

Current liabilities:		
Accounts payable		$ 72,430
Dividends payable		25,000
Total current liabilities		97,430
Owner's equity:		
Capital stock	$110,000	
Retained earnings	46,410*	156,410
Total liabilities and owners' equity . . .		$253,840

* January 1 balance $35,210 + Net income $36,200 − Dividend $25,000 = December 31 balance $46,410.

Chapter 3

1. *b.* 1.

Accounts Receivable	2,500,000	
Revenue from Sales		2,500,000

2.

Cash	2,400,000	
Accounts Receivable		2,400,000

3.

Inventory	1,600,000	
Accounts Payable		1,600,000

4. Accounts Payable 1,525,000
      Cash.   1,525,000

5. Cost of Goods Sold. 1,550,000
      Inventory   1,550,000

6. Salaries Expense. 380,000
      Salaries Payable.   380,000

7. Salaries Payable 385,000
      Cash.   385,000

8. Miscellaneous Expenses 130,000
      Accounts Payable.   130,000

9. Accounts Payable 125,000
      Cash.   125,000

10. Prepaid Rent 132,000
      Cash.   132,000

11. Rent Expense ($132,000/2 + $60,000) 126,000
      Prepaid Rent.   126,000

12. Equipment 80,000
      Cash.   80,000

13. Depreciation Expense. 88,000
      Accumulated Depreciation   88,000

14. Cash 32,000
      Accumulated Depreciation. 82,000
        Equipment.   100,000
        Gain on Sale of Equipment.   14,000

15. Dividends Declared. 80,000
      Dividends Payable   80,000

16. Dividends Payable. 75,000
      Cash.   75,000

d. C1. Revenue from Sales 2,500,000
        Gain on Sale of Equipment 14,000
          Income Summary.   2,514,000

C2. Income Summary 2,274,000
        Cost of Goods Sold   1,550,000
        Salaries Expense   380,000
        Miscellaneous Expense.   130,000
        Rent Expense   126,000
        Depreciation Expense   88,000

C3. Income Summary 240,000
        Dividends Declared   80,000
        Retained Earnings   160,000

a, c, & d. (000 omitted to save space)

Cash

Bal.	230	(4)	1,525
(2)	2,400	(7)	385
(14)	32	(9)	125
		(10)	132
Bal.	340	(12)	80
		(16)	75

Accounts Receivable

Bal.	350	(2)	2,400
(1)	2,500		
Bal.	450		

Inventory

Bal.	300	(5)	1,550
(3)	1,600		
Bal.	350		

Prepaid Rent

Bal.	60	(11)	126
(10)	132		
Bal.	66		

Equipment

Bal.	860	(14)	100
(12)	80		
Bal.	840		

Accumulated Depreciation

(14)	82	Bal.	410
		(13)	88
		Bal.	416

Accounts Payable

(4)	1,525	Bal.	130
(9)	125	(3)	1,600
		(8)	130
		Bal.	210

Salaries Payable

(7)	385	Bal.	10
		(6)	380
		Bal.	5

Dividends Payable

(16)	75	Bal.	15
		(15)	80
		Bal.	20

Capital Stock

| | | Bal. | 850 |

Retained Earnings

		Bal.	385
		(C3)	160
		Bal.	545

Revenue from Sales

| (C1) | 2,500 | (1) | 2,500 |

Cost of Goods Sold

| (5) | 1,550 | (C2) | 1,550 |

Salaries Expense

| (6) | 380 | (C2) | 380 |

Miscellaneous Expenses

| (8) | 130 | (C2) | 130 |

Rent Expense

| (11) | 126 | (C2) | 126 |

Depreciation Expense

| (13) | 88 | (C2) | 88 |

Dividends Declared

| (15) | 80 | (C3) | 80 |

Gain on Sale of Equipment

| (C1) | 14 | (14) | 14 |

Income Summary

| (C2) | 2,274 | (C1) | 2,514 |
| (C3) | 240 | | |

e.
SATURN STORES, INC.
Income Statement
For the Year Ended December 31, 19x2

Revenue from sales..............		$2,500,000
Cost of goods sold		1,550,000
Gross margin		950,000
Operating expenses:		
Salaries	$380,000	
Rent........................	126,000	
Depreciation	88,000	
Miscellaneous................	130,000	724,000
Operating income		226,000
Gain on sale of equipment........		14,000
Net income		$ 240,000

SATURN STORES, INC.
Balance Sheet
As of December 31, 19x2
(in thousands of dollars)

Assets			Liabilities and Owners' Equity		
Current assets:			Current liabilities:		
Cash		$ 340	Salaries payable.............		$ 5
Accounts receivable		450	Accounts payable		210
Inventory..................		350	Dividends payable		20
Prepaid rent...............		66	Total current liabilities...		235
Total current assets.....		1,206	Owners' equity:		
Equipment	$840		Capital stock	$850	
Less: Accumulated			Retained earnings	545	
depreciation	416		Total owners' equity.....		1,395
Net equipment		424	Total liabilities and		
Total assets		$1,630	owners' equity......		$1,630

2. *a.* The change in the cash balance is irrelevant because it is affected by many transactions in addition to payments to merchandise suppliers. The cost of merchandise purchased is equal to the cost of goods sold *less* the portion represented by the decrease in the inventory:

$$\text{Purchases} = \$700 - \$35 = \$665$$

Merchandise Inventory

Bal.	150	Cost of goods	
Purchases	665	sold	700
Bal.	115		

b. The amount of cash paid to suppliers is the cost of purchases *less* the portion unpaid and therefore added to accounts payable:

$$\text{Payments} = \$665 - (\$90 - \$80) = \$655$$

Accounts Payable

Payments	655	Bal.	80
		Purchases	665
		Bal.	90

3. *a and c.*

Cash

Bal. 3/1	13,200	(4)	61,300
(3)	60,000	(6)	7,500
Bal. 3/31	4,400		

Accounts Payable

(4)	61,300	Bal. 3/1	65,000
		(1)	46,500
		Bal. 3/31	50,200

Accounts Receivable

Bal. 3/1	72,000	(3)	60,000
(2a)	57,000		
Bal. 3/31	69,000		

Sales Revenue

		Bal. 3/1	130,000
		(2a)	57,000
		Bal. 3/31	187,000

Merchandise Inventory

Bal. 3/1	92,000	(2b)	36,000
(1)	46,500		
Bal. 3/31	102,500		

Cost of Goods Sold

Bal. 3/1	79,000		
(2b)	36,000		
Bal. 3/31	115,000		

Salaries and Wages Payable

(6)	7,500	Bal. 3/1	450
		(5)	7,200
		Bal. 3/31	150

Salaries and Wages Expense

Bal. 3/1	14,500		
(5)	7,200		
Bal. 3/31	21,700		

b.

1. Merchandise Inventory.......................... 46,500
       Accounts Payable   46,500

2. Accounts Receivable 57,000
       Sales Revenues   57,000

   Cost of Goods Sold 36,000
       Merchandise Inventory   36,000

3. Cash... 60,000
       Accounts Receivable.......................   60,000

4. Accounts Payable............................. 61,300
        Cash   61,300

5. Salaries and Wages Expense 7,200
        Salaries and Wages Payable   7,200

6. Salaries and Wages Payable.................... 7,500
        Cash   7,500

d. Each account balance was determined by adding its debits, adding its credits, and determining the amount by which the larger sum exceeded the smaller.

Cash on hand was $4,400.

Accounts Receivable of $69,000 signifies the amount owed to Kelly by its customers.

Merchandise Inventory of $102,500 identifies the cost of goods on hand and available for sale.

Salaries and Wages Payable of $150 represents the amount Kelly owed its employees for services already performed.

Accounts Payable of $50,200 is the amount Kelly owed suppliers and other providers of goods and services.

Sales Revenues of $187,000 is the cumulative sales value of merchandise sold since the beginning of the year.

Cost of Goods Sold of $115,000 is the cost to Kelly of the merchandise it sold (for $187,000) since the beginning of the year.

Salaries and Wages Expense contains the $21,700 in salaries and wages earned by Kelly's employees since the beginning of the year.

4. *a.* Truck 10,000
            Cash   10,000

Depreciation Expense............................. 2,000
    Accumulated Depreciation   2,000

b.

Truck			Accumulated Depreciation		
1/1/x6	10,000			12/31/x6	2,000
				12/31/x7	2,000
				12/31/x8	2,000
Bal.	10,000			Bal.	6,000

c. Cash 2,500
    Accumulated Depreciation........................ 6,000
    Loss on Sale of Truck 1,500
        Truck....................................   10,000

5. 1. Merchandise Inventory.................... (+A)   5,000
           Notes Payable .... (+L)   5,000

       2. Cash..................................... (+A)   4,000
           Accounts Receivable.................. (−A)   4,000

       3. Accounts Payable....................... (−L)   6,000
           Cash .... (−A)   6,000

       4. Salaries Expense .... (−OE)   1,000
           Salaries Payable .... (+L)   1,000

       5. Salaries Payable .... (−L)   900
           Cash .... (−A)   900

       6. Cash.................................... (+A)   50,000
           Note Payable .... (+L)   50,000

       7. Accounts Receivable .... (+A)   8,000
           Sales Revenue....................... (+OE)   8,000

           Cost of Goods Sold .... (−OE)   6,000
           Merchandise Inventory .... (−A)   6,000

       8. Land.................................... (+A)   7,000
           Cash .... (−A)   7,000

       9. Dividends Declared...................... (−OE)   3,000
           Dividends Payable................... (+L)   3,000

      10. Office Supplies Expense .... (−OE)   60
           Accounts Payable .... (+L)   60

      11. Accounts Receivable .... (+A)   100
           Cash .... (−A)   100

6. *a* and *c.* To save space, the journal entries (part *b*) are not listed here. They can be identified easily from the numerals in parentheses in the T-accounts that follow.

Cash					Capital Stock		
Bal.	12,510	(7b)	44,400			Bal.	50,000
(2)	296,000	(8)	248,850			(10)	60,000
(10)	60,000					Bal.	110,000
Bal.	75,260						

Accounts Receivable					Retained Earnings	
Bal.	23,060	(2)	296,000		Bal.	35,210
(1)	301,000					
Bal.	28,060					

Merchandise Inventory			
Bal.	67,200	(1)	181,000
(3)	246,300		
Bal.	132,500		

Sales Revenues		
	(1)	301,000

Equipment		
Bal.	36,140	
(4)	3,800	
Bal.	39,940	

Cost of Goods Sold		
(1)	181,000	

Accumulated Depreciation		
	Bal.	17,120
	(9)	4,800
	Bal.	21,920

Salaries Expense		
(7)	43,000	

Rental Expense		
(5)	15,000	

Accounts Payable			
(8)	248,850	Bal.	35,180
		(3)	246,300
		(4)	3,800
		(5)	15,000
		(6)	21,000
		Bal.	72,430

Depreciation Expense		
(9)	4,800	

Salaries Payable			
(7b)	44,400	Bal.	1,400
		(7a)	43,000
		Bal.	0

Miscellaneous Expenses		
(6)	21,000	

Dividends Payable		
	(11)	25,000

Dividends Declared		
(11)	25,000	

d.

Sales Revenues	301,000	
Income Summary		301,000
Income Summary.................................	264,800	
Cost of Goods Sold		181,000
Salaries Expense		43,000
Rental Expense.............................		15,000
Depreciation Expense		4,800
Miscellaneous Expense......................		21,000
Income Summary................................	36,200	
Retained Earnings		36,200
Retained Earnings..............................	25,000	
Dividends Declared		25,000

1. *a.* 2. Asset, Accounts Receivable, +$500,000; Owners' Equity, +$500,000. These amounts overstate the actual effects; these overstatements are corrected in item 5.

3. Asset, Cash, +$510,000; Asset, Accounts Receivable, −$510,000.

4. No change in assets, liabilities, or owners' equity.

5. Asset, Accounts Receivable, −$11,200; Owners' Equity, −$11,200 [$11,200 = $28,200 − ($25,000 − $8,000)].

b. 2. Accounts Receivable............................ 500,000
     Sales Revenues.............................   500,000

3. Cash 510,000
     Accounts Receivable   510,000

4. Allowance for Uncollectibles 8,000
     Accounts Receivable   8,000

5. Bad Debts...................................... 11,200
     Allowance for Uncollectibles..................   11,200

c. Accounts receivable, gross........................... $932,000
     Less: Allowance for uncollectibles   28,200
     Accounts receivable, Net $903,800

d. $11,200.

2. *a.* 11/14   Interest paid, two months at 14 percent of $6,000 .. $140.00
       12/14   Interest accrued, one month at 14 percent of
                  $6,000 ....   70.00
       12/31   Interest accrued for 17 days:
                  $17/360 \times 14\% \times ($6,000 + $70 − $4,000) ....$ 13.69
          Total interest expense.............................. $223.69

b. Interest Expense................................. 13.69
     Interest Payable...............................   13.69

c. Interest Expense................................. 10.46
     Interest Payable 13.69
     Note Payable.................................... 2,070.00
     Cash...   2,094.15

3. *a.* $83,500 − ($55,000 − $40,000) = $68,500.

b. Liability for Service Warranty......................... 40,000
     Cash...   10,000
     Inventory   30,000

     Warranty Expense 68,500
     Liability for Service Warranty   68,500

4. *a.* The missing amounts can be calculated in the following sequence:

C = rent expense = $21,600
D = gross sales revenue = $317,300
A = sales on account = D = $317,300
B = collections and write-offs = $82,400 + $317,300 − $96,700 = $303,000
E = cost of goods sold = $206,200
F & G = estimated bad debts = $4,500
H = write-offs of accounts receivable = $3,300 + $4,500 − $5,100 = $2,700
J = amortization of prepaid rent = C = $21,600
I = prepaid rent, January 1 = $21,600 + $7,500 − $24,800 = $4,300
K = cost of goods sold = E = $206,200
L = ending inventory = $31,800 + $194,900 − $206,200 = $20,500

b. Adjusting entries: C, F, J, and perhaps E and K

5. *a.* 1. Allowance for Uncollectibles 165
        Accounts Receivable 165

2. Bad Debts.................................... 785
        Allowance for Uncollectibles................. 785
    [$91,600 − $165 − $89,315 − ($1,500 − $165)]

3. Cost of Goods Sold........................... 347,060
        Purchases 344,500
        Inventory 2,560
    [$89,000 − $86,440 = $2,560]

4. Inventory...................................... 975
        Accounts Payable........................... 975

5. Insurance Expense 700
        Prepaid Insurance.......................... 700

6. Depreciation Expense......................... 1,240
        Accumulated Depreciation 1,240

7. Interest Expense 400
        Interest Payable 400

8. Salaries and Wages Expense.................... 240
        Salaries and Wages Payable................. 240

b.

THE GUYTON COMPANY
Adjusted Trial Balance
December 31, 19x3

	Debits	Credits
Cash	$ 30,900	
Notes receivable	17,700	
Accounts receivable	91,435	
Allowance for uncollectibles		$ 2,120
Inventory of merchandise..........	87,415	
Prepaid insurance................	1,725	
Other prepayments	1,340	
Land	16,000	
Building and equipment...........	45,800	
Accumulated depreciation		9,340
Accounts payable		19,775
Salaries and wages payable........		240
Interest payable..................		400
Mortgage payable		45,000
Capital stock		150,000
Retained earnings................		53,720
Sales revenues...................		400,000
Bad debts.......................	785	
Interest revenue..................		480
Cost of goods sold	347,060	
Advertising expense	1,200	
Salaries and wages expense	16,640	
Depreciation expense.............	1,240	
Insurance expense	700	
Miscellaneous selling expense	5,800	
Property tax expense	3,300	
Miscellaneous general expense.....	8,435	
Interest expense	3,600	
Totals........................	$681,075	$681,075

c.

THE GUYTON COMPANY
Income Statement
For the Year Ended December 31, 19x3

Sales revenue		$400,000
Less: Estimated bad debts.........		785
Net sales revenue		399,215
Interest revenue..................		480
Total revenue		399,695
Expenses:		
Cost of goods sold	$347,060	
Salaries and wages expense	16,640	
Depreciation expense.............	1,240	
Insurance expense	700	
Advertising expense	1,200	
Miscellaneous selling expenses	5,800	
Property tax expense	3,300	
Miscellaneous general expense.....	8,435	
Interest expense	3,600	
Total expenses.................		387,975
Net income.......................		$11,720

THE GUYTON COMPANY
Balance Sheet
December 31, 19x3

Assets

Current assets:

Cash......................		$ 30,900
Notes receivable..............		17,700
Accounts receivable...........	$91,435	
Less: Allowance for uncollecti-		
bles....................	2,120	89,315
Inventory of merchandise.......		87,415
Prepaid insurance.............		1,725
Other prepayments............		1,340
Total current assets.........		$228,395

Plant assets:

Land........................		16,000
Building and equipment........	45,800	
Less: Accumulated deprecia-		
tion....................	9,340	36,460
Total plant assets..........		52,460
Total assets.............		$280,855

Liabilities and Owners' Equity

Current liabilities:

Accounts payable..............	$ 19,775	
Salaries and wages payable.....	240	
Interest payable...............	400	
Total current liabilities......	20,415	

Long-term liability:

Mortgage payable..............	45,000	
Total liabilities...........		$65,415

Owners' equity:

Capital stock.................	150,000	
Retained earnings.............	65,440	
Total owners' equity......		215,440
Total liabilities and own-		
ers' equity...........		$280,855

Chapter 5

1.

STRONG CABINETS, INC.
Schedule of Manufacturing Costs and Cost of Goods Sold
For the Year Ended December 31, 19x2

Materials costs:		
Materials on hand, January 1, 19x2..........	$ 80,000	
Materials purchased.....................	400,000	
Cost of materials available for use..........	480,000	
Less: Materials on hand, December 31, 19x2 .	90,000	
Cost of materials used.................		$ 390,000
Factory labor cost..........................		450,000
Other factory costs:		
Depreciation.............................	16,000	
Rent....................................	84,000	
Miscellaneous	130,000	230,000
Total factory cost......................		1,070,000
Add: Work in process, January 1, 19x2		110,000
Total cost in production....................		1,180,000
Less: Work in process, December 31, 19x2.....		80,000
Cost of goods finished.....................		1,100,000
Add: Finished goods inventory, January 1, 19x2		70,000
Cost of goods available for sale		1,170,000
Less: Finished goods inventory, December 31,		
19x2....................................		120,000
Cost of goods sold...................		$1,050,000

2.

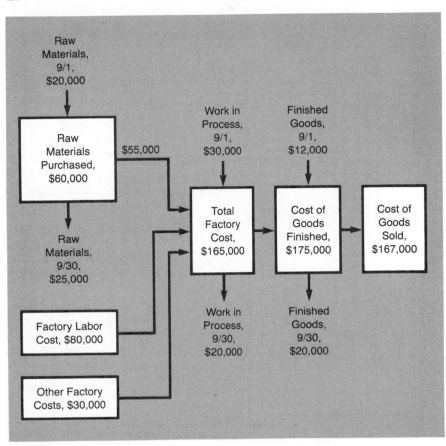

3. *a* and *c.*

Materials Inventory				Work in Process Inventory			
Bal. 9/1	20,000		55,000	Bal. 9/1	30,000		175,000
	60,000				55,000		
					80,000		
					30,000		
Bal. 9/30	25,000			Bal. 9/30	20,000		

Finished Goods Inventory				Cost of Goods Sold			
Bal. 9/1	12,000		167,000		167,000		
	175,000						
Bal. 9/30	20,000						

b. Materials Inventory............................... 60,000
    Accounts Payable.............................   60,000

Work in Process Inventory 55,000
    Materials Inventory............................   55,000

Work in Process Inventory 80,000
    Wages and Salaries Payable   80,000

Work in Process Inventory 30,000
    Accounts Payable, etc..........................   30,000

Finished Goods Inventory.......................... 175,000
    Work in Process Inventory......................   175,000

Cost of Goods Sold................................ 167,000
    Finished Goods Inventory   167,000

4. *a.*

KING MANUFACTURING COMPANY
Schedule of the Cost of Goods
Manufactured and Sold
For the Month Ended October 31, 19xx

Factory materials:
  Materials inventory, October 1 .... $11,650
  Purchases 4,500
  Materials available 16,150
  Materials inventory, October 31 8,900
    Materials issued 7,250
Factory labor......................... 5,100
Depreciation 400
Other factory costs.................... 1,820
Total factory cost..................... 14,570
Work in process, October 1 8,320
Total costs in production 22,890
Work in process, October 31 10,240
Cost of goods finished 12,650
Finished goods inventory, October 1...... 11,100
Cost of goods available................. 23,750
Finished goods inventory, October 31..... 9,250
    Cost of goods sold $14,500

b.

Materials Inventory				**Work in Process**		
Bal.	11,650	(2)	7,250	Bal.	8,320	(6)	12,650
(1)	4,500			(2)	7,250		
Bal.	8,900			(3)	5,100		
				(4)	400		
				(5)	1,820		
				Bal.	10,240		

Finished Goods					Accounts Receivable		
Bal.	11,100	(7)	14,500	Bal.	xxx		
(6)	12,650			(8)	19,350		
Bal.	9,250						

Accumulated Depreciation				Salaries and Wages Payable			
		Bal.	xxx			Bal.	xxx
		(4)	500			(3)	7,700

Accounts Payable				Cost of Goods Sold			
		Bal.	xxx	(7)	14,500		
		(1)	4,500				
		(5)	3,555				

Sales Revenues				Selling and Admin. Expenses			
		(8)	19,350	(3)	2,600		
				(4)	100		
				(5)	1,735		

c.

KING MANUFACTURING COMPANY
Income Statement
For the Month of October 19xx

Sales revenues		$19,350
Less: Cost of goods sold	$14,500	
Selling and administrative expenses.	4,435	18,935
Net income		$ 415

5. *a.* Production costs:

Materials	$290,000
Labor	140,000
Depreciation	15,000
Other	135,000
Total	$580,000

b.

Production costs (part *a*)	$580,000
Less: Ending work in process	115,000
Cost of goods finished	$465,000

c.

Cost of goods finished (part *b*)	$465,000
Add: Beginning finished goods inventory	5,000
Cost of goods available for sale.	470,000
Less: Ending finished goods inventory.	85,000
Cost of goods sold.	$385,000

d. Sales revenues $525,000
   Expenses:
       Cost of goods sold $385,000
       Selling and administrative salaries   59,000
       Depreciation on office equipment   2,000
       Other selling and administrative
           expenses   29,000
       Income taxes   24,000   499,000
   Net income . . . . $ 26,000

e. Retained earnings, beginning of month . . . . $ 40,000
   Add: Net income   26,000
   Less: Dividends declared . . . .   (35,000)
       Retained earnings, end of month . . . . $ 31,000

f. Purchases $360,000
   Less: Usage   290,000
   Inventory on hand . . . . $ 70,000

Chapter 6   **1.** *a.* Present value of outlay . . . .   −$ 35,000
              Present value of receipts: 0.3220 × $100,000 = ...   +   32,200
                  Net present value . . . .   −$ 2,800

          b. Present value of 1/1/x1 outlay . . . .   −$ 80,000
              Present value of 1/1/x6 outlay: 0.5674 × $20,000 . . . .   −   11,348
              Present value of receipt of $10,000 per period for six peri-
                  ods: 4.1114 × $10,000 . . . .   +   41,114
              Present value of receipt of $20,000 per period for 10 peri-
                  ods starting six periods hence: (6.9740 − 4.1114) ×
                  $20,000 . . . .   +   57,252
                  Net present value . . . .   +$ 7,018

          c. Present value of 1/1/x1 outlay: 1.0000 × $20,000 . . . .   −$ 20,000
              Present value of next 10 outlays: 5.6502 × $20,000 . . . . .   − 113,004
              Present value of receipt: 0.2567 × $250,000 (*n* = 12) . . .   +   64,175
                  Net present value . . . .   −$ 68,829

       2. *a.* Table 2, $r = 0.10$, $n = 5$ 3.7908

$$\text{Annual payment} = \frac{\$1,000,000}{3.7098} = \$263,796.56$$

b.

Year	Payment of Interest*	Total Payment	Repayment of Borrowing	Amount Owed, End of Year†
1	$100,000.00	$263,796.56	$163,796.56	$836,203.44
2	83,620.34	263,796.56	180,176.22	656,027.22
3	65,602.72	263,796.56	198,193.84	457,833.38
4	45,783.34	263,796.56	218,013.22	239,820.16
5	23,982.02	263,796.56	239,814.54	5.62‡

* 10% of amount owed, end of previous year.
† Amount owed, beginning of year, minus payment this year.
‡ Rounding error. This can be eliminated by using the formula at the top of Table 2 to derive a multiplier of 3.7907868 and an annual payment of $263,797.48.

c. Table 2, $r = 0.05$, $n = 10$ 7.7217

$$\text{Semiannual payment} = \frac{\$1,000,000}{7.7217} = \$129,505.16$$

This is less than half the annual payment in part *a* because the amount borrowed gets repaid more rapidly.

d. Table 2, $r = 0.10$, $n = 5$ 3.7908

$$\text{Amount borrowed} = 3.7908 \times \$200,000 = \$758,160$$

3. *a.*

July 1, 19x7 payment....................		$16,000.00
Next four payments.....................	$15,000	
Table 2, $r = 0.05$, $n = 4$	×3.5460	53,190.00
Last five payments......................	4,000	
Table 2, $r = 0.05$, $n = 5$	×4.3295	
Present value at 7/1/x8	17,318	
Table 1, $r = 0.05$, $n = 4$	×0.8227	14,247.52
Present value at 7/1/x7 (cost of the equipment)................		$83,437.52

b.

Balance, 7/1/x7 ($83,437.52 − $16,000)		$67,437.52
Interest rate per quarter: 0.20/4	×	0.05
Interest expense, 7/1/x7 − 9/30/x7		3,371.88
Payment, 10/1/x7...............................		(15,000.00)
Loan reduction, 10/1/x7...........................		(11,628.12)
Loan balance, 7/1/x7		67,438.00
Loan balance, 10/1/x7 − 12/31/x7..................		55,809.40
Interest rate per quarter..........................	×	0.05
Interest expense, 10/1/x7 − 12/31/x7		$ 2,790.47

Total interest expense, 19x7:		
7/1/x7 − 9/30/x7................................		$ 3,371.88
10/1/x7 − 12/31/x7..............................		2,790.47
Total		$ 6,162.35

4. *a.* Table 2, *r* = 0.07, *n* = 50

	13.8007	
	× $600,000	$ 8,280,420
Table 1, *r* = 0.07, *n* = 1	0.9346	
	×$5,000,000	4,673,000
		$12,953,420

b. Table 2, *r* = 0.14, *n* = 25

	6.8729	
	×$1,200,000	8,247,480
Table 1, *r* = 0.14, *n* = 1	0.8772	
	×$5,000,000	4,386,000
		$12,633,480

c. Initial payment

		$ 1,200,000
Table 2, *r* = 0.14, *n* = 24	6.8351	
	×$1,200,000	8,202,120
Table 1, *r* = 0.14, *n* = 1	0.8772	
	×$5,000,000	4,386,000
Total		$13,788,120

5. *a.*

Year	Cash Flow	Multiplier (Table 1)	Present Value
1	$150,000	0.8929	$133,935
2	230,000	0.7972	183,356
Total			$317,291

b.

0	$150,000	1.0000	$150,000
1	230,000	0.8929	205,367
Total			$355,367

c. Income = $355,367 − $317,291 = $38,076.
(This can also be obtained, with a $1 rounding error, by taking 12 percent of $317,291 = $38,075.)

d.

Present value, end of year 2.........................	$230,000
Present value, beginning of year 2	205,367
Income, year 2	$ 24,633

e. The richer opportunity elsewhere reduces the value of this asset slightly without changing the future cash flows. These cash flows then provide a greater annual income because they start from a smaller present-value base.

Year	Cash Flow	Beginning of Year 1		Beginning of Year 2	
		Multiplier (Table 1)	Present Value	Multiplier (Table 1)	Present Value
1........	$150,000	0.8696	$130,440	1.0000	$150,000
2........	230,000	0.7561	173,903	0.8696	200,008
Total ...			$304,343		$350,008

Income = $350,008 − $304,343 = $45,665 in year 1.
Income = $230,000 − $200,008 = $29,992 in year 2.

Chapter 7

1. *a.* We start with two basic calculations:
   1. The profit on a unit is $25 − $12 − $6 = $7.
   2. The inventory should be listed at sale price less future selling costs, $25 − $6 = $19.

   Effect of producing one unit:
     Cash decreased by $12.
     Inventory increased by $19.
     Owners' equity increased by $7.

   Effect of shipping one unit:
     Cash decreased by $6.
     Inventory decreased by $19.
     Receivables increased by $25.

   Effect of collecting $25:
     Cash increased by $25.
     Receivables decreased by $25.

   b.

	First Year	Second Year
Revenue	$1,500,000	$1,875,000
Cost of goods sold	720,000	900,000
Selling expense...........	360,000	450,000
Administrative expense.....	200,000	200,000
Net income............	$ 220,000	$ 325,000

2. *a.*

Gross revenues..............		$500,000
Bad debts		10,000
Net revenue................		490,000
Manufacturing costs		350,000
Gross margin		140,000
Other expenses:		
Selling	$80,000	
Administrative............	50,000	130,000
Income before taxes.........		$ 10,000

b. Inventory would be reported at $4.90 a unit, a total of $49,000.

    c. Gross margin on a delivery basis would be 90,000 units × ($5.00 − $0.10 − $3.50) = $126,000. The company, therefore, would report a $4,000 *loss* before income taxes.

    d. Inventory would be reported at $3.50 a unit (average manufacturing cost), or $35,000 total. This is $14,000 less than the amount reported under the production basis.

Note: information on depreciation and production payments would be relevant if you had been asked to calculate the cash flow; it has no bearing on the measurement of income in an accrual-basis accounting system.

3. *a.* The gross value of this shipment is $1 million plus the present value of the second $1 million. From Table 1 in Appendix A, we find that the present value of $1 one year later at 12 percent is 0.8929. Revenue therefore is $1,000,000 + $892,900 = $1,892,900.

    b. The $892,900 should have appeared as a current account receivable. An equivalent solution would have been to report a gross receivable of $1 million, less an allowance for unearned interest of $1,000,000 − $892,900 = $107,100. The net receivable in either case would be shown as $892,900.

Chapter 8   **1.** *a.*

Year	LIFO Cost Goods Sold	LIFO Ending Inventory	
19x1	55,000 × $3.10 = $170,500	10,000 × $3.00 = $ 30,000	
		5,000 × 3.10 = 15,500	
		$ 45,500	
19x2	68,000 × $3.50 = $238,000	10,000 × $3.00 = $ 30,000	
		5,000 × 3.10 = 15,500	
		2,000 × 3.50 = 7,000	
		$ 52,500	
19x3	80,000 × $3.75 = $300,000	10,000 × $3.00 = $ 30,000	
		5,000 × 3.10 = 15,500	
		2,000 × 3.50 = 7,000	
		10,000 × 3.75 = 37,500	
		$ 90,000	
19x4	70,000 × $3.80 = $266,000	10,000 × $3.00 = $ 30,000	
	2,000 × 3.75 = 7,500	5,000 × 3.10 = 15,500	
	$273,500	2,000 × 3.50 = 7,000	
		8,000 × 3.75 = 30,000	
		$ 82,500	

Year	FIFO Cost of Goods Sold	FIFO Ending Inventory
19x5	75,000 × $4.00 = $300,000	10,000 × $3.00 = $ 30,000
		5,000 × 3.10 = 15,500
		2,000 × 3.50 = 7,000
		8,000 × 3.75 = 30,000
		5,000 × 4.00 = 20,000
		$102,500
19x6	70,000 × $4.25 = $297,500	10,000 × $3.00 = $ 30,000
	5,000 × 4.00 = 20,000	5,000 × 3.10 = 15,500
	5,000 × 3.75 = 18,750	2,000 × 3.50 = 7,000
	$336,250	3,000 × 3.75 = 11,250
		$ 63,750
19x7	85,000 × $4.40 = $374,000	10,000 × $3.00 = $ 30,000
		5,000 × 3.10 = 15,500
		2,000 × 3.50 = 7,000
		3,000 × 3.75 = 11,250
		15,000 × 4.40 = 66,000
		$129,750
19x8	95,000 × $4.50 = $427,500	(Same as 19x7) = $129,750

b.

Year	FIFO Cost of Goods Sold	FIFO Ending Inventory
19x1	10,000 × $3.00 = $ 30,000	15,000 × $3.10 = $ 46,500
	45,000 × 3.10 = 139,500	
	$169,500	
19x2	15,000 × $3.10 = $ 46,500	17,000 × $3.50 = $ 59,500
	53,000 × 3.50 = 185,500	
	$232,000	
19x3	17,000 × $3.50 = $ 59,500	27,000 × $3.75 = $101,250
	63,000 × 3.75 = 236,250	
	$295,750	
19x4	27,000 × $3.75 = $101,250	25,000 × $3.80 = $ 95,000
	45,000 × 3.80 = 171,000	
	$272,250	
19x5	25,000 × $3.80 = $ 95,000	30,000 × $4.00 = $120,000
	50,000 × 4.00 = 200,000	
	$295,000	
19x6	30,000 × $4.00 = $120,000	20,000 × $4.25 = $ 85,000
	50,000 × 4.25 = 212,500	
	$332,500	

19x7 . . . . .   20,000 × $4.25 = $ 85,000   35,000 × $4.40 = $154,000
                 65,000 ×   4.40 =   286,000
                                   $371,000

19x8 . . . . .   35,000 × $4.40 = $154,000   35,000 × $4.50 = $157,500
                 60,000 ×   4.50 =   270,000
                                   $424,000

2. *a* and *b.* Inventory, January 1   0
       Purchases . . . .   8,500 units, $29,840
       Sales . . . .   6,000 units
       Inventory, December 31 . . . . .   2,500 units

	FIFO	LIFO
Inventory, December 31:		
(1,800 × $4.05) + (700 × $4)	$10,090	
(1,000 × $3.00) + (1,500 × $3.25)		$ 7,875
Cost of goods sold:		
Purchases ($29,840) − 12/31 inventory	19,750	21,965
Gross margin:		
Sales ($30,000) − Cost of goods sold	10,250	8,035

 c. LIFO would reduce income before taxes by $2,215 ($10,250 − $8,035) and net income by $1,661.25 [$2,215 × (1.0 − 0.25)]; it would increase cash flow by $553.75 ($2,215 × 0.25).

3. *a.* Item by item:

	Lower of Cost or Market	
Product	Per Unit	Total
A	$ 8	$ 80,000
B	15	300,000
C	20	600,000
D	8	320,000
Total		$1,300,000

Pooled inventory:

Product	Total Cost	Total Market
A	$ 100,000	$ 80,000
B	300,000	320,000
C	600,000	690,000
D	400,000	320,000
Total	$1,400,000	$1,410,000

Lower of cost or market is $1,400,000.

 b. The pooled-inventory approach increases the net income by $100,000 ($1,400,000 − $1,300,000).

c. The answer depends on what the financial statements are intended to convey. The item-by-item method is the most "conservative" and should be used if the objective is to have the balance sheet show the smallest inventory total consistent with the accrual basis of accounting. The pooled-inventory method should be used if the objective of the lower-of-cost-or-market rule is simply to protect investors against an overstatement of the amount recoverable from inventories as a whole. Finally, if the objective is to produce an inventory amount that best predicts future cash flows, the answer will depend on which amount is more likely to be related to this quantity.

4. *a.*

	FIFO		LIFO	
	Tons	**Cost**	**Tons**	**Cost**
Inventory, 1/1/x2 ..	15,000	$ 1,875,000	15,000	$ 1,875,000
Purchases, 19x2 ..	100,000	13,000,000	100,000	13,000,000
Goods available....	115,000	14,875,000	115,000	14,875,000
Inventory, 12/31/x2........	20,000	2,700,000	15,000	1,875,000
			5,000	650,000
			20,000	2,525,000
Cost of goods sold	95,000	$12,175,000	95,000	$12,350,000
Inventory, 1/1/x3 ..	20,000	$ 2,700,000	20,000	$ 2,525,000
Purchases, 19x3 ..	90,000	12,600,000	90,000	12,600,000
Goods available....	110,000	15,300,000	110,000	15,125,000
Inventory, 12/31/x3........	5,000	700,000	5,000	625,000
Cost of goods sold	105,000	$14,600,000	105,000	$14,500,000

b. The involuntary liquidation increased reported income before taxes by $150,000. The liquidation amounted to 15,000 tons, but the first 5,000 of these were liquidated voluntarily. The involuntary part of the liquidation caused the transfer from the LIFO inventory of 10,000 tons at $125. The effect on reported income was:

10,000 tons at current prices of $140	$1,400,000
10,000 tons at inventory price of $125	1,250,000
Net effect on reported income............	$ 150,000

c. The effect is to increase the cost of the inventory by $200,000 over the level that would have prevailed if there had been no involuntary liquidation:

Base quantity, 5,000 tons.................. $ 625,000
19x4 layer, 10,000 tons................... 1,450,000

Total 2,075,000
LIFO cost of 15,000 tons, 12/31/x2 1,875,000

Net effect on inventory .... $ 200,000

d.

	Pretax Income Difference	Tax Effect at 50%	
19x2............	$175,000	$87,500	FIFO pays more tax
19x3	(100,000)	(50,000)	LIFO pays more tax
19x4............	25,000*	12,500	FIFO pays more tax

* Calculation:	FIFO	LIFO
Beginning inventory...............................	$ 700,000	$ 625,000
Purchases...	14,500,000	14,500,000
Goods available...................................	15,200,000	15,125,000
Ending inventory..................................	2,175,000	2,075,000
Cost of goods sold................................	$13,025,000	$13,050,000

5. *a.* Goods on hand at time of price increase: 11 units
Price increase: $90 − $85 = $5 a unit
Holding gain arising during 19x3: 11 units × $5 = $55

b,c,d.

	FIFO Cost	LIFO Cost	Current Cost
Cost of goods available:			
Beginning inventory	$ 525	$ 380	$ 595
Purchases (13 × $85)	1,105	1,105	1,105
Holding gain (11 × $5)			55
Cost of goods available...........	1,630	1,485	1,755
Cost of ending inventory:			
FIFO (6 × $85)	510		
LIFO (4 × $50 + 2 × $60)...........		320	
Current cost (6 × $90)			540
Cost of goods sold	1,120	1,165	1,215
Sales revenue (14 × $100)...........	1,400	1,400	1,400
Gross margin.......................	280	235	185
Holding gain			55
Net income........................	$ 280	$ 235	$ 240

e and *f.*
Inventory, January 1, 19x3:

Current cost.....................	$ 595	$ 595
Reported cost	525	380
Unrealized holding gain	70	215
Holding gain for the year............	55	55
Holding gains available	125	270
Unrealized holding gains:		
FIFO: 6 × ($90 − $85)..............	30	
LIFO: 6 × $90 − $320..............		220
Realized holding gains*..............	$ 95	$ 50

* Alternative calculation:

Current cost of goods sold	$1,215	$1,215
Reported cost of goods sold..................	1,120	1,165
Realized holding gains	$ 95	$ 50

g. In both FIFO-cost and LIFO-cost balance sheets, the inventory asset and the retained earnings component of owners' equity are understated by the amount of the unrealized holding gain, if current cost is taken as the measurement benchmark.

h. When prices are rising sharply and the volume of sales relative to the size of the inventory is low, as in this case, a large proportion of the FIFO cost of goods sold will be measured at prior-year prices, giving rise to the realization of holding gains. Under LIFO, in contrast, even when a liquidation takes place, most of the cost of goods sold will be measured at current prices and the realized holding gains will be smaller.

i. A $30 holding loss was realized (included in reported income) in 19x2 because the LIFO method moved some units to the income statement at the late-in-the-year price ($85) even though these units were sold when the current cost was only $75. This didn't happen in 19x3, however. Instead, the LIFO cost of goods sold included four units at $85 and one unit at $60 when the current cost of goods sold was *higher,* $90. Each of these had the effect of a *liquidation,* bringing older, lower unit costs into the income statement. The realized holding gain on the final five units sold was:

$$4 \times (\$90 - \$85) = \$20$$
$$1 \times (\$90 - \$60) = \underline{30}$$
$$\text{Total} \ldots\ldots\ldots \underline{\underline{\$50}}$$

6. *a.* Current cost of goods sold:

January 1–May 15, 55,000 × $2	$110,000
May 16–December 31, 35,000 × $2.20	77,000
Total	$187,000
Current-cost, ending inventory, 60,000 × $2.20	$132,000

    b. Holding gain:

        Inventory on May 16: 50,000 − 15,000 = 35,000 units.
        Price increase: 20 cents a unit.
        Holding gain = 35,000 × $0.20 = $7,000.

    c. Current-cost margin:

Revenues:

January 1–May 15, 55,000 × $3	$165,000
May 16–December 31, 35,000 × $3.10	108,500
Total	273,500
Cost of goods sold (from part a)	187,000
Current-cost margin	$ 86,500

7. *a.*

Current cost of goods sold (as in problem 6)	$187,000
Inventory holding gain	0
Current-cost margin (as in 6)	86,500

    b. The conclusion is that Company A benefited by having an inventory position when prices went up. Company B had to rely entirely on its merchandising operations to generate income. The purpose of this question is to emphasize a very simple point which is often overlooked: Companies without inventories have no inventory holding gains and losses, no matter what inventory-costing method is used.

8. *a.*

	Units	Cost
Beginning inventory	50,000	$ 97,500
Purchases:		
January 1–May 15	40,000	80,000
May 16–December 31	60,000	132,000
Goods available	150,000	309,500
Ending inventory	60,000	132,000
Cost of goods sold	90,000	$177,500

    b.

	January 1	December 31
Current cost of inventory (from problem 6)	$100,000	$132,000
FIFO cost of inventory (from part a)	97,500	132,000
Unrealized holding gain	$ 2,500	$ —

c. Inventory holding gain included in net income:

Current cost of goods sold (from problem 6) $187,000
FIFO cost of goods sold (from part a).   177,500
  Inventory profit. . . . . $ 9,500

This $9,500 is the sum of the $7,000 holding gain for the year (problem 6, part *b*) and the $2,500 change in the unrealized holding gain between the beginning and end of the year (problem 8, part *b*). It is included in gross margin and is not identified separately in the income statement.

Chapter 9

1. *a.* Straight-line depreciation:
Depreciable cost = $30,000 − $1,500 = $28,500.
Rate = 1/5 = 20%.
Depreciation = 20% × $28,500 = $5,700 a year.

b and *c.*

	DDB Depreciation		**SYD Depreciation**	
Year	**Beginning Balance**	**Depreciation at 40%**	**Fraction of Depreciable Cost**	**Depreciation**
1	$30,000	$12,000	5/15	$9,500
2	18,000	7,200	4/15	7,600
3	10,800	4,320	3/15	5,700
4	6,480	2,592	2/15	3,800
5	3,888	1,555	1/15	1,900

d. Implicit-interest depreciation:

Year	**Beginning Book Value**	**Cash Flow**	**Imputed Interest @ 10%**	**Depreciation**
1	$30,000	$7,668	$3,000	$4,668
2	25,332	7,668	2,533	5,135
3	20,197	7,668	2,020	5,648
4	14,549	7,668	1,455	6,213
5	8,336	7,668	834	6,834

2.

	Each Machine	**All Machines**
Asset cost:		
Purchase price.	$16,250	$ 97,500
Freight.	700	4,200
Handling	200	1,200
Installation:		
Labor.	800	4,800
Materials	100	600
Total.	$18,050	$108,300

If the bookkeeping system is loosely designed, the installation materials and perhaps even some of the installation labor might be expensed. In theory, though, they should be capitalized.

3. *a.* Original cost.. $50,000
     Accumulated depreciation 4 × $2,500   10,000
       Book value $40,000

  b. Equipment... 6,000
       Cash...   6,000

  c. Depreciation Expense.................................. 2,875
     Accumulated Depreciation..........................   2,875

The life of the machine wasn't extended, and the $40,000 + $6,000 = $46,000 book value had to be depreciated during the remaining 16 years of the asset's expected useful life.

  d. Original cost: $50,000 + $6,000 .... $56,000
     Accumulated depreciation:
       4 × $2,500 .... $10,000
       12 × $2,875 34,500
       Overhaul............................... (12,000)   32,500
       Book value............................. $23,500

Depreciation = $23,500/9 = $2,611 a year.

4. *a.* The conventional answer here is that an accelerated depreciation formula should be used, because cash flows are likely to decline rapidly as the textbook ages. If the time value of money is considered, an argument can be made for implicit-interest depreciation, but with sharply declining cash flows, this could be approximated by a diminishing-charge method or possibly by straight-line.

  b. If we look at textbook A only, the accelerated methods will lead to lower reported income in the first two years and higher reported income in the last two years than straight-line depreciation would show. If we look at *all* the company's textbooks as a group, however, the effect of the choice depends on the rate of growth. If the company is growing, accelerated depreciation would reduce reported income in all years, unless the company stopped bringing out new textbooks in any quantity for a year or two. The assets' book value would be greater under straight-line depreciation than under any accelerated method.

5. *a.*

Year of Purchase	Historical Book Value	Multiplier	Replacement Cost
19x0	$ 60,000	180/100	$108,000
19x2	24,000	180/110	39,273
19x5	44,000	180/150	52,800
Total	$128,000		200,073

Less: Historical cost 128,000

Unrealized holding gain .... $ 72,073

b.

Year of Purchase	Historical Cost Depreciation	Multiplier	Replacement-Cost Depreciation
19x0	$10,000	190/100	$19,000
19x2	3,000	190/110	5,182
19x3	4,000	190/150	5,067
Total	$17,000		$29,249

c. Realized holding gain = $29,249 − $17,000 = $12,249. The historical-cost income statement classifies the $12,249 realized holding gain as an *undisclosed* component of operating income. The current-cost income statement excludes this amount (because it actually arose in previous years), but reports the entire 19x9 holding gain (part *e*'s $20,691) on a separate line.

d.

Year of Purchase	Historical Book Value	Multiplier	Replacement Cost
19x0	$ 50,000	200/100	$100,000
19x2	21,000	200/110	38,182
19x5	40,000	200/150	53,333
Total	$111,000		191,515

Less: Historical cost 111,000

Unrealized holding gain .... $ 80,515

e. Realized holding gain (part *c*) $12,249

Increase in unrealized holding gain:

December 31 (part *d*).................... $80,515

January 1 (part *a*)........................ 72,073   8,442

Total holding gain $20,691

Chapter 10

1. *a.* The face value is $1 million, the payments each year will be $120,000, and the amount paid equals the present value of the future payments using a yield-to-maturity rate of 14 percent, or 7 percent every six months, compounded semiannually.

   b. $866,700, because the price must be less than the maturity value to produce a yield in excess of the coupon rate.

   c. The term is 20 years (the multiplier of 86.67 is found in the 20-year column, 14.0 percent row of Table 6).

   d. Interest expense = 14%/2 × $866,700 = $60,669.

Interest Expense....................................	60,669	
Cash..		60,000
Discount on Bonds..............................		669

   e. Outstanding loan balance = $866,700 + $669 = $867,369.
   Interest expense = 14%/2 × $867,369 = $60,716.

Interest Expense....................................	60,716	
Cash..		60,000
Discount on Bonds..............................		716

   f.
Bonds payable, maturity value	$1,000,000
Less: Unamortized bond discount	131,915
Liability to bondholders	$ 868,085

2. *a.*
Income before depreciation and taxes		$6,000,000
Depreciation.........................		850,000
Income after depreciation..............		5,150,000
Income tax: Current ($4,750,000* × 50%)..	$2,375,000	
Deferred ($5,150,000 × 50% −		
$2,375,000)..............	200,000	2,575,000
Net income..........................		$2,575,000

   * Current taxable income = $6,000,000 − $1,250,000 = $4,750,000.

   b.
Depreciation Expense	850,000	
Accumulated Depreciation....................		850,000
Income Tax Expense...........................	2,575,000	
Income Taxes Payable		2,375,000
Deferred Income Taxes		200,000

3. *a.*
Amount of each deferred payment....................	$ 4,000
Present value multiplier (Appendix A, Table 2,	
r = 0.12, *n* = 4).................................	× 3.0373
Liability	12,149
Cash paid immediately.................................	4,000
Asset..	$16,149

b. Depreciation expense: $16,149/5 .... $3,230
   Interest expense: 0.12 × $12,149 1,458

   Total $4,688

c. Book value of asset: $16,149 − $3,230 .... $12,919
   Book value of liability: $12,149 − ($4,000 − $1,458) .... $ 9,607

Note: In practice, this method would be used only if the lease qualified as a *capital lease* which occurs only when the "lease transfers substantially all of the benefits and risks incident to ownership."

4. a. Although this can be solved by using the mathematical formula, Table 2 in Appendix A makes it simpler:

   P = A × multiplier: $100,000 = A × 3.4331
                              A = $29,128 a year.

b.

Year	Interest	Loan Reduction	End-of-Year Balance
1	$14,000	$15,128	$84,872
2	11,882	17,246	67,626
3	9,468	19,660	47,966
4	6,715	22,413	25,553
5	3,577	25,551	0

c. Cash 100,000
     Notes Payable 100,000

   Interest Expense 14,000
   Notes Payable 15,128
     Cash 29,128

5. a. This is a three-year annuity of 30 × $100 = $3,000.
     Its present value two years from now is 2.5771 × $3,000 = $7,731.30.
     Its present value now is 0.8573 × $7,731.30 = $6,628.04.
   b. Amortization is a two-year annuity equivalent to $6,628.04.

   Annuity = $6,628.04/1.7833 = $3,716.73

   c. Pension expense:

   Amortization of past service cost $3,716.73
   Current service cost:
     Present value, one year from end of this year, of
     three-year annuity of $100; 2.5771 × $100 = $257.71
     Present value, end of this year: 0.9259 × $257.71 = .. 238.61

   Total pension cost $3,955.34

Chapter 11

1. *a.* Shares issued: par value $160,000 (160,000 × $1).
Additional paid-in capital $480,000 [160,000 × ($4 − $1)].
Added to retained earnings: $441,600 − $0.20 × 960,000 = $249,600.
The owners' equity at December 31, 19x1:

Common stock, 960,000 shares.......	$ 960,000
Additional paid-in capital	780,000
Retained earnings	749,600
Total	$2,489,600

b. The book value of the common equity wasn't diluted because the new shares were issued at $4, whereas the book value of the earlier shares was only $2 ($1.6 million/800,000 shares). The market value *may* have been diluted, if investors estimated that the company's return on the $4 was likely to be less than the return each previous share had been expected to earn before the new issue was offered for sale.

2. Retained earnings would decrease by $30,000, the total par value of the common stock would increase by $10,000, and additional paid-in capital would increase by $20,000.

3. *Purchase of treasury stock:* decreased cash by $3,000 and decreased owners' equity by $3,000. It is classified temporarily as a negative component of the owners' equity.

Dividend declaration: decreased retained earnings by $0.30 × 99,900 = $29,970; increased the liability, dividends payable, by this same amount.

Dividend payment: decreased both the asset, cash, and the liability, dividends payable, by $29,970.

Sale of treasury stock: increased cash by $4,000 and increased owners' equity by this amount, canceling the $3,000 negative component and adding $1,000 to additional paid-in capital.

4. *a.* Income available for common stock = $312,000 − $50,000 = $262,000. Primary earnings per share = $262,000/100,000 = $2.62.
b. Equivalent common shares = 100,000 + 2 × 10,000 = 120,000. Fully diluted earnings per share = $312,000/120,000 = $2.60.

Chapter 12

1. *a.* Cantara's ownership interest in Denby was large enough to require the use of the equity method. Cantara therefore should include 25 percent of $30,000 = $7,500 in its reported income for 19x1.
b. Cantara's investment can be calculated as follows:

Purchase price (2,500 × $30)............................	$75,000
Equity in 19x1 retained earnings* (2,500 × $1.40).........	3,500
Total..	$78,500

* Equity in net income: ¼ × $30,000..	$7,500
Less: Dividends received: 2,500 shares × $1.60...........................	4,000
Equity in retained earnings	$3,500

2. *a.*

Purchase price.............................		$ 92,000
Essex's owners' equity	$110,000	
Pilot's percentage	×80%	
Book value acquired		88,000
Goodwill		$ 4,000

b.

Essex's owners' equity	$110,000
Minority percentage.......................	×20%
Minority interest.........................	$ 22,000

3. *a.* The problem is to find the yield rate that a market price of $87,590 would provide on bonds with $100,000 face value—which translates into $87.59 for a bond with $100 face value. The yield rate is found by consulting Table 6 of Appendix A, which shows the yield rates of 12 percent bonds at various prices and maturities. Durant's bonds had 15 years to maturity at the time of purchase, so the answer is in the 15-year column of Table 6. The $87.59 price is found in the 14.0 percent row of the 15-year column. The anticipated yield to maturity therefore was 14 percent.

b.

Investments	87,590	
Cash		87,590

c. Carrying the calculations to the nearest dollar produces the following amounts:

June 30: 14%/2 × $87,590.............	$ 6,131
December 31: 14%/2 × $87,721*	6,140
Total interest revenue	$12,271

* $87,590 + $131 amortization of bond discount ($6,131 − 12%/2 × $100,000).

d. Table 6 in Appendix A indicates that the market value of a 12 percent, $100 bond 10 years from maturity when the yield rate is 15 percent is $84.71, and $89.41 when the yield is 14 percent. The proceeds therefore were $84,710, and the loss was $4,700 ($89,410 − $84,710).

e.

Cash...	84,710	
Loss on Sale of Investment........................	4,700	
Investments		89,410

4. *a.* Present value of cash flows = $15,000/0.10 = $150,000
Book value of net assets   100,000
    Unrecognized goodwill . . . . $ 50,000

b. When Barth acquired the tangible assets of Bolton, it is supposed to record these assets at their *fair value,* often based on an appraisal. It should recognize $145,000 − $125,000 = $20,000 as the cost of purchased goodwill.

5. *a.* The amount payable by Alcon has no effect on consolidated net income. The eliminating entry is:

Accounts Payable 35,000
    Accounts Receivable   35,000

The investment income represents dividends paid by Nonon during the year. Since this will be replaced on the consolidated income statement by Nonon's revenues and expenses, and since the dividends weren't paid to outsiders and therefore don't belong on a consolidated statement, the following elimination is appropriate:

Investment Income 50,000
    Dividends Declared   50,000

Sales revenue is overstated by $250,000, inventory is overstated by $30,000, and the cost of goods sold is overstated by $220,000. (The actual cost of goods sold was $180,000 − $70,000 = $110,000. Alcon showed a cost of goods sold of $250,000 − $100,000 = $150,000, and Nonon showed a cost of goods sold of $180,000, a total of $330,000. The difference between these two totals is $220,000.) The entry is:

Sales Revenues 250,000
    Inventory   30,000
    Cost of Goods Sold   220,000

b.
ALCON CORPORATION AND SUBSIDIARY
Consolidated Income Statement
For the Year Ended December 31, 19x1

Sales revenues	$5,750,000
Cost of goods sold	3,480,000
Gross margin	2,270,000
Other expenses	1,700,000
Net income	$ 570,000

6. *a.*

Company X income as reported................		$55,000
Less: Dividends received (0.8 × $10,000)........		8,000
Operating income		47,000
Add: Equity in Company Y's income:		
Company Y dividends	$10,000	
Increase in Y's retained earnings............	5,000	
Company Y's income......................	15,000	
Company X's interest.....................	×80%	12,000
Net income................................		$59,000

b. $80,000 + 12,000 − $8,000 = $84,000.

c.

Company X..	$ 47,000
Company Y..	15,000
Combined income..................................	62,000
Minority interest (0.2 × $15,000)	3,000
Consolidated net income	$ 59,000

d.

Company Y owners' equity..........................	$105,000
Minority percentage	×20%
Minority interest..................................	$ 21,000

Chapter 13

1. *a.* Transactions were:

Purchases of plant and equipment for $1,700.

Sale of plant and equipment for $300.

Depreciation of $900.

b. To be added back to net income to derive cash flow from operations:

Depreciation, $900.

Loss on retirements, $400.

To be listed with other sources of cash:

Sale of plant and equipment, $300.

To be listed as a use of cash:

Purchase of plant and equipment, $1,700.

2. Sources of cash:
   Operations:

Net income...........................	$ 8,243	
Add: Depreciation	5,501	
Decrease in inventory	1,486	
Increase in accruals payable...........	4,296	
Increase in taxes payable	4,534	
Deferred taxes ($4,899 − $4,362)	537	
Less: Increase in accounts receivable	(17,331)	
Decrease in accounts payable.........	(2,468)	
Cash flow from operations.................	4,798	
Issue common shares (A)....................	12,047	
Sale of plant assets (B)	83	
Issue bonds	7,000	$23,928

Uses of cash:

Preferred dividends.........................	80	
Retire preferred stock ($1,347 − $1,123) + $37 .	261	
Purchase plant assets.....................	18,082	
Purchase marketable securities	1,005	19,428
Increase in cash		$ 4,500

(A)	Change in common stock.................		$ 175
	Change in additional paid-in capital	$11,835	
	Add: Retirement of preferred stock	37	11,872
	Proceeds from issuance of common		$12,047

(B)	Change in plant assets	$17,682	
	Purchase...............................	18,082	
	Cost of sold asset		$ 400
	Change in accumulated depreciation	5,184	
	Depreciation expense	5,501	
	Debit due to sale		317
	Book value of sold asset		$ 83

3.

	Income Statement	Noncash Elements	Cash Flow
Revenues/collections:			
Cash sales (0.3 × $325,400)	$ 97,620		$ 97,620
Credit sales/collections:			
Credit sales (0.7 × $325,400). . . .	227,780		227,780
Less: Bad debts	(4,100)*	$(3,800)*	(300)
Add: Decrease in accounts receivable		14,300	14,300
Net collections from credit sales			241,780
Net sales/collections	321,300		339,400
Equity in Wilson Corporation's earnings	12,000	12,000	—
Net revenues/collections . .	333,300		339,400
Expenses/payments:			
Cost of goods sold	178,600		
Add: Increase in inventory		5,400†	
Less: Increase in accounts payable		(11,300)	
Payments to suppliers			172,700
Salaries expense	68,800		
Add: Decrease in salaries payable		4,100	
Payments to employees			72,900
Depreciation expense	14,900	14,900	—
Insurance expense	1,000		
Add: Increase in prepaid insurance		1,400	
Payments for insurance			2,400
Research and development	2,500		2,500
Patent amortization	1,800	1,800	—
Interest expense	21,300		
Add: Bond premium amortization		2,700	
Interest payments			24,000
Income tax expense	16,300		
Less: Deferred portion		3,100	
Change in current taxes payable		0	
Income tax payments			13,200
Total expenses/operating cash payments	305,200		287,700
Net income/cash flow from operations	$ 28,100		$ 51,700

* With no write-offs, collections would have been equal to credit sales plus the decrease in gross receivables. Part of the $14,300 decrease in gross receivables, however, was due to write-offs of specific accounts. The company provided $4,100 for bad debts, but the increase in the allowance for uncollectibles was only $3,800. The write-off of gross receivables therefore was the remaining $300 ($4,100 − $3,800).

† Purchases = Cost of goods sold + Increase in inventory = $178,600 + $5,400 = $184,000.

4. 1. $7,000 use
2. $24,000 source and $3,000 add-back to income
3. $10,000 source
4. $6,500 source and $6,500 use
5. $7,000 source and $17,000 use
6. $2,200 add-back to income
7. $265,000 source
8. $4,500 source and $4,000 use
9. $2,400 subtraction from income*
10. $20,000 source and $300 add-back to income

* "Decreases in accounts payable" is a subtract-from adjustment to income.

Chapter 14

1. *a.*

Current cost, December 31, 19x10	$27,000
Current cost, December 31, 19x9	23,000
Nominal holding gain	$ 4,000

Current cost, December 31, 19x10		$27,000
Current cost, December 31, 19x9	$23,000	
Inflation multiplier	× 225/198	26,136
Real holding gain		$ 864

Current cost, December 31, 19x11	$30,000
Current cost, December 31, 19x10	27,000
Nominal holding gain	$ 3,000

Current cost, December 31, 19x11		$30,000
Current cost, December 31, 19x10	$27,000	
Inflation multiplier	× 270/225	32,400
Real holding loss		$ 2,400

2. *a.*

	January 1	December 31
Cash	$10	$15
Accounts receivable	20	40
Total monetary assets	30	55
Accounts payable	5	7
Notes payable	10	30
Bonds payable	10	10
Total monetary liabilities	25	47
Net monetary position	$ 5	$ 8

b.

	Nominal Dollars	Multiplier	Constant Dollars	Purchasing Power Loss
Net monetary position, January 1	$5	200/180	$5.56	$0.56
Net monetary transactions	+3	200/190	3.16	0.16
Total			8.72	
Net monetary position, December 31	$8	200/200	8.00	
Purchasing-power loss				$0.72

3. *a.* Present value of cash flows:

$250,000 × 6.1446	$1,536,150
$1,500,000 × .3855	578,250
Total	$2,114,400

VALENTINE COMPANY
Value-Based Balance Sheet
As of January 1, 19x1

Current assets:

Cash	$ 100,000
Accounts receivable	300,000
Inventories (2.5 × $200,000)	500,000
Total current assets	900,000
Plant assets	1,200,000
Goodwill	444,400*
Total assets	$2,544,400

Current liabilities:

Accounts payable	$ 80,000
Notes payable	70,000
Total current liabilities	150,000
Bonds payable (0.8 × $350,000)	280,000
Total liabilities	430,000

Owners' equity:

Common stock	650,000
Retained earnings	1,464,400†
Total owners' equity	2,114,400
Total liabilities and owners' equity	$2,544,400

* Present value		$2,114,400
Net tangible assets:		
Total tangible assets	$2,100,000	
Total liabilities	430,000	1,670,000
Goodwill		$ 444,400

† $2,114,400 − $650,000 = $1,464,400

b. Present value, December 31, 19x1:

$260,000 × 6.1446	$1,597,600
$1,600,000 × .3855	616,800
Total	2,214,400
Present value, January 1, 19x1 [from (a)]	2,114,400
Increase in present value	100,000
Cash dividend	90,000
Net income	$ 190,000

VALENTINE COMPANY
Value-Based Income Statement
For the Year Ended December 31, 19x1

Sales revenues		$2,000,000
Cost of goods sold		1,550,000
Gross margin		450,000
Depreciation	$ 80,000	
Other operating expenses	230,000	
Interest expense	10,000	
Income tax expense	100,000	420,000
Income before value adjustment		30,000
Value adjustment		160,000
Net income		$ 190,000

4. *a.* Cost of goods sold (600 × A780) × 60 percent × $8.50 — $2,386,800

Foreign currency exchange gain or loss:

October 30: A117,000 × ($8.50 − $8.20)	$ 35,100
December 31: [(600 × A780) − A117,000 = A351,000]	
× [$8.75 − $8.50 = $0.25]	(87,750)
Foreign currency exchange loss	$ 52,650

b. Cost of goods sold (600 × A780) × 40 percent × $8.50 — $1,591,200

Foreign currency exchange gain:

January 8: A351,000 × ($8.75 − $8.55)	$ 70,200

Chapter 15

		19x3	19x4	19x5	19x6
1. *a.*	Number of shares (000) . .	50,000	50,000	52,000	52,000
	Earnings available for				
	common stock (000) . .		$96,000	$101,300	$99,100
	Earnings per share		$1.92	$1.95	$1.91
b.	Book value per share . . .	$16.60	$17.52	$18.60	$19.51
c.	Average common equity				
	(000)		$853,000	$921,650	$990,850
	Return on common				
	equity		11.3%	11.0%	10.0%

2. *a.* 1. Debt decreases while equity remains unchanged; the debt/equity ratio therefore will fall.

2. Cash increases and then decreases by the same amount; cur-

rent liabilities also remain unchanged. The current ratio will not be affected.

3. Since total assets have decreased, the ratio of sales to total assets (asset turnover) will increase.

b. 1. If the capitalized amount is equal to the book value of the building before the sale-leaseback, total debt will remain unchanged and the debt/equity ratio will be unaffected. If the capitalized amount is less than the former book value, the debt/equity ratio will fall.

2. If the first lease payment falls within the next 12 months or the next operating cycle, the present value of that payment will appear as a current liability. The current ratio therefore will fall.

3. Again, the effect depends on the amount capitalized. If this amount is equal to the book value of the building before the sale-leaseback, total assets will remain unchanged and the asset-turnover ratio will be unaffected. If a smaller amount is capitalized, asset turnover will increase.

3. *a.*   Return on assets $= \dfrac{\text{Earnings before interest and taxes (EBIT)}}{\text{Total assets}}$

Because this equation contains two unknowns, we must start by deriving one of them.

Return on common equity $= \dfrac{(\text{EBIT} - \text{Interest}) \times (1 - \text{Tax rate})}{\text{Common equity}}$

Again we have two unknowns, but we know that the common equity equals total assets minus total liabilities and that liabilities are 25 percent of the common equity. Putting these together, we find that:

Common equity $= \$100,000/1.25 = \$80,000$

This permits the calculation of EBIT:

$$7.2\% = \frac{\text{EBIT} - \$2,000}{\$80,000} \times 0.55$$

EBIT $= \$10,473 + \$2,000 = \$12,473$

Return on assets (before taxes) $= \$12,473/\$100,000 = 12.47\%$.
Return on assets (after taxes) $= 12.47\% \times (1 - 0.45) = 6.86\%$.

b. Since the aftertax return on assets is less than the return on common equity, the use of leverage succeeded in increasing the rate of return on the common equity.

4.

Net sales	$13,851,000*
Cost of goods sold.	3,749,100†
Gross margin	10,101,900
Selling and administrative expenses	4,454,700‡
Income before tax	5,647,200
Income tax expense.	1,694,160
Income from continuing operations.	3,953,040

Discontinued operations:

Loss from discontinued operations, net of $9,000 tax effect.	$ (21,000)	
Gain on disposal of discontinued operations, net of $255,000 tax effect	595,000	574,000
Income before extraordinary items		4,527,040
Loss from uninsured flood damage, net of $720,000 tax effect		(1,680,000)
Income before effect of accounting changes.		2,847,040
Cumulative effect of a change in an accounting principle, net of $157,500 tax effect		367,500
Net income		$ 3,214,540

* $14,275,300 − $424,300.
† $3,866,700 − $117,600.
‡ $4,791,400 − $336,700.

Chapter 16

1. *a* and *b*. The first step is to calculate total cost at each volume. The second step is to extrapolate this schedule backward, to estimate total cost at zero volume. This is the estimated total fixed cost. The third step is to subtract this amount from estimated total cost at each volume—the difference is total variable cost. The final step is to divide this total by the number of units to get average variable cost. Average fixed cost is calculated in the same manner, by dividing total fixed cost by the number of units:

Volume (units)	Total Cost		Total Variable Cost	Average Variable Cost	Average Fixed Cost
0	$10	(est.)	$ 0	—	—
1	11		1	$1.00	$10.00
2	12		2	1.00	5.00
3	13		3	1.00	3.33
4	14		4	1.00	2.50
5	15		5	1.00	2.00
6	16		6	1.00	1.67
7	17		7	1.00	1.43
8	18		8	1.00	1.25
9	20		10	1.11	1.11
10	23		13	1.30	1.00

c. This calls for an estimate of incremental cost: total cost at 10 units ($23) less total cost at 9 units ($20), or $3.

2. The only relevant number is opportunity cost, reflecting the cash flows Smith will receive in the future. None of the past prices is relevant to this decision because Smith can do nothing now to change them. The $6 price was an opportunity cost in 19x5. Her decision not to sell then was the same as a decision to buy 200 shares at that price at that time. It no longer has any more relevance, however, than the $15 and $20 historical purchase prices. Even the $8 price has no relevance because the $10 tender offer makes that the effective floor under the market price; it can't go lower as long as the tender offer is in effect, and it will go higher only if enough shareholders believe that the stock is worth more than $10.

3. a. The first step is to identify the alternatives. One alternative is to operate trucks A and B; the other is to operate truck A and use the independent trucker. The second step is to decide which costs will be totally unaffected by the choice (sunk costs). In this case, all the fixed costs are irrelevant to the decision because they will be unaffected by it. (Both trucks will be in service during the whole period under either alternative.)

	Trucks A and B	Truck A and Independent
Truck A:		
Driver	$15 × 40 = $ 600	$15 × 40 = $ 600
Gas and oil	$0.20 × 400 = 80	$0.20 × 600 = 120
Maintenance	$0.08 × 400 = 32	$0.08 × 600 = 48
Truck B:		
Driver	$15 × 40 = 600	—
Gas and oil	$0.22 × 600 = 132	—
Maintenance	$0.10 × 600 = 60	—
Independent	—	780
Total	$1,504	$1,548

Since the use of both company trucks will reduce total cash outflows by $44 ($1,548 − $1,504), this alternative should be selected.

b. By disposing of truck B, the company could save the following annual cash outflows:

Fixed:	
Garage space	$ 800
Registration and insurance	1,500
Maintenance	500
Variable:	
Driver: $15 × 650	9,750
Gas and oil: $0.22 × 650 × 15	2,145
Maintenance: $0.10 × 650 × 15	975
Total	$15,670

If the independent trucker's charges would exceed $15,670, the company would find it profitable to keep truck B in service. At any lower price, the company should use the independent. (Depreciation was ignored in this calculation because it didn't represent a cash flow to be affected by the decision. If keeping the truck would affect its salvage or resale value, this effect would have to be considered, as we'll see in Chapter 21.)

Chapter 17

1. *a.* Contribution margin per unit: $40 − $30 = $10.
   Fixed cost to be covered: $16,600.
   Break-even volume: $16,600/$10 = *1,660 units.*

   b. Average variable cost per unit = $30 + ($10,000 + $2,500)/2,000
   = $36.25.
   Contribution margin per unit = $40 − $36.25 = $3.75.
   Fixed cost to be covered: $2,300 + $1,800 =$4,100.
   Break-even volume: $4,100/3.75 = *1,093.3 units.*

   c. If all costs are proportionally variable, then production is justified if only one unit can be sold, as long as the contribution margin per unit is positive. In this case, if all costs are proportionally variable, average variable cost will be $30 + ($16,600/2,000) = $38.30, and the contribution margin will be $1.70.

   Generalizing from this, we can say that the higher the proportion of fixed costs in the cost mix at a specified volume, the higher will be the break-even volume.

2. Total cost if proposal is approved: 25 × $14,000 =$350,000
   Total cost if proposal is rejected: 10 × $15,500 = <u>155,000</u>
   Incremental cost . . . . <u>$195,000</u>

   The proposal is acceptable.

3. Fixed costs are sunk costs with respect to this decision; all variable costs are incremental. Contribution margins per hour of scarce capacity are as follows:

	A	B	C
Price	$4	$6	$10
Variable cost	2	4	6
Contribution margin per unit	2	2	4
Hours per unit	2	1	5
Contribution margin per hour . . .	$1	$2	$0.80

Capacity should be allocated first to product B, which has the highest contribution margin per hour, then to product A, and finally to product C, which has the lowest hourly contribution. The resulting production schedule is:

Product	Units	Hours
B	40	40
A	25	50
C	2	10
Total		100

4. *a.*

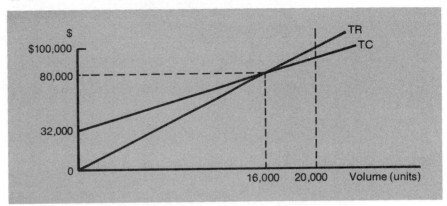

b. Break-even point: $32,000/($5 − $3) = 16,000$ units.
Margin of safety: $20,000 − 16,000 = 4,000$ units.
Anticipated profit:

Revenues at $5	$100,000
Variable costs at $3	60,000
Fixed costs	32,000
Income before taxes.	$ 8,000

c. 1. Break-even point: $32,000/($5.50 − $3) = 12,800$ units.
Margin of safety: $18,000 − 12,800 = 5,200$ units.
Anticipated profit:

Revenues at $5.50.	$ 99,000
Variable costs at $3	54,000
Fixed costs	32,000
Income before taxes.	$ 13,000

2. The effect of the price increase is to increase the spread between total cost and total revenue at any given volume. When volume is measured in physical units, as it is in this case, this increased spread is reflected in the profit-volume chart as a steeper slope for the total revenue line. The revised chart is shown here:

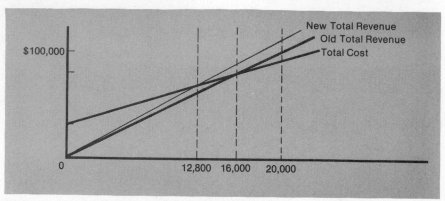

3. Profit target: 1.1 × $8,000 (from *b*) .... $ 8,800
   Total fixed costs 32,000
     Needed contribution margin $40,800

   Target volume = $40,800/$2.50 = 16,320 units.

d. 1. Break-even point: $36,000/($4.60 − $3) = 22,500 units.

   2. Profit target: 1.1 × $8,000 (from *b*) .... $ 8,800
      Total fixed costs 36,000
        Needed contribution margin $44,800

   Target volume = $44,800/$1.60 = 28,000 units.

5. *a.*

	Contribution Margin per Unit	Present Program		Proposed Program	
Product		**Volume**	**Profit Contribution**	**Volume**	**Profit Contribution**
A..................	$2.00	30,000	$60,000	40,000	$ 80,000
B..................	0.75	40,000	30,000	32,000	24,000
Total contribution margin			90,000		104,000
Fixed costs			72,000		81,700
Income before taxes			$18,000		$ 22,300

The proposal looks desirable.

b.

Product	Contribution Margin per Unit	Units Sold	Profit Contribution
A.....................	$1.90	35,000	$66,500
B.....................	0.65	45,000	29,250
Total contribution margin.....			95,750
Fixed costs			72,000
Income before taxes			$23,750

This alternative is even better than the one in part *a*. A good question to ask now, however, is what would happen if more selling effort (as in part *a*) were devoted to the redesigned and repriced products; this might produce even better results.

6. Revenue at lower prices (90 percent × $15,000). . . . $13,500

Cost of doing the work:

Labor: 600 hours × $8	$4,800	
Additional labor: 80 hours × $8	640	
Materials.	6,000	
Other processing costs: 600 hours × $2	1,200*	
Total		12,640
Incremental profit		$ 860

* If costs vary with labor input rather than with service output, this cost should be $1,360; the decision remains the same.

The incremental cost of doing the work is less than the incremental revenue. Therefore, the shop should reduce its prices and improve its service, and thereby keep the business.

Chapter 18

1. *a.* This company has two separate—and very different—products, each of which is likely to be the focus of pricing and other managerial decisions. This would require adding a "product" dimension to the cost account structure, at least in manufacturing.

An organizational classification probably would be useful as well. The company's activities are classified into three major functions: manufacturing, marketing, and administration. Each probably has two or more organizational subdivisions (the factory has vacuum assembly, two or more duct work production centers, a maintenance shop, a parts department, and a manager's office, at a minimum). Management probably would find an organization breakdown useful, both for reporting on department performance (which we haven't discussed yet) and for increasing the accuracy of product-costing data.

Finally, some object-of-expenditure accounts probably should be further subdivided. Wages costs, for example, even if departmentalized, cover different kinds of employee services, and management may need to know how much each kind of service costs. Freight costs, too, should be divided between inbound and outbound freight. Furthermore, the "miscellaneous" category may be too large, covering up differences in the behavior of the various cost elements in this category.

b. One plausible explanation is that Zebra has been growing rapidly and has been managed by a small group of managers who have participated in its growth and know its secrets. When the company was small, direct observation substituted for detailed reporting.

And for managers who know the operations well, less formal information is necessary than for the new managers a growing company will have to add.

2. *a* and *b*.

	Average Cost	
Department	Variable	Full
A	$0.60	$0.80
B	1.60	2.00
C	0.64	1.04
D	0.40	0.72

Product	Full Cost		Variable Cost	
PDX ..	$0.80 + $2.00	= $2.80	$0.60 + $1.60	= $2.20
QYK ..	$0.80 + $1.04 + $0.72 =	2.56	$0.60 + $0.64 + $0.40 =	1.64

   c. Relative costs (PDX/QYK):
   Full cost: $2.80/$2.56 = 1.09.
   Variable cost: $2.20/$1.64 = 1.34.
   The reason for the difference in these ratios is that QYK is processed in departments that have a heavier mix of fixed costs than department B, where PDX is processed.

3. *a.*

		Labor Ratio		Apportionment
PDX	12,500	12,500	18.18%	$ 5,000
QYK	37,500 × 1.5	56,250	81.82	22,500
Total		68,750	100.00%	$27,500

	Unit Service Cost	Direct Full Cost	Total Cost
PDX	$ 5,000/12,500 = $0.40	$2.80	$3.20
QYK	$22,500/37,500 = 0.60	2.56	3.16

   b. Average service cost per unit = $27,500/50,000 = $0.55 a unit.
   Allocation:
      To PDX = $0.55 × 12,500 = $ 6,875.
      To QYK = $0.55 × 37,500 = 20,625.
   Allocated unit cost:
      PDX: $2.80 + $0.55 = $3.35.
      QYK: $2.56 + $0.55 = $3.11.

   c. The sales manager's proposal increases the apparent profitability of QYK by $0.05 a unit ($3.16 − $3.11), or $1,875 a month. This increase is spurious, however, because the problem states that a unit of QYK is responsible for more costs of the service centers than a unit of PDX. The proposal to change the allocation method should be rejected. "Fairness" has no meaning in this context. It ought to describe a causal relationship, but the sales manager probably has in mind obtaining a cost result that will enable sales of QYK to appear to be profitable. Good managerial accounting can't be built on this kind of unstable foundation.

4. *a.*

Finished	10,000
Ending work in process: 2,000 × 0.25	500
Moving average divisor	10,500
Beginning work in process: 4,000 × 0.5	2,000
Equivalent production	8,500

b. Average cost, current month = $76,500/8,500 = $9.00.

c. Costs to be distributed:

Beginning work in process: 4,000 × 0.5 × $8.60	$17,200
Costs, current month	76,500
Total	$93,700

Unit cost distributor = $93,700/10,500 = $8.9238 a unit.

Cost distribution:

Finished goods: 10,000 × $8.9238	$89,238
Ending work in process: 2,000 × 0.25 × $8.9238	4,462
Total	$93,700

Chapter 19

1. *a.* Overhead rate = $900,000/100,000 = $9 a direct labor-hour. Cost of Job No. 423:

Materials	$ 800
Labor	400
Overhead ($9 × 60)	540
Total	$1,740

Actual overhead	$106,000
Absorbed overhead (10,000 × $9)	90,000
Underabsorbed overhead	$ 16,000

2. *a.*

Materials:		Work in process:	
Beginning inventory	$10,000	Beginning inventory	$ 15,000
Purchases	16,000	Additions:	
	26,000	Direct materials	18,000
Issues	18,000	Direct labor	48,000
Ending inventory	$ 8,000	Overhead:	
		5,000 × $4	20,000
			101,000
		Completions	80,000
		Ending inventory	$ 21,000

b. Beginning finished goods inventory.................. $ 20,000
   Completions.. 80,000

                                              100,000
   Ending finished goods inventory..................... 23,000

     Cost of goods sold .... $ 77,000

c. Actual overhead.................................... $ 17,000
   Absorbed overhead: 5,000 × $4 20,000

     Overabsorbed overhead .... $ 3,000

3. First calculate plantwide and departmental overhead rates:

			Hours		
Product	**Output**	**Dept. 1**	**Dept. 2**	**Dept. 3**	**All Depts.**
A............	40,000	80,000	40,000	40,000	
B............	40,000		80,000	80,000	
C............	10,000	20,000	30,000	30,000	
Total hours		100,000	150,000	150,000	400,000
Overhead........		$400,000	$300,000	$100,000	$800,000
Overhead rate		$4.00	$2.00	$0.67	$2.00

Then calculate unit overhead cost for each product:

	Product A		Product B		Product C	
	Hours	**Cost**	**Hours**	**Cost**	**Hours**	**Cost**
Department rates:						
Department 1........	2	$ 8.00	—		2	$ 8.00
Department 2........	1	2.00	2	$4.00	3	6.00
Department 3........	1	0.67	2	1.34	3	2.01
Total unit cost		$10.67		$5.34		$16.01
Plantwide rate........	4	$ 8.00	4	$8.00	8	$16.00

As this shows, the effect on the unit costs of product A and B is substantial, and the department overhead rates presumably indicate more accurately the amount of resources used to support production of the product. If production and sales are not equal, the difference will also affect reported income.

4. *a. Step 1:* Allocate building costs ($5,000):

Office	Storeroom	Maintenance	Able	Baker
750	500	250	2,000	1,500

Step 2: Allocate office costs, including share of building costs ($6,370 + $750). Hours spent in building and office departments should not be included in the allocation base because the building

department's costs have already been allocated and the office department can't allocate costs to itself. The allocation base therefore is 8,900 labor-hours, and the allocation is:

Storeroom	Maintenance	Able	Baker
240	400	4,480	2,000

Step 3: Allocate storeroom costs ($2,260 + $500 + $240):

Maintenance	Able	Baker
150	1,050	1,800

Step 4: Allocate maintenance costs ($6,000 + $250 + $400 + $150). Only 400 maintenance hours enter into the calculation. The 10 hours used in the office must be ignored because that department's costs have already been allocated. The allocation is:

Able	Baker
2,550	4,250

The cost allocation schedule now shows the following:

	Building	Office	Store-room	Mainte-nance	Able	Baker
Direct overhead	$5,000	$6,370	$2,260	$6,000	$ 2,770	$ 3,100
Allocations:						
Building	(5,000)	750	500	250	2,000	1,500
Office		(7,120)	240	400	4,480	2,000
Storeroom			(3,000)	150	1,050	1,800
Maintenance				(6,800)	2,550	4,250
Total					$12,850	$12,650
Normal volume (direct labor-hours)............					5,000	2,000
Overhead rate					$2.57	$6.325

b.

	Job 123	Job 321
Able at $2.57 an hour	$12.85	$ 5.14
Baker at $6.325 an hour	12.65	31.62
Total	$25.50	$36.76

5. *a.* Full-costing overhead rates:
Department A: $25,000/5,000 = $5 a direct labor-hour
Department B: $60,000/10,000 = $6 a pound

Job order costs:

	Job 1	Job 2
Direct materials	$2,400	$ 4,800
Direct labor:		
Department A	1,620	900
Department B	420	280
Overhead:		
Department A at $5	900	500
Department B at $6	2,880	9,000
Total	$8,220	$15,480
Unit cost	$13.70	$15.48

b. Variable costing overhead rates:
Department A: $15,000/5,000 = $3 a direct labor-hour
Department B: $20,000/10,000 = $2 a pound

Job order costs:

	Job 1	Job 2
Direct materials	$2,400	$4,800
Direct labor:		
Department A	1,620	900
Department B	420	280
Overhead:		
Department A at $3	540	300
Department B at $2	960	3,000
Total	$5,940	$9,280
Unit cost	$9.90	$9.28

c. Variable unit cost of job 2 is less than that of job 1; full cost was greater for job 2 than for job 1. The main reason is that job 2 used much more of department B's capacity than job 1, and department B has a much higher proportion of fixed costs than department A. Total profit is thus much more sensitive to variations in sales of product Y (job 2) than to variations in sales of product X.

Chapter 20	**1.** *a.*	Division A	Division B	Division C	Total
	Profit Plan				
	Sales revenues	$1,000	$3,000	$2,100	$6,100
	Divisional expenses:				
	Cost of goods sold	650	1,650	1,260	3,560
	Marketing.	150	500	300	950
	Administrative	150	300	200	650
	Total	950	2,450	1,760	5,160
	Division margin.	$ 50	$ 550	$ 340	940
	Headquarters expenses				400
	Net income				$ 540
	Cash Budget				
	Revenues.	$1,000	$3,000	$2,100	$6,100
	Less: Increase in receivables . .	10	200	50	260
	Collections	990	2,800	2,050	5,840
	Cost of goods sold.	650	1,650	1,260	3,560
	Add: Inventory increase.	50	100	50	200
	Purchases	700	1,750	1,310	3,760
	Less: Increases in payables . . .	15	50	80	145
	Payments to suppliers	685	1,700	1,230	3,615
	Division marketing costs	150	500	300	950
	Division administration (expense less depreciation)	145	285	180	610
	Total divisional disbursements	980	2,485	1,710	5,175
	Division cash flow	$ 10	$ 315	$ 340	665
	Head-office disbursements:				
	Central administration				390
	Equipment.				130
	Dividends.				350
	Total head-office disbursements.				870
	Net decrease in cash				$ (205)

b. Anticipated cash balance: $290 − $205 . . . . $ 85
    Minimum cash balance: 5% × $6,100   305
    Cash shortage. $220

Since the company has only a $100 line of credit, the proposed plan is not financially feasible.

2. *a.* Expected disbursements:

Sales	$2,400,000
Net income before taxes	95,000
Total expenses	2,305,000
Depreciation	48,000
Cash expenses	2,257,000
Accounts payable decrease	20,000
Inventory increase	17,000
Income taxes	93,000
Dividends	30,000
Additions to plant	125,000
Total expected disbursements	2,542,000

Expected collections:

Sales	$2,400,000	
Accounts receivable decrease	35,000	
Total expected collections		2,435,000

Expected excess of disbursements over collections	107,000
Cash balance, January 1, 19x2	54,000
Expected cash deficit, December 31, 19x2	$53,000

b. Management might seek ways of improving the current profit margin. Because material and labor costs are rising, competitors' costs may be increasing too, and a price increase might be feasible. Significant cost reductions or changes in product mix, however, probably cannot be realized soon enough to do much for the 19x2 cash flow, except possibly as mentioned below.

Other than a possible price increase, management would seem to have two main options: (1) reduce "discretionary" expenditures on such items as plant and equipment, dividends, or special programs now included under expenses; or (2) obtain additional cash by borrowing. The planned capital-expenditure program is very large, but may be entirely necessary to effect the planned changeover in product lines. Stock sales may be difficult to make because reported income is now low, so the choice is really between borrowing and cutting back.

Unless the capital budget has a good deal of slack in it, the company would seem to be ripe for some kind of borrowing. One possible source is to increase accounts payable instead of reducing them—inventories are increasing, after all—but this will provide only $37,000, even if the entire increase in inventory can be financed this way. The cash balance cannot be reduced to zero, either, and the company would seem to need at least $50,000 in funds. Passing the dividend would yield only $30,000 of this.

Chapter 21

1. Each of these proposals has the same average annual cash flow after the initial outlay is made ($1,750), but present value ranges from a small negative sum to +$3,311, and the internal rate of return varies from 9.7 percent to 15.5 percent:

a.

Time	Cash Flow	10 Percent Factor	Present Value at 10 Percent	Present Value at X Percent	Internal Rate of Return
				12%	
0........	−$10,000	1.0000	−$10,000	−$10,000	
1–10.....	+ 1,750/yr.	6.1446	+ 10,753	+ 9,888	
Net present value ..			+$ 753	−$ 112	11.7%

b.

Time	Cash Flow	10 Percent Factor	Present Value at 10 Percent	Present Value at X Percent	Internal Rate of Return
				13%	
0........	−$10,000	1.0000	−$10,000	−$10,000	
1–10.....	+ 1,500/yr.	6.1446	+ 9,217	+ 8,139	
1–5	+ 500/yr.	3.7908	+ 1,895	+ 1,759	
Net present value ..			+$ 1,112	−$ 102	12.7%

c.

Time	Cash Flow	10 Percent Factor	Present Value at 10 Percent	Present Value at X Percent	Internal Rate of Return
				11%	
0........	−$10,000	1.0000	−$10,000	−$10,000	
1–5	+ 1,500/yr.	3.7908	+ 5,686	+ 5,544	
6–10	+ 2,000/yr.	2.3538	+ 4,708	+ 4,387	
Net present value ..			+$ 394	−$ 69	10.9%

d.

Time	Cash Flow	10 Percent Factor	Present Value at 10 Percent	Present Value at X Percent	Internal Rate of Return
				9%	
0........	−$10,000	1.0000	−$10,000	−$10,000	
1–10.....	+ 1,350/yr.	6.1446	+ 8,295	+ 8,664	
10......	+ 4,000	0.3855	+ 1,542	+ 1,690	
Net present value ..			−$ 163	+$ 354	9.7%

e.

					15%
0........	−$10,000	1.0000	−$10,000	−$10,000
1–15.....	+ 1,750/yr.	7.6061	+ 13,311	+ 10,233

Net
present
value ..   +$ 3,311   +$ 233

					16%
0........	−$10,000			−$10,000
1–15.....	+ 1,750/yr.			+ 9,757

Net
present
value ..   −$ 243   15.5%

2. Payment period:

a. $10,000/$1,750 = 5.7 years (6 years if payments come in annually).

b. $10,000/$2,000 = 5 years.

c. Unpaid after five years: $10,000 − 5 × $1,500 = $2,500.
Number of years to pay back this amount: $2,500/$2,000 = 1.25 years.
Total payback period: 5 + 1.25 = 6.25 years (7 years with annual payments).

d. $10,000/$1,350 = 7.4 years (8 years with annual payments).

e. $10,000/$1,750 = 5.7 years (6 years with annual payments).

Average return on investment:

	Average Cash Flow	Average Depreciation	Average Income	Average Investment*	Average Return (Percent)
a.	$1,750	$1,000	$ 750	$5,000	15%
b.	1,750	1,000	750	5,000	15
c.	1,750	1,000	750	5,000	15
d.	1,350	600	750	7,000	10.7
e.	1,750	667	1,083	5,000	21.7

* These averages are halfway between the initial investment and the end-of-life salvage value.

3. *a.* Pretax analysis:

Immediate cash flow (time = 0):
To make: Cost of new machine................	−$7,000
To buy: Proceeds from sale of old machine	+ 1,500
Difference (incremental cash flow)	−$8,500

Annual cash flow (time = 1–7):
To make: Out-of-pocket production costs, at $0.20....................................	−$1,200
To buy: Purchase costs, at $0.50	− 3,000
Difference (incremental cash flow)	+$1,800 a year

b. Aftertax analysis:

Investment outlay (time = 0):
To buy: Proceeds from sale of old machine . . . . +$1,500
        Tax [40% of ($1,500 − $2,000)] . . . . +   200*
Net proceeds from sale. . . . . + 1,700
To make: Cost of new machine. . . . . − 7,000
      Difference (incremental cash flow) . . . . −$8,700

* A tax credit is equivalent to a cash inflow.

Annual cash flow (years 1 through 7):

| Year | Pretax Cash Flow | Tax Depreciation | | | Taxable Income | Tax | Aftertax Cash Flow |
		Old Machine	New Machine	Total			
1.	+$ 1,800	$ 500	$1,050	$1,550	$ 250	$ 100	$ 1,700
2.	+ 1,800	500	1,540	2,040	(240)	(96)	1,896
3.	+ 1,800	500	1,470	1,970	(170)	(68)	1,868
4.	+ 1,800	500	1,470	1,970	(170)	(68)	1,868
5.	+ 1,800	—	1,470	1,470	330	132	1,668
6.	+ 1,800	—	—		1,800	720	1,080
7.	+ 1,800	—	—		1,800	720	1,080
Total	+$12,600	$2,000	$7,000	$9,000	$3,600	$1,440	$11,160

4. *a.* Cost of machine $100,000
Less: Tax reduction on portion expensed
    (0.4 × $50,000) . . . . (20,000)
Add: Working capital required 10,000
     Total . . . . $ 90,000

b.

	Year 1	Year 2
1. Before-tax reduction in operating costs	$20,000	$20,000
2. Tax depreciation: $50,000 × (15% and 22%). .	7,500	11,000
3. Taxable saving (line 1 − line 2).	12,500	9,000
4. Tax (line 3 × 0.4)	3,750	3,600
5. Aftertax cash flow (line 1 − line 4).	$16,250	$16,400

5. *a.* Initial cash flow:

New facility:
Installed cost		$65,000
Less tax effect, expensed portion		
(40% × $15,000)		6,000
Net cash outlay, new facility		59,000
Replaced facilities:		
Market value...........................	$10,000	
Tax basis..............................	32,000	
Taxable loss	22,000	
Tax credit at 40%......................	8,800	
Net proceeds, old facilities		
($10,000 + $8,800)		18,800
Incremental initial cash outlay........		$40,200

Annual cash flows:

The pretax incremental cash inflow is $19,800 a year ($17,775 + $2,500 − $475). The $2,500 incremental depreciation shown in the table of savings isn't a difference in cash inflows and should be ignored. The $475 indicated saving in general factory management costs is illusory; these costs are fixed in total and are unlikely to change in response to changes in the amount of labor used.

Calculation of aftertax cash flows:

		Tax Depreciation					
Years from Now	*(1)* Pretax Cash Flow	*(2)* Present Facility	*(3)* New Facility	*(4)* Difference	*(5)* Taxable Income *(1) − (4)*	*(6)* Income Tax *(5)* × 40%	*(7)* Aftertax Cash Flow *(1) − (6)*
0.........	[as calculated above]						−$40,200
1.........	+$ 19,800	$ 4,000	$ 7,500	$ 3,500	$ 16,300	$ 6,520	+ 13,280
2.........	+ 19,800	4,000	11,000	7,000	12,800	5,120	+ 14,680
3.........	+ 19,800	4,000	10,500	6,500	13,300	5,320	+ 14,480
4.........	+ 19,800	4,000	10,500	6,500	13,300	5,320	+ 14,480
5.........	+ 19,800	4,000	10,500	6,500	13,300	5,320	+ 14,480
6.........	+ 19,800	4,000	—	(4,000)	23,800	9,520	+ 10,280
7.........	+ 19,800	4,000	—	(4,000)	23,800	9,520	+ 10,280
8.........	+ 19,800	4,000	—	(4,000)	23,800	9,520	+ 10,280
9.........	+ 19,800	—	—	—	19,800	7,920	+ 11,880
10.........	+ 19,800	—	—	—	19,800	7,920	+ 11,880
Total	+$198,000	$32,000	$50,000	$18,000	$180,000	$72,000	+$85,800

b. Calculation of present value:

Years from Now	Aftertax Cash Flow	12% Multiplier	Present Value
0	−$40,200	1.0000	−$40,200
1	+ 13,280	0.8929	+ 11,858
2	+ 14,680	0.7972	+ 11,703
3	+ 14,480	0.7118	+ 10,307
4	+ 14,480	0.6355	+ 9,202
5	+ 14,480	0.5674	+ 8,216
6	+ 10,280	0.5066	+ 5,208
7	+ 10,280	0.4524	+ 4,651
8	+ 10,280	0.4039	+ 4,152
9	+ 11,880	0.3606	+ 4,284
10	+ 11,880	0.3220	+ 3,825
Net present value			+$33,206

The proposal should be accepted.

Chapter 22

1. Steering control information might consist of advance booking data on individual flights and on individual origin/destination pairs. These data, combined with similar historical information, might be used to signal the need to expand or curtail individual portions of the service, to discontinue service at some airports altogether, or to expand the size of ground crews in some locations.

   Other information that might serve steering control purposes would be data on the costs and revenues of individual flights, individual origin/destination pairs, and individual origin or destination points; and data on operating statistics such as fuel consumption, maintenance cost, on-ground costs in comparison to plan, and maintenance turnaround time in Chicago.

   Scorecard information would consist largely of comparisons, by responsibility, of actual costs and revenues with the amounts budgeted, perhaps adjusted for variations in external conditions.

2. *a.*

	Actual	Budgeted
Income	$ 63,000	$ 70,000
Investment	700,000	665,000
Return on investment	9.0%	10.5%

b.

	Actual	Budgeted
Income	$ 63,000	$ 70,000
Investment charge at 12%	84,000	79,800
Residual income (loss)	$ (21,000)	$ (9,800)

c. Neither the ROI percentages nor the residual income numbers are relevant to managerial evaluation because of the changes in the allocated amounts and the changes in traceable investments and depreciation, none of which is controllable in any meaningful sense. Using budgeted amounts to replace the actual amounts reported for these elements, we can calculate a revised residual income number as follows:

Working capital (actual).....................		$200,000
Traceable plant and equipment (budgeted).....		420,000
Allocated investments (budgeted).............		95,000
Adjusted investment		$715,000
Income as reported.........................		$ 63,000
Less: Change in depreciation	$2,000	
Change in allocations	5,000	(7,000)
Add: Tax on the changes....................		3,500
Adjusted income...........................		59,500
Carrying charge (12% × $715,000).............		(85,800)
Adjusted residual income (loss).............		$ (26,300)

This indicates that the division manager's performance was actually a good deal worse than the initial comparisons indicated. One problem is that investment in working capital exceeded the plan by $50,000. Sales volume was $100,000 less than the budgeted amount (evidenced by the decrease in the allocation of head-office costs), so this wouldn't justify the increase in working capital. Furthermore, the decrease in sales volume was accompanied by a $10,500 aftertax decrease in divisional income (from $70,000 to $59,500). The sources of this decrease should be investigated to see how much of it was within the division manager's control.

d. The ratio of profit contribution to traceable investment is 13.8 percent ($63,000 income plus 50 percent of $40,000 in head-office charges, divided by $600,000 traceable investment). This indicates that the division may be paying its way. It is close enough to the minimum, however, to justify asking how many costs in the head office and how many investments administered by the head office are attributable to this division. If a study finds that attributable costs and investments in the head office are large enough to push the division's attributable return-on-investment substantially below 12 percent, then top management should analyze the division's incremental cash flows, both now and in the future when major capital investments are being considered. The purpose: to find out whether withdrawal would be desirable.

3. a. The memorandum should stress the following points:
   1. If the alternative is idleness, the only incremental costs may be the variable costs of 90 cents a pound, and this is far less than the proposed transfer price. Hull's profit will be 70 cents more for every pound of X it processes for the Hingham Division.

Without these 50,000 pounds, product X would show a loss of $20,000 after deducting its share of division fixed costs; with this production, the pretax income would be $15,000. This can be summarized in the following schedules for the Hull Division:

	If Hingham Buys from Hull @ $1.60	If Hingham Buys Outside
Sales outside (100,000 pounds)	$200,000	$200,000
Sales—Hingham (50,000 pounds)	80,000	—
Total sales	280,000	200,000
Product-traceable costs:		
Variable manufacturing costs	135,000	90,000
Sales commissions	10,000	10,000
Depreciation	20,000	20,000
Other traceable costs	40,000	40,000
Total traceable costs	205,000	160,000
Product profit contribution	75,000	40,000
Share of division fixed costs	60,000	60,000
Income before taxes	$ 15,000	$ (20,000)

2. If the Hull division will retain idle workers on the payroll to avoid losing a skilled work force, the incremental cost could be even less than 90 cents a pound because some labor costs would be sunk.

3. Even if the traceable fixed costs increase in steps, it is unlikely that these could be high enough to make an incremental loss. At the present volume they average only 27 cents a pound.

4. The Hull Division manager should recognize a longer-term problem—if cheaper substitutes are available, this may indicate a serious competitive weakness for the long run.

b. Some economists establish such a strict set of necessary conditions for the use of negotiation that they are almost never met. If you are willing to use the criteria established in this chapter, however, negotiation should be appropriate here. Hull has access to outside customer markets; Hingham has access to outside suppliers. If Hull were busy, the company might even be better off to have Hingham buy outside. If profit decentralization is to mean anything, we must rely on the division managers to identify situations of this type.

Chapter 23   1. *a.*

	Product A	Product B	Total
Equivalent units:			
Finished units................	5,000	10,000	
Ending inventory	300	600	
	5,300	10,600	
Beginning inventory............	500	500	
Total.....................	4,800	10,100	
Standard direct-labor cost per unit ..	×$ 2	×$ 1	
Total standard direct-labor cost.....	$9,600	$10,100	$19,700
Actual direct-labor cost...........			23,500
Direct-labor spending variance			$ 3,800 unfavorable

b.

Standard direct-labor cost		$19,700
Actual hours × standard rates......		22,000
Labor usage variance		$ 2,300 unfavorable
Actual hours × actual rates		23,500
Labor rate variance		1,500 unfavorable

c.

Ending inventory:		
Product A: 600 × ½ × $2........		$ 600
Product B: 1,200 × ½ × $1		600
Total......................		$ 1,200

2.

Actual cost of materials purchased:		
95,000 × $2.05	$194,750	
Standard cost of materials purchased:		
95,000 × $2.00	190,000	
Materials price variance..................		$ 4,750 unfavorable
Actual quantity of materials used:		
61,000 × 1.5 × $2........................	183,000	
Standard quantity of materials used:		
61,000 × 1.6 × $2........................	195,200	
Materials usage variance..................		12,200 favorable
Materials spending variance		$ 7,450 favorable

3. *a.*

	Month 4			Month 5		
	Actual	**Budget**	**Variance**	**Actual**	**Budget**	**Variance**
Controllable:						
Nonproductive time	$ 800	$1,000	$ 200	$1,200	$ 750	$(450)
Other indirect labor	3,700	4,000	300	3,600	3,500	(100)
Operating supplies	650	600	(50)	430	450	20
Total controllable	5,150	5,600	450	5,230	4,700	(530)
Noncontrollable:						
Depreciation	2,100	2,000	(100)	2,150	2,000	(150)
Building service charges . .	770	700	(70)	730	700	(30)
Total	$8,020	$8,300	$ 280	$8,110	$7,400	$(710)

b. Only the first three overhead cost items listed are likely to be of any significance in evaluating the cost-control performance of the department supervisor, and, of these, nonproductive time and other indirect labor have the greatest impact. Depreciation and building service charges are noncontrollable and have no bearing on managerial evaluation in this department.

c. Labor costs did not go down with decreasing volume. There are many possible reasons for this. This may merely be a time lag—management may have decided not to cut the labor force to meet the volume reduction in the hope that volume would recover quickly. This should be examined more critically if volume continues at these newer lower levels. We cannot ignore any one month's reports, but we need to examine them in the context of a longer period of time. Even two months is likely to be too short a period for random forces to have averaged themselves out.

The other item in which the variance has increased is depreciation, and this should be labeled as noncontrollable.

Chapter 24

1. Actual overhead. $19,900
Budgeted overhead:
$10,000 + 4,200 × $2.50 20,500
Overhead spending variance. . . . . . . $ 600 favorable
Standard overhead: 4,200 × $4.50. 18,900
Overhead volume variance . . . . 1,600 unfavorable
Total overhead variance. . . . . $1,000 unfavorable

2. *a.* Overhead rate:
Fixed costs: $4,680/9,000 = $0.52 per standard direct labor-hour
Total: $0.52 + $1.15 = $1.67 per standard direct labor-hour.
Standard overhead cost:
(10,500 hrs. + 3,600 hrs. − 4,000 hrs.) × $1.67 = $16,867.
b. Month-end balance: 3,600 hrs. × $1.67 = $6,012.

c.
Actual overhead	$17,400	
Budgeted at standard hours		
(10,100)	16,295	
Spending variance		$1,105 unfavorable
Standard overhead	16,867	
Volume variance		572 favorable
Total overhead variance		$ 533 unfavorable

3. *a.*
Actual overhead	$17,400	
Budgeted overhead at 10,800		
actual hours	17,100	
Spending variance		$ 300 unfavorable
Budgeted overhead at 10,100		
standard hours	16,295	
Labor efficiency variance		
(700 hours × $1.15)		805 unfavorable
Standard overhead	16,867	
Volume variance		572 favorable
Total overhead variance		$ 533 unfavorable

b. The three-variance method is appropriate here because the need for overhead costs is determined by the number of *actual* direct labor-hours. The spending variances therefore should measure departures of actual costs from the budget based on actual hours, and this is the hallmark of the three-variance method.

The two-variance method was appropriate in problem 2, part *c*, because the need for overhead costs there was determined by the number of *standard* direct labor-hours. The spending variance therefore was correctly measured as the departure of actual overhead cost from the budget based on standard hours.

4. *A:* $22,500/4,500 = $5.
B: $22,500 + $1,300 = $23,800.
C: $1,300 unfavorable − $1,500 unfavorable = $200 favorable.
D: $23,800 + $200 = $24,000; or $22,500 + $1,500 = $24,000.
E: $1,500/(5,000 − 4,500) = $3 × 5,000 = $15,000.
F: $5 − $3 = $2.
G: $15,000 + $2 × 5,000 = $25,000.

5. *a.*
Historical evaluation:
  Overexpenditure = $16,200 − $16,000 . . . . . $ 200

Cost overrun:
  Actual cost of progress achieved. $16,200
  Budgeted cost of progress achieved.   12,000
    Overrun to date $4,200

Slippage:
  Actual time . . . . 2 months
  Budgeted time of progress achieved. . . . . 1½ months
    Slippage to date. . . . .   ½ month

Projection:
Cost overrun:
  Revised budget $60,000
  Original budget 48,000
    Projected cost overrun 12,000
  Overrun to date 4,200
    Projected additional overrun . . . . $ 7,800

Slippage:
  Revised time table . . . . 7 months
  Original time table . . . . 6 months
    Projected slippage . . . . 1 month
  Slippage to date. ½ month
    Projected additional slippage . . . . ½ month

Rate of expenditure:
  Original budget . . . . $8,000 a month
  Revised budget:
    Estimated total cost. $60,000
    Costs to date 16,200
      Estimated remaining costs . $43,800
    Projected rate: $43,800/5 . . . . 8,760 a month
Projected increase in rate of
  expenditure. . . . . $ 760 a month

    b. Possible responses:

        1. Abandon the project.
        2. Increase the rate of expenditure to try to complete the project at the originally scheduled time.
        3. Stretch out the project, possibly to reduce future costs and possibly to spread out the drain on the company's cash resources.
        4. Appoint a new project manager.

    The main criterion for choosing among the first three of these is the anticipated net benefit (benefit minus research costs, stated at present value). For this purpose, management should ask for new estimates of benefit from the marketing or economic research staff, together with estimates of the costs of different research configurations.

The criterion for evaluating the manager's performance is *effectiveness*. The variances to date should be studied to see why progress has been slow and estimated future costs have been increased. If this analysis seems to indicate incompetence, then a new manager should be found.

Index

*This book has been set Quadex 202, in 10 and 9 point
Primer, leaded 2 points. Part numbers are 24 point
Avant Garde Medium and part titles are 36 point Avant
Garde Bold. Chapter numbers are 24 point Avant Garde
Medium and chapter titles are 24 point Avant Garde
Bold. The size of the type page is 36 picas by 47 picas.*